ISBN 978-1-332-77283-4
PIBN 10440972

This book is a reproduction of an important historical work. Forgotten Books uses state-of-the-art technology to digitally reconstruct the work, preserving the original format whilst repairing imperfections present in the aged copy. In rare cases, an imperfection in the original, such as a blemish or missing page, may be replicated in our edition. We do, however, repair the vast majority of imperfections successfully; any imperfections that remain are intentionally left to preserve the state of such historical works.

1 MONTH OF
FREE
READING

at

www.ForgottenBooks.com

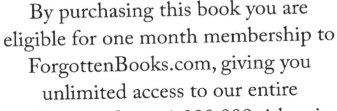

By purchasing this book you are eligible for one month membership to ForgottenBooks.com, giving you unlimited access to our entire collection of over 1,000,000 titles via our web site and mobile apps.

To claim your free month visit:

www.forgottenbooks.com/free440972

English
Français
Deutsche
Italiano
Español
Português

www.forgottenbooks.com

Mythology Photography **Fiction**
Fishing Christianity **Art** Cooking
Essays Buddhism Freemasonry
Medicine **Biology** Music **Ancient**
Egypt Evolution Carpentry Physics
Dance Geology **Mathematics** Fitness
Shakespeare **Folklore** Yoga Marketing
Confidence Immortality Biographies
Poetry **Psychology** Witchcraft
Electronics Chemistry History **Law**
Accounting **Philosophy** Anthropology
Alchemy Drama Quantum Mechanics
Atheism Sexual Health **Ancient History**
Entrepreneurship Languages Sport
Paleontology Needlework Islam
Metaphysics Investment Archaeology
Parenting Statistics Criminology
Motivational

AN

AINU-ENGLISH-JAPANESE DICTIONARY

(Including a Grammar of the Ainu Language.)

BY THE

Rev. JOHN BATCHELOR F. R. G. S.

Author of The Ainu of Japan—The Ainu and
their Folk-lore—Sea-girt Yezo, etc.

アイヌ。英。和辭典

及

アイヌ語文典

SECOND EDITION

TOKYO

Published by the METHODIST PUBLISHING HOUSE, Ginza, Tokyo

London KEGAN PAUL, TRENCH, TRUBNER, Co.

1905

PL
495
Z5B3
1905

Printed at
The Tokyo Tsukiji Type Foundry
Tokyo, Japan

Horobetsu

Dec: 15th, 1919.

Dear Dr. Montandon,

Many thanks for the measurements. I am glad you have met with such large success in the short time you were here.

I have made many inquiries but find that the Ainu have never heard of a "spear-thrower" and I have never heard of a name for one among them.

The first word you mention is the Japanese ohyo, the Ainu is at, "elm fibre", of which they make their native cloth. The other word is iyangarapte or irangarapte, and equals "How-do-you-do".

I am at the dictionary daily and it is steadily growing. If the Japanese Government cannot take 500 copies I shall be unable to print it as I have spent all my money on the Ainu and have none left. It will be a pity to leave it unpublished and there is no one living I could trust to see the proofs through the press. But I hope Government will take it up, unless they do the old work must suffice, and that would be great pity.

Mrs Batchelor and the daughter join with me in sending very kindest regards and best wishes for the coming Xtmas-tide and New Year.

Yours very Sincerely

Jno Batchelor

DEDICATION.

Dedicated by permission to His Excellency Baron Yasukata Sonoda, Governor General of Hokkaidō, in grateful remembrance of sympathy shown in the publication of this work.

ヌ又得サル所ナカルヘシ抑々アイヌノ本邦ニ於ケル關係太

一萬三千餘語自今アイヌ語ヲ研究スル者之ニ出テ求メハ則

二文ヲ以テシ名ケテアイヌ和英辭典ト曰フ集錄スル所實ニ

ヲ之レカ編著ヲ企テ年ヲ歷テ茲ニ其業ヲ卒ヘ配スルニ英和

ノ信賴ヲ受ク君世ノ爲メニ完全ノアイヌ辭書ナキヲ憂ヘ自

其語ニ通シ併セテ風俗ヲ審ニシ致義其間ニ行ハレ深ク彼等

ク其部落ヲ跋涉シ屢々彼族ト同棲シ困苦其ニ嘗メ遂ニ能ク

ス其初來ルヤ先ツアイヌ語ヲ學ヒ以テ布敎ニ便セントシ普

友人バチラー君本道ニ在ルコト殆ント將ニ三十年ナラント

アイヌ和英辭典序

著ノ世ニ出ルヲ喜ヒ為メニ一言ヲ叙スト云爾

ル、ミナラス本道ノ政ニ從フ者亦坐右ノ一寶ナリ余深ク此

多ク其命名ヲ傳フ然ラハ則チ本書ノ成ル獨リ學界ニ稗益ス

タ古シ殊ニ本道ノ如キハ久シク彼ノ占居セシ處地物ノ稱呼

明治三十八年九月

従三位男爵　園田安賢

TRANSLATION.

My Friend Mr. Batchelor has resided in Hokkaido for the space of nearly thirty years. When he first came to this island he almost at once commenced to study the Ainu language with the object of preaching the Gospel. He has visited nearly all the native villages and has at times lived entirely among the Ainu making light of the hardships which had to be endured. In course of time Mr. Batchelor gained a free command of the native tongue as well as a full knowledge of the customs of the people. As a consequence Christianity has been widely spread among them and he has gained their full confidence. Mr. Batchelor has felt the great need of a Dictionary and other books on the language, and at last, after many years of hard labour has compiled the present work entitled—AN AINU-ENGLISH-JAPANESE DICTIONARY:—which work contains some 13,000 words. It is thought that this book will fully meet the requirements of any students of the Ainu language. The relation between the Ainu and Japanese dates from very ancient times, particularly so in respect of this island which they still occupy. Here too the names of many places retain the original Ainu words. Hence the completion of the present work is of much scientific interest as well as of great practical use. In writing this Preface I desire to express my deep interest in the publication of the present work.

Sept., 1905.

Y. SONODA,
Baron of the Junior Third Court Rank.

PREFACE.

Sixteen years have elapsed since the publication of the compiler's last Ainu Dictionary, and during that period of time he has had the work constantly before him correcting and enlarging it. It was not his original intention to print a new dictionary and the work of revision was only done by way of recreation and for the purposes of his private work as a Missionary among the Ainu. But inasmuch as the first edition has been long out of print, and during the last decade more than five hundred friends have asked for copies, he has thought it advisable to once more place the results of his studies before the public in the form asked for. And, in doing this the Author desires to express his best thanks to the following Gentlemen. First, to His Excellency Baron Sonoda, Governor General of Hokkaidō, for the great interest and sympathy he has shown in the publication of this work and to whom it has been respectfully dedicated. Next to Mr. K. Yamada, sometime Chief Inspector of Schools for the Hokkaidōchō, for the cordial assistance he has rendered in recommending the book to all Japanese educationalists throughout the Empire. Then to his great Friend Dr. Miyabe Professor of Botany in the Agricultural College of Sapporo for his great kindness in supplying him with, as well as examining and correcting, all the scientific names of trees and plants found in this volume ; and to Mr. S. Nozawa, of the Fisheries Bureau, Hokkaidōchō, for so cordially doing the like in the various branches of zoölogy. Next the Author thanks his Friend Mr. S. Fujimura, likewise of the Fisheries Bureau, for so readily consenting to read his manuscripts and for correcting the

Japanese before sending the work to the Press. And lastly, but by no means least, very heartily does he thank his old Friend and Fellow Student of the Ainu Language—Professor K. Jimbō, of The Imperial University, Tōkyō, for undertaking the arduous task of assisting in reading the proofs, and for his suggestions with regard to the *kana* writing and other matters such as pointing out printers errors, mistranslations and other oversights. It was a very great advantage to have one to read the proofs who has studied the languages in which the book is written, and whose native tongue is one of them.

As the work was printed by a Japanese firm at Tōkyō, nearly a thousand miles from the writer's home in Sapporo, the table of errata will be found to be considerably larger than it would have been had he been in a position to see the proofs oftener. This must be the excuse for so long a list, for which, also, every apology is made. The errata belonging to the Dictionary part will be found at the end of the Dictionary, while those appertaining to the Grammar will be found at the end of the book.

Sapporo, August, 1905.

INTRODUCTION.

Whatever may be thought to the contrary, on account of the remoteness of the subject from ordinary topics, no sooner does one take up the study of Ainu in real earnest than he finds that the collection of words and arranging them in the form of vocabulary has by no means been neglected. For, to say nothing of those tabulated by Japanese (the *Moshiogusa* to wit), since the year 1730, when *Philipp Johann von Strachlenberg* of Stockholm published his *Der Word- und Destliche Theil von Europa und Asia*, quite a number of lists of words have appeared. Yet amid all the present writer has seen he does not feel that he can do better than refer the student to M. M. Dobrotvorsky's *Ainsko-Russkiŭ Slovar (1875)*. This is undoubtedly a good work but by no means in every case safe. A steady perusal of the book has proved to the present Author that there are several matters to be particularly guarded against in it. Such as, for example, the following.

(1.) Dobrotvorsky has introduced many foreign words unnoted into his *slovar* which examination proves cannot be traced to any known Ainu root. While on the other hand he has wrongly defined the word under examination. Note, for examples, some of the foreign words brought in. Dobrotvorsky gives *jo*, "lock." But this is pure Chinese or Japanese, the Ainu having no native locks or keys. He also gives *enu*, собáка, but this is clearly the Japanese word inu (イヌ) "dog." Why he should have put it in one is at a loss to know for the Ainu have two words of their own for "dog," viz. *seta* and *reyep*. Again, he has given *Cha-pan*, "earthenware:" but this is evidently the Japanese *chawan*, " tea-cup "! But perhaps one of the most beautiful disguises appears in the word Итчири, " Верста "! But this when turned into honest Roman letters, is just *ichi-ri*, Japanese (イ チ リ) *ichi ri* " one *ri*," pure and simple.

(2.) Then, again, the Russian alphabet has been employed in writing Ainu ; yet, whatever may be said for the beauties and perfection of this method when writing Russian, it is quite certain that it is not adapted for Ainu ; the ordinary Roman, as pronounced on the continent of Europe, is much better. Russian is distinctly a gutteral language, *which the Ainu is not;* the latter language resting more (so to speak) on the vowels than on the consonants. Thus, for example, Dobrotvorsky represents plain *ho* by ro, ra, or xo, and xa. There is also a difficulty in the hard mute ъ. Nor is this all. There is also a great difficulty in the uses of щ (*shtch*) and such like consonants. To cut the matter short, it is the Author's opinion, gained by practice, that the Russian way of writing is quite misleading when applied to the Ainu language.

But Dobrotvorsky's work is interesting in quite another way, inasmuch as it connects Yezo Ainu with that formerly spoken in Saghalien* and about the peninsula of Kamtchatka. Let us take one interesting example only by way of illustration of this. At Usu, in Southern Yezo, the present Author often heard the native name of a certain fish which he could not define in English. But Dobrotvorsky gives the very same word as used in the north, and which further study proves to be the dolphin. In like manner the work gives Варантука which we are told is " a kind of fish." At Usu, again, the same word is used, and there *warantuka*

---

* *Saghalien* is a Russian corruption of the Ainu name *Sakarin-moshiri*, i.e. " Navy plateau country."

is *Stickœs, sp.* But perhaps the most important thing about the book is that Dobrotvorsky suspects the Ainu language of being an inflected one, while the grammar following this dictionary clearly proves it now to be so and in some cases shows *how* it has become so.

Passing by many smaller vocabularies the largest to appear previous to my own Ainu-English-Japanese Dictionary (1889) (of which the present volume is a much enlarged and thoroughly revised edition) is that published (unread) by the Rev. J. Summers in Vol. XIV. Part II. page 186 *et seq.*, of the Transactions of the Asiatic Society of Japan 1886. It is a great pity Mr. Summers had not a better working knowledge of the Ainu language, his vocabulary being admittedly founded on the efforts of others. As, for example, Dixon ; Dening ; Klaproth ; Scheube ; Siebold ; Batchelor ; Dobrotvorsky ; Pfizmaier ; Davidoff ; and such works as the Yezo Gosen and the Matsumai Mss. This collation and quotation of Authors has not made the work any more valuable for, alas, many of their oversights and mistakes have also been copied. Summer's vocabulary has some 3,000 words in it, while at the end are found 63 sentences (by no means exact) in the Saru dialect.

It appears to be supposed that the present writer is the first independent British worker in this line. But such is not the case. The Author cannot allow this work to go to press without mentioning the fact that Mr. W. Dening, formerly of the Church Missionary Society at Hakodate, was the first Englishman to really take up the work of studying Ainu in thorough earnest. Mr. Dening's vocubulary, containing some 925 words and 38 phrases, will be found in vol. I. of *The Chrysanthemum* (now defunct). Though published in 1881 the words were collected five years previously. My own first efforts in Ainu studies commenced in 1877. Would that Mr. Dening had staid among us here to complete a work so important and so well begun.

Since the publication of the Author's Dictionary in 1889 the only original work of a vocabulary description presented to the public appears to be that printed conjointly by Profs. Jimbō and Kanazawa both of the Imperial University of Tōkyō. This little work is called *Ainu go kwaiwa jiten* (アイヌ語會話字典), and was published in the 31st year of Meiji. Both words and phrases are in Ainu and Japanese only and therefore useless to all who do not read Japanese.

In the year 1896 Prof. S. Kanasawa (above referred to in connection with Prof. Jimbō) published " A Revision of the *Moshiogusa*, an Ainu vocabulary " in vol. XIX. July—September No. 2 Journal of the Tōkyō Geographical Society. I have looked this vocabulary through and also studied the Moshiogusa word for word as given by Dr. Pfizmaier in his *Untersuchungen uiber den Bau der Ainu sprache.* The result is that I cannot help thinking that it would have been far better had the Prof. reprinted the Moshiogusa just as it stands, for this revision very much partakes not only of the nature of editorship (which I deny the Author any right to assume), but also of changing (and that very clearly) of a Northern way of speaking into a Southern ; thus destroying a very important link. Perhaps such a statement from me requires proof (which I am fully prepared to give if necessary and will do if required), but for the present (not to take up too much space) I ask that the following few examples only be accepted as one kind of proof. Thus :—The Moshiogusa gives リ イ (*ri-i*) which Prof. Kanazawa revises into plain リ (*ri*) thus cutting off the final イ (*i*). Ought this to be allowed in philological science? For one I most emphatically protest that it should not be.

Ri (リ) is an adjective meaning " high," while *ri-i* (リ イ) is an abstract noun meaning " the heights," both in Saghalien and Yezo. I do not therefore see where the revision (properly so called) comes in. It deserves some other name. Again, the Moshiogusa gives ウンジポ (*unjipo*) for " fire ;" Mr. Kanazawa revises this into *unji* only, thus omitting the final ポ (*po*). But the Ainu of Yezo at the present day use *unjipo* when addressing the fire upon the hearth as a goddess, the particle *po* implying respect and reverence. Not to multiply instances, however, I will take one more example only. The Moshiogusa gives イ エ ポ コ (*iyepoko*) which the Prof. revises into *iyepokba guru*, thus substituting *ba* for *o* and adding *guru* ! I cannot understand such science as this. It is not philology. What is it, I wonder ! …………But *iyepok-o* is an adjective of the singular number and of the objective case meaning in plain English " bearing the hatred of others,"* while *iyepokba guru* is a noun plural of the person and singular of the object meaning " one who is hated by others." Mr. Kanazawa's work is one rather of industry than of true science, and the task he set before himself is one which would naturally require a long and varied experience among the Ainu themselves and in the various Northern and Southern districts in which they have lived before being performed. It is a work rather to be dreaded than undertaken lightly.

It will be found that in this Dictionary the Ainu word has been written in Japanese *Kana* as well as with the Roman letters. This was done at the last moment owing to the request of friends for the sake of any who do not read the Roman form. I was rather sorry at being asked to do this because Ainu cannot be properly represented by

---

* (But at the same time implying that he *dos'nt mind it at all* !)

kana. Still, for the sake of my friends request, I have waved my scruples on this point and fallen in with the wish. But it must be remembered that the Roman is the text and not the *kana*.

Wherever it has been found necessary to employ a word of Chinese or Japanese* origin through lack of an Ainu equivalent such word has been given. But where this is the case it has for the most part been marked, and where it has not those who know Japanese will of course be able to see which is Ainu and which Japanese. E.g. *Umma* "a horse ;" *hitsuji* " sheep ;" *ishan-tono* " a doctor." It is more than possible also that some of the Japanese translation may not quite fit the English, but here again I would remind the reader that the text is Ainu-English, and not Ainu-Japanese. Like the *kana* writing, so also the *Japanese* was an after-thought it being the compiler's original intention to write the work in Ainu-English only.

---

* (But in some cases it is very difficult to determine which is Ainu, Japanese, or Chinese or *vise versa*.)

LIST OF ABBREVIATIONS.

a. or *adj.*	Stands for	...Adjective.	
abla.	,,	,,	...Ablative.
adv.	,,	,,	...Adverb.
aux. v.	,,	,,	...Auxiliary verb.
conj.	,,	,,	...Conjunction.
dat.	,,	,,	...Dative case.
e.g.	,,	,,	...Example.
Eng.	,,	,,	...English.
exlam.	,,	,,	...Exclamation.
gen.	,,	,,	...Genitive case.
geo.	,,	,,	...Geographical.
i.e.	,,	,,	...Id est.
imper.	,,	,,	...Imperative mood.
instrv	,,	,,	...Instrumental.
interj.	,,	,,	...Interjection.
intr.	,,	,,	...Intransitive.
Jap.	,,	,,	..Of Japanese origin.
lit.	,,	,,	...Literally.
loc.	,,	,,	...Locative particle.
met.	,,	,,	...Metaphor.
n.	,,	,,	...Noun.
nom.	,,	,,	...Nominative case.

obj.	Stands for	...Objective case.	
obj. pro.	,,	,,	...Objective pronoun.
part.	,,	,,	...Particle.
pass.	,,	,,	...Passive voice.
per. pro	,,	,,	...Personal pronoun.
phr.	,,	,,	...Phrase.
pl.	,,	,,	...Plural.
post.	,,	,,	...Postposition.
poss. pro.	,,	,,	..Possessive pronoun.
prep.	,,	,,	...Preposition.
pro.	,,	,,	...Pronoun.
reflex pro.	,,	,,	...Reflexive pronoun.
rel. pro.	,,	,,	...Relative pronoun.
sing.	,,	,,	...Singular.
syn.	,,	,,	..Partly synonymous words.
v.i.	,,	,,	...Intransitive verb.
v.t.	,,	,,	...Transitive verb.
——	,,	,,	...Repetition of the word under which it occurs.

LIST OF ERRATA TO PART I.

PAGE.

6. Foot note for Sakarin write sahrin & for navy write wavy.
7. Top line write *Stichœus* for *Stickœs.*
21. Under AIORO write Lateolabrax for Lateolabrap. And for Kamni write Kamui.
24. Under AKIANCHI strike out one *s* in "ssalmon." Also under AKKITEK write pecten for "*p*cten."
29. Second line from top. Write no*t* for "no" in the left hand column.
30. Under the 3rd AN write an-eyaiiraige for an-eyaiirage.
34. Last word left hand column write Korachi for koraeki.
45. Under ARI write iri-au for iri-au. Also write ARI-AN for ARI-AU.
51. Under at strike out the second *i* in "squirriel."
57. For AUWONNUM*Y*ERE write AUWONNUM*G*ERE. Also write choose for chose.
63. For CHIPEN-KUTE-KINA write CHIPE*U*-KUTE-KINA.
67. Second line from top of right column write "favour" for "favowr."
69. Under CHIKOTPA write *pl* of *ch*ikote for *ch*ikote. Also write Chikob*cp* for Chikobop.
73. Write CHIORA*UG*E for CHIORANGE and for Aorange write Aorauge.
75. Write Chipiyeto-sei for Chipiyeto-sie.
114. For Eramutusaoke write Eramutasaske.
129. Under EWAK write *E*iwak for *R*iwak.
136. For HAKMA-HAMAKA write HAKMA-HAKMAKA.
140. Under HAUKOTPARE write after *Syn* Peutange for Peutauge.
151. In the last line but one, left column, write HOSHIKI for HSONIKI.
218. Under KATUWENDE write "ashamed" for *a*s-shamed.
273. Under MUKSHIT write *Kotukka* for *Kotkuka.*
290. In the illustration under NITOKOT write nitokot for notokot.
292. Under NI-YAU write *N*itek for *K*itek.
301. Under NUPURU write after "water" the word *or*, and strike out the "or" after "Wine."
302. Under NUSHUYE write b*y* for b*e.*
308. Under OISHIRU write "salmon" for salmen.
314. Under OMAP write T*o* for T*e.*
334. Under *Pakashnu* write Kopao for K*a*pao.
355. For PON-NU-PAN-NU write PON-NU-PON-NU, and for PONSHINSEP write PONSHIN*G*EP.
370. In the illustration under RATASKEP change the *d* into *p* in the first *ras-taskep.*
373. Write quie*t* for quite under RENE.
381. Write RU*TT*UMI for RU*K*UMI.
387. For SAMBE-MURUMRUSE write SAMBE-MURUMURUSE.
388. Under Samoro-nimam write in the last line Governo*ur* for governor.
402. For S*h*iki-poro-chep write **Shlkl-poro-chep.**
427. Under sh*i*ta write *S*eta for *C*eta.
434. For Susu-man-chiku*m* write Susu-man-chiku*ni.*
444. Under Tekun-shipship write horse*tail* For horse*t.*
455. For Tuiru*k*umi write Tuiru-*h*umi.
478. Under woroge write mo*a*t for *mast.*

PART I.

AN
AINU-ENGLISH-JAPANESE
DICTIONARY.

アイヌ—和—英—辭　典*

A (ア).

A, ア, 此 (ア) A ハ他動詞ニ加ヘル時ハ自動詞ヲ作リ得ルナリ. 例セバ、ヌエ、書ク、アヌエ、記サレタ. A passive prefix to verbs. Thus, *Nuye,* "to write;" *anuye,* "to be written." *Raige,* "to kill;" *araige* "to be killed." The old form still used among the Saghalin Ainu and also among those inhabiting the central districts of Yezo is *an.* Thus, *annuye,* "written;" *an-raige,* "killed." *Set akara!* "Is the table to be prepared?" But this *a* or *an* is not always prefixed to the word it governs, other words may intervene between them. Thus, for *wakka atare,* "water was caused to be drawn," we hear, *awakka tare;* and for *akushiobas,* "to be helped," we hear *ka hi-a-obas.*

A, ア, 此 (ア) A ヲ動詞ニ加フル時ハ時トシテ過去ヲ示スナリ. 例セバ、アナケレ、終リシ. Sometimes *a* or *an* represents past time only. Thus; *aokere,* "it has been finished," *anki ruwe ne,* "it has been done," or "it was finished" or "done."

A, ア, 時トシテコノ (ア) A ヲ實格代名詞ノ直キ前ニ置クトキハ自動詞ノ第一人稱單數或ハ複數トナルナリ. 例セバ、

---

* On comparing the English and Japanese titles of this work a discrepancy will be at once observed by those who read these two languages, for while the work is called "An Ainu-English-Japanese Dictionary" in English, the Japanese title reads "An Ainu-Japanese-English Dictionary." The explanation is two-fold. 1stly, Originally the Mss. were in Ainu and English only, the Japanese being added afterwards at the request of Japanese friends. 2ndly, After going to press the order was changed by placing the Japanese before the English. But the work is essentially Ainu-English so that wherever any discrepancy should appear between the Ainu and Japanese the real sense must be settled by the English. Moreover, it will be found that many more examples have been given in English than in Japanese, while in some instances only sufficient Japanese has been written to give the bare key to the word defined in English.

アエンキック、我ハ打タレシ. アウン
キック、吾々ハ打タレシ. When used
immediately followed by the obj.
per. pro. en, " me," or *un,* " us,"
and a verb, it, together with the
pronoun should be translated by
" I am " and " we are " respectively ; for thus is formed the 1st
per. sing. and pl. of the passive
voice to verbs. Thus :—*a-en-kık,*
" I am struck ;" *a-un-kık,* " we
are struck." But when *a en* or *a
un* are used before verbs made
transitive by the addition of *e*
they should be translated by
" me " and " us." Thus :—*a en
epotara ki ruwe ne,* " they feel
anxiety about me " (lit : " I am
being felt anxiety about); *a un
emik,* " they bark at us " (lit : " we
are barked at ").

A, ア, コノ (**ア**) A ノ後ニ *ne* トイフ語
チナクトキハ第一人稱代名詞ノ複數ト
ナルナリ. 例セバ、エレンアネワ、吾
々三人. When followed by *ne,*
a represents the 1st per. pl. pro.
thus :—*E ren a ne wa,* " we
three." This mode of expression
is the same as *ren chi ne,* "we
three." But it should also be
remembered that under certain
conditions *eren a ne wa* may
mean "they three." Cfo. also *etun
a ne wa* with *tun chi ne,* " we two."
Literally translated *eren a ne wa*
is, " we being three." **Syn : chi;
anokai; chiutara ; chiokai utara ;** this latter sometimes being
corrupted into **chokai utara.**

A, ア, 或時 (**ア**) A ハ代名詞單數第一
人稱チ示スモノナリ. ケセバ、トカブチ
ウンアルアネルエネ、我レハ十勝ノ人

ナリ. Sometimes *a* is used for
the 1st per. sing. pro. " I."
As, *Tokapchi un guru a ne ruwe
ne,* " I am a Tokapchi man."
*Ashinuma anak nei guru kot'turesh
a ne ruwe ne,* " I am that
person's younger sister." Under
certain conditions of context
these illustrations might be translated in the 3rd person. **Syn :
Ku-ani.**

A, ア, 時ニ *Koro* ナル動詞ト共ニ用
キルトキハ (A) **ア,** ハ第三人稱複數、人
代名詞トナル. 例セバ、アコロブリキア
ムベ、彼等ノ持來タリタルモノ). Pre-
fixed to *koro,* " to possess," the
3rd per. pl. pro. " they " is
formed. Thus, "the things they
brought " is, *akoro ariki ambe.*
Such is the idiom but the words
mean in fact, " having the things
they came."

A, ア, 時ニ *Koro* (持) ト共ニ用キル
トキハ第一人稱複數持格代名詞トナル
例セバ、アコロ ベ、我儕ノモノ. By
prefixing *a* to the verb *koro,*
" to have," the 1st per. pl.
poss. pro. " our " is obtained.
Thus :—*Akorobe,* " our things."
Akoro michi, " our father." But
where there is no danger of ambiguity the *koro* may be dropped.
As :—*Shipakari, a uni wa ekbe,*
" only think ; they came from our
home ! " **Syn : Chikoro.**

A, ア, 時ニ *Koro* ノ前ニ A チ加フル
トキハ第一人稱單數持格代名詞トナル
ナリ、假セバ、アコロサポ、吾ガ姉、But
when used with *koro, a* sometimes represents the 1st per. sing.

poss. pro. "my." Thus, *akoro sapo*, "my elder sister." *akoro yupo*, "my elder brother."

A, ア, 時トシテ A ハ第二人稱持格單數代名詞トナルナリ、例セバ、アアクタ リ、汝ノ弟等。 Sometimes *a* is found for the 2nd per. sing. per. pro. "your," and as such is short for *aokai* or *anokai*, "you" and "ye." Thus :—*aakutari*, "your younger brothers." The full way of writing this would be *a-koro akihi utari*. See *aakutari* and *aaktonoge*.

A, ア, 時トシテ A ハ第二人稱單數代名詞ニ用キラルルコトアリ。 Sometimes *a* represents the 2nd per. sing. per. pro. "you." As :—*Tukkari kotan wa ek a ruwe he an?* "Have you come from *Tokkari?*" The more usual way however of using such phrases is by substituting *e* for *a*, *e* being a contraction of *eani*, "you."

A, ア, 時トシテ A ハ第三人稱單數代名詞ニ用キラル。 A is sometimes used for the 3rd per. sing. per. pro. "he," "she"; and even sometimes as the rel. pro. "who." *A-e-hotuyekara*, "he is calling you." *T' du an a guru*, "the person who was here."

A, ア, 時トシテ A ハ動詞ノ後ニ用キラル其時ハ疑問或ハ確答ノ義ナリ。 Used after verbs *a*, sometimes hardened into *ya*, expresses interrogation, and sometimes affirmation. Thus. *an a?* "Is there"; *an a*, "there is," which is intended being determined by the tone of voice. **Syn : ta a? ta an?**

A, ア, 齒、肉又ノ股、支流。 A tine. A tooth. A prong of a fork, spear, or harrow. Thus :—*Re a ush op*, "a trident."

A, ア, 誰、タレ、何、ナニ、所ノ、トコロ ノ。 *rel. pro.* Who. Which. As :— *E kik a guru nen ne ruwe?* "Who struck you."

A, ア, 嗚呼、*inter.* Ah. Oh. Alas. As :—*A ku kon nishpa*, "Ah, my master"! *A e seta*, "Ah, you dog"; **Syn : Aa.**

A, ア, 然、シカリ、*adv.* Yes. **Syn : E. Ruwe ne wa. Kon ne.**

A, ア, 一個、一方、全ク、*adj.* and *adv.* One. One of a pair. Entirely. Wholly. Thoroughly. Quite. As :— *A-shik*, "one eye"; also *ara-shik*. **Syn : Ara ; at.**

A, ア, 坐スル、(單數)。 *v.i. (sing).* To sit. As :—*Kina kata a*, "to sit on a mat. *Mo no a*, "sit still." *A wa an*, "to be sitting." *A kane an*, "he is sitting."

A, ア, 燃エル。*v.i.* To burn. As :— *Abe a*, "the fire is burning." **Syn : Rui. Paraparase.**

A, ア, 豐饒ナル、ユタカナル、盛ナル、サ カンナル。 *adj.* and *v.i.* To be in plenty. Luxurious. To be.

Aa, アヽ, 嗚呼、アヽ。 *interj.* Ah. Ah. Alas. See *A.*

Aahupkoropo, アヽフプコロポ, 養子、モラヒコ。 *n.* An adopted child. **Syn : Aeahupkoropo. Ahupkoropo.**

Aainukoro, アヽイヌコロ *v.i.* and *adj.* 敬ハレル、大切ニ思ハレル。 To be

treated with respect. Honoured.
Revered. Important. Held in esteem.

Aainukorobe, ア・イヌコロベ 大切ニ
思ハレルモノ. *n.* A thing of importance. A thing of value.

Aakkari, ア・ッカリ, 優リタル. *adj.*
Surpassed. Passed by. As:—*Hoshiki no an chip aakkari an na,*
"the ship which went out first has
been passed."

Aaktonoge, ア・クトノゲ, 弟、(尊敬
スル語). *ph.* "My younger brother." " Your younger brother."

Aakutari, ア・クタリ, 弟等. *ph.*
"your " or "my "or "our younger brothers." From *aokai, aki,*
and *utari.*

Aani, ア・ニ, 運バル、、持タル、. *adj.*
Held. Carried. Led. As:—*Aani
pon guru,* "the little fellow who
is being carried."

Aani-ushike, ア・ニウシケ, 手、(物ヲ
握ム柄) 例セバ、シュアニウシケ、鍋
ノ手. *n.* A handle. A place to
take hold of. As:—*Shu aani u-
shike,* "a pot handle." *Apa ushta
aani ushike,* "a door handle."

Aanka, ア・ンカ, 出來上リシ、置カル
レ、頁ケシ. *v.i.* Made. Finished.
Defeated. Placed. Put.

Aanno, ア・ンノ, 頁ケタル. *v.i.* and
adj. Over-come. Defeated. **Syn:**
Aannu. Aapkara.

Aannokara, ア・ンノカラ, 頁カサレ
ル. *v.i.* To be over-come or defeated. **Syn: Aannoka. Aapkara.**

Aanno-raige, ア・ンノライゲ, 爭フテ
殺サレレ. *v.i.* To be killed in contest. **Syn: Anno-a-raige. Annu-
a-raige. Annu-a-koiki.**

Aannu, ア・ンヌ, 頁カサレレ. *v.i.* To
be defeated.

**Aannu-no-hachire, ア・ンヌノハチ
レ,** 爭フテ頁カサル. *v.i.* To be over-
thrown in contest.

Aannu no hachiri, ア・ンヌノハチリ,
爭フテ頁カサル. *v.i.* To be overcome
in contest.

Aannu-no-koiki, ア・ンヌノコイキ, 鬪
フテ殺サレレ. *v.i.* To be killed in
contest.

Aannu-no-ye, ア・ンヌノエ, 議論シテ
頁ケル. *v.i.* To get the worst of
it in argument.

Aapkara, ア・ブカラ, 頁カサル、腐レ.
v.i. To be defeated. To have become rotten through exposure to
the elements.

Aapkarabe, ア・ブカラベ, 腐ッタ物.
Anything rotten.

Aapte, ア・ブテ, カチ落ス、落膽スル、
弱イ、例セバ、アアプテアスアブカシエ
アイカプ、弱イカラ步メヌ. *v.i.* and
adj. To be very weak. To have
lost one's strength. As:—*Aapte
gusu apkash eaikap,* "he cannot
walk through weakness."

Aara, ア・ラ, 全ク、悉ク、假セバ、アア
ライサム、全ク無シ. *adv.* Entirely.
Quite. Thoroughly. As:—*Aara
iam,* "it has entirely gone."
Syn: Ara. Aara.

Aara, ア・ラ, 美麗ナル、ウツクシキ.
adj. Beautiful. Pretty. Neat.
Syn: Atomte.

Aara-ushtek, ア・ラウシテク, 斷絕
シタ. *v.i.* Exterminated. Extinguished.

Aara-ushtekka, ア・ラウシュテッカ,
斷絕スル. *v.t.* To exterminate.
To extinguish.

Aashi, ア・シ, 閉シラレル・ *v.i.* To be shut. Closed. Set up (as a door in a door-way or a post).

Aashiri, ア・シリ, 他人、ホカノヒト・ *n.* Other persons. Strangers.

Aashiri-oreshpa-utara, ア・シリ オレシパウタラ, 孤兒、ミナシゴ、(複數)・ *n.* Orphans. Lit: " persons brought up by others."

Aashiri-oresu-guru, ア・シリオレス グル, 孤兒、ミナシゴ、(單數)・ *n.* An orphan.

Aashte, ア・シテ, 立タシメル、設立サ レル・ *n.* To be established. To be set up.

Aatama, ア・タマ, 難産ノ時ノ咒・ *n.* Name of a ceremony in which any woman suffering from hard labour is made to partake of a certain food in order to procure parturition.

Aba or abaha, アバ, アバハ, 親類、(單數)・ *n.* A relation. **Syn: Iriwak.**

Apa or apaha, アバ, アバハ,

Aba or abahautara, アバ, アバハウタラ, 親類、(複數)・ *n.* Relations. **Syn: Uiriwak utara.**

Apa or apahautara, アバ, アバハウタラ,

Abe, アベ, 試、カコツケ、假偶・ *n.* Pretence. Appearance. **Syn : Ap.**

Abe, アベ, 火、例セバ、アベアレ、火ヲ燃 ヤ・ *n.* Fire. *Abe are,* "to kindle a fire." *Abe-erau,* "to cover up fire with ashes." *Abe erepo,* "to rake fire together." *Abe kuru,* "to approach the fire." *Abe oraitek,* "the fire is dying out." *Abe-pakakse,* "the fire crackles." *Abe-pat-patke,* "the fire sputters."

Abe-rui, "the fire burns." *Abe ukopoye,* "to stir a fire." *Abe ush,* "the fire is out." Sometimes pronounced **api.**

Abe-chikuni, アベチクニ, 薪、タキギ・ *n.* Fire-wood. **Syn : Abe-ni.**

Abe-bashui, アベバシュイ, 火箸、ヒバ シ・ *n.* Fire-tongs.

Abe-etok, アベエトク, 上坐、カミザ・ *n.* The head of a fire-place.

Abe-etumbe, アベエツムベ, 蛾、夜ノ 蝶、ガ・ *n.* A kind of large butterfly moth. (Lit : " Fire-borrowers ").

Abe-kamui, アベカムイ, 火女神・ *n.* The goddess of fire. **Syn : Kamui huchi; Iresu kamui; Unchi kamui.**

Abe-kes, アベケス, 燒ヶ木・ *n.* A fire brand. By some *Abe-kis.*

Abe-keshi, アベケシ, ネッポ・ *n.* Dragonet. **Callionymus sp.*

Abe-kis, アベキス, 燒ヶ木・ *n.* Same as *abe-kes.*

Abe-koro, アベコロ, 託言スル、カコ ツケル、マネル・ *v.i.* To pretend to be. To ape. Simulate. **Syn : Ap-koro.**

Abe-kot, アベコツ, 爐、ロ・ *n.* The hearth. The bed of the fire.

Abe-mau, アベマウ, 火熱、カネツ・ *n.* Fire heat.

Abe-meri, アベメリ,

Abe-merimeri, アベメリメリ, 火花、ヒバナ・ *n.* Fire sparks.

Abe-miru, アベミル,

Abe-nep-koro humi-an-tashum, ア ベチプコロフミアンタシュム, 熱病、チ ツピャウ・ *n.* Fever. (Lit: the dis-

---

• There are three species of the Callionymus in Yezo.

ease which feels like fire). **Syn :
Sesekmau tashum.**

Abe-ni, アベニ, 薪、タキギ. *n.* Fire-
wood. **Syn : Abe-chikuni.**

Abe-ni, アベニ, エゾサンザシ、ヤチザ
クラ. *Cratægus chlorosarca, Max.*

Abe-nipek,
アベニペック, 火光、ヒノヒカリ. *n.*
Abe-nupek, Firelight.
アベヌペック,

Abe-nui, アベヌイ, 火焰、ホノホ、例セ
バ、アベヌイコテレケ、火ガ付ク. *n.* A
tongue of fire. A flame of fire.
As :—*Abe-nui kotereke,* "to catch
fire."

Abe-oi, アベオイ, 竃、カマド、爐、ロ.
n. A Fire-place. A Furnace.
Syn : Abe-sokot.

Abe-op, アベオブ, 火鉢、ヒバチ. *n.* A
Fire-box. A brasier.

Abe-o-usat, アベオウサッ, 熾ツテ居レ
炭. *n.* Live coals.

Abe-push, アベブシ, 火ガ跳ネル. *ph.*
The fire jumps.

Abe-sakunto, アベサクント, 偽造青銅
ニセカラカネ. *n.* A kind of spurious
bronze. Metal which has been
subjected to fire to give it the
colour of bronze ; usually an old
sword guard.

Abe-sam,
アベサム,
Abe-sami,
アベサミ. 爐邊. *n.* The hearth.
Abe-samu, The fire-side.
アベサム,
Abe-sham,
アベシャム,

Abe-sam-karabe, アベサムカラベ, ロ
セン、(灰ナラシ). *n.* A hearth-rake.
Syn : Abe-sam kara kirai.

Abe-sam kara kirai, アベサムカラ

キライ, ロセン、(灰ナラシ). *n.* A
hearth-rake.

Abesamta, アベサムタ, 爐邊ニ、ロバ
タニ. *adv.,* By the fire-side. As :
—*Abe samta an,* "it is by the
fire."

Abe-seseki,
アベセセキ, 火熱、ヒノネツ. *n.* Fire
Abeseseku, heat. **Syn : Sesek
アベセセク,** mau.

Abe-shinda, アベシンダ, 爐. *n.* A
Fire place.

Abe-shotki, アベシヨッキ, 爐ノ中、(火
チオク所). *n.* The very centre of
a fire bed. The particular place
in the centre of a fire in which the
fire goddess is supposed to dwell.

Abe-sokot, アベソコッ, 爐、ロ. *n.* A
furnace. A fire-place. **Syn : Abe
oi.**

Abe-usat, アベウサッ, 熱灰、アツイハイ
n. Hot cinders. As :—*Abe-o-usat,*
"living coals."

Abe-ututta, アベウツッタ, 爐ノ下坐郎
チ西端. *n.* The lower or western
end of a fire place.

Abi, アビ, 磨リ痕、スリキズ. *n.* A
place caused by rubbing.

Abo, アポ, 母、ハヽ、又ハ父、チヽ. (方言).
n. Mother in some districts and
Father in others. **Syn : Habo.**

Abu, アブ, 海氷、ウミノコホリ. *n.* Sea-
Apu, アブ, ice.

Acha, アチヤ, 小細ニ切ラレ、挽キ割
ラレル、例セバ、チエプアチヤオケレ、
魚切ラレタ. *v.i.* To be cut up into
fine pieces. To be sawn up as
wood. As :—*Chep acha okere,*
"the fish has been cut up."

Acha, アチヤ, 父、チヽ、叔父、チヂ、老
人、トショリ. *n.* An uncle. Father.
Also used as a term of respect

when addressing old men. **Syn:** **Achapo; achipo.**

Achapo, アチヤポ, 叔父、ヂヂ、父、チ チ、老人、トショリ. *n.* An uncle. See *acha.*

Achi, アチ, 熟シタル. *adj.* Cooked. Ripe.

Achi, アチ, 他ノ、外ノ. *adj.* Other. Strange. Belonging elsewhere.

Achi, アチ, アル(復數)・ *v.i.* Are. *Pl.* of *an* "to be."

Achike, アチケ, 陰門. The vagina. The word to be used by a physician is *chinuina-korobe.* **Syn: Chinu-nuke ambe.**

Achikka, アチッカ, 滴タル. *adj.* and *v.i.* To drop. Dropped as water. *v.t. chikka.*

Achikka, アチッカ, 神ニ捧酒スル禮. *n.* The ceremony of offering libations to the gods and ancestral spirits. **Syn: Icharapa an.**

Achikka an, アチッカアン, 神ニ捧酒ス ル禮ヲ爲スコト. *v.i.* To perform the *Achikka* ceremony.

Achiku ure, アチクルレ, Achiukurure, アチウクルレ, } 流レヲ塞ク、(河ナド). *v.t.* To obstruct the current of a river (as by logs of wood).

Achipiyere, アチビイェレ, 訴ラル、咎 ラレ. *v.i.* To be accused. To be reminded of one's faults.

Achipiyere guru, アチビエレグル, 私生子. *n.* A bastard. **Syn: Apiya. Achiye. Chiappise.**

Achipo, アチポ, 叔父、老人、父. *n.* Uncle. Father. An old man.

Achisei, アチセイ, 他ノ. *adj.* Other. Strange. Belonging elsewhere. Of another house. **Syn: Atchisei.**

Achisei un guru, アチセイウングル, 他ノ人、(單數). *n.* A stranger. A person of another house or village. **Syn: Achi-un-guru. Atchi-un-guru.**

Achisei un utara, アチセイウンウタ ラ, 他ノ人、(復數)・ *n.* Strangers, (pl: of *achisei un guru*).

Achiu, アチウ, 刺込ム、サシコム. *v.t.* To stick in. To drive in.

Achiukurure, アチウクルレ, Achikurure, アチクルレ, } 流レヲ塞ク、(河ナド ノ). *v.i.* To obstruct the current of a river (as by logs).

Achi-un-guru, アチウングル, 他人、(單數). *n.* A stranger.

Achi-un-utara, アチウンウタラ, 他人、(復數). *n.* Strangers.

Achiye, アチエ, 私生子・ *n.* A bastard. **Syn: Apiya. Chiappise.**

Ae, アエ, 食セラル. *v.i.* To be eaten. *Ae wa isam,* "it has been eaten up." The transitive form is *e,* "to eat."

Aeahupkarapo, アエアフッカラポ, 貰 ヒ子、モラヒコ. *n.* An adopted child. **Syn: Ahupkarapo.**

Aeankes, アエアンケス, 惡マル、. *v.i.* and *adj.* To be disliked. Hated. Despised. The transitive form is *Eankes.* **Syn: Etunne.**

Aearamuye, アエアラムイェ, 端折、ヘ ショル. *v.t.* To tie the clothes back as for walking or running. **Syn: Ayoaramuye.**

Aeatukopashbe, アエアツコバシュベ, Aeatukopashtep, アエアツコバシュテプ, } 吐キ出スモノ. *n.* Vomit. (Lit: "matter made to run forth by vomiting)."

Aeatup, アエアトゥプ, 吐キ出スモノ. *n.* Vomit.

Aechake, アエチャケ, 泥ダラケナル、汚レタル. *adj.* Muddy. Dirty. **Syn: Kapa.**

Aechakkep, アエチヤッケプ, 不潔ナルモノ. *n.* A dirty thing. Dirt. Anything repulsive.

Aechararase, アエチャララセ, 靜ニ進ミ行ク. *v.i.* To glide along. To slip along. To go along stealthily. To go along and leave a trail behind one as drops of water falling from a bucket. **Syn: Anechararase. Aeochararase.**

Aechikopoye, アエチコポエ, 擾亂サレタル、カキミダサレタル. *adj.* Mixed. Stirred up.

Aehababu, アエハババプ, **Aehapapu,** アエハパプ, 分ケ與フル. *v.i.* To be given out in small portions. As: *Amam aehapapu,* "to apportion food sparingly." **Syn: Aeyukke.**

Aehababuno, アエハババプノ, 吝ミテ. *adv.* Sparingly. In a sparing manner. **Syn: Aeyukke.**

Aehatatne, アエハタノ子, 無事ニ護ラレル、例セバ、カムイホサリアングスアエハタッチルエ子、神様ノ御助ケニテ無事ニ護ラルル. *v.i.* To be kept free from harm. As:—*Kamui hosari an gusu aehatatne ruwe ne,* "I have, by the providence of God, been kept free from harm."

Aehomatu, アエホマツ, 驚クベキ、驚カサレタル. *adj.* and *v.i.* Wonderful. Marvellous. Surprising. Extraordinary. To be surprised, startled, or frightened.

Aehoshipire, *(sing.),* アエホシピレ, **Aehoshippare,** *(pl.)* アエホシッパレ, 戻サレル、モドサル. *v.i.* To be sent back. To be returned.

Aehotke amip, アエホッケアミプ, 寝衣、ネマキ. *n.* Sleeping clothes. Night clothes.

Aehotkep, アエホッケプ, 寝間着、ネマキ. *n.* Same as *aehotke amip.*

Aehuye, アエフエ, 何々ナ……待ツ. *v.t.* To await. **Syn: Atere.**

Aeikapa, アエイカパ, 話ノ材料、ハナシノタネ, *n.* The matter or substance of a speech or lecture As:—*Upakuma aeikapa wa ye,* "give the matter of the address."

Aeikosamba, アエイコサムバ, 眞似タル、眞似ノ, *v.i.* and *adj.* Imitated. Like. **Syn: Aeyukara.**

Aeimau-anu, アエマウアヌ, 甚ダ怖ロシイ. *adj.* Very dreadful. (Lit: to have one's breath taken away).

Aeishiramnep, アエイシラムチプ, 必要ナル物, *n.* Needs. Wants. Necessities. **Syn: Kon rusuibe.**

Aeishokori, アエイショコリ, 信仰, *n.* Faith. Belief.

Aeishokorobe, アエイショコロベ, 信仰スルモノ、信經, *n.* Creed. What one believes.

Aeishungere, アエイシユンゲレ, 信ツラレヌ, *v.i.* To be disbelieved. To be treated as a lie.

Aeishungerep, アエイシユンゲレプ, 信ジラレヌ物. *n.* Disbelief. A thing disbelieved.

Aeiwange-eikapbe, アエイワンゲエアイカノベ, 無用ノ物、怠惰名, *n.* An idle fellow. A useless thing or person.

Aeiwange-ushike-isam, アエイワンゲウシケイサム,
Aeiwange-ushike-ka-isam, アエイワンゲウシケカイサム,
無用ナル、怠惰ナル・ *adj.* and *n.* Useless. Objects of no value.

Aeiyokunnure, アエイヨクンヌレ, 奇妙ナル、驚クベキ・ *v.i.* and *adj.* Wonderful. Marvellous. Surprising.

Aeiyokunnurep, アエイヨクンヌレプ, 奇妙ナモノ、驚クベキモノ・ *n.* Something wonderful. A marvellous thing.

Aeiyonnupba, アエイヨンヌプバ, 告發サレル・ *v.i.* To be accused of a crime. To be had up before a court.

Aeiyonnupba-guru, アエイヨンヌプバグル, 被告人・ *n.* A person accused of a crime. A person upon trial.

Aekap, アエカプ, 挨拶、アイサツ・ *n.* A greeting. A salute.

Aekatki, アエカッキ, 避ケル・ *v.t.* To avoid. **Syn:** Eshishi.

Aekatnu, アエカッヌ, 甘、ウマキ・ *adj.* Delicious. Nice. Pleasant. Pleasing to the taste.

Aekatnup, アエカッヌプ, 甘キモノ・ *n.* Anything pleasing to the taste.

Aekimatek, アエキマテク, 恐怖スル・ *v.i.* and *adj.* Afraid. Fearful. Struck with fear.

Aekimatekbe, アエキマテクベ, 恐怖スベキモノ・ *v.* A thing to be afraid of. A fearful thing.

Aekiroroan, アエキロロアン・ 面白キ、綺麗・ *adj.* Pleasant. Nice. Pretty. Interesting and pleasing to the sense of sight.

Aekiroroambe, アエキロロアムベ, 綺麗ナモノ、面白キモノ・ *n.* Anything pleasant, pretty, nice.

Aekiroro-an-i, アエキロロアンイ, 綺麗ナコト、面白キコト・ *n.* Pleasantness.

Aekiroro-anka, アエキロロアンカ, 喜バセル・ *v.t.* To interest. To please.

Aekosamba, アエコサムバ, 眞似タレ・ *v.i.* and *adj.* Imitaetd. **Syn:** Aeyukara.

Aekotekot, アエコテコツ, 氣絶シテ後生キル・ *v.i.* To faint away and revive. (Lit: "died and died ").

Aekoiki, アエコイキ, 叱カラレタ、打タレタ・ *adj.* Scolded. Smitten.

Aemaka, アエマカ, 暇ナダサレタ、棄テラレタ、(單數)・ *v.i.* and *adj.* To be cast off. Abandoned. Thrown away. Discharged.

Aemakap, アエマカプ, 投棄ラレタルモノ・ *n.* Refuse. Rubbish. Anything cast away.

Aemakatesu, アエマカテス, 外カラ中ノ内ニ曲ゲレ・ *v.i.* and *adj.* Turned up towards the inside from the outside.

Aemakba, アエマッバ, 投ゲ棄テラレタ、(複數)・ *v.i.* and *adj.* Cast off. *Pl:* of *aemaka.*

Aemakbap, アエマクバプ, 投棄ラレメモノ、(複數)・ *n.* Refuse. Rubbish. Waste. (*pl.*)

Aemarapto-kara, アエマラプトカラ, 何々……以テ響應ヲ設ケル、例セバ、ラメスケプアエマラプトカラ、野菜ト果實ヲ以テ響應ナスル・ *v.t.* To use in a feast. As:— *Rataskep aemarap-*

to *kara,* " to make a feast of vegetables, herbs, and fruits (with no meat or fish.)

Aemina, アエミナ, 笑ハル. *v.i.* and *adj.* To be laughed at. Ridiculed.

Aeiminap, アエィミナップ, 笑ハルベキモノ. *n.* An absurdity. A laughable thing.

Aemina-no, アエミナノ, 笑ハレベキ. *adj.* Absurdly. Laughably. Ridiculously.

Aen, アエン, 第一人稱、單數代名詞、我チ、例セバ、アエンキキ、私ハ打タレタ. *per. pro.* 1st per. sing. pass. voice or the obj. case, "I am." As:—*A-en-kik* "I am struck" (lit: " I was an object struck ").

Aeneusara, アエチウサラ, 喜バサル. *v.i.* To be pleased. Made glad. To be caused to rejoice.

Aeneusarabe, アエチウサラベ, 喜バシキ話. *n.* Pleasing stories. Gladdening news.

Aeninuibe, アエニヌイベ, 枕. *n.* A pillow. **Syn: Chieninuibe.**

Aenishte, アエニシテ, 制セラル. *v.i.* To be governed.

Aenishte, アエニシテ, 何々チ耐ヘ能フ. *v.i.* and *adj.* To be able to endure.

Aenkoisamka, アエンコイサムカ, 損スル. *v.t.* To suffer loss. To be made to lose as in a bargain.

Aenupetne, アエヌベッチ, 喜ブ. *v.i.* To be rejoiced over. To be pleased with.

Aenupetnere, アエヌベッチレ, 喜バセル. *v.i.* To be made to rejoice over. To be made pleased or happy.

Aenupurube, アエヌブルベ, 守護神、オマモリ. *n.* A charm used to keep off illness or bad luck. - **Syn: Chikashinninup, Aeshiship.**

Aenuwap, アエヌワプ, 分娩. *v.i.* and *n.* Birth.

Aenuwap-toho, アエヌワップトホ, 誕生日, *n.* A birth-day.

Aeochararase, アエオチヤララセ, 痕チ殘ス. *v.i.* To go along and leave an intermittent trail behind one as water dropped from a bucket. **Syn: Aechararase. Anechararase.**

Aeoichiure, アエオイチウレ, 交合. *v.i.* To have sexual intercourse.

Aeokbe, アエオッベ, 衣類チ乾ス竿. *n.* A towel horse.

Aeok-ushi, アエオッウシ, 着物. *n.* Clothing. **Syn: Amip.**

Aeoma, アエオマ,⎫ 傾ケル. *v.i.* To
Aioma, アイオマ,⎭ lean over. To bend over. **Syn: Eshir'eoma.**

Aeomare, アエオマレ, 對話スル. *v.t.* To hold intercourse with.

Aeomoshiroi, アエオモシロイ, 喜ブ. *v.i.* To be pleased with. To be delighted with. **Syn: Aenupetne.**

Aeomoshiroire, アエオモシロイレ, 喜バサレル. *v.i.* To be made pleased.

Aeoramsakka, アエオラムサッカ, 廢スル、止メル. *v.t.* To abolish. To make void. To bring to nothing. **Syn: Aepande.**

Aeoripak, アエオリパク, 怖ロシイ.
adj. Dread. Dreadful. **Syn:**
Ashitoma.

**Aeoshikpekarep, アエオシクベカ
レプ,** 目標、メジルシ. *n.* An object aimed at.

Aeoshirokbe, アエオシロクベ, 邪寛、
ジャマ. *n.* A hindrance.

Aeoshirokokbe, アエオシロコックベ,
邪寛、ジャマ. *n.* A hindrance. (Lit:
"something knocked against").

Aep, アエプ, 食物、ショクモツ、例セバ、
アエプケマン、饑饉. *n.* Food. As :—
Aep keman, "a scarcity of food";
aep nuye an, "an abundance of
food."

Aepakashnu, アエバカシヌ, 牧ヘラ
レタ. *adj.* Taught. Instructed.
Warned.

**Aepakashnu-wa-an, アエバカシヌ
ワアン,** 牧ヘラレタ、滅メラレタ. *adj.*
Taught. Instructed. Warned.

Aerange, アエバンゲ, 嫌ハレタ. *adj.*
Abominated. Hated. Disliked.
Syn: Aetunne. Aeangesh.

Aepange-i, アエバンゲイ, 憎悪、嫌ハ
レタコト. *n.* An abomination.
Hatred. Anything disliked. **Syn:**
Aetun-ne-i.

Aepangep, アエバンゲプ, 嫌ハレタモ
ノ. *n.* A thing hated. **Syn: Ae-
turnep.**

Aepante, アエバンテ, 無クスル. *v.t.*
To abolish. To bring to nothing.
(Lit: To make weak or "insipid.")
**Syn: Katchakte. Aeoram-
sakka.**

Aepanup, アエバヌプ, 女ノ朝于. *n.*
A woman's head dress. **Syn:**
Chipanup.

Aep-chari, アエプチヤリ, 食物ヲ粗末
ニスル. *v.t.* To waste food. Im-
providence in the matter of food.
Syn: Aepkoshini.

Aep-chari-guru, アエプチャリグル, 大
食家、タイショク. *n.* A glutton.
One who wastes food.

Aepekarep, アエベカプ, 目的、メア
テ. *n.* An object aimed at.

Aep-hapapu, アエプハパプ, 小食ナ
ル, *v.i.* To eat sparingly. To be
sparing in the matter of food.

Aep-itusare, アエップイツサレ, 食ヲ
施ス, *v.t.* To bestow food (as on
a beggar.)

**Aep-koibe-isam-guru, アエプコイベ
イサムグル,** 大食家、タイショク. *n.*
A glutton.

Aep-koshini-guru, アエプコシニグル,
速ク又ハ多量ニ食スル人. *n.* A fast
or wasteful eater. A great eater.
A glutton.

Aep-op, アエプオプ, 辨当、ベンタウ.
n. A food wallet.

Aep-rapapsep, アエプラパプセプ, 食
ベ残シ. *n.* Crumbs. Remnants of
food. (Lit: "Food dropped down).

Aepuntek, アエプンテク, 満足スル、喜
ブ, *v.i.* and *adj.* To be happy.
Contented. **Syn: Akopuntek.**

Aepusukara, アエプスカラ, 浮ブ、(例
セバ死魚ノ水面ニ浮ブガ如キナイフ).
v.i. To come to the top (as dead
fish to the surface of water).

Aeramasu, アエラマス, 喜ブ、ヨロコ
ブ. *v.t.* and *v.i.* To be pleased
with. To consider delightful, interesting, or admirable.

Aeramasu-i, アエラマスイ, 面白キ、オ
モシロキ. *adj.* and *n.* Interesting.
Of interest. Interest.

Aeramasu-nonno, アエラマスノン
ノ, 綺麗ナ者、キレイナモノ. *n.* A
handsome person (Lit: "an
admirable flower)."

Aeramchuptek, アエラムチュプテク,
災害ノ、ヲザハイノ. *adj.* Troubled.
Calamitous.

Aeramchuptekbe, アエラムチュプテ
クベ, 災害、ハザハイ. *n.* A calamity.

Aeramu-hokasush, アエラムホカスシュ,
or
Aeramu-hokasusu, アエラムホカスス,
不満足、フマン
ゾク. *adj.* and
v.i. To be
dissatisfied.

Aeramu-hopunini, アエラムホプニ
ニ, 情チ動ス. *v.i.* To have the
feelings stirred up.

Aeramu-nishte, アエラムニシュテ, 惨
酷ノ、ヒドイ. *adj.* Cruel. Hardhearted. As:—*Aeramu-nishte guru*, "a cruel person."

Aeramu-sarak, アエラムサラク, 心痛
スル. *v.i.* To be in trouble. To
be in adversity. To suffer mental
pain. To grieve. To be men-
tally agitated.

Aeramusarakbe, アエラムサラクベ,
心配. *n.* Trouble. Adversity.

Aeramu-sarakka, アエラムサラッカ,
心配サセル. *v.i.* and *adj.* Troubled.

Aeramu-shinne, アエラムシンチ, 満
足ニ思フ、決心シタ、例セバ、クキア
エラムシンチ、私モ成シテ 仕舞ツタ.
v.i. To be satisfied. To have
determined. Finished. As:—
Ku ki aeramu-shinne, "I have
finished doing it." This word
appears to carry the idea of
contentment in it sometimes and
as such equals the word *yaiyainuwere*.

Aeramushitne, アエラムシチ, 心配
シテ居ル. *adj.* Troubled. Comfort-
less. To be in pain.

Aeramu-usausak, アエラムウサウ
サク, 曖昧ナル、アイマイナル. *adj.*
Ambiguous. Confusing.

Aeramu-usausakka, アエラムウサ
ウサッカ, 瞞着セラレタ、ダマサレタ.
adj. and *v.i.* To be confused.
Syn : Eramu-kachipeutekka.

Aerannak, アエランナック, 無用、イラ
ナイ、障碍、ジヤマ. *v.i.* Not wanted.
To be a hindrance.

Aerannakbe, アエランナックベ, 無用
物、イラナイモノ、障阻物、ジヤマモノ.
n. A nuisance. A hindrance.
Something not wanted.

Aerannakka, アエランナッカ, 欲セヌ、
好マヌ. *v.t.* To dislike. To think
a nuisance.

Aeraratkire, アエララッキレ, 降サレ
タ、下サレタ. *v.i.* To be taken down.
To be lowered.

Aeratkip, アエラッキプ, 褌ノ端. *n.*
The ends of a loin cloth. **Syn :
Tepa.**

Aerayap, アエラヤップ, 美イ、賞讃スベ
キ. *adj.* Beautiful. Pleasant. Pleasing. Praiseworthy.

Aerayapka, アエラヤップカ, 美ク恩フ.
adj. and *v.i.* To be made to admire. To consider beautiful.

Aerikomare, アエリコマレ, 増大ス
ル. *v.t.* To augment. To enlarge.

Aerusaikari, アエルサイカリ, 待チ伏
セスレ、先チ領スル、豫メ圍カル. *v.t.*
To go to forestall. To forlay.
To surround or get round.

Aesaman, アエサマン, 冤法、マホフ.
n. Sorcery. **Syn : Niwok.**

Aesamanki, アエサマンキ, 寛法ヲ施ス. *v.i.* To practice sorcery. **Syn.: Niwokki.**

Aesanasapte, アエサナサプテ, 敬フヘキモノ. *n.* Something to be treated with reverence.

Aesanniyo, アエサンニヨ, 考ヘ定メラル、算敷セラル丶. *v.i.* To have settled or determined. To be treated as. To be reckoned up.

Aesanniyop, アエサンニヨプ, 精算書、考ヘ. *n.* An account. A thought. A consideration.

Aesapamuyep, アエサパムイェプ, 頭巾、ヅキン. *n.* A head-cloth.

Aeshinap, アエシナプ, 秘密、ヒミツ、隱クレタモノ. *n.* A secret. A hidden thing. Anything tied up so as to conceal it. A parcel.

Aeshikkoingara, アエシッコインガラ, 僞善スル. *adj.* and *v.i.* To act the hypocrite. **Syn : Shikoingarara.**

Aeshimoshmare, アエシモシュマレ, 知ラザル振リチスル. *v.t.* To ignore. To pretend not to know a person.

Aeshinnuye, アエシンヌエ, 記サレタ、錄サレタ. *v.i.* To be written. **Syn : Anuye.**

Aeshirikuran, アエシリクラン, 面白イ、可笑イ. *adj.* Comical. Funny.

Aeshiritomtomop, アエシリトムトモプ, 飾物、カザリモノ. *n.* A jewel. An ornament. **Syn : Aeyaitomtep.**

Aeshirun, アエシルン, 惡シキ. *adj.* Bad. Reprobate.

Aeshirun-guru, アエシルングル, 惡人. *n.* A bad person. A reprobate.

Aeshiship, アエシシプ, 守護、マモリ. *n.* A charm. **Syn : Aenupurube. Chiko-shinninup.**

Aeshitaigi, アエシタイギ, 叩ク、打ツ. *v.i.* To be beaten. Struck.

Aeshitchari, アエシッチヤリ, 散ッタ. *adj.* Scattered. Dispersed. **Syn : Chieshitchari.**

Aeshiyuk-amip, アエシユクアミプ,
Aeshiyuk-be, アエシユックベ, 晴着、ハレギ. *n.* The best clothes. The clothes worn at festivals.

Aeshopki-ainu, アエシヨプキアイヌ, 饗應ニ列ラナリシ人. *n.* Men sitting at a feast. **Syn : Aneshopki-ainu.**

Aetashumbe, アエタシユムベ, 病ノ原因. *n.* Any cause of illness.

Aeteshkara, アエテシユカラ, 雇ハル. *v.i.* To be sent on business. To be employed by another. To be sent for.

Aetomsam, アエトムサム, 身體、カラダ. *n.* The body. As :— *Ete un aetomsam kohosari yan,* " turn the body this way."

Aetoitap, アエトイタプ, 農產物、ヤクサンブツ. *n.* Garden produce. Things planted in the garden.

Aetoranne, アエトランネ, 能ハズ、例セバ、イベアイトランネ、食スルコト能ハズ. *v.i.* To be unable to do. Not liking to do. As :— *Ibe aetoranne,* " to be unable to eat." *Iki aetoranne,* " to be unable to do." *Mokoro poka iki aetoranne,* " I was even unable to sleep."

Aette, アエッテ, 與ヘタル. *v.i.* To be given. Sent. Handed over.

Aetunne, アエトゥンネ, 嫌忌サレタ. *v.i.* and *adj.* Abominated. Hated. Disliked. **Syn : Aepange. Akowen.**

Aetunne-i, アエトゥンチイ, 忌ムコト. *n.* Dislike. Hatred. Abomination. **Syn : Aepange-i.**

Aetunnep, アエトゥンチブ, 忌ムモノ. *n.* Abomination. A thing hated. **Syn : Aepangep.**

Aeuitaknup, アエウイタクヌブ, 誓約、タイヤク. *n.* A covenant. A promise.

Aeukote, アエウコテ, 結ビ合ハス. *v.i.* To be tied together.

Aeuminare, アエウミナレ, 喜バサレタ. *v.i.* (*pl.*) To be made to laugh. To be made pleased with. **Syn : Aenupetne.**

Aeunbe-ne, アエウンベ子, 天罰ニテ死ス. *v.i.* To die as a punishment for one's evil deeds.

Aeunupe-o,
アエウヌベオ,
Aeinupe-o,
アエイヌベオ,
for the dead. 葬儀ノトキノ饗應ノ食物. *n.* The food provided in feasts

Aeurammakka, アエウラムマッカ, 喜バサル. *v.i.* To be made happy with. To be pleased with. **Syn : Aenupetne.**

Aeurep, アエウレブ, 施與、ホドコシ. *n.* Alms. **Syn : Eungeraitep.**

Aeutonotoush, アエウトノトウシュ, 醉ハセル. *v.i.* To be affected by strong drink. To be drunk.

Aewangep, アエワンゲブ, 道具、ドウグ. *n.* Tools. Implements.

Aewangep-ushike-isam, アエワンゲブウシケイサム, 無用ナルモノ. *ph.* Useless. Abject.

Aewange-ushike-ka-isam, アエワンゲウシケカイサム, 無用ナレ. *ph.* Useless. Abject.

Aeyai-kamui, アエヤイカムイ, 祭ル神. *n.* The stronger and higher powers who are worshipped. The gods and demons who are supposed to be worthy of worship.

Aeyaikikip,
アエヤイキキブ,
Aeyaikikipbe,
アエヤイキキブベ,
dangerous thing. 危キモノ. *n.* Dangers. A

Aeyaikikip-i, アエヤイキキブイ, 危キコト. *n.* Danger. Dangerous places, events, or states.

Aeyaikikip-no, アエヤイ キキブノ, 危ウシ. *adv.* Dangerously. With danger.

Aeyaikikip-no-iki, アエヤイキキノブノイキ, 冒險、大膽ニ、例セバ、アエヤイキキノイキグル、大膽ナル人. *adv. ph:* Adventurously. In a dangerous manner. As:—*Aeyaikikip no iki guru*, "an adventurous person."

Aeyaikittaktaku, アエヤイキッタックタク, 欲スレド能ハズ. *v.i.* To desire to have, be or do, but yet not able to realize the wish. As:—*Nei guru naa shiknu kuni akon rusui koroka, tane aeyaikittaktaku wa an ambe ne ruwe ne,* "he desires to live longer but is unable."

Aeyainu,
アエヤイヌ,
Aeyanu,
アエヤヌ,
Aeyannu,
アエヤンヌ,
腐敗サレタ. *adj.* Spoiled.

Aeyaipishi-ambe,
アエヤイピシアンベ,
Aeyapushup,
アエヤプシュブ,
knowledgement. Things one confesses. 皆白、イヒアラハシ. *n.* A confession. Ac-

**Aeyairamattep, アエヤイ ラマッテ
ブ**, 目的、モクテキ. *n.* Anything
aimed at. **Syn : Aeoshikpekarep.**

**Aeyairamokotep, アエヤイ ラモコテ
ブ**, 道具. *n.* Tools. Implements.
Utensils.

**Aeyaisambepokashterep, アエヤイ
サムベポカシテレッブ**, 憫レナルモノ.
n. A pitiable or miserable object.

**Aeyairamshitne, アエライ ラムシツ
子**, 困ラセル. *v.i.* To suffer.

**Aeyairamshitnere, アエヤイ ラムシ
ツチレ**, 人チ困マラセル. *v.t.* To
make suffer.

Aeyaitomtep, アエヤイトムテブ, 人
ノ飾リニスルモノ. *n.* Personal ornaments. **Syn : Aeshiritomo-
tomop.**

**Aeyaiyattasa-kunip, アエヤイヤッ
タサクニブ**, 供物、ソナヘモノ. *n.* A
return present. A gift given in
acknowledgement of some favour.
A sacrifice. An offering to a god
or to the names of the dead.

**Aeyaiyattasap, アエヤイヤッタサ
ブ**, 供物、ソナヘモノ. *n.* A sacrifice.
Syn : Aeyaiyattasa-kunip.

**Aeyaiyukki, アエヤイユッキ,
Aeyaiyupki, アエヤイユッキ,**
定期川ノ為ニ備フル
モノ. *v. i.* Set
apart for some
special purpose.

Aeyam, アエヤム, 大切ニ思フ. *v.t.* To
take care of. To treat as of
importance. **Syn : Aehatatne.**

Aeyam, アエヤム, 大切ナル. *adj.* Important. Of consequence.

Aeyambe, アエヤムベ, 大切ナルモノ. *n.*
A thing of importance. A thing
to be taken care of.

Aeyam-no, アエヤムノ, 大切ニ. *adv.*
With care. Carefully.

**Aeyannu, アエヤンヌ,
Aeyainu, アエヤイヌ,** 害ハレタ. *v.i.* Spoiled.

**Aeyapte, アエヤプテ,
Aeyayapte, アエヤヤプテ,** 為スコトチ好マヌ、例
セバ、アエヤヤプテ
グスショモカラ、好
マヌユエ為サヌ. *adj.* and *v.i.* Disinclined to do a thing. Inex-
perienced. Not to like doing.
As :—*Aeyayapte gusu shomo kara,*
"he did not do it because he
disliked it." *Ki kuni aeyayapte,*
"he would not do it." **Syn :
Aniugesh.**

Aeyopanerep, アエヨパチレッブ, 外套.
n. A coat. **Syn : Ashkakamurep.**

Aeyukara, アエユカラ, 眞似ラレタ.
adj. and *v.i.* Like. Imitated. **Syn :
Aeikosamba.**

Aeyukke, アエユッケ, 分ケ與ヘル、少
シク與ヘル、節約スル、例セバ、チイア
マムアエユブケロエイワンゲヤン、節
約ニ食物チ用キテクレ. *v.t.* To give
out anything a little at a time.
To portion out. To use sparingly. To use with care. As :—
*Nei amam aeyupke wa eiwange
yan,* "use the food with care."

Aeyukke-no, アエユッケノ, 節約シ
テ.例セバ、アエユッケノアンクニブチ、
注意シテ川キベキモノナリ. *adv.* Spa-
ringly. Grudgingly. In a sparing manner. With care. Carefully. *Aeyukke no an kunip ne,*
"it is a thing to be used carefully." **Syn : Aehabapu.**

Afuraye, アフラエ, 洗濯セラレタ. *v.i.*
and *adj.* Washed. To be washed.

Afuraye-ambe, アフラエアムベ, 洗フ
コト. *n.* Ablutions. A washing.
Things washed.

Afuraye-i, アフラエイ, 洗ヒ. *n.* Ablutions. A washing.

Afurayep, アブライェブ, 洗ツタモノ. *n.* Things washed.

Aha, アハ, キンマメ、ヤブマメ. *n.* The hog-peanut. *Amphicarpœa Edgeworthii, Benth.* var. *japonica, Oliver. Aha* is applied to both the nut and vine though more properly *aha* is the nut and *ahara* the vine. **Syn : Eha.**

Ahacha, アハチヤ, キンマメノハナ. *n.* The flower and pod of the hog-peanut.

Ahara, アハラ, キンマメノクキ. *n.* The vine of the hog-peanut.

Aheshui, アヘシユイ, 坐眠スル、井子ムリスル. *v.i.* To sleep in a sitting posture. **Syn : Aeshuiba.**

Ahekote, アヘコテ, 結バレタ. *adj.* Tied up. Possessed.

Aekoteguru, アエコテグル, 夫、オツト. *n.* One's husband.

Aekote-nishpa, アエコテニシパ, 主人、天子、王. *n.* Master. King. Emperor.

Ahi, アヒ, 此ノ字ハ awa ト同シ、在ツテ. *part.* Same as a-i. Being. **Syn : Wa.**

Ahonnokka, アホンノッカ, 馴ラス. *v.t.* To tame.

Ahori-pet, アホリベツ, 堀割、ホリワリ. *n.* A canal.

Ahui, アフイ, Ahun-i, アフンイ, 入口、入ルコト. *n.* An entrance. An entering in. As:—*Ahui shiri soyui shiri shomo anukara,* "I neither saw him going in nor coming out."

Ahun, アフン, 入ル(單數)、例セバ、チセイオルンアレン、内ニ這入ル. *v.i.* (*sing*). To enter. To go in. As:—*Chisei orun ahun,* "to enter a house." The plural form is *ahup.*

Ahun-apa, アフンアパ, 内ノ戸. *n.* An inner doorway. **Syn : Ahunturupa.**

Ahun-chuppok, アフンチェツポク, 西ノ方. *n.* The west. **Syn : Moshirigesh. Moshiri-pok. Chup-pok.**

Ahunde, アフンデ, Ahunge, アフンゲ, 入レル(單數). *v.t.* (*sing*). To put in. To bring in. To admit.

Ahunge-i, アフンゲイ, 入レルコト(單數). *n.* A bringing in. Admittance.

Ahungere, アフンゲレ, 入レサセル(單數). *v.t.* To send in through another. To cause another to admit.

Ahun-i, アフンイ, 入口、入ルコト. *n.* An entrance. A place of access. **Syn : Ahun-ushike.**

Ahunka, アフンカ, 布ノヌキ糸. *n.* The woof of cloth. The threads which run across cloth. As:—*Attush oro ahunka omare,* "to put the woof into cloth."

Ahunka-nit, アフンカニ, 糸卷キ、例セバ、アフンカニツオロイヨ、糸卷ニ糸ヲ卷ク. *n.* A spool used in weaving. As:—*Ahunka-nit oro iyo,* "to wind thread on a weaving-spool."

Ahun-mindara, アフンミンダラ, 中敷、土間. *n.* A small bare place just inside a hut upon which to leave one's foot-gear when entering. **Syn : Rutom.**

Ahunpara. アフンパラ, 地獄ノ入口. n. The entrance to hades.

Ahun-pururugep, アフンプルルゲプ, 家ニ吹キ込ミシ雨雪塵ノ如キモノ. n. Snow, rain or dust blown into a house by the wind.

Ahunrasambe, アフンラサムベ, 梟、フクロウ. n. An owl of any kind.

Ahun-tonchi-kama-ni, アフントンチカマニ, 戸ノ塵、トノズリ. n. A door-sill.

Ahun-turupa, アフンツルパ, 内ノ戸. n. An inner-doorway. **Syn: Ahunapa.**

Ahun-ushike, アフンウシケ, 入口, n. An entrance. A place of entering in. **Syn: Ahun-i.**

Ahup, アフプ, 入ル(複數). v.i. To enter (pl).

Ahupkara, アフプカラ, 貰フ、例セバ、マチアフプカラ、妻チ貰フ. v.t. To receive. To accept. To marry. As:—Amip ahupkara, "to receive some clothes." Machi ahupkara, "to take a wife."

Ahupkarabe, アフプカラベ, 貰ヒ物, n. Something received. A present.

Ahupkara-guru, アフプカラグル, 乞兒、物チ貰フ人、コヤキ. n. A recipient. A beggar. **Syn: Iyahupkara-guru.**

Ahupkara-po, アフプカラポ, 貰兒、モライコ. n. An adopted child.

Ahupte, アフプテ, 入レル(複數). v.t. (pl). To send in. To put in. To bring in. To admit.

Ahupte-i, アフプテイ, 入レルコト, n. An admittance. A bringing in.

Ahuptere, アフプテレ, 入レサセル(複數). v.t. To send in by another (pl).

Ahuptere-i, アフプテレイ, 他人ニ入レサセルコ. n. A sending or bringing in by another.

Ai, アイ, 河ノ細支流. n. A tributary of a river.

Ai, アイ, 刺、トゲ. n. Thorns of plants.

Ai, アイ, 矢、例セバ、アイラプ、矢ノ羽根. n. An arrow. As:—Ai-rap, "feathers of arrow shafts." Ai-rum, "an arrow-head."

A-i, アイ, A-hi, アヒ, } 此ノ字ハ AWA ト同シ、在リテ. part. This particle is a kind of past tense factor equalling "did," "was." As:— Shomo ene ku inu kuni ku ramu ahi, tan orushpe ku nu, "I did not expect to hear such news as this I have now heard." A-hi is in some instances interchangeable with awa. **Syn: an.**

A-i, アイ, A-hi, アヒ, } 此ノ字ハ順序又ハ時刻チ指スモノナリ. part. Sometimes this particle is used as an adverb of time. As:—Ki kusu ne a-i, "the time it ought to be done." Tane ku oman kuni a-i epa ruwe ne, "It is now time for me to go."

Aiai, アイアイ, 嬰兒、赤子、アカゴ. n. A baby. An infant.

Aiai-iyomap, Same as Aiai-o-umbe.

Aiainukoro, アイアイヌコロ, 満足ニ思フ. v.i. To be contented. **Syn: Yaiyainuwere. Yaiyainukoro.**

Aiai-o-umbe, アイアイオウムベ, 兒守カ兒チ負フトキ背ノ上ニ兒チ垂セシムル木. n. A piece of wood tied to a sling used for carrying children. The sling itself is called *pakkai-tara.*

Aibashi-kene-ni, アイバシケチ二, ハナヒリノキ. *n.* *Leucothoe Grayana.* *Max.*

Aibe, アイベ, 鮑、(樺太アイヌ二テ蝎蚌). *n.* The sea-ear. *Haliotis tuberculata.* Among the Saghalin Ainu *aibe* is "oyster;" so also is *Piba.*

Aibep, アイベプ, 食器. *n.* Eating utensils such as cups, plates, spoons and chopsticks.

Aichinka, アイチンカ, 矢ノ部分ヲ結ブ絲. *n.* Bark thread used for tying the different parts of arrows together.

Ai-chiure, アイチウレ, 矢ノ根二付ケル骨. *n.* The "foot" or bone head of an arrow to which the arrow point is fixed.

Aichoko-ibe, アイチヨコイベ, **Aichikor-ibe, アイチコ.イベ,** } アカエイ. *n.* Stingray. *Dasyatis akajei, M. & H.* **Syn : Aikot-chep.**

Aieninui, アイエ二ヌイ, 臥ス、伏ス. *v.i.* To lie down to rest. To lie down to sleep.

Aieninuibe, アイエ二ヌイベ, 枕、マクラ. *n.* A pillow. **Syn : Aininuibe. Chieninuibe.**

Ai-epishki, アイエピシキ, 射ル、矢ヲ以テ撃ツ. *v.t.* To shoot at with arrows.

Aige, アイゲ, ナガラ、其後、例セバ、オマンアイゲシ、ツチヤキルエ子、歩キナガラ獣ヲ唱フ. *post.* As. Thereupon. And so. As :—*Oman aige shinotchaki ruwe ne,* "he sings as he goes along." *Nei orushpe ku ye, aige, utara obitta en emina nisa*

ruwe ne. "I told the news, whereupon the people all laughed at me."

Aihatatne, アイハタッチ, 看護セラレル. *v.i.* To be taken care of (as a person). **Syn : Aehatatne.**

Aikakushte-amip, アイカクシテアミブ, 外套、上着, *n.* An overcoat.

Ai-kanchi, アイカンチ, 矢筈、ヤハズ. *n.* A notch in the end of an arrow for the bow-string.

Aikannit, アイカン二ツ, 矢ノ根二付ク骨. *n.* The bone part of an arrow.

Aikap, アイカブ, 能ハズ. *v.i.* and *adj.* To be unable. Awkward. Unskilful. **Syn : Appene.**

Aikap, アイカブ, ホタテガイ. *n.* The pecten.

Aikap-sama, アイカブサマ, 右ノ方. *adv.* On the left hand side. With the left hand. Sometimes an awkward person.

Aikap-sei, アイカブセイ, エゾ二シキ. *n.* A pecten shell. *Pecten lactus Gould.*

Aikarakara, アイカラカラ, 仕上レ、出来上ル. *v.i.* Finished. Done. Also "to do."

Aikarip, アイカリブ, スノキ, *n.* *Vaccinium hirtum, Th.*

Aikashup-ni, アイカシュブ二, イヌッゲ. *n.* *Ibex crenata, Th.*

Aikne, アイク子, 二分シタ、例セバ、アイクチツエ、二ツ二切ル. *adv.* Asunder. In two. As :—*Aikne tuye,* "to cut in two;" "to separate joint from joint."

Aikoikarabe, アイコイカラベ, 見本、手本. *n.* An example. A copy. Something to be imitated.

Aikoisamba, アイコイサムバ, 眞似ラ
レタ. *v.i.* and *adj.* Like. Imitated.

Aikoisambap アイコイサムバプ, 眞
似ラレタモノ. *n.* Something imitated.

Aikorep, アイコレプ, 贈物、賜物、オク
リモノ. *n.* A present. A gift.

**Aikosama,
アイコサマ,**
Aikosama, 眞似スル. *v.t.* To im-
アイコサムバ, itate.
**Anikosamba,
アニコサムバ,**

Aikoshi, アイコシ, 渡ス. *v.t.* To betray. **Syn: Ekoshi.**

Aikot-chep, アイコツチェプ, アカエイ.
n. Sting ray. *Dasyatis akajei,*
M. & H. **Syn : Aichokoibe.**

Aikup, アイクプ, 飲ミ器. *n.* Drinking utensils.

Aikushte-amip, アイクシテアミプ,
上着. *n.* A coat. An outer garment.

Aimakanit, アイマカニト, 矢ノ根ニ
付ク骨. *n.* The bone part of an
arrow to which the head is attached.

Aimokirika, アイモキリカ, 無情、憐
レナル. *adj.* Miserable. Abject.

**Aimokirika-shukup, アイモキリカ
シュクプ,** 不憫ナル生活. *v.i.* To live
in a very miserable fashion. To
live miserably.

Aina-ni, アイナニ, ヘニバナ、ヘクタ
ボク. *n. Lonicera Maximowiczi,*
Rupr.

Ainan-pone, アイナンポ子, 脛骨、胞
骨、ニノウデ. The shin-bone. The
bone between the elbow and wrist.

Aine, アイ子, 其處、其後、其時、例セバ、
ラムオトクリホツヱカラ、アイ子エセ

サルエ子、長イ間呼ンデ漸ク應ヘタ.
post. Thereupon. After a while.
Hardly. Upon which. At last.
As:—*Ramneto ku hotuyekara, aine,*
ese nisa ruwe ne. "I called him
for a very long time and at last
he answered."

A-ine, 此字ハ時トシテ過去ヲ示ス
アイ千, 語ナリ. *part.* This
A-hine, particle indicates the
アヒ千, past or perfect tense. As:—*Tap*
seenne otta ku apkash kuni ku ra-
mu a-ine koroka tap ku apkash
nisa ruwe ne. "I did not expect
to walk thus far yet I have come
here."

Ai-kot-chep, アイコットチェプ, アカエ
ヒ. *n.* Stingray. *Dasyatis akajei.*
(*M. and H.*)

Aininuibe, アイニヌイベ, 枕、マクラ.
n. A pillow. **Syn : Chiennuibe.**
Aieninuibe.

Ainu, アイヌ, 人、人間、友、父、夫、アイヌ
ト云フ人種. *n.* Man. A man. The
race of people called *Ainu*. Com-
rade. Father. Husband.

Ainu-ataye, アイヌアタイェ, 殺人ノ罰
金. *n.* A fine for murder. **Syn :**
Kewe-tak.

Ainu-bata, アイヌバタ, 悲哀ノ辭、カ
ナシイカナ、ホシイナー, *exol :* Ah
me! Expression of desire and dis-
sappointment.

Ainu-buri, アイヌブリ, 人ノ習慣. *n.*
The habits or customs of man in
general or of the Ainu in particular.

Ainu-ep, アイヌエプ, 化物、バケモノ、
怪物. *n.* A hobgoblin (supposed to
walk backwards.)

Ainu-eshpa, アイヌエシバ, 人ヲ知ラサル爲ネフ. *v.i.* To ignore a person.

Ainu-ikiri, アイヌイキリ, 人ノ時代、多クノ人. *n.* An age; A generation. A crowd of men.

Ainu-ikiri-ka-oma-buri, アイヌイキリカオマブリ, 原罪. *n.* Original sin.

Ainu-katu-ehange, アイヌカツエハンゲ, 死ニ近キ. *ph.* To be near dying (Lit:—Nearing a person's form). **Syn: Rai-etokooiki.**

Ainu-kina, アイヌキナ, ヤブタバコ, *n. Carpesium abrotanoides, L.*

Ainu-kirikuru, アイヌキリクル, 人ヲ笑フ、嘗レ. *v.t.* To mock. To make fun of. To laugh at a person. **Syn: Eoya-itak.**

Ainu-koapkash, アイヌコアブカシ, 姦淫. *v.i.* A woman to commit adultery with a man.

Ainu-koiwak, アイヌコイワク, 通フ (結婚ノ目的ヲ以テ男ノ家ニ), *v.i.* To visit one's husband. To pay attentions with a view to marriage. To visit one's intended or spouse.

Ainukoro, アイヌコロ, 敬フ. *v.t.* To reverence. To honour. To treat with respect.

Ainu-kut, アイヌクツ, 人ノ咽喉. *n.* A man's throat.

Ainu-kutoro-humi, アイヌクトロフミ, 談話ノォト. *n.* The sound of men talking.

Ainu-kuwa, アイヌクワ, 男ノ墓標. *n.* A man's grave mark.

Ainu-moshiri, アイヌモシリ, アイヌノ住ム國. *n.* Ainu-land. **Syn: Ya-un-moshiri.**

Ainu-muk, アイヌムク, ヤキノゲジ. *n. Lactuca squarrosa, Miq.*

Ainu-noka, アイヌノカ, 人ノ寫眞. *n.* The photo of a human being. A picture as a man. **Syn: Ainu-nokaha.**

Ainu-rak-guru, アイヌラッグル, アイヌノ元ノ名. *n.* Said by some ainu to be the ancient name of this race. **Syn: Aioina-rak-guru.**

Ainu-san-i,
アイヌサニ,
Ainu-sanikiri,
アイヌサニキリ, } アイヌノ子孫. *n.* Ainu posterity. Of ainu descent.
Ainu-santek,
アイヌサンテク,

Ainu-sat-chiri, アイヌサッチリ, カハテフ、ヤマセミ. *n.* A kind of large grey kingfisher. Oriental spotted kingfisher. *Ceryle guttata (Vigors).*

Ainu-shikashishte, アイヌシカシシテ, 人ヲ無頓着ニ扱フ. *v.t.* To treat people with indifference.

Ainu-shikashishte-guru, アイヌシカシシテグル, 人ヲ知ラザルフリスル人, *n.* One who treats others with indifference.

Ainu-shitchiri, アイヌシッチリ, 鳥ノ名. *n.* The same as *Ainu-satchiri.*

Ainushkare-no, アイヌシカレノ, 驚クベク. *adv.* Wonderously.

Ainu-shut, アイヌシュツ, アイヌノ先祖. *n.* The Ainu ancestors. **Syn: Ainu-ekashi.**

Ainu-topa,
アイヌトバ,
Ainu-topaha, } アイヌノ集會、群衆ノ人. *n.* A crowd of men. An assembly of people.
アイヌトバハ,

Ainu-topake, アイヌトパケ, 酋長. *n.*
A chief. Captain. Leader.

Ainu-tukap, アイヌツカブ, 幽靈. *n.*
A ghost. The manes of the dead
(supposed to be of a white colour).

Ainu-utor-humi, アイヌウトルフミ,
人ノ歩ム音. *n.* The sound of men
walking. **Syn: Apkash utor'-
humi.**

Ai-o, アイオ, 刺アル. *adj.* Thorny.
Syn: Aiush.

Aioina-kamui, アイオイナカムイ, ア
イヌノ先祖ノ名. The name of the
ancestor of the Ainu.

Aioma,
アイオマ, 凭レカカレ. *v.i.* To lean
Aeoma, over.
アエオマ,

Aioro, airo, ayoro, アイロ, スズキ.
n. Lateolabrap japonicus. (*T. & S.*)
Syn: Shimechike. Shunchike.

Aipone, アイボ子, 股骨, モモホネ. *n.*
The thigh bones.

**Aipone-tanne-guru, アイボ子タン
子グル,** 長ケ高キ人. *n.* A tall person.

Aiporo-sak, アイボロサク, 慚愧ナレ、
ハヅカシキ. *adj.* To be ashamed.
Syn: Iporohachiri.

Aiporo-sakka, アイボロサッカ, 愧カ
シムレ. *v.t.* To make ashamed.

**Airamkatchaushka, アイラムカッチ
ヤウシカ,** 或事ヲ侭サヌヤウニ勧メラ
レタ. *adj.* and *v.i.* To have been
dissuaded from something.

Airamye, アイラムイェ, 譽ムベキ、崇ム
ベキ. *adj.* and *v.i.* Adorable.
Adored. Praised.

Airap-kina, アイラブキナ, クサソテ
ツ、コ、ミ、(方言). *n.* The fertile
fronds of the basket-fern or *Onoclea germanica, Willd.*

Airu, アイル, 有ル、感ズル、音スル. *v.i.*
To be. To feel. To sound. As:—
Chikuikui ap-koro humi airu an,
"I feel as though I was being
nibbled."

Aisa, アイサ, 海鳥ノ類. *n.* A kind
of bird of the duck species having
a tuft of feathers on its head.

**Aisarakka-kamni, アイサラッカカ
ムニ,** 過ツテ矢チ以テ打タルヽコト、過
ツテ矢ニ當ル事. *n.* A being ac-
cidentally shot by arrows.

Aiseisekka, アイセイセッカ, 溫メル、
熱セラル. *v.i.* To be heated.
Madehot.

Aishikikiri, アイシキキリ, 矢ノ根ノ穴.
n. The eye in the end of an
arrow head in which the shaft is
fixed.

Aishikoshirepa, アイシコシレバ, 到
着シタ. *v.i.* (*pl*). To have arrived
at a place.

Aishiri-ekot, アイシリエコツ, 死ス
ル. *v.i.* To die.

**Aishirubare-guru, アイシルバレグ
ル,** 狂人、惡鬼ニ付カレタル. *n.* A
maniac. A person possessed by
the devil.

Aishitomare, アイシトマレ, 畏ロシ
イ、囂々シイ. *v.i.* and *adj.* Dreadful. Noisy. Said to noisy children.

Aishumam, アイシュマム, 粟ノ類. *n.*
A kind of millet.

Ai-shup, アイシュブ, 矢ニ用ユル篠. *n.*
The reed shaft of an arrow.

Aitakepishte, アイタケピシテ, 樣
言スル、クリゴトスル. *v.i.* To re-
peat one's self. To be voluble.
Loquacious.

Aitakepishtep, アイタケピシテブ,
樣言、クリゴト. *n.* A heap of words.

Loquacity. As :—*Tapan tu itak re itak aitakepishtep nekon a ambe ne ruwe ta an?* "what means this great heaping up of words"?

Aitam-niukeshte, アイタムニウケシテ, 刀チ以テ禦ク. *v.i.* To defend with a sword. To render difficult by means of a sword.

Aitek, アイテク, 遣ラル、雇ハレ、. *v.i.* To be sent. To be employed by another. **Syn : Auitek.**

Aituyere, アイツイェレ, マデニ往ク、取ラル、切リ割ラル、. *v.i.* To go as far as. To be taken. To be cut off.

Ai-ush, アイウシ, 刺アル. *adj.* Thorny. **Syn : Ai-o.**

Aiush-kuttara, アイウシクッタラ, アザミノ類. *n.* A thistle. **Syn : Antsami.** *Cnicus sp.*

Ai-ush-ni, アイウシニ, ハリギリ. *Acanthopanax ricinifolium.*

Ai-ush-samambe, アイシサマムベ, サソカレイ. *n. Ceidoderma asperinnus,* (*T. & S.*)

Aiush-top, アイウシトプ, タマザ、. *n. Arundinaria panicueata, Fr. et Sav.*

Aiwak, アイワク, 放棄セラル、埋ラル. *v.i.* To be cast away. Buried. To return from one's work.

Aiwak-gusu-atere, アイワクグスアテレ, 待ツ. *v.t.* To await.

Aiwakte, アイワクテ, 放棄スル、埋ル、埋葬スル. *v.t.* To bury the dead. To throw away.

Aiyo, アイヨ, 充満スル、例セバ、ネイウツルアイヨワエンコレ、何卒其ノ間チ充タセヨ. *v.t.* To fill up. As :— *Nei uturu aiyo wa en kore,* "please fill up the spaces."

Aiyo, アイヨ, Aoko, アオコ, 縫箔. *n.* Pieces of material let into garments for ornament. As : — *Aiyo ekara,* "to ornament a dress."

Aiyoitakushi, アイヨイタクシ, Aiyoitakshi, アイヨイタッシ, 詛ハレタル. *adj.* and *v.i.* To be accursed. Cursed.

Aiyonitasare, アイヨニタサレス, 改名. *v.i.* To change one's name.

Aiyonitasare-rehei, アイヨニタサレレヘイ, Auoniutasare-rehei, アウオニウタサレレヘイ, 改名. *n.* An alias.

Aiyunin, アイユニン, 苦痛アル、クツウアル. *v.i.* and *adj.* To be in great bodily pain. To be in distress.

Ak, アク, 弟、ナトチト. *n.* A younger brother. **Syn : Aki. Akihi.**

Ak, アク, 射ル. *v.i.* To shoot with an arrow.

Aka, アカ, 水. *n.* Water. **Syn : Wakka.**

Akakoro, アカコロ, 甚多、頗多. *adv.* Very many. **Syn : Poronno.**

Akakotare, アカコタレ, 開ク、分ケル. *v.t.* To open. To divide.

Akam, アカム, 指環、ユビワ. *n.* A ring.

Akam, アカム, ウバユリチ以テ造リシ圓キ菓子. *n.* A round cake usually made of arrow-root and having a hole in the centre.

Akam, アカム, ゴツコ. *n.* The sea-snail.

Akama, アカマ, 見落ス、過ギ越ス. *v.t.* To drop out (as a word in a sentence). To jump over. To pass over.

Akamkoreumbe, アカムコレウムベ, 魚名. *n.* Same as *Akamkotchep.*

Akamkotchep, アカムコツチェブ, ゴ
ツコ. *n. Liparis Agassizii, Put-
num.* Seasnail.

Akam-saye, アカムサイェ, 過卷ク、ウ
ブマク. *v.i.* To be coiled up in
rings as snakes are sometimes
found doing.

**Akam-ukopoyebe, アカムウコポイェ
ベ,** 筥、ヘラ. *n.* A stick used for
stirring the pot when arrow-root
cakes are being boiled.

Akamure, アカムレ, 蔽ハル. *v.i.* To
be covered up.

Akan, アカン, 造ラレタ. *v.i.* To be
made. Done. *Same as akara.*

A-kane, アカチ, 坐シテ. *part.:* Sitting. To be in a sitting posture.

Akaparaka, アカパラカ, 有漏抜、ウ
ロヌク. *v.t.* To thin out. **Syn:**
Akapare.

Akara, アカラ, 造ラレタレ. *v.i.* To be
made. To have finished doing a
thing.

Akara-eashkai, アカラエアシカイ,
出來能フ. *adj.* Achievable. Able
to be done.

Akarakara, アカラカラ, 給ス、縫スル.
v.t. To do. To do fancy needlework.

Akarakarape, アカラカラベ, 縫箔.
n. Fancy needle-work. **Syn:**
Chikarakarabe.

Akari, アカリ, 出來事. *n.* A thing
done. An action performed. The
way to perform an action.

Akaru, アカル, 出來事. *Same as a-
kari.*

Aka-san-nai, アカサンナイ, 水ノア
ル谷. *n.* A valley with water in
it.

Akashi, アカシ, チョット當タル. *v.t.*
To hit slightly.

A-kasu, アカス, 餘リ多ク. *adj.* Too
much. Too many.

Akatchiu, アカッチウ, 刺サレタル、刺
サル. *v.i.* and *adj.* To be stuck.
Pierced.

Akatchiu-guru, アカッチウグル, 愛
ラシカラヌ人. *n.* An unamiable
person. One who cannot be tru-
sted.

Akateomare, アカテオマレ, 愛密ア
ル. *adj.* Amiable. Loveable.

Aka-ush, アカウシ, 水ダラケ. *adj.*
Containing water. Watery. **Syn:**
Wakka-ush.

Akbe, アクベ, 陷穴、罠、ワナ. *n.* A
trap. A rat trap. (This is really
a spring-bow which is often set
in the trail of the larger animals
or in the runs of rats). **Syn:**
Akku.

Akbe-imok, アクベイモク, 罠ノ餌、例
セバ、アクベイモクオマレ、罠ニ餌ヲ設
ク. *n.* A trap bait. As :—*Akbe
imok omare* or *Akbe imok unu,*
"to bait a trap."

Akbe-ande, アクベアンデ, 罠ヲ掛ル.
v.i. To set a trap.

Akbe-imok, アクベイモク, 罠ノ餌. *n.*
A trap bait.

Akbe-shuat, アクベシュアツ, 罠ニ餌ヲ
付ケル器ノ名. *n.* The wood catch
placed in a trap to loosen that
portion of wood which sets the
bow-string free.

Akbe-yokore, アクベヨコレ, 罠ヲ掛
ル. *v.i.* To set a trap.

Akem-karabe, アケムカラベ, 針仕事.
n. Needle-work.

Akerekeri, アケレケリ, 削ラレル. *v.i.* and *adj.* To be scraped.

Akes, アケス, 屑、西ノ方. *n.* Dregs. The western end of a place or thing. The lower end of a place or thing. **Syn: Keshi. Kes. Kesh.**

Akesoro, アケソロ, 小屋ノ西方ノ入口ニ. *adv.* At the entrance or lower end of a hut.

Akes-un, アケスウン, 小屋ノ西方ノ入口ニ. *adv. Same as Akesoro.*

Akeure, アケウレ, 削ラレタル. *adj.* Hewn. Planed.

Aki, アキ,
Akihi, アキヒ, 弟. *n.* A younger brother.
Akpo, アッポ,

Aki, アキ, 出來タル. *v.i.* and *adj.* Done. Finished.

Akianchi, アキアンチ, 鮭、サケ. *n.* Ssalmon. **Syn: Shibe. Kamui chep.** (*Jap.*)

Aki-eashkai, アキエアシカイ, 出來ル. *adj.* Achievable. Can be done.

Akihi, アキヒ,
Aki, アキ, 弟. *n.* A younger brother.
Ak, アク,

Akihi-utara, アキヒウタラ, 弟等. *n.* Younger brothers.

Akimokkara, アキモッカラ, 出先ニテ變死ス. *v.i.* To be killed away from one's home as by accident.

Akka,
アッカ, 然レドモ. *conj.* Although.
Akkai,   **Syn: Yakka.**
アッカイ,

Akka, アッカ, 水. *n.* Water. Same as *Wakka* and *aka.*

Akka-shum,
アッカシュム, 水ノ泡. *n.* Water
Akka-sum, foam.
アッカスム,

Akkanne, アッカンネ, 清明ナル. *adj.* Clean. Same as *Ashkanne.*

Akkari, アッカリ, 過ゲル、優ル. *post.* Than. Surpassing. Expression of the comparative degree.

Akkari-kara, アッカリカラ, 過ル、勝ル. *v.t.* To surpass. To do better or worse than. (Preceded by the objective case).

Akkari-ki, アッカリキ, 過ル、勝ル. Same as *Akkari-kara.*

Akke,
アッケ, ホタテガイ. *n.* A scallop.
Akke-tek, *Pecten yezoensis, Jay.*
アッケテク

Akkesh, アッケシ, 牡蠣、カキ. An oyster. *Ostræ agigas, Thunt.*

Akketek,
アッケテク, ホタテカイ. *n.* Scallap.
Akke, *Pekten yezoensis.*
アッケ, *Jay.*

Akku, アック, 羂、ワナ. *n.* A trap. See *Akbe.*

Ak-nishpake, アクニシパケ, 弟. *n.* A younger brother.

Akno, アクノ, 弓術ニ秀デシ. *adj.* Clever at shooting arrows.

Akno-guru, アクノグル, 射手. *n.* Archers. An archer.

Ako-apa-ashi, アコアパアシ,
Ako-apa-seshke, アコアパセシケ, 閉込メル. *v.t.* To shut in.

Akoekomo, アコエコモ, 先ヲ曲ゲル. *v.t.* To clinch.

Akoerayap, アコエラヤプ, 驚キ且喜ブ. *v.i.* To be agreeably surprised.

Akoewara, アコエワラ, 吹キ開ケラレル. *v.i.* To be blown to.

Akoewara-ewara, アコエワラエワラ, 吹キツケラレル. *v.i.* To be blown away to. To be blown to.

Akohepitare, アコヘピタレ, 眞直グニナル. *v.i.* To rise up as from a bending position.

Akoiki, アコイキ, 博タル、殺サレ. *v.i.* To get killed. To be struck.

Akoipishi, アコイピシ, 裁判セラレタ. *v.i.* To be judged.

Akoipishi-gusu-atak, アコイピシグスアタク, 呼出サル、(裁判ナドヘ). *v.i.* To be arraigned. To be had up for judgement.

Akoipishi-gusu-atakte, アコイピシグスアタゝテ, 呼出ス. *v.t.* To arraign. To bring before a court.

Akoisamka, アコイサムカ, 無クスル. *v.t.* To destroy. To bring to nothing. Sometimes also used intransitively.

Akokarakari, アコカラカリ, 包マレル、包マレタル. *v.i. and adj.* Rolled up. Wrapped up.

Akokatpakbe, アコカッパクベ, 悪人. 邪人. *n.* A bad person. A sinner.

Akokatpak-guru, アコカッパクグル, 悪人、邪人. *n.* A bad person. A sinner. **Syn: Katpak-ki-guru.**

Akokemachichi, アコケマチチ, 寝マッテ疑ル. *v.i.* To lie with one's legs curled up. As:—*Shotki kuruka akokemachichi,* "he is lying upon his bed with his legs curled up."

Akokemi-an, アコケミアン, 罕ナル、少キ. *v.i.* To be scarce.

Akomuyep, アコムイェプ, 死人ト共ニ埋メル衣服. *n.* The ordinary clothing buried with the dead.

Akonere, アコ子レ, 破壊セラレタ、(單數), *v.i. and adj. (sing).* Wrecked. Smashed up.

Akonerepa, アコ子レパ, 破壊セラレタ、(複數). *v.i. and adj. (pl).* Wrecked. Smashed up.

Akopan, アコパン, 嫌ハレタ、忌マレタ. *adj.* Hated. Abhorred.

Akopangere, アコパンゲレ, 嫌ハレタル. *adj.* Hated. Abhorred. **Syn: Aepangere.**

Akopao, アコパオ, 叱カラル. *v.i.* To be scolded. To be punished. **Syn: Akosakaikara.**

Akpo, アクポ, 弟. *n.* A younger brother.

Akopuntek, アコプンテク, 喜ブ. *v.i.* To be pleased. To rejoice. **Syn: Akoyainuchaktek. Akoyairenga.**

Akopuntekte, アコプンテゝテ, 喜バセル. *v.t.* To please another. To make another rejoice.

Akoram-niukesh, アコラムニウケシ, 承認セズ. *v.t.* To dissent from.

Akore, アコレ, 貰フ. *v.t.* To receive. To take.

Akore-guru, アコレグル, 貰ッタ人. *n.* A recipient.

Akor'ewen, アコﾙエウェン, 惡ク遇ス
ﾙ. v.t. To treat badly.

Akcro, アコロ, 私ノ、我々ノ、汝ノ、彼
等ノ. pro. My. Our. Your. Their.

Akoroashpa, アコロアシバ, 聞エヌ
フリス. v.i. To be deaf to.

Akorobe, アコロベ, 人ノモノ. n. One's
belongings.

Akcrokaiki, アコロカイキ, 然レドモ.
adv. Although.

Akoropap, アコロバブ, 人ノ物. n.
One's belongings.

Akosakaikara,
アコサカイカラ,
Akosakayokara,
アコサカヨカラ,
Akopas.
} 叱カラレル. v.i.
To be scold-
ed.   Syn :

Akoshiratki, アコシラツキ, 護ラレ
ﾙ. v.i. To be taken care of.

Akoshiratkip, アコシラツキブ, 守リ
主、マモリヌシ. n. One's guardian
angel.

Akcshinninup, アコシンニヌブ, 守護
袋、マモリブクロ. n. A charm.

Akoshituriri, アコシツリリ, 延バサ
レタ、例セバ、ショツキクルカアシツ
リリ、寝臺ノ上ニ長ク延ベラレタ. v.i.
To be stretched out lengthwise.
As :—Shotki kuruka akoshituriri.
"He is stretched out lengthwise
upon his bed."

Akowen, アコウェン, 嫌ハレタﾙ. adj.
and v.i. Abhorrent. Hated. despised. Syn : Aetunne.

Akoyoyamokte, アコヨヤモクテ, 困
ﾏﾙ. v.i. To be troubled. As :—
Kamui kuroro akoyoyamokte. "To
be troubled by the deities."

Akpo, アクポ, 弟. n. A younger
brother. Syn : Aki.

Akshinot, アクシノツ, 射遊、矢ヲ射ﾙ
アソビ. n. A game of archery.

Aktonoge, アクトノゲ, 弟. n. A
younger brother. Syn : Aki.

Akusa, アクサ, 渡舟ス. v.t. To ferry
across a river.

Akusa-guru, アクサグﾙ, 船頭(河渡場
ノ)、渡守. n. A ferry-man.

Akusa-ushi, アクサウシ, 渡場. n. A
ferry.

A-kush, アクシ ナレドモ. adv. Although.

Akuwakore, アクワコレ, 物質ヲ與フ、
シチヱツ、例セバ、イタクグスアクワコ
レ、言葉ノ爲ニ實物ヲ與ヘﾙ. v.t. To
give as a pledge. Also "to set
up a mark to a grave." As :—
Itak gusu akuwakore. "To give
as a pledge to one's word." Rai-
guru akuwakore, "to set up a post
for the dead."

Am,
アム,
Ami,
アミ,
Amihi,
アミヒ,
} 爪、ツメ. n. Finger or toe
nails. The claws of birds
and animals. Am-ras,
nail-parings."

Ama, アマ, 置ク. v.t. To put. To
place. To put away. As :—Shi-
ri-kata ama, "to place on the
ground."

Ama, アマ, 焼キタﾙ. v.i. and adj.
Roasted.

Ama, アマ, 有ﾙ、在ﾙ. v.i. To be.

Ama-an, アマアン, 有リシ. past part.
Was. Syn : Ama-kane-an.

Amaka, アマカ, 開カレタ. v.i. and
adj. Opened. Syn : Makke.

Amakaraye, アマカライエ, 開ケタﾙ、
晴レタﾙ.adj. Open. Clear. Syn :
Aomakaraye.

Amakiri-uwekote, アマキリウウェコテ, Amokiri-uwekote, アモキリウウェコテ, 箕坐スル, アグラカク. *v.i.* To sit cross-legged.

Amaktono, アマクトノ, Amaktonoge, アマクトノゲ, 弟. *n.* A younger brother.

Amam, アマム, Amama, アママ, 農產. *n.* Garden produce, such as rice, millet, wheat, barley.

Amam-chikap, アマムチカプ, Amam-e-chikap, アマムエチカプ, Amam-chiri, アマムチリ, Amam-e-chiri, アマムエチリ, 雀, スヾメ. *n.* A sparrow.

Amam-e-itangi, アマメイタンギ, Amam-itangi, アマムイタンギ, Amam-o-itangi, アマムオイタンギ, 飯茶椀. *n.* A rice cup. A cup used for eating rice or millet out of.

Amamkoho, アマムコホ, 粉、コ. *n.* Flour.

Amam-mosh, アマムモシ, 蝿ノ名. *n.* A kind of small fly.

Amam-muru, アマムムル, 粟麥類ノカラ. *n.* Millet or rice husks.

Amampo-kikiri, アマムポキキリ, 螽斯、キリギリス. *n.* A grasshopper. **Syn: Amamepo.**

Ama-ni, アマニ, 梁、ハリ. *n.* A beam of wood.

Aman-ni, アマンニ, 梁、ハリ. *n.* The long poles to which the lower ends of the side-rafters of a hut are tied. **Syn: Sopesh-ni.**

Amapa, アマパ, 置ク(複數). *v.t.* To put. To place. (*pl*).

Amu-shi, アムシ, 爪チ以テツカム. *v.t.* To take hold of with claws.

Amatak, アマタク, Amatak-tono, アマタクトノ, Amatak-tonoge, アマタクトノゲ, 妹. *n.* A younger sister. **Syn: Mataki. Turesh.**

Ama-u, アマウ, 物チ置イタ場所. *adv.* The place where something has been put. **Syn: Ama-ushi.**

Amba, アムバ, 運フ、(複數). *v.t.* To carry.

Amba, アムバ, 浮樣、ウキ. *n.* The floats attached to the tops of fishing nets.

Ambai, アムバイ, 蟹、カニ. Same as *Ambayaya.*

Ambari, アムバリ, 網針、アバリ. A netting needle.

Amba-wa-apkash, アムバワアプカシ, 持ツテ歩ム. *v.i.* To go along carrying something. (*pl*).

Ambayaya, アンバヤヤ, Ampayaya, アンパヤヤ, 蟹、カニ. *n.* A crab.

Ambe, アムベ, 火. *n.* Same as *Abe,* Fire. **Syn: Unchi.**

Ambe, アムベ, Anbe, アンベ, 物、モノ. *n.* A thing. Article. Object. The matter of a subject.

Ambe, アムベ, 眞ニ. *adv.* Truly. Indeed. Is. It is so. As:—*Ambe he?* "Is it so?"

Ambochichi, アムボチチ, Ampochichi, アムポチチ, 摘ム. *v.t.* To pinch. (*sing.*) To scratch.

Ambochitpa, アムボチッパ,摘ム(複數). *v.t.* To pinch. (*pl*). To scratch.

Amchayaya, アムチヤヤヤ, Ampayaya, アムパヤヤ, } 爪ヲ以テ握ム. *v. t.* To hold in the claws.

Amchayaya-wa-kishma, アムチヤヤヤワキシマ, 爪ヲ以テ握ム. *v.t.* To hold in the claws.

Am-etu, アムエツ,爪ノ端、ツメノハシ、例セバ、チイケルサムベタネアムエツパクノアン、彼ノ脈ハ殆ント休ム. *n.* The ends of the finger-nails (Met : "A very little;" "very sparingly;" "faintly;" "almost finished." As :—*Nei guru sambe tane ametu pak no an*, that person's pulse have nearly finished beating."

Ami, アミ, Amihi, アミヒ, } 爪、ツメ. *n.* Claws. Finger or toe-nails. **Syn : Am.**

Ami, アミ,着タ. *v.i.* & *adj.* Clothed. Dressed. To be wearing.

Amichi, アミチ, 我等ノ父. *pro.* Our father.

Amichi-ainu, アミチアイヌ,我が父、我等ノ父. *pro.* Our father.

Ami-iyok, アミイヨク, 竊ム. *v. t.* To steal.

Ami-iyok-guru, アミイヨクグル, 盗人、ヌスビト. *n.* A thief. **Syn : Ikka-guru.**

Amikekara, アミケカラ, 刺身ニ切ル. To cut in thin slices. To slit fish down the middle, cut off the heads and take out the back-bone.

Am-iki, アムイキ,爪ヲ以テヒツ搔ク. *v.t.* To scratch.

Am-ikiri, アムイキリ, 知ル、識ル. *v. t.* Same as *amkiri*. To know. To recognize.

Amip, アミプ,着物、キモノ. *n.* Clothing. Attire. Dress. A garment.

Amip-numsam, アミプヌムサム, 前襟、マイエリ. *n.* The front edge of a garment.

Amip-shirika, アミプシリカ, 着物ノオモテ. *n.* The upper or outside of a garment.

Amip-shiripok, アミプシリポク, 着物ノウラ. *n.* The inside or underside of a garment.

Amiri-yaoshkep, アミリヤオシケプ,メクラグモ. *n.* The fatherlonglegs. **Syn : Ami-tanne yaoshkep.**

Ami-tanne-yaoshkep, アミタンチヤオシユケプ,メクラグモ、クモ. *n.* The father-long legs.

Amiyok, アミヨク, 盗ム、ヌスム. *v.t.* To steal.

Amiyok-guru, アミヨクグル, 盗人、ヌスビト. *n.* A thief.

Amke, アムケ, 掃フ、(複數). *v.t.* To brush off as grass seeds or rubbish from one's clothes.

Amke, アムケ, 整理スル、カタヅケル. *v.t.* To put away (*pl of the object*).

Amkire, アムキレ, 紹介スル、知ラセル. *v.t.* To cause to know. To introduce one person to another.

Amkiri, アムキリ, 知ル、識ル、シル. *v.t.* To know. To be acquainted with. **Syn : Amikiri.**

Amkiri-guru, アムキリグル, 知人、シリアイ. *n.* An acquaintance.

Amkit, アムキツ, 鷲ノ啼キ聲、ワシノナキコエ. *n.* The cry of an eagle.

Amkokishima, アムコキシマ, 爪又ハ手ヲ以テツカム. *v.t.* To seize with the hands or claws.

Amkokomo, アムココモ, 爪又ハ手チ以
テ掴ム. *v.t.* To seize with the hands
or claws. **Syn: Amkosaye.**

Amkosaye,
アムコサイ 爪チ以テ握ム. *v.t.* To
Amkosayo, seize with the hands
アムコサヨ, or claws.
Amkoshayo,
アムコシヤヨ,

Amma, アムマ, 置ク. *v.t.* To put.
To place. **Syn: Ama.**

Amma, アムマ, 有リテ. *part.* Being.
Same as *an-wa.*

Am-nishu, アムニシュ, 足ナキ臼. *n.*
A kind of footless mortar.

Amo, アモ, 安息、イコフ. *v.i.* To be
at peace. To be at rest.

Amoini, アモイニ, 腕、(前部)、ウデ.
Same as *amunini, n.* The fore-
arm.

Amomka, アモムカ, 浮ブ、ウカブ. *v.i.*
and *adj.* To float. To drift.
Floating. Afloat. As:—*Amomka
chip,* "a floating boat."

Amore, アモレ, 閑セヌ、カマハヌ、息
マセル. *v.t.* To let alone. To let
rest. To quiet.

Ampayaya, アムパヤヤ, 蟹、カニ. *n.*
A crab. **Syn: Hotempoyaya.
Hotemtemu.**

Ampiri, アムピリ, 爪チ以テカキシ痕.
n. A scratch. A wound left by
a scratch.

Ampiri-o, アムピリ, 爪ナ以テカク、
搔ク、ヒツ爬ク. *v.t.* To scratch. To
wound with the nails or claws.

Amras, アムラス, 爪ノ切屑、ツメノキ
リクズ、例セバ、アムラスバクノイサ
ム、少シモ有ラヌ. *n.* Nail-parings.
Met: a very small portion. " A

jot or tittle." As :—*Amras pak
no isam,* "there is no the least
bit."

Amse, 坐、椅子、イス、ザ. *n.* A
アムセ, seat. A throne. From
Amset, *a-se.*
アムセツ,

Amsho, 家ノ床、イヘノユカ. *n.* The
アムシヨ, entire floor of a house.
Amso, **Syn: Sho. So.**
アムソ,

Amshokkara, アムショッカラ, 敷物、
シキモノ、(床或ハ腰掛ニ用ユ). *n.* A
small mat made of large rushes
and used to spread over the floor
as a seat. **Syn: Shokkara. A-
putki.**

Amsho-shut, アムシヨシュツ, 床端、
ユカノハシ. *n.* The edge of a floor.
Syn: Sho-shut.

Amu, アム, 爪、ツメ. *n.* The finger
nails (*pl*).

Amuchichi, アムチチ, 爪チ以テヒツ
搔ク、(單數). *v.t.* To scratch. (*sing*).

Amuchitpa, アムチツパ, 爪チ以テヒ
ツ搔ク、(複數). *v.t.* To scratch.

Amunin, 腕、ウデ、(前部). *n.* The
アムニン, lower part of the
Amunini, arm. The fore-arm.
アムニニ,

Amuraiba, アムライバ, 手チ他人ノ頭
上ニ置キテ愛情チ表ス挨拶. *v.i.* To
fondle a person by rubbing his
head.

Amusa, アムサ, 手チ他人ノ頭上ニ置
キテ愛情チ表スル挨拶. *v.i.* To stroke
the head as in salutation.

Amushbe, アムシベ, 蟹、カニ、蝦、エ
ビ. *n.* A crab. Any animal, large
or small, having claws.

An, **アン,** 有ル、アル. *v.i.* To be. There is.

An, **アン,** 一、イチ、全ク、マツタク. *adj.* and *adv.* One. One of a pair. Quite. Entirely. Contracted from *ara*.

An, **アン,** 此ノ An ハ時トシテ最上級ノ意又ハ強聲ヲ表スモノナリ. *part.* Sometimes used as a superlative or intensifying particle. As:— *Aneongami an-eyaiirage,* "to respect and thank profoundly."

An, **アン,** 此ノ An ハ時トシテ動詞ノ前ニ加フル時ハ自動詞ニスルカアリ. *part.* Used before some verbs *an*, like *a*, has a past and passive signification. As:— *An-raige,* "he was killed."

An, **アン,** 全ク、マツタク. *adv.* Quite. As:— *An-rai,* "quite dead."

An, **アン,** 夜、ヨ. *n.* Night. **Syn:** Anchikara,

An-ai, **アンアイ,** 變ラヌ、同、オナジ. *adv.* Changeless. The same.

An-aige, **アンアイゲ,** シナガラ. *ph.* In the act of. About to be. As:— *Tane ariki an an-aige,* "As they are just now coming."

An-aine, **アンアイ子,** 漸、ヨツヤク、乍、ナガラ、理ナキ、例セバ、アンアイ子ウパキタ、漸ク段々ニ. *ph.* Hardly. With difficulty. Whilst. Without provocation or cause. As:— *An-aine uwepakita,* "hardly and by degrees." *An-aine en kik,* "he struck me without provocation." *Ikushta ek an an-aine hotuyekara,* "he called to him whilst he was coming yonder."

Anaishiri, **アナイシリ,** 死人ノ靈. *n.*

A departed spirit. The manes of the dead.

Anak, **アナク,** and **Anakne,** **アナク子,** 此詞ハ日本ノ(ハ)ニ同ジ. *part.* *Anak* serves to isolate or emphasize a word or subject, and may in a sense be regarded as a sign of the nominative case. When followed by *ne* it renders the whole sentence to which it is applied a substantive clause. Often it is not translated but in some instances it must be, the context alone determining by what phrase or word it should be represented. The words "as for;" "in reference to;" "as regards," are among the most apt English equivalents. It very nearly represents the Japanese *wa*, ハ、.

Anak-ka, **アナッカ,** トハ云ヘドモ. The same as *an yakka*, "although there is."

Anak-ki-koroka, **アナッキコロカ,** ケレドモ、然レトモ. *ph.* Even though it is. Nevertheless.

Anak-ne, **アナク子,** ハ、アナグヲ見ル可シ. See *anak*.

Anakoroka, **アナコロカ,** 有ルナレド. *ph.* Although there is.

An-an, **アンアン,** 有ル、有リシ. *aux v.* There was. There is.

An-anchikara, **アンアンチカラ,** 或ル夜. *adv.* One evening.

An......an-gesh shiriki, **アン...アンゲシシリキ,** 殆ンド、幾ンド. *ph.* Nearly. As:—*An otke an-gesh shiriki,* "it was nearly speared." **Syn: Naa** followd by a passive.

Anankoro, **アンアンコロ,** 有ルナラン.

aux. There will be. Same as *an nangoro.*

Anapa, アナパ, 親戚、シンセキ. *n.* Relation. **Syn: Apa-utara.**

Anare, アナレ, 勝、カツ. *v.t.* To defeat. **Syn: Annokara.**

Anasak, アナサク, 無キ、持タヌ. *adv.* Without. Not being; not having.

Anasap, アナサブ, 默許スレ. *v.i.* To connive at. **Syn: Kashieshina.**

Anat-ni, アナツニ, イヌガヤ、ヒヤウブ (方言). *n. Cephalotaxus drupacea, S. et Z.*

Anbe, アンベ,
Ambe, アムベ, 物、モノ. *n.* An article. A thing. An object. Truth. Fact. As:—*Ambe ne,* " it is truth."

Anchi, アンチ, 石炭、セキタン. *n.* Coal.

Anchi, アンチ, 黑キ石. *n.* A kind of black flint. Obsidean.

Anchikara, アンチカラ, 夜、ヨ. *n.* Night. **Syn: Kunne-to. Anikara.**

Anchikara-chup, アンチカラチュプ, 月、ツキ. *n.* The moon.

Anchikara-ibe, アンチカライベ, 夕飯、ユウメシ. *n.* Supper.

An-chup, アンチュプ, 月、ツキ. The moon.

Ande, アンデ, 置ク、取テ置ク. *v.t.* To put. To place. To set on one side. To put away. **Syn: Unu. Anu. Ama.**

Ande, アンデ, 止メル、巳メル. *v.i.* and *v.t.* To cease. To set down. To let alone. **Syn: Moshima no oka.**

Andepa, アンデパ, 止メル、巳メル、(複数). *v.t.* To put or place. *Il* of the person.

Andere, アンデレ, 巳メサセル、置カセル. *v.t.* To cause to cease. To make put down. To cause another to set on one side.

Ane, ア子, 私、我、ツレ. *pro.* I. **Syn: Ku, Kuani.**

Ane, ア子, 小キ、細キ、例セバ、アチアムベ、小サキモノ. *adj.* Small. Thin. Tiny. As:—*Ane ambe,* "a tiny thing." *Ane pon top,* "a tiny thin bamboo."

Ane-kane, アチカチ, 針金、ハリガチ. *n.* Wire. Thin mettle.

Anekarara, アチカララ, 仕上リ、爲シ了ッタ、成就シタ. *v.i.* Done. Made. Finished. **Syn: Aekarakara.**

Anekempo, アチケムポ, ナメクヂ. *n.* A slug. **Syn: Kina-mokuriri.**

Anekik, アチキク, 搏、ウツ. *v.t.* To flog. To strike. Also flogged. Struck.

Anekosama, アチコサマ, 眞似スル、(單數). *v.t.* To imitate (*sing*).

Anekosamba, アチコサムバ, 眞似ス ル、(複數). *v.t.* To imitate (*pl*).

Anekoyaiiraige-an-na, アチコヤイイライゲアンナ, 眞ニ難有キ. *ph.* Hearty thanks.

Ane-kut, アチクツ, 狭キ帶. *n.* A small girdle.

Aneongami, アチオンガミ, 深ク尊敬スレ、フカクソンケイスル. *v.t.* To pay profound respects.

Aneopetcha, アチオペッチヤ, 小サキ口アル河. *n.* A river with a narrow mouth.

Aneoshkoro, アチオシコロ, 重ンズル、貴トブ、尊トブ. *v.t.* To prize, desire, or seek after earnestly.

Aneru, アチル, 細道、ホソミチ. *n.* A trail. A bridle-path.

Ange, アンゲ, 今為サントス. *adv.* To be about to do. As:—*Ki ange shiriki*, "he came near doing it."

Angesh, アンゲシ, 欲セヌ. *v.t.* To dislike. **Syn: Kopan. Pange. Kowen.**

Angura, アングラ} 樰、塀、ヘイ、カコヒ. *n.* A

Ankura, アンクラ} fence. A hedge.

Anguru, アングル, 者、人. *n.* A person.

An-gusu, アングス, 故ニ. *part.* Because. **Syn: Gusu.**

An-gusu-ne-na, アングスネナ, アルガ故ニ. *ph.* Because there is.

An-hike, アンヒケ, 或時ニ、或者. *adv.* When a thing is. The thing that is.

Ani, アニ, 如、ゴトシ. *adv.* As. So. As:—*Ani korachi*, "as it is;" "like that." As:—*En otta ani korachi ku koramkon na*, "I ask that it may be so to me."

An-i, アンイ, 出来上ツタ事. *n.* Something done. Something which is. As:—*Epirikare an gusu ene iki-an-i ne*, "this thing was done for your benefit."

An-i, アンイ, 居ル所. *n.* Abode. The place where something is. **Syn: An-ushike.**

Ani, アニ, 攢フル、タヅサエル. *v.t.* To hold or carry in the hands. To lay hold on.

Ani, アニ, 此字チ加フル時ハ命令ノ意チ作ス、例セバ、エクワイエアニ、來タリテ話セ. *part.* Sometimes used at the end of a sentence as an imperative particle. As:—*Ek wa ye ani*, "come and tell me." *Ni-*

shatta ek ani, "Come to-morrow." **Syn: Hani.**

Ani, アニ, 時ニ. *adv.* When. Then.

Ani, アニ, 以テ. *part.* By. With. By means of. **Syn: Ari.**

Ani, アニ, 彼、彼女、其ハ. *pro.* He. she. It.

Ani-ambe, アニアムベ, 持テ歩ク物、携フルモノ. *n.* Anything one is carrying.

An-ibe, アンイベ, 夕飯、ユフメシ. *n.* Supper.

Anika-aiki, アニカアイキ, 如シ、左様ニ上手、實ニ巧ミナレ、例セバ、アニカアイキエアシカイ、上手ニ出來ル. *adv.* So. So clever. Very clever. As:—*Ani-ka aiki eashkai*, "he can do it so cleverly."

Anikara, アニカラ, 夜、ヨ. *n.* Night. **Syn: Anchikara.**

Anikkotama, アニッコタマ, 圍ム、カコム、(單數). *v.t.* To surround. (*sing*).

Anikkotamba, アニッコタムバ, 圍ム、カコム、(複數). *v.t.* To surround. (*pl*).

Anikomeuba, アニヒコメウバ, 堀出ス、(複數). *v.t.* To grub up as trees (*pl*).

Anikomewe, アニヒコメウェ, 掘出ス、(單數). *v.t.* To grub up as trees (*sing*).

Anikoreuba, アニコレウバ, 刀チ以テ撃ツ、(複數). *v.t.* To strike with a sword (*pl*). Really "to bend."

Anikorewe, アニコレウェ, 刀チ以テ撃ツ、(單數). *v.t.* To strike with a sword (*sing*), Really "to bend."

Aninap, アニナプ, 煉リヌル食物. *n.* Jam. Anything smashed. As:—*Anina-kapato*, "preserves made of the *Nuphar Japonicum*." *Anina-nikaop*, "jam made of fruit." "Fruit preserves." *Anina-niseu*, "mashed acorns."

Aniniap, アニニアブ, 餌. *n.* A bait drawn along the bottom of rivers or the sea as a decoy for fish. **Syn : Apniniap.**

Aninka, アニンカ, 吸込ム. *adj. & v.i.* To be absorbed. From *nin*, " to shrink up."

Anipa, アニパ, 持ツ、貰テ行ク (複數). *v.t.* To carry. *Pl :* of the person.

Anirukushte, アニルクシテ, 活動ス ル、カツドウスル. *v. i.* To become actively excited. To stretch out the arms and legs in anger. **Syn : Anurukushte.**

Anishka, アニシカ, 貴重ナル. *adj.* Valuable. Difficult to spare. **Syn : Aotupekare.**

Anishuk, アニシュク, 招カレレ. Called. Invited.

Aniugesh, アニウゲシ, 欲セヌ、好マ ヌ、爲スコトヲ好マヌ. *v.i.* To dislike to do a thing. To be disinclined to act. **Syn : Aeyapte.**

Ani-utara, アニウタラ, 運途スル人. *n.* Carriers. Bearers.

Ani-utara, アニウタラ, 彼等. *pro.* They. Those persons. **Syn : Nei-utara.**

Ankan, アンカン, 間、アイダ、乍、ナガ ラ. *adv.* Whilst. As :—*Ieiwange ankan.* "Whilst using it."

Ankara, アンカラ, 爲シタル. Same as *akara*, "made ;" "finished ;" "to be done."

Ankerai, アンケライ, 貸フ. *v.t.* To receive.

Ankes, アンケス, 曉、アカツキ. *adv.* Daybreak. Early morning.

Ankes-pakita, アンケスパキタ, 拂曉、 ヨアケガタ. *adv.* The very first dawn of early morning.

Anki, アンキ, 扇、アフギ. *n.* A fan. **Syn : Aungi.**

Anki, アンキ, 有ルベシ. *aux.* About to be. Will be.

Ankik, アンキク, 打タレ. *v.i.* To be struck. Same as *akik.*

Anko, アンコ, ナレバ、時ニ. *adv.* If. Should. When.

Ankoiki, アンコイキ, 打タル. Same as *akoiki* "to be beaten ;" also "a battle," "a fight."

Ankomonash, アンコモナシ, 忙カシ キ. *adj.* Busy. In great haste.

Ankomonashte, アンコモナシテ, 急 ガス. *v. t.* To hasten.

Ankorachi, アンコラチ, 此ノ通リ、例 セバ、エイェイタクアンコラチ、汝ノ云 フ通リ. *ph.* Like this. Thus. In this way. In accordance with. Openly. Above-board. As :—*E ye itak an-korachi*, "as you say."

Ankoirushka, アンコイルシカ, 他人 ノ怒ヲ受クルコ. *v. i.* To suffer the wrath of another. **Syn : Akoiru-shka.**

Ankoro, アンコロ, 若シ、時ニ、アルベ キ時. *adv.* When. If. Should. About the time of.

Ankoro-iki, アンコロイキ, 然レドモ. *adv.* Although.

Ankoroka, アンコロカ, 有リテモ. *adv.* Although there is.

Ankoro-ka-iki, アンコロカイキ, 然レ ドモ. *adv.* Although.

Ankoro-kusu-ne, アンコロクス子, 有 ルベシ. *ph.* There will be.

Ankura, アンクラ, 園、塀、カコヒ、ヘイ. *n.* A fence. A hedge. **Syn : Angura. Chashi.**

Ankusa-guru, アンクサグル, 渡守、ワタシマモリ. *n.* A ferry-man. **Syn : Akusa-guru.**

Ankushkerai, 助ヶニヨリ. *adv.* **アンクシケライ,** By the help of. **Ankushkeraipo,** Owing to. By **アンクシケライポ,** favour of. As : — *E an kushkeraipo ku shiknu ruwe ne,* "it is by your favour I am now alive." *Kem-ush an, awa, chep ankushkerai shiknu ash ruwe ne,* "there was a famine, but owing to the fish we are alive."

Ankushtashi, アンクシタシ, 助ヶニヨリ. *adv.* By the help of. Owing to. **Syn : Ankushkerai.**

Anna, アンナ, Anne, アンヌ, Anno, アンノ, Annu, アンヌ, 健康ナル、スコヤカナ. *adj.* Healthy. In good health. **Syn : Iwange-no-an.**

Anna-ambe, アンナアムベ, Anne-ambe, アンチアムベ, Anno-ambe, アンノアムベ, Annu-ambe, アンヌアムベ, 健康、スコヤカ. *n.* Health. A person in health.

Anne-ikippo, アンチイキッポ, Anno-ikippo, アンノイキッポ, 其通、ソノトウリ. *adv.* In the same way. After the same manner. So. **Syn : Nei-no-koroeki.**

An-ni, アンニ, 立木、タチキ、幹、ミキ. *n.* A standing tree. The trunk of a tree.

Annitne-kamui, アンニッチカムイ, 極悪ノ悪鬼、ゴクアシキアクマ. *n.* The worst of the demons.

Anno, アンノ, 勝、カツ. *v.t.* To defeat.

Anno-i, アンノイ, 勝利. *n.* A Defeat.

Anno-ikippo, アンノイキッポ, Anne-ikippo, アンチイキッポ, 其通、ソノトウリ. *n.* So. After the same manner. In the same way.

Anno-kara, アンノカラ, 勝、カツ. *v.t.* To defeat. To over-come. **Syn : Annu-kara.**

An-noshike, アンノシケ, 夜中、ヨナカ. *n.* Midnight.

An-noshike-paketa, アンノシケパケタ, 丁度夜中、チョウドヨナカ. *adv.* The very middle of the night.

Annu, アンヌ, 勝ツ. *v.t.* To defeat.

Annu-kara, アンヌカラ, 勝、カツ. *v.t.* To defeat. To over-come.

Annu-kippo-kara, アンヌキッポカラ, 競フ、キソフ. *v.i.* To vie with. To strive with. To compete. As:— *Nei ambe iki gusu toan ainu tura ku annu-kippokara kusu ne,* "I will strive with him in doing business."

Annu-no, アンヌノ, 無代價ナル. *adj.* Free of cost. Also, "having been defeated."

Annu-no, アンヌノ, 敗北シタル、廢レタル. *adj.* Defeated. Beaten. Overcome.

Annu-no-hachire, アンアノハチレ, 勝ツ. *v.t.* To defeat in contest.

Annu-no-hachiri, アンヌノハチリ, 敗ケル. *v.i.* To be defeated in contest.

Annu-no-koiki, アンヌノコイキ, 勝ツ. *v.t.* To defeat. To over-come in strife.

Annu-no-ye, アンヌノイェ, 沈黙サセル. *v.t.* To put to silence.

Annupa, アンヌパ, 饒カナ レ. *adj.* To be in plenty. Plentiful.

Annu-tuiba, アンヌツイバ, 戦ニテ殺ス. *v.t.* To slay in battle.

An-nuye, アンヌイェ, 記サレタ レ. *adj.* Written.

An-ohoro, アンオホロ, 延ハサレタ、永ク保ツ. *v.t.* and *v.i.* To be lengthened. To have been kept for a long time. To lengthen.

Anokai, アノオカイ, 汝、我々、汝等. *pro.* You. Ye. We. **Syn: Aokai.**

An-omare, アンオマレ, 中ニ入レラレタ レ. *adj.* Having been put in. Containing. **Syn: Aomare.**

Anomi, アノミ, 拝スル. *v.t.* To worship.

Anonoye, アンノイェ, 覘フ、狙フ、チラフ. *v.t.* To take aim at.

Anonoyep, アノノイェブ, 覘ハレタ物. *n.* An object. **Syn: Atukambe.**

Anore, アノレ, 彩色シタル、イロツケタレ. *adj.* Coloured. **Syn: Iroaush.**

Anotange-kara, アノタンゲカラ, 刀チ以テ撃タレ. *v.i.* To be struck with a sword.

Anoye, アノイェ, チザレタレ. *adj.* Contorted. Twisted.

Anrai, アンライ, 殺サレタ、死ンダ. *v.i.* Slain. Quite dead.

Anraige, アンライゲ, 殺サレタ. *v.i.* To have been killed.

Anrakoro, アンラコロ, クロユリ. *n.* The black lily. *Fritillaria Kamtschatensis, Gawl.*

Anramasu-ushuyeshuye, アンラマスウシュイェシュイェ,
Anramasu-uweshuye, アンラマスウウェシュイェ, 喜ブ. *v.i.* and *adj.* To be pleased. To be happy.

Anramush, アンラムシ, 親切ナレ. *adj.* Kind.

Anrapoki, アンラポキ, 敗ケレ、殺サレル、例セバ、ヤイキキプナ、エアンラポキアカリクスチナ. 注意セヨ汝敗ケルゾ. *v.i.* To be defeated. To be killed. To be made to submit to another. As:—*Yaikikip na, eanrapoki akari kusu ne na,* "be careful, you will be defeated by me."

Anramu-ochiu, アンラムオチウ, 許ス、ユレス, *v.t.* To permit. To allow. To concede.

Anrawechiu, アンラウェチウ, 殺ス、勝ツ. *v.t.* To kill. To defeat.

Anreika-kara, アンレイカカラ, 承知スル、誉メル. *v.i.* To assent. To put the hands up to the head as a sign of assent. To praise.

An-reske-po, アンレスケポ, 他人ニ養育サレタ子供. *n.* Children brought up by persons other than their parents. **Syn: Aoreshpa utara.**

Anro, アンロ, ……ナラシメヨ、……デアラシメヨ. *imper of an.* Let be.

Anruki, アンルキ, 呑込ム. *v.t.* To swallow.

Anruru, アンルル, エゾノ西海岸. *adj.* The western shores of Yezo. As:— *Anruru un atui,* "the western sea."

Antek, アンテク, 鳥渡、チョット. *adv.* Just. Only. For a little while.

Antsami, 　アザミノ類. *n.* Thistles. *Chicus sps.* **Syn :** **Aiush-kuttara.**
アンツァミ,
Anzami,
アンザミ,

Antuki, **アンツキ**, 小豆、アツキ. *n.* A kind of small red bean.

Antunanga, **アンツナンガ**, 逢フ、遭フ、アフ. *v.t.* To meet.

Anturashi, **アンツラシ**, 昇、ノボル (複數). *v.i.* To ascend a ladder, mountain, or a river together.

Anu, **アヌ**, 置ク. *v.t.* To put. To place.

Anu, **アヌ**, 聞エル. *v.i.* To be heard. Also *ph.:* " I hear," and " do you hear."

Anu, **アヌ**, 分カル、尋ヌル. *v.t.* To understand. To inquire. As :— *Michi orota anu,* "to inquire of one's father."

Anuepare, **アヌエパレ**, 全ク告知ラセル. *v.t.* To fully tell. To repeat a tale. **Syn : Anure-epare.**

Anuirototo, **アヌイロトト**, 全ク無クスル. *v.i.* To be quite destroyed.

Anuitashi, **アヌイタシ**, 聞キシ. *v. i.* To have heard. **Syn : Nu-okere.**

Anukan, **アヌカン**, 現ハレ. *v.i.* To appear. Same as *anukara.*

Anukan-no, **アヌカンノ**, 鮮カニ、アザヤカ=. *adv.* Clearly. Distinctly. Whilst seen.

Anukantek, **アヌカンテク**, 見ル. *v. t.* To see.

Anukara, **アヌカラ**, 夜、ヨル. *n.* night.

Anukara, **アヌカラ**, 見エル. *v.i.* To be seen. To appear. Also " to see."

Anukar'etoranne, **アヌカレトランネ**, 見タクナイ. *ph.* " Not caring to see."

Anukarahumi-wen, **アヌカラフミウェン**, 見ニクキ. *adj.* Unsightly.

Anukara-i, 　見エルモノ. *n.* An object or place seen or looked at. The direction in which one is looking.
アヌカライ,
Anukah'i,
アヌカリ,

Anukara-kopan, **アヌカラコパン**, 見タクナイ. *ph.* " To dislike to look at."

Anuktekka, 　何々チ喜ブ、何々チ樂ム. *v.i. & adj.* To take pleasure in a thing. To delight in. Pleasant.
アヌクテッカ,
Anuptekka,
アヌプテッカ,

Anumge, **アヌムゲ**, 撰バレタ. *v.i. & adj.* Chosen out.

Anumse, **アヌムセ**, 多クノ. *adj.* Many. Numerous.

Anumunu, **アヌムヌ**, 塞ガルル. *v.i.* To be stopped up. **Syn : Chinum-unu.**

Anun, **アヌン**, 他人. *n.* Another person.

Anun-itak, **アヌンイタク**, 外國語. *n.* Strange words. Foreign talk.

Anun-kopaki, **アヌンコパキ**, 他人チ敵ト思フ. *v.t.* To look upon another as an enemy.

Anun-korobe, **アヌンコロベ**, 他人ノ物. *n.* Another person's belongings.

Anun-nishpa, **アヌンニシパ**, 外ノ人、汝. *n.* The other person. Sometimes " you."

Anuno, **アヌノ**, 解ル樣ニ. *adv.* Intelligibly. Understandingly.

Anunukep, **アヌヌケプ**, 貴重ナル物. A precious thing.

Anun-utara, **アヌンウタラ**, 他人、タニン. *n.* Strangers. Other persons.

Anupa, **アヌパ**, 置ク(複數). *v.t.* To place (*pl*).

Anupiwe, アヌピウェ, 膌ツ. *v.t.* To conquer. **Syn: Annokara.**

Anure, アヌレ, 知ラサレル. *v.i.* To be told. Made known.

Anure-epare, アヌレエパレ, 聞カセレ. *v.t.* To tell.

Anurukushte, アヌルクシテ, **Anirukushte, アニルクシテ,** } 慎激テシ手足ヲ伸張スレ. *v.i.* To stretch out the arms and legs as in anger.

Anru-oka, アンルオカ, 畢ハル. *v. i.* To finish (as a meal).

An-ushike, アンウシケ, 住所、スマイ. *n.* One's abode. An abiding-place. The place where anything is. **Syn: An-i.**

Anushuk, アヌシュク, **Anishuk, アニシュク,** } 招カレレ. *v.i.* To be called. To be invited.

Anushuye, アヌシュイェ, 手招キスレ. *v. t.* To call by beckoning to. **Syn: Tekparuparu. Inushuye.**

Anutureshi, アヌツレシ, 昇ル、ノボル. *v.i.* To ascend a river together. Same as *antureshi*.

An-wa, アンワ, 有ル、アリテ. *ph.* and *part.* It is. Being.

An-wa-ne-yakne, アンワチヤク子, 然レドモ. *ph.* Yet. Although.

An-yakne, アンヤク子, 有ルナラバ. *conj.* If there is.

Ao, アオ, 騎フレル、中ニ在ル. *v.i.* To be ridden. Contained in.

Aoattuye, アオアッツイェ, 切リ落トス. *v.i.* To be cut quite off or through.

Aoho, アオホ, **Aiyo, アイヨ,** } 縫箔、メイハク. *n.* Pieces of cloth let into a garment for ornament.

Aoho-ekara, アオホエカラ, 縫箔スレ. *v. i.* To ornament a dress.

Aoingara, アオインガラ, 覗ク、ノゾク. *v. t.* To peep at.

Aoingara, アオインガラ, 青天、アナソラ. *n.* The heights above. The open skies. **Syn: Nishoro. Nishkotoro.**

Aoingara-moshiri, アオインガラモシリ, 青天、アチゾラ. *n.* The heights. The firmament. The open sky. The heavens.

Aoitakshi, アオイタクシ, **Aoitakushi, アオイタクシ,** } 詛ハレ. *v.i.* To be cursed.

Aoka, アオカ, **Aokai, アオカイ,** } 汝. *pro.* You. **Syn: Anokai. Eani. E-shiroma.**

Aokai-utara, アオカイウタラ, **Aokai-utare, アオカイウタレ,** **Aokai-utari, アオカイウタリ,** } 汝等. *pro.* Ye. you.

Aokai-yaikota, アオカイヤイコタ, 汝自身. *pro.* You yourself.

Aokbare, アオクバレ, 攻メラル、容メラレ. *v.i.* Rebelled against. Persecuted.

Aokbare-guru, アオクバレグル, 容メラレタ人. *n.* A person rebelled against or persecuted.

Aokere, アオケレ, 畢リシ、シマフ. *v. i.* Finished. Completed. Done with.

Aokerep, アオケレプ, 畢リシ事. *n.* A thing done. Anything accomplished.

Aokettektek, アオケッテクテク, 終リシ、仕上ッタ. *v.i.* Finished. Done. Completed.

Aokushke, アオクシケ, 潜ル、水クゞル. *v.i.* To dive.

Aomakaraye, アオマカライェ, 開キタ ル. *adj.* Open.

Aomonnure, アオモンヌレ, 譽メラレ タ レ. *adj.* Praised.

Aonai, アオナイ, 窪, クボミ. *n.* A gully.

Aonga, アオンガ, 浸ス、ヒタス. *v.t.* To put to soak. To soak thoroughly. **Syn : Ionga.**

Aongami, アオンガミ, 拜マレル. *v. i.* To be adored. Worshipped.

Aop, アオプ, 器, ウツス. *n.* A vessel, bag or box in which anything is put.

Aopanerep, アオパチレプ, 上着. *n.* A coat. **Syn : Ashka-**
Aeyopanerep, アエヨパネレプ, **kushtep. Ash-kakamurep.**

Aopentari, アオペンタリ, 傾ケル、斜メニセラレ. *v.i. & adj.* To be tilted up. To be raised up a little. **Syn : Aotari.**

Aopepipkere, アオペピプケレ, 脹ラセレ. *v.t.* To cause to swell up (as by putting water into a dry tub.

Aorakere, アオラケレ, 減スル、消ユル. *v.i.* To diminish. To die out. To cease. To lower. **Syn : Ramka. Arakere.**

Aorauge, アオラウゲ, 當ラズ、遲レル. *v.i.* and *v.t.* To miss. To be behind-hand. **Syn : Chiorauge.**

Aosama, アオサマ, 蔽ヒ重ヌレ. *v.i.* To be doubled back or over.

Aoripet, アオリベツ,
Ahoripet, アホリベツ, 壕、堀割、ホリワリ. *n.* A canal.
Auri-pet, アウリベツ,

Aoreshpa-utara, アオレシパウタラ, 孤兒、ミナシゴ、貰子、モライコ. *n.* Orphans. Adopted children. Children brought up by people other than their parents.

Aosh, アオシ, 欲シガル、貴重ニ思フ. *v.i.* and *adj.* To be followed. Sought after. Valued. Prized. Desired.

Aoshikiru, アオシキル, 迂回スル、メグレ. *v.t.* To skirt or go round (as a mountain).

Aoshiraye, アオシライェ, 進マセタ. *v.i.* Moved along.

Aoshiri-nukara, アオシリヌカラ, 見エズナル迄見送ル, *v.t.* To watch out of sight.

Aoshkoro, アオシコロ, 貴バレタレ. *adj.* Prized. Valued.

Aosura, アオスラ, 放棄セラレタレ、(單數). *v.i.* and *adj.* Abandoned. Cast off (*sing*).

Aosurupa, アオスルパ, 放棄セラレタ ル、(複數). *v.i.* and *adj.* Cast off. Abandoned (*pl*).

Aota, アオタ, 隣人. *n.* The next door. As :—*Aota an guru,* "the next door neighbour."

Aotari, アオタリ, 蔽ヒ重ナリタル. *v.i.* and *adj.* To be tilted up. **Syn : Aopentari.**

Aota-un-guru, アオタウングル, 隣人、(單數). *n.* The next door neighbour.

Aota-un-utara, アオタウンウタラ, 隣人、(複數). *n.* The next door neighbours.

Aotupekare, アオツペカレ, 吝嗇ナル. *adj.* Difficult to spare. **Syn : Anishka.**

Aotushetaye, アオツシェタイェ, 罰ノ 爲ニ髪ヲ釣リル上ゲラル. *v.i.* To be hung up by the hair of the head as in punishment.

Aotuwashi, アオツワシ, 勇敢ナレ. *adj.* Bold. Fearless. **Syn: Rametok-koro.**

Aoyaitak, アオヤイタク, 嘲ラル、アザケラレ. *v.i.* To be derided. Made a fool of. Mocked.

Aoyanenep, アオヤ子チブ, 嘲笑セラレタモノ. *n.* A butt for derision. A person made fun of.

Aowemushi, アオウェムシ, 貧シキ、憐レナレ. *adj.* Poor. In bad condition.

Ap, アブ, 釣針、ツリバリ、銛尖. *n.* A fishhook. The head of a fish-spear.

Ap, アブ, 物、モノ. *n.* An article. A thing. As:— *Ine nei ap,* "Where is that thing." **Syn: Ambe.**

Ap, アブ, 眞似スル振リ. *n.* Pretence. **Syn: Abe. Abe-koro.**

Ap, アブ, 有ルベキ、有ルヤウ、例セバ、エククス子アブ、來ル筈デス. *part.* Preceded by the words *kusu ne, ap* signifies that something was intended or ought to be done. As:— *Ek kusu ne ap,* "he ought to have come." *Chi ki kusu ne ap,* "we intend to do it."

Ap, アブ, 此語ハ過去ヲ示スニ用ユルナリ、例セバ、イベアブ、食セシ. *part.* Sometimes *ap* is used to express past time. As:— *Ibe ap,* "he has eaten." *Ran ap,* "he has gone down."

Apa, アバ, 漏ル. *v.i.* To leak. **Syn: Apekush.**

Apa, アバ, 入口、海ノ方ヨリ見タレ 河口、例セバ、アバアシテ、戸ヲ閉メル. *n.* A door-way. A gateway. An entrance. The open mouth of a river looked at from the sea. As:— *Apa ashte,* "to shut a door." *Apa chaka or maka,* "to open a door." *Apa shi,* "to shut a door." *Apa-ushta,* "a door."

Apa-chip, アバチブ, 戸磨板、敷居. *n.* A door-sill. The grooved piece of word for a door to slide along in.

Apakashnu-guru, アバカシヌグル, 囚人、メシウド. *n.* A prisoner. A person undergoing punishment.

Apan, アバン,
Apani, アバニ, 此. *pro.* This. **Syn: Tapan. Tapani.**

Apanne, アバン子, イカイ. *n.* An edible kind of mussel.

Apakikkara, アバキッカラ, 防禦スル、戸ヲ守ル. *v.i.* To defend one's door-way.

Apakoashi, アバコアシ,
Apakoseshke, アバコセシケ, 戸ヲ閉ジテ出入ヲ断ツ. *v.t.* To shut the door to. To shut in or out.

Apangere, アバンゲレ, 嫌ハレタル. *v.i. and adj.* Abhorent. Hated. Despised. **Syn: Aetunne.**

Apa-otbe, アバオッベ, 戸ノ前ニ掛ケル蓆. *n.* A mat hung in a doorway.

Apapo, アバボ, 花ノ名. *n.* Some kind of flower.

Apapok, アバボク, 裏ニ. *adv.* Behind. As:— *Chisei apapok,* "behind the house."

Apapu, アパプ, 叱カラレル、ワビス
ル. *v.i.* To be scolded. To apologize. **Syn: Akosakayokara.**

Apara, アパラ, 害スル、罪スレ. *v.t.*
To injure. To condemn. To lay
a fault upon another. **Syn:
Epara.**

Aparakoatte, アパラコアッテ, 詛ハ
レタル、叱カラレタル. *adj.* Accursed. Scolded. **Syn: Akosakayokara.**

Aparu, アパル, 扇ク、アオグ. *v.t.* To
fan. To blow by means of a
fan or any such like instrument.

Aparu, アパル, 入口、闞、シキミ. *n.*
The threshhold.

Apa-shem, アパシェム, 玄關、ゲンカン.
n. An entrance porch.

Apa-shi, アパシ, 戸ヲ閉メレ. *v.i.* To
close a door.

Apa-shta,
アパシタ, }戸、ト. *n.* A door.
Apa-ushta,
アパウシタ,

Apashte, アパシテ, 勝ツ、論ジテ勝ツ.
v.t. To defeat. To silence in argument.

Apashte, アパシテ, 走ラセル、逃ガス.
v.i. To be made to run. To be
driven away.

Apatu, アパツ, 散リタル、吹キ散ラサ
レタル. *adj.* Scattered. Blown
about.

Apaushbe, アパウシベ, 戸、ト、戸ノ前
ニ掛ケタル蓆. *n.* A door. A mat
hung before a doorway.

Apa-ushke, アパウシケ, 入口. *n.*
A door-way.

Apa-ushta, アパウシタ, 戸、ト. *n.*
A door. **Syn: Apashta.**

Apa-utara, アパウタラ, 親類、(複數).
n. Relations.

Ape-keshui, アペゲシュイ, ネツボ. *n.*
Dragonet (*Callionymus curvico-
rinis, Cuv. & Val.*)

Api, アピ, 擦疵、スリキズ. *n.* A
wound caused by chaffing.

Api, アピ, 拔ク、(刀ナドチ). *v.t.* To
draw out as a sword from its
sheath. As:—*Tam api,* "to draw
a sword."

Apikuira,
アピクイラ, }潛ンテ行ク、隱レテ
Apikuira-kara, 行ク. *v.i.* To go
アピクイラカラ,
along stealthily. As:—*Hau-shut
oroge apikuira,* "he went along
stealthily following the voice."

Apikuira-no, アピクイラノ, 潛ンデ、
例セバ、アピクイラノオマンワネイユ
クライゲニサ、潛ンデ住ツテ鹿チ殺シ
タ. *adv.* Stealthily. As:—*Apikuira no oman wa nei yuk raige
nisa,* "he went along stealthily
and killed the deer."

Apiri,
アピリ, }獸ノ足跡、擦疵、スリキズ.
Apirihi, *n.* The trail of an
アピリヒ, animal. A foot-print.
A chaffing. A wound left by
rubbing.

Apiru, アピル, 拭ヒタル、擦ル. *v.i.*
and *adj.* Wiped. Rubbed. Chaf-
fed.

Apiya, アピヤ, 私生子. *n.* A bastard.
A half-cast. **Syn: Chiappise.**

Apiye-guru, アピイェグル, 私生子. *n.*
A bastard. A half-cast.

Ap-ka, アプカ, 釣絲、ツリイト. *n.* A
fishing line.

Apka, アプカ, 雄鹿、ヲジカ. *n.* A male
deer. A buck.

Apkara, アブカラ, 取ル、貫フ. *v.t.* To take. To receive. **Syn: Ahupkara.**

Apkara, アブカラ, 勝、カツ. *v.t.* To defeat.

Apkara, アブカラ, 天氣ニ當テ腐ル. *v.i.* To become rotten through exposure to the weather.

Apkash, アブカシ, 步行スル、アルク. *v.i.* and *adj.* To walk. On foot.

Apkash-komon-nukuri, アブカシコモンヌクリ, 蹌踉スレ. *v.i.* To falter in walking.

Apkash-shiniuka, アブカシシニウカ, 步ミチ欲セズ. *v.i.* Indisposed to walk.

Apkash-shinukuri, アブカシシヌクリ, 步キ難キ. *v.i.* To find a difficulty in walking either through old age or indisposition.

Apkash-utor-humi, アブカシウトルフミ, 步音. *n.* The sound of foot steps.

Apka-topa, アブカトバ, 雄鹿ノ群、オシカノムレ. *n.* A herd of male deer.

Apkoro, アブコロ, 如ク見エル、恰モ *adv. ph.* As though. It appears. Like. As:—*Chish apkoro iki,* "he appears to be crying." *Eraman ap koro iki,* "he seems to understand."

Apkot-ni, アブッコニ, 用意ノ整ヒタル釣竿、ツリサチ. *n.* A fishing rod ready prepared for fishing.

Apniniap, アブニニアブ,
Apniniop, アブニニオブ, } 魚ヲ捕ル餌. *n.* A kind of fish decoy. **Syn: Chininiap.**

Apnini-furep, アブニニフレブ, 木ノ實ノ種類. *n.* Some kind of nut.

Apninisei, アブニニセイ, 木ノ實ノ皮. *n.* A nut shell.

Apnit, アブニツ, 釣竿、ツリザチ、銛、鉾ノ類. *n.* A fishing rod. Also a kind of spear. **Syn: Perainit. Tush-ni.**

Aponki, アボンキ,
Apunki, アブンキ, } 扇、アフギ. *n.* A fan. **Syn: Yaiparaparup.**

Apohotonoge, アボホトノゲ, 我ガ子ヨ、(嘆稱ノ辭). *ph.* My dear child.

Apoknare, アボクナレ, 面ヲ俯セテ、カホチフセテ, *adv.* Face-downwards.

Aponde, アボンデ, 減ゼラレ. *v.i.* Reduced. Made small or little.

Aporose, アボロセ, 何々ト名付ケラレタレ. *v.i.* and *ph.* Called by the name of. Called. Named. He who is named. That which is called.

Aporosep, アボロセブ, 何々ト名付ラレタルモノ. *n.* Things that are called or named. As:—*Seta ari aporosep,* "the things called dogs."

Appene, アッペ子, 拙手(ヘタ)ナル. *adj.* Clumsy. Awkward. **Syn: Aikap. Katchak.**

Apsai-ni, アブサイニ, 銛ノ先、モリノサキ. *n.* A piece of wood to which hooks are attached when fishing.

Apsai-pit, アブサイピツ, 銛ニ付クレ石. *n.* A stone attached to an *apsai-ni* to keep it under water.

Apte, アブテ, 弱キ. *adj.* Weak. Powerless.

Apto, アブト, 雨、アメ. *n.* Rain.

Apto-ash,
アプトアシ, 雨降ル. *v.i.* To rain.
Apto-ashpa, It rains.
アプトアシパ,

Apto-ashte-guru, アプタアシテグ
ル, 雨ヲ降ラセル人. *n.* A rain-
maker.

Apto-chikap, アプトチカプ, チドリ、
ムナグロ. *n.* The golden plover.
Charadrius fulvus, Gm.

Apto-hauge, アプトハウゲ, 段々ニ霽
レテユク. *v.i.* To gradually cease
raining.

Apto-nishoro, アプトニショロ, 降リ
サウナ空、(雨ノ). *n.* Rainy skies.

Apto-okake-an, アプトオカケアン,
雨ガ止ンダ. *ph.* It has finished
raining. **Syn : Apto-tui.**

Apto-ran,
アプトラン, 雨ガ降ル. *v.i.* It is
Apto-rui, raining.
アプトルイ,

Apu,
アプ, 海氷、ウミノコホリ. *n.* Sea-
Abu, ice.
アブ,

Apui-kotoro, アプイコトロ, 耳ノ内
面. *n.* The inside surface of the
ears.

Apunki, 扇、アフギ. *n.* A fan.
アプンキ,
Aonki, **Syn : Aungi. Yaipa-**
アオンキ, **raparup.**

Apun-no, 靜カニ、溫和ニ. *adv.*
アプンノ, Gently. Softly. As :
Hapun-no, —*Apun no mokoro,*
ハプンノ,
"good night" (lit. "sleep gently.") *Apun no paye,* "good bye"
(lit. go gently).

Apun-no-apun-no, アプンノアプン
ノ, 甚靜カニ、頗溫和ニ. *adv.*
Very gently. Very softly.

Apushke, アプシケ, 獣ニ裂カル. *v.i.*
To be torn by an animal.

Aputki, アプツキ, 席莚、シキムシロ. *n.*
A mat made of rushes used for
laying on a floor. **Syn : Shokkara.**

Ara, アラ, 有レ、例セバ、アパシアラ、戸
ヲ閉メレ. *aux. v.* Imperative form
of the verb "to be," used as an
auxilliary to other verbs. As :—
Apa shi-ara, "shut the door."
Syn : Yara.

Ara, アラ, 開キタル. *adj.* Open.

Ara, アラ, 全ク. *adv.* Entirely.
Quite. Only. Nothing but. As :
—*Ishirikurantere, ara mim patek,*
"dear me, it is nothing but fat."

Ara, アラ, 鋏、ハサミ、(蟲ナド). *n.*
Forceps.

Ara,
アラ, ハサミムシ. *n.* An
Ara-kikiri, earwig.
アラキキリ,

Ara, アラ, 一、壹足ノ一、例セバ、アラシ
ク、獨眼、片眼. *adj.* One. One of a
pair. As :—*Ara-shik,* "one-eye."
Syn : Oara.

Ara, アラ, 側、脇、傍、ワキ. *n.*
Side. As :—*Ar'ita,* "the side
boards of a boat."

Ara, アラ, 遲キ、緩キ、ノロキ. *adj.*
Late. Slow.

Ara, アラ, 綺麗ナル、キレイナル、美シ
キ. *adj.* Pretty. Beautiful. As :
—*Ara chisei,* "a beautiful house."

Ara, アラ, 裝飾ス. *v.t.* To beautify. To ornament. As :—*Chisei ara,* "to ornament a house."

Ara-attap-ne, アラノタプネ, 空シ
キ手デ、カラテデ. *adv.* Empty-
handed.

Arage, アラゲ, 物ノ半分. *adj.* Half of anything. Partly. In part. As :—*Keutum arage pirika kamui an, keutum arage wen kamui an,* "they are deities partly good and partly evil."

Araguru, アラグル, 綺麗ナコト. *n.* Beauty.
Arakuru, アラクル, Glory. Majesty.

Araige, アライゲ, 殺サレタ. *v.i.* Killed.

Araka, アラカ, 痛ム、イタム. *v.i.* To ache. To be in pain.

Araka-i, アラカイ, 苦痛、痛ム處. *n.* An aching. An aching place.

Arakap, アラカプ, 苦痛、イタミ. *n.* An aching. Something which aches.

Arakare, アラカレ, 苦痛サセル. *v.t.* To give pain to. To agonize.

Arakat-oroge-chiepoknare, アラカトロゲチエポクナレ, 落膽サセレ *v.t.* To dishearten. To cause to lose spirit.

Arake, アラケ, 半分、ニツノ一ツ. *adj.*
Arage, アラゲ, Half. One of two.
As:—*Chep arake,* "half a fish." *Keire arake,* "one shoe."

Arake-chiraige-tashum, アラケチライゲタシュム, 中風、チカブ. *n.* Paralysis.

Arakere, アラケレ, 減ズル. *v.i.* To diminish. To cease to be. To lower. **Syn:** Ramka. **Aorakere.**

Araki, アラキ, 來ル(復敷). *v.i.* (pl). To come. **Syn:** Ariki.

Arakikiri, アラキキリ, ハサミムシ. *n.* An earwig.

Arakirisamtek-omare, アラキリサムテクオマレ, 箕坐スル、アグラカク. *v.i.* To sit crosslegged.

Arakke, アラッケ, 酒、サケ. *n.* Wine. Sake. Strong drink.

Arakotomka, アラコトムカ, 無論、疑ハズ. *adv.* Without doubt. Doubtless.

Arakotomka, アラコトムカ, 己チ飾ル. *v.t.* To ornament one's self.

Arakuntukap, アラクンツカブ, 極惡ノ惡寬. *n.* The very worst of the demons.

Arakuru, アラクル, 美シキコト. *n.* Beauty.
Araguru, アラグル, Glory. Majesty.

Arakurukashi, アラクルカシ, 丁度上ニ. *adv.* Exactly above.

Arakushkonna, アラクシコンナ, 甚ダ急ニ. *adv.* Very suddenly.

Arakuwan-no, アラクワンノ, 眞直ニ、前ニ. *adv.* In front. Straight ahead.

Aramaken, アラマケン, 何々ニ笑フ. *v.t.* To amuse. To laugh at.

Aramakenbe, アラマケンベ, 面白キコト. *n.* An amusing thing.

Aramaukese, アラマウケセ, 傍ニ、カタハラニ. *adv.* By the side of.

Aramepakare, アラメパカレ, 思フ、考ヘル. *v.t.* To think. To consider. To calculate. To weigh in the mind.

Aramoi-sam, アラモイサム, 北、キタ. *n.* The north. **Syn:** Oyanruru.

Aramoisam, アラモイサム, 入海、イリウミ. *n.* A bay.

Arani-wano, アラニワノ, 先キニ、以前ニ. *adv.* Previously to. **Syn:** Ekanai-wano.

Araoraye, アラオライェ, 下ゲル. *v.t.* To lower. To let down.

Arapa, アラバ,
Arupa, アルバ, 往、ユク. *v.i.* To go.

Arapare, アラバレ,
Arupare, アルバレ, 行カシム. *v.t.* To send. **Syn: Omande.**

Arapekere-kamui, アラペケレカムイ, 極善ノ神. *n.* The best of the deities.

Ararapa, アララバ, 詰メ込ム、搖リ込ム. *v.t.* To press down. To shake down.

Ararirari, アラリラリ, 踏ミ固ムレ. *v.t.* To shake or trample down. To press down. To harden by trampling on.

Arasatchepare, アラサッチェバレ, 開ラク、(風ニ衣服ナドノ飛ビ開ク). *v.t.* To fly open, as the parts of a dress.

Arasereke, アラセレケ, 半分、ハンブレ. *n.* The half of anything.

Arashka, アラシカ, 空手ノ、カラテノ、持タズ. *v.i.* and *adj.* To be empty handed. Not carrying.

Arashne, アラシ子, 共ニ、皆共ニ. *adv.* Altogether.

Arashuianda, アラシュイアンダ, 或時ニ、或處ニ. *adv.* Once upon a time. At a certain time or place.

Arashui-ne, アラシュイ子,
Arashui-no, アラシュイノ, 一回. *adj.* Once. **Syn: Ari-shui.**

Arashui-range, アラシュイランゲ, 一一ニ. *adv.* One at a time.

Arashunketu, アラシュンケツ, 草絲. クサイト. *n.* A grass band or cord.

Arataraka, アラタラカ, 愚カナル、ムチヤクチヤナル. *adj.* Silly. Senseless. Delirious. Slovenly. Careless. **Syn: Etaraka. Aretaraka.**

Aratchi, アラッチ, 溫和ノ、オダヤカナル. *adj.* Quiet. Peaceable.

Aratchire, アラッチレ, 穩ニスル、安心サセル. *v.i.* To be pacified. To be acquitted of a crime.

Arauratki-no, アラウラッキノ, 唯タ、此ノミ. *adv.* Only. Only this and nothing else.

Araushtek, アラウシテク, 消エル、鏖殺サレレ. *v.i.* To be extinguished. Exterminated. Massacred.

Araushtekka, アラウシテッカ, 消ス、無クスル. *v.t.* To extinguish. To massacre. To exterminate.

Arawa(n), アラワ,
Aruwa(n), アルワ, 七ツ. *adj.* Seven.

Arawan-hotne, アラワンホツ子, 百四十. *adj.* One hundred and forty.

Arawan-ikashima-hotne, アラワンイカシマホツ子, 二十七. *adj.* Twenty seven.

Arawan-ikashima-ine-hotne, アラワンイカシマイ子ホツ子, 八十七 *adj.* Eighty seven.

Arawan-otutanu, アラワンオツタヌ, 第七. *n.* The seventh. (For the numerals see Grammar *Chapter vii*).

Arawe, アラウェ, 泡、アワ. *n.* Froth. The scum of a boiling pot.

Are, アレ, 火ヲ付ケル. *v.t.* To kindle. To light. As:—*Abe are*, "to light a fire."

Are, アレ, 坐ラセル、置ク、(網ナド). v. t. To cause to sit. To set (as a fisher-man his nets).

Are, アレ, 全ク、強ク. adj. Quite. En-
Ari, アリ, tirely. With force.

Are, アレ, 置ク. v. t. To put. To place. **Syn : Ande.**

Are-abe, アレアベ, 燃ユル火. n. A flaming fire.

Areika, アレイカ, 喜ブ. v. i. To be pleased with. **Syn : Erayap.**

Areikop, アレイコブ, 名ヅケル. v. i. To be named.

Areka, アレカ, 承知スル、誉メラレル. v.i.
Areika, アレイカ, and v. t. To give assent to. To be praised. To second. To encourage.

Arakushkonna, アラクシコンナ, 急ニ. adv. Very
Arekushkonna, アレクシコンナ, suddenly. In a moment.

Arepokara, アレポカラ, 海ニテ死ス. v.t. To die at sea.

Arerakari, アレラカリ, 曝サレタル、晒ラサレタル. adj. Aired. Exposed to the wind.

Arerakari-ki, アレラカリキ, 晒ス、サラス. v.t. To air in the wind.

Areshirikush, アレシリクシ, 通過ス ル、トウリユク. v. i. To pass by.

Areshirikush-guru, アレシリクシグ ル, 通行人、訪問者. n. A passer by. A visitor. A caller.

Ari, アリ, 持ツテ、例セバ、マレクア リチブエコイキ、銛ヲ以テ魚ヲ捕ル. post. By means of. With. For. As :—*Marek ari chep koiki*, " to kill fish with a spear." *Ari ya*

etaye an tush, " A rope used for drawing a net." **Syn : Ani.**

Ari, アリ, 燃エル. v. i. To be alight.

Ari, アリ, 皮ハゲタル. adj. Skinned. **Syn : Iri-au.**

Ari, アリ, 遅キ. adj. Late. Tardy. Slow. **Syn : Ara.**

Ari, アリ, 其ノ. pro. That. That which. As :—*Ahup yan, ari hawash*, " he says you are to enter. *Seta ari ayep*, " that which is called a dog."

Ari, アリ, 全ク、強ク. adv. Quite. Severely. Entirely. With force. **Syn : A. Ara.**

Ari-au, アリアウ, 其ノ、彼等. pro. That. Those. As :—*Ari an itak ani ye nisa ruwe ne*, " he spoke with those words."

Arikari-chisei, アリカリチセイ, 家ノ 骨組. n. The framework of a house. The roof over a pit-dwellig. **Syn : Chisei-niye. Chirikari-chisei.**

Ariki, アリキ, 來ル、(複數). v. i. To come (pl. of ek).

Ariki-an, アリキアン, 來タ. v.i. past. Have come.

Ariashin-no, アリアシンノ, 一度、又. adj. Once. Again.

Ariki-ash-shiri, アリキアシシリ, 來 リツ、. v. i. Coming. They are coming.

Arikiki, アリキキ, 育ツル、ツダツ、例セ バ、ルプネパクノアリキキ、大人トナル マデ育テル. v. t. To bring up. To rear. As :—*Rupne pak no arikiki*, " to bring up to manhood. *Arikiki tuikata*, " during adolescence."

Arikiki-no, アリキキノ, 全力ヲ以テ. *adv.* With all one's might. With might and main. **Syn: Shiari-kiki-no,**

Ari-kiki-tuikata, アリキキツイカタ, 生長スル間. *ph.* During adolescence.

Arikinne, アリキン子, 全ク、其ク. *adv.* Quite. Thoroughly. **Syn: Arara. Earakinne.**

Arikiri, アリキリ, 甚ダ. *adj.* Very much. Intensely.

Arikko, アリッコ, カ ラ マ ツ サ ウ. *n.* The feather columbine. *Thalictrum aquilegifolium, L.*

Arikko-kuttara, アリッコクッタラ, アリツコ二同ジ. *n.* The same " as *Arikko.*

Arimu, アリム, 鼠、ネヅミ. *n.* A rat or mouse. **Syn: Eremu.**

Arikomare, アリコマレ, 懸ル、カケル. *v. t.* To hang up. To put on a high place.

Arikoraye, アリコライェ, 上ゲル. *v.t.* To raise. To shift from a lower to a higher position.

Arip, アリプ, 屋根. *n.* A roof. A covering. As: *Chisei arip*, " the roof of a house."

Aripekunne, アリペクン子, 小刀. *n.* A small knife.

Arishirikush, アリシリクシ, 訪問スル. *v. t.* To call upon in passing. To look in upon.

Arishui, アリシュイ, 一度. *adj.* Once. **Syn: Arashui.**

Arita-omap, アリタオマプ, 海二テ漁スル船. *n.* A small boat with boards fixed to its sides used for sea-fishing.

Aro, アロ, 甚ダ早キ. *adj.* Very early. Premature. As: — *Aro-paikara.* " very early in the spring."

Arohokamginno, アロホカムギンノ, 折角、故意二. *adv.* Purposely. On purpose. **Syn: Hokamgin-no.**
Arokamgim-no, アロカムギムノ,

Aro-nochiu, アロノチウ, 夕ノ明星、ユウノメウゼウ. *n.* The evening star. **Syn: Aronuman-nochiu.**

Aro-numan, アロヌマン, 暮方、クレカタ. *n.* Twilight. Late in the evening.

Aro-numan-nochiu, アロヌマンノチウ, 夕ノ明星. *n.* The evening star. **Syn: Aro-nochiu.**

Aronnu, アロンヌ, 殺ロサレタ、(複數). *v.i.* Killed. *Pl: of Raige.*

Aronnu-wa-isam, アロンヌワイサム, 殺ロサレタ. *ph.* Killed and done away with.

Aropaikara, アロパイラカ, 早春. *n.* Very early spring.

Aroramboso, アロラムボソ, 疑懼スル. *v. i.* To be agitated with fright. **Syn: Aramboso.**

Arorokishne-no, アロロキシチノ, 秘密二、ナイショ二. *adv.* Secretly. Privately.

Aroshinep, アロシチプ, 第一. *n.* The first one. Primier.

Aru, アル, 時トシテ此字ヲ動詞二加フルトキハ複數ノ働キヲナスナリ. *part.* Sometimes used as a plural prefix to verbs.

Aruchire, アルチレ, 充分二煮エヌ. *adj.* Under-cooked.

Arukirika-samtek-o, アルキリカサムテクオ, 箕坐スル、アグラカク. *v.i.* To sit tailor-fashion. To sit cross legged.

Arupa, アルパ, 行ク、(單數). *v.i.* To go.
Arapa, アラパ, (*sing.*)

Arupakbe, アルパクベ, 同ジク、同ジ程. *adv.* Alike. In the same degree.

Arupare, アルパレ, 遣ス、途ル. *v.t.* To send.
Arapare, アラパレ,

Arushantuka-aukoamba, アルシャンツカアウコアムバ, 配列スル. *ph.* To hang in orderly rows. To set in orderly array.

Arushito, アルシト, ウバユリノ菓子. *n.* A round cake made of arrow-root. **Syn: Akam.**

Arushka, アルシカ, 憤怒ヲ受ケルモノ ニナッタ. *v.i.* To have become an object of anger.

Arutam, アルタム, 刀、カタナ. *n.* A sword. **Syn: Tam. Emush.**

Arutam-euk-guru, アルタムエウッグル, 俘虜、トリコ. *n.* A captive.

Arutereke, アルテレケ, 跳子マツル、駻ル. *v.i.* To jump about. **Syn: Tereke-tereke.**

Aruterekere, アルテレケレ, 跳子サセル、駻子サセル. *v. t.* To cause to jump about. To make frisk about (as animals).

Arutoro, アルトロ, 北、キタ. *n.* The north.

Arutu, アルツ, 舶來シタル. *adj.* Imported. **Syn: Chikusa. Chiyange.**

Arutu-ashkoro, アルツアシコロ, 日本酒. *n.* Japanese *sake*. **Syn: Chikusa-ashkoro. Chiyange-ashkoro.**

Aruwohumse-chiu, アルウォフムセチウ, 蛇ヲ見シ雀ガ
Aruwomsei-chiu, アルウォムセイチウ, 群カリ集マリテ悲鳴スル聲. *n.* The peculiar warbling sparrows make when they see a snake. **Syn: Niwenhoripi.**

Asakara, アサカラ, 麻、アサ、イラクサ. *n.*
Asangara, アサンガラ, Hemp. Nettles. **Syn: Hai.**

Asam, アサム, 底、ソコ、基石、ドダイ、例セバ、チセイアサマ、家ノ
Asama, アサマ, 土臺. *n.* Bottom. Foundation. As:—*Chisei asama,* "the foundation of a house." *Ure-asama,* "the sole of the foot."

Asam-kotoro, アサムコトロ, 底內面、ソコノウチメン. *n.* The inside surface of the bottom of anything. As·—*Pet asam-kotoro,* "the surface of a river's bottom."

Asam-sak, アサムサク, 底ナシノ. *adj.* Bottom-less.

Asam-sak-i, アサムサクイ, 底ナキ所. *n.* A bog. The abyss.

Asangara, アサンガラ, 麻、アサ、イラクサ. *n.*
Asakara, アサカラ, Hemp. **Syn: Hai.**

Asangi, アサンギ, 青キ、綠、ミドリ. *adj.* Blue. Green.

Asapa-muyep, アサパムイェプ, 頭巾、ヅキン. *n.* A head cloth. **Syn: Aesapa-muyep.**

Asarama, アサラマ, 撰擇スル、エラブ. *v.t.* To choose.

Asari, アサリ, 上ヲ向イテ開ラキタル.

adj. Opened out. Open to the skies. The open skies.

Ase, アセ, 坐席、腰掛、コシカケ. *n.* A seat. A stool or chair. **Syn: Aset. Amset. Set.**

Aseika, アセイカ, 湯ニ浸タス. *v.t.* To steep in hot water. To scald.

Aseireka, アセイレカ, 油ニテアゲル、煠ク. *v.t.* To fry in hot water or fat.

Asesekka, アセセッカ, 熱スレ. *v. t.* To heat. To make hot.

Aset, アセツ, 腰掛、コシカケ, *n.* A stool ; seat ; a chair.

Ash, アシ, 立ツ、起キアガル. *v.i.* To stand. To appear. To arise.

Ash, アシ, 吹ク, To blow (as wind). To descend (as rain). **Syn : Rui.**

Ash, アシ, 此ノ ash チ受動詞ニ付加スル時ニハ複敷自己代名詞ニ爲ルナリ、例セバ、アリキアシ、吾々ハ來ル. *part.* When added to intransitive verbs *ash* indicates the 1st per. pl. As :—*Ariki ash,* "we come." *Paye ash,* "we go." When added to intransitive verbs it indicates the action of the first person upon the second. As :—*Kuani echi nure ash kusu ne,* " I will tell you " ; *e kore ash na,* " I give it to you." *Seta chi-ronnu ash okere,* " we have killed the dogs."

Ash-ash, アシアシ. 歩ムダリ止マツタリスレ. *v. i.* To go a little way and then stop. **Syn : Eyokkot.**

Ashbe, アシベ, 魚ノ脊鰭. *n.* The first dorsal fin of the larger kinds of fish. On the smaller kinds of fish this is called. " *Mekka-ushbe.*"

Ashi, アシ, 立タセル. *v.t.* To set up. To put. To hang over. As :—

Shu abe kata ashi, " Set the kettle over the fire."

Ashi-ai, アシアイ, 毒矢、ドクヤ. *n.* Arrows with poison attached. *See oha-ai.*

Ashureka, アシュレカ, 去ル. *v.i.* To leave. To go away. To depart.

Ashika, アシカ, 布ノ絲. *n.* Thread in cloth.

Ashikipet, アシキベツ, 指、ユビ. *n.* A finger. A toe. **Ruwe ashikipet,** " the thumb " ; **pon-ashikipet,** " the little finger " ; **itangi-kem-ashikipet,** " the index finger."

Ashikipet-orun-kani, アシキベツオルンカニ, 指環、ユビワ. *n.* A finger ring.

Ashikipettu, アシキベッツ, 指、(複數). *n.* The fingers (*pl*).

Ashikipettu-orun-kani, アシキベッツオルンカニ, 指環 (複數). *n.* Rings for the fingers.

**Ashikne,
アシクネ,
Ashiknep,
アシクネプ,** } 五. *adj.* Five.

Ashikne-hotne, アシクネホツネ, 百、數ニ關スル事ハ第七章ニアリ. *adj.* A hundred. (For the numerals see Grammar *cpt. vii*).

Ashiknen, アシクネン, 五人. *n.* Five men.

Ashikne-otutanu, アシクネオツタヌ, 第五. *adj.* The fifth.

Ashikne-shine-wan-hot, アシクネシチワンホツ, 千. *adj.* A thousand.

**Ashikne-shuine,
アシクネシュイネ,
Ashikne-shuino,
アシクネシュイノ,** } 五度. *adj.* Five times.

Ashiknure, アシクヌレ, 救助セラル.
v.i. To be saved. To be made to
live.

Ashikopa, アシコバ, 似タレ. *adj.*
Resembling.

Ashikoraye, アシコライェ, 貰フ、受ケ
レ. *v.t.* To receive. **Syn : Akore.**

Ashikore, アシコレ, 生ル. *v.i.* To be
born.

Ashimbe, アシムベ, 罰金、バツキン. *n.*
A fine.

Ashimbe-sange, アシムベサンゲ, 罰
金チ出ス. *v.t.* To pay a fine.

Ashimbe-sangere, アシムベサンゲレ,
罰金チ課ス. *v.t.* To fine.

Ashimbe-turu, アシムベツル, 列ニス
ル、並ベレ. *v.i.* To be arranged in
a row.

Ashin, アシン, 出デ行ク. *v.i.* To go
out. To come out.

Ashin, アシン, 新シキ. *adj.* New.
Syn : Ashiri.

Ashinge, アシンゲ, 迯リ出ス、拔出ス.
v.t. To send out. To root out.
To pluck out. To pull out or up.

Ashinkop, アシンコプ, 繩ノ引輪、ナ
ワノコカシワ、結目、ムスビメ. *n.* A
noose. A knot.

Ashinkop-nere, アシンコプチレ, 引
輪スル、結ビコブツクル. *v.t.* To
make into a knot.

Ashin-no, アシンノ, 新シク. *adv.*
Newly. Again. Afresh. For the
first time.

Ashin-no-kara, アシンノカラ, 新ニ
スレ. *v.t.* To renew. To do over
again.

Ashinru, アシンル, 雪隱、セツイン. *n.*
A water-closet. **Syn : Soine-ru.
Osoine-ru.**

Ashinuma, アシヌマ, 自ラ、自身. *pro.*
One'self. I. **Syn : Kuani. Yaikata.**

Ashiokte, アシオクテ, 衝キ當ル、引掛
ケル、ヒキカケル. *v.t.* To strike
against. To get hooked up in.

Aship, アシブ, 咲ク、(單數). *v.i.* To
flower. To blossom. (*sing*).

Ashippa, アシッバ, 咲ク、(複數). *v.i.*
To flower. To blossom. (*pl*).

**Ashiramkore-guru, アシラムコレグ
ル,** 友、知己、トモ. *n.* A friend. An
acquaintance.

Ashirekatta, アシレカッタ, 急ニ仆レ.
To fall down suddenly.

Ashiri, アシリ, 新シキ、次ギ. *adj.* New.
The next. As :—*Ashiri-pe*, " a
new thing"; *Ashiri-pa*, "a new
year." **Syn : Ashiri-an.**

Ashirikara, アシリカラ, 改ムル. *v.t.*
To make over again. To renew.
Syn : Ashin-no-kara.

**Ashirikashurare,
アシリカシュラレ,**
**Ashirikashomare,
アシリカショマレ,** }
歴シ出ス、オシダ
ス. *v.i.* To be
crowded out.

Ashiriki, アシリキ, 改ムル. *v.t.* To do
again. To renew. **Syn : Ashirikara.**

Ashishirikire, アシシリキレ, 退ク.
v.i. To retire.

Ashiseturuka, アシセツルカ, 背ノ上
ニ. *adv.* Over one's back. On
one's back. **Syn : Asei. Akai.**

Ashit, アシツ, 新シキ. *n.* New. Next.
Syn : Ashiri.

Ashitoma, アシトマ, 恐ロシキ、オソ
ロシキ. *adj.* Awful. Dreadful.
Fearful.

Ashitoma-i, アシトマイ, 恐ロシキ處、墓、ハカ. *n.* A grave. A dreadful thing or place. **Syn: Tushiri.**

Ashitomap, アシトマブ, 恐シキモノ. *n.* A dreadful thing. Something to be afraid of.

Ashitomarep, アシトマレブ, 恐シキモノ. *n.* A thing to make one fear. An appalling thing or circumstance.

Ashituk-kirau, アシツッキラウ, 鹿ノ新シキ角. *n.* The new horns of deer.

Ashiu, アシウ, 一度. *adj.* Once. **Syn: Arashiu.**

Ashkai, アシカイ, 能フ、伎倆アル、精巧ナル. *adj.* Able. Clever. Adroit. Capable. **Syn: Ri-no.**

Ashkai-no, アシカイノ, 上手ニ. *adv.* Ably. Cleverly. Adroitly.

Ashkai-samma, アシカイサムマ, 右ノ方. *adv.* The right hand side.

Ashkakamarep, アシカカマレブ, Ashkakushtep, アシカクシテブ, 外着、上着. *n.* A coat.

Ashkanne, アシカンチ, Akkanne, アッカンネ, 清潔ナル、純粹ノ. *adj.* Clean. Pure. **Syn: Turu-sak.**

Ashkanne-ne-kara, アシカンチ子カラ, Ashkanne-no-kara, アシカンチノカラ, 清ムル. *v. t.* To cleanse. **Syn: Turu-sakte.**

Ashkannere, アシカンチレ, 清ムレ. *v.t.* To cleanse.

Ashke, アシケ, 手. *n.* The hand. **Syn: Teke.**

Ashke-auk, アシケアウク, 殺サル. *v. i.* To be killed. To have one's life taken by hand.

Ashke-kotoro, アシケコトロ, 掌、タナゴヽロ、手ノヒラ. *n.* The palm of the hand.

Ashketesh, アシケテシ, 櫛、クシ. *n.* A comb.

Ashkeuk, アシケウク, 殺ス. *v.t.* To kill.

Ashke-ukom, アシケウコム, 拳、コブシ. *n.* The fists.

Ashkoro, アシコロ, 手一パイ. *n.* A handful.

Ashkoro, アシコロ, 舶來ノ酒類、例セバ、アルツアシコロ、輸入シタ酒. *n.* Wine or spirits of any kind. As:—*Arutu ashkoro,* "imported wine."

Ashkororo, アシコロロ, 手イツパイ. *n.* A handfull.

Ashnap, アシナブ, Asnap, アスナブ, 櫂. *n.* An oar. **Syn: Assap.**

Ashne, アシ子, 五. *adj.* Five. **Syn: Ashikne.**

Ashni, アシニ, 墓標、ハカジルシ. *n.* A memorial set up to mark a grave. A grave stone.

Ashni-pusa, アシニブサ, 女ノ墓標ニ付ケレ總. *n.* A tassle hung on a woman's grave mark.

Ashnu, アシヌ, 早キ、其キ、上手ナル、例セバ、シユクプアシヌ、早ク生ズル. *adj.* Quick. Well. Clever. Good. *Shukup-ashnu,* "of quick growth." *Hoyupu-ashnu,* "a good runner." *Ashnu-guru,* "a clever person."

Ashpa, アシバ, 聾、ツンボ、例セバ、アシバキサライツタヌレ、聾者ノ眞似スル. *adj.* Deaf. As:—*Ashpa kisara itutanure,* "to turn a deaf ear to."

Ashpa, アシバ, 降ル、(複數). *v.i.* To descend. To come down. (*pl. of ash*).

Ash-ratchako, アシラッチャコ, 標燈、タチランプ. *n.* A standing light. A light set up as a guide.

Ashrekut, アシレクツ, 第一項椎. *n.* The top of the spine. Atlas.

Ashrukonna, アシルコンナ, 建ツ. *v.i.* To stand (as a house). To be built up.

Ashte, アシテ, 立タセル. *v.t.* To set up. To make stand.

Ashui, アシュイ, 一度. *adj.* Once. Syn: **Ashiu. Arashuine.**

Ashuttasa, アシュッタサ, 供養スレ. *v. t.* To perform certain rites for the dead.

Ashuye, アシュイェ, 手招キスル、搖スル. *v. t.* To call by beckoning to. To shake about. Syn: **Ashuye-shuye. Korenna-shuye.**

Ashwambe, アシワンベ, 陰核. *n.* Clitoris.

Asnap, アスナブ, 櫂、カイ. *n.* An oar.

Asoro, アソロ, 底、跡、臀、シリ. *n.* Bottom. Hinder-most. The posteriors. Syn: **Asoro.**

Asoye, アソイェ, 穴ヲ穿ツ. *v.t.* To bore a hole.

Asoyep, アソイェブ, 錐、キリ. *n.* A gimlet.

Assa, アッサ, 漕ク. *v.t.* To row. Syn: **Assap-koro.**

Assap, アッサブ,
Asnap, アスナブ, } 櫂、カイ. *n.* An oar.

Assap-chikiri-ush, アッサブチキリウシ, 水カキ足. *n.* Web-footed.

Assuru, アッスル, 評判、噂、名聲. *n.* Fame.

Assuru-an, アッスルアン, 有名ナル. *adj.* Famous.

Assuru-ash-hawe-o, アッスルアシハウェオ, 名高クナル. *v.i.* To have become famous.

Assurunure, アッスルヌレ, 披露スル、イヒフラス. *v.t.* To make known.

Asura-ni, アスラニ, 披露ス、イヒアラス、言ヒ知ラセル. *v.t.* To make famous. To make known. To narrate. To describe.

Asuru-oroge-hopuni, アスルオロゲホブニ, 言ヒ布ラサル. *v.i.* To spread about as a rumour.

Asurube, アスルベ, 熊ノ耳. *n.* A bear's ear.

At, アツ, 二分ノ一、半分. *adj.* One of a pair. One. Half. As:—*At-kema,* "one foot." *At-tem,* "half a mile." (lit: "half a stretch of the arms).

At, アツ, 楡ノ皮絲、絲、イト、紐、ヒモ. *n.* Elm fibre. A string. A thong. A loot-lace.

At, アツ, 物ノ柄. *n.* The handle of anything. The sash of a bag. Syn: **Atu. Atuhu.**

At, アツ, 鼯鼠、ムサビ. *n.* A kind of grey flying-squirriel. *Pteromys leucogenys, Temn.*

At, アツ, 輝ル. *v. i. & adj.* Shining. Light. To shine. Syn: **Tom.**

At, アツ, 豐カナル、多數ナル. *v. i. & adj.* Plentiful. To be numerous.

At, アツ, 出ヅル、(蒸氣又ハ煙ノ). *v.i.* To come forth as steam or smoke.

At, アツ, 有ル、(複數). *v. i.* Are. (*pl. of an*).

Atak, アタク, 迎ヘラレル. *v. i.* To be sent for. To be fetched.

Ataku-kara, アタクカラ, 結塊スル、カタメル. *v.i. & adj.* Agglomerated. **Syn: Taku-akara.**

At-amba, アタムバ, 絲ヲ以テ導ク、(復数). *v.t.* (*pl.*) To lead by a string.

Atane, アタ子, 蕪、カブ. *n.* Turnips.

At-ani, アタニ, 絲ヲ以テ導ク、(單數). *v.t.* (*sing*). To lead by a string.

Atap, アタプ, 搖ルヽ(舟ノ). *v.i.* To roll about as a ship at sea.

Atap, アタプ, 地ヨリ掘リ出サレタモノ. *n.* Anything dug out of the ground. **Syn : Ata-ambe.**

Atarabe, アタラベ, **Atarobe, アタロベ,** アイヌノカバン、(草ヲ以テ造リ物チ入レテ運ビ寢ルトキハ其ノ上ニフス). *n.* A pallet. Couch. Mattress. A travelling bag. (used to sleep on at night.) **Syn : Atarakina.**

Atarimaye, アタリマイェ, 用、關係、持前. *n.* One's rights. One's own business. One's own affairs. As:— *Ku atarimaye gusu, iteki isaikako yan,* "don't interfere for this is my business." **Syn : Yaikota gusu-an-kunip.**

Atari-tari, アタリタリ, ダクック、(馬上ナトニテ). *v.i.* To be shaken up and down as in a saddle when riding.

Atarope, アタロベ, アイヌノカバン、(草ニテ造リ物チ入レテ運ブ又寢ヌル時其上ニ横ハル. Same as **Atarabe.**

Atat, アタツ, 細カニ切ラレル. *v.i.* To be cut up into small pieces. *Atat-chep,* "fish cut up into small pieces and dried."

Atau, アタウ, 物ノ置キ場所. *adv.* A place where something is or has been placed (*pl.*)

Ataye, アタイェ, 直段、チダン. *n.* Price. As:—*Ataye kara,* "to pay." *Ataye eraratikire,* "to beat down in price." **Syn : Aro.**

Ataye-arapare, アタイェアラバレ, 拂フ、ハラウ. *v.t.* To pay.

Ataye-eraratkire, アタイェエララッキレ, 直引スル. *v. t.* To beat down in price.

Ataye-hauge, アタイェハウゲ, 安價ナル. *adj.* Cheap. **Syn : Ataye-pan. Oro-pan.**

Ataye-kore, アタイェコレ, 拂フ、支辨スル. *v.t.* To pay. **Syn : Ataye-sange. Ataye-omande. Oro-omande.**

Ataye-nupuru, アタイェヌプル, 高價ナル. *adj.* Expensive. Dear. **Syn : Ataye - yupke. Oro - nu puru.**

Ataye-pan, アタイェバン, 安價ナル. *adj.* Cheap.

Ataye-sange, アタイェサンゲ, 支辨スル、ハラフ. *v.t.* To pay.

Ataye-ye, アタイェイェ, 直ヲ付ケル. *v. t.* To price.

Ataye-yupke, アタイェユプケ, 高價ナレ. *adj.* Expensive. Dear.

Atchei, アッチエイ, 外ノ、異レル. *adj.* Other. Strange.

Atchi, アッチ, 不潔ナル、穢キ. *adj.* Dirty. Filthy. As:—*Atchi an na,* "it is dirty."

Atchisei, アンチセイ, 他ノ家. *n.* Another house. A stranger's dwelling.

Atchisei-un-guru, アッチセイウングル, 異人. *n.* Strangers.

Atchiu, アッチウ, 鎗ヲ投ゲル. *v.t.*
To thrust. To throw a spear.

Atchiu-ashnu, アッチウアシヌ,
Atchiu-no, アッチウノ, } 鎗投ゲノ上手ナル. *adj.* Clever at throwing a spear.

Ateineka, アテイチカ, 濕ヲス、水ヲ掛ケル. *v.t.* To water. To moisten.

Atemka, アテムカ, 水ヲ掛ケテ息ヲ吹キ返サセレ. *v.t.* To revive (by sprinkling water upon).

Atere, アタレ, 待ツ. *v.t.* To await. **Syn : Aehuye. Etere.**

Aterekere-terekere, アテレケレ テレケレ, 子供ヲ搖スル. *v. t.* To dangle up and down as a child.

Atesep, アテセブ, 織物、チリモノ. *n.* Anything woven.

Ateshkara-kore, アテシカラコレ, 傳言スル、コトヅケル. *v.t.* To send a message by a person.

Ateshko, アテシコ, 他人ニ傳言セラル、例セバ、アラパグルアテシコルスイ、其人ニ傳言シタイ. *v.t.* and *v.i.* To send a message by another. To be employed on an errand by another. As :—*Arapa guru ateshko rusui,* "I wish to send a message by him." **Syn : Teshkara.**

Ateuina, アテウイナ, 繋ク、ツナグ. *v.t.* To tie up.

Atkochi, アッコチ, 魚ノ尾、尾鰭. *n.* A fish's tail The caudal fin of a fish.

Atkoro-guru, アッコログル, 蛸、タコ、章魚. *n.* Octopod. **Syn : Atuina.**

At-ni, アツニ, オヘヨウ. *n.* Mountain elm. *Ulmus montana, Sm. var. laciniata, Trautv.*

At-ni-koro, アツニコロ, 木ノ叉ニテ支ヘレ. *v.i.* To be tied up to a tree. To fix in the fork of a tree. **Syn : Oknikoro.**

Atomte, アトムテ, 美シキ. *adj.* Beautiful. Pretty. Neat. **Syn : Aara. Irammasure.**

Atomte-no, アトムテノ, 美麗ニ. *adv.* Beautifully. Neatly. Prettily. Well. **Syn : Irammakaka.**

Atomte-no-kara, アトムテノカラ, 綺麗ニスル、瓦クスル. *v.t.* To do well. To make pretty. To beautify.

Atpa, アツパ, 案内者、大將、アンナイジャ. *n.* A leader. A general. A captain. As :—*Yuk atpa,* "a leader deer." *Utara atpa,* "a captain of a gang of men."

Atpa, アツパ, 前ニ. *post.* The head or beginning. At the front of anything.

Atpake, アツパケ, 始、ハシメ. *n.* Beginning. Commencement. As :— *Atpake otta,* "in the beginning." *Atpake un,* "at the beginning." *Atpake wano,* "from the beginning."

Atpaketa, アツパケタ, 始メニ. *adv.* In or at the beginning.

Atpata, アツパタ, 先頭ニ、マツサキニ. *adv.* At the head.

At-saranip, アツサラニプ, 楡ノ皮ヲ以テ造リシ袋. *n.* A kind of bag made of elm fibre.

Attapne, アッタプ子, 空(カラ)手ニテ. *adv.* Empty handed. Having nothing.

Attashnure, アッタシヌレ, 一口ニ呑ム. *v.t.* To drink up at once without resting. To swallow quickly (as any kind of noxious medicine).

Atte, アッテ, 輝カス、點ラス、説明スル、トキアカス、例セバ、ヌペキアツテ、輝カス. *v.t.* To make shine. To send forth. To explain. To increase. As:—*Nupeki atte*, "to send forth light." *Yuk atte, chep atte,* "to make deer and fish increase."

Atte, アッテ, 懸ケル、起タシムレ. *v.t.* To hang up. To suspend. As:—*Horikashi atte,* "to suspend from." To set up.

Atte-kane, アンテカ子, 懸カッテアル. *adv.* Hanging. In a suspending position.

Attem, アッテム, 腕牛廣、ハンヒロ. *n.* Half the distance one can attain by stretching the arms out.

Attereke, アッテレケ, 飛躍スル、ハネル. *v.i.* To jump or hop about as a frog.

Attereke-tereke, アッテレケテレケ, 飛躍スル、トブ. *v.i.* To jump or hop about as a frog. Frequentative of *Attereke*.

Attomsama, アットムサマ, 迄、マデ. *adv.* As far as. To. As:—*En-attomsama eushi,* "he came to me."

Attune-no-an, アッツ子ノアン, 冷遇セラル. *v. i.* and *adj.* To be slighted. To be treated in a slighting manner.

Attush, アッツン, オヒョッノ皮チ以テ造ラレシ衣服. *n.* A kind of cloth made from the inner bark of mountain elm trees. A garment made of mountain elm bark cloth.

Attush-aiyo, アッツシアイヨ, 楡ノ皮チ以テ造リシ衣服ニ附ケタル縫箔. *n.* Pieces of Japanese stuff let into *attush* for ornament.

Attush-bera, アッツシベラ, 杼、オサ. *n.* A flat piece of wood used in making cloth.

Attush-kara, アッツシカラ, 織レ. *v.t.* To weave *attush*.

Attush-karabe, アッツシカラベ, 織機. *n.* A loom.

Atu, アツ, **At,** アツ, **Atuhu,** アツフ, 柄、飾帯. *n.* A handle. The sash of a bag. A lace. Thong. Reins.

Atu, アツ, 吐キ出ス. *v.t.* To vomit. *Atu-kopase,* "to vomit very much."

Atu-amba, アツアムバ, 絲チ以テ導ク. *v.t.* To lead by a string. (*pl*).

Atuhu, アツフ, 柄. *n.* A handle. The sash of a bag.

Atui, アツイ, 海、ウミ. *n.* The sea. The ocean. As:—*Atui-tomotuye,* "to cross the seas." *Atui turimimse; atui turu turimimse* and *atui kunrakkunrak,* "the roaring of the sea. **Syn: Rep.**

Atui-epirika, アツイエピリカ, 船ニ強イ. *v.i.* To be a good sailor.

Atui-ewen, アツイエウェン, 船病. *n.* Sea-sickness.

Atui-gesh, アツイケシ, 海ノ西岸. *n.* The western part of the sea.

Atui-ka, アツイカ, 海上、海面. *adv.* Over the sea. Also the surface of the sea.

Atuikata-kaikai, アツイカタカイカイ, 跳海. *n.* A short choppy sea. **Syn: Rera-kaikai.**

Atui-kor'ekashi, アツイコレカシ, 海神. *n.* The gods of the sea.

Atui-koro, アツイコロ, 航海スル. *v.i.* To go to sea. To go a voyage.

Atui-kom, アツイコム, シヤコ. *n.* A kind of *stomapoda,* (*Squilla sp.*). **Syn : Okom. Rokom.**

Atui-kurukashi, アツイクルカシ, 海面. *n.* The surface of the sea.

Atuina, アツイナ, Atuinao, アツイナオ, Atuihre, アツイン子, } 蛸、タコ、章魚. *n.* An octopod. **Syn : Atkoro guru. Atuinne.**

Atui-ochiuchiu, アツイオチュウチウ, イソヒヨドリ. *n.* Eastern blue rock thrush. *Monticola cyanus solitaria* (*Mulb*).

Atui-orun-ahunrasambe, アツイオルンアフンラサムベ, 海鳥ノ名. *n.* A kind of sea bird said to resemble an owl.

Atui-pa, アツイバ, 海ノ東岸. *n.* The eastern portion of the sea. Also sometimes called, *atui-pake.* As :— *Atui-pa ne atui-gesh ne,* " from one end of the sea to the other." Also, *Atui pa pakno atui-gesh pakno,* " to the ends of the sea."

Atui-seppa, アツイセッバ, ハスノハガイ. *n.* Sand-cake. (*Laganum, sp.*). **Syn : Ruru-seppa.**

Atuita, アツイタ. 十、(動物ヲ敷フレ時ニノミ用ユ.) *adj.* Ten. (Used only in counting animals). As :— *Tu atuta* " twenty animals."

Atui-tomotuye, アツイトモツイ エ, 航海スル. *v.i.* To go a voyage. To cross the seas.

Atui-turimimse, アツイツリミムセ, Atui-turu-turimimse, アツイツルツリミムセ, } 海ノ響キ *n.* The roaring of the sea.

Atu-kopase, アツコバセ, 甚ダ多ク吐出ス. *v.i.* To vomit very much.

Atupepeotke, アツベベオッケ, 捕縛セラレ. *v.i.* To be taken prisoner.

Atupepeuk, アツベベウク, 捕縛セラレ. *v.i.* To be bound prisoner.

Aturainu, アツライヌ, 失ハレタレ. *adj.* and *v.i.* Lost. Gone astray. To have lost one's way. **Syn : Shitturainu.**

Aturainu-ambe, アツライヌアムベ, 失フタ物. *n.* Something lost.

Aturainu-wa-an, アツライヌワアン, 失ハレタレ. *adj.* Lost. Gone astray. **Syn : Shitturainu-wa-an.**

Atura-wa, アツラワ, 共ニ. *adv.* Together with.

Aturika, アツリカ, 經絲、タテイト. *n.* The warp in cloth.

Atusa, アツサ, 裸體ナレ、ハダカナレ. *adj.* Naked.

Atushi, アツシ, 縛レ. *v.t.* To bind with a cord.

Atushpa, アツシバ, 裸體ニスル. *v.t.* To strip naked.

Atuyaokkarapbe, アツヤオッカラブベ, 慈惠、アハレミ. *n.* Compassion.

Au, アウ, Awe, アウェ, Awehe, アウェヘ, } 木ノ叉、川ノ叉、鹿ノ角ノ叉、例セバ、ベッアウ、河ノ枝. *n.* Branches or forks of trees. Branches or forks in deer's horns. River branches. As :— *Au-ush-kirau,* " horns with branches." *Pet au,* " the branch of a river." *Ni awe,* " the branches of a tree."

Auitek-guru, アウイテッグル, 僕、シモベ. *n.* A servant.

Aukashiu, アウカシウ, 助ヶ合フ. *v.t.* To help one another.

Aukoamba, アウコアムバ, 運ブ. *v.t.* To carry (*pl. of the object*).

Aukomaktekka, アウコマクテッカ, 共ニ喜ブ. *v.i.* To feel mutual satisfaction. To be mutually happy. To rejoice together.

Aukonuchattekka, アウコヌチヤッテッカ, 共ニ喜ブ. *v.i.* To mutually rejoice. To be merry. To rejoice together.

Aukomi, アウコミ, 着ル. *v.i.* To be clothed with. To be wearing (*pl. of the object*).

Aukomomse, アウコモムセ, 曲ッタ、曲ル、屈ム. *adj.* and *v.i.* Bent. Humped. To stoop. To bow in thanks.

Aukonumba, アウコヌムバ, 壓ス、オス. *v.i.* To be pressed upon. To be thronged.

Aukopa, アウコバ, 他人ノ言葉ヲ曲グル. *v.t.* To wrest (as one's words).

Aukopa, アウコバ, 似ル. *v.i.* To be like. To resemble one another. **Syn: Uanukopa. Aukosamba.**

Aukopa-eaikapbe, アウコバエアイカブベ, 互ニ異ル物. *n.* Something incomparable. Things differing from one another.

Aukoramu-oshma, アウコラムオシマ, 一致スル. *v. i.* To be in accord. To agree. To be agreable.

Aukoramu-oshmap, アウコラムオシマブ, 約束、一致. *n.* An agreement. Accord.

Aukoratchire, アウコランチレ, 赦サレ. *v.i.* To be pardoned. To be forgiven. To be pronounced innocent.

Aukosamba, アウコサムバ, 相似レ. *v. i. & adj.* To resemble one ano-

ther. Like. Alike. **Syn : Uanukopa. Aukopa.**

Aukoshina, アウコシナ, 結ビ合セレ. *v.t.* To tie together.

Aukotama, アウコタマ, 合同スレ. *adv.* Collectively. Also *v. t.* To take in a collective manner. To add together.

Aukotunere, アウコツチレ, 互ニ取リ廻シテ見ル. *v. t.* To pass to one another to look at (as a treasure).

Aukowende, アウコウェンデ, 親ミチ破ブレ. *v. t.* To stir up strife. To set at variance.

Aumshup, アウムシュブ, 先祖傳來ノ品物. *n.* Heirlooms. Things handed down from father to son.

A-un, アウン, 吾々チ. *pro.* We. The first person plural passive voice to verbs. As :—*A-un-kik,* " we are struck."

A-un, アウン, 吾々ノ. *pos. pro.* One's own. As :—*A-un-chisei,* " one's own house.

A-un-guru, アウングル, 隣人. *n.* A neighbour. **Syn : Aota-an-guru.**

Aungeraitere, アウンゲライテレ, 貰フ. *v. t.* To receive (as a prize).

Aungi, アウンギ,　**Aunki, アウンキ,** 扇. *n.* A fan. **Syn : Apunki. Yaiparaparu.**

Aunnumba, アウンヌムバ, 壓セラレ. *v. i.* To be pressed together. To be squeezed.

Aunochiubare, アウノチウバレ, 死セリ. *v. i.* To have died.

Auoniutasare, アウオニウタサレ, 改名スレ. *v.i.* To change one's name. **Syn : Aiyonitasare.**

Auoshmare, アウオシマレ, 生長シ タレ. *v.i.* To have become fully grown. As:—*Okkaiyo shiripo auoshmare,* "to have become a man." *Shiwentep shiripo auoshmare,* "to have become a woman." **Syn: Rupne. Shukup-okere.**

Aupshi, アウブシ, 逆ニ、サカサマニ. *adv.* Upside down.

Aupshire, アウブシレ, 倒ニスル. *v. t.* To turn upside down.

Aupushi, アウブシ, 貫通スル. *v.i.* To be strung together as onions or chestnuts.

Aure, アウレ, 與ヘル. *v. t.* To give.

Aureechiu, アウレエチウ, 蹴ク、尊敬 スレ. *v.i.* To be reverential. To stumble.

Aureerutu, アウレエルツ, 足ニテ物ヲ 排スレ, *v. t.* To push on one side with the foot.

Ausatuye, アウサツイエ, 細カニ切ラ レ. *v.i.* To be cut in pieces.

Aush-kina, アウシキナ, フタマタイチ ゲ. *n. Anemone dichotoma, L.*

Aushtekka, アウシテッカ, 鏖殺セラレ. *v.i.* To be massacred.
Aushtekka-wa-isam, アウシテッカワイサム,

Autara, アウタラ,
Autare, アウタレ, 親戚. *n.* Relations. **Syn: Apa-utara.**
Autari, アウタリ,

Autasa-ashte, アウタサアシテ, 不和ニ スレ、親睦ヲ破ル. *v. t.* To set at variance. To set up crosswise.

Automotnoka, アウトモッノカ, 無知ナ ル. *adj.* and *v.i.* Unlearned. Not to know. To be ignorant.

Autunashi, アウツナシ, 搗ク. *v.t.* To pound in a mortar (*pl. of the person*).

Auturashi, アウツラシ, 共ニ登ル. Same as *Anuturashi.* (*pl.*) To ascend a river in company with.

Auwa, アウワ, ホウジロカモ. *v.t.* Goldeneye. *Fuligula clangula, Linn.*

Auwatore, アウワトレ, 整フ、正シカル. *v.i.* To be in order. To be correct. As:—*Itak auwatore wa ye,* "to speak correctly."

Auwatori, アウワトリ, 籍ヲ轉ズル. *v.t.* and *v.i.* To be registered. To register. To be set apart. To enrole.

Auwatori-kambi, アウワトリカムビ. 戸籍簿. *n.* A register.

Auwechiure, アウウェチウレ, 摩レ合 フ. *v.i.* To come into contact with one another.

Auweunu, アウウェウヌ, 出來上レル. *adj.* Complete.

Auwonnumyere, アウウォンヌムイェ レ, 撰擇スル. *v.t.* To chose out.

Auwonnuyetasare, アウウォンヌイェ タサレ, 譯スル. *v.t.* To translate.

Awa, アワ, 或時ハ此ノ語ハ過去ヲ示シ 或時ハ又ノ意義ナリ. *part. Awa* expresses past time, and indicates that one thing having been done another was commenced. This particle never finishes a subject. It is also sometimes like the adverb "as," and sometimes like the conjunctions "and," "also."

A-wa, アワ, 燃エテイル. *adj.* Ablaze.

Awa-kina, アワキナ, 草、クサ. *n.* Grass. Growing grass.

Awe, アウエ, 又、マタ. *n.* Forks of trees. Tributaries of rivers.
Awehe, アウェヘ, Branches on the horns of deer. **Syn: Au.**

Awekatta, アウェカッタ, 突入スレ. *v.i.* To rush in.

Awendarap, アウェンダラブ, 夢、ユメ. *n.* A dream.

Awendarapte, アウェンダラブテ, 夢ミ レ. *v.i.* To be caused to dream.

Awepetetne, アウェペテツ子, 言ヒ能ハ ズ. *v.i.* To be unable to speak (as through cold or parched or stiff lip).

Awoshi, アウォシ, 結合スレ.*v.t.* To tie together.

Awotereke, アウォテレケ, 急ギテ入レ. *v.i.* To rush suddenly in (as into a house.)

Aya, アヤ, 木理、モクメ、掌ノ條. *n.* Grains in wood. The lines of the hands.

Ayai-epirikare, アヤイエピリカレ, 利 己スレ、私ヲ益スル. *v.i.* To have done one's self good. To have gained something for one's self.

Ayaikikip, アヤイキキブ, 危險ナレ. *adj.* Dangerous.

Ayaikikipbe, アヤイキキブベ, 危險 ナル者. *n.* Anything dangerous. Dangers. A dangerous person.

Ayaikikip-i, アヤイキキビ, 危險ナル コト. *n.* Dangers. Dangerous times or places. As :—*Ayaikikip- ikoekari,* " to meet with dangers."

Ayaishishire-ushi, アヤイシシレウ シ, 隠レ處. *n.* A shelter.

Ayaita-o, アヤイタオ, 灸點スル. *v. t.* To apply the moxa.

Ayatuka, アヤツカ, ……デ有ルナレド. *ph.* Though it is. Though he is.

A-yakne, アヤク子, ……デ有ルナラバ. *ph.* If it was. If he was.

Ayaku, アヤク, 破レタル. *adj.* Burst.

Ayangep, アヤンゲブ,   **Ayange-kunip,** アヤンゲクニブ,   供物. *n.* A sacri- fice. An offer- ring.

Ayapo, アヤポ, 嗚呼、アヽ. *exclam.* Oh! An exclamation of pain. **Syn : Itasasa. Ayo.**

Aye, アイェ, 稱セラル、名付ケラレ. *v.i.* To be called. To be named. As :—*Ainu ari aye utara,* " the people called Ainu." **Syn : Aporose.**

Aye-hi, アイェヒ, 言ハレシコト. *n.* Speech. Anything said, or spoken. The way of calling or saying. **Syn : Itak-hi.**

Ayemonetoko, アイェモチトコ, 甚ダ、 多ク、酷烈ニ. *adv.* Severely. Very much. **Syn : Niwen-no. Yupke- no.**

Ayep, アイェブ, 稱セラレタレ、例セバ、 セタアリアイエブ、犬ト云ハレルモノ. *ph.* Things called. That which is called. Also a noun ; a speech. Anything said. As :—*Seta ari ayep,* " the things called dogs." *Nei ayep anak ne wen,* " that was a bad speech."

Aye-wairure, アイェワイルレ, 言語ヲ 誤マラレル. *v.i.* To be caused to make a mistake in speaking. **Syn : Itak-pitaksakka.**

Ayo, アヨ, 嗚呼、アヽ. *exclam.* Oh. An exclamation of pain. As :— *Ayo habo, habo,* " oh mother, mother." **Syn : Ayapo. Itasasa.**

Ayoaramuye, アヨアラムイェ, 裳チカ ヽ. *v.t.* To tie the clothes back (as when one wishes to work or run). **Syn : aeasamuye.**

Ayokitanne, アヨキタン子, 流ル(潮ノ).

v.i. To flow, as the tide. **Syn:** **Shirara-pesh. Shiraraika.**

Ayokitakne, アヨキタク子, 退ク、ヒ ク (潮ノ). *v.i.* To ebb, as the tide. **Syn: Shirara-ha.**

Ayomnere, アヨムチレ, 中止スル(罰チ 恐レテ). *adj.* and *v.i.* To be kept from doing something by fear of punishment.

Ayoro, アヨロ,
Aioro, アイオロ,
Airo, アイロ, } スズキ. *n.* A kind of perch. *Lateolabrax japonicus, T. and S.*

Ayupnishpake, アユプニシバケ,
Ayupnishpakehe, アユブニシバケヘ, } 兄、アニ. *n.* One's elder brother.

B.

No initial sentence in Yezo Ainu ever properly commences with a *b*. But in composition *p* is often *nigoried* into *b*. For every word therefore having the sound of *b* the reader is referred to the same under *p*.

C (チ).

Cha, チャ, 大ナル、群衆ノ、多數ノ. *adj.* Great. Many.

Cha, チャ,
Chaha, チャハ, } 長ヶ短キ樹木. *n.* Under-wood. Spray wood. Twigs.

Cha or chash, チャ, チャシ, 圍、カコ イ、塀、ヘイ. *n.* A Fence. Hedge.

Cha, チャ, 茶. *n.* Tea.

Cha, チャ, 頭、口、顔. *n.* The head. The mouth. The face.

Cha, チャ, 細カニ切ル、摘ミ切ル、例セ バ、フムベチャ、鯨チ切レ. *v.t.* To cut up. To cut or pinch off as the heads of wheat, millet, barley etc. As:—*Humbe cha,* "to cut up a whale;" *Amam push cha,* "to pinch off heads of millet."

Cha, チャ, 平ニ敷ク. *v.i.* Spread out flat.

Cha, チャ, 時トシテ單數名詞ニ付加ス ル時ハ複數ニナスナリ. *part.* Some-times heard used as a plural suffix to verbs and nouns.

Cha, チャ, 海岸、河岸. *n.* The shores of the sea. The low banks of rivers. **Syn: Sa.**

Chabe, チャベ, 猫. *n.* A cat. Also often called *Meko.* These words are also often heard among the Japanese of Yezo.

Chacha, チャチャ, 老人、例セバ、チャ チャウタラウウエランガラブアンナ、老人等ヨ吾汝等ノ安否チ問フ. *n.* An old man. As:—*Chacha utara,* "old men." *Chacha utara uwe-rangarap an na,* "old men, I salute you."

Chacha, チャチャ, 鋸チ以テ切ル、例セ バ、ニチャチャ、木チ鋸ル. *v.t.* To saw. To cut. As:—*Ni chacha,* "to cut wood."

Chacha-komon, チャチャコモン, 鋸 屑、ノコクズ. *n.* Saw-dust.

Chaha, チャハ, 篠 (コ ユ ダ). *n.*
Twigs.

Chaipuni, チャイプニ, 荷物ヲ運ブ船.
n. A large boat of Japanese
make. A cargo boat.

Chairak, チャイラク, } 徐カニ走ル(犬狐
Chairakchairak, チャイラクチャイラク, } ナドノ). *v.i.*
To trot a-
long in a gentle manner, as a dog
or fox. **Syn: Sambas. Tanta-
riki no oman.**

Chak, チャク, 急ニ出ル. *v.i.* To pop
out ; to come suddenly out.

Chak, チャク, 肥満ナル、フトリタル、脂
コキ. *adj.* Fat, soft, flabby.

Chak, チャク, 無、ナシ. *adv.* Without.
Not having. This word is sometimes used as a negative adjectival
ending, and often appears in
compounds. Thus :— *Katchak,*
" weak in ability "; (lit : without tact). **Syn : Sak.**

Chaka, チャカ, 汚穢ナル、キタナキ.
adj. Dirty. Filthy. As :—*Chaka
itak,* " filthy speech." **Syn :
Ichaka. Ichakkere.**

Chaka, チャカ, 開ク、ヒラク. *v.t.* To
open. As :—*Apa chaka,* " to
open a door." **Syn : Maka.
Sarare.**

Chakchak, チャクチャク, ミソサヽイ.
n. Japanese wren. *Troglodytes
fumigatus, Tem.*

Chake, チャケ, 厭フ、好マヌ. *v.t.* To
disdain. To dislike.

Chakekoshne, チャケコシ子, 誹ル、
ノヽシル. *v.t.* To slander.

Chakka, チャッカ, 陥ル、罠ニカヽル.
v.i. To be caught in a snare.

Chakke, チャッケ, 開キタル. *adj.*
Open.

Chakkere, チャッケレ, 穢キ. *adj.*
Dirty. Filthy. **Syn : Chaka.
Ichakkere.**

Chakkerep, チャッケレブ, 穢キ物. *n.*
A dirty thing.

Chakkosamba, チャッコサムバ, 掃フ、
晴ル、(複數). *v.i.* To clear away
(as clouds). To disperse. (*pl*).

Chakkosambare, チャッコサムバレ,
掃フ、(複數). *v.t.* To clear away.
To disperse (*pl*).

Chakkosanu, チャッコサヌ, 掃フ、晴ル.
(單數). *v.i.* To clear away (as
clouds). To disperse (*sing*). To
die away as sound.

Chakkosanure, チャノコサヌレ, 掃フ、
(單數). *v.t.* To clear away. To
disperse. (*sing*).

Chakoro, チャコロ, 饒舌ノ、オシヤベ
リノ. *adj.* Talkative.

Chakoko, チャココ, 學ブ、習フ. *v.t.*
To learn. **Syn : Eyaipakashnu.
Eyaihannokkara.**

Chaktako, チャクタコ, 行燈、ランプ、
提燈. *n.* A lamp. Lantern.
Syn : Ratchako.

Chakte, チャクテ, 放ツ、(係蹄ナドチ).
v.t. To let off as a gin or snare.

Chama-ku, チャマク, 弭弓、オトシユ
ミ. *n.* A spring-bow. **Syn : Ku-
ari-ku. Ku-ama-ku. Chiari-ku.**

Chamon, チャモン, 上唇、ウヘノクチ
ビル. *n.* The upper lip.

Chamse, チャムセ, 物ヲ食スルトキノ
嚙ム音、例セバ、パロチャムセフミ、物
ヲ食スルトキノ音. *v.i.* To make a
noise (as in eating). To crunch
audibly with the mouth. As :—

Paro chamse humi, "the noise . made by eating."

Chamse-chamse, チャムセチャムセ, 物ヲ食スルトキノ噛ム音. *v.i.* The frequentive or intensified form of *chamse.*

Chanan, チャナン, 少シ、僅ニ、或時. *adj.* and *adv.* A little. A few. Sometimes. **Syn : Pon no. Uturuta an range.**

Chanan-no, チャナンノ, 粗末ナル. *adj.* Badly. Slovenly. **Syn : Shusan no.**

Chanchan, チャンチャン, 一歩ヲ進ムル. *v.i.* To take a step forward.

Chanse, チャンセ,} 物ヲ食スル時ノ噛ム音. **Chanchanse, チャンチャンセ,}** *adj.* The same as *chamse* and *chamchamse.*

Chanup, チャヌブ, 目的、終局. *n.* An object. An end. **Syn : Ikkewehe.**

Chapish, チャピシ, 耳語スル、サヽヤク. *v.i.* To whisper.

Chapish-chapish, チャピシチャピシ, 耳語スル、サヽヤク. *v.i.* An intensified or frequentive form of *Chapish.*

Chara, チャラ,} 口、クチ. *n.* The mouth. **Charo, チャロ,}** **Syn : Charo. Para. Paro.**

Charage, チャラゲ, 散ラサレタル. *v.i.* and *adj.* To be scattered. **Syn : Apatu.**

Charagere, チャラゲレ, 散ラス. *v.t.* To scatter. **Syn : Patu.**

Charange, チャランゲ, 議論スル、呵カル. *v.i.* To storm. To argue. **Syn : Rutke.**

Charapa, チャラバ, 取積ス、混雑スル、亡ボス、例ヘバ、チセイチャラバ、家ヲ取リ積ス. *v.t.* To put into confusion. To pull down. As :— *Chisei charapa,* "to pull down a house."

Charapa-charapa, チャラバチャラバ, 混雑スル、亡ボス. *v.i.* An intensified form of *charapa.*

Chararage, チャララゲ, 散ラサレタル. *v. i.* and *adj.* Scattered. **Syn : Charage.** But *chara* means "to be scattered" of oneself while *chararage* means to have been scattered by another.

Chararase, チャララセ, 急下スル、流レスグ. *v.i.* To slip down. To flow along. To shoot down rapids. To slide down a mountain side.

Charase, チャラセ, 動夕、振フ. *v. i.* To move. To shake.

Chari, チャリ, 散ラス. *v.t.* To sprinkle. To scatter about. **Syn : Patu. Patu-patu.**

Chari, チャリ, 點火セル. *adj.* Lighted. As :—*Chari-abe,* "a lighted fire." **Syn : Chi-ari.**

Chari-chari, チャリチャリ, 散ラス. *v.t.* An intensified form of *chari,* "to sprinkle" or "scatter."

Charo, チャロ,} 口. *n.* The mouth. The **Chara, チャラ,}** mouth of a valley, glen, or stream. **Syn : Paro.**

Charo-an, チャロアン, 雄辯ナル. *adj.* Eloquent.

Charo-nunnun, チャロヌンヌン, 接吻スル. *v.t.* To kiss. To suck the lips.

Charopen, チャロペン, 悪口ノ、罵詈的. *adj.* Abusive.

Charopende, チャロペンデ, 罵ル、ノ
ノシル、惡口スル、反對スル. *v.t.* To
abuse. To scold. To speak against.

Charototke, チャロトッケ, 音ヲ爲ス、
唱フ、物ヲ言フ、啼キ聲ヲ爲ス. *v.i.* To
make a noise (as in weeping).
To be fluent. To speak or say.
To sing (as a bird). **Syn: Chaurototke. Chauchauotke.**

Charuge-sande, チャルゲサンデ, 繼續
進行スル. *v.i.* To be continually
going.

Charumbe, ⎫ 舌、シタ. *n.* The
チャルムベ, ⎬
Parumbe, ⎭ tongue.
バルムベ,

Charushbe, チャルシベ, コロツプ、木
栓. *n.* A cork or stopper.

Charuwatore, チャルワトレ, 整ハレ.
v.i. To be put in order. Arranged. To be set in rotation.
To be put in rows. **Syn: Saru-
watore.**

Chash, チャシ, ⎫
Pash, パシ, ⎬ 走ル. *v.i.* To run.

Chashash, チャシヤシ, 速ク走ル. *v.i.*
To run swiftly.

Chashchash, チャシチャシ, 速ク.
adv. Quickly.

Chashi, チャシ, 圍、塀、城. *n.* A fence.
An enclosure. A castle. A
fortress.

Chashikara, ⎫ 圍フ、カコフ. *v.t.* To
チャシカラ, ⎬ enclose. To fence
Chashkara, ⎬ in.
チャシカラ, ⎭

Chashka, チャシカ, 急ガス. *v.t.*
To hasten.

Chash-no, チャシノ, 走リテアル、走
ルル. *adj.* Running.

Chashnu, チャシヌ, 早ク. *adj.*
Quick.

Chashnu, チャシヌ, 準備セラレタル.
adj. Prepared. Beautified. Made.
ready.

Chashnu-i, チャシヌイ, 準備セラレ
タル所. *n.* A place prepared. A
beautiful place.

Chashnu-no, チャシヌノ, 早ク. *adv.*
Quickly. **Syn: Tunashi-no.**

**Chashnu-mimdara, チャシヌミム
ダラ,** 家ノ庭. *n.* The region immediately outside a house. An
open yard.

Chashnure, チャシヌレ, 準備スル.
v.t. To prepare. To set in order.
To make ready.

Chashnutara, チャシヌタラ, 明カナ
レ、晴レタレ. *adj.* Clear. Open (as
weather). **Syn: Shitchashnu-
tara.**

Chashte, チャシテ, 早メル. *v.t.* To
hasten. To accelerate. **Syn:
Tunashka. Tunashte.**

Chataraye, チャタライェ, 推察スル.
v.t. To surmise. To guess. **Syn:
Pataraye.**

Chatchari, チャッチャリ, 散ラス. *v.t.*
To sprinkle. To scatter. **Syn:
Chari-chari.**

Chauchawatke, チャウチャワツケ,
能辯ナレ. *v.i.* and *adj.* To be
fluent. **Syn: Chaurototke.
Charototke.**

Chaunaraye, チャウナライェ, 入ル.
v.i. To come in. To enter (as
rays of light through a window).

Chaurototke, チャウロトッケ, 能辯ナ
レ. *v.i.* To be fluent. **Syn:
Chauchawatke.**

Chawawa, チャワワ, 揉ム. *v.t.* To
rub between the hands (as wheat
or maize). **Syn: Kisakisa.**

Chayaya, チヤヤヤ, 支へ持ツ. *v.t.* To hold up (as claws).

Che, チェ, 家、イヘ. A house. **Syn: Chisei.**

Cheachiu-shiyeye, チェアチウシイェイェ, 顛癇、テンカン. *n.* Fits. **Syn: Pitke-tashum.**

Cheappe, チェアッペ, 私生兒. An illegitimate child. **Syn: Chiappise.**

Chearaita, チェアライタ, 無シ、當ラズ. *v.i.* To be untouched. To escape untouched or unseen. To be without (as without a beard or whiskers). As:—*Rek kuru poka chearaita,* "a young fellow without whiskers." **Syn: Chieahaita.**

Cheka, チェカ, 家根. *n.* The roof of a house.

Chep, チェブ, 魚、例セバ、チェブコイキ 魚チ捕ル、漁スレ. *n.* Fish. Called *chiep* in some districts. *Chep atkochi,* "a fishes'tail." *Chep koiki,* "to fish." *Chep rupi,* "a shoal of fish." *Chep tui,* "fish entrails." *Chep up,* "The soft roe of fish." *Chep mim,* "the flesh of fish." *Chep ram,* "fish scales."

Chep-chiporo, チェブチポロ, 魚ノ卵. *n.* The spawn of any kind of fish with the exception of that of herrings. Herring spawn is called *homa.*

Chep-ehapuru, チェブエハブル, 早ク 饑レ. *v.i.* To become soon hungry.

Chep-enishte, チェブエニシテ, 饑チ堪へレ. *v.i.* To be able to endure hunger well.

Chepen-kute-kina, チェベクテキナ, アヤメ. *n.* *Iris sibirica, L.*

Chep-furukappo, チェブブルカッポ, 古キ魚ノ皮. *n.* Old fish-skins.

Chep-kap, チェブカブ, 魚ノ皮. *n.* Fish-skins.

Chepkap-hosh, チェブカブホシ, 魚皮製ノ靴. *n.* Leggings made of fish-skin.

Chep-mokrap, チェブモクラブ, 魚ノ腹ノ鰭. *n.* The pectoral fins of fishes.

Chep-motot, チェブモトツ, 魚ノ脊骨. *n.* The back-bone of a fish.

Cheppo, チェッポ, 若魚、小魚. *n.* A young fish. Little fish.

Chep-ram, チェブラム, 鱗、ウロコ. *n.* Fish scales.

Cheshikiraine, チェシキライチ,
Chieshikiraine, チエシキライチ, } 憐レム. *v.t.* To pity.

Cheuko, チェウコ, 雙子、フタゴ. *n.* Twins.

Cheure, チェウレ, 足、足ノ指. *n.* A foot. The toes.

Chi, チ, 吾々. *pro.* We. The first person *pl.* pronoun. **Syn: Chi utara. Chi okai utara.**

Chi, チ, 此ノ字チ他動詞ノ前ニ加フル時ハ自動詞ニナシ又ハ形容詞トナル、例セバ、チベレバニ、割リシ木. *part.* When the particle *Chi* is prefixed to some nouns and active verbs it has a kind of adjectival and passive force. As:—*Mipi,* "clothing," *chi-mipi,* "ready made clothes." *Pereba,* "to cleave." *Chipereba ni,* "cleft wood."

Chi, チ, 汚レタレ. *adj.* Wet dirt. Mud. Filth.

Chi, チ, 熟シタレ、枯レタル. *adj.* Cooked. Ripe. Dry. Dead. Withered.

Chi, チ, 時トシテ此ノ字ヲ名詞ニ付加スレトキハ複數ノ働キヲナス. *part.* Sometimes used as a plural suffix to nouns. As *pe,* " water;" *pechi,* " waters."

Chi, チ, 陰部. *n.* The privates.

Chiai,
チアイ, 木栓、セン. *n.* A cork.
Chiaye, A stopper.
チアイェ,

Chiai, チアイ, 合フ. *v.i.* To be at one. United. Conjoined.

Chiai-ush-chep., チアイウシチェプ, イトウオ. *n.* Nine spined stikleback. *Pygosteus steindachneri. Jor.* and *Sny.*

Chiama, チアマ, 置カレタレ. *adj.* Set. Placed.

Chiama-ku, チアマク, 弭弓、オトシコミ. *n.* A spring-bow.

Chiama-ya, チアマヤ, 大綱. *n.* A large fish-net.

Chiani-ku, チアニク, 弓. *n.* An ordinary bow.

Chiannure, チアンヌレ, 忘レ易カレ. *v.i.* To be forgetful. Absent minded.

Chiapakore, チアパコレ, 優待スレ. *v.t.* To treat hospitably.

Chiappise, チアッピセ, 私生子. *n.* A bastard.

Chiari, チアリ, 火ヲ點シタレ. *adj.* Lighted. Kindled. As :— *Chiari abe,* " an already lighted fire."

Chiari-ku, チアリク, 弭弓. *n.* A spring-bow.

Chiaye, チアイェ, 木栓、セン. *n.* A cork. A stopper. **Syn : Konkochi.**

Chichap, チチャプ, アヅマザ. *n.* *Arundinaria (Sasa) nipponica, Mak. et Shib.*

Chichari, チチャリ, 散サレタレ. *adj. v.i.* Scattered. Dispersed.

Chicharichare, チチャリチャレ, 散ラス. *v.t.* To scatter.

Chichatchari, チチャッチャリ, 散サレタレ. *adj.* Scattered. **Syn : Achatchari.**

Chichikeu, チチケウ, 幽霊. *n.* An apparition. Spectre.

Chichip, チチプ, 痛、ウヅク事. *n.* Shooting pains.

Chichipiyere, チチピイェレ, 親ノ過失ヲ想ハス. *v.t.* To remind one of the faults of his parents.

Chichira, チチラ, 魚ノ名、(ウナ). *n.* A kind of fish (*Jap. Una*).

Chieappise, チエアッピセ, 私生子. A bastard. A half-breed.

Chieattuye, チエアッツイェ, 男用ノ匙. *n.* A man's spoon.

Chiehaita, チエハイタ, 持タヌ、無シ. *v.i.* To be without. Not having. **Syn : Chieraita.**

Chiehomatu, チエホマツ, 愕ク、驚ク. *v.i.* To be surprised at. Startled.

Chiehorokakep, チエホロカケプ, 幣ノ名. *n.* Name of a kind of *inao* or willow offering to the gods.

Chieikip, チエイキプ, 庖丁、小刀. *n.* A knife. Chopper. **Syn : Makiri.**

Chieishunge, チエイシュンゲ, 詐僞. *n.* A deception.

Chieishungerep, チエイシュンゲレプ, 詐僞. *n.* A deception. A lie.

Chiekot, チエコツ, 怒ッテ死ス. *v.i.* To die of anger. To kill one's self in wrath. **Syn : Kem-ekot. Yaichep-ekote.**

Chi-e-kunip, チエクニプ, 糧食. *n.* Necessary food. **Syn : E kuni aep.**

Chiemetup, チエメツブ, 饗應ノ時ニ婦人ニ分與スル酒. *n.* A portion of wine given to women at some of the Ainu feasts. **Syn: Emetup.**

Chieninuibe, チエニヌイベ, 枕、マクラ. *n.* A pillow.

Chieoma, チエオマ, 付キ立ツ. *v. i.* Sticking into. **Syn: Aeoma.**

Chieomare, チエオマレ, 混淆スル、交雑スレ. *v. t.* To mix with. To hold intercourse with. **Syn: Ukopakaunu.**

Chieotke, チエオッケ, 觸レル、當ル. *v.t.* To touch. To strike against. **Syn: Chiekik. Tomooshma.**

Chiepanup, チエパヌブ, 女ノ頭巾. *n.* A woman's headdress. **Syn: Chipanup.**

Chieshikiraine, チエシキライ子, 憫レム、憐憫スレ. *v.t.* To pity.

Chieshinnuye, チエシンヌイェ, 錄サレタル、記サレタル. *adj.* Written. **Syn: Anuye an. Eshinnuye.**

Chieshirikikkik, チエシリキッキク, 雷ヘテ鳴ル、(風ガ戸ヲ打ツ如ク). 搖ガス、強ク響ク. *v.i.* To bang as a door by the wind. To rattle. To jar.

Chieshitchari, チエシッチヤリ, 散リシ、撒布シタル. *v.i.* and *adj.* Scattered. Dispersed. **Syn: Aechitchiare.**

Chieshungere, チエシュンゲレ, 詐謀スレ、欺ク. *v. t.* To practice deception. **Syn: Aeshungerep.**

Chieshungerep, チエシュンゲレブ, 虚言、ウソ. *n.* A lie. A deception. **Syn: Aeshungerep.**

Chiesonere, チエソ子レ, 眞ニ、誠ニ. *adv.* Truly.

Chiesorore-guru, チエソロレグル, 客人. *n.* A visitor. **Syn: Areshirikush guru.**

Chietattari, チエタッタリ, 扇グ、上下ニ動ク、(鳥尾ノ如ク). *v.i.* To move up and down (as the tail of a bird).

Chietaye-sei, チエタイェセイ, ホタテガイ. *n.* Scallop. *Pecten yessoensis, Jay.*

Chietu, チエツ, 岬、鼻. *n.* A sharp cape. The nose. A projection.

Chieturi, チエツリ, 戸棚. *n.* A cupboard. A-room protruding from the sides or ends of a house.

Chieukaramu, チエウカラム, 晩熟ナ. *v. adj.* Of late maturity.

Chieuko-an, チエウコアン, 雙子ヲ生ム. *v.i.* To bear twins.

Chieuramtekuk, チエウラムテクク, 窘ム レ、苦ム レ、迫害スル. *v.t.* To persecute. **Syn: Keshke.**

Chieure, チエウレ, 足、足ノ指. *n.* The toes. The feet.

Chifuye, チフイェ, 煎ス、焼ク、炊ク. *n.* Same as *Chihuye.* "to burn."

Chifuye, チフイェ, アマニウ、(方言). *n.* Same as *Chihuye* and *Chishuye, Angelca edulis, Miyabe.*

Chihauge, チハウゲ, 靜カナル、徐カナル. *adj.* Soft. Silent.

Chihaye, チハイェ, 失ハル. *v.i.* To be lost. **Syn: Aturainu.**

Chihayere, チハイェレ, 失フ. *v.t.* To lose. **Syn: Turainu.**

Chiheshui, チヘシュイ, 坐眠スル. *v.i.* To sit and sleep.

Chihetuku, チヘツク, 出ル、生長セラレタ. *v. i.* To come out. To have grown.

Chihetukure, チヘツクレ, 現ハル. v.i. To appear. To rise (as clouds).

Chihokambare, チホカムバレ, 六ケ敷キ. adj. Difficult.

Chihoki, チホキ, 商品. n. Merchandise.

Chihoma, チホマ, 害ナ受ケル. v.i. To suffer hurt.

Chihotke, チホツケ, 褌. n. A loin cloth. Syn: Tepa.

Chihuye, チフイ, アマニゥ、(方言). n. A kind of plant used for food. *Angelica edulis, Miyabe.* Also called *chifuye* or *chishuye.*

Chiinrarakka, チインララッカ, 滑ル. adj. Slippery. Syn: Rarak.

Chiiriwak-kore, チイリワッコレ, 親類ノ如ク二待遇スル. v.t. To treat as a relative.

Chiishitomare, チイシトマレ, 愕カサル、驚カサル. v.i. To be frightened.

Chi-itakte, チイタクテ, 占フ、預言スル. v.i. To divine. To be seized with a spirit of divination. To prophesy.

Chiitarare, チイタラレ, 變ズル. v.i. To change.

Chiitasare-guru, チイタサレグル, 狂氣ナルモノ. n. A maniac. A person out of mind. An imbecile.

Chik, チク, 滴ル. v.i. To drop as water. To drip.

Chikai, チカイ, 曲リタル. adj. Winding. Crooked.

Chikai-anu, チカイアヌ, 死ス、感覺ナ失フ、例セバ、チカイアヌヲライ、急二死ス. v.i. To die. To faint through an accident. To faint away. This word is also sometimes used as an adverb; "suddenly," "unexpectedly." As:—

Chikai anu wa rai, "to die suddenly." Syn: Ekushkonna sambe-toranne.

Chikai-chish, チカイチシ, 細ク曲リタル道路. n. A winding narrow path. A precipitous rugged place. Syn: Wenshiri. Chish. Nangashke chiukush.

Chikambe, チカムベ,
Chikamge, チカムゲ,
樹木又ハ塀ナド二積止マリシ雪. n. Snow settled upon trees or fences. Syn: Hashka-omap.

Chikap, チカプ, 陰莖、(賤語). n. Slang for *Chi* or *chiye,* the privates.

Chikap, チカプ, 鳥、例セバ、チカプチシ、鳥ノ啼聲. n. A bird of any kind. As:—*Chikap chish,* "a bird's song. *Chikap etu* and *chikap etukepushbe,* "a bird's bill." *Chikap hawe ash,* "the bird sings." *Chikap ishi,* "a bird's tail." *Chikap saye,* "a flight of birds."

Chikap-hup, チカプフプ, ゴエフマツ. n. *Pinus pentaphylla Mayr.*

Chikap-kanchi, チカプカンチ, 鳥ノ翼. n. Bird's wings.

Chikap-ka-oreu-ni, チカプカオレウ二, 樓木、トマリギ. n. A roost. .

Chikap-kina, チカプキナ, ヒメクワンザウ. n. *Hemerocallis Dumortieri, Morr.*

Chikap-konkoni, チカプコンコニ, 鳥ノ羽毛. n. Feathers.

Chikap-kutchi, チカプクッチ, ミヤママタ、ビ. n. *Actinidia kolonukta, Max.*

Chikap-muk, チカプムク, キジカクシ. n. *Asparagus schoberioides, Kunth.*

Chikap-nok, チカプノク, 卵. n. Eggs.

Chikap-pero-ni, チカブペロ二, Chikao-pero-ni, チカオペロ二, オホナラ. n. A kind of oak. Quercus crispula, Bl. **Syn: Shi-peroni.**

Chikappo, チカッポ, 木造流行病除ケノ神符. n. A kind of charm made of elder used to drive away sickness and contagious disease.

Chikappo-mau, チカッポマウ, タカネヘラ. n. Rosa acicularis, Lindl.

Chikappo-peroni, チカッポペロ二, オホナラ. n. Quercus crispula, Bl.

Chikap-rap, チカブラブ, Chikap-rapu, チカブラブ, 烏ノ翼. n. Bird's wings. By some, " feathers."

Chikappui, チカッブイ, エンコウサウ. n. Caltha palustris, L. var. sibirica, Regel.

Chikap-set, チカブセツ, 烏ノ巣. n. A bird's nest.

Chikap-setaini, チカブセタイ二, Chikap-seta-ni, チカブセタ二, アヅキナシ. n. Pyrus Miyabei, Sarg. **Syn: Setaini.**

Chikap-shungu, チカブシュング, アカェソ、シンコマツ. n. A kind of fir tree. Picea Glehni, Fr. Schm.

Chikaptekkup, チカッテツクプ, 烏ノ翼. n. Wings.

Chikap-toma, チカブトマ, キナナノアマナ. n. The yellow star of Bethlehem. Gagea lutea Rœm. et Sch.

Chikap-uru, チカブウル, 鳥皮ニテ造リシ衣服. n. A garment made of bird-skins. Also ". bird-skins."

Chikarakarabe, チカラカラベ, 縫箔. n. Fancy needle-work. An embroidered dress.

Chikashnukara, チカシヌカラ, 好運ナレ. v.i. To be fortunate. To have special favour from the gods. To be blessed.

Chikashnukarape, チカシヌカ ラペ, 恩惠、寶. n. A treasure. A blessing.

Chikaye, チカイェ, Chikai, チカイ, 曲リタル. adj. Winding. Crooked. As:—Chikaye ru, " a winding path."

Chikaye-chish, チカイェチシ, Chikai-chish, チカイチシ, 險シキ曲リ途. n. A winding, precipitous, rugged place. **Syn: Wenshiri. Nangashke chiukush.**

Chichik, チチク, 滴ル. v.i. To drop as water.

Chikemekarabe, チケメカラベ, 縫箔. n. An embroidered dress. **Syn: Chikarakarabe.**

Chikere, チケレ, 觸ルヽ、接スル. v.t. To touch. **Syn: Temba.**

Chiki, チキ, 若シ、時二、例セバ、クオマンチキクカラクスネ、若シ往クナラバ爲スベシ. post, If. When. As:—Ku oman chiki ku kara kusu ne, " I will do it if (or "when") I go." Nukat'chiki nure wa un kore, " if you see it let us know."

Chiki-ne-wa, チキ子ワ, 若シ左樣ナラ、例セバ、アンチキ子ワピリカ、其ノ通リ. ナラバ宜ロジイ. ph. If it is so. Ne wa with chiki does not finish a sentence, something else always follows. As:—An chiki ne wa pirika, "if it is so, then it is well."

Chikiri, チキリ, 脚、足、アシ. n. The legs. By some "the feet." As:—Chikiri asam, "the soles of the feet." **Syn: Kema.**

Chikiri, チキリ, 堆、塊. *n.* A lump. A heap.

Chikiri-ashikipet, チキリアシキベツ, 足ノ指. *n.* The toes.

Chikiribe, チキリベ, 縫箔. *n.* Ornamental clothes. Clothes ornamented with fancy needlework. **Syn : Chikarakarabe. Chikemekarabe.**

Chikisa-kara, チキサカラ, 木ト木チ 磨擦シテ火チ作ル. *v.i.* To make fire by rubbing sticks together.

Chikisa-ni, チキサニ, アカタモ. *n.* The elm tree. *Ulmus campestris, Sm.* The wood and roots of this tree are used especially for producing fire.

Chikisa-ni-karush, チキサニカルシ, タモギタケ. *n.* A kind of mushroom (*Pleurotus*) which grows on the stems of fallen elm-trees. It is used as food by the Ainu. *Pleurotus ulmurius, Bull.*

Chikisap, チキサブ, 縫スル、ヒウチス ル. *v.i.* To strike fire with a flint and steel.

Chikisap, チキサブ, 斜面、小山ノ坂ノ 面. *n.* A slope. A hill-side. **Syn : Huru-kotoro.**

Chikishirototo, チキシロトト, 擦ル、 爬ク. *v.i.* To rub an itching spot.

Chikka, チッカ, 滴ラス. *v.t.* To drop as drops of water. To let drip. **Syn : Chikte.**

Chikkiri, チッキリ, ネツキウチノ遊 戯. *n.* Name of a game somewhat resembling draft. (see *ukonittupte*).

Chikko, チッコ, 老夫. *n.* An old man.

Chikoapushke, チコアブシケ, 負傷ス ル. *v.i.* To be wounded. To be torn as by a bear. **Syn : Piri-ao.**

Chikobap, チコバブ, コガネムシ. *n.* A beetle.

Chikoe, チコエ, 副ヘテ食フ. *v.t.* To eat with. As :—*Emo shum chikoe,* " he eats fat with the potatoes."

Chiko-hummore, チコフムモレ, 靜ニ ナル、默スレ. *v.i.* To be quiet. To become silent. To stand still and listen.

Chikoikip, チコイキブ, 生物、(魚鳥獸 ノ類). *n.* Animals of any kind whether of land or sea.

Chikokarakari, チコカラカリ, 仕上ガ ル、縺レル. *v.i.* To have become entangled. To be done.

Chikokari, チコカリ, 縺レル. *v.i.* Same as *Chikokarakari.*

Chikokatpak, チコカッパク, 罪惡. *n.* Sins. Misdemeanours. Evil acts done.

Chikokatpak-ki, チコカッパクキ, 罪 チ犯ス. *v.i.* To commit sins.

Chikokatpakte, チコカッパクテ, 罪チ 犯カサセル、罪スレ. *v.t.* To make sin. To fix sins upon a person. To condemn.

Chikokoi, チココイ, 腎臟. *n.* The kidneys.

Chikonoiba, チコノイバ, 流レ滴レ. *v.i.* To run round. To trickle as blood from a wound. To run as grease from a candle.

Chiko-okere, チコオケレ, 徒爾ナラ シム、終ル. *v.t.* To bring to naught. To finish.

Chi-koro, チコロ,
Chikot, チコツ, } 吾等ノ. *pro.* Our.

Chikoro-chimakani, チコ ロチマカ 二, チシベツ、ギスカザカ. *n. Gymnocanthus intermedius, T. & S.*

Chikosamtek, チコサムテク, 汚點ア ル、疣ナ ル. *adj.* Spotted. Having dirty spots. **Syn : Chikotachi.**

Chiko-seshke, チコセシケ, 閉ヅ ル、塞 ガ ル、閉塞ガ レ. *v.i.* Closed. Shut up.

Chikoshinninup, 神符 (身 ニ付 ケ ル **チコシンニヌプ,** マ モ リ). *n.* A **Chiko-shinnuka,** charm. An **チコシンヌカ,** amulet.

Chikoshiripire, チコシリビレ, 物ナ 戻サ ル ト . *v.i.* To be caused to return something.

Chikotachi, チコタチ, 汚點ダ ラ ケ ナ レ. *adj.* Spotted. **Syn : Chikosamtek.**

Chikote, チコテ, 縛ク、(單數). *v.t.* To tie up (as a horse) *sing.*

Chikotpa, チコッパ, 縛ク、(複數). *v.t. Pl.* of *chikote.*

Chikte, チクテ, 滴ラス. *v.t.* To drop. To allow to drip (as water).

Chikuba, 嚙マ レ ト. *v.i.* To be **チクバ,** bitten by an animal. **Chikubaba,** To be set upon (as **チクババ,** by an animal). **Syn : Akubaba. Shitashke.**

Chikuba-kikiri, チクバキキリ, コ ガ ネ ム シ ノ類. *n.* A beetle. **Syn : Chikobap. Chikubap.**

Chikubap, チクバプ, 黑キコガネムシ ノ類. *n.* A beetle. **Syn : Chikobop.**

Chikube-ni, チクベ二, イ メ ン ジュ、 エ ン ジュ. *n.* A kind of flowering shrub. *Cladrastis amurensis, Benth. var. Buergeri, Max.* This

shrub is used as a medicine and charm against disease.

Chikuikui, チクイクイ, 嚙 ミ 碎. *v.i.* To be gnawed. **Syn : Akuikui.**

Chikuni, チク二, 樹木、例セバ、チ ク 二 ハ ム、木ノ葉. *n.* Wood and trees of any kind. As :—*Chikuni awe,* " branches of trees." *Chikuni ham,* " leaves of trees." *Chikuni sempirike,* " the shade of trees." *Chikuni shinrit,* " the roots of trees." *Chikuni shuppa kara,* " to make a bundle of wood." *Chikuni tek,* " branches of trees." *Chikuni retara kami,* " the white wood in trees found near the bark." *Chikuni raun kami,* "the heart of a tree." **Syn : Ni.**

Chikuni-awe, チク二アウェ, 木ノ枝. *n.* The branches of a tree.

Chikuni-ikpui, チク二イクブイ, 木 ノ心. *n.* The heart of a tree. **Syn : Chikuni-osshi. Chikuni kunne kamihi. Chikuni raun kami.**

Chikuni-kunne-kamihi, チク二クン 子カミヒ, 木ノ心. *n.* Same as above.

Chikuni-nirek, チク二二レク, 地衣. *n.* Lichens.

Chikuni-muye, チク二ムイェ, 薪ノ束. *n.* A faggot of wood. A bundle of wood.

Chikuni-osshi, チク二オッシ, 木ノ心. *n.* The heart of a tree. **Syn : Chikuni kunne kamiki.**

Chikuni-pe, チク二ベ, 木ノ汁液. *n.* Sap of a tree.

Chikuni-pon-ikoro, チク二ポンイコ ロ, 寶物ノ木刀. *n.* Small wooden treasures of the shape of ancient swords.

Chikuni-potoki, チクニポトキ, 木像. *n.* A wooden idol.

Chikuni-ras, チクニラス, 木屑、キクツ. *n.* Shavings. Chips of wood. Syn: Koppa.

Chikuni-shikai, チクニシカイ, 木釘. *n.* A wooden peg. Syn: Ni shikai.

Chikuni-tokum, チクニトクム, 木ノ節. *n.* A knot in a tree. A knob on a tree.

Chikuni-tope, チクニトペ, 木ノ液汁. *n.* Tree sap. Syn: Chikuni-pe.

Chikuni-tumama, チクニツママ, 木ノ幹. *n.* Trunks of trees.

Chikup, チクプ, 飲ムコト. *n.* A drinking. A sitting to drink. Syn: Ikup.

Chikurure, チクルレ, 來ル、過グル. *v.i.* To come. To pass. To cross (as a bird the heavens).

Chikusa, チクサ, 輸入ノ、例セバ、チクサアシコロ、輸入ノ酒: *adj.* Imported. As:— *Chikusa ashkoro,* "imported wine."

Chikusa-ashkoro, チクサアシコロ, 酒. *n.* Sake. Rice wine. Syn: Chirutu ashkoro; this word means "Imported wine."

Chikush, チクシ, 過ギラレ. *v.i.* To be passed over.

Chikushi, チクシ, 途、道、ミチ. *n.* A path. A road.

Chikush-ru, チクシル, 途、道、ミチ. *n.* A path. A road.

Chikuwaikara, チクワイカラ, 癲癇チ患フ. *v.i.* To be afflicted with apoplexy or fits.

Chikuwan-turi, チクワンツリ, 眞直ニ突出ル. *v.i.* To stick out straight.

Chima, チマ, 炙キタレ. *adj.* Roasted. Roast. Toasted. As:—*Chima chep,* "roasted fish." Syn: Ama.

Chima, チマ, 痂、カサブタ. *n.* Scales. Dead skin.

Chimaire-kamui, チマイレカムイ, 日本皇帝、知事. *n.* The Emperor of Japan. A governor. Syn: A-hekote. Nishpa.

Chimakani, チマカニ, カジカノ總稱. *n.* A kind of sculpin. Also called ten-chimakani and pet-kotch-imakani.

Chimakanit, チマカニツ, 炙キ串. *n.* A roasting spit.

Chima-kina, チマキナ, ウド. *n.* The spikenard plant. *Aralia racemosa, L. var. sachalinensis, Reg.* Used by the Ainu both as a vegetable and medicine.

Chima-o, チマオ,⎫ 痂アル、カサブタアル.
Chima-ush, チマウシ,⎭ *adj.* Scabby.

Chimaktekka, チマクテッカ, 悦ブ. *v.i.* To rejoice.

Chimaukara, チマウカラ, 火傷スル. *v.i.* To scald or burn one's self.

Chimayamaya, チマヤマヤ, 痒(カユ)ガル. *v.i.* To itch.

Chimba, チムバ, 手探レ、例セバ、ムンチムバワフナラ、草ノ中チ手マ探グル. *v.t.* To feel for. To search after by feeling. As:—*Mun chimba wa hunara,* "to search after by feeling in the grass."

Chimba-chimba, チムバチムバ, 手探レ. *v.t.* An intensified form of *chimba.*

Chimemke, チメムケ, 短ク切ル、剪ル. *adj.* and *v.i.* Cut close. Shaven.

As :—*Sapa chimemke,* " to have the hair shaven off or cut close." *Chimemke sapa,* "a shaven head."

Chimeshmesu, チメシメス, 荒ヶ〆レ、鋸歯狀ノ. *adj.* Jagged. **Syn:** **Notako-notako.** **Uturuuturu chimeshmesu.**

Chimi, チミ, 手探ル. *v.t.* To feel after. To search after by feeling. This word is the singular form of *Chimba.*

Chimi-chimi, チミチミ, 手探ル. *v.t.* An intensified form of *chimi.* To feel after. To search out. When applied to human beings this word has a bad meaning. Thus, *Ainu chimi-chimi,* " to search out a man" i.e. "to pick out his faults."

Chimip, チミブ, **Chimipi,** チミピ, 着物. *n.* Attire. Clothing. As :— *Ku goro chimip,* " my clothes."

Chimondum, チモンヅム, 力、チカラ、權威、ケンイ. *n.* Strength. Power. Authority.

Chimondum-kore, チモンヅムコレ, 強ムル、權威ヲ與フル. *v.t.* To strengthen. To give authority to a person.

Chimoyemoye, チモイェモイェ, 動ク. *v.i.* To move.

Chimoyomoyo, チモヨモヨ, 僅ナル、稀ナル. *adj.* Few. Scarce.

Chimutbe, チムツベ, 頸掛玉、記章. *n.* A necklace. A badge.

Chin, チン, 擴ゲル. *v.t.* To spread out. To stretch out.

Chin, チン, 骨盤、足. *n.* The pelvis. The top of the legs.

Chinana, チナナ, 乾魚. *n.* Fish which has been cleaned and dried in the sun unsalted and with the heads left on. See *satchep.*

Chinanarange, チナナランゲ. 仆ル、欺カレ. *v.i.* To fall down. To be deceived. To be put out of countenance.

Chinene, チ子子, 痙攣ノ類、ケイレンノルイ. *n.* A kind of cramp. Pins and needles. *Chinene* attacks the hands, arms, feet and legs. **Syn:** **Tukunne.**

Chingara, チンガラ, 乾スタメ二擴ゲル. *v.t.* To spread out skin to dry.

Chingeu-pone, チンゲウボチ, **Chinkeu-pone,** チンケウボチ, 骨盤. *n.* The pelvis.

Chingi, チンギ, 端、ハシ、境、サカイ. *n.* Edge. Border. Hem. Lappet. *Same as chinki.*

Chinika, チニカ, 一步、脚、例セバ、チニカプニ、一步ヲ進メル. *n.* A step. The legs. As :— *Chinika puni,* " to take a step." *Chinika turi,* " to stretch the legs." *Chinika takne guru,* " a person who takes short steps." *Chinika tanne guru,* " a person who takes long steps."

Chininiap, チニニアブ, 釣餌. *n.* A kind of decoy used in catching river trout. **Syn:** **Apniniap.**

Chininuibe, チニヌイベ, 枕. *n.* A pillow. **Syn:** **Chieninuibe.**

Chinirarapare, チニララバレ, 俯シテ坐ス. *v.i.* To sit with bended head as in deep respect or thought. **Syn:** **Hepokiush.**

Chinisap, チニサブ, 急ギテ. *adv.* In haste. As :—*Chinisap karabe,* " a thing done in haste."

**Chinishteramkore, チニシテラムコ
レ,** 壓制スレ、虐ゲル. *v.t.* To oppress. To be hard upon.

**Chinishteramkorep, チニシテラム
コレプ,** 壓制、無殘. *n.* Oppression.
Hardness of heart.

Chinita, チニタ, 夢、ユメ. *n.* A
dream. A nightmare. **Syn:
Wendarap.**

**Chinita-ki,
　チニタキ,**
**Chinita-koro,
　チニタコロ,**
**Chinita-nukara,
　チニタヌカラ,** } 夢ミレ. *v.i.* To
dream. To
have night-
mare.

Chinitankashure, チニタンカシュレ,
競フ. *v.i.* To race. **Syn: Uwetushmak.**

Chiniukesh, チニウケシ, 出來ヌ、能ハ
ヌ. *v.i.* To be unable.

Chinkanokush, チンカノクシ, 後ニ
仆レ. *v.i.* To fall backwards.

Chinkanpayotne, チンカンパヨツチ,
後ニ仆レテ足ヲ開ク、劇シク步ム、強ク
步ム、(怒リシトキノ如ク). *v.i.* To
fall over backwards with out-
stretched legs.

**Chinka-paye-turituri, チンカパイェ
ツリツリ,** 濶步スル、(怒シガ如ク).
v.i. To stride along (as in anger).

Chinki, チンキ, 着物ノ端. *n.* The
edge or lappet of any part of a
garment. *Same as chingi.*

Chinkotoro, チンコトロ, 下股. *n.*
The under part of the thighs.

Chinna, チンナ, 壕、溝、ミゾ. *n.* A
ditch. **Syn: Chirinnai. Pechiri.**

Chinna, チンナ, 骨盤. *n.* The pelvis.
The top of the legs.

Chino, チノ, 熟シタレ. *adj.* Ripe.
Cooked.

Chinomi, チノミ, 拜神、又ハ秡拜物. *n.*
The worship of the gods. Also
worshipped.

Chinore, チノレ, 欺ク. *v.t.* To deceive. To counterfeit. As :—
Ohinore itak ki, "to deceive by
word of mouth."

Chinorep, チノレプ, 僞物、ニセモノ. *n.*
An imitation. A deception.

Chinot, チノツ, 腮、アゴ. *n.* The chin.
A blunt cape.

Chinowainure, チノワイヌレ, 殆ンド
殺サレ. *v.i.* To be nearly killed.
To come near meeting with an accident.

Chinoye, チノイェ, 拗(ネヂ)レタル、飾
ラレタレ. *adj.* Twisted. Curled.
Trimmed. Ornamented.

Chinoye-tat, チノイェタツ, 樺ノ木ニテ
作リシ室內用ノ燈火. *n.* Birch bark
twisted so as to form a torch or
light.

Chinru, チンル, 雪下駄、カンジキ. *n.*
Snow-shoes. **Syn: Teshma.**

**Chinuchakchakka, チヌチャクチャッ
カ,** 競爭スル. *v.i.* To strive. **Syn:
Uwetushmak.**

**Chinuchanuchakka, チヌチャヌチ
ャッカ,** 競爭スル. *v.i.* To strive.
To vie.

Chinukara, チヌカラ, 見ラレル. *v.i.*
To be seen.

Chinukarabe, チヌカラベ, 見エル物.
n. Something to see. Anything
to look at.

Chinumumu, チヌムム, 塞ガレ. *v.i.*
To be stopped up. **Syn: Anu-
mumu.**

Chinunuke-ike, チヌヌケイケ, 陰門.
n. Vagina. **Syn: Achike. Samambe. Nuina-korobe.** All

but *nuina-korobe*, are considered slang.

Chin-uturu, チンウツル, 骨盤ノ上部. *n.* The fleshy part of the pelvis.

Chinuye-pira, チヌイェピラ, 文字チ書シアル岩. *n.* A rock having inscriptions upon it.

Chioboshmamba, チオボシマムバ, 可笑シキ. *adj.* Ridiculous. Funny. **Syn: Aitakboso.**

Chioikare, チオイカレ, 上チ越サル丶. *v.i.* To be passed over, as a tree or house by a bird.

**Chi-oka, チオカ,
Chi-okai, チオカイ,
Chi-okai-utara, チオカイウタラ,** 吾々. *pro.* We.

**Chi-oka-gusu, チオカグス,
Chi-okai-gusu, チオカイグス,** 吾等ノ爲ニ. *ph.* For us. On our behalf.

**Chiokapapa, チオカパパ,
Chokapapa, チョカパパ,** 前ニ屈ム (大ニ笑フトキノ如ク). *v.i.* To lean forward (as in laughing heartily). **Syn: Chiorewewe.**

Chiokaukap, チオカウカプ, 縫箔シタ衣服. *n.* An embroidered dress. **Syn: Chikemekarabe.**

Chiomap, チオマプ, 愛セラレタル. *adj.* Beloved.

Chiopentari, チオペンタリ, 顛仆スル. *v.i.* To fall down with the heels in the air.

Chiorange, チオランゲ, 下ル. *v.i.* To come down. To descend.

**Chiorewewe, チオレウェウェ,
Chorewewe, チョレウェウェ,** 前ニ屈ム、(甚ダ笑フトキノ如ク). *v.i.* To lean forward (as in

laughing heartily). See *Chiotesusu.* **Syn: Chiokapapa.**

Chiorange, チオランゲ, 當ラズ. *v.i.* and *v.t.* To miss. To be behind hand. **Syn: Aorange.**

Chioshka-saranip, チオシカサラニプ, 木皮チ以テ作ラレシ籠. *n.* A kind of basket ornamented with coloured bark or reeds.

Chioshke-sapa, チオシケサバ, 旋毛 (ツムジ)チ綴ル. *v.i.* To have the hair plaited on the top of the head.

Chiotanne, チオタンチ, 爐様、ロブチ. *n.* The wooden framework used round a hearth or fire-place. **Syn: Inumbe.**

Chiotanne-turi-guru, チオタンチツリグル, 爐邊ノ人、親シキ人. *n.* A very dear friend. A close friend. A person upon whom one depends (lit: "a hearth framework person"). A metaphorical phrase indicating love, trust, endearment or friendship; the *chiotanne* of a hearth being supposed to embrace one of the most important and sacred places in a hut. **Syn: Chiotanne ainu.** (Masc). **Chiotanne mat.** (Fem).

**Chiotari, チオタリ,
Chotari, チョタリ,** 後ロヘ蹴ル. *v.i.* To kick out from behind as a horse. **Syn: Hoketu.**

**Chiotesusu, チオテスス,
Chotesusu, チョテスス,** 反身シテ笑フ. *v.i.* To lean back (thrusting the stomach forward) as when laughing heartily. As:—*Mina gusu chiotesusu chiorewewe,* "to be bent back and forth in laughing."

Chioushikara, チオウシカラ, 置カレ *v.i.* To be placed. To be set (as a house upon a hill).

Chioyange, チオヤンゲ, 漂着ス ル. *v.i.* To be cast ashore as a wreck or dead fish.

Chioyapte, チオヤプテ, 舟ヲ陸ニ引上 ゲル. *v.t.* To drag a boat to shore.

Chioyaush, チオヤウシ, 舟揚場. *n.* A beaching place for boats.

Chip, チプ, 舟、例セバ、チプアリアレ ラ、船ニテ送ル. *n.* A boat. A ship. As :— *Chip ari arura,* " to send by boat." *Chip atap,* " the boat rolls." *Chip chiwende,* " a shipwreck." *Chip erau oma,* " the boat sinks with the waves." *Chip erik oma,* " the boat rises with the waves." *Chip iyapte,* " to unload a boat." *Chip kan ita,* " the top board of a boat," bulwarks." *Chip kiri,* " the ribs of a boat." *Chip koiyange,* " a boat to be cast a-shore." *Chip kuta,* " to turn a boat upside down." *Chip nanta,* " the bows of a boat." *Chip o,* " to sail in a boat"; " to work a boat." *Chip o guru,* " a sailor "; " a boatman." *Chip okanchi,* "a rud-der." *Chip orowa no yan,* also, *Chip orowa no oashin,* " to land "; " to go out of a boat." *Chip orun ahun,* " to board a boat." *Chip orun ichipo,* " to load a boat." *Chip osoro,* " a boat's stern." *Chip otta kusa,* " to load a boat." *Chip paruru,* "the top edging of a boat." *Chip sapa,* " the bows of a boat." *Chip sei,* " the skeleton of a boat." *Chip sange,* " to land a boat." *Chip sanita,* " the deck of a ship."

Chip shua, " to be sea-sick." *Chip-shikeka,* " a boat's deck." *Chip umta,* " a boat's stern." *Chip wende,* " to be wrecked." *Chip yange,* " to haul a boat a-shore."

Chip, チプ, 陰門、(下等ノ語). *n.* A slang word for the vagina.

Chipa, チパ, 切リカ丶ル. *v. t.* To strike at with a sword.

Chipachipa, チパチパ, 望ム. *v.t.* To hope for. To long for. As :— *Ku keutum ta ku chipachipa kane hum ash,* " I feel a longing for something in my heart." *Nishat-ta yuk kam ku e kuni ku chipa-chipa ruwe ne,* " I hope to have some venison to eat to-morrow." It should be noted that *kuni* generally precedes the word *chipa-chipa* as illustrated in the last of the preceding examples.

Chipahau-ushka, チパハウウシカ, 云 フ、告ゲル. *v.t.* To say. To tell. As :— *Usakatneka chipahau-ushka,* " he says various things." **Syn : Opahau-ush.**

Chipanup, チパヌプ, 女ノ頭巾. *n.* A kind of headdress worn by women at feasts when they wait upon the men. **Syn : Chiepa nup. Aep-anup.**

Chiparase, チパラセ, 現ハル. *v.i.* To appear. To be depicted as anger upon the countenance.

Chiparasere, チパラセレ, 現ハス. *v.t.* To make appear. To show as anger upon the countenance.

Chipaske, チパスケ, 黒燒ノ. *adj.* Burnt black.

Chipaskuma-koro, チパスクマコロ,

悸ク. *v.i.* To be surprised or startled. As :—*Ingara chipaskuma koro*, "to be startled or startled at seeing something."

Chipaskuma-koro, チパスクマコロ, 傳說ヲ告グル. *v.i.* To recite traditions. To tell of ancient things.

Chipasusu, チパスス, 散レ、例セバ、ユク チ パスス ワ キ ラ ワ パイェ、鹿ハ散リ 走レリ. *v.i.* To disperse. To scatter. As :—*Yuk chipasusu wa kira wa paye*, "the deer scattered and ran away." **Syn: Uko-opiu. Eukopi-eukopi kira.**

Chipasusure, チパススレ, 散ラス. *v.t.* To disperse. To scatter. **Syn: Uko-opiure. Eukopieukopi wa kirare.**

Chipat, チパツ, 魚ノ肛門. *n.* A fishes anus.

Chipatuye, チパツイェ, 舟ヲ下ス. *v.i.* To launch a boat.

Chipekare, チペカレ, 入ル、出レ. *v.i.* To go in or out. As :—*Koro uni chipekare*, "he entered his home."

Chipereba-ni, チペレバニ, 割木. *n.* Cleft wood. Fuel.

Chipeshishte, チペシシチ, 進ム. *v.i.* To go along. To proceed.

Chipeukote-kina, チ ペ ウ コテキナ, アヤメ. *n.* Iris sibirica L. By some called *Chipeukute*.

Chipiyak, チピヤク, 鴫、シギ. *n.* A snipe.

Chipiyeba, チピェバ, 貝ノ名. *n.* A kind of shell fish.

Chipiye-guru, チピィェグル, 雜種. *n.* A half-caste. **Syn: Apiye guru.**

Chipiyep, チビイェブ, 雜種. *n.* A half-breed. The child of an Ainu and Japanese.

Chipiyep-korobe, チビイェブコロベ, 雜種. *n.* A half-breed. A term of reproach.

Chipiyere, チビイェレ, 古キ罪ヲ願ハセル. *v.t.* To remind a person of his faults.　　　[*n.* Winkles.

Chipiyeto-sie, チビイェトセイ, 貝ノ名.

Chip-ni-susu, チプニスス,
Chip-susu, チプスス, } ヤマネコヤナギ、パツ コヤナギ. *n.* A kind of willow. *Salix Caprea L.*

Chip-o, チブオ, 漕グ. *v.t.* To row.

Chipo-eto, チポエト,
Chipo-yeto, チポイェト, } 巻貝ノ名. *n.* Any kind of gastropoda. **Syn: Chipiyeto-sei.**

Chipoka, チポカ, 子ヲ産ムコト. *n.* Child-birth.

Chipoka-ekahuye, チポカエカフイェ, 子ヲ取上グル、(產婆ノ). *v.t.* To nurse a woman during child-birth.

Chipoka-ekahuye-guru, チポカエカ フイェグル, 產婆. *n.* A person who nurses another during child-birth. A mid-wife.

Chipon-ninap, チポンニナプ,
Chiporo-ninap, チポロニナプ, } 魚ノ子ヲ粉ニスル道具. *n.* A fish-roe crusher.

Chipon-nina-pon-nima, チポンニ ナポンニマ, 魚ノ子ヲ碎ク小サキ道具. A small wooden tray or dish with a spout, used for smashing up fish roe.

Chipori, チポリ,
Chipoyo, チポロ, } 魚ノ卵、(鯡ヲ除ク). *n.* The spawn of any kind of fish excepting herrings. Herring spawn is called *homa*.

Chiporo-ande, チポロアンデ, 產卵ス ル(魚). *v.i.* To spawn.

Chiporo-ninap, 魚ノ子 チ粉醬スル道
チポロニナプ, 具. *n.* A fish-
Chipon-ninap, roe crusher.
チポンニナプ,

Chiposhpare, チポシパレ, 照リ渡ル.
v.i. To shine through as light.
To pierce through.

Chipoyan-i, チポヤニ, 上陸場、埠頭. *n.*
A landing place.

Chipta-chikap, チプタチカプ, クマゲ
ラ. *n.* Great black woodpecker.
Picus martius, Linn. Syn: Chip-
tachiri.

Chirai-chep, チライチェプ, イトウ. *n.*
Blakiston trout. *Hucho blakistonii,*
(*Higd*).

Chiraima-chiri, チライマチリ, オシ
ドリ. *n.* Manderin duck. *Anas
galericulata, Linn.*

Chirairep, チライレプ, 遺産相續品. *n.*
Heirlooms. Syn: Eikeshkorobe.

Chirama, チラマ, 最下ノ、低キ. *adj.*
Low. The lowest.

Chiramamtep, チラマムテプ, 熊、ク
マ. *n.* A bear. The general name
for bears. Special names are as
follows:—*Shiyuk,* "a he bear."
Kuchan, "a she bear." *Hokuyuk,* "a man eating bear." *Peurep* are cubs in their first year.
Riyap are cubs in their second
year. *Chishurap* are cubs in
their third year. After the third
year a-cub is called *Chiramantep,
kamui,* or *kim un kamui.*

Chiramrarire, チラムラリレ, 保護ス
ル. *v.t.* To take care of. To
preserve. To keep safe and happy. Syn: Koshiratki. Chishikrarire.

Chirangeashkoro, チランゲアシコロ,

栗類ニテ造ラレシ酒. *n.* A kind of
drink made from millet. This
is a pure native drink and is said
to have been used by the Ainu
before Japanese *sake* was introduced.

Chirarakka, チララッカ, 滑カナル.
adj. Slippery. Syn: Chiinrarakka.

Chirarire, チラリレ, 後ヨリ往ク、從フ.
v.t. To go after. Syn: Kashirari oman.

Chirashnuka, チラシヌカ, 色取リタ
ル、彩色シタル、例セバ、チラシヌカサ
ラニプ、彩色セラレタル籠. *adj.* and
v.i. To be striped with colours.
To be of various colours. As:—
Chirashnuka saranip, "a basket
ornamented with various paterns."

Chiratchitkere, チラッチッケレ, 懸カ
ル. *v.i.* To be suspended. To
hang. Syn: Aratkire.

Chiratchitkerep, チラッチッケレプ, 懸
リシモノ. *n.* Anything suspended
(as a pot over a fire, a lamp from
a ceiling, clothes from a line, etc.).
Syn: Aratchitkerep.

Chire, チレ, 煮過ギル、炙キスギル. *v.t.*
To overcook. To burn. To cook.
As:—*Amam shuye wa chire,* "put
the rice on and cook it."

Chire, チレ. 日光ニ晒ラス、例セバ、ム
ンシュクスチレ、草ヲ枯ラス. *v.i.* To
expose to the sun. To put to dry
in the sun. Also *v.i.* "to be
scorched." This word is always
preceded by *shukus,* "sunshine";
but is never applied to drying fish.
As:—*Mun shukus chire,* "to make
hay." *Shukus chire wa ku kapu*

pichitche, "my skin is peeling through exposure to the sun."

Chirekte, チレクテ, 彈ズル. *v.t.* To play (as a musical instrument).

Chirekte-huttara, ヨブス、マサウ、ポ
チレクテフッタラ, ウナ. *n. Senecio sagittatus,*
Chirekte-kuttara, *cio sagittatus,*
チレクテクッタラ, *Schultz Bip.* Also called by some *pet-kutu; wakka-kuttara; rek-kuttara.*

Chirektep, チレクテプ, 樂器ノ類、音ヲ發スルモノ. *n.* A musical instrument of any kind.

Chirekte-top, チレクテトプ, 笛. *n.* A flute.

Chirepnaoshkep, チレブナオシケブ, 綱、ツナ、繩. *n.* A cord used for tying up boxes and for general purposes.

Chiri, チリ, 溝、管. *n.* A ditch. Tube. Pipe. **Syn: Pechiri.**

Chiri, チリ, 鳥. *n.* A bird of any kind. This word, though used in some districts as *chikap* is in others, very often occurs in compounds. Thus:—*Kapa-chiri,* "an eagle." *Retat'-chiri,* "a wild swan." *Amame-chiri,* also *amame-chikap,* "a sparrow."

Chirikari-chisei, チリカリチセイ, 家ノ骨組. *n.* The frame-work of a house. **Syn: Chisei Niye.**

Chirikipuni, チリキプニ, 直立スル(山ノ如シ). *v.i.* To stand up (as a large house or high mountain).

Chirikoraye, チリコライェ, 回復スル、晴ラス、強メル、上ゲル、陸ラスル. *v.t.* To revive. To clear away. To strengthen. To raise. To lift up.

Chirinnai, チリンナイ, 細流ノ川、水管、溝. *n.* A very small stream.

Chirinnaine-san, チリンナイチサン, 跡ヲ殘ス、(蛇、蝸牛ノ步ミシ如ク). *v.i.* To go along and leave a continuous trail behind as a snake or worm.

Chiri-po, チリポ, 小鳥. *n.* A little bird. A young bird of any kind.

Chiripui, チリプイ, エンコウサウ. *n. Caltha palustris L. var. sibirica, Reg.*

Chiriri, チリリ, 漏レル、滴ル. *v.i.* To trickle. To drip (as water). To slip through.

Chironnup, チロンヌプ, 狐、キツネ. *n.* A fox. In some places called *furep* which means "a red thing," "a red animal." The proper names for foxes are:— *Chironnup, shumari,* and *shitumbe. Shitumbe* is generally applied to the black fox. The word *chironnup* enters into the names of other two animals, viz., *Upas chironnup,* "ermine." (lit: snow fox), so called because in winter, its hair is said to change in colour from black to white; and *Wor'un chironnup* "a river otter" (lit: water fox). The usual name for "river otter" however is *Esaman.* The skulls of foxes are used for divination by the Ainu men.

Chironnup-kina, チロンヌプキナ, キミカクサウ. *n.* Lily of the valley. *Convallaria majalis, L.*

Chirosh, チロシ, 熊祭ニ用キル尖ノ鈍キ矢. *n.* Blunt arrows used to irritate bears in the bear feasts. **Syn: Akshinot pon ai. Akshinot pon guru.**

Chiroshki, チロシキ, 引ク、(幕ナドチ).

v.t. To draw (as window curtains or blinds).

Chiroshne-chep, チロシ子チェブ, 魚ノ類. *n.* Sea-poachers (including several species).

Chiroshnu-cheppo, チロシヌチェッ朮, 魚ノ類. *n.* A kind of small salt water fish. Probably the white-bait.

Chirui, チルイ, 高慢ナル、倨傲ナレ、狡猾ナル. *adj.* Boast-full. Haughty. Sly.

Chirutu-ashkoro, チルツアシコロ, 日本酒. *n.* Japanese *sake.* **Syn: Chikusa-ashkoro. Tonoto.** The word *Tonoto* really means "official milk."

Chisaure-ramu, チサウレラム, 冷遇スレ. *v.t.* To treat slightingly. **Syn: Chituperamu.**

Chisei, チセイ, 家、イへ、例セバ、カムイチセイ、熊ノ穴. *n.* A house. A hut. An abode. A bear's den. A wasp's nest. As:—*Kamui chisei,* "a bear's den." *Soyai chisei,* "a wasp's nest." *Chisei asam,* "the foundation of a house." *Chisei erupshike,* "the front of a house." *Chisei honto,* "the back of a house." *Chisei kara,* "to build a house." *Chisei kes,* "the west end of a house where the rubbish is thrown." *Chisei kipip,* "the thatch of a house." *Chisei kipip kara,* "to thatch a house." *Chisei kitai* or *kitaige,* "the roof of a house." *Chisei koro guru,* "a householder." *Chisei koro inao,* "household offerings of willow shavings to the gods." *Chisei koro katkimat,* "the mistress of a house." *Chisei semohonto,* "the back of a house." *Chisei orowa no soine,* "to go out of a house." *Chisei niye,* "the framework of a house." *Chisei orun ahun,* "to enter a house." *Chisei oshike chashnure,* "to set a house in order." *Chisei oshiketa so kara,* "to, prepare for a guest." *Chisei pa,* "the east end of a hut." *Chisei pana,* "the west end of a hut." *Chisei pan etupok,* "the upper corner of the west end of a hut." *Chisei pena,* "the east end of a hut. *Chisei pen etupok,* "the upper end of the east end of a hut." *Chisei rorogeta,* "the outside of the east end of a hut." *Chisei rupshi,* "the front of a house." *Chisei soi,* "the site of a house." *Chisei sokashi,* "the sloping sides of the roof of a house." *Chisei sopa,* "the treasure corner of a hut." *Chisei tai,* "a village" or "a hamlet." *Chisei ta turesh,* "the younger daughter of a house." *Chisei tumama,* "the wall of a house." *Chisei uhuye,* "a conflagration." *Chisei un,* "at home." *Chisei un ahun,* "to go indoors." *Chisei un ahupte,* "to take indoors." *Chisei urupshik,* "the outside of the east end of a hut." *Itunnap chisei,* "an ant's nest." *Chisei nokipip,* "the eaves of a house."

Chiseikoash, チセイコアシ, 家或ハ熊ノ穴ヲ圍ム. *v.t.* To compass. To surround a bear's den in order to shoot the bear when it comes out.

**Chisei-kor'ewen-guru, チセイコレ
ウェングル,** 二三度獨身ニ成リシ男女.
n. A twice or thrice made widow
or widower.

Chisei-maka-ni, チセイマカニ, 小舎
ノ屋上ノ棟. *n.* The upper beams
of a hut. Rafter braces.

Chisei-nomi, チセイノミ, 新宅祝. *n.*
Prayer made for the prosperity of
a houshold, or a feast made on
the occasion of taking up one's
abode in a new house.

Chisei-nomi-an, チセイノミアン, 新
宅ヲ祝フ. *v.i.* To hold a house
warming feast.

Chisei-paraka, チセイパラカ, 天井、
屋根裏. *n.* The inside of the roof
of a house. Ceiling.

Chisei-uhuyeka, チセイウフイェカ, 家
ニ火ヲ放ツ. *v.t.* To set a house on
fire. To commit arson.

**Chisei-uhuyeka-i, チセイウフイェカ
イ,** 放火, ヒツケ. *n.* A house-
burning. Arson.

Chisei-un, チセイウン, 家ニ、内ニ. *adv.*
At home. Indoors. Towards
home. Towards a house.

Chisei-upshoro, チセイウプショロ,
家ノ内. *n.* The inside of a house.
The main part of a hut (lit:
house-bosom).

Chiseshke, チセシケ, 閉メル. *v.t.*
To close up. To stop.

Chish, チシ, 哭ク、例セバ、チシハウェ、泣
漪. *v.i.* To cry. To weep. To
sing (as a bird). As :— *Chish
hawe* " a weeping." " A crying "
or " wailing." *Chish koro*, " weeping," " whilst weeping." *Chish
sessereke*, " to sniffle as in weep-

ing." *Chish kokarakarase* also
chish korimimse, also *chish koshishirapa*, " to cry " or " to
weep."

Chish, チシ, 喰シキ道路. *n.* A steep
winding path. A precipitous path.
**Syn : Wen-shiri. Chikaye-chi-
sh. Ekayechish. Nangashke.**

Chishchish, チチシ, 水滴. *n.* A
drop of water.

Chishikeraine, チシケライネ, 憐ム.
v.t. To pity. **Syn : Chieshike-
raine.**

Chishikoseshke, チシコセシケ, 布列
スル、擴ガル、ナラブ. *v.i.* To be
spread out (like a town).

Chishikrarire, チシクラリレ, 護ラレ
ル. *v.t.* To take care of. To preserve. To keep safe and well.
This word is often used with *chiramrarire*, " to keep safe and
happy," in prayer.

Chishimemokka, チシメモッカ, 喧嘩
ヲ仕向ケル. *v.t.* To pick a quarrel. To challenge to fight. **Syn :
Ishimemokka.**

Chishinap, チシナプ, 罰金. *n.* A
fine. **Syn : Ashimbe.**

Chishipusure, チシプスレ, 急ニ現ハ
レ. *v.i.* To appear suddenly. To
come suddenly into view. **Syn :
Ekushkonna anukara.**

Chishirianu, チシリアヌ, 有ル. *v.i.*
To be. **Syn : An. Okai.**

Chishirikirap, チシリキラプ, 悲シム、
憂フル. *v.i.* To be sorry.

Chishirikirapte, チシリキラプテ, 悲
シマシムル. *v.t.* To make sorry.

**Chishirikokarakara, チシリコカラ
カラ,** 卷ク. *v.t.* To wind round.

Chishitomap, チシトマブ, 妖怪、魑魅. *n.* A bogie.

Chishitoshito, チシトシト, 縮ミタル. *adj.* Curled.

Chishituriri, チシツリリ, 續ク. *v.i.* To be continuous in a line or succession (as the descendants of a people). Thus :—*Huchi santek e-kashi santek chishituriri utara chi ne ruwe ne,* "we are the lineal descendants of the ancient fathers and mothers." **Syn : Shituri.**

Chishkara, チシカラ,
Chishkan, チシカン, } 泣ク. *v.i.* To weep.

Chish-konchi, チシコンチ, 獨身者ノ頭巾. *n.* A kind of bonnet worn by widows and widowers. As :— *Chish konchi eush,* or *chish konchi koro,* "to wear a widow's bonnet."

Chishne, チシ子, 縁ヲ刻ミタル、鋸齒狀ノ. *adj.* Indented.

Chishne, チシ子, 臼ノ幹、瓶ノ首. *n.* The stem of a mortar. The neck of a bottle.

Chishne-nishu, チシ子ニシュ, 幹ノアル臼. *n.* A mortar with neck or stem.

Chishpo, チシポ, 針刺、ハリサシ. *n.* A needle cushion formerly worn attached to the neck of a women's dress.

Chishrimimse, チシリミムセ, 跳子踊ル、身體ヲ動搖スル、(子供ガ子守ノ背ニテ爲ス如ク). *v.i.* To dance or move about when crying (as children sometimes do).

Chish-sessereke, チシセッセレケ, 吸泣スレ. *v.i.* To weep inwardly. To sniffle. To weep a little silently.

Chishte, チシテ, 泣カス. *v.t.* To make cry.

Chishurap, チシュラブ, 三歳ノ熊. *n.* A three year old bear's cub.

Chishuye, チシュイェ, アマニウ. *n.* *Angelica edulis, Miyabe.* Also called *chihuye* in some places. *Chishuye kuttara,* "the old stems of the Angelica."

Chishuye, チシュイェ, 煮ル. *v.t.* To cook by boiling.

Chisoikatta, チソイカッタ, 急ギテ家ヨリ出ヅル. *v.t.* To go out of doors in haste. To get out of a carriage in a hurry.

Chisoinaraye, チソイナライェ, 出ヅル、外出スル、(家ヨリ). *v.i.* To go out. To pass out of a door.

Chita, チタ, 掘リ出サル. *v.i.* Dug up. Extracted from the earth.

Chitakte, チタクテ, 預言スレ. *v.i.* To divine. To be made to speak (as by the gods). **Syn : Chiitakte.**

Chitarape, チタラペ, 袋. *n.* A satchel. A bag. A kind of sedge mat used for carrying bundles, usually ornamented with strips of work or rushes. **Syn : Itara. Onikapunbe.**

Chitekkamure, チテッカムレ, 手ニテ蔽フ. *v.t.* To spread the hands over. To cover over with the hands.

Chitennep, チテンチブ, 赤子、嬰兒. *n.* A young baby. **Syn : Teinep.**

Chiterekere, チテレケレ, 踊レ、跳ル. *v.i.* To prance. To jump about. To dance.

Chitokba, チトクバ, 粗末ナル、飾ナキ. *adj.* Unornamented. Not decorated. Sloven. Common. As :—

Chitokba ai, " an ordinary undecorated arrow.

Chitokitoki, チトキトキ, 飾ラレタレ、縫ヒモラレタレ. *adj.* Ornamented. Having patterns.

Chitomte, チトムテ, 美シキ、飾ラレタレ. *adj.* Beautiful. Ornamented. As :—*Chitomte ai,* " an ornamental arrow" (used at bear feasts).

Chitomte-no-an, チトムテノアン, 綺麗ナルレ. *adj.* Luxurious. Beautiful. Glorious. Decked out with beautiful things.

Chitomtep, チトムテプ, 綺麗ナルモノ. *n.* Beautiful things. Ornaments. Glory. Majesty.

Chitoratekka, チトラテッカ, 昏睡病. *n.* Coma. Lethargy. **Syn : Katu-toranne.**

Chitoshke, チトシケ, 嗚呼、(嘆息ノ語). *interj.* An expression of disgust (said by the Ainu to be a Japanese word).

Chitput, チツプツ, 魚ノ腎鰭. *n.* The anal fin of a fish.

Chituima, チツイマ, 遥カニ、遠クニ、例セバ、チツイマツリ、遠クニマデ延ビレ. *adv.* Far. Distant. As : —*Chituima turi,* " stretching a long way."

Chituirep, チツイレプ、**Chiturep,** チツレプ, カガイモ. *n.* A climbing plant, the roots and pods of which are used as food. *Metaplexis Stauntoni, Roem. et Sch.*

Chiturep-chippo, チツレプチッポ, 同上. *n.* Same as above.

Chitunash, チツナシ, 迅カニ、急ニ. *adv.* Quickly. In haste. **Syn : Tunashi.**

Chitunashka, チツナシカ, 急ガセル. *v.t.* To hasten.

Chituperamu, チツペラム, 軽視スレ、粗略ニ扱フ. *v.t.* To slight. To treat slightingly. **Syn : Chisaure-ramu.**

Chiturichippo, チツリチッポ, カイモノ殻. *n.* The seed pod of the *chituirep.*

Chiturusere, チツルセレ, 急ニ出レ、急ニ現ハル. *v.i.* To spring out suddenly. To appear suddenly (as an animal in the forest).

Chiturusere, チツルセレ, 外レル(関節ナドノ). *v.i.* and *adj.* To be dislocated. To be out of joint. Displaced. **Syn : Epittek.**

Chitush-kokarakari, チツシコカラカリ, 縫ルレ. *v.i.* To become entangled as a rope. Thus :— *Umma chitush-kokarakari range gusu ku pita kushki,* "I will set the horse free because its rope gets entangled."

Chiu, チウ, 苦痛スル、火傷スル. *v.i.* To tingle. To be scalded. To burn.

Chiu, チウ, 河流、例セバ、チウハウゲ、静カナル流レ. *n.* The current of a stream or river. A current in the sea. As :—*Chiu hauge,* "a gentle current." *Chiu rui,* " a strong current." **Syn : Chiwe.**

Chiuchiu, チウチウ, 鶺鴒、セキレイ. *n.* The wagtail. **Syn : Ochiuchiu.**

Chiuchiubare, チウチウバレ, 散ラサレル. *v.i.* To be scattered about.

Chiuitek-guru, チウイテクグル, 召使. *n.* A servant.

Chiukokarakari, チウコカラカリ, 縺
ル、カラマレ. *v.i.* To become
mixed up. To be twisted as
thread in a needle. **Syn: Hochikarakari.**

Chiukoi, チウコイ, 堆積、塊、カタマリ.
n. A heap. A lump.

Chiukomau, チウコマウ, ホ、ヅキ. *n.*
The winter cherry. *Physalis Al-
kekenji, L.*

**Chiukomoyemoye, チウコモイェモ
イェ,** 縺レル. *v.i.* Moved together.
Twisted.

Chiukonumumu, チウコヌムム, 塞カ
レ. *v.i.* To be stopped up.

Chiukopayere, チウコパイェレ, 搔廻
ス、混ズル、搔雜セル.. *v.t.* To stir
up. To mix. **Syn: Koyak-
koyak.**

Chiukopoye, チウコポイェ, 搔廻サレ
ル、混スル、困却スル. *v. i.* To be
mixed with. To intermingle. To
be stirred up. To be troubled.
To be in doubt. To be perplexed.
Syn: Chiutumashure.

**Chiukopoye-keutum-koro, チウコ
ポイェケウツムコロ,** 二心チ懷ク、誠實
ナラザル、狐疑スル. *v.i.* and *adj.* To
be double faced. Insincere. To
have the mind stirred with doubts,
fears, or troubles.

Chiukotaptapu, チウコタブタブ, 團
メル. *v.t.* To roll up into a ball.

Chiukush, チウクシ, 泣ク、涙チ流ス.
v.i. To weep. To shed tears. As:
—*Ku nangashike chiukush ruwe
ne,* "I have tears running down
my face." **Syn: Chish.**

Chiukururu, チウクルル, 流レチ塞ケ
(木草ナドチ以テ). *v. i.* To be
obstructed as the current of a
stream by logs or posts.

Chiunno-tashum, チウンノタシュム,
敗血病. *n.* The scurvy.

Chiun-chisei, チウンチセイ, 己ノ家、
吾家. *n.* One's own home.

Chiupiri, チウビリ, 渦流. *n.* An
eddy in a stream.

Chiupuni, チウブニ, 渦流ノ戻リ水.
n. The back waters of an eddy.

Chiure, チウレ, 足、足ノ指. *n.* The
foot. The toes. **Syn: Cheure.**

Chiuri, チウリ, ホツキガイ. *n.* Clams.

Chiurip, チウリブ, 薯蕷、ヂチンジョヤ.
n. *Dioscorea japonica, Thumb.*

Chiurito, チウリト, 海扇. *n.* Cockles.

Chiurori, チウロリ, 渦流. *n.* An
eddy. A whirlpool caused by
water from a height. The water
in an eddy which goes downwards.

Chiurui, チウルイ, 潮流、シオナガレ.
n. A sea current.

Chiushi, チウシ, 上二塗ル. *v. t.* To
spread on. As:—*Shum chiushi
wa e,* "he spreads fat on and
eats it."

Chiutek, チウテク, 使用スル. *v.t.* To
serve.

Chiutek-guru, チウテ〻グル, 召使. *n.*
A servant.

Chiutumashbare, チウツマシバレ, 惑
フ、困ル. *v. i.* To be perplexed.
To be in trouble. **Syn: Chuko-
poye.**

Chiutumashure, チウツマシュレ, 困
ル、疑フ. *v.i.* To be in doubt,
trouble, or perplexity. **Syn:
Chiukopoye.**

Chiwash, チワシ, 魚ノ群. *n.* Shoals
of fish. As:—*Chiwash ek,* "shoals

of fish are coming." **Syn : Chep rupi. Chep rup.**

Chiwash, チワシ, 川口. *n.* The mouths of rivers. **Syn : Pet putu.**

Chiwash-ekot-mat, チワシスコツマツ, 川口ノ女神. *n.* The goddesses of the mouths of rivers.

Chiwe, チウェ, 河流. *n.* The current of a stream or river. As :— *Chiwe moire*, "a slow current." *Chiwe tunash*, "a swift current." **Syn : Chiu.**

Chiuoro, チウオロ, 晒サヌ布. *n.* Undressed or unbleached cloth.

Chiwende, チエンデ, 破船スル. *v. i.* To be wrecked. **Syn : Mimam. Awende.**

Chiyaikorushka, チヤイコルシカ, Chiyaikorushkara, チヤイコルシカラ, 憫ム. *v. t.* To have mercy on.

Chiyange, チヤンゲ, 輸入セラレタル. *adj.* Imported. As :— *Chiyange ashkoro*, "imported wine." **Syn : Arutu. Chikusa.**

Chiyange-ashkoro, チヤンゲアシコロ, 日本酒. *n.* Japanese *sake* (lit : imported wine). **Syn : Arutu-ashkoro. Akusa-ashkoro.**

Chiye, チイェ, 陰部. *n.* The private parts. **Syn : Chi.**

Chok, チョク, 下、シタ. *adv.* Under. Beneath. **Syn : Tok.**

Chokai, チョカイ, 我、私. *pro.* I. From chiokai, "we." *Chokai* is principally used by those Japanese who speak a little Ainu, but never by the Ainu when talking together. It is pigeon Ainu and should be avoided.

Chokapapa, チョカパパ, Chiokapapa, チオカパパ, 屈ム. *v. i.* To lean forward (as in laughing heartily).

Cho, チョ, 錠. *n.* A lock (Japanese).

Chokka, チョッカ, 日本ノ村. *n.* A Japanese village in contradistinction to an Ainu village. (from the Japanese *Choka*).

Chokoko, チョココ, Chokokoi, チョココイ, 腎、鳥ノ砂膽. *n.* The kidneys. The gizard of a bird.

Chomba, チョムバ, 枡、マス. *n.* A measure.

Chopara, チョバラ, Chotara, チョタラ, 嘆爾ノ語. *excl.* An exclamation of exultation. Hurrah. **Syn : Parasekoro.**

Chopchopse, チョブチョブセ, 接吻、キッス. *n.* A kiss.

Chopchopse-kara, チョブチョブセカラ, 接吻スル. *v.t.* To kiss.

Chopiat, チョビアツ, 逃走スル. *v. i.* To run away. To escape. **Syn : Kurinin.**

Chorauge, チョラウゲ, Chiorauge, チオラウゲ, 不成效、人後ニ落ツル. *v.t.* and *v.i.* To be unsuccessful. To be behind-hand. To miss. **Syn : Orauge. Aorauge.**

Chorewewe, チオレウェウェ, Chiorewewe, チョレウェウェ, 前ニ屈ム. *v. i.* To lean forward (as in laughing heartily). **Syn : Chiokapapa.**

Choropok, チョロポク, Koropok, コロポク, 下ニ. *adv.* Under. (According to Ainu habits of thought this word is conceived of as a noun).

Choropoketa, チョロポケタ, 下ニ·
adv. Beneath. Underneath. Under.

Choropoki, チョロポキ, 下ニ. *adv.*
Beneath. Underneath. Under.

Choropokiketa, 下ニ. *adv.* Under.
チョロポキケタ, Beneath. Un-
Choropoketa, derneath. Just
チョロポケタ, underneath.

Choropok-un, チョロポクウン, 下ニ、
シタニ. *adv.* Under. Underneath.
Beneath.

Chotari, チョタリ, 後ロヘ蹴ル. *v. i.*
Chiotari, チオタリ, To kick from
behind (as a horse). **Syn: Hoketu.**

Chotcha, チョッチャ, 當ル、剌ス (單數).
v.t. (*sing*) To shoot and hit. To
sting.

Chotchapa, チョッチャパ, 當ル、剌ス.
(複數). *v.t.* (*pl*) Same as above.

Chotesusu, チョテスス, 後ヘ反ル. *v.i.*
To lean back (as in laughing
heartily).

Cho-un-guru, チョウングル, 囚人. *n.*
A prisoner. *Cho,* is the Japanese
word *jo,* "a lock." Hence *cho-
un-guru,* literally means, "the
person under the lock."

Cho-un-kamui, チョウンカムイ, 天皇、
皇帝. *n.* The Emperor of Japan.
(*Cho* is a Japanese word meaning
chief, and *kamui* is a title of
respect).

Chu, チュ, 河流. *n.* A river current.

Chuchu, チュチュ, 芽、メ. *n.* A bud.

Chueshuye, 顔ニ見ハス. *v. i.* To
チュエシュイェ, betray (as temper
Chiuweshuye, in the face). As:
チュウェシュイェ,

—*Ipot'tum kon'na chueshuye,* "to
betray temper in the countenance."

Chuk, チュク,
Chuk-an, チュクアン, 秋. *n.* Au-
Chuk-pa, チュクパ, tumn.
Chuk-unpa, チュクウンパ,

Chukpes, チュクペス, 下腹. *n.* The
lower part of the abdomen. **Syn:
Chupkes.**

Chunchupeushte, チュンチュペウシテ,
合成スル(金屬ナドチ)、マセモノスル.
v.t. To alloy (as metal).

Chup, チュプ, 發光體、太陽、月(時ニ用
ユ)、例セバ、チュプアフン、日沒. *n.*
A luminary. The sun. Moon.
A month. As:—*Chup ahun,*
"the sun is setting." *Chup
chisei,* "the halo round the
moon." *Chup hetuku,* "the sun
is rising." *Chup kes,* "sunset."
Chup keseke, "the end of a
month." *Chup kiai,* "the rays
of the sun." *Chup nin,* "the
waning of the moon." *Chup
nupek,* "sunlight." *Chup orush
guru,* "the man in the moon."
Chup pishno, "monthly." *Chup
pok,* the west." *Ohup poro,* "full
moon." *Chup rai,* "an eclipse."
Chup ram, about sunset." *Chup
ri,* "about nine or ten a.m."
Chup sapa "the beginning of a
month." *Chup shikari,* "full
moon." *Chup ta,* "monthly."

Chup-bera, チュプベラ, 女用ノ匙. *n.*
A spoon used by women.

Chup-chisei, チュプチセイ, 月ノ笠. *n.*
The halo round the moon.

Chup-ewen, チュプエウェン, 月經. *n.*
Menses.

Chup-ka, チュプカ, 東. *n.* The east. As :—*Chup-ka un utara*, "the Ainu who live on the east coast of Yezo. **Syn : Moshiripa.**

Chup-kamui, チュプカムイ, 日、月. *n.* The sun or moon.

Chup-kari, チュプカリ, 日向ニ、ヒナタニ. *adv.* In the sun. Places where the sun shines.

Chupke, チュプケ, 目ヲ閉ヅル. *v.i.* To close the eyes.

Chup-kes, チュプケス, 鳩尾(ミツオチ). *n.* The pit of the stomach. **Syn : Chukpes.**

Chupki, チュプキ, 威光、光輝、美麗. *n.* Glory. Brightness. Beauty. **Syn : Araguru. Nupeki.**

Chup-kosanu, チュプコサヌ, 閉メル. *v.t.* To close. To shut (as the eyes).

Chupo-hetuku-hi-moshiri, チュポヘツクヒモシリ, 東、日ノ出. *n.* The east. The sun-rise.

Chupoka, チュポカ, 出産. *n.* Childbirth. As :— *Chupoka ne wa shotki otta naa an ruwe ne*, "she has had a child and is still in bed."

Chuppe, チュプペ, 月經. *n.* Menses.

Chuppok, チュッポク, 西. *n.* The west.

Chup-sam-oma, チュプサムオマ, 日向ボコリスレ. *v.i.* To bask in the sun.

Chup-tom, チュプトム, 日光、晴天. *n.* Sunshine. Clear weather.

Chupoka-ekahuye-guru, チュポカエカフイェグル, 産姿. *n.* A midwife.

Chupotomush, チュポトムシ, 日光ニ. *adv. ph.* In the sunshine.

Chupu, チュプ, 折リカヘス. *v. t.* To turn back as a cloth. To fold. As :—*Set kashiketa an senkaki emko chupu wa wakka set kata ande*, "turn the table-cloth back and set the water upon the table."

Chupu, チュプ, } 閉メレ. *v.t.* and *v.i.*
Chupu-chupu, チュプチュプ, } To shut. To close (as the eyes). To be blinded (as by a flash of light). To flash about as light. **Syn : Kochupuchupu.**

Chuputuru, チュプツル, 月ト月トノ期間. *n.* The space of time between moons.

Chup-wen, チュプウェン, 月經. *n.* Menses. **Syn : Chup-ewen. Chuppe.**

Churup-chup, チュラプチュプ, 第一月. *n.* The month of January.

D.

As *d* never appears to commence a sentence in Yezo Ainu and is therefore only heard in composition it always appears in this work, when used initially, under *t*. デー (D) ハ文ノ始メニハ用ヰザレドモ文ノ中間ニハ用ヰラル、而シテデー (D) ハ文ノ始ニアルトキハティー (T) ト發音ス.

E (エ).

E, エ, 汝、此字ヲ動詞ニ附加スルトキ
ハ人代名詞二人稱單數トナルナリ、例
セバ、エオマン、汝往ク. *pro.* You.
Used before verbs in general the
particle *e* is the second person
singular of the personal pronoun
" you." As : — *E kik,* " you
strike." *E oman,* " you go."
Syn : Eani. Aokai.

E, エ, 汝ノ、實名詞ノ前ニ用ユルトキ
ハ物主格トナルナリ、例セバ、エサパ、
汝ノ頭. (ii.) *pro.* Your. When
used before nouns *e* is the poss.
pronoun " your." As : — *E sapa,*
" your head." *E makiri,* " your
knife." **Syn : E koro.**

E, エ, 汝ノ、物主格トシテ此ノ字ヲ用
ユルトキハ屢々 koro ナル動詞カ直
ク其後ニ來ル、例セバ、エコロハ
ボ、汝ノ母、エコロミチ、汝ノ
父. (iii.) *pro.* When *e* is used
as the possessive pronoun it is
often immediately followed by the
verb *koro,* " to possess." As : —
E koro habo, " your mother." *E
koro michi,* " your father." *E
korobe ne* hawe ? " are these your
things ? "

E, エ, 持ツ、自動詞ノ後ニ在ルトキハ他動
詞ニ變セシム、例セバ、キラ、逃クル、エ
キラ、持ツテ越クル. (iv.) *part.* Prefixed to intransitive verbs *e* has
the power of changing them into
transitives. As : — *Kira,* " to run."
Ekira, " to run away with." *Mik,*
" to bark." *emik,* " to bark at."

Nupetne, " to rejoice." *Enupetne,*
" to rejoice over."

E, エ, 動詞ニ此字ヲ加フルトキハ何タ
ヲ以テシタトノ意ニナル、例セバ、タ
ムエライゲ、刀チ以テ殺ロス. (v.)
part. When prefixed to some
transitive verbs *e* sometimes expresses the means by which an
action was done and may be
translated by the words " with,"
" by." Thus : — *Raige,* " to kill,"
tam eraige, " to kill with a
sword."

E, エ, 他動詞ニ此ノ字ヲ加フルトキハ受
動詞トナス.チ得ルナリ、例セバ、アイヌ
セタエイツカ、人カ犬ヲ盗ンダ. (vi.)
part. Prefixed to some transitive
verbs *e* represents the objective
case of the preceding noun. As :
— *Seta eikka,* " the dog stole it ; "
ainu seta eikka, the man stole the
dog."

E, エ, 形容詞ノ前ニ此ノ字ヲ加フルト
キハ動詞トナスコトヲ得ルナリ、例セ
バ、ヒリカ、善キ、エヒリカ、利益ス
ル、ニシテ、固イ、エニシテ、忍ビ能
フ. (vii.) *part.* Prefixed to adjectives *e* has a verbalizing power.
As : — *Nishte,* " hard ; " *enishte,*
" to be able to endure." *Pirika,*
" good ; " *epirika,* " to be bent on
gain."

E, エ, 內ニ、方ヘ、例セバ、エキムン、
山ヘ向フ. (viii.) *prep.* In. To.
Towards. When used as a preposition *e* is prefixed to nouns.

Thus : — *Ekim-un*, "in" or "towards the mountains."

E, エ, ヨリ、カラ、數チ算スル場合ニ於テ省減ノ意味ニ用井ラル、例セバ、ワンエツホツネ、四十ヨリ十チ減ス (卽チ三十). (ix.) *part.* From. When used with the numerals the particle *e* signifies subtraction. Thus :— *Wan e tu hotne*, "thirty" (lit : ten subtracted from two score). *Wan e re hotne*, "fifty," (lit : ten subtracted from three score).

E, エ, 此ノ字チ時チ示ス副詞ノ前ニ用テ keta 或ハ geta チ其後ニ加ヘレトキハ其時ノ確實ナルコチ證スルモノナリ. (x.) *part.* The particle *e* placed before with *keta* often changed into *geta* placed after adverbs of time, expresses definiteness or exactness. Thus :—*Nei tohota*, "on that day;" *nei etohogeta*, "on that very day." *Nei an-chikarata*, "on that night;" *Nei eanchikarageta*, "on that very night." *Nei pahata*, "in that year;" *nei epahageta*, "in that very year."

E, エ, 膿汁、(ウミ)、液、火山灰. *n.* Matter. Pus. Humour. Fine pumice dust. Ashes.

E, エ, 然リ、左様. *adv.* Yes. **Syn : A. Hawe-ne. O. Oun. Ruwe. Ruwe-un. Ruwe-ne.**

E, エ, 嗚呼. *interj.* Ah. Oh. Alas.

E, エ, 食スレ. *v. t.* To eat. **Syn : Ibe.**

Eachiu, エアチウ, 銛チ投ゲル. *v.t.* To cast a spear at anything. **Syn : Kachiu. Katchiu.**

Eahun, エアフン, 入ル、ハイル. *v.i.* To go into. To enter into.

Eahunpururugep, エアフンプルルゲプ, 家ニ吹込ミシ塵雪雨ナド. *n.* Snow, rain, or dust blown into houses by the wind.

Eaikap, エアイカプ, 出來ヌ、能ハヌ. *v.t.* Unable to do a thing.

Eaikap-no, エアイカプノ, 不完全ナル、未熟ノ. *adj.* Abortive.

Eak, エアク, 狙ヒ擊ツ. *v.t.* To shoot at.

Eameokte, エアメオクテ, 盗ム. *v.t.* To steal. To keep back that which ought to be given to another, (lit : " to hook in with the finger-nails).

Eami, エアミ, ミヤマカケス. *n.* Brandts jay. **Syn : Metot eami.**

Eamkiri, エアムキリ, 知ル、覺エレ. *v.t.* To know. To recognize. **Syn : Kiri.**

Eanasap, エアナサプ, ヤット、離シク. *adj.* Quiet.

Eanchikarageta, エアンチカラゲタ, 丁度其夜. *adv.* That very night. That particular night.

Eane, エアチ, 淡キ、細キ. *adj.* Thin. High or squeaky as the voice.

Eane-hau, エアチハウ, 細キ聲. *n.* A thin voice. Ischnophonia.

Eane-no-po, エアチノポ, 困難ニ、ヤット. *adv.* Hardly. With great difficulty.

Eaneramu-pashkosamba, エアチラムパシコサムバ, 喜ブ. *ph.* To be glad. To rejoice. **Syn : Eramu-pashkosamba.**

Eangesh, エアンゲシ, 厭フ、好マヌ. *v.t.* To dislike. **Syn : Kopan.**

Eani, エアニ,｝淡キ、細キ、例セバ、エ
Eane, エアチ,｝アニハウ、細キ聲. *adj.* Thin. High or squeaky as

a voice. Thus :—*Eani hau*, " a squeaky voice."

Eani, エアニ, 汝. *pro.* You. **Syn :** E. Aokai. Eani-un.

Eani e koro, エアニエコロ, 汝ノ、例 セバ、エアニエコロセタ、汝ノ犬. *poss. pro.* Your. As :—*Eani e koro seta*, " your dog."

Eani-un, エアニウン, 汝. *pro.* Yóu.

Eani-yaikota, エアニヤイコタ, 汝、汝 自身. *pro.* You. Yourself.

Eanruru, エアンルル, 西海岸へ、例セ バ、エアンルルンクオマン、私ハ西海 岸へ往ク. *ph.* To the west coast. As :—*Eanruru'n ku oman*, " I am going to the west coast."

Eanun-no, エアヌンノ, 随意ニ、無代價 ニ. *adv.* Freely. Without price. **Syn :** Ataye-sak-no. Oro-isam-no.

Eanru-no-koro, エアンヌノコロ, 所 有スレ. *v.t.* To possess.

Eanuramu hemususu, エアヌラム ヘムスス, 善イト思フ. *v.t.* To think good or wise. To be delighted with.

Eara, エアラ, 全ク. *adv.* Entirely. Quite.

Eara, エアラ, 一ツ、例セバ、エアラコ 一枚着物、ソンデ. *adj.* One. As :— *Eara kosonde*, " one garment."

Earaka, エアラカ, 食傷スル、例セバ、 カルシエアラカ、木ノ子ニテ食傷スル. *v. i.* To be hurt by. As :— *Karush earaka*, " hurt by eating mushrooms."

Earakush, エアラクシ, 渡ル、例セ バ、チカプチュプエアラクシニサルウェ 子、鳥ガ月チカスメテ渡リシ. *v.i.* To pass across. As :—*Chikap chup*

earakush nisa ruwe ne, " the bird passed across the moon."

Earamatke-no, エアラマッケノ, 疾 ク、例セバ、エアラマツケノオマン、疾 ク往ク. *adv.* Quickly. As :— *Earamatke no oman*, " to go quickly." *Earamatke no ye*, " to say quickly." **Syn :** Tunashi-no. Eattunne-no. Chashnu-no.

Earamoisam, エアラモイサム, 海岸 ノ草ノ生セシ部分. *n.* That part of the sea shore where vegetation meets the sand.

Earasaine-no, エアラサイ子ノ, 一捲 キ、(縄ノ如ク)、直チニ. *adv.* In one coil (as a rope). Once only. At once. **Syn :** Arashui-ne.

Earasamne, エアラサム子, 十、(魚チ 数フル時ノ語). *adj.* Ten (used only in counting fish).

Earautor'un, エアラウトルン, 他ノ所 ニ. *adv.* Elsewhere.

Earikinne, エアリキン子, 全ク、綺麗 ニ、瓦ク. *adv.* Thoroughly. Well. Entirely. Quite.

Easara, エアサラ, 注文スル、命ズル. *v.t.* To order (as anything from a shop).

Eashinge, エアシンゲ, 出ス、例セバ、 イタクエアシンゲ、モノ〉云フ. *v. t.* To send forth. To send out. As :— *Itak eashinge*, " to speak," " to say " (lit : to send out words).

Eashin-no, エアシンノ, 又、再ビ、例 セバ、エアシンノカラ、改メテ爲ス. *adv.* Again. Afresh. Newly. As :—*Eashin no kara*, " to do over again," " to alter," " to remake."

Eashirane, エアシラ子, 知ラル. *v.i.* To be made known. To be noised abroad.

Eashiri, エアシリ, 嗚呼、例セバ、エアシリアエキロロアン、嗚呼如何ニ面白カラズヤ！ *interj.* Dear me! How very! Just so! The exact meaning of this word can only be determined by the context. As:—*Eashiri aekiroro an,* "how very interesting!" *Eashiri, shui ek a!* "dear me has he come again!"

Eashiri, エアシリ, 此ノ如キ揚合ニ、例セバ、ヤクエアシリ、若シ左様デアリシナラ. *adv.* It being so. In that case. *Yak eashiri,* "if it is so."

Eashiri, エアシリ, 成程、其ノ通リ. *adv.* Just so. Exactly. **Syn:** **Eashittap-ne. Son-no.**

Eashirika, エアシリカ, 誠ニ. *adv.* Verily. Certainly. **Syn: Son-no-un.**

Eashiriki-kushki, エアシリキクシキ, アラヂメナラヌ、アル筈、例セバ、ツッヒシチエアシリキクシキ、ニツアルハズ. *ph.* There must be. There ought to be. As:—*Tuppish ne eashiriki kushki,* "there must be two," "there ought to be two."

Eashittap, エアシッタブ, Eashittapne. エアシッタブチ, 嗚呼. *interj.* Dear me! Just so! Exactly. Certainly. The full form of this word is *eashiri tap ne.*

Eashka, エアシカ, 甚ダ、多ク. *adv.* Very. Much. Very much. In a great degree.

Eashkai, エアシカイ, 爲シフ能フ、出来ル. *v.i.* To be able to do.

Eashkai-guru, エアシカイグル, 俊倆アル人. *n.* A clever person. An adept.

Eashkai-no, エアシカイノ, 上手ニ、巧妙ニ. *adj.* Cleverly. Ably.

Eashkaire, エアシカイレ, 學ブ、例セバ、カンビエアシカイレ、讀ミ書キヲ學ブ. *v.t.* To learn. As:—*Kambi eashkaire,* "to learn to read and write."

Eassa, エアッサ, 造ル. *v.t.* To make (as clothes.)

Easuru-anu, エアスルアヌ, Eassuruanu, エアッスルアヌ, 知ラルヽ. *v.i.* To be made known. To be noised abroad.

Easuru-ash, エアスルアシ, Easuru-ashte, エアスルアシテ, 有名ナル、名高キ. *adj.* Famous.

Easuru-ashte, エアスルアシテ, Eassuru-ashte, エアッスルアシテ, 知ラセレ、報告スル. *v.t.* To make known. To advertise.

Easuru-nu, エアスルヌ, Eassuru-nu, エアッスルヌ, 知ラレ、報告セラル. *v.i.* To be made known. To be advertised.

Eat, エアツ, 在ル、居ル、懸ケテアル. *v.i.* To be. To dwell. To be hung up as a pot over a fire. To stand (as a country or people).

Eat, エアツ, 適合スル、同意スル. *adj.* Agreeing with.

Eatpake, エアツバケ, 原始、例セバ、エアツバケタ、始メニ. *n.* The beginning. A commencement. As:—*Eatpaketa,* "in the beginning," "At the commencement."

Eatpakegeta, エアツバケゲタ, 丁度其ノ始メニ. *adv.* At the very beginning.

Eattarage, エアッタラゲ, 遺棄ス レ.
v.t. To forsake. To leave alone.
Syn : Moshima-no-okai.

Eattarashi, エアッタラシ, 能ハザル、
不適當ナレ、粗暴ナル. adj. and v.i.
To be unable. To be unfaithful.
Incapable. To slight.

Eattekta, 其他、一方デハ. adv.
エアッテクタ,
Eattekehata, ph. On the other
エアッテケハタ, hand. Besides.

Eattereke-ne, エアッテレケ子, 捷ク、
容易ニ. adv. Easily. Quickly.
With great ease. **Syn : Isaika-
no.**

Eattunne-no, エアッツン子ノ, 速ク、
止マラズシテ、例セバ、エアッツンネノ
アッカシ、速ク歩ム. adv. Quickly.
Without stopping. All at one
time. As :—*Eattunne no apkash*,
"to walk quickly," or "without
stopping." *Eattunne no kara*,
"to do quickly," or "all at one
time." **Syn : Earamatke-no.
Tunashi-no.**

Eattunne-no, エアッツン子ノ, 一人デ.
adv. By itself. Alone. Only.
Syn : Shinep-ne-an.

Eatu, エアツ, 吐出ス. v.t. To vomit.

Eatukopash, エアツコパシ, 吐キ出ス.
v.t. To vomit. To be sick.

Eauwa, エアウワ, 水鳥ノ名. n. Same
as Auwa.

Ebitta, エビッタ, 全ク、凡テ、例セバ、
モシレビッタ、萬國. adj. All. The
whole. The aggregate. Throughout the whole. As :—*Moshir'
ebitta*, "all countries ; " i.e. "the
whole world."

Eboso, エボソ, 成程、相デアル. interj.
Just so. Indeed. So it is. It
appears so. As :—*Eboso, nei
guru ihoshki katu ne wa ku nukara*,
"just so, that man appears to
me to be drunk." **Syn : Eposo.**

Eboso-gusu, エボソグス, 誠ニ、實ニ.
adv. Verily. Indeed. Just so.
Just as. **Syn : Eposo-gusu.**

Ebui, エブイ, 芽. n. A bud.

Ebuike, エブイケ, 花. n. A flower.

Ebuike-pirasa, エブイケピラサ, 花
ガ開ク. v.i. To flower.

Ebuiushbe, エブイウシベ, 榀、タル'キ.
n. The rafters at the ends of a
hut, which are put up crosswise
as a kind of foundation for the
others near them to lean upon
and be fastened to.

Echake, エチャケ, 不作法ナレ、例セ
バ、子ノ子ヤッカショモエチヤケヮピリ
カグンチ、彼ハ不作法チセザル其
キ人デ有. v.t. To do slovenly. To
act in an unseemly manner. As :
—*Nep ne yakka shomo echake wa
pirika gun'ne*, "he is a good
person who never does unseemly
acts." **Syn : Ichake.**

Echakoko, エチャココ, 敎ヘル. v.t.
To teach.

Echakurash, エチャクラシ, 枝アル流
木. n. A floating log with branches
attached.

Echanchauge, エチャンチヤウゲ, 輕
ク當ル、チョット觸ル丶. v.t. To
glance. To touch but not hurt.
To touch slightly.

Echararase, エチャララセ, 進ム、例
セバ、テクワボエチヤララセ、手ノ助
チ以テ進ム. v.i. To move along.
To skim along (as a fish upon

the surface of water). . As:—
Tek wa po echararase, "he moved
along by the help of his hands."

Echi, エチ, 汚シタレ、穢キ. *adj.* and
v.i. To be soiled. To be stained.

Echi, エチ, 汝等、例セバ、エコロコタン
オルンエチルラクスチナ、汝等ヲ本國
ヘ途ルベシ. *pro.* Ye. *Echi* is sometimes used as the sing. objective
pronoun "you." As:—*E koro kotan orun echi rura kusu ne na*, "I
will send you home to your
country." *Ek, echi kouwepekennu*,
"come here, I have something
to ask you." **Syn: Echiutara.**

Echi, エチ,⎫ 柄、嘴(瓶ナドノ). *n.* A
Etu, エツ,⎬ spout. A handle.

Echianupkorobe, エチアヌプコロベ,
慎重ニスル、心チ留メル. *v.i.* To be
careful. To keep in mind.

Echichiuka, エチチウカ, 避クル. *v.t.*
To avoid. **Syn: Eshishi.**

Echikiki, エチキキ, 注キ出ス. *v.t.* To
pour out.

Echikikippo, エチキキッポ, シジウカ
ラ・ *n.* Manchurian great tit.
Parus atriceps minor, (*S. & T.*).

Echi-koro, エチコロ, 汝等ノ. *poss.*
pro. pl. Your.

Echinge, エチンゲ, 龜. *n.* A turtle.

Echi-okai, エチオカイ, 汝等. *per. pro.*
pl. Ye.

Echi-okai-utara, エチオカイウタラ,
汝等. *per. pro. pl.* Ye. **Syn:**
Echi-tari. Echi-utari.

Echip, エチプ, 自分ノモノ、例セバ、
チコレチプ子、其ハ我等ノモノナリ. *n.*
One's own personal belongings.
One's goods. As:—*Chikor echip*

ne, "they are our goods." **Syn:**
Kukorobe.

Echip-ika, エチプイカ, 渥ニサラハレ
ル(船上ノ物ヲ). *v.i.* To be washed
overboard.

Echi'tari, エチタリ, 汝等. *per. pro.*
pl. Ye. Short for *echi utari.*

Echi-utara,⎫
エチウタラ,⎬ 汝等. *per. pro. pl.* Ye.
Echi-utare,⎪
エチウタレ,⎭

Echiokunnure, エチオクンヌレ, 他人
ノコトチ心配スル. *v.i.* To feel concern for another.

Echiriri, エチリリ, 流レ滴ル、物ニ副
フテ滴ル. *v.i.* To trickle down.

Echiuka, エチウカ, 避クレ. *v.t.* To
avoid. **Syn: Eshishi.**

Echiukurure, エチウクルレ, 壓ク.
v.t. To obstruct the current in
a stream by driving in posts or
casting in logs or any other ob-
structions.

Echiure, エチウレ, 物ニ當ル、衝突ス
レ. *v.i.* To come into contact with.
To strike against.

Echiush, エチウシ, 口ノアル、例セバ、
エチウシバッチ、口ノアル椀. *adj.*
Having a spout. As:—*Echi ush
batchi*, "a bowl with a spout."

Echopnure, エチョプヌレ, 接吻スル.
v.t. To kiss. **Syn: Chopchopse-
kara.**

Echopopo, エチョポポ, 入レル. *v. t.*
To put into. **Syn: Omare.**

Echuchari, エチュチャリ, イハツツジ.
n. Vaccinium praestans, Lamb.

Echuppok, エチュッポク, 西. *n.* The
west.

Echutko, エチュツコ, 間違フ、例セ
バ、タンベアナッキタアンベエチュツコ
ノアン、此ト彼レト違フ. *v.i.* To dif-

fer. To mistake. As:—*Tambe anak ne ta ambe echutko no an,* "this differs from that." **Syn: Uweshinnai-no-an.**

Echutko-no, エチュツコノ, 間違ツテ. *adv.* Differently. Mistakenly.

Echutko-no-ki, エチュツコノキ, 破ル、違反スル、例セバ、エカムバクテイ エチュツコノキ、其ノ約束テ破リシ. *v.t.* To break (as a promise). To do differently. As:— *Ekambakte-i echutko no ki,* "he broke his word."

Echutku-nu, エチュツクヌ, 同キ. *adj.* The same.

Edo, エド,
Eto, エト, } エヅミツハギ. *n. Lythrum Salicaria, L.* (See Endo).

Eembe, エエムベ,
Eenbe, エエンベ, } 利器、又物. *n.* Any sharp instrument as a knife or sword.

Een, エエン, 銳キ、例セバ、エエンマキリ、銳キ小刀. *adj.* Sharp. As:— *Een makiri,* "a sharp knife."

Eenarishpa, エエナリシパ, 嚙ム、嚙ンデ引張ル. *v.t.* To bite at (as at one's sleeve). To pull (as one's sleeve with the teeth). To pull with the teeth.

Eenbe, エエンベ,
Eembe, エエムベ, } 利器. *n.* Any sharp instrument as a knife or sword.

Eenka, エエンカ,
Eenke, エエンケ, } 磨ガ. *v.t.* To sharpen.

Eenkashikegeta, エエンカシケゲタ, 丁度上ニ. *post.* Exactly above. Just over.

Eepaketa, エエパケタ, 又、其次キ. *adv.* Again. Next. Upon this. After that. Besides.

Eeripak, エエリパク, 諸共ニ. *adj.* Together with. At the same-time.

Eese, エエセ, 答ヘル. *v.t.* To answer.

Eeshiri,
エエシリ, } 以前. *adv.* Previously.
Eshiri,
エシリ, } Before.

Eeshiri-an, エエシリアン,
Eshiri-an, エシリアン, } 以前ノ、例セバ、エエシリンアアプ、以前ノモノ. *adj.* Above-mentioned. Previous. As:—*E-eshiri an ap,* "the previous one." **Syn: Senramsekoro.**

Eetasa, エエタサ, 更ニ、ヨリ多ク、甚ダ、例セバ、エエタサシリポプケ、甚タ熱キ. *adj.* More. Than. Too much. Very. Extremely. As: —*Eetasa shiripopke,* "it is extremely hot." **Syn: Eitasa.**

Eha, エハ, ギンマメ、ヤブマメ. *n.* The Hog-Peanut. *Amphicarpœa Edgeworthii, Benth. var. japonica, Oliv.* **Syn: Oha.**

Eha, エハ, 臍ノ緒. *n.* The navel string.

Ehabapu, エハバプ,
Ehapapu, エハパプ, } 節儉シテ用ユル、貯フル. *v.t.* To keep back. To save. To use sparingly. To be careful of (as of food).

Ehaita, エハイタ, 避クレ. *v.t.* To avoid. **Syn: Eshishi. Shikiru.**

Ehaita-no-oman, エハイタノオマン, 避クレ、過ギ越ス. *ph.* To avoid. To go past.

Ehaitare, エハイタレ, 除ケサセレ. *v.t.* To cause to miss. To cause to avoid.

Eham, エハム, 止メル、塞ク. *v.t.* To oppose. To stop. **Syn: Etokotuye.**

Ehange, エハンゲ, 近ヨル. *adj.* and *v.i.* To be near at hand. To draw near.

Ehangeko, エハンゲコ, 遠ク. *adv.* Far. Distant. Far away.

Ehangeko-no-an, エハンゲコノアン, 遠ク. *adv.* Distant. To be far away. That which is far away.

Ehange-no, エハンゲノ, Ehange-no-an, エハンゲノアン, 近キニアル、例セバ、エハンゲノアンエカシ、近キ先祖. *v.i.* To be near at hand. To be close. As:—*Ehange no an ekashi,* "one's near ancestors" in contradistinction to *mak un ekashi,* "one's ancient ancestors."

Ehange-no-oman-i, エハンゲノオマンイ, 近ヨルコト. *n.* A drawing near.

Ehangere, エハンゲレ, 近カヨラセル. *v.t.* To cause to come nigh.

Ehapi, エハピ, 蔑ミスレ、輕ンズル. *v. i.* To slight.

Ehapuru, エハプル, 堪エ能ハヌ. *v. i.* Unable to endure.

Ehariki-sam, エハリキサム, 左ノ方. *adv.* On the left.

Ehariki-so-un, エハリキソウン, 爐邊ノ左方. *adv.* The left hand side of a fire-place.

Ehatatne, エハタツチ, 守ル. *v.t.* To watch over. To keep free from harm. To take special care of. **Syn: Eyam.**

Ehaukashiu, エハウカシウ, Ehaukashu, エハウカシュ, 大聲ニテ言フ. *v.i.* To speak with a loud voice. **Syn: Haukore. Kunitara.**

Ehaukatki, エハウカツキ, 姦通スル. *v.t.* To commit adultery.

Ehaye, エハイェ, 足ラザル. *v.i.* To come short of. To be insufficient. **Syn: Eikohaye.**

Ehetche, エヘツチェ, 答ヘレ. *v.t.* To return an answer to. To respond to.

Eheuba, エヘウバ, 凭リカヽル. *v. i.* To lean over. To lean on one side.

Eheuge, エヘウゲ, 凭リカカレ. *v.i.* and *adj.* To be bent. To lean on one side. To lean over.

Eheugere, エヘウゲレ, 曲ケル. *v.t.* To bend.

Eheuheuge, エヘウヘウゲ, 動搖スル(舟ノ). *v. i.* To roll or lean on one side as a ship at sea.

Ehoat, エホアツ, 臍ノ緒. *n.* The string leading from a child to its mother' navel.

Ehochari, エホチャリ, 泯費スル. *v.t.* To waste. **Syn: Aretaraka-kara.**

Ehochatchari, エホチャツチャリ, 散ラス、徒ニ費ヤス. *v.t.* To scatter. To waste.

Ehoma, エホマ, 踊ノ名. *n.* The name of a dance. A dance in which the word *ehoma* is continually repeated.

Ehomatu, エホマツ, 驚ク、(馬ノ如ク). *v.t.* To shy at (as a horse). To start at.

Ehonkanteshke, エホンカンテシケ, 肥エタル腹ノ. *adj.* Abdominous. **Syn: Honi-poro.**

Ehontom-ne-guru, エホントムネグル, 愚人. *n.* A fool. A stupid person. **Syn: Haita-guru.**

Ehopiru, エホピル, 離ルル、去ル. *v.t.* To leave. Go away from.

Ehopiye, エホビイェ, 飛上ガル、例セバ、メコアナク子チカプ エホビイェ、猫ガ鳥ニ對ツテ飛上ガル. *v.t.* To spring upon. To spring out of. As:— *Meko anak ne chikap ehopiye,* "the cat sprang upon the bird."

Ehopuni, エホプニ, 脹レ上ル、(腫物ノ如ク)・ *v.i.* To come up as boils or blisters. To arise.

Ehorari, エホラリ, 伏ス、寝ル、例セバ、アイアイシンダウプショロゲエホラリ、子供ハ搖リ籠ニ伏シテチル. *v.i.* To recline. To lie (as a child in its cradle). As:—*Aiai shinda upshoroge ehorari,* "the child is lying in the bosom of the cradle." **Syn: Hotke.**

Ehoroka, エホロカ, 後ヘ. *adv.* Backwards.

Ehoroka-no, エホロカノ, 後ノ方ニ、例セバ、エホロカノアプカシ、後ヘ行ク. *adv.* In a backward manner. Backwards. As:—*Ehoroka no apkash,* "to walk backwards."

Ehoroka-rapush-chikap, エホロカラブシチカプ, 日本人ヲ指セル暗語. *n.* A secret term used by the Ainu of the Japanese when the subject spoken of is present and the Ainu do not wish him to know that he is the subject of conversation. (lit: "the bird with its wings turned backward).

Ehosatara, エホサタラ, 浪費ス. *v.t.* To waste.

Ehose, エホセ, 反對ノ方ヲ見ル. *v.i.* To look away from. To look in an opposite direction.

Ehoshi, エホシ, 彼地此地. *adv.* The other way about.

Ehoshki, エホシキ, 不足ニ思フ. *v.i.* To be dissatisfied. **Syn: Shomo aeramushinne. Rampokashte.**

Ehoshippare, エホシッパレ, 戻ス. *v.t.* To send back. To return.

Ehumkotui, エフムコツイ, 小キ蛾ノ類. *n.* A kind of small black gnat.

Ehunara, エフナラ, 羨ム、貪ル. *adj.* and *v.t.* To begrudge. Stingy. Greedy. To keep back. To withhold. To desire.

Ehureppo, エフレッポ, ヤマツヽジ. *n.* *Rhododendron indicum, Sweet, var. Kaempferi, Max.*

Ehuru-hemesu, エフルヘメス,
Ehuru-tasa, エフルタサ,
Ehuttasa, エフッタサ, } 小山ニ登ル. *v.i.* To ascend a hill.

Ehuru-hose, エフルホセ, 小山ヲ降ル. *v.i.* To descend a hill. **Syn: Ehuru ran. Ehuru pesh.**

Ehuru-pesh, エフルペシ,
Ehuru-ran, エフルラン, } 小山ヲ下ル. *v.i.* To descend a hill.

Ehuru-pesh-kina, エフルペシキナ, コタニヲタリ. *n.* *Scolopendrium vulgare, Sm.*

Ehuru-tasa, エフルタサ,
Ehuttasa, エフッタサ,
Ehuru-mesu, エフルメス, } 小山ニ上ル. *n.* To ascend a hill.

Ehuye, エフイェ, 待ツ (單數). *v.t.* (*sing*). To await. To wait for. **Syn: Atere.**

Ehuyepa, エフイェバ, 待ツ、(複數). *v.t.* To await. To wait for. (*pl*).

Eihok, エイホク, 賣ル. v.t. To sell. Syn: Eiyok.

Eika, エイカ, 溢ル. v.i. To run over.

Eikan-no, エイカンノ, 豊カニ. adv. Abundantly. Bountifully. Syn: Nuye an no.

Eikapa, エイカパ, 談話ノ種ヲ得ル. v.i. To get matter for a speech.

Eikare, エイカレ, 溢ルルマテ充ス. v.t. To fill to overflowing.

Eikashu, エイカシュ, 過キル、優ル. v.t. To surpass. To go beyond.

Eikashnukara, エイカシヌカラ, 與ヘル. v.t. To give. To bestow.

Eikaun, エイカウン, 餘リ多キ. adv. and v.i. Too much. Than. More. To be more. Syn: Eetasa. Eitasa. Kasu no.

Eikaun-rusui, エイカウンルスイ, 競フ、爭フ. v.t. To emulate. To have a desire to surpass.

Eikaunu, エイカウヌ, 我意ヲ張ル、爲シ過ギル、超エル. v.t. and v.i. To be selfwilled. To overdo. To prefer to do. To surpass.

Eikaunu-no, エイカウヌノ, 過キテ爲ス、我ママニスル. v.t. and v.i. To do over-much. To do in a selfwilled manner.

Eikeshkore, エイケシコレ, 相續サセル. v.t. To cause to inherit.

Eikeshkoro, エイケシコロ, 相續スル. v.t. To inherit.

Eikeshkorobe, エイケシコロベ, 遺産動産. n. Heirlooms. Things inherited from another. Syn: Chirairep.

Eikeshui, エイケシュイ, 寒テル、怒ツテ見返ル. v.t. To turn away from anything in anger. To abandon. To forsake.

Eikishma, エイキシマ, 摑ム. v.t. To seize.

Eikka, エイッカ, 盗ム. v.t. To steal. Syn: Ikka.

Eikohaye, エイコハイェ, 不足スレ. v.i. To be insufficient. Syn: Ehaye.

Eikoiki, エイコイキ, 鬪フ. v.t. To fight.

Eikoisamba, エイコイサムバ, 倣フ、眞似スル. v.t. To imitate. Syn: Koikara.

Eikoshi, エイコシ, 手渡ス. v. t. To hand over. To betray. Syn: Ekoshi.

Eikotuntek, エイコツンテク, 反響ヌル. v.i. To resound.

Eikushtek, エイクシテク, 餘リ、過分ノ、例セバ、エイクシテクポロ、餘リ大キイ. adj. Too much. Surpassingly. As:—Eikushtek poro, "too large." Eikushtek pon, "too small." Eikushtek pirika, "too good." Syn: Mashkin.

Eimek, エイメク, 當分スル、分配スル. v.t. To allot. To apportion. To divide. Circulate.

Eingush, エイングシ, 懼レル. v.i. To be afraid. Syn: Ishitoma.

Einore, エイノレ, 混ズル. v.t. To adulterate. Syn: Ukopoye.

Einupitara, エイヌピタラ, 好マヌ、用キヌ、厭フ. v.t. To not want or like. To eschew. To hate. Syn: Etunne.

Einure, エイヌレ, 火ヲ點ズル. v.t. To light (as a lamp). Syn: Uhuyeka.

Eipak, エイパク, 足ル. v.i. To be sufficient. Syn: Pakno.

Eipake, エイバケ, 端、ハシ. n. The edge. Syn: Paruruge. Kanetuhu.

Eipakige, エイバキゲ, 端、ハシ. n. The edge. Edges. Syn: Eipake.

Eipak-shomoki, エイバクショモキ, 不足スレ. v.i. To be insufficient. Syn: Ehaye. Eikohaye.

Eipokun, エイポクン, ヨリモ少ナキ. v.i. To be less than.

Eipokun-no, エイポクンノ, ヨリモ少ナク. adv. Not so much. Less.

Eipok-unu, エイポクウヌ, 好マズ、口惜ム. v.t. To dislike. To regret.

Eiramnukuri, エイラムヌクリ, 為スコトナ好マヌ、例セバ、クエツンエイラムヌクリ、余ハ借リルコトナ好マヌ. v.t. To dislike to do. Not to care to do. As:—Ku etun eiramnukuri, "I do not care to borrow it." Ye eiramnukuri, "to dislike to tell." Syn: Eutchike. Iramnukuri.

Eiram-kotoro-mewe, エイラムコトロメウェ, 響メル、鼓舞スル、励マス. v.t. To encourage.

Eirawe, エイラウェ, 為シタガル、殺シタガレ. v.t. To desire to do. To wish to kill. Syn: Irawe.

Eiripak, エイリバク, 均シキ. adj. Even. Equal. Syn: Uwe-iripak.

Eiripakno-kara, エイリバクノカラ, 均シクスレ. v.t. To make equal. To make even.

Eirusa, エイルサ, 貸ス、(単数). v.t. To lend. (sing). Syn: Shosere.

Eirusa-guru, エイルサグル, 貸人. n. One who lends.

Eirushpa, エイルシバ, 貸ス (複数). v.t. To lend. (pl). Syn: Shoserepa.

Eisamta, エイサムタ, 傍ニ. adv. By the side of. Close to. Syn: Samaketa.

Eishikashpari, エイシカシバリ, 貪ル. v.t. To covet. Syn: Ibeporore. Yaikoshipuinere.

Eishiramne, エイシラムネ, 欲スル. v.t. To wish for. To desire. To want. Syn: Kon rusui.

Eishiramnep, エイシラムネブ, 必要. n. Needs. Desires. Wants. Syn: Kon rusuibe.

Eishokon, エイショコン, Eishokoro, エイショコロ, 信ズル. v.t. To believe.

Eishokor-i, エイショコリ, 信仰. n. Faith.

Eishokor-i-tumashnure-buri-akire, エイショコリツマシヌレブリアキレ, 信ナ堅クスレ. v.t. To confirm (Introduced by the Compiler).

Eishokor-i-tumashnure-buri-akire-katu, エイショコリツマシヌレブリアキレカツ, 按手式. ph. The order for Confirmation (Introduced by the Compiler).

Eishungere, エイシュンゲレ, 信セヌ. v.t. To disbelieve.

Eitak-amkire, エイタクアムキレ, 約束スレ. v.t. To promise.

Eitasa, エイタサ, 餘リニ. adv. Too much. Than. More. Syn: Eetasa. Eikaun. Kasu no.

Eitoko, エイトコ, 始メニ. adv. At the beginning.

Eiwak, エイワク, 帰ル. v.i. To return to one's home (as from work).

Eiwange, エイワンゲ, 用サル. *v.t.*
To use. To make use of. **Syn:**
Ewange.

**Eiwange-chieikip, エイワンゲチエイ
キプ,** 道具. *n.* Tools.

Eiwange-kunip, エイワンゲクニプ,
道具. *n.* Tools.

Eiwangere, エイワンゲレ, 用キサセ
ル. *v.t.* To cause to use.

Eiyok, エイヨク, 賣ル. *v.t.* To sell.
Syn: Ehok.

Eiyokbe, エイヨクベ, 賣品、貨物. *n.*
Merchandise.

Eiyonuppa, エイヨヌッパ, 訴フレ. *v.t.*
To accuse of a crime. To complain about.

**Eiyonuppa-ambe, エイヨヌッパアム
ベ,** 告訴. *n.* A complaint. An
accusation.

Eiyoinimba, エイヨイニムバ, 反響ス
ス. *v.i.* To echo. To resound.
To have a noise in the head.
Syn: Shiri-eiyunimba. Tuntek.

Ek, エク, 來ル、(單數). *v.i.* To come.
(*sing*).

Eka, エカ, 捻ル、ヨル. *v.t.* To make (as
a rope). To twist. As:—*Tush
eka,* "to make a rope,"

Ekai, エカイ, 周圍ニ. *adj.* Round.
Round about.

Ekaechish, エカエチシ,
Ekaichish, エカイチシ, 山、岩ナドノ險シク凸凹
シタルトコロ. *n.*
Rugged places. A
sharply pointed rock. A mountain pinnacle or peak.

Ekai, エカイ, 周圍ノ. *adj.* Round.

Ekai-nupuri, エカイヌプリ, 火山. *n.*
A volcano (extinct or active).

Ekakari, エカカリ, 上縫スレ. *v.t.* To
sew over (as in making button
holes).

Ekakoyaske, エカコヤスケ, 割レタレ.
adj. Cracked (from top to bottom).

**Ekamasu-chitarabe, エカマスチタ
ラベ,** 袋. *n.* A bag for carrying
clothes etc., when travelling.

Ekambak, エカムバク, 警戒. *n.* A
warning.

**Ekambak-isam-no, エカムバクイサ
ムノ,** 唐突ニ、不圖. *adv.* Without
warning.

Ekambakte, エカムバクテ, 前以テ
テ知ラセル、豫示スル. *v.t.* To forewarn. To make known. **Syn:**
Shietok. Ashongokushte.

Ekambakte-i, エカムバクテイ, 前以テ
知ラセルコト、豫示、豫約. *n.* A fore-
warning. A promise.

Ekambakte-ki, エカムバクテキ, 豫示
スレ、約束スル. *v.t.* To forewarn.
To promise.

**Ekambakte-no-an-itak, エカムバク
テノアンイタク,** 約束、豫示. *n.* A
warning. A promise.

Ekamparasasa, エカムバラササ, 匣
平ナル口チ持ツ器具. *adj.* Any vessel with a flat lip.

Ekanai, エカナイ. 以前ニ. *adv.* Previously. Before. Anciently. **Syn:**
Etokota.

Ekanai-ita, エカナイイタ,
Ekanaita, エカナイタ, 以前ニ. *ph.* At a previous time. **Syn:**
**Etokota. Makui-
shiri. Arani-wano.**

Ekanai-wano, エカナイワノ, 其ノ以
前ニ. *ph.* From before that time.
From ancient times. **Syn: Ma-
kui-shiri-wano.**

Ekannayukara, エカンナユカラ, 同
ジ. *adv.* Like. **Syn: Ukorachi.**

Ekanok, エカノク, 出迎フ、例セバ、エカノククスオマン、出迎ニ往ク. *v.t.* To go to meet. As:—*Ekanok gusu oman,* "to go to meet."

Ekap, エカブ, 挨拶スル、會釋スル. *v.t.* To greet. To salute.

Ekarakara, エカラカラ, 爲ス. *v.t.* To do. This word very often occurs in legends in place of *kara* and *ki*.

Ekari, エカリ, 迎ヘラルヽ、出來上レ. *v.i.* and *v.t.* To be met. To put forth (as strength). To be done. To be finished. **Syn: Karaokere. Kiroro yupu wa ki.**

Ekari, エカリ, 周リ、邊リ、例セバ、チセイエカリ、家ノ周リ. *post.* Around. By. Along. As:—*Chisei ekari,* "around the house." **Syn: Kari. Okari.**

Ekari, エカリ, 流浪スレ. *v.i.* To wander about. **Syn: Ekeshneoman.**

Ekarire, エカリレ, 圍フ. *v.t.* To inclose. **Syn: Nikkotama.**

Ekari-wa-oman, エカリワオマン, 巡ル、例セバ、トエハリワオマン、彼ハ湖ヲ廻リシ. *ph.* To go round. As:—*To ekari wa oman,* "he went round the lake."

Ekashi, エカシ, 祖先、老人. *n.* An ancient. A grandfather. Ancestors. A title of respect to middle-aged men. *Mak un ekashi,* "one's remote ancestors." *Ehange no an ekashi,* "one's near ancestors." *Ekashi uruoka hoppa itak,* "the traditions handed down from the ancients."

Ekashpa-umbe, エカシパウムベ, 冠. *n.* A crown made of shavings.

Ekashish, エカシシ, 卑ム、惡ム. *v.t.* To despise. To hate.

Ekashuppo, エカシュッポ, 蝌蚪(オタマジャクシ). *n.* Tadpoles.

Ekasu, エカス, 向へ、外ニ、超エテ. *adv.* Beyond. **Syn: Kasu no oman.**

Ekataiirotke, エカタイイロッケ, 好ム、愛スレ. *v.t.* To like. To be fond of. To love. **Syn: Katsomare.**

Ekatchaush, エカッチャウシ, 厭フ、好マヌ. *v.i.* To feel antipathy towards. To be displeased with. **Syn: Eramu ekatchaush.**

Ekatki, エカッキ, 接近スル. *v.t.* To approach. To go to. **Syn: Karange no oman.**

Ekatki, エカッキ, 除ケレ、避クル. *v.t.* To avoid. **Syn: Eshishi. Aekatki.**

Ekatnu, エカッヌ, 好ム、愛スル. *v.t.* To like. To be fond of. To love. **Syn: Konoburu.**

Ekatta, エカッタ, 遍急ニ、暴力ヲ以テ. *adv.* In haste. With violence.

Ekatupase, エカツパセ, 拒ム、嫌フ. *v.t.* To refuse. To dislike. To be disinclined to do something. As:—*Oman ekatupase,* "to dislike to go." **Syn: Nukuri.**

Ekaya-ni-ika, エカヤニイカ, 船ノ柱ヨリ落ツレ. *v.i.* To fall from a ships mast. **Syn: Okaya-nipichi.**

Ekaye, エカイ, 調子. *n.* A tune. **Syn: Kaye.**

Ekaye-chish, エカイェチシ, 山ノ險シキ所. *n.* Very steep mountain peaks. Precipitous places. **Syn: Ekaichish.**

Ekashinne-no, エカシン子ノ, 此方
彼方ニ、例セバ、エカシンネノアブカシ、
アチコチ歩ク. *adv.* To and ˙ fro.
Hither and thither. As:—*Eka-
shinne no apkash,* "to walk to and
fro." **Syn : Ekeshne. Epish-
kan un.**

Eke, エケ, 上ヲ掬ヒトル. *v.t.* To
skim. As :—*Tope eke,* " to skim
milk."

Ekeshne, エケシ子, 此方彼方ニ、例セ
バ、エケシチインガラ、アチコチ見廻
ス. *adv.* To and fro. Hither and
thither. About. As :—*Ekeshne
apkash,* "to walk hither." *Ekeshne
ingara,* " to look about hither and
thither." *Ekeshne shiri uwande,* "to
look about very carefully." **Syn :
Ekeshinne no. Epishkan-un.**

**Ekeutum-konna-tanak-tanak, エケ
ウツムコンナタナクタナク,** 氣ヲ落ス、
落膽スレ. *ph.* To lose heart. To
faint. To faint and come to frequently.

**Ekike-ush-bashui, エキケウシバシュ
イ,** 鬚ヲ上ゲノ棒(祭ノ時ニ用ユル). *n.*
A ceremonial moustache-lifter ;
i.e. a moustache-lifter having
shavings left attached to it.

Ekimne, ユキム子, 山ヘ行ク. *v. i.*
To go to the mountains to work
or hunt.

Ekimne-un, エキムヂウン, 山ニ. *adv.
ph.* To the mountains.

Ekim-un, エキムウン, 山ニ. *adv. ph.*
To the mountains.

Ekimopkara, エキモプカラ, 山ニテ
計ラズモ慘死スル. *v. i.* To meet
with a violent death in the moun-

tains (as from any accident).
Syn : Sarak kamui.

Ekira, エキラ, 携テ走ル. *v. t.* To
run away with.

Ekohaye, エコハイェ, 不足スル. *v. i.*
To be insufficient. **Syn : Eikohaye. Upak shomoki.**

Ekohoppa, エコホッパ, 去ル、離ル、
(複數). *v.t.* To leave. To depart
from (*pl*).

Ekohopi, エコホピ, 去ル、離ル、(單數).
v.t. To leave. To depart from.
(*Sing*). **Syn : Orowa no oman.**

Ekohopi-notkush, エコホピノックシ,
疎ンズル、遠ザカル、嫌フ. *v.t.* To
look upon with disfavour. To
eschew. To dislike. To disapprove. **Syn : Akopan. Kutnoye.**

Ekohopi-shikiru, エコホピシキル, 轉
顧スル. *v.i.* To turn away from.

**Ekohopi-wa-oman, エコホピワオマ
ン,** 去ル、離ル、. *v. t.* To leave.
To go away from.

Ekohoshipire, エコホシピレ, 質ニ置
ク. *v.t.* To pawn.

Ekoimokokoro, エコイモココロ, 贈
ル、呈スル. *v.t.* To take a present
to another. To present to. **Syn :
Eikrap-kore.**

Ekoimokorobe, エコイモコロベ, 贈
物. *n.* A present.

Ekoimare, エコイオマレ, 水ヲ汲ミ
出ス. *v.t.* To pour out.

Ekoirak-koirak, エコイラクコイラク,
動搖セシムル. *v.t.* To shake up as
anything in a bottle. To agitate
(as water). **Syn : Koyakoyak.**

Ekoisamka, エコイサムカ, 無クスル、
空クスレ. *v.t.* To bring to naught.
To destroy. **Syn : Isamka.
Uhaye-wa-isamka.**

Ekokomge, エココムゲ, 凭レル、倚リ
カヽレ. *v. t.* To lean upon (as
upon a table). **Syn: Kokonge.**

Ekokomo, エココモ, 縁ヲ付ケル、折リ
込ム. *v. t.* To bind (as a dress).
To fold over (as in sewing).

**Ekokomo-wa-ukaukau, エココモワ
ウカウカウ,** 縁ヲ付ケル. *v. t.* To
bind.

Ekomo, エコモ, 折リ込ム. *v.t.* To
fold over.

Ekomomse, エコモムセ, 玉ニマク.
纏レル. *v.i.* Twisted into a lump
or ball. Turned.

Ekonishuye, エコニシュイェ, 振リ當
テル. *v. t.* To swing against.
Syn: Shuyeshuye wa eok.

**Ekonnukan-nukare, エコンヌカン
ヌカレ,** 敎ヘレ. *v.t.* To teach. To
instruct.

Ekonramu, エコンラム, 心、胸. *n.*
The heart. The mind. Feelings.
Syn: Keutum.

Ekonramu-shitne, エコンラムシツ子,
怒ラセレ. *v.i.* To be aggravated.
To be much irritated. To be in
great trouble.

**Ekonramu-shitnere, エコンラムシツ
子レ,** 痛マセル. *v. t.* To agonize.
To give pain to.

Ekonramu-tanak, エコンラムタナク,
苦眠スル. *v.i.* To have troubled
sleep. To have bad dreams.

**Ekonramu-tanak-shitne, エコンラ
ムタナクシツ子,** 甚タ煩累スル、苦悶シ
テ眠レヌ. *v. i.* To be in great
straits. To be unable to sleep
for great trouble.

Ekopash, エコパシ, 倚リ掛ル、凭ル.
v.i. To lean against. As:—*Tuma-*

ma epokash, "to lean against a
wall."

Ekopashte, エコパシテ, 凭ラセカケ、例
セバ、ネイオカイベチクニエコパシテ、
其ヲ木ニ凭ラセテクレ. *v. t.* To set
against. To rest upon. As:—
Nei okaibe chikuni ekopashte yan,
"set that thing against the tree."

Ekoraininne, エコライニン子, 出來
カタキ. *adv.* Difficult of accomplishment.

Ekoramkoro, エコラムコロ, 乞フ. *v.t.*
To beg for. To ask for.

Ekorobe, エコロベ, 汝ノモノ. *n.* Your
belongings.

Ekoshi, エコシ, 委託スル、手渡ス. *v.t.*
To leave to the care of another.
To hand over. To betray. **Syn:
Aikoshi.**

Ekot, エコツ, 死ヌ、例セバ、メエコツ
ト、凍死スル. *v.i.* To die. As:—
Me ekot, "to die of cold." *Popke
ekot,* "to die of heat." **Syn:
Rai.**

Ekotan-koro, エコタンコロ, 住居ニス
ル. *v. t.* To make a home of.
As:—*Nupuri uturu ekotankoro,*
"to make one's home among the
mountains."

Ekote, エコテ, 殺ロス. *v.t.* To kill.
Syn: Raige.

Ekotekot, エコテコツ, 度々氣ヲ失フ.
v.i. To faint away repeatedly.

Ekotewen, エコテウェン, 苦ムンデ死
ヌ. *v. i.* To die hardly. To die
a painful death.

Ekotpoka, エコッポカ, 近ヨレ. *v. t.*
To approach. To get at.

Ekotpoka-ewen, エコッポカエウェン,
近ヨル能ハズ. *v. i.* To be unable

to approach. Unable to draw near to.

Ekotpoka-ewen-itara, エコッポカエウェンイタラ, 近ヨルコト能ハズ. *ph.* and *v.i.* To be unable to touch. To be unable to approach.

Ekottanu, エコッタヌ, 注意スル、関係スル、例セバ、イテキエコッタヌ、関セズニナケ. *v.t.* To pay attention. To have a care for. To interfere. As:—*Iteki ekottanu,* "do not interfere;" "take no notice of it."

Ekottanu, エコッタヌ, 注意アレ. *adj.* Attentive.

Ekottanu-wa, エコッタヌワ, 注意シテ. *adv.* Attentively.

Ekottanu-shomoki, エコッタヌショモキ, 忽カセニスレ. *v.t.* To neglect. To take no notice of a thing. To let alone.

E-kunip, エクニプ, 食物. *n.* Food. Necessaries of life.

Ekte, エクテ, 來タラセル. *v.t.* To cause to come.

Ekunneyot, エクンチヨツ, 眩スル(急ニ暗處ニ入リ). *v.i.* To be dazzled with darkness (as upon entering a dark room fresh from the light).

Ekurok, エクロク, 黒キ. *adj.* Black. Of a dark colour. **Syn: Kunne.**

Ekurok-o, エクロコ, 黒キ. *adj.* Black.

Ekushkonna, エクシコンナ, 突然ニ. *adv.* Abruptly. Suddenly. Immediately. **Syn: Imontabire.**

Ekushna, エクシナ, 通過スル、例バ、ナッケエクシナ、貫ク. *v.i.* and *adj.* To pass through. Open. Uncovered (as one's thoughts).

As:—*Otke ekushna,* "to pierce through." **Syn: Oboso.**

Ekushna-etaye, エクシナエタイ, 貫キ取ル. *v.t.* To draw through.

Ekushnare, エクシナレ, 貫キ通ス. *v.t.* To send through. To open (as the heart to another). To push through. To make known.

Ekusuri-kara, エクスリカラ, 治療スル. *v.t.* To doctor. As:—*Ku shikihi ekusuri-kara rusui,* "I desire to doctor my eyes."

Emaka, エマカ, 逐グル、棄テ. *v.t.* To discharge. To abjure. To cast away. (*Sing*). **Syn: Osura.**

Emakba, エマクバ, 逐グル、棄テ. *v.t.* To discharge. To cast away. To abjure. (*Pl. of Emaka*).

Emaknaguru, エマクナグル, 後方ニ. *adv.* Backward.

Emaknatara, エマクナタラ, 開ク. *v.t.* To open up. To light up. To clear away. As:—*Shukustoikunne chisei upshoro emaknatara,* "a bright light lit up the inside of the house."

Emauri, エマウリ, 種々ノイチゴナドノ名. *n.* A general name for black-berries, strawberries and raspberries.

Emaukush, エマウクシ, 鼻ヲ通シテ云フ. *v.i.* To speak through the nose.

Emawanu, エマワヌ, 甚タ怖ロシキ. *adj.* Very dreadful.

Emetapunin, エメタプニン, 寒ク見エレ. *v.i.* To look cold.

Emetup, エメツプ, 祭ノ時女ニ與ヘル酒. *n.* A portion of wine given to women at a feast. **Syn: Chimetup.**

Emik, エミク, 吠ヘル. *v.t.* To bark at.

Emina, エミナ, 笑フ. *v.t.* To laugh at.

Emina-e-sapse, エミナエサブセ, 嘲笑スレ. *v.t.* To deride. To scorn. **Syn : Emina-sapse.**

Emko, エムコ, 半分. *adj.* Half. A part. The ends of anything. As :—*Emko e tup,* "one and a half." *Emko e rep,* "two and a half."

Emko-gusu, エムコグス, 此ノ故ニ. *post.* Therefore. For this reason.

Emkoisamka, エムコイサムカ, Enkoisamka, エンコイサムカ, 所有物ヲ失フ. *v.i.* To suffer the loss of one's belongings.

Emko-sama, エムコサマ, 此ノ故ニ. *post.* Therefore. **Syn : Tambegusu.**

Emkota, エムコタ, 直ニ. *adv.* Soon. Very quickly. Now. **Syn : Tunashi no.**

Emo, エモ, 馬鈴薯 (ツヤガタライモ). *n.* Potatoes. As :—*Emo otomire,* "to earth up potatoes."

Emoinatara, エモイナタラ, 懸カル. *v.i.* To hang about (as clouds or smoke over a city.)

Emokoro-koshikururu, エモコロコシクルル, 眠ラレヌ. *v.i.* To be unable to sleep. To turn about in one's sleep.

Emomnatara, エモムナタラ, 有ル、居ル、安全ニアル. *v.i.* To be. To be serene. To rest upon. To be at rest.

Emonasap, エモナサブ, 遅キ. *adj.* Late. Slow. **Syn : Muchimasap. Moire.**

Emonashnu, エモナシヌ, 速キ. *adj.* Quick. Early. Fast. **Syn : Tunashi no. Hemban no. Muchimashnu.**

Emoni, エモニ, 漁スレ、獵スル、例セバ、エモニピリカ、瓦キ漁. *v.t.* To hunt. To fish. As :—*Emonipirika,* "to be saccessful in hunting or fishing." *Emoni-wen,* "to be unsuccessful in hunting or fishing."

Emonush, エモヌシ, 忙ハシカル. *v.i.* To be busy. As :—*Nep-nep ku emonush* " I am busy about a variety of things." **Syn : Mon an.**

Emoshma, エモシマ, 別々ニ、例セバ、エモシマノイキ、別々ニスレ. *adv.* Differently. Separately. As :—*Emoshma emoshma no iki* "to do separately or differently."

Emoshma-no-ande, エモシマノアンデ, 度外ニ置ク. *v.i.* To apostatize. To put in another place.

Emoshma-no-an-guru, エモシマノアングル, 物ヲ度外ニ置ク人. *n.* An apostate.

Emotontori-ush-chikap, エモトントリウシチカプ, ウミアイサ. *n.* Red-breasted merganser. *Mergus serrator, Linn.* **Syn : Aisa.**

Empuina, エムブイナ, 頭ヲ前ニ垂レ. *v.t.* and *v.i.* To fall or knock down head first.

Empuinare, エムブイナレ, 頭ヲ前ニ垂レサスル. *v.t.* To cause to knock or fall down head first.

Emu-emu, エムエム, 摑ム. *v.t.* To lay hold of anything with the hands (as a child a table when trying to climb upon it).

Emuka-oshma, エムカオシマ, 頭ヲ前ニ垂ル. *v.i.* To fall down head foremost.

Emukne, エムクネ, 残ラズ. *adj.* All. The whole.

Emukne-no, エムクチノ, 全ク. *adv.* Wholly. In their entirety.

Emukne-no-an, エムクチノアン, 其レノミ. *ph.* That is all.

Emukne-no-isam, エムクチノイサム, 皆失セタリ. *ph.* They are all gone. There are none. They are entirely gone. There is not one left. **Syn: Obitta isam.**

Emukne-no-okere, エムクチノオケレ, 皆仕舞フ. *ph.* They have all come to naught. They are all finished.

Emush, エムシ,
Emushi, エムシイ, } 刀、例セバ、エムシアフンゲ、刀ヲ挟ニ納メル. *n.* A sword. As :—*Amut emushi anochautekka,* " I drew the sword I wore " (used in legends). *Emush-ahunge,* " to sheathe a sword " *Emush etaye,* " to draw a sword." *Emush eyaikikikara,* " to fence " or " to defend one's self with a sword." *Emush mekka,* " the back of a sword," also *emush mekkashike. Emush mut,* " to wear a sword." *Emush notaku,* " the edge of a sword." *Emush shitom-ush,* " to wear a sword." **Syn : Tam. Rangetam.**

Emush-at, エムシアツ, 刀ノ紐. *n.* A sword sash.

Emush-ibe, エムシイベ, 刀ノ刃. *n.* A sword blade.

Emush-nip, エムシニプ, 刀ノ柄. *n.* A sword hilt.

Emush-po, エムシポ, 短刀. *n.* A dirk, generally fixed on ancient Ainu quivers. A small wooden Ainu treasure. A small sword.

Emush-seppa, エムシセッパ, 刀ノ鍔. A sword guard.

Emush-shirika, エムシシリカ, 刀ノ鞘. *n.* A sword sheath.

En, エン, 我ヲ. *pro.* Me. Objective case of *Ku,* "I." The objective *en* is often found in Ainu where in English the nominative "I" is used. Thus :—*En pakno isam,* " not so much as I." *En shirine,* " instead of me."

Enangara, エナンガラ, 逢フ、安否ヲ問フ. *v.t.* To meet. To greet.

Enankurukashi, エナンクルカシ, 面、顔. *n.* The countenance. The face.

Enankurukashi-epukitara, エナンクルカシエブキタラ, 感ヲ面ニ見ハス. *ph.* To look pleased or angry.

Enankurukashi-parase, エナンクルカシバラセ,
Enankurukashi-parasere, エナンクルカシバラセレ, } 怒レル如シ. *ph.* To look angry.

Enan-o-guru, エナンオグル, 二心ノ人. *n.* A double-faced person. **Syn: Tu-nan-o-guru.**

Enanrapoki-ekari-na, エナンラポキエカリナ, 我汝ノ高慢ヲ制セン. *ph.* " I will take down your countenance ; " i.e. I will lower your pride. So found in legends, where this phrase is sometimes used as a challenge.

Enchararage, エンチャララゲ, 刺ア
レ. *adj.* Prickly.

Encharashne, エンチャラシ子, 喧嘩
スレ、爭鬪スレ. *v.i.* To quarrel.

**Enchiki-maimai, エンチキマイマ
イ,** ガンコウラン. *n.* The crowberry. *Empetrum nigrum,* L.
Called also *Ichikimaimai.*

**Endo,
エンド,
Edo,
エド,
Eto,
エト,** } エゾミソハギ. *n.* A kind of
herb used as food. *Lyth-
rum Salicaria,* L.

Endrum, エンドルム, 鼠. *n.* A rat
or mouse. **Syn: Erum.**

Ene, エ子, 其ノ、斯ノ如シ、其ノ通リ、例
セバ、エ子アムベ、其ノモノ. *adv.*
Thus. So. In this or that manner.
What. Such. As:—*Ene ponbe
he?* "so small"? *Ene porop he?*
"is it so large"? *Hembara ne
yakka ene moire range,* "he is always thus late." *Shomo ka ene
hawash kuni aramu a-hi,* "I had
no idea that such things had been
said." *Ene ikichi ainu poronno
okai,* "there are many Ainu who
do that sort of thing." *Ene shiri
buri an rok,* "there are those
kinds of customs." *Ene ambe,*
"that thing," "such a thing"
(used in a bad sense). *Ene okaibe,* "that fellow" "that rascal."
Iresu ruwe ene oka-hi, "he was
reared after this wise."

**Ene-akari-ka-isam, エ子アカリカイ
サム,** 仕方ガナイ. *ph.* There is no
help for it.

Ene-ani, エ子アニ, 斯ノ如ク. *adv.*
Thus. So. Like this or that.

Ene ani ne, "it is so "it is as
you say."

Ene-ene, エ子エ子, 左様. *adv.* So, so.
Just so.

Eneka, エ子カ, ドウニカ. *adj.* Somehow. Anyhow.

**Ene-hawashi,
エ子ハワシ,
Ene-hawe-okai,
エ子ハウェオカイ,** } 彼ハ斯ノ如ク言ヒ
シ. *ph.* He
spake thus.
He said this. He spake after this
or that manner. Thus it is said.

Ene-neika, エ子子イカ, 其ノ通リ. *adv.*
In that way. So. Thus. As:
— *Ene neika shomo ahi,* "it has
never been so before.

Ene-pakno, エ子パクノ, 其レ程. *ph.*
To that degree. To this or that
extent.

**Enenge-ni,
エ子ンゲニ,
Eninge-ni,
エニンゲニ,** } タラノキ. *n.* The Angelica tree. *Aralia
sinensis,* L. The
leaves of this plant are used as
food by the Ainu. The Ainu of
Tokachi call this tree *Shuat-ni.*

Enekaiki, エ子カイキ, 然而シテ. *adv.*
It being so.

Eneturu pakno, エ子ツルパクノ, 其
レ程. *ph.* To such a degree. So.
As:—*Nei guru anak ne eneturu
pakno wen ruwe he an?* "was he
so bad?"

Eneusara, エ子ウサラ, ヲ喜ブ. *v.t.*
To take pleasure in. To rejoice
over. To get one's living by.

Eni-ika, エニイカ, 木ヨリ墜ツル. *v.i.*
To fall from a tree. **Syn: Onipichi.**

Enikuruki, エニクルキ, 頁傷スル、害
セラル. *v.i.* To be wounded. To

be hurt. **Syn : Yayapushkere. Yaiyeshikorap.**

Eninge-ni, タラノキ. *n.* See *En-*
エニンゲニ, *enge-ni.* The Ange-
Enengi-ni, lica tree.
エチンギニ,

Enininge, エニニンゲ, 遅キ. *adj.*
Slow. Dull. As :—*Shukup eni-ninge,* "of slow growth."

Eninui, エニヌイ, 枕スル、休ム、眠ル.
v. i. To lay the head upon a pillow. To take a rest. To sleep.

Eninuibe, エニヌイベ, 枕. *n.* A pillow. **Syn : Aininuibe. Chi-eninuibe.**

Eninuite, エニヌイテ, 寝サスル、休マ
セル. *v.t.* To put to rest. To put to bed.

Enikokomo, エニココモ, 杖チ以チ打
ツ. *v.t.* To strike with a stick.

Eni-omare, エニオマレ, 杖チ以テ打ツ.
v.t. To strike with a stick.

Enishomap, エニショマプ, 案ズル. *v.t.*
To feel anxious about.

Enishpane, エニシバネ, 司ドル. *v.t.*
To lord over.

Enishpeush, エニシベウシ, 唾. *n.*
Salivation. Also to drivel.

Enitatke, エニタッケ, 風チヒク、(感
冒). *v. i.* To be afflicted with a stuffy cold in the head. To sniffle as when one has a cold in the head. **Syn : Omke.**

Enitomom, エニトモム, 眠ム、注意シ
テ見ル. *v.i.* To stare at. To look at carefully. To look into. **Syn : Enutomom.**

Eniuchinne, エニウチンネ, 他人チ軽
ンズル. *v.t.* To show dislike to another. To treat in a slighting manner. To drive away. To eject. **Syn : Eangesh.**

Eniwa, エニワ, 禿タル. *adj.* Bare
(as a mountain). **Syn : Cha-sak. Atusa.**

Enka, エンカ, 上. *post.* Over. Above.

Enkaoiki, エンカオイキ, 恩ム、祝スル.
v.t. To bless. **Syn : Nunuke. Inunuke.**

Enkashike, エンカシケ, 上. *post.*
Over. Above.

Enkashike-keta, エンカシケケタ, 丁
度上. *post.* Exactly over.

Enkashike-peka, エンカシケペカ, 上.
post. Over.

Enkashiketa, エンカシケタ, 上. *post.*
Over. Upon.

Enkata, エンカタ, 上. *post.* Upon.
Over.

Enkoisamka, 損失スル. *v. i.* To
エンコイサムカ, suffer the loss of
Emkoisamka, one's goods.
エムコイサムカ,

Enkoro, エンコロ, 目ト目ノ間、鼻梁、
(ハナメシラ). *n.* The space between the eyes. The bridge of the nose.

Enkoro-itak, エンコロイタク, 鼻ニ掛
ケテ言フ. *v.i.* To speak through the nose.

Enomi, エノミ, 神酒チ以テ神ニ祈ル.
v.t. To worship with libations.

Enon, エノン, 何處ヘ. *adv.* Whither.
Syn : Ine un.

Enopek-ush, エノペクウシ, 眩ム. *v.i.*
To be dazzled with light.

Enueshkari, エヌエシカリ, 左樣ヘ思
掛ケナカッタ. *ph.* I did not expect it.

Enuitasa, エヌイタサ, 當ラズ. *v.t.*
To miss (in walking).

Enukara, エヌカラ, 鈍キ、例セバ、エ
メカラマキリ、鈍キ小刀. *adj.* Dull

(as a knife). Thus :— *Enukara makiri*, "a dull knife."

Enumitanne, エヌミタン子, ヨノミ. *n.* A kind of berry. *Lonicera coerulea, L.*

Enumnoya, エヌムノヤ, ヤマガラ. *n.* Japanese tit. *Parus varius, T. and S.* **Syn : Numnoya-chip.**

Enumnumge, エヌムヌムゲ, 豊カナ ル. *adj.* Plentiful. Abundant.

Enunui,
エヌヌイ, 眠ル. *v.i.* To sleep.
Enunuye,
エヌヌイェ,

Enup, エヌブ, 不便ナル. *adj.* Inconvenient.

Enupek-ush, エヌペクシ, 眩ム. *v.i.* To be dazzled with the light as when one enters the light from a dark room. **Syn : Enopek-ush.**

Enupitara, エヌピタラ, 嫌フ、遮クル、 賤ムム. *v.t.* To eschew. To be tired of. Not to desire. To hate. To despise. To forbid. To dislike. The degree of intensity is to be gathered from the context. **Syn : Kereroshke.**

Enushkari, エヌシカリ, 愕ク. *v.i.* To be surprised at. To be amazed.

Enutomom, エヌトモム, 見ル. *v.t.* To look at or into. To stare at. To look at carefully. As :— *Hoka noshike enutomom*, "to look into the fire (as in deep thought)." **Syn : Enitomom.**

Eochayaige, エオチャイゲ, 繁茂ス ル. *v. i.* To stand and spread out thickly as branches of trees.

Eoha, エオハ, 空ニナル. *v.i.* To become empty.

Eohare, エオハレ, 空ニスレ. *v.t.* To empty. **Syn : Ohare.**

Eoikushi, (*s*)
エオイクシ, 着ル、擴クル. *v. t.* To clothe. To
Eoikushpa, (*pl*)
エオクシバ, spread over.

Eok, エオク, 當レ、(單數). *v.t.* To knock or kick against. (*s*).

Eokok, エオコク, 打チ當ル、(複數). *v.t.* To knock or kick against. (*pl.*).

Eokokte, エオコクテ, 打チ當ラセル. *v.t.* To cause to knock or kick against. (*pl.*)

Eokte, エオクテ, 引掛ル. *v.t.* To hook in. To draw in by means of a hook. To hang up. To fix on. As :— *Tara ibe sapa eokte*, "to fix the headpiece of a sling (used for carrying bundles) upon the head." (*sing.*)

Eoma, エオマ, 倚リカヽル、凭ルヽ、例 セバ、カンニエオマ、杖ニ依ル. *v.t.* To lean upon. As :— *Kanni eoma*, "he is leaning upon his staff."

Eomken, エオムケン, 捕ル能ハズ、漁セ ヌ. *v.i.* To be unable to catch. To be unsuccessful in the chase or at fishing.

Eomoshiroi, エオモシロイ, 喜バレル、 愛セラレル. *v.t.* To take delight in. To be fond of. To be delighted with. **Syn : Enupetne.**

Eomoshiroire, エオモシロイレ, 喜バレ ル、愛セラレル. *v.i.* The same as *Eomoshiroi*.

Eonne,
エオン子, 手顔チ洗フ. *v.t.* To wash
Ewonne, the face and hands.
エウォン子, **Syn : Yashke.**

Eopetoko, エオペトコ, 刺ス. *v.t.* To prick. To pierce. **Syn : Otke.**

Eorauge, エオラウゲ, 間ニ合ハヌ. *v.t.* To miss (a sa train). To get behind.

Eoripak, エオリパク, 尊敬スル. *v.t.* To honour.

Eoro, エオロ, 甚ダ、例セバ、エオロハンゲコ、甚ダ遠キ. *adj.* Very. Exceedingly. As:—*Eoro hangeko.* "very distant;" "afar."

Eorura, エオルラ, 送ル. *v.t.* To send. **Syn: Omande.**

Eoshikpekare, エオシクペカレ, 覗フ、狙フ. *v.t.* To take aim at.

Eoshikpekarep, エオシクペカレプ, 狙ハレタル物、目的. *n.* A thing aimed at. **Syn: Aeyairamattep.**

Eoshirok, (s)
エオシロク, 妨ゲル. *v. t.* To
Eoshirokok, (pl) hinder.
エオシロコク,

Eoshittesu, エオシッテス, 輕觸シ去ル、滑ル. *v.t.* To glance off. To slip.

Eoshkoni, エオシコニ, 追付ク. *v.t.* To overtake.

Eoshiwen, エオシウェン, 自分ノ爲メニ保ツ、藏ス、例セバ、イタクエオシウェン、知ラサヌ. *v.i.* To keep to one's self. As:—*Itak-eoshiwen,* "not to tell." *Yaikota korobe eoshiwen,* "to keep one's belongings to himself."

Eot, エオツ, 適合セル、一致セル. *adj.* Agreeable. Agreeing with. **Syn: Eat.**

Eotara, エオタラ, 突キ立ツ. *v.t.* To stick out of. To pierce. To hit. **Syn: Eroshki.**

Eotashish, エオタシシ, 早クスル、急がス. *v.t.* To hasten. To hurry.

Eoteknup, エオテクヌプ, 富、豊多. *n.* Riches.

Eotke, エオツケ, 付ケル. *v.t.* To stick into. To thrust into.

Eotui, エオツイ, 終ル. *v.t.* To bring to an end. To finish.

Eotuibe, エオツイベ, 終リシモノ. *n.* Things brought to an end.

Eotuyetuye, エオツイェツイェ, 持ツテ往ク. *v.t.* To carry away, (as in theft). To take away. **Syn: Eikka wa oman. Koro wa oman.**

Eotuyetuye, エオツイェツイェ, 振動ス ル、扇ク、掃フ. *v.t.* To shake. To fan. To brush. **Syn: Paruparu.**

Eoyaitak, エオヤイタク, 嘲リ笑フ. *v.t.* To make fun of. To laugh at derisively. To make a dupe of another. To mock. **Syn: Ainukirukiru.**

Eoyashimge, エオヤシムゲ, 翌日. *adv.* The next day. The day after.

Ep, エプ, 食物、例セバ、エプカイサム、食物がナイ. *n.* Food. As:—*Ep ka isam,* "there is no food. **Syn: Aep. Ibe ambe.**

Epa, エパ, 迄、滿ツル、(時期ナドノ). *v.i.* and *adv.* To be fulfilled (as time). As far as. As:—*Naa shomo nei ushike epa shomoki,* "before one's time."

Epa, エパ, 當タル、及ブ、例セバ、クエパエアイカプ、私ハ及ブコトが出來ナイ. *v.t.* To reach to. To attain to. As:—*Ku epa eaikap,* "I cannot reach it." *Epa pakno ku mokoro kusu ne,* "I shall sleep as much as I can."

Epakashi, エパカシ, 敎訓. *n.* Teaching. Doctrine. Instruction.

Epakashnu, エパカシヌ, 敎ヘル. *v.t.* To teach. To instruct. **Syn: Eyaihannokkare.**

Epakashnu-i, エパカシヌイ, 敎訓. *n.*

Instruction. Doctrine. **Syn: Epakashnu ambe. Epakashi.**

Epakashnu-nishpa, エパカシヌニシパ, 教師. *n.* A teacher. One who instructs.

Epakashnure, エパカシヌレ, 教ヘサセル. *v.t.* To cause another to teach.

Epakokomo, エパココモ, 杖ヲ以テ頭ヲ打ツ. *v.t.* To knock on the head with a stick.

Epanchokkai-nep, エパンチヨツカイ子ブ, 黥(イレズミ)ナキ女. *n.* An untattooed woman.

Epange, エパンゲ, 　**Eepange, エエパンゲ,** 　終リニ. *adv.* At the end. At the finish.

Epange, エパンゲ, 好マヌ、嫌フ. *v.t.* To not want. To hate. To dislike. **Syn : Etunne.**

Epanu-ki, エパヌキ, 過失ヲ數フ. *v.t.* To find fault with.

Epara, エパラ, 吹ク. *v.i.* To blow.

Epara, エパラ, 罪ヲ負ハス、害ヲ被ラス. *v. t.* To lay a fault upon another. To condemn. To injure another. To cause to catch (as a disease).

Eparatek-sei-yuk, エパラテクセイユク, 角枝ノ落チシ鹿. *n.* A deer with deformed antlers. There is a superstition to the effect that whoever kills one of these animals is certain to die shortly afterwards.

Eparoahunkanit, エパロアフンカニツ, 織機ノ絲卷. *n.* A weaving spool.

Eparorokashi-kuyushitara, エパロロカシクユシタラ, 嚙ミ碎ク. *v.t.* To

chew. To masticate. As :—*Aep eparorokashi kuyushitara*, "to masticate one's food."

Epaukoiki, エパウコイキ, 爭鬪スル、喧嘩スル. *v.i.* To quarrel. **Syn : Upaure.**

Epaure, エパウレ, 爭論スル. *v.i.* To dispute. To quarrel. **Syn : Epaukoiki.**

Epaushi, エパウシ, 頭ニ被ル. *v.i.* To be wearing upon the head.

Epaushire, エパウシレ, 頭ニ卷ク. *v.t.* To put round the head as a sling for carrying bundles.

Epeka, エペカ, 當タル、ニ付テ、正ダス. *v. t.* To refer to. To hit. To adjust. As :—*Nei ambe e epeka kuni ne kara*, "adjust it."

Epeka-no-ye, エペカノイェ, ニ付テ言フ. *v.t.* To allude to.

Epekara, エペカラ, 　**Epekare, エエペカレ,** 　狙フ、指サス、正タス. *v.t.* To aim at. To point at. To adjust.

Epekereyot, エペケレヨツ, 眩ム. *v.i.* To be dazzled with light (as in coming from a dark room into the bright sunlight).

Epenge, エペンゲ, 　**Eepenge, エペンゲ,** 　根原ニ、源ニ、始メニ. *adv.* At the source. In the beginning.

Epesap, エペサブ, 小刀ノ類. *n.* The name of a kind of flat knife.

Epesh, エペシ, 浸ミ通ル. *v. i.* To soak through. **Syn : Oboso.**

Epesh, エペシ, 川上ニ. *adv.* Towards the source of a river. **Syn : Pet turashi.**

Epesh, エペシ, 長サ. *n.* The length.

Epetchiu, エペッチウ, 眠ク. *v.i.* To

stumble. To stumble through striking the foot against an object. **Syn : Ureepetchiu.**

Epetchiure, エペツチウレ, 蹶カセル. *v.t.* To cause to stumble.

Epetke, エペツケ, 野兎. *n.* A hare. **Syn : Isepo. Oshuke.**

Epetke, エペッケ, 三口、鉄唇、兎唇、(ミックチ). *adj.* Hare-lipped.

Epettuye, エペッツイェ, 裂ル. *v.t.* To slit.

Epetpetke-chep, エペツペッケチェプ, イカ. *n.* Cuttle-fish.

Epikot, エピコツ, 仕上ラザレ. *adv.* Unfinished.

Epikot-attush, エピコツアッツシ, 仕上ラザル着物. *n.* Cloth in the process of being made.

Epikot-kina, エピコツキナ, 織リツ、アル薦. *n.* Mats in process of being made.

Epinise-itangi, エピニセイタンギ, 飯杓子. *n.* A laddle used for taking food out of a pot.

Epirika, エピリカ, 儲ケル. *v.t.* To gain. To acquire. **Syn : Yaiepirikare.**

Epirika-ambe,
エピリカアムベ, } 利益. *n.* Gain.
Epirika-i,
エピリカイ, }

Epirikap, エピリカプ, 利益. *n.* An advantage. A thing gained. **Syn : Eyaiepirikarep.**

Epirikare, エピリカレ, 儲ケル. *v.t.* To gain. To acquire.

Epiru, エピル, 掃キ出ス. *v.t.* To brush out. To beat out. To beat the sick with bunches of grass or twigs to drive out demons of sickness.

Epiru, エピル, 摘ミ出ス. *v.t.* To pick out (as fish from the meshes of a net).

Epishi, エピシ, 海岸ヘ向フ、例セバ、エヒシサプ、我等ハ海岸ニ行ク. *adv.* To or towards the sea-shore. As :— *Epishi sap*, "we are going to the sea-shore."

Epishka-un, エピシカウン, 彼處此處、例セバ、エヒシカウンホサリヮインガラ、彼處此處ヲ見レ. *adv.* Here and there. This way and that. About. Hither and thither. As :—*Epishka un hosari wa ingara*, "to look this way and that." *Epishka un nukara*, "to look about." **Syn : Epishne.**

Epishne, エピシネ, 海岸ニ向フ. *adv.* Towards the sea-shore.

Epitche, エピッチェ, 禿ゲタル. *adj.* Bald. **Syn : Otop-sak.**

Epitche-nonno, エピッチェノンノ, タンポポ. *n.* The dandelion. *Taraxacum officinale, Wigg. var. corniculatum, Koch et Ziz.* **Syn : Honoinoep.**

Epittek, エピッテク, 外レシ、脱臼スル、例セバ、タプスツエピッテク、肩ガ外レシ. *v.i.* and *adj.* Displaced. To be out of joint. To be displaced or dislocated. As :—*Tapsutu epittek*, "the shoulder is dislocated." *Apa epittek*, "the door has got out of its groove." **Syn : Chiturusere.**

Epittekka, エピッテッカ, 取外ヅス. *v.t.* To displace. To unfasten. To put out of joint.

Epokba, エポクバ, 責メレ、詈メル、憎ム. *v.t.* To persecute. To hate. To oppose. To contravene. This

word is preceded by *otta*. **Syn:**
Epoppa.

Epokba-guru, エポクバグル, 敵. *n.*
An enemy. A persecutor. An
adversary.

Epokbap, エポクバプ, 敵. *n.* An
adversary.

Epoki, エポキ, 下方へ. *adv.* Downwards.

Epokikomo, エポキコモ, 下方ヘ疊ム、
折込ム. *v.t.* To fold down.

Epoki-komomse, エポキコモムセ, 下
ノ方ヘ引キ掛ル. *v.i.* To be hooked
downwards.

Epokituye, エポキツイェ, ヨリ少キ.
adj. Less than.

Epoko, エポコ, 短氣ナル、喧嘩ヲ好ム.
adv. Waspish. Snappish. Quarrelsome.

Epoppa, エポッパ, 嫌フ、憎ム、窘メレ.
v.t. To hate. To persecute. To
oppose. **Syn: Epokba.**

Eporose, エポロセ, 食慾ナル. *v.i.*
and *adj.* Avaricious. Covetous.
Greedy.

Eposo, エポソ, 實ニ、成程. *adv.* Same
as *Eboso*. Just so. Indeed.

Eposo-gusu, エポソグス, 誠ニ、成程·
Verily. Just so. Just as. Indeed.
Syn: Eboso gusu.

Epotan-ni, エポタンニ, オホバイボタ
ノキ. *n.* The privet. *Ligustrum
medium, Fr. et Sav.*

Epotara, エポタラ, 心配スル、案ズル.
v.t. To feel anxiety for another.
To feel anxious about. To be
troubled about. To miss (as a
friend). As:—*Kuani isam yakun
ku utara a en epotara ki ruwe ne,*
"if I am not there my relations

will feel anxious about me."
Syn: Enishomap.

Epotara, エポタラ, 病者ノ爲メニ祈ル、
治療スル. *v.t.* To pray for the
sick. To treat a disease.

Epotara-guru, エポタラグル, 醫師.
n. A doctor. One who prays
for the recovery of a sick person.
One who treats the sick in any
way with a view to recovery.

Epotpochi, エポツポチ, プシダマ. *n.*
Lonicera Morrowie, A. Gray.

Epui, エプイ, 芽. *n.* A bud.

Epuige, エプイゲ, }
Epuike, エプイケ, } 花. *n.* A flower.

Epuige-shipirasa *(sing)*, **エプイゲシ
ピラサ,** 花咲ク. *v. i.* To blossom.
To flower.

Epuige-shipiraspa *(pl)*, **エプイゲシ
ピラスパ,** 花咲ク. *v. i.* Same as
above.

Epuike-hepirasa *(sing)*, **エプイケヘ
ピラサ,** 花咲ク. *v. i.* Same as
above.

Epuike-hepiraspa *(pl)*, **エプイケヘ
ピラスパ,** 花咲ク. *v. i.* Same as
above.

Epuike-pirasa *(sing)*, } 花咲ク. *v. i.*
エプイケピラサ, } Same as
Epuike-piraspa *(pl)*, } above.
エプイケピラスパ, }

Epuina-no, エプイナノ, 面ヲ伏セル、
例セバ、エプイナノハチリ、面ヲ伏シ
テ仆レタ. *adv.* Face downwards.
As:—*Epuina no hachiri,* "to fall
upon the face."

Epuinepi, エプイチビ, 堆積、塊. *n.*
A heap of anything. A lump.
Syn: Eputanashpe.

Epuinepushbe, エプイ子ブシベ 堆積、塊. *n.* Same as above.
Upunepushbe, ウプチブシベ,

Epuinepi-kara, エプイ子ビカラ, 積ム. *v.t.* To heap up. To make into a heap.

Epuinepushbe, エプイ子ブシベ, 堆積、塊. *n.* A heap of anything. A lump.

Epukitara, エプキタラ, 表ハス、顯ハス(怒リナドチ). *v.t.* To show (as temper).

Epunepush, エプ子ブシ, 積ム. *v.t.* To heap up. To stack (as hay).

Epungau, エプンガウ, カハイモ. *n.* *Metaplexis Stauntoni, Roem et Sch.* Syn : Chituirep.

Epunepushbe, エプチブシベ, Epuinepushbe, エプイチブシベ, 堆積、塊. *n.* A heap of anything. A lump.

Epungi, エプンギ, 番人. *n.* A watchman. Syn : Shiruwe guru.

Epungine, エプンギ子, 守ル、治ムル. *v.t.* To govern. To watch over. To take care of. To look after.

Epungine-guru, エプンギ子グル, 司ドル人、統治者. *n.* A governor. A ruler. A watchman. A caretaker.

Epunginep, エプンギチブ, 司守人、統治者. *n.* Same as *Epungine guru.*

Epuni, エプニ, 上ゲル. *v.t.* To lift up. To raise. To set up on end. To lift up to. *e.g. Pase kamui shik epuni,* " he lift his eyes up to the true god."

Epuruse, エプルセ, 水チ吹ク. *v.t.* To squirt. To blow out of the mouth (as water).

Epusu, エプス, 出ヅル. *v.i.* To come out of. To come up.

Eputanashpe, エプタナシベ, 堆積、塊. *n.* A lump of anything. Syn : Epuinepi.

Epyukke, エプユッケ, 吝嗇スレ. *v.i.* To be stingy. Syn : Ibeunara.

Erai, エライ, 垂下スル. *v.i.* To droop as wheat when blown down by the wind or caused to fall through abundance or excessive weight.

Eraiba-pushi. エライバブシ, ハマベンケイサウ. *n.* *Mertensia maritima, Don.*

Eraikotne-pirika, エライコツ子ビリカ, 信ズベキ. *adj.* Reliable.

Eraikotne-wen, エライコツ子ウェン, 信セラレヌ. *adj.* Unreliable.

Eraininne, エライニン子, 成就ニ六ヶ敷シキ、成就シ難キ. *v.i.* Difficult of accomplishment. Syn : Aki hokamba.

Erainiukesh, エライニウケシ, 助ケル. *v.t.* To help. To act faithfully towards. To persevere in. As :—*Echi kotchaketa erainiukesh ku ki na,* " I will persevere on your behalf." Syn : Eranniukesh.

Erairai, エライライ, プヨ. *n.* A kind of very tiny black fly. A midge.

Erakoro, エラコロ, 食傷スレ. *v.i.* To be affected by. As :—*Buta kam erakoro,* " he was made sick by eating pork."

Eraman, エラマン, 了解スル、知ル. *v.t.* To understand. To know. Syn : Eramu an.

Eramambe, エラマムベ, 知ラレタルコト. *n.* Anything known.

Eramande, エラマンデ, 知ラセル. *v.t.* To make known or understood.

Eraman-no, エラマンノ, 明カニ、知リシ、熟考シテ. *adv.* Knowingly. Advisedly. With wisdom. Wisely.

Eramanre, エラマンレ, 獵スル. *v.t.* To hunt. **Syn: Iramande.**

Eramante, エラマンテ, 知ラセル. *v.t.* To make known.

Eramashu, エラマシュ, 喜バセル. *v.t.*
Eramasu, エラマス, To regard with pleasure. To be pleased with. To admire.

Eramashu-no, エラマシュノ, 喜コンデ、樂シク.
Eramasu-no, エラマスノ, *adv.* Admiringly. Pleasurably. In a pleasing manner.

Eramashure, エラマシュレ, 喜バセレ. *v. t.* To
Eramasure, エラマスレ, give pleasure to. To make another pleased.

Eramchuptek, エラムチュプテク, 悲ム、苦痛スレ.*v.i.* To be in sorrow or distress.

Eramchuptekbe, エラムチュプテクベ, 悲歎、困難. *n.* Sorrow. Distress. Trouble. Affliction.

Eramchupush, エラムチュプシ, 淋シキ. *v.i.* To feel lonely. **Syn: Mishmu.**

Eramkatchiush, エラムカッチウシ, 好マヌ、嫌フ.*v.t.* To hate. To dislike. To be averse to. To be disgusted with. **Syn: Etunne.**

Eramisam, エラミサム, 分ラヌ. *v.i.* Not to understand or know.

Eramishkare, エラミシカレ, 分ラヌ. *v.t.* Same as above.

Eramkoeshkari, エラムコエシカリ, 愕ク. *v. t.* To be surprised at. To wonder at. **Syn: Enushkari.**

Erampekamam, エラムペカマム, 心悶エル、心配
Erampekamama, エラムペカママ, スル. *v.i.* To be in trouble. **Syn: Aeshirikirap an.**

Erampekamambe, エラムペカマムベ, 煩累、苦悶. *n.* Troubles.

Erampeutek, エラムペウテク, 分ラヌ. *v.i.* To not understand. Not to know.

Erampokiwen, エラムポキウェン, 哀レナレ. *adj.* Miserable. Pitiable.

Erampokiwen-ki, エラムポキウェンキ, 憐ム. *v.t.* To pity. To have mercy upon.

Erampokiwen-wa-kore, エラムポキウェンワコレ, 憐ム. *v. t.* To pity. To take pity on. To have mercy upon.

Erampopash-kosamba, エラムポパシコサムバ, 喜ブ. *v. i.*
Erampopash-kosanu, エラムポパシコサヌ, To be pleased. To feel rejoiced. **Syn: Yainuchattek.**

Eramu, エラム, 了解スル、曉ル. *v. t.* To understand. To know. To apprehend.

Eramu-an, エラムアン, 了解スル、曉ル. *v. t.* To understand. To know. *Eramu an na mungi na,* "a. phrase meaning that one thoroughly understands."

Eramuchakbe, エラムチャクベ, 好マザルコト、放棄セラレタルコト. *n.* A thing which discourages. A

. ˙thing eschewed. Anything disliked.

Eramu-ekatchaush, エラムエカッチャウシ, 嫌フ. *v.i.* To feel antipathy towards another. To be displeased with. **Syn: Ekatchaush.**

Eramuhauge, エラムハウゲ, 親切ニ遇スレ. *v.t.* To show kindness towards.

Eramuhokasush, 不満足ナレ. *adj.*
エラムホカスシ,
Eramuhokasusu, and *v.i.* Dissatisfied. To
エラムホカスス, be dissatisfied.

Eramuhokasush-no, エラムホカスシノ, 不満足ニ. *adj.* In a dissatisfied manner.

Eramuhokasusu-no, エラムホカススノ, 不満足ニ. *adj.* Same as above.

Eramu-hopunini, エラムホプニニ, 胸ヲ腰ガス. *v.t.* To stir up the heart or mind.

Eramu-ikatchaush, エラムイカッチャウシ, 好マヌ、憎ム、例セバ、カムイアナクネウェンブイエラムイカッチヤウシ神ハ悪シキ仕業ヲ嫌フ. *v.t.* To dislike. To look upon with disfavour. To look upon with displeasure. To disapprove of. As :—*Kumui anak ne wen-buri eramu-ikatchaush,* "God looks upon evil deeds with disfavour."

Eramu-ikurukuru, エラムイクルクル, 心配スル、煩フ. *v.i.* To be troubled. To be in trouble. **Syn: Yaikowepekere.**

Eramukittararage, エラムキッタララゲ, 怖レル、懼レル. *v.i.* To be afraid. To be in dread. To be struck with awe. **Syn: Kimatek. Ishitoma.**

Eramukachipeutekka, エラムカチペウテッカ, 思ヒ亂レシ、攪亂セシ. *adj.* and *v.i.* To be confused by another. Confused. Confounded. **Syn: Aeramu-usausakka.**

Eramukachipeutek-no, エラムカチペウテクノ, 混雜ナル. *adj.* Confusedly. As :—*Eramukachipeutek no ye,* "to talk confusedly."

Eramunin, エラムニン, 向フ見ズノ、注意セヌ. *adj.* and *v.t.* Rash. Careless. To neglect. Not to acknowledge. To treat as a stranger. To slight. **Syn: Eramu-unun. Ramueunin.**

Eramu-nin-no, エラムニンノ, 不注意ニ、粗末ニ. *adv.* Carelessly. Negligently.

Eramu-sam, エラムサム, 了解セヌ. *v.i.* Not to understand.

Eramu-unun, エラムウヌン, 忘レル. *v.t.* To forget. To over-look.

Eramush, エラムシ, 了解スル、名高キ、例セバ、エラムシグル、有名ナル人. *adj.* Known. Recognized. Learned. As :—*Eramush guru,* "a person who knows." **Syn: Aramush.**

Eramushbe, エラムシベ, 知ラレタイコト. *n.* A thing known.

Eramushkare, 了解セヌ. *v.t.* Not
エラムシカレ, to understand.
Eramushkari, Not to know.
エラムシカリ,
Syn: Erampeutek.

Eramushkarep, 知ラヌコト. *n.*
エラムシカレプ, Things one does
Eramushkarip, not know or
エラムシカリプ, understand. **Syn: Erampeutekbe.**

Eramutasaoke, エラムタサオケ, ヲ
悩マス. *v.t.* To be vexed with.

Eramutunash, エラムツナシ, 曉リ早
キ、銳敏ナレ. *adj.* Acute. Quick-
witted. Quick of understanding.

Eramutunash-i, エラムツナシイ, 銳
敏ナル. *n.* Quick-wittedness.
Acuteness.

Eramu-unun, エラムウヌン, 注意セ
ヌ. *v.i.* To take no notice of.
To be careless. To be forgetful.
Syn : Eramunin.

Eramu-unun-no, エラムウヌンノ, 不
注意ニ. *adv.* Carelessly. Forgetfully.

Eramu-usausak, エラムウサウサク,
混雜ナレ、攪亂セレ. *adj.* Con-
fusing.

**Eramu-usausakbe, エラムウサウサ
クベ,** 混雜ナルモノ、錯亂. *n.* Something confusing.

**Eramu-usausakka, エラムウサウサ
カ,** 混亂スレ. *v.t.* To confuse.

**Eramu-usausak-no, エラムウサウ
サクノ,** 紊レテ、混亂シテ. *adv.* Con-
fusingly. In a confusing manner.
As :—*Eramuusausak no ye,* " to
tell in a confusing manner."

Eranniukesh, エランニウケシ, 辛棒
ナレ、助ヶ. *n.* Help. Persever-
ance. **Syn : Erainiukesh.**

Eraokatta, エラオカッタ, 浸ス. *v.t.*
To dip into. To throw into
water. **Syn : Erauokatta.**

Eraomare, エラオマレ, 謙ダスラセレ、
下ダス. *v.t.* To lower. To humble.

Eraot, エラオツ, 斜ナレ. *adj.* Slanting. **Syn : Sekumtarara.**

Erapurap, エラプラプ, 蝴蝶、蛾. *n.* A
butterfly. A moth. **Syn : Kamakata. Heporap.**

Erarak, エララク, 沈ミタル. *adj.*
Sunken.

Eraratki, エララツキ, 垂下スレ. *v.i.*
To hang down. To be low. To
be bent down. To slant.

Eraratkire, エララツキレ, 曲ゲル、下
ダス. *v.t.* To bend down. To
lower. To send down. To make
to slant.

Eraraye, エララィェ, 平ニスレ(桝ニテ
穀物ヲ舛ルトキノ如ク). *v.t.* To level
off (as grain in a measure.)

Erashka, エラシカ, 切ル. *v.t.* To
cut. To trim by cutting (as
paper).

Eratkip, エラツキプ, 褌. *n.* A loin-
cloth. **Syn : Tepa.**

Erau, エラウ, 埋メル. *v.t.* To bury.
To cover up. As :—*Abe erau,*
" to cover up fire " in order to
preserve it.

Eraukushte, エラウクシテ, 沈マセレ.
v.t. To dip into. To sink into.

Eraunkuchi, エラウンクチ,
Eraunkut, エラウンクツ, ⎱ 下喉. *n.* The lower
part of the throat.

**Eraunkuchi-kamui-noye, エラウン
クチカムイノイェ,** 唸ル、口吟ム. *ph.*
To hum. To speak deep down
in the chest. To make melody
in the heart (lit : to sing to
God from the lower part of the
throat). See *Onnu-onnu.*

Erauokatta, エラウオカッタ, 沈メレ.
v.t. To sink. To dip into.

Erawekatta, エラウェカッタ, 沈メレ.
v.t. To sink. Ta dip into.

Erayap, エラヤプ, ヲ喜プ. *v.i.* To
be pleased with. To express
pleasure in. **Syn : Areika.**

Erayapka, エラヤブカ, 喜ハセレ. *v.t.* To please. Also an *interj.* of pleasurable surprise.

Eraye, エライェ, 知ラヌ. *v.t.* Not to know. To be ignorant. of. As:—*Nei ambe oara ku eraye ruwe ne,* "I do not in the least understand that."

Erayekotne, エライェコツ子, 不足ニ思フ. *v.i.* To be dissatisfied. **Syn: Aeramushinne shomoki.**

Ere, エレ, 食ハセル. *v.t.* To feed. **Syn: Ibere.**

Ere, エレ, 延バス、伸バス. *v.t.* To stretch out.

Ereba, エレバ, Erepa, エレバ, 置ク、(網ノ如ク). *v.t.* To set (as a net in the sea). **Syn: Turupa.**

Eregus, エレグス, Eregush, エレグシ, 大口魚、(タラ). *n.* A codfish.

Erekasu, エレカス, 甚ダ、例セバ、エレカスヒリカルウェ子、其レハ甚ダ善イ. *adj.* Very. As:—*Erekasu pirika ruwe ne,* "it is very good."

Erem, エレム, 鼠. *n.* A rat. As: *Erem akbe,* "a rat trap." **Syn: Eremu. Erum.**

Eremtambu, エレムタムブ, Eremutambu, エレムタムブ, 疣、イボ. *n.* A wart. Papilloma.

Erem-kina, エレムキナ, オホバコ. *n.* The plantain. *Plantago major, L. var. asiatica, Dcne.* **Syn: Eeremu-kina. Erumkina.**

Eremu. エレム, 鼠. *n.* A rat. **See Erem.**

Eremu-kina, エレムキナ, オホバコ. *n.* The plantain. *Plantago major, L. var. asiatica, Dcne.*

Eremuosara. エレムオサラ, 死人ノ着物ヲ結ブ飾ノ紐. *n.* A peculiar kind of ornament used to decorate the cords which are used in burying the dead.

Eren, エンレ, 三人. *n.* Three persons. As:—*Eren a ne wa,* "we three."

Erengaine, エレンガイ子, 勝手ニ、随意ニ. *adv.* As one likes. According to one's own desires.

Erep, エレブ, 四個ト半. *adj.* Four and a half.

Erepa, エレバ, Ereba, エレバ, 置ク、(網ヲ海中ニナク如ク). *v.t.* To set (as a net in the sea).

Erepo, エレポ, 掻キ集メテ埋メル、例セバ、アベエレポ、火ヲ埋メル. *v.t.* To rake up. As:—*Abe erepo,* "to rake up the fire."

Ererashuye, エレラシュイェ, 跟蹌(ヨロメク)、搖レル. *v.i.* To totter. To shake (as in the wind). To be unable to stand (as a drunken man).

Ereunui, エレウヌイ, 曲リノ内方. *n.* The inside of a bend. *Met:* "out of sight." As:—*Ereunui ta ande,* "put it out of sight" (lit: place it in the bend). **Syn: Oahunge-i.**

Erikikuru, エリキクル, 上ニ坐ス. *v.i.* To sit upon. To ride upon.

Erikitari, エリキタリ, 上方ヘ向キシ. *adj.* Pointing upwards.

Erikitesu, エリキテス, 上方ニ向テ傾ク. *v.i.* To slant upwards.

Erikomare, エリコマレ, 上ゲル. *v.t.* To exalt. To raise the price of anything.

Erikomara-ichen, エリコマレイチェン, 口銭. A commission on goods sold.

Eritne-shukup, エリッチシュクプ, 養ハル、青テラレレ. *v.i.* To be reared. To grow up gradually.

Erok, エロク, 内ニ在レ. *v.i.* To dwell in. To be in. As:—*Kotan erokbe kamui an, moshiri erokbe kamui tapan na,* "there are gods who dwell in villages, and gods who dwell in countries."

Eroki,
エロキ,
Heroki, } 鰊 (ニシン). *n.* Herrings.
ヘロキ, *Clupea harengus Linn.*
Heruki,
ヘルキ,

Erokroki, エロクロキ, ヨイカ、カスイドリ. *n.* The night-jar. *Caprimulgus jotaka, T. & S.*

Erorunne, エロルンネ, 上坐ノ方. *adv.* Towards the upper end of the fireplace. As:—*Erorunne euturunne hosari wa ingara,* "he turned his head and looked towards the upper and lower ends of the fireplace."

Eroshki, エロシキ, 立タセレ. *v.t.* To set up. To stick up as posts. To shoot at and hit with an arrow. As:—*Ai eroshki,* "he shot and hit it with an arrow."

Eruimakanu, エルイマカヌ, 路ヲ除ケレ. *v.i.* To make way for.

Erum, エルム, 鼠. *n.* A rat. **See Erem.**

Erumakanu, エルマカヌ, 路ヲ遜ヅル. *v.i.* To get out of the way so as to let another pass. (Lit: to open up a way). **Syn: Horuenene.**

Erumaknere, エルマクネレ, 路ヨリ除ケレ. *v.t.* To turn out of a way.

Erum-kina, エルムキナ, オホバコ. *n.* The plantain. *Plantago major, L. var. asiatica, Dcne.*

Erupshi, エルブシ, 前面. *n.* Front. As:— *Chisei erupshi,* "the front of a house."

Erupshige,
エルブシゲ, } 前面. *n.* Front.
Erupshike,
エルブシケ,

Erupshiketa, エルブシケタ, 前ニ. *adv.* In front of.

Erupshikeketa, エルブシケケタ, 丁度前ニ. *adv.* Exactly in front of.

Erurikiraye,
エルリキライェ, } 頭ニ巻ク. *v.t.* To tie round the head as for the purpose of tying the hair back.
Erurikirayeba,
エルリキライェバ,

Erusa, エルサ, 貸ス. *v.t.* To lend.

Erusaikari, エルサイカリ, 圍ム. *v.t.* To surround. **Syn: Nikkotama.**

Erutompak, エルトムパク, 路程. *adv.* Part way.

Esaman, エサマン, 水獺, (カハチソ). *n.* An otter. *Lutra vulgaris, Erxb.*

Esaman-ki, エサマンキ, 覡術、(河獺ノ頭ヲ以テ). *n.* Sorcery. Divination by means of a river otter's head.

Esaman-sapa, エサマンサバ, 河獺ノ頭. *n.* An otter's head (*met*—"to be forgetful").

Esambe-kese, エサムベケセ, 心中ヨリ、熱心ニ. *adv.* From the heart.

Esambe-keseta, エサムベケセタ, 心中ニ、心ノ底ニ. *adv.* At the bottom of the heart.

Esanaguru, エサナグル, }
Esanakuru, エサナクル, } 前方、例セバ、エサナクルオマン、前ニ進ム. *adv.* Forward. As :— *Esanakuru oman,* " to go forward."

Esana-sap-guru, エサナサプグル, 乱暴ナル人. *n.* A wanton person. A riotous person.

Esanniyo, エサンニヨ, 考ヘル、算フル. *v.t.* To consider. To account. To reckon. To determine.

Esanniyop, エサンニヨプ, 計算、勘定. *n.* An account. A consideration. Anything settled.

Esapane, エサバ子, 司ドル、治ム、支配スル. *v.t.* To govern. To lead. To superintend. To act as chief or head.

Esapane-guru, エサバ子グル, 司者、統治者. *n.* A governor. A head. A leader. A chief.

Esapanep, エサバ子プ, 司者、統治者. *n.* Same as *Esapane guru.*

Esapse, エサブセ, 嘲笑スレ. *v.t.* To ridicule. To laugh at.

Esapse-itak, エサブセイタク, 嘲笑スレ. *n.* Ridicule. **Syn : Eoya-itak.**

Esara, エサラ, 開キタレ. *adj.* Open.

Esara-no, エサラノ, 開キテ. *adv.* Openly.

Esara-chish, エサラチシ, 大聲デ泣ク. *v.i.* To cry aloud.

Esarasara, エサラサラ, 知ラセル. *v.t.* To make known. **Syn : Nure.**

Esash, エサシ, 音スル、響ク. *v.i.* To make a low rumbling sound. As :— *Riri esash humi,* the sound of the rumbling waves.

Esau, エサウ, 前齒. *n.* The front teeth.

Esau-tarara, エサウタララ, 出齒ノアル. *v.i.* To have projecting teeth.

Esaush, エサウシ, 前面ニ. *adv.* In front. **Syn : Kotchaketa.**

Ese, エセ, 答フル、例セバ、エセワエネイタクヒ、彼レハ答ヘテ日ク. *v.t.* To answer. As :— *Ese wa ene itak-hi :*— " he answered and spoke thus."

Ese-itak, エセイタク, 答. An answer. **Syn : Itasa itak.**

Esep, エセプ, 答. *n.* An answer.

Esere, エセレ, 答サセレ. *v.t.* To cause another to answer.

Esereponnu, エセレポンヌ, 抜ク. *v.t.* To draw out as a knife from its sheath. **Syn : Etaye.**

Eseshke, エセシケ, 閉ヅル、塞ク. *v.t.* To shut. To stop up.

Eshaot, エシャオツ, 持ツテ走ル. *v.t.* To run away with. **Syn : Kira.**

Eshi, エシ, 來ル. *v.i.* To come.

Eshi, エシ, 犬ニ用ユル間投詞、(汝閉ヂヨ). *excl :* A word used principally to quiet dogs, though sometimes used when addressing persons, (lit : you shut up).

Eshikari, エシカリ, 塞ガレタ、通セヌ. *v.i.* To be stopped. Pressed. As :— *Osshi eshikari,* " to be constipated."

Eshikari, エシカリ, 捕レ、攫ム. *v.t.* To catch (as an animal or fowl). To seize. As :— *Niwatori-chikap eshikari wa raige yan* " catch a fowl and kill it."

Eshikarun, エシカルン, 記憶スル. *v.t.* To call to mind. To remember. To keep in mind. To feel anxious about.

Eshikarun-i, エシカルンイ, 思想、思案. *n.* Thought. Remembrance. Anxiety for. **Syn: Yaikataka-rap.**

Eshikarun-no, エシカルンノ, 記憶其キ. *adj.* Having a good memory. Also *adv.* Knowingly. **Syn: Ra-mu-shikarun no.**

Eshikarun-shomoki-no, エシカルンショモキノ, 思ハズニ. *ph.* Accidentally. Forgetfully. Not remembering. Absent-mindedly.

Eshikashke, エシカシケ, 否ム. *v.t.* To deny.

Eshikipop, エシキポプ, 眺メラレ. *v.i.* To be stared out of countenance. **Syn: Enitomom.**

Eshikiraine, エシキライ子, 憐 レム、例セバ、ピリカノエンエシキライ子ワウンコレ、何卒我チ憐メ. *v.t.* To compassionate. To pity. As:—*Pirika no en eshikiraine wa un kore,* "please look upon me with compassion."

Eshikerimrim, エシケリムリム, Eshkerimrim, エシケリムリム, 片栗 (カタクリ). *n.* The dogtooth violet. *Erythronium denscanis, L.*

Eshiknak, エシクナク, Eshiknaki, エシクナキ, 物チ見メ、(心シテ見メ)、例セバ、子イアンペウェンワクスエシクナキヤン、其レハ悪シキモノ故見ナイデクレ. *v.i.* To be blind to a thing. Not to see a thing. To take no notice of. To be purposely blind to a thing. To purposely not look at. As:—*Nei ambe wen wa gusu eshiknaki yan,* "don't look at it for it is bad." *Eneturu pakno wenbe ne gusu ku*

eshiknaki nisa ruwe ne, "it was so bad that I purposely did not look at it."

Eshikoingara, エシコインガラ, 見ラレレ. *v.i.* To be seen. As:—*Moshima guru orowa no eshikoingarā kuni ne,* "in order to be seen of others." **Syn: Anukara.**

Eshikoingare, エシコインガレ, 見セレ. *v.t.* To show to another. **Syn: Nukare.**

Eshikonukare, エシコヌカレ, 見セル. *v.t.* To show to another.

Eshikop, エシコプ, 両親、親. *n.* Parents.

Eshikop-sak-guru, エシコプサクグル, 孤兒、(單數). *n.* An orphan.

Eshikop-sak-utara, エシコプサクウタラ, 孤兒、(複數). *n.* Orphans.

Eshikopuntekka, エシコプンテッカ, 此ノ人チ以テ他ノ者チ喜バセル. *v.t.* To cause another to please a third party. As:—*Shinuma heikachi koro habo eshikopuntekka ruwe ne,* "he caused the lad to please his mother." **Syn: Nupetnere.**

Eshikte, エシクテ, 充ツル. *v.t.* To fill. **Syn: Eikare.**

Eshimge, エシムゲ, 翌日. *adv.* The next day.

Eshimon-sam, エシモンサム, 右ノ方. *adv.* Towards the right hand side.

Eshina, エシナ, 否ム、秘密ニスル. *v.t.* To deny. To bind up. To keep secret. To hide (as one's faults). **Syn: Shikaeshina yara.**

Eshina-shomoki, エシナショモキ, 陽ハニ. *adv.* Above-board. Openly. Frankly.

Eshinakara, エシナカラ, 隠ス、秘密 ニスレ. v.i. To keep secret.

Eshini, エシニ, 業ヲ止メル、死ス、延引 スル. v.i. To retire from work. To abdicate. To adjourn. To die.

Eshinire, エシニレ, 退カス、止メル、猶 豫スレ. v.t. To adjourn. To cause to retire.

Eshiniuka, エシニウカ, 疲レル. v.i. To get tired of a thing. To feel indisposed. **Syn : Shingi.**

Eshinnukuri an, エシンヌクリアン, 出來ズ、能ハズ、厭フ. v. i. To be unable. To feel a disinclination to do something.

Eshinnuye, エシンヌイェ, 記サレシ. v.i. To be written. **Syn : Anuye. Chieshinnuye.**

Eshinot, エシノツ, 持ッテ遊ブ. v.t. To play with.

Eshinotbe, エシノツベ, 遊具、玩弄物. n. A plaything.

Eshipa,) 聞カヌ振スル、不滿足ニ思フ.
エシパ,{
Eshpa, } v.i. To be dissatisfied
エシパ,) with. Not to listen. To pay no attention to. To turn a deaf ear to a person. To treat with indifference. Not to look at. As:—Ainu eshipa, "to treat the man with indifference."

Eshipa-itak, エシパイタク, 聞キタク ナキコト. n. Things one desires not to hear.

Eshipakashnu, エシパカシヌ, 該博 ナル、博學ナル. adj. Learned.

Eshipattuye, エシパッツイェ, 運動スレ. v.i. To drill. To exercise. To determine to do something with diligence.

Eshipopkep, エシポプケプ, 兵器. n. Arms. Implements of war.

Eshiramgiri,) 知ル. v.t. To know.
エシラムギリ,{ To know one's
Eshiramkiri, } way. To recognize
エシラムキリ,) a person. **Syn : Eamkiri.**

Eshireoma, エシレオマ, 凭ル. v.i. To lean over.

Eshirepa, エシレパ, 到着スル. v.t. To arrive at a place.

Eshiri,)
エシリ,{ 以前ニ. adv. Previously.
Eeshiri, } Before.
エエシリ,)

Eshiri-an, エシリアン,) 以前ニ、例
Eeshiri-an, エエシリアン,} セパ、エ
シリアンアプ、以前ニ在リシモノ. adj. Above mentioned. Previous. As: —Eshiri an ap, "the previous one."

Eshirieok, エシリエオク, 引掛ケル. v.t. To hook on to. To hook in.

Eshirikoshi, エシリコシ, 外レル. v.i. To swerve. To go off the track.

Eshirikoshi-henoye, エシリコシヘノ イェ, 一方ニ、外レル. v.i. To swerve to one side.

Eshirika, エシリカ, 投棄テレ. v.t. To cast down. **Syn : Oshiripichi.**

Eshirikatta, エシリカッタ, 投棄テレ. v.t. To throw down to the ground with violence.

Eshirikik, エシリキク, 撃チ倒ス. v.t. To knock down.

Eshirikirap, エシリキラプ, 苦ム. v.i. To suffer trouble. To suffer affliction. **Syn : Ramupekamam.**

Eshirikopash, エシリコパシ, 倚リ掛 カレ. v. i. and adj. To lean against. Leaning against.

Eshirikopashte, エシリコパシテ, 立テ掛ケレ. *v.t.* To set against.

Eshirikokari, エシリコカリ, 卷ク. *v.t.* To twist. To wind.

Eshiriokte, エシリオクテ, 懸ケレ. *v.t.* To hang up. **Syn: Shiriokte.**

Eshiriotke-otke, エシリオッケオッケ, 搖ブリ込ム. *v.t.* To shake down as grain in a measure.

Eshiri-pichi, エシリピチ, 外レル. *v.i.* To slip off. To go off the track.

Eshiroko, エシロコ, 蹶ク、當タレ. *v.i.* To strike against. To stumble.

Eshirok-shirok, エシロクシロク, 蹶ク. *v.i.* To stumble and hesitate (as in speaking). To strike against. To kick. **Syn: Shirok-shirok.**

Eshiru, エシル, 磨ク、摩ル. *v.t.* To rub.

Eshishi, エシシ, 除ケレ. *v.t.* To avoid. To pass by. To eschew. **Syn: Ehaita.**

Eshishiknakte, エシシクナクテ, 知ラヌフリスレ. *v.t.* To ignore. To pretend not to know. **Syn: Aeshimoshmare.**

Eshishire, エシシレ, 除ケサセレ. *v.t.* To cause to avoid.

Eshishiriki, エシシリキ, 辭スル. *v.t.* To abdicate.

Eshishirikire, エシシリキレ, 職ニ就カス. *v.t.* To establish in business. To enthrone. To abdicate in favour of another.

Eshisho-un, エシショウン, 爐ノ右方. *adv.* By the right hand side of a hearth.

Eshishte, エシシテ, 除ケサセル. *v.t.* To cause to avoid.

Eshishuye (*sing*), **エシシュイェ, Eshishuyeba** (*pl*). **エシシュイェバ,** 搖ブル、動ク. *v.t.* To swing. To shake. To wave.

Eshitaige, エシタイゲ, Eshitaigi, エシタイギ, 投ゲル. *v.t.* To throw to. To cast to.

Eshitapka, エシタプカ, 肩ノ上ニ. *adv.* Upon the shoulders.

Eshitapka-ani, エシタプカアニ, 肩ニテ運ブ. *v.t.* To carry on the shoulders.

Eshitchiu-shirikomuru-kosamba, エシッチウシリコムルコサムバ, 烈シク仆ル、打チ仆サレ. *ph.* To fall heavily. To be knocked down (as in contest).

Eshittat-oseshke, エシッタツオセシケ, 歩ムトキニ踐ム木ナドガ割レル音スル. *v.i.* To make a noise of cracking and snapping as walking through dry twigs or reeds.

Echittauge, エチッタウゲ, 打切ル. *v.t.* To chop.

Eshkari, エシカリ, 取ル、摑ム. *v.t.* To catch (as a bird, animal or fish.)

Eshkari, エシカリ, 塞ガレタ. *v.i.* To be stopped up.

Eshkerimrim, エシケリムリム, Eshikerimrim, エシケリムリム, 片栗(カタクリ). *n.* Dog tooth violet. *Erythronium dens-canis, L.*

Eshna, エシナ, 嚔(クサメ)スル. *v.i.* To sneeze.

Eshochupu, エショチュプ, 饗應ヲ仕舞フ. *v.i.* To get up from a feast. To clear away the mats upon which visitors to a house have been sitting.

Eshokka, エショッカ, カハカザ.カ. *n.* A kind of fresh water fish. Bull-head. *Cottus pollux,* Gthr. **Syn:** **Pon chimakani. Pet kotchimakani.**

Eshokshoki, エショクショキ, 鳥ノ名. *n.* Any kind of wood-pecker.

Eshorokanni, エショロカンニ, ミツメ ウツギ. *n.* *Staphylea Bumalda,* *S. et Z.*

Eshoshipi, エショシビ, 再婚スレ. *v.t.* To remarry.

Eshouk, エショウク, 懸買スレ. *v. t.* To buy upon trust. · To contract a debt. **Syn: Shose kara.**

Eshpa, エシバ, ⎫ 忽セニ思フ、冷淡ニ
Eshipa, エシバ, ⎭ 扱フ. *v. i.* To treat with indifference. To ignore. See *Eshipa.*

Eshunangara, エシュナンガラ, 輕ク スレ. *v. t.* To lighten. **Syn:** **Pekereka.**

Eshunangare, エシュナンガレ, 輕ク サセレ. *v.t.* To cause to lighten.

Eshunge, エシュンゲ, 詐ル、偽ル. *v.t.* To lie to.

Eshungere, ⎫ 信セヌ、詐リト思フ.
エシュンゲレ, ⎬ *v.t.* To disbelieve.
Eishungere, ⎪ To consider false.
エイシュンゲレ, ⎭
Syn: Eumbipka.

Eshopki, エショブキ, 坐チ遁グル. *v.t.* To make room for another to sit down.

Esonki, エソンキ, 損失スル. *v.t.* To lose as in a bargain.

Esonnere, エソンネレ, 確メレ. *v. t.* To confirm.

Eshuyeshuye, エシュイェシュイェ, モ ノチ搖ル. *v.t.* To waive.

Esoine, エソイ子, 大便ニ行ク. *v. i.* To go to ease one'self.

Esoine-ru, エソイチル, 便所. *n.* A water-closet. (This is a polite word).

Esoro, エソロ, 下ダレ. *v. i.* To descend. To go down (as a stream). To go down towards the lower end of anything. As: —*Pet esoro san,* "to descend to the mouth of a river." **Syn:** **San.**

Esoro, エソロ, ⎫長サ. *n.* Length.
Esoroho, エソロホ, ⎭ **Syn: Epesh.**

Esoshipi, エソシビ, 亡兄弟ノ妻チ娶ル. *v.t.* To take a deceased brother's widow to wife.

Esoye, エソイェ, 動搖スル. To roll about.

Esum (*sing*)**, エスム,** ⎫溺死スル.*v.i.*
Esumba (*pl*)**, エスムバ,** ⎭ To be drowned. To drown.

Esum-wa-rai (*sing*)**, エスムワライ,** 溺死シタル. *adj.* Drowned.

Esumba-wa-rai (*pl*)**, エスムバワラ イ,** 溺死シタレ. *adj.* Drowned.

Esumka, エスムカ, 溺死サセレ. *v. t.* To drown.

Esumka-wa-rai, エスムカワライ, 溺 死スル. *v.i.* To be drowned.

Esumka-wa-raige, エスムカワライ ゲ, 溺死サセレ. *v.t.* To drown.

Etakasure, エタカスレ, ヨリモ、甚ダ、 例セバ、タンゲルエタカスレウェンゲン ネ、此ノ人ハ甚ダ悪シキ人ナリ. *adv.* and *adj.* Than. Surpassing. Very. Too much. Surpassingly. Exceedingly. As:—*Tan guru etakasure wen gun'ne,* "this is an exceedingly bad person." *Nei*

guru etaksure nishpa ne guru,
" that is a very rich person."

Etakupbe-ne, エタクブベ子, 球、毬.
n. A ball. **Syn : Takuchi.**

Etamani, エタマ二, 途ヲ掃フ. *v.t.*
To clear the way to a place.
To clear a space as with a
sword.

Etamba, エタムバ, 此處. *adv.* This
way. Here.

Etamba-un, エタムバウン, 此處. *adv.*
This way. Here. **Syn : Ekush-
un.**

Etara, エタラ, 突込ム. *v. t.* To
pierce. To stick into. To stand
out of. To hit. **Syn : Eotara.**

Etaraka, エタラカ, 粗末二、目的ナキ.
例セバ、エタラカイタク、無駄ナ話.
adj. and *adv.* Without purpose.
Having no object in view. Unnecessarily. Aimlessly. Carelessly. Careless. Aimless. Rashly. As:—*Etaraka itak,* " aimless
talk." *Iteki etaraka nepka kar'an,*
" do nothing carelessly." *Iteki
etaraka un nishomap yan,* " do
not be unnecessarily anxious
about us."

Etaraka-iki, エタラカイキ, 粗末二ナ
ス. *v.t.* To do carelessly. To do
by chance. To do rashly. As :
—*Etaraka iki ku ak aige, chikap
ku chotcha,* " though I shot carelessly I hit a bird."

Etaraka-iki-kara, エタラカイキカラ,
粗末二ナス. *v.t.* To do carelessly.
To slight.

Etaraka-kara, エタラカカラ, 輕ンズ
ル. *v.t.* To slight.

Etaraka-ki, エタラカキ, 徒費スル、注
意セヌ、例セバ、イテキタンアエバエタ

ラカキ、此ノ食物ヲ費スナカレ. *v. t.*
To waste. To be careless of.
As:—*Iteki tan aep etaraka ki,*
" do not waste this food." **Syn :
Koatcha.**

Etaraka-no, エタラカノ, 忽カ二、
徒費スレ. *adv.* Slightingly. Carelessly. Unnecessarily.

Etaratara, エタラタラ, モノ二就イ
テ立ツ. *v.i.* To stick out of.

Etasa, エタサ, 横切リテ. *adv.* Across.
Back again. Athwart. From
one to the other.

Etashpa, エタシバ, 横切レ. *adv.*
Across. Athwart. *Pl. of Etasa.*

Etashpe, エタシベ, 海馬. *n.* A sea-
lion. *Otaria stelleri, Less.*

Etashum, エタシュム, 疾フ. *v.t.* To
suffer with or from. As:—*Chikiri etashum,* " to suffer with a
bad leg."

Etashumbe, エタシュムベ, 病原. *n.*
A cause of illness.

Etaye, エタイェ, 引出ス、抜ク. *v. t.*
To draw out. To abduce. To
extract. To pull away from. To
pull off. As:—*Apa kotuk na, pon
no etaye yan,* " it is sticking to
the door, pull it away " (or "pull
it off.")

Etayetaye, エタイェタイェ, 引去レ、抜
ク. *v.t.* To pluck out. As :—*Tu-
yuk kishki etayetaye,* " he plucked
out two hairs from the deer."

Etere, エテレ, 期待スレ. *v. t.* To
wait. To wait for. **Syn : Ehuye.**

Eterekere, エテレケレ, 置ク. *v.t.*
To put on. To place. As:—
Ashiseturuka eterekere, " he put
it on his back."

Eteshkara, **エテシカラ**, 途ル. v.t. To send to. To send with a message.

Etesu, **エチス,** 上向ス レ. v.i. To
Eteshu, **エテシュ,** turn up. **Syn : Aemaka-tesu.**

Etesure, **エテスレ**, 上向ニ ス ル. v.t. To make turn up. To cause to glance off.

Eteun, **エテウン**, 此處. adv. Here. This way.

Eteye, **エテイ**エ, 塞グ (單數). v.t. To choke.

Eteyepa, **エテイ**エバ, 塞グ (複數). v.t. To choke. (pl.)

Eto, **エト,** ナキフタコウジュ. n.
Edo, **エド,** A kind of edible
Endo, **エンド,** herb. (see Endo).

Etoi, **エトイ**, 禿ゲタル、赤裸ナル. adj. Bald. **Syn : Otop-sak.**

Etoitoshpa, **エトイトシバ**, 萌出ル. v.i. To sprout out from the earth.

Etoikoninde, **エトイコニンデ**, 爲シテ見ル. v.t. To assay.

Etoipukka, **エトイブッカ**, 土チ蔽フ、例セバ、エモエトイブツカ、芋チ植ル. v.t. To earth up. To put earth to. As :—Emo etoipukka, " to earth up potatoes." **Syn : Otoipukka.**

Etoita, **エトイタ**, 植エル、播種スル. v.t. To plant. To sow.

Etok, **エトク**, 源. n. Source. Origin. Head. Top. Limit. As :—Pet etok, " the source of a river." Hoka etok, " the head of a fire-place."

Etoko, **エトコ**, 以前ニ、前面ニ. adv. Before. Formerly. Previously.

In front of. As :—En etoko, " in front of me."

Etoko-an, **エトコアン**, 以前ノ、例セバ、エトコアンオヌマン、一昨日. adj. Before. As :—Etoko an onuman, " the day before yesterday." **Syn : Hoshiki.**

Etoko-aseshke, **エトコアセシケ,** 妨グ、防グ. v.t. To
Etoko-atuye, **エトコアツイ**エ, prevent. To hinder. To forbid.

Etoko-kush, **エトコクシ**, 前ニ進ム. v.i. To go forward. To cross in front of one.

Etoko-numne, **エトコヌム子**, 待伏セ ス ル. v.i. To lie in wait. **Syn : Etoko-ush.**

Etokota, **エトコタ,** 前面ニ、以前ニ.
Etokta, **エトクタ,** adv. In front of. At the head of. Before. Previously.

Etoko-ush, **エトコウシ**, 待伏セスル. v.i. To lie in wait. **Syn : Etoko-numne.**

Etokoushbe, **エトコウシベ,** 前ニアルモノ、例セバ、
Etokushbe, **エトクシベ,** ペッエトクシベ、水源ニ在ルモノ. n. Things at the source or head of anything or place. As :—Pet etokushbe, " things at the river's source." (sometimes used as a metaphor for " mountains.")

Etokooiki, **エトコオイキ**, 準備スル. v.t. To prepare. To make ready. To be at the point of death. As :—Rai etokooiki, " to be at the point of death."

Etokoseshke, **エトコセシケ**, 防グ、妨ゲル、禁ズル. v.t. To hinder. To

prevent. To forbid. To stop. **Syn: Etokotuye.**

Etokotuye, エトコツイェ, 防ケ、妨ケ ル、築スル. *v.t.* To hinder. To prevent. To forbid. To stop. To circumvent. **Syn: Etoko-seshke.**

Etokoush, エトコウシ, 待伏スル. *v.i.* To lie in a wait. **Syn: Etoko numne.**

Etokoush, エトコウシ, Etokush, エトクシ, 爲サントス、例セバ、クキエ トコウシ、我ハナスベシ *Auxil. v.* About to do. As:—*Ku ki etokoush,* "I am about to do it." *Oman eto-kush,* "he is about to go."

Etokush, エトクシ, 用意スル、豫備ス ル. *auxil. v.* To get ready. To make preparation. About to do. With the words *nekon a ka,* "must." As:—*Nekon a ka akara etokush ruwe ne,* "I must do it somehow or other."

Etomka, エトムカ, 上ニ照ラス. *v.t.* To make to shine upon. **Syn: Kotomka.**

Etomne, エトムネ, 好漁ノ又ハ、好獵ノ. *adj.* Successful in hunting or fishing.

Etomo, エトモ, 研ガク、習フ. *v.t.* To smooth out. To arrange. To polish.

Etomochine, エトモチネ, 愚鈍ノ、迷 蒙ノ. *adj.* Stupid. Silly. Imbecile. Absurd.

Etomochine-no, エトモチネノ, 蒙愚 ニ. *adv.* Stupidly. Absurdly.

Etomochinep, エトモチネプ, 背理、 妄誕、痴漢. *n.* An absurdity. A stupid person.

Etonne, エトンネ, 嫉フ、憎ム. *v.t.* To envy. To hate. **Syn: Etunne.**

Etopara, エトパラ, 追ヒ出ス. *v.t.* To get rid of. To drive out. To send out of the way. As:— *Chisei orowa no etopara,* "he drove him out of the house."

Etoranne, エトランネ, 爲スコトヲ好 マヌ. *v.t.* To dislike to do. Not caring to do.

Etoro, エトロ, 鼻汁. *n.* Mucus.

Etoroki, エトロキ, 鼾ヲカク. *v.i.* To snore.

Etoropo, エトロポ, 水母. *n.* Jelly fish. Medusa. **Syn: Tonru-chep. Humbe-etoro.**

Etororat, エトロラツ, 鼻汁. *n.* Mu-cus from the nose.

Etororatki, エトロラツキ, 鼻汁ヂ垂ラ ス. *v.i.* To have a running at the nose.

Etororatkip, エトロラツキプ, 鼻垂、 ハナタラシ. *n.* A dirty nosed person.

Etoru, エトル, 鐘、例セバ、エトルフミ アシ、鐘ガ鳴ツテオル. *n.* A bell. As:—*Etoru humi ash,* "the bell rings." *Etoru humi ashte,* "to ring the bell."

Etoruratki-nonno, エトルラツキノン ノ, ナルコユリ. *n.* Solomon's Seal, (lit: "bell hanging flower.") *Polygonatum giganteum, Dietr, var. falcatum, Maxim.* In some places the "lily of the valley."

Ette, エッテ, 與ヘル、手渡ス. *v.t.* To give. To hand over. To assign.

Etu, エツ, Etuhu, エツフ, 鼻、柄、鳥ノ嘴、刃物ノ尖先. *n.* The nose. A spout. A handle. The bill of a bird. The point of a knife or sword. As :—*Etu kapke guru,* " a person with a flat nose." *Etu kara,* " to clean the nose." *Etu kemnu,* "a bleeding at the nose." *Etu mekka,* "the bridze of the nose." *Etu mekka riri,* " to be proud." *Etu mesu,* " to cut off the nose," (as in punishment for crime). *Etuni,* " to blow the nose." *Etu piruba,* " to wipe the nose." *Etu pesh ingara,* "to look down the nose." **Syn : Chietu.**

Etu,
エツ, 鼻. *n.* A spout. A handle.
Echi, **Syn : Echi. Chietu.**
エチ,

E-tup, エツブ, 一ット 半分. *adj.* One and a half.

Etuchikore-itak, エツチコレイタク, 怒言. *n.* Words of anger. Angry words. **Syn : Irushka itak.**

Etuchikere-itak-ki, エツチケレイタクキ, 怒リテ言フ. *v. i.* To speak angrily.

Etuchikereppo, エツチケレッポ, 廿日鼠. *n.* A mouse.

Etuiriten-amam, エツイリテンアマム, 稗ノ類. *n.* A kind of millet.

Etukange, エツカンゲ, 列ベル. *v.t.* To set in order.

Etukarip, エツカリプ, 口籠、口網、(犬馬ナドノ). *n.* A muzzle.

Etu-kishima, エツキシマ, 驚ク、愕ク、(直譯：鼻ヲ摘ム). *v.i.* To be surprised (lit : to seize the nose).

Etu-masmasa, エツマスマサ, 嗅ク. *v.t.* To smell. To sniffle. **Syn : Hura nu.**

Etupe, エツベ, 水鼻. *n.* Drops of water sometimes seen hanging

from the nose. As :—*Etupe-chikke,* " a running at the nose."

Etupechikka, エツペチッカ, 鼻垂ル. *v.i.* To have a running at the nose.

Etupe-chikkap, エツペチッカプ, 鼻垂、ハナタラシ. *n.* A person with a dirty nose. A person having drops of water hanging from the nose.

Etupui, エツプイ, 鼻孔. *n.* The nostrils.

Etuk, エツク, 突キ出ツル、出ツル. *v.i.* To extend beyond. To come out. To protrude. To sprout forth. As :—*Ruye kasu no etuk,* " it extends beyond the line."

Etukepushbe, エツケプシベ, 鳥ノ嘴. *n.* A bird's bill.

Etukka, エツッカ, 出ス. *v.t.* To push out. As :—*Mokoriri kirawe etukka ruwe ne,* " the snail pushes out its horns."

Etukkare, エツッカレ, 突キ出ス. *v.t.* To push out (as the head out of a window).

Etumam, エツマム, 身體. *n.* The body. As :—*Etumam noshke,* " the waist or middle of the body." **Syn : Shituman.**

Etumamkashi, エツマムカシ, 身ニ着ケル、(衣ヲ着ル如ク)、帯スル. *v.i.* To have upon the body. To be clothed with (as with armour). To wear round the waist).

Etumekka, エツメッカ, 鼻梁. *n.* The bridge of the nose.

Etumekkarire, エツメッカリレ, 高慢スル、鼻ヲ高クスル. *v.i.* To be proud (lit : to carry the nose high).

Etun, エツン, 借ル. *v.t.* To borrow.

Etun, エツン, 二人. *n.* Two persons. **Syn: Tu niu.**

Etunangara, エツナンガラ, 逢フ. *v.t.* To meet.

Etu-ni, エツニ, 鼻ヲ拭フ. *v.t.* To wipe the nose.

Etunip, エツニプ, 口嘴ノアル器具. A vessel with a spout. A basin with a spout. A cup with a spout to it. **Syn: Etunnup. Etunup.**

Etunne, エツンネ, 憎ム、好マヌ. *v.t.* To abhor. To hate. To despise. To reject. To dislike. To abominate. To be unable. As:— *Nei ainu ku etunne,* "I dislike that person." *Mokoro etunne,* "to be unable to sleep." *Ibe etunne* "to dislike to eat." **Syn: Akowen.**

Etunne-i, エツンチイ, 倦厭、憎悪. *n.* Abhorrence. Hatred.

Etunnup, エツンヌプ, 口嘴ノアル器具. *n.* A vessel with a spout. A cup with a spout to it. A basin with a spout. **Syn: Etunip.**

Etu-pe, エツペ, 鼻汁. *n.* Nose water.

Etu-petneka, エツペツチカ, 鼻汁ヲ垂ラス. *ph.* A running at the nose.

Etu-pi, エツピ, 鼻汁. *n.* Mucus from the nose.

Etu-noyanoya, エツノヤノヤ, 鼻ヲ摩スル. *v.i.* To rub the nose.

Etunup, エツヌプ, 口嘴ノアル器具. *n.* See *Etunnup.*

Etu-pui, エツプイ, 鼻孔. *n.* The nostrils. **Syn: Etupuike.**

Eturamkoro, エツラムコロ, 卑怯ナル. *adj.* Cowardly. **Syn: Katchak koro. Ishitoma-tektek.**

Eturi-echiu, エツリエチウ, 支フレ、撐スレ. *v.t.* To support. To shove up.

Eturi-echiu, エツリエチウ, 悸トカス. *v.i.* To start back at anything. **Syn: Eshishi.**

Eturu, エツル, 迄. *adv.* As far as. As much as. Unto. To. As:— *En uturu pakno,* "as much as I."

Eturupak, エツルパク, 同ジホドノ. *adj.* To be equal. Equal. **Syn: Uwepak.**

Eturupakno, エツルパクノ, 間ニ、迄. *adv.* Whilst. During. As far as. To the extent of.

Eturupak-shomoki, エツルパクショモキ, 匹敵セザル、劣レレ. *adj.* Unequal.

Etushingari, エツシンガリ, 鼻ヲ摩スル. *v.i.* To rub the nose with the palm of the hand and to sniffle. Also, to make a snorting noise with the nose. To snort or grunt (as a pig).

Etushmak, エツシマク, 競フ. *v.t.* To strive with. To compete.

Etushnatki, エツシナツキ, 貫キ通ス. *v.t.* To permeate. To fill with. To extend to. To gush forth. As:—*Iruka ne. koro tonoto hura chisei upshoro etushnatki,* "in a short time the smell of the wine permeated the whole house."

Etushpitchire, エツシピッチレ, 蓄フル、保存スレ. *v.t.* To reserve.

Etushtek, エツシテク, 愚カナル、思慮ナキ. *adj.* Foolish. Thoughtless.

Etushtek, エツシテク, 急ギチ、動シデ. *v.i.* To be in a great hurry. To be excited. To get excited.

Etushtek-no, エツシテクノ, 愚ニ、急 ニ. *adv.* Foolishly. Hurriedly Thoughtlessly.

Etutanne-kikiri, エツタン子キキリ, 蚊. *n.* A mosquito (lit: long nosed insect).

Etutkopak, エツッコパク, 別チ告ゲレ. *v.t.* To bid farewell.

Etututturi, エツツッツリ, 嗅ゲ. *v. i.* To snuff. To snif at.

Eu, エウ, 兩親. *n.* Parents.

Euainukoro, エウアイヌコロ, 敬フ. *v.t.* To honour. To respect. To reverence. **Syn: Kooripak.**

Eubitte, エウビッテ, 結ビ目. *n.* A knot. **Syn: Eukobitte.**

Eubitte-kara, 結ビ目スレ. *v.t.* To
エウビッテカラ, knot. To tie a
Eubitte-ki, knot.
エウビッテキ,

Euchike, エウチケ, 出來ナイ、仕事チ 厭フ. *v.i.* To be unable, awkward or incapable. To feel disinclined to do a thing.

Euchoroshte, エウチョロシテ, 傍ニ 置カレ、. *v. i.* To be placed by the side of.

Eukashiu, エウカシウ, 助ケ合フ. *n.* *v.t.* To help one another.

Euko, エウコ, 駝背(モムシ). *n.* A hunchback.

Euko, エウコ, 共ニ結メレル. *v.i.* To be joined together. To conjoin.

Eukobitte, エウコビッテ, 結目. *n.* A knot.

Eukobitte-kara, 結フ. *v.t.* To tie a
エウコビッテカラ, knot. To knot.
Eukobitte-ki,
エウコビッテキ, **Syn: Eubitte**
kara. Eubitte ki.

Eukoiki, エウコイキ, 喧嘩スル、爭鬪 スル. *v.t.* To fight together.

Eukonda, エウコンダ, 木ノ又. *n.* The fork of a tree.

Eukoitak, エウコイタク, 告知スル、言 フ. *v. t.* To tell to. To speak with.

Eukopa, エウコパ, 扭(子ザル)、例セバ、 クイェイタクエウコパ、私ノ言葉チ扭 ル. *v.t.* To wrest. As:—*Ku ye itak eukopa,* "he wrests my words."

Eukopashte, エウコパシテ, 撑フレ. *v.t.* To shore up. To keep from falling.

Eukopi, エウコビ, 分ルヽ、離間スレ. *v.i.* To part asunder. To separate. To divide.

Eukopi-eukopi, エウコビエウコビ, 散 亂スレ. *v.i.* To scatter (as frightened animals).

Eukopi-no, エウコビノ, 分レテ、別々 ニ. *adv.* Dividedly. Separately.

Eukopire, エウコビレ, 分ケル、別々ニ ズレ. *v.t.* To part asunder. To separate. To divide.

Eukopi-wa, エウコビワ, 分レテ、別々 ニ. *adv.* Separately. Dividedly. As:—*Eukopi wa oman,* "to go separately."

Eukoramkoro, エウコラムコロ, 相談 スル、協議スレ. *v.i.* To take counsel together. To hold a consultation. To consult together.

Eukoyairap, エウコヤイラブ, 譽メレ. 頌揚スレ. *v.t.* To praise.

Eukot, エウコツ, 姦淫スル. *v.i.* To have illicit intercourse.

Eukotama, エウコタマ, 共ニ、合セテ. *adv.* Altogether. Together.

Eukotama-no, エウコタマノ, 合セテ. *adv.* Unitedly.

Eukote, エウコテ, 結ビ合ハス. *v.t.* To tie together.

Eukoturire, エウコツリレ, 迄ニ伸バス. *v.t.* To hold out to.

Eukoyupekere, エウコユペケレ, 論ズル. *v.t.* To discuss. To reason about.

Eumarapto-koro, エウマラプトコロ, 祭ヲ行フ. *v.i.* To hold a feast.

Eumashnu, エウマシヌ, 集ムル、蓄ヘル. *v.t.* To collect. To store up. To put away.

Eumashtekka, エウマシテッカ, 充ツル. *v.i.* To fill. To become very abundant. As :— *Chep ne manup pet iwaro shoka eumashtekka,* "all the rivers were filled with fish."

Eumbipka, エウムビブカ, 信セヌ. *v.t.* To disbelieve.

Eumina, エウミナ, 笑フ. *v.t.* To laugh at. To deride. (*pl*).

Euminare, エウミナレ, 笑ハセル. *v.t.* To make laugh. (*pl*).

Eumontasa, エウモンタサ, 酬ユレ、返ス. *v.t.* To do in return. To render. **Syn : Hekiru.**

Eumpirima, エウムピリマ, 裏切(ウラギリ)スレ、内應スレ. *v.t.* To betray. To make known secretly.

Eun, エウン, ニ、迄. *prep.* To. Unto.

Eun, エウン, 彼ニ. *prep.* To him. To her. To it. At him. Towards him. As :— *Nei guru eun shomo shinuma nukara,* "he did not look at. him."

Eun, エウン, 刺ス、入レル、例セバ、タムシリカエサン、刀チサヤニ刺ス. *v.i. & adj.* To stick in. Sticking in.

Containing. To have. To possess. To be in. To be. As :— *Tam shirika eun,* "the sword is in the sheath."

Eun, エウン, 悪ク感ズレ. *v.t.* To affect in a bad way.

Eunbe, エウンベ, 悪ク感ズルモノ、兇兆. *n.* Something which affects one in a bad way. An ill-omen.

Eungerai, エウンゲライ, 受取ル、貰フ. *v.t.* To receive (as a present). To accept. To take (as alms). **Syn : Ahupkara.**

Eungeraite, エウンゲライテ, 與ヘレ. *v.t.* To give (as alms). To cause to accept. **Syn : Ahupkare.**

Eunini-an-guru, エウニニアングル, **Euninu-an-guru,** エウニヌアングル, 饗應ノ客. *ph.* Guests at a party.

Eunkashi-no, エウンカシノ, 熱心ニ、額ニ. *adv.* Earnestly. Mostly. **Syn : Yokkata.**

Eunkeshke, エウンケシケ, 責メル. *v.t.* To persecute.

Euomare, エウオマレ, 逢フ、歡迎スル. *v.t.* To meet. To welcome. To put in upon.

Euomashnu, エウオマシヌ, 包ム、荷造リスレ. *v.t.* To pack up.

Eupakte, エウバクテ, 果タス、完成スレ. *v.t.* To complete. To fill up.

Eupeka, エウペカ, 向ヒ合フテ坐ス. *v.i.* To face one another. As : —*Eupekarok,* "to sit facing one another."

Eupoppokinne, エウポッポキンチ, 結合シタレ. *adj.* Joined together.

Eupshire, エウブシレ, 反覆スレ. *v.t.* To turn bottom upwards. To turn upside down.

Euramtekuk, エウラムテクク, 襲フ、追求スレ. *v. t.* To attack. To pursue.

Eurarapa, エウララバ, 壓迫スル、雍塞スレ. *v. i.* To press upon. To crowd upon.

Eure, エウレ, 與ヘレ. *v.t.* To give. To bestow.

Euruki, エウルキ, 呑ミ込ム. *v.t.* To swallow.

**Eusama, エウサマ,
Eusamanu, エウサマウン,
Eusamamba, エウサマムバ,** 二重. *adj.* Double.

Eush, エウシ, ヘ行ク、ヨリ來ル. *v.i.*
Eushi, エウシ, To come to. To go to. As:—*Nei kotan attomsama eush,* "he came as far as that village."

Eush, エウシ, 刺ス、貫ク. *v.t.* To
Eushi, エウシ, pierce. To stick on or into. To set up (as a post).

Eutashpa, エウタシバ, 為シ合フ. *v.t.* To do one to another.

Eutastasa, エウタスタサ, 口答ヘスル. *v.t.* To contradict. **Syn : Itastasa.**

Eutchike, エウッチケ, 為スコトヲ好マヌ、例セバ、イェエウッチケ、話シタクナイ. *v. i.* To dislike to do a thing. As:—*Ye eutchike,* "he dislikes to tell." **Syn : Eiramnukari.**

Euturunne, エウツルンチ, 下坐ニ. *adv.* Towards the lower end of the hearth.

Euyaikopuntek, エウヤイコブンテク, 共ニ喜フ. *v. i.* To take mutual delight in. To rejoice over together.

Euyepnu, エウィェブヌ, 相談スル、同意スレ. *v.i.* To hold council. To agree. **Syn : Eukoramkoro.**

Ewak, エワク, 家ヘ歸ヘル. *v.i.* To
Riwak, リワク, go home. To return to one's home.

Ewakokomke, エワココムケ, 上ニ向イテ、曲ガレル. *adj.* Turning upwards. Bent upwards.

Ewakshiroroge, エワクシロロゲ, 罨キ場. *ph.* A place in which anything is (heard only in traditions). **Syn : Otta an i.**

Ewara, エワラ, 口チ以テ吹ク. *v. t.* To blow with the mouth. **Syn : Uku.**

Ewara-ewara, エワラエワラ, 口ニテ吹ク. *v.t.* An intensified form of *ewara,* "to blow with the mouth."

Ewekatkara, エウェカツカラ, 試ミレ. *v.t.* To tempt to do a thing. As:—*Tonoto ewekatkara,* "to tempt to drink wine."

Ewekatu, エウェカツ, 共ニ. *adv.* Mutually.

Ewen, エウェン, 損失スル. *v.t.* To lose (as in a bargain). To do with difficulty. To be unable to do properly. To do but poorly.

Ewende, エウェンデ, 敗ル、壊ス. *v.t.* To spoil.

Ewonne, エウォンチ, 手足チ洗フ. *v.t.*
Eonne, エオンチ, To wash the face and hands. **Syn : Yashke.**

Ewonne-wakka, エウォンチワッカ, 洗ヒ水. *n.* Washing water.

Eyai, エヤイ, 汝自身. *rel. pro.* Yourself. Your own.

Eyai, エヤイ, 拜スル、例セバ、エヤイカムイ、拜スベキ神. *v. t.* To worship. As:—*Eyai kamui,* "the gods who are worshipped."

Eyaiashishka, エヤイアシシカ, 悔ヒ改ムル. *v.t.* To repent of a thing.

Eyaichichitakte, エヤイチチタクテ, 白狀スレ、懺悔スレ. *v.i.* To acknowledge. To confess.

Eyaiekatu-wen, エヤイエカツウェン, 失禮スレ. *v.t.* To insult. **Syn: Osamatki itak.**

Eyaiepirikare, エヤイエピリカレ, 利得スル、儲ケレ. *v.t.* To gain through one's own exertions. To do good to one's self.

Eyaieshikorap, エヤイエシコラプ, 惱ム. *v.t.* To suffer from a disease. As:—*Chikiri eyaieshikorap,* "to suffer with a bad leg." **Syn: Nikuruki.**

Eyaieshinge, エヤイエシンゲ, 自分ノモノト詐レ、僭越スル. *v.t.* To arrogate. To claim falsely.

Eyaihaitare, エヤイハイタレ, 避クレ. *v.t.* To avoid (lit : to cause one's self to avoid). **Syn: Eyaishishire.**

Eyaihannokkara, エヤイハンノッカラ,
Eyaihonnokkara, エヤイホンノッカラ, 學プ. *v.t.* To learn. **Syn: Eyaipakashnu. Chakoko. Yaieashkaire.**

Eyaikatanu, エヤイカタヌ, 敬フ. *v.t.* To respect.

Eyaikatekara, エヤイカテカラ, 戀ヒ煩ヒスレ. *v.i.* To be love-sick.

Eyaikoemaka, エヤイコエマカ, 棄テル. *v.t.* To throw away. To abandon.

Eyaikopuntek, エヤイコプンテク, 喜プ. *v.t.* To rejoice over.

Eyaikoramkoro, エヤイコラムコロ, 爲スコトヲ翼フ. *v.i.* To desire to do. As:—*Toi kara eyaikoramkoro,* "he desires to do his garden."

Eyaikoshiramshui (s), エヤイコシラムシュイ, 思フ、考フ. *v.i.* To think. To consider.

Eyaikokoshiramshuiba, (pl), エヤイココシラムシュイバ, 思フ、考フ. *v.i.* Same as above.

Eyaimonpok-tushmak, エヤイモンポクツシマク, 忙ハシ. *v.i.* To hasten to do anything. To work hard.

Eyainu, エヤイヌ, 感ズル、經驗スル. *v.i.* To experience. To feel.

Eyainu, エヤイヌ, 壞ス. *v.t.* To spoil.

Eyaipakashnu, エヤイパカシヌ, 習フ、自ラ制スレ. *v.t.* To learn. To restrain one's self. **Syn: Eyaihannokkara.**

Eyaipaye, エヤイパイェ, 懺悔スレ. *v.t.* To confess.

Eyaipushi, エヤイプシ, 白狀スル、懺悔スル. *v.t.* To acknowledge. To confess.

Eyaipuship, エヤイプシプ, 白狀スルコト、懺悔スルコト. *n.* A confession. An acknowledgment.

Eyairamatte, エヤイラマッテ, 注意シテ狙フ. *v.t.* To take careful aim.

Eyairamatte, エヤイラマッテ, 忍フ. *v.t.* To endure. To suffer. To be patient over. **Syn: Yaishiporore.**

Eyairamikashure, エヤイラミカシュレ, 妬ム、羨ム. *v.t.* To envy. To desire to surpass. **Syn: Ukeshkean.**

**Eyairamkashure, エヤイラムカシュ
レ,** 競爭スル、努力スレ. *v.i.* To endeavour to defeat. To strive with.

**Eyairamkikkara, エヤイラムキッカ
ラ,** 眠フ、拒ム. *v.t.* To refuse to take.

Eyairamkuru, エヤイラムクル, 欲ス
レ. *v.t.* To have a desire for.
To wish to obtain. To try to
get hold of.

**Eyairamkuru-shitotkere, エヤイラ
ムクルシトツケレ,** 取ラント試ムル.
v.t. To endeavour to obtain. As:
—*Nei shintoko ku eyairamkuru shitotkere,* "I will endeavour to
obtain those treasures."

Eyairamnuina, エヤラムヌイナ, 葬ル、
埋メル. *v.t.* To bury. **Syn:**
Ueyairamnuina.

Eyairanniukes, エヤイランニウケス,
殆ンド醉タレ. *adj.* Nearly in-
toxicated.

Eyairenga, エヤイレンガ, 好ム、喜バ
セル. *v.t.* To like. To cheer.
To be pleased with. To pay
respects to. To rejoice over.
Syn: Enupetne.

**Eyairenga-enupetnep, エヤイレン
ガエヌペツチブ,** 好物. *n.* A thing
acceptable. Anything one is
pleased with.

**Eyaisambepokash, エヤイサムベポ
カシ,** 憐レナレ. *adj.* Pitiable.

**Eyaisambepokashte, エヤイサムベ
ポカシテ,** 憐レニスル. *v.t.* To
make pitiable.

Eyaisarama, エヤイサラマ, 他人ニ爲
サレ. *v.t.* To give to another
to do.

Eyaishikarunde, エヤイシカルンデ,
思ヒ起ス. *v.i.* To recall to mind.

Eyaishiknuina, エヤイシクヌイナ,
目ヲ蔽フ. *v.i.* To cover the eyes.

Eyaishishire, エヤイシシレ, 避クレ.
v.t. To avoid. To wrest (as
words). As:—*Kotan eyaishishire,*
"to avoid a town." *Nei guru
ku ye itak eyaishishire ruwe ne,*
"he wrests my words."

Eyaitoki, エヤイトキ, 驚カス. *v.t.*
To alarm.

Eyaitompuni, エヤイトムブニ, 馬鹿
ニスル. *v.t.* To make a fool of.
Syn: Eoyaitak.

Eyaitupa, エヤイツパ, 好ンデ爲ル.
adj. Willing.

Eyaituba, エヤイツパ,⎫切望スル、欲
Eyaitupa, エヤイツパ,⎰ スレ、希フ.
v.i. To be eager to do. To desire.
To wish. To be ambitious of
doing.

Eyaitubap, エヤイツパブ,⎫欲スル人、
Eyaitupap, エヤイツパブ,⎰目的. *n.*
One desirous of doing. One eager
to do. An object. Something
one aims at.

Eyaitupekare, エヤイツペカレ, 節制
セレ. *adj.* Abstemious.

Eyaiyattasa, エヤイヤッタサ, 呈スル、
與フ. *v.t.* To offer (as wine and
inao to the gods).

Eyaiyukki, エヤイユッキ,⎫仕舞ツテ匿
Eyaiyupki, エヤイユブキ,⎰ ク. *v. t.*
To set on one side. As:—*En
gusu nei ambe eyaiyupki yan,*
"place that on one side for me."

Eyam, エヤム, 注意深キ、其キ. *adj.*
Careful. Well. **Syn: Ehatatne.**

Eyambe, エヤムベ, 注意深キ人. *n.*
A careful person.

Eyamno, エヤムノ, 謹ンデ、其ク. *adv.*
Carefully. Well.

Eyanu, エヤヌ, 敗ル、壞ス. *v.t.* To spoil. **Syn : Eannu. Eyainu.**

Eyapkire, エヤプキレ, 捨レ、棄レ. *v.t.* To cast away.

Eyapte, エヤプテ, 六ケ敷キヤウニスレ. *v.t.* To render difficult.

Eyasara, エヤサラ, 他人ニサセレ. *v.t.* To get done by another person.

Eyasara, エヤサラ, 尖ラス、研グ. *v.t.* To sharpen. ¡ As :—*Noko eyasara,* " to sharpen a saw."

Eyaske, エヤスケ, 割レテ. *adv.* Cracked.

Eyayapte, エヤヤプテ, 爲スチ好マヌ、經驗ナキ. *v.t.* and *v.i.* To be in-experienced. To dislike to do. To be unable to do through inexperience. To feel troubled about anything. As :—*Ku eyayapte gusu ku kara eaikap,* "I cannot do it for I have had no experience." *Nei ambe uk eyayapte,* "I do not like to accept it."

Eyayattasa, エヤヤッタサ, } 神ニ幣ト酒トヲ獻スレ.
Eyaitattasa, エヤイタッタサ, } *v.t.* To offer as *inao* and wine to the gods.

Eyeyapte, エイェヤプテ, 爲スチ好マヌ、經驗ナキ. *v.t.* and *v.i.* Same as *Eyayapte.*

Eyok, エヨク, 賣レ. *v. t.* To sell. **Syn : Eiyok.**

Eyokbe, エヨクベ, 賣品. *n.* Merchandise.

Eyoki, エヨキ, 止マレ. *v.i.* To stop. To cease.

Eyokire, エヨキレ, 止メレ. *v. t.* To stop.

Eyoko, エヨコ, 狙フ、待伏セスル. *v.t.* To take aim at. To stand ready to shoot at. To lie in wait for.

Eyokkot, エヨッコツ, 一步進ンデハ停ル. *v.i.* To go a little way and then stop. **Syn : Ashash.**

Eyomak, エヨマク, 屬ヲ解ク、棄ツレ. *v.t.* To send away. To discharge.

Eyomne, エヨムネ, 罰スル. *v.t.* To deter from doing something by punishment. To punish.

Eyongoro, エヨンゴロ, 待チ伏サスレ. *v. t.* To lie in wait for. As :— *Neko anak ne erum eyongoro wa hopiye kuni korachi an ruwe ne,* "the cat is lying in wait ready to spring upon the rat."

Eyukara, エユカラ, 眞似レ. *v. t.* To imitate. To mock. To do in the same way as another. **Syn : Ikoisamba.**

Eyukke, エユッケ, 蓄ヘル. *v. t.* To store up (as food). To take great care of. To use sparingly.

Eyukke-kishima, エユッケキシマ, 攫マリ着ク. *v.t.* To cling to.

F (フ).

The letter *f* resembles the true labial in sound, it being softer than the English labiodental *f*. It is always slightly aspirated as though, indeed, it were *h*. 此處ニ記サレタル f ハ眞ノ f ノ音ニ非ズシテ少シク h ニ似タリ

Fu, フ, 生、ナマ、例セバ、フアマム、生米、ナマゴメ. *adj.* Raw. Green. Uncooked. As:—*Fu amam*, "uncooked rice." *Fu kam*, "raw meat." *Fu ni*, "green wood."

Fuchi or **Huchi, フチ. フチ**, 火. *n.* Fire. **Syn: Abe. Unchi. Fuji.**

Fukashtaro, フカシタロ, 蒸ス. *v.t.* To put to soak. To steam. To cook by steaming (a very common word but of Japanese origin). **Syn: Sat-shuke.**

Fukinane, フキナ子, 常盤草、トキワグサ、青キ、緑（ミドリ）ナル. *n.* Evergreen grasses. *Adj.* Green.

Fukuru, フクル,
Pukuru, プクル, 手袋、袋. *n.* Gloves. A bag. A pocket.

Fura, フラ,
Hura, フラ, 香、香氣. *n.* A smell. Scent.

Fura-at, フラアツ, 臭氣ヲ發スル. *v.i.* To stink.

Fura-nu, フラヌ, 嗅グ. *v.t.* To smell.

Fura-wen, フラウェン, 惡臭、汚臭. *n.* A bad smell. A stench.

Furaye, フライェ, 洗フ、(單數). *v.t.* To wash. **Syn: Yashke. Oshopshopo.**

Furayeba, フライェバ, 洗フ、(複數). *v.t.* To wash (*pl. of furaye*).

Furayep, フライェプ, 沐浴. *n.* Ablutions. **Syn: Afuraye-i. Yashkep.**

Fure, フレ, 赤イ. *adj.* Red.

Fure-ai-ush-ni, フレアイウシニ, タチイチゴ、サンザシバイチゴ. *n.* *Rubus crataegifolius, Bunge.* Also called *Yuk-emauri* and *kamui-furep*.

Fure-chikap, フレチカプ, 鳥ノ名、(鴨ノ類). *n.* A kind of wild duck inhabiting the sea principally, but found in rivers during rough weather.

Fure-echinge, フレエチンゲ, アカウミカメ. *n.* A turtle. *Chelonia caouna, Wagl.*

Fure-hat, フレハツ, テツセンゴミシ. *n.* *Schizandra chinensis, Bail.*

Fureka, フレカ, 赤ク染メレ. *v.t.* To dye red.

Fure-kani, フレカニ, 銅. *n.* Copper.

Fure-kani-ikayop, フレカニイカヨプ, 銅飾リノ筒. *n.* A quiver ornamented with copper.

Furep, フレプ, シロバナヘビイチゴ. *n.* Wild strawberry. *Fragaria elatior, Ehrh.*

Furep, フレプ, 狐、キツ子、赤キモノ. *n.* A red thing of any kind. A fox.

Fureppo, フレッポ, エゾスクリ. *n.*

A wild red currant. *Ribes petraeum Wulf. var. tomentosum, Max.*

Furere, フレレ, 赤クスレ. *v.t.* To make red.

Fure-shiriki-o, フレシリキオ, 赤キ模様アル. *ph.* Having red patterns.

Fure-shiripuk, フレシリブク, 赤キ色ノアル魚. *n.* A kind of red-coloured rock-trout.

Fure-shisam, フレシサム, 外國人. *n.* Foreigners. Europeans or Americans. As :—*Fure shisam chip,* "a foreign ship."

Fure-soi, フレソイ, アカゾイ、キンキン、メヌケ. *n.* Name applied to several species of red-coloured rock fishes (*Sebastodes*).

Furetamkere, フレタムケレ, 電. *n.* Lightning. **Syn: Imeru.**

Fure-toi, フレトイ, 赤キ土. *n.* Clay.

Fure-tom, フレトム, 赤キ. *adj.* Red.

Furi, フリ, 大キナル鳥、(或人鷲ナリト云フ). *n.* A kind of very large bird said by some to be an eagle.

Furu, フル, } 小山、坂. *n.* A hill. An
Huru, フル, } acclivity.

Furu-an, フルアン, } 坂多キ、峭シキ. *adj.* Ac-
Huru-an, フルアン, } clivous.

Furu-kuru, フルクル, 晴レカカリタレ雨雲. *n.* A passing rain-cloud.

Furukap, フルカプ, }
Furukappo, フルカッポ, } 死体ノ皮骨、傳説ニ由レバ、フルカプハ昔ノ時ニ善キ食物ヲ指シテ日ノ事アリ、例セバ、チェプフルカッポ アイヌアエオレス、此人ハ美味ナル魚ニテ育テラレタリ. *n.*

The skin and bones of anything dead and decomposed. In legends furukap is sometimes used of good food, and may be translated by delicious ; thus :— *Chep furukappo ainu aeoresu,* "the man was brought up on delicious fish."

Fushko, フシコ, 古昔ノ、古キ. *adj.* Ancient. Antique. Old. Stale.

Fushko-ne, フシコ子, 昔ニ、古クナレ. *adv.* Anciently. Also *v.i.* To have become stale.

Fushko-okai, フシコオカイ, 昔ノ. 原始ノ. *adj.* Aboriginal. Old. Ancient.

Fushko-okai-utara, フシコオカイウタラ, 原人、古人. *n.* The ancients. Aborigines.

Fushkotoi, フシコトイ, 古キ. *adj.* Ancient. Old.

Fushkotoita, フシコトイタ, }
Hushkotoita, フシコトイタ, } 昔ニ、昔時. *adv.* Anciently. In ancient times.

Fushkotoi-wa, フシコトイワ, 昔カラ、幼少ノ時ヨリ. *adv.* From olden times. From early childhood.

Futtat or **Huttat,** フッタツ, フッタツ, クマザサ. *n.* Bamboo grass. Arundinaria.

Fushtotta, フシトッタ, 釣道具ヲ入レル袋. *n.* A skin bag used for carrying fishing tackle.

Fuyehe or **huyehe,** フイェヘ, 頬. *n.* The cheeks.

Fuyetok, フイェトク, }
Fuyetop, フイェトプ, } 笛. *n.* A flute.

Fuyetop-rekte, フイェトプレクテ, 笛ヲ吹ク. *v.i.* To play a flute.

H （ハ）.

Ha, ハ, 減ズル、退ク(潮ノ如ク). *v.i.* To ebb (as the tide). To diminish. To grow less (as water in a river). To recede. To decrease in size or volume. To grow less (as in boiling). To go down a river into the sea (as fish). To withdraw.

Haaure, ハアウレ, 足面(アシノカフ). *n.* The instep.

Habo, ハボ, 母. *n.* Mother. **Syn : Unu. Totto.**

Hachako, ハチャコ, 赤子. *n.* A baby. **Syn : Tennep.**

Hacham, ハチャム, サクラドリ. *n.* Starling.

Hachimaki, ハチマキ, 手拭 (頭ヲ裹ムニ用コ.). *n.* A towel. (*Jap*).

Hachire, ハチレ, 仆ス. *v.t.* To make fall down. To make tumble. **Syn : Hokushte.**

Hachiri, ハチリ, 仆ル、(單數). *v.i.* (*Sing*). To fall down. To tumble.

Hachiripa, ハチリパ, 仆ル、(複數). *v.i.* (*pl*). To fall down.

Hai, ハイ, 嗚呼、嘆息ノ語、例セバ、ハイクサバ、嗚呼私ノ頭. *interj.* Oh ! An exclamation expressive of pain. As :—*Hai ku sapa,* " oh, my head " !

Hai, ハイ, 大麻、蕁麻、絲. *n.* Hemp. Nettle. String. As :—*Hai karo,* " to make string." *Hai-tush,* " a hempen rope."

Haina, ハイナ, 繩(ナワ). *n.* A line.

Hainakani, ハイナカニ, 針金. *n.* Wire.

Haipungara, ハイプンガラ, ツルウメモドキ. *n.* A kind of creeping plant, *Cela-trus articulatus Th.*

Haita, ハイタ, 不足ナル、例セバ、クラナアシネプハイタ、鞍一ツ不足ナリ. *v.i.* To come short of. To decrease. To be insufficient. As : —*Kura naa shinep haita,* " there is one saddle short."

Haita, ハイタ, 外ヅス (的ヲ). *v.i.* To miss (as a mark).

Haita-guru, ハイタグル, 愚人、痴漢. *n.* A fool.

Haitapa, ハイタパ, 減ズル. *v.i.* To decrease. (*pl*.)

Hak, ハク, 口. *n.* The mouth. Used only in traditions and now nearly obsolete.

Hakakse, ハカクセ, 靜カニ. *adj.* and *v.i.* Softly. Silently. As :— *Hakakse itak,* " to speak softly ;" " to whisper."

Hake, ハケ, 此方ノ側. *adv.* This side. As :—*Hake-wa,* from this side of (a place).

Hakegeta, ハケゲタ, Hagegeta, ハゲゲタ, 此方ノ側、此處. *ad.* This side of. Here. This side.

Hakeiketa, ハケイケタ, Hake-ita, ハケイタ, 此方ノ側、例セバ、ペトホケイケタ、河ノ此方側. *adv.* This side of. As :—*Pet hakeiketa,* " this side of the river."

Haketa, ハケタ, | 此處、此邊. *adv.* Here.
Hake-ita, ハケイタ, | This side.

Hakma-hakma, ハクマハクマ, 徐カ ニ、耳語スル. *adj.* and *v.i.* Silent. To whisper. To speak very softly. **Syn : Pinu-no-ye.**

Hakma-hamaka, ハクマカクマカ, 耳語スル. *v.i.* To whisper. To speak very softly. Same as *Hakmahakma*.

Ham, ハム, 木ノ葉. *n.* Leaves of trees.

Ham, ハム, 否. *adv.* No. Not.

Hambe, ハムベ, 父. *n.* Father. **Syn : Michi. Ona. Onaha.**

Hamne, ハムネ, 全ク、殘ラズ. *adj.* Whole. Entire.

Hamne-an, ハムネアン, 全ク、殘ラズ. *adj.* Whole. Entire.

Hamne-no, ハムネノ, 有リノマヽ、其ノ儘、全ク. *adv.* As they are. Untouched. Left alone. Wholly. Entirely.

Hamne-ruki, ハムネルキ, 呑込ム. *v.i.* To swallow. To swallow whole.

Hamo, ハモ, 鱧、ハモ. *n.* A salt-water eel. Said to be of Japanese origin.

Hamoki, ハモキ, | 伏ス. *v.i.* To lie down
Hamuki, ハムキ, | (as an animal). To be asleep.

Hampukuchotchap, ハムブクチョッチャブ, | 蜻蛉 (トンボ).
Hankuchotchap, ハンクチョッチャブ, | *n.* Dragon flies.

Hamu, ハム, | 木ノ葉. *n.* Leaves. **Syn:**
Hamuhu, ハムフ, | Ham.

Hamu. ハム, 靜カニ. *adj.* Gently. **Syn : Hapunno.**

Hange, ハンゲ, 近ク、例セバ、ハンゲ ノエク、近ヨル. *adj.* Near. As : —*Hange no ek,* "to come near." *Hange esoine,* "to go to make water." (Polite.)

Hange-a, ハンゲア, 小便スル、(女ニ用ユ). *v.i.* To make water (only used of women).

Hange-ike, ハンゲイケ, 此方、例セバ、ナムクシナイコタンハンゲイケ、ナムクシナイ村ノ手前. *adv.* This side of. As :—*Yamkushnai kotan hange-ike,* "this side of *Yamkushnai.*" **Syn : Hekageta.**

Hangeiketa, ハンゲイケタ, 此方. *adv.* This side of.

Hangeko, ハンゲコ, 遠キ、例セバ、ハンゲコノアン、其ハ遠シ. *adj.* Far. Afar. Distant. As :—*Hangeko no an,* "it is far away." **Syn : Tuima no.**

Hani, ハニ, | 此ノ字チ動詞ノ後ニ加フルトキ
Ani, アニ, | ハ願意又ハ命令チ表ハシ又ハ多ク答チ求ムルノ語トナルナリ、例セバ、オマンワイェハニ、往キテ彼ニ告ゲヨ. *part.* After verbs this particle often indicates request or command. It is a kind of softening factor and is very much used when the speaker expects to be answered. As :— *Oman wa ye hani,* "go and tell him ;" *E,* "yes" (I will.)

Hanku, ハンク, 臍. *n.* The navel.

Hankuchotchap, ハンクチョッチャブ, 蜻蛉 (トンボ). *n.* Dragon flies.

Hankupkara, ハンクブカラ, 拳チ固メル. *v.i.* To square the fists with the third knuckle of the second finger protruding.

Han-ne, ハンネ, 否、然ラズ. *adv.* No ; it is not. **Syn : Seenne.**

Hannokara, ハンノカラ, 教ュル、訓練スル. *v.t.* To teach. To break in (as a horse). **Syn : Epakashnu.**

Haphap, ハプハプ, 離有、(婦人及ビ小兒主トシテ此語チ用ユ). *adv.* Thank you (used principally by women and children).

Hapi, ハピ, 愚ナルコトチナス、嘲笑スル. *v.i.* To act foolishly or unwisely. *v.t.* To deride. To laugh at. **Syn : Eoya-itak.**

Haprapchup, ハプラプチュプ, 三月. *n.* The month of March.

Hapun, ハプン, 柔カキ、(ハプルノ略). *adj.* Short for hapuru, "soft."

Hapun-no, ハプンノ, or **Apun-no, アプンノ**, 静カニ. *adv.* Gently.

Hapun-no-oman, ハプンノオマン (*sing*). or **Hapun-no-paye, ハプンノハイ**, (*pl*). 左様ナラ. *ph.* Goodbye. Adieu. (lit : go gently).

Hapun-rui, ハプンルイ, 砥石. *n.* A soft whetstone.

Hapuru, ハプル, 柔カキ、静カナル. *adj.* Soft. Gentle. Quiet.

Hapuruka, ハプルカ, 柔カニスル. *v.i.* To make soft. **Syn : Pewanka.**

Hapuru-pone, ハプルポネ, 軟骨. *n.* Gristle. Cartilage.

Hara, ハラ, ハナドウ. *n.* *Heracleum lanatum, Michx.*

Harakika, ハラキカ, or **Harikika, ハリキカ**, 縄. *n.* Rope. Cord.

Haraki, ハラキ, 積荷. *n.* A load (as of wood). **Syn : Nishke an. Nina.**

Haraki, ハラキ, 左側ノ. *adj.* The leftside of anything or any where. On the left. **Syn : Hariki.**

Haram, ハラム, 蜥蜴(トカゲ). *n.* A lizard.

Harara-shinot, ハララシノツ, 踊リノ名(婦人ノ踊リニシテ鳥ノ羽打キチ真似スル). *n.* The name of a woman's dance, in which those who take part imitate birds flapping their wings.

Hariki, ハリキ, 左、例セバ、ハリキテク、左手. *n.* The left. As :— *Hariki tek,* "the left hand."

Harikika, ハリキカ,
Harakika, ハラキカ, } 絲、繩. *n.* Cord. Rope.

Harikimon, ハリキモン, 左ノ方. *adv.* The left hand side. On the left hand side.

Hariki-sam, ハリキサム, 左側ニ. *adv.* On the left hand side.

Hariki-so, ハリキソ,
Hariki-sho, ハリキショ, } 爐ノ左方(東ノ窓ヨリ見タル)、客ノ坐スル場所. *n.* The left hand side of a hearth looking in from the east window. This is the place where visitors sit.

Harikiso-inumbe, ハリキソイヌムベ, 爐ノ左ノ端(東方ヨリ見タル). *n.* The left edge of the hearth (looking in from the east).

Harikiteksam, ハリキテクサム, 左ノ方. *adv.* On the left hand side.

Haro, ハロ, 肥ヘタル、例セバ、肥大ノ人. *adj.* Fat. As :—*Haro-guru,* "a fat person."

Harokoro, ハロコロ, 肥ヘタル. *adj.* Fat. Stout. Corpulent. **Syn:** **Mimush.**

Haro-sak, ハロサク, 瘠セタル. *adj.* Lean. Thin. **Syn: Sattek.**

Harotke, ハロツケ, 滑リ落チレ. *v. i.* To slip down.

Haru, ハル, 食物、野菜. *n.* Food. Stores. Vegetables. Provisions. A luncheon basket. Herbs. Very often the young shoot of the cow-parsnip.

Harubere, ハルベレ, 破裂スル、割レル. *v.i.* To burst. To split. **Syn:** **Yaske.**

Haru-koro, ハルコロ, 糧ヲ齎ラス. *v.i.* To take provisions with one (as when on a journey or at work).

Haru-oboso, ハルオボソ, 亂費スル. *v.t.* To waste (as food). **Syn: Aep koatcha.**

Hasa, ハサ, 開ク、開キタル. *v.i.* and *v.t.* To be open. To open the mouth. As:—*Ishirikurantere, nei chikoikip ru turainu wa hasa kane chish wa okai,* "dear me! the animal has lost its way and is crying with its mouth open." **Syn: Pasa. Maka.**

Hash, ハシ, 下生ノ樹、灌木. *n.* Underwood. Shrubs. Scrubwood.

Hash-inao, ハシイナオ, 幣ノ一種. *n.* A kind of *inao* made of scrubwood.

Hash-inao-koro-kamui, ハシイナオコロカムイ, 梟. *n.* The screech owl.

Hashipo, ハシポ, イソツヽジ. *n.* *Ledum palustre, L. var. dilatatum, Wapl.*

Hashipo-keushut, ハシポケウシュツ, エゾムラキツヽジ. *n.* *Rhododendron dahuricum, L.*

Hashka, ハシカ, 痲疹、ハシカ. *n.* The measles.

Hashka-omap, ハシカオマプ, 樹木ニ積リシ雪. *n.* Snow which has settled on trees and fences. **Syn: Chikambe. Chikamge.**

Hashop, ハショプ, 叢林. *n.* A copse of small trees.

Hashtai, ハシタイ, 林. *n.* A clump of trees. A forest. **Syn: Nitai.**

Hashtumane, ハシツマ子, 害ヲ蒙ラズ (輕キ物ニ觸レタルトキノ如ク). *v. i.* To be left uninjured as when struck with some light instrument.

Hat, ハツ, 葡萄. *n.* Grapes.

Hatat, ハタツ, 細カニ切リテ干シタル魚. *n.* Fish cut up into slices and dried.

Hatcho, ハッチョ, 可愛ラシキ、綺麗ナル. *adj.* Pretty. Lovely. **Syn:** **Eramasu.**

Hatcho-nonno, ハッチョノンノ, 子供ヲ親愛スル語. *ph.* A term of endearment used when addressing children. A pretty child.

Hatopok, ハトポク, 脇ノ下. *n.* The arm-pits.

Hat-piye, ハツピイェ, 葡萄ノ種子. *n.* Grape pips.

Hat-pungara, ハツプンガラ, ヤマブドウ. *n.* Grape vines. *Vitis Coignetiæ Pulliat.*

Hattara, ハッタラ, 淵(フチ). *n.* Deep water. A deep pool of water.

Hatto-an, ハットアン, 禁ジタル. *adj.* Forbidden.

Hattoki, ハットキ, Hattoho-ki, ハットホキ, 妨クレ、此語ノ前ニハ毎ニクニナル語アリ、例セバ、エククニハットホキ、人ノ来ルテ邪魔スル. *v.t.* To prevent. This word is generally preceded by *kuni*. Thus :— *Ek kuni hattoho ki,* "to prevent one's coming."

Hau, ハウ, 聲. The voice. The voice of either man, animals, fowls or any other living creatures. *Hau* may also be applied to the voice of God. **Syn: Hawe.**

Hau, ハウ, Hau-ash, ハウアシ, Hawe-ash, ハウェアシ, 話ス、音スル. *v.i. & n.* To speak. To say. To sing. A noise. Sound.

Hauge, ハウゲ, 靜ナル、柔キ、安キ、遲キ、例セバ、アプトハウゲ、靜ナル雨. *adj.* and *v.i.* Gentle. Soft. Light. Weak. Cheap. Quiet. Slow. To be unable to do a thing. As :—*Apto hauge,* "a gentle rain." *Hauge ainu,* "a weak man.' *Ma-hauge,* "to swim slowly"; "to be unable to swim fast."

Hauge-hauge, ハウゲハウゲ, 甚ク靜ナル. *adj.* and *v.i.* Very gentle. Very soft. Very quiet. To be very gentle.

Hauge-hum, ハウゲフム, 低囁、サヤメキ. *n.* A low murmuring sound.

Hauge-ki, ハウゲキ, 告知スル、音フ、唸ク. *v.i.* To say. To tell. To hum as a wasp. To make a rumbling sound with the voice.

Hauge-no, ハウゲノ, 靜カニ. *adv.* Gently. Quietly. Softly. As :—*Hauge no ki,* "to do a thing gently." *Hauge no itak,* "to speak softly."

Hauge-no-humuse, ハウゲノフムセ, 唸ル. *v.t.* To make a murmuring sound.

Hauge-no-rui-no, ハウゲノルイノ, 靜カニ又荒ク、高ク又低ク(音聲チ). *ph.* Gently and roughly or softly and loudly.

Haugere, ハウゲレ, 柔和ニスル. *v.t.* To assuage. To render weak or soft. To compose.

Hauge-turan-no-uru-uruk, ハウゲツランノウルウルク, 聲チ震ハセル(話フトキニ). *ph.* To make the voice quiver as in singing.

Hauge-turan-no-uyuiki, ハウゲツランノウユイキ, 聲チ震ハセテ歌フ. *ph.* The same as *hauge turan no uru-uruk.*

Haukakonna-charototke, ハウカコンナチャロトツケ, 啼ク(鳥ナドノ). *v.i.* To sing as birds.

Haukorehawe-charotke, ハウコレハウェチャロツケ, 啼ク(鳥ナドノ). *v.i.* Same as above.

Hau-hokka, ハウホッカ, Hau-okka, ハウオッカ, 呼ブ. *v.t.* To call to.

Hauki, ハウキ, 話ス、哭ク. *v.i.* To speak. To cry aloud. To say. **Syn : Itak.**

Haukore-kunitara, ハウコレクニタラ, 叫ブ. *v.i.* To shout. **Syn: Ehaukashu.**

Haukoro, ハウコロ, 嘶ク、啼ク(鳥血獸ナドノ). *v.i.* To neigh as a horse. To crow as a cock. To sing, as a bird.

Haukotantariki, ハウコタンタリキ,
歩ミナカラ話ス、哮ヘ、. v. i. To
speak as one walks along. To
yelp as a dog.

Haukotpare, ハウコツパレ, 助ケヲ呼
ブ. v.i. To call for help. Syn：
Kimakhau. Peutauge.

Hauokka, ハウオッカ,) 呼ブ. v. t.
Hau-hokka, ハウホノカ,) To call
to. Syn：Hotuyekara.

Haurutotke, ハウルトッケ, クスグレ.
v.t. To tickle. Syn：Hairotke.

Hawash,) 言フ、知ラセル、例セバ、タ
ハワシ,} チアフフアリハワシ、今這
Hawashi,) 入テモ宜ロシイト言ヒマ
ハワシ,
ス. v.t. To say. To tell. As：—
Tane ahup ari hawash, "he says
you are to enter now." Syn：
Hawe ash.

Hauturumbe,) 使、天使、中保者. n. An
ハウツルムベ,} angel. A messen-
Hauturunbe,) ger. A middle
ハウツルンベ.) man. Mediator.

Hauturun-guru, ハウツルングル, 全
上. n. Same as Hauturunbe.

Hau-shut, ハウシュツ, 聲ノスル方.
adv. The direction of the voice.

Hawe, ハウェ, 尋問ノ語ナリ、例セバ、
アンハウェ、其處ニ在リマスカ、エヌレ
ハウェ、彼ニ話シマシタカ. part. This
word is often used as an interrogative particle. As：—An hawe？
is there"？ E nure hawe？ "have
you told him"？ Nen ta hawe an？
who is there"？

Hawe, ハウェ, 話ス. v.i. To speak.
To say. Syn：Ye.

Hawe, ハウェ,) 聲、例セバ、ハウェ
Hawehe, ハウェヘ,) ルイ、高聲. n.

The voice. As：—Hawe rui, "a
loud voice."

Hawe-an, ハウェアン,) 言フ. v.t. To
Hawe-ash, ハウェアシ,) speak. To
Say. To tell. Syn：Itak.

Hawe-ashte, ハウェアシテ, 聲ヲ出ス、
啼ク (蛙ナド). v. t. To call out.
To say. To croak as a frong.

Hawe-eamkiri, ハウェエアムキリ, 聲
デ聞キ分ケレ. v.t. To recognize a
voice.

Hawe-ki, ハウェキ, ブンブン云フ
(蜂ナド). v.i. To hum as a wasp.
Syn：Hau-ki. To make a noise
with the voice.

Hawe-kiri, ハウェキリ, 聲デ聞キ分ケ
ル. v.t. To recognize a voice.
Syn：Hawe-eamkiri.

Hawe-ne, ハウェ子, 然リ. adv. Yes.
Syn：Ruwe. Ruwe un. Ruwe
ne wa. E. A. O un.

Hawe-ne-yakun, ハウェ子ヤクン, 左
様デアルナラバ. ph. If it is so.
Syn：Nei no ne chiki.

Hawe-sange, ハウェサンゲ, 高音デ話
ス、哮ル. v.i. To speak loudly.
To roar as an animal.

Hawe-roise, ハウェロイセ, 哮ル、聲
ヲ上ゲル. v.i. To make a noise
with the voice. As：—Haweroise
guru, "a noisy person."

Hayango, ハヤンゴ, 火薬包子、紙筒
(ハヤゴツ). n. A cartridge. (Jap).

Hayashitai ハヤシタイ, 林. n. A
forest. Syn：Nitai.

Haye, ハイェ, 嗚呼. excl. Oh！ An
exclamation expressive of pain.
Syn：Hai.

Haye, ハイェ, ヨリモ少キ. v. i. To
be less than.

Haye, ハイェ, カジキ魚ノ鼻. n. The

prolonged upper jaw of a common sword-fish.

Hayokbe, ハヨクベ, 武具. *n.* Armour. **Syn : Hayokne.**

Hayokbe-kirau, ハヨクベキラウ, 兜ノ鍬形. *n.* The horns on a helmet.

Hayokne, ハヨク子, 武具. *n.* Armour.

He, ヘ, 呼吸. *n.* The breath.

He, ヘ, 口氣、疑問ノ語ニシテアン (an) ナル語ニ癪クチ例トス、エクレ ウエヘアン、彼ハ來タカ. *part.* This particle expresses interrogation, and is often though by no means always, followed by the verb *an* " to be." Thus :—*Ek ruwe he an?* " has he come ? " *Tane he?* " now ? " *Achapo he?* " is it my uncle ? "

He, ヘ, 何、何ンダ. *adv.* What ?

He, ヘ, 向フ. *adv.* Facing. Towards. In front. Surface.

Heashi, ヘアシ, 元始、起原. *n.* The beginning. The commencement.

Heaship, ヘアシプ, 始メシモノ. *n.* A thing which has been commenced.

Heashire, ヘアシレ, 始マル、出ス. *v.t.* To commence. To send forth. To publish as a book.

Heashpa, ヘアシパ, 始メル(複數). *v.i.* To commence (*pl.*)

Hebashi, ヘバシ, 海岸ニ向テ. *adv.* Towards the sea-shore. **Syn : Hesashi.**

Hebera, ヘベラ, ⎫ 川上ヘ向フ、内地
Heberai, ヘベライ, ⎭ ヘ向ケ. *adv.* Up a stream or river. Towards the interior of a country. **Syn : Opishne.**

Hechaka, ヘチャカ, 晴レル、例セバ、ニシクルヘチャカ、雲晴レル. *v.i.* To clear away as a fog. To become clear. As :—*Nishkuru hechaka,* " the clouds are clearing away." **Syn : Hechawe.**

Hechawe, ヘチャウェ, 發出スル(弓銃ナドノ). *v.i.* To go off as a gun. To become unstrung as a bow. To become unravelled. To clear away as a fog. To get torn. To clear away as clouds.

Hechawe-kani, ヘチャウェカニ, 銃ノ引金. *n.* The trigger of a gun.

Hechawe-ni, ヘチヤウェニ, 弩ノ彈キ止メ. *n.* The trigger of a crossbow. That portion of a bow or trap which causes the string to be let loose from the place which holds it.

Hechawere, ヘチヤウェレ, 放ツ、射ル. *v.t.* To let off a gun or bow. To undo. To pull to pieces. To pick to pieces.

Hechimi, ヘチミ, 別レタル、分割シタル. *adj.* Parted. Divided.

Hechimi-kara, ヘチミカラ, 頭髮チ牛ョリ分ケル. *v.i.* To have the hair parted in the middle.

Hechimisara, ヘチミサラ, オホノカヒ. *n.* Mussel. *Mya arenaria, Linn.*

Hechirasa, ヘチラサ, 咲ク(單數). *v.i.* To blossom (*sing*).

Hechirasa, ヘチラサ, ⎫ 髮ノ亂レル. *v.i.* To
Hechirasasa, ヘチラササ, ⎭ be rough as the hair. **Syn: Herisarisa.**

Hechirasasare, ヘチラササレ, 髮チ束ス. *v.t.* To make rough as the hair.

Hechiraspa, ヘチラスバ, 咲ク（複數）. *v.i.* To blossom. (*pl*).

Hechiri, ヘチリ, 遊ビ. *n.* Amusement. Play. Fun. **Syn: Shinot.**

Hechiri, ヘチリ, 遊ブ. *v.i.* To play. To jump about.

Hechirin, ヘチリン, 鳴ル、音スル.*v.i.* To jingle. To rattle.

Hechirin-kani, ヘチリンカニ, 金輪、(犬馬ナドノ首ニ付ケテ音ヲ發セシム). *n.* Metal rings fastened to animals and so arranged as to jingle when they move.

Hechirin-kut,ヘチリンクツ, 金輪ノ付キタル上帶. *n.* A waistband with metal rings attached.

Heheba,
ヘヘバ,⎫覗キ見ル. *v. t.* To peep
Heheuba,⎰ at.
ヘヘウバ,

Hehem, ヘヘム, 引張ル. *v.t.* To pull.

Heikachi, ヘイカチ,⎫少年. *n.* A
Hekachi, ヘカチ, ⎰ lad. A boy. In some places this word is applied to both boys and girls. Generally, however, boys only are called *heikachi*. (*Sing*) The plural being *heikat'tara* or *heikachi utara*.

Heikachi-koro, ヘイカチコロ, 男兒ヲ守リスル、養育スル. *v.i.* To nurse a male child.

Heikachi-koro-guru, ヘイカチコログル, 男兒守、乳母. *n.* A nurse.

Heikachi-ram-koro, ヘイカチラムコロ, 子供ラシキ. *adj.* Childish. Childlike.

Heikat'tara,
ヘイカッタラ,⎫子供等. *n.* Lads.
Heikachi-utara,⎰ Boys.
ヘイカチウタラ,

Heise, ヘイセ,
Heisepa, ヘイセバ,⎫氣息、呼吸. *n.*
Hesepa, ヘセバ,⎰The breath.

Heise-heise, ヘイセヘイセ, 忙シク呼吸スレ. *v.i.* To breathe quickly. To be out of breath as in running.

Heise-ki, ヘイセキ, 呼吸スレ. *v.t.* To breathe.

Heise-mawe, ヘイセマウェ, 氣息、呼吸. *n.* The breath.

Heisepa, ヘイセバ,⎫呼吸. *n.* The
Heise, ヘイセ, ⎰breath.

Heiseturiri, ヘイセツリリ, 大息スル、嘆ブレ. *v.i.* To sigh. **Syn: Tanne heisei omande.**

Hekachi, ヘカチ, 少年. *n.* Same as *Heikachi*, "a lad."

Hekai, ヘカイ, 古キ、老ヒタレ、熟シタレ. *adj.* Old. Ancient. Ripened.

Hekai-hokushte, ヘカイホクシテ, 老死スレ. *v.i.* To die of old age.

Hekai-oro, ヘカイオロ, 死シタレ.*adj.* Dead.

Hekatpa, ヘカツバ, 生レル(複數). *v.i.* To be born. (*pl.*)

Hekatu, ヘカツ, 生レル (單數). *v. i.* To be born (*sing*).

Hekatup, ヘカツプ, 生レタルモノ. *n.* That which is born.

Hekature, ヘカツレ, 子ヲ産ム. *v. t.* To bear a child. To bring forth.

Heki, ヘキ, 故ニ. *adv.* Because. For the reason that. **Syn: Wa gusu.**

Heki, ヘキ,⎫爲シ能ハズ. *aux. v.*
Hekiya, ヘキヤ,⎰To be unable to do. **Syn: Eaikap.**

Hekim, ヘキム, 森. *n.* A forest.

Hekimo, ヘキモ, 森ニテ. *adv.* In the forest.

Hekiru, ヘキル, 避ク ル、背向ク. To turn away from. **Syn : Shitutanure.**

Hekiya, ヘキヤ, 爲シ能ハヌ. *aux. v.*
Heki, ヘキ, To be unable to do.

Hekomba, ヘコムバ, 歸ル(複數). *v.i.* To return. **Syn : Hoshippa.** (*pl.*)

Hekomo, ヘコモ, 歸ル(單數). *v.i.* To return. **Syn : Hoshipi.**

Hekota, ヘコタ, 向フ. *adv.* Facing. Towards. **Syn : Hesashi.**

Hekota-hosare, ヘコタホサレ, 振向ク. *v.i.* To turn towards.

Hekote, ヘコテ, 傍ニ. *adv.* By the side of.

Hekote, ヘコテ, 結フ、繋グ. *v.t.* To tie up;" and "tied up."

Hekote-guru, ヘコテグル, 夫婦. *n.* A husband or wife.

Hekututu, ヘクツツ, エゾネギ. *n.* Chives. *Allium schœnoprasum, L.* **Syn : Shikutut.**

Hemak, ヘマク, 後ニ. *adv.* Behind. After.

Hemaka, ヘマカ, 終了スル、成遂グル. *v.t.* To finish. Also "to have done."

Hemakaraiba, ヘマカライバ, 川上ヘ歸ル. *v.i.* To return towards a river's source. To return from a journey.

Hemakari, ヘマカリ, 歸ル(重ニ海岸ヨリ). *v.i.* To return (especially from the sea-shore.

Hemakashi, ヘマカシ, 裏ヲ表ニ、後ヲ先ニ. *adv.* Wrong side before. Before.

Hemanda, ヘマンダ, 何. *adv.* What? As :—*Heikachi hemanda kara*

gusu kimta oman a? "what has the lad gone to the mountains for?" *Hemanda ye?* "what does he say"? *Hemanda ta a?* "what is it?" **Syn : Nep.**

Hemanda-gusu, ヘマンダグス, 何故. *adv.* Why? As:—*Hemanda gusu tambe nei no an a?* "why is this so?" **Syn : Nep gusu.**

Hematu, ヘマツ, 屈シタル. *v.i.* Twisted. To be cramped. To be drawn out of position.

Hemban, ヘムバン, 早ク. *adj.* Quick. **Syn : Tunashi.**

Hemban-nisap, ヘムバンニサプ, 急ニ. *adv.* Very suddenly.

Hemban-no, ヘムバンノ, 早ク. *adv.* Quickly. **Syn : Tunashi no.**

Hembara, ヘムバラ, 何時. *adv.* When.

Hembara-kane, ヘムバラカ子, 何時. *adv.* When.

Hembara-ne-yakka, ヘムバラ子ヤッカ, 常ニ. *adv.* Always. At any time. As :—*Hembara ne yakka ene moire range,* "he is always thus late."

Hembara-pakno-ne-yakka, ヘムバラパクノ子ヤッカ, 何時マデモ. *adv.* For ever. How long soever. Aye.

Hembarata, ヘムバラタ, 何時. *adv.* At what time. When.

Hemeshpa, ヘメシパ, 登ル、上ル (複數).
Hemespa, ヘメスパ, *v. t.* (*pl.*) To ascend. To go up. To climb a mountain.

Hemesu, ヘメス, 登ル、上ル (單數).
Hemeshu, ヘメシュ, *v. t.* (*sing*). To ascend as a mountain. To climb. To go up.

Hemge, ヘムゲ, 又ハ………トモ、例セ
バ、マヘムゲシュエヘムゲ、煮テモ焼イ
テモ. *post.* Either. Or. As:—
Ma hemge, shuye hemge, "either
roasted or boiled." **Syn: Hene-
ki.**

Hemhem, ヘムヘム, モ亦、ト. *post.*
And. Also.

Hemhem……hemhem, ヘムヘム, ト
(アレトコレトノ如ク). *post.* Both.
And.

Hemhem-ki……hemhem-ki, ヘム
ヘムキ, ト、モ. *post.* Either……
or. Both……or. Both……and.

Hemoimoi, ヘモイモイ, 動ク. *v.i.*
To move.

Hemoi, ヘモイ, 海ニ居ル鮭類 (来タ川
ニ上ラヌ). *n.* Salmon found in
the sea before entering the rivers.
Syn: Keneu.

Hemoi-ke, ヘモイケ, 鮭類ノ脂. *n.*
The fat of salmon.

Hemoi-up, ヘモイウプ, 鮭ノ精蟲. *n.*
The soft row of salmon.

Hempak, ヘムパク, 幾何. *adv.* How
many. As:—*Hempak be,* "how
many." *Hempak no,* "how
much." *Hempak hot an ruwe ta
an?* "how many score are there?"

Hempututu,⎱片意地ナ. *v.i.* To
ヘムプツツ,⎰be sulky. **Syn:**
Hepututu,⎰
ヘプツツ,⎰**Patukuku.**

Hene, ヘ子, ト、或ハ、モ. *post.* And.
Either.

Hene……hene, ヘ子, 何モ. *post.*
Both……and. Either.

Henekkere, ヘ子ッケレ, ハヒマツ、ヒ
ネキリマツ. *Pinus pumila, Regel.*
Syn: Todonup.

Henene, ヘ子子, 折曲ツテ往ク. *v.t.*
To go crookedly. As:—*Ru henene,* "to go out of a path."

Heneu, ヘ子ウ, マスノスケ. *n.* King
salmon.

Heneuba, ヘ子ウバ, 倚リ懸ル. *v.i.*
To lean over.

Henne, ヘン子, 否. *adv.* No.

Henne-nep, ヘン子プ, 何モナシ.
adv. There is nothing.

Henne-nep-ka, ヘン子プカ, 何モ
ナシ. *adv.* Nothing.

Henoye, ヘノイヌ, 眠ル. *v.i.* To
doze. To sleep.

Henoye, ヘノイヌ, 曲リタル、捻レタ
ル. *adj.* Crooked. Twisted.

Hense-tashum,⎰
ヘンセタシュム,⎰喘息. *n.* Asthma.
Heise-tashum,⎰
ヘイセタシュム,⎰

He-o, ヘオ, 浮ビ出ツル. *v.i.* To dive
out of (as from water when
diving). To come to the surface.

Hepshi, ヘプシ,⎰川下、例セバ、ヘバ
Hebashi, ヘバシ,⎰シウンオマン、川
テ下ダル. *adv.* Down stream. As:
—*Hebashi un oman,* "to follow
a stream down."

Hepeku, ヘペク, 燃エル. *v.i.* To
flare. **Syn: Paraparase.**

Hepenki, ヘペンキ, 生長スル. *v.t.*
To rear. To bring up. Also
" source "; " origin."

Hepenki-kotan, ヘペンキコタン, 故
郷. *n.* One's native place.

Heperai, ヘペライ, 川上ヘ、例セバ、
ヘペライワオマン、川ヲ上レ. *adv.*
Up a stream. As:—*Heperai wa
oman,* "to follow a stream up."

Hepere, ヘペレ, 熊ノ子. *n.* A bear's cub.

Hepere-chep, ヘペレチェブ, 魚ノ名. *n.* Name of a fish. *Azuma em-nion, Jor & Sny.* (Same as *Nikappana*).

Hepere-kot, ヘペレコツ, 熊ノ子ヲ生長セシムル檻. *n.* A cage made to bring up bear cubs in.

Hepere-kot-urai-ni, ヘペレコツウライ二, 熊祭リノ時ニ熊ヲ繋ク柱. *n.* The pole to which bear cubs are tied during a bear feast.

Hepere-pusaru, ヘペレプサル, 熊祭ノ時熊ニ與フル食物ナ入レル袋. *n.* A bag containing food offered to bears before being killed.

Hepere-sat-chep, ヘペレサツチェブ, 熊祭ノ時熊ニ與フル干魚. *n.* An offering of dried fish made to bears when killed in the bear feast.

Hepeu, ヘペウ, オヒヨウ. *n.* Halibut. *Hypoglosus hypoglosus, Linn.*

Hepirasa, ヘピラサ, 咲ク(單數). *v.i.* To blossom (*sing*).

Hepiraspa, ヘピラスバ, 咲ク(複數). *v.i.* To blossom (*pl*).

Hepita, ヘピタ, 放ツ(銃又ハ弓ナドノ). *v.i.* To rise up from a bent position. To let go. To set off (as a trap or gun).

Hepita-ni, ヘピタ二, 落シニ用ユル彈キ木. *n.* A bent piece of wood used as a spring in traps; also a trap for snaring animals and birds.

Hepitoto, ヘピトト, 大キナル小刀. *n.* A large knife. **Syn: Makiri.**

Hepokichiu, ヘポキチウ, 身ヲ屈メレ(禮拜ノトキ). *v.i.* To bow one's self as in worship.

Hepokiki, ヘポキキ, 低頭スル. *v.i.* To bow the head. To bow down.

Hepokipoki, ヘポキポキ, 首肯スル. *v.i.* To nod the head.

Hepokitekka, ヘポテテッカ, **Hepoktekka,** ヘポクテッカ, 屈メレ、低頭スル. *v.i.* To bow down. To bow the head.

Hepoki-ush, ヘポキウシ, 身ヲ曲ゲル、(禮拜スルトキ). *v.i.* To bow one's self as in worship.

Hepoko, ヘポコ, 嫌惡スル. *v.t.* To despise. To abhor.

Hepoktekka-heteshtekka, ヘポクテッカヘテシテッカ, 上下スル. *ph.* To rise and fall as anything upon the sea. To bow and rise.

Heporap, ヘポラブ, 蝶又ハ蛾. *n.* A butterfly or moth.

Heporap-wata, ヘポラブワタ, 繭、マユ. *n.* Cocoons.

Hepuni, ヘブ二, 見上ゲル. *v.i.* To look up. To turn the eyes upward.

Hepuru, ヘブル, 長ク縺レタル毛(獸類ナドノ). *v.i.* and *adj.* To have long rough hair as some animals. Long-haired.

Hepututu, ヘブツツ, 拗ネル. *v.i.* To be sulky. **Syn: Hempututu. Pattukuku.**

Hera, ヘラ, 跛ノ、アシナヘタル. *adj.* Maimed. Lame. Crippled. **Syn: Yaiewen.**

Heraske, ヘラスケ, 裸體ノ. *adj.* Naked. Bare. Striped.

Herasa, ヘラサ, 下ダス. *v.t.* To send down. **Syn: Arange.**

Herashi, ヘラシ, 下方ヘ. *adv.* Downwards. Towards the sea shore. From above.

Herashi-ratki, ヘラシラツキ, 弔ツル ス、懸クレ. *v.i.* To be suspended.

Herashi-ratkire, ヘラシラッキレ, 掛 ケル. *v. t.* To hang down. To suspend.

Herashnu, ヘラシヌ, 輝ラス. *v.i.* To shine. **Syn : Heri at.**

Herashnure, ヘラシヌレ, 磨ク、輝 ラス. *v.t.* To shine. To polish. **Syn : Heri atte.**

Here, ヘレ, 輝キ. *n.* Brightness.

Heregush, ヘレグシ, タラ(大口魚)、エ レグシニ同シ. *n.* Same as *eregush*, a cod fish.

Herehereke, ヘレヘレケ, 輝ケル、照 レル. *adj.* Shining. Bright.

Hererush, ヘレルシ, 照ラス. *v.i.* To shine.

Hererushte, ヘレルシテ, 照ラス. *v.t.* To shine.

Heri-at, ヘリアツ, 照ラス. *v.i.* To shine.

Heri-atte, ヘリアッテ, 照ラス. *v. t.* To shine.

Herikashi, ヘリカシ, 上方. *adv.* Upwards.

Herisarisa, ヘリサリサ, 蓬髪. *v.i.* To be rough as the hair. **Syn : Hechirasasa.**

Heroki, ヘロキ,⎫
Heruki, ヘルキ,⎬ ニシン. *n.* A herring. *Clupea*
Eroki, エロキ,⎭ *harengus, Linn.*

Heron, ヘロン, 貧乏ナル、貧シキ. *adj.* Poor. Destitute.

Heru, ヘル, 同ジ、唯、ホンノ、例セ バ、ヘルアイヌ、同等ノ人、ヘルアン アパラアニパテク、ホンノ口ベカリ(不 誠實)、ヘルアイヌ、同ジ人間. *adj.* The same. Of the same kind. Merely. Only. Just. Simply. As :—*Heru ainu,* "the same class of people." *Heru an a paro ani patek,* "just with the mouth only," i.e. "insincerely."

Heruki, ヘルキ,⎫
Heroki, ヘロキ,⎬ ニシン. *n.* A herring, *Clupea*
Eroki, エロキ,⎭ *harengus, Linn.*

Hesashi, ヘサシ, 海岸ノ方ヘ. *adv.* Towards the sea-shore. **Syn : Hebashi.**

Hesashi, ヘサシ, 此處、又ハ爐ニ向フ、 例セバ、ヘサシナヌキル、顔ヲ此方ヘ 向ケヨ. *adv.* Here. Facing the fire. This way. As :—*Hesashi nanu kiru,* "turn the face this way." **Syn : Sa ta. Teda. Hekota.**

Hese, ヘセ, 嘆息スル. *v.i.* To breathe. To sigh.

Hese-hum-pirika, ヘセフムピリカ, 快ヲ感スル. *v.i. ph.* To feel better in health.

Hesei-turiri, ヘセイツリリ, 暑キトキ 又ハ疲レタルトキニ大息スル. *v.i.* To blow as when hot or tired. **Syn : Tanne hushta arapare.**

Hese-mau, ヘセマウ, 氣息. *n.* The breath. **Syn : Hesepa.**

Hesepa, ヘセパ,⎫
Heisepa, ヘイセパ,⎬ 口氣、氣息. *n.* The breath.
Heise, ヘイセ,⎭

Heshi, ヘシ, 北西ノ海. *n.* The north-western seas.

Heshi, ヘシ, 小湖. *n.* A pond. A small lake.

Heshiu, ヘシウ, 寢ル. *v.i.* To sleep.

Heshuiba, ヘシュイバ, 坐眠スル. *v.i.* To sleep in a sitting posture. To sit and sleep. **Syn: Aheshui.**

Heshuri, ヘシュリ, 出家、神主、又ハ禿頭. *n.* A buddhist or shinto priest. Also any person whose head has become bald through disease.

Heshuye-shuye, ヘシュイェシュイェ, 動搖スル(風ニ樹ノ動クガ如ク). *v.i.* To waive about as trees in the wind.

Heta, ヘタ, 現場又ハ現時ヲ顯スニ用ユル語ナリ、例セバ、モコンラポケタヘタ、丁度寢テ居タトキ. *part.* This word is sometimes used to express the very time or place. Thus:—*Mokon' rapoketa heta,* "at the very time he was asleep." *Nupuri kitaigeta heta chikuni okai,* "there are trees upon the very top of the mountain."

Hetak, ヘタク, 此ノ語ハ掛弊ニシテ見ヨ、サア、ヤレ、ナド、言フガ如シ. *interj.* This word expresses urgency, desire, defiance, vigilance or solicitude, each particular meaning being determined by the tone of voice and subject. Behold! Come. Now then. Look out. Dear me! Oh dear! As:—*Hetak, akoro chisei orun paye rusui,* "oh dear! I desire to go to our house." *Hetak, nishpa ek wa ibe,* "now master come and eat."

Hetaptapu, ヘタプタプ, 立膝シテ眠ル. *v.i.* To lie down with the head resting in the arms and the legs drawn up.

Hetari-araka, ヘタリアラカ, 刺撃スル、(ヅキヅキト痛ム). *n.* Shooting pains.

Hetari-ni, ヘタリニ, 垂木ノ下端ニ縛リ付ケル棒(桁ニ仝シ). *n.* The long poles to which the lower ends of the end rafters of a but are tied. See also *Aman-ni.* **Syn: Hotari-ni.**

Hetarire, ヘタリレ, 立タセル. *v.t.* To set up. To make stand.

Hetche, ヘツチェ, 答ヘル、諾スル. *v.i.* and *n.* To answer affirmatively. An answer. To respond to. To give a word of assent. **Syn: Ese.**

Hetchi, ヘツチ, 獣ヲ唱フトキ用ユルトキノ語. *n.* A peculiar exclamation made by the Ainu when singing some kinds of songs. An exclamation of assent.

Heteshtekka, ヘテシテッカ, 頭ヲ上ゲル. *v.i.* To lift up the head. To hold the head up.

Heteshu, ヘテシュ, 頭ヲ上ゲル. *v.i.* To hold the head up. To lift up the head. **Syn: Hetari.**

Hetke-hetke, ヘツケヘツケ, 抜キ差シスル、(刀ノ如ク). *v.t.* To draw out and push in as a sword.

Hetokush, ヘトクシ, Etokush, ヘトクシ, 將ニ、例セバ、イサムヘトクシ、今將ニ滅セントス. *v.i.* About to be. As:—*Isam hetokush,* "about to come to nothing." "About to lose sight of."

Hetopo, ヘトポ, 又、歸ル. *adv.* Again. Back. **Syn: Ehoroka.**

Hetopo-hetopo, ヘトポヘトポ, 度々. *adv.* Again and again. Frequently.

Hetopo-hetopo-oman, ヘトポヘトポオマン, 往来スル. *ph.* To go backwards and forwards.

Hetopo-shiknu, ヘトポシクヌ, 甦生ス
ル. *v.i.* To return to life.

Hetopo-shiknure, ヘトポシクヌレ, 甦
ラス. *v.t.* To raise to life.

Hetukba, ヘツクバ, 生長スル、出ヅル.
v.i. To grow. To come forth.
Pl. of Hetuku.

Hetukbap, ヘツクバプ, 生長スルモノ.
n. Things which grow.

Hetukbare, ヘツクバレ, 生ヤス、出ス、
生ム、(複數). *v.t.* (*pl.*) To make
grow. To send forth. To produce.

Hetuku, ヘツク, 生長スル、(單數). *v.i.*
(*Sing*). To grow. To come forth.
To be born. To rise as the sun.

Hetukure, ヘツクレ, 生ヤス、生ム. *v.t.*
To make grow. To send forth.
To give birth to.

Heturashte, ヘツラシテ, 共ニ住フ、
(兄弟ノ如ク=). *v.i.* To live with
another (as with a sister or brother).

Heturu, ヘツル, 屈ム. *v.t.* To bend.
To stoop.

Heuge, ヘウゲ, 屈ム、曲ル. *v.i.* To
be bent. To be crooked. **Syn:**
Ohoge.

Heugere, ヘウゲレ, 屈メル、曲ゲル. *v.t.*
To bend. **Syn: Ohogere.**

Heune, ヘウ子, 弱キ、柔カキ. *adj.*
Supple. Sleek. Tender. Weak.

Heunenep-koro, ヘウ子子プコロ, 弱
キ、柔カキ. *adj.* Supple. Sleek.
Weak.

Heush, ヘウシ, 着ケレ. *v.t.* To put
on as a hat. To draw on as
boots.

Heye, ヘイエ, 顏. *n.* The countenance. Face.

Hi, ヒ, or **I, イ,** 此語ヂ動詞又ハ形容
詞ニ附加スルトキハ名詞トナスヂ得、
例セバ、エイショコロ、信仰スレ、エイ
ショコロイ、信仰. *part.* Suffixed
to verbs or adjectives this particle has the power of changing
them into substantives. As:—
Eishokoro, " to believe." *Eisho-
koro-i,* "belief." *Pirika,* "good."
Pirika-i, " a good thing." See *I.*
Syn: Ambe.

Hi, ヒ, 左様. *adv.* Yes. So.

Hike, ヒケ, or **Ike, イケ,** 此ノ語ヂ
動詞ニ付加フレトキハ、ニ就テ、又ハ、
ニ關シテノ意トナルナリ、例セバ、クヌ
ヒケ、我聞クコトニ關シテハ. *part.*
This particle is used as a suffix
to verbs, and signifies " as regards," " with reference to which."
Thus, *ku nu hike,* " as regards
what I hear." *Ku nukar'hike,*
" with refernce to what I see."

Hike, ヒケ, 物. *n.* An article.
Thing.

Hinta-ne, ヒンタ子, 何ナリヤ. *adv.*
What is it? **Syn: Nep ta.**

Hinta-ta, ヒンタタ, 何ナリヤ. *adv.*
What is it?

**Hitsuji, ヒツジ, Hitsuji-chikoikip,
ヒツジチコイキプ,** 羊. *n.* Sheep.
A sheep. (*Jap.*)

**Hitsuji-epungine-guru, ヒツジエプ
ンギ子グル,** 羊牧者. *n.* A shepherd.
(lit: sheep watcher.)

**Hitsuji-reshpa-guru, ヒツジレシバ
グル,** 牧羊者. *n.* A shepherd (lit:
sheep rearer).

Hitsuji-topa, ヒツジトバ, or **topaha, トバハ,** 羊ノ群. *n.* A flock of
sheep.

Ho, 木, 陰門. *n.* The anus. Vagina. The posteriors.

Ho, 木, ヨリ、離レタル、後ロ. *adv.* Off. Away from. Back. Behind.

Ho, 木, 呼ブ. *v.t.* To call.

Ho-atak, ホアタク, 呼ビ戻ス. *v.t.* To fetch by calling. **Syn: Hotuye-kara.**

Hoashtari, ホアシタリ, 跛ノ、アシナヘタレ. *adj.* Lame. Maimed.

Hobashi, ホバシ, 海岸ヨリ. *adv.* From the sea-shore.

Hochahocha, ホチャホチャ, 跳子踊ル. *v.i.* To hop.

Hochaku, ホチャク, 糞、下痢スル. *n.* Manure. Also to suffer from diarrhea.

Hochatchari, ホチャッチャリ, 姦淫ス ル. *v.i.* To commit adultery.

Hochatchari-guru, ホチャッチャリグ ル, 姦通者. *n.* An adulterer or adulteress.

Hochauchau, ホチャウチャウ, **Hochawachawe,** ホチャワチャウェ, 跳躍スル、三脚ニテ歩ム、(跛ノ犬馬ノ如ク). *v.i.* To hop. To walk on three legs as a lame horse or dog.

Hocheppo, ホチェッポ, 魚ノ名. *n.* *Elxis nikkomis. Jor. and Sny.*

Hochiarana, ホチアラナ, 下ダレ. *v.i.* To descend. **Syn: Ran.**

Hochihi, ホチヒ, 合計数. *n.* A sum.

Hochikachika, ホチカチカ, 跳ル (魚ノ如ク). *v.i.* To splash about. To flounder as a fish.

Hochikarakari, ホチカラカリ, **Hochikom,** ホチコム, 縮ル、縺レル. *v.i.* To crumple up. To be twisted or tangled. **Syn: Chiukarakari.**

Hochika-hochika, ホチカホチカ, 跳ル. *v.i.* To flounder as a fish.

Hochikok, ホチコク, ヨタカ. *n.* Goatsucker.

Hochikom, ホチコム, **Hochikarakari,** ホチカラカリ, 縮レタレ、縺レタル. *v.i.* To crumple up. To become twisted. To become intangled.

Hochin, ホチン, 股ノ下. *n.* The under part of the thighs. **Syn: Chin-kotoro.**

Hochin-uturu, ホチンウツル, 骨盤. *n.* The pelvis.

Hochin-uturu-kushte, ホチンウツルクシテ, 跨リテ. *adv.* Astride.

Hochipakara, ホチバカラ, 子ヲ搖レ. *v.t.* To dandle up and down as a child.

Hochipki, ホチブキ, 搖レ、例セバ、アパウシタカタホチブキ、彼ハ門扉ニヨリテ垂搖シテ居ル. *v.i.* To swing. Thus:—*Apa-ushta kata hochipki,* "he is swinging on the gate."

Hochiukarapa, ホチウカラバ, 浮ビ、深フ. *v.i.* To float about as in the back water of an eddy.

Ho-eimek, ホエイメク, 遊女ノ務チスル. *v.t.* To act the harlot.

Ho-eimek-guru, ホエイメクグル, 姦淫スル人. *n.* An adulterer.

Hokot, ホコツ, 深キ. *adj.* Deep. **Syn: Ohoro.**

Hoinu, ホイヌ, 貂、テン. *n.* A marten. Sable.

Hoishtaritari, ホイシタリタリ, 跛ノ ル. *adj.* Lame. Maimed. **Syn: Hera.**

Hoito, ホイト, 乞食. *n.* A beggar. **Syn: Iyahup-guru. Iyekari-guru.**

Hoito-ki, ホイトキ, 乞フ. *v.t.* To beg. **Syn: Iyahupkara.**

Hoiyaku, **ホイヤク**, 墮胎. *n.* An abortion. A miscarriage. Same as *Honyaku.*

Hoiyo, **ホイヨ**, 夜鷹ノ類. *n.* Some kind of night hawk.

Hoiyo, **ホイヨ**, Hoiyo-ki, **ホイヨキ**,} 姦淫スル. *v.t.* To commit adultery. To wish evil to another. To desire to harm. To do evil.

Hoiyo, **ホイヨ**, 惡シキ,放蕩ナル. *adj.* Bad. Abandoned. Evil. Wicked.

Hoiyop, **ホイヨブ**, 放蕩ナル人. *n.* An abandoned person. A person bent on mischief. An adulterer. An utterly wicked person. One who prays that evil may overtake another. One who steals the religious symbols of another. A person who commits sacrilege.

Hoiyo-tusu, **ホイヨツス**, 惡シキ預言. *n.* Evil prophecies.

Hok, **ホク**, 買フ. *v.t.* To buy.

Hoka, **ホカ**, 爐. *n.* A fireplace.

Hoka-etok, **ホカエトク**, 爐ノ上座. *n.* The head of a fireplace. That part of the inside of a hut nearest the head of a fireplace.

Hokamba, **ホカムバ**, 六ケ敷. *adj.* Difficult.

Hokamburi, **ホカブリ**, Hokkamburi, **ホノカブリ**,} 女ノ帽子. *n.* A woman's bonnet.

Hokannashi, **ホカンナシ**, 上方ニ、外方ニ. *adv.* The upper. The outer.

Hoka-o, **ホカオ**, 火上ニ置ク、例セバ、パスパスコカオ、炭ヲ繼グ. *v.t.* To put on a fire. As:—*Paspas hoka-o,* "to put charcoal on a fire."

Hoketu, **ホケツ**, 後ヘ蹴ル. *v.i.* To kick out from behind as a horse. **Syn: Chotari. Chiotari.**

Hoketuketu, **ホケツケツ**, 爬キ掴ル、(鳥ノ如ク). *v.t.* To scratch (as fowls).

Hokeura, **ホケウラ**, 肪胱. *n.* A bladder.

Hoki, **ホキ**, 筵術ヲ使フ、例セバ、メホキ、寒氣ヲ呼フ. *v.t.* To call for by enchantments. As:—*Me-huki,* "to call for cold." *Apto hoki guru,* "a rain maker."

Hokiru-kiru, **ホキルキル**, 搖レル. *v.i.* To sway too and fro.

Hokke, **ホケ**, 伏ス. *v.i.* Same as *Hotke,* "to lie down."

Hokomkokte, **ホコムコクテ**, 立膝ス ル. *v.i.* To raise the knees up towards the chin.

Hokorakorak, **ホコラコラク**, Okorakorak, **オコラコラク**,} 鳴ル. *v.i.* To rattle. To rattle together as things loose in a box.

Hoku, **ホク**, 夫、オット. *n.* A husband.

Hoku-koiwak, **ホクコイワク**, 己レノ夫ニ逢フ. *v.i.* To go to visit one's husband.

Hokukura, **ホククラ**, or Hokure, **ホクレ**, 掛聲ニ用ユル語. *excl.* An exclamation of urging, defying, or calling the attention to anything. This word is generally placed at the beginning of a sentence.

Hokure, **ホクレ**, 貪食スル、例セバ、ホクレイベ、食リテ食スル. *adv.* Greedily. Excessively. As:—*Hoku-*

re ibe, "to eat greedily." *Hokure iku*, "to drink greedily."

Hokush, ホクシ, 仆レ、落ツレ. *v.i.* To tumble over. To capsize. Collapse. **Syn : Hachiri. Horak.**

Hokushte, ホクシテ, 仆ス. *v.t.* To knock over. To turn over. To knock down. To upset.

Hokuyuk, ホクユク, 人チ食スル熊. *n.* A man-eating bear. A bear which steals horses or cattle. The opposite is called *Noyuk*. **Syn : Wenyuk.**

Hokuyuk-emauri, ホクユクエマウリ, クロイチゴ. *n. Rubus occidentalis*, L. var. *japonicus, Miyabe.*

Hom, ホム, 木ノ節. *n.* A knot in wood.

Hom, ホム, 節、フシ. *n.* A flaw in cotton or weaving threads. A knot in a piece of wood. A joint of the body. A variation of *kom*.

Homa, ホマ, 鰊ノ子. *n.* The hard spawn of herrings.

Homaka, ホマカ, 晴レル. *v.i.* To clear away. (as weather).

Homaka, ホマカ, 後ロ. *post.* Back. Behind. Aft. Backward. After. A little way off. As :—*Homaka chanchan*, "to step back." **Syn : Makta.**

Homakachiwe, ホマカチウェ, 流レ戻レ. *v.i.* To be washed back by the current of a river.

Homakaita, ホマカイタ, 遠ク. *adv.* Distant. Yonder. There. As:— *Homakaita no ande*, "put it yonder."

Homaka-no, ホマカノ, 後、アト. *adv.* After. Behind.

Homakochiwe, ホマコチウェ, 後ニ流ル. *v.i.* To move backwards.

Homakashi, ホマカシ, 後. *post.* Back. Behind.

Homakorobe, ホマコロベ, 海鳥ノ名. *n.* Name of a kind of sea-bird.

Homakushta, ホマクシタ, 後. *adv.* Abaft. Behind.

Homan-no, ホマンノ, 微カニ、模糊トシテ. *adv.* Dimly. Indistinctly.

Homara, ホマラ, 困迷スル、眩スレ. *v.i.* To be dizzy. To see dimly.

Homara, ホマラ, 温和ナル. *adj.* Gentle. As:—*Keutum homara guru*, "a gentle person."

Homara-no-po, ホマラノ木, 微ニ、不分明ニ. *adv.* Indistinctly.

Homare, ホマレ, 眩暈セシムル、錯乱セシムレ. *v.t.* To make dizzy. To confuse.

Homaretara, ホマレタラ,
Homaritara, ホマリタラ, } 微ニ、僅ニ、静ニ. *adv.* Dimly. Slightly. A little. Gently.

Homatu, ホマツ, 驚ク. *v.i.* To be startled. To be taken aback. To shy (as a horse).

Homatu-matu, ホマツマツ, 驚ク. *v.i.* To be frightened.

Homature, ホマツレ, 愕カス. *v.t.* To startle. To amaze. To astonish.

Homeru, ホメル, 痛ム. *v.i.* To be hurt. To be distorted.

Homerure, ホメルレ, 傷メル. *v.t.* To distort. To wound.

Honeinonno-tak, ホ子イノンノタク, 懐妊セレトキノ祝. *n.* A ceremony performed on or about the time of conception.

Hon-ekot, ホンエコツ, 産死スレ. v.i. To die of child-birth. **Syn :** Hon ewen wa rai.

Hone-kunne-chep, ホ子クン子チェブ, バセ類ノ總稱. n. Gobies (including several species).

Honene, ホ子子, 午後ノ三時頃. adv. The middle of the afternoon. **Syn : Chup ram.**

Honeugoro, ホ子ウゴロ, 下腹. The lower part of the abdomen.

Hon-ewen-wa-rai, ホンエウェンワラ イ. v.i. See hon-ekot.

Hongesh, ホンゲシ, 眞中. n. The middle.

Honi, ホニ, 腹. n. The belly. The abdomen. The stomach. As :— Honi araka, " the stomach ache."

Honi-araka, ホニアラカ, 腹痛. n. Cholic.

Honi-nini, ホニニニ, 匍匐スレ. v.i. To crawl upon the stomach. **Syn : Reye. Honoyanoya wa arapa.**

Honoinoep, ホノイノエブ, タンボボ. n. Dandelion. Taraxacum officinale, Wigg. var. corniculatum, Koch et Ziz.

Honi-un, ホニウン, 腹ノ. adj. Abdominal.

Honi-un, ホニウン,⎫ 妊娠スル. v. i.
Honun, ホヌン, ⎭ To have conceived a child. **Syn : Shinnaikat-iye-unu.**

Honi-un-no, ホニウンノ, 腹部ニ. adv. Abdominally.

Honkoro, ホンコロ, 妊娠スル. v. i. To conceive. To be pregnant. **Syn : Yaiapase.**

Honne-no, ホン子ノ, 長キ. adj. Long. **Syn : Ohonno. Ohoro.**

Honnere, ホン子レ, 罪ヲ免ス. v. t. To acquit. To absolve. **Syn : Tushi honnere.**

Honnere-i, ホン子レイ, 赦免. n. Acquittal.

Honoi-noyep, ホンノイノイェブ, タン ボボ. n. The dandelion. **Syn : Epetchi nonno. Honoinoep.**

Honoise, ホノイセ, 唸ル、吠エレ. v.i. To growl as a dog. To snarl. To hum (as in a song).

Honoye, ホノイェ, 方寄ル、偏スル. v.i. To lean on one side. To lean over. To be twisted out of place. **Syn : Heneuba.**

Honoye-noyep, ホノイェノイェブ, タ ンボ. n. A dandelion.

Honoyere, ホノイェレ, 方寄ラセレ. v.t. To tip over. To make lean.

Hontom, ホントム,⎫ 半分. port. Half. By.
Hontomo, ホントモ,⎭ In. On. As :—Pa hontom e tu pa, "a year and a half." Hontom e rep, " two and a half." Hontom e tup, " one and a half."

Hontomo-paro-chep, ホントモパル チェブ, シコ、ヒシコ. n. Anchovy. Engraulis japonicus. Tem. & Schl.

Honu, ホヌ, 腹這ニ伏ス. v.i. To lie down flat on the stomach and drag ones self along by the hands. **Syn : Reye.**

Honyaku, ホンヤク, 牛産、流産スル. n. and v.t. An abortion. A miscarriage. To abort.

Honyakure, ホンヤクレ, 流産サセレ. v.t. To produce abortion.

Hoparata, ホパラタ, 無禮ナスレ. v. t. To insult in an indecent manner. Hoparata is a kind of insult resorted to particularly by women, and consists in throwing up the hinder part of their garments and whipping the postoriors at a person. This performance is generally acted in secret and behind a person's back.

Hopash, ホパシ, 仆レシ. *v. t.* To fall.

Hopashi, ホパシ, } 海岸ヨリ. *adv.* From
Hobashi, ホバシ, } the sea-shore.

Hopashte, ホパシテ, 倒レシ. *v.t.* To fell.

Hopayapaya, ホパヤパヤ, } 苦シム. *v. i.* To struggle. To
Hopayepaye, ホパイェパイェ, } stretch out the arms and legs as a kicking baby or an animal in its death struggles.

Hopechina, ホペチナ, 坐ス(單數)、(日本人ノ樣ニ). *v.i. (sing).* To sit upon the heels.

Hopechina-rok, ホペチナロク, 坐ス、(複數). *v. i. . (pl).* To sit upon the heels.

Hopentari, ホペンタリ, 仆ス. *v. t.* To knock over.

Hopera, ホペラ, } 海岸ヘ往ク. *adv.*
Hoperai, ホペライ, } To go to the sea-shore. From the interior.

Hopirasa, ホピラサ, 開キシ(ツリ返ル迄ニ). *adj.* and *v.i.* Opened out backwards.

Hopita, ホピタ, }
Hopiuba, ホピウバ, } 早ク走ル. *v. i.* To run
Hopiwe, ホピウェ, } fast.

Hopiuba, ホピウバ, 精勵スレ、努力スル (複數). *v.t.* To do with a will. To do with might. To pull by placing the foot against an object (*pl.*) **Syn: Hopiwe.**

Hopiwe, ホピウェ, ホプイメノ(單數). *v.t.* Same as *Hopiuba* (*sing*).

Hopiye, ホピイェ, 早ク走ル. *v.i.* To run fast.

Hopokna, ホポクナ, 横ニ立テラル. *v.i.* To be set on its edge (as a basket or box). To be tipped on one side.

Hopoknare, ホポクナレ, 斜メニ立タセル. *v.t.* To tilt on one side. To set on its edge (as a basket or box).

Hopoknashi, ホポクナシ, 下. *adv.* Underneath. Below. Under.

Hopoknashi-kotoro, ホポクナシコトロ, 下方ノ面. *n.* The under surface of anything.

Hoporap, ホポラプ, 蝶. *n.* Same as *heporap,* "a butterfly."

Hopoye-rera, ホポイェレラ, 旋風. *n.* A whirl-wind. **Syn: Shipoye-poye rera. Wen rera. Rera-shiu.**

Hoppa, ホッパ, 殘ス. *v.t.* To leave behind.

Hopse, ホプセ, 吸フ. *v.t.* To sip up.

Hopsehopse, ホプセホプセ, 吸フ. *v.t.* To sip up.

Hopse-hopse-kara, ホプセホプセカラ, 吸フ. *v.t.* To sip up.

Hopse-kara, ホプセカラ, 吸フ. *v.t.* To sip up.

Hopumba, ホプムバ, 飛ブ、上ガル (複數). *v. i.* To fly. To get up. To arise. (*Sing. of hopuni*).

Hopuni, ホプニ, 飛プ、上ガル (單數).
v. i. To fly. To get up. To
arise. To set out on a journey
(*pl. Hopumba*).

Hopunki, ホプンキ,
Opunki, オプンキ, ⎱ 左様、然リ、ハイ. *adv.*
⎰ Yes. So.

Hopurap, ホプラプ, 蝶. *n.* A butterfly.

Horak, ホラク, 壞レル、折レル. *v. i.*
To break. To snap off as dead
wood. To tumble down as a
house.

Horak-hum, ホラクフム, 折レル音.
n. The sound of breaking wood.

Horakte, ホ ラ ク テ, 仆ス. *v.t.* To
push over. To knock down.

Horaochiwe, ホラオチウェ, 仆ル、下
レ、落ツル. *v. i.* To fall down.
To come down. To drop off. To
descend. **Syn: Raotereke.**

Horap, ホラプ,
Orap, オラプ, ⎱ ヤマシヤクヤク. *n. Pæonia*
⎰ *obovata, Max.*

Horararase, ホラララセ, 沈ム. *v. i.*
To sink into.

Horari, ホラリ, アル、ナレ. *v.i.* To
be. To exist. **Syn: An. Rari.**

Horashi, ホラシ, 下. *adv.* Beneath.
Under. Underneath.

Horatutu, ホラツツ, 辷ル. *v.i.* To
slide. **Syn: Oninkot. Harotke.
Charase.**

Horatutu-ushi, ホラツツウシ, 辷ル
所. *n.* A slide. **Syn: Oninkot
an-i.**

Horawashi, ホラワシ, 下、例セパ、ホ
ラワシアミプ、下衣. *adv,* Under.
Beneath. As :—*Horawashi amip,*
"an under garment."

Hore, ホレ,
Horehore, ホレホレ, ⎱ 來イ來イ. *excl.* Come !
⎰ come !

Horika, ホリカ, 下ノ方ニ. *adv.*
Downwards.

Horikashi, ホリカシ, 下ノ方ニ. *adv.*
Downwards.

Horiki, ホリキ, 上ノ方ニ. *adv.*
Upwards.

Horikiraye, ホリキライェ, 衣ヲ褰ケレ
(單數). *v.t.* To tuck up the clothes.
To pull up the garments (as for
work).

Horikirayepa, ホリキライェパ, ホリ
キライェノ(複數). *pl.* of *Horikiraye.*

Horikitai, ホ リ キ タ イ, 上. *adv.*
Over. The space above.

Horiko, ホリコ, 上. *adv.* Over.
Overhead.

Hiripi, ヒリピ,
Horippa, ホリッパ, ⎱ 飛プ、躍ル. *v.i.* To jump.
⎰ To dance.

Horippa-shinot, ホリパシノツ, 踊ノ
名. *n.* The name of a dance.

Horohorose, ホロホロセ, 襲撃スレ.
v.t. To set upon as a dog.

Horohorose-kara, ホロホロセカラ,
襲撃サセル. *v. t.* To set a dog
upon.

Horoka, ホ ロ カ, 後ヘ向ク. *adv.*
Turned backwards. Backwards.
Back.

Horoka-ai-ush-ni, ホロカアイウシニ,
ナニウコギ. *n.* A kind of thorny
tree. *Acanthopanax divaricatum,*
S. et Z.

Horoka-apkash, ホロカアプカシ, 後
ヘ歩ム、後退スレ. *v. i.* To walk
backwards.

Horoka-chiu, ホロカチウ, 渦. n. An eddy. A back-water.

Horokaika, ホロカイカ, 眞直ニ. adv. Straightway. As:—*Horokaika hoshipi,* "to return straightway." *Horokaika tereke ahun,* "to rush in." Syn: Nuni.

Horoka-ingara, ホロカインガラ, 顧ル. v.i. To look back.

Horoka-moi, ホロカモイ, 渦. n. An eddy.

Horokareyep, ホロカレイェブ, サリカニ. n. A crayfish.

Horokashi, ホロカシ, 下ニ. adv. Downwards.

Horoka-shipi, ホロカシピ, 後ヘ往ク. v.i. To go backward.

Horoka-shuwat, ホロカシュワツ, 木製ノ鉤. n. A wooden hook.

Horokasuwat, ホロカスワツ, 同上. n. Same as above.

Horoka-tom, ホロカトム, 反照、反射. n. A reflection.

Horoka-tuyo-tuyo, ホロカツヨツヨ, 振リ反ル. v.i. To face about. To turn round. Syn: Hosari.

Horokeu, ホロケウ, 狼、オホカミ. n. A wolf.

Horokeu-kene, ホロケウケ子, ミヤマハンノキ. n. A kind of alder. *Alnus viridis, DC. var. sibirica, Rgl.*

Horopse, ホロブセ, 吸フ、呑ム. v.t. To sip up. To drink.

Horopse-kara, ホロブセカラ, 吸フ、呑ム. v.t. To sip up.

Hororose-kara, ホロロセカラ, 襲撃サセル(犬ノ如ク). v.t. To set at as a dog. To cause to attack.

Horose, ホロセ, 腐敗シタル. adj. Stale. Stinking. Addled. Rotten. Syn: Munin.

Horutu, ホルツ, ニヽル(地ニリノ如ク). v. i. To slip as land. Syn: Meshke.

Hosamun, ホサマム, 振向ク. v.i. To turn the head.

Hosare, ホサレ, 廻ル. v.t. To turn round.

Hosari, ホサリ, 神ノ攝理. n. Providence. As:—*Kamui hosari an gusu ene ani ne,* "it is so by the providence of God."

Hosari, ホサリ, 後振向ク、例セバ、ホサリツインガラ、後ヲ振向イテ見ル. v.i. To turn the head. To turn about. As:—*Hosari wa ingara,* "to look back," "to look round."

Hosarire, ホサリレ, 他人ノ頭ヲ振向カセル. v.t. To turn the head of another. To cause to turn round.

Hose, ホセ, 下ル、例セバ、エフルホセ、小山ヲ下ル. v. i. To descend. As:—*Ehuru hose,* "to descend a hill." Syn: Ran. San. Pesh.

Hose, ホセ, 聲ヲ搦ゲテ答フ. v.t. To answer by calling to.

Hose, ホセ, 倒ス. v. t. To fell as trees. As:—*Chikuni hose,* "to cut down trees.

Hosh, ホシ, } 脚胖. n. Leggings.
Hoshi, ホシ, }

Hosh-at, ホシアツ, 脚胖ノ紐. n. Legging strings.

Hosh-hosh, ホシホシ, 犬ヲ掛ラセル. v.t. To set a dog at any one.

Hoshike, } 以前、例ヘバ、ホシキヌマ
ホシケ, } ン、一昨日. adv. Last.
Hoshiki, } Previous. Before.
ホシキ, } Antecedent. As:—*Hoshiki numan,* "the day before yesterday." *Hoshiki sak ne,* "the year before last."

Hoshiki, ホシキ, 待ツ. *v.i.* To wait. **Syn : Oshke.**

Hoshiki-an, ホシキアン, 前者ノ、例セバ、ホシキアンヌマン、一昨日. *adv.* The previous one. As :— *Hoshiki an numan,* "the day before yesterday." *Hoshiki an sakne pa,* "the year before last."

Hoshiki-hoshiki, ホシキホシキ, マテマテ. *ph.* Wait, wait.

Hoshiki-no, ホシキノ, 以前ニ. *adv.* Previously.

Hoshiki-teine, ホシキテイ子, バイケイサウ. *n. Veratrum album, L. var. grandiflorum, Max.*

Hoshipi, ホシビ, 還ル(單數). *v.i.* To return. (*Sing*).

Hoshipire, ホシビレ, 戻ス. *v.t.* To send back.

Hoshippa, ホシッパ, 還ル(複數). *v.i.* To return. (*pl*).

Hoshippare, ホシッパレ, 返ス、戻ス. *v.t.* To send back. To return. (*pl*).

Hoshipshipi, ホシブシビ, 廻ル、例セバ、ホシブシヒワインガラ、後チ見ル. *v.i.* To turn round. As :— *Hoshipshipi wa ingara,* "to look back." **Syn : Okshut no.**

Hoshiptektek, ホシブテクテク, 早ク還ル. *v.i.* To return quickly.

Hosura, ホスラ, 無禮チ働ク. *v.i.* To act in an indecent manner. To insult another by exposing one's self.

Hot, ホツ, } **Hotne, ホツ子,** } 二十. *adj.* Twenty. A score.

Hota-hota, ホタホタ, 輾轉スル、ノタウチマワレ. *v.i.* To wallow. **Syn: Yaikirukiru. Shishiripa.**

Hotakba, ホタクバ, 蹴ル. *v.t.* To kick the feet out. To struggle. **Syn : Hopayepaye.**

Hotakutaku, ホタクタク, 爬キ掘ル. *v.i.* To lie down and scratch up the earth (as fowls).

Hotanu, ホタヌ, } **Hotanukara, ホタヌカラ,** } 訪問スレ、見舞フ. *v. t.* To visit a sick person. To call upon a person in trouble. This verb is usually immediately followed by *gusu* and the verb *arapa,* "to go." As :— *Nei tashum guru ku hotanukara gusu ku arapa kusu ne,* "I will go and visit the sick person." *Chihotanukara iyekarakara wa ikore yan,* "please pay us a visit."

Hotari, ホタリ, 倒ル、破裂スル. *v.i.* To tumble down. To burst as a volcano. **Syn : Opush.**

Hotari-ni, ホタリニ, 家ノ垂木ノ下端ニ結ブ木 (桁ナリ). *n.* The long poles to which the lower ends of theend rafters of a hut are tied. **Syn: Hetari-ni.** See also **Amanni.**

Hotempayaya, ホテムパヤヤ, カニ. *n.* A crab. **Syn : Ambayaya.**

Hotemtemu, ホテムテム, カニ. *n.* A crab.

Hotemu, ホテム, 横ニ歩ム. *v.i.* To move along sidewise.

Hotke, ホツケ, } **Hokke, ホッケ,** } 伏ス、寝ニ就ク. *v.i.* To lie down. To go to bed.

Hotke-wa-an, ホツケワアン, 寝テイレ. *adv.* Abed. In bed.

Hotkere, ホツケレ, 寝サセレ. *v.t.* To lay down. To put to bed.

Hotku, ホツク, 身ヲ屈メル. *v.i.* To stoop down.

Hotku-hotku, ホツクホツク, 屈メレ. *v.i.* To stoop down.

Hotoki-maimai, ホトキマイマイ, クロミノウケヒスカゲラ、日ノミ. *n.* A kind of honeysuckle. *Lonicera coerulea,* L. **Syn: Ho. Enunitanne.**

Hotopo, ホトポ, 再ビ歸ヘル. *adv.* Back again. **Syn : Hetopo.**

Hottoro, ホットロ, 額. *n.* The forehead. **Syn : Heputuru.**

Hottoro-gesh, ホットロゲシ, 額ノ下部. *n.* The lower part of the forehead.

Hotui, ホツイ,
Hotuye, ホツイェ, } 呼ブ. *v.t.* To call.

Hottoro-pa, ホットロバ, 額ノ上部. *n.* The upper part of the forehead.

Hotuse, ホツセ, 引ク. *v.t.* To draw. **Syn : Nimba.**

Hotuyekara, ホツイェカラ, 呼ブ. *v.t.* To call. To call to. As :—*Nei guru hotuyekara yan,* "call him." *Nei guru hotuyekar'an,* "call him."

Hotuyepakara, ホツイェバカラ, 呼ブ. To call. (*pl*).

Hoyashi, ホヤシ, 海濱、河畔. *n.* The seaside. A river side. The brink of the sea or a river.

Hoyashi-ikaobas, ホヤシイカオバス, 溺死スル人ヲ救フ. *v.t.* To go to save one from drowning.

Hoye, ホイェ, 惡シキ業ナチナス. *v.t.* To do evil deeds. To act sinfully.

Hoyecheppo, ホイェチェッポ, 魚ノ名. *n.* A kind of fish. *Elxis nikkonis,* Jor and Sny.

Hoyuptektek, ホユブテクテク, 速ク飛ビ去ル. *v.t.* To fly away quickly.

Hoyupu, ホユブ, 走ル(單數). *v.i.* To run. (*sing*).

Hoyuppa, ホユッバ, 走ル(複數). *v.i.* To run. (*pl*).

Huchi-kema, フチケマ, 燃木 (モヘサシ). *n.* A fire-brand.

Huchi, フチ,
Huji, フヂ, } 祖母. *n.* Grandmother. An old woman. Female ancestors. Fire. *Kamui huchi,* "the goddess of fire."

Hui, フイ,
Hube, フイベ, } 獸ノ腹中ノ脂肪. *n.* The inside fat of animals of the larger kinds. By some "the liver."

Hui-ni, フイ二, 落葉松 (カラマツ). *n.* Larch. **Syn : Hup-ni.**

Hum, フム, 碎片、塊. *n.* A piece of anything.

Hum, フム, 音. *n.* A sound. **Syn : Humi.**

Humba, フムバ, 磨リ耗ラス、細二切ル. *v.t.* To grate. To cut into very fine pieces. To cut up. **Syn : Nokan no tuyeba.**

Humba-humba, フムバフムバ, 細二切レ. *v.t.* To cut up in fine pieces.

Humbe, フムベ, クヂラ. *n.* A whale.

Humbe-e, フムベエ, 鯨ノ白肉. *n.* Blubber.

Humbe-etoro, フムベエトロ, クラゲ. *n.* Jelly-fish. Medusa. **Syn : Toponra. Tonru-chep. Etoropo.**

Humbe-ki, フムベキ, 鯨ノ白肉. *n.* Whale blubber.

Humbe-reki, フムベレキ, 鯨鬚. *n.* Whale-bone.

Humbe-rika, フムベリカ, 鯨ラノ白肉. *n.* Blubber.

Humhum-okkai-kamui, フムフムオッカイカムイ, シマフクロゥ. *n.* Blakiston's eagle owl.

Humbe-rit, フムベリツ, 鯨ノ腱. *n.* Whale's sinews.

Humge, フムゲ, 搖ル. *v.t.* To dangle or swing about. **Syn: Koshuyeshuye.**

Humhumse, フムフムセ, 羽音スル、(鳥ナドノ). *v.i.* To make a whirling sound as birds in flight.

Humi, フミ, 様子、音、形. *n.* Appearance. Sound. State. Form. By way of. As:— *Wen humi an,* "it appears to be bad." *Poro humi an,* "there is a great sound." *Yainu humi wen,* "to feel out of sorts." *Nukara humi wen,* "ugly." *Ingar'an humi ne ya, wendarap an humi hene ya, aeramushkare,* "whether by way of a dream, or by sight, I know not." *Chikuikui ap koro humi airu an,* "I feel like being gnawed."

Humi, フミ, 何ント、(感嘆)、例セバ、ネッポロフミ、何ト大キナモノダラウ. *interj.* How! Dear me, how! As:—*Nep poro humi,* "how great." *Nep wen humi,* "how bad." *Shiri seisek humi,* "dear me, how very hot it is!"

Humirui, フミルイ, エゾヤマドリ、エゾライテフ. *n.* The hazel-hen.

Humkan, フムカン, 音、音スレ. *n.* A sound. *v.i.* To make a noise. **Syn: Humiash.**

Humnanda, フムナンダ, or **Humnanta,** フムナンタ, 同所ニ. *adv.* At one place. By the side of. Together. As:— *Humnanda ibe,* "to eat together."

Humnanda-ande, フムナンダアンデ, 同所ニ置ク. *v.t.* To put in one place. To put together.

Humnanta, フムナンタ, 同所ニ. *adv.* In one place. Together.

Humnan-un, フムナンウン, 同所ニ. *adv.* In one place. Together.

Humne, フムネ, 時々. *adv.* Sometimes. At intervals.

Hum-niukeshte, フムニウケシテ, 能ハヌ. *v.i.* To be unable. **Syn: Eaikap.**

Hum-ochikap, フムオチカプ, 梟. *n.* An owl.

Humotanne, フモタンネ, 遠響. *n.* A long rumbling sound.

Humrarire, フムラリレ, 止マレ. *v.i.* To settle upon. To come upon.

Humrikikatta, フムリキカッタ, 音シテ上ル. *v.i.* To ascend with a sound.

Humse, フムセ, 音ヲ發スル. *v.i.* To gruff. To grunt. To growl. To sound. To make a noise.

Humse-chikap, フムセチカプ, コイサキ. *n.* Night-heron. *Nycticarix nycticarap, Linn.*

Humse-humse, フムセフムセ, 鳴ラス、例セバ、キサラフムセフムセ、耳ガ鳴ル. *v.i.* To sound. To make a noise. As:—*Kisara humsehumse,* "to have a noise in the ears."

Humuturu, フムツル, 端、ハシ. *n.* The ends of such things as string and cotton.

Hunak, フナク, or **Kunak,** クナク, 何々スルト、例セバ、アラパクナクイエ、彼ハ往クト云ヘリ. *pro.* That. As:

—*Arapa hunak ye*, " he says that he will go."

Hunaketa, フナケタ, 彼所. *adv.* There. That place.

Hunakta, フナクタ, 何所. *adv.* Where? As:—*Hunakta an ruwe he an!* "where is he."

Hunakta-un, フナクタウン, 何所ヘ. *adv.* Whither?

Hunakta-wa, フナクタワ, 何所ヨリ. *adv.* Whence?

Hunak-un, フナクウン, 何所ヘ. *adv.* Whither. As:—*Hunak un arapa!* "where are you going."

Hunak-wa, フナクワ, 何所ヨリ、何所. *adv.* Whence? Where. As:— *Hunak wa e korobe an!* " where did you get it?"

Hunapak, フナパク, 仕合ナル、幸福ナル. *adv.* Fortunately.

Hunara, フナラ, 尋ヌル、探ス (單數). *v.t.* To search for. To seek. (*sing*).

Hunarapa, フナラパ, 尋ヌレ、探レ. *v.t.* To search for. (*pl*).

Hunda, フンダ, 筆. *n.* A written form. (*Jap: Fude*). As:—*Shiroshi hunda*, " a passport."

Hunki, フンキ,
Hunka, フンカ, } 草又ハ灌木ノアル海濱. *n.* That part of the seashore upon which grass and low shrubs grow.

Hunna, フンナ, 誰. *pro.* Who. *Hunna e korep an!* " who gave it to you." **Syn: Nenta-an.**

Hunna-koro, フンナコロ, 誰ノ、(持格). *pro.* Whose. As:—*Hunna korope an!* " whose is it?"

Hunsebe, フンセベ, *n.* Same as *hunse-chikap.*

Hup, フプ, 腫物. *n.* A swelling. A boil. An abcess. As:—*Huphetuku*, " to have boils."

Hup-oma, フプオマ. 腫物アル. *v.i.* To have boils.

Hup-ni, フプニ, トドマツ. *n.* Sakhalien fir. *Abies sachalinensis, Masters.*

Huppokush-mun, フッポクシムン, ツメメナモト. *n.* *Clintonia udensis, Trautv. et Mey.*

Hupsei, フプセイ, or **Hupiusei, フピウセイ**, ジンカサガヒ. *n.* Limpets. Patella.

Hura, フラ, or **Huraha, フラハ**, 香氣、例セバ、チマウフラ、熟果ノ香、ニワフラ、善キ香. *n.* A smell. As: —*Chi-mau hura*, " the smell of ripe brier fruit.' *Niwa hura*, " a nice ripe smell." *Nitoro hura*, " the smell of over-ripe brier fruit." *Nitokot hura*, " a smell of something decomposing."

Hura-at, フラアツ, 惡臭チ發スル. *v.i.* To stink.

Hura-nu, フラヌ, 嗅ク. *v.t.* To smell.

Hurakrakkara, フラクラッカラ, or **Hurarakka, フララッカ**, 嗅ク. *v.t.* To smell.

Hurarui, フラルイ, 强キ匂ヒノ、例セバ、フラルイアイヌ、强キ香ノアル人. *adj.* Having a strong smell. As: —*Hurarui ainu*, " a strong smelling man."

Hurarui-chep, フラルイチェプ, キコウリウナ. *n.* Same as *Nuiras* Smelt. *Osmerus dentex, Steind.*

Hurarui-kina, フラルイキナ, or **Hurarui-mun, フラルイムン**, ギャウジャニンニク、キトビル. *n.* *A kind of Garlic. Allium victorsalis, L.*

Sometimes stuffed in the pillows of the sick to drive out disease. **Syn : Pukusa.**

Hura-wen, フラウェン, 悪臭. *n.* A bad smell. A stink.

Hura-wen-kina, フラウェンキナ, カリガチサウ. *n.* *Caryopteris divaricata, Max.*

Huru-an, フルアン, or **Furu-an, フルアン,** 坂アル. *adj.* Acclivious.

Huru, フル, or **Furu, フル,** 小山、坂. *n.* A hill. An acclivity.

Hussa, フッサ, 病ヲ吹キ掃フ、(人ノ病ヲ癒ス爲メニスルコト). *v.i.* To blow upon the sick as a charm to drive away disease.

Hussa-omande, フッサオマンデ, 大息スル. *v.i.* and *v.t.* To sigh. To blow. To puff. To blow at. **Syn: Hussa shiukosamba.**

Hussei, フッセイ, —吹キ. *v.i.* and *n.* To blow. A puff. The cere-

mony of blowing upon the sick. See the next word.

Hussei-omande, フッセイオマンデ, or **Hussei-shiukosamba, フッセイシウコサムバ,** 吹ク. *v.t.* To blow at. Also *v.i.* To sigh. To puff.

Hut, フツ, 驚嘆ノ詞. *interj.* An exclamation of surprise.

Hutne, フツ子, 窄キ. *adj.* Narrow.

Huttat, フツタツ, スヾタケ. *n.* Bamboo grass. Arundinaria. *Sasa borealis, Max. et Shib.* Sometimes pronounced as though it were *futtat. Huttat takusa,* "a bunch of bamboo grass."

Huyehe, フイェへ, 煩、顏、容貌. *n.* The cheeks. The Face. Countenance. Also pronounced. *fuyehe.* **Syn: Heye.**

Huyuine, フユイ子, 全ク. *adj.* Entirely. Through and through.

I (イ).

I, イ, 此ノイ (I) ヲ動詞ノ前ニ置クトキハ其ノ意義ヲ强クス、例セバ、ヌ、聞ク、イヌ、注意シテ聞ク. (*i*). When the vowel *I* is prefixed to some verbs it has the power of intensifying their meaning. As :—*Nu,* "to hear," *iuu,* "to listen. *Chimichimi,* "to search after," *ichimi-chimi,* "to search diligently after."

I, イ, 時トシテ此ノイ (I) ハ 自己代名詞ノ第三人稱單數ニ用井ラル、例セバ、カムイイイツレンワグアスネイノイタクルウェネ、神ヨリ詫宣ヲ受ケテカクノ如キコトヲ云フ. (*ii*). Sometimes the particle *I* stands for the third per-

son singular personal pronoun, objective case. As :—*Kamui i ituren wa gusu nei no itak ruwe ne,* "he speaks so because he is inspired by God." *Ikurukashike,* "upon him." *Nep ipon aiai,* "what a small child it is." *Seta inoshpa ruwe ne,* "the dog is chasing him." *Akoro sapo ireshpa ruwe ne,* "my elder sister brought him up."

I, イ, 此ノイ (I) ハ時トシテ人代名詞ノ第一人稱複數物主格トナルナリ、例セバ、イパクスネ、彼レハ我々チ見付ケルナラン. (*iii*). Sometimes the vowel *I* stands for the first person plural objective case of the personal pronoun, "us." Thus:—*Ipa kusu ne*, "he will find us." *Ikik an*, "he struck us."

I, イ, 此ノイ (I) ハ時トシテ人代名詞ノ第一人稱單數物主格トナルナリ、例セバ、イユプテ、我ニ與ヘヨ。(*iv*). Sometimes the vowel *I* stands for the first person singular objective case of the personal pronoun. As:—*Iyupte*, "give it to me." *Iere*, feed me." **Syn : En.**

I, イ, 此ノ字ヲ實名詞ノ前ニ置クトキハ第三人稱單數物主格トナルナリ、例セバ、イポネグル、彼レノ子供。(*v*). Sometimes, when *I* is prefixed to nouns, it represents the third person singular possessive pronoun, "his" or "her." As:—*Ipo ne guru*, "his" or "her child."

I, イ, 此ノ字ヲ形容詞又ハ動詞ニ付加スルトキハ實名詞ニ變セシムルチ得、例セバ、ピリカ、宜シイ、ピリカイ、善キコト、オケレ、仕上ル、オケレイ、仕上.(*vi*.) When suffixed to adjectives and verbs *I* has the power of changing them into nouns. Thus:—*pirika*, "good," *pirika-i*, "goodness." *Okere*, "to finish," *okere-i*, "the finish." *Akara*, "to be done," *Akari*, "a thing done," "a thing to be done." *Ene akari ka isam*, "nothing can be done" (i.e. there is no help for it).

イ, 此ノ字ヲ ne ニ付加フルトキハ指示代名詞トナルナリ、例セバ、ネイアンベ、其ノ物。(*vii*). When suffixed to *ne* the particle *I* makes with *ne* the demonstrative pronoun, "that," "those." Thus:—*Nei ainu*, "that man." *Nei utara*, "those persons." *Nei ambe*, "that thing."

I, イ, 此ノ字ヲタ (ta) ナル語ニ付加シイタ (ita) トスルトキハ場所或ハ時チ指示ス、例セバ、ネイイタ、其ノ時、或ハ其ノ所。(*viii*). When *I* is prefixed to the word *ta*, thus making it *ita*, "time" or "place" is expressed. Thus:—*Nei ita*, "at that time or place."

I, イ, 文章中ニ單獨ニ置カルヽトキハ時或ハ場所チ指示スレナリ、例セバ、ネイイオロ、其所ヨリ、其時ヨリ。(*ix*). When standing alone in a sentence, the vowel *I* often signifies "time" or "place." Thus:—*Nei i oro*, "from there;" "thence", "from that time."

I, イ, 時トシテイ (I) ノ後ニワノ、ワ、又ハ、オロワ、(カラ、ヨリ、ノ意) 又ハ。オッタ、オロン、(ニ、又ハ、ヘ、ノ意) 等ノ語カ續クトキハ凡テ地名ノ後ニ用井ラルヽナリ、例セバ、サツポロイワノ、札幌ヨリ。(*x*). The particle *I* is often heard suffixed to the names of places when followed by the post-positions *wano*, *wa*, *orowa*, "from" or *otta*; *orun*, *orota*, "to." Thus:—*Satporo*, *i wano*, "from Satporo" *Pirator' i otta*, "to Piratori." When so used *i* appears as the equivalent of *kotan*, "town," "place," or "village."

I, イ, テクサマタ (傍、ソバ) ト云フ副詞ニ付加ヘルトキハ此ノイ (I) ハ時トシテ我レチ、我レノ、ナル意トナル。(*xi*). When prefixed to the adverb *teksamata*, "by the side of," *i* sometimes represents the pronoun *en*, "me." As:—*Iteksamata*, "by my side."

I, **イ**, 此ノイ (I) ハカラフト、又ハ沙流地方ニ於テハ時トシテ n ノ代リニ用井ラル、例セバ、ポイ、チポント云フガ如シ. (xii). In speaking *I* will often be heard for *n* particularly in the Saru and Saghalien dialects As: — *Poi* for *pon*, " small," " little."

I, **イ**, イート云フ叫聲. An onomatopœa for a squeal.

Ibe, **イベ**, 食スル、例セバ、イベアエラムシンヂ、食フテ仕マフ. *v.t.* To eat. As: — *Ibe aeramushinne*, " to have been satisfied with food."

Ibe-ambe, **イベアムベ**, 食物. *n.* Food. Syn: Aep.

Ibe-ap, **イベアプ**, 吝マズニ食物ヲ與フル. *adj.* and *v.i.* To be kind in giving away food.

Ibe-erok, **イベエロク**, 食スル爲メニ坐ス、(複數). *v.i.* To sit down to eat.

Ibehe, **イベヘ**, 食物、果實、言語ノ意味、原素、力、刀劍ノ又. *n.* Food. Fruit. Bulbs. The meaning of a word. Essence. A sword or knife-blade. Strength.

Ibe-hunara, **イベフナラ**, 吝嗇、シワキ. *v.i.* To be stingy.

Ibe-bashui, **イベバシュイ**, 箸、ハシ. *n.* Chop-sticks.

Ibe-mondum, **イベモンヅム**, 食慾. *n.* The appetite.

Ibe-op, **イベオプ**, 鎗. *n.* Spears.

Ibep, **イベプ**, 食器. *n.* Eating utensils.

Ibepa, **イベパ**, 食スル. *v.t.* (*pl*). To eat.

Ibeporore, **イベポロレ**, 食婪ナル. *adj.* and *v.i.* Avaricious. Greedy. Coveteous. Syn: Ibe-shikashure. Eporore. Eishikashpari.

Ibere, **イベレ**, 食ベサセレ. *v.t.* To feed.

Iberekut, **イベレクツ**, 食道. *n.* The œsophagus.

Ibe-rok, **イベロク**, 大食スレ. *v.t.* To be given to much eating. To sit and eat.

Ibe-rui, **イベルイ**, 食ヲ食レ. *adj.* and *v.i.* Greedy. To be a great eater. To be greedy.

Ibe-sak, **イベサク**, 乏シキ、無意味ナル、漁獵ニ幸ノナキ. *adj.* and *v.i.* To be poor. To be unlucky in the hunt or at fishing. Absurd. Meaningless.

Ibe-sakbe, **イベサクベ**, 笑フ可キコト、背理. *n.* An absurdity.

Ibe-sak-no, **イベサクノ**, 荒唐ニ. *adv.* Absurdly.

Ibe-sarakorobe, **イベサラコロベ**, ナナガザメ. *n.* Thresher shark. *Alopecias vulpes*, (*Gmelin*.)

Ibeshikashure, **イベシカシュレ**, 食レ. *v.t.* To covet. To be greedy over.

Ibeshikashure, **イベシカシュレ**, 食レ. *adj.* and *v.i.* To be coveteous. Greedy. Avaricious.

Ibetam, **イベタム**, 刀、カタナ、劍. *n.* A sword.

Ibeunara, **イベウナラ**, 鄙吝スレ. *v.i.* To be stingy. Syn: Epyupke.

Ibe-ush, **イベウシ**, 肥エタル、大粒ノ、例セバ、イベウシアマム、大粒ノ米. *adj.* Well-favoured. Full. Fat. As: — *Ibe-ush amam*, " full corn."

Icha, **イチャ**, 摘ミ採ル、鯨ノ肉ヲ切ル. To gather. To pick off. To cut up whale's flesh. Syn: Ipushtuye.

Ichaka, イチャカ, 不潔ナル、無遠慮ナル. *adj.* Dirty. Immodest.

Ichakka, イチャッカ, 急＝起チ上ル. *v.i.* To start up suddenly.

Ichakkere, イチャッケレ, 不潔ナル. *adj.* Dirty.

Ichakoko, イチャココ, 教ヘル、馴ラス. *v.t.* To train. To teach. A hole. A ditch.

Ichan, イチャン, 鱒鮭ノ卵ヲ産ミ付ケル水中ノ塚. *n.* The hole salmon make in the beds of rivers in which to deposit their spawn. A spawning bed.

Ichan-chup, イチャンチュブ, 新月. *n.* The new moon.

Ichaniu-chep, イチャニウチェブ, 鱒(マス). *n.* Sea trout. *Oncorhynchus masou, Brevoort.*

Ichanui, イチャヌイ, 鱒(マス). *n.* Same as above.

Ichankot, イチャンコツ, ヤマベ. *n.* Young sea trout.

Ichanui, イチャヌイ, 鱒. *n.* A salmon-trout.

Ichanui-cheppo, イチャヌイチェッポ, 鱒ノ子. *n.* A small salmon-trout.

Icha-piba, イチャピバ, 貝ノ名(アイヌハ此ノ貝ヲ以テ穀物ノ穂ナドヲ切リ採ル＝用ユ). *n.* A kind of shell used for cutting off the ears of corn during harvest. **Syn：Icha-sei.**

Icharapa-an, イチャラパアン, 神酒ヲ獻ズル儀式. *n.* The ceremony of offering libations to the gods. The ceremony of house-warming. **Syn：Achikka an. Shinnurappa.**

Icharapo, イチャラポ, シャク、コシャク. *n.* The wild chervil. *Anthriscus sylvestris, Hoffm.*

Ichari, イチャリ, 篩(フルイ). *n.* A round wicker basket. A sieve.

Ichari-kina, イチャリキナ, (イチャラポ、ト同ジ). *n.* Same as *Icharapo.*

Icha-sei, イチャセイ, 穀物ヲ刈入レル＝用ユル貝. *n.* Shells used for cutting off the ears of corn in harvest. **Syn：Icha-piba.**

Ichashkara, イチャシカラ, 呪フ、トリック. *v.t.* To curse. To bewitch. **Syn：Ishirishina.**

Ichawetenge, イチャウェテンゲ, 命ズル. *v. t.* To command. **Syn：Ipawetenge.**

Ichen, イチェン, 錢. *n.* Money.

Ichikimaimai, イチキマイマイ, ガンカウラン、コケノミ. *n.* The crowberry. *Empetrum nigrum, L.*

Ichimichimi, イチミチミ, 懇＝探ス. *v. t.* To search diligently after. To act inquisitively.

Ichotcha, イチョッチャ, 剌ス. *v.t.* To sting (as a wasp).

Ichuptasarep, イチュブタサレブ, 赤楊樹ノ皮ノ煎汁ナリ産後＝服用ス. *n.* The name of a decoction made from alder bark and taken after child-birth.

Ien-peka, イエンペカ,
Iyen-peka, イイェンペカ, ｝上ヘ. *adv.* Over.

Ienupitara, イエヌピタラ, 輕ンズル. 拒絶スル. *v. t.* To slight. To reject.

Ifurere, イフレレ, 赤ク染メル. *v. t.* To dye red.

Ihabo, イハボ, 父. *n.* Father. **Syn：Michi.**

Ihaita-keutum, イハイタケウツム; 惡心. n. A bad heart or mind.

Ihanokka, イハノッカ, 呼ブ、起コス. v.t. To call. To wake up.

Ihenkotpa, イヘンコツパ, 點頭スル、愛スル、可愛ガレ. v. i. To nod to a person. To endeavour to attract the attention of a small child by nodding. To love. To fondle. To comfort.

Ihewe, イヘウェ, 横風ニテ帆走スル. v.t. To sail with a side wind. To tack as a ship.

Ihok, イホク, 賣買スレ. v.t. To buy or sell.

Ihokbe, イホクベ, 商品. n. Merchandise.

Ihokkorobe, イホノコロベ, 賣品. n. Same as above.

Ihoma, イホマ, 憐憫. n. Compassions. Tender mercies.

Ihoroshutke, イホロシュツケ, ガ急セル. v.t. To hurry. Syn: Iunashka.

Ihoserekere, イホセレケレ, 困難スレ. v. i. To be in trouble. Syn: Iyoyanumare. Yaikowepekere.

Ihoshki, イホシキ, 酩酊スレ. v.i. To be drunk.

Ihumba, イフムバ, 細カニ切リタレ. adj. Cut. To mince.

Ihumge, イフムゲ, 喧シキ. adj. Noisy.

Ii, イイ, 成程. interj. Indeed. Oh. Syn: Ohaine.

Ik, イク, 關節、章節、脊骨、例セバ、ポチイクプイ、神經弓. n. A joint of the body. A division. A chapter. A verse. The backbone. As:—Pone ik-pui, "the neural canal of the backbone."

Ik, イク, 百. adj. A hundred. Syn: Ashikne hotne.

Ika, イカ, 理. n. A reason.

Ika, イカ, 溢レル、沸騰スル. v.i. To run over. To overflow. To bubble up. To pass from one to another. To be full.

Ika, イカ, 注意ノ語、例セバ、イカエチハチンナ、氣チ付ケヨ汝ハ墜落セン. excl. and adv. Be careful lest. Look out! Mind! Lest. As:— Ika! echi hachin na, "be careful or you will fall." Syn: Ikiya.

Ika, イカ, 爲スナカレ、例セバ、イカエチエナ、食フナカレ、イカエオマンナ、行ク勿レ. v.i. Do not. As:—Ika echi e na, "don't eat them." Ika e oman na, "do not go." Syn: Iteki.

Ika, イカ, 步ミ. n. A stride. A step.

Ika, イカ, 飛跳ル. v. i. To take leaps and bounds.

Ikabiuki, イカビウキ, 助ケル. v. t. To help. To assist.

Ikaehotanu-guru, イカエホタヌグル, 番人、病者チ見舞フ人. n. A watchman. One who visits the sick.

Ikaetunnai, イカエツンナイ, 疾走スル(馬ノ如ク). v.i. To gallop very fast.

Ikaeyoko, イカエヨコ, 看病スル. v.t. To nurse the sick. To watch over. To keep watch.

Ikaeyoko-guru, イカエヨコグル, 看病人. n. A sick-nurse. Syn: Ikahuye guru. See also Chipoka ekahuye guru.

Ikahuye, イカフイエ, 看病スル. v. t. To nurse the sick.

Ikahuye-guru, イカフエグル, 看病人. *n.* A sick nurse.

Ika-ika, イカイカ, 沸ク(湯ノ如ク). *v.i.* To bubble up (as boiling water).

Ika-koro, イカコロ, 跨ケル、跨ケ. *v.t.* To step over. To gallop (as a horse). **Syn: Kama-kush.**

Ikanepeka, 為スベカラズ、例セバ、
イカ子ペカ, イカネペカエキナ、其
Iki-neipa, レナシテハナラヌ、イ
イキイバ, カネペカエオマンナ、
Ikineipeka, 汝ハ行クベカラズ. *v.*
イキイペカ, *i.* Must not. As :—*Ikanepeka e ki na*, "you must not do so." *Ikanepeka e oman na*, "you must not go."

Ikanepeka-shomo, イカ子ペカショモ, セネバナラヌ、例セバ、イカネペカシ ヨモエイエナ、言ヒナサイ. *ph.* Must. As :—*Ikanepeka shomo e ye na*, "you must say it."

Iki-neipeka-shomoki, イキ子イペカ ショモキ, 同上. *ph.* Same as above.

Ikani, イカニ, 眞珠. *n.* A pearl.

Ikaobas, イカオバス, 助ケル、救フ. *v.t.* To help. To save.

Ikaoiki, イカオイキ, 助ケル、救フ. *v.t.* To help.

Ikaononkara, イカオノンカラ, 番ス ル. *v.i.* To stand guard.

Ikaononkara-guru, イカオノンカラ グル, 番人. *n.* A guard.

Ikaoshke, イカオシケ, 與ヘル. *v.t.* To give. To bestow.

Ikapa, イカバ, 上ヘ. *adv.* Over. Above. *(pl)*.

Ikarakara, イカラカラ, 縫箔スレ、仕 事スル. *v.t.* To embroider. To work.

Ikaraku, イカラク, 甥、姪. *n.* A nephew.

Ikarapopchep, イカラポプチェプ, ヘ リフア. *n.* Same as *Ikarekocheppo*. Porcupine fish.

Ikarari, イカラリ, 縫ヒ付ケレ. *v.i.* To sew into. To sew one thing upon another. The narrow line seen upon a border in fancy needlework. To patch.

Ikarashki, イカラシキ, 執着スレ. *v.t.* To have a care for. To dislike to part with. To be attached to a thing. Loath to part with.

Ikare, イカレ, コボス、轉ゲル、例セ バ、プイカレ、倉庫ヨリ轉ゲ出ル. *v.t.* To spill. To roll out. To over fill. As :—*Pu ikare*, "to roll out of a godown."

Ikarekocheppo, イカレコチェッポ, ヘ リフア. *n.* Porcupine fish. *Diodon holocanthus, Linn.*

Ikarip, イカリプ, 粉碎スレ. *v.t.* To grind. To pound.

Ika-ru, イカル, 山ノ頂ノ途. *n.* A path along the top of mountains or hills.

Ikashi, イカシ, 上ニ. *adv.* Upon.

Ikashima, イカシマ, 過剰ノ. *adj.* Over. Above. Plus. . More than.

Ikashima, イカシマ, 餘ル、過ギレ、 例セバ、ムンギアホクワイカシマイチ エン、參チ買フテ餘リシ錢. *v.t.* and *adv.* To surpass. To exceed. Above. Over. As :—*Mungi ahok wa ikashima ichen*, "the money which remained after buying the wheat."

Ikashimap, イカシマプ, 残餘. *n.* Remnants. Remainder.

Ikashimare, イカシマレ, 加ヘル. *v.t.* To enhance.

Ikashimare-i, イカシマレイ, 残リモ ノ. *n.* Surplus. That which remains.

Ikashiu, ⎫ 助ケレ、例セバ、ニツネカ
イカシウ, ⎬ ムイオツタイカシウケル
Ikashui, ⎪ オカイ、惡冤ニ助ケル人
イカシュイ, ⎭ ガアレ. *v.t.* To help. To cast in one's lot with. To side with. As:—*Nitne kamui otta ikashiu guru okai,* "some persons side with (lend themselves to) the devil."

Ikashma, イカシマ, 餘ル、過ギル. Same as *Ikashima,* "to exceed."

Ikashmare-i, イカシマレイ, 附加. *n.* An Accession.

Ikashpaotte, イカシパオッテ, 命ズル. *v.t.* To command. To give commandments.

Ikashpaotte-i, イカシパオッテイ, 命 令. *n.* Commandments.

Ikashum, イカシュム, 餘リモノ、殘リ モノ. *n.* Surplus. That which is left ever.

Ikateomare-ambe, イカテオマレアム ベ, 同情. *n.* Sympathy.

Ikateomare-guru, イカテオマレグル, 朋友、親友. *n.* A friend. A hospitable person. A sympathizer.

Ikateomare-ki, イカテオマレキ, 同情 ヲ寄セル. *v.t.* To sympathise with.

Ikatkara, イカツカラ, 馬鹿ニスレ. *v.t.* To make a fool of. To deceive.

Ikaun, イカウン, 外ニ. *adv.* Besides.

Ika-unu, イカウヌ, 重ネル、氣儘ニ振 舞フ. *v.t.* To put in upon. To add to. To act wilfully. To act contrary to another's will.

Ika-ushi, イカウシ, 山路、ヤマミチ. *n.* A path over a hill.

Ikayop, ⎫
イカヨブ, ⎬ 矢筒. *n.* A quiver.
Ikayup, ⎪
イカユブ, ⎭

Ikayop-pakkai, イカヨブパッカイ, 矢 筒ヲ頁フ. *pl.* To carry a quiver of arrow.

Ike, イケ, 物、此語ハ屢關係代名詞トシ テ、所ノ物ノ意ヲ示ス、例セバ、チイ イカシュムイケユクノウクグルオツタ クコレナ、我ハユクノウクニ殘セシ所 ノ物ヲ與ヘシ、又、クヌカリケ我ガ見 シ物. *n.* An article. A thing. That. This word is often used as the relative pronoun "that which." As:—*Nei ikashum ike Yuk-no-uk guru otta ku kore na,* "I gave that which was left to *Yuk-no-uk.*" *Ku nukar' ike,* "that which I saw was." **Syn: Ambe.**

Ike, イケ, 其時ニ. *adv.* At that time.

Ikehumshu, イケフムシュ, 出來ゴト. *n.* An accident. **Syn: Ikeuhumshu.**

Ikem, イケム, 舐ル. *v.t.* To lick.

Ikema, イケマ, イケマ. *n.* A plant used both as a medicine and for food. *Cynanchum caudatum, Maxim.*

Ikema-chippo, イケマチッポ, イケマ ノ莢(サヤ). *n.* The pod of the *ikema* or *Cynanchum caudatum, Maxim.* **Syn: Penup.**

Ik emnu, イケムヌ, 復讎スレ、代理ス ル. *v.t.* To avenge. To take the part of another. **Syn: Ikotki.**

Ikemumbe, イケムムベ, 食指. *n.* The

index finger. **Syn : Itangi kem ashikipet.**

Ikera, イケラ, 甘キ. *adj.* Sweet. Nice.

Ikera, イケラ, 戀人. *n.* One's sweetheart.

Ikera, イケラ, 搔痕. *n.* A scratch.

Ikera-kara, イケラカラ, 爬ク. *v.t.* To make a scratch.

Ikere, イケレ, 爬ク、足ニテ攪混スレ. *v. t.* To scrape or scratch. To shuffle with the feet.

Ikereru, イケレル, 殆ント醉フ. *v. i.* To be just on the point of intoxication.

Ikerikarap, イケリカラブ, 神經痛症ノ一種ニテ毛根ヲ冒カス. *n.* A kind of neuralgia which attacks the roots of the hair.

Ikerokpa, イケロクバ, 足ヲ以テ攪混スレ. *v.i.* To shuffle with the feet.

Ikesamba, イケサムバ, 追フ. *v.t.* To chase. To run after. To follow. **Syn : Itomkot. Iyokot.**

Ikesh-koro, イケシコロ, 相續スル. *v.t.* To inherit.

Ikesh-koro-guru, イケシコログル, 相續人. *n.* An heir.

Ikeshui, イケシュイ, 怒ル、慎ル、例セバ、イケシユイワオマン、慎ツテ行ク. *v.i.* To be angry. As :—*Ikeshui wa oman,* "to go away in anger."

Ikeu, イケウ, 遁レ. *v. i.* To run away. **Syn : Kira. Shaot.**

Ikeuhumshu, イケウフムシュ, 出來ゴト. *n.* An accident. **Syn : Ikehumshu.**

Ikeure, イケウレ, 削ル. *v.t.* To hew.

Ikeutum-wende, イケウツムウェンデ, 爭ヒ起コス. *v.i.* To stir up strife.

Iki, イキ, 爲ス (單數)、例セバ、ネンタイキルウェチ、誰ガナセシヤ. *v.t.* To do (sing). As :—*Nen ta iki ruwe ne,* "who did it ?"

Ikia, イキア,
Ikiya, イキヤ, ソレ、ソノ、カレ、ソコ、例セバ、イキアアイヌ、ソノ人、イキアブ、彼奴 (輕蔑ノ意ヲ含ム). *pro.* That. Him. He. There. A word generally implying contempt. As :—*Ikia ainu,* "that man." *Ikiap,* "that fellow."

Iki-aetoranne, イキアエトランネ, 能ハズ、例セバ、モコロポカイキアエトランネ、睡眠スルコト能ハズ. *ph.* Unable to do. As :—*Mokoro poka iki-aetoranne,* "to be unable to sleep."

Ikichi, イキチ, 爲ス、例セバ、エチイキチアイヌポロンノオカイ、其樣ナコトナスル人ガ多クアレ. *v. t.* To do. As :—*Ene ikichi ainu poron no okai,* "there are many men who do that kind of thing."

Ikihi, イキヒ, 既ニ爲セシコト、例セバ、マカナクイキキ、何ナナサレシヤ. *n.* Something which has been done. As :—*Makanak ikihi,* what was being done ? "

Ikikse, イキクセ, 縮少シタレ. *v.i.* To become crumpled.

Ikimaukushte-ikip, イキマウクシテイキブ, 行動ニテモノチタトヘルコト. *n.* A parable expressed in action.

Ikineipeka, イキネイペカ, 氣ヲ付ケヨ、爲サザル可カラズ. *adv.* Look out. Be careful. Verily. Certainly. Must. Without doubt.

Ikinnimara, イキンニマラ, 一部分、例セバ、イキンニマラキキカラワアンデ、部分ヲ殘シテ置ク. *adv.* and *n.* In part. A part. As :—*Ikinnimara kikikara wa ande,* "to keep back a part of anything."

Ikipniukesh, イキブニウケシ, 忠實ナ
ル. *adj.* Faithful. To act faithfully. Also, unable to do a thing.
Awkward.

Ikirare, イキラレ, 逐フ. *v. t.* To
frighten away.

Ikiri, イキリ, 数、文字、代、縫目、順
序. *n.* A number. A letter. A
figure. Order. Generation. Line.
A seam. *Ainu ikiri,* " a generation." As :—*Ikiri-hechawere,* "to
pick out a seam. *Ikiri-ikiri an
no,* " in order."

Ikiri-ikiri-an, イキリイキリアン, 順
序ニ. *adv.* In order.

**Ikiri-ikiri-an-no, イキリイキリアン
ノ,** 順序的ニ. *adv.* Orderly.

Ikiri-kara, イキリカラ, 縫フ. *v.i.*
To seam. To sew.

Ikirimimunhi, イキリミムンヒ, 魚ノ
側線. *n.* The lateral line of fishes.

Ikiri-pake, イキリバケ, 酋長. *n.*
Chief. Head.

Ikiri-paketa, イキリバケタ, 上ニ、頂
上ニ、先頭ニ. *adv.* At the top.
At the head.

Ikiroro-ande, イキロロアンデ, 美麗ナ
ル、美シク思フ. *adj.* and *v.i.* To
consider pretty, nice, beautiful or
fine. **Syn : Irayapka.**

Ikiroro-anka, イキロロアンカ, 綺麗ナ
ル、美クシキ. *adj.* and *v.i.* Pretty.
Nice. Beautiful. Fine. As :—
Nep ikiroro anka, " how beautiful."

Ikiru, イキル, 顛覆サセル. *v. i.* To
be overturned.

Ikisakani, イキサカニ, 錐、ボルト錐.
n. An awl. An auger. A drill.

Ikisha-kani, イキシャカム, 同上. *n.*
Same as above.

Ikisa-ni, イキサニ, 木製ノ錐. *n.* A
wooden gimlet or awl. A drill.

Ikisap, イキサプ, 錐. *n.* A drill.
awl.

Ikishima, イキシマ, 爭鬭スル人々ヲ
引キ分ケレ. *v.t.* To part persons
who are quarrelling.

Ikitara, イキタラ, ナ シ マ ザ. *n.* A
kind of bamboo. *Sasa kurilenis,
Mak. et Shib.*

Ikiya, イキヤ, 氣ヲ付ケヨ. *excl.* and
adv. Mind ! Be careful lest !
Look out !

Ikiyap, イキヤプ, or Ikiap, イキアプ,
奴、物、惡漢、(第三者ニ對シテ用ユ レ
輕蔑ノ語). *n.* A fellow. A thing.
An article. A rascal. A term
of contempt applied to a third person. As :—*Nei a ikiyap sange wa
en nukare,* " show me that thing."

Ikka, イッカ, 盗ム. *v.t.* To steal.
To abduct. **Syn : Eikka.**

Ikka-guru, イッカグル, 盗人. *n.* A
thief.

Ikkapa, イッカバ, 盗ム. *v. t.* To
steal (*pl*).

Ikkeu, イッケウ, 脊椎. *n.* The spine.
The backbone. Vertebrae. **Syn :
Ikki.**

**Ikkeu-kamui-koro-tashum, イッケ
ウカムイコロタシェム,** 脊髓症. *n.*
Spinal disease. **Syn : Yashitukkari.**

**Ikkewe, イッケウェ, or Ikkewehe, イ
ッケウェへ,** 脊骨、言語ノ意義、山ノ端.
n. The backbone. The spine. The
vertebrae. The meaning of a
word. A ridge of mountains. As:
— *Ikkewe-komo,* " to bend the
back." *Ikkewe turi,* " to straighten the back.

Ikkewe-an, イッケウェアン, 強キ、意味深重ナル. *adj.* Strong. Full of meaning. Powerful.

Ikkewehe, イッケウェヘ, 脊骨. *n.* The spine. The backbone. See *Ikkewe*.

Ikkewe-rauge, イッケウェラウゲ, 駝背(セムシ)ノ. *adj.* Humpbacked. **Syn : Ikkewe-komge.**

Ikkewe-sak, イッケウェサク, 弱キ、無意味ノ. *adj.* Weak. Meaningless. Absurd.

Ikkewe-sakbe, イッケウェサクベ, 背理、妄誕. *n.* An absurdity.

Ikkewe-sak-no, イッケウェサッノ, 理ニ戻リテ、謬リテ. *adv.* Absurdly.

Ikki, イッキ, 脊椎. Same as *ikkeu.*

Ikmaure, イクマウレ, 噯氣(オクビ)チスレ. *v.i.* To belch. To eructate. To make manners.

Ikne-no, イク子ノ, 眞直ニ. *adv.* Straightly.

Iko, イコ, 共ニ. *adv.* Together with.

Iko, イコ, 甚、多キ、例セバ、イコワヤシヌ、甚タ、怜悧ナレ. *part.* Very. Much. Very much. This particle is sometimes prefixed to verbs to express superlativeness or intensity. Thus : — *Wayashnu,* "wise," *iko - wayashnu,* "very wise."

Iko-ande, イコアンデ, 他人ニ預ケレ. *v.i.* To commend to the care of another.

Iko-arakomo, イコアラコモ, 痛ム. *v.i.* To suffer pain. **Syn : Yairamhekomo.**

Ikoba, イコバ, 間違ツテ取ル、取リ違へル. *v.t.* To take by mistake. To mistake. To mistake one for another.

Ikoep, イコエプ, 副食物. *n.* Any kind of food eaten with rice or millet.

Ikohonne, イコホンチ, 臆病ニ、懼レテ. *adv.* Cowardly. **Syn : Uchike. Turamkoro.**

Ikohonoye, イコホノイェ, 罰スレ. *v.t.* To punish. To punish with sickness. **Syn : Paragoatte.**

Ikohummore, イコフンモレ, 靜ニスル、默スレ. *v.t.* To silence. To quiet.

Ikoiki, イコイキ, 烈シク叱カル. *v.t.* To scold severely. To fight. As : —*Tono orowa no aikoiki,* "he was severely reprimanded by the official."

Ikoingara, イコインガラ, 祝福チ授ケル. *v.t.* To bless.

Ikoisamba, イコイサムバ, 眞似スレ. *v.t.* To imitate.

Ikoitupa, イコイツバ, 欲スル、羨ム. *v.t.* To wish for. To be jealous of. To envy.

Ikokandama, イコカンダマ, 騙ス、瞞着スル. *v.t.* To deceive. To cheat.

Ikokanu, イコカヌ, 注目スル、傾聽スル. *v.i.* To look about. To be on the alert. To listen. To be attentive. To witness.

Ikokanu-wa-nu, イコカヌワヌ, 傾聽スル、注意シテ聞ク. *v.t.* To listen attentively.

Ikokanu-guru, イコカヌグル, 證人、立合人. *n.* A witness. An attentive person.

Ikokatpak-ki, イコカツパクキ, 罪チ犯ス. *v.t.* To sin.

Ikokka-guru, イコッカグル, 愚者. *n.* A fool. **Syn: Haita-guru.**

Ikokuba, イコクバ, 強ク、嚙ム. *v. t.* To bite severely.

Ikokut, イコクツ, オホイタドリ. *n. Polygonum sachalinense, Fr. Schm.*

Ikokuttara, イコクッタラ, 同上. *n.* same as above.

Ikombap, イコムバプ, 幼蟲. *n.* A caterpillar. **Syn: Ikonkap.**

Ikombap-wata, イコムバプワタ, 昆蟲ノ繭. *n.* A cocoon.

Ikomikom, イコミコム, 這フ(毛蟲ノ如ク). *v.t.* To go along as a caterpillar.

Ikomui, イコムイ, 虱ヲ探ス. *v.t.* To search for lice.

Ikon, イコン,
Ikoni, イコンニ, } 痛ム、病氣ニナル. *v.i.* To suffer pain. To be ill.

Ikoniko, イコニコ, 痛ム. *v. i.* To ache. To be in pain.

Ikonire, イコニレ, 苦痛サセル. *v. t.* To agonize. To make suffer.

Ikoni-tupiri, イコニツピリ, 重傷. *n.* A painful wound. A severe wound.

Ikoni-ushpa, イコニウシパ, 急ニ痛ム. *v. i.* To be seized with pain.

Ikonkap, イコンカブ, 幼蟲. *n.* A caterpillar. **Syn: Ikombap.**

Ikonnu, イコンヌ, 凶事ヲ未前ニ戒シム. 呪フ. *v.t.* To give warning of something bad to come. To bewitch. To cause misfortune.

Ikonnu-guru, イコンヌグル, 覚法使、凶兆. *n.* A witch. A thing of ill omen. A thing which causes misfortune.

Ikonnup, イコンヌプ, 覚術使. *n.*

One who forewarns of something bad to come. A witch. **Syn: Ishinnerep.**

Ikopan, イコバン, 叱ル. *v.t.* To scold. **Syn: Kopao.**

Ikopopke, イコポプケ, 溫カナル、例セバ、イコポプケアミプ、溫カナル着物. *adj.* Warm. As: — *Ikopopke amip,* "warm clothing."

Ikopopke-samau-ni, イコポプケサマウニ, 腐朽セル聚木. *n.* Heaps of rotten wood such as harbor snakes and the like reptiles.

Ikopuntek, イコプンテク, 喜ンデ事ヲスル. *v.i.* and *v.t.* To be very much pleased. To do with pleasure. To greet. As: — *Ku ikopuntek,* I am very much pleased." **Syn: Yairenga.**

Ikoramu-hoshki, イコラムホシキ, 懶怠ナル者ヲ勵マス. *v.t.* To hurry one who is lazy. To scold for being lazy.

Ikoramkore, イコラムコレ, 願ハス. *v.t.* To cause to ask for.

Ikoramkoro, イコラムコロ, 乞フ、願フ. *v.t.* To beg. To ask for.

Ikoramnukara, イコラムヌカラ, 誘惑スル. *v.t.* To tempt.

Ikoramnukara-ambe, イコラムヌカラアムベ, 誘惑. *n.* Temptation.

Ikoramnukarape, イコラムヌカラベ, 誘惑者. *n.* The tempter.

Ikorampa, イコラムパ, 叱ル. *v.t.* To scold. **Syn: Kopao.**

Ikorampoktuye, イコラムポクツイェ, 棄テ置カレル. *v.i.* To be let alone. To be taken no notice of. To be treated in an indifferent manner.

To be cut off from the favour of God. As:—*Kamui ikorampoktuye gusu kemush iki ruwe ne,* " this famine has arisen because the gods are unfavourable."

Ikoramu, イコラム, 疑フ. *v.t.* To suspect.

Ikor'atara, イコラタラ, 刀ノ紐. *n.* A sword sash. **Syn: Emush-at.**

Ikore-guru, イコレグル, 物ヲ與フル人. *n.* A person who gives anything away. A giver.

Ikoro, イコロ, 寶. *n.* Treasures. Precious things. Riches (Usually an old sword or wooden imitations of swords.

Ikoro-an, イコロアン, 富祐ナレ. *adj.* Rich.

Ikoro-koro, イコロコロ, 富祐ナレ. *adj.* Rich. **Syn: Oteknu.**

Ikoro-koro-guru, イコロコログル, 富人. *n.* A rich person.

Ikorokoshini, イコロコシニ, 耗ラス、涙費スレ. *v.t.* To waste. **Syn: Aibe-samka.**

Ikoro-nishpa, イコロニシパ, 富人. *n.* A rich person.

Ikosaksak, イコサクサク, 不満足ニ思フ. *v.t.* To be dissatisfied with.

Ikosan, イコサン, 急病ニ罹レ. *v.i.* To be suddenly attacked with illness. To be suddenly seized with pain. The fever stage in ague.

Ikosange, イコサンゲ, カヲ出ス. *v.t.* To put forth as strength.

Iko-sapane-guru, イコサパ子グル, 同等ノ人. *n.* Persons of the same office or rank.

Ikosaure, イコサウレ, 親切ニ待遇スレ. *adj.* To be kind to. To deal gently with. Not to be hard upon.

Ikoshina, イコシナ, 繃帯スレ. *v.t.* To bind up. As:—*Piri ikoshina,* " to bind up a wound."

Ikoshunge, イコシュンゲ, 詐ル. *v.t.* To lie to. To cheat. To gull.

Ikotama, イコタマ, 共ニ. *adv.* Together. **Syn: Uturu.**

Ikotarara, イコタララ, 手ノ上ニ置キテ差出ス. *v.t.* To hold out in the hand.

Ikotchane, イコッチャ子, 仲裁スレ. *v.t.* To mediate.

Ikotchane-guru, イコッチャ子グル, 仲保者. *n.* A mediator.

Ikotchanep, イコッチャブ, 仲保者. *n.* A mediator. A go-between.

Ikotke, イコツケ, 他ノ人ヲ瞀ムル爲ニ罪ナキモノヲ罰スル、對手ニ己レノ復讐ノ念ヲ知ラシムル爲メ第三者ヲ當ル. *v.t.* To punish an innocent person in order to warn others. To warn or punish anyone that others may take warning. To make an example of. To avenge one's self on a third party to show the state of one's feelings towards the person upon whom vengeance ought according to right to have been taken.

Ikotki, イコツキ, 同上. *v.t.* Same as above.

Ikotunash, イコツナシ, 迅速ナレ. *adj.* Very fast.

Ikotuntek, イコツンテク, 病メイ. *v.i.* To be ill.

Ikowayashnu, イコワヤシヌ, 智慧勝レタレ. *v.t.* To surpass in wisdom. To be very wise.

Ikowende, イコウェンデ, 損ズル、破壞スレ. *v.t.* To spoil. To smash up.

Ikoyairenga, イコヤイレンガ, 誉メレ. v.t. To praise. To cheer. **Syn:** Eyairenga.

Ikoyorikipuni, イコヨリキブニ, 段段ニ見エテ來ル、(旅行ノ時遠山ナトノ). v.i. To come into sight as a distant mountain when travelling.

Ik-pui, イクブイ, 神經弓孔. n. Neural canal of vertebræ.

Ikra, イクラ,
Ikura, イクラ,} 關節、章句. n. A joint. A verse.

Iku, イク, 飲ム、喫スル(酒煙草ナドヲ). v.t. To drink strong drink. To smoke.

Iku-ambe, イクアムベ, 飲料. n. Drink.

Iku-an, イクアン, 吸飲ノ. adj. Drinking.

Ikuapushke, イクアブシケ, 破レル、裂クレ. v.i. To break.

Ikuapushkere, イクアブシケレ, 破ル、裂ク. v.t. To break.

Ikuba, イクバ, 嚙ム. v.t. To bite. **Syn:** Shiri-kuba.

Ikubaba, イクババ, 同上. v.t. Same as above.

Iku-bashui, イクバシュイ, 鬚髯ヲ上ゲル棒. n. A moustache-lifter.

Ikui, イクイ, 嚙ム. v.t. To chew. **Syn:** Kui-kui.

Ikui-kui, イクイクイ, 嚙ム. v.t. To chew. **Syn:** Notmoimoye. Kui-kui. Chamse. Chamchamse.

Ikui-nimak, イクイニマク, 白齒. n. The grinders. The molars.

Ikui-nimaki, イクイニマキ, 同上. n. Same as above.

Ikuira, イクイラ, 窃カニ歩ム. v.i. To go along steathily or noiselessly.

Syn: Humi mo apkash. Syn: Kuira. Ipikuira.

Iku-komanakte, イクコマナクテ, 酒ヲ慕フテ眠ル能ハズ. v.t. To be unable to sleep on account of inordinate desires for strong drink.

Ikunnere, イクンネレ, 黒ク染メレ. v.t. To dye black.

Ikunneyot, イクンネヨツ, 眩キ. v.i. To be dazzled with darkness as when coming fresh indoors from the light.

Ikunpone, イクンポ子, 踝. n. The ankle bone. **Syn: Tokumbone.**

Ikup, イクブ, 酒器. n. Drinking utensils, as cups, moustache-lifters, etc.

Ikura, イクラ, or Ikra, イクラ, 關節、章節. n. A joint. A division. A verse.

Ikure, イクレ, 飲マセレ. v.t. To give to drink.

Ikurianda, イクリアンダ, 嘲ル. v.t. To laugh at. To deride.

Ikurok, イクロク, 坐シテ飲ム、大酒スル. v.i. and adj. To sit and drink. To be much given to drinking.

Ikurube, イルクベ, 鰻. n. Eel. *Anguilla japonica, Schlegel.* **Syn:** Ukurube.

Ikurukuru, イクルクル, 痛ム. v.i. To be in pain. Sometimes used like *Ikururu.* **Syn:** Araka.

Ikururu, イクルル, 陳痛. n. The pangs of childbirth (especially the pangs immediately antecedent to the actual birth of a child). **Syn: Kapuhu. Ikurukuru.**

Ikurushna, イクルシナ, 眞直ニ. adj. Straight.

Ikurusui, イクルスイ, 渇シタレ. *v.i.* To be thirsty.

Ikusa, イクサ, 河ヲ渡ス. *v.t.* To ferry across a river. *Pl. Ukushpa.*

Ikusa-guru, イクサグル, 渡守. *n.* A ferry-man.

Ikusa-i, イクサイ, 渡場. *n.* A ferry. *Pl. Ukushpa-ushi.*

Iku-sakayo, イクサカヨ, 暴酒スレ. *v.t.* To revel.

Ikushbe, イクシベ, 柱、戸ノ枠. *n.* A post. A door post. A column. Pillar.

Ikushketa, イクシケタ, 向ニ. *adv.* Beyond. That side of.

Ikushke-peka, イクシケベカ, 向ニ. *adv.* Beyond.

Ikushta, イクシタ, 向ニ、彼處ニ. *adv.* Beyond. There. Over yonder.

Ikushun, イクシュン, 向ニ、横切スレ. *adv.* Beyond. Across.

Ikush-wano, イクシワノ, 彼處ヨリ. *adv.* Thence.

Ikuso, イクソ, 列坐シテ酒ヲ呑ムコト. *v.i.* To sit in lines by the hearth to drink.

Ikutasa, イクタサ, 酒宴. *n.* A drinking feast.

Ikutuni, イクツニ, 涎衣. *n.* A bib.

Ima, イマ, 焼ク. *v.t.* To roast.

Ima-ni, イマニ, 焼串. *n.* A piece of wood upon which to stick fish or flesh to roast. A roasting spit.

Ima-nit, イマニツ, 焼串. *n.* A roasting spit.

Imanit-tai, イマニッタイ, 焼串、(複数). *n.* A large number of roasting spits.

Ima-onit, イマオニツ, 焼串. *n.* A roasting spit.

Imakake, イマカケ, 一ツ置キ、例セバ、シチトイマカケ、一日オキ. *adv.* Every other. As :—*Shine to imakake,* "every other day."

Imakake, イマカケ, 然ル後、下、後ロ. *post.* Then. After. Thence. Below. Behind. As :—*Set imakake,* "behind the table."

Imakaketa, イマカケタ, 後ニ. *adv.* Afterwards. Thenceforth. After that.

Imakake-un, イマカケウン, 後ニ. *adv.* Afterwards.

Imakanu, イマカヌ, 間隙ヲ設ケレ. *v.t.* To open up or clear a space. As :—*Ru imakanu,* "to open up a way."

Imashkin, イマシキン, ヨリ多ク、例セバ、ポンイマシキンポン、何々ヨリ小サキ、ポロイマシキンポロ、何々ヨリ大キイ. *adv.* Much more. Rather. As :—*Pon imashkin pon,* "smaller." *Poro imashkin poro,* "larger."

Imek, イメク, 食物ヲ分カツ. *v.t.* To serve out food. To portion out.

Imek-guru, イメクグル, 食物ヲ分カッ人. *n.* A person who serves out food. One who portions out anything.

Imeru, イメル, 電光. *n.* Lightning.

Imi, イミ, 日本風ノ着物. *n.* Generally Japanese clothing. Clothes made after Japanese fashion. Sometimes any clothes.

Imok, イモク, 餌、(罠ノ). *n.* A trap bait.

Imokirika, イモキリカ, 惡シキ. *v.i.* and *adj.* Abject. Miserably bad. To live in utter misery.

Imok-omare, イ モクオマレ, 羂 ニ 餌 チナク、鉤ニ餌ナ附ケレ. *v.t.* To bait a trap. To bait a fish hook.

Imommuye, イ モムムイ ェ, 贖 フ. *v.t.* To atone. To propitiate. To give as a present.

Imompekari, イ モ ムペ カ リ, 憐ム. *adj.* To take pity on. To have mercy on. **Syn : Erampokiwen wa kore.**

Imompekari, イ モ ムペ カ リ, 同上. *adj.* Same as above.

Imomtabire, イ モムタビレ, 急ヶ. *v.t.* To hurry. To hasten. To be busy.

Imontabire-kashpa, イ モンタビレカ シバ, 甚々急ヶ. *v.i.* To be exceedingly busy.

Imontabire-no, イ モンタビレノ, 急ニ. *adv.* Abruptly.

Imontasa, イ モンタサ, 復讐. *v.t.* To retalliate. To revenge.

Imu, イ ム, 狂セ ル、ヒステリヤ. *adj.* and *v.i.* A kind of hysteria. Rabid. Mad. To be attacked with sudden fits of hysteria.

Imuki, イ ムキ, 同上. *adj.* and *v.i.* Same as above.

Imu-bakko, イ ムバッコ, ヒステリヤニ カ、ツタ老婦人. *n.* Any old woman subject to fits of *imu* or hysteria.

Imu-imu, イ ムイ ム, 烈シキヒステリ ヤ. *adj.* and *v.i.* An intensified form of *imu*.

Imu-imu-ki, イ ムイ ムキ, 同上. *adj.* and *v.i.* Same as above.

Imut, イ ムツ, 刀. *n.* A sword. As: —*Imut mut*, To wear a sword.

Imut-shitoki, イ ムツシトキ, 女ノ珠ノ 首飾 り. *n.* A woman's bead necklace.

Ina, イ ナ, 何々セ ラ レヌ樣ニ注意セヨ、 例セバ、子イ セタニウェンセネタグスイ ナアエクバアンナ、彼レハ悪イ犬ダカ ヲ嚙マレナイ樣ニ用心セヨ. *v.i.* Take care lest. Be careful lest. As:— *Nei seta niwen seta ne gusu ina ae-kuba an na*, "as that is a savage dog take care lest it bite you" (lit: take care lest you are bitten). *Iyai-kipte, ina e kubaba an na ; oyakta arupa, yaikipte na*, "you are in danger, take care lest it bite you, get out of the way, it is dangerous." **Syn: Ika.**

Ina, イ ナ, 傳言、傳說、願、歌. *n.* A message. Tradition. Request. A song.

Inakarap, イ ナカラブ, 祝スレ. *v.t.* To salute.

Inambe, イ ナムべ, 何レ. *adj.* Which.

Inambe-gusu-ne-yakun, イ ナムべ グス子ヤクン, 如何トナレバ、故ニ. *adv.* For. Because. For this reason.

Inan, イ ナン, 何レ、何. *adj.* Which. What. As:—*Nei guru inan kotan un guru ne ruwe he an ?* " to what village does that person belong " ? *Nei guru inan kotan wano ek a ?* " which town does he come from."

Inani, イ ナニ, 何處. *adv.* Where.

Inankayo, イ ナンカヨ, 草木ノ莖. *n.* The stem of a plant.

Inao, イ ナオ, 幣. *n.* Whittled pieces of willow, lilac and other wood which are stuck in the ground as offerings to the gods. *Inao* bear some mark or sign by which the gods may know who is the offerer.

In the Ainu idea, no greater sin can be committed than that of stealing and hiding the *inao* of another person, the idea being that the gods, finding themselves without *inao*, will withdraw their favour from those who ought to have offered them. No worse name can be given to an Ainu than *Inao sak guru*, "the man without *inao*."

Inao-chipa, イナオチバ, 多クノ幣. *n.* A cluster of *inao*. The place at the east end of a hut where the *inao* are placed.

Inao-ke, イナオケ, 幣チ造ル. *v.i.* To make *inao*.

Inao-kema, イナオケマ, 幣ノ柄. *n.* Pieces of wood to which *inao* are tied.

Inao-kike, イナオキケ, 幣ノ削リカケ. *n.* The shavings which are left attached to *inao*. Pieces of willow shaving which are sometimes hung in Ainu huts.

Inao-korashkoro, イナオコラシコロ, 栗ニテ造リシ酒. *n.* A kind of liquor distilled from millet.

Inao-kotchep, イナオコッチェブ, 鮭或ハ鱒ノ子. *n.* Young salmon.

Inao-netoba, イナオネトバ, 幣ノ柄. *n.* A piece of wood to which *inao* are sometimes tied.

Inaoru, イナオル, 熊送リノ式場ニテ被ル冠. *n.* A kind of crown worn by the men at bear feasts. **Syn:** **Sapa-unbe. Ekashpa-unbe.**

Inaotumbu, イナオツムブ, 幣チ匿ク箱. *n.* A box filled with *inao* shavings.

Inauni-kina, イナウニキナ, クルマバ サウ. *n.* Wood-ruff. *Asperula odorata*, L.

Inauni-susu, イナウニスス, 同上. Same as above.

Inde, インデ, 目眵、メヤニ. *n.* A gummy discharge from the eyes.

Ine, イネ, 何處、例セバ、イチチイアブ、其ノモノハ何處ニ在ルカ. *adv.* Where? As:— *Ine nei ap*, "where is that thing?"

Ine, イネ, 四. *adj.* Four.

Ine, イネ, **Hine**, ヒネ, 行動チ示ス、例セバ、エクイチ、來ル、オマンイチ、往ク、イルカイエクイネチ、彼人ハチヨイト來タノ *part.* This word is expressed by the English participle "ing." Thus :—*Ek ine*, "coming." *Oman ine*, "going." *Irukai ek ine ne!* "he has come for a short time?"

Inean, イチアン, 何方ノ. *adj.* Which of two.

Ine-apkushta, イチアブクシタ, 嗚呼、オヤ、如何ニ、例セバ、マー此様ニ魚カ澤山ニ、イチアブクシタチエブボロンノアン・ *interj.* Dear me! How great. How surprising. As :— *Ine apkushta chep poron no an*, "dear me, what a number of fish." **Syn: Karainepta un.**

Ineaush-pekambe, イチアウシベカムベ, オニビシ. *n.* *Trapa quadrispinosa*, Roxb.

Ine-hotne, イチホツチ, 八十. *adj.* Eighty. Four-score.

Ine-hotnep, イチホツチブ, 八十個. *n.* Eighty things.

Ine-ikashima-wan, イチイカシマワン, 十四. *adj.* Fourteen.

Ine-otutanu, イチオツタヌ, 第四. *adj.* The fourth.

Ine-rere, イ子レレ, 四、例セバ、イ子レ レコ、四日. Four. As:—*Ine rere-ko,* "four day."

Ine-reyunashi, イ子レユナシ, 四人ニ テ臼ク. *v.i.* Four persons to pound in a mortar. *See Utunashi. Yaitunashi. Autunashi. Reunashi.*

Ine-rokbe, イ子ロクベ, オヤ、(嘆息ノ 辭)· *interj.* Same as *ineapkushta.* Dear me ?

Ine-sambanu, イ子サムバヌ, 四角ノ. *adj.* Square. Four-sided.

Ine-shuine, イ子シュイ子, 四度. *adj.* Four times.

Ine-shuine-o, イ子シュイ子オ, 同上. Same as above.

Ine-un, イ子ウン, 何處へ、例セバ、イ 子ウンエチマン、何處へ行クカ. *adv.* Whither. As:—*Ine-un e oman,* "whither are you going."

Ingan, インカン, 見ル. *adv.* Same ·as *ingara.*

Ingan-no, インガンノ, 遠目カ利ク. *adv.* Long-sighted. Of good sight.

Ingan-rui, ンガルイ, 穿鑿好キナレ. *adj.* Curious. Inquisitive.

Ingaprapu, ンガブラプ, 眉ヲ動カ ス. *v.i.* To work the eyebrows up and down.

Ingara, ンガラ, 見ル. *v.i.* To look at. To see.

Ingara-poka, インガラポカ, 無意味 ニ眺メル、何トナク見ル. *ph.* Merely to see. Merely to look at. Just to look.

Ingi, イ ン ギ, 皆、凡テ. *adj.* All. Universal.

Inichu, イニチュ, 疑フ. *v.i.* To be suspicious.

Inine-itangi, イニ子イタンギ, 杓子ニ 用ユル椀. *n.* To scoop out. A cup used as a ladle.

Inini, イニニ, 噛ム. *v.t.* To bite at (as a fish at a bait).

Inini-ap, イニニアプ, 銛、モリ. *n.* A kind of fish spear to which a bait is tied.

Inisapushka-an, イニサプシカアン, 驚カサレ、急ガセレ. *adj. and v.i.* To be startled suddenly. To be suddenly surprised. To hurry.

Inise, イニセ, 杓子. *n.* A dipper. A ladle. Also *v.t.* To ladle out drink.

Inisei-ya, イニセイヤ, 投網. *n.* A small hand net.

Initne-ike, イニツ子イケ, 惡覨、惡鬼. The devil. A demon.

Inkush, イニクシ, 懼ル、戰慄スル. *v.i.* To fear. To tremble through fear. To call out in fear. **Syn: Ishitoma.**

Inne, イン子, 許多ナレ、多數ノ. *adj.* Multitudes. Many. Numerous.

Inne-no, イ ン子ノ, 群集ノ. *adj.* In crowds.

Inne-topaha, イン子トパハ, 多數ノ、 群集ノ. *adj.* Very many. A great multitude.

Inne-utara, イン子ウタラ, 群集. *n.* A multitude.

Inoka, イノカ, 蛇ノ形ニ造ラレタル偶 像. *n.* An idol made in the shape of a snake for divination, cursing and worship.

Inokoshke, イノコシケ, 嫉ム. *v.i.* To be jealous of. **Syn: Eyaitunnap.**

Inomi-chup, イノミチュプ, 一月. *n.* January. The month of libations; possibly so called from the Japanese custom of paying visits and drinking at the new year.

Inonchip, イノンチブ, 愚弄スル、醜弄 スレ. *v. t.* To baffle. **Syn: Unkeshke.**

Inonchirube, イノンチルベ, 醜弄セラ レタル人. *n.* A person baffled in something he desired to do or have.

Inon, イノン, 祈禱. *n.* Prayer.

Inonno, イノンノ, 同上. *n.* Same as above.

Innono-itak, イノンノイタク, 祈ル. *v.i.* and *n.* To pray. Prayer.

Inonno-itak-hi, イノンノイタクヒ, 祈 禱. *n.* Prayer.

Inonno-itak-i, イノンノイタクイ, 同 上. *n.* Same as above.

Inore, イノレ, 欺ク. *v.t.* To deceive. **Syn: Chinore. Kokandama.**

Inonre-itak-ki, イノンレイタクキ, 偽 ル. *v. i.* To lie to. **Syn: Koshunge.**

Inoshketa, イノシケタ, 丁度眞ン中. *adv.* In the very centre.

Inoyenoye, イノイェノイェ, 捻ル. *v.t.* To twist.

Inotu, イノツ, 生命. *n.* Life.

Inraprapu, インラプラプ, 眨シクテ瞬 キスレ. *v i.* To blink or wink with the eyes. **Syn: Shik-ukochupchupu.**

Inrapu, インラプ, 同上. *v.i.* Same as above.

Inu, イヌ, 聴ク. *v.t.* To listen. To hear. To listen attentively. As: —*Ku pishi wa ku inu*, "I will make enquires."

Inu-ewen, イヌエウェン, 聴キ違ヘレ. To mistake in hearing.

Inukuri, イヌクリ, 能ハヌ、下手. *adj.* and *v.i.* Unable. Awkward. Incapable. To be incapacitated through sickness or old age. To dislike to do. **Syn: Aikap. Kopan.**

Inukuri-an-korokai, イヌクリアン コロカイ, 御氣ノ毒ナレトモ. *ph.* I am sorry to trouble you, but.

Inuma, イヌマ, 自分ノ寶物. *n.* One's treasures and ornaments.

Inumba, イヌムバ, 漉ス (複數). *v. t.* To strain.

Inumbe, イヌムベ, 爐緣. *n.* The wooden framework round a fireplace.

Inumbe-ibe, イヌムベイベ, タチウオ. *n.* Silver fish. *Trichiurus haumela Forskal.*

Inumbe-saushbe, イヌムベサウシベ, 爐ノ中ニアル杭 (主トシテ物ヲ削ル台 ニ用ユ). *n.* A little post stuck at each corner of the fireplace used as a chopping-block.

Inumechiri, イヌメチリ, 鷹ノ類. *n.* A kind of hawk.

Inumu, イヌム, 漉ス (單數). *v. t.* To strain (*sing*).

Inun, イヌン, 獵ノタメ野宿スル. *v. i.* To stay away from home in pursuit of one's lively-hood as when fishing or working in a distant garden.

Inun-chisei, イヌンチセイ, 山小屋. *n.* A fisherman's hut.

Inuni-chiri, イヌニチリ, 小鷹ノ𩀌. *n.* A kind of hawk. **Syn: Onumechiri.**

Inu-no, イヌノ, 合點早キ、晤リ早キ. *adj.* Quick of apprehension. Quick-witted.

Inunukashiki, イヌヌカシキ, 憐憫、慈悲. *n.* Mercy. Pity. Compassion.

Inunukashiki-wa-kore, イヌヌカシキワコレ, 憐ム. *v.t.* To have mercy upon. To pity.

Inunuke, イヌヌケ, 祝福. *n.* Blessings.

Inunuke-ambe, イヌヌケアムべ, 祝福. *n.* Blessings.

Inunuke-ash, イヌヌケアシ, 我ハ汝チ憐ム. *ph.* I pity thee. What a pitiable object!

Inunuke-ne, イヌヌケ子, 惠マレタレ、幸運ナレ. *adj.* Blessed. Fortunate.

Inup, イヌプ, 聞キシコト. *n.* A thing heard.

Inupitara, イヌピタラ, 欲セス、嫌フ. *v.t.* To feel dislike to. To dislike. **Syn: Kopan. Epange.**

Inupukushish, イヌプクシシ, 外出チ好マス. *v.i.* To dislike to go out. **Syn: Soine kopan.**

Inusa-inusa, イヌサイヌサ, 傳説ノ名. *n.* The name of an Ainu legend of a famine.

Inushiramare, イヌシラマレ, 抑ヘ、制止スレ. *v.t.* To control. To hold in. To restrain.

Inushuye, イヌシュイェ, 呼フ、手招ス. *v.t.* To call. To beckon.

Inushuyep, イヌシュイェプ, 旗. *n.* A flag.

Inuye, イヌイェ, 文身スレ、彫刻スレ. *v.t.* To tattoo. To carve wood. **Syn: Shinuye.**

Iokbare, イオクバレ, 無謀ナコトチスル、反謀スル. *v.t.* To rebel. To oppose.

Iokbare-guru, イオクバレグル, 反逆人. *n.* A rebel. One who goes against another.

Ioman, イオマン, 早ク往ク. *v.i.* To go quickly. **Syn: Tunashino oman.**

Iomande, イオマンデ, 送ル. *v.t.* To send away. To kill an animal in sacrifice.

Iomompekere, イオモムペケレ, 憐ム. *adj.* To have mercy upon. To take pity on.

Ionga, イオンガ, 潤カス、浸ス. *v.t.* To put to soak. To soak thoroughly. **Syn: Aonga.**

Ioriki-kut-koro, イオリキクツコロ, 腰ニ帯ス. *v.i.* To gird up the loins. **Syn: Orikut koro.**

Ionga-kuttara, イオンガクッタラ, ハンゴンサウ. *n. Senecio palatus, Pall.*

Ioripakka, イオリパッカ, 恐ロシキ. *adj.* Dreadful. As:—*Ioripakka ta hau an,* "how dreadful." **Syn: Ashitoma.**

Ioromamekara, イオロマメカラ, 不平チ言フ、愁訴スレ. *v.i.* To complain. **Syn: Iyaishirikara.**

Iotutanu, イオツタヌ, 其ノ次、第二. *adj.* The next in order. The second.

Ioyapa, イオヤパ, 明後年. *adv.* The year after next.

Ioyashimge, イオヤシムゲ, 明々後日. *adv.* The third day from to-morrow.

Ipa, イパ, 蹣跚、チドリアシ. *v.i.* To reel about as a drunkard.

Ipakarip, イパカリプ, 秤、衡、ハカリ. *n.* Balances. Scales. Weights.

Ipakashi, イバカシ, 教訓. *n.* Doctrine. What one teaches.

Ipakashnu-chisei, イバカシヌチェセイ, 獄舍、學校. *n.* A prison. A house of correction. A school.

Ipakashnu-guru, イバカシヌグル, 教師. *n.* A teacher.

Ipaketa, イバケタ, 然ルトキ. *adv.* Then. As :—*Nei ipaketa,* " at that time." **Syn : Ita.**

Ipakke-ni, イバッケニ, 鹿ヲ呼ブ笛. *n.* A kind of musical instrument used for decoying deer. **Syn : Irektep.**

Ipanchierep, イバンチエレブ, 他人ニ恨ミヲ抱キテ不潔ナルモノヲ食セシムル人. *n.* An evil minded person who spites another by giving him filthy food to eat. **Syn : Pauchikoro-guru.**

Ipaotenge, イバオテンゲ, 命スル. *v.t.* To command. **Syn : Ipawetenge.**

Ipara, イバラ, 傳染スル. *v. i.* To transmit (as a disease). To catch a disease. **Syn : Koturuse.**

Iparo-maka-ni, イバロマカニ, 熊ノ口ニ入レル木. *n.* The piece of wood thrust into the mouths of bears and other animals when killing them in sacrifice.

Iparo-shuke, イバロシュケ, 人ノ爲メニ食物ヲ調理スル. *v.t.* To cook for another. As :—*En iparo-shuke wa en kore,* " please cook me some food."

Ipatuye-chiuchiubare, イバツイェチェウチウバレ, モガク. *v. i.* To flounder about. To writhe (as an animal in its death-struggles).

Ipawe, イバウェ, 命令. *n.* A command. **Syn : Ikashpaotte.**

Ipawetenge, イバウェテンゲ, 命ズル. *v.t.* To command. **Syn : Kashpaotte.**

Ipawetenge-i, イバウェテンゲイ, 命令. *n.* Commandments.

Ipikuira, イビクイラ, 密カニ歩ム. *v.i.* To go along stealthily. **Syn : Kuira. Okuira.**

Ipirimuye, イビリムイェ, 償フ. *v. t.* To make amends. To make amends for some wounds or harm rendered. **Syn : Immomuye.**

Ipiru, イビル, 毛換リヌ, レ. *v. i.* To moult as a bird. To lose one's hair.

Ipishi, イビシ, 裁判スレ. *v. t.* To judge.

Ipishi-aesanniyo-i, イビシアエサンニヨイ, 裁判. *n.* Judgement.

Ipishiship, イビシシブ, 蕁麻、オホバイラクサ. *n.* Nettles. *Urtica dioica,* L. var. *platyphylla, Wedd.*

Ipishishte, イビシシテ, 切割ク. *v.t.* To rip up (as a bear before skinning it).

Ipishki, イビシキ, 數. *n.* Number.

Ipishki-wa-ingara, イビシキワインガラ, 數フレ. *v.t.* To count.

Ipishki-wa-nukara, イビシキワヌカラ, 數ル. *v.t.* To count.

Ipita, イビタ, 放ス. *v.t.* To let loose.

Ipokash, イボカシ, 醜キ. *adj.* Ugly.

Iporo, イボロ,} 顔付、樣子、例セバ、イ
Ipot, イボツ,} ボツツムコンナ、顔色ニ、イボツツムコンナナシュイェシュイェ、顔色ヲ變スレ. *n.* The countenance. Aspect. As :—*Ipot'tum konna,* " in the countenance." *Ipot'*

tum konna shuye-shuye, "to change the countenance."

Iporo-chiuk, イポロチウク, 顔色ヲ變ス ル. *v. i.* To change colour in the countenance through internal excitement. As:—*Fure iporochiuk,* "to blush," "to turn red."

Iporo-hachire, イポロハチレ, 恥カシ ムレ. *v.t.* To make ashamed.

Iporo-hachiri, イポロハチリ, 恥シキ、 立腹スル. *v.i.* To be ashamed. To be angry.

Iporo-ningi, イポロニンギ, 願フ心ノ. *adj.* Of a bitter temper.

Iporo-pirika, イポロピリカ, 顔色ヨ キ. *v.i.* To look happy or pleased. Good-looking.

Iporo-pirikare, イポロピリカレ, 喜 バセレ. *v.t.* To please.

Iporose, イポロセ, 名ケラレタレ. *v.t.* Called. Named.

Iporo-shikaunure, イポロシカウヌ レ, 怒リテ顔ニ現ハス. *v.i.* To show anger in the face. To look displeased.

Iporo-shiu, イポロシウ, 願フ心ノ. *adj.* Of a bitter temper. (lit: of a bitter countenance). **Syn: Iporo-ningi.**

Ipot, イポツ, 顔付キ. *n.* Same as *Iporo,* "the countenance."

Ipuni, イプニ, 給事スル. *n.* To wait upon as servants or helpers in a feast.

Ipuni-guru, イプニグル, 給事. *n.* A servant.

Ipush-tuye, イプシツイェ, 摘ミ採レ. *v.t.* To pluck off. To pinch off (as heads of millet at reaping time.

Irachitkere, イラチツケレ, 懸ケル. *v.t.* To hang up (as a picture or ornament).

Iramande, イラマンデ, 獵スル、漁スレ. *v.t.* To hunt. To fish.

Iramande-guru, イラマンデグル, 獵 師、漁師. *n.* A hunter.

Iramasure, イラマスレ, 美クシキ、嘆 賞スヘキ. *adj.* Beautiful. Admirable.

Iramasure-no, イラマスレノ, 美クシ ク. *adv.* Admirably. Prettily.

Iramatshuye, イラマツシュイェ, 考ヘ ル、熟考. *v.i.* To think. To consider. To revolve in one's mind. **Syn: Ramepakari.**

Irambotarare, イラムボタラレ, 嘆ガ シイナ. *excl.* You noisy one! Noisy.

Iramchuptekka, イラムチュプテッカ, 恐レル. *v.i.* To feel timid. To be afraid. **Syn: Ishitoma.**

Iramepakari, イラメパカリ, 思慮アレ. *adj.* Thoughtful.

Irami, イラミ, 崖、ガケ. *n.* Precipices.

Iramikachaushka, イラミカチャウ シカ, 失望スレ. *v.i.* To be disappointed.

Iramisaika, イラミサイカ, 僅少ノ、温 和ナレ. *adj.* A very little. Gentle. Easy. **Syn: Pon no.**

Iramisaikare, イラミサイカレ, 平易ニ スル、少クスレ. *v.t.* To make easy. To make less.

Iramisamka, イラミサムカ, 騙取スレ. 欺ク. *v.t.* To obtain by fraud. To deceive.

Iramishkare, イラミシカレ, or **Iramushkare, イラムシカレ,** 了解セヌ. *v.t.* Not to understand. **Syn: Eramushkare. Erampeutek.**

Iramkara, イラムカラ, シラセレ、怒
ラセル、泣カセル. v.t. To tease.
To make angry. To make cry.
To poke fun at. Syn: Ramukara.

Iramkare, イラムカレ, 悔ム. v.i. To
feel regret.

Iramkatchaushka, イラムカッチ
ャウシカ, 他人ノ爲サントスルコトナ止
メサセレ. v.t. To disuade from a
project or action.

Iramkittarara, イラムキッタララ, 懼
レル. v.i. To be in fear. Syn:
Kimatek.

Iramkoiki, イラムコイキ, 勸メレ. v.t.
To exhort. To persuade. To im-
portune. Syn: Onishnishi.

Irammakaka, イラムマカカ, 全ク、悉
ク、好ク、例セバ、イラムマカカウウエベ
ケンヌ、充分ニ調ヘル. adv. Tho-
roughly. Decorous. Carefully.
Quite. Nicely. Well. As:—
Irammakaka uwepekennu, "to enquire carefully." Syn: Roramne.

Irammokka, イラムモッカ, 遊戲スレ.
v.i. To play. To have some fun.
To tease. To poke fun at.

Iramno, イラムノ, 共ニ. adv. Together. As:—Iramno paye, "to
go together." Syn: Ukoiram
no.

Iramnukuri, イラムヌクリ, 爲ルコト
ナ好マヌ. v.i. To dislike to do.
To feel diffident. To be averse
to.

Irampokiwen, イラムポキウェン, 憫ム
ベキノ. adj. Pitiable.

Irampokiwen-wa-kore, イラムポキ
ウェンワコレ, 恤ム. v.t. To pity.
To have mercy upon.

Irampoye, イラムポイェ, 戲レル. adj.
Sportful. Playful. Noisy.

Iramsarakka, イラムサラッカ, 心配
ナ掛ラレル. v.i. and adj. To be
troubled.

Iramshitnere, イラムシツ子レ, 此レ
ハ此レハ(嘆息ノ辭、耐ヘ忍ハレヌノ意
ナ表ス). excl. Dear me! Dear!
dear! An exclamation expressive
of impatience.

Iramtoinere, イラムトイ子レ, 悲イカ
ナ、(嘆息ノ辭). excl. How sad!
What a trial! An exclamation
expressive of sorrow and com-
miseration. As:—Nei guru rai,
awa, iramtoinere ta hau! "how
sad! the man has died."

Iramtuiba, イラムツイバ, 臆病ナル、
恐ロシキ、例セバ、イラムツイバタハ
ウアシア、何ント恐ロシイデハナイカ.
v.i. and adj. To be timid. To be
frightened. As:—Iramtuiba ta hau
ash a; "what a frightful thing."!

Iramu, イラム, 考慮スレ. v.i. To be
thought of. To be considered.
Syn: Aramu.

Iramuikurukuru, イラムイクルクル,
關係スル. v.i. To be concerned
about.

Iramuok, イラムオク, 悲ム. v.i. To
be sorry. To be distressed.

Iramuokka, イラムオッカ, 悲マセレ.
v.t. To make sorry. To distress.

Iramye, イラムイェ, 譽メレ. v.t. To
praise. To applaud.

Iramyep, イラムイェブ, 稱賛. n. Acclamation.

Irangarap, イランガラブ, 挨拶. n. A
salutation. This word is often
pronounced Iyangarap by those

Japanese who speak a little Ainu. It is pigeon ainu and should be avoided.

Irangarap-itak, イ.ランガラプイタク, 挨拶ノ語. *n.* The words of a salutation. A salutation.

Irangarapte, イ ラ ンガラプテ, 如何 デスカ、(訪問ノ辭). *adv.* How do you do.

Irannakka, イランナッカ, 障碍物. *n.* A nuisance. A hindrance. *v.i.* To have no need of.

Irappa, イラッパ, 先祖ニ酒チ獻ゲルノ儀式. *n.* The ceremony of offering libations to the dead. **Syn:** **Icharapa an.**

Irapokkari, イラポノカリ, 貧シキ. *adj.* Poor. **Syn: Yaieshinniukesh.**

Irara, イララ, 惡戲ノ、イタヅラナ. *adj.* Naughty. Saucy. Sly.

Irarap, イララプ, 惡戲スル者. *n.* A sly creature. A naughty creature.

Irarape, イララペ, 惡戲スルコト、狡猾. *n.* A naughty thing. Naughtiness.

Irarape-ki, イララペキ, 惡戲チスレ. *v.t.* To do naughty things.

Irapungara, イラプンガラ, アマチヤヅル. *n.* *Gymnostemma cissoides, Benth.*

Irara-wa, イララワ, 狡猾ニ、イタヅラ =. *adv.* Slily. Naughtily.

Irat, イラツ, 失フ、外ツス(的チ). *v.t.* To lose. To miss. **Syn: Aturainu.**

Iraugetupa, イラウゲツパ, 仕事チスル. *v.t.* To do business. To pursue as a business.

Irawe, イラエ, 爲シタキ、殺シタキ. *v.t.* To desire to attack. To desire to

do. To wish to kill. As :—*Pirika buri ku irawe ne,* "I desire to do good things." *Chiramantep ku irawe ruwe ne,* "I desire to kill a bear." **Syn : Ramande.**

Irayapka, イラヤプカ, 美シト思フ、驚クベキ哉、(嘆息ノ辭). *v.t.* and *excl.* To consider beautiful or nice. Dear me! how beautiful. I am surprised. This exclamation always gives assent to the subject exciting it, it indicates assent but never denial.

Iraye, イライェ, 殺ロス. *v.t.* To kill. To have good sport. As :—*Tande iraye poro,* "lots have been killed today."

Iraye-guru, イライェグル, 殺害者. *n.* A person who has killed something. A killer. A successful hunter.

Irekte-chiri, イレクテチリ, ハヤブサ. *n.* A falcon. *Falco peregrinus, Tunst.*

Irektep, イレクテプ, 鹿チ呼ブ笛. *n.* A musical instrument used for decoying deer. **Syn : Ipakke ni.**

Irenga, イレンガ, 意思、厚意、意向.. *n.* Will. Favour. Disposition. Mind. A law. Rule. Business As :—*Pirika irenga,* "good will." *Wen irenga,* "a bad disposition." *Kamui irenga,* "the favour of God." *Tono-irenga,* "Government business."

Irenga-atte, イレンガアッテ, 厚意チ以テ遇スル. *v.t.* To treat with good will. To favour.

Irenga-koro, イレンガコロ, 世話ニナル. *v.i.* To enjoy the favour of another.

Irenga-ratchire, イレンガラツチレ, 調停スル. *v.t.* To reconcile.

Irenga-sange, イレンガサンゲ, 惠ム. 親切ニスル. *v.t.* To favour. To treat with good will.

Irenga-uturu-eapkash, イレンガウ ツルエアブカシ, 仲保スル. *v.i.* To act as a go - between.

Irenga-uturu-eapkash-guru, イレ ンガウツルエアブカシグル, 仲保人. *n.* A go-between. **Syn: Iyuturu oma guru.**

Irenga-wende, イレンガウェンデ, 爭ヒ ヲ惹起ス. *v.t.* To stir up strife.

Irenga-ye, イレンガイェ, 調停スル. *v.t.* To reconcile.

Ireshpa, イレシバ, 生長スル、(複數). *v.t.* To bring up. To rear. (*Pl. of the person*).

Ireske, イレスケ, 生長スル. *v.t.* To bring up. (*Pl of the object*).

Iresu, イレス, 生長スル. *v.t.* To bring up. To sustain.

Iresu-guru, イレスグル, 他人ヲ生長 セシムル人. *n.* One who brings another up.

Iresu-habo, イレスハボ, 母、養母. *n.* One's mother. A foster-mother. **Syn: Iresu totto.**

Iresu-huchi, イレスフチ, 火ノ女神. *n.* The goddess of fire. A foster-mother. **Syn: Onne huchi. Kamui huchi.**

Iresu-kamui, イレスカムイ, 神、(人ヲ 養フ). *n.* God, the sustainer (lit : foster-god).

Iresu-michi, イレスミチ, 父、養父. *n.* One's father. Foster-father.

Iresu-shinda, イレスシンダ, 神ニ付 ケル名ニシテ我搖籃卽チ養育ノ搖籃 ノ義ナリ. *n.* A term applied to

God. " The bringer up." " the sustainer." " Our cradle " (lit : Foster-cradle.).

Iresu-totto, イレストット, 母、養母. *n.* One's mother. Foster-mother.

Iresu-yubi, イレスユビ, 兄. *n.* Elder brother. Foster elder brother.

Iretaraka, イレタラカ, 漂白スレ、晒 ラス. *v.t.* To bleach.

Iri, イリ, 一家族ノモノ. *v.i.* To be of the same family. As :— *Shine iri guru,* " persons of the same family."

Iri, イリ, 皮ヲ剝ク、毛チ拔キ採ル. *v.t.* To skin. To pluck out as feathers. **Syn : Risei. Ri.**

Iri-an, イリアン, 皮剝キタレ. *adj.* Skinned. **Syn : Ari.**

Iri-guru, イリグル, 親類. *n.* Relations.

Irikuwan-no, イリクワンノ, 前ニ、前 頭ニ、卒先シテ. *adv.* Straight ahead. In front.

Iririp, イリリブ, ナホパイラクサ. *n.* Stinging nettles. *Urtica sisica, L. var platyphybla Wedd.*

Irishik-pui, イリシクブイ, 家族ニ似 タル顔付. *n.* Family likeness.

Iritak, イリタク, 親類、兄弟. *n.* Relations. Brothers and sisters.

Iriwak, イリワク, 血緣、兄弟. *n.* Blood relations. Brothers. As : — *Tu iriwak ne orowa shine tureshnu,* " two brothers and one sister."

Iriwak-ne-guru, イリワクチグル, 親 類、兄弟、姊妹. *n.* Brothers. Relations. Sisters.

Iro, イロ, or **Iroho, イロホ,** 色. *n.* Colour.

Irosome, イロソメ, 彩色シタル. *adj.* Coloured. **Syn : Iroaushi. A-nore.**

Iroaushi, イロアウシ, 彩色シタレ. *adj.* Coloured.

Iro-eshiknak, イロエシクナク, 色盲ノ. *adj.* Colour-blind.

Iroikeshne, イロイケシ子, 段々ニ、次々ニ. *adv.* One after another. By degrees.

Iroki, イロキ, 光ル、色チ有ツ. *v.i.* To shine. To have colour.

Ironne, イロン子, 厚キ. *adj.* Thick. (Used only of inanimate objects).

Ironne-samambe, イロン子サマムベ, クロガシラ. *n.* A kind of plaice. *Parophrys. sp.*

Ironne-tat-ni, イロン子タツニ, 樹木ノ名. *n.* A kind of birch.

Irorokeshne, イロロケシ子, 傍ニ. *adv.* By the side of.

Iroshki, イロシキ, 魂祭ル. *n.* The ceremony of offering food to the manes of the dead.

Iru-etoko, イルエトコ, 前面ニ、前ニ. *adv.* In front of. Before. **Syn : Kotchaketa.**

Iruike, イルイケ, 磨ク、鋭クスル. *v.t.* To sharpen. **Syn : Eenka.**

Iruka, イルカ,
Irukai, イルカイ, 暫時. *adv.* For a little while. For a short time. In a little while. After a short time.

Irukai-tomta, イルカイトムタ, 暫時ニシテ. *adv.* In a short time. After a little while. Just for a moment. For a short time.

Iruka-ne-koro, イルカ子コロ, 暫クシテ. *adv. ph.* After a short time. A little afterwards. Shortly.

Irukuru, イルクル, 難産. *n.* The pangs of child-birth.

Irup, イルプ,
Irupi, イルプイ, 糟粕. *n.* Dregs. Sediment. The remains of the arrowroot plant after the flour has been extracted.

Irura, イルラ, 送ル. *v.t.* To take or send away. To see one off as when going on a journey.

Irusa, イルサ, 貸ス. *v.t.* To lend.

Irushka, イルシカ, 怒ル. *v.i.* To become angry.

Irushka-chep, イルシカチェプ, フグノ總稱. *n.* Puffer. Swell fish. Name applied to several species of *Gn. Spheroides.*

Irushka-i, イルシカイ, 忿怒. *n.* Anger. Wrath.

Irutasa, イルタサ, 此處ヨリ彼處へ. *adj.* From one to the other.

Irutashpa, イルタシバ, 互ノ. *adj.* Mutual.

Irutashpa-no, イルタシバ, 互ニ. *adv.* Mutually.

Irushkare, イルシカレ, 怒ヲス. *v.t.* To make angry. To stir to anger. To aggravate.

Iruwe, イルウェ, 熊ノ足跡. *n.* A bear's foot-print.

Isa, イサ, 古キ、熟シタレ、皺ノヨリタル. *adj.* Old. Ripe. Harvest time. Wrinkled. Aged.

Isa, イサ, キーキート叫フ、鹿ノ鳴聲. *v.i.* To squeak. A deer's call.

Isa-wa-okere, イサワオケレ, 熟シタル. *v.i.* and *adj.* To have become quite ripe as fruit.

Isaika, イサイカ, 容易ナル. *adj.* Easy.

Isaikako, イサイカコ, 干渉スレ、口出シスル. *v.t.* To interfere. To speak when not spoken to.

Isam, イサム, or Isham, イシャム, 非ス、無シ、全ク無シ、居ラヌ、例ヘバ、オマンワイサム、往キテ居ラヌ、エワイサム、食ベテ仕舞フテナイ. *v.i.* Not to be. It is not. To be absent. In some cases the word *isam* expresses "entirety," and may be translated by "away." Thus :—*oman wa isam,* "he has gone away." *Koro wa oman wa isam,* "he has taken it away." *E wa isam,* "it has all been eaten." *Rai wa isam,* "he has died." *Isam kotom an,* "there appears not to be," "it looks as if there were none." When immediately followed by the verb *isam* may be translated by not As :—*Naa ek isam,* "he has not yet come."

Isama, イサマ, 無シ. *v.i.* Same as *Isam.*

Isama-ni, イサマニ, 横桁、支柱. *n.* A cross-beam. A tie beam. Brace.

Isambe, イサムベ, 有ラヌ、無クナッタ. *n.* and *v.t.* It is not. To have died.

Isami, イサミ, 何モナイ、例セバ、ネプカオッタ イェブカイサミ、汝ハ其レニ對シテ何モ言フ處ハナイ. *v.i.* and *n.* It is nothing. There is nothing. Absence. As :—*Nep ka otta yep ka isami,* "there is nothing you can say to it," *i. e.* "you have nothing to answer."

Isam-isam, イサムイサム, 早ク終リニナル. *v.i.* To come quickly to an end.

Isamka, イサムカ, 癈スル、滅絶スル. *v.t.* To abolish. To annihilate.

To annul. To assuage. To abrogate. **Syn: Oyak un omande. Oyakta omande.**

Isamka-i, イサムカイ, 癈止. *n.* Abolition.

Isam-no-po, イサムノポ, 否、アラズ. *ph.* No, there is not.

Isamta, イサムタ, ニ次ク : *adv.* Next to.

Isapa-kik-ni, イサパキクニ, 鮭、鱒ナドチ捕ヘテ撲殺ス爲メニ用ユル柳ノ棒. *n.* A willow stick used for killing salmon after they have been captured.

Isapte, イサプテ, 給事スル. *v.t.* To wait upon as in a feast. **Syn: Ipuni.**

Isapte-guru, イサプテグル, 給事人. *n.* A waiter. **Syn: Ipuni-guru.**

Isapte-mat, イサプテマツ, 給事婦. *n.* A waitress.

Isapte-atchike, イサプテアツチケ, 大キナル盆. *n.* A large tray. A waiter.

Ise, イセ, 鳴ク. *v.i.* To squeak. To call out. To squeal.

Ise-hawe-ash, イセハウェアシ, 鳴ク、鹿ノ呼聲. *v.i.* To squeal. The call of a deer.

Iseise, イセイセ, 啼ク. *v.i.* To squeak.

Iseku, イセク, 分娩ノ間際ニ乳房ノ脹レル事チ云フ、(人畜共ニ用キラレ). *v.i.* To swell up with milk as the breasts of animals just before having young. This word is also applied to women. **Syn: Topeseku.**

Isempiroitak, イセムピロイタク, 讒謗スル. *v.t.* To back-bite. To speak evil of another. **Syn: Ohaige-kara.**

Isenram-ari, イセンラムアリ, 前ニ云
ヘレ如ク. *ph.* The aforesaid. That
which was spoken of before. **Syn:**
Senramsekoro.

Isenrambe, イセンラムベ, 屢、此語ハ
毎ニ間投詞ニ用キラレオヤオヤノ意チ
表ス. *adv.* Again and again.
Continually. Always. Dear-dear!
This word is always used as a
kind of interjection. As :—*Isen-
rambe-hau,* "saying it again."

Isenramte, イセンラムテ, 同上. *adv.*
Same as above.

Isenramte-shiri, イセンラムテシリ,
何時デモ同ジコトチスレ. *ph.* Al-
ways doing the same thing.

**Isenramte-shiri-ki, イセンラムテ
シリキ,** 同上. *ph.* Same as above.

Isepo, イセポ, 兎、エチコウサキ、シロ
ウサキ. *n.* A hare. *Lepus var
iabilis. Pall.* **Syn: Epetke.
Oshuke. Raikuma.**

Isepo-keromun, イセポケロムン, チ
シマスゲ. *n.*   *Carex Buxbaumi.
Wahl.*

Isepo-saraki, イセポサラキ, ヒロハ
ノドジョツナギ. *n.* *Glyceria aqua-
tica, Sm.*

**Iseremak-inonno, イセレマクイノン
ノ,** 呪フ. *n.* A prayer that another may receive harm. A prayer for a curse.

Iseremak-oitak, イセレマクオイタク,
謗レ. *v.t.* To backbite. **Syn:
Ohaigekara.**

Iseremak-ush, イセレマクウシ, 助ケ
レ. *v.t.* To help. **Syn: Ikao-
biuki.**

Isese, イセセ, 啼ク. *v.i.* To squeal.
Syn: Ise.

Isesekka, イセセノカ, 温タメレ. *v.t.*
To heat.

Ishan-tono, イサントノ, 醫師. *n.* A
doctor. (*Jap*).

Ishi, イシ, 鳥ノ尾. *n.* A bird's tail.

Ishikamare, イシカマレ, 置ク. *v.t.*
To put. To set down.

Ishikari, イシカリ, 同轉ス レ. *adj.*
Winding. Tortuous.

Ishikari, イシカリ, 閉塞、便秘(病ノ). *n.*
Constipation. Stopped up.

Ishikashpere, イシカシペレ, 貪レ、羨
ム. *v.t.* To covet. **Syn: Ikeshika-
shure.**

Ishikekara, イシケカラ, 瞬キスル.
v.i. To wink the eyes.

Ishikipipka, イシキピプカ, 恥チテ頭
チ垂レル. *v.i.* To be unable to
look up for shame. To hang the
head in shame.

Ishikoba, イシコバ, 意匠、目的、待ツ.
n. Design. Intent. Also. *v.i.*
To wait.

Ishiksamnere, イシクサムチレ, 脇目
ニテ見ル. *v.i.* To look out of the
corners of the eyes.

Ishimekuttara, イシメクッタラ, ナツ
ユキサウ、オニシモツケサウ. *n.*
Filipendula kamtschatica, Max.

Ishimemokka, イシメモッカ, 喧嘩仕
掛ケレ. *v.i.* To pick a quarrel
with. To challenge to fight. **Syn:
Chishimemokka.**

Ishimne, イシムチ, 明日. *adv.* To-
morrow. The day following. As:
—*Ishimne hike an gusu ne na,*
"we will go on with it tomorrow."

Ishine, イシチ, 共同シテ. *adj.* Conjointly. Together.

Ishineka, イシチカ, 蠱惑スル. *v.t.*
To bewitch.

Ishinere, **イシチレ**, or Ishinnere, **イシンチレ**, 形ヲ變ズレ. *v.i.* To assume the form of some other being. To act the witch. **Syn : Shinere. Yaitasare.** Same as above.

Ishinerep, **イシチレプ**, or Ishinnerep, **イシンチレプ**, 幽霊. *n.* A phantom or ghost. A witch.

Ishiorore, **イシオロレ**, 驚ク. *v.i.* To be surprised. **Syn : Iyokunure.**

Ishiororeka, **イシオロレカ**, 驚カス. *v.t.* To surprise.

Ishi-oush, **イシオウシ**, 驕慢ナコトヲ言フ. *v.t.* To speak proudly.

Ishiraineka, **イシライチカ**, 待伏セス レ. *v.i.* To crouch. **Syn : Yongororo.**

Ishiramka, **イシラムカ**, 可愛ガル. *v.i.* To fawn.

Ishiramkore, **イシラムコレ**, 愛スル. *v.t.* To love. To care for.

Ishiri, **イシリ**, カヲ用キテ. *adv.* With might. Severely.

Ishiriki, **イシリキ**, ノ代リニ. *adv.* Instead of. **Syn : Shirine.**

Ishiri-kootke, **イシリコオツケ**, 強ク刺ス. *v.t.* To spear very much, or thoroughly.

Ishirikurantere, **イシリクランテレ**, マー (嘆息ノ辭). *interj.* Dear me ! Oh dear ! As :—*Ishirikurantere nep poro!* "dear me how large!" *Ishirikurantere, ukuran etutanne kikiri túmi sange,* "dear me, how the mosquitoes waged war last night." *Ishirikurantere, ara mim patek,* "dear me ! it is nothing but fat."

Ishirishina, **イシリシナ**, 蠱惑スル. *v.t.* To bewitch. **Syn : Ichashkara.**

Ishiriro, **イシリロ**, 荒キ鼻息ヲスレ (奔馬ノ如ク). *v.i.* To snort (as a horse).

Ishiru, **イシル**, 摩リ剝ク. *v.t.* To abrade. To rub off. To grate. As :—*Tush ishiri wa tui,* "the rope has worn asunder." *Ku teke ishiru wa meshke,* "I have rubbed the skin off my hand." *Shuop ush-i ishiru wa pitche,* "the paint has been rubbed off the box." *Nei numa ishiru wa tonto ne,* "that skin has had the hair rubbed off and has become bare."

Ishirubare, **イシルバレ**, 惡氣ニ取付カレル. *v.i.* To be possessed with a devil. To be afflicted with cleptomania. To be a maniac. **Syn : Nitne Kamui shikatkare.**

Ishirubarep, **イシルバレプ**, 狂人. *n.* A maniac.

Ishirup, **イシルプ**, 鑢、鑢. *n.* A file.

Ishitaigi, **イシタイギ**, 織ル. *v.t.* To weave. To make cloth.

Ishitoma, **イシトマ**, 懼レル. *v.i.* To be afraid. **Syn : Kimatek.**

Ishitomare, **イシトマレ**, 驚カス. *v.t.* To frighten.

Ishitoma-ship, **イシトマシブ**, 織物スルトキ用ユル腰當テ. *n.* A flat piece of wood bent so as to fit the lower part of the back and used in weaving cloth.

Ishitomatektek, **イシトマテクテク**, 臆病ナル、恐ロシキ. *adj.* Fearful. Cowardly. **Syn : Eturamkoro.**

Ishiu, イ シウ, 不断 ニ、常 ニ. *adv.* Ordinarily.

Ishkari, イ シカ リ, 閉塞 セ シ. *v.i.* Stopped up.

Ishnichi, イ シニチ, 脊椎ノ下端. *n.* The lower end of the spine.

Ishpoki, イ シポキ, カレイノ一種. *n.* A kind of flounder.

Isho, イ ショ, 豊饒ナル. *adj.* Plenteous. Sport. Lucky. Also game, as bears, deer, etc. As :—*Isho koro guru*, "a lucky sportsman." *Ainu moshiri chikoikip isho pirika moshiri ne*, "Ainu land is a place where there are plenty of animals." *Isho koven*, "unlucky in sport." *Tanto isho pirika*, "to-day we have had good sport." *Isho nuikesh*, "unfortunate in hunting."

Isho, イ ショ, 前面ニ. *adv.* In front of. Ahead.

Isho-itak, イ ショイタク, 見聞シタルコト ヲ語ル. *v.t.* To tell what one has seen and heard. To report upon. To say. To report. **Syn : Uweneusara.**

Isho-itak-ambe, イ ショイタクアムベ, 報告. *n.* A report. News.

Isho-itak-an, イ ショイタクアン, 報知. *n.* News.

Isho-itakka, イ ショイタッカ, 知セル、話ス. *v.i.* To tell. To say,

Isho-kapiu, イ ショカピウ, アホウドリ. *n.* Albatross. **Syn : Shikambe. Oshkambe. Onne-chikap.**

Ishon, イ ション, or **Ison, イ ソン,** 豊饒ナル. *adj.* and *v.i.* Plenteous. good sport. Clever. Lucky. Fortunate.

Isho-sange-kamui, イ ショサンゲカム イ, 梟(フクロ). *n.* An owl.

Isho-seta, イ ショセタ, 橇ヲ曳クトキ先頭ニ立ツ犬. *n.* A leader sleigh dog.

Ishu, イ シュ, 生涯. *n.* One's lifetime. A lifetime. One's life. **Syn : Ishu tuika.**

Ishu, イ シュ, 有ル、存在スル. *v.i.* and *adj.* To be. To exist. To live. Living. Perfect health. Strong. As :—*Ishu Kamui*, "the living God." *Ishu an*, "it is alive." *Ishu rapoketa*, "during one's lifetime."

Ishu-i, イ シュイ, 生命、生涯. *n.* Life. A lifetime.

Ishu-ramat, イ シュラマツ, 生霊. *n.* A living soul.

Ishu-tuika, イ シュツイガ, 一生涯. *n.* A lifetime. During one's life.

Iso, イ ソ, 裸岩. *n.* Large bare rocks.

Ison, イ ソン, or **Ishon, イ ション,** 器用ナル、巧ナル、運ノ善キ. *adj.* and *v.i.* Clever. Lucky. Plenteous. Fortunate. To have good sport.

Isonbe, イ ソンベ, 多ク漁セシ人. *n.* A successful hunter or fisher.

Isoye, イ ソイエ, 箕ニテル. *v.t.* To shake the husks off a winnow after winnowing.

Isoyep, イ ソイエブ, 箕. *n.* A winnow. **Syn : Muye.**

Isoyep, イ ソイエブ, 錐(キリ). *n.* A gimlet.

Ita, イ タ, 板. *n.* A board.

Ita, イ タ, 何時. *rel. pro.* When.

Itak, イタク, or **Itakki, イタッキ,** 言語. *n.* A word. Language. Speech.

Itak, イ タク, 話ス、云フ. *v.i.* To speak. To say. To acknowledge.

To tell. As :— *Tu itak kainon
yaikoruki*, " to swallow one's
words." *Itak hau konna charototke*,
" to speak fluently." *Itak awatore
wa ye*, " to speak without making
any mistakes."

Itak-ambe, イタカクアムベ, 言葉. *n.*
A word.

**Itakamkirara-ye, イタカムキララ
イェ,** 紹介スル. *v.t.* To introduce. To
make known.

Itakamkire, イタカムキレ, 約束スレ.
v.t. To promise.

Itak-ande, イタクアンデ, 言ヒ置ク.
To leave word.

Itak-apak-guru, イタクアパクグル,
訥辯家. *n.* A bad speaker.

Itakbe, イタクベ, 彈キ弓ノ柄. *n.* The
stem of a spring-bow.

**Itak-chihoshipire, イタクチホシピ
レ,** 命令ヲ取消ス. *v.t.* To counter-
mand.

Itak-eashinge, イタクエアシンゲ, 話
ス、云フ. *v.i.* To speak. To say.

Itak-eoshiwen, イタクエオシウェン,
氣ニ障ヘテ物チ云フ、間違ヘテ報知ス
ル. *v.i.* To speak disagreeably. To
be diffident in speaking. To mis-
inform.

Itak-eyukara, イタクエユカラ, 口眞
似スル. *v.t.* To mock. To imitate
one's speech.

**Itak-hau, イタクハウ, or Itak-ha-
we, イタクハウェ,** 話シ聲. *n.* The
tone of voice in speaking. What
one says.

**Itak-hau-konna-charototke, イタ
クハウコンナチャロトツケ,** 流暢ニ語
ル. *ph.* To speak fluently. Fluent.

Itak-hi, イタクヒ, or Itak-i, イタク

イ, 演說、又談話. *n.* A speech. Acknowledgement. A message.

Itak-ibehe, イタクイベヘ, 言葉ノ意
味. *n.* The meaning of a word or
speech.

Itak-ikkewehe, イタクイッケウェヘ,
言葉ノ意味. *n.* The meaning of a
word or speech.

**Itak-inuni, イタクイヌニ, or Itak-
ununi, イタクウヌニ,** 吃ル. *v.i.*
To stammer in speaking.

Itak-kashi, イタクカシ, 不從順、忤フ
(サカラウ). *v.t.* To disobey.

Itak-keshkara, イタクケシカラ, 罰金
ヲ拂フ、(複). *v.i.* To pay a fine
(*pl*).

**Itak-koshinonruki, イタクコシノン
ルキ,** 吃ル. *v.i.* To falter in
speaking.

Itak-koshishuye, イタクコシシュイェ,
身振リスル、(話シスル時). *v.i.* To
sway about when talking.

Itak-kutchama, イタククッチャマ, 話
シ聲. *n.* The tone of one's voice.
A dialect. Pronounciation.

**Itak-maukushte-itak, イタクマウク
シテイタク,** 譬喩. *n.* A parable. A
hidden speech.

**Itak-maukushte-uwepekere, イタ
クマウクシテウウェペケレ,** 譬喩. *n.* A
fable.

Itak-ne-manup, イタクネマヌプ, 話
ノ種子. *n.* The matter of a speech.
A speech. Words.

Itak-nini, イタクニニ, 吃ル. *v.i.* To
stutter.

Itak-oikap, イタクオイカプ, 罰金. *n.*
A fine. **Syn : Ashimbe.**

Itak-oikap-sange, イタクオイカブサ
ンゲ, 罰金ヲ拂フ. v.t. To pay a
fine. Syn: Ashimbe sange.

Itak-omare, イタクオマレ, 話ノ仲間
入リナスレ. v. t. To join in conversation.

Itakpa, イタッパ, 話ス. v.i. To speak
(*pl of the person*).

Itak-ramachi, イタクラマケ, イタク
ラマトニ同ジ. n. Same as itak-ramat. Syn: Itak-ibehe.

Itak-ramat, イタクラマツ, 言語ノ意
味. n. The meaning of a word or
speech.

Itak-rui-guru, イタクルイグル, 多辯
者. n. A great talker or speaker
(not necessarily a phrase of evil
import).

Itak-san-i, イタクサンイ, 命令. n. A
command. An order from a superior. As:—*Tono orowa no ene
itak san-i*, "thus orders the government."

Itakshikushte-itak, イタクシクシテ
イタク, 比喩談. n. An illustration.

Itak-sura, イタクスラ, 末期ノ言葉、遺
言. n. The last words of a dying person. A person's last wishes
or commands. Syn: Hoppa-itak.

Itak-taknere, イタクタク子レ, 略言ス
ル. v.t. To abbreviate.

Itak-teksama, イタクテクサマ, 再ビ、
マタ. adv. Again. Besides.

Itak-tomte, イタクトムテ, 面白キ話ノ.
adj. Of pleasant speech.

Itak-tomte-guru, イタクトムテグル,
面白ク談話スル人. n. A person who
speaks in a pleasing manner.

Itak-tomtere, イタクトムテレ, 言葉ヲ
飾ル. v.t. To polish up one's manner of talking.

Itak-tunash, イタクツナシ, 早口ニテ
言フ. adj. and v.i. To talk quickly. To speak without due thought
As:—*Itak-tunash wayasap*, "a
quick talker is unwise."

Itaku, イタク, 話. n. A speech. The
plural of *itak*.

Itak-ununin, イタ,ウヌニン, イタキ
ノ複數. v.i. To stammer in talking.

Itak-uwetore-kambi, イタッウエト
レカムビ, 辭典. n. A dictionary.

Itan, イタン. 槌. n. Hammer.

Itanchiki, イタンチキ, 床. n. Floor.

Itangi, イタンギ, 椀. n. A cup.

Itangi-kem-ashikepet, イタンギケ
ムアシケペツ, 親指. n. The index
finger. So called because it is
generally used for scraping out
remnants of food from the eating
utensils. Syn: Ikemumpe.

Itara, イタラ. 袋. n. A bag. A
satchel. Syn: Chitarabe.

Itaraka, イタラカ, 僅ニ、不知不識ニ.
adv. Imperceptibly. Just. Slightly.

Itara-kamas, イタラカマス, 手荷物
n. Luggage. Syn: Shike.

Itaratara, イタラタラ, グラグラスル.
adj. Shaky.

Itasa, イタサ, ノ代リニ、ノ返シニ、
例セバ、イタサカレ、贈物ニ對シテ返禮
スル. adv. In return. In answer
to. As:—*Itasa kare*, "to do"
or "give in return for something
received."

Itasa, イタサ, 變リ易キ、定リナキ、例
セバ、イタサレラ、變リ易キ風. adj.
Changeable. As:— *Itasa ·rera,*
"a changeable wind."

Itasa-itak, イタサイタク, 答. *n.* and *v.t.* An answer. To answer.

Itasare, イタサレ, 交換スル. *v.t.* To exchange.

Itasasa, イタササ, 苦痛ノ嘆息. *excl.* An exclamation of pain. **Syn:** **Ayapo.**

Itasayupkep, イタサユブケプ, 嵐. *n.* A storm.

Itashka-o, イタシカオ, 袖チカ丶ゲル. *v.i.* To tie up (as one's sleeves). To turn up one's sleeves.

Itashko, イタシコ, 袖チ巻上ゲル. *v.t.* To turn up one's sleeves. To tie up (as one's sleeves).

Itata, イタタ, 打ツ、(鎚ニテ)、打切レ. *v.t.* To hammer. To chop.

Itata-ni, イタタ二, 俎. *n.* A chopping block. **Syn: Itaugi ni.**

Itaya-pu, イタヤブ, 板造ノ倉. *n.* A store-house made of boards.

Itauge-ni, イタウゲ二, 俎. *n.* A chopping block.

Itashtasa, イタシタサ, 失禮スル、抗辯スル. *v.i.* To be saucy. To contradict.

Itastasa, イタスタサ, 同上. *v.i.* Same as above.

Itaugi, イタウギ, 打切ル. *v.t.* To chop.

Itek, イテク, 雇ハレル. *v.i.* To be employed. To be sent.

Iteki, イテキ, 勿スナ. *aux. v. & adv.* Do not. *Iteki* is imperative. As:—*Iteki nep ye,* "do not say anything." *Iteki mashkin no shikte,* "do not fill it too full." *Iteki nekon a ka iki,* "do not meddle with it." *Iteki nei peka,* "by no means." Followed by *kuni ne, iteki* forms a supplication ; Thus :

—*Iteki aehomatu kuni ne ki wa en kore,* "grant that I may be afraid of nothing."

Itekika, イテキカ, 禁ズル. *v.t.* To prohibit. **Syn : Hattoki.**

Itekka-kara, イテッカカラ, 禁ズレ. *v.t.* To prohibit.

Iteme, イテメ, 伸ビスル. *v.i.* To stretch out at full length.

Iteme-ni, イテメ二, 梁. *n.* The beams in the upper part of a hut. **Syn : Umangi-ni.**

Iteme-kikiri, イテメキキリ, 尺蠖. *n.* The looper caterpillar.

Itemi-kikiri, イテミキキリ, 同上. *n.* Same as above.

Itere, イテレ, 待ツ. *v.t.* To await. To wait for.

Itese, イテサ, 織. *v. t.* To weave. To spin.

Iteseka, イテセカ, 織絲. *n.* The strings used in weaving mats.

Itese-ni, イテセ二, 織機ノ或部ノ名. *n.* An instrument used in spinning or weaving cloth.

Iteye-ni, イテイ二, 機槌オトシ. *n.* A kind of snare, so constructed that the top shall fall down upon any animal going under it.

Itomkokanu, イトムコカヌ, 預ケ丶、依托スル. *v.t.* To commit to the care of another. To let another do. Also *v.i.* Not to be able to do without the consent of another.

Itomkot, イトムコツ, 從フ、追フ. *v.t.* To follow. To pursue. **Syn : Iyokot. Ikesamba.**

Itomne, イトムチ, 羨ム. *v.t.* To envy. **Syn : Eyaitunnap.**

Itomnukara, イトムヌカラ, 結婚スレ. *v.t.* To marry. To live together as husband and wife. **Syn: U-tomnukara.**

Itomnukara, イトムヌカラ, 夫婦. *n.* Husband and wife. **Syn: Um-urek guru.**

Itomnukara-utara, イトムヌカラウタラ, 夫婦等. *n.* Husbands and wives. Also "Husband and wife."

Itomo, イトモ, 平和. *n.* Peace.

Itomo-itak, イトモイタク, 和睦スル. *v.i.* To make peace.

Itomushi, イトムシ, 腹鰭. *n.* The ventral fins of fishes.

Itomot-guru, イトモツグル, 巧ナル獵者. *n.* A clever or successful hunter. **Syn: Etomne guru.**

Itomo-un-puyara, イトモウンプヤラ, 南窓. *n.* A window on the south side of a house.

Itoppa, イトッパ, 己ノ印. *n.* One's personal mark or sign.

Itoshinni, イトシンニ, ホザキシモツケ、エゾハギ. *n.* Spiræa salicifolia, L. var. lanceolata, Torr. et Gray. **Syn: Nitat-shingep.**

Ittone, イット子, 往復スル. *v.i.* To go and return. To go and come back at once.

Ituiba, イツイバ, 切リ落ス、殺ロス. *v.t.* To cut off. To kill.

Ituibapuibe, イツイバブイベ, 惡人ノ子. *n.* Son of a bad man. A name given to the children of very bad parents. Also sometimes applied to bad young people irrespective of their parents. The offspring of a person who has been killed.

Itui-rui, イツイルイ, 荒砥. *n.* A rough whetstone.

Ituye-rui, イツイェルイ, 荒砥. *n.* Same as above.

Ituituye, イツイツイェ, 簸ル. *v.t.* To winnow.

Ituituye-i, イツイツイェイ, 箕場、ウチバ. *n.* A winnowing place.

Itukarige-sak-no, イツカリゲサッノ, 恐レナク、憚リナク. *adv.* Without diffidence. Without fear.

Itukari-sak-no, イツカリサクノ, 恐レナク、憚リナク. *adv.* Without difficulty. Without fear.

Itumama-ni, イツママニ, 織機ノ部分. *n.* A piece of straight wood used in weaving.

Itumashire, イツマシレ, 混製スレ. *v.t.* To adulterate.

Itunnap, イツンナツプ, 蟻、例セバ、イツンナプチセイ、蟻ノ巣. *n.* An ant. As:—*Itunnap chisei*, "an ant's nest."

Itupeshnu-kusu-ne-utara, イツペシヌクス子ウタラ, 會葬者. *n.* Attendants at a funeral. Mourners.

Itura, イツラ, 導ク. *adj.* Led. As:—*Itura guru*, "a person led."

Ituren, イツレン, 神詫チ受ケル、默示チ受ケレ. *v.i.* To be inspired. To be actuated by some internal impulse.

Ituren-kamui, イツレンカムイ, 守護神. *n.* One's guardian angel.

Iturupukte, イツルプクテ, 眩ク、近眼. *adv.* Dimly. Short-sightedly.

Itusare, イツサレ, 與ヘル. *v.t.* To give. To bestow. As:—*Aep itusare guru*, "a person who gives food to a beggar."

Itushtek, イツシテク, 獸類ニ取リ付カ

レル. *v.i.* To be possessed by an animal. To be bewitched by an animal. To be mad.

Itushtekka, イツシテッカ, 急イデモノチサセレ. *v.t.* To cause one to do anything with haste.

Itushtek-korachi, イツシテッコラチ, 馮カレタル様子、狂ハシク. *adv.* As one possessed. Madly.

Itushtek-no, イツシテクノ, 激シク、取リ付カレタ如ク、迅早ニ. *adv.* With severity. Madly. With great haste and determination, (generally used in a bad sense).

Itutande, イツシテンデ, 知ラヌ振リチスル. *v.i.* To take no notice of. To turn a deaf ear to. As:— *Ashpa kisara itutanure,* or *ashpa kisara itutande,* "to turn a deaf ear to."

Itutanure, イツタヌリ, 同上. *v.i.* Same as above.

Ituyashkarap, イツヤシカラプ, 愛スレ可愛ガレ. *v.t.* To love. To fondle.

Ituye, イツイェ, or **Itui, イツイ,** リ切落トス、虐殺スレ. *v. t.* To cut off. To massacre. As:— *Kotan ituye,* "to massacre a village."

Ituye-sere-hum, イツイェセレフム, 物チ切断スル音. *n.* The noise made in cutting anything asunder.

Ituyerui, イツイェルイ, 荒砥. *n.* A rough whetstone.

Iturui, イツルイ, 同上. *n.* Same as above.

Iukotama, イウコタマ, 共ニ. *adv.* Together. (*Obj*).

Iun, イウン, 傷ツケル、痛メル、例セバ、ツイイウン、腹ガ痛ム. *v.i.* To hurt. To be in pain. As:—*Tui iun,* "to suffer from the stomach ache."

Iunin, イウニン, 病、疼痛、苦痛. *n.* Sickness. Disease. Pain. As:—*Iunin tununi,* "to groan with pain." Also *v.i.* To suffer. To be in pain.

Iuninka, イウニンカ, 患マシム. *v.t.* To make suffer.

Iunin-itak, イウニンイタク, 鋭キ言葉. *n.* Burning words. Heart-searching words. Words which reach the heart. Effective speech.

Iun-iun, イウンイウン, 甚疼痛ニ患ム. *v.i.* To suffer great pain.

Iunu, イウヌ, 着ル、例セバ、レクチイウヌ、頃ニ着師レ. *v.t.* To put on as a necklace. As:—*Rekuchi iunu,* "to put upon the neck."

Iutek, イウテク, 仕ヘル. *v.t.* To serve. As:—*Kamui iutek,* "to serve God."

Iwa, イワ, 岩、岡. *n.* Land as opposed to rivers. Rocks.

Iwai, イワイ, 給料. *n.* Wages. Salary. **Syn: Pumma.**

Iwayehe, イワイェヘ, 同上. *n.* Same as above.

Iwak, イワク, 往ク、例セバ、クウニタクイワク、我ハ家ニ往クナリ. *v.t.* To go. To go away. To return from work. As:—*Ku uni ta ku iwak,* "I am going home."

Iwak, イワク, 密通スレ. *v.i.* To have illicit intercourse. Intercourse between the sexes.

Iwak-an, イワクアン, 家ニ還ツタ. *v.i.* To have gone home (as from work).

Iwakikin-ni, イワキキンニ, ナ、カマ

ド. *n.* Mountain Ash. *Pyrus aucuparia, Gœrtn. var. japonica, Max.*

Iwakte, イワクテ, 送ル、埋ル. *v.t.* To send away. To cause to go. In some places, "to bury."

Iwan, イワン, 六. *adj.* Six. **Syn: Iwan otutanu.**

Iwanatushbe, イワナツシベ, 陶器. *n.* A kind of earthen vessel.

Iwanbe, イワンベ, 六. *n.* Six.

Iwanbe-ikashima-wanbe, イワンベイカシマワンベ, 十六. *adj.* Sixteen.

Iwanbe-otutanu, イワンベオツタヌ, 第六. *adj.* The sixth. **Syn: Iwan ikinne.**

Iwange, イワンゲ, 壮健ナル. *v.i.* and *adj.* In good health. Healthy.

Iwange-no, イワンゲノ, 壮健ニ. *adv.* Healthy. In good health.

Iwange-no-an, イワンゲノアン, 壮健ニナル. *v.i.* To be in good health.

Iwange-no-okai, イワンゲノオカイ, 壮健ナル. *v.i.* (*pl*). To be in good health.

Iwangere, イワンゲレ, 癒ル. *v.t.* To heal. To make well.

Iwangeuba, イワンゲウバ, 壮健ナル. (*pl.*) *v.i.* To be well in health.

Iwa-ni, イワニ, アチダモ. *n.* Ash tree. *Fraxinus longicuspis, S. et Z.*

Iwan-ikinne, イワンイキンネ, 第六. *adj.* The sixth.

Iwanrekut-koro-guru, イワンレクツコログル, 偽チ言フ人. *n.* A liar (lit. a person with six throats).

Iwanshuine, イワンシュイ子, 六度. *adj.* Six times.

Iwarasupa, イワラスパ, サハアザサキ. *n. Hydrangea Hortensis, DC. var. acuminata, A. Gray.*

Iwashi, イワシ, イワシ. *n.* Sardine. (Japanese). *Cupanodon melanostictus, (Fos).*

Iwasoko-ni, イワソコニ, 同上. *n.* Same as *Iwarasupa.*

Iwatarapbe, イワタラブベ, 赤子、嬰兒. *n.* A small child. A very young baby.

Iwatarappe, イワタラッベ, 小兒、赤子. *n.* A child. **Syn: Poho. Pon aiai. Tennep.**

Iwatope-ni, イワトペニ, メイケツカヘデ、ハナイタヤ. *n.* A kind of maple. *Acer japonicum, Th.* Also, *Acer palmatum, Th.*

Iwau, イワウ, 硫黄. *n.* Sulphur.

Iwayehe, イワイェヘ, 給料. *n.* Wages. Salary. A bribe.

Iwende, イウェンデ, 呪フ. *v.t.* To curse. To cause to become bad.

Iwendep, イウェンデブ, 惡鬼、惡寃. *n.* Demons. Things which harm people. The devil. **Syn: Nitne Kamui. Wen kamui.**

Iwentep, イウェンテブ, 同上. *n.* Same as above.

Iwok, イウォク, 病チ追フ. *n.* A ceremony for charming disease out of the sick.

Iworo, イウォロ, 山、例セバ、イチロシヨクルカ、山ノ上. *n.* Mountains. As: —*Iworo shokuruka*, "over the mountain tops." *Iworo shokata*, "on the whole mountain."

Iworo, イウォロ, 全ク、皆ナ、例セバ、ヘテイチロ、諸川、レプウンイチロ、海一面ニ. *adj.* The whole. As:— *Pet iworo*, "the whole river" or "all the rivers." *Rep un iworo*, "the whole sea." *Ya un iworo*, "the whole earth.

Iworush-ande, イヲルシアンデ, 重
子テ中ニ入レル. v.t. To be put into
one another.

Iyahunge, イヤフンゲ, 家ニ入レル. v.t.
To take into a house.

Iyahup, イヤフプ, 受ケル、貰フ. v.t.
To receive. Syn: Ahupkara.

Iyahup-guru, イヤフプグル, 貰フ人、
乞食. n. A recipient. A beggar.
Syn: Hoito guru. Ahupkara
guru.

Iyai, イヤイ, 危キ、恐シキ、例セバ、イ
ヤイアン、ソッハ危イゾ. v.i. and adj.
Danger. Fearful. As:—Iyai an,
"there is danger." Iyai hawe ne
an, "fearful talk."

Iyai-iyai, イヤイイヤイ, 注意セヨ. ph.
Be careful. Take care.

Iyaiiraigere, イヤイイライゲレ, 難有.
adv. Thank you.

Iyaiiraigere-iongamire, イヤイイラ
イゲレイオンガミレ, 難有、我レ汝ノ
安否ヲ問フ. ph. Thank you; I
salute you.

Iyaikipte, イヤイキプテ, 甚ダ危キ.
v.i. To be very dangerous.

Iyaikoirushkare,
イヤイコイルシカレ,
Iyaikorushkare,
イヤイコルシカレ,
静ニナル、穏
ニナル. v.i.
To be sere-
ne. To be calm. To be even
tempered. Also to be trouble-
some. This word is generally
used in an imperative sense, and
when a person has been suffering
from some trouble, or when one
is afraid he has given trouble.
It then seems to form part of a
salutation. The word means:—
"I am afraid I have made you
angry." Thus:—Irangarapte, iya-

ikoirushkare, "how do you do, may
you be calm."

Iyainumare, イヤイヌマレ, 懼レル、
例セバ、イナイヌマレイヨシセレ
ケレハウアシア、何ト恐シキ話
デナイカ. v.i. To be afraid. To
be in dread. Also sometimes used
as an interjection "how shocking!" Thus:—Iyainumare, iyoshserekere hau ash a! "how shocking, what dreadful talk"!

Iyaipirare, イヤイピラレ, 失望スル.
v.i. To have one's hopes frustrat-
ed. To be disappointed.

Iyaitupa, イヤイツパ, 欲スル. v.t.
To desire.

Iyaishirikara, イヤイシリカラ, 哀訴
スル、失望ヲ述ベル. v.i. To com-
plain. To be disappointed.

Iyama, イヤマ, 種ヲ播ク、(バラマキス
ル). v.t. To sow seed broadcast.
Syn: Iyare.

Iyangarap, イヤンガラプ, or Irangarap, イランガラプ, 挨拶ノ語. n.
A salutation.

Iyangarap-itak, イヤンガラプイタク,
or Irangarap-itak, イランガラプ
イタク, 挨拶ノ語. n. A salutation.
The words of a salutation.

Iyangarapte, イヤンガラプテ, 如何
デスカ. adv. How do you do. This
word is a corruption of the word
Irangarapte.

Iyapapu, イヤパプ, 兔シテ乞フ. v.t.
To beg one's pardon.

Iyapi, イヤピ, 羽キ. adj. Weak.
Invalid. Lame.

Iyapi-guru, イヤピグル, 柔羽ナル人.
病人. n. A weak person. A lame
person. A sick person. An invalid.

Iyapo, イヤボ, 苦痛ノ聲. *excl.* An exclamation of pain.

Iyapo, イヤボ, or **Iyabo, イハボ,** 父、(或地方ニテノ母).*n.* Father. **Syn: Michi. Ona.** In some places "mother."

Iyara, イヤラ, 他ノ、外ノ、例セバ、イ ヤラコタンタ、外ノ村ニ. *adj.* Other. Different. As:—*Iyara kotan ta,* "in other villages." **Syn: Moshima an.**

Iyare, イヤレ, 種ヲ播ク. *v.t.* To sow seed broadcast. **Syn: Iyama.**

Iyashinȝe, イヤシンゲ, 償フ、返報ス レ. *v.t.* To make compensation. To give as compensation for some evil done. To compensate. A fine paid for something wrongfully done.

Iyashke-ani, イヤシケアニ, 饗應ノ席 ニ導ク. *v.t.* To be led to a feast. To be brought into a house of feasting. **Syn: Ashke auk.**

Iyashke-uk, イヤシケウク, 饗筵ニ招 ク. *v.t.* To invite to a feast.

Iyashke-uk-shongo, イヤシケウクシ ョンゴ, 招待. *n.* An invitation to a party or feast.

Iyatte, イヤッテ, 飾ル. *v.t.* To ornament. To hang up ornaments.

Iyaukotte, イヤウコッテ, 吃ル、發音. *n.* and *v.i.* To lisp. Pronunciation. To stammer. A stammering pronunciation. As:—*Iyaukotte pirika,* "of good pronunciation." *Iyaukotte-wen,* "of bad pronunciation."

Iye, イイェ, 知ラセレ. *n.* To tell.

Iye-e-ine, イイェエイ子, 四ッ. *adj.* Four.

Iye-e-ine-ikinne, イイェエイ子イキン 子, 第四. *adj.* The fourth.

Iye-ere, イイェエレ, 三. *adj.* Three.

Iye-ere-ikinne, イイェエレイキン子, 第三. *adj.* The third.

Iye-itak, イイェイタク, 言フ、話スル. *v.t.* To tell.

Iye-ka-hunara, イイェカフナラ, 待望 ム. *v.t.* To wait expectantly for. To await with anxiety.

Iyekamge, イイェカムゲ, 知ラセル.*v.t.* To make known.

Iyekarakara, イイェカラカラ, 出來タ ル. *v.i.* To be done. **Syn: Anekarakara.**

Iyekari, イイェカリ, 乞フ. *v.t.* To beg.

Iyekari-guru, イイェカリグル, 乞食. *n.* A beggar. **Syn: Hoitoguru.**

Iyeninuite, イイェニヌイテ, 寝カス.*v.t.* To put to bed.

Iyemaune, イイェマウ子, 混スレ. *v.i.* To mix. **Syn: Ikopoyege.**

Iyeniuchinne, イイェニウチン子, 喧嘩 サセル. *v.t.* To cause to quarrel. To set at variance.

Iyen-peka, イイェンペカ, or **Ien-peka, イエンペカ,** 上ニ. *adv.* Over. As:—*Chikap anak ne un iyen-peka kush,* "the birds cross over us."

Iyenuchupkichiure, イイェヌチュプキ チウレ, 光リニ眩スル. *v.t.* To be dazzled by the rays of the sun.

Iyenupe-o-guru, イイェヌペオグル, 會 葬者. *n.* Mourners for the dead.

Iyeokok, イイェオコク, 蛇ニ噛マルレ. *v.i.* To be bitten by a snake. **Syn: Aeokokte.**

Iyepa, イイェバ, 出來ル、オチ恃ム、例 セバ、イエバチキポンノアブカシヤク

ヒリカ、汝ハ出來ルト思フナラバ爲シ
テ見ヨ. *adj.* Able. To feel able.
As :—*E iyepa chiki pon no apkash yak pirιk ι,* "you had better
walk if you feel able.

Iyepoko, イイェポコ, 惡念ナㇽ. *adj.*
Evil-minded. Of bad intent.

Iyepokun, イイェポクン, 惡念ナㇽ.
adj. Evil-minded. Of bad intent.

Iyepokun-guru, イイェポクングㇽ, 惡
念ナㇽ人. *n.* An evil-minded person.

Iyepe-ainu, イイェベアイヌ, 花婿. *n.*
A bride-groom. **Syn : Itomnukara guru.**

Iyepe-habo, イイェベハボ, 姑. *n.*
The mother of one's wife.

Iyepe-mat, イイェベマツ, 花嫁. *n.*
A bride.

Iyepe-michi, イイェベミチ, 繼父. *n.*
A father in law.

Iyepe-totto, イイェベトット, 繼母. *n.*
A mother-in-law.

Iyepeise, イイェベイセ, 壯健ナㇽ. *adj.*
To be in good health.

Iyeramuhauge, イイェラムハウゲ,
親切ナㇾ. *adj.* Kind.

Iyeramu-nishte, イイェラムニシテ,
無慘ナㇽ, 殘忍ナㇾ. *adj.* Cruel.

Iyerikiteshpa, イイェリキテシバ, 捧
ゲ持ツ. *v.t.* To hold up.

Iyeshikeraine, イイェシケライ子, 助
ヶㇽ, 救フ, 惠ム. *v.t.* To help. To
favour.

Iyetapkara, イイェタブカラ, 踊. A
dance.

Iyetaptapu, イイェタブタブ, 被ㇽ. *v.t.*
To cover as the head. To wrap
up the head. To hide the head

under the wings as birds. Thus :
—*Chikap iyetaptapu kane mokoro
wa okai,* "the birds are sleeping
with their heads covered." *Ku
sapa araka gusu, ku iyetaptapu
ruwe ne,* "as I have a headache
I have wrapped it up."

Iyetaye, イイェタイェ, 拔キ出ス. *v.t.*
To draw out.

Iyetokoiki, イイェトコイキ, 準備スㇽ.
v.t. To prepare.

Iyetoko-ush, イイェトコウシ, 待伏セ
テスㇾ. *v.t.* To ambush. To lie
in wait for.

Iyetokta, イイェトクタ, 前ニ. *adv.* In
front of.

Iyetuima-samun-samun, イイェツ
イマサムンサムン, 共ニ歩ク. *v.i.* To
walk together. To walk side by
side.

Iyetunangara, イイェツナンガラ, 逢
フ. *v.t.* To meet.

Iyetushmak, イイェツシマク, 豫期ス
ㇽ. *v.t.* To anticipate. To forestall.

Iyeutanne, イイェウタン子, 偕ニアㇽ.
v.i. To be in company with. To
be together with. **Syn : Tura
no.**

Iyo, イヨ, 入ㇾㇽ. *v.i.* To put into.

Iyo, イヨ, 充ツㇽ. *adj.* Full. Filled.

Iyo-ai, イヨアイ, 毒矢. *n.* A poisoned arrow. **Syn : Iyo-rum.**

Iyo-aship, イヨアシブ, 疥癬. *n.* The
dry eczema. The itch. **Syn :
Maiyaige tashum.**

Iyo-attush, イヨアッツシ, 日本ノ布ニ
テ飾リシ衣服. *n.* A cloth garment
trimmed with Japanese stuff.

Iyochi, イヨチ, 眩暈スル. *adj.* Perplexed. Dizzy.

Iyochishbare, イヨチシバレ, 損ジル. *v.t.* To spoil.

Iyohai, イヨハイ, 驚愕ノ言葉. *excl.* An exclamation of surprise. Dear me! Dear, dear! Oh dear.

Iyohaichish, イヨハイチシ, or **Iyohaiochish, イヨハイオチシ,** 歌. *n.* A psalm. A song.

Iyohaikara, イヨハイカラ, 謗ル. *v.t.* To backbite. To slander. **Syn: Isempiroitak.**

Iyohaiochish, イヨハイオチシ, 歌. *n.* A psalm or song.

Iyoira, イヨイラ, 忘レル. *v.t.* To forget.

Iyok, イヨク, 鈎ニ引キ掛ケラル. *v.i.* To be caught in a hook. To be hooked.

Iyokake-un, イヨカケウン, 直キ後、引續イテ. *adv.* Immediately after. Afterwards.

Iyokane, イヨカ子, 後ロ. *adv.* Behind.

Iyokane-emushpo, イヨカ子エムシポ, 小刀. *n.* A small sword very much valued by the Ainu as a treasure.

Iyokatushmak, イヨカツシマク, 敵チ追フ. *v.t.* To follow an enemy up. To attack an enemy in the rear.

Iyokeshupkachiure, イヨケシュブカチウレ, 足迄ノ着物チ着ル. *v.i.* To be clothed down to the foot.

Iyokbe, イヨクベ, 鎌. *n.* A sickle. This word is sometimes corrupted into *iyopbe.*

Iyokot, イヨコツ, 從フ. *v.t.* To follow. **Syn: Ikesamba. Itomkot.**

Iyokoto, イヨコト, 痘痕. *n.* Pock marks.

Iyokte, イヨクテ, 引掛ケル、刈入レル. *v.t.* To hook in. To get with a hook. To reap.

Iyokunnure, イヨクンヌレ, 驚カス. *v.i.* To be surprised. **Syn: Ishiorore.**

Iyokunure, イヨクヌレ, 同上. *v.i.* Same as above.

Iyokush, イヨクシ, 裏返ヘス. *v.t.* To turn inside out. **Syn: Okush.**

Iyomai, イヨマイ, 陰門、陰茎. *n.* The privates. The penis.

Iyomande, イヨマンデ, 熊祭リ. *n.* A bear feast. A feast in which any animal is killed.

Iyomande, イヨマンデ, 屠殺シテ人ニ贈ル、犠牲ニスル. *v.t.* To kill and send as a present to another person. To kill as a bear for a feast. To sacrifice (as an animal).

Iyomap, イヨマブ, 物ノ入リシ器具. *n.* A vessel or instrument in which anything is placed. As :—*Aiaiiyomap,* "a cradle" (lit: "the instrument in which the baby is placed.")

Iyomap, イヨマブ, 愛スル、可愛ガル. *v.t.* To fondle. To love.

Iyomap-guru, イヨマブグル, 可愛ガル人. *n.* One who fondles another.

Iyomare, イヨマレ, 注グ (酒ナドチ). *v.t.* To pour out as wine into a cup.

Iyomare-guru, イヨマレグル, 給仕. *n.* A waiter at a drinking feast.

One who distributes wine at a feast.

Iyomomo, イヨモモ, 光ニ眩スル. *v.i.* To be dazzled with the sun or any bright object.

Iyonitasare, イヨニタサレ, 變ヘル、例セバ、レイヘイイヨニタサレ、改名スル. *v.t.* To change. As:—*Reihei iyonitasare*, "to change one's name."

Iyonnupba, イヨンヌブバ, 僞證スル、誹ル. *v.t.* To bear false witness. To speak evil of another.

Iyonnupba-guru, イヨンヌブバグル, 僞證. *n.* A false witness. An accuser.

Iyonnupba-itak, イヨンヌブバイタク, 寃罪. *n.* A false accusation.

Iyonuitasa, イヨヌイタサ, 返報スル. *v.t.* To do in return. To return as good for evil or evil for good.

Iyookunnure, イヨオクンヌレ, 甚シク驚ク. *v.i.* To be very much surprised.

Iyokunnure, イヨクンヌレ, 同上. *v.i.* Same as above.

Iyoomaoma, イヨオマオマ, 慰メラレル. *v.i.* To be comforted.

Iyoomaoma-an-i, イヨオマオマアンイ, 樂境. *n.* A place of comfort. A comfortable place.

Iyo-omare, イヨオマレ, 二個ノ荷物ヲ重子テ負フ. *v.t.* To carry two bundles upon the back, one upon the shoulders and the other lower down the back.

Iyop, イヨブ, 器、袋、箱. *n.* A vessel. A bag. A box.

Iyopakkai-ushi-guru, イヨパッカイウシグル, 子守. *n.* A nurse.

Iyopanere, イヨパチレ, 帶ナシニ衣物ヲ着ル. *v.i.* To wear the clothes loose without the girdle.

Iyopannatte, イヨパンナッテ, 同上. *v.i.* Same as above.

Iyopbe, イヨブベ, 鎌. *n.* A sickle. **Syn: Iyokbe.**

Iyopok-omare, イヨポクオマレ, 二個ノ荷物ヲ重子テ負フ. *v.t.* To carry two bundles upon the back, one upon the other.

Iyopsura, イヨブスラ, 鉾ヲ投ゲレ. *v.t.* To cast a spear.

Iyorakse, イヨラクセ, 不足ナレ. *adj.* Insufficient. **Syn: Eikohaye.**

Iyorapte, イヨラブテ, 上ニ降ル、圖ラズ出合フ. *v.i.* To descend upon. To chance upon.

Iyorande, イヨランデ, ニ降ル、例セバ、ペツラントムイヨランデ、河邊ニ下ダル. *v.t.* To chance upon. To come down to. As:—*Pet rantom iyorande*, "to come down to a river."

Iyoriki-puni, イヨリキブニ, 舉ゲラレル、攪拌スレ. *v.i.* To be raised up. To be pleased. To be stirred up as in anger. To be lifted up. To be stirred up. As:—*Rera iyoriki puni*, "he was lifted up by the wind."

Iyoro-itak, イヨロイタク, 談ノ仲間入リチスル、話ノ邪覽ナスレ. *v.i.* To join in conversation. To interfere when others are talking. **Syn: Tomo-un itak.**

Iyororope, イヨロロベ, 歐ニ用ユル言葉(喵トシタル意義アルニ非ズ). *interj.* An excl: of pleasure. A word sometimes heard in songs, but which does not appear to have any special meaning.

Iyo-rum, イ ヨ ル ム, 毒矢. *n.* A poisoned arrow. **Syn: Iyo-ai.**

Iyorun, イヨルン, 乞フ、願フ. *v.t.* To beg. **Syn: Ikoramkoro.**

Iyorun-ki, イ ヨ ル ン ギ, 同上. *v.t.* Same as above.

Iyorun-guru, イヨルングル, 乞食. *n.* A beggar.

Iyorushpe-nu, イヨルシペヌ, 話ヲ聞ク. *v.t.* To hear the news.

Iyoshi, イ ヨ シ, 後 =. *adv.* After. Afterwards.

Iyoshi-no, イ ヨ シ ノ, 後 =. *adv.* Afterwards. By and by.

Iyoshi-un, イ ヨ シ ウ ン, 後 =. *adv.* By and by.

Iyoshikpekare, イヨシクペカレ, 狙フ、覘フ. *v.t.* To aim at.

Iyoshserekere, イヨシセレケレ, 恐ル ル、例セバ、イヤイヌマレイヨシセレ ケレハウアシア、驚クベキカナ、ナン ト恐シキ話ナラズヤ. *v.i.* and *adj.* To be afraid. To be in fear. Fearful. Dreadful. As :—*Iyai-numare, iyoshserekere hau ash a!* " how shocking, what dreadful talk " !

Iyotaipeshte, イヨタイペシテ, 仔細ニ 問フ. *v.t.* To make very close inquiries. To thoroughly search by making inquiries. **Syn: Tomte no uwepekenu.**

Iyotta, イヨッタ, 最多ナル、例セバ、イ ヨッタピリカ、最モ善キ. *adj.* Most. Superlatively. This word is used before adjectives to give the superlative degree. Thus :—*Iyotta piriku,* " most good." *Iyotta wen,* " most bad."

Iyotupekare, イヨツペカレ, 吝キ. *adj.* Stingy. Miserly. **Syn: Yaiotupekare.**

Iyounumpekare, イヨウヌムペカレ, 助ケル. *v.t.* To assist one in trouble. To advise.

Iyoyamokte, イヨヤモクテ, 愕ク. *v.i.* To be astonished. To marvel. To wonder.

Iyoyange, イ ヨ ヤ ンゲ, 上ゲル. *v.t.* To lift up. To offer to a superior.

Iyukoikire, イユコイキレ, 爭ヲ起ス、 害ヲ爲ス. *v.t.* To make mischief. To stir up strife. **Syn: Iyuturu-pao. Iyukowende.**

Iyukoikire-guru, イユコイキレグル, 惡戯者、不和ヲ起サスル人. *n.* A mischief maker. A person who sets others at variance with one another.

Iyukomi, イユコミ, 重子著スル. *v.i.* To wear much clothes.

Iyukowende, イユコウェンデ, 爭ヒヲ 起ス. *v.t.* To make mischief. To stir up strife. **Syn: Iyukoikire.**

Iyukowende-guru, イユコウェンデグ ル, 不和ヲ起サスル人. *n.* A person who sets others at variance with one another.

Iyun, イ ユン, 內ニ. *post.* In.

Iyuninka, イユニンカ, 損害スル、痛ミ ヲ與ヘル. *v.t.* To damage. To hurt. To give pain to.

Iyun-wa-rai, イユンワライ, 塞グ、呼 吸ヲ止メル、例セバ、レクチポチイユン ワライ、彼ハ喉ニ骨ヲ立テテ塞死シタ. *v.i.* To choke. As :—*Rekuchi pone iyun wa rai,* " he died through having a bone in his throat."

Iyupokba, イユポクバ, 惡ム、迫害ス ル. *v.t.* To hate. To persecute.

Iyurui, イユルイ, 墓、埋メレ所. *n.*
A grave. **Syn: Tushiri. Tu-
rushiru. Hayashitai.**

Iyuta, イユタ, 臼ク. *v.t.* To pound
millet or rice.

Iyuta-ni, イユタニ, 杵. *n.* A pestle.

Iyutaratuye, イユタラツイェ, 親類ヲ
殺ロス. *v.t.* To kill one's relations. *v.i.* To run amuck. **Syn:
Yaiutaratuye.**

Iyutari, イユタリ, 親類、仲間. *n.*
Relations. Friends. Comrades.

Iyutasa-ashte-guru, イユタサアシ
テグル, 不和ヲ起サスル人. *n.* A
person who sets others at variance with one another.

Iyuturu, イユツル, 間. *adv.* Among.
Between.

Iyuturu-eapkash-guru, イユツルエ
アブカシグル, 使者. *n.* An am-
bassador. **Syn: Hauturunguru.**

Iyuturu-oingara-guru, イユツルオ
インガラグル, 看守スル人. *n.* One
who watches between others.

Iyuturu-oma-guru, イユツルオマグ
ル, 仲立人. *n.* A go-between.
**Syn: Irenga uturu eapkash
guru.**

Iyuturupao, イユツルパオ, 害ヲ起ス.
v.t. To make mischief. **Syn:
Iyukoikire.**

Iyuturupao-guru, イユツルパオグル,
害ヲ起ス人. *n.* A mischief maker.

K (ケ).

K, ク, 我、ワレ、(此ノ字ヲ動詞ノ前ニ付
ケ加フレトキハ第一人稱代名詞トナル
ナリ、例セバ、ケアシカイ、私ニ出來マ
ス、語ノ本體ハクアニ、ナレドモカニ、
ク、ト訛リテ終ニ此處ニ示セルモノ
トナレリ. *pro.* This letter is often
prefixed to verbs as the first person singular personal pronoun
"I," particularly in the Saru
district and when the verbs begin
with a vowel. As:—*Keashkai* for
Ku eashkai, "I am able." *Koira*
for *ku oira,* "I forget." The full
form of this word is *Kuani,* then
kani, then *ku,* and lastly *k* as
here.

Ka, カ, (i). 此ノ語ハ自動詞ニ附加シテ他
動詞ト成スカアリ、例セバ、イサム、無
イ、イサムカ、無クスル. *part.* *Ka* is
suffixed to some intransitive verbs

to make them transitive. Thus:
—*Isam,* "there is none," *isamka,*
"to bring to nothing." *Kotuk,*
"to adhere," *kotukka,* "to stick
on." *Nin,* "to decrease," *ninka,*
"to make decrease."

Ka, カ, (ii). 此語ハ時ニヨリ名詞ニ附加
ヘテ他動詞ヲ作ルコトアリ、例セバ、ペ
ケレ、光リ、ペヅレカ、輝カス. *part.*
Ka is also sometimes heard suffixed to nouns to give them a
transitive verbal force. Thus:—
Pekere, "light," *pekereka,* "to
lighten."

Ka, カ, (iii). 時トシテ此ノ字ハ語意ヲ
輕クスル爲メニ用井ラル、此場合ニハ
動詞必ズ之ニ從フ、例セバ、セエンチカ
キ、我ハ爲シマセン. *part.* Some-
times the particle *Ka* is used as
a kind of softening factor, and

as such, cannot always be translated into English; when so used, however, it is always followed by the verb. Thus :—*Seenne ka ki*, " I have not done it." *Ku meraige ka ki*, "I am cold." *Seenne ku oman ka ki*, "I have not been." *Kimta oman aige naa shomo hoshipi ka ki*, " he went to the mountains and has not yet returned."

Ka, カ, (iv). 又、然レドモ. *post*. Also. Although. And. As :— *Kuani ka ku oman kusu ne*, "I also shall go." In some places this word is pronounced *kai*, but when *i* is added the meaning is slightly different inasmuch as it gives to *ka* a kind of substantive meaning. **Syn: Ne yakka.**

Ka, カ, 上、ウヘ. *n*. The top of anything. As :—*Pira ka*, "the top of a cliff." *Ka ta*, "on the top." *Ka un*, " on the top," " towards the top."

Ka, カ, 然レドモ、デモ. *post*. Although. Even. So.

Ka, カ, 絲、例セバ、カタク、絲丸. *n*. Thread. Cotton. String. As :— *Ka-tak*, "a ball of thread or string."

Ka, カ, 虱ノ卵. *n*. Nits. Louse eggs.

Ka......ka, カ......カ, 夫レモ此レモ、夫レデモナイ此デモナイ、例セバ、クアニ カシヌマカウツラオマンルウェ子、彼モ 我モ共ニ行ク、クアニカショモ子エア ニカショモ子汝デモナイ我デモナイ、 *post*. Both......and. Neither...... nor. When used with a negative

ka.........ka is also negative, but when used with an affirmative it is affirmative also. As:— *Kuani ka shinuma ka utura oman ruwe ne*, "both he and I are going." *Kuani ka shomo ne, eani ka shomo ne*, "neither you nor I." **Syn: Ne yakka.........ne yakka.**

Kaanu, カアヌ, 鳥チ捕ル羂. *n*. A kind of bird-trap consisting of a bent piece of wood and string.

Kabiuki, カビウキ, 助ケル、救フ. *v.t.* To help. To save. To assist. **Syn: Kaobiuki.**

Kabiuki-wa-kore, カビウキワコレ, 助ケル、救フ. *v.t.* To help.

Kacharashnu, カチャラシヌ, 健康ナ ル. *adj*. Healthy.

Kachimbe, カチムベ, 草ノ名. *n*. A kind of grass.

Kaeobiuki, カエオビウキ, 助ケル、救 フ. *v.t.* To help. To save.

Ka-etuki, カエツキ, 織出シ. *n*. The surplus end of the threads used in weaving cloth.

Kagara, カガラ, 海鳥ノ類. *n*. A kind of large sea duck. **Syn: Menan. Shuke.**

Kai, カイ, 又、而シテ. *post*. Also. See *Ka* (iv).

Kai, カイ, 背ニデ運ブ. *v.t.* To carry on the back. **Syn: Pakkai.**

Kaibe, カイベ, Kaipe, カイベ, 磯ノ白 涎. *n*. The surf of the seas. Breakers.

Kaika, カイカ, 絲チ造ル. *v.i.* To make string.

Kaikai, カイカイ, 呼ブ、(犬ナド). *v.t.*

To call as a dog. As:—**Seta kaikai.**

Kaikai, カイカイ, 涯荒キ海、例セバ、アツイカタカイカイ、海上ノ涯荒レル. *n.* A short choppy sea. As:—*Atui kata kaikai,* "the choppy surface of the sea." **Syn: Rera kaikai.**

Kaikiri, カイキリ, 交尾スル、(馬ヤ鹿ナドノ). *v.i.* To rut (as deer). **Syn: Ukokaikiri.**

Kaikuma, カイクマ, 柴. *n.* Spray wood. A hare.

Kainon, カイノン 呑ム. *v.t.* To swallow.

Kaipe, カイペ, 白涯、(暗邊＝折レル). *n.* Same as *kaibe,* "breakers."

Kaisash, カイサシ, 咳キ. *n.* A low murmur. A rumbling sound. As:—*Itak kaisash,* "the murmuring sound of talking."

Kaisei, カイセイ, 死骨、尻. *n.* A corpse.

Kaishikut-kesh, カイシクツケシ, 喉頭. *n.* The top of the throat.

Kaishikut-kesh-makaraye, カイシクツケシマカライエ, 咳バライ、(訪問ノ時家ニ入ラヌ先ニ咳バライシテ禮トナス). *v.i.* To clear one's throat as when about to enter a house.

Kaita, カイタ, 錨. *n.* An anchor. A variation of *Kaite.*

Kaite, カイテ, 錨、例セバ、カイテアマ、錨ヲ下ロス. *n.* An anchor, *Kaite ama,* "to cast anchor." *Kaite ande,* "to cast anchor." *Kaite pusu,* "to weigh anchor." *Kaite yange,* "weigh anchor." *Kaite range,* "to cast anchor." *Kaite*

rende, "to cast anchor." *Kaite tush,* "an anchor rope."

Kaka, カカ, 子ヲ負フ. *v.t.* Same as *Kakka.* To carry an infant on the back. Used chiefly by children. **Syn: Pakkai.**

Kakapo, カカポ, 姉. *n.* An elder sister. **Syn: Saha. Sápo.**

Kakewe, カケウェ, 魚ノ頭上ニアル肉. *n.* The meat on the top of a fish's head. **Syn: Repe.**

Kakewe, カケウェ, 守ル、防ク、例セバ、トイカケウェ、畑ヲ守ル. *v.t.* To defend. To keep guard over. As:—*Toi-kakewe,* "to guard one's garden." **Syn: Kikikara.**

Kake, カケ, 槌. *n.* A hammer.

Kaki, カキ, 翳ス、例セバ、テクカキワインガラ、手ヲ翳シテ見ル. *v.t.* To hold the hands up to the forehead. Thus:—*Tek kaki wa ingara,* "to look at by shading the eyes with the hands."

Kakka, カッカ, 子ヲ負フ. *v.t.* To carry a child on the back. **Syn: Pakkai.** Used chiefly by children.

Kakkankawak, カッカンカワク, 歌ノ名. *n.* The name or refrain of a song.

Kakko, カッコ, or **Gakko, カッコ,** 學校. *n.* A school. *(Jap.)*

Kakkok, カッコク, 子規、杜鵑. *n.* The common cuckoo. *Kakkok hau,* "the cuckoo's note."

Kakkok-amam, カッコクアマム, オホバタチシマラン. *n. Streptopus amplexifolius, DC.*

Kakkok-kina, カッコクキナ, アヤメ. The iris. **Syn: Chepeukute-kina.**

Kakkok-nonno, カッコクノンノ, ヒメ クワンザウ. *n.* *Hemerocallis Dumortieri, Morr.*

Kakkum, カックム, 水桶. *n.* A bucket for drawing water.

Kakse, カクセ, 咳バライ. *v.i.* To clear the throat.

Kakse-kakse, カクセカクセ, 咳バライ. To make a noise with the throat as in spitting up phlegm. To clear the throat.

Kam, カム, 肉. *n.* Flesh. Meat.

Kam, *adv.* Over. Above. Upper. **Syn: Kan.**

Kama, カマ, 鐵瓶. *n.* A kettle. (*Jap*).

Kama, カマ, 飛越ヘル、上チ越ス、例セ バ、カマテレケ、飛ビ越ヘル、カマイン ガラ、越シテ見ル. *v.t.* To step across. To go over. As:—*Kama tereke*, "to jump across." *Kama etaye*, "to draw over or across." *Kama eyapkiri*, "to throw over or across." *Kama ingara*, "to look across." *Kama kush*, "to pass over." *Kama turi*, "to stretch across." *Kama wa oman*, "to go across or over."

Kama-hairuru, カマハイルル,
Kama-haururu, カマハウルル,} 肉ノ羹. *n.* A stew. Soup made from meat.

Kama-hau, カマハウ, 肉ノ羹. *n.* A stew made of meat cut into slices.

Kama-hau-kara, カマハウカラ, 肉 羹チ造ル. *v.t.* To make a meat stew.

Kama-haururu, カマハウルル,
Kama-hairuru, カマハイルル,} 肉ノ羹物. *n.* A meat stew. Soup made from meat.

Kamakap, カマカブ, 織機. *n.* A weaving loom.

Kamakara, カマカラ, 織機. *n.* A weaving loom.

Kamakata, カマカタ, 蝶. *n.* A butterfly. **Syn: Erapurapu. Haporap.**

Kamakush-marapto, カマクシマラ ブト, 過越ノ祝、(キリスト教ノ). *n.* The Passover feast. (Introduced by the compiler).

Kamanata, カマナタ, 大庖丁. *n.* A large knife. **Syn: Nata.**

Kamaso, カマソ, 扁平ナル岩. *n.* A flat rock. A broad flat rock.

Kamasu, カマス, 包ミ、叺、カマス. *n.* A wrapper. A parcel. (*Jap.*)

Kamasu, カマス, 叺ニ包ム. *v.t.* To make into a parcel.

Kamasu-kara, カマスカラ, 叺チ造ル. *v.t.* To make a parcel.

Kamasu-oroomare, カマスオロオマ レ, 叺ニ入レル、畳ム. *v.t.* To put into a wrapper. To fold up. Also, *kamasu oro iyo*, "to put into a wrapper." "To wrap up."

Kamba-ush-bashui, カムバウシバシ ユイ, 鬚髯チ上ゲル棒、(祭リノトキニ用 ユ). *n.* The festive ceremonial moustache-lifter. **Syn: Iku-pa- shui.**

Kamba-ush-reki, カムバウシレキ, 口 髯. *n.* The moustache.

Kambi, カムビ, 紙、手紙. *n.* Paper. A letter.

Kambi-chikap, カムビチカブ, 凧、 (鳥ノ形ニ造ランシ). *n.* A kite.

Kambi-nuye, カムビヌイ, 書ク. *v.t.* To write. To write a letter.

Kambi-nuye-guru, カムビヌイェグ ル, 記者. *n.* A scribe.

Kambi-nuyep, カムビヌイェブ, 筆. *n.* A pen. A pencil.

Kambi-nuyep, カムビヌイェブ, アヤメ. n. *Iris sibirica, L.*

Kambi-sosh, カムビソシ, 書籍. n. A book. As:—*Kambi-sosh oro-oitak,* "to read a book."

Kamdachi, カムダチ, 麹. n. Rice steamed and otherwise prepared for brewing purposes. Malt.

Kamdachi-sak-guru, カムダチサクグル, 愚人. n. A fool.

Kam-e-ewen, カムエエウェン, 食傷 (肉食シテ). v.i. To be hurt by eating meat.

Kameyarape, カメヤラペ,
Kameyarope, カメヤロペ, 遺恨ノ為メニ不潔ナルモノヲ食ハセル人. n. One who makes another eat filth or the bad parts of an animal out of spite. **Syn: Pauchikoro-guru.**

Kamiash, カミアシ, or Kamiyashi, カミヤェシ, 毒蛇、(時トシテ人ヲ罵冒スレニ用ユル). n. A poisonous snake. A dead body. A demon.

Kamiyashi-tashum, カミヤシタシュム, 惡氣ニ取付カレタ病. n. Demonaical possession.

Kamkashke, カムカシケ, 皮膚、身體ノ外部. n. The skin. The surface of the body.

Kambe, カムベ, 水面、例セバ、カンペ グルカ、水上ニ. n. The surface of water. As:—*Kambe-kuruka,* "on the water."

Kamoi, カモイ, 化膿セル腫物、梅毒. n. A running sore. Syphilis.

Kampara, カムパラ, 外方. adv. Without. Outside of.

Kamporo, カムポロ, 緣. n. The rim of anything.

Kamu, カム, 上ニ置カレい、蔽フ. v.i. and adj. To be placed upon, as a lid upon a pot. To cover. To overshadow.

Kamui, カムイ, 神. n. A god. A bear. A title applied to anything great, good, important, honourable, bad, fierce or awful; hence used of animals and men, gods and devils. (I). Used as a prefix *Kamui* my be regarded as an adjective. Thus:—*Kamui rera,* "a great or good wind." *Kamui nonno,* "a beautiful flower." *Kamui nishpa,* "a great or dread master." (II). Used as a suffix *Kamui* may be regarded as a noun. Thus:—*Abe kamui,* "fire god." *Rera kamui,* "wind god." *Rep un kamui,* "sea gods." *Nitne kamui,* "devils."

Kamui-aikarip, カムイアイカリブ, ウコンウツキ. n. *Diervilla Middendorffiana, Carr.*

Kamui-amam, カムイアマム, ミノゴメ、サ、ノミ. n. *Beckmannia erucaeformis, Host.* Also used for the grain of bamboo.

Kamui-chep, カムイチェブ, 鮭. n. Common salmon of Japan. **Syn: Shibe.**

Kamui-chikappo, カムイチカッポ, シマフクロウ. n. Blakiston's eagle owl. **Syn: Kamuiekashi.**

Kamui-chip, カムイチブ, 厄病ヲ追ヒ攘フ為メニイナオヲ積ミテ流ス船、(アイヌノ迷信ニ用ユ). n. A boat with *inao* and straw images placed in it and sent floating down a river or out to sea for the purpose of carrying away disease.

Kamui-chiitakte, カムイチイタクテ, 神托ヲ受ク. v.i. To be inspired.

Kamui-chisei, カムイチセイ, 熊ノ穴巣. *n.* A bear's den. **Syn : Kamuiset.**

Kamui-ekashi, カムイエカシ, シマフクロウ. *n.* Blakiston's eagle owl.

Kamui-emauri, カムイエマウリ, ヲラジロイチゴ. *n.* *Rubus phoenicolasius, Max.* Sometimes called *yuk-emauri.* Also *Rubus occidentalis, L. var. japonicus, Miyabe.*

Kamui-enenge-ni, カムイエチンゲニ, Kamui-eninge-ni, カムイエニンゲニ, タラノキ、クロイチゴ. *n.* The angelica tree, *Aralia sinensis, L.*

Kamui-hurep, カムイフレブ, タチイチゴ. *n.* *Rubus crataegifolius. Bunge.* Also called *yuk-emauri.*

Kamui-hauturun-guru, カムイハウツルングル, 天使. *n.* An angel. **Syn : Kamui hauturunbe. Kamui uitekbe. Kamui shongo guru.**

Kamui-kosari, カムイコサリ, 神ノ攝理. *n.* The providence of God.

Kamui-huchi, カムイフチ, 火ノ女神. The goddess of fire. **Syn : Onne huchi. Iresu huchi. Abe kamui.**

Kamui-hum, カムイフム, 雷. *n.* Thunder. **Syn : Kamui turu humse hum.**

Kamui-humbe, カムイフムベ, シヤチ鯱. *n.* The killer whale. *Orca gladiator, Lacep.*

Kamui-irushkatashum, カムイイルシカタシュム, 中風. *n.* Paralysis.

Kamui-kambi-sosh, カムイカムビソシ, 聖書. *n.* The bible.

Kamui-kene-ni, カムイケチニ, ミヤマハンノキ. *n.* A kind of alder.

Alnus viridis, DC. var. sibirica, Rgl. **Syn : Horokeukene.**

Kamui-keu-kina, カムイケウキナ, ハクカ. *n.* The peppermint. *Mentha arvensis, L. var. piperascens,* Also called *Toi-orush-mun.*

Kamui-kiri-samata, カムイキリサマタ, 神ノ前、神ノ知ル所. *ph.* Before God. In the knowledge of God.

Kamui-koitukka-chep, カムイコイツッカチュブ, 魚ノ名. *n.* Some kind of fabulous fish.

Kamui-koingara, カムイコインガラ, 惠マレタル. *adj.* Blessed. Lucky.

Kamui-korametok, カムイコラメトク, Kamui-ramotok, カムイラモトク, 大瞻ナル. *ph.* and *adj.* Very brave.

Kamui-kotan, カムイコタン, 天. *n.* Heaven.

Kamui-kuroro, カムイクロロ, 神ニ困ラセラル. *ph.* and *v.i.* To be troubled by the gods.

Kamui-kuru, カムイクル, 密雲(白又ハ黒). *n.* Thick black or white clouds.

Kamui-moshiri, カムイモシリ, 天. *n.* Heaven.

Kamui-nomi, カムイノミ, 神酒ヲ獻ズルコト. *n.* The ceremonies of drinking to and worshipping the gods.

Kamui-noya, カムイノヤ, イハヨモギ. *n.* A kind of mugwort. *Artemisia sacrorum, var. latiloba, Ledeb.* Also used for *Artemisia japonica, th,* チトコヨモギ and *A. Stelleriana, Bess.* シロヽモキ.

Kamui-nupek カムイヌペク, or ni-pek, ニペク, 神ノ恩寵. *n.* The

favour of the gods. The glory of the gods.

Kamui-oposam, カムイオポサム, 熊チ愛撫スル辭、(熊祭ノ時用ニ). *ph.* A term of affection applied to bear cubs just before killing them in sacrifice. Dear little divinity.

Kamui-otopush, カムイオトプシ, 縮毛. *adj.* Curly-headed.

Kamui-otta-oman, カムイオッタオマン, 死ス. *v.i.* To die. **Syn : Rai. Isam. Ekot. Moshiri hoppa.**

Kamui-oroitak, カムイオロイタク, 祈ル. *v.i.* To pray. **Syn : Inonno-itak.**

Kamui-pa, カムイパ, 神罰. *n.* Punishment of the gods. Also, a year of calamity.

Kamui-pak-buri, カムイパクブリ, 神ノ病チ以テ罰スル、惡行. *n.* Evil deeds which the gods punish with sickness. Henious crimes.

Kamui-pungara, カムイプンガラ, ノブダウ. *n. Vitis heterophylla, Th.*

Kamui-rametok, カムイラメトク,
Kamui-korametok, カムイコラメトク, 大膽. *n. ph.* and *adj.* Very brave.

Kamui-rangetam, カムイランゲタム, 立派ナル刀. *n.* The sword of the gods. A beautiful sword.

Kamui-ratashkep, カムイラタシケプ,
Kamui-rataskep, カムイラタスケプ, 果實. *n.* All kinds of fruits which grow on trees.

Kamui-san-nan, カムイサンナン, 美シキ顔. *n.* A beautiful face. **Syn : Shiretokkoro.**

Kamui-set, カムイセツ, 熊ノ穴. *n.* A bear's den. **Syn : Kamui-chisei.**

Kamui-shongo-akore-guru, カムイションゴアコレグル, 天使. *n.* An angel.

Kamui-shongo-guru, カムイションゴグル, 天使. *n.* An angel.

Kamui-shongo-koro-guru, カムイショゴコログル, 天使. *n.* A angel.

Kamui-shotki, カムイショツキ, 爐ノ中央ニアル灰 (火ノ女神ノ處ナリト云フ). *n.* The ashes in the very centre of a fireplace, supposed to be the birth place of the goddess of fire.

Kamui-shu, カムイシュ, 陶器. *n.* An earthen pot. **Syn : Toi-shu.**

Kamui-shupki, カムイシュプキ, ヨシ. *n.* A kind of large reed.

Kamui-soroma, カムイソロマ, センマイ. *n.* The flowering fern. *Osmunda regalis, L.*

Kamui-tashum, カムイタシュム, 皰瘡. *n.* The small-pox. **Syn : Oripak tashum.**

Kamui-tat-ni, カムイタツニ, タケカンバ. *n.* A kind of birch. *Betula Ermani, Cham.*

Kamui-turu-humse-hum, カムイツルフムセフム, 雷. *n.* Thunder. **Syn : Kamui hum.**

Kamui-tusare, カムイツサレ, 神恩. *n.* God's help or favour. **Syn : Kamui irenga.**

Kamui-uitekbe, カムイウイテクベ, 天使. *n.* An angel. **Syn : Kamui hauturunbe.**

Kamui-yukara, カムイユカラ, 傳說. *n.* Traditions.

Kamuktek, カムクテク, 閉ヅル、(眼チ). *v.t.* To shut as the eyes. As :— *Shik kamuktek,* "to shut the eyes."

Kamukamup, カムカムプ, 提緒ヲ附
ケタル箱、又ハ、籠. *n.* A small
box with strings attached to it
as a handle to carry it by. Also
a basket with a lid made of
grass.

Kamure, カムレ, 蔽 フ、蓋 フ. *v.t.*
To cover over.

Kan, カン, 爲ス. *v.t.* To do. To
make. Short for *kara.*

Kan, カン, 上. *adv.* Up. Top. Over.
Syn : Ka. Kam.

Kana, カナ, 鉋. *n.* A plane.

Kana, カナ, 絲卷. *n.* A reel of
cotton.

Kana, カナ, 願フ. *v.t.* To ask for.
Thus :—*Shinuma shine ichi en
kore kuni nishpa orowa no kana
ruwe ne,* "he asked his master
for a yen."

Kana-iki, カナイキ, 鉋カケル. *v.t.*
To plane.

Kanasayep, カナサイエプ, 絲卷. *n.*
An instrument for winding thread
upon. A reel.

Kana-op, カナオプ, 絲卷. *n.* A reel.
Syn : Kanasayep.

Kanat-ni, カナツニ, イタガヤ. *n.*
Cephalotaxus drupacea, S. et Z.

Kanbashui,
**　　　カンバシュイ,**
Kamba-ush-bashui,
**　　カンバウシバシュイ,**
鬚ヲ擧ゲル箸,
（酒ヲ飲ムトキ）. *n.* A
festive ceremonial moustache
lifter also called *Kike ush bashui.*

Kanchi, カンチ 櫂. Oars. Sculls.

Kanchikama-ni, カンチカマニ, サン
セゥ. *n.* *Zanthoxylum piperitum,*
DC. The leaves and fruit of this
shrub are used as a condiment to
food.

Kando, カンド, 天. *n.* Heaven.
The sky. As :—*Kando koro
Kamui,* "God the possessor of
Heaven."

Kando-kotoro, カンドコトロ, 天、蒼
穹. *n.* The skies. The vault of
heaven.

Kando-moshiri, カンドモシリ, 天國.
n. Heaven.

Kane, カネ, 鐵. *n.* Metal. Iron.
Kani, カニ, Money.

Kane, カネ, 此ノ字ヲ動詞ノ後ニ加フレ
トキハ副詞トナス.ヲ得、例セバ、アプ
カシカネ、步キナガラ. *part.* This
word is sometimes suffixed to
verbs to change them into
adverbs or adverbial phrases.
As :—*Apkash kane.* "whilst walking." *Ki kane,* "whilst doing."
Ramma kane, "always."

Kane, カネ, ド、而シテ、又、モ、例セバ、カ
ニネヲエアニカネ、私ト汝ト. *part.*
Sometimes *kane* is used as the
conjunction "and" or "even"
"both" or "also." As :—*Kani
newa eani kane,* "you and I."

Kanetuhu, カネツフ, 尖端. *n.*
Edges. The point of a knife,
needle or sword. **Syn : Paruruge.**
Eipake.

Kango-ani-utara, カンゴアニウタラ,
柩ヲ昇ク人. *n.* The bearers of a
corpse at a funeral. *Kango* in the
Japanese *kago.*

Kani, カニ, 我. *pro.* I. **Syn :**
Kuani. Ku. K.

Kani, カニ, 金屬、錢. *n.* Metal.
Kane, カネ, Money.

Kani-kik-guru, カニキクグル, 鍛冶師.
n. A black-smith.

Kani-penere, カニペネレ, 金ヲ鍛ユレ、

v.t. To melt metal. To heat iron to a red or white heat.

Kani-pon-kasa, カニポンカサ, 甲. *n.* A helmet. A crown or hat of metal.

Kani-shikai, カニシカイ, 鐵釘. *n.* An iron nail. A nail made of metal.

Kani-toitap, カニトイタプ, 鋤. *n.* A spade.

Kani-tuchi, カニツチ, 金槌. *n.* An iron hammer. From Japanese *Kanazuchi.*

Kani-wakka-kep, カニワッカケプ, 金杓子. *n.* A metal water ladle.

Kanit, カニツ, 梭. *n.* A shuttle.

Kankan, カンカン, 大腸. *n.* The large intestines.

Kankan, カンカン, 腸詰(料理ノ説). *n.* Sausages.

Kankapkapeka, カンカプカペカ, 偽善. *n.* Hypocrisy.

Kankapkapeka-iki, カンカプカペカイキ, 偽善ヲ行フ. *v.i.* To act the hypocrite.

Kankapkapeka-iki-guru, *n.* **カンカプカペカイキグル**, 偽善者. *n.* A hypocrite.

Kankitai, カンキタイ, 冠毛(頭ノ). *n.* The hair upon the top of the head. The crown. Roof of a house. **Syn: Chisei sapa.**

Kanna, カンナ, 雷. *n.* Thunder. **Syn: Kamui hum.**

Kanna, カンナ, 再. *adv.* Again.

Kanna, カンナ, 上ノ、例セバ、カンナノツケ゚、上顎. *post.* Upper. Over As :—*Kanna notkeu*, " the upper jaw." *Kanna papush*, " the upper lip."

Kanna-kanna, カンナカンナ, 屢々. *adv.* Again and again. Often.

Kanna-kamui, カンナカムイ, 雷神. *n.* The thunder god.

Kanna-kamui-hum, カンナカムイフム, 雷. *n.* Thunder.

Kanna-kamui-humi-ash, カンナカムイフミアシ, 雷鳴スレ. *v.i.* To thunder. **Syn: Kamui turimimse hum.**

Kanna-kara, カンナカラ, 再ビヌル. *v.t.* To do over again.

Kanna-moshiri, カンナモシリ, 地上ノ世界、即チ生物界ニシテボクナモシリ即チ死物界ニ對シテ云フ. *n.* The upper world, *i.e.* the world of living beings. This word is used in contradistinction to *Pokna moshiri,* " Hades."

Kanna-shui, カンナシュイ, 又. *adv.* Again.

Kanni, カンニ, 杖. *n.* A stick. A walking-stick. A club. A staff.

Kannit, カンニツ, 矢ニ用井ル骨. *n.* The bone part of an arrow.

Kan-nitai, カンニタイ, 大樹. *n.* Large trees. Large timber.

Kan-niukesh, カンニウケシ, 拙手ナル. *adj.* Awkward. To be unable to do.

Kan-rok, カンロク, 爲ス. *v.t.* To do.

Kanshiri, カンシリ, 體ノ前部. *n.* The forepart of the body, i.e. the bosom and face. As :—*Kanshiri kata echopnure,* " to kiss the bosom and face of a child."

Kantori-kamui, カントリカムイ, 雨雪ノ神. *n.* The god who makes it snow and rain.

Kapa, カパ, 泥ダラケナル. *adj.* Muddy. Dirty. **Syn : Aechake.**

Kaobiuki, カオビウキ, 助ケル、救フ. *v.t.* To help. To save.

Kap, カブ, 皮一外部. *n.* The skin. The outer covering of anything. **Syn : Kapu.**

Kapachiri, カバチリ, 鷲. *n.* Eagle.

Kapacheppa, カバチェッパ, 魚ノ名. *n.* The land locked blue-back salmon.

Kapai, カバイ, ムカゴイラクサ. *n.* A kind of nettle. *Laportea bulbifera, Wedd.*

Kapakapa, カバカバ, 甚シク泥ダラケ ナル. *adj.* Very muddy. Very dirty.

Kapap, カバブ, 蝙蝠. *n.* A bat. A flitter-mouse.

Kapara, カバラ, 薄キ. *adj.* Thin.

Kapara-amip, カバラアミブ, 縫箔セ シ着物. *n.* An ornamented garment. **Syn : Kapari-mip.**

Kapara-kam, カバラカム, 肋ノ肉. *n.* The diaphragm. Midriff.

Kapara-kasa, カバラカサ, 兜、笠. *n.* A helmet. A hat.

Kaparape, カバラペ, 奇麗ナル. *adj.* Handsome. Pretty. As:—*Kaparape itangi kaparape otchiki,* " a pretty cup and tray."

Kapara-samambe, カバラサマムベ, ソウハチ. *n.* ·*Hippoglossoidis sp.*

Kaparui, カバルイ, カレイノ一種. *n.* A kind of flat fish.

Kapari-nup, カバリヌプ, 縫箔セシ着 物. *n.* An ornamented garment **Syn : Kapara-amip.**

Kaparush, カバルシ, 岩. *n.* Rock.

Kapato, カバト, カハホネ. *n.* A kind of yellow water-lily. The *Nuphar japonicum DC.* This plant is used as an article of food.

Kapat-tat-ni, カバノタッニ, シラカン バ. *n.* A kind of birch tree.

Betula alba, L. var. vulgaris, DC. **Syn : Petat-ni.**

Kapiu, カピウ, 鷗頬ノ總稱. *n.* Seagull.

Kapiu-sei, カピウセイ, ウチムラサキ. *n. Saxicava arctica, Linn.*

Kapke, カブケ, 扁キ、平ナル. *adj.* Flat. As:—A *Etu-kapke guru,* " a flat-nosed person."

Kappa, カッパ, 水神. *n.* A water nymph. **Syn : Shokai.**

Kappara, カッパラ, 茸. *n.* A toadstool.

Kapshi, カブシ, 倒ス. *v.t.* To overthrow.

Kaptek, カブテク, 平タキ、重キ. *adj.* Flat. Heavy, as dough. Level.

Kaptek-nere, カブテクチレ,
Kaptek-no-kara, カブテクノカラ,
}平タクスル. *v.t.* To flatten. To make level.

Kapu, カブ, 皮. *n.* Bark. Skin. **Syn : Kap.**

Kapuhu, カブフ, 産ノ苦ミ. *n.* The pangs of child-birth.

Kapu-kara, カブカラ, 皮ヲ剥ク. *v.t.* To bark a tree. To skin. To peel. To flay. **Syn : Kapu soso. Soshpa. Kapuri.**

Kapu-noye, カブノイェ, 捻(ツメ)ル. *v.i.* To pinch.

Kapu-pitak-tashum, カブピタクタ シュム, 濕疹. *n.* Eczema. **Syn : Iyoship.**

Kapu-ri, カブリ, 剥ク. *v.t.* To flay. To skin. To bark a tree. To peel. **Syn : Kapu kara.**

Kapu-risei, カブリセイ, 拔ク、(鳥ノ毛 ナド). *v.t.* To pluck as a fowl. To skin.

Kapu-soso, カブソソ, 皮ヲ剥ク. *v.t.* To bark a tree. To skin.

Kara, カラ, 造ル、爲ス、例セバ、イキリ、縫目、イキリカラ、縫フ、ナムケ、風邪、ナムケカラ、風チ引ク. *v.t.* To make. To do. To act. To achieve. To build. To accomplish. The word *kara* is often used as an auxiliary to verbalized nouns. Thus:— *Ikiri*, "a seam," *ikiri kara*, "to sew." *Omke*, "a cold"; *omke kara*, "to take cold." *Kara wa ingara*, "to try. To attempt"

Karabe, カラベ, ミツヒキ. *n.* *Polygonum virginianum*, *L*.

Kara-i, カライ, 功名. *n.* Achievement.

Kara-imi, カライミ, 仕上リタル着物. *n.* Ready made clothes.

Karaka-chiri, カラカチリ, 鶉、ウヅラ、*n.* A quail. *Cotunus japonica*, *T. and S*.

Karakara, カラカラ, 梳ル、掃除スル、*v.t.* To tidy. To comb as the hair. To do.

Karakara, カラカラ, 爲ス. *aux. v.* To do. This word is often heard in prayer. As:—*A en kore kuni ne karakara wa en kore*, "grant that it may be given me."

Karakarase, カラカラセ, 轉落ル. *v.i.* To run off (as water off a duck's back). To slip off.

Karakarasere, カラカラセレ, 轉バス. *v.t.* To roll away. To cause to run off.

Karakari, カラカリ, 包ム. *v.t.* To roll up. To wrap up. **Syn: Kokarakari.**

Karakat, カラカツ, 器量. *n.* Ability. **Syn: Kara mondum.**

Kara-kiroro, カラキロロ, 器量. *n.* Ability.

Karakisa, カラキサ, 木チ磨擦シテ火チ造ル. *v.t.* To make fire by rubbing sticks together.

Kara-koyaikush, カラコヤイクシ, 爲シ能ハザル. *v.i.* To be unable to do or make.

Karaku, カラク, 甥、姪. *n.* A nephew. A niece.

Karaku-ne-guru, カラクチグル, 甥、姪. *n.* A nephew. A niece.

Kara-mondum, カラモンヅム, 器量. Ability.

Karamu, カラム, 大切ニスル. *v.t.* To take great care of. **Syn: Eyam no koro.**

Karange-no-ek, カランゲノエク, 接近スル. *v.t.* To approach. To draw near to.

Kara-ni, カラニ, 火チ造ル爲メニ用ユル木. *n.* Sticks used for producing fire.

Karan-karan-karan, カランカランカラン, 金屬ノ打合ヒテ生スル音. *inte·j.* An onomatopœia expressive of the jingling sound caused by metal knocking together.

Kara-okere, カラオケレ, 成シ畢ル. *v.t.* To finish. To accomplish.

Karara, カララ, 爲サセル. *v.t.* To cause to make. To make another do.

Kararat, カララツ, ハシソカラス. *n.* Carrion crow. *Corvus corone*, *Linn*. **Syn: Shirari-kokari.**

Karari, カラリ. 上ニ置カル. *v.i.* To be placed upon. To rest upon.

Kara-shuma, カラシュマ, 燧石. *n.* A flint used for striking fire. **Syn: Kattashuma.**

Karauto, カラウト, 寳箱. *n.* A treasure box. A money box. **Syn : Mat-shuop.**

Kare, カレ, 爲サセル. *v.t.* To cause to make or do **Syn : Karara.**

Kar-i, カリ, 功蹟. *n.* Achievement.

Kari, カリ, ...ニョッテデ、例セバ、オヤルカリ、他ノ道ヨリ行ク、ブヤラカリインガラ、窓越ニ見ル. *post.* By. Through. Along. As :— *Oya ru kari,* " to go by another road." *Pet kari oman,* " to go along a river." *Puyara kari ingara,* " to look at through a window." *Kari omande yara-hi isam,* " there is no-one to send it by."

Kari, カリ, 輪行スル. *v.i.* To go in a circle.

Kari, カリ, 通ル. *v.t.* To go by. To pass along.

Karimba-ni, カリムバニ, ヤマザクラ. *n.* A cherry tree. *Prunus Pseudo-Cerasus, Lindl.*

Karimba-tat, カリンバタツ, サイハダカンバ. *n.* *Betula Maximowicziana, Regel.*

Karip, カリブ, 輪. *n.* A hoop. A ring.

Karip-pashte, カリブパシテ, 輪ヲ投ゲル. (遊戯ノ名). *v.t.* To throw a hoop from one to another as children in play. The game of throwing a small hoop which is caught by thrusting a stick through it whilst it is in full motion.

Karire, カリレ, 廻同ス. *v.t.* To send round in a circle.

Karishiri, カリシリ, 瞥見スル. *v.t.* To get a glimpse of a thing.

Karisia, カリシア, 敎會. *n.* The Christian Church. (This word has been introduced by the compiler).

Karop, カロブ, 燧道具. *n.* Flint and steel used for making fire.

Karu, カル, 凸凹アル. *adj.* Uneven. Rough. Turbulent. Lumpy.

Karu, カル, 燧袋. *n.* A flint and steel box or bag. **Syn : Piuchi-op.**

Karush, カルシ, 茸. *n.* Mushrooms. Fungi.

Kasa, カサ, 笠、傘. *n.* A hat. An umbrella.

Kasa-rantup, カサランツブ, Kasa-rantupep, カサランツペブ, 笠ノ紐. *n.* Hat strings.

Ka-saye, カサイエ, 卷絲. *n.* A coil of string or rope. A noose.

Ka-sayep, カサイェブ, 絲卷. *n.* An instrument upon which to wind cotton or thread. A spool. A reel.

Kash or kashi, カシ, 又ハ **カシ,** 小屋、納屋. *n.* A lodge, A hunter's or fisherman's lodge.

Kashi, カシ, 上、ニ、例セバ、チクニカシオニカオブ、木上ニ結ヒタル果實. *post.* Upon. On. As :— *Chikuni kashi o nikaop,* " the fruit which is borne upon the tree."

Kashi, カシ, 效驗ナキ. *v.i. and adj.* To be inefficient. To be ineffective, Ineffectual.

Kashiakik, カシアキク, 病ヲ治スル爲メ木ノ枝又ハ草ヲ以テ病人ヲ打ツ. *v.t.* To beat sick persons with boughs of trees or bunches of grass to cure them of disease.

Kashi-a-obas, カシアオバス, 救ハレ、助ケラレ ル. *v.i.* To be saved. To be

Kashi-a-obiuki, カシアオビウキ, helped.

Kashi-butu-unu, カシブツウヌ, 蓋フ、隱ス. *v.t.* To cover up. To keep secret. To put a lid on anything.

Kashichiobiuki, カシチオビウキ, 助ケ ル. *v.t.* To help. As:—*Kashi- chiobiuki aekarakara gusu ek an na.* "I have come to help you."

Kashi-chiukush, カシチウクシ, 上ヲ 流レル. *v.i.* To flow over as water over stones or a fallen tree.

Kashi-e-obas, カシエオバス, 助ク、救フ. *v.i.* To save. To help.

Kashi-e-obiuki, カシエオビウキ,

Kashieshina, カシエシナ, 黙許スレ. *v.t.* To connive at. **Syn : Anasap.**

Kashi-ikiri-kush, カシイキリクシ, リ ス、キネヅミ. *n.* A squirrel. *Sciurus lis, Temm.*

Kashi-iush, カシイウシ, 惡シキ天氣. *n.* Unpropitious weather. **Syn : Kashiush.**

Kashi-iyo, カシイヨ, 増ス. *v.t.* To put in upon. To augment. To add to.

Kashi-iyop, カシイヨブ, 増加. *n.* Addition.

Kashi-iyop-wa-ye, カシイヨブワイ ェ. 針小棒大ニスル. *v.t.* To exaggerate.

Kashi-kamu, カシカム, 蓋フ、蔽ハ ル. *v.t.* To cover. To over-shadow.

Kashike, カシケ, 上、上 =. *post.* Upon. Above.

Kashike-kik, カシケキク, 何物ニテモ 其上ヲ打ツ、(例セバ、病人ノ病チ追ヒ 掃フタメ). *v.t.* To strike the top

of anything. To beat a sick person with the smaller branches of trees or bunches of grass as a charm to drive away disease and evil spirits. **Syn : Epiru.**

Kashike-omare, カシケオマレ, 上ニ 置ク. *v.t.* To put upon. **Syn : Kashi-iyo.**

Kashiokok, カシオコク, 蹴. *v.t.* To kick against. (*pl*),

Kashike-peka, カシケペカ, 上 =. *adv.* Above. In the heights.

Kashiketa, カシケタ, 上 =. *adv.* Upon. Above.

Kashiketa-anuye, カシケタアヌイ ェ, 以上ノ如ク. *adj.* Above mentioned. Written above.

Kashikewe, カシケウェ, 守ル. *v.t.* To defend, To take care of. **Syn : Ka-kewe.**

Kashi-kush, カシクシ, 越エル. *v.t.* To pass over. As:—*Chisei kashi- kush,* "to pass over a house." *Ya- ikota katpak kashi kush wa moshima guru katpak patek esanniyo,* "he passes over his own faults and thinks only of those of others." *Koro buri kashi kush guru,* "a person who does not think of his own deeds."

Kashinda, カシンダ, 鳥ヲ取ル罠. *n.* A kind of bird snare.

Kashinkop, カシンコブ, 罠. *n.* A snare made of string.

Kashiobas, カシオバス, 救フ、助ケレ. *v.t.* To save. Te help. **Syn : Kashiobiuki.**

Kashiobiuki, カシオビウキ, 救フ、助ケ ル. *v.t.* To save. To help.

Kashioiki, カシオイキ, 人ノ爲メ二準備 ス ル. *v.t* To provide for the wants of others.

Kashiok, カシオク, 蹴 ル. *v.t.* To kick against (*sing*).

Kashiokara, カシオカラ, 禁ズル. *v.t.* To forbid. To warn not to do a thing. To bridle. To punish for doing something wrong. **Syn : Hattoki.**

Kashiokba, カシオクバ, 蹴 ル. *v.t.* To kick against (*pl*). **Syn : Kashiokok.**

Kashiomare, カシオマレ, 上二置ク、 訴フル. *v.t.* To put upon. To accuse. To add to. **Syn : Kashike-omare.**

Kashiomarep, カシオマレプ, 増加. *n.* An addition.

Kashioniwen, カシオニウェン, 僞善ナ ル. *adj.* Hypocritical. To pretend to know nothing about a thing. **Syn : Yaiko-oniwen. Shieram- peutekre.**

Kashiorai, カシオライ, 相次テ死ス. *v.t.* To die one after another.

Kashi-ose, カシオセ, 與フ. *v.t.* To bestow. To give. To take and give to another. **Syn : Ika-oshke.**

Kashi-ota, カシオタ, 灌ク. *v.t.* To anoint. To sprinkle over.

Kashi-oyoko, カシオヨコ, 守ル. *v.t.* To keep under one's eye. **Syn : Epungine.**

Kashiramu, カシラム, 助手スル. *v.t.* To take one's part. **Syn : Kashi- kewe.**

Kashirarapa, カシララバ, 壓シ付ケ ル. *v.t.* To press down.

Kashirari, カシラリ, 直キ後. *adv.* Immediately after. Behind. As:— *Kashirari wa ek,* " he is following

behind." Also *v.t.* To press upon.

Kashirarire, カシラリレ, 後二. *adv.* Afterward.

Kashish, カシシ, 防ク、碍ク. *v.t.* To prevent.

Kashi-seshke, カシセシケ, 蓋フ. *v.t.* To cover over. To shut down.

Kashitomuship, カシトムシプ, 織機 ノ名. *n.* An article worn round the body by women when weav- ing cloth, and which holds the threads tight and straight.

Kashiu, カシウ, 救フ、助ケル. *v.t.* To help. To assist. **Syn : Ikashiu.**

Kashiunno, カシウンノ, 上二. *adv.* Over. Above. To be over.

Kashiush, カシウシ, 惡キ天氣. *adj.* Bad weather. **Syn : Shiri-wen.**

Kashkamui, カシカムイ, 資. *n.* Treasures. Things one prizes very highly. Life. Strength.

Kashkamui-koro, カシカムイコロ, 繁昌スル. *v.i. and adj.* To be prosperous. To be in good health. Fortunate. Lucky. **Syn : Mau- kopirika.**

Kashkamui-oshitchiu, カシカムイ オシッチウ, 幸運ナル、仕合セニナル. *adj. and v.i.* Fortunate. Lucky.

Kashkamui-sak, カシカムイサク, 死 ヌ、運ガ惡イ. *v.i.* To die. To be unprosperous. To be sick.

Kashkep, カシケプ, 雪搔キ. *n.* A snow-shovel. **Syn : Upas-kep.**

Kashkun, カシクン, 其他. *adv.* Be- sides that. **Syn : Kashike-un.**

Kashnukara, カシヌカラ, 仕合ニナ ル、神恩チ受ケル. *v.t.* To be lucky. To have special favour from the gods. To be fortunate.

Kash-okake, カシオカケ, 後. *adv.* Afterwards.

Kashpa, カシバ, 過多ニ、例セバ、ボプケ カシバナ、餘リ熱イ. *adv.* Too much. As:—*Popke kashpa na,* " it is too hot." **Syn: Mashkin no.**

Kashpaotte, カシバオッテ, 命ズル. *v.t.* To command. To adjure. Also *n.* A command.

Kashpaotte-i, カシバオッテイ, 命令. *n.* A commandment.

Kashperenga, カシペレンガ, 惠ミ、 助ケ. *n.* Favour. Help. Good will.

Kashu, カシュ, 匙. *n.* The spoon. **Syn: Kasu.**

Kashu, カシュ, 直ク後. *adv.* Immediately after. Close upon. As:— *Itak kashu,* " immediately one has done speaking," " even before one has finished talking."

Kashu, カシュ, **Kashiu, カシウ,** **Kashui, カシュイ,** 徒渉スル、例セバ、ベッカ シュウ 河チ徒渉スル. *v.t.* To wade through. To scoop up. As:—*Pet kashiu.* " to wade through a river."

Kashui, カシュイ, 餘リ、例セバ、ボロカ シュイ、餘リ大イナル. *adv.* Too. As:—*Poro kashui,* " too large." *Pon kashui,* " too small." *Pirika kashui,* " too good." **Syn: Mashkin no.**

Kashumbe, カシュムベ, カスベ、ガン キエイ. *n.* Skate. *Raja kenojei, M. and H.* **Syn: Uttap. Futtap.**

Kashup, カシュブ, 杓子. *n.* A ladle. A large spoon.

Kashup-ni, カシュブニ, **Kasup-ni, カスブニ,** マユミ. *n.* Spindlewood. *Evonymus europaea, L.* var. *Hamiltoniana. Max.*

Kashupni-samanbe, カシュブニサマ ンベ, *n.* *Kareius scutifer (Stewd).*

Kashure, カシュレ, 過多ニ. *adv.* Too much. Very much.

Kaskep, カスケブ, 雪搔キ. *n.* A snow-shovel. A Scoop. **Syn: Upas-kep.**

Ka-soya, カソヤ, **Ka-soyai, カソヤイ,** ハチ. *n.* A kind of small bee.

Kasu-no, カスノ, 餘リ、過分. *adv.* More. Too much. Above. Over. As:—*Kasu no ka shomo ne, pokashnu ka shomo ne,* " neither more nor less." *Kasu no koro wa ek,* " bring more."

Kasushne, カスシ子, 容易ナル. *adj.* Easy. **Syn: Isaika.**

Kat, カツ, 器量、仕方、心、感覺. *n.* Ability. Form. Shape. Tact. Acumen. The heart. The feelings.

Kata, カタ, 上ニ、例セバ、シリカタ 地ノ上ニ. *adv.* Upon. On the top of anything. As:—*Shiri kata,* " upon the ground."

Kataiirotke, カタイイロツケ, 愛スル. *v.t.* To love. To be fond of. **Syn: Omap.**

Katairotke-guru, カタイロツケグル, 親友、朋友. *n.* A friend. **Syn: Kateomare guru.**

Katak, カタク, 絲玉. *n.* A ball of thread or fibre.

Katam, カタム, キンバイサウ. *n.* *Trollius patulus, Salisb.*

Katam-sara, カタムサラ, サ丶ハ ラ.
n. A plain of arundinaria.

Katap, カタブ, モ丶只丶又丶サエモ. *adv.*
Even. Either. Only. **Syn:
Poka.**

Katap-katap, カタブカタブ, カ.....カ丶
例セバ丶 アイヌカタブカムイカタブ人
カ神カ. *adv.* Either......or. As:—
Ainu katap kamui katap. "either
a man or a god." **Syn: Hene.
......hene.**

Katawa-ne, カタワ子, 不具ナ ル. *adj.*
Deformed.

Katchak, カノチャク, 能力ナキ丶 弱キ丶
貧シキ. *adj.* Weak. Powerless.
Without tact. Abject. Poor.
Incapable. Stupid. **Syn: Okirasap.** Irapokkari.

Katchak-be, カッチャクベ, 弱キモノ丶
貧シキモノ. *n.* A weak creature.
An abject.

Katchak-koro, カッチャクコロ, 臆病ナ
ル. *adj.* Cowardly. Unable.

**Katchak-mondum, カッチャクモンド
ム,** 弱キ. A weak disposition.
Infirmities.

Katckak-wa, カッチャクワ, 弱キ. *adj.*
Abjectly.

Katcham,
カッチャム, 心丶性. *n.* The heart.
Katchama, The mind. Nature.
カッチャマ,

Katchi, カッチ, 火ヲ造ル木. *n.* Fire-
sticks.

Katchiu, カッチウ, 鎗ヲ投ゲル. *v.t.* To
cast or thrust a spear at anything. **Syn: Kachiu. Eachiu.**

Katchiu, カノチウ, 責メル丶 蔑ミスル.
v.t. To persecute. To take no
notice of. To treat with indif-

ference. **Syn: Shikashishte.
Epokba.**

Katchiyai-ni, カッチヤイニ, 火ヲ作 ル
トキニ用ユル木. *n.* The stick which
is turned by the hands when
making fire.

Kateomare-guru, カテオマ レグル,
親友丶朋友. *n.* A friend. **Syn:
Katairotke guru.**

Katekara, カテカラ, 馬鹿ニスル丶欺ク.
v.t. To make a fool of. To
deceive. **Syn: Ikatkara. Ramu-
samka.**

Kateush, カテウシ, 惡鬼 ニ付カレル.
v.i. To be possessed by a devil.

Katken, カッケン, カヤガラス. *n.*
Dipper. **Syn: Katten.**

Katkimat, カノキマツ, 主婦. *n.* Mistress of a house.

Katkoro, カツコロ, 安全ニアル丶壯健
ニアル丶才能アル. *v.i.* To be well
and happy. To have ability.

Kat-moire, カツモイ レ, 遲鈍ナ ル. *adj.*
Slow. Dull. **Syn: Katu-moire.
Noratchitara.**

Kat-o, カツト, 上手ナル丶巧ミナル. *adj.*
Clever. Expert.

Kat-o-guru, カツトグル, 上手ナル者.
n. An adept. A clever person.
An expert.

Katorik, カ トリク, 公ナル. *adj.*
Catholic. Universal. (Introduced by the compiler).

Katpak, カツバク, 罪. *n.* Sins.
Syn: Chikokatpak. Wenburi.

Katpak-atusare-ambe,
カツバクアツサレアムベ,
Katpak-atusare-i,
カツバクアツサレイ,
罪ヲ赦スコト. *n.* Absolution.

Katpak-ki, カツパッキ, 罪ヲ犯ス. *v.t.* To commit sin.

Katpakkore, カツバッコレ, 有罪ト定ム. *v.t.* To condemn. **Syn: Tumu-maukush.**

Katpak-koro, カツバッコロ, 罪アル. *v.t.* and *v.i.* To have sins. To sin. To be a sinner. **Syn: Chikokatpak an.**

Katpak-koro-guru, カツバッコログル, 罪人. *n.* A sinner.

Katpak-obosore-ambe, カツバクオボソレアムベ,
Katpak-obosore-i, カツバクオボソレイ, 罪ヲ赦スコト. *n.* Absolution. **Syn: Katpak tusare ambe.**

Katpak-tusare, カツバクツサレ, 罪ヲ赦ス. *v.t.* To forgive sins. To absolve.

Katpak-tusare-i, カツバクツサレイ, 罪ノ赦シ. *n.* Absolution.

Katta, カッタ, 此ノ字ヲ動詞ニ付加スレトキハ急激ノ意ヲ表ス. *part.* A verbal ending implying hurry and violence. Same as *Ekatta*.

Katten, カッテン, カヮガラス. *n.* Dipper. (*Cinclus Pallasi, Tem.*) **Syn: Katken.**

Kattuima, カッツイマ, 遠キ. *adv.* Far. Distant.

Katu, カツ, or **Katuhu, カツフ,** 仕方、形、顔、有樣、法. *n.* Mode. Shape. Figure. Form. Face. Method. Appearance. Countenane. Way. *Katu* is sometimes added to verbs to change them into nouns. Thus: —*An katu*, "existence." *Katu rengaine*, "according to circumstances." *Katu ene ani*, "this is the way of it."

Katu-chakakke, カツチャカッケ, 無異 安全ナル. *v.i.* To be well and happy. To feel serene. To be comfortable. **Syn: Nupetne.**

Katue, カツエ, 懐姙スル. *v.i.* To be pregnant.

Katu-humi-pirika, カツフミピリカ, 善キ、丁寧ナル、壯健ナル. *adj.* Good. Well behaved. To be in good health.

Katu-humi-wen, カツフミウェン, 惡キ、無禮ナル、病氣ナル. *adj.* Bad. Badly behaved. To be in bad health.

Katu-ikashishba, カツイカシシバ, 弱キ、疲レタ、懶キ. *v.i.* To be weak, tired, lazy or decrepit.

Katuiush, カツイウシ, 狂スル. *v.i.* and *adj.* Crazy. Mad. Unreasonable. **Syn: Keutum chiitasare. Etomochine. Etomochinne.**

Katu-kara, カツカラ, 嘲ヶル. *v.t.* To mock. **Syn: Eoyaitak.**

Katukara, カツカラ, 直ス、正ス. *v.t.* To straighten out. To put right.

Katukarakaran, カツカラカラン, 用意スル、仕度ス. レ. *v.t.* To prepare. To make ready. **Syn: Ushipinire.**

Katukari, カツカリ, 席ヲ織ルニ用ユル絲. *n.* The strings of which mats are made.

Katukari, カツカリ, 立入ル. *v.t.* To interfere. To act the busybody. **Syn: Shiayapkire.**

Katukari-guru, カツカリグル, 周旋人. *n.* A busy-body.

Katukarikari, カツカリカリ, 短氣ナル. *v.i.* and *adj.* To be impatient. **Syn: Ramukarikari.**

Katumki, カツムキ, フトキ. *n.*
Bulrush. *Scirpus lacustris, L.*

Katu-moire, カツモイレ, 遅鈍ナル.
adj. Slow. Dull of comprehension. **Syn: Noratchitara.**

Katunashka, カツナシカ, 助ケル、救
フ. *v.t.* To help. To rescue. To
assist. **Syn: Kaobiuki.**

Katun-katun, カツンカツン, 悪戯ナ
ル. *adj.* Mischievous.

Katupase, カツパセ, 懶キ、怠レ、粗末
ナル. *adj.* Idle. Lazy. Sloven.
To dislike to do. Disinclined.
Syn: Katu-toranne.

Katupirika, カツピリカ, 奇麗ナル、揃
フテアル. *adj.* Nice. In order.
Tidy. Pretty.

Katurenga, カツレンガ, 命ズル. *v.t.*
To command. To enjoin.

Katu-rengaine, カツレンガイ子, 事
宜ニ由リテ. *adv.* According to
circumstances. As one desires.
As it may happen.

Katu-shineatki, カツシ子アツキ, 果
敢ナル. *v.i.* To be determined.
Stable. Resolute. **Syn: Ramu-
oshitchiu.**

Katu-toranne, カツトラン子, 懶キ.
adj. Lazy. Idle. Dull. Sloven.
Syn: Katupase.

Katu-turushno, カツツルシノ, 冷淡
ニ. *adv.* Indifferently.

Katu-utura, カツウツラ, 控目ナル.
v.i. Diffident. **Syn: Ramu-utura.**

Katuwa, カツウェ, ヒナノウスツボ. *n.*
Scrophularia alata, A. Gray.

Katu-wen, カツウェン, 醜キ. *adj.*
Ugly. **Syn: Ipokash.**

Katu-wende, カツウェンデ, 馬鹿ニス
ル. *v.t.* To make a fool of. To
make ashamed. **Syn: Yaini-
koroshmare.**

Katwende, カツウェンデ, 馬鹿ニスル.
v.t. To make a fool of. To make
as-shamed. This word is the same
as *katu-wende;* but *katu-wende*
always becomes *katwende* after
the objective pronoun *i* "us."
Thus:—*Nei guru i katwende,*
"that person is making fools of
us."

Kaukau, カウカウ, 霰. *n.* Hail.

Kaukau-ash, カウカウアシ, 霰フル.
v.i. To hail.

Kaukau-pas, カウカウパス, 霰フル.
v.i. To hail.

Kaure, カウレ, 脆キ. *adj.* Brittle.

Kawausei, カワウセイ, 朽チル. *n.*
Dry-rot.

Kaya, カヤ, 帆. *n.* A sail.

Kayaisei, カヤイセイ, 發音スル、鳴ル.
v.i. To sound. To rattle. As:
—*Kitchi-kayaisei,* "the death rat-
tles."

Kaya-koro, カヤコロ, 帆掛ケル. *v.i.*
To set sail.

Kaya-ni, カヤニ, 帆柱. *n.* A mast.

Kaya-shishte, カヤシシテ, 帆ヲ揚ゲ
ル. *v.t.* To spread a sail. To set
sail.

Kaye, カイェ, 破壊スル. *v.t.* To break.

Kaye, カイェ, 調子、譜. *n.* A tune.
**Syn: Ekaye. Shinotcharewe.
Kutkayekai.**

Kawause, カワウセ, 脆キ. *adj.*
Brittle. Crisp.

Ke, ケ, 此ノ字ヲ自動詞ノ語尾ニ加レト
キハ他動詞トナル、例セバ、ライ、死ヌ、
ライゲ、殺ロス. *part. Ke,* softened
into *ge,* is suffixed to some in-

transitive verbs to make them transitive. Thus:—*Rai*, "to die;" *raige*, "to kill." *San*, "to descend;" *sange*, "to send down;" "to take down."

Ke, ケ, 或時ハ Ke (ケ) ハ動詞ノ目的ヲ複數ニスル. *part.* *Ke* sometimes forms the plural of the object of verbs. Thus:—*shuye*, "to cook" (*sing*); *shuke*, "to cook" (*pl. obj.*).

Ke, ケ, 所. *loc. part.* Place. Locality; sometimes pronounced as if it were *ke-i*.

Ke, ケ, 婦女ノ用ユル間投詞. *interj.* Exclamation of surprise used by women and girls.

Ke, ケ, イザ、例セバ、ケウク、イザ取レ. *interj.* Here. As:—*Ke, uk*, "here, take it."

Ke, ケ, 掬フ. *v.t.* To skim. To scoop. To laddle up. (This word must never be used of skimming milk or the fat off soup, in such cases *eke* is the word used).

Ke, ケ, 幣ヲ造ル. *v.t.* To make *inao*.

Ke, ケ, 所. *adv.* Place.

Ke, ケ, 脂肪. *adj.* Fat. Grease.

Kean-no, ケアンノ, 誠ニ. *adv.* Truly. Just so.

Keannakun, ケアンナクン, ハイ、成程. *adv.* Just so. Yes. Exactly. **Syn: Ruwe un.**

Kechi, ケチ, 呻吟スル. *v.t.* To groan. To moan as in illness. **Syn: Nuwap.**

Keiki, ケイキ, 膕ヒカヽミ. *n.* The under-part of the knees.

Keiperi-pe, ケイペリペ, 淵. *n.* Shallow rapid water cf a river bed. **Syn: Utka.**

Keirat, ケイラツ, 鞋ノ紐. *n.* Sandal thongs. Boot laces or strings.

Keirat-muye, ケイラツムイェ, or **Keirat-shina**, ケイラツシナ, 鞋ノ紐ヲ結ブ. *v.i.* To lace up one's boots.

Keire, ケイレ, 皮靴. *n.* Salmon or deer-skin boots. Boots. Shoes.

Keire-shiru, ケイレシル, 靴摺レ. *v.i.* To hurt one's foot with a boot. To be wrung by one's boots.

Keire-ush, ケイレウシ, 靴ヲ穿ツ. *v.t.* To wear boots.

Keirekap-chep, ケイレカプチェプ, 魚ノ頭ト脊骨ヲ去リテ干シタルモノ. *n.* Fish with their heads cut off, the backbone taken out, and then dried.

Kek, ケク, 私ガ來ル. *v.i.* To come. I am coming. **Syn: Ku-ek.**

Kekaihi, ケカイヒ, 饑饉. *n.* A famine. A scarcity. **Syn: Keman.**

Keke, ケケ, サア、サア. *exclam.* Here, here.

Kekeshi, ケケシ, 存在、命. *n.* Existence. Life.

Kekirit, ケキリツ, 踵ノ腱. *n.* The tendons of the heels. As:—*Kekirit tuye*, "to cut the tendons of the heels as in punishment for murder."

Kekke, ケッケ, 破壞スル. *v.t.* To break. **Syn: Kaye.**

Kekon, ケコン, **hetak**, ササ, 今無、有リマセン. *adv. ph.* Here, now. Come, come. Now, be quick.

Kem, ケム, 嘗ル. *v.t.* To lick. As:—*Kem wa inu*, "to taste." **Syn: Kemkem.**

Kem, ケム, 血. *n.* Blood. *Kem-shito*, "a clot of blood." *Kem-kara*, "to bleed."

Kem, ケム, 針. *n.* A needle. *Kempui,* "the eye of a needle." *Kem oho unu,* "to thread a needle."

Kema, ケマ, Kemaha, ケマハ, 脚. The legs. The feet.

Kema-koni, ケマコニ, 跛ナル. *adj.* Lame. **Syn : Hera.**

Kema-koshne-guru, ケマコシチグル, キツネ. *n.* A fox. *Canis japonicus, Gray.*

Kema-koshne-guru-marapto, ケマコシチグルマラプト, 狐ノ骨チ以テ罪人チトフ. *n.* Ceremony of finding out a culprit by means of the skull of a fox. **Syn : Shitumbe marapto.**

Kemaratki-ningari, ケマラッキニンガリ, 耳環. *n.* Ear rings.

Kema-ure, ケマウレ, 足ノ裏、足. *n.* The lower part of the extremities. The feet. The soles of the feet.

Kema-ush, ケマウシ, 足ノアル. *adj.* Having legs.

Kemaush-inao, ケマウシイナオ, 幣. *n. Inao* (*i.e.* whittled pieces of wood) which have sticks tied to them to make them longer.

Kembe, ケムベ, 食指. *n.* The index finger.

Kem-eki, ケムエキ, Kem-iki, ケムイキ, 縫フ. *v. t.* To sew. To do needlework.

Kem-ekot, ケムエコツ, 餓死スレ. *v.i.* To die of starvation. To starve. **Syn : Chiekot. Yaichepekote.**

Kem-ewen, ケムエウェン, 餓死シタル. *adj.* Starved. Lean through want of food.

Kemi-an, ケミアン. 稀有ナル. *adj.* Rare. Precious.

Kemihi, ケミヒ, 血. *n.* Blood. **Syn : Kem.**

Kemihi-ush, ケミヒウシ, 血ダラケ. *adj.* Bloody. **Syn : Kem-ush.**

Keminakarushka, ケミナカルシカ, 厳格ナル. *v.i.* To be grave.

Kemi-ush, ケミウシ, 饑饉. *adj.* A famine. **Syn : Kem-ush.**

Kem-kara, ケムカラ, 出血スレ. *v. i.* To bleed.

Kemkem, ケムケム, 咶ル、嘗ル. *v.t.* To lick.

Kem-nu, ケムヌ, 出血スル. *v.i.* To bleed.

Kemnu, ケムヌ, 復讐スル. *v. t.* To requite. To avenge. To take the part of another.

Kem-nure, ケムヌレ, 出血サス. *v.t.* To make bleed.

Kem-o, ケムオ, 血ダラケナル. *adj.* Bloody.

Kem-oho-unu, ケムオホウヌ, 絲チ針ニ通ス. *v.t.* To thread a needle.

Kem-op, ケムオプ, 針箱. *n.* A needle-case.

Kemorit, ケムオクツ, 血統. *n.* Line of descent. Family blood.

Kemot, ケモツ, 血ダラケナル. *adj.* Bloody. Blood-shot. As :—*Kemot shik,* "blood-shot eye."

Kemotot, ケモトツ, 血塊. *n.* A blood bladder caused by accident. A clot of blood.

Kempana, ケムパナ, 血點. *n.* Spots of blood.

Kem-pui, ケムプイ, 針ノメド. *n.* The eye of a needle.

Kemram, ケムラム, 饑饉. *n.* A scarcity. A famine.

Kemrampa, ケムラムパ, 饑饉年. *n.* A season of famine.

Kemrit, ケムリツ, 脈. *n.* Veins.

Kem-shito, ケムシト, 血塊. *n.* Congealed blood. Clots of blood.

Kem-ush, ケムウシ, 血ダラケナル. *adj.* Bloody.

Kem-ush, ケムウシ, 饑饉ガアル. *v.i.* A famine to exist. ("There is" or "was" a famine).

Kem-ush-rok-okai, ケムウシロクオカイ, 饑饉ガアル. *v.i.* A famine to exist. ("There is" or "was a famine.")

Kem-wa-inu, ケムワイヌ, 味フ. *v.t.* To taste.

Ken, ケン, ヒルガホ. *n.* Bindweed. *Calystegia Sepium, Br.* **Syn:** **Kittesh.**

Kenash, ケナシ, 林野. *n.* A plain of trees.

Kenashioromap, ケナシオロマプ, エンレイサウ. *n.* *Trillium Smallii, Max.*

Kenashka-ushbe, ケナシカウシベ, 洪水. *n.* A flood.

Kene, ケ子, 河ニ登ラントスル鮭. *n.* Same as *Keneu.*

Kene-karush, ケ子カルシ, ㆑キダケ. *n.* *Pleurotus sp.*

Kene-ni, ケ子ニ, ヤマハンノキ. *n.* The black alder. *Alnus incana, Willd.*

Kene-ni-karush, ケ子ニカルシ, ㆑キダケ. *n.* *Pleurotus sp.*

Keneu, ケ子ウ, マスノスケ. *n.* *Oncorhyncha sp.*

Keni, ケニ, 芽. *n.* A sprout. A bud.

Keni-hetuku, ケニヘツク,}
Kene-hetuku, ケ子ヘツク,} 芽ザス. *v.i.* To sprout. To bud.

Kenituk, ケニツク, or Kenetuk, ケ子ツク, 芽ザス、萌ス. *v.i.* To sprout. To bud.

Kenitup, ケニツプ, or Kenetup, ケ子ツプ, 芽. *n.* A sprout. A bud.

Kennatara, ケンナタラ, 勉メテ見ル. *v.i.* To look at intently.

Kenru, ケンル, or Kereru, ケレル, 家. *n.* A house. Home. Abode. As:—*Kamui koro kenru,* "the home of the Gods," "a church" or temple."

Kenuma, ケヌマ, 身體ノ毛. *n.* The hair of the body.

Keoro, ケオロ, 腦. *n.* The brain.

Kep, ケプ, 物ヲ掬ヒ取ル器具、(雪搔キ水アカトリ等). *n.* A scoop.

Kep, ケプ, 掬ヒ出ス、剝ク. *v.t.* To peel. To bark. To scoop. **Syn:** **Soshpa.** As:—*At kep gusu oman,* "he has gone to bark elms."

Kep, ケプ, 急ニ破開スル. *v.i.* To burst suddenly open.

Keparapara, ケパラパラ, or Kiparapara, キパラパラ, オニノヤガラ. *n.* A kind of leafless orchid. *Iridæa sp.* **Syn:** **Unintek;** **Unitek.**

Keparapara-ohaukop, ケパラパラオハウコプ, イハノリ. *n.* *Porphyra suborbiculate, Kjellm.* (A kind of red sea-weed.

Keperibe, ケベリベ, 淵. *n.* Deep smooth water.

Kepkep, ケプケプ, or Kepkepu, ケプケプ, 嚙切ル、啄㆑. *v.t.* To gnaw. To peck as a bird.

Kepuru, ケプル, 裸ナル、(毛ナキ). *adj.* Bare. Hairless as leather.

Kepuru-kara, ケプルカラ, モヲ抜ク、

(獸ノ皮ヨリ). *v. t.* To pluck the hairs out of an animal's skin.

Kepush, ケブシ, 刀又ハ鎗ノ鞘. *n.* A sheath of a sword or spear. **Syn: Shirika.**

Keputuru, ケブツル, 額. *n.* The forehead.

Kera, ケラ, 味. *n.* Flavour. Taste. As :—*Kera an,* "sweet." *Kera pirika,* "of good taste;" "good flavour." *Kera wen,* "nasty;" "bad flavoured."

Kerai, ケライ, 其通リ成程、例セバ、ケ ライニシバネ、成程、主人ノ樣ダ. *adv.* Just so. Just like. Indeed. As: —*Kerai, nishpa ne,* "just like the master." *Kerai, Kamui itak ne,* "they are indeed the words of God." *Kerai, tan guru wen gun'-ne,* "this is indeed a bad person."

Kerai, ケライ, 惠ミ、助ケ. *n.* Grace. Favour. Help.

Kerainepta-un, ケライ子ブタウン, 何 ントマー、(驚嘆ノ詞). *interj.* Dear me! How many! As:—*Kerai-nepta un yuk chikoikip at shiri an a !* "dear me, what a number of deer there are to be sure!"

Kera-ru, ケラル, 甘キ. *adj.* Sweet. Nice.

Kere, ケレ, 當ル、搖ル. *v.t.* To touch. To brush against. **Syn: Tomo-ooshma.**

Kerekap, ケレカブ, 干鮭. *n.* Salmon cut down the centre, the back-bone taken out and spread out flat and dried. The skins of the fish so treated are used for boots.

Kere-kere, ケレケレ, or **Keri-keri, ケリケリ,** 嚙ム、啄ム、擦ル. *v.t.* To gnaw. To scrape.

Kerepnoye, ケレブノイェ, 毒氣頓ル猛 烈ナル附子. *n.* A kind of *Aconitum* having very virulent poisonous properties.

Kerero, ケレロ, ユキザ丶. *n.* *Smilacina japonica, A. Gray.*

Kereroshki, ケレロシキ, 好マヌ. *v.t.* To dislike. **Syn: Enupitara.**

Kereru, ケレル, or **Kenru, ケンル,** 家 *n.* A house.

Keri-keri, ケリケリ, or **Kere-kere, ケレケレ,** 嚙ム、擦リ磨ク、啄ク. *v.t.* To scrape. To gnaw.

Kerop, ケロブ, 靴下. *n.* Stockings. Socks.

Kerumun, ケルムン, ヤマアハ. *n.* *Calamagrostis Epigejos, Roth.*

Kerup, ケルブ, 目. *n.* The eyes. **Syn: Shiki.**

Kes, ケス, or **Kese, ケセ,** 終リ、例セ バ、トケス、日ノ終リ、即チタ. *n.* The end. The finish. As:—To kes, "the end of the day," *i.e.* "evening." *An kes,* "the end of the night," *i.e.* "early morning."

Kes, ケス, 各、皆、例セバ、ケサンチカ ラ、毎夜. *adj.* Every. Each. As: — *Kes anchikara,* "every night." *Kes chup ta,* "monthly." *Kes pa,* "annually." *Kes to,* "daily." *Kesto kesto,* "daily."

Kes, ケス, or **Kesh, ケシ,** 燒棒杭. *n.* A brand of fire. As:—*Abe kes,* "a firebrand."

Kes, ケス, 點. *n.* A spot. As:— *Kes-o,* "to have spots."

Keseamba, ケセアムバ, 追フ. *v.t.* To pursue. To hunt. **Syn: Noshpa. Keseamba wa oman.**

Keseke, ケセケ, 終リ. *n.* The end. The finish. Remainder. **Syn: Okese.**

Keseta, ケセタ, 終リニ. *adv.* At the end.

Kesh, ケシ, or **Gesh, ゲシ,** 下、終リ. *adj.* Lower. The end. The bottom. Probably a variation of *kes.* As :—*Set-gesh,* " the foot of the table."

Kesh, ケシ, 色ノ線、點. *n.* A stripe (in colour). A spot.

Keshirekari, ケシレカリ, 故郷又ハ兩親ヲ離レル. *v.i.* To leave one's parents or village. To wander about. **Syn: Kotan ekari.**

Keshirekari-guru, ケシレカリグル, 流浪者. *n.* A wanderer.

Keshke, ケシケ, 迫害スル. *v.t.* To persecute. **Syn : Epokba.**

Kesh-o, ケシオ, 斑(マダラ)ナル. *adj.* Spotted. Striped.

Keshup, ケシュプ, 踵. *n.* The heel. The lower part of the heel. As :—*Keshup apkash,* " to walk on the heels."

Keskes, ケスケス, 點. *n.* Spots.

Keskes-o, ケスケスオ, 斑、マダラナル. *adj.* Spotted.

Keso, ケソ, 斑點アル. *adj.* Spotted.

Kesorap, ケソラプ, 鸞鳥ノ名、(孔雀鷹若クハ鷲ノ類ナラン乎). *n.* A fabulous kind of big bird, perhaps a peacock, or hawk, or eagle. (Lit : Speckle-winged). The bird of Paradise.

Kesto, ケスト, 毎日. *adv.* Daily.

Ketchimuige, ケッチムイゲ, 踵ノ上部. *n.* The upper part of the heel. The heel tendons. As :—*Ketchimuige kotuye,* " to cut the heel tendons (as in punishment for murder).

Ketketchep, ケツケッチェプ, 蛙. *n.* A frog.

Ketu, ケツ, 擦ル. *v.t.* To scrape.

Kettok, ケットク, 病ノ名(風ホロシ). *n.* A kind of itching rash caused by exposure to the cold winds.

Ketu-hash, ケツハシ, カラスシキミ. *n. Daphne chinensis, Lam.,* var. *breviflora, Max.*

Ketunchikara, ケツンチカラ, 伸シテ干ス、(皮ノ如ク). *v.i.* To spread out dry as the skins of animals. **Syn : Chinkara.**

Ketush, ケツシ, or **Ketushi, ケツシ,** 女ノ寶箱. *n.* A woman's treasure bag or box. **Syn : Shut-ketu-shi.**

Keu, ケウ, 死人、骸骨. *adj.* and *n.* Dead. A corpse. A dead body. (Said to have originally meant life.)

Keu-ataye, ケウアタイェ, 殺人ニ對スル罰金. *n.* A fine for murder.

Keu-chimaush, ケウチマウシ, 頭部ノ腫物、白禿風シラクモ. *adj.* To have a scabby head.

Keu-uk, ケウウク, 人ヲ殺ス. *n.* To murder. **Syn : Keuk. Keweuk.**

Keuk, ケウク, 人ヲ殺ス. *v. t.* To murder.

Keuk-guru, ケウクグル, 人殺シ. *n.* A murderer.

Keukata, ケウカタ, 故. *part.* Because. So. As. Why. For the reason that. As :—*Nep keu kata pon an gusu,* " it was because I was so small." *Nep keukata nei no e ki ya?* " Why did you do so " ?

Keukimui, ケウキムイ, 冠頭、ツムジ. *n.* The crown of the head.

Keukosanu, ケウコサヌ, 物ノ割レ音. *v.i.* To give forth a very great noise as something breaking.

Keura, ケウラ, 味. *n.* Taste. Flavour.

Keurap, ケウラプ, 譽メル. *v.t.* To praise.

Keure, ケウレ, 削ル. *v.t.* To plane. To peel off. To sharpen as a pencil or stick. To shave off. To hew.

Keure, ケウレ, 破レ易キ. *adj.* Brittle.

Keurotke, ケウロツケ, 鳴ル. *v.i.* To sound. To rumble. To rattle as thunder.

Keush-keush, ケウシケウシ, 石ノ落ツル音. *n.* The rattle of stones rolling down the side of mountains.

Keushut, ケウシュツ, 叔父、老人、男ノ先祖. *n.* and *adj.* Uncle. Ancient. Old. Male ancestors. Male relations. **Syn : Acha.**

Keutum, ケウツム, 心、意志、感. *n.* The mind. Heart. Will. Affections. As:—*Keutum arage pirika kamui an, keutum arage wen kamui an,* "there are gods with partly good and partly evil dispositions."

Keutum-atte, ケウツムアッテ, 志チ立テル、決心スル. *v.i.* To fix the mind on. To be determined.

Keutum-atte-no, ケウツムアッテノ, 目的チ定メテ. *adv.* With a purpose.

Keutum-chashnu, ケウツムチャシヌ, 堅忍ナレ. *adj.* Patient. **Syn :**

Keutum oshitchiu.   Ramushiroma.

Keutum-chiutumashbare, ケウツムチウツムシバレ, 心ノ混雑ナル、迷フ. *v.i.* To be perplexed. **Syn : Sambe chiutumashire.**

Keutum-isam-guru, ケウツムイサムグル, 愚人、痴漢. *n.* A fool. **Syn : Haita guru. Etomochine. Paka ne guru.**

Keutum-koshne, ケウツムコシチ, 忍堪弱キ. *adj.* Impatient. **Syn : Ramu-koshne.**

Keutum-murumuruse, ケウツムムルムルセ, 憤怒スル. *v.i.* To boil over with anger. **Syn : Sambe-murumuruse.**

Keutum-nin-ush, ケウツムニンウシ, 困ラレテレ. *v.i.* To be troubled. **Syn : Oknatara.**

Keutum-okere, ケウツムオケレ, 學識アレ. *adj.* Learned. **Syn : Oramush.**

Keutum-oshitchiu, ケウツムオシッチウ, 安全ナル、穩カナレ. *adj.* Complacent. Quiet. Firm. To be determined.

Keutum-oupeka, ケウツムオウペカ, 正直ナル. *adj.* Upright. Righteous.

Keutum-raine, ケウツムライチ, 悲哀ナレ. *adj.* Sorrowful.

Keutum-ramuoshma, ケウツムラムオシマ, 面白キ、適合スル. *adj.* Agreeable. Acceptable. To agree with.

Keutum-ramuoshma-i, ケウツムラムオシマイ, 受納. *n.* Acceptance.

Keutum-ritetke, ケウツムリテッケ, 親切ナレ. *adj.* and *v.i.* Kind. Of a kind disposition. **Syn : Ramu-hauge.**

Keutum-sak, ケウツムサク, 思考ナキ、愚人. *adj.* and *n.* Thoughtless. A fool.

Keutum-ukopoyege, ケウツムウコポイェゲ, 二心ヲ持ツ. *adj.* Fickle. Double-faced.

Keutum-urenga, ケウツムウレンガ, 同心ノ. *adj.* United. **Syn : Ukoramuoshma.**

Keutum-usaraye, ケウツムウサライェ, 赦ス. *v.t.* To pardon. To forgive.

Keutum-utumashi, ケウツムウツマシ, 心ノ定マラサレ. *adj.* Unstable. Doubtful.

Keutum-utumkush,
ケウツムウツムクシ,
Keutum-uturukush,
ケウツムウツルクシ,
好マザル、氣ニ合ハザル. *v.i.* To be disagreeable. **Syn : Kuroma keutum koro.**

Keutum-yupke, ケウツムユプケ, 危暴ナル. *adj.* Wild. Severe. Bold. Audacious. **Syn : Sambe yupke.**

Keu-wen, ケウウェン, 頭ノ腫物、白禿瘡シラクモノ. *adj.* To have scabs on the head.

Kewe, ケウェ, or **Keu, ケウ,** 死骸、人頭. *n.* A dead body. A corpse. Also the head.

Kewe, ケウェ, 身長、例セバ、ケウェポロケル、丈ノ高キ人. *n.* Stature. As:— *Kewe poro guru,* "a large stout person." *Keweram,* "short of stature." *Kewe ri,* "tall."

Kewe, ケウェ, 追ヒ出ス、追ヒ捨フ. *v.t.* drive out. To expel. To drive away.

Kewe-ataye, ケウェアタイェ, 殺人罪ノ罰金. *n.* A fine for murder. **Syn : Ainu ataye.**

Kewechari, ケウェチヤリ, 追ヒ散ラス. *v.t.* To scatter by driving (as animals or birds).

Kewe-tak, ケウェタク, 殺人罪ノ罰金. *n.* A fine for murder. **Syn : Ainu ataye. Kewe ataye.**

Kewe-uk, ケウェウク, 殺ロス、首ヲ切ル. *v.t.* To kill. To behead.

Keworo, ケウォロ, 力量. *n.* Strength. **Syn : Tumu.**

Keworo-sak, ケウォロサク, 弱キ. *adj.* Strengthless. Weak. **Syn : Tumsak.**

Keyannakun, ケヤンナクン, or **Keyannakari, カヤンナカリ,** 成程、其ノ通. *adv.* Indeed. Just so. So. Exactly. **Syn : Ohaine.**

Keyam, ケヤム, 大危険ニアル. *v.i.* To be in great danger.

Ki, キ, ヨシ又ハアシノ總稱. *n.* A general name for rushes and reeds.

Ki, キ, 脂、アブラ. *n.* Fat.

Ki, キ, 虱. *n.* A louse.

Ki, キ, 事ヲ爲ス、例セバ、キホプニ、急キテ起キ上レ. *v.t.* To do anything. To accomplish. To act. To achieve. When preceding another verb *ki* has the sense of "hurry," "severity." or "urging" in it. Thus:—*Ki hopuni,* "to get up in a hurry." **Syn : Kara. Iki.**

Ki-abe-gusu, キアベグス, 然レドモ. *adv.* Yet. Although. **Syn : Yakka.**

Ki-ai, キアイ, 光線、焔、反射. *n.* A blaze. A ray of light. Reflection.

Kiai-ush, キアイウシ, 閃メク. *v.i.* To sparkle. To blaze.

Kiapa, キアバ, 粟. *n.* Millet. **Syn:** **Piapa.**

Kichi, キチ, 爲ス(複數). *v.t.* To do. *Pl. of Ki.*

Kichimomne,) マガレイ. *n.* A kind
キチモムチ, (of flounder. *Li-*
Kuchimomne, (*manda yokohamœ,*
クチモムチ,) *Gthr.*

Kichirakotba, キチラコツバ, 輾ル.*v.i.* To creak as cart wheels or oars in rowing a boat. To tick as a clock. **Syn: Rek.**

Kichitche, キチンチェ, 時計ノ運轉スル ニ似タル音、輾ル. *v.i.* To tick as a watch or clock. To creak as cart wheels or oars in rowing a boat.

Ki-i, キイ, 爲シタル事、成就. *n.* Achievement.

Kik, キク, 打ツ、叩ク. *v.t.* To strike. To hit. To knock. To beat.

Kikararip, キカラリプ, 梁. *n.* A joist. A beam.

Ki-kat, キカツ, 才能. *n.* Ability.

Kike, キケ, 鉋屑. *n.* Shavings.

Kike-chinoye-inao, キケチノイェイナオ, 幣ノ名. *n.* A kind of fetich with curled shavings attached.

Kikeparase-inao, キケパラセイナオ, 幣ノ名. *n.* Kind of fetich having the shavings spread out.

Kiketa, キケタ, ト雖モ、ナレドモ. *post.* Although. **Syn: Yakka.**

Kike-ush, キケウシ, 削リカケノ付キタ ル. *adj.* Having shavings attached.

Kike-ush-bashui, キケウシバシュイ, 削リカケノ付キタル髥上ゲ器. *n.* A ceremonial moustache-lifter-i.e. a moustache-lifter having shavings

on it and used especially in religious ceremonies.

Kik-humbe, キクムベ, 楯. *n.* A shield.

Kiki, キキ, 引キ搔ク. *v.t.* To scratch.

Kikiaraye, キキアライェ, 贖ル. *v.i.* To be redeemed.

Kikikara,) 防グ、守護スレ. *v.t.* To
キキカラ, (defend. To keep
Kikkara, (back. As:— *Wen guru*
キッカラ,) *an gusu en kikikara wa en kore,* "please defend me because of that bad person." *Ku goro pumma ikinnimara kikikara wa ande nisa,* "he kept back part of my wages."

Kiki-kiki, キキキキ, 引キ搔ク. *v.t.* To scratch.

Kikin-ni, キキンニ, エゾハミヅザグ ラ. *n.* The bird cherry. *Prunus Padus, L.*

Kikinraichep, キキンライチェプ, 蛹 (サナギ). *n.* A chrysalis.

Kikituye, キキツイェ, 防グ. *v.t.* To ward off. To keep away.

Kikiraye, キキライェ, 贖フ. *v.t.* To redeem.

Ki-kiroro, キキロロ, 才能. *n.* Ability.

Kikiri, キキリ, 蠅、其他昆蟲. *n.* Insects and flies.

Kikkara,) 防グ、守ル、例セバ、アパキッ
キッカラ, カラ、戸ヂ守ル. *v.t.* To
Kikikara, (defend. As:—*Apa*
キキカラ,) *kikkara,* "to defend a door." *Moshiri kikkara,* "to defend a country." *Kotan kik-kara,* "to defend a village," as from disease by charms of various kinds.

Kikkik, キッキク, 驚愕ノ聲(殊ニ婦人ノ). *excl.* An exclamation of surprise. Used principally by women and girls.

Kikkik, キッキク, 打ツ, 蹴ル. *v.t.* To strike. To beat. Frequentive form of *kik.* **Syn : Shirikik.**

Ki-koyaikush, キコヤイクシ, 爲シ能ハズ. *v.i.* Unable to do.

Kim, キム, 山脈、(複數). *n.* The mountains.

Kimak-hau, キマクハウ, 驚ノ聲、救助ヲ叫ブ聲. *n.* A frightened tone of voice. A cry for help.

Kimak-no, キマクノ, 速ニ、迅速ニ、例セバ、キマクノアッカシヤン、速ニ歩メ. *adv.* Fast. Quickly. As:— *Kimak no apkash yan,* "walk fast." **Syn: Pikan no. Pikan-kane.**

Kimatek, キマテク, 恐レル、性急、注意スル. *v.i.* To be careful. To be afraid. To be in a hurry. To be in fear. Startled. **Syn : Ishitoma.**

Kimat-no, キマツノ, 早ク. *adv.* Quickly. **Syn: Tunashino.**

Kimbui, キムブイ, 鹿ノ角. *adv.* Deer's horns. Antlers.

Kimbui-etu, キムブイエツ, 角ノ尖. *n.* Points of horns.

Kimbuikes, キムブイケス, 鹿角ノ最端. *n.* The points or extreme ends of a deer's horns.

Kimge-sama, キムゲサマ, 山際ニテ、山ノ側テ. *adv.* By the sides of the mountains. **Syn : Nupuri kotoro.**

Ki-mondum, キモンヅム, 才能、技巧アル事. *n.* Ability.

Kimoppe, キモッペ, 野獸、狐. *n.* Wild beasts. A fox.

Kim-oro, キモロ, 山間ニテ. *adv.* Among the mountains.

Kimta, キムタ, 山ノ中ニテ、山間ニテ. *adv.* In the mountains. Among the mountains.

Kimui, キムイ, 頭ノ頂、冠. *n.* The top of the head. Crown.

Kimui-oshmaki, キムイオシマキ, 襟首. *n.* The nape of the neck. **Syn : Oksutu.**

Kimumbe, キムムベ, 野獸. *n.* Wild beasts.

Kim-un, キムウン, 山中ニ、山ニ. *adv.* In the mountains. To the mountains.

Kimunge, キムンゲ, 山中ノ大湖. *n.* A very large mountain lake.

Kimun-kunau, キムンクナウ, フクジユサウ. *n. Adonis amurensis, Regel et Radd.*

Kimum-upeu, キムムペウ, カハラバウフウ. *n. Peucedanum terebinthaceum, Fisch.*

Kim-ushpu, キムウシプ, 山中ノ貯藏庫、(狩人ガ一時假ニ建テタル). *n.* A temporary store house put up by hunters when hunting in the mountains.

Kina, キナ, 大ナル草ノ總稱、又燈心草、或ハ疎剛ナル草ニテ造レル蓆. *n.* A general name for grasses of the larger kinds. Also, a mat made of coarse grass or rushes.

Kina-emauri, キナエマウリ, シロバナノエンレイサウ. *n. Trillium kamtschaticum, Pall.*

Kina-kara, キナカラ, 草ヲムシレ. *v.t.* To weed. To pull up weeds.

Kina-mokoriri, キナモコリリ, タニシ. *n.* A kind of gastropod. **Syn: Anekempo.**

Kinanbo, キナンボ, } マンホウ、ウキ
Kinapo, キナボ, } キ. *n.* Sunfish. Head-fish. *Mola mola, Linn.*

Kina-okeura, キナオケウラ, クイナ. Water-rail. *Rallus aquaticus indicus.* (*Blyth*). **Syn: Okeura.**

Kina-pe, キナベ, 露. *n.* Dew.

Kinapo, キナボ, ウミガメ. *n.* A turtle.

Kinapo-tambu, キナボタムブ, 龜ノ甲. *n.* Tortoise-shell.

Kinaraita, キナライタ, キンミヅヒキ. *n.* *Agrimonia pillosa, Ledeb.*

Kinaratashkep, キナラタシケブ, 草 (食用ニ供セシ名稱ノ). *n.* Herbs. Any kind of grass fit for food.

Kina-saranip, キナサラニブ, 草ニテ造レル袋. *n.* A kind of bag made of grass.

Kinashut, キナシュツ, 捲キタル蓆. *n.* A mat rolled up.

Kinashut-kari, キナシュツカリ, 蛇ニ憑カレ. *v.i.* To be possessed by a snake. **Syn: Tokkom parachi.**

Kinashut-un-guru, } アヂタイショウ.
キナシュッウングル, } *n.* A snake.
Kinashutunbe, } *Elaphis vir-*
キナシュツンベ, } *gatus, Schleg.*
Syn: Okokko.

Kinashut-orowa-no, キナシュツオロワノ, 力ノ限リ. *adv.* With all one's might. **Syn: Ramuoshi wano. Toiko.**

Kina-surugu, キナスルグ, ツルブシ. *n.* *Aconitum volubile, Pall.* var. *japonicum. Max.*

Kinatush, キナツシ, 藁繩. *n.* Straw rope.

Kinatuye-hosh, キナツイェホシ, 脚胖 (草又木皮製). *n.* Summer leggings made of grass or bark.

Kinin, キニン, 姦淫スレ. *v.t.* To commit adultery. **Syn: Omoinu.**

Kinkai, キンカイ, 荷物. (*Jap*). *n.* Luggage. Goods. **Syn: Shike. Itara kamasu.**

Kinkinne-upas, キンキンチウバス, 雪ノ小片. *n.* Small flakes of snow.

Kinnatara, キンナタラ, 盛装ニ坐スル (饗應ノ時ナトニ). *v.i.* To sit well clothed as at a feast.

Kinne-ni, キンチニ, キンギンボク. *n.* *Lonicera Morrowii, A. Gray.*

Ki-no, キノ, 賢キ、巧捷ナル. *adj.* Able. Clever. Adroit. Apt. **Syn: Eashkai.**

Kinop, キノブ, 肝臓. *n.* The liver. **Syn: Yukram.**

Kinrakara, キンラカラ, 怒ル、發狂スル. *v.t.* To be angry. To be mad or crazy. As:—*Kinrakara wa ye,* "to speak in anger." **Syn: Irushka.**

Kinra-koro, キンラコロ, 同上. *v.i.* To be angry.

Kinra-ne-ekohetari, キンラチエコヘタリ, 怒ツテ振リ向ク. *v.i.* To turn round in anger.

Kinratara, } 美装シテ坐ス(宴ニ臨ム
キンラタラ, } トキノ如ク). *v.i.* To
Kinnatara, } sit well clothed as
キンナタラ, } at a feast.

Kinup, キヌブ, } 平原、蘆. *n.* A
Kinupka, キヌブカ, } plain of reeds.

Kinupsho, キヌブショ, 蘆原. *n.* A plain of reeds.

Ki-o, キオ, 多虱ノ. *adj.* Lousy.

Kioka, キオカ, 取リ盡クサレシ. *adj.* Cleared. As a garden

of its vegetables. **Syn: Kioka-ke.**

Ki-otchike, キオッチケ, 蘆製ノ盆. *n.* A tray made of reeds.

Kip, キプ, 行動、仕上ゲタ物. *n.* An action. A thing done. **Syn: Ki-hi.**

Kiparapara, キバラバラ, 海草ノ一種. A kind of seaweed.

Kipip, キピプ, 注意スル、疑慑スレ. *v.i.* To be careful. To fear.

Kip-niukesh, キプニウケシ, 忠義ナル. *adj.* Faithful.

Kira, キラ, 走セ去ル. *v.i.* To run away.

Kirai, キライ, 櫛. *n.* A comb. •

Kirau, キラウ, 角、鹿角. *n.* Horns. Antlers.

Kirau-awe, キラウアウェ, 鹿ノ枝角. *n.* Branches of a deer's horns. **Syn: Kirau konda.**

Kirau-ush-chimakani, キラウウシチマカニ, コセカヂカネ. *n.* A kind of stone-sculpin. *Ceratocottus diceras (Pallas).*

Kirawe, キラ ウェ, 角、鹿ノ角. *n.* Horns. Antlers.

Kirawe, キラウ, 髄. *n.* Marrow. **Syn: Kiri.**

Kirawe-o-pone, キラウェオポ子, 髄骨. *n.* A marrow bone.

Kire, キレ, 爲サシム. *v.t.* To cause to do.

Kiri, キリ, 髄. *n.* Marrow. **Syn: Kirawe.**

Kiri, キリ, 知ル、認識スル. *v.t.* To know. To recognize. **Syn: Amkiri.**

Kiri, キリ, 脛、脚. *n.* The legs. The feet.

Kiri-guru, キリグル, 知己. *n.* An acquaintance.

Kirikewe, キリケウェ, 脚ノ骨. *n.* The bones of the legs. **Syn: Chikiri-pone.**

Kirikiru, キリキル, 嘲フ、笑フ. *v.t.* To mock. To laugh at. To make fun of. **Syn: Eyaipuni.**

Kiripa, キリバ, 顚覆スレ、搔キ雜セル. *v.t.* To turn over. To stir. Properly *kirupu.*

Kiripiru, キリピル, 脫ゲ、(靴ナドチ). *v.t.* To cast off (as boots).

Kiripu, キリプ, 脂肪. *n.* Fat.

Kiripu-o, キリプオ,
Kiripu-ush, キリプウシ,
Kiri-ushte, キリウシテ, } 肥滿ナル. *adj.* Fat.

Kiri-ushte, キリウシテ, 肥ヤス. *v.t.* To fatten.

Kirisam, キリサム, 側ニ. *adv.* By the side of one. **Syn: Samata.**

Kiri-samta, キリサムタ, 側ニ. *adv.* Close by. Near one's feet.

Kiri-wen, キリウェン, 瘠セタル. *adj.* Thin. Lean.

Kirok, キロク, 其事チ爲ス. *v.t.* To be doing anything.

Kironnu, キロンヌ, 充チタル、滿足シ タル. *adj.* Full. Satisfied.

Kironnure, キロンヌレ, 充タス、滿足 セシムル. *v.t.* To fill. To satisfy.

Kiroro, キロロ, 力、才能. *n.* Power. Strength. Ability. **Syn: Okira.**

Kiroro-an, キロロアン, 强キ. *adj.* Strong. Powerful.

Kiroro-ashnu, キロロアシヌ, 强キ. *adj.* Strong. Able-bodied. **Syn: Tumashnu.**

Kiroro-ekot, キロロエコツ, 氣絶ス レ、死 メ レ. *v.i.* To faint. To lose one's strength. To die.

Kiroro-koro, キロロコロ, 強キ、有爲ナ レ. *adj.* Strong. Able.

Kiroro-rui, キロロルイ, 強キ・ *adj.* Strong. Of great strength.

Kiroro-sange, キロロサンゲ, 全力チ以テ. *adv.* With all one's might.

Kiroro-yuptek-no, キロロユブテク ノ, 力強ク. *adv.* Powerfully.

Kiroro-yupu-wa, キロロユブワ, 全力 チ以テ. *adv.* With all one's might. **Syn : Shiarikiki no.**

Kiru, キル, 顛覆ス ル、轉バス. *v.t.* To turn over. To roll over.

Kiru-kiru, キルキル, 顛覆ス レ、(キ ル ノ語意ヨ リ強キ). *v.t.* An intensified form of *kiru.* Applied to human beings this word has an evil sense. Thus :—*Ainu kiru-kiru,* " to turn a man over and over," i.e. to search out a person's faults.

Kiru-osh, キルオシ, 腰. *n.* The loins.

Kirupa, キルバ, 顛覆ス ル、轉バス、(複 數). *v.t.* To turn over. To roll over. *Pl. of kiru.*

Kiruruge, キルルゲ, 間ニ. *adv.* A-mongst. **Syn : Uturu. Tumu-geta.**

Kirurugeta, キルルゲタ, 間ニ. *adv.* Amongst.

Kisa, キサ, 錐揉ス ル、手チ揉ム、(アイヌ ガ木チ以テ火チ起スガ如シ). *v.t.* To rub in the hands as fire-sticks when producing fire. To make a hole with an awl.

Kisa, キサ, 皮チ剝ク. *v.t.* To peel. **Syn : Kapu kara.**

Kisa-kisa, キサキサ, 揉ム、錐揉ミスレ. *v.t.* To rub in the hands as an awl or fire-stick. To bore with an awl. **Syn : Kisa.**

Kisan-nin, キサンニン, 耳ノ中央ノ部 分. *n.* That part of the ear between the lobe and top.

Kisanrap, キサンラブ, 耳ノ上部. *n.* The upper part of the ears. **Syn : Kisara sap,**

Kisara, キサラ, 耳、例セバ、クイェ
Kisaraha, キサラハ, イタクエキサ ラ ナッタアフンゲ、我言チ汝ノ耳ニ挿 メヨ. *n.* The ears. As :—*Ku ye itak e kisara otta ahunge,* " put my words into your ears." *Ashpa kisara itutanure,* " turn a deaf ear to it." *Kisara mayaiye* " to have itching ears " (*met,* to desire to bore : also, to be spoken about).

Kisara-hap, キサラハブ. 耳朶. *n.* The lobe of the ear. **Syn : Kisara top.**

Kisarapeot, キサラペオツ, マヒヅレ サウ. *n. Maianthemum bifolium, DC.*

Kisara-pui, キサラブイ, 耳ノ穴. *n.* The ear-holes.

Kisarapui-o, キサラパイオ, 耳朶ニ穴 チアケレ. To bore a hole in the ears.

Kisara-sap, キサラサブ, 耳ノ上部. *n.* The upper part of the ears. **Syn : Kisanrap.**

Kisara-top, キサラトブ, 耳朶. *n.* The lower part or lobe of the ear. **Syn : Kisara-hap.**

Kisara-turu, キサラツル, 耳垢. *n.* Ear-wax.

Kisashke, キサシケ, 惡寒ガスル、(雨又ハ寒氣ノ爲). *v.i.* To be chilled with rain and cold as :—*Ku kisashke humi ash,* "I feel chilled."

Kisassara, キサッサラ, 沼地 (高キ蘆ノ繁茂セレ). *n.* A plot of thick tall reeds.

Kisat-tarara, キサッタララ, 動物ノ如ク耳朶チ竪テル. *v.i.* To prick up the ears as an animal when listening.

Kisattarara-pekambe, キサッタララベカムベ, ヒ シ. *n.* *Trapa bispinosa, Roxb.*

Kisat-turu, キサッツル 耳垢. *n.* Earwax.

Kiseri, キセリ, 煙管. *n.* A tube. A tobacco pipe.

Kiseri-otop, キセリオトプ, 煙管筒. *n.* A tobacco pipe case.

Kiseri-uhuika, キセリウフイカ, 煙管ニ火チ點ズル. *v.t.* To light a pipe.

Kisesseri, キセッセリ, アイヌノサビ. *n.* A kind of bitter cress. *Cardamine yezoensis, Max.* This plant is used as an article of food. **Syn : Nisesseri, Risesseri,**

Kishikin-ni, キシキンニ, クロウメモドキ. *n.* Buckthorn. *Rhamnus japonicus, Max.*

Kishima, 捕 ル、押 ル. *v.t.* To lay
キシマ,
Kis ma, hold of. To seize. To
キシマ,
arrest. To take hold.
To curb.

Kishinkishin,
キシンキシン, カゼカノ一種. *n.* A
Kishunkishun, kind of sculpin.
キシュンキシュン,

Kishirekari-guru,
キシレカリグル, 浮浪人. *n.* A
Keshirekari-guru, wanderer.
ケシレカリグル,

Kishki, キシキ, 獸ノ毛. *n.* The hair of animals. As :—*Tu yuk kishki aetayetaye,* "two hairs were plucked out of the deer."

Kishma, キシマ, 捕ル、捉ム. *v.t.* To seize. To hold. To clasp. To catch.

Kishunkishun,
キシュンキシュン, ケシベツ ギスカゼ
Kishinkishin, カ. *n.* A kind
キシンキシン, of sculpin.
Gymnocanthus intermedius, T. & S.

Kitai, キタイ, 頂上、物ノ頂邊. *n.* The top of anything. Summit.

Kitaige, キタイゲ, 物ノ頂邊. *n.* The top of anything.

Kitaigeta, キタイゲタ, 物ノ頂邊ニ於テ. *adv.* On the top of anything.

Kitai-oma-ni, キタイオマニ, 棟木. *n.* The ridge-pole of a house.

Kitat, キタッ, シラカンバ. *n.* White birch. *Betula alba, L. var. vulgaris. DC.*

Kitaiomani, キタイオマニ, 柾、栩. *n.* Roof shingles. Roof poles. Rafters.

Kitchi, キッチ, 槽、盤. *n.* A manger. A trough.

Kite, キテ, 銛ニ用ユル骨. *n.* The bone part of a fish spear, or harpoon to which the iron point is fixed.

Kite-not, キテノツ, 銛ノ穗尖. *n.* The iron point of a fish spear, or harpoon.

Kite-nimaki, キテニマキ, 犬齒. *n.* The dog teeth.

Kittesh, キッテシ, ヒルガホ. *n.* The
Kitesh, キテシ, Bindweed.

Calystegia Sepium, Br.   **Syn:**
Ken.

Kito, **キト**, ギャウジャニ ンニク. *n.*
Allium victorialis, L.   **Syn:**
Kitu. Pukusa.

Kiu, **キウ**, ヒメイズイ. *n.*   *Polygonatum humile, Fisch.*

Kiuta-chup, **キウタチュブ**, 四月. *n.*
The month of April called by
some *Mokiuta-chup.*

Kiyanne, **キヤン子**, 年長ナル、最年長
ナレ. *adj.* Eldest. Elder.

Kiyanne-mat, **キヤン子マツ**, 姉娘. *n.*
An elder daughter.

Kiyanne-po, **キヤン子ポ**, 長子. *n.* An
elder child.

Kiyannere, **キヤンチレ**, 主トスル、長
子ノ待遇チスレ. *v.t.*   To make
chief. To treat as an elder child.

Ko, **コ**, 粉. *n.* Flour. Powder.
Koho, **コホ**,   Anything ground
fine.

Ko, **コ**, 日(常ニ他語ト組合ス). *n.* A
day. Only heard in combination
with other words. As:—*Tut ko.*
"two days"; *rereko,* "three
days."

Ko, **コ**, 若シ、然ルニ. *post.* When. If.
Whilst. As:—*Tan kusuri ni ko
anak ne e riten ruwe ne,* "you will
get better if you drink this
medicine."

Ko, **コ**, 此語分詞ナレドモ動詞ノ先ニ附
セラレ前置詞トシテ歴々用キウル、例
セバ、キラ、走ル、コキラ、ヘ走ル. *part.*
This word is often used as the
preposition "to" and is prefixed
to verbs. Thus:—*Kira.* "to run
away," *ko-kira,* "to flee to." *Ye,*
"to say," *ko-ye,* "to say to."
Ko-ongami, "to worship."

Ko, **コ**, 此語文章ノ始ニ於テハ無寛味ナ
リ、日本語ノ發語、イザニ似タリ. *part.*
Sometimes the word *ko* is heard
at the beginning of a sentence,
and has no special meaning. It
is so used merely to give the
speaker time to think.

Ko, **コ**, 此語チ接尾語ニ用ユル時ハ、時ト
シテ、遠キチ示ス、例セバ、ハンゲ、
近キ、ハンゲコ、遠キ. *part.* Used
as a suffix to some words *ko*
gives the sense of distance. As,
hange, near; *hange-ko,* "far
away."

Ko, **コ**, ウチニノ意味ナリ. *prep.* In.
As:—*Ko-apa ashi,* "to shut in."

Koapa-ashi,   **コアパアシ,**
Koapa-seshke, **コアパセシケ,** 閉ヂ
込ム、又ハ閉メ出ス. *v.t.* To shut in
or out. As:—*Kamui chisei otta
a-ko-apa ashi,* "she is shut in
the church."

Koarikire, **コアリキレ**, 來ラス(複數).
To cause to come to. (*Pl.*)

Koaruwe-un, **コアルウェウン**, 全キ、全
部ノ. *v.i. and adj.* To be entire.
Whole.   **Syn: Ramne no.**

Koash, **コアシ**, 圍ム、例セバ、チセイコ
アシ、熊ノ穴又家チ圍ム. *v.t.*   To
surround. As:—*Chisei koash,*
"to surround a bear's den," or
a "house."

Koasarani, **コアサラニ**, 知ラセレ. *v.t.*
To make known to.

Koatcha, **コアッチャ**, 漬ス、侮辱スレ、
冷遇スル、呪フ、浪費スル. *v.t.* To
blaspheme. To treat slightingly.
To treat badly. To accurse. To
waste. To curse. **Syn: Yai-
ikiri.**

Koatcha-wa-an, コアッチャワアン, 呪
レシ. *adj.* Accursed.

Kochan, コチャン,｜厭フ、欲セザ レ.
Kopan, コパン,｜ *v.t.* To dislike. Not to want.

Kochanup, コチャヌプ, 物體、望ンダ
物. *n.* An object. A thing looked forward to.

Kochanup-koro, コチャヌプコロ, 目
指ス. *v.t.* To have as an object.
To keep in view.

Kocharapa, コチャラパ, 分配スレ. *v.t.*
To distribute. **Syn : Kochatcha-
ri.**

Kochare-ewen, コチャレエウェン, 誹ル.
v.t. To revile.

Kochaotke, コチャオッケ, 突キ出ス(顔
ナドヲ戸口ナドヨリ). *v.t.* To put
through (as the face and head
through a door-way).

Kochi, コチ, 足跡. *n.* A footprint.
A path or trail. As :— *Chikiri
kochi,* "a footprint." **Syn: Kot.**

Kochi-kara, コチカラ, 地ナラシスレ.
v.t. To make level as a plot of
land to build a house upon.
Syn : Kotchi kara.

Kochikok, コチコク, ヨタカ、カスイド
リ. *n.* Japanese Goatsucker.
Caprimulgus jotaka, T. & S.

Kochimpuni, コチムプニ, 歩ム、散歩
スレ. *v.i.* To walk.

Kochupchupu, コチュプチュプ, 盲ス
ル(光ナドニテ)、瞬ク、閃ク. *v.i. and*
v.i. To be blinded as by light. To
blink the eyes at. To flash about.
To send forth flashes of light.

Kochuppa, コチュッパ, 捲ク、(複數).
v.t. (pl.) To roll up.

Kochupu, コチュプ, 捲ク、(單數). *v.t.*
(*sing*). To roll up.

Koeachiure, コエアチウレ, 打ツ(釼ニ
テ切ル). *v.t.* To strike as with a
sword.

Koehange, コエハンゲ, 近ヅク. *v.t.*
To draw near. to.

Koekari, コエカリ, 相逢フ. *v.t.* To
meet with.

Koekushna, コエクシナ, 通リ抜ケレ、
通ス. *v.t.* To pass through. To
traverse.

Koeratchitke, コエラッチッケ, 懸ル、下
ガル. *v.i.* To hang down.

Koerikoma, コエリコマ, 登ル. *v.t.*
To ascend.

Koeshikeraine, コエシケライ子, 憐ム.
To pity. As :—*Nei ainu ku
koeshikeraine gusu aki na,* "I
do it because I pity the man."
Syn : Erampokiwen wa kore.

Koetaye, コエタイェ, ヨリ引ク. *v.t.* To
pull from.

Koetun, コエツン, 借用スレ. *v.t.* To
borrow from.

Koewechiu, コエウェチウ, 合フ、逢フ
(網ノ端ト端トガ合フテ魚ヲ圍ム). *v.i.*
To meet. As the ends of a net
round fish.

Kohaitakashpa, コハイタカシパ, 醜
キ面チスレ. *v.i.* To make a very
ugly face. To be very repulsive
in one's looks.

Ko-hawe-ashte, コハウェアシテ, 呼
ブ、訪フ. *v.i.* To call to. To call
upon.

Kohemachichi, コヘマチチ, 仰グ. *v.i.*
To throw the head back.

Koheraye, コヘライェ, 似ル. *v.t.* To
resemble. To be like.

Koho, コホ, 粉. *n.* Flour.

Kohoetetke, コホエテッケ, 懸ケテ垂
レル. *v.i.* To hang out or down.

Kohonoye, コホノエ, 罰スル. *v.i.* To
punish. **Syn: Paragoatte.**

Kohoshipire, コホシピレ, 物ヲ人ニ返
ス. *v.t.* To return anything to
another.

Kohoshupkarapa, コホシュブカラパ,}
Kohoshupkare, コホシュブカレ,}
近付ク. *v.t.* To go near to. To
touch (as wind) but to do no
harm.

Kohummumatki, コフムマツキ,}
Kohumumatki, コフムマツキ,} 風
ナドノ張リタル縄ニ觸ル、音. *n.* The
whirring sound or whistle of the
wings of birds in flight, or as
wind through the ropes of a ship.

Kohuye, コフイエ, 焦ゲル. *v. t.* To
burn as food in a saucepan.
Syn : Shu-kohuye.

Koi, コイ, 海波. *n.* The waves of
the sea. **Syn: Ruyambe.**

Ko-ihok, コイホク, 賣ル. *v.t.* To sell
to. **Syn: Otta eok.**

Koikara, コイカラ, 倣フ、寫ス. *v.t.*
To imitate. To copy. **Syn :
Ikosamba.**

Koikara-guru, コイカラグル, 弟子. *n.*
A disciple.

Koikashke, コイカシケ, 東ニ當リ. *adv.*
To the eastward.

Koikature, コイカツレ, 急行スル. *v.i.*
To speed along. To go along in
a hurry. **Syn : Chashnu no
arapa.**

Koikayupu, コイカユブ, 非常ニ急ギ行
ク. *v.i.* To go very fast.

Koiki, コイキ, 叱ル、魚ノ如ク捕エル、
戰フ、殺ス. *v.t.* To scold. To
catch as fish. To fight. To kill.

Koingara, コインガラ, 比ベル. *v.t.*
To compare.

Ko-iokbare, コイオクバレ, 反亂ヲ起
ス. *v.t.* To rebel against.

Koiomare, コイオマレ, 酌ス. *v.i.*
To pour out for another. As :—
Sake en e-koiomare yan, "pour me
out some *sake.*

Koipak, コイパク, 罰スル、叱ル. *v.t.*
To punish. To scold.

Koipishba, コイピシバ, 尋ヌル、判斷
スル. *v.t.* To enquire. To ask.
To judge, As :—*En koipishba,* "he
enquired of me." *Pl of koipishi.*

Koipishi, コイピシ, 判斷スル、檢査ス
ル. *v.t.* To judge. To enquire
into.

Koipokita, コイポキタ, 西ニ當リ. *adv.*
To the westward.

Koipokun, コイポクン, 西ニ當リ. *adv.*
Westwards.

Koipuni, コイプニ, 與フ. *v.t.* To
give. **Syn: Kore.**

Koira, コイラ, 我失念セリ. *v.t.* I
forget. **Syn: Ku oira.**

Koiraiiraige, コイライイライゲ, 謝ス.
v.t. To thank.

Ko-iramye, コイラムイエ, 讚ムレ. *v.t.*
To praise.

Koireika, コイレイカ, 讚ムレ. *v.t.*
To praise. As :—*Kamui koireika,*
"to praise God."

Ko-irushka, コイルシカ, 怒ル. *v.t.*
To be angry with. As :—*Iteki
oman, e oman yak ne nei guru e
ko-irushka kusu ne na,* "do not

go, for if you do he will be angry with you."

Koisam, コサイム, or **Koisamka, コイサムカ,** 全滅セシム. *v.t.* To bring to nothing. To annihilate.

Koisamkokka-eshitchiure, コイサムコッカエシッチウレ, 座スレ. *v.i.* To sit upon the knees Japanese fashion.

Koishitoma, コイシトマ, 恐ル. *v.t.* To be afraid of.

Koi-shum, コイシュム, 泡. *n.* Foam. Froth.

Koitakkashi, コイタッカシ, 從ハヌ、違背スル. *v.t.* To disobey. As:— *Kamui irenga koitakkashi,* " to disobey the will of God."

Koito, コイト, or **Kuitop, クイトブ,** 雁、がン. *n.* A goose.

Koiwak, コイワク, 娶ル或ハ嫁チ取ル. *v.i.* To take a wife or husband.

Koiyange, コイヤンゲ, 涙ニ、打チ上ゲラレ. *v.i.* To be tossed up by the waves.

Koiyange-ni, コイヤンゲニ, 涙ニ打チ上ゲラレタル木、漂着木. *n.* Wood tossed up by the waves.

Koiyangep, コイヤンゲブ, 難船. *n.* A wreck.

Kokakse, コカクセ, 汚ス. *v.t.* To dirty. To besmear.

Kokandama, コカンダマ, 欺ク. *v.t.* To deceive. **Syn: Ikoshunge.**

Kokarakarase, コカラカラセ, 為ス. *aux. v.* To do. As:—*Chish kokarakarase,* " to cry."

Kokarakari, コカラカリ, 捲ク. *v.t.* To roll up. To wind round.

Kokaramotte, コカラモッテ, 失スレ. *v.i.* To reject. To miss. **Syn: Epotara. Emaka.**

Kokararase, コカララセ, 着レ. *v.t.* To clothe.

Kokarase, コカラセ, 群ガル. *v.i.* To swarm. To congregate. **Syn: Kotoise.**

Kokari, コカリ, 捲ク. *v.t.* To roll up. To wind.

Kokatpak-guru, コカツパッグル, 罪人. *n.* A sinner. **Syn: Chikokatpak guru.**

Kokatun-ki, コカツンキ, 洒落レレ. *v.i.* To do or say funny things for amusement.

Kokekke, コケッケ, 折ル、(木ナドヲ). *v.t.* To break (as wood).

Ko-keutum-koro, コケウツムコロ, 適フ、偏ル. *v.i.* To be in accord with. To be partial to.

Ko-keutum-oshitchiure, コケウツムオシッチウレ, 己チ制スル. *v.i.* To restrain one's self. **Syn: Yaishikkashma.**

Kokik, コキク, 打ツ. *v.t.* To strike.

Kokikkik, コキッキク, 屢バ打ツ. *v.t.* To strike frequently.

Kokina-kara, コキナカラ, 草チトレ. *v.t.* To weed. As:—*Atane kokina-kara,* "to weed turnips."

Kokininpashte, コキニンパシテ, 饒舌ナレ. *v.t.* To talk much. To act wickedly with another.

Kokira, コキラ, 逃ゲル. *v.t.* To flee to.

Kokirau-puni, コキラウプニ, 角ノ如ク手チ頭上ニ置キテ坐ス. *v.i.* To sit with the hands over the head like horns.

Kokka, コッカ, 膝. *n.* The knees.

Kokkaea, コッカエア, 跪ク、(卑敬). *v.i.* To kneel. To sit upon the knees.

Kokkaerok, コッカエロク, 跪ク(複數). *v.i.* To kneel. (*Pl of kokkae a*).

Kokkaeshirotke, コッカエシロツケ, 跪ク. *v.i.* To kneel.

Kokkapa, コッカパ, 膝頭. *n.* The knee-cap.

Kokkasapa, コッカサパ, 膝頭、膝. *n.* The knee. The knee cap.

Kokko, コッコ, 爲スクレ、打捨テ置ケ. *v.i.* Do not. Let it alone. This word is equal to *iteki*, but is only used by little children.

Kokko, コッコ, ゴツコ. *n.* Sea snail. (*Jap*). *Liparis agassizii, Putnam*.

Kokkop, コッコブ, 死體. *n.* A corpse. **Syn : Kaisei.**

Koko, ココ, 婿. *n.* Son-in-law. Brother-in-law.

Kokomge, ココムゲ, 凭ル. *v.i.* To lean upon.

Kokomgere, ココムゲレ, 凭ラセレ. *v.t.* To make lean upon.

Kokomomatki, ココモマツキ, 屈シテ行ク. *v.i.* To go along in a stooping posture.

Kokou, ココウ, 婿. *n.* A son-in-law.

Kokou-ne-guru, ココウチグル, 婿. *n.* A son-in-law.

Kokuruse, コクルセ, 亂スレ、混同サス.レ. *v.i.* To be confused. To be confounded.

Kokurusere, コクルセレ, 亂ス、混同サセレ. *v.t.* To confuse. To confound.

Kom, コム, 葉. *n.* Leaves.

Kom, コム, 節瘤、指ノ節、小山. *n.* The knuckles. A knob. Hillock. Knotty. Knobby.

Komaunukuri, コマウヌクリ, 恐レレ. *v.t.* To be afraid of. **Syn : Koishitoma.**

Kombu, コムブ, or **Komboo,** コムボ, 昆布、コンブ. *n.* A kind of brown sea-weed. *Laminaria*.

Kombururu, コムブルル, 疎キ(モナドノ). *adj.* Rough, as hair.

Kombu-samambe, コムブサマムベ, タカノハカレイ. *n.* *Platichthys stellatus. Pallas*.

Komeshpa, コメシバ, 切リ落ス(複數). *v.t.* (*pl*). To clip off.

Komesu, コメス, 切リ落ス(單數). *v.t.* (*sing*). To clip off.

Komge, コムゲ, 曲ゲタレ. *adj.* Bent. Twisted. Contracted. Concave. **Syn : Reuge.**

Komge-kani, コムゲカニ, 緊釘(カスガヒ). *n.* A clamp.

Komgep, コムゲブ, 曲リタルモノ. *n.* Something bent, or twisted.

Komgep-makiri, コムゲブマキリ, (彫刻用ノ)小刀. *n.* A knife used for carving.

Komkomse, コムコムセ, 縮レタル、荒キ. *adj.* Curled. Rough. **Syn : Chiukonoyenoye.**

Kom-ni, コムニ, カシハ. *n.* Oak. *Quercus dentata, Th.* **Syn : Tunni.**

Kom-ni-karush, コムニカルシ, シヒタケ. *n.* *Lepiota sp.*

Komo, コモ, 引キ入ル、緊迫スル、撚レタレ. *v.t.* To draw in. To compress. Also, distorted. Twisted.

Komna, コムナ, 曲ゲル、捻ル. *adj.* Winding. Twisted. Entangled. Crooked. Gnarled.

Komomse, コモムセ, 押シ合ヒ、痙攣スレ. *v.i.* To be cramped. Drawn.

Komon, コモン, 塵埃. *n.* Dirt. Refuse. Dust. As :— *Chacha komon,* " saw-dust."

Komontuchi, コモンツチ, 人魚ノ寶. *n.* Riches said to be possessed by the mermaids.

Kompo, コムポ, 昆布、コンブ. *n. Laminaria.* Seaweed.

Komrani, コムラニ, } 落葉スル. *v.i.*
Kom-tuye, コムツイェ, } To shed leaves.

Komui, コムイ, 摘ミ出ス、(頭ヨリ虱チ摘ミ出ス). *v.t.* To pick out (as lice from the head).

Komun, コムン, 塵. *n.* Litter. Dust. Dirt.

Komuye, コムイェ, 捲キ付ル. *v.t.* To bind round.

Kon, コン, 持ツ. *v.t.* To possess. To have. This word is a contraction from *koro.* It is used as the possessive pronoun "his" "your," " their etc. Thus :— *E kon reihei,* " your name." *Ku kon nishpa,* "my master." See *Koro.*

Konam, コナム, 落葉. *n.* Fallen leaves.

Ko-nan-epuni-wa-orun-ingara, コナンエプニワオルンインガラ, 厚意チ以テ見ル. *v.t.* To look upon with favour.

Konchi, コンチ, 帽子. *n.* A hat. A cap. As :— *Konchi-eush,* " to put a cap on."

Konda, コンダ, 双子. *n.* Twins. **Syn : Chieuko.**

Konda, コンダ, 樹ノ節、鹿ノ枝角. *n.* A knot in a tree. A branch in a deer's horn.

Konde, コンデ, 與フ. *v.t.* To give. **Syn : Kore.**

Kone, コネ, 壞レタレ. *adj.* Broken. Smashed.

Kongane, コンガネ, 黄金. *n.* Gold.

Kongane-ikayop, コンガネイカヨプ, 金飾ノ瓶. *n.* Quivers having gold ornamentation.

Konge-ni, コンゲニ, ツリバナ. *Evonymus oxyphyllas, Miq.*

Koni, コニ, 痛ム. To ache. To be in pain. As :— *Tui koni,* " the stomach ache." **Syn : Araka.**

Koniki, コニキ, 一所ニタヽム. *v.t.* To fold together.

Koniki, コニキ, 粉々ニ、微塵ニ. *adj.* In pieces. **Syn : Humne humne an.**

Konin, コニン, 小クナル(月ノ如). *v.i.* To wane as the moon.

Koninka, コニンカ, 減ズル. *v.t.* To make less.

Konish-oshirikonoye, コニシオシリコノイェ, 雲ニ包マル. *v.i.* To be enveloped in clouds.

Konishtapapa, コニシタパパ, 擴ル、(雲ナド). *v.i.* To spread over (as clouds over a place).

Konitata, コニタタ, 抱ク(病人ナドチ). *v.t.* To hold in the hands as a sick person.

Konitatke, コニタツケ, 連ナレ、一所ニナル. *v.i.* To be joined.

Koniwen, コニウェン, 攻撃スル. *v.t.* To rush upon. To attack. **Syn : Kopiuki.**

Koniwok, コニウォク, 卽人(狐頭ノ占ニ依ツテ斯ク定メラレタル人). *n.* The person pointed out as a culprit by augury with the fox's head.

Konkai, コンカイ, 大ナル桶. *n.* A vat. A large tub.

Konkitai-ushbe, コンキタイウシベ, 帽子ノ總(フサ). *n.* The tassel on the top of a hat.

Konkochi, コンコチ, 栓. *n.* A stopper. A cork. **Syn : Chiai.**

Konkon-upas, コンコンウパス, 大ナル雪片. *n.* Large flakes of snow.

Konkoni, コンコニ, or **Konkon, コンコン,** 羽毛、綿毛. *n.* Feathers. Down.

Konna, コンナ, ヨリ、カラ、ノ意ナレド時トシテハ反對ニ、中、中ニ、等ノ意チ示ス事アリ. *adv.* From. After. Also sometimes used in an opposite sense. In. Into. **Syn : Orun. Syn : Orowa,**

Konna, コンナ, 內側ニ、中ニ. *adv.* Inside. Into.

Konne, コンチ, 然リ、實ニ然リ. *adv.* Yes. Just so.

Konne-konne-o, コンチコンチオ, 實ニ然リ、然リ. *adv.* Just so, just so. Yes.

Konniki, コンニキ, 破レタル、裂ケタル、(或レ木ノ大ナル葉ノ如). *adj.* Tattered. Torn (as the large leaves of some plants and trees. In pieces. Ragged. Jagged. As : —Otu konniki orekonniki orange-range, " to hang down in tatters." **Syn : Nikihi.**

Konru, コンル, 氷. *n.* Ice. **Syn : Apu.**

Kon-rusui, コンルスイ, 望ム、持タント願フ. *v.t.* To wish for. To desire to have.

Kontukai, コンツカイ, 小使. *n.* A public servant in rank next below the third or lowest · chief of a village. The three titles of the chiefs were-*So-ottena*, the head chief ; *ottena*, the second or ordinary chief ; and *so-kontukai*, the third or lowest chief. The *kontukai* ranked below these three dignitaries. (Of Japanese origin).

Konu-ewen, コヌエウエン, 誤解スル、能ク聞カズシテ分ラヌ. *v.t.* To misunderstand. Not to hear perfectly. To ˌbe unable to understand through having heard imperfectly.

Konukara, コヌカラ, 比ベル. *v.t.* To compare.

Konukoshne, コヌコシチ, 憎ム. *v.t.* To hate. To be angry with.

Konumbara-sange, コヌムバラサンゲ, 攻擊スレ. *v.t.* To attack. To fall on. As :—*Nei guru i konumbara sange nisa*, " he attacked him." **Syn : Kopiuki.**

Konumbara-sap, コヌムバラサブ, 攻擊スル(複數). *v.t.* To attack. *Pl :* of *konumbara sange.*

Konuptek, コヌブテク, 好ム. *v. t·* To like. To appreciate. To be fond of. **Syn : Konupuru.**

Konupure, コヌブレ, or **Konupuru, コヌブル,** 好ム. Same as *Konuptek.* To like.

Ko-ochiupashte, コオチウパシテ, 急ギ行ク. *v.t.* To go to in a hurry. **Syn : Chashnu no otta arapa.·**

Ko-okai, コオカイ, 集マル. *v.i.* To be together. To be congregated together. **Ko-okaire,** " to cause to congregate."

Ko-ok-turiri, コオクツリリ, 首筋チ前方ニ伸ベル(重キモノチ負ヒシ時ノ

如ク). *v.i.* To stretch the neck forward (as through carrying a heavy burden). **Syn: Okkeu turiri.**

Ko-ok-uoru-ushi, コオクオルウシ,
Ko-ok-uoru-chiure, コオクオルチウレ, 曲ッテ坐ル. *v.i.* Sitting in a bent position. **Syn: Okkeu nini.**

Koomam, コオマム, 枯葉. *n.* Dead leaves.

Ko-oman, コオマン, 行ク、交ハレ. *v.i.* To go to. To associate with.

Koomande, コオマンデ, 贈ル、與フ. *v.t.* To send to. To give.

Ko-omap, コオマブ, 愛スレ. *v.t.* To love.

Koongami, コオンガミ, 崇拜スル. *v.t.* To worship.

Ko-opsura, コオブスラ, 槍ヲ投ゲ付ケ ル. *v.t.* To cast a spear at. **Syn: Kachiu.**

Kooraoma, コオラオマ, 下ル. *v.i.* To descend.

Ko-oripak, コオリパク, 敬スレ. *v.t.* To honour. **Syn: Eoripak.**

Kooroshutke, コオロシュッケ, 諫ル、勸 メル. *v.t.* To exhort. To coax. **Syn: Onishnishi.**

Kop, コブ, 灌木ノ生ズル小丘、小山. *n.* A small hill. Also a copse.

Kopahaunu, コパハウヌ, 交際スル、物 語ル、聽聞スレ. *v.t.* To hold intercourse with. To speak of. To hear of.

Kopak, コパク, 非難スル、叱スレ. *v.t.* To blame. To scold.

Kopakbe, コパクベ, 平均スル. *v.t.* To make equal.

Kopake, コパケ, or **Kepakke, コパ ッケ,** 側ニテ. *adv.* By the side of. Near to. **Syn: Samata.**

Kopakeat, コパケアツ, 一致スレ. *v.i.* and *adj.* To agree with. Agreeable to.

Kopake-sama, コパケサマ, 迄ハ. *adv.* As far as. To. Unto. The outskirts of a place.

Kopaketa, コパケタ, or **Kopakta, コ パクタ,** 側ニテ. *adv.* By the side of. Near to. As:—*I kopaketa an na,* "it is by the side of you."

Kopakketa, コパッケタ, ニ就イテ、於 テ. *adv.* About. At. In. As: —*Onuman kopakketa ku hopuni,* "I shall start in the evening."

Kopaktuye, コパクツイェ, 近ヅクチ望 ム. *v.t.* To desire to go near. **Syn: Samketa oman rusui.**

Kopan, コパン, or **Kochan, コチャ ン,** 嫌フ、憎ム. *v.t.* To dislike. To abhor. To abominate.

Kopange, コパンゲ, 嫌フ、憎ム. *v.t.* To dislike. To abhor. To abominate.

Kopante, コパンテ, 嫌ハシム、憎マシ ム. *v.t.* To cause another to dislike.

Kopao, コパオ, 叱スレ. *v.t.* To scold. To chide.

Kopashirota, コパシロタ, 叱スル、怒 鳴ル. *v.t.* To scold. To storm at. To speak angrily to. To recite the evil deeds of another. **Syn: Kopao.**

Kopecha, コペチャ, or **Kopetcha, コ ペッチャ,** 鴨ノ總稱. *n.* A wild duck. This word was formerly applied to tame or domesticated as well as to wild ducks, but for tame ducks the Japanese word *ahiru* has now been adopted.

Kopenram-turi, コペンラムツリ, 鵄首スル、首ヲ差伸シブ. *v.i.* To stretch out the neck.

Kopiubapiuba, コピウバピウバ, 驅ヒ、逐フ. *v.t.* To drive. To chase.

Kopiuki, コピウキ, 攻撃スレ. *v.t.* To attack. To fall upon. To rush at. **Syn : Koniwen.**

Kopiwe, コピウェ, 押ス、壓ス、垷内へ追ヒ込ム、投ゲル. *v.t.* To push. To press. To drive into a corral. To throw at. As :—*Shuma kopiwe,* " to stone." *Umma kopiwe yan,* " drive the horses into the corral."

Kopiye-kara, コピイェカラ, 投ゲル. *v. t.* To throw at. As :—*Shuma ari kopiye kara,* " to throw stones at."

Koponchi, コポンチ, 腐リシ物ノ疎キ塵. *n.* The coarse dust of decayed matter. Coarse earth dust is called *toitoi-koponchi,* and fine earth dust *toitoi-mana.*

Koponchi-mana, コポンチマナ, 腐リシ物ノ細カキ塵. *n.* The fine dust of decayed matter.

Koponchi-ne, コポンチ子, 碎ケテ塵トナレ. *v.i.* To crumble into dust.

Kopoye, コポイェ, 交ゼレ. *v.t.* To mix. To stir.

Kopoyege, コポイェゲ, 交ジル、雜ジル. *v.i.* To be mixed. To be stirred.

Koppa, コッパ, 削リ屑、木片 (コツパ). *n.* Chips. Shavings. **Syn : Chikuni ras.**

Kopuni, コプニ, 食ハセル. *v. t.* To give to eat. To offer to eat.

Kopuni, コプニ, 熊祭ノ時屠リタル熊ニ捧ゲル供物. *n.* The ceremony of offering cakes etc, to slain animals.

Kora, コラ, or **Koro, コロ,** 彼ノ、私ノ、彼ノ女ノ、彼等ノ、其ノ. *poss pro.* His. My. Her. Their. Its.

Korachi, コラチ, ノ如ク、(又思フノ意味ニモ用キラレ). *adv.* Like. As. After the same manner. In accordance with. According to. According. This word is also sometimes used with the sense of " to think." As :—*Irushka kuni ku nukara korachi,* " I thought it looked as though he was angry."

Korachi-anno, コラチアンノ, 其故ニ. *adv.* Accordingly.

Korak, コラク, 決シテ……ナラヌ. *adv.* Never. Not. As :— *Ene neika korak shomo ahi,* " it has never been so before."

Korambashinne, コラムバシン子, 交際スレ. *v.t.* To associate with. To hold communion with. **Syn : Uotta payekai.**

Koramkon, コラムコン, 乞フ. *v.t.* Same as *Koramkoro.* To ask for. To beg.

Koramkoro, コラムコロ, 乞フ. *v. t.* To beg. To ask.

Koramnukara, コラムヌカラ, 迷ハス、試ミル. *v.t.* To tempt. To allure.

Koramnukara-i, コラムヌカライ, 誘惑. *n.* Temptations. Allurements.

Koramnukarape, コラムヌカラペ, 誘惑者. *n.* A tempter.

Korampoktuye, コラムポクツイェ, ⎫
Koramputuye, コラムブツイェ, ⎭
賛成セヌ、省ミヌ. *v.t.* To disapprove of. To disregard. To pay no attention to. **Syn : Shomo ekottanu.**

Koramu, コラム, or **Kuramu, クラム,** 思フ、疑フ、(此語ノ前ニ「クニ」ナル語用井ラレ). *v.t.* To suspect. To think. This word is always preceded by *kuni*. As :— *Nei guru anak ne nei ambe eikka kuni koramu,* "I suspect that man of having stolen it."

Kor'an, コラン, コロ、アン、ノ略ニシテ、動詞ト共ニ用キラレ、時ハ、現在チ示ス. This word is short for *Koro an,* and is often used with verbs to express present time. **Syn : Shiri ki.**

Koraonaka-puni, コラオナカブニ, ⎫
Koranaka-puni, コラナカブニ, ⎭
立テレ. *v.i.* To be set up on end. **Syn : Epuni.**

Korara, コララ, or **Koran, コラン,** 贈ル. *v.t.* To give. To cause another to give. As :— *Kuani tambe ekorara ash na,* "I give this to you." **Syn : Koraye.**

Korara-guru, コララグル, 施與者. *n.* A giver.

Korare-guru, コラレグル, 被與者. *n.* A receiver of a present.

Koraye, コライェ, 與フ. *v.t.* To give. **Syn : Korara.**

Kore, コレ, 與フ、奥へ. *v.t.* To give. To administer. To assign.

Kore-an, コレアン, 奥へヲレシ. *adj.* Given.

Koreika, コレイカ, 讃メレ. *v.t.* To praise.

Korenna-shuye, コレンナシュイェ, 振リ廻ス. *v.t.* To shake about. **Syn : Ashuye-shuye.**

Korere, コレレ, 奥へシムレ. *v.t.* To cause another to give.

Koreuba, コレウバ, 曲ゲレ、(複數). *v.t.* To bend. (*pl*).

Korewe, コレウェ, 曲ゲレ (單數). *v.t.* To bend. (*sing*).

Korikoshma, コリコシマ, 攀ゲ登ル. *v.t.* To climb up. **Syn : Nimu.**

Korimimse, コリミムセ, 爲ス、(動詞ノ意味チ強ムルニ用ユ). *v. aux.* To do. This auxiliary intensifies the meaning of a verb. As :— *Chish korimimse,* "to cry much."

Korishpa, コリシパ, 根コギニスル. *v.t.* To root up.

Koro, コロ, 所有スル、得ル. *v.t.* To possess. To obtain. **Syn : Kot. Kotcha.**

Koro, コロ, 或ル動詞ノ前ニ「コロ」チ付スル時ハ其動詞チ副詞、又ハ副詞句ニ爲スカアリ、例セバ、「ヌコロ」聞ク間ニ、又ハ聞ク時ニ. *part.* When immediately following some verbs, *koro* has the power of turning them into adverbs or adverbial phrases. Thus :— *Nu-koro,* "whilst hearing;" or "when he heard." *Ariki-koro,* "when coming;" or when he "came."

Koro, コロ, コロコニノ略、フキ. *n.* An abbreviation of *Koroko-ni,* Petasites.

Koro, コロ, ⎫ 私ノ、君ノ、彼ノ女ノ、彼
Goro, ゴロ, ⎬ ノ、彼等ノ、我等ノ. *poss.*
Kon, コン, ⎭ *pro.* My. Your. Her.

His. Their. Our. As:—*Ku go-robe*, " my thing."   *E koro habo,* " your mother."   *Chi kon nishpa,* " our master."

Korochare, コロ チャ レ, 與フ. *v.t.* To give.

Korobe, コロへ, 所有物. *n.* Belongings.

Koroham, コロハム, フキノハ. *n.* The blade of the *Petasites.*

Koro-hine, コロヒチ, 所有セル. *adj.* Having.

Koroka, コロカ, 若シモ、ト雖、併シ. *post.* If. Although. But.

Koro-kor'an, コロコラン, 所有セル. *partic.* To be possessing.

Koroko-ni, コロコニ, フキ. *n.* *Petasites japonicus, Miq.* **Syn : Makayo.**

Koroka-omap, コロカオマプ, シロバナノエンレイサウ. *n.* *Trillium kamtschaticum, Pall.*

Korokorose, コロコロセ, 鳴ル (鈴ナドノ). *v.i.* To rattle. To jar. **Syn : Okorakorak.**

Korokorosere, コロコロセレ, 鳴ル. *v.t.* To rattle. To jar.

Koropa, コロバ, 與フ(複數). *v.t.* To bestow (*pl*),

Koropare, コロバレ, 與フ. *v.t.* To give. To bestow.

Koropok, コロポク, 下ニ. *adv.* Under. Beneath. **Syn : Choropok.**

Koropok-guru,

Koropok-un-guru, コロ ポク グル, コロポクングル,

穴居人(アイヌモ又其他ノ人モ)ノ名、此語ノ意味ハ郎チ、下ニ住フ人ノ義ナリ. *n.* The name of such people, *Ai-*

nu or others, who dwell is pits during the winter months for warmth.   *Koropok* is local for *choropok,* " under ;" " beneath " Hence the name means " pit-dwellers.

Koropokta, コロポクタ, 下. *adv.* Beneath.

Koropok-un, コロポクン, 下. *adv.* Beneath.

Koro-wa, コロワ, 所有スル、ニ依テ、チ以テ、例セバ、コロワエク、持テ來イ. *adj.* Having. By means of. With. As :— *Koro wa ek,* " bring it." *Chikuni koro wa ku raige,* " I killed it with a stick."

Koruenempa, コルエチムパ, 道ニ外レル、(複數). *v.i.* (*pl*). To turn out of a road or path. To get out of the way. **Syn : Erumakanu.**

Koruenempare, コルエチムバレ, 道チ外ス. *v.t.* To turn out of a road or path. **Syn : Erumakanure.**

Koruenene, コルエチネ, 道ニ外レル、(單數). *v.i.* (*sing*). To turn out of a road or path. **Syn : Erumakanu.**

Koruenenere, コルエチ子レ, 道チ外ス. *v.t.* To turn out of a road or path.

Kosa, コサ, カラハナサウ. *n.* Hops. The roots of hops are used by the Ainu as an article of diet. *Humulus Lupulus, L.*

Kosa-ra, コサラ, カラハナサウノ蔓. *n.* Hop-vine.

Kosakaikara, コサカイカラ, 叱スル、面責スル. *v.t.* To scold. To reprove. **Syn : Panakte.**

Kosakaiyokara, コサカイヨカラ, 面責スル、叱レ. *v.t.* To reprove. To scold.

Kosakaiyokarakara, コサカイヨカラカラ,
Kosakaiyokara-ki, コサカイヨカラキ,
非難スル、叱ル、騒ガス、争論スル. *v.t.* To scold. To reprove. To make an uproar. To rebuke. To quarrel with.

Kosamba, コサムバ, 比較スル. *v.t.* To liken.

Kosankokka-eshitchiure, コサンコッカエシッチウレ, 坐ル. *v.i.* To sit upon the knees Japanese fashion.

Kosantek, コサンテク, 粘着スル、着ク. *v.i.* To stick to. To adhere. **Syn: Kotuk.**

Kosaraye, コサライュ, 分配スル. *v.t.* To divide among others. **Syn: Usaraye.**

Kosat-nan-kapu-ukaiukai, コサツナンカプウカイウカイ, 皺寄リタル顔ヲ持ツ. *v.i.* To have a wrinkled face (as an old person).

Kosaunu, コサウヌ, 薄クスル(スープノ如ク). *v.t.* To make thin as soup. To dilute. As :—*Ruru kosaunu.* **Syn: Ko-usei.**

Koshikerana-atte, コシケラナアッテ, 見下ス. *v.i.* To look down at.

Koshikiraine, コシキライ子, 憐ム. *v.t.* To pity. **Syn: Erampoki-wen wa kore.**

Koshikiru, コシキル, 顧ル、振向ク. *v.t.* To turn round to.

Koshikkan-aine-aine-aicharara, コシッカンアイ子アイ子アイ チャララ, 瞋立顔スル. *v.i.* To look fierce. To look very angry.

Koshikkote, コシッコテ, 看守スル、熟視スル. *v.t.* To look at intently. To watch.

Koshimbu, コシムブ, or **Koshimpuk, コシムブク,** 人魚. *n.* A mermaid.

Koshimonruki, コシモンルキ, 吃ル. *v.i.* To falter in talking. To stammer.

Koshina, コシナ, or **Koshina-shina, コシナシナ,** 縛リ上ゲル、縛リ付グル. *v.t.* To tie to. To tie up.

Koshinewe, コシチウェ, 共ニ樂シム、共ニ遊ブ. *v.i.* To take pleasure with. To sport with. To play. **Syn: Tura no shinot.**

Koshini, コシニ, 浪費スル. *v.t.* To waste. As:—*Ikoro koshini,* "to waste one's goods." **Syn: Etaraka isamka. Koatcha.**

Koshinip, コシニブ, 浪費、浪費セラレシ物. *n.* Waste. A thing wasted.

Koshinnukuri, コシンヌクリ, 恐ル、恐レテ爲スチ好マヌ. *v.t.* To be afraid of. To dislike to do through fear or reverence.

Koshinniukesh, コシンニウケシ, ナスチ得ズ. *v.i.* To be incapable. To be unable to do a thing. As.—*Kishima koshimniukesh,* "to be unable to catch."

Koshipashnu, コシバシヌ, 輝ク、清澄ナレ. *adj.* and *v.i.* Bright. Clear. As:—*Shik koshipashnu,* "to have bright eyes." *Koshipashnu wakka,* "clear water." *Kando kotoro koshipashnu,* "the sky is clear." **Syn: Pekashnu.**

Koshipashnu, コシバシヌ, 惡クセラ、惡キ. *adj.* To be badly done by. Bad. **Syn: Shipashnu.**

Koshiratki, コシラツキ, 看守スル、番ス レ. *v.t.* To take care of. To watch over. To guard.

Koshirepa, コシレバ, 到着スル. *v.i.* To arrive at.

Koshiruwande, コシルワンデ, 檢査ス レ. *v.t.* To examine. **Syn : Uwande.**

Koshishirapa, コシシラバ, 爲ス. *v. aux.* To do. As :—*Chish koshishirapa,* " to cry."

Koshishuye, コシシュイェ, 搖ル、例セ バ、イタクコシシュエ、語ル時ニ身體チ 搖ル. *v.i.* To waive or sway about. As :—*Itak koshishuye,* " to sway about when talking."

Koshishuye, コシシュイェ, 搖ブレ (子供チ). *v.t.* To dandle or swing about, at a child. **Syn: Humge.**

Koshi-uturu-karire, コシウツルカリ レ, 知ラヌ振リスレ. *v.t.* To ignore. To take no notice of. **Syn : Shiramsamte.**

Koshiwiwatki, コシウェワツキ, 風ノ 吹ク音、又ハ鳥獸ノ飛ビ走ル音. *n.* The whirring sound of the wind. The sound made by birds flying or animals rushing along. *Rera pash hum koshiwiwatki,* " the sound of rushing wind."

Koshmat, コシマツ, 嫁. *n.* A daughter-in-law.

Koshmat-habo, コシマツハボ, 姑. *n.* Mother-in-law. **Syn : Iyepehabo. Iyepetoto.**

Koshne, コシチ, 輕キ. *adj.* Light.

Koshne-no-kara, コシチノカラ, 輕ク スレ. *v.t.* To lighten.

Koshui, コシュイ, 再ビ、又. *adv.* Again. **Syn : Shui.**

Koshune-kara, コシュチカラ, 照ス. *v.t.* To lighten. To show a light to. **Syn : Pekereka.**

Koshunge, コシュンゲ, 虛言スレ. *v.t.* To lie to. **Syn : Ikokandama.**

Koshuyep, コシュイェブ, Kosuwep, コスウェブ, Kusuwep, クスウェブ, Kusuyep, クスイェブ, キヂパト. *n.* A Turtle dove. *Turtur gebastis, Temm.*

Koskoso, コスコソ, Koskoso, コスコソ, コソソ, 手チ以テ重ミチ試ミレ. *v.t.* To feel the weight of anything.

Kosonde, コソンデ, 小袖. *n.* A cloak made of Japanese material.

Kosuwep, コスウェブ, Kosuyep, コスイェブ, Kusuwep, クスエブ, Kusuyep, クスイェブ, キヂパト. *n.* Turtle dove.

Kot, コツ, 所有スル、(此語ハ、コロノ約 語ナリ). *v.t.* To possess. This word is a contraction of *koro.* As :— *Ku kot chisei,* " my house."

Kot, コツ, Kot-ne-hi, コツチヒ, 堀、小谷、孔. *n.* A dip in the ground. A small valley. Also, a ditch. A grave. A hole. A dyke.

Kot, コツ, 墓(人又ハ他ノ者ノ葬ラレシ 所). *n.* A grave. **Syn : Tushirikot. Iyurui-kot. Ashitoma-i.**

Kot, コツ, 宅地. *n.* A house plot. **Syn : Kotchi. Kochi.**

Kotama, コタマ, 共ニ. *adv.* Together. With. Augmented. **Syn: Aukotama.**

Kotamge, コタムゲ, 凡テ. *adj.* Altogether.

Kotan, コタン, 村、所、市、例セバ、コタ ンブリ、所ノ風俗. *n.* A village. A place. A city. A town. As:— *Kotan buri,* "the customs of a place." *Kotan kara Kamui,* "the Creator." *Kotan ekari guru, kotan shaot guru,* "a fugitive." *Kotan koro sapo moshiri koro sapo,* "the name of the morning star, considered to be a goddess." *Kotan pa,* "the east end of a town or village." *Kotan gesh,* "the west end of a town, village, or place." *Kotan tek* "the district round a village." *Kotan ukoturuge,* "the borders of a village or district." *Kotan un utara,* "the inhabitants of a place."

Kotan - shitchire-moshiri-shitchire, コタンシッチレモシリシッチレ, 九 耶列官源ノ義經ノ名. *n.* A name sometimes given to Okikurumi or Kurō-hangwan Minamoto no Yoshitsune.

Kotan-shitchire-moshiri-shitchire-pon-oibepi-poro, コタンシッチ レモシリシッチレポンオイ ヘ ビポ ロ, 辨慶ノ名. *n.* A name sometimes given to Wariune kuru, the henchman of Kurohongwan Minamoto no Yoshitsune.

Kotan-uni, コタンウニ, 酋長ノ小舎. *n.* The chief hut in a village.

Kotanu-shaot-guru, コタヌシャオツ グル, 脱走者、浪人. *n.* A fugitive.

One who runs away from his village.

Kotcha, コッチャ, 持ツ、(複数). *v.t.* To possess. *Pl of koro.*

Kotcha, コッチャ, 前. *post.* Before. In front of. Ahead.

Kotchake, コッチャケ, 前. *post.* In front of. Ahead.

Kotchaketa, コッチャケタ, 前. *post.* In front of. Before.

Kotchaketa-shiri, コッチャケタシリ,
Kotchaketa-shirihine, コッチャケタシリヒ子,
他人ノ爲ニスレ. *v.t.* To do for another.

Kotchaot, コッチャオツ, 前、前面. *post.* Before. In front of. **Syn: Ratchaot.**

Kotchaot-guru, コッチャオツグル, 前 驅者、豫報者. *n.* A fore-runner. **Syn: Ratchaot guru.**

Kotchapa, コッチャパ, 前、前面. *post.* To front. Ahead.

Kotchi, コッチ, 場所、穴、葬ル所. *n.* A plot of land. A grave. A hole. Site.

Kote, コテ, 縛ル、結ビ合ス. *v.t.* To tie up with anything. To tie on to. As:—*Tush-kote,* "to tie up with a rope."

Kotekot, コテコツ, 度々氣絕スル. *v.i.* To faint repeatedly. To become repeatedly unconscious. **Syn: Ekotokot.**

Kotekramyupu, コテクラムユブ, シ ガミ著ク. *v.t.* To cling to. **Syn: Tekramyupu. Eyupkekishina.**

Ko-tereke, コテレケ, 火ガツク、飛ビ付ク. *v.t.* To jump to. To catch as fire. As:—*Abe-nui kotereke* "to catch fire."

Kotereke-tereke, コテレケテレケ, 飛ビ付ク、飛ビ移ル. *v.t.* To jump to. To leap to as fire from house to house in a conflagration.

Kotki, コツキ, 他人ヲ戒ムル為ニ無罪ノ者ヲ罰スル. *v.t.* To punish an innocent person in order to warn others. *See Ikotke.*

Kotne, コツ子, 凹イ. *adj.* Depressed. Hollow.

Kotne-hi, コツ子ヒ, 壕、凹地. *n.* A ditch. A hollow place. A depression in the earth.

Koto, コト, 琴. *n.* A harp. (*Jap*).

Kotoise, コトイセ, 集合スル. *v.i.* To congregate. To come together. **Syn: Kokararase. Uwekarapa.**

Kotom, コトム, 美シキ. *adj.* Pretty. Good-looking. **Syn : Tomte.**

Kotomaan, 明カ=. *adv. and v.i.* **コトマアン, Kotomnan, コトマン,** Apparently. To appear to be. As:—*Seta kotom an ruwe ne,* "it is apparently a dog."

Kotom-no, コトムノ, 美事=. *adv.* Prettily. Beautifully. **Syn : Tomte no.**

Kotoro, コトロ, 側、物ノ堺. *n.* The sides of anything. A boundary. As:—*Nai-kotoro,* "the sides of a stream" or "glen." *Nupuri kotoro,* "the sides of a mountain."

Kotorush-ni, コトルシニ, コシアブラ. *n.* Name of a tree.

Acanthopanax sciadophylloides, Fr. et Sav.

Kotpara, コツパラ, 首環、襟. *n.* A collar.

Kotpara, コツパラ, 胸. *n.* The chest. The bosom. **Syn : Penram.**

Kotpoketa, 前. *adv.* Before. As:— **コツポケタ, Kotpokita, コツポキタ,** *Nei guru un kotpoketa shirepa nisa ruwe ne,* "he arrived there before us."

Kotpokiketa, コツポキケタ, 前. *adv.* Before. Same as *Kotpoketa.*

Kotuikosama, コツイコサマ, 下ル、降ル、(單數). *v.i.* (*sing*). To come down. To descend. **Syn: Ran.**

Kotuikosamba, コツイコサムバ, 下ル、降ル、(複數). *v.i.* (*pl*). To come down. To descend. **Syn: Rap.**

Kotuikosanu, コツイコサヌ, 下ル、降ル. *v.i.* To come down. Same as *Kotuikosama.*

Kotuituige, コツイツイゲ, 發スレ、陰顯スル. *v.i.* To issue. To come out. To give forth. To appear and disappear at intervals. As:—*Erum anak ne shui orowa etuhu kotuituige,* "the rat pops its head in and out of its hole."

Kotuk, コツク, 粘着スレ、着ク. *v.i.* To adhere. To stick to. **Syn : Kosantek.**

Kotuk-wa, コツクワ, 粘氣アレ. *adj.* Adhesive.

Kotukka, コツッカ, 附着サセレ. *v.t.* To stick on. To agglutinate.

Kotuk-kotuk, コツクコツク, 附着シ易キ. *adj.* Sticky. Agglutinative.

Kotumi, コツミ, 戰、軍、イクサ. *n.* A fight. A war.

Kotumi-koro, コツミコロ, 戰フ. *v.t.*
To war with. To fight. To
give battle.

Koturuse, コツルセ, 傳染スレ. *v.t.*
To catch as a disease. To pass
from one to another as a disease.

Kotushmak, コツシマク, 暗殺スル、殺
ス. *v.t.* To assassinate. To kill.

Kotushtek-no, コツシテクノ, 急ギテ、
嚴格ニ. *adv.* In haste. With
severity. Hurriedly. As:—*Ko-
tushtek no ki,* "to do in haste."

Kotususatki, コツススサツキ,
Kutususatki, クツススサツキ, 震フ、戰慄スレ. *v.i.*
To trouble. To
shake. To quiver.

Kotusuyupu, コツスユプ, 力ノ限リチ
出シテスル. *v.t.* To do with all
one's might. To put forth all
one's power. **Syn: Kiroro yupu
wa ki.**

Kotuwatuwak, コツワツワク, 疥癬チ
生ウタル、瘦セタレ、柔キ. *adj.*
Mangy. Thin. Poor. Soft.

Kotuyashi, コツヤシ, 保ツ、家族ノ中
ニ保存スル. *v.t.* To hold. To keep
in one's family. To hand down
in the same family.

Ko-uainukoro, コウアイヌコロ, 敬ス
ル、崇ムル. *v.t.* To honour. To
treat with respect. **Syn: Eoripak.**

Kouk, コウク, 取ル、例セバ、ネイイチ
エンアエンコウク、其錢ハ私カラ取ツ
タノデス. *v.t.* To take from. As:—
Nei ichen a en kouk, "the money
was taken from me."

Koumam, コウマム,
Koomam, コオマム, 朽葉(クチバ)、枯葉(カレ
ハ). *n.* Dead leaves.
Decaying leaves.

Kourepuni, コウレプニ, 步ム. *v.i.*
To walk. **Syn: Apkash.**

Ko-usei, コウセイ, 薄クスル、(スープ
ノ如ク). *v.t.* To make thin as
soup. As:—*Ruru kousei,* "to
make soup thin."

Kouwekari, コウウェカリ, 集マレ. *v.i.*
To assemble. **Syn: Uwekarapa.**

Kouwekarire, コウウェカリレ, 集ムル. *v.i.*
To assemble.

Kowen, コウェン, 憎ム、嫌フ. *v.t.* To
hate. To dislike. To abbor.
To abominate. **Syn: Etunne.**

**Koyaikeutum-ochitchiure, コヤイ
ケウツムオチッチウレ,** 自制スレ、心ニ
銘スル. *v.i.* To keep ones'self in.
To hold ones'self in. To restrain
ones'self. To hold fast in the
heart or mind.

Koyaikush, コヤイクシ, 出來兼ル、拙
實ナレ. *v.i. and adj.* To be unable to do. Unskilful. Awkward.
Impossible. As:—*Mokoro koyaikush,* "to be unable to sleep."
Syn: Kara eaikap. Eaikap.

Koyaimonakte, コヤイモナクテ, 睡
ラレヌ、(激昂ノ爲). *v.i.* To be
unable to sleep through excitement.

Koyainurat, コヤイヌラツ, 睡度キ.
v.i. To be sleepy. **Syn: Mokon
rusui.**

Koyainurattet, コヤイヌラッテツ,
睡メキ. *v.i.* Sleepy. **Syn: Mokon
rusui.**

Koyainutumu, コヤイヌツム, 人事不
省ニナル、忘レル. *v.i.* To become
unconscious. To forget. **Syn:
Ramu-unun.**

Koyairamkikkara, コヤイラムキッカラ, 能力ナキ為メ事ヲ中止スレ. *v.i.* To cease through inability to do a thing. To be incapable. To be unable. As:—*Kishima koyairamkikkara*, "to be unable to catch." **Syn: Koshinniukesh.**

Koyaisanasange, コヤイサナサンゲ, 傍ニ行ク. *v.i.* To go to the side of. **Syn: Samake un arapa.**

Koyaishinire, コヤイシニレ, 退ク、休ム. *v.i.* To retire. To rest. To withdraw as from business or war. **Syn: Eshini.**

Koyakoya, コヤコヤ, 掻キ廻ス. *v.t.* To stir up. To shake up.

Koyakkoyak, コヤッコヤク, Koyakoyak, コヤコヤク, 掻キ廻ェ. *v.t.* To stir up. To shake up. **Syn: Chiukopoyere. Eko-irakkoirak.**

Koyan-chep, コヤンチェブ, 鰤、ブリ. *n. Yellow tail. Seriola quinqueradiata, J. & S.*

Koyapkiri, コヤブキリ, 投ゲル. *v.t.* To throw at.

Koyaspa, コヤスパ, 裂キ取ル. *v.t.* To tear from.

Ko-ye, コイェ, 知ラセレ. *v.t.* To say to. To tell.

Ko-ye-ap, コイェアブ, 彼ニ語リシ事. *ph.* That which was said to him. **Syn: Otta aye ambe.**

Koyome, コヨメ, 暦. *n.* An almanac. *(Jap).*

Koyupke, コユブケ, 強キ. *adj.* Strong. Firm.

Koyuptektek, コユブテクテク, 活潑ナル、勉強ナレ、勉強スレ. *v.i. and adj.* To be active. Industrious.

To be industrious. **Syn: Yuptek. Niwashnu.**

Ku, ク, 飲ム、喫煙スル. *v.t.* To drink. To smoke.

Ku, ク, 私、(名詞ノ前ニ附ク時ニハ私ノ). *pro.* I. When used before nouns, "my."

Ku, ク, 弓、例セバ、クカ、弦. *n.* A bow. As:—*Ku ka*, "a bow string." *Ku mun noshike*, "the middle of a bow." *Ku pita*, "to unstring a bow."

Kuama-ku, クアマク, 弩. *n.* A spring-bow. **Syn: Kuare-ku. Chare-ku. Chama-ku.**

Kuani, クアニ, 私、(動詞ノ前ニテハ k. 又ハ ku). *pro.* I. Before verbs *k* or *ku*.

Kuani-yaikota, クアニヤイコタ, 私、私自身. *pro.* I. Myself.

Kuare, クアレ, 弩ヲ仕掛ル. *v.t.* To set a spring bow.

Kuare-ku, クアレク, 弩. *n.* A spring bow. **Syn: Chiare-ku, Chama-ku.**

Kuba, クバ, 噛ム (單數). *v.t. (sing).* To bite. To hold with the teeth.

Kubaba, クバパ, 噛ム、(複數). *v.t. (pl).* To bite. To hold with the teeth. **Syn: Shirikuba. Ikuba. Chikubaba.**

Kucha, クチャ, Kuchachisei, クチャチセイ, Kuchanchisei, クチャンチセイ, 獵小舎、漁舎. *n.* A hunter's or fisherman's lodge. A lodging place.

Kucha-kotchisei, クチャコッチセイ, 獵小舎. *n.* A hunter's lodge.

Kuchan, クチャン, 牝熊. *n.* A she-bear.

Kuchihi, クチヒ, 帯. *n.* A band. A belt.

Kuchikanna, クチカンナ, 饒舌ナレ、多辯ナル、不誠實ナレ. *adj.* Talkative. Insincere. To talk big. Impure. Deceitful. Naughty. Fickle. **Syn: Iyukoikire.**

**Kuchi-momne-samambe,
       クチモム子サマムベ,
Kichi-momne-samambe,
       キチモム子サマムベ,**
マガレイ. *n.* A kind of flounder. *Limanda yokohamœ, Gthr.*

Kuchishikiru. クチシキル, 浮氣ナレ、變リ易キ. *adj.* Fickle. Changeable. **Syn: Kuchikanna.**

Kuchiwa, クチワ, 轡. *n.* A horse's bit. (*Jap*).

**Kugoro,
  クゴロ,
Kukot,
  クコツ,** 私ノ. *pro. per.* My. Mine.

Kui, クイ, シコタンマツ、ゲイマツ. *n.* The kurile larch. *Larix dahurica, Turcz, var. japonica, Max.*

Kuikui, クイクイ, シキ類ノ總稱. *n.* A curlew. A sandpiper. Snipe.

Kuikui, クイクイ, 噛ム. *v.t.* To gnaw.

Kukerekep-ni, クケ レケプニ, . *n.* Same as *Nipesh-ni.*

Kui-karush, クイカルシ, エブリコ. *n.* *Polyporus officinalis, Fr.* **Syn: Shui-karush.**

Kuira, クイラ, 潜シテ行ク. *v.i.* To go along stealthily. To steal up to. *Kuira wa oman chiki yuk raige eashkai nangoro,* "if you go along stealthily you may kill a deer." **Syn: Ipikuira.**

**Kuito,
  クイト,
Kuitop,
  クイトプ,** 雁、ガン. *n.* Wild geese.

Kuitop-kina, クイトプキナ, ヒメ クヮンザウ. *n.* Day lily. *Hemerocallis Dumortieri, Morr.*

Kukeu-pone, クケウポ子, 肩胛骨. *n.* The shoulder-blade.

Kukewe, クケウェ, 肩、(特ニ肩ノ前部). *n.* The shoulders, especially the fore-part. *Clavicula.*

**Kukka,
  クッカ,
Kupka,
  クプカ,** 鶴嘴. *n.* A mattock.

Kuma, クマ, *n.* A deep roaring sound.

Kuma, クマ, 物乾竿. *n.* A pole for drying clothes upon.

Kumadaki, クマダキ, 妹. *n.* A younger sister. **Syn: Turesh. Mataki. Machiribe.**

Kumane, クマ子, 連山ノ嶺. *n.* A ridge-like mountain top. As:— *Kumane tapkop,* "a mountain-top ridge."

Kumatai, クマタイ, 物干竿、(複數). *n.* (*pl*). Drying poles. (*Sing*). *Kuma.*

Kumi, クミ, 黴(カビ). *n.* Mildew.

Kumi-ush, クミウシ, 黴(カビ)ノ生エタ レ. *adj.* Mouldy. Mildewy.

Kumsei, クムセイ, 鳴ル. *v.i.* To rattle (as wind in the stomach).

Kunak, クナク, ト、例セバ、アラパクナ クイェ、行クト云ヒマス. *pro.* That. Thus:— *Arapa kunak ye,* "he says that he will go." *Heikachi tane ek kunak ye,* "the lad says that he will come now." **Syn: Sekoro. Ani. Ari.**

**Kunau-nonno, クナウノンノ, フクジ
ユサウ.** *n.* *Adonis amurensis,
Regel et Radd.*

Kunchiru, クンチル, 大道、公道. *n.*
A broad road. A broad highway.

**Kunda, クンダ, 鞦(シリガヒ)ニ付ケタ
ル木製ノ輪.** *n.* The reels on a
crupper.

Kungashi, クンガシ, 日本製ノ小舟. *n.*
A small boat of Japanese make.

Kungi, クンギ, 釘. *n.* A nail (*Jap*).

**Kuni, クニ, 爲、ノ爲ニ、例セバ、クク
クニタムバコ、我喫スル爲ノ烟草.** *post.*
For. In order that. That. In
order to. Probably. As :—*Ku ku
kuni tambako*, "the tobacco for
me to smoke.' *Nishatta oman
kuni ku ramu*, "I think that he
will go to-morrow." *Ye kuni ku
ek ruwe ne*, "I have come in
order to tell you." *E an kuni
chisei*, "a house for you to live
in." *Ek kuni tere*, "wait for
him to come."

Kuni-gusu, クニグス, ノ爲ニ. *post.*
For. In order to. For purpose
of.

**Kuni-ne, クニネ, ノ爲メニ、又爲、ヤウ
ニ、例セバ、ショモソユムバクニネク
カラ、私ハソレが出ナイヤウニ致シマ
ス.** *post.* In order that. In order
to. So that. For the purpose
of. As :—*Shomo soyumba kuni
ne ku kara*, "I will make it so
that they cannot get out." *Iteki
homatu kuni ne kara yan*, "do it
so as not to frighten him."

**Kunipe-koro-yainu,
クニペコロヤイヌ,
Kunibe-koroyainu,
クニペコロヤイヌ,** 預期スル. *v.t.*
To antici-
pate. To

expect. **Syn : An kusu ne ari
yainu.**

Kunip, クニプ, 義務. *n.* Duty.
This word expresses duty or need
or purpose. As :—*Ki kunip*,
"that which one ought to do."

Kunkashi, クンカシ, 日本製ノ小舟. *n.*
A Japanese boat. **Syn : Mochip.**

Kunna, クンナ, 黒キ. *adj.* Black.
Dark.

Kunnatara, クンナタラ, 黒キ. *adj.*
Black. Dark. **Syn : Ekureok.**

Kunne, クンネ, 黒キ. *adj.* Black.
Dark. As :—*Kunne shiriki-o*
"having black patterns."

Kunne-chup, クンネチュプ, 月. *n.*
The moon.

**Kunne-echinge, クンネエチンゲ, ア
オウミカメ.** *n.* Green turtle.
Chelonia viridis, T. & S.

**Kunne-emaure, クンネエマウレ, ク
ロイチゴ.** *n.* *Rubus occidentalis,
L. var. japonicus, Miyabe.*

Kunne-i, クンネイ, 黒色、暗黒、暗處.
n. Blackness. Darkness. A
dark place.

Kunne-ibe, クンネイベ, 夕食. *n.* Supper. The evening meal.

Kunneiwano, クンネイワノ, 朝. *adv.*
Morning.

**Kunneiwano-ibe, クンネイワノイベ,
朝飯.** *n.* Breakfast. The morning
meal.

**Kunne-kina-emauri, クンネキナイ
マウリ, エンレイサウ.** *n.* *Trillium.
Smallii, Max.*

Kunne-mata, クンネマタ, 仲冬. *n.*
Mid-winter.

Kunne-nino, クンネニノ, ノナ. *n.*
The sea-urchin.

Kunne-nishat, クンチニシャツ, 朝マ
ダキ、早昧. *adj.* Very early morning.

Kunne-no-kara, クンチノカラ, 黒ク
スレ、悪口ス、レ. *v.t.* To blacken.
To slander.

Kunnep, クンチプ, 黒染ノアツシ、黒色
ノ物. *n.* Attush dyed black.
Anything black.

**Kunne-reushi-oman, クンチレウシ
オマン,** 休息セズニ夜行スル. *adv.* To
travel all night without stopping
for rest.

Kunne-shiknum, クンチシクヌム, 瞳.
n. The pupil of the eye.

Kunne-soi, クンチソイ, クロツイ. *n.*
Sebastodes Schlegeli, (*Hilgd*).

Kunne-tamhere, クンチタムヘレ, 稲
妻. *n.* Lightning. **Syn: Imeru.**

Kunne-to, クンチト, 夜. *n.* Night.

Kunne-tom, クンチトム, 黒色ナル.
adj. Of a black colour.

Kunneyot, クンチヨツ, 眩ズル (暗ノ為
ニ). *v.t.* To be blinded by darkness.

Kunnu, クンヌ, 黒キ. *adj.* Black.
Syn: Ekureok.

Kunnu-itak, クンヌイタク, 宜敷カラ
ザル話. *n.* A curse.

Kuntukapap, クンツカパプ, 海魚ノ一
種ニテ角アリテ扁平ナルモノナ
リト云ヒ傳ヘ漁夫等ノ最モ恐レ
ヽモノナリ. *n.* A kind of flat
salt-water fish said by some to
have horns, and of which the
Ainu fishermen are extremely
afraid. Probably devil-fish.

Kupka, クブカ, Kukka, クッカ, 大ナル鍬嘴. *n.* A large
mattock. As:—*Kupka
nichi,* "the handle of a
mattock."

Kure, クレ, 飲マセル. *v.t.* To give
to drink.

Kureanda, クレアンダ, Kureande, クレアンデ, 誹ル、嘲ル. *v.t.* To
laugh at. To deride.
**Syn: Eoya itak
ki.**

Kuri, クリ, 雲. *n.* A cloud. **Syn:
Nishkuru.**

Kuri, クリ, Kurihi, クリヒ, 陰. *n.* A shadow.

Kurimukere, クリムケレ, Kurimukhere, クリムクヘレ, 隠ス、捨テル. *v.t.*
To hide. To do
away with. To
make away with. As:—*To-an
raitush tunashimo kurimukere yan,*
"make haste and hide the cord
with which he hung himself."

Kurimukmuke, クリムクムケ, 隠ス.
v.t. To hide away.

Kurimonto, クリモント, 沼地. *n.* A
bog.

Kurinin, クリニン, 逃ル. *v.t.* To
escape. To run away. **Syn:
Chopiat.**

Kurokok, クロコク, 暗黒、黒色. *n.*
Blackness. Darkness.

Kurokok-buri, クロコクブリ, 悪事、罪.
n. Bad deeds. Sins.

Kuroma, クロマ, 腸. *n.* The bowels.
Syn: Serima.

Kuroma-kokuruse, クロマコクルセ,
迷ハス. *v.i.* To be confounded.

**Kuroma-keutumkoro, クロマケウト
ムコロ,** 不愉快ナル. *v.i.* To be
disagreeable.

Kuroro, クロロ, ニテ. *adv.* Through.
By. As:—*Ainu kuroro akoyayo-*

mokte, kamui kuroro akoyayomokte, "he was troubled both by men and gods."

Kuroro, クロロ, 要素、意志、心. *n.* Essence. Will. Heart. Mind. *Kamui kuroro akooripak kunip ne,* "the will of the gods is to be respected."

Kuru, クル, Guru, グル, Gur, グル, 人、者、鳥獣無生物ニモ應用セラル、例セバ、タンチカブアナクネソンノアオシクルネ、此鳥ハ大層欲シガラレマス. *n.* A person. This word is also sometimes applied to animals, fowls or inanimate objects. As:—*Tan chikap anak ne son no aosh guru ne,* "these fowls are very much sought after," or "prized."

Kuru, クル, 陰雲. *n.* A shadow. Shade. A cloud. **Syn: Kurihi.** Sempirike.

Kuru, クル, 近ク. *v.i.* To draw near. As:—*Abe kuru,* "to draw near to a fire."

Kuruise. クルイセ, 鳥ノ一種. *n.* A kind of bird.

Kuruka. クルカ, 上、上ニ. *adv.* Above. Upon. As:—*Wakka kuruka,* "upon the water." **Syn: Kashiketa.**

Kurukashi, クルカシ, 物ノ上面、上ニ. *n. and adv.* The upper surface of anything. Upon. On the top of.

Kurukashike, クルカシケ, 上ニ、頂ニ. *adv.* Upon. On the top of. As:—*Set kurukashike osoroushi,* "to sit upon a chair."

Kurukashike-aukomomse, クルカ

シケアウコモムセ, 其他ニ、ソレカラ. *adv.* Besides which. Upon which.

Kuruka-shikama, クルカシカマ, 惠ム、守ル. *v.t.* To bless. To be kind to. To preserve.

Kuruki, クルキ, 鰓. *n.* The gills of fish. The region of the tonsils.

Kurukituk, クルキツク, 喉ニ於ケル潰瘍. *n.* An abscess in the throat.

Kuruko-hopuni, クルコホプニ, 氣絶ス. *v.i.* To faint. To lose consciousness.

Kurukokonna-shiknatara, クルコ コンナシクナタラ, ウツ・ニナレ. *v.i.* To fall into a trance.

Kurukush, クルクシ, 痙攣ス. *v.i.* To twitch.

Kuruman, クルマン, 陰. *n.* A shadow. **Syn: Kuruhi.**

Kurumat, クルマツ, 日本婦人. *n.* A Japanese woman.

Kurumi, クルミ, 日本男子. *n.* A Japanese man.

Kurun-kane, クルンカ子, 薄黒キ. *adv.* Slightly darkened as one's skin with newly growing whiskers. As:—*Kurun-kane an ainu,* "a young man."

Kurunni, クルンニ, ドロ、デロ. *n.* Balsam poplar. *Populus suaveolens, Fisch.*

Kuruppe, クルッペ, 白霜. *n.* The white frost.

Kuruppe-chiai, クルッペチアイ, 白霜ノ片. *n.* Flakes of white frost.

Kuruppe-an, クルッペアン, 霜降ル. *v.i.* To freeze as in a white frost. To rime.

Kurushut, クルシュツ, Kurushutuhu, クルシュツフ, 草木ノ幹. *n.* The stems of weeds and trees.

Kusa, クサ, Kusaha, クサハ, 渡船スレ. *v.i.* To ferry across a river. As:— *Echi kusa shisam mochip o wa ek kor' an,* "the Japanese is coming in a rowboat to ferry you across."

Kusan, クサン, 驚テ示ス聲. *exclam.* Exclamation of surprise. Oh. Oh dear. Dear me. Thus:— *Kusan, nep poro erum ku raige,* "dear me, what a large rat I killed."

Kush, クシ, 栗ノ殻. *n.* Shells or burs of chestnuts. **Syn: Push.**

Kush, クシ, 渡ル、横切レ. *v.t.* To pass over. To cross. To cross as a river. To traverse. As:— *Kush wa oman,* "to walk across." *Kush wa omande,* "to send across.',

Kushkerai, クシケライ, 故ニ、御蔭テ. *adv.* Owing to. By the favour of.

Kushketa, クシケタ, 向フ. *adv.* Beyond.

Kushki, クシキ, 為サレトス、成ラントス. *part,* About to be or do.

Kushna, クシナ, 通シテ、例セバ、クシナエタエ、通シテ引ク. *adv.* Through. As:—*Kushna etaye,* "to draw through." *Kamui anak ne chikoro keutum kushna nukara,* "God sees through our hearts." *Kushna otke,* "to pierce through."

Kushnare, クシナレ, 突貫ス. *v.t.* To thrust through.

Kushne-no, クシチノ, 通シテ. *adv.* Through.

Kushta, クシタ, 彼方、向フ. *adv.* Yonder. Beyond. **Syn: Okushun.**

Kushte, クシテ, 伸バス、(馬ニ乗ル時ノ足ノ如ク). *v.t.* To stretch out as the legs in sitting astride a horse. To stretch over. To cross over.

Kusu or gusu, クス, 又ハ **グス,** 故ニ、為ニ、例セバ、ワツカタグス.オマン、水クム為ニ行ケリ. *post.* Because. As:—To. In order to. For. For as much as. As:—*Wakka ta gusu oman,* "he has gone to draw water." *Nu gusu ku ek,* "I have come in order to hear." This word also expresses the idea that a thing ought to be done. As:—*Ki kusu ne ap,* "he ought to have done it." *Ingara gusu,* "in order to look." *Kusu an orushpe,* "tidings of."

Kusu-eun, クスエウン, 幸ニシテ. *adv.* Fortunately. As:—*Kusu eun ku uk,* "fortunately I got it."

Kusu-ne, クスネ, 未來ヲ指ス詞. *part.* The sign of future time. As:— *Ku ek kusu ne,* "I shall come." *Kusu ne gusu,* "as it is about to be."

Kusuri, クスリ, 温泉、藥. *n.* Hot springs. Medicine.

Kusuwep, クスウェプ, Kusuyep, クスイェプ, Kosuwep, コスウェプ, Kosuyep, コスイェプ, キジバト. *n.* Turtle dove. *Turtur orientalis, Lath.*

Kut, クツ, 喉. *n.* The throat. As:—*Kut makela mina,* "he laughs in his throat."

Kut, クツ, 帶. *n.* A girdle. A waistband. As:—*Kut koro,* "to fasten one's waistband." *Kut-nokte*, " to buckle one's belt."

Kut, クツ, or **Kute, クテ,** 岩、断崖. *n.* Crags. Rugged places. Cross valleys. As :— *Range kut*, " crags which hang downwards." *Rikun kut*, " crags which point upwards.

Kuta, クタ, 醗ス、棄テル. *v.t.* To spill. To throw away. To upset. As :—*Nani puyara kari kuta*, " he threw it straight out of the window." *Tope ehok guru rupush shiri kata oshittesu wa hachiri, orowa, tope kuta*, " the milkman slipped upon the frozen earth and spilt the milk."

Kutapa, クタパ, 醗ス、覆ス(複數). *v.t.* (*pl*). To spill. To upset.

Kutcham, クノチャム, or **Kutcha-ma, クッチャマ,** 喉頭、語ノ發音、方言. *n.* The top of the throat. The pronounciation of a word. A dialect. As :—*Shine kutcham koro*, " to pronounce or speak in the same way." *Kutcham pirika*, " to speak clearly." *Kutcham wen*, " to speak hoarsely."

Kutcharo, クッチャロ, 喉頭. *n.* The same as *kutcham*.

Kutchi, クッチ, 喉. *n.* The throat.

Kutchi, クッチ, コクヮ、サルナシ實ノ. *n.* The fruit of the *Actinidia arguta, Planch*. This fruit is eaten by the Ainu, and is greatly relished by bears.

Kutchi-hayaisei, クッチハヤイセイ, 人ノ死セントスル時、喉ノ鳴ル事. *n.* The death rattle.

Kutchike. クッチケ, 陰莖. *n.* The penis. **Syn : Iyomai.**

Kutchi-pungara, クッチブンガラ, コクヮ、サルナシ. *n.* *Actinidia arguta, Planch.*

Kutchi-tui, クッチツイ, 断崖. *n.* Crags. Rugged places. **Syn : Kut.**

Kutchup, クッチュプ, 帶ヲ織ルニ用ュル小木片. *n.* A small piece of wood used for weaving girdles.

Kute, クテ, 断崖. *n.* Crags. See *Kut*.

Kuteai, クテアイ, 坐ス. *v.i.* To sit. **Syn : A.**

Kutek, クテク, 獣ヲ罠ニ導ク爲ノ園、又鳥ノ罠. *n.* A kind of fence made for the purpose of leading animals into snares. Also a snare to catch birds.

Kutkamakap, クッカマカプ, 帶ヲ織ル小サキ機. *n.* A small loom used for weaving girdles.

Kutkan, クッカン, 喉ヲ刺激スル. *v.i.* To have an irritation in the throat. **Syn : Kutpishishi.**

Kutkesh, クツケシ, 喉. *n.* The throat. As :—*Kutkesh ka makaraye*, " to clear the throat (so as to let the inmates of a house know when one is at hand).

Kutkoro, クツコロ, 帶スル. *v.i.* To gird. To fasten one's girdle on.

Kut-koro-kamui, クツコロカムイ, 断岩ノ神. *n.* The demons of crags and cross valleys.

Kutnoye, クツノイェ, 嘉セヌ. *v.t.* To look upon with disfavour. To dislike. To eschew. To disapprove. **Syn : Ekohopi. Notkush-Akopan.**

Kutpishishi, クツピシシ, 喉ヲ刺激ス
ル. *v.i.* To have an irritation in
the throat. **Syn : Kutkan.**

Kutpokechiu, クツポケチウ, 佩ケ. *v.t.*
To wear in the belt (as a sword).
To stick in the belt.

Kuttara, クッタラ, 空虚ナ レ莖. *n.*
The hollow stem of any kind of
plant.

Kuttara-amam, クッタラアマム, ウ
ラシロタデ. *n. Polygonum Weyri-
chii, Fr. Schm.*

Kutte, クッテ, 腮ヲ上ゲル. *v. i.* To
hold the chin up. To raise the
chin.

Kuttesu, クッテス, or **Kuttesuru, ク
ッテスル,** 腮ヲ上ゲル. *v.i.* To hold
the chin up. To look up.

Kuttoko, クットコ, or **Kuttoku, クッ
トコ,** 倒ニスル. *adv.* Upside down.
The wrong side up.

Kuttokoitak, クットコイタク, 囈語.
n. Wandering speech. Senseless
talk.

Kuttokoye, クットコイェ, 囈語スル. *v.t.*
To wander in one's talk. To
speak so as not to be understood.
To speak in riddles. To talk rubbish. As :—*Kuttoko aye hawe an
wa,* " he is just talking rubbish."

Kuttom, クットム, or **Kuttomo, クッ
トモ,** 喉. *n.* The pharynx.

**Kuttom-meshra-meshra, クットム
メシラメシラ,** 喉カラ高ク語ル. *v. i.*
To speak loudly out of the throat.
To make a great noise with the
throat. To speak gruffly.

Kuttom-ushbe, クットムウシベ, 帯ニ
サス大庖丁. *n.* A long knife worn
in the belt. *Kuttom ushbe esere*

ponnu, " to draw one's knife out
of the sheath."

Kuttu, クッツ, 断岩. *n.* Crags. Jagged rocks.

Kutu, クツ, 陷網(ウライ). *n.* A kind
of wickerwork fish trap. A weir.

Kutususatki, クツサツキ, or **Kotu-
susotki, コツスソツキ,** 震フ、戦慄ス
ル. *v.i.* To tremble. To quiver.
To shake.

Kuwa, クワ, 杖、墓標. *n.* A staff.
Cudgel. Club. Crutch. A walking
stick. A tombstone. As :—*Ainu
kuwa* " a man's tomb-stone ;
shiwentep kuwa, " a woman's tomb-
stone or grave mark."

Kuwa, クワ, 質、假セバ、タムベアナク
ネイタククワネ、是ハ余ノ言質ナリ.
n. A pledge. As :—*Tambe anak ne itak kuwa ne,* " this is the
pledge of my word."

Kuwaisho, クワイショ, 會所. *n.* The
Japanese Government offices
which were formerly established
in Yezo (*Jap*).

Kuwakore, クワコレ, 質ヲ與ヘル. *v.i.*
To give as a pledge.

Kuwanno, クワンノ, 眞直ナル. *adj.*
Straight.

Kuwash, クワシ, 眞直ナル. *adj.* Upright. **Syn : Oupeka.**

Kuyatatke, クヤタツケ, 鳴ル. *v. i.*
To rattle. As :—*Ashke kuyatatke,*
" to have a rattling in the stomach."

Kuyekaichup, クイェカイチュプ, 十二
月. *n.* The month of December.

Kuyoe, クヨエ, or **Kuyoi, クヨイ,** 鰾.
n. An air bladder of fish.

M (マ).

Ma, マ, 燒ク、例セバ、マカ△、燒肉、チエ プマヤン、魚ヲ燒ケ. *v.t.* To roast. As:— *Ma kam,* "roast meat." *Chep ma yan,* "roast the fish."

Ma, マ, 半島、小島、沼湖、(河又ハ海ニ續 ク). *n.* A small spit of land in a river or the sea. A peninsula, or tiny island. As applied to water "a lagoon." Also, *adj.* Dry :

Ma, マ, 泳グ. *v.i.* To swim.

Ma-chikap, マチカプ, 水鳥. *n.* Water fowls.

Machi, マチ, 妻、例セバ、マチアフプカ ラ、娶ル. *n.* A wife. As:—*Machi ahupkara,* "to marry." **Syn : Mat ahupkara.**

Machi-sak-guru, マチサクグル, 獨身 者. *n.* A bachelor. **Syn : Mat sak guru.**

Machiribe, マチリべ, 從弟、從妹. *n.* Cousin. Also by some, "younger sister."

Machitke, マチツケ, 痙攣シタル. *adj.* and *v.i.* To be convulsed. Cramped. To have one's joints drawn up as in pain. **Syn : Hematu.**

Machiya, マチヤ, 町、例セバ、マチヤ ゲシ、町ノ西端、マチヤバ、町ノ東端. *n.* A street. A Japanese city. A town. As:—*Machiya gesh,* "the west end of a street." *Machiya pa,* "the east end of a street." From Japanese *machi,* "town or street," and Ainu *ya,* land.

Mai, マイ, 内障眼、ソコヒ、例セバ、マイ オマシク、眼白内障アル. *n.* A cataract. As:—*Mai oma shik,* "eyes having cataract in them."

Maimaige, マイマイゲ, 死ニ瀕セル. *adj.* Nearly dead. At death's door. **Syn : Rai-ehange. Wen-ehange.**

Maire, マイレ, or **Maire-ki, マイレキ,** 伺候スル. *v.i.* To go to pay respects to (as to a governour).

Mairototke, マイロトツケ, 痒シ、例セ バ、クサパマイロトツケ、我ガ頭痒 シ. *v.i.* To itch. As:—*Ku sapa mairototke,* "my head itches." **Syn : Mayaige.**

Maitari, マイタリ, or **Mantari, マン タリ,** 前掛. *n.* An apron. A pinafore. (*Jap.*)

Maiyaige, マイヤイゲ, or **Mayaige, マヤイゲ.** 痒シ. *v.i.* To itch. **Syn : Mairototke.**

Mak, マク, 何、例セバ、マクエキ、何ヲ 爲シ居ルヤ. *adj.* What. As:— *Mak e ki,* "what are you doing." Same as *Makanak.*

Mak, マク, 後方、例セバ、マクワノ、後 方ヨリ. *n.* The wake. Rear. The back-ground. As:—*Mak wano,* "from behind." **Syn : Oshmake.**

Maka, マカ, 開ケレ. *v.t.* To open. **Syn : Sarare.**

Makachinkan-roshki, マカチンカンロシキ,
Makachinkan-tari, マカチンカンタリ,

足チ揚ゲテ仰向ニ寝ル. *v. i.* To lie flat upon the back with the legs in the air.

Makachinkan-tara-kosamba, マカチンカンタラコサムバ, 足チ延シテ仰向ニ寝ル. *v.i.* To lie stretched upon the back with the legs extended.

Maka-hokush, マカホクシ, 後方ニ仆ル. *v.i.* To fall backwards.

Makahokushte, マカホクシテ, 後方ニ仆ス. *v.t.* To knock down backwards.

Maka-hotari, マカホタリ, or **Makotari, マコタリ,** 小サキ木兎. *n.* The little horned owl.

Makan, マカン, 如何様ナル、例セバ、マカンカッコロベ、如何ナル形. *adv.* What kind. Such a kind. As:—*Makan kat korobe,* "what kind of shape."

Makanak, マカナク, 何ト、例セバ、タンコタン レイヘイ マカナク アイェ レウェアン、此村ノ名ハ何ナリヤ、マカナク アタィエ アン、價ハ何ナルヤ、マカナク ハウェ アンルウェアン、何ト彼ハ云ヒシカ. *adv.* What. As:—*Tan kotan reihei makanak aye ruwe an?* "what is the name of this village." *Makanak ataye an,* "what is the price?" *Makanak hawe an ruwe an,* "what did he say?" **Syn: Nekon a.**

Makananda, マカナンダ, 或時、例セバ、マカナンダアンマカナンダイサム、或ル時ハアリ、又或時ハナシ. *adv.* Sometimes. See *Makan ne koro*). As:—*Makananda an, makananda isam,* "sometimes there is and sometimes there is not."

Makangane, マカンガネ, 格別ニ、特ニ. *adv.* Particularly. In a special manner. Beyond measure.

Makanit, マカニツ, 矢ノ根ニ付ク骨. *n.* The bone part of an arrow to which the head is affixed.

Makan-ne-koro, マカン子コロ, 或時ニ是、又或ル時ニ其、例セバ、マカン子コロ タプ コラチ イエ マカン子コロ ネイ ネイ ノ コラチ イエ、時トシテ彼ハ是チ云ヒ、又時トシテ彼ヲ云フ. *adv.* Sometimes this, sometimes that, now this now that. As:— *Makan ne koro tap korachi ye, makan ne koro nei no korachi ye,* "sometimes he says this and sometimes that." **Syn: Makanda.**

Maka-ni, マカニ, 梁. *n.* A cross beam.

Makan-ruru, マカンルル, 北海. *n.* The northern sea.

Makanu, マカヌ, 開ク、晴レル、例セバ、レ マカヌ、道ガ開ケタ. *v.i.* To clear. To open. As:—*Ru makanu,* "the way is open."

Makaotari, マカオタリ, or **Maka-hotari, マカホタリ,** コミミヅク. *n.* Short-eared owl.

Makap, マカプ, 内地ヘ行ク. *v.i.* To go inland. **Syn: Pene un paye.**

Makapa, マカパ, 開. *v.t.* To open (*pl*).

Makaraye, マカライェ, 開ク、晴レル. *v.i.* To clear. To open.

Makaro, マカロ, マダイワウ、ギシギシ、スイバノ類. *n.* Docks and Sorrels. *Rumex acetosa, L.*

Makayo, マカヨ, フキノトウ. *n.* The flower-shoot of the *Petasites japonicus, Mig.*

Maketa, マケタ, 後方ニ於テ. *adv.* In the background. Behind. **Syn : Oshmaketa.**

Makip, マキブ, 何、例セバ、マキプイキ、彼ハ何テ爲シ居ルヤ. *adv.* What. As :—*Makip iki,* " what is he doing."

Makiri, マキリ, 小刀. *n.* A knife.

Maketari, マケタリ, 損スル、負ケル. *v.i.* To lose. To lose at play.

Makiri-ibe, マキリイベ, 小刀ノ刃. *n.* A knife blade.

Makiri-nip, マキリニブ, 小刀ノ柄. *n.* A knife handle.

Makiri-saya, マキリサヤ, 小刀ノ鞘. *n.* A knife sheath.

Makke, マッケ, 開ケタル、割レタレ. *v.i.* and *adj.* To be opened. To be split asunder. Open.

Makkosamba, マッコサムバ, 治マル (喧嘩ナドノ). *v.i.* To be cleared up as a quarrel. To be cleared away as clouds.

Makmaka, マクマカ, 開ク. *v.t.* To open.

Makmakbe, マクマクベ, 輝ク、閃ク、例セバ、イメルマクマクベ、稲妻ガ閃ク. *v.i.* To glitter. To flash as light. As :— *Imeru-makmakbe,* " the lightening flashes."

Maknaraye, マクナライ, 逐ヒヤル. *v.t.* To drive away. To clear out of the way. To dispel.

Maknarutu, マクナルツ, 逐ヒヤレ. *v.t.* To dispel. To clear out of the way. (*pl*). **Syn : Maknaraye.**

Maknatara, マクナタラ, 明カナル、顯レタレ. *adj.* Clear. To be opened out to view. Open as the skies. As :— *Kando kotoro maknatara,* " a clear sky."

Makne, マク子, 故ニ、例セバ、マクネ ガス、何等ノ理由ニヨリテ. *adv.* Wherefore. Why. As :—*Makne gusu* "for what reason." **Syn : Nep gusu.**

Mak-peka, マクペカ, 後ノ方ニ. *adv.* In a backward position or direction.

Makta, マクタ, 後、他所、例セバ、マクタウカオ、收藏ス、マクタアレ、除キ去ル. *adv.* Behind. Away. As :—*Makta ukao,* " to put away." *Makta are,* " to clear away (as food etc.").

Makta-ekashi, マクタエカシ, 太古ノ民. *n.* The very ancient people.

Makta-makta, マクタマクタ, 場所テ アケヨ. *adv.* Back, back. Make room.

Makui-shiri, マクイシリ, 太古ノ. *adv.* Very ancient. In olden times. **Syn : Fushkotoi.**

Makun, マクン, 後ニ、太古ニ、例セバ、マクンエカシ、初代ノ先祖. *adv.* Behind. In the rear. Ancient. As :—*Makun ekashi,* " the early ancestors."

Makun-apa, マクンアバ, 子宮. *n.* The womb. **Syn : Po-apa. Po- pukuru. Sange apa.**

Makun-amunin, マクンアムニン, 二ノ腕. *n.* That part of the arm next the shoulder. **Syn : Mak un tek.**

Makun-tapsutu, マクンタブスツ, 肩ノ上部. *n.* The top of the shoulder.

Mama-habo, ママハボ, 繼母. *n.* Step- mother.

Mama-michi, ママミチ, 継父. *n.* Step-father.

Mama-po, ママポ, 継子. *n.* A step-child.

Mamba, マムバ, 側ニ置ク、包ム. *v.t.* To set on one side. To do up, as goods for transportation.

Mame, マメ, 豆、例セバ、マメケプシェベ、豆ノ莢、マメニ、豆ノ手栄、マメヌム、豆チ剥ク、マメプンガラ、豆ノ蔓. *n.* Beans. As :—*Mame kepushbe,* "a bean pod." *Mame ni,* "bean sticks ; " sticks placed for runner beans to climb upon." *Mame num akara,* "to shell beans or peas." *Mame pungara,* "bean vines." (*Jap*).

Mame-kikbe, マメキクベ, 連枷. *n.* A flail used for beating out beans. **Syn: Pai.**

Mamta, マムタ, 愛スル詞、綺麗ナル、善キ. *adj.* A term of endearment used principally when speaking to children. Pretty. Lovely. Charming.

Mana, マナ, 座埃. *n.* Dust. As :— *Toi mana,* "earth dust."

Manaita, マナイタ, or **Manaita-chikuni,** マナイタチクニ, 俎板. *n.* A board for cutting up food upon. **Syn: Moshkara.** (*Jap*).

Mantari, マンタリ, or **Maitari,** マイタリ, 前掛. *n.* An apron.

Maramarage, マラマラゲ, 緩キ、外レ ダル. *adj.* Loose. Disconnected.

Maramarase, マラマラセ, マラマラゲ ニ同ジ. *adj.* Same as *maramarage*

Marapto, マラプト, 祭、例セバ、マラプ トアン、祭スル. *n.* A feast. *Marapto an,* "to keep a feast."

Marapto-aainukoro-guru, マラプト アアイヌコログル, 祭ノ司. *n.* The governor of a feast. **Syn: Marapto koro guru.**

Maratto, マラット, 熊ノ頭、熊祭. *n.* A bear's head. A bear feast.

Maratto-iwak, マラットイワク, 眼上 ノ麦粒腫(モノモライヒ). *n.* A sty on the eye-lid.

Maratto-sapa, マラットサパ, 熊ノ頭 骨、(拝スル為メ屋外ニ掛ケル). *n.* A bear's skull which is placed outside the huts for worship.

Marek, マレク, 魚銛. *n.* A hook used for spearing fish.

Marek-op, マレクオプ, 魚銛ノ柄. *n.* A long piece of wood to which a fish spearing hook is fixed.

Marek-shu or **shui,** マレクシュ, 又ハ シュイ, 魚叉チ取リ付ケル小キ木. *n.* A small piece of wood to which a hook used for spearing fish is attached.

Marek-torara, マレクトララ, 魚銛 チ柄ニ結ビ付ル皮. *n.* A piece of skin used to tie a *marek* to its handle.

Marotke, マロツケ, 緩キ、外レシ. *n.* and *adj.* Loose. Disconnected.

Marotke-chiporo, マロツケチポロ, 鮭 ノ筋子、(卵子). *n.* The ripe row of salmon.

Masa, マサ, 柾、例セバ、マサイコロ、柾 ニテ飾ラレシ寶物. *n.* Shingles. Thin slices of wood. As :—*Masa ikoro,* "treasures ornamented with thin slices of wood." *Masa ikayop,* "quivers, ornamented with thin slices of wood."

Masa, マサ, 開ク、顕ス. *v.t.* To open. To display.

Masara, マサラ, 海濱ノ草生ヘシ處.
n. The back part of the sea
shore upon which grass and weeds
grow. That part of a river bank
where vegetation commences. The
part immediately behind this upon
which shrubs grow is called *hun-
kika.*

Masara-orunbe, マサラオルンベ, エ
ゾスカシユリ *n.* *Lilium dahuricum, Gawl.* The bulbs of this
lily are used as an article of food.

Masasa, マササ, 開ケサセル. *v.t.* To
cause another to open.

Masaske, マサシェ, 擴ゲタレ. *adj.*
Opened out. Spread out. **Syn:
Maske.**

Mashki-no, マシキノ, or **Mashkinno,** マシキンノ, 過多、イテキマシユキ
ノシクテ、餘リ一盃ニ滿スヲヿ、マシユ
キンノポン、餘リ小サキ. *adv.* Too
much. Over. Above. Too. As:
—*Iteki mashki no shikte,* "don't
fill it too full." *Mashkin no pon,*
" too small." Mashkin no poro,
" too great."

Maske, マスケ, 擴ゲタル、開ケタル. *adj.*
Spread out. Open. Bare.

Masmasa, マスマサ, 開ク. *v.t.* To
open. **Syn: Makmaka.**

Mat, マツ, 兎罠. *n.* A kind of trap
used for catching hares.

Mat, マツ, 女、妻、雌. *n.* A female.
A wife. A woman.

Mata, マタ, or **Mata-pa,** マタパ, or
Mata-un-pa, マタウンパ, 冬. *n.*
Winter.

Mataburip, マタブリプ, 熊手. *n.* A
rake. **Syn: Shirikerekerip.**

Mat-ahupkara, マツアフプカラ, 娶レ.
v.t. To marry a wife.

Mataki, マタキ, 妹. *n.* A younger
sister. **Syn: Machiribe. Turesh.**

Matambushi, マタムブシ, 男ノ頭巾.
n. A kind of thick head gear
worn by men. **Syn: Sapa-shi-
na ambe.**

Matapa, マタパ, 女ノ親類. *n.* Female
relatives.

Matapa, マタパ, 冬. *n.* Winter.

Matatambu, マタタムブ, マタタヒ.
n. *Actinidia polygama, Planch.*
The fruit of this plant is used as
an article of food by the Ainu.

Matariya, マタリヤ, 冬籠スル (單數).
v.i. To spend the winter at a
place. (*sing*).

Matariyapa, マタリヤパ, 冬籠リスレ
(複數) *v. i.* To spend the winter
at a place. (*pl.*)

Matcharashne, マッチャラシ子, or
Macharashne, マチャラシ子, 乾キテ
コナゴナニナリタレ. *adj.* In separate particles. Dry and loose (as
earth dried up by the sun.)

Matchep, マッチェプ, キンマス. *n.*
Silver salmon. *Oncorhynchus ki-
sutch (Walb.)*

Mat-eramunishte, マテラムニシテ,
妻ヲ虐待スレ. *v.i.* To ill-use one's
wife. **Syn: Mat-shikeshte. Mat-
kor'ewen.**

Matkachi, マッカチ, 娘. *n.* A girl.
A female child.

Matkachi-utara, マツカチウタラ, 娘
達. *n.* Girls.

Mat-karaku, マツカラク, 姪. *n.* A
niece.

Matkat'tara, マツカッタラ, 娘達. *n.*
Girls. Young female children.
Syn: Matkachi-utara.

Mat-ko-iwak, マッコイワク, 妻又ハ 許嫁ヲ間訪スル. *v.i.* To visit one's intended wife. To pay attentions to a young lady with a view to marriage. To go to visit one's wife.

Mat-kor'ewen, マッコレウェン, 妻ヲ 虐待スル. *v.i.* To ill-treat one's wife.

Matkosanu, マッコサヌ, 蹶起スレ. *v.i.* To leap up from a sitting or lying posture.

Mat-kuwa, マックワ, 女ノ墓標. *n.* A woman's grave mark.

Matn'au, マッナウ, 北風. *n.* The north wind. **Syn: Matne-au.**

Matne, マッチ, 女ノ、牝ノ. *adj.* A female whether of man or beast.

Matne-au, マッチアウ, 北風. *n.* The north wind. **Syn: Matn'au.**

Matne-hekachi, マッチヘカチ, 娘、女 ノ子. *n.* A girl. A female child. **Syn: Matkachi.**

Matne-mitpo, マッチミツポ, 孫娘. *n.* A grand daughter.

Matnep, マッチプ, 女性. *n.* A female.

Matne-po, マッチポ, 娘. *n.* A daughter. A female child.

Matne-noya, マッチノヤ, ヨモギ. *n.* Mugwort. *Artemisia vulgaris, L.*

Matne-top, マッチトプ, シャッタンチ ク. *n.* The blotched bamboo.

Mat-sak-guru, マツサクグル, 独身者. *n.* A bachelor.

Matrure, マツルレ, 娶ル. *v.t.* To take to wife.

Mat-shikeshke, マツシケシケ, 妻ヲ 虐待スレ. *v.i.* To ill-treat one's wife. **Syn: Mat-kor'ewen. Mat-eramunishte.**

Mat-shuop, マツシュオプ, 女ノ資函、銭 函. *n.* A woman's treasure box. A box in which a woman stores her nicknacks. A money box.

Mau or **Mawe,** マウ, 又ハ マウ二, 状 態. *n.* State. Condition.

Mau, マウ, or Mawe, マウェ, 空氣、呼 吸、風、例セバ、マウエドツク、風前二. *n.* Air. Breath. Wind. As:— *Mau etok,* "before the wind."

Mau, マウ, 玫瑰ノ實、ハマナスノミ. *n.* The fruit of the *Rosa rugosa, Thunb.* Hips.

Mau, マウ, 力、味、品性. *n.* Strength. Vigour. Force. Stamina. Taste. Flavour, Character.

Maukopirika, マウコピリカ, 幸ナレ、 好運ナレ. *adj.* Lucky. Fortunate. **Syn: Riri-kopirika. Kashika-mui koro. Seremak koro. Kashkamui oshitchiu.**

Maukopirikaki, マウコピリカキ, 好運 ナル. *v.i.* To be lucky or fortunate.

Maukowen, マウコウェン, 不幸、不幸二 ナレ. *adj.* and *v.i.* Unlucky. To be unfortunate. **Syn: Okash-kamui sak.**

Maukush, マウクシ, 透ル、(風ノ如シ)・ *v.t.* To pass through as the wind. To permeate. To penetrate.

Mau-ni, マウ二, ハマナス. *n.* Beach rose. *Rosa rugosa, Thunb.*

Maun-maun, マウンマウン, 舌ヒ曲ケ ル、變心スレ. *v.i.* To prevaricate. To be fickle. **Syn: Ramkosh-kashke.**

Mau-noyere, マウノイェレ, 腔ヲ躱ハ ス. *v.i.* To avoid as a sword sweep. To jump away as from one striking with a sword.

Mau-nu, マウヌ, 強キ、強キ香味アル. *adj*. Strong. Having strong flavour.

Maupere, マウペレ, 風ニ折レル. *v.i.* To be broken with the wind. **Syn : Mau kaye.**

Maurotki-chiporo, マウロツキチポロ, 成熟セレ魚卵. *n.* Fish roe having each egg separate. **Syn : Marotke chiporo.**

Mau-sak, マウサク, 弱キ. *adj*. Weak.

Maushipirasa, マウシピラサ, 流行ス ル (病ノ如シ). *v.i.* To spread as disease.

Maushiko, マウシコ, 活澄ナル. *adj*. Full of life. Bright eyed.

Maushiro, マウシロ, or Maushoro, マウショロ, 口笛ヲ吹ク. *v.i.* To whistle.

Maushok, マウショク, 欠スル. *v.i.* To yawn.

Maushok-chierarapa, マウショクチエララバ,
Maushok-yaierarapa, マウショクヤイエララバ,
屡〻欠スレ. *v.i.* To yawn frequently.

Maushoro, マウショロ, or Maushiro, マウシロ, 口笛ヲ吹ク. *v.i.* To whistle.

Mawari-kambi, マワリカムビ, 旅行券. *n.* A passport. **Syn : Shiroshi kambi.** (*Jap*).

Mawe, マウェ, 味、要素、状態、例セバ、マウェユプケチャ、強キ茶. *n.* Taste. Flavour. Essence. State, condition. As : — *Mawe-yupke cha*, "strong tea."

Mawe-an, マウェアン, 強キ香ノスル. *adj*. Of strong flavour.

Mawe-arapare, マウェアラバレ, 乾カ ス、曝ス. *v.t.* To air. To dry. **Syn : Maw-omare.**

Mawe-tui, マウェツイ, 死ス. *v.i.* To die.

Mawe-yupke, マウェユプケ, 強キ、香味 アレ. *adj*. Strong. Of strong flavour.

Maw-omare, マウヲマ, 乾カス、曝ス. *v.t.* To air. To dry. **Syn : Satke. Mawe-arapare.**

Mayaige, マヤイゲ,
Mayaike, マヤイケ, } 痒ガル、例セバ、
クチキリマヤイゲ、我脚痒シ. *v.t.* To itch. As :—*Ku chikiri mayaige*, "my leg itches." *Kisara maiyaige*, "To have itching ears. To desire to hear. To be talked about." **Syn : Mairototke.**

Mayaige-tashum, マヤイゲタシュム, 疥癬. *n.* The itch.

Mayamaya, マヤマヤ, or Mayemaye, マイェマイェ, 痒ガレ. *v.i.* To itch. To be irritated.

Mayaya, マヤヤ, 刺激スル、例セバ、レ クチマヤヤ、咽喉ヲ刺激スレ. *v.t.* To irritate (as parts of one's body). As :— *Rekuchi mayaya*, "to irritate one's throat."

Mayeat, マイェアツ, 鳴ル、音スレ. *v.i.* To sound. To make a noise. **Syn : Maikosamba.**

Mayemaye, マイェマイェ, or Mayamaya, マヤマヤ, 痒ガル. *v.i.* To itch. To be irritated.

Mayun, マユン, 愉快ナル音ノスレ. *adj*. Of pleasing sound.

Mayun-mayun, マユンマユン, 鳴リ 響ク. *v.i.* To sound. To ring. To resound. **Syn : Uwetunuise.**

Mayun-no, マユンノ, 鳴リ響キテ. *adv.* Resounding. Ringing.

Me, メ, 寒サ、例セバ、メエコツ、凍死スル. *n.* Cold. Coldness. As:— *Me ekot,* "to die of cold," "to starve with cold."

Me-an, メアン, 寒キ (天氣ニノミ用ユ). *adj.* Cold. (Spoken of the weather only.)

Mechakko, メチャッコ, 髑髏、頭蓋骨. *n.* A skull. The cranium.

Megane, メガ子, 眼鏡、例セバ、メガネコロ、眼鏡チカケレ. *n.* Spectacles. (*Jap*). As:—*Megane koro,* "to wear spectacles."

Mehuru, メフル, 腎臓、(魚ノ脊膓). *n.* Kidney of fish.

Mek, メク, 部分. *n.* A division.

Mek, メク, 猫ノ鳴聲. *n.* An onomatopœa for a cats-mew.

Me-kamui-koro, メカムイコロ, リウマチス二罹ル. *v.i.* To be afflicted with rheumatics.

Me-kamui-tashum, メカムイタシム, リウマチス. *n.* Rheumatism.

Mekare, メカレ, 分ツ. *v.t.* To divide.

Mekka, メッカ, 物ノ背(ムネ). *n.* The back edge of anything.

Mekkashike, メッカシケ, 刀背、山ノ端、家ノ棟. *n.* The back of a fish, knife, or sword. The ridge of a mountain or house.

Mekkaushbe, メッカウシベ, 小魚ノ背鰭. *n.* The dorsal fin of the smaller fishes. This fin on the larger kinds of fishes is called *Ashbe.*

Mekkaushike, メッカウシケ, 魚ノ背、刀ノ背. *n.* The back of a fish knife, or sword.

Meko, メコ, 猫. *n.* A cat.

Mekoashi, メコアシ, 粟ノ一種. *n.* A kind of millet.

Mekoparachi, メコパラチ,
Mekoparagoat, メコパラゴアツ,
Mekopachiko-an, メコパチコアン,
Mekoparat, メコパラツ,
Mekoparoat, メコパロアツ, 猫ニ崇ラレレ. *v.i.* To be possessed or bewitched by a cat as a punishment for some evil done to the feline family.

Mekoro, メコロ, 冷キ. *adj.* To be cold.

Mekse, メクセ, 猫ガ鳴ク. *v.i.* To mew.

Mem, メム, 沼、湖. *n.* A pond. Lake. Swamp.

Meman, メマン, 凉キ. *adj.* Cool.

Membiru, メムビル, (ノビル). *n.* A wild garlic. See *mempiro.*

Memka, メムカ, 一軒ノ小村. *n.* A hamlet of one house.

Memke, メムケ, 削ル. *v.t.* To shave.

Mempa, メムパ, 差出口スル、話ノ腰チ折ル. *v.i.* To cut off one's speech. To commence speaking and leave off before having finished.

Mempiro, メムピロ,
Mempiru, メムビル, ノビレ. *n.* A wild garlic. *Allium nipponicum, Fr. et Sav.*

Mena, メナ, 池. *n.* A pond. A puddle of water. **Syn: Mem.**

Menasaru, メナサル, ハマエンドウ. *n.* Beachpea. *Lathyrus maritimus, Bigel. var. Thunber gianus, Miq.* **Syn: Noiporo-kina. Menash-mame.**

Menash, メナシ, 東風. *n.* The east wind.

Menash-kikiri, メナシキキリ, 小蠅ノ一種. *n.* A kind of small fly.

Menashuke, メナシュケ, ホウジロガ
モ. *n.* Golden eye (sea-fowl).
Fuligula clangula, (Linn).

Meni, メニ, 小雨、霧. *n.* Fine rain.
Mist.

Meni-ash, メニアシ, 霧降ル. *v.i.* To
drizzle as fine rain.

Menoko, メノコ, 婦女、雌. *n.* A
woman. A female. This word
is of Japanese origin and may
be designated pigeon Ainu. The
proper Ainu words for woman are
Mat-ainu and *shiwentep.*

Menu, メヌ, 寒クナル、寒サチ感ズル.
v.i. To be cold. To feel the
cold. **Syn: Meraige.**

Meraige, メライゲ, 寒クナル、寒サチ
感スル. *v.i.* To be cold.

Meraoma-ni, メラオマニ, バッコヤ
ナギ. *n.* The goat willows. *Salix
baprea, L.*

Meri, メリ, 閃メク、煌ク. *n.* A
twinkle. A bright flash of light
or fire. **Syn: Miru.**

Meri-at, メリアツ, 燦ク、輝ル. *v.i.*
To twinkle (as the stars). To
shine.

Meri-meri, メリメリ, 火花、例セバ、ア
ベメリメリ、火花. *n.* A spark.
As :—*Abe meri-meri,* " a spark
of fire."

Meri-merige, メリメリゲ, 燦ク. *v.i.*
To twinkle as the stars.

Meshke, メシケ, 壊レ. *v.t.* To
break. To rub off. To creak.

Meshpa, メシバ, 切リ去ル、壊ル、例
セバ、キサラメシバ、罰トシテ耳チ
切リ去ル. *v.t.* To cut off. To
break. To clip. As :—*Kisara
meshpa,* " to cut off the ears as
in punishment for crime."

Mesmeske, メスメスケ, 壊レテ. *adv.*
Broken up.

Mesu, メス, 切リ去ル、壊リ去ル、取リ
去ル、壊ル、例セバ、エツメス、罰ト
シテ削ル. *v.i.* To cut off. To
break off. To take off. To break.
As :—*Etu mesu,* " to cut off the
nose as in punishment for crime."
*Nei akamkotchep tumashnu gusu
shuma wano mesu eaikap,* " he
cannot take the sea-snail off the
stone on account of its strength."
Pl. Meshpa.

Mesuya, メスヤ, 寒サニ弱ハル. *v.i.*
To become weak through exposure to the cold.

Metarop-notorap, メタロフノトラブ,
鰓、蓋骨. *n.* Operculum.

Metat, メタツ, タケカンバ. *n.*
Betula Ermanni, Cham.

Metot, メトツ, 山ノ端、山地. *n.* A
ridge of mountains. Mountainous places.

Metoteami, メトテアミ, ミヤマカケ
ス. *n.* Brand's jay. *Garrulus
brandti, Ever.*

Metotshiri, メトツシリ, 山ノ端. *n.* A
ridge of mountains.

Metumbeka, メツムベカ, 極寒. *n.*
The very cold weather.

Me-un, メウン, 寒ク、寒サニ感ズル.
v.i. and adj. To be cold. Cold.
Syn: Meraige.

Meunatara, メウナタラ, 美シク.
例セバ、トアンチクニロシキルウェ
メウナタラ、其等ノ樹木ハ美シク其處
ニ生セリ. *adv.* Beautifully.
Newly. In a beautiful manner.
As :—*To an chikuni roshki ruwe
meunatara,* " those trees stand
there in a beautiful manner."
Syn: Teshnatara.

Meuren-chep, メウレンチェブ, ギンマ ス. *n.* Silver salmon. Same as *Mat-chep.*

Mi, ミ, 着ル、例セバ、アミプミ、衣ヲ 着ル. *v.t.* To clothe. To wear. As:—*Amip mi,* "to put on clothes."

Mi-ambe, ミアムベ, 衣類. *n.* Clothes. **Syn: Amip.**

Michi, ミチ, 父・ *n.* Father. **Syn: Ona. Iyapo. Hambe.**

Michipa, ミチバ, ミツバ、ミツバセリ. *n. Cryptotaenia japonica, Hassk.*

Mik, ミク, 吠ル、例セバ、セタミク、犬 ガ吠ユレ. *v.i.* To bark. As:— *Seta mik,* "the dog barks."

Mike, ミケ, 薄キ片. *n.* Thin slices. **Syn: Nike.** Also *v.t.* To cut with slices.

Mike-mike, ミケミケ, 輝ク、燦ク、例 セバ、イメルミケミケ、稲妻ガ閃ク. *v.i.* To glitter. To flash as lightning. As:—*Imeru mikemike,* "the lightning flashes." **Syn: Mak makke.**

Mike-rui, ミケルイ, 薄片ニスル. *v.t.* To cut into thin slices. **Syn: Nikerui.**

Mimdara, ミムダラ, or **Mindara,** ミ ンダラ, 塵塚. *n.* A rubbish heap.

Mimdara, ミムダラ, or **Mindara,** ミ ンダラ, 庭、牧場. *n.* A yard. A clear space in front of the Ainu huts. Also a place where animals feed. A pasture.

Mim or **mimi,** ミム, 又ハ ミミ, 脂肪、 魚肉、例セバ、イシリクラシテレ、ア ラミムパテク、オヤオヤ、脂肪許デ ナイカ、チェブミム魚肉. *n.* Fat. The flesh of fish. As:—*Ishiri kuratnere, ara mim patek,* "dear

me! it is nothing but fat." *Chep mim,* "fish flesh."

Mimi-pene, ミミペチ, 柔キ肉ノ. *adj.* Soft fleshed. Flabby.

Mim-ush, ミムウシ, 肥エタル、強壯ナ ル. *adj.* Fat. Stout.

Mim-ushka, ミムウシカ, 肥ヤス. *v.t.* To fatten.

Mim-ushte, ミムウシテ, 肥ヤス. *v.t.* To fatten.

Mina, ミナ, 笑フ、例セバ、ミナヒ子、ミ ナカ子、笑ヒテ. *v.i.* To laugh. As:—*Mina hine; mina kane,* "laughing."

Mina-mina, ミナミナ, 抱腹スル. *v.i.* To laugh heartily.

Mina-ne-manup, ミナ子マヌブ, 笑フ 人. *n.* A laughing person.

Minapa, ミナバ, 笑フ(複数). *v.i.* To laugh. (*pl*).

Minare, ミナレ, 娯マセル、宥ス. *v.t.* To amuse.

Minchi, ミンチ, ミツ. *n. Pilea pumila, A Gray.* The richweed. **Syn: Moshi-kina.**

Mintuchi, ミンツチ, 人獸ノ類. *n.* A kind of fabulous animal said to be half human and half animal and to inhabit lakes and rivers. A sort of evil dispositioned mermaid who causes many accidents in rivers, ponds, and lakes. These mermaids are said to have bodies like those of human beings while they have hoofs instead of hands or feet. They are also said to disembowel and devour human beings when they catch them. The Ainu threaten children with mermaids to keep them from going near rivers. There are also said to be good mermaids or *pirika mintuchi*, really faries inhabiting the mountains, and these are said to benefit people with their help.

Mintuchi-sani, ミンツチサニ, 人魚ノ子孫、最悪ノ嘲. *n.* A descendant of a mermaid. A very bad term of reproach.

Mip, ミプ, 衣類. *n.* Clothing. **Syn : Amip.**

Mire, ミレ, 着ル. *v.t.* To clothe.

Miru, ミル, 燦キ. *n.* A twinkle. A sparkle.

Miru-at, ミルアツ, Meri-at, メリアツ, } 燦ク. *v.i.* To twinkle (as the stars). To sparkle.

Mirumiru, ミルミル, 燦ク. *v.i.* To sparkle. To shine. To twinkle.

Mishmu, ミシム, Nishmu, ニシム, } 寂シキ、寂シク感ズル. *adj. and v.i.* Lonely. To feel lonely.

Mitpo, ミッポ, 孫. *n.* A grandchild.

Mo, モ, 沈黙、平和. *n.* Silence. Peace. **Syn : Ratchitara.**

Mo, モ, 不活潑ナル、静ナル、鈍キ. *adj.* Sluggish. Quiet. Slow. Gentle. Also " small " as in the word *moashikipet,* " the little finger."

Moashikepet, モアシケペツ, 小指. *n.* The little finger.

Mochip, モチプ, 持符(船ノ一種). *n.* A row-boat.

Mochup, モチュプ, 五月. *n.* The month of May also called *Shikiuta-chup.*

Mohonto, モホント, 後、例セバ、チセイ、モホント、家ノ後. *adv.* Behind. Back. As :—*Chisei mohonto,*

" the back of a house." **Syn : Oshmak.**

Moi, モイ, 平地、海灣、稍カナル所. *n.* (*Geog*). Smooth, level, or flat places. Also a bay in the sea or a smooth, level, quiet place among the mountains. When applied to the sea, this word signifies a bend in the shore, where the water is quiet and sheltered from the winds. It is almost equivalent to " harbour " and " sound ; " particularly may this word be applied to a " land-locked harbour." When applied to rivers, *moi* also signifies a sheltered bend where the waters are quiet.

Mo-i, モイ, 平和、平和ナル處. *n.* Peace. A place of peace.

Moimoi, モイモイ, 動カス、搖リ動カス. *v.t.* To move. To shake.

Moimoige, モイモイゲ, 震ハス、動カス. *v.i.* To tremble. To move.

Moinatara, モイナタラ, 擴ガル、(雲ガ山ノ上ナド二). *v.i.* To be spread out as clouds over the mountains or as smoke over a town. To lie extended as a city.

Moire, モイレ, 遲キ、鈍キ. *adj.* Slow. **Syn : Katu moire.**

Moireka, モイレカ, 緩メル. *v.t.* To slacken.

Moirepa, モイレバ, 遲キ、鈍キ、(複數). *adj.* Slow (*pl*).

Moire-no, モイレノ, 緩二. *adv.* Slowly.

Moiretara, モイレタラ, 緩二. *adv.* Slowly.

Moishutu, モイシュツ, 打ツ. *v.t.* To flog. To strike with the hand. To beat. **Syn : Monshutu.**

Moishutu, モイシュツ, 意味、理由、例セ バ、イタクモイシュツ、詞ノ意味. *n.* Meaning. Reason. As:—*Itak moishutu,* "the meaning of a word." **Syn: Ikkewehe.**

Moitek, モイテク, 港口ノ土地. *n.* The land immediately at the entrance to a harbour.

Moiwa, モイワ, 坂. *n.* A gradual sloping hill or mountain. Also a little hill. **Syn: Pon huru.**

Mokiuta-chup, モキウタチュブ, 四月. The month of April.

Mokkeu, モッケウ, 鰓蓋骨. *n.* The operculum of fishes.

Mokon, モコン,
Mokoro, モコロ, } 眠レ. *v.i.* To sleep.

Mokonnoye, モコンノイェ, 死ス. レ. *v.i.* To be dead. To be fast asleep.

Mokon-rawere, モコンラウェレ, 睡タ イ. *v.i.* To desire to sleep. **Syn: Mokon-rusui.**

Mokon-rusui, モコンルスイ, 睡クナレ. *v.i.* To be sleepy. To desire to sleep. **Syn: Mokon-rawere.**

Mokore, モコレ, 寝カス. *v.t.* To put to sleep.

Mokori, モコリ, 寝所. *n.* A sleeping place. **Syn: Mokoro ushi. Hotke ushi.**

Mokoriri, モコリリ, 巻貝ノ總稱. *n.* A snail. Periwinkles. Whelks. The name of any kind of whelk-shaped shell.

Mokoriri-sei, モコリリセイ, 巻貝ノ皿. *n. Siphonalia signum, Reeve.*

Mokoro-an, モコロアン, 寝ル. *v.i.* To sleep.

Mokoro-an, モコロアン, 睡リテ. *adv.* Asleep.

Mokoro-koinu, モコロコイヌ, 安眠チ 妨ゲラル. *v.i.* To be disturbed in one's sleep.

Mokoro-koitak, モコロコイタク, 寝言 テ云フ. *v.i.* To talk in one's sleep. **Syn: Monna-itak.**

Mokoro-komosh, モコロコモシ, 睡遊 スル. *v.i.* To walk in one's sleep.

Mokoro-komosh-guru, モコロコモシ グル, 睡遊人. *n.* A somnambulist.

Mokoro-kotushmak, モコロコツシ マク, 寝者チ打ツ. *v.t.* To murder one while sleeping.

Mokoro-pokai-hike, モコロポカイヒ ケ, 熟睡スル人、寝坊. *n.* A great sleeper. **Syn: Mokonrui guru.**

Mokot, モコツ, 寝ル、例セバ、モコッツイ カタ、寝レル間ニ. *v.i.* Same as *mokoro.* As:— *Mokot' tuikata,* "whilst sleeping"; "during rest."

Mokrap, モクラブ, 胸鰭. *n.* The pectoral fins of fishes.

Mom, モム, 流ル、流テ下ル. *v.i.* To flow as a river. To float down a stream. To float.

Mom, モム, 漂フ. *adv.* Adrift. Afloat.

Moma, モマ, スモヽ. *n.* Plums. *Prunus communis, Huds.*

Momambe, モマムベ, 牝鹿. *n.* A doe (deer).

Moma-ni, モマニ, スモヽノ木. *n.* A plum tree.

Momauta-chup, モマウタチュブ, 六 月. *n.* The month of June, by some called *shinan-chup.*

Moma-yarape, モマヤラベ, 着テ居レ 衣類. *n.* The clothes one wears.

Momnatara, モムナタラ, 一杯ニナレ. *v.i.* To be full to the very brim.

Momde, モムデ, 浮ベレ. *v.t.* To set afloat.

Momka, モムカ, 浮ベル. *v.t.* To cause to float.

Momok, モモク, 普通ノ、凡俗ノ. *adj.* Common. Vulgar. **Syn : Pashta.**

Momok-aeiwange-itak, モモ𛀁アエイワンゲイタク, 俗語. *n.* Colloquial.

Momok-itak, モモキタク, 俗語. *n.* Colloquial. Ordinary language. Vulgar talk.

Momok-momok-aeiwangep, モモク モモクアエイワンゲブ, 苦力、人夫. *n.* A coolie. An ordinary servant.

Mompok, モムポク, 下、下 ニ. *adv.* Under. Beneath.

Mompoketa, モムポケタ, ヨリ少ク、例 セバ、エンモムポケタパアン、我ヨリ年少. *adv.* Less than. As :—*En mompoketa pa an,* " of less years than I " ; i.e. " younger than I."

Mon, モン, 仕事、勞働. *n.* Business. Labour. Work. **Syn : Moni. Mongo.**

Monak, モナク, 寐ラレヌ. *v.i.* and *adj.* To be unable to sleep. To be awake. Dull. Tired. Sleepy.

Monak, モナク, 無職ノ. *adv.* Without business or work.

Monak, モナク, 扨テ、例セバ、モナク、ネイノキコウェン、應、若シ汝斯ク爲サバ、其ハ惡シカル可シ. *interj.* Now. As :—*Monak, nei no ki ko wen,* " now, if you do so it will be bad."

Mon-an, モンアン, 多忙ナル. *v.i.* and *adj.* Busy.

Monasap, モナサブ, 緩慢ニ仕事スレ. *adj.* Slow at work. **Syn : Katumoire.**

Monashnu-no, モナシヌノ, 速ニ. *adv.* Quickly.

Monawere, モナウェレ, 口許リニテ實行セヌ. *v.i.* To talk of doing something, but not to do it. **Syn : Yairawere.**

Mondum, モンヅム, 力、權威、才能、健康. *n.* Power. Authority. Ability. Strength. Health. **Syn : Ki mondum. Ki kiroro. Kara kat. Ki kat.**

Mondum-kore, モンヅムコレ, 強メレ、權威ヲ與ヘル. *v.t.* To authorize. To strengthen.

Mondum-pirika, モンヅ ピリカ, 健全トナル、例セバ、ソチエツムピリカワヘエイキ、汝正シク健全ナルヤ. *v.i.* To be in good health. As :—*Sone e tumu pirika wa he, e iki,* " are you really better in health." **Syn : Tumu pirika.**

Mondum-pirika-ki, モンヅムピリカ キ, 全快スレ. *v.i.* To recover from sickness.

Mondum-wen, モンヅムウェン, 病氣スル. *v.i.* To be in ill health.

Mongeshna, モンゲシナ, 漸次、例セバ、ポロンノエヤイハンノッカラヤッカモンゲシナエラムペウテク、彼ハ勉メテ學ビシカバ、些力解スルナリ. *adv.* By degrees (used in a negative phrase). As :—*Poron no eyaihannokkara yakka mongeshna erampeutek,* " although he studies hard he understands less."

Mongesh-ta, モンゲシタ, 仕事ヲ終ル. *v.t.* To finish what one is doing.

Mongo, モンゴ, 仕事. *n.* Business. Work. **Syn : Mon. Moni.**

Mongo-an, モンゴアン, 爲ス可キ仕事ガアレ. *v.i.* To have business to transact. **Syn : Moni-an.**

Mon-hauge, モンハウゲ, 閑ナレ. *v.i.*
Not busy. Not having much to
do. **Syn: Moni-saure.**

Moni, モニ, 仕事. *n.* Labour. Work.
Business. **Syn: Mongo.**

Moniamuye, モニアムイェ, 順フ、償フ.
v.i. To be atoned for. To be
redressed.

Moni-an, モニアン, 爲ス汋キ仕事ヲ持
ツ. *v.i.* To have business to
transact.

Moni-saure, モニサウレ, 仕事ニ下手
ナル. *adj.* Weak handed at work.
Not busy.

Monichashnu-no, モニチャシヌノ, 妨
ナシニ、速ニ. *adv.* Without impediment. Quickly.

Monimuye, モニムイェ, 償フ、報酬ヲ與
ヘレ. *v.t.* To redress. To re-
munerate.

Moni-yupke, モニユブケ, 仕事ニ上手
ナル. *adj.* Strong handed at
work.

Monna-itak, モンナイタク, 寐言ヲ云
フ. *v.i.* To talk in one's sleep.
Syn: Mokoro-koitak.

Mo-no, モノ, 靜ニ. *adv.* Quietly.
Silently.

Mo-no-an, モノアン, 靜マル、安全ナ
ル、例セバ、モノアンノロク、默坐ス
ル. *v.i.* To be at peace. To
be quiet. As:—*Mo-no an no
rok,* "to sit in silence."

Mopas, モパス, 駈ル. *v.i.* To canter.
Syn: Chaira.

Monraige, モンライゲ, 働ク、例セバ、
チイタエモンライゲ、君ハ何處ニテ働
クナ. *v.i.* To work. As:—*Neita
e monraige?* "where do you
work"?

Mon-saure, モンサウレ, 閑ナル. *v.i.*
Not busy. Not much to do.
Syn: Mon-hauge.

Monshutu, モンシュツ, 打ツ、手ニテ
打ツ. *v.t.* To beat. To strike
with the hand. **Syn: Moishutu.**

Montabi, モンタビ, 忙シキ. *v.i.* To
be busy. To be engaged.

Montabire, モンタビレ, 忙シキ. *v.i.*
To be busy. **Syn: Unisapka
an.**

Mon-ush, モンウシ, 多忙. *adj.* Busy.

More, モレ, 靜ムレ. *v.t.* To quiet.
To compose. **Syn: Haugere
Ratchire.**

More, モレ, 毒矢ノ根ヲ包ム木ノ葉. *n.*
Any kind of leaf in which arrow
poison is wrapped.

Moreu, モレウ, 縫ノ模様. *n.* The
turns and twists in fancy needlework. Paterns of embroidery.

Mori, モリ, 小山. *n.* A little hill.
A hillock. A slope.

Moru, モル, 鬢ノ毛. *n.* The hairs
which grow on the temples.

Moru-enka, モルエンカ, 蟀谷 (コメカ
ミ). *n.* The temples.

Mosa,
モサ,
Mose,
モセ, ⎫
Mose, ⎬ イラクサノ纖維. *n.* The
モセ, ⎭ bast fibres of nettles.
Also "nettles" in some
places.

Mose,
モセ, ⎫ 刈ル. *v.t.* To reap.
Mose-kara, ⎬ To mow.
モセカラ, ⎭

Mose-hai, ⎫ イラクサ. *n.* Stinging-
モセハイ, ⎬ nettles. *Urtica dioica,*
Mouse, ⎭ *L.* var. *platyphylla,*
モウセ,

Wedd. Also "the inner bark or bast fibres of nettles." **Syn:** **Ipishiship.**

Mosem, モセム, 玄關. *n.* An antichamber. A porch.
Moshem, モシェム,

Mosh, モシ, 蠅. *n.* A fly.

Mosh, モシ, 醒ㇽ. *v i.* To wake up.

Moshikarabe, モシカラベ, ツクガネ ニレジン. *n.* *Adenophora verticillata, Fisch.*

Moshi-kina, モシキナ, ミヅ. *n.* *Pilea pumila, A. Gray.* The richweed. **Syn: Minchi.**

Moshima, モシマ, 他ノ. *adj.* Another. Other. Besides.

Moshima-an-ike, モシマアンイケ, 他 ノ者. *n.* The other one. **Syn: Naa moshimap. Naa oyap.**

Moshima-kotan-ta, モシマコタンタ, 他ノ村ニ. *adv.* Abroad.

Moshima-no-okai, モシマノオカイ, 捨置ク. *v.t.* To let alone.
Moshima-okai, モシマオカイ,

Moshimap, モシマブ, 他ノ. *adj.* Other. Others.

Moshimap, モシマブ, 他ノ者. *n.* Another one.

Moshima-shui, モシマシュイ, 再ビ、 其他ニ. *adv.* Again. Besides.

Moshir' or Moshiri, モシル, 又ヘ、モ シリ, 國、世界、モシリ、ハ文章ニ於 テ、歴モシル、トナル、例セバ、モシ ルホツボ、死ス. *n.* A country. The world. *Moshiri* often becomes *moshir'* in composition. As:— *Moshir' hoppa*, "to die." *Oya moshir' un guru*, "a foreigner." *Moshiri pake, moshiri gesh,* "the

whole world." *Moshiri shikapne-ka no* "the whole world," "The surroundings of a country."

Moshiri-buri, モシリブリ, 習慣、風俗. *n.* The ways, customs or manners of a people.

Moshiri-chup-ka, モシリチュブカ, 東. *n.* The east. **Syn: Moshiripa. Moshiri etok.**

Moshiri-chup-pok, モシリチュブポク, 西. *n.* The west. **Syn: Moshirigesh. Moshiri emko.**

Moshiri-emko, モシリエムコ, 西. *n.* The west.

Moshiri-etok, モシリエトク, 東. *n.* The east.

Moshiri-gesh, モシリゲシ, 西. *n.* The west.

Moshiri-hoppa, モシリホッパ, 死スル、此世ヲ逝ル.
Moshirioppa, モシリオッパ, *v.i.* To die. To leave the world.

Moshiri-ikkewe-chep, モシリイッケ ウェチェブ, 世界ヲ脊負ヒタル魚. *n.* The name of the fish upon the back of which the world is supposed to rest. **Syn: Tukushish.**

Moshiri-ko-ishu-ambe, モシリコイ シュアムベ, 生涯. *n.* One's life.

Moshiripa, モシリパ, 東. *n.* The east. **Syn: Moshiri chuppok. Moshiri etok.**

Moshir-un-guru, モシルングル, 外 國人. *n.* A foreigner.

Moshir-un-utara, モシルンウタラ, 一國ノ住民. *n.* The inhabitants of a country.

Moshit, モシツ, 世界. *n.* The world. The same as *moshiri.*

Moshitpa-tata, モシ、ブタタ, 地上、空中. *n.* Above the earth. The open expanse above.

Moshiu-kina, モシウキナ, ナホバモンキゥ. *n.* *Angelica refracta, Fr. Schm.* **Syn : Yakara-kina.**

Moshkara, モシカラ, 俎板. *n.* A tray used for cutting up food and also for carrying fish in. **Syn : Manaita.**

Moshkara, モシカラ, 物ヲ置ク爲ニ草ヲ敷ク. *v.i.* To spread out grass to lay anything upon. To be laid out like lumps of grass. To be mown down like grass.

Mosh-wa-an, モシワアン, 覚醒シタル. *adj.* Awake.

Moso, モソ. 醒マス、起ス. *v.t.* To waken. To rouse up from sleep.

Mosomoso, モソモソ, 俎. *n.* Maggots. **Syn : Mososhpe.**

Mosomoso, モソモソ, 醒マス、起ス. *v.t.* To rouse up from sleep.

Mososhpa, モソシバ, 醒マス、(複數). *v.i.* To arouse. (*pl*).

Mososhpe, モソシペ, 俎. *n.* Maggots. **Syn : Mosomoso.**

Mososhpe-kut, モソシペクツ, クカイサゥ. *n.* *Veronica sibirica, L.*

Mososo, モソソ, 起上レ. *v.t.* To rouse up.

Motarap, モタラブ, **Notarap,** ノタラブ, 魚ノ頬肉. *n.* The cheeks of fish.

Moteki, モテキ, **Motekki,** モテッキ, 幸ニシテ、仕合ニ. *adv.* Fortunately. Luckily. **Syn : Kusu eun.**

Moto or motoho, モト, 又ヘ、モトホ, 起元、原始、土著ノ者. *n.* Origin. Beginning. Native.

Moto-kotan, モトコタン, 故郷. *n.* One's native place.

Motoma, モトマ, 少キ蓆. *n.* A small mat.

Motontori, モトントリ, 鷄冠、髻(マゲ). *n.* A top-knot. A crest or tuft of feathers seen on the heads of of some kinds of birds. A tress.

Motontori-kara, モトントリカラ, 髻ヲ結ブ. *v.i.* To do the hair Japanese fashion.

Motot, モトツ, 魚ノ脊髓. *n.* The backbone or ventral column of fishes.

Mototchi-ikiri, モトッチイキリ, 魚ノ脊椎骨. *n.* Vertebra of fishes.

Motta, モッタ, 釿(舟ヲ刳ルニ用ユ). *n.* A kind of adze used for hollowing out boats. **Syn : Tenua.**

Mouru, モウル, 女ノ下着. *n.* A woman's under dress. A chemise. Shift.

Moyo, モヨ, 少ナキ. *adj.* A few. **Syn : Shipuine.**

Moyoike, モヨイケ, 蠢ク. *v.i.* Same as *moyomoyo.*

Moyomoyo, モヨモヨ, 蠢ク. *v.i.* To move as swarms of maggots in putrified fish or meat. **Syn : Ukopaiyaige.**

Moyuk, モユク, 狢、▲ジナ. *n.* A kind of racoon. *Canis procyonoides, Gray.*

Moyuk-soyai, モユクソヤイ, 土蜂. *n.* A humble bee.

Mu, ム, 傾ク、匍フ. *v.t.* To slant upwards or downwards. To creep.

Mu, ム, 縫フ. *v.t.* To sew. **Syn:** Kem-eki.

Mu, ム, 塞ガル、例セバ、キサラム、耳ガ塞ガレ. *v.i.* and *adj.* To be stopped up. Blocked up As:—*Kisara mu,* "to have the ears stopped." **Syn: Omu.**

Muchattek, ム チャッ テ ク,
Nuchatktek, ヌ チャッ ク テ ク, 悦ブ. *adj.* and *v.i.* To rejoice. To feel happy.

Mochimasap, モチマサブ, or **Muchinusap,** ムチヌサブ, 綏キ、鈍キ. *adj.* Slow. **Syn: Moire. Katu-moire.**

Muchimashnu, ムチマシヌ, or **Nuchimashnu,** ヌチマシヌ, 速ナレ. *adj.* Quick. **Syn: Emonashnu. Tunash.**

Mui, ムイ, 結フ、束メレ. *v.t.* To tie. To bind. To make into a bundle.

Mui, ムイ, 束、例セバ、ムイネアカラ、束子レ. *n.* A bundle. As:—*Mui ne akara,* "to be made into a bundle."

Mui, ムイ, 簸. *n.* A winnow.

Mui, ム イ, 山ヨリ海ノ方ヘ向イテ見ル時ハ、少シク低下シ、且次第ニ幅廣ク傾キ、又海ノ方ヨリ山ノ方へ向イテ見ル時ハ其ノ反對ニ見ユル場所. *n.* A place which slants gradually outwards and slightly downwards towards the sea when looked at from the mountains and *vice versa* when looked at from the sea.

Mui-kara, ムイカラ, 簸ル. *v.t.* To winnow.

Muimamba, ムイマムバ, 旅仕度スレ. *v.i.* To prepare for a journey.

Muimuye, ムイムイェ, 掃ヒ去ル. *v.t.* To brush away. To sweep off.

Muk, ムク, バアソブ. *n. Codonopsis ussuriensis, Hemsl.* The root of this plant is used for food by the Ainu.

Muk, ムク, 塞ガレタレ. *adj.* Stopped up. Bunged up.

Muk, ムク, 秘密ナル. *adj.* Secret. Hidden.

Mukara, ムカラ, 斧. *n.* An axe.

Mukara-eiki, ムカラエイキ, 斧ニテ截レ. *v.i.* To chop with an axe.

Mukecharase, ムケチャラセ, 匍フ. To crawl along. To work one's self along upon the side or stomach. **Syn: Mukereye.**

Mukechirase, ムケチラセ, 拂フ、掃フ. *v.i.* To sweep. **Syn: Munuye.**

Mukechirasep, ムケチラセブ, 箒. *n.* A broom. **Syn: Munuyep.**

Mukekashi, ムケカシ, ツリガネニンジン. *n. Adenophora verticillata, Fisch.*

Mukereye, ムケレイェ, 匍フ. *v.t.* To crawl along. To work one's self along upon the side or stomach. **Syn: Mukecharase.**

Muke-upshoro, ムケウブショロ, 腰卷. A woman's loin cloth.

Mukkane, ムッカ子, 圓キ. *adj.* Round.

Mukkane-chikuni, ムッカ子チクニ, or **Mukkane-ni,** ムッカ子ニ, 圓キ竿. *n.* A round pole.

Mukke, ムッケ, 秘密ナル. *adj.* Mysterious. Secret. As:— *Kamui mukke itak,* "the mysteries of God." *Keutum mukke guru,* "a person who keeps matters secret."

Mukkere, ムッケレ, 隱ス、秘密ニスル. *v.t.* To hide. To keep secret. **Syn: Oraunu.**

Mukkosamba, ムッコサムバ, 塞ガレ
ル. *v.i.* To be stopped up.

Mukkot, ムッコツ, 恐ル、例セバ、ケゥ
ツムオロゲムッコツカネコトマン、彼
ハ心ニ懼チ抱ク如ク二見ユル. *v.i.* To
be in fear. As :—*Keutum oroge
mukkot kane kotoman,* " he appears
to have fear in his heart."

Mukku, ムック, or **Mukkuri, ムックリ,**
樂器ノ名、ビヤボン. *n.* A kind of
musical instrument made of wood,
and somewhat resembling a "Jew's
harp."

Mukkuri-rekte, ムックリレクテ, ムク
リチ彈ズレ. *v.i.* To play upon the
mukkuri.

Mukmuk, ムクムク, 塞ガレシ. *adj.*
Stopped up.

Mukmukke, ムクムッケ, 塞グ. *v.t.* To
stop up.

Mukmukpa, ムクムクバ, 塞グ、例セ
バ、キサラムクムクバタン、汝ノ耳チ塞
グ、卽チ聽ク勿レ. *v.t.* To stop up.
As :— *Kisara mukmukpa yan,*
"stop up your ears ;" i.e. "do
not appear to hear."

Mukramama, ムクラママ, 縮ム. *v.i.*
To cringe.

Mukshit, ムクシツ, バツプ、例セバ、ム
クシツコツカ、バツプチアテル. *n.*
A poultice. As :—*Mukshit kotkuka,*
"to poultice."

Mukuribe, ムクリベ, ナツメゥナキ. *n.*
A lamprey. **Syn : Ukuribe.**

Mumi, ムミ, 組合、級. *n.* A company. A class.

Mun, ムン, 草、雜草. *n.* Grass.
Weeds.

Munchiri, ムンチリ, アバ. *n.* Millet. *Setaria germanica, Trin.*

Mungi, ムンギ, 小麥. *n.* Wheat.

Munin, ムニン, 朽チタレ. *adj.* Rotten. Addled. **Syn : Horose.**

Munin-shiyeye, ムニンシイェイェ,
or **Munin-tashum, ムニンタシュム,**
癩病. *n.* Leprosy.

Mun-konchi-koro, ムンコンチコロ,
無住ノ家屋ノ如ク荒レタレ. *adj.* To
become desolate as a deserted
house (lit. to wear a grass bonnet).

Mun-kuta-ushi, ムンクタウシ, 堆肥.
n. A manure heap. **Syn : Mun-
ush mimdara.**

Munnuye, ムンヌイェ, 拂フ. *v.i.* To
sweep.

Munnuyep, ムンヌイェブ, 箒. *n.* A
broom.

**Munnuyep-nochiu, ムンヌイェブノチ
ウ,** 慧星. *n.* A comet.

Mun-pe, ムンペ, 露. *n.* Dew. **Syn :
Kinape.**

Mun-ra, ムンラ, 草ノ葉. *n.* A blade
of grass.

Munsamambe, ムンサマムベ, シマカ
レイ. *n.* *Yebrias yebrinus.* F. &
S.

Mun-tuitui, ムンツイツイ, 病氣ノ呪ニ
衣チ打ツ. *v.t.* To beat one's
clothes as a charm against sickness.

**Mun-ush-mimdara, ムンウシミムダ
ラ,** 堆肥. *n.* A manure heap.

Murayeba, ムライェバ, 禮トシテ人ノ
頭チ撫デル. *v.t.* To stroke the head
as in salutation.

Muri, ムリ, ハマニンニク、チンキ. *Elymus mollis, Trin.*

Muriri, ムリリ, 葬式ノ時死體ニ結ブ紐. *n.* A band used for tying up the dead for burial. **Syn: Mururi.**

Muru or **Muruhu, ムル,** 又ハ **ムルフ,** 糠. *n.* Chaff. Husks. Bran.

Murumuruse, ムルムルセ, 怒ル. *v.i.* To be angry. To boil up with anger.

Mururi, ムルリ, 死體及ビ其ト共ニ葬ル品物ヲ結ブ縄. *n.* A lace or cord used for tying up the dead and the paraphernalia buried with them. **Syn : Muriri.**

Musa, ムサ, 他人ノ頭ヲ撫デル (禮義トシテ). *v.t.* To stroke the head of another person in salutation. **Syn: Uruiruye. Umusa.**

Muse, ムセ, イラクサ. *n.* Same as *Mose,* " nettles."

Muse-chiri, ムセチリ, ツツドリ. *n.* Himalayan cuckoo. *Cuculus intermedius.*

Mut, ムツ, 帯フ(刀チ)、頸ニカケレ. *v.t.* To wear as a sword. To wear round the neck. As :—*Emush mut* " to wear a sword." *Emut omushi anochautekka,* " he drew the sword which he wore." **Syn : Unu.**

Mutbe, ムツベ, 刀、武器. *n.* Swords, Arms.

Muye, ムイェ, 束. *n.* A bundle.

Muyemanba, ムイェマンバ, 包装スル. *v.t.* To pack up one's things.

N (ナ).

N, ン, 數詞ノ後ニ附ケ加フレバ N ハ、ニウ(人)ノ略ナリ. *n.* When found suffixed to numerals *n* is a contraction of *Niu,* " a person." See *Niu.*

Na, ナ, 此詞ヲ働詞ノ後ニ加フル時ハ文意ノ終リタルチ示ス. *part.* This particle is often placed after a verb when a subject is supposed to be finished or a sentence concluded. It is a conclusive or affirmative particle.

Na, ナ, 運フ、荷フ、例セバ、ニナクスオマン、彼ハ木ヲ取リニ行ツタ. *v. t.* To carry. As:—*Ni na gusu oman,* " he has gone to fetch wood."

Na, ナ, 水. *n.* Water. As:—*Nai,* " a stream." *Na-rai,* " a ditch."

Naa, ナア, 猶、若シ否定ノ詞ト共ニ用ユレバ、未ダノ意味ナリ、此詞ハ又形容詞ノ前ニ付ケ加ヘテ、比較級ヲ構成ス、例セバ、ナアポン、ヨリモ少ク. *adv.* Yet. More. With a negative " not yet." This word is often used before adjectives to express the comparative degree. Thus :—*Naa pon,* " smaller." *Naa poro,* " larger." As :— *Naa an,* " there is more." *Naa arashuine,*

" once more." *Naa ek isam*, "he has not yet come." *Naa isam*, "there is no more." *Naa moshima*, " yet again." "Again." *Naa okai*, " there are more." *Naa pon no*, " a little more" *Naa shinep*, " one more." *Naa shomo*, " not yet."

Naa-anak, ナアアナク, 受動ノ働詞ニ接續スルトキハ殆ンドノ意味トナル、例セバ、ナアアナクアオツケ、殆ンド槍ニテ剌サレントシタリキ. *adv.* When followed by a passive verb-"nearly." As:—*Naa anak aotke*, "it was nearly speared." **Syn: An......an-gesh shiriki. Naa-nipo.**

Naani, ナ ア ニ,
Naanihungo, ナアニフンゴ, 殆 ン ド.
Naanipo, ナ ア ニ ポ,
adv. Almost. Nearly.

Na-anun-neyakka, ナアヌン子ヤッカ, 何處ニモ. *adv.* Anywhere. Everywhere. **Syn: Nei ta ne yakka. Inani un ne yakka.**

Naa-samata, ナアサマタ, 其他、再ビ、又. *adv.* Besides. Again. Also.

Naa-shirankoro, ナアシランコロ, 暫ラクシテ. *adv.* Presently. A little later.

Nahun, ナフン, 只今、數日以前. *adv.* Just now. A few days ago. Just a little while ago. **Syn: Take. Ahunak.**

Nahun-po, ナフンポ, 今、即時. *adv.* Now. Just now. Now again.

Nai, ナイ, 流、河、谷. *n.* A stream. A river; (in saghalien "a large river").—A valley either with or without water.

Naibutchi, ナイブッチ, 河口. *n.* A river's mouths. (*pl*).

Naikosamba, ナイコサムバ,
Naikosanu, ナイコサヌ, 鳴ル、音スレ、例セバ、タムヒフムカンナイコサメ、刀チ抜クトキノ音. *v.i.* To make a noise. To sound. As:—*Tam pi humkan naikosanu*, "the sound of drawing swords."

Nai-yau, ナイヤウ, 支流. *n.* Tributaries of a stream.

Nak, ナク, 場所、何處、幾何. *n. and adj.* Place. Where. What. How much.

Nak, ナク, 否ラズ、ナシニ、例セバ、シクナク、盲目、目ガ無イ. *adv.* Not. Without. As:—*Shik-nak*, "without eyes;" "blind." **Syn: Sak.**

Nakan, ナカン, 何處へ. *post.* Whither.

Nakkane, ナッカ子, 幾何. *post.* How much?

Nak-oro, ナコロ, 何處へ. *post.* To where?

Nak-ta, ナクタ, 何處ニ. *adv.* Where. **Syn: Hunakta.**

Naktek, ナクテク, 丁度、何處デ、丁度何程カ. *post.* Just where. Just how much.

Nak-wa, ナクワ, 何處カラ、例セバ、ナクワエク、何處ヨリ彼ハ來リシカ. *adv.* Whence. As:—*Nak wa ek*, "whence has he come?"

Nak-we, ナクウェ, 何處カラ. *adv.* Whence. **Syn: Nak-wa.**

Nam, ナム, 冷キ、例セバ、ナムワッカ、新鮮ナル水、又ハ冷水、之ニ對シテヒツルワッカ、ハ俤溜セル水ナリ. *adj.* Cold as water or one's feet or hands. Fresh or cool (as fresh water). Thus:—*Nam wakka*, "fresh or cool water." Fresh water in contradistinction to stagnant water is called *pituru wakka*.

Namde, ナムデ, 冷ス. *v.t.* To set to cool. To cool. **Syn : Tuwarage. Tuwaraka.**

Nami-oyan, ナミオヤン, 魚ノ如ク寄ル. *v.i.* To crowd together as fish in water.

Namka, ナムカ, 冷ス. *v.t.* To make cool.

Namshu, ナムシュ, or **Namshun, ナムシュン**, 蛆. *n.* Maggots. Grubworms.

Nan, ナン, 顔. *n.* The face. As :—*Nan kokik*, " to slap the face."

Nanapo, ナナポ, 直チニ. *adj.* Immediately.

Nanchi-chup, ナンチチュプ, 七月. *n.* The month of July by some called shimauta-chup.

Nanchimi, ナンチミ, 娼妓、淫賣婦. *n.* A secret whore or whoremonger. A secret harlot.

Nanepuriwen, ナチプリウェン, 憐ム. *v.t.* To pity.

Nanga, ナンガ, 顔. *n.* The face.

Nangashke-chiu-kush, ナンガシケチウクシ, 落葉スレ. *v.i.* To shed leaves.

Nangeu, ナンゲウ, 頬骨. *n.* The cheekbones.

Nange, ナンゲ, or **Nanke, ナンケ**, 刈ル、例セバ、ヌンナンゲ、草ヲ刈ル. *v.t.* To mow. As :—*Mun nange*, " to mow grass."

Nangon, ナンゴン, ナンゴロ ニ 同ジ. Same as *nangoro*.

Nangora, ナンゴラ, 多分、大抵、例セバ、子コンアキナンゴラ、彼ハ大抵何ヲ爲スナランカ. *adv.* Perhaps. It is most likely to be so. As :— *Nekon a ki nangora?* " What will he most likely do."

Nangoro, ナンゴロ, 未來及ビ未來ノ實現ヲ示ス助詞. *aux. v.* This word expresses the future tense and also a future probability, " there probably will be." *Ek nangoro*, " he will probably come," or " he will come."

Nangoro-wa, ナンゴロワ, 多分、大抵 *adv.* Perhaps. Probably. Most likely. Being likely.

Nan-hepuni, ナンヘプニ, 顔ヲ上ゲル. *v.t.* To hold up the face.

Nani, ナニ, 直チニ、速ニ、然ル時ニ. *adv.* Immediately. Quickly. At once. Then. Without stopping.

Nani-no-po, ナニノポ, 直チニ. *adv.* Immediately. At once.

Nani-hungo, ナニフンゴ,
Naanihungo, ナアニフンゴ, 殆ド. *adv.*
Nanipo, ナ ニ ポ,
Almost. Nearly.

Nani-nani, ナニナニ, 直チニ. *adv.* Very quickly. At once. Immediately. Directly after.

Nani-po, ナニポ, 殆ド. *adv.* Nearly. **Syn : Naanihungo.**

Nan-iporo, ナンイポロ, 顔色. *n.* The complexion of the face.

Nani-rai, ナニライ, 頓死. *n.* A sudden death.

Nani-ruki, ナニルキ, 鵜吞ニスル. *v.t.* To swallow without biting. To swallow whole.

Nankan-tushte, ナンカンツシテ, 顔ヲシカメル. *v.i.* To screw up the face.

Nan-kotchaketa, ナンコッチャケタ, 面前ニ. *adv.* Before the face of. In the presence of.

Nan-kotchaketa-pirasa, ナンコッチャケタピラサ, 示ス、顯ス、前ニ擴ケル. *v.t.* To reveal. To make known. To spread out before one.

Nanta, ナンタ, 船首. *n.* The bow of a ship or boat.

Nan-tarara, ナンタララ, 顔ヲ擡ケル. *v.t.* To hold up the face. **Syn: Nan-hepuni.**

Nan-shik-tarara, ナンシクタララ, 見上ケル (不意ノ音響ニ驚キタルトキノ如ク). *v. t.* To look up (as when startled by any unexpected noise).

Nanu, ナヌ, or **Nanuhu, ナヌフ,** 顔. *n.* The face.

Nanu-iporo, ナヌイポロ, 顔、貌、カホカタチ. *n.* The countenance.

Nanu-isam, ナヌイサム, 耻ヅル. *v.i.* To feel ashamed. To be put out of countenance. **Syn: Yaikatuwen. Yainikoroshma.**

Nanu-wen-chep, ナヌウェンチェプ, トウ〻ッカヂカ. *n.* Sculpin. *Hemilepidotus gilberti, Jor. & Eny.*

Nanu-wen-chimakani, ナヌウェンチマカニ, トウ〻ッカヂカ. *n.* A kind of sculpin. *Hemilepidotus gilbertii, (Tilesius).*

Nanu-wen-kikiri, ナヌウェンキキリ, 青蠅 (蚊ニ似タル尾ヲ持ツ). *n.* A kind of small blue fly having a woolly tail resembling mildew.

Narai, ナライ, 塚. *n.* A ditch. **Syn: Pechiri.**

Nasa, ナサ, 裂ク. *v.t.* To tear. **Syn: Yasa.**

Nashke, ナシケ, 碎ク. *v.i.* Slit. Cracked.

Nata, ナタ, 尖ノ無キ大ナイフ. *n.* A kind of large pointless knife.

Nata, タナ, 誰ノ. *adj.* Whose.

Naugep, イウゲプ, or **Naukep, ナウケプ,** 鉤、釣針. *n.* A crook. A hook.

Naukepsaine, ナウケプサイ子, 搔キ分ケル (木ノ茂リタル枝ナドチ). *v.t.* To hook or hold on one side as branches of trees as when one is passing through a forest.

Naye, ナイェ, 條(スヂ)、標(シルシ)、例セメ、マキリアニナイェカラ、小刀ニテ標ヲ付クル. *n.* A line or mark. As: —*Makiri ani naye kara,* "to make a mark with a knife."

Ne, 子, ...ニナル、アル、例セバ、ペ子、水ニナル. *v.i.* To become. To be. Is. As:—*Ainu ku ne,* "I am an Ainu." *Pe ne,* "to become water." *Koponchi ne,* "to become dust." This word is often used as an affirmative particle; it follows nouns and is itself generally followed by *ruwe ne.* As:—*Seta ne ruwe ne,* "it is a dog." *Chep ne ruwe ne,* "it is a fish."

Ne-gusu, チグス, 故ニ、例セバ、ソンノチグス、眞ナルガ故ニ. *post.* For. Because. As:—*Son no ne gusu,* "because it is true."

Nei, 子イ, 其、彼、彼ノ女. *pro.* That. The. He. She. It.

Nei-a, チイア, 其、左樣、例セバ、チイアケル、其人、チイアァ、其物、チイアヤクアィェ、左樣ト云ハル. *pro.* That. So. As:—*Nei a guru,* "that person." *Nei a ap,* "that thing." *Nei a yak aye,* "so it is said."

Nei-ambe, チイアムベ, 其物. *n.* That thing. That person.

Nei-a-orota, チイアオロタ, 然ル時ニ. *adv.* Then. Upon that.

Nei-a-yakka, チイアヤッカ, 而シテ、又、ト雖モ、例セバ、キヤチイヤッカ、其ハ爲サレタレド. *post.* And. Also. Although. As:—*Ki wa nei a yakka*, "although it is done."

Nei-a-yakka……ne-yakka, チイアヤッカ……チヤッカ, …モ……又……モ. *post.* Both…and, when used with an affirmative ; neither……nor, when used with a negative.

Nei-a-yak-ne, チイアヤクネ, or **Nei-a-yakun, チイアヤクン**, 若シ、ト雖モ. *post.* If. Although.

Nei-hi-samata, チイヒサマタ, 其ノ他ニ. *adv.* Beside that. Besides.

Nei-ita, チイイタ, 然ル時ニ、其時ニ、例セバ、チイトホシュゲトホ、其次ノ日. *adv.* Then. At that time. As:—*Nei toho shimge toho*, "the following day."

Nei-ka, チイカ, 其如ク、其様ニ. *adv.* So. In that way.

Neikehuike, チイケフイケ, or **Neikene-yakka, チイケチヤッカ**, 總テ、何處デモ. *adj.* All. Every-where.

Neikeseima, チイケセイマ, 總テ、全ク. *adj.* All. Entirely.

Neina, チイナ, 歌、謠. *n.* A song. A chant.

Neina-chikap, チイナチカブ, 鳴鳥ノ一種. *n.* Some kind of singing bird.

Nei-no, チイノ, ……ノ如ク、例セバ、チイノカヲ、似セル、倣做スル. *adv.* So. As. Thus. Like that. As:—*Nei no kaia*, "to imitate, to do like."

Nei-no-an, チイノアン, 左様ニ、……ノ如、即チ. *adv.* So. Thus. Like this or that. It is so.

Nei-oro-pakno, チイオロバクノ, 如何程遠キカ. *ph.* How far ?

Nei-orota, チイオロタ, 然ル時、其處、チイオロタアン、其ハ其處ニアルカ. *adv.* Then. There. As:—*Nei orota an !* " is it there ? "

Nei-orun, チイオルン, 何處、何. *adv.* Where. What. Of what place. As:—*Nei orun guru e ne*, what place do you belong to ?

Nei-pak-no, チイバクノ, 如何程遠ク. *ph.* How far.

Nei-pak-no-nei-wa-ne-yakka, チイバクノチイワチヤッカ, 何處デモ、何時デモ、例セバ、ネイバクノチイヮチヤッカクオイラクニプショモタバンナ、其ハ余ガ決シテ忘レサル物ナリ. *ph.* Every-where and at all times. As:—*Nei pakno nei wa ne yakka ku oira kunip shomo tapan na*, "it is a thing I shall never forget.

Nei-pak-no-ne-yakka, チイバクノチヤッカ, 或ル處マデ. *ph.* As far as one likes. To any distance. Everywhere. Anywhere.

Nei-pak-no-nei-wa-ne-yakka, チイバクノチイワチヤッカ, 何處デモ、何時デモ. *ph.* Everywhere. At all times. Important.

Nei-pak-no-ne-yakka……shomo, チイバクノチヤッカ……ショモ, 決シテ……セヌ、例セバ、チイバクノチヤッカクオイラクニプショモタバンナ、其ハ余ガ決シテ忘レザル物ナリ. *ph.* Never. As:—*Nei pakno ne yakka ku oira kunip shomo tapan na*, "it is a thing I shall never forget."

Neita, 子イタ, 何處. *adv.* Where.

Neita-korak, 子イタコラク, 曾テナシ. *adv.* Never before. **Syn : Ene neita shomoki a hi.**

Neita-korak-ayayamkire, 子イタコラクアヤヤムキレ, 全ク知ラザリシ者. *ph.* A thing one has never known before.

Neita-ne-yakka, 子イタ子ヤッカ, 何處テモ. *adv.* Anywhere. Everywhere.

Neita-pakno-newa-ne-yakka, 子イタパクノ子ワ子ヤッカ, 何時ニテモ、常ニ. *adv. ph.* Always.

Nei-ushpe, 子イウシペ, 音信. *n.* Any news. News from any place.

Nei-utara, 子イウタラ, 彼等、彼等. *pro.* They. Them.

Nei-wa, 子イワ, 何處ヨリ、例セバ、子イヤエク、汝ハ何處ヨリ來レルカ. *adv.* Whence. As:—*Nei wa ek,* "where have you come from?" **Syn : Nak wa.**

Neko, 子コ, 若シ、時ニ、例セバ、エクチク、若シ彼米ラバ. *post.* If. When. As:—*Ek neko,* "if he comes."

Nekon-a, 子コナ, 何ノ、例セバ、子コナアカラ、何シタモノダラウ. *adv.* What kind. What. As:—*Nekon a akara,* "what is to be done." *Nekon a iki wa gusu,* "what to do." *Nekon a ataye an,* "what is the price." *Nekon a hawe an,* "what did he say." *Nekon a akara kuni guru ta a?* "what ought to be done with him? "what shall we do with him." *Nekon a a-*

kara kunip ta an a? "what is to be done with it." **Syn : Makanak.**

Nekon-a-poka, 子コナポカ, 何卒. *adv.* Please. Somehow or other.

Nekon-ka, 子コンカ, 如何ニ. *adv.* How. Somehow.

Ne-manup, 子マヌプ, 呼稱セラル、物、例セバ、セタ子マヌプ、此者ハ犬ト稱セラル. *ph.* The object called. As :—*Seta ne manup,* "the object called "dog."

Nekon-ka-newa, 子コンカ子ワ, 何卒. *ph.* Please (often used in prayer).

Nekon-ne-yakka, 子コン子ヤッカ, 併. ナレドモ. *post.* However.

Nen, 子ン, or **Neni,** 子ニ, 誰、例セバ、タムベチンキヤ、誰が此ヲ爲セシカ. *pro.* Who. Somebody. As :—*Tambe nen ki ya?* "who did this?"

Nenchike, 子ンチケ, 獨樂, コマ. *n.* A top. **Syn : Tumu.**

Nenka, 子ンカ, 誰カ、何者カ. *adj.* Somebody. Some one or other.

Nen-korope, 子ンコロペ, 誰ノ. *poss. pro.* Whose. **Syn : Hunna korobe.**

Nen-ne, 子ン子, 誰、例セバ、タムベキケルチンチヤ、此ヲ爲セシハ誰ナルカ. *adv.* Who. As:—*Tambe ki guru nen ne ya?* "who is he that has done this?"

Nen-ne-kuru-ka, 子ン子クルカ, 誰テモ. *n.* Anybody. **Syn : Nen ne yakka.**

Nen-ne-yakka, 子ン子ヤッカ, or **Nen-nen-ne-yakka,** 子ン子ン子ヤ

ッカ, 各人、誰デモ. *n.* Everybody. Anybody.

Nenta, チンタ, 誰、例セバ、チンタイキ ルウェアン、誰カ此チ ナ セ シカ. *pro.* Who. As:—*Nenta iki ruwe an?* " who did it." *Nenta hawe an?* " who is there? "

Nep, チブ, or **Nepi, チピ**, 何、菜物、或 物、例セバ、ヘイカチ ネブ カラ グ スキム タ ナマンア、此若者ハ何ノ爲ニ 山 ニ 行キシカ、イ テキ ネ プ イェ、何事モ云 フ ナ カ レ、ネブ ア エ ホ マ ツ ア ン ナ、彼ハ 或ル物チ恐ル. *adv.* What. Something. Anything. As:—*Heikachi nep kara gusu kimta oman a?* " what has the lad gone to the mountains for?" *Nep shinotcha e ki rusui ya?* " what hymn do you wish to sing?" *Iteki nep ye,* " do not say anything." *Nep aehomatu an na,* "he is afraid of something."

Nep-gusu, チブグス, 何故、例セバ、チ ブ グ ス アイヌ イタ クエア シ カ イ、如 何ニ 彼ハ アイヌ語チ話シ得ルカ、チ ブ グ ス タ ム ベ チ イ ノ ア ン ア、何故ニ然 ル ヤ. *adv.* Why. Wherefore. How. *Nep gusu Ainu itak eashkai?* " how is it he can speak Ainu?" *Nep gusu tambe nei no an a?* " why is this so." **Syn:** **Hemandagusu.**

Nep-ne-ka, チ ブ チ カ, 或 物. *post.* Something.

Nep-irenga-koro-gusu, チブイレン ガコログス, 何 故 ニ. *ph.* Why. For what reason. Wherefore.

Nep-ka, チブカ, 或物. *n.* Something. Something or other.

Nepka-ambe, チブカアムベ, 或物ノ. *adj.* Something or other.

Nepka-sak-no, チブカサクノ, 無一物 ノ、例セバ、チブカサクノクエク、余ハ 何物チモ持チ來ラズ、チブカショモク イェ、余ハ何モ云ハ ザ リ キ. *adj.* Having nothing. As:—*Nep ka sak no ku ek,* "I have brought nothing." *Nep ka shomo ku ye,* "I said nothing."

Nepki, チブキ, 業、職、務、例セバ、チ ク タ エ チ ブ キ、何處デ汝ハ働クカ. *n. & v.t.* Business. Work. To do work or business. As:—*Nakta (neita) e nepki?* "where do you work?" *Soita nepki kor'an,* "he is doing something out of doors." *Ku arapa wa nepki,* "I will go and do something."

Nepki-ne, チブキ子, 或物、何カ、例セ バ、チブキ子ブキ、何事カチ爲シ居レリ. *n.* Something or other. As:— *Nep ki ne aki,* " to be doing something or other." *Nepki isam,* "he is doing nothing."

Nepkor'ambe, 子 ブ コ ラ ム ベ, 斯 ク、ノ如ク、例セバ、 エ ア ニ チブ コ ラ ム ベ、汝ノ如ク. *adv.* Such. So. So......as. Thus:—*Eani nepkor'ambe,* "such as you." *Eani nep pon kor'ambe,* "so small as you." *Kuani nepkoro oira gusu,* "a person who forgets like me."

Nepkoro, チブコロ, 如ク、例セバ、チブ コロ カ子、恰モ其ノ如ク. *adv.* Like. As. Resembling. As:—*Nepkoro kane,* "As it is." " Like."

Nepkoro-okai, 子ブコロオカイ, 斯ク、 ノ如ク、エ ア ニ ア エ チ ブ コ ロ オ カ イ イ ベ ル ウェ グ ル チ イ イ タ ア ン ア、他ニ汝 ノ如キ大食者アリ. *adv.* Same as *nepkor'ambe.* As:—*Eani a e nepkoro okai ibe ruwe guru nei ita* *an a !* "Is there another such a big eater as you?"

Nep-ne, チブチ, 否定ノ動詞ニ伴ハザ ル時ハ、或物ノ意味、若シ夫レニ伴フ トキハ、何モナシノ意味ナリ、例セ バ、チブチアラム、汝ハ何チ考へ居レ カ、チブチアラムカショモキ、其ハ考 フルノ物ニアラズ. *post.* Followed by a verb without a negative this word means "anything," something;" but when followed by a negative it means "nothing," "a thing of no importance." Thus :—*Nep ne aramu !* "are you thinking of anything?" *Nep ne aramu ka shomoki,* "it is nothing to be thought of," or "it is not worth even a thought," i.e. it is of no importance. What is it?

Nep-ne-gusu, チブチグス, 何故ニ. *post.* Why. For what reason.

Nep-nep, チブチブ, 種種ノ、種々ノ物、 例セバ、チブチブグ エモヌシ、余ハ種 々ノ事ニ関シテ多忙ナリ. *adj.* and *n.* Various. Many. Various things. As :—*Nep-nep ku emonu- sh,* "I am busy about a variety of things."

Nep-ne-yakka, チブチヤッカ, or **Nep-nep-ne-yakka, チブチブチ ヤッカ,** 何デモ、例セバ、チブチエブチ ヤッカ、何ノ魚ニテモ. *n.* Anything. Everything. In any case. By all means whatsoever. As :— *Nep chep ne yakka,* "what fish soever," *Nep ne yakka ibe emoka shomoki,* "he eschews no food." i.e. "he eats everything."

Nepshui-shui, チブシュイシュイ, 繰返 シ繰返シ、度々. *post.* Again and again.

Neppo, チッポ, 片小. *n.* A little bit of something.

Neppu, チブ, 漂木ノ堆積. *n.* Heaps of drift wood.

Nep-ta, チブタ, 何、例セバ、チブタ レイ ヘイアン、其ノ名ハ何カ. *pro.* What. As :—*Nep ta reihei an,* "what is it called." "What is its name." *Nep ta an !* "what is it." *Tambe nep ta an !* "what is this."

Neptapa, チブタバ, 其ハ何カ. *ph.* What is it?

Nere, チレ, 似合ハス、模擬スレ、…… トシテ遇スル、例セバ、アエヤイカム イチレ、禮拜ス可キ神トシテ遇スレ. *v.t.* To cause to become. To imitate. To treat as. As :—*Ae- yai-kamui nere,* "to treat as gods to be worshipped."

Ne-rok-okai, チロクオカイ, 間違タル. *v.i.* To have mistaken one for another. To be mistaken in see- ing. **Syn : Nei ambe.**

Ne-shiri, チシリ, ノ如リ見ユ. *v.i.* It seems. It indicates. It appears as.

Neshkoni, チシコニ, 栗ノ木、ナニゲ ルミ. *n.* Walnut tree. *Juglans Sieboldiana, Maxim.*

Net, チツ, 平穏ナル水面. *n.* The smooth surface of water.

Net, チツ, 漂木. Drift wood. **Syn: Nit.**

Net, チツ, 人形、身體. *n.* An ef- figy. Body. An idol. As :—*Ainu net* "the body or effigy of a man." **Syn : Noka. Inoka.**

Neto, チト, 平穏ナル天氣. *n.* Still calm weather.

Neto-an, チトアン, 平穩ナル海. *adj.* A calm sea. **Syn: Notoan.**

Netoba, チトバ, or **Netobake,** チトバケ, 體. *n.* The body. Trunk. **Syn: Tumama.**

Neto-wen, チトウェン, 荒海ノ. *adj.* A rough sea. **Syn: Noto wen.**

Neum-poka, チウムポカ, 如何ニカシテ. *adv.* Somehow or other. In some way or another.

Neun, チウン, 種々ノ、何ナルカ. *adj.* What is it. What. Various.

Neun-an-gusu, チウンアングス, 何故ニ. *ph.* For what reason. What can it be.

Neun-neun, チウンチウン, 種々ノ、多クノ. *adj.* Various. Many.

Neun-ne-yakka, チウンチヤッカ, 何處カニ、何處デモ. *adv.* Anywhere. Everywhere. By all means. **Syn: Neita ne yakka.**

Neun-shi-no-nei-ya, チウンシノチイヤ, 何處ヘ行キシカ. *ph.* Where has it gone.

Neusara, チウサラ, 物語ル. *v.i.* To tell tales. **Syn: Uweneusara.**

Neusara-ambe, チウサラアムベ, 音信. *n.* News. A chat. Gossip.

Neusara-guru, チウサラグル, 講談師. *n.* A storyteller.

Newa, チワ, 而シテ、又. *post.* And. Also.

Newa......newa, チワ......チワ, モ......モ、例セバ、クアニチワエアニチワ、我モ汝モ. *post* Both......and. As :—*Kuani newa eani newa*, " both you and I."

Neyakka, チヤッカ, ト......ト. *post.* Both ; and. Also.

Ni, ニ, 吹ク (鼻チ). *v.t.* To blow (as the nose).

Ni, ニ, 服用スル、飲ム、例セバ、タンクスリニコアナクチツナシノエリテンクスチ、君若シ此藥チ飲マバ、君ハ速ニ癒エン. *v.t.* To drink as medicine, tea; soup or hot water. As :—*Tan kusuri ni ko anak ne tunashi no e riten kusu ne*, " if you drink this medicine you will get better soon."

Ni, ニ, 延ビル. *v.i.* To stretch out.

Ni, ニ, 樹、例セバ、ニエオクテ、樹ニ懸ル. *n.* A general name for trees or wood. As :—*Ni eokte*, " to hang upon a tree." *Ni ham*, " the leaves of trees." *Ni ibehe*, " the fruit of trees," *Ni ka omare*, " to lay upon a bush." *Ni periba*, " to cleave wood." *Ni-wakka*, " the sap of trees."

Ni, ニ, or **Niu,** ニウ, 人. *n.* A person.

Niasara, ニアサラ, 熊ノ尾、尾骶骨. *n.* A bear's tail. The lower end of the spine. Coccyx.

Nibu, ニブ, ⎱ 山中ノ食物庫. *n.* A
Nipu, ニブ, ⎰ storehouse in the mountains.

Nichihi, ニチヒ, 柄. *n.* The handle of anything.

Nichimba, ニチムバ, ⎱ 柄. *n.* The
Nichiepa, ニチエバ, ⎰ handle of any tool or utensil.

Nichitne, ニチツ子, 疲勞、痙攣. *n.* The cramp. To be stiff from work or exercise. To be tired.

Ni-eanu-no, ニエアヌノ, 速ニ. *adv.* Fast.

Ni-hamu, ニハム, 木ノ葉. *n.* The leaves of trees.

Niham-muninkap, ニハムムニンカブ, 細雨. *n.* Very fine rain.

Niharu, ニハル, 寄生樹、ヤドリギ. *n.* Mistletoe. *Viscum album, L.* Sometimes used as a medicine and sometimes as food.

Nihorak-chup, ニホラクチュプ, 九月. *n.* The month of September.

Ni-ikiri, ニイキリ, 荷ノ木. *n.* A load of wood.

Nikambe, ニカムベ, 菌ノ一種. *n.* The white leathery layers of the fungus mycolium found between the bark and wood of dead oak, elm or ash trees.

Nikanoisep, ニカノイセプ, 樹木ニ纏繞スルキヅタノ類. *n.* Any tree-climbing plant.

Nikanoige-pungara, ニカノイゲブンガラ, 樹木ニ纏繞スルキヅタノ類. *n.* Any tree-climbing vine.

Nikaop, ニカオプ, 木ノ實. *n.* The fruit of trees.

Nikap, ニカプ, 病メル、例セバ、ニカプアイヌ、病人. *adj.* Sickly. Ill. As:—*Nikap ainu,*" a sick man.

Ni-kap, ニカプ, 樹皮、特ニ楡ノ皮. *n.* The bark of trees, especially the bark of elm trees. **Syn: Nikapu.**

Nikap-attush, ニカプアッツシ, 楡ノ皮ニテ造レル布. *n.* Cloth made from elm bark.

Nikappa, ニカッパ,} カズナギノ
Nikappana, ニカッパナ,} 一種. *n.* A kind of blenny. (*Ayuma Emnion Jor. of Eg*):

Nikap-umbe, ニカプムベ, 飾ノアル蓆ノ一種. A kind of ornamented mat. **Syn: Okitarunbe.**

Nikara, ニカラ, 梯子、楷段、チイクル ニカラシリカハチリ、彼ハ梯子ヨリ轉ゲ墜チタリ. *n.* A ladder. Stairs. As:—*Nei guru nikara shirika hachiri,* "he tumbled down stairs."

Nikashup, ニカシュプ、木匙. *n.* A wooden spoon.

Nikat-turashi-hemesu, ニカッツラシヘメス, 梯ヲ昇ル. *v.t.* To go up a ladder.

Nikaun-emauri, ニカウンエマウリ, タケイチゴ. *n.* *Rubus crataegifolius Bunge.*

Nike, ニケ, 薄キ片ニ切ル. *n.* and *v.t.* Slices. To cut into thin slices.

Nikeiruru. ニケイルル,} 狭キ路、径.
Nikeururu, ニケウルル,} *n.* A narrow road. A bridle-path. A foot-path.

Nikema, ニケマ, 樹幹. *n.* The trunk of a tree.

Nikerui, ニケルイ, 薄キ片ニ切ル. *v.t.* To cut into thin slices.

Nikerui-chep, ニケルイチェプ,} 二ツ割ニシタル干魚. *n.* Fish
Mikerui-chep, ミケルイチェプ,} having their heads cut off, their backbone taken out, split down the middle as far as the tail and dried in the sun.

Nikeururu, ニケウルル, ニケイル ニ同ジ. *n.* Same as Nikeiruru.

Niki, ニキ, 疊ム. *v.t.* To fold up.

Niki,
ニキ,}
Nikihi,} 襞(ヒダ). *n.* Tucks. Plaits.
ニキヒ,}

Niki-an, ニキアン, 襞(ヒダ)トリタル. *adj.* Plaited. Having tucks. As:—*Niki an amip,* "plaited garments."

Nikikara, ニキカラ, 疊ム. *v.t.* To fold up. **Syn: Ukoniki kara.**

Nikkotama, ニノコタマ, 圍ム. *v.t.* To surround.

Nikoniko, ニコニコ, 縮レタレ. *adj.* Curled (as hair). Crumpled.

Nikorange, ニコランゲ, 收穫スル、取リ下ス. *v.t.* To gather as beans in harvest. To take down from above.

Nikoro, ニコロ, 抱ク. *v.t.* To embrace. To fold in the arms.

Nikoro, ニコロ,
Nikorobe, ニコロヘ, } 內部. *adv.* Inside.

Nikororose, ニコロロセ, キツヽキガ木ヲ喙ク音. *n.* Sound made of the wood-pecker when pecking at trees.

Nikotuk, ニコツク, フクロウ. *n.* Owl.

Nikuru, ニクル, 木ノ蔭、又ハ影. *n.* The shade or shadow of trees.

Nikuru-ki, ニクルキ, 不意ノ災ニ逢フ、惱ム. *v.i.* To meet with an accident. To suffer. **Syn: Yai-iuninka.**

Nima, ニマ,
Nimaha, ニマハ, } 木ノ盆. *n.* A wooden tray. A charger. A bowl.

Nimakaka, ニマカカ, 齒ヲ現ス（犬ノ如ク）. *v.t.* To show the teeth.

Nimaki, ニマキ, 齒、例セバ、ニマキアラカ齒痛. *n.* The teeth. As :— *Nimata araka*, the toothache.

Nimaki-kutu, ニマキクツ, ツバメガモト. *n. Clintonia udensis, Trautv. et Mey.*

Nimaki-ukerere, ニマキウケレレ, 切齒スル. *v.i.* To gnash the teeth. **Syn : Sei-kui.**

Nimaki-uturu-iyun, ニマキウツルイユン, 齒ノ間ニ挾マレ. *v.i.* To lie between the teeth (as a fishbone).

Nimaki-uturu-kara, ニマキウツルカラ, 小楊子ヲ使フ, *v.i.* To pick the teeth.

Nimakka-ni, ニマッカニ, サハフタギ. *n. Symplocos crataegoides, Ham.*

Nimak-kotuk. ニマッコツク, サイハイラン. *n. Cremastra Wallichiana, Lindl.* An orchid.

Nimara, ニマラ,
Nimaraka, ニマラカ, } 半、半分. *adj.* Half. **Syn : Upak sereke.**

Nimaraha, ニマラハ, 朋友、親類. *n.* Friends. **Syn : Utara nimaraha. Ekatairotke guru. Eshiramkiri guru.**

Nimba. ニムバ, 牽ク、引キズル. *v.t.* To draw. To lead as a horse. To drag along.

Nimu, ニム, 攀ヅル. *v.t.* To climb. **Syn : Turashi.**

Nin, ニン, 溶ケル、減ズル. *v.t.* To melt. To become less as water in a river. To abate. To become absorbed. To change. To vary. **Syn : Shi-etaye.**

Nin, ニン, 木ノ瘤. *n.* A wen. An unnatural lumpy formation often seen upon trees.

Nin. ニン, 筋、肉. *n.* The muscles of the body.

Nina, ニナ, 粉碎スル. *v.t.* To pulverize. To crush.

Nina, ニナ, ヒラメ. *n.* A kind of sole. *Paralichthys olivaceus, Linn.*

Ninacha, ニナチァ, ミゾクサ. *n.* A kind of flounder. *Hipppglossoides* sp.

Nina-chep, ニナチェブ, ヒラメ. *n.* *Taralichitiys clioaceus, T. and S.*

Nina-chi, ニナチ, ミゾクサ. *n.* *Hippoglossides* sp.

Nina-kikiri, ニナキキリ, 螢. *n.* A glow-worm. **Syn : Ninakeppo. Ninckeppo. Ninninkeppo.**

Nina-kippo, ニナキッポ, } 螢. *n.* Fire flies.
Nina-kippo, ニナキッポ, } Glow-worms.

Ninara, ニナラ, 小山、高臺、小山ノア ル原野. *n.* Table-land. Small hills. Flat plains with low mountains in them. A terrace.

Ninaye, ニナイェ, 神ヨリノ罰トシテ十 代存命セリト言ヒ傳ヘラル、アイヌノ 名. *n.* The name of an Ainu who is said to have lived for ten generations and could not die, as a punishment from God.

Nin-chup, ニンチュブ, 半月. *n.* The waning moon. cresent.

Ninekeppo, ニ子ケッポ, 螢. *n.* A glow-worm. **Syn : Ninakeppo. Ninninkeppo.**

Ninge, ニンゲ, 膽. *n.* Gall.

Ningeu, ニンゲウ, 首骨. *n.* The collar bones.

Ningeu-paroho, ニンゲウパロ木, 咽 喉部. *n.* The region of the throat.

Ningeu-ohesarahi, ニンゲウオヘサラ ヒ, 鳩尾、ミズオチ. *n.* The pit of the stomach.

Nin-guru, ニングル, 侏儒、小人. *n.* A dwarf.

Nini, ニニ, 神經痛. *n.* Nerve pains. Sympathetic pains in the body.

Nini-ashi, ニニアシ, ウツク（火傷ノ爲 ニ）. *v.i.* To have shooting pains in the various parts of the body caused by a boil or wound.

Nini, ニニ, 延バス、引ク. *v.t.* To stretch out. To draw. **Syn : Turi.**

Ninka, ニンカ, 吸收スル. *v.t.* To absorb. To sap up.

Ninka-i, ニンカイ, 吸收. *n.* Absorption.

Ninkari, ニンカリ, 耳環. *n.* An earring.

Ninninkeppo, ニンニンケッポ, 螢. *n.* Glow-worms. Also called **Ninekeppo. Ninakeppo.**

Ninninu, ニンニヌ, 縫フ. *v.t.* To stitch.

Nino, ニノ, 海膽（ウニ）. *n.* The sea-urchin.

Nino-e-chep, ニノエチェブ, ハコトコ ナメアブラヲ. *n.* A kind of rock trout. **Syn : Rumaibe.**

Nino-okai, ニノオカイ, } クルマユリ. *n. Lilium avena ceum, Fisch.*
Ninoka, ニノカ, } **Syn : Niyokai.**

Ninokararip, ニノカラリブ, ヒトデ. *n.* A star fish. **Syn : Otakara-rip.**

Ninoropoki, ニノロポキ, } 膕（ヒカガミ）. *n.* The
Nioropoki, ニオロポキ, } under part of the knee.

Ninu, ニヌ, 珠ヲ繋ケ、魚ヲ竿ニ掛ケ ル. *v.t.* To thread as beads or chestnuts. To string on a pole as fish.

Ninum, ニヌム, } 殻果、胡桃ノ果. *n.* Nuts.
Ninumi, ニヌミ, } By some "walnuts" especially.

Nin-wa-isam, ニンワイサム, 吸收シ
タル. *adj.* Absorbed.

Nioropoki, ニオロポキ. 膕. *n.* The
under part of the knee. Same
as *Ninoropoki.*

Ni-osshi, ニオ�ノシ, 木ノ心材. *n.* The
heart of a tree.

Nip, ニブ, 刀又ハ小刀ノ柄. *n.* The
handle of a sword or knife.

Ni-pe, ニペ, 木ノ汁. *n.* The sap of
trees.

**Nipek,
ニペク,
Nupek,
ヌペク,** 焰、光明、例セバ、アベニペク、火焔. *n.* A flame. Brightness. Splendour. As :—
Abe nipek, " a flame of fire."
Syn: Nipeki. Nupek. Nupeki.

Nipeki-at, ニペキアツ, 光レ、輝ク.
v.i. To shine.

Nipek-atte, ニペカッテ, 輝カス、光
ラセル. *v.i.* To make shine.

Nipeknu, ニペクヌ, 燃ユル. *v.i.* To
flare. **Syn: Nupeknu. Paraparase. Hepeku.**

Nipokkep, ニポッケブ, 下生ノ樹. *n.*
Under-wood.

Nipesh-ni, ニペシニ, シナノキ. *n.*
Linden-tree. *Tilia cordata Mill,
vav, japonica, Miq.*

Niptani, ニブタニ, 肉置場(山中ニテ獲
物多キトキ一時之ヲ貯藏スル處).
n. A wooden platform the Ainu
make in the mountains upon
which to store meats. A meat
store.

Niramram, ニラムラム, 樹ノ表皮. *n.*
The surface bark of trees.

**Niras,
ニラス,
Nirash,
ニラシ,** 木片. *n.* A wood splinter.

Nire, ニレ, 藥、茶、汁、又ハ、湯水ヲ與
ヘル. *v.t.* To give medicine, tea,
soup or hot water to drink.

Nire, ニレ, 墨ニ用ユル色. *n.* A
kind of dye with which the
Ainu women tattoo themselves.
The tree of whose bark this dye
is produced is called *Iwa ni.*

Nireki, ニレキ, サルヂガセ. *n.* Usnea
longsisima, *L.*

Nirewe, ニレウェ, 切齒スル. *v.i.* To
gnash the teeth. **Syn: Niyoro
kara. Nimakaka. Seikui.**

Nirush, ニルシ, 齦、例セバ、カンナニ
ルシ、上齦. *n.* The gums. As :—
Kanna nirush " the upper gums."
Pokna nirush, " the lower gums."

Nirush, ニルシ, 苔類. *n.* All sorts,
of mosses and lichens growing
on the trunks of trees.

Nirush-kara, ニルシカラ, 齒ヲ露
出スル(腹ノ立ツ時ノ如ク). *v.t.* To
shew the teeth at one (as an
angry dog).

Nirush-tarara, ニルシタララ, 齒ヲ露
出スレ. *v.i.* To shew the teeth at
one (as an angry dog).

Nisa, ニサ, 凹地、洞、空洞. *n.* A
hollow place. A hole in a tree.

Nisa, ニサ, 過去ヲ示ス助動詞. *aux. v.*
This word is used after verbs to
indicate past time. **Syn: Okere.**

Nisako, ニサコ, 直チニ、直グ後ニ、
只今. *adv.* Presently. In a
short time. After a little while.
For a short time. As :—*Nisako
ku oman,* " I am going in a
little time." **Syn : Naa shiran-
koro. Naa okaketa.**

Nisao, ニサオ, 空虚ナル、例セバ、ニサ ナチクニ、空虚ナル木. *adj.* Hollow. As:—*Nisao chikuni,* "a hollow tree."

Nisap, ニサブ, Nisapi, ニサピ, 脛骨. *n.* The shin bone of human beings. The shin bone of animals is called *ainan pone.* **Syn:** **Nisapi-pone.**

Nisapka, ニサブカ, 早ムル. *v.t.* To quicken.

Nisap-no, ニサブノ, 速ニ、突然、直ニ. *adv.* Quickly. In a hurry. Suddenly. All at once. **Syn:** **Tunashno. Chashnu no.**

Nisap-no-nisap-no, ニサブノニサブ ノ, 甚速ニ、甚突然ニ. *adv.* Very quickly. In a very great hurry. Very suddenly.

Nisashnu, ニサシヌ, 健康ナル. *adj.* Healthy. **Syn: Shukupashma. Iwange no an.**

Nisat, ニサツ, 黎明ニ. *adv.* Daybreak. Early morning. **Syn:** **Pekennisat.**

Nisato, ニサツ, 黎明ニ. *adv.* The morning twilight.

Nisat-saot-nochiu, ニサツサオツノチ ウ, 曉星. *n.* The morning star.

Nisatta, ニサッタ, Nishatta, ニシャッタ, 明日. *adv.* To-morrow.

Nisatta-onuman, ニサッタオヌマン, Nishatta-onuman, ニシャッタオヌマン, 明晩. *adv.* To-morrow evening.

Nise, ニセ, 掬ヒアゲル. *v.t.* To dip up. To ladle out.

Nisei, ニセイ, 断崖. *n.* A precipice. A very steep valley. A gorge.

Nisei, ニセイ, 掬ヒ上ゲル、例セバ、ヒシ ヤコアニニワツシ、ナロワノワッカニ セイ、柄杓ニテ手桶ノ水ヲ汲上ゲル. *v.t.* To dip up. To ladle out. As:—*Pishako ani niwatush orowa no wakka nisei,* "to dip water out of a bucket with a ladle."

Nisei-omke, ニセイオムケ, 風邪(胸ノ). *n.* A cold on the chest. **Syn:** **Nishu omke.**

Nisesseri, ニセッセリ, Kisesseri, キセッセリ, Risesseri, リセッセリ, アイヌッサピ. *n.* A kind of water cress. *Cardamine yezoensis, Max.* This plant is used as an article of food. Horse—raddish.

Niseu-num, ニセウヌム, 檞ノ實. *n.* An acorn.

Niseupe-nonno, ニセウペノンノ, ウ ラベニイチゲ. *n. Anemone Rad-deana. Regel.*

Niseu-shu, ニセウシュ, カシノミノカ ラ. *n.* An acorn-cup.

Nish, ニシ, 雲、天、空. *n.* Clouds. The heavens. The air. **Syn:** **Nishkuru.**

Nishashin, ニシャシン, 曙光ノ. *adj.* The coming appearance of the dawn.

Nishatek, ニシャテク, 黎明. *adv.* Very early in the morning. The cock crowing.

Nishat-shaot-onchiu, ニシャツシャオ ツノチウ, 曉星. *n.* The morning star. Called also *Nisat-saot nochiu.*

Nishatta, ニシャッタ, Nisatta, ニサッタ, 明日. *adv.* To-morrow.

Nishetok-wen, ニシェトクウェン, 薄暗朝キ. *n.* A gloomy morning.

Nishike, ニシケ, 塵、木ノ束. *n.* A buudle of wood.

Nishikep, ニシケブ, 甲蟲ノ一種. *n.* A kind of beetle.
Nishikeppo, ニシケッポ,

Nishike, ニシケ, 木ヲ運ブ. *v.i.* To carry wood. **Syn: Haraki.**
Nishke, ニシケ, Nina.

Nishiromare, ニシロマレ, 拘束スル. *v.t.* To curb or hold in.

Nishiu, ニシウ, 磨臼. *n.* A millstone.

Nishka, ニシカ, 吝ム、例セバ、アコレクニニシカ、遣リ吝ム. *adv.* Hard to spare. Difficult to part with. As:—*Akore kuni nishka,* "difficult to give."

Nishka, ニシカ, 蒼穹. *n.* The skies. The heavens above the clouds.

Nishke, ニシケ, 伴フ. *v.t.* To take in company. **Syn: Shiren. Tura.**

Nishke, ニシケ, 木ヲ運ブ. *v.i.* To carry wood.
Nishike, ニシケ,

Nishkotoro, ニシコトロ, 空. *n.* The skies. The firmament.

Nishkuran, ニシクラン, 曇ル. *ph.* It is cloudy.

Nishkuru, ニシクル, 雲、例セバ、ニシクルヘチャカ、雲が晴レル. *n.* The clouds. As:—*Nishkuru hechaka,* "the clouds are clearing away."

Nishkuru-un, ニシクルウン, 暗ク且ツ曇レル. *adj.* Dark and cloudy. **Syn: Shirikuru-un.**

Nishkuttu, ニシクッツ, 雲ノ層. *n.* Strata or piles of clouds.

Nishmu, ニシム, 寂シキ、淋シガル. *adj. v.i.* Lonely. To feel lonely.
Mishmu, ニシム, Weary.

Nishmukamui, ニシムカムイ, 惡寛. *n.* The devil.

Nish-oshitchui, ニシオシッチュイ, 雲ノ柱、例セバ、ニシオシッチウィイマカケウングルクネルウェ子、余ハ雲外ヨリノ人ナリ. *n.* Pillars of clouds. As:—*Nish-oshitchiwi imakake un guru ku ne ruwe ne,* "I am a person from beyond the clouds."
Nish-ochitchiwi, ニシオシチッチウィ,

Nishoshichiu-moshiri, ニショシチウモシリ, 天. *n.* The place of clouds. The heavens.

Nishomap, ニショマブ, 心配スレ. *v.i.* To be anxious about. To long for. **Syn: Epotara.**

Nishoma-o, ニショマオ, *v.i.* To feel anxiety about.

Nishoro, ニショロ, 蒼穹. *n.* The firmament. The heights above.

Nishoro-okake-an, ニショロオカケアン, 晴レル. *v.i.* To clear up (as weather).

Nishoro-uwande, ニショロウワンデ, 天氣ヲ見ル. *v.i.* To examine the skies to see what the weather is likely to be.

Nishoro-wen, ニショロウェン, 曇ル. *adj.* Cloudy.

Nishorun-kotan, ニショルンコタン, 遠國. *n.* Far off countries. Distant lands.

Nishpa, ニシパ, 主人、富者、貴下. *n.* Master. Lord. Sir. A rich person. A title of respect.

Nishpake, ニシパケ, 主人、時トシテ人ノ親族ニ對スル尊稱、例セバ、エユピニシパケ、君ノ御令兄. *n.* Master. Lord. Sir. Sometimes applied as a title of respect to a person's relations. As:—*E yupi-nishpake,* "your respected elder brother."

Nishpa-koshungep, ニシパコシュンゲプ, 富人ヲ欺ク者、例セバ先キニ晴天ニシテ後ニ曇天. *n.* A deceiver of the rich. Spoken of a day which begins clear and fine and then turns out badly. See *Wen-guru koshungep.*

Nishpuk, ニシブク, アブラコ. *n.* Rock trout. *Hexagrammus aluraco. Jor. and Duy.*

Nish-ram, ニシラム, 曇天、低キ雲. *adj.* Lowering clouds. Cloudy weather.

Nishshi, ニシシ, 厚ク. *adv.* Thickly. Densely.

Nishte, ニシテ, 固キ. *adj.* Hard.

Nishte-no-kara, ニシテノカラ, 固メル. *v.t.* To harden.

Nishu, ニシュ, 脚アル木ノ臼. *n.* A wooden mortar having a foot to it.

Nishu-chishbe, ニシュチシベ, 臼ノ胴. *n.* The middle part of a stem of a mortar.

Nishuk, ニシュク, 救ヲ呼ブ. *v.t.* To call another as a help. **Syn：Shikashuire. Shikapashte.**

Nishuk, ニシュク, 手招ギスル. *v.t.* To beckon. To call by beckoning.

Nishumaune, ニシュマウ子, 強キ、美シキ、安ヲカナル. *adj.* Strong. Beautiful. Safe. Same as *nishuwamne.*

Nishu-omke, ニシュオムケ, 風邪(胸ノ). *n.* A cold on the chest. **Syn：Nisei omke.**

Nishuwamne, ニシュワム子, 強キ、美ハシキ、安ヲカナル. *adj.* Strong. Beautiful. Safe.

Nisosh, ニソシ, 木ノ皮ノ層. *n.* A layer of bark. A wooden platter.

Nit, ニツ, 腐朽シタル(濕レテ). *adj.* Rotten. The wet rot. Clammy.

Nit, ニツ, 棘、光レル木片(漂木). *n.* A thorn. A sharp piece of wood. A splinter. Drift-wood. **Syn：Net.**

Nitai, ニタイ, 森林. *n.* A forest. A clump of trees. **Syn：Hashitai.**

Nitai-karabe, ニタイカラベ, 風. *n.* Wind.

Nitai-sak-chikapsak-moshiri, ニタイサクチカプサクモシリ, 荒地. *n.* A barren land. A desert.

Nitan, ニタン, 脚ノ早キ. *adj.* Swift of foot. **Syn：Tunash.**

Nitan-koro, ニタンコロ,
Nitan-no, ニタンノ, 速ニ、早ク. *adj.* Swiftly.

Nitat, ニタツ, 沼地ニ樹ノ生シタル部分. *n.* The wooded part of a swamp.

Nitarango, ニタランゴ, 甚ダ、早ク. *adj.* Very swift.

Nitata, ニタタ, 看護スル、(單數). *v.t.* (*sing*). To hold in the hands as a sick person. To nurse the sick.

Nitat-kene-ni, ニタツケ子ニ, ハレ
ノキ. *n. Alnus miaritima, Nutt.*

Nitatpa, ニタツパ, 看護スル、（複数）.
v.t. pl. To nurse the sick. To
hold in the hands as a sick
person.

Nitatraurau, ニタッラウラウ, 天南星
ノ一種其ノ球根ハ附子ト共ニ熊鹿等ヲ
殺スニ用ユル毒ヲ製ス. *n.* A kind of
herb the bulb of which is sometimes used mixed with aconite as
a poison for killing bears and
deer. Jack in the pulpit.

Nitat-shingep, ニタツシンゲブ, ホザ
キシモツケ. *n. Spiræ salicifolia,
L. var. lanceolata, Torr. et Gray.*
Syn : Itoshin-ni.

**Nitattara-pekambe, ニタッタラペカ
ナベ,** ヒシ. *n. Trapa bispinosa
Roxb.*

Nitat-tope-ni, ニタットペニ, クロビ
イタヤ. *n. Acer Miyabei, Max.*

Nitek, ニテク, 木ノ枝. *n.* Branches
of trees. **Syn : Ni-yau.**

Nitemaka, ニテマカ, 木ノ片ヲ以テ開
ケル、例セバ、パロニテマカ、魚ヲ干
ストキニ、木ノ片ヲ以テ口ヲ開ケル.
v.t. To open with a piece of
wood. As :—*Paro nitemaka,* "to
open the mouth with a piece of
wood as in drying fish."

Nitesh, ニテシ, 筏. *n.* A raft.

Nitne, ニツ子, 固キ、堅キ、重キ、悪キ.
adj. Hard. Tough. Stiff.
Heavy as dough. Bad. Evil.
Rotten.

Nitne-hike, ニツ子ヒケ, 蝮（マムシ）.
n. A viper. **Syn : Takne hike.**

Nitne-kamui, ニツ子カムイ, 悪鬼.
n. The devil. Evil spirits.
Syn : Nitnep.

**Nitne-kamui-shikatkare,
ニツ子カムイ シカツカレ,**
**Nitne-kamui-shikatkari,
ニツ子カムイ シカツカリ,**
**Nitne-kamui-shikatirushi,
ニツ子カムイ シカチルシ,**
鬼ニ憑レル. *v.i.* To be possessed
with a devil. **Syn : Katush.
Wen-ituren-koro.**

Nitnep, ニツ子ブ, 強堅ナル物、悪鬼. *n.*
A tough thing. An evil spirit.
The devil.

Nitnep-parat, ニツ子ブパラツ, 依憑.
n. Demonania.

Nitokkari, ニトッカリ, 眩暈スル.
Giddy.

Nitok, ニトク, 木片. *n.* A splinter.

Nitokot, ニトコツ, 例セバ、ニトコツ
フラ、腐臭、腐リタレ. *adj.* Decom-
posed. Rotten. Used chiefly of
decomposing flesh. As :—*Notokot
hura,* "a rotten smell"; "stinking."

Nitomoshma, ニトモシマ, 叩ク、搔キ
ムシル（轉ク）. *v.t.* To knock. To
graze.

Nitoro, ニトロ, 熟シ過ギタル玫瑰ノ實.
n. Over ripe brier fruit.

Nitoro, ニトロ, 美味ナル、例セバ、ニト
ロフラアンアエプ、甘サウニ匂フ食物.
adj. Sweet. Nice. Delicious.
Appetizing. Used of food principally. As :—*Nitoro hura an aep,*
"food with a sweet or appetizing
smell."

Nitotkari, ニトッカリ, 眩暈スル. *adj.*
Giddy. **Syn : Nitokkari.**

Nit-otke, ニトツケ, 棘デ刺ス. *v.t.*
To prick with a thorn.

Nitpa, ニツパ, 柄. *n.* The handles of
tools or utensils.

Nitpo, ニッポ, 小ナレ沙魚. *n.* A small kind of shark.

Nitpo, ニッポ,
Mitpo, ミツポ, } 孫. *n.* A grandchild.

Nitumam, ニツマム, 幹. *n.* Trunks of trees.

Nitun, ニツン, 森. *n.* A forest.

Nitush, ニツシ, 桶. *n.* A tub. A vat.

Niu, ニウ, 人、(數ヘル時ニノミ用キ、一人、二人等ノ如シ、又略シテ N トナル事アリ)、例セバ、シヂン、一人、ツン、二人. *n.* A person. This word is only used with the numerals, and may be said to resemble in some extent the so called "classifiers" of Chinese. *Niu,* "man" is sometimes contracted to n only. Thus:— *Shinen,* "one person." *Tun,* "two persons."

Niuchire, ニウチレ, 不愉快ナル. *adj.* Disagreeable.

Niuchire-atte, ニウチレアッテ,
Niuchire-kara, ニウチレカラ, } 人チ不愉快ニスル行ヒ. *v.i.* To act in a provoking manner towards. To behave in a disagreeable manner towards another.

Niukesh, ニウケシ, 拙劣ナル、無能ナル、不運ナル、爲スチ好マヌ. *adj.* and *v.i.* Awkward. Incapable. Unable to do a thing. Unfortunate. To dislike to do a thing.

Niurotki, ニウロツキ, 不味ナル、歉ノ生セシ. *adj.* Insipid. Nasty. Of bad taste. Stale. Mouldy. **Syn:** Kera wen.

Niurototo, ニウロトト, 燒キ盡ス. *v.t.* To burn up.

Niush-niush, ニウシニウシ, 骨ガ痛ム. *v.i.* To have a pricking and aching sensation in the bones.

Niwa, ニワ, 熟セル、美味ナル. *adj.* Very ripe. Sweet. As:—*Niwa hura,* "a sweet smell." *Niwa hura an aep,* "a sweet smelling, appetizing dish."

Niwa, ニワ, 迅速. *n.* Quickness. Speed.

Ni-wakka, ニワッカ, 樹ノ汁. *n.* Tree sap.

Niwasap, ニワサブ, 緩キ、怠リタル. *adj.* Slow. Tardy.

Niwashnu, ニワシヌ, 活澄ニ、勤勉ニ. *v.i. adj.* Lively. Diligent. Active. To be industrious. **Syn:** Yuptek. Koyuptektek.

Niwatori-chikap, ニワトリチカプ, 鷄. *n.* The domestic fowl. A cock or hen. This is a hybrid compound, *niwatori* Japanese, and *chikap* Ainu.

Niwatush, ニワツシ, 手桶. *n.* A bucket. A water butt.

Niwen, ニウェン, 峻酷ナル、荒キ. *adj.* Austere. Wild. Fierce.

Niwenhoribi, ニウェンホリビ, 變死人ニ對シテ行フ一種ノ儀式. *n.* The ceremonies performed upon the death by accident of a person. This ceremony consists in the men and women forming single file and marching as near to the place of accident as possible at the same time emitting a peculiar grunt as each step is taken. The men march with drawn swords or long knives in the right hand; when the left foot is placed upon the ground the sword is stretched out, and when the right foot is set down it is drawn in. Perfect time is kept in this performance. Also the noise sparrows make when they see a snake, see *Aruuokumse-chiu.*

Niwen-no-kire, ニウェンノキレ, 強迫 ス ル. *v.t.* To coerce.

Niwenrek, ニウェンレク, 高聲ノ話. *n.* The sound of high or loud talking. The peculiar noise sparrows make when they see a snake or adder.

Niwok, ニウォク, 狐ノ髑髏(占ニ用ユル) 又ハ此チ以テ占ヒ得シ判斷. *n.* The skull of a fox kept for purposes of augury. Discovery by augury by a fox's skull. Augury. Divination. **Syn : Aesaman.**

Niwok-ki, ニウォッキ, 狐ノ髑髏ニテ占 フ. *v.i.* To perform augury with a fox's head. **Syn : Aesaman ki.**

Niwok-ki-guru, ニウォッキグル, 占者、 巫人. *n.* The augurer. A diviner.

Niwok-ki-marapto, }
ニウォッキマラプト, }
Niwok-marapto, }
ニウォクマラプト, }
狐ノ髑髏ニテ罪 人チ判スル儀 式. *n.* The ceremony of discovering a culprit by means of augury with a fox's skull. **Syn : Shitumbe marapto. Kema koshne guru marapto.**

Niya, ニヤ, 萌芽、萌エ出ツル、例セバ、 ニヤツク、萌エ出ツル. *n.* Buds.

Also *v.i.* To become green (as trees. As :—*Niya tuk,* "to bud forth."

Niyap, ニヤプ, 焔、例セバ、アベヤプ 火焔. *n.* A flame. As :—*Abe niyap,* a flame of fire."

Niyarakap, ニヤラカプ, 木ノ皮. *n.* The bark of trees.

Ni-yau, ニヤウ, 木ノ枝. *n.* The branch of a tree. **Syn : Ki-tek.**

Niye, ニイェ, 物ノ骨組. *n.* The framework of anything.

Niye, ニイェ, 齒ニテ支ヘレ. *v.t.* To hold with the teeth.

Niyehe, ニイェヘ, 莖、例セバ、ムンニイ ェヘ、草葉ノ莖. *n.* A stalk. As :— *Mun niyehe,* "the stalk of a blade of grass.

Niyekara, ニイェカラ, 切齒スル. *v.i.* To grind the teeth as in pain or anger.

Niye-nishte, ニイェニシテ, 死ニ難キ. *adj.* Difficult to die. Tenacious of life.

Niye-rishpa, ニイェリシパ, 齒ニテ支ヘ レ. *v.t.* To hold in the teeth.

Niyokai, ニヨカイ, クルマユリ. *n.* *Lilium avenaceum, Fisch.*

Niyoki-eremu, ニヨキエレム, 長キ耳 アル鼠. *n.* A rat having long ears.

Niyoro-kara, ニヨロカラ, 切齒ヌル. *v.i.* To gnash the teeth. **Syn : Sei-kui. Nirewe.**

Niyuk, ニユク, 栗鼠. *n.* A squirrel.

No, ノ, 詞ノ後ニ付キテ、形容詞チ副詞 ニ副詞チ形容詞ニ變更スル分詞. *part.* A particle placed after adjectives to change them into adverbs, or after adverbs to change them into adjectives.

No, ノ, 英語ノ ing ノ如ク用ヒラレ、進行ノ意味チ表ス. *part.* Sometimes used like "ing." As:—*Nukan,* "to see" *Nukan no*; "seeing."

Nochautekka, ノチャウテッカ, 抜ク、(刀ノ如ク). *v.t.* To draw as a sword. **Syn: Emush etaye.**

Nochi, ノチ, 口、顎、例セバ、ノチモイモイゲ、顎チ動カス. *n.* The mouth. The jaws. As:—*Nochi moimoige,* "to move the jaws.

Nochi-iush, ノチイウシ, 癲癇. *n.* Epilepsy. Fits.

Nochipon, ノチポン, 小量ノ. *adj.* A small quantity. A little.

Nochipon-no, ノチポンノ, 倹約シテ. *adv.* Sparingly.

Nochiu, ノチウ, 星. *n.* Stars. As:— *Nochiu makke-makke,* "the stars twinkle."

Nochiu-o-kando, ノチウオカンド, 星空. *n.* The starry heavens.

Nochiu-tom-ush-ningari, ノチウトムウシニンカリ, 白キ硝子ノ玉アル耳環. *n.* Earrings with white glass beads.

Noibe, **ノイベ,**
Noipe, **ノイベ,** 腦. *n.* Brains.

Noibe-rat, ノイベラツ, 腦漿分. *n.* The watery substance of the brain.

Noiboro, **ノイボロ,**
Noiporo, **ノイポロ,** 前額、腦 (場合ニ依リテ). *n.* The forehead. In some places also "brain." Where *noiporo* is used for brain, the forehead is called *noiporo pone.*

Noige, ノイゲ, 綯レレ、捻レル. *v. i.* Twisted.

No-iki, ノイキ, 眞似スル. *v.t.* To imitate. To do like.

Noikisama, ノイキサマ, 頬ノ鬚. *n.* The side whiskers.

Noine, ノイ子, 恰モ、例セバ、タンウコランアプトアシノイチアン、今夜雨降ルガ如ク見ユ. *adv.* As if. As though. To have the appearance of. This word is generally followed by the verb *an,* "to be," and expresses the potential mood. Thus:—*Tan ukuran apto ash noine an,* "it looks as if it will rain to-night." *Ek noine an,* "he appears to be coming." *E omke kara noine an,* "you appear to have caught cold." *Noine hum ash,* "it sounds as if it were." *Shomo an noine hawe ash,* "there seems not to be."

Noi-poro-kina, ノイポロキナ, クサフゲ. *n.* A kind of vetch. *Vicia Cracea L. var japonica Miq.* **Syn: Mena saru. Menash mame.**

Noitek, ノイテク, 疲ル. *v.i.* To become tired. **Syn: Shingi.**

Nok, ノク, 卵、睾丸. *n.* An egg. The testicles.

Noka, ノカ, or **Nokaha, ノカハ,** 像、地圖、畵. *n.* An image. A map. A picture. **Syn: Inoka net.**

Nokan, ノカン, 小キ. *adj.* Small. Little.

Nok-anu, ノカヌ, 卵チ産ム. *v.i.* To lay an egg.

Nok-itangi, ノキタンギ, 卵チ入レル器. *n.* An egg cup.

Noki-konru, ノキコ ンル, 垂氷. *n.* Icicles.

Noki-poro, ノ キポロ, 病ノ名. *n.* Hernia. Rupture.

Nok-kapu, ノッカプ, 卵ノ殻. *n.* An egg shell. **Syn : Nok-sei**

Nok-karari, ノッカラリ, 卵ヲ抱ク. *v.i.* To sit upon eggs (as a bird).

Nok-koro, ノッコロ, 卵ヲ産ム. *v.i.* To lay eggs.

Noko, ノコ, 鋸. *n.* A saw. (*jap*).

Noko-konchi, ノココンチ, 鋸屑. *n.* Sawdust.

Nokoshke, ノコシケ, 妬ム、羨ム. *v.i.* To be jealous. **Syn : Eyaieitunnap.**

Nok-po,　⎫ 蛋白、卵黄、睪丸. *n.* The
ノクポ,　⎬ white of an egg.
Nok-pi,　　The centre of the yolk
ノクピ,　⎭
of an egg. Testicles.

Nok-sei, ノクセイ, 卵殻. *n.* An egg shell. **Syn : Nok kapu.**

Nokuyak, ノクヤク, アマツバメ. *n.* A swift.

Nomi, ノミ, 幣又ハ神酒ヲ奉ル式. *n.* *v.t.* The ceremony of offering *inoa* or libations of wine (often both) to the gods. To worship. *Nomi* does not of necessity include prayer, but simply the mere fact of offering, for *inao* are often placed in the ground without any prayer being said and still this act is called *nomi*. *Chisei nomi*, "a house-warming."

Nomi-nit, ノミニツ, ミツバウツギ. *n.* *Staphylea Bumalda, S. et Z.*

Nomo, ノモ, 平穏、静粛. *n.* Peace. Quietness.

Nomo-irenga, ノモイレンガ, 平和、好意. *n.* Peace. Good-will.

Non, ノン, 唾. *n.* Saliva. Spittle. As :—*Non ashinge*, " to spit."

Nona, ノナ, 海膽. *n.* The sea-urchin.

Nonekarip, ノ子カリプ, ヒトデ. *n.* A star-fish. **Syn : Otakarip.**

Nonishatta, ノニシャッタ, 早昧. *adv.* Early-morning.

Nonno, ノンノ, 花. *n.* A flower.

Nonno, ノンノ, 悦ノ叫. *exclam.* An exclamation of pleasure. **Syn : Ononno.**

Nopuyapuya, ノプヤプヤ, 痘痕 (アバタ). *adj.* Pock-marked.

Nonuina, ノヌイナ, 隱ス. *v.t.* To hide. **Syn : Nuina.**

Nopakan, ノパカン, 晴天. *n.* Clear good weather.

Noram, ノラム, 温厚ナル. *adj.* Gentle.

Noratchitara, ノラッチタラ, 緩キ、鈍キ、温厚ナル. *adj.* Slow. Dull. Gentle. **Syn : Moiretara.**

Noru, ノル, 熊ノ足跡. *n.* A bear's foot-print. **Syn : Iruwe.**

Noshikarikari, ノシカリカリ, 眩暈シタル. *adj.* Giddy.

Noshike,　⎫
ノシケ,　⎬ 中央. *adv.* Middle.
Noshki,　　
ノシキ,　⎭

Noshiketa, ノシケタ, 中央. *adv.* Middle. Halfway. In the midst.

Noshike-un, ノシケウン, 中央. *adv.* In the middle.

Noshpa, ノシバ, 從フ、追蹤スル. *v.t.* To follow. To chase. To pursue. To run after. As :—*Noshpa wa oman*, " he pursued him." **Syn : Keseamba.**

Not, ノ ツ, ロ一杯. *n.* A mouthful.
As :—*Shine-not*, " one mouthful."

Not,
ノツ, 顎、岬. *n.* The jaws. A
Notu, blunt cape.
ノツ,

Nota, ノタ, 顔. *n.* The face. **Syn :**
Nan.

Nota, ノタ, 海面、例セバ、ノタヒリカ、
靜波海. *n.* The surface of the sea.
As:—*Nota pirika*, " a calm sea."
Nota wen, " a rough sea."

Notak, ノタク, 銳キ刄尖. *n.* The edge
of any sharp tool. The edge of
a knife or axe or board.

Notakam, ノタカム, 頰. *n.* The
cheeks.

Notakam-bone, ノタカムボ子, 頰骨.
n. The cheekbone.

Notakne, ノタク子, 傍＝. *adv.* Upon
its side. To be turned upon its
side.

Notako-notako, ノタコノタコ, 鋸齒
狀ノ. *adj.* Jagged.

Notaku, ノタク, 銳キ刄ヲ持チタル. *adj.*
Having a sharp edge.

Notakup, ノタクブ, 諸種ノ道具. *n.*
Tools of any kind.

Notarap,
ノタラブ, 鰓(アキト). *n.* Fish gills.
Motarap, The cheeks of fish.
モタラブ,

Notarup, ノタルブ, 平手デ打ツ. *v.t.*
To box the ears. To slap the
face.

Notasam, ノタサム, 岬. *n.* A cape.

Not-echiu, ノテチウ, 食氣ガ退マヌ、
イベノテチウ、食シ得ズ. *v.i.* To
have lost one's appetite. As:—*Ibe
not-echiu*, " to eschew one's food."
" To be unable to take food."

Notekpake, ノテクバケ, 最上ノ. *adj.*
The very best. Most good.

Notenai, ノテナイ, 南、例セバ、ノテナ・
イレラ、南風. *n.* The south
As :—*Notenai rera*, " the south
wind."

Notese,
ノテセ, 鳩ノ如ク其ノ子ヲ哺フ. *v.t.*
Noteshke, To feed as a pigeon
ノテシケ, its young.

Notetuye, ノテツイェ, 嚙ミ切ル. *v.t.*
To bite off.

Notka, ノッカ, 弩＝付ケル繩此＝觸ル
レバ發矢ス. *n.* The string attached to spring bows, which when
touched lets off the arrow.

Notkarari-ainu, ノッカラリアイヌ,
枕人、(男性、愛シ又ハ信頼スル人ノ儀
ナリ). *n.* A pillow man. A person one loves or relies on.

Notkarari-guru, ノッカラリグル, 枕
人(男女性). *n.* A pillow person. A
person in whom one trusts. A
friend.

Notkarari-mat, ノッカラリマツ, 枕
人(女性). *n.* A pillow woman.

Notkeu, ノッケウ, 顎、例セバ、カンナノツ
ケウ、下顎. *n.* The jaws. As :—
Kanna notkeu, " the upper jaw."
Pokna notkeu, " the lower jaw."

Notkeu-mokurap, ノッケウモクラブ,
n. Pectral fins of fishes.

Notkiri, ノツキリ, 頤(オトガヒ). *n.*
The chin.

Notkush, ノツクシ, 顏ヲソムケル. *v.t.*
To turn the head away from.
Syn : Oyakun kiru.

Not-maka-ni, ノツマカニ, 枕(バイ)、猿
轡(サルグツワ). *n.* A gag. A
A plug of wood often put into

the mouth of the dying to keep it from closing.

Not-moimoye, ノツモイモイェ, 噛ム. v.t. To chew. **Syn: Kui-kui. Ikui-kui. Chamse.**

Noto, ノト, 海面. n. The surface of the sea. **Syn: Nota. Neto.**

Notokkari, ノトッカリ, 眩暈スル. adj. Giddy. Faint. To be in a swoon.

Notonoho. ノトノホ, 酋長. n. A chief. A head. **Syn: Nishpa.**

Not-omare, ノトマレ, 寄リ懸カレ. To lean upon as upon a stick. Lit :—" to place the chin upon."

Not-oro-ikui. ノトロイクイ, 反芻ス レ. v.i. To chew the cud.

Notosam, ノトサム, 岬. n. A cape.

Nottatawause, ノッタタワウセ, 震フ、歯チガタカセレ. v.i. To shiver. The teeth to chatter. **Syn: Wauwause.**

Notu, ノツ, } 頤、岬. n. The jaws. A
Not, ノツ, } cape.

Not-uturu, ノツウツル, 魚ノ舌. n. A fish's tongue.

Noya, ノヤ, ヨモギ. n. Mugwort. *Artemisia vulgaris, L.*

Noya-noya, ノヤノヤ, 揉ム、剝ク、例セバ、ムンギプシテケヘオッタノヤノヤ、手ニテ麥ノ穂チ揉ム. v.t. To rub. To peel. To strip by rubbing. As :—*Mungi push tekehe otta noyanoya,* "to rub ears of wheat in the hands."

Noyap, ノヤプ, } 横顔、例セバ、ノヤヒタン
Noyapi, ノヤビ, } チグル、長顔ノ人. n. The side of the face.

The profile. As :—*Noyapi tanne guru,* "a person with a long face."

Noyaparaka-tashum, ノヤパラカタシュム, 耳腺炎. n. Face-ache. The mumps.

Noya-surugu, ノヤスルグ, 毒ノ一種. n. A kind of poison.

Noye, ノイュ, 廻ス、絢ム、捻ル. v.t. To turn. To twist. To wind. To wring. To turn over.

Noye, ノイェ, 負ケル、死スル、例セバ、トノトノイェ、酒ニ負クレ. v.i. To be overcome with a thing. To be dead. As :—*Tonoto noye,* "to be overcome with wine." *Mokon noye,* "to be overcome with sleep" "to be dead."

Noyuk, ノユク, 瓦熊、人及ビ家畜ナトチ襲掠セザレ. n. A good bear. i.e. A bear which does not attack people or steal animals. *Noyuk,* is the opposite of *hokuyuk.*

Nu, ヌ, 名詞ノ後ニ付ク時ハ、多ク、豐ニ、ノ意味チ有ス、例セバ、チエプヌ、魚ノ豐ニ、ユクヌ、鹿ノ多キナドノ如シ. part. Suffixed to nouns *nu* has the force of *nuye an,* "to be abundant." As :—*Chepnu,* "an abundance of fish." *Yuknu,* "plenty of deer." *Nu is therefore a plural suffix.* Suffixed to verbs *un* has the force of *eashkai,* "to be able"; to be clever." As :—*Ok,* "to shoot"; *oknu,* "able to shoot" *i.e.* "an archer."

Nu, ヌ, 聞ク、尋ヌル、此ノ動詞ハ普通、オッタ、ナル語ニ續ツク、例セバ、エンオッタヌ、彼ハ余ニ尋子タリ. v.t. To hear. To enquire. To listen. This verb is generally preceded by *otta*. As:—*En otta nu*, "he enquired of me." *Nu utara, n.* Hearers. An audience.

Nu, ヌ, 涙. *n.* Tears. **Syn : Nupe.**

Nu-an, ヌアン, 澤山ナレ、豐ナレ. *adj.* Plenteous. Abundant. **Syn : Nuye an. Nu-ush.**

Nuap, ヌアブ, 病ニ呻吟スル. *v.i.* To groan as in sickness. **Syn : Nuwap.**

Nuashnu, ヌアシヌ, 眞面目、シラフ. *adj.* Sober.

Nube, ヌベ,
Nupe, ヌピ, 涙、例セバ、ヌベグスシクナッ カチ、涙ニ曇ル. *n.* Tears. As:—*Nube gusu shiknak kane.* "blinded by tears." **Syn : Nu.**

Nucha-guru, ヌチャグル, 露國人. *n.* A Russian.

Nuchak, ヌチャク, 幸ナル. *adj.* Pleased. Happy. **Syn : Nuchat.**

Nuchat, ヌチャツ, 幸福ナレ、悦ベレ. *adj.* Same as *Nuchak*. Pleased. Happy.

Nuchatka, ヌチャツカ, 幸福ニスレ. *v.t.* To make happy. **Syn : Nuchat-tekka.**

Nuchatte, ヌチャッテ, 悦バス、幸福ニス レ. *v.t.* To please. To make happy

Nuchattek, ヌチッテク, 悦ビタル、幸福 ナル. *adj.* Pleased. Happy.

Nuchattekka, ヌチッテッカ, 悦バス、幸 福ニスレ. *v.t.* To make happy.

Nuchimashnu, ヌチマシヌ, or **Mu-chimashnu, ムチマシヌ,** 活澄ナレ. *adj.* Active. Agile. Abrupt.

Nuchimashnu-i, ヌチマシヌイ, 活澄. *n.* Activity.

Nuchimashnu-no, ヌチマシヌノ, 活 澄. *adv.* Actively. Quickly.

Nuchimashnure, ヌチマシヌレ, 速ニ スレ. *v.t.* To accelerate.

Nu-ewen, ヌエウェン, 聞取り難キ. *adj.* Hard of hearing.

Nu-eyaituba, ヌエヤイツバ, 好奇心チ 持ツ、穿鑿好キナレ. *adj.* Curious. Inquisitive.

Nugesh, ヌゲシ, クロカモノ類. *n.* A kind of black coloured duck.

Nui, ヌイ, 火焰. *n.* A flame of fire.

Nuikara, ヌイカラ, 梳ク (髪ナドチ)、 掃ク、拂フ. *v.t.* To comb as a horse's mane. To currycomb. To groom. To brush.

Nuikarape, ヌイカラベ, 刷子. *n.* A brush. A currycomb.

Nui-kotereke, ヌイコテレケ, 火ガツ ク. *v.i.* To catch fire.

Nuina, ヌイナ, 隱ス. *v.t.* To hide away.

Nuina-korobe, ヌイナコロベ, 生殖器 (男女共). *n.* The private parts of both male and female.

Nuinak, ヌイナク, 隱ル. *v.t.* To hide one's self.

Nuina-no, ヌイナノ, 竊ニ. *adv.* Secretly. **Syn : Arorokishne no.**

Nuina-shomoki-no, ヌイナショモキ ノ, 公然. *adj.* Above board. O-penly. **Syn : Anukan no.**

Nuipe, ヌイベ, or **Numbe, ヌムベ,** 護 謨. *n.* Gum.

Nuira, ヌイラ, キュクウナ. *n.* Smelt. *Aemerus dentex, Stimd.*

Nuisam, ヌイサム, 衽. *n.* The front edge of a dress or coat.

Nui-uk, ヌイウク, 火ガツク、例セバ、チセイヌイウク、家ニ火ガツク. *v.i.* To catch fire. As:—*Chisei nui uk,* "the house caught fire."

Nukan, ヌカン, 見ル. *v.t.* To see. Short for *Nukara.*

Nukande, ヌカンデ, ニ示スレ. *v.t.* To show.

Nukan-no, ヌカンノ, 公然ル. *adv.* Openly. Above-board. Seeing.

Nukan-nukara, ヌカンヌカラ, 看病スレ. *v.t.* To nurse as a sick person. To look well after. To take care of. **Syn: Nitata.**

Nukanro, ヌカンロ, 見セヨ. *v.t.* Let us see.

Nukara, ヌカラ, 見ル. *v.t.* To see.

Nukara-eramushkare, ヌカラエラムシカレ, 未見ザリシ. *v.i.* Not to have seen.

Nukara-ewen, ヌカラエウェン, 視力ノ弱キ、朧ニ見エル. *v.i.* To see badly. Not to see clearly. To have bad sight.

Nukara-humi-wen, ヌカラフミウェン, 醜キ、見ヤウトモセズ. *adj.* and *v.i.* Ugly. Unsightly. Not caring to see.

Nukara-no, ヌカラノ, 好ク見ル、明カニ見ル. *v.t.* To see well. To see clearly.

Nukara-tek, ヌカラテク,
Nukattek, ヌカッテク, 瞥見スル. *v.t.* To get a glimpse of anything. **Syn: Iruka nukara.**

Nukara-uonnere, ヌカラウオンチレ, 見シ. *v.i.* To have seen.

Nukare, ヌカレ, 表示スル. *v.t.* To show.

Nukat, ヌカツ, 見ル. *v.t.* Same as nukara, "to see."

Nukattek, ヌカッテク, 瞥見スレ. *v.t.* To get a glimpse at.

Nukesh-chiri, ヌケシチリ, シノリガモ. *n.* Harlquin duck. *Fuligula histrionica,* (*Linn*).

Nukki, ヌッキ, 泥ダラケノ. *adj.* Muddy. **Syn: Nukki.**

Nuko-okai, ヌコオカイ, 豐富ナル. *adj.* Very plenteous. **Syn: Nuye an.**

Nukoshne, ヌコシチ, 暴キ、殘忍ナレ、短氣ナレ. *adj. and v.i.* Wild. Rough. To be soon angry. Short-tempered. **Syn: Purikanda. Puri-o. Puri-yupke.**

Nukuri, ヌクリ, 嫌フ. *v.t.* To dislike. As:—*Me nukuri,* "to dislike the cold." *Apto nukuri,* "to dislike the rain." **Syn: Kopan.**

Nukuri-ibe, ヌクリイベ, 八ツ目鰻. *n.* A lamprey.

Num, ヌム,
Numi, ヌミ, 水滴、丸球. *n.* A drop. A ball. As:— *Wakka num,* "a drop of water.", *Shik num,* "the eye-ball."

Num, ヌム, 乳頭. *n.* The nipples of the breast.

Numa, ヌマ,
Numaha, ヌマハ, 毛. *n.* Hair of any kind.

Numa-kiru, ヌマキル, 脱毛スル. *v.t.* To shed the coat (as an animal).

Numan, ヌマン,
Numan-i, ヌマンイ, 昨日、例セバ、ヌマンアリキシリカイサム、彼等昨日ヘ來ラザリキ. *adv.* Yesterday. As:—*Numan ariki*

shiri ka isam, "they did not come yesterday."

Numan-ibe, ヌマンイベ, 夕飯. *n.* The evening meal.

Numan-onuman, ヌマンオヌマン, 昨夜. *adv.* Last evening.

Numarashtara, ヌマラシタラ, 物ヲ運ブニ用フル皮紐. *n.* A leather thong used for carrying purposes.

Numa-shosho, 毛ヲ抜ク. *v.i.* To **Nu**ma**-shosho,** ヌマションショ, take the hair ヌマショウショ, out of a skin with a knife. To pluck.

Numa-shut, ヌマシュツ, 底豆(ヨコマメ). *n.* A corn. A wort. A blister.

Numat, ヌマツ, 紐帶. *n.* The strings to fasten a dress.

Numat-koro-sei, 具ノ名. *n.* The **ヌマツコロセイ,** name of a **Numat-kot-sei,** kind of bi- **ヌマツコツセイ,** valve. The name of a shell often used by children to ornament their dress strings.

Numa-ush-kikiri, ヌマウシキキリ, 毛蟲. *n.* A caterpillar.

Numba, ヌムバ, 搾出ス. *v.t.* To squeeze. To press out. To rub together. To press.

Nume-chiu, ヌメチウ, 急ニ攻撃スル、(鳥ノ生餌ヲ啄ムトキニノミ用ユ). *v.t.* To attack suddenly. Used only of birds attacking their prey. To strike with the breast bone as hawks are said to do their prey.

Numge, ヌムゲ, 撰ブ、指名スル. *v.t.* To choose. To appoint.

Numi, ヌ ミ, 總ベテ. *adj.* All. **Syn: Obitta.**

Numi, ヌミ, 身長(ミノタケ)、果實、穀物. *n.* Stature. A berry. A grain. As :—*Numi rupne ota,* "coarse-grained sand."

Numi-pon, ヌミポン, 短キ、例セバ、ヌミポングル、小人. *adj.* Short. As :—*Numi pon guru,* "a small person."

Numi-poro, ヌミポロ, 丈高キ. *adj.* Tall.

Numko-sange, ヌムコサンゲ, 圍ム. *v.t.* To besiege.

Numne, ヌム子, 圓キ. *adj.* Round.

Numne, ヌム子, 圍ム. *v.t.* To besiege. To surround.

Numne-an, ヌム子アン, 番スル、待伏ス、圍ム、先取スル. *v.i.* To watch. To lie in wait. Also to forestall. To surround.

Numnoya-chip, ヌムノヤチプ, ヤマガラ. *n.* Japanese tit. *Parsus varius, T. and S.* **Syn : Enumnoya.**

Numnoye, ヌムノイ, ヤマガラ. *n.* Japanese tit. **Syn : Enummoye.**

Numpe, 糊. *n.* Gum. Paste. **ヌムベ,** Glue. Size. A soft **Nuipe,** wen. Boss. A swelling. **ヌイベ,**

Numpe-aushi, ヌムベアウシ, 糊ヅケス ル. *v.t.* To paste.

Numpe-omap, ヌムベオマブ, 糊壺. *n.* A paste pot.

Numsam, ヌムサム, 衣類ノ前襟. *n.* The front edges of a dress or coat.

Num-ush, ヌムウシ, 疎キ粒ノ. *adj.* Coarse grained. As : *Num-ush ota,* coarse sand.

Nun, ヌン, 吸收スル. *v.t.* To absorb. To suck. **Syn: Shikonun.**

Nunnu, ヌンヌ, 吸フ. *v.t.* To suck.

Nunnun, ヌンヌン, 吸フ. *v.t.* To suck. To absorb. **Syn: Shikonunnun.**

Nu-no, ヌノ, 明白ニ聞ク. *v.t.* To hear well.

Nunuke, ヌヌケ, 惠ム. *v.t.* To bless. **Syn: Kaoiki.**

Nunumaunu, ヌヌマウヌ, 強キ. *adj.* Strong.

Nup, ヌプ, 聞キシ事. *n.* A thing heard.

Nup, ヌプ, 平原丘、頂ノ平キ山. *n.* A plain. Table-land. Field. A fen. **Syn: Nuponne.**

Nupa, ヌパ, 聞ク (複數). *v.t.* To hear (*pl*).

Nupe, ヌベ, ギヤウジヤニンニク. *n.* A kind of wild garlic. *Allium victorialis, L.* **Syn: Pukusa.**

Nupe, ヌベ,
Nupehe, ヌベヘ, }涙. *n.* Tears. **Syn: Nu.**

Nunaibe, ヌナイベ, ハゴトコ. *n.* *Agrammus agrammus, Schlegel.*

Nupek, ヌベク,
Nupeki, ヌベキ,
Nupeki-hi, ヌベキヒ, }光、光明. *n.*
Nipek, ニベク,
Nipeki-hi, ニベキヒ,
Light. Brightness.

Nupek-at, ヌベクアツ, 光ル. *v.i.* To shine. Shining.

Nupeki-at-kamui, ヌベキアツカムイ, 輝ケル神、眞ノ神. *n.* The shining God. The true God.

Nupeki-atte, ヌベキアッテ, 照ス. *v.t.* To cause to shine.

Nupetne, ヌベツ子, 樂シキ. *adj.* Joyful. Pleased.

Nupetne-an, ヌベツ子アン, 樂シキ. *v.i.* To be joyful. To rejoice.

Nupetnere, ヌベツ子レ, 樂シマシム. *v.t.* To please.

Nupettek, ヌベッテク, 十分醒メタレ. *v.i.* To be wide awake.

Nupittek, ヌピッテク, 眞面目ニナル. *v.i.* To become sober.

Nupka, ヌプカ, 平原. *n.* A plain. Field. Table-land. **Syn: Nup.**

Nupka-ushi, ヌプカウシ, ス、キカヤ. *n. Miscanthus japonicus, Benth.*

Nupki, ヌプキ, 泥ダラケナル、濁水ノ如ク濃厚ナレ. *adj.* Muddy. Thick, as dirty water.

Nupki, ヌプキ, オニガヤ. *n. Miacanthus, sp.*

Nupkina, ヌプキナ, キミカケサウ、スズラン. *n.* Lily of the Walley. *Convallaria maialis, L.*

Nupki-at, ヌプキアツ,
Nupki-ot, ヌプキオツ, }泥ダラケノ. *adj.* Muddy.

Nupkire, ヌプキレ, 泥ダラケニスレ. *v.t.* To make muddy.

Nupkurun-ni, ヌプクルンニ, ハコヤナギ. *n.* Poplar. *Populus tremula, L. var. villosa, Wesm.* Also called *Yai-ni.*

Nuponne, ヌポン子, 平原. *n.* A plain. **Syn: Nup.**

Nupoppet, ヌポッペツ, 汗. *n.* Sweat. Perspiration.

Nup-pukusa, ヌッブクサ, キミカケサウ. *n.* Lily of the vallen. *Convallaria majalis, L.*

Nupure, ヌプレ, 好ム. *v.t.* To like. To be fond of.

Nupshingep, ヌプシンゲプ, ノ ハ ギ. *n. Lespedeza bicolor, Turcy.*

Nup-shungu, ヌプシュング, キ ジ カ ク シ. *n. Asparagus schoberioides, Kunth.*

Nupuri, ヌプリ, 山、例セバ、ヌプリヘ メス、山ニ登ル. *n.* A mountain. As:—*Nupuri hemesu,* "to ascend a mountain." *Nupuri kitai,* "the top of a mountain." *Nupuri kotoro,* "the sides of a mountain." *Nupuri ran,* "to descend a mountain."

Nupun-noya, ヌプンノヤ, イ ハ ヨ モ ギ. *n. Artemisia sacrorum, Ledeb. var. latiloba, Ledeb.*

Nupuri-esoro, ヌプリエソロ, 麓. *n.* The foot of a mountain.

Nupuri-esoro-ran, ヌプリエソロラ ン, 下山スル. *v.i.* To descend a mountain.

Nupuripa, ヌ プ リ バ, 山ノ前面. *n.* The forepart of a mountain. We final *pa* is not to be confounded with *ka,* "top."

Nupuri-pesh, ヌプリペシ, 麓. *n.* The foot of a mountain.

Nupuripo, ヌ プ リ ポ, 小山. *n.* A small mountain.

Nupuri-shut, ヌプリシュツ, 麓. *n.* The foot of a mountain.

Nupuri-shuttomo, ヌプリシュットモ, 麓ヨリ少シク上ノ處. *n.* A little above the foot of a mountain.

Nupuri-tapka, ヌプリタプカ, 山ノ頂. *n.* The top of a mountain.

Nupuri-uturu, ヌプリウツル, 谷. *n.* Valleys.

Nupuru, ヌプル, 貴重ナル、例セバ、カム イ、ヌプルモンカシ、神ノ貴キ業ニ ヨ リ. *adj.* Precious. Estimable. As:—*Kamui nupuru mon-kashi,* "by the estimable (or precious) works of God."

Nupuru, ヌプル, 濃厚ナ ル(酒又ハ水ノ). *adj.* Thick or dirty or strong as water. Wine or. Black. Very dark. As:— *Nupuru tonoto,* "strong wine."

Nupuru, ヌプル, 預言スレ. *v. t.* To prophesy.

Nupuru-guru, ヌプルグル, 預言者. *n.* A prophet. **Syn: Uweingara guru.**

Nupuruka, ヌプルカ, 黒クスレ. *v. t.* To blacken.

Nupuru-moshiri, ヌプルモシリ, 天. *n.* Heaven.

Nu-rapapse, ヌラパプセ, 落涙スル. *v.i.* To shed tears.

Nure, ヌレ, 語ル、親シム、宣言スル. *v.t.* To tell. To acquaint. To announce. To apprise. This form of the verb takes *otta* before it.

Nusa, ヌサ, 幣ノ集合. *n.* The clusters of *inao* which the Ainu place outside their east windows or upon the seashore as offerings to the gods.

Nusakesak, ヌサケサク, 眞面目. *n.* Sober. **Syn: Nuashnu.**

Nusatam, ヌサタム, 疫病ヲ祓フ爲ニ用 ユル幣. *n.* A kind of *inao* waved over the sick to drive away disease. **Syn: Takusa.**

Nushimamne, ヌシマムネ, 強キ、安 全ナレ. *adj.* Strong. Safe.

Nushimamne-no, ヌシマムネノ, 強 ク、安全ニ、例セバ、ヌシマムネノカ ラ、堅固ニ述テレ. *adv.* Strongly. Safely. As:—*Nushimamne no kara,* "to build strongly."

Nushimaune-no, ヌシマウチノ, 強ク.
adv. Strongly. In a strong manner. As :—*Nushimaune no akara*,
" is it made or done strongly."

Nushuk, ヌシュク, or **Nishuk-ni-
shuk, ニシュクニシュク**, 手招スレ. *v.
t.* To beckon. To call. To pray
to God.

Nushinne-no, ヌシンチノ, 快ヨク.
adv. Comfortably.

Nushiromare, ヌシロマレ, 制御スレ.
v.t. To control.

Nushuye, ヌシュイェ, 手招ギスレ. *v.t.*
To beckon. To call be beckoning.

Nuso, ヌソ, 橇. *n.* A sleigh.

Nusumaunu-no, ヌスマウヌノ, 強ク.
adv. Strongly. In a strong manner. **Syn : Nushimaune no.**

Nutap, ヌタプ, 山間ノ平野. *n.* A
level place between mountains.

Nutap, ヌタプ, 川ノ彎曲セル個處ノ
內部. *n.* The inside of a bend in
a river. An isthmus.

Nutokkari, ヌトッカリ, 眩暈スレ. *v.i.*
To be giddy. To feel dizzy. **Syn :
Ramukari. Ramukari-kari.**

Nu-ush, ヌウシ, 豐ナレ. *adj.* Plenteous. Abundant· **Syn : Nuye
an. Nuye ush.**

Nuwap, ヌワプ, 呻ク. *v.i.* To groan.

To call out in pain. To give
birth.

Nuwashi, ヌワシ, or **Nuashi, ヌアシ**,
眞面目ナル. *adj.* Sober.

Nuyasa, ヌヤサ, 割ル(單數). *v.t.* To
break in or through. To split
(*sing*).

Nuyaske, ヌヤスケ, 割レレ. *v.i.*
Broken through. Split.

Nuye, ヌイェ, 書ク、彫刻スル、入墨スル.
v.t. To write. To tattoo. To
carve.

Nuye-an, ヌイェアン, 豐ナル. *adj.*
Plenteous. **Syn : Nu an. Shiri
eshik. Nu ush.**

Nuyaspa, ヌヤスパ, 割レ(複數). *v.t.*
To break in or through (*pl*).

Nuye-an-i, ヌイェアンイ, 豐饒. *n.*
Abundance. **Syn : Shiri eshik-
be.**

Nuye-an-no, ヌイェアンノ, 豐ニ.
adv. Abundantly.

Nuye-ita, ヌイェイタ, 寫字板、石板. *n.*
A writing tablet.

Nuyep, ヌイェプ, 幕、刷毛. *n.* A pen.
A broom. A brush.

Nuyere, ヌイェレ, 書カセレ. *v. t.*
To cause to write.

Nuye-ush, ヌイェウシ, 豐ナル. *adj.*
Plenteous. Abundant. **Syn :
Nuye an.**

Nuyuk, ヌユク, 火ガツク. *v.i.* To
catch fire.

〇 (オ).

O, オ, 名詞ノ後ニ付ク時ハ、形容詞ノ力
チ有ス、例セバ、アイオニ、剌アル木.
Suffixed to nouns the particle *o*

has an adjectival force. As :—
Ai-o ni, " thorny wood." *Uruki-
o*, " lousy."

O, オ, ヨリ、カラ、例セバ、オキムウシ、山カラ. *prep.* From. Off. A seperative particle. As:— *O-kim un,* "from the mountains." *O-pish ne,* "from the sea-shore." (See *E, prep.*).

O, オ, 入ル、、例セバ、シュオロワッカオ、水チ鍋ニ入ル. *v.t.* To put in. As: *Shu oro wakka o,* "to put water into a saucepan."

O, オ, 乗馬スル、乗ル. *v.t.* To ride. To sail in a boat.

O, オ, 實チ結ブ. *v.t.* To bear fruit as a tree.

O, オ, 鑿ル、開ク、例セバ、シクオ、目チ開ク. *v.t.* To bore. To open. As:— *Shik o,* "to open the eyes." *Shui o,* "to bore a hole."

O, オ, 突キ出ル. *adj.* and *v.i.* To project. Projecting. To stick out.

O, オ, 含ム、例セバ、トノトオイタンギ、此ノ盃ニハ酒が有レ. *v.i.* To be inside. Contained in. As:— *Tonoto o itangi* "the, cup with wine in it."

O, オ, 有ル、存在スレ. *v. i.* To be. To exist.

O, オ, 何物ニテモ底ノ外部、例セバ、オウフイシュ、底ノ燒ケシ鍋. *n.* The outside bottom of anything. As:— *O uhui shu,* "a pot with the bottom burnt." *O uhui nikap attush,* "an old burnt garment."

O, オ, 陰部、特ニ肛門ノ邊. *n.* The private parts, particularly the region of the anus.

O, オ, 河口. *n.* The mouth of a river.

O, オ, 穴、例セバ、オブシチクニ、穴ノアイタル木. *n.* A hole. As:—*O push chikuni,* "wood with holes bored in it."

Oa, オア, 蛙. *n.* A frog. **Syn: Oterekep. Tereke ibe. Otereke-ibe.**

Oa, オア, 一對ノ一ツ、此ノ語ハオアラ(*o a r a*) ノ略ナルオアツ (*o a t*) ノ代リニ用ヒラル、例セバ、オアチキリ、一足. *adj.* One of a pair. This word is sometimes used for *oat* which is a contraction of *oara.* Thus:— *Oa chikiri* for *oatchikiri* short for *oara chikiri,* "one foot."

Oahunge, オアフンゲ } 樽曲シタル物
Oahungi, オアフンギ, } ノ内側. *n.* The inside of a bend, **Syn: Ereunui.**

Oai, オアイ, 集會所. *n.* A meeting place.

Oaikanchi, オアイカンチ, ハサミムシ. *n.* An earwig. **Syn: Oai-ush kikiri.**

Oai-ush-kikiri, オアイウシキキリ, ハサミムシ. *n.* An earwig.

Oan, オアン, 全ク、例セバ、オアンライゲ、全ク殺ス. *adv.* Thoroughly. Quite. Entirely. Outright. This word is a contraction from *oara.* Thus:— *Oanraige,* "to kill outright;" for *oara raige.*

Oan-nikap, オアンニカブ, 臆病者、賤シキ物、死體、重病人. *n.* A cowardly person. A worthless being. A corpse. A very sick person.

Oanruru, オアンルル, 四海岸ヨリ. *adv.* From the western shores of the sea.

Oara, オアラ, 二ツノ一ツ、一對ノ一ツ. *adj.* One of a pair. One of two.

Oara, オアラ, 全ク、オアラエン、全ク惡シキ. *adv.* Entirely. Quite. Very. Thoroughly. As:— *Oara wen,* "very bad," or "abominable." *Oara aetunne,* "very much hated."

Oara-araki, オアラアラキ, 半. *adj.* A half.

Oara-kanchi-ush, オアラカンチウシ, ハサミムシ. *n.* A earwig. **Syn:** Oai kanchi. Oaiush-kikiri.

Oashin, オアシン, 出テ行ク、入リ來ル. *v.i.* To go out. To come out.

Oashinge, オアシンゲ, 逐リ出ス、取リ出ス. *v.t.* To send out. To take out. To root out.

Oaship, オアシブ, 出入スレ. *v.i.* To come or go out. To issue forth (*pl.*)

Oashiuka-amip, オアシウカアミブ, 亙キ衣類. *n.* Good clothes. **Syn:** Aeshiyuk amip.

Oat, オアツ, ニツノーツ、此ノ語ハオアラノ略ナリ、例セハ、オアツチキリ、一足(片足). *adj.* One of two. This word is short for *oara.* As:— *Oatchikiri* for *oara chikiri,* "one foot." *Oat-teke,* "one hand."

Oat, オアツ, ニツノーツ. *adj.* One of two.

Oatuimaka, オアツイマカ, 河ノ廣キ口. *n.* The broad open mouth of a river.

Oatu-wakka, オアツワッカ, 動物ノ精液. *n.* Animal semen.

Oau-ush-kikiri, オアウウシキキリ, ハサミムシ. *n.* An earwig. **Syn:** Oaikanchi.

Obakanere, オバカチレ, 愚ニスル、馬鹿ニスレ、例セハ、チイクルイクワサケオバカチレ、大酒ノ爲ニ愚トナル. *v.t.* To make a fool of. To deprive one of his senses. As:—*Nei guru iku wa sake obakanere,* "through drinking wine has made a fool of him."

Obitta, オビッタ, 總ベテノ、全體ノ. *adj.* All. The whole.

Obiyo, オビヨ, 聲か嗄レレ. *v.i.* To have lost the voice as in a heavy cold. **Syn:** Shiunuomke.

Oboru, オボル, 最惡シキ非難ノ語. *n.* A very evil term of reproach.

Oboshpa, オボシパ, 通ツテ行ク. *v. t.* To go through. *Pl.* of *oboso.*

Oboshpare, オボシパレ, 通ツテ行カセレ. *v.t.* To cause to go through. *Pl.*

Oboso, オボソ, 通シテ、例セハ、オボツウンインガラ、通シテ見ル. *post.* Through. As:— *Oboso un ingara,* "to look through."

Oboso, オボツ, 通ツテ行ク、浸ミ透ス. *v.t.* To go through. To soak through.

Obosore, オボソレ, 無クスル、治療スレ、爲スヤウニスル、通シテ行カシム. *v.t.* To allay. To alleviate. To cease to do (as evil). To cause to go through.

Ochako, オチャコ, 横行ナレ. *adj.* Presumptuous. Given to loose ways.

Ochakot, オチャコツ, 強盗シテ暮ス. *v.t.* To live in debauchery.

Ochakot-guru, オチャコツグル, 強盗. *n.* A debauchee.

Ochi, オチイ, 突進スレ. *v.i.* To dart. To whirl. To rush.

Ochiai-ush-mun, オチアイウシムン, クロコリ. *n.* *Fritillaria Kamtchatensis, Gawl.*

Ochichiwi, チチチウィ, 立ツ、積ミカサ ナル. *v.i.* To stand up on end. To be piled up. **Syn: Ochiuchiu.**

Ochike, オチケ, 盆. *n.* A tray. **Syn: Nima. Otckike.**

Ochikiki, オチキキ, 空ヶ盡ス. *v.t.* To empty to the very last drop. To drain.

Ochikirui, オチキルイ, 放蕩ナレ. *adj.* Lewd. Corrupt.

Ochinkama, オチンカマ, 踏ミ越ス. *v.t.* To step over.

Ochinakkari, オチナッカリ, 日本人. *n.* A Japanese.

Ochinkapa, オチンカバ, 足ヲ伸バシテ 坐スレ. *v.i.* To sit with the legs stretched out.

Ochipa, オチバ, 突進スレ、渦ク. *v.i.* (*pl.*) To dart. To whirl. To rush.

Ochipep, オチベプ, 滑ナル. *adj.* Even. Plain. Smooth.

Ochipumi, オチブミ, 足趾ヲ付ケレ. *v.t.* To follow a trail.

Ochishbare, オチシバレ, 破損サセレ. *v.t.* To spoil. To damage.

Ochiu, オチウ, or Hochiu, ホチウ, 姦 淫. *n.* Adultery.

Ochiubare, オチウバレ, 死ス. *v.i.* To die.

Ochiuchiu, オチウチウ 積ミカサナレ、 立ツ. *v.i.* To be set up on end. To be piled.

Ochiunoye, オチウノイェ, 交接ヲ欲シ テ死ス. *v.i.* To die through strong desire to have sexual intercourse.

Ochiuchiu-chikap, オチウチウチカ プ, 鶺鴒(セキレイ). *n.* A wagtail. **Syn: Chiuchiu. Ochiu-chiri.**

Ochiuchiue, オチウチウエ, 強迫. *n.* Compulsion.

Ochiupashte, オチウバシテ, 交接スレ. *v.i.* To have sexual intercourse.

Ochiwe, オチウェ, 追ヒヤレ. *v.t.* To drive away. As:—*Ochiwe wa isamka,* "to drive clean away."

Ochopcho, オチョプチョ, 魚ノ尾. *n.* A fish's tail.

Ochopkokomge, オチョプココムゲ, 縮マレ(寒サニ). *v.i.* To shrink up as a person or dog in the cold.

Oeshikari, オエシカリ, 塞グ. *v.t.* To be closed up as the mouth of a river.

Ochukko-eshikari, オチュッコエシカ リ, 尿閉. *n.* Stoppage of the urine. Ischury.

Ochupka-un, オチュプカウン, 東ノ方. *n.* The region of the East.

Oha, オハ, 空ナル、例セバ、オハチセ イ、空屋. *adj.* Empty. As:— *Oha chisei,* "an empty house." *Oha shiure,* "to take care of an empty house."

Oha-ai, オハアイ, 無毒ノ矢. *n.* Arrow without any poison attached. **See. Ashi-ai.**

Ohai-araiko-tenge, オハイアライコ テンゲ, 泣ク(子供ガ母ヲ慕ヒ). *v.t.* To weep as a child after its mother.

Ohaige-kara, オハイゲカラ, 誹ル. *v.t.* To backbite. To abuse. **Syn: Sempirioitak.**

Ohaige-kara-i, オハイゲカライ, 讒謗. *n.* Abuse. Slander.

Ohai-ingara, オハイインガラ, 見送ル. *v.i.* To look after one.

Ohaine, オハイ子, 實ニ. *adv.* Indeed. Just so.

Ohaine-kane, オハイ子カ子, 實ニ. *adv.* Indeed. Just so.

Ohaita, オハイタ, 塞ガル、適合セズ. *v.i.* To be warded off. Not to fit.

Ohaitare, オハイタレ, 逃ガス. *v.t.* To cause to escape. To defend from. To ward off. To make not fit. To cause to avoid.

Ohaiyokke, オハイヨッケ, or Oha-yokke, オハヨッケ, 吐氣ヲ催ス、噯氣スレ. *v.i.* To belch. To eructate. To retch.

Ohak, オハク, 淺キ. *adj.* Shallow.

Ohare, オハレ, 空ニスレ. *v.t.* To empty.

Ohariki-so-un, オハリキソウン, 爐ノ右側、卽チ、アイヌノ家ノ戸口ヨリ見テ. *adv.* On the right hand side of a fireplace. (Looking in from the porch door of an Ainu hut).

Oharu, オハル, 澄ミタル汁. *n.* A clear soup.

Ohasama, オハサマ, 鞦 (シリガヒ). *n.* A crupper.

Oha-shinotcha, オハシノツチャ, 調子. *n.* A tune.

Oha-shirun, オハシルン, 空屋ヲ守レ. *v.i.* To take care of an empty house.

Oha-shiure, オハシウレ, 空屋ヲ守ル. *v.i.* To take care of an empty house.

Ohau, オハウ, 魚肉又ハ獸肉ト野菜トヲ混合シテ煮タル食物. *n.* A fish or meat stew with vegetables intermixed.

Ohau-kina, オハウキナ, ガジャウサウニリンサウ、フクベラ. *n.* *Anemone*

---

flaccida, Fr. Schm. **Syn: Pukisa kina.**

Ohau-not, オハウノツ, 烝ル爲ニ用意セラレシ肉又ハ植物. *n.* A lump of meat or vegetables cut ready to stew.

Ohau-not-kara, オハウノツカラ, 肉又ハ魚ヲ煮ル. *v.i.* To make a meat or fish stew.

Ohayokke, オハヨッケ, or Ohaiyok-ke, オハイヨッケ, 吐氣ヲ催ス. *v.i.* To retch.

Ohetke, オヘツケ, 翻ル、コボル、例セバ、エツワノショモチヤオヘツケヤ、茶ハ土瓶ノ口ヨリ翻レシヤ. *v.i.* To be spilled. To run out. As:—*Etu wano shomo cha ohetke ya?* "Won't the tea run out of the spout?"

Ohetu, オヘツ, 翻ス、コボス. *v.t.* To spill. To shed. To empty.

Ohetuku, オヘツク, 出デ來レ. *v.i.* To come out of.

Oheuge, オヘウゲ, 曲リタレ. *adj.* Crooked. Bent.

Oheugesak-i, オヘウゲサクイ, 精確. *n.* Accuracy.

Oheuge-sak-no, オヘウゲサクノ, 精確ナレ、眞直ナル. *adj.* Accurate. Straight. **Syn: Oupeka.**

Oheugere, オヘウゲレ, 曲ゲル. *v.t.* To bend. **Syn: Henoyere.**

Oheuge-shomoki, オヘウゲショモキ, 精確ナレ、眞直ナレ. *adj.* Accurate. Straight. Right.

Oheuge-shomoki-no, オヘウゲショモキノ, 精確ニ、眞直ニ. *adv.* Accurately. Straightly. Rightly.

Oho, オホ, 縫箔. *n.* A kind of fancy needle-work.

Ohoge, オホゲ, 曲リタレ. *adj..* Crooked. **Syn: Oheuge.**

Ohoikara, オホイカラ, 縫箔スレ. *v.i.* To do a kind of fancy needlework.

Ohokara-kem, オホカラケム, 縫針. *n.* A sewing needle.

Ohon-no, オホンノ, 長キ間、永々. *adv.* For a long time.

Ohonto, オホント, 家ノウシロ. *n.* The back of a house. **Syn: Osorogesh. Okesh. Apapok.**

Ohontoki, オホントキ, 肛門. *n.* The anus.

Ohontom, オホントム, 側ニ. *adv.* By the side of.

Ohooho, オホオホ, or **Ohuohu, オフオフ,** 案内ヲ頼ム一種ノ聲. *n.* A peculiar noise made by women as a warning before entering a house or room.

Ohoro, オホロ, 永々. *adv.* For a long time.

Ohorukara, オホルカラ, 縫箔スレ. *v.t.* To embroider.

Ohuiyoro-ne, オフイヨロ子, 如何デセウカ、此ノ語ハ否定ノ意味ヲ示ス. 例セバ、オフイヨロネ、ネイアシウェンテプセシマヶコロヤヶアアエラムペウテヶ、彼ノ女ハ生キテ居ルカ死ンダカ如何デセウ. *adv.* How will it be? This word carries with it a negative idea. As:— *Ohuiyoro ne, nei a shiwentep seremak koro yak a aerampeutek,* "How it will be with that woman, whether she will live or not I know not, the probability being that she will die. *Ohuiyoro ne, shiknu kuni aponde,* "how will it be, I think he will not live."

Ohurukotuibe-mun, オフルコツイベムン, カラハナサゥ. *n.* Hops. *Humulus lupulus, L.*

Oibe, オイベ, 元素、持續力. *n.* Essence. Durance. Stamina.

Oibe-an, オイベアン, 永ヶ續キタル. *adj.* To have stamina or endurance. To last a long time.

Oibe-chawan, オイベチャワン, 飯椀. *n.* An eating cup. **Syn: Oibesei.**

Oibep, オイベブ, or **Oibepi, オイベピ** 食器、飯椀. *n.* Eating utensils. An eating cup.

Oibe-sak, オイベサク, 弱キ、弱クナル. *adj.* and *v.i.* To be weak. **Syn: Tum-sak.**

Oibe-sam, オイベサム, 浪費スル. *v.t.* To do away with quickly. To waste. To waste away. **Syn: Oisam.**

Oibesamka, オイベサムカ, 浪費スレ. *v.t.* To waste. **Syn: Oisamka.**

Oibe-sei, オイベセイ, 食器、皿. *n.* An eating vessel. A plate.

Oika, オイカ, 越エテ、例セバ、オイカホプニ、飛ビ越エテ. *post.* Over. As: —*Oika hopuni,* "to fly over." *Oika ingara,* "to look over." *Oika kama,* "to step over." *Oika tereke,* "to jump over."

Oikara, オイカラ, クズ. *n.* A kind of climbing liguminous plant. *Pueraria Shunbergiana, Benth.* Used for tying purposes. The small inner fibre is sometimes used for securing thread.

Oikaru, オイカル, 燃(ヨ)レタル、縺(ム ス)ヒタル. *adj.* Twisted. Entwined.

Oiki, オイキ, 胴ル. *v.t.* To touch. To meddle with.

Oiki-oiki, オイキオイキ, 胴ル. *v.t.* To touch. To meddle with.

Oikush, オイクシ, 漏レル. *v. i.* To leak. (As a tub or bucket). **Syn : Opekush.**

Oikush-un, オイクシウン, 向フ二. *adv.* Beyond.

Oimatturinne, オイマッツリン子, 長ク延フ. *v.i.* To be stretched out lengthwise as in lying down. To be stretched out. **Syn : Omatturinne.**

Oimek, オイメク, 恐ル. *v.i.* To fear. To be afraid.

Oina, オイナ, 古代ノ、傳説ノ. *adj.* Ancient. Traditional.

Oina, オイナ, 昔話チ ス. レ. *n.* and *v.t.* To relate ancient traditions.

Oina-mat, オイナマツ, ノブキ. *n. Adenocaulon adhaerecens, Maxim.*

Oina-otta, オイナオッタ, 古代、例セバ、オイナオッタアンブリ、古代ノ習慣. *adv.* In ancient times. As :— *Oina otta an buri,* "an ancient custom." *Oina otta tambe korachı hawashanu ruwe ne na,* "such is the ancient news we have heard." *Oina otta tapne shiriki yak aye,* "it is said that it was so done in ancient times."

Oingara, オインガラ, 覗ク、又覗キ込ム. *v.t.* To peep through. To look through.

Oinuye, オイヌイェ, 達スル. *v.i.* To reach to. To attain to (as water from a river to a road on shore).

Oioi-ki, オイオイキ, 喝采 ス レ. *v.t.* To acclaim.

Oioiki-i, オイオイキイ, 喝采. *n.* An acclamation.

Oioioioi, オイオイオイ, 驚愕又ハ稱讚ノ叫ビ、例セバ、オイオイオイオイエアニネプネヤッカエカラコイラムマカカエ

カンレウェネ、臆爲ス事毎二君ハ善シ *excl.* An exclamation of surprise or admiration. As :—*Oioi oioi, eani nep ne yakka e kara ko irammakaka e kan ruwe ne,* "ah, what ever you do you do you do well."

Oiporoboso, オイポロボソ, 顏色チ變ヘル、(苦痛、心配、病氣等ノ爲)、蒼クナル. *v.i.* To change countenance as through pain, trouble, or sickness. To turn pale.

Oira, オイラ, 忘ル、(單數). *v.t.* To forget. (*sing*).

Oirapa, オイラパ, 忘ル (複數). *v.t.* To forget. (*pl.*)

Oisam, オイサム, 浪費スル. *v.i.* To waste away. **Syn : Oibesam.**

Oisamka, オイサムカ, 浪費スレ. *v. t.* To waste. **Syn : Oibesamka.**

Oishiru, オイシル, 産卵後鮭. *n.* A very old salmon. A salmon which has died of old age. Spent salmen.

Oitak-sak, オイタクサク, 免チ願フ、言ヒ、違フ. *v.t.* To beg pardon. To make a mistake in talking or by word of mouth.

Oitak-sakka, オイタクサッカ, 言ヒ違ハセレ. *v.t.* To cause to make a mistake by word of mouth.

Oitak-sakte, オイタクサクテ, 詫チ云ハセレ. *v.t.* To make beg pardon.

Oitakushi, オイタクシ, 呪フ. *v.t.* To curse.

Ok, オク, 惡シキ、兇惡ナル. *adj.* Trouble. Evil. Badness. Severe in a bad sense.

Ok, オク, 襟頭 (エリクビ). *n.* The nape of the neck. Atlas. The neck. **Syn : Okkeu.**

Ok, **オク**, 心、感情. *n.* The heart. The feelings.

Ok, **オク**, 鬱悶スル、フサグ. *v.i.* To be low-spirited. To be cast down. Troubled.

Oka or okai, **オカ**, 又ハ **オカイ**, 有リ、住フ. *v.i.* To be. To dwell. To be at a place.

Okachupu, **オカチュブ**, 引キ戻ス. *v.t.* To take back. **Syn: Oka-uk.**

Okai, **オカイ**, 有ル、住ム. *v.i.* To be. To dwell. To be at a place. To abide. Both *sing* and *pl.*

Okaibe, **オカイベ**, 存在物. *n.* An existing thing.

Okai-ushike, **オカイウシケ**, 住居、在所、アリカ. *n.* An abode. A place where anything is.

Okakara, **オカカラ**, 長キ. *adj.* Lengthwise.

Okake, **オカケ**, 後、其後. *adv.* After. Subsequently. Cleared away. As:—*Shiriokake an*, " the weather has cleared up."

Okake-an, **オカケアン**, 終リ. *n.* A finish. An end.

Okake-anka, **オカケアンカ**, 終ラセル. *v.t.* To make to finish or stop.

Okake-an-koro, **オカケアンコロ**, 其後. *adv.* Afterwards. After that. Then.

Okake-chishne, **オカケチシチ**, 傷痕、キズアト. *n.* A mark left on the body as by illness. A sore place. A scar.

Okakere, **オカケレ**, 終ラセレ. *v.t.* To make stop or finish.

Okaketa, **オカケタ**, 其後. *adv.* Afterwards.

Okake-un, **オカケウン**, 其後. *adv.* Afterwards.

Okakuira, **オカクイラ**, 窃ニ後ヲ追フ. *v.t.* To follow after stealthily. **Syn: Okapikuira.**

Okamge-no, **オカムゲノ**, 適當ニ、突然ニ. *adv.* On purpose. Purposely. Suddenly. Advisedly. **Syn: Shiokamge no. Okamgiri.**

Okamgiri, **オカムギリ**, 適當ニ、突然ニ. *adv.* On purpose. Purposely. Suddenly.

Okamoi-koro, **オカモイコロ**, 梅毒ヲ患フ. *v.i.* To be afflicted with syphilis. **Syn: Pana-etashum.**

Okanchi, **オカンチ**, 舵、カヂ. *n.* A ship's rudder.

Okanka, **オカンカ**, 継蟲、(サナダムシ). *n.* A tape worm.

Okankotokke, **オカンコトッケ**, 傾キタル、參差タレ. *adj.* (*geo*). Declivious. Rugged.

Okan-natki, **オカンナッキ**, 圍樂スル、マドキスレ. *v.t.* To sit in a circle.

Okapikuira, **オカピクイラ**, 竊ニ後ヲ追フ. *v.t.* To follow stealthily after.

Okari, **オカリ**, 周リニ. *post.* About. Around.

Okarira, **オカリレ**, 取リ廻ス. *v.t.* To put round.

Okashkamui-koro, **オカシカムイコロ**, 健全トナル、病氣ヨリ恢復スル. *v.i.* To be in health. To revive from sickness. **Syn: Seremakkoro.**

Okashkamui-sak, **オカシカムイサク**, 病トナル、病ム、力ヲ落ス、病ガ篤ク

ナル、不仕合セニナル. *v.i.* To be in
bad health. To lose strength.
To grow worse in sickness. To
be unfortunate.

Okasu, オカス, or **Oukasu, オウカス,**
甚ダ、大ニ、例セバ、タネオカスヒ
リカ、彼ハ今甚ダ善シ. *adv.* Very.
In a great degree. To a great
extent. Much. Very much. As:
—*Tane okasu pirika,* " he is now
much better."

Okata, オカタ, 後ニ、例セバ、エンオカ
タ、我が後ニ. *adv.* After. Behind.
As:—*En okata,* " after me." **Syn:**
Okake.

Oka-uk, オカウク, 取リ戻ス. *v.t.* To
take back. **Syn: Oka-chupu.**

Okaya-ni-pichi, オカヤニピチ, 檣ヨ
リ落ツ. *v.i.* To fall from a mast.
Syn:**Ekaya-ni ika.**

Okaye, オカイエ, 斷レタル、チギレタレ.
adj. Broken off.

Okbare, オクバレ, 不孝チスル、敵スル.
v.t. To treat one's parents slightingly or unfilially. To rebel
against. To fight against. **Syn:**
Uokbare. Iyokbare.

Ok-chish, オクチシ, 泣ク(哀ノ爲). *v.t.*
To weep for sorrow.

Okekarip, オケカリプ, 襟、頸環. *n.* A
collar.

Ok-ekot, オケコツ, 悲シガル. *v.i.*
To be very sorrowful. To be
very cast down. To die of sorrow.

Okep, オケプ, 兇鳥. *n.* Name of a
very rare bird said to be of ill
omen.

Okep, オケプ, 惡シキ音信. *n.* Bad
news.

Okep-koro-guru, オケプコログル, 兇
報ヲ齎ラセシ人. *n.* A bearer of
evil tidings.

Okep-shongo, オケプションゴ, 兇報.
n. Bad news.

**Okep-shongo-koro-guru, オケプシ
ョンゴコログル,** 兇報ヲ齎ラセシ人. *n.*
One who brings bad news.

Okere, オケレ, 終ル、爲シ遂グル. *v.t.*
To finish. To accomplish.

Okere-i, オケレイ, 終リ. *n.* The
finish. Accomplishment. The
end.

Okerep, オケレプ, 終リ. *n.* Accomplishment.

Okerepa, オケレパ, 終ル、(複數). *v.i.*
Finished. To be done. *Pl* of *o-
kere.*

Okes, オケス, 尻、底. *n.* The posteriors. The rump. The bottom.
Syn: Osoroho.

Okese, オケセ, or **Okesegeta, オケ
セゲタ,** 終リニ、後、例セバ、イノンノ
イタクオケセゲタ、祈ノ後. *adv.* At
the end of. After. As:—*Inonno-itak okesegeta,* " after prayers.'

Okettektek, オケノテクテク, 終リシ.
v.i. To have finished. To have
prepared.

Okeuba, オケウバ, 追ヒヤル. *v.t.* To
drive away. *Pl.* of *okewe.*

Okeura, オケウラ, コバン. *n.* A
moor-hen.

Okewe, オケウエ, 追ヒヤレ. *v.t.* To
drive away.

Okikurumi, オキクルミ, アイヌチ文明
ニ導キシ人(源ノ義經ヲ指スナラン)、ア
イヌノ傳説ニヨレバ、義經ハ樺太島ニ

テ殺サレタリト. *n*. The name of a person said by the Ainu to have been a great civilizer of the race. Most likely this person was the Japanese hero Kurōhangwan Minamoto no Yoshitsune who fled from Japan to Yezo in the twelfth century of our era to avoid the sword of his elder brother. He is said by the Ainu to have been killed by Ainu in Saghalien.

Okikurumi-turesh-machi, オキクルミツレシマチ, オ キ ク ル ミ ノ 妻. *n*. The wife of Okikurumi.

Okimne, オキム子, 山 ヨ リ. *adv*. From the mountains. *O* is a preposition meaning "from." (See *O prep*. and compare *E, prep*).

Okim-un, オキムウン, 山 ヨ リ. *adv*. From the mountains.

Okimumpe, オキムンベ, 洪水. *n*. A flood.

Ok-iporo, オキポロ, 愁色. *n*. A sad countenance.

Okira, オキラ, 力. *n*. Strength.

Okirasap, オキラサベ, 弱 キ. *adj*. Weak.

Okirashnu, オキラシヌ, 強 キ. *adj*. Strong.

Okisashke, オキサシケ, 濡 レ テ 汚 レ シ. *adj*. Wet and dirty (as an infant).

Okishka, オキシカ, 兎、鹿、又熊ノ尾. *n*. The tail of a hare, deer, or bear.

Okitak, オキタク, 悲シキ話. *n*. Sad or sorrowful talk. **Syn : Okneitak.**

Okitarumbe, オキタルムベ, 飾澁ノ類. *n*. A kind of ornamental mat. **Syn : Nikapumbe.**

Okkai, オッカイ, 男ノ、雄ノ、牡ノ. *adj*. Male.

Okkai-apa, オッカイアパ, 男ノ親類. *n*. Male relations.

Okkai-bo, オッカイボ, 青年. *n*. A young man.

Okkai-karaku, オッカイカラク, 甥. *n*. A nephew.

Okkai-ko-iwak, オッカイコイワク, 情夫ノ許ヘ通フ. *v.i*. To visit one's intended husband. To pay attentions to a young man with a view to marriage.

Okkai-mitpo, オッカイミッポ, 孫(男). *n*. A grandson.

Okkai-poho, オッカイポホ, 男ノ子、息子. *n*. A male child. A son.

Okkai-shiripo-auoshmare, オッカイシリポアウオシマレ, 成人シタ. *ph*. To have become a man.

Okkai-tomo-un-patek, オッカイトモウンパテク, 常ニ男ト共ニ居ル. *v.i*. To be always with men.

Okkaiyo, オッカイヨ, 男、青年. *n*. A male. A young man.

Okkashi, オッカシ, Okkashita, オカシタ, ヨ リ 多 ク、ヨ リ. *adv*. More than. Some more. More besides. Than.

Okkeu, オッケウ, 脊ノ上部、襟頭、頸、例セバ、 オッケウ カタチ ニ ララパレ、脊チ曲ゲ坐スル. *n*. The upper part of the back. The nape of the neck. The neck. As :— *Okkeu kata chinirarapare*, "to sit with bended back or neck as in great respect." *Okkeu nichitne*, "an aching neck"

Okkeu nini, "to stretch out the neck." *Okkeu nitne,* "a stiff neck." *Okkeu nitturinne,* "to hold the head up." *Okkeu ukao,* "to draw the neck in." *Okkeu ukotuntek,* "to have an aching neck."

Okkeu-kashi-apirikare, オノケウカシアビリカレ, 持參金ナヤレ. *v.t.* To give a dowry to a person with his daughter when given in marriage.

Okko, オノコ, 友、麼呼ビカケニ用ユ. *n.* Friend. Often used in addressing a person. **Syn : Ikatairotke guru.**

Okkeumaka-atte, オノケウマカアッテ, 倒ニ吊ルス. *v.t.* To hang with the face looking upwards.

Oknatara, オクナタラ, 哀シム. *v.i.* To be sad or sorrowful.

Ok-ne-iporo-oma, オクネイポロオマ, 俯ス、俯シタレ、悲シキ顏スル. *v.i.* and *adj.* To have a cast down appearance.

Ok-ne-itak, オクネイタク, カナク、悲シゲナル話. *n.* Spiritless, gloomy or sorrowful talk.

Oknetop, オクネトブ, ネマガリダケ. *n. Sasa paniculata, Mak. et Shib.* A kind of bamboo. **Syn : Pinnetop.**

Oknikoro, オクニコロ, 木ノ叉. *n.* The fork of a tree. An indentation.

Oko, オコ, 捉ム、鉤ニテ捕フ. *v.t.* To catch on to. To hook on to.

Okoi, オコイ, 海波ヨリ. *adv.* Out of the waves of the sea.

Okoika-un, オコイカウン, 東ヨリ. *adv.* From the east. **Syn : Ochupka-un.**

Okoipok-un, オコイポクウン, 西ヨリ. *adv.* From the west.

Okokke, オコッケ, 吊ルス (複數). *v. t.* To hang up. (*pl*).

Okokko, オコッコ, 蛇. *n.* A snake. **Syn : Ashitomap.**

Okokko-akam, オコッコアカム, トグロ打ツタル蛇. *n.* A curled up snake.

Okom, オコム, 海豚 (イルカ). *n.* A dolphin. **Syn : Rokom. Tannu.**

Okomomse, オコモムセ, 辭議スル、禮スル. *v.i.* To bow as in salutation or deep respect.

Okorakorak, オコラコラク, 鳴レ (箱中ノ物ノ如ク). *v.i.* To rattle as things in a box.
Hokorakorak, ホコラコラク,

Ok-pirikare, オクピリカレ, 幸ナラシム. *v.t.* To please. To make happy.

Okshiri, オクシリ, 荒蕪ノ地. (*geo*). Bad land.

Okshut-no, オクシュツノ, 後チミル、例セバ、ショモオクシユツノエクニサルウェネ、彼ハ後チ見ズシテ來レリ. *adv.* A looking back. As :—*Shomo okshut no ek nisa ruwe ne,* "he came without looking back."

Okshutu, オクシュツ, **Oksutu, オクスツ,** 襟頭. *n.* The nape of the neck. **Syn : Kimui oshmaki.**

Okte, オクテ, 哀シマスレ. *v. t.* To make sorrowful.

Oktomne-an, オクトム子アン, 死者チ悲シム. *v.i.* To sorrow for ·the dead.

Okturiri, オクツリリ, 首ヲ延ス. *v.i.* To stretch the neck out.

Okuikoeshkari, オクイコエシカリ, 尿閉、例セバ、オクイコエシカリツ エコツ、尿ノ塞リテ死ス. *n.* Stoppage of the water. As:—*Okuikoeshkari wa ekot,* "to die of stoppage of the water."

Okuima, オクイマ, 尿スル. *v.i.* To urinate. To make water. **Syn:** **Yaichinani. Ru-kari.**

Okuima-kina, オクイマキナ, ツリフネ サウ. *n. Impatiens, Textori, Miq.* A kind of Touch-me-not.

Okuru-kina, オクルキナ, ギバウシ. *n. Funkia ovata, Spreng.*

Okunnure, オクンヌレ, 悲シム. *v.i.* To feel grieved about.

Okunushike, オクヌシケ, 險阻ナル 場所. (*geo*). A craggy place.

Okush, オクシ, 裏ガヘス. *v.t.* To turn inside out. **Syn: Iyokush.**

Okush-un, オクシウン, 向フニ. *adv.* Beyond. **Syn: Kushketa.**

Okuwan-no, オクワンノ, 前ニ. *adv.* Ahead. In front of. Towards the front. **Syn: Arakuwan-no. Irikuanno.**

Ok-yoni, オクヨニ, 老年ノ爲ニ腰曲ル. *v.i.* To shrink up through old age.

Om, オム, 股. *n.* The thigh.

Oma, オマ, 風メレ、例セバ、オマココ モマットキ、風ミテ行ク. *adj.* Stooping. As:—*Oma kokomomatki,* "to go along in a stooping manner."

Oma, オマ,
Omai, オマイ, } 含ム. *v.i.* To be inside. Containing. Having. Holding. With.

Omai, オマイ, 行ク. *v.i.* To go. Same as *Oman.*

Omai, オマイ, 寝床、露塞. *n.* A bed. A platform. A place where something has been put.

Omairenga, オマイレンガ, 規則、法律、命令. *n.* Rules. Laws. Commands

Omai-so, オマイソ, 爐邊ノ方. *n.* The floor of a hut along the sides of a fireplace. The sides of a room or chamber.

Omaka, オマカ, 仕末スル. *v.i.* To clear away. To open up.

Omakano, オマカノ, 後. *adv.* Behind. By some *Homaka no.*

Omakatektereke, オマカテクテレケ, 蹣跚スル(醉ヒタル人ノ如ク). *v.i.* To reel as a drunken person. To walk crookedly.

Omakirush, オマキルシ, バッタ. *n.* A locust.

Oman, オマン, 行ク、進ム、(單數). *v.i.* (*sing*). To go. To advance. To proceed. The plural of this word is *paye.*

Oman-an, オマンアン, 行ケリ. *v.i.* Gone.

Omande, オマンデ, 送ル. *v.t.* To send. *Pl. Payere.*

Omanru, オマンル, 道路. *n.* A path.

Oman-rukot, オマンルコット, 道路. *n.* A worn path. A road. A trail.

Oman-so, オマンソ, 爐邊、ロバタ. *n.* That part of the floor of a hut along the sides of a fireplace.

Oman-tekkoro, オマンテッコロ, 少シ ク行キテ、行キツツ. *ph.* Having gone a little way. Whilst going.

Omaoma, オマオマ, 慰ムル. *v.t.* To comfort.

Omap, オマブ, 愛スル. *v.t.* Te love. **Syn: Katairotke.**

Omare, オマレ, 入ルル. *v.t.* To put into.

Omatturinne, オマッツリン子, 長ク延ビレ. *v.i.* To be stretched out lengthwise as in lying down.

Omau, オ マ ウ, 味、元素、風. *n.* Flavour. Taste. Essence. The wind.

Omau-kaun, オマウカウン, 風ノ上ニ. *adv.* To the windward.

Omaukush-ni, オマウクシニ, コブシ. *n. Magnolia Kobus. DC.* Also called *Opke-ni.*

Omaunure, オマウヌレ, 恐ル. *v.i.* To be afraid.

Omau-pokun, オマウポクン, 風下ニ. *adv.* To the leeward. **Syn: Opara pok un.**

Omau-sak, オマウサク, 無味ナル、穩ナル. *adj.* Tasteless. Flavourless. Calm.

Om-chikiri, オムチキリ, 後足. *n.* The hind feet of animals.

Omihi, オミヒ, 後脚. *n.* The hind legs of animals.

Omke, オムケ, 喘息、風邪、例セバ、オムケオシマ、風邪ニ罹ル. *n.* A cold. Asthma. As.—*Omke oshma*, "to catch a cold."

Omke-kara, オムケカラ, 風邪ニ罹ル. *v.i.* To take cold.

Omkepo, オムケポ, 咳スル. *v.i.* To cough.

Om-mekka, オムメッカ, 股ノ前部. *n.* The top or front part of the thigh.

Omoikoro,
オモイコレ, 姦濫スル. *v.t.* To commit
Omoinu, adultery.
オモイヌ,

Omoinu-ambe, オモイヌアムベ, 姦淫. *n.* Adultery.

Omoinu-guru, オモイヌグル, 姦淫者. *n.* An adulterer.

Omoinu-shiwentep, オモイヌシウェンテブ, 姦婦. *n.* An adulteress.

Omomo, オモモ, 善ク. *adv.* Well. Thoroughly. Nicely. **Syn: Uwatori.**

Omommomo-no, オモムモモノ, 速ニ、容易ニ、善ク. *adv.* Swiftly. Easily. Nicely. Well.

Omommomo-wa-ye, オモムモモワイェ, 平易ニ語ル. *v.i.* To say in an easy manner. To tell in a simple manner.

Omompekare, オモムペカレ, 厚ク敬フ. *v.t.* To treat with great defference.

Omonchina, オモンチナ, 轡頭 (オモカヒ). *n.* A horse's headstall. A bridle.

Omonku, オモンク, 手綱 (タヅナ). *n.* A bridle.

Omonnure, オモンヌレ, 誇張スレ、阿諛スル. *v.t.* To boast. To flatter. **Syn: Panore.**

Omonre, オモンレ, 讃スル. *v.t.* To praise. **Syn: Reika. Iranuye. Ramye.**

Omoyepush, オモイェプシ, 毛冠 (トサカ) アル. *adj.* Crested.

Om-poki, オムポキ, 股ノ下部. *n.* The under part of the thigh.

Omtui-pok, オムツイポク, 股ノ下部. *n.* The under part of the thigh.

Omu, オム, 塞ガル、例セバ、ヘツブツ
オム、河口ハ塞レリ. *v. i.* To be
stopped up. As:— *Pet butu
omu,* "the river's mouth is stopped up." *Ku kiseri omu wa
tambako ku eaikap,* "my pipe is
stopped up and I cannot smoke."
Syn: Mukkanne.

Omuken, オムケン, 捕フル能ハズ. *v.i.*
To be unable to catch.

Omumbe,
オムムベ, 股引. *n.* Trousers.
Omunbe,
オムンベ,

Omusa, オムサ, 昔漁期ノ終リニ日本人
ノ役人ノ長ガ會所ニテアイヌノ爲ニ開
ク宴會. *n.* A feast given in
ancient times to the Ainu at the
end of the fishing season, and
when the officials were on circuit
duty.

Om-utoro-sama, オムウトロキマ, 股
ノ下部. *n.* The under part of the
thighs.

On, オン, 腐ル(皮膚又ハ魚ナドノ). *v.i.*
To rot as skins or fish. **Syn: Horose. Apkara.**

On, オン, 熟シタル、食シ得ラル、例セ
バ、ミミナン、此魚ハ食フニ堪ユ. *adj.*
Ripe. Fit for eating. Cakes
prepared for food. As:—*Mimi
on* "the fish is fit to be eaten."

Ona, オナ, 父. *n.* Father. **Syn:
Onaha. Michi. Iyapo.**

Onashi, オナシ, 髑髏. *n.* Skull.
Cranium.

Ona-shiri, オナシリ, 父ノ代リニ. *ph.*
Instead of a father. To act as
a father towards.

Ongami, オンガミ, 挨拶スル、拜ム. *v.t.*
To salute. To worship. To bow
to. To adore.

Onikapunbe,
オニカプンベ, 木ノ皮又ハ蓙チ以
テ飾リタル蓙.
Onikapun-kina,
オニカプンキナ, *n.* A small
sedge mat ornamented with strips
of bark or rushes.

Oninkaot, オニンカオツ, 進ム(舟ノ水
面ニ於ケルガ如シ). *v.i.* To slip
along as a boat upon the surf
of the sea or down a stream.

Oninkaot, オニンカオツ, 滑ル、スベル.
v.i. To slide. To skate. **Syn:
Horatutu.**

Oninkot ani, 滑リ場所. *n.* A slide.
オニンコタニ, **Syn: Horatutu**
Oninkot-ushi, **ushi.**
オニンコツシ,

**Oninumba-hawe-ash, オニヌムバハ
ウェアシ,** 鳴ク(羊ノ如ク). *v.i.* To
bleat like a sheep.

Onipichi, オニピチ, 木ヨリ落ツル. *v.i.*
To fall from a tree.

Onishboso, オニシボソ, 隕石、電撃セ
ラル. *n. and v.i.* A meteorllite.
To be struck with lightning.

Onishboso, オニシボソ, 死ス. *v.i.* To
die.

Onishbosore, オニシボソレ, 殺ス. *v.t.*
To kill.

Onishnishi, オニシニシ, or **Onishni-
shu, オニシニシュ,** 諫ム、忠告スル.
v.t. To exhort. To advise. To
persuade. To abet. To coax.
Syn: Kooroshutke.

Onishnishi-i, オニシニシイ, 忠告、勸告.
n. Exhortation. Advice.

Onna, オンナ, or **Onnai, オンナイ,** 内
部. *n.* The inside.

Onnaige, オンナイゲ, 内部. n. The inside.

Onnaigeta, オンナイゲタ, 内ニ. adv. Inside.

Onnaige-un, オンナイゲウン, 内ニ. Inside.

Onne, オン子, 老ヒタル、貴キ、古代ノ、例セバ、オンネエコツ、老ヒテ死ス. adj. Old. Prized. Valued. Aged. Ancient. As:—Onne ekot, "to die of old age." Onne kotan. "an ancient town," "a capital." Syn: Onne koro.

Onne-chikap, オン子チカブ, 信天翁、海鶏.・ n. The albatross. Syn: Oshkanibe. Shikambe. Ishokapiu.

Onne-chikuni, オン子チクニ, 接骨木、ニハトコ. n. The elder tree. Sambucus racemosa, L.

Onne-huchi, オン子フチ, 火ノ女神. n. The goddess of fire. Syn: Kamui huchi. Abə huchi. Abe kamui Iresu huchi.

Onne-koro, オン子コロ, 老フル. v.t. To become old. To be aged.

Onnep, オン子ブ, ォツトセイ. n. A large fur seal. Syn: Uneu. Callorhinus ursina, Linn.

Onne-paskuru, オン子パスクル, ワタリガラス. n. Raven. Corvus corax Linn.

Onnere, オン子レ, 知ル、(單數). v.t. To know. Syn: Uwonnere. (sing).

Onnerepa, オン子レバ, 知ル(複數). v.t. To know (pl).

Onnu-onnu. オンヌオンヌ, 吟ズル、クチズサム. v.i. To make a noise inwardly. To hum. To make melody in the heart. To speak to one's self. See Eraunkuchi. Kamui noye.

Onon, オ ノ ン, 何處ヨリ. adv. Whence. As :—Nishpa, onon e ek? "Master, whence have you come?" Syn: Hunak wa.

Ononno, オノンノ, 悦ノ呌. exclam. An exclamation of pleasure. Syn: Nonno.

Onruika, オンルイカ, 口吟スレ、クチズサスミル. v.i. To make a humming sound with the voice. To crone.

Ontaro, オンタロ, 樽. n. A tub or bucket.

Onturep, オンツレブ,
Onturep-kam, オンツレブカム,
Onturep-tak. オンツレブタク,
ォ ホゥ パ ユリ. n. Dried lily-root cakes. Cakes made from the Lilium Glehni, Fr. Schm.

Onuitasa, オヌイタサ,
Onutasa, オヌタサ,
Onkitasu, オンキタス,
外ス、見落ス. v.t. To miss. To pass by without seeing. Syn: Uakkari. Uonuitasu. Enuitasa.

Onuman, オヌマン, 夕. adv. Evening. Syn: Shiri onuman.

Onuman-ibe, オヌマンイベ, 夕飯. n. Supper. The evening meal.

Onutasa, オヌタサ,
Onuitasa, オヌイタサ,
Onitasu, オニタス,
見失フ、見落ス. v.i. To miss. To pass by without seeing. Syn: Uokkari.

Ooho, オオホ, 深キ. adj. Deep.

Ooitak, オオイタク, 會話スレ. v.i. To converse together.

Oosorushi, オオソルシ, 坐ル. *v.i.* To sit upon.

Op, オブ, 鎗. *n.* A spear. *Op-seshke ka,* "a string used to tie a spear to the shaft."

Op, オブ, ニ於テ. *adv.* In. Same as *un.*

Op, オブ, 器. 例セバ、シユム オツ、油器. *n.* A box. A vessel in which to put anything. As:—*Shum op,* "a vessel for carrying or holding oil." **Syn: Shuop.**

Opagoat, オバゴアツ, 姦淫者. *n.* An adulterer.

Opahau-ush, オバハウウシ, 惡シキ風聞. *adv.* Of bad fame. **Syn: Chipahau-ushka.**

Opanguash-chikoikip, オバングアシチコイキプ, 前脚短ク後脚長キ動物. *n.* An animal with short fore and long hind legs.

Openrene, オベンレ子, 身體ノ下部ニ弱ミヲ感ズル. *v.i.* To feel weak about the lower part of the body.

Openrene, オベンレ子, 身體ノ上部ニ弱ミヲ感ズル. *v.i.* To feel weak about the chest and upper part of the body.

Oparapokun, オバラポクン, 風下、カザシモ. *adv.* The leeward. **Syn: Omau pok un.**

Opasopash, オバソバシ, 走セ廻ル. *v.i.* To run about.

Opatasse, オバタッセ, 下痢. *n.* Diarrhoea.

Opatache, オバタッチ, 下痢. *n.* Diarrhoea. **Syn: Opichitche. Opikikise.**

Opatttek, オバッテク, 噴火スル、破裂ス ル. *v.i.* and *adj.* To burst as a volcano. Burst open.

Opattekka, オバッテッカ, 破裂サスル. To burst open. To break into. **Syn: Opush.**

Opechiri, オベチリ, 漏レ. *v.i.* To leak.

Opechiri, オベチリ, 弩チ仕掛ケル. *v.i.* To set a spring bow.

Opekin-aruki-wa-isam, オベキンアルキワイサム, 忘ル. *ph.* To forget.

Opekush, オベクシ, 漏ル. *v.i.* To leak (as a tub or bucket). **Syn: Oikush.**

Opentari, オベンタリ, 根コギニスル、顛倒スル. *v.i.* To be rooted up. To fall down with the heels in the air. **Syn: Chiopentari.**

Opere, オベレ, 少女. *n.* A little girl.

Operekep, オベレケプ, 女ノ子. *n.* A female child.

Opesa, オベサ, 問ヲ多クカケル. *v.i.* To be inquisitive. To make inquiries.

Opesa-opesa, オベサオベサ, 問ヲ多クカケル. *v.i.* To be very inquisitive.

Opesh, オベシ, 聽ク、問フ. *v.i.* To listen. To act in an inquisitive manner. To inquire into. **Syn: Iyopesh.**

Opesh, オベシ, 傳ハリ下レ. *v.i.* To run down as rain down the trunk of a tree.

Opetkaushi, オベツカウシ, 渡船塲. *n.* A ford in a river.

Opetke, オベツケ, 疎襤、ボロ. *adj.* Ragged. Torn.

Opetpetke, オペツペツケ, 汚穢ナル醜 種ノ. *adj.* Ragged and dirty. **Syn: Oshitratanne.**

Opichi, オビチ, 滴ラス、オトス、緩 ムレ、取リ落ス. *v.t.* To drop. To loose. To allow to slip out of the hand.

Opichitche, オビチノチェ, 下痢病. *n.* Diarrhoea. **Syn: Opikikise. Opatatche.**

Opikikise, オビキキセ, 下痢病. *n.* Diarrhoea.

Opikin, オビキン, Opokin, オポキン, 補助スル、助ケル. *v.t.* To do for another. To assist. **Syn: Opukun.**

Opio-omke, オビオオムケ, 重キ風邪. *n.* A heavy cold.

Opirasa, オビラサ, 擴ケカケル. *v.t.* To spread over.

Opirika, オビリカ, 多クノ、甚ダ多ク ノ. *adj.* Many. Very many (used only of good things as deer or bears or fish). Very plentiful.

Opiri-sak, オビリサク, 健康ノ、無疵ノ、 完全ノ. *adj.* Without blemish. Sound. Whole.

Opishne, オビシ子, 海岸ヨリ. *adv.* From the sea-shore.

Opita-shiri, オビタシリ, 解キタレ. *adj.* Undone. Loose.

Opke, オブケ, 放屁スル. *v.i.* To break wind.

Opke-ni, オブケニ, コブシ. *n. Magnolia Kobus, D.C.* Also called *Omaukush-ni.*

Opne-top, オブ子トツブ, ネマガリダケ. *n. Sasa paniculata Mak. et Shib.*

Opoi, オポイ, 不誠實ナル. *adj.* Insincere.

Opoisam, オポイサム, 小サキ. *adj.* Small. Little.

Opoktara, オポクタラ, 疎キ、アラキ. *adj.* Jagged. Stripped up (as bark).

Opokun, オポクン, Opukun, オブクン, 補助スレ. *v.t.* To do for another. To assist.

Opombake, オポムバケ, アマガヘル. *n.* Tree frog.

Opunki, オブンキ, 其通リ、仰ノ如ク、 然リ. *adv.* Just so. As you say. So it is. Yes. Indeed.

Opopmau, オポプマウ, 熱. *n.* Fever.

Opuruse, オブルセ, 埋マル. *v.i.* To sink into.

Opush, オブシ, 破裂スル、開ク. *v.t.* To burst open. To break into. **Syn: Opattekka.**

Opush, オブシ, 穴アル、鑿ル. *adj. and v.i.* Having holes. Bored. As: *Opush chikuni,* "wood with holes bored into it."

Opushbe, オブシベ, 叉(銛チ此上ニ乗 セテ投グル者). *n.* A kind of rowlock used to send spears through when spearing fish.

Oputuye, オブツイェ, 押シヤル(舟チ濱 ヨリ出ス如ク). *v.t.* To push off as a boat from the shore.

Ora, オラ, アシカノ尾. *n.* The tail of a sea-lion.

Orage, オラゲ, Orake, オラケ, アラズ、シカラズ. *v.i.* Is not. To come to nothing. To become extinct.

Orai, オライ, 善良ナル、温順ナレ. *adj.* Good. Gentle. Humble.

Orai, オライ, 動物ノ如ク吃驚スレ. *adj.* Shy as animals. Quickly startled. To be absent as game when looked for.

Orai, オライ, 馬ノ如ク吃驚スル、逃脚チ早クスル. *v.t.* To shy at as a horse. To flee from in haste. To start at quickly.

Oraibe, オライベ, 尿チ堪ヘ能ハヌ人、寐小便スル人. *n.* A person who cannot hold his water. One who wets the bed.

Orai-ka, オライカ, 謙ラセル、命令スレ. *v.i.* To make humble. The command.

Orai-tashum, オライタシュム, 病ノ名 (尿チ堪ヘ能ハヌ). *n.* A disease the chief feature of which is that one cannot hold his water.

Oraitek, オライテク, 爛スブル、例セバ、アベオライテク、火ガ爛ル. *v.i.* To smoulder. To be just at the point of going out. As:—*Abe oraitek,* "the fire smoulders."

Orake, オラケ, Orage, オラゲ, 消滅スル. *v.i.* To become extinct. To come to nothing.

Orakse, オラクセ, 満足セヌ、例セバ、イベ オラクセ、食ニ満足セヌ. *v.i.* To be dissatisfied. To wish for more. To be insufficient. As:— *Ibe orakse,* "to be dissatisfied with one's food."

Oramatu, オラマツ, 學問アル、例セバ、オラマツグル、學者. *adj.* Learned. As:—*Oramatu guru,* "a learned person. **Syn : Eramatu.**

Oramboso. オラムボソ, 怖レ迷フ. *v.i.* To be agitated with fright.

Orambosore, オラムボソレ, 驚カス. *v.t.* To frighten.

Oramnure, オラムヌレ, 惡シト思フ. *v.t.* To think bad. To consider a thing bad.

Oram-sak, オラムサク, 愚ナル、惰弱ナレ. *adj.* Stupid. Imbecile.

Oram-sakka, オラムサツカ, 睡ム、馬鹿ニスル. *v.t.* To despise. To make a fool of.

Oramtaisak, オラムタイサク, 迷ヘル. *adj.* Bewildered.

Oramsakka, オラムサッカ, 輕ンズル、(上ノ人ニ對シテ). *v.t.* To behave disrespectfully towards one's betters.

Oramush, オラムシ, 學問アル. *adj.* Learned. **Syn : Eramush.**

Orap, オラブ, ヤマシヤクヤク. *Paeonia obovata,* Maxim. Also called by some *Horap.*

Orange, オランゲ, 横タハラセル、蟠ラス. *v.t.* To allow to lie down.

Orarai, オララ イ, 空ナル、荒レタレ. *adj.* Empty. Desert.

Oraugi, オラウギ, Orauge, オラウゲ, 遲キ、運クナレ、外レレ. *adv.* and *v.i.* Late. To miss. To be too late.

Oraunu, オラウヌ, 秘スル. *v.t.* To keep secret as one's thoughts and actions. **Syn : Eshina.**

Orau-oshma, オラウオシマ, 脚ガ深ク蹈ミ込ム. *v.t.* To sink into.

Oraurauge, オラウラウゲ, 埋マレ. *v.i.* To sink into.

Oraurauge-i, オラウラウゲイ, 低濕ノ地. *n.* A bog.

Oren, オレン, ニ、マデ. *post.* To Syn : Are-un. **Arun.**

Orene, オレ子, 弱クナル、立タレヌ又ハ步マレヌ. *v.i.* To become weak. To be unable to walk or stand.

Orep-un, オレブウン, 海ヨリ. *adv.* From the sea.

Orep-unbe, オレブウンベ, 海嘯、ツナミ. *n.* A tidal wave.

Oreshpa, オレシバ, 育テル(複數). *v. t.* To bring up. (*pl*). **Syn : Shukupte.**

Oresu, オレス, 育テル(單數). *v.t.* To bring up.

Oretopo, オレトポ, 歸ル. *v.i.* Tore turn. **Orohetopo, オロヘトポ,** Syn : **Hekomba.**

Ori, オリ, 堀リ出ス. *v.t.* To dig out.

Oriki-kut-horo, オリキクツコロ, 裙ヲ端折ル. *v.i.* To gird up one's loins. To gather up one's skirts.

Orikipuni, オリキフニ, 擡ゲル. *v.t.* To lift up.

Orikiraye, オリキライェ, 裳チカヽグレ. *v.t.* To hold the garments up high as in crossing a river.

Orampakte, オラムパクテ, 脅ス. *v.t.* To threaten.

Orampeshbare, オラムペシバレ, Orampechishte, オラムベチシテ, 深キ感動ヲ以テ考ヘル. *v.i.* To think about with deep feeling. To speak of in a very feeling manner.

Orikitesu, オリキテス, 下方ニ傾ク. *v.i.* To slant downwards.

Orikutkoro, オリクツコロ, 裙ヲ端折ル. *v.i.* To gird up the loins. Same as *oriki kut koro.*

Oripak-an, オリパクアン, 丁寧ニスル. *v.i.* To be polite. To be reverential. To be humble.

Oripak-an-no, オリパクアンノ, 謙遜シテ、例セバ、オリパクツライコラムコロ,余ハ謙遜シテ願フ. *adj.* Humbly. As :—*Oripak tura ikoramkoro,* "I humbly beg you."

Oripak-o, オリパクオ, 謙遜スル. *v.i.* To be humble or reverential.

Oripak-shiyeye, オリパクシイェイェ, or **Oripak-tashum, オリパクタシュム,** 疱瘡、虎烈剌. *n.* The smallpox. Cholera. **Syn : Kamui tashum.**

Orishimne, オリシム子, 明日. *adv.* Tomorrow. **Syn : Nishatta.**

Orit, オリツ, 突起シタル血管. *n.* Protruding veins.

Orito, オリト, 突起シタル血管ノ. *adj.* Being protruding veins.

Orito-tashum, オリトタシュム, 膨大シタル血管. *n.* Varicose veins.

Oro, オロ, 甚ダ. *adv.* Very. **Syn : Eoro.**

Oro, オロ, 入ツテアレ. *v.i.* To be in. At, or by. To be contained in. At. Inside of. Situated in. *Oro* governs the word as follows. As :—*Chisei oro,* "in the house."

Oro, オロ, 代價、豐富、例セバ、オロヌプレ、高價ノ. *n.* The price of any thing. Abundance. As :—*Oro nupuru,* "dear ; " *oro isam no,* "without price."

Oro-an-no, オロアンノ, 代價ヲ以テ、多クノ、例セバ、オロアンノコレ、多ク與フ. *ph.* With a price. Much. As :—*Oro an no kore,* "to give abundantly."

Oro-fushkone, オロフシコ子, 甚ダ古キ. *adv.* Very anciently. **Syn: Otdeeda.**

Oroge, オロゲ, 水路ニ依テ到着スル. *v.i.* To arrive at a place by water.

Oroge, オロゲ, 内部、内ニ、例セバ、ケヅムオロゲパラセ、胸ノ燃ユル. *adj.* Inside. In. As :—*Keutum oroge parase,* " to have a burning in the mind ; " Thus :—*Irushka keutum aekeutum oroge parase,* " to burn with anger." **Syn: Oshke.**

Oroge, オロゲ, 岩ノ下ノ穴. *n.* A hole under a rock.

Oroge-nina, オロゲニナ, 木製ノ盆. *n.* A kind of wooden tray.

Orogesh, オロゲシ, 子孫. *n.* Descendants. **Syn: Santek.**

Oro-hangeko, オロハンゲコ, 甚ダ遠キ. *adv.* Very distant.

Oro-isam-no, オロイサムノ, 無代價ニテ、無報酬ニテ、例セバ、オロイサムノコレ、與フ. *ph.* Without a price. Without remuneration. As :— *Oro isam no kore,* " to give."

Oro-iyo, オロイヨ, 入レル、、捲キ付ケル、例セバ、トツクリオロイヨヤン、瓶ニ注入セヨ. *v.t.* To put in. To wind on. As :—*Tokkuri oro iyo yan,* " pour it into the bottle." *Ahun-ka-nit oro iyo,* " to wind thread on a spool."

Oroke, オロケ, ノ如ク. *adv.* As. Like as. So.

Orokesh, オロケシ, or **Orogesh, オロケシ,** 子孫. *n.* Descendants.

Orokeweuse-hawe-ash, オロケウェウセハウェアシ, 鳴ク(羊ノ如ク)、叫ユ

ル. *v.i.* To bleat as a sheep. To roar. **Syn: Oninumba hawe ash.**

Orokotuye, オロコツイェ, 切リ下ゲレ. *v.t.* To cut down-wards. To cut perpendicularly.

Oro-kush, オロクシ, 横切ル. *v.i.* To cross.

Oroma, オロマ, 脂. *n.* Fat. Suet.

Oromam, オロマム, or **Oroman, オロマン,** 怒ル、不平チ云フ. *v.i.* To be angry. To be cross. To grumble.

Oromande, オロマンデ, 呻ク、ウメク. *v.i.* To groan.

Oromawepe, オロマウェペ, 呻ク聲. *n.* A gruff' voice.

Oromawe-soshma, オロマウェソシマ, 呻キテ語ル. *v.i.* To speak gruffly.

Oromun, オロムン, ハンゴンサウ. *n.* *Senecio palmatus, Pall.* Also called *Pekambe-kuttara.*

Oro-oiki, オロオイキ, 觸ル、、. *v.t.* To touch. To meddle with.

Orooitak, オロオイタク, 讀ム. *v.t.* To read.

Oro-omande, オロオマンデ, 呻ク、ウメク. *v.i.* To groan.

Oro-omap, オロオマブ, 物チ入レル器、例セバ、ルホントムタレウシアンコ、アエブオロオマブ、旅ニ用ユル辨當. *n.* A vessel in which to put things. As :—*Ru hontomta reushi an ko, aep oro omap,* " a vessel in which to put food for when one rests on a journey."

Oro-omare, オロオマレ, 入レル. *v.t.* To put into.

Oro-onurep, オロオヌレプ, 物ヲ入レ
ル器. *n.* A vessel in which to
put things.

Oro-oya-chiki, オロオヤチキ, 如何ニ
キ、實ニ、同時ニ. *ph.* Indeed. At
the same time.

Oro-pakno, オロパクノ, 其處マデ.
adv. ph. So far. That far.

Ororumbe-ne, オロルムベネ, 戰爭ノ
原因. *n.* An occasion for war or
a quarrel.

Orosama, オロサマ, 又、再ビ、其他.
adv. Again. Besides. **Syn :**
Samata.

Orosama, オロサマ, 内ニ、其内ニ、總
テ. *adv.* and *adj.* Amongst. All.

Oroshine-anda, オロシネアンダ, 嘗テ.
adv. Once upon a time. On a
certain occasion.

Orota, オロタ, 内ニ. *adv.* In. Inside. In which. By. To. **Syn :**
Otta.

Orota-an, オロタアン, 含ム、増加スル.
v.i. To be in. To accrue.

Orota-okai, オロタオカイ, 含ム、増加
スレ. *v.i.* To be in. To accrue.

Orota-ye, オロタイェ, 呼ビ掛ケレ、語
ル. *v.t.* To accost. To tell. To
say to.

Orowa, オロワ, 其時、依テ、而シテ、カ
ラ、例セバ、オヤプオロワパカネアカ
ラ、彼ハ彼等ニ愚弄セラレタリ. *post.*
Then. By. And. From. As :
— *Oyap orowa paka ne akara,* "he
was made a fool of by them."

Orowa-no, オロワノ, 後ニ、其時、カラ、
依テ. *adv.* After. Then. From.
By. Also. And.

Orowa-no-po, オロワノポ, 其時ヨリ、
其後. *adv.* And then. After that.

Orowa-aibe-sei, オロワアイベセイ, 淺
キ皿. *n.* A platter. An eating
shell or bowl.

**Orowa-no-yaiisamka, オロワノヤイ
イサムカ,** 自殺スル、缺席スレ. *v.i.*
To absent one's self. To kill one's
self. (*See Yaiisamka*).

Orun, オルン, ニ、ニ於テ、ニマデ、例セ
バ、オルンアフン、入ル. *post.* To.
In. Unto. As :— *Orun ahun,*
"to enter."

Orura, オルラ, 途ル. *v.t.* To send.

Orush, オルシ, 含ム. *v.i.* To be in.
Syn : Otta an. Otta okai.

Orushpe, オルシペ, 音信、報知、話. *n.*
News. Tidings. A tale. An
anecdote. A story.

Oru-unu, オルウヌ, 追蹤スル. *v.t.* To
follow a trail.

Osa, オサ, 砂. *n.* Sand. **Syn :** Ota.

Osa, オサ, 織機、杼. *n.* A loom.

Osakange, オサカンゲ, 呼ビ寄セル.
v.t. To send one person to another.
To call to one. To bid.

Osamatki, オサマツキ, 反對ノ、好マシ
カラヌ. *adj.* Contrary. Disagreeable. Sidewise.

**Osamatki-keutum-koro, オサマツキ
ケウツムコロ,** 好マヌ、不愉快ナル.
v.i. and *adj.* To be disagreeable.
Disagreeable.

Osampichi, オサムピチ, 不意ニ落ス.
v.t. To let suddenly fall on one
side.

Osan-osan, オサンオサン, 下ル、降ル.
v.i. To come down to.

Osap, オサプ, 下ル、下リ. *v.i.* To descend. A descent.

Osau-sau, オサウサウ, 緩メル. *v.t.* To loosen.

Osau-usauke, オサウウサウケ, 緩キ. *adj.* Loose.

Ose, オセ, 叫ュル. *v.i.* To roar. To cry.

Ose-kamui, オセカムイ, エゾイヌ. *n.* A wolf. *Canis familiaris* (*Yesso-ana*).

Osemkere, オセムケレ, 靜ニ、秘密ニ. *adv.* Quietly. Secretly.

Osemkere-ki, オセムケレキ, 秘密ニ爲ス、靜ニナス、例セバ、オセムケレオマン、秘密ニ行ク. *v.t.* To do quietly or in secret. As:— *Osemkere omar*, "to go quietly or in secret."

Osempiri, オセムピリ, 後ノ、隱レタル、目ニ見エヌ. *adj.* Behind. Hidden. Out of sight.

Ose-puni, オセプニ, 揚ゲル. *v.t.* To lift up. To elevate.

Osh オシ, or **oshi, オシ,** 後、次. *adv.* Wake. After. Next. Behind.

Osh-an, オシアン, 次ノ. *adj.* The next.

Osh-ek, オシエク, 次ノ、從フ. *adj.* and *v.t.* The next. To come next in order. To follow.

Osh-oman, オシオマン, 從フ. *v.t.* To follow.

Oshikama, オシカマ, 後ヨリ. *adv.* From behind.

Oshikarimba, オシカリムバ, 環. *n.* A circle. A ring.

Oshike, オシケ, or **Oshikehe, オシケ** ヘ, 内ニ、胃. *adv.* and *n.* Inside. The stomach.

Oshiketa, オシケタ, 内ニ. *adv.* Inside.

Oshike-op, オシケオプ, 臟、ゾウ. *n.* The entrails.

Oshike-un, オシケウン, 内ニ. *adv.* Inside.

Oshikiru, オシキル, 迂囘スレ. *v.t.* To go round; as round a mountain.

Oshikkote, オシッコテ, 讚ムル、愛スレ. *v.t.* To take a fancy to. To admire. To love.

Oshikkote-guru, オシッコテグル, 戀人. *n.* One's sweetheart.

Oshikkurukote, オシノクルコテ, 讚歎シテ見ル. *v.t.* To look at with admiration.

Oshiknuka, オシクヌカ, 感歎シテ見レ. *v.t.* To look at with admiration.

Oshikoni, オシコニ, 追ヒ付ク、儲ケレ、獲ル. *v.t.* To overtake. To earn. To get.

Oshikpekare, オシクペカレ, 狙フ. *v.t.* To take aim.

Oshikshuye, オシクシュイエ, 見廻ス. *v.t.* To turn the eyes about. To look about.

Oshimonsam, オシモンサム, 右手ノ方ニ. *adv.* At the right hand side.

Oshinnu, オシンヌ, 安全ナル、善キ. *adj.* Safe. Good. Beautiful.

Oshioun, オシオウン, 傾秘. *v.i.* Constipation. **Syn: Osshi-eshikari.**

Oshipi, オシピ, 反對ニ、アベコベニ. *adv.* Wrong end first.

Oshiraiba, オシライバ, 行ク、(複數).
(*Pl.*) *v.i.* To go to. To move
along. To go.

Oshiraye, オシライェ, 行ク、(單數).
(*Sing*) *v.i.* To move along. To
go.

Oshiri, オシリ, 地、席. *n.* The earth.
Ground. A place where one sits
or lies.

Oshirikatanu, オシリカタヌ, 眠ラレヌ.
v.i. To be unable to rest or sleep.

Oshirikonoye, オシリコノイェ, 包マ
ル、(雲ナド二). *v.i.* To be enveloped (as with clouds). To settle
down.

Oshirikopa, オシリコパ, 到着スレ. *v.i.*
To arrive at. To come to.

Oshirikosat, オシリコサツ, 乗リ揚ゲ
レ、座礁スル、(舟ガ淺瀬ヤ岸ナド二)、
例セバ、チプオシリコサツルウェチ、小
舟ガ乗リ揚ゲタ. *v.t.* To ground
as a ship or boat. As:—*Chip
oshirikosat ruwe ne,* "the boat is
aground."

**Oshiripichi, オシリピチ, or Oshiri-
pitba, オシリピツバ,** 打チ倒ス. *v.t.*
To knock down.

Oshiripotki, オシリポツキ, アリ、フク
ラゲ. *n.* Yellow tail. *Seriola
quinqueradiata, T. & S.*

Oshiri-sempiri, オシリセムピリ, 後
二、道二外レタル、秘密ノ場所二. *adv.*
Behind. Out of the way. In a
secret place.

**Oshiri-sempiri-unu, オシリセムピリ
ウヌ,** 隱ス. *v.t.* To hide away.
Syn: Nuina.

Oshirokka, オシロッカ, 止マレ. *v.t.*
To detain. To stay.

Oshiroma, オシロマ, 住居スレ. *v.t.*

To dwell at a place. **Syn: Shiroma.**

Oshirumuke, オシルムケ, 見エズナレ
迄見送レ. *v.t.* To watch one till
he goes out of sight.

Oshirush, オシルシ, 跛ノ、不具ノ. *adj.*
Lame. Maimed.

Oshish, オシシ, 底、地面. *n.* Bottom. Ground. As:—*Oshishte,*
"on the ground."

Oshish-oun, オシシオウン, 家ノ口ヨ
リ見テ左方ノ爐邊. *adv.* On the left
hand side of a fireplace looking
in from the porch door of a hut.

**Oshitteshu, オシッテシュ, or Oshitte-
su, オシノテス,** 滑リコロブ、例セバ、ト
ペエホクグルルプシシリカタオシッテ
シュ、オロワ、コロトペクタ、乳賣ガ凍
リシ地二滑ツテ乳チ醗シタ. *v.i.* To
slip down. As:—*Tope ehok guru
rupush shiri kata oshitteshu, orowa,
koro tope kuta,* "the milkman
slipped upon the frozen earth and
spilled his milk."

Oshitchiu, オシッチウ, 決定セラル、決
心セラレ. *v.i.* To be decided. To
be determined.

Oshitchiu-no, オシノチウノ, 決然.
adv. Decidedly.

Oshitchiure, オシッチウレ, 決定ス、決
心スレ. *v.t.* To decide. To determine.

**Oshitkurukote, オシックルコテ, or
Oshikkurukote, オシックルコテ,**
熱視スル、愛ラシゲ二見ル. *v.t.* To
watch carefully. To look at with
favour. To look lovingly upon.
Syn: Oshikunu.

Oshitratomne, オシツラトム子, 穢キ

襤褸. *adj.* Ragged and dirty. **Syn: Opetpetke.**

Oshittesu, オシツテス, 滑ル. *v.i.* To slip.

Oshiun, オシウン, or **Oshi-oun, オシオウン**, 便秘ニ苦ム. *v.i.* To suffer from constipation. To be costive.

Oshkambe, オシカムベ, アホウドリ. *n.* The albatross. **Syn: Onnechikap. Shikambe. Isho-kapiu.**

Oshke, オシケ, 胃、身體ノ内部、物ノ内部、例セバ、オシケアラカ、胃ニ痛ミアリ. *n.* The inside of the body. The inside of anything. As:—*Oshke araka*, "to have the stomach ache."

Oshke, オシケ, 網チアム、又修繕スル、織ル. *v.t.* To make or mend nets. To net. To weave.

Oshkewe, オシケウェ, 性質、氣、品性. *n.* The disposition. Temper. Character. Turn of mind.

Oshkoni, オシコニ, 追ヒ付ク、(單數). *v.t.* To over-take.

Oshkonika, オシコニカ, 追フ. *v.t.* To pursue. To strive to catch.

Oshkonipa, オシコニパ, 追ヒ付ク、(複數). *v.t.* To overtake (*pl*).

Oshma, オシマ, 穴ニ陷ル、入ル. *v.i.* To fall into a hole. To go in. To get in. To enter (as a rat into a trap).

Oshma, オシマ, 罹ル、例セバ オムケ オシマ、風邪ニ罹ル. *n.* To take (as a cold). As:—*Omke oshma*, to catch a cold.

Oshmake, オシマケ, 後、例セバ、オシマケワ コッチャケワ、前ニモ後ニモ. *post.* Behind. As:—*Oshmake wa kotchake wa*, "both before and behind." **Syn: Homokashi.**

Oshoprotki, オショプロッキ, ブリ. *n.* Yellow tail. *Seriola quinqueradiata, T. & S.* **Syn: Koyanchep.**

Oshopshopo, オショプショポ, 濯グ、スヽグ. *v.t.* To rinse. To wash out.

Oshotki, オショッキ, or **Osotki, オソッキ**, 寢床. *n.* A bed. A sleeping place.

Oshoyumbe, オショユムベ, 幻、マボロシ. *n.* An apparition.

Oshpara-ni, オシパラニ, 接骨木、ニハトコ. *n.* The elder tree. *Sambucus racemosa, L.* Used as a medicine at childbirth; also as a charm against disease. **Syn: Onne-chikuni. Soko-ni.**

Oshtari, オシタリ, 下痢. *n.* Diarrhoea.

Osh-uk, オシウク, 引キ戻ス. *v.t.* To take back.

Oshuke, オシュケ, シロウサギ. *n.* A hare. *Lepus variabilis, Pall.* **Syn: Kaikuma. Oshukep. Isepo. Epethe.**

Osoine-ru, オソイチル, 雪隱. *n.* The water closet. This a better word to use than *Ashinru.* **Syn: Esoine ru.**

Osoma, オソマ, 人糞. *n.* Human excrement. Fœces. Dung.

Osoro, オソロ, 下腹. *n.* The abdomen. **Syn: Panake.**

Osoroka, オソロカ, 後ヨリ、尻ヨリ、下ヨリ. *adv.* From the posteriors. From behind. From below.

Osoro-un, オソロウン, 下腹ノ. *adj.* Abdominal.

Osoro-un-no, オソロウンノ, 下腹ノ. *adv.* Abdominally.

Osoro-gesh, オソロゲシ, 寄添ヘ レ. *adj.* Close by the side of.

Osoro-gesh, オソロゲシ, 家ノ裏. *n.* The back of a house. **Syn : Chisei ogesh.**

Osoroma, オソロマ, 大便ニ行ク. *v.i.* To go to stool.

Osoyoshma, オソヨシマ, 突然ニ走リ出ス. *v.i.* To rush suddenly out of doors. To gush out. To drop out. As :—*Niwatush asama osoyoshma,* "the bottom dropped out of the bucket."

Ossereke, オッセレケ, 悲シム、澁面ス ル、容易ニ怒ル. *v.i.* To be sorry. Morose. Surly. Stern. Gruff. Snappish.

Osshi, オノシ, 木ノ心、キノシン. *n.* The heart of a tree. The inside of anything. Core.

Osshi-eshikeri, オノシエシケリ, 便秘. *n.* Constipation. **Syn : Oshioun.**

Osshiwen, オッシウェン, 爲スチ好マヌ. *v.i.* To dislike to do a thing.

Osura, オスラ, 投ゲ棄テル、(單數). *v.t.* To throw away. (*sing*).

Osurupa, オスルパ, 投ゲ棄テル、(複數) 例セバ、ナスルパランゲプ、投ゲ棄ラレ シ物. *v.t.* To throw away. (*pl*). As :—*Osurupa rangep,* " things to be thrown away." *Pl.* of *osura*.

Ot, オツ, 葬ル爲ニ布ニ卷カレシ死體. *n.* A corpse rolled up in mats ready for burial. *Ot ani chikuni,* "a

pole used in carrying corpses to their burial."

Ot, オツ, 甚ダ、此語ハオロノ略ナリ、例 セバ、オツデエダ、太古ニ. *adv.* Very. This word is contracted from *oro*. Thus :— *Ot-deeda* for *oro teeda*, "in very ancient times."

Ot, オツ, 有ル、(複數). *v.i.* To be. *Pl.* of *o*.

Ota, オタ, 灌ギカチレ. *v.t.* To pour upon.

Ota, オタ, 砂. *n.* Sand.

Ota, オタ, 嫌フ、不用ナル. *v.t.* To dislike. To not want. **Syn: Kopan. Irannakka.**

Otachimakani, オタチマカニ, カチ カノ一種. *n.* A kind of sculpin.

Otakkoro, オタッコロ, 短キ. *adj.* Short.

Otakne, オタクネ, 短キ. *adj.* Short.

Otamba, オタムバ, 此ノ方、例セバ、ル イカオタムバ、橋ノ此方. *adv.* This side of. As :—*Ruika otamba,* "this side of the bridge." **Syn: Hakeita.**

Otakoro, オタコロ, 砂ノ. *adj.* Sandy. Gritty.

Otamba-un, オタムバウン, 是レヨリ. *adv.* Hence. From this side.

Otanne, オタンネ, 長キ. *adj.* Lengthwise.

Otanne-ni, オタンネニ, 竿. *n.* A pole. A perch.

Otapana, オタパナ, 細砂. *n.* Fine sand.

Otara, オタラ, 突キサス、突キサシタル. *v.i.* and *adj.* To stick into. Sticking in.

Otasam, オタサム, 海岸. *n.* The seashore.

Otarop, オタロブ, テフザメ. *n.* A sturgeon. *Acipenser mikadoi, Hilgd.*

Otashish, オタシシ, 歸ラント欲スル. *v.i.* To desire to return.

Otasashke, オタサシケ, 悩ム、苦シム. *v.i.* To suffer. To feel pain.

Otatoshka, オタトシカ, 砂濱. *n.* A bank of sand.

Ota-tope-ni, オタトペニ, カラコギカ ヘデ. *n. Acer Ginnala, Maxim.* A kind of maple.

Ota-shipship, オタシブシブ, スギナ. *n.* Field horse-tail. **Syn: Tehun shipship.** *Equisetum arvense, L.*

Ota-ush, オタウシ, 砂ノ. *adj.* Sandy.

Otchari-sak, オッチャリサク, 古ク破レ タレ. *adj.* Old and worn out.

Otchike, オッチケ, 盆. *n.* A tray.

Otchine, オッチ子, 無能ナル、弱キ. *adv.* Incapable. Without tact. Weak. Feeble.

Otchinep, オッチ子ブ, 無能ナル人. *n.* An incapable person.

Otchiwe, オッチウェ, 弱キ. *adj.* Weak.

Otdeeda, オッデエダ, 大古ノ. *adv.* In very ancient times.

Otekna, オテクナ, 攻撃スレ. *v.t.* To attack. To set upon. **Syn: Piuki. Chorauge.**

Oteknu, オテクヌ, 富ミタレ. *adj.* Rich.

Otekomare, オテコマレ, 抱擁スル、抱キ着ク. *v.t.* To embrace. To take into the arms. To cuddle.

Otekpeshbare, オテクペシバレ, 髮チ 撫テレ、撫テテ延ス. *v.t.* To stroke the beard. To smooth out anything long as straws or pieces of string or fibre.

Otek-sak, オテクサク, 貧シキ、貧ナル. *adj.* Poor. **Syn: Irapokkari.**

Otereke, オテレケ, 蹴ル、踏ミ捩ル. *v.t.* To kick. To trample upon.

Otettereke, オテッテレケ, 踏ミ捩ル. *v.t.* To trample upon.

Otke, オッケ, 刺ス、貫ク. *v.t.* To prick. To pierce.

Otke-otke, オッケオッケ, 屢刺ス. *v.t.* To prick often or much.

Otke-ekushna, オッケエクシナ, 貫キ 通ス. *v.t.* To pierce through.

Otoiboshpa, オトイボシバ, 地チ通シ テ行ク. *v.i.* To go downwards through the earth.

Otoinure, オトイヌレ, 掘ル(土チ)、例セ バ、エモ オトイヌレ、芋チ掘ル. *v.t.* To earth. As:—*Emo otoinure,* "to earth potatoes." **Syn: Oto-ipukte.**

Otoipukka, オトイプッカ, 築ク (土堤 チ). *v.t.* To bank up.

Otoipukte, オトイプクテ, 掘リ上ゲル (土チ)、築ク (土堤チ). *v.t.* To earth up. To bank up.

Otompui, オトムブイ, 肛門. *n.* The anus. **Syn: Yoropui.**

Otompui-kina, オトムブイキナ, クサ ノヌ. *n.* The common Celandine. *Chelidonium majus, L.*

Otonno-itak, オトンノイタク, 聲ノ低 ク聞エル事、竊ニ語ル. *n.* A low

murmuring of voices. A slow speaking. Also *v.i.* To speak slowly.

Otonoikari, オトノイカリ, Otonaikari, オトナイカリ, 朝寝スル、寝過ス. *v.i.* To sleep late. To oversleep one's self. **Syn: Hopuni-moire.**

Otonrim, オトンリム, 大砲ナドノ音、例セバ、オトンリムオツク、轟音. *n.* A thumping sound. The report of guns. As:—*Otonrim otuk,* "the sound of thumping."

Otop, オトブ, 頭髪. *n.* The hair of the head.

Otop-konchi-koro, オトブコンチコロ, 哀悼スル、哀悼ノ爲髪ヲ下ゲル. *v.t.* To mourn for the dead. To let the hair hang down as in mourning for the dead.

Otop-sak, オトブサク, 禿ゲタレ. *adj.* Bald.

Otraisambe, オツライサムベ, 心案乱ス. レ. *v.i.* To be mystified.

Otta, オッタ, ニレ、迄、依テ、例セバ、エンオッタヌ、彼ハ余ニ訊ネタリ. *post.* In. To. Unto. By. Of. Among. With the verb *nu,* "to hear," or inquire" *otta* is used like the English word "of." As:—*En otta nu,* "he inquired of me." *Amip otta uk,* "he took them from his dress." *Kamui otta shikaobiukire,* "to be saved by God." **Syn: Orota.**

Ottaanushike, オッタアヌシケ, 物ノ有ル場所. *ph.* The place where it is.

Otta-oman-i, オッタオマンイ, 入口、玄関. *n.* Entrance. Access. A going to.

Otta-omare, オッタオマレ, 入レ、. *v.t* To put into.

Otta-ye, オッタイェ, 向ツテ云フ. *v.t.* To address.

Otteeda, オッテエダ, 甚ダ古キ、大古ノ. *adv.* Very anciently. In very ancient times.

Ottem-itak, オッテミタク, 憐ム. *v.i.* To commiserate. **Syn: Omaoma-itak.**

Ottena, オッテナ, 酋長. *n.* The ordinary chief of a village. See *Kontukai.*

Otubera, オツベラ, 杓子. *n.* A ladle. A spoon.

Otuiba, オツイバ, 切リ倒ス. *v.t.* To cut down.

Otuk, オツク, 轟々タル音ヲ出ス. *v.i.* To give forth a thumping sound.

Otuk, オツク, 突キ出ツル. *v.i.* To stick out of.

Otukonniki-ore-konniki, オツコンニキオレコンニキ, 襤褸ガ下ル. *ph.* To hang down in rags.

Otumine, オツミ子, 戦因. *n.* An occasion for war. **Syn: Oukoiki-ne. Ororumbe ne.**

Otupekare, オツペカレ, 吝嗇ナル. *adj.* Miserly. Stingy.

Oturai-sambe-ekote-kara, オツライサムベエコテカラ, 強ムル、勤ムル、身ヲ隠ス、恍惚スレ、例セバ、アイヌカッチ アイヌカラ クニ オツライ サムベアエコテ カラ、彼ヲ恍惚タラシムル爲余ハ姿ヲ隠セリ. *v.t.* To endeavour. To mystify. To do with all one's might. To render one's self invisible. As:—*Ainu kat ne ainu-kara kuni oturai-sambe ae-*

kate kaia, "I rendered my form invisible so as to mystify him."

Otusanashke, オツサナシケ, 兩手チ
擦ム一種ノ挨拶. *n.* The salutation
of rubbing the hands.

**Otusanashkeuwenoye, オツサナシ
ケウウェノイェ,** 兩手チ擦ンテ挨拶スレ.
v.t. To salute by rubbing the
hands.

Otusashuishiri, オツサシュイシリ, 永
遠ニ. *adv.* For ever. As:—
*Otusashuishiri wa no otusashui-
shiri pakno,* "from everlasting to
everlasting." **Syn: Shashuishiri.**

Otush-etaye, オツシエタイェ, 拷問(ゴ
ウモン)スレ,(髪ノ毛チ取ツテ吊リ下
ゲル). *v.t.* To hang up by the
hair of the head as in punishing
or making a person confess a
fault.

**Otushshiwenpa-shiritatpa, オツシ
シウェンパシリタツパ,** 叱スレ. *v.i.*
To scold.

Otutapkanru, オツタプカンル, 踊リ、
且ツ手チ拍ツ. *v.i.* To dance and
clap the hands.

Otutapkara, オツタプカラ, 多ク踊レ.
v.i. To dance much.

**Otutapkara-oretapkara, オツタプ
カラオレタプカラ,** 踊リクルフ. *v.i.*
To dance very much.

Otuwashi, オツワシ, 怜悧ナル故ニ撰
フ. *v.t.* To chose on account of
one's cleverness. **Syn: Asarama.**

Otuye, オツイェ, 切リ去ル. *v.t.* To
carry cut off.

Otuye, オツイェ, 海鳥ノ一種. *n.* A
kind of sea-fowl.

Otuyetute, オツイェツテ, 煽グ、アホグ.
v.t. To fan. **Syn: Paruparu.**

Otuyetuye, オツイェツイェ, 持チ去ル
(盗ミテ持チ去ルヤウニ). *v.t.* To
carry away (as one's property in
theft).

Ouguru, オウグル, 切リ目多クスル. *v.t.*
To cut very much. To cut not
quite through.

Ouhaita, オウハイタ, 合ハヌ. *v.i.*
Not to fit.

Ouhuika, オウフイカ, 焦ゲル. *v.t.*
To burn (as food on the bottom
of a saucepan).

Oukasu, オウカス,⎫ 甚グ、大ニ、例セ
Okasu, オカス,⎭ バ、オウカスピ
リカ、彼ハ大ニ善シ. *adv.* Very.
In a great degree. As:—*Oukasu
pirika.* "He is much better."

Oukashui, オウカシュイ, 増減スレ(腫
物ノ如ク). *v.t.* To increase or
decrease as a boil.

Oukoiki-ne, オウコイキ子, 爭論原因.
n. An occasion for quarrelling.
Syn: Ororumbe ne.

Oukot, オウコツ, 結合シタル. *adj.*
Joined together.

Orukotokne, オルコトク子, 深谷. *adj.*
A deep, difficult valley.

Oun-no, オウンノ, 此時ヨリ、初ヨリ、
例セバ、タンパアシリチュプ オウンノ、
本年一月ノ始. *adv.* From the time
of. At the commencement of.
As:—*Tampa ashiri chup oun no,*
"at the beginning of the first
month of this year."

Oupak, オウパク, 適スレ. *adj.* Fit.

Oupak-no, オウパクノ, 通常ニ. *adv.*
Fittingly.

Oupeka, オウペカ, 廉直ナル、正キシ. *adj.* Upright. Righteous. Straight. Accurate.

Oupeka-i, オウペカイ, 正確. *n.* Accuracy.

Oupeka-no, オウペカノ, 正確ニ. *adv.* Accurately. Aright. Properly.

Oupekare, オウペカレ, 改直スル、修繕スル. *v.t.* To set to rights. To mend. To adjust.

Oupshoro-omare, オウブショロオマレ, 懐中スル. *v.t.* To place in the bosom.

Oupshorota, オウブショロタ, or **Oupshotta, オウブショッタ,** 懐中ニ、例バ、オウブショッタオマレ、彼女ガ懐中ニ入レタ. *adv.* In the bosom. As:— *Oupshotta omare,* " she put it in her bosom."

Ouri, オウリ, 掘リ出スル. *v.t.* To dig up.

Ousakarire, オウサカリレ, 隔日. *adv.* Alternate days. **Syn: To shikamare.**

Ousamo, オウサモ, 溝(戸ナドノ). *v.i.* To make a groove.

Ouse, オウセ, 只. *adv.* Only. Merely. Just.

Oush, オウシ, 附着スル. *v.i.* To be stuck on.

Oush-no-an, オウシノウン, 附屬スル所ノ、例セバ、オウシノアンイタクオロオイタク、私ハ附屬セル物讀ム可シ. *adj.* Adhering to. Sticking on. As:— *Oush no an itak ku oro-oitak,* " I will read the remainder."

Oushi, オウシ, 突キ刺ス. *v.i.* To stick in.

Oushi, オウシ, 席、生レシ場所、何物カ有ル所. *n.* A seat. A birthplace. The place where anything is.

O-ushike, オウシケ, 近ク、添ヒテ、於テ、例セバ、チセイオウシケ、家ニ近ク. *adv.* Near to. Close by. At. Place where. As:— *Chisei o-ushike,* " close by the house." *Chikuni o-ushike,* " at the foot of the tree."

O-ushiketa, オウシケタ, 傍ニ. *adv.* By the side of.

Owata, オワタ, 水. *n.* Water.

Oworo-koash, オウォロコアシ, 水面ニ達セル滑ナル表面ヲ有スル崖又ハ岩. *n.* A cliff or rock with a smooth surface running straight down into a river or stream of water.

Oya, オヤ, 他ノ、外國ノ、次ノ、異リタル. *adj.* Other. Another. Alien. Next. Different.

Oya-chiki, オヤチキ, 其他、實ニ、又. *adv.* Besides. Indeed. Again.

Oya-itak, オヤイタク, 反語. *n.* Irony.

Oyakne, オヤクネ, 過去、ヨリ、カラ. *adv.* Past. Off. From.

Oyak or **oyake, オヤク,** 又ハ **オヤケ,** 外ニ、其ノ他ノ所ニ、外側ニ. *adv.* Without. Elsewhere. Outside.

Oya-kotan-ta, オヤコタンタ, 外ノ處ニ. *adv.* Abroad.

Oyak-ta, オヤクタ, 外ノ處ニ、彼方ヘ. *adv.* Abroad. Away.

Oyakta-ande, オヤクタアンデ, 他ノ處ニ置ク、無クスル. *adv.* To place

elsewhere. To adduce. To abrogate.

Oyakta-oman, ヤヤクタオマン, 他ノ處ヘ行ク. *v.i.* To go elsewhere.

Oyak-un, オヤクウン, 他處ニ. *adv.* Elsewhere.

Oyak-un-omande, オヤクウンオマンデ, 他處ヘ途ル、無クスル. *v.t.* To send to another place. To adduce. To abrogate.

Oya-moshiri-ta, オヤモシリタ, 外ノ處ヘ. *adv.* Abroad.

Oya-moshiri-un-guru, オヤモシリウングル, 外國人. *n.* A foreigner.

Oya-mokoro-ki, オヤモコロキ, 死ス. *v.i.* To die. **Syn: Rai.**

Oyamokte, オヤモクテ, 奇ナル、驚ク. *adj. and v.i.* Odd. Funny. Unusual. Strange. To be surprised at. This word is sometimes used as an interjection indicative of surprise or wonder.

Oyan, オヤン, 乗ラシムレ. *v.t.* To cause to ride. *Naa shomo ku oman gusu nei ku goro umma oyan rusui,* "as I cannot go yet, I wish to let him ride my horse.

Oyange, オヤンゲ, 打ナ上ゲル (浪風ニヨリテ). *v.t.* To cast ashore.

Oyanruru, オヤンルル, 北ノ海. *n.* The north sea. **Syn : Aramoi-sam.**

Oyap, オヤブ, 他ノ者. *n.* Another one. A different one.

Oyap, オヤブ, 上陸スル. *v.i.* To land from a boat.

Oya-pa, オヤパ, 來年. *n.* Next year.

Oyapa-eoyapaka, オヤパエオヤパカ, 翌々年. *adv.* The year after next.

Oyapi. オヤビ, 蛇、惡寬. *n.* A snake. A demon.

Oyapkopoye, オヤブコポイェ, 混消ス. *v.t.* To adulterate.

Oyaporo-guru, オヤポログル, 日本人、他人種ノ人. *n.* A Japanese. A person of another race.

Oyaramat, オヤラマツ, 亡魂. *n.* A departed spirit.

Oyaramkore, オヤラムコレ, 知ラヌ人トシテ待遇スル. *v.t.* To treat as a stranger.

Oyasa, オヤサ, 切リ下ゲレ. *v.t.* To cut downwards.

Oyashi, オヤシ, 精靈、鬼、善又ハ惡靈. *n.* A spirit. A good or evil spirit. A demon.

Oyashkep, オヤシケブ, 女ノ子. *n.* A female child. **Syn: Operekep.**

Oyashim, オヤシム, 明後日. *adv.* The day after to-morrow.

Oyashima, オヤシマ, 明後日. *adv.* The day after to-morrow.

Oyashim-shimge, オヤシムシムゲ, 明々後日、シアサッテ. *adv.* The second day from tomorrow.

Oyashiri, オヤシリ, 異リタル、惡シキ. *adj.* Different. Bad.

Oyatorokoro-samambe, オヤトロコロサマムベ, カレイノ一種. *n.* A kind of flounder.

Oya-ukuran, オヤウクラン, 明晩. *adv.* To-morrow evening.

Oyokane, オヨカチ, or **Oyokaush, オヨカウシ**, 殘リ. *n.* Remainder.

Oyopero-ni, オヨペロニ, ハクウンボク. *n.* *Styrax Obassia,* Sieb. et Zucc.

Oyumakun-atui, オユマクンアツイ, 東ノ海. *n.* The eastern sea.

Oyupupke, オユプブケ, 惡クナル、(病氣、又ハ病人ノ). *v.i.* To grow worse as a disease or sick person.

Oyupupu, オユブブ, 搔キマワス、諫ㇾ. *v.i.* To stir up. To exhort. To incite.

Oyuyukechiri, オユユケチリ, 啄木鳥ノ一種. *n.* A kind of woodpecker.

P (ピ).

P, ブ, 此語ガ形容詞及ビ動詞ノ後ニ付ク時ハ、其チ名詞トナスカチ有ス.例セバ.ポロ、大ナル、ホロプ、大ナル物. Used as a suffix to adjectives and verbs *p* has the power to turn them into nouns. Thus :—*Poro,* " large "; *porop,* " a large thing." *Kashiobiuki,* " to help "; " to save ; *kashiobiukip,* " a helper," " a saviour." *P* so used is contracted from *pe,* " a thing," " an article."

Pa, パ, 有リ (複數三人稱)、重ニ動詞ノ接尾ニ用ユ、例セバ、ホシピ(單數)ホシッパ(複數)歸ル. *n.* The 3rd pers. pl. of *an* to be ; " they." Used chiefly as a suffix to. Thus :—*Hoshipi* (Sing) *hoshippa* (pl), " to return." *Kore* (Sing), *korepa,* (pl) " to give."

Pa, パ, 充チタレ、例セバ、ワツカシチバ、水一杯. *adj.* Full. As :— *Wakka shine pa,* " a cupful of water."

Pa or **paha, パ,** 又ハ **パハ,** 時季、齡、例セバ、パイカラパ、春季. *n.* A season. Age. A year. Thus : —*Paikara pa,* " the season of spring." *Sak pa,* " the season of summer." *Mata pa,* " winter." *Nei pakno e paha an a?* what is your age " ? *Pa pirika,* " a year of plenty. *Pa wen,* " a bad year for crops or hunting or fishing." *Pa yupke,* " a rough season or year." *Pa emko,* " half a year." *Pa koshipashnu,* " to have one's garden produce destroyed by birds or animals."

Pa, 圍體ノ首長、東、例セバ、ウタラパ、酋長. *n.* The head of the body. A chief. The east. Thus :—*Utarapa,* " a chief," " a lord." *Moshiri-pa,* " the east." *Set pa,* " the head of a table." **Syn: Pake. Sapa.**

Pa, パ, 發見スレ. *v.t.* To find.

Pa or **paha, パ,** 又ハ **パハ,** 蒸氣、煙、鯨ノ吐ク水煙. *n.* Steam. Smoke. The water which whales blow out. *Pa at,* " to emit steam or smoke."

Pa or **paba, パ,** 又ハ **パバ,** 罰、疱瘡. *n.* Punishment. Small-pox. **Syn: Kamui-pa. Pak.**

Pa-ashin, パアシン, 煙筒、煙出シ. *n.*

A chimney. A going off of steam or smoke.

Pa-akari, バアカリ, 煙ベラル、煙ベラレタル. *v.t. and adj.* To be smoked.

Pa-ashinbe, バアシンベ, 頁ス(負債アル人ヲ). *v.i.* To let one off (as a debtor). To forego one's rights.

Pa-ashinge, バアシンゲ, 水ヲ噴ク(鯨ノ如ク). *v.t.* To blow or send out water as a whale.

Pa-ashingep, バアシンゲプ, 煙筒. *n.* A chimney.

Pachi, バチ, or **Patchi, バッチ,** 木鉢、鉢. *n.* A basin. A wooden bowl.

Pachiko-an, バチコアン, 罰セラル. *v.i.* To be punished.

Pachingara, バチンガラ, or **Patchingara, バチンガラ,** ガヤガカ. *n.* Sibastodes Taczanowskii (Steind).

Paenrum, バエンルム, 唇ノ眞中. *n.* The middle of the lips.

Pagoat, バゴアツ, 惡シキ、輕蔑セラレレ. *adj.* Wicked. Bad. One spoken against. One who is under-going some punishment from fiends or the higher powers.

Pahau, バハウ, 風說、ウハサ、例セバ、カムイタシュムアンノイチバハウアン、疱瘡アリトノ噂アリ. *n.* A rumour. As:—*Kamui tashum an noine pahau an,* " it is rumoured that there is small-pox."

Pahenenu, バヘチヌ, 尋ヌレ. *v.t.* To inquire. **Syn: Patemtemu ki. Uwepekenu.**

Pai, バイ, サヽ. *n.* Bamboo grass.

Pai, バイ, 連枷、(カラサホ)、例セバ、バ イアニシリキク連枷ニテ打ツ. *n.* A flail. As :—*Pai ani shirikik,* " to thrash with a flail." **Syn : Mamekikbe.**

Pai, バイ, 行ク (複數). *v.t.* To go. (*pl*). **Syn : Paye,**

Paige, バイゲ, チクチクスレ. *v.i.* To prick or twitch as " pins and needles."

Paikara, バイカラ, 春. *n.* The spring of the year. **Syn : Paikaru.**

Paikara-pa, バイカラバ, 春季. *n.* The season of spring.

Paikara-un-pa, バイカラウンパ, 春季. *n.* The season of spring.

Paipai-chiri, バイバイチリ, シジウカラ. *n.* A tit. *Parus atriceps minor, Hokrsfield.*

Paiyaige, バイヤイゲ, 震フ、寒ガレ. *v.i.* To shiver. To feel cold.

Pak, バク, 罰. *n.* Punishment.

Pak, バク, 叱スレ. *v.t.* To scold.

Paka, バカ, 愚人. *n.* A fool. **Syn : Yairampeutek guru.**

Pakakse, バカッセ, 爆音(火ノハネル)、例セバ、アベバカクセ、火ガ爆ル. *v.i.* To crackle as a fire. To creak with a noise (as ice). As:—*Abe pakakse,* " the fire crackles " **Syn : Push.**

Pakararip, バカラリプ, 草製ノ帽子. *n.* A hat made of grass.

Pakari, バカリ, 計レ、量ル、格ス. *v.t.* To measure. To weigh. To kill.

Pakari, バカリ, 煙ス. *v.t.* To smoke (as fish).

Pakari-kane, バカリカチ, 分銅. *n.* Weights.

Pakashnu, バカシヌ, 罰スレ、訓戒ス
ル. *v.t.* To admonish. To punish.
Syn: Kapao.

Pakashnu-i, バカシヌイ, 訓戒. *n.*
Admonition.

Pakashnu-wa-kashpaotte, バカシ
ヌワカシパオッテ, 嚴命スレ. *v.t.* To
adjure.

Paka-un-guru, バカウングル, 愚人.
n. A fool. A hybrid compound
Paka being a Japanese word.

Pak-buri, バクブリ, 罰ス可キ行爲、惡
行. *n.* Evil deeds. Deeds worthy
of punishment.

Pake, バケ, 頭. *n.* The head. **Syn:
Pa. Sapa.**

Pakekai, バケカイ, 死人ト共ニ埋メル
食器. *n.* The bowls, cups and
trays buried with the dead.

Pake-koshne, バケコシ子, 譏ル.
v.t. To backbite. To talk of
others. **Syn: Kuchikanna.**

Pake-moire, バケモイレ, 訥辯ナレ.
adj. Slow of speech. Ineloquent.
Syn: Pawe-moire.

Pakenuma-ush, バケヌマウシ, 貝ノ
一種. *n.* A kind of shellfish.

Pake-omap, バケオマブ, 籠ノ一種.
n. A kind of basket used for
carrying bundles. **Syn: Chita-
rape.**

Pake-rui, ハケルイ, 多辯ナレ. *adj.*
Talkative.

Pakesara, バケサラ, 慢ズル、高慢ナ
レ. *v.i. and adj.* To be proud.
Syn: Shiokunnure.

Pakesara-wa, バケサラワ, 高慢ニ.
adv. Proudly.

Pakes-upas, バケスウパス, 忘レ雪.
n. The last snow of the season.

Paketa, バケタ, 首ニ、始ニ. *adv.* At
the head. In the beginning.

Paketaketa, バケタケタ, 多言スル.
v.i. To jabber.

Paketara, バケタラ, or **Pakesara,**
バケサラ, 慢ズル、高慢ナル. *adj.
and v.i.* To be proud. Proud.
Haughty.

Paketaraki, バケタラキ, 高慢ニ振舞
フ. *v.i.* To act proudly.

Pake-tunash, バケツナシ, 早口ノ.
adj. Quick in speaking. Quick
in answering.

Pake-usaot, バケウサオツ, 言ヒ間違
フ. *v.i.* To make a mistake in
talking. **Syn: Itak-oira.**

Paki, バキ, or **Pakihi,** バキヒ, 時.
Time.

Paki, バキ, エビ. *n.* A prawn.

Pakiri, バキリ, 庖丁. *n.* A knife.
Syn: Makiri.

Pakisaraha, バキサラハ, 口ノ邊. *n.*
The sides of the mouth.

Pakkai, バンカイ, 背負フ. *v.t.* To
carry on the back as a child.

Pakkaibe, バンカイベ, 背負フ、道具.
n. A sling used for carrying
children on the back.

Pakkaitara, バッカイタラ, 背負フ道
具ノ繩ノ部分. *n.* The cord parts
of the sling used for carrying
children on the back. **Syn:
Pakkai-tupa.**

Pakkai-tupa, バッカイツバ, 背負フ道
具ノ繩ノ部分. *n.* The same as
pakkai-tara.

Pakko, パッコ, 老婦. *n.* An old woman. **Syn: Huchi.**

Pakno, バクノ, 迄、此ノ如キ、充分ニ. *adv.* Until. As far as. Such as. Than which. Sufficient. Adequate. This word expresses the utmost limits.

Pakoat, バコアツ, 叱ラレレ. *v.i.* To be scolded. **Syn: Akosakayokara.**

Pako-enratki, バコエンラツキ, 叱ル、不親切ニ取扱フ. *v.t.* To scold. To treat unkindly. **Syn: Pakoshipashnu. Pashitaige. Wenkoenratki. Wenkoshipashnu.**

Pakokanu, バコハヌ, 窃ニ聞ク、立聞スレ. *v.t.* To listen secretly. To go eavesdropping.

Pa-koro-kamui, バコロカムイ, 鳥ノ名、又ハ疱瘡、虎烈剌病ノ神. *n.* The red-cap. Also the demon of such diseases as small-pox and cholera.

Pako-shipashnu, バコシバシヌ, 叱スル. *v.t.* To scold. *See Pakoenratki.*

Pakte, バクテ, 計ル、ハカル. *v.t.* To measure.

Pakuchiuchiu-chep, バクチウチウチブ, カハハギ. *n.* File fish. *Stephanolepis cirrhifer, T. & S.*

Pan, バン, 腰, 下, 例セバ, バンイッケウェ, 脊椎骨ノ下部. *adj.* Same as *pana*, Lower. As:—*Pan ikkewe,* "the lower part of the spine."

Pan, バン, 口、クチ. *n.* Same as *paro*, the mouth but only so used in certain conditions. As:—*Pan-rakte,* "to taste."

Pan, バン, 弱キ、無味ナル、新鮮ナル、例セバ、バンロッカ、新鮮ナル水. *adj.* Weak. Flavourless. Insipid. Fresh. As:—*Pan wakka,* "fresh water." *Pan-shippo,* "flavourless salt."

Pan, バン, パン. *n.* Bread.

Pana, バナ, 塵. *n.* Dust. **Syn: Mana.**

Pana, バナ, 下ニ、例セバ、ペッバナタ、河下ニ向ヒ. *adv.* Below. Nether. As:—*Pet pana ta,* "towards the mouth of the river."

Pana-e-tashum, バナエタシュム, 梅毒. *n.* Syphilis. **Syn: Okamui-tashum. Kamoi-tashum.**

Panake, バナケ, 後、下. *n.* The behind. Bottom. **Syn: Osoro.**

Panake-an, バナケアン, 下腹ノ. *adj.* Abdominal.

Panake-un-no, バナケウンノ, 下腹ノ. *adv.* Abdominally.

Panakte, バナクテ, 罰スル. *v.t.* To punish. **Syn: Aapapu.**

Panare, バナレ, 偽善. *n.* Hypocrisy.

Panare, バナレ, 偽善チ行フ. *v.i.* To be hypocritical.

Panata, バナタ, 處ノ下端. *adv.* The lower end of a place.

Pancho, バンチョ, 大工. *n.* A carpenter.

Pandane, バンダ子, ハン種、麹. *n.* Barm. Yeast. (*Jap*).

Pane-tupok, バ子ツボク, 西ノ簷. *n.* The eaves of the west end of the roof of a house.

Pange, バンゲ, 好マヌ. *v.t.* To dislike. To feel disinclined to. Not to like or want. To abominate. **Syn: Kowen.**

Pange-i, バンゲイ, 嫌恩. *n.* Abomination. **Syn: Aetunne-i.**

Pange-pet, パンゲペツ, 下流. *n.* The lower part of a river.

Pannikotoro, パンニコトロ, 上顎. *n.* The roof of the mouth. The palate.

Pannok, パンノク, 西ノ簷. *n.* The west end of the roof of a hut.

Panore, パノレ, 僞ル、欺ク、媚フ. *v.t.* To lie. To deceive. To flatter.

Panore-i, パノレイ, 媚ビ、賞讃. *n.* Flattery. Adulation.

Panore-guru, パノレグル, or **Panore-itak-guru,** パノレイタックグル, 阿諛者. *n.* A flatterer.

Panrakte, パンラクテ, 味フ. *v.t.* To taste.

Panrekte, パンレクテ, 嘯ク. *v.i.* To whistle. **Syn : Maushoro.**

Pantak, パンタク, or **Pantaku,** パンタク, パンノ一塊. *n.* A loaf of bread.

Pa-ore-mina, パオレミナ, 微笑ス. *v.i.* To smile.

Pa-pon, パポン, 若キ. *adj.* Young.

Pa-poro, パポロ, 老ヒタル. *adj.* Old. **Syn : Isa. Onne. Onne-koro.**

Paptisma, パプテスマ, 洗禮. *n.* Baptism. (This word was introduced by the compiler).

Paptisma kore, パプテスマコレ, 洗禮ヲ授ク. *v.t.* To baptize.

Paptisma-uk, パプテスマウク, 洗禮ヲ受ク. *v.t.* To receive baptism.

Papush, パプシ, or **Chapush,** チャプシ, 唇、例セバ、カンナパプシ、上唇. *n.* The lips. As :—*Kanna papush,* "the upper lip." *Pokna papush,* "the lower lip." *Papush*

turiri, "to pout the lips." See **Patoi. Patchake.**

Par, パール, 口、クチ、例セバ、ヘルパルアニ、ホン口先ニテ. *n.* The mouth. (Contracted from *para* or *paro*). As :—*Heru par'ani,* "with just the mouth," i.e. "insincerely."

Para or. **paroho,** パラ, 又ハ パロホ, 口、クチ. *n.* The mouth. *Para nunnun,* "to suck the lips as in rearing bear cubs." *Para rui guru,* "a loud speaker." *Para sange* "to speak." *Para seshke,* "to stop or cover the mouth." *Para shinuye,* "to tattoo the lips." *Para ukotukka,* "to shut the mouth." *Para yupke,* "to speak severely." **Syn : Charo.**

Para, パラ, 廣キ、例セバ、パラル、大道. *adj.* Broad. As :—*Para ru,* "a broad road. The highway."

Paraka, パラカ, 天井. *n.* A ceiling. The inside of the roof of a house.

Parakankan, パラカンカン, サナダムシ. *n.* Tape worm.

Parakara, パラカラ, 澁キ、苛キ、熱キ. *adj.* Acrid. Pungent. Hot.

Paraki, パラキ, 秋蟲、ダニ. *n.* A tick.

Parakina, パラキナ, ミヅバセウ. *n.* A kind of swamp arum. *Lysichiton kamtschatensis, Schott.*

Parakoat, パラコアツ, 神罰ヲ受クレ. *v.i.* To be punished by God.

Parakoatte, パラコアツテ, 呪フ、罰スレ. *v.t.* To accurse. To curse. To punish.

Parakomonak, パラコモナク, 食慾ノ

爲眠ヲレヌ. *v.i.* To be unable to sleep through intense desire for food. **Syn : Paroko-shomo-mo-koro.**

Parakosamba, バラコサムバ, 嗅 ク. *v.t.* To smell. **Syn : Hura nu.**

Parakoyakoya, バラコヤコヤ, 曖昧ニ言フ、ソドクドイフ. *v.i.* To speak indistinctly. To babble. (*sing*). For the plural see *Uhautaroise.*

Paramuriri, バラムリリ, 死軆ヲ棺ニ結フ. *n.* String used in lacing a corpse to its bier.

Paraparak, バラパラク, 絶叫スレ. *v.i.* To cry loudly. **Syn : Rai-paraparak. Rayaiyaise.**

Paraparase, バラバラセ, 風前ニ飛ブ、燃ユル. *v.i.* To fly before the wind. To burn. To be ablaze. To spread out as flame of fire. **Syn : A. Rui. Uhui.** As :— *Abe paraparase,* "the fire burns."

Paraparasere, バラバラセレ, 燃ヤス. *v.t.* To make burn.

Paraparase-wa, バラバラセワ, 燃ユル所ノ. *adj.* Ablaze.

Parapok, バラポク, ト見エル、例セバ、メナシハラポクアン、東風吹クト見ユル. *v.i.* To appear. To seem. This word is spoken chiefly of the weather. As :— *Menash parapok an,* "it seems as though there will be an east wind."

Parapok, バラポク, 陰、後、場所. *v.i.* and *n.* To appear. Shadow. Shade. Behind. Lieu.

Parasatchep, バラサッチエブ, 多言者、ナシヘリ. *n.* A chatterbox.

Parase, バラセ, 風前ニ飛ブ、漂フ. *v.i.* To fly before the wind. To drift.

Parase, バラセ, Pararase, バララセ, 燃ユル、例セバ、アベパララセ、火ガ爆子ル. *v.i.* To burn. To burn up in thousands of sparks as spray wood or thorns. As :— *Abe pararase,* "the fire sends off sparks." See *uhuye.*

Parasekoro, バラセコロ, 喜ノ叫. *excl.* Hurrah.

Paratakup, バラタクブ, 多言者、ナシヤヘリ. *n.* A chatterbox.

Paratek, バラテク, or **Parateke, バラテケ,** 手. *n.* The hands.

Paratek-yuk, バラテクユク, or **Eparatek-sei-yuk, エバラテクセイユク,** 叉角ノ失セタル鹿、此ヲ殺ス者ハ其後久シカラズシテ死ストノ迷信アリ. *n.* A deer with deformed antlers. There is a superstition to the effect that whoever kills one of these animals is certain to die soon after.

Parato, バラト, 幅廣キ河口 (沼ノ如キ). *n.* An estuary.

Paraure, バラウレ, 足ノ面、アシノカウ. *n.* The instep.

Paraure-ekomomse, ハラウレエコモムセ, 畸形脚. *n.* Club-footed.

Paretoko, バレトコ, 道ヲ備フル、準備スル、計畫スル、例セバ、チイケルアライケクニバレトコヤイカラシリアン、其人ヲ殺ス計畫アリ. *v.i.* To prepare the way for. To get ready to do. To plot. To scheme. As : *Nei guru araige kuni paretoko yaikara shirian,* "there is a plot on foot to kill that person."

Parara, バララ, 感動、神来. *n.* Influence. Inspiration.

Pariri, バリリ, 神来ス ル. *v.i.* To be inspired. *n.* Air.

Paro, バロ, 口. *n.* Same as *Para.* **Syn: Charo.**

Paro-a-o-shuke, バロアオシュケ, 御馳走ス ル. *v.i.* To be entertained with food.

Paroka, バロカ, 上顎. *n.* The roof of the mouth.

Paroko-shomo-mokoro, バロコショモモコロ, 食欲ノ為ニ寐ラレヌ. *v.i.* To be unable to sleep through intense desire for food. **Syn: Parakomonak.**

Paronitemaka, バロニテマカ, 枝ヲ含マス、木片ヲ以テ口ヲ開ク. *v.t.* To gag. To open the mouth with a piece of wood.

Paronnata, バロンナタ, 自ラ語リ、又ハ自ラ聞ク、例セバ、バロンナタヌ、自ラ聞ク. *v.i.* To speak or hear for one's self. As:—*Paronnata nu,* "to hear for one's self. *Paronnata itak,* "to speak for one's self.

Parononot, バロノノツ, 口水ノ出ヅル、食欲ノ為涎ヲ流ス. *v.i.* To water at the mouth as in anticipation of something nice to eat or drink.

Paro-oiki, バロオイキ, 他人ノ為ニ食物ヲ備フ. *v.t.* To provide food for another.

Paro-o-shuke, バロオシュケ, 馳走ス ル. *v.t.* To entertain a guest with food.

Paropetetne, バロペテツチ, 吃者、ドモリ、吃ル、ドモル. *n.* and *v.i.* Impeded utterance. Ischnophony (used especially of those who can-

not speak for cold). **Syn: Awepetetne.**

Paroshopshopo, バロショブショボ, 含嗽ス ル. *v.i.* To gargle.

Paroshuke, バロシュケ, 煮ル、料理ス ル. *v.i.* To stew. To cook food. To cook for.

Paro-un, バロウン, 能辯ナレ. *adj.* Eloquent.

Paru, バル, 飛散ス ル. *v.i.* To fly about as dust or chaff.

Paru, バル, 拂フ、又ハ打ツ(蠅ナドチ). *v.t.* To brush or knock off as a fly from the forehead or nose.

Parumbe, バルムベ, 舌. *n.* The tongue. (lit. *Paro-un-be,* "the thing in the mouth).

Paruparu, バルバル, 扇. *n.* A fan.

Paruparu, バルバル, 扇ク. *v.t.* To fan.

Paruparuge, バルバルゲ, 端. *n.* Edges.

Parure, バルレ, 飛散セシムル、風ヲ扇イデ起ス. *v.t.* To make fly about as dust. To cause wind as in waving anything.

Paruruge, バルルゲ, 端. *n.* Edges. **Syn: Eipake. Kanetuhu.**

Pas, バス, 黒キ. *adj.* Black.

Pas, バス, **Paspas,** バスバス, 石炭、木炭、火絨(ホクチ). *n.* *coal.* Charcoal. Cinders. Tinder.

Pasa, バサ, 開口ス ル. *v.t.* To open the mouth. **Syn: Hasa.**

Pasamok, バサモク, 鳥ニ寃セラレ. *v.i.* To be bewitched by birds.

Pasani, バサン, イカ. *n.* Cuttlefish. Calamary.

Pasa-pasa, バサバサ, 屢〻開口スル.
v.i. To open the mouth frequently.

Pasare, バサレ, 開口ス,レ. *v.t.* To
open the mouth.

Pase, バセ, 重キ、眞ナル、重要ナル、
例セバ、バセオルシベ、重要ナル報道.
adj. Heavy. True. Important.
As:— *Pase orushpe,* "important
tidings."

Pase-kamui, バセカムイ, 眞神. *n.*
The true God.

Pase-ni, バセニ, サハシデ. *n.* Car-
pinus cordata, Bl.

Pase-no-kara, バセノカラ, 重カラシ
ムレ. *v.t.* To make heavy.

Pase-no-po, バセノポ, 甚ダ多ク、熱心
ニ、大事ナレ、例セバ、バセノポクヤイ
ライゲナ、多謝ス. *adv.* Very much.
Earnestly. As:— *Pase no po ku
yaiiraige na,* "I thank you very
much. **Syn: Pasetara.**

Pasetara, バセタラ, 甚ダ多ク、熱心ニ、
大事ナル. *adv.* Same as pase no
po.

Pash, バシ, 入墨、イレズミ. *n.* Tattoo.

Pash, バシ, 駈スル(馬ノ如ク). *v.i.* To
gallop as a horse. To run.

Pa-shinap, バシナブ, 頭巾(女ノ). *n.*
A head dress (woman's).

Pashirota, バシロタ, 叱スル. *v.t.* To
storm at. To scold.

Pashitaigi, バシタイギ, 叱スル、言ニ
テ不親切ニ取扱フ. *v. t.* To scold.
To treat unkindly by word of
mouth.

Pashta, バシタ, 俗ノ、通常ノ、惡シキ、
荒キ. *adj.* Vulgar. Common. Bad.

Worthless. Useless. Careless.
Rough. Ugly.

Pashta-no, バシタノ, 不注意ニ、荒ク、
惡ク. *adv.* Carelessly. Roughly.
Badly.

Pashte, バシテ, 駈シラスレ. *v.t.* To
make gallop. To send along fast
as in throwing a hoop. To make
run.

Pashui, バシュイ, 箸、例セバ、イクバシュ
イ、鬚テ上ゲル棒. *n.* Sticks used at
meals instead of knives and forks.
As:— *Iku bashui,* "a moustache
lifter." *Pera bashui,* "a spoon."
Uren bashui, "chopsticks." *Abe
bashui,* "fire tongs."

Paskuma, バスクマ, 敎ユル、例セバ、
エチエポバスクマ エ チ ミッポ バスク
マ、汝ノ子モ孫モ敎ヘ日. *v.t.* To instruct. To teach. As:— *Echi
po paskuma echi mitpo paskuma,*
"instruct both your children and
grandchildren.

Paskuru, バスクル, 鴉. *n.* A crow
or rook.

Paskuru-kamui, バスクルカムイ, カ
ラスヘビ. *n. Tropinodotus mar-
tensi, Hilgd.*

Paskuru-okokko, バスクルオコッコ,
カラスヘビ. *n.* Same as above.

Paskuru-topo, バスクルトポ, ハマグ
リ. *n. Meretrix meretrix, Linn.*

Paskuttara, バスクッタラ, ナンバン
ハコベ. *n. Cucubalus baccifer,
L. var. japonicus, Miq.*

Paskuru-toho-sei, バスクルトホセイ,
or **Paskutto-sei, バスクッセイ,**
ハマグリ. *n.* A kind of shell-fish.
Meretrix meretrix, Linn.

Pasna, パスナ, 燒屑､灰燼. *n.* Cinders.

Pas-op, パスオブ, 火絨箱(ホグチバコ). *n.* A tinderbox.

Paspas, パスパス, 木炭､黒キ火絨. *n.* Charcoal. Black cinders.

Passanna, パッサンナ, イカ. *n.* The ink-fish. Calamary.

Pasushke, パスシケ, 混亂シテ逃グレ. *v.i.* To flee in disorder.

Pata, パタ, 蟋蟀､キリギリス､蝗､イナ ゴ. *n.* A grasshopper or locust. **Syn : Takataka.**

Patachinne, パタチン子, 早口ニ語ル. *v.i.* To talk very rapidly. To gabble. To babble.

Pataoata, パタオアタ, 蟋蟀､キリギリ ス､蝗､イナゴ. *n.* Same as *pata*.

Patapatakse, パタパタクセ, 跳ル､(火 ノ花ノ如ク). *v. i.* To snap off or jump about (as fire or splinters) with a crackle.

Patapata, パタパタ, or **Patupatn, パ ツパツ,** 簸ル､ヒル. *v.t.* To winnow.

Pataraye, パタライェ, 推量スル. *v.t.* To surmise. To guess.

Patchake, パッチャケ, 唇. *n.* The lips. **Syn : Papush.**

Patche, パッチェ, 飛散スレ(雪ノ如ク). *v.i.* To fly about as snow or dust or spray. To explode as a volcano or bottle.

Patchi, パッチ, or **Pachi, パチ,** 鉢. *n.* A wooden basin.

Patchinu, パッチヌ, 釘拔. *n.* Pinchers. Tongs.

Patchingara, パッチンガラ, or **Pachingara, パチンガラ,** ガヤガヤ. *n.*

A kind of rockfish. *Sebastodes taczanowskii,* (*Steind*).

Patek, パテク, 只. *adj.* Only.

Patemtemu-ki, パテムテムキ, 訊子 ル､聞キタガリ､見タガル、穿鑿スレ. *v.t.* To make inquiries. To act in an inquisitive manner. **Syn: Uwepekennu. Pa-hene-nu.**

Patemtemu-ki-guru, パテムテムキ グル, 穿鑿好ノ人、センサクズキノヒ ト. *n.* An inquisitive person.

Patoi, パトイ, 唇ノ表面. *n.* The surface of the lips. The lips. **Syn: Papush.**

Patpatke, パツパツケ, 跳ヌル(火ノ如 ク)、涌ク. *v.i.* To crack off and fly about. To bubble up as boiling water. To jump about (as fire in many splinters from a log). Thus :—*Abe patpatku,* "the fire-jump. **Syn: Pop.**

Pattakupi, パッタクピ, 嘵舌家､オシヤ ベリ. *n.* A chatterbox.

Pattukuku, ヌッツクク, スチル. *v.i.* To be sulky. To pout the lips.

Patukuku, パツクク, スチレ. *v. i.* The same as *pattukuku.*

Patu, パツ, 飛散スル.*v.i.* To scatter. To fly about. To jump about as fat in fire.

Patupatu, パツパツ, 鰭(ハ子)ル. *v. i.* To flounder as fish. To scatter.

Pauchi, パウチ, 食物ニ毒チ入レル事､ 例セバ、パウチオシユケ、毒食チ料理ス ル. *n.* To put poison in one's food. As :—*Pauchi o-shuke,* "to prepare a poisoned meal." *Pauchi e yara,* "to give one poisoned food to eat."

Pauchi-kina, バウチキナ, オホバセ
ンキウ. *n. Angelica refracta, Fr.
Schm.*

Pauchikoro-guru, バウチコログル,
極惡人、殊ニ毒害ヲ企ツル如キ人.
n. A very evil minded person
specially a woman who spites
another by administering poisoned
food. **Syn : Kameyarape,** or
Kameyarope.

Paumbe, バウムベ, 鉢卷. *n.* A head
band.

Paunguru, バウングル, 賢人、酋長. *n.*
A wise person. A chief.

Pau-pau, バウバウ, 狐ノ鳴聲ヲ示ス語.
n. An onomatopoeia for the bark
of foxes.

Pawe, バウェ, 話. *n.* Speech.

Pawe-moire, バウェモイレ, 語ルニ遲
キ. *adj.* Slow of speech. **Syn :**
Pake-moire.

Pawe-otke, バウェオツケ, 速ニ、例セ
バ、アバノシキバウェオツケ、急ギ家ニ
入ル. *adv.* Quickly. Hurriedly.
As :—*Apa noshki pawe otke*, " to
enter a hut in a hurry." **Syn :**
Tunashino.

Pawetenge, バウェテンゲ, 命令スル.
v.t. To give commandment.

Pawetenge-i, バウェテンゲイ, 命令.
n. A commandment.

Paweteshu, バウェテシュ, 證スル. *v.i.*
To bear witness.

Paweteshu-guru, バウェテシュグル, 證
據人. *n.* A witness.

Paweteshu-i, バウェデシュイ, 證據. *n.*
Witness. Testimony.

Pawetok-an, バウェトクアン, 賢キ、
學問アル、能辯ナル. *adj.* Wise.
Learned. Eloquent.

Pawetok-koro, バウェトクコロ, 賢キ、
學問アル、總明ナル、能辯ナル. *adj.*
Wise. Learned. Astute. Eloquent.

**Pawetok-koro-guru, バウェトクコロ
グル,** 賢人. *n.* A wise person.

Payaya, バヤヤ, 握ム、ツカム、(獸其爪
ヲ以テ). *v.t.* To hold up as an
animal its claws. **Syn : Ambayaya.**

Paye, バイェ, 行ク. *v.i.* To go. To
advance. To proceed. *Pl.* of *o-
man* or *arupa.*

Paye-ash, バイェアシ, 我等行ク. *ph.*
We go.

Payekai, バイカイ, 旅行スル. *v.i.* To
travel.

Payekai-guru, バイェカイグル, 旅人.
n. A traveller.

Payere, バイェレ, 送ル. *v.t.* To send.

Paye-takup, バイェタクブ, 行キタレ
ド目的ヲ達セズ. *v.i.* To go somewhere but see no one. To go
somewhere with a special object
in view, but to be unable to accomplish the object.

Pe, ペ, 物. *n.* An article. A thing.
Syn : Ambe.

Pe, ペ, or **Pehe, ペヒ,** 濁水、霧、例セ
バ、ハッペ、葡萄汁. *n.* Water,
principally undrinkable water.
Thick water. Mist. Fine rain.
Melting snow. Sap. Juice. As :
—*Hat pe*, " grape juice.

Pecha, ペチャ, 河. *n.* A river.
Syn : Petcha.

Pechan, ペチャン, 瘠セタル. *adj.*
Thin. Slight. **Syn : Narai.**

Pechara, ペチャラ, 巾アル水(卽チ、海

岸ニ沿フ河ノ如ク). n. The broad, spread out water such as the broadened mouths of some rivers along the sea coast.

Pechi, ペチ, 河. n. A river. **Syn: Pet.**

Pechicha, ペチチャ, 水溜. n. Puddles of water.

Pechinne, ペチンネ, 濕リタル. adj. Wet through.

Pechiri, ペチリ, 濠、濕地. n. A ditch. A water conductor. A damp place.

Pei, ペイ, 泡沫、アブク. n. A bubble. A water-bladder

Peikosanu, ペイコサヌ, 音スル、(柔キ物ヲ切リ、又ハ貫キタルガ如キ). v.i. To sound as if something soft was being cut or pierced.

Pechish, ペチシ, 水ノ. adj. Aqueous. Containing water.

Peka, ペカ, ニ依テ、例セバ、ヤペカ、陸ニヨリ. adv. By. As:—*Ya peka*, "by land."

Peka, ペカ, 向ツテ. adv. Facing. Towards.

Peka, ペカ, 捕ル. v.t. To catch (as a ball).

Peka, ペカ, 側、部分、場所、例セバ、テペカ、此處ニ. adv. Side. Part. Place. As:—*Te peka*, "here." *To ani peka*, "there."

Pekakarabe, ペカカラベ, アメンボウ n. A water fly. *Hydrometra sp.*

Pekama, ペカマ, 浮ブ、漂フ. v.i. To float.

Pakambe, ペカムベ, ヒシ. n. Water caltrops. *Trapa bispinosa, Roxb.*

Pekambe-kuttara, ペカムベクッタラ,

ハンゴンサウ. n. *Senecio palmatus, Pall.* Also called *Oromun.*

Pekange, ペカンゲ, 漂フ、浮ブ. v.i. To float. **Syn: Pekama.**

Pekangere, ペカンゲ, 浮バスル. v.t. To make float.

Pekaonit, ペカオニツ, 布ヲ織ルニ絲ヲ分ケル機械. n. Same as *Pekaotni.*

Pekaotbe, ペカオツベ, 布ヲ織ルニ絲ヲ分ケル機械. n. Same as *Pekaotni.*

Pekaotni, ペカオツニ, 同上. n. An instrument used for separating threads in making cloth. **Syn: Pokaonit. Tambu.**

Pekashnu, ペカシヌ, 純粋ノ、例セバ、ペカシヌワッカ、清水. adj. Pure. Unmixed. As:—*Pekashnu wakka*, "pure water." **Syn: Posokayatki.**

Peken-nishat, ペケンニシヤツ, 黎明. n. Daybreak.

Pekennupe, ペケンヌペ, 涙. n. Tears. **Syn: Nupe.**

Peken-rera, ペケンレラ, 追手、順風. n. A good or favourable wind. **Syn: Pirika rera.**

Pekep, ペケプ, 柄杓. n. A water ladle.

Pekep-chikap, ペケプチカプ, ハクテフ. n. Hooper swan. *Oygnus musicus, Bechst.* **Syn: Pekere chikap.**

Pekepkere-chikap, ペケプケレチカプ, ウヅラ. n. A quail. *Coturnix communis, Bonn.*

Pekere, ペケレ, 光. n. Light.

Pekere-ash, ペケレアシ, or **Pekere-ashnu, ペケレアシヌ,** 光ル. v.i. To be light.

Pekere-ashnu-i, ペケレアシヌイ, 聖地、美ナル處. n. A beautiful place.

Pekere-buri, ペケレブリ, 善行. n. Good deeds. Righteous acts.

Pekere-chikap, ペケレチカプ, or Pe-kep-chikap, ペケプチカプ, 鵠. n. A swan. **Syn : Retat chiri.**

Pekere-chup, ペケレチュプ, 太陽. n. The sun.

Pekere-keutum, ペケレケウツム, 淸キ心. n. A pure heart.

Pekere-nishat, ペケレニシャツ, 黎明. n. Daybreak. **Syn: Peken ni-shat.**

Pekere-kamui, ペケレカムイ, 善神. n. The good gods. **Syn : Piri-ka kamui. Arapekere kamui.**

Pekere-mata, ペケレマタ, 初冬・ n. The early part of the winter.

Pekere-sam, ペケレサム, 晝. adv. In day light. In the day-time. In the light.

Pekettosa, ペケットサ, 獸ノ腹ノ毛無キ處. n. The bare place in the skins of animals under the belly.

Pekiri, ペキリ, 泡、汁. n. Froth or scum. Soup. Broth.

Peko, ペコ, or Beko, ベコ, 牛. n. A bull or cow. Ox.

Pekse, ペクセ, 牛. v.i. To low as oxen.

Pen, ペン, 源、上、谷ノ上方. adj. Source. The upper part of a valley.

Pena, ペナ, 上ニ. adv. Upper. Above. **Syn : Penge.**

Penake, ペナケ, 咽喉. n. The throat. **Syn : Rekuchi.**

Penake, ペナケ, 上. adj. Upper.

Penaketa, ペナケタ, 上ニ. adv. Upper. Up above. The upper place.

Penata, ペナタ, 場所ノ上. n. geo. The upper part of a place.

Pende, ペンヂ, 尖端、例セバ、ウレペンテ、趾尖. n. The points of certain things. As :— *Ure-pende,* "the points of the toes."

Pene, ペネ, 消化スレ. v.t. To digest.

Pene, ペネ, 小雨. n. Fine rain. **Syn : Apto.**

Pene, ペネ, 水ノ、溶ケタル、消化スル. adj. & v.i. Aqueous. Watery. To melt as snow. To become thawed. To digest. Fluid.

Peneka, ペネカ, 濕リタル. adj. Wet. Aqueous.

Penere, ペネレ, 激熱スル、ゲキチッスレ. v.t. To heat to the degree of redness or whiteness as in heating metal.

Penetupok, ペネツポク, 屋根ノ東ノ方. n. The upper or east end of the roof of a house.

Penge, ペンゲ, 上ニ、例セバ、ペンゲペッ、上流. adv. Upper. As :— *Penge-pet,* "the upper part of a river."

Pengirechiu-pangirechiu, ペンギレチウパンギレチウ, 統卒スル. v.t. To govern. To rule over. **Syn : Epungine. Esapane.**

Pengisep, ペンギセプ, 弧角線. n. The groin

Peni, ペニ, 内地、例セバ、ペニウンパイエアン、内地ヲ旅スル. adv. Inland. The interior of a country. As :

—*Peni un paye an,* " to travel inland."

Peni-un-guru, ペニウングル, 山人、田舎人. *n.* Mountaineers. Countryman.

Pennok, ペンノク, 屋根ノ東部. *n.* The upper or east end of the roof of a hut.

Penoye, ペノイェ, 絞ル. *v.t.* To wring out as wet clothes.

Penram, ペンラム, 胸. *n.* The chest.

Pensai, ペンサイ, 帆船. *n.* A junk or sailing ship.

Penup, ペヌプ, イケマ. *n.* A kind of plant whose root is used both as food and for medicine. It is also put in pillows as a charm against disease. *Cynanchum caudatum, Maxim.* **Syn: Ikema.**

Peoshish, ペオシシ, 河床. *n.* The bed of a river.

Peot, ペオツ, 濕リタル. *adj.* Wet. Damp. Containing water.

Peot-humi, ペオツフミ, 音、(パサト云フ音). *n.* A heavy thud. A cracked sound.

Peot-kando, ペオツカンド, 霧. *n.* Fogs. Misty clouds. **Syn: Urarakando.**

Pep, ペプ, or **Pepe,** ペペ, 濕リタル. *adj.* Damp watery. Boggy.

Pepero, ペペロ, ユキザサ. *n.* A liliaceous plant. *Smilacina japonica, A. Gray.*

Pepesh, ペペシ, 毛ノ如ク眞直ニ. *adj.* Straight as hair.

Pepuni, ペプニ, 水ニ擧ゲラル. *v.i.* To be lifted up by water.

Pera, ペラ, 梭. *n.* A shuttle.

Pera, ペラ, or **Bera,** ベラ, **Perabashui,** ペラバシュイ, 匙. *n.* A spoon.

Perai, ペライ, 釣スル. *v.t.* To fish with rod and line.

Perai-ap, ペライアプ, 釣針. *n.* A fish hook.

Perai-kara, ペライカラ, 釣スル. *v.i.* To fish with rod and line.

Perai-nit, ペライニツ, 釣竿. *n.* A fishing rod. **Syn: Tushni ; apkotni.**

Perai-shok, ペライショク, アンコゥ. *n.* Fishing frog. *Lophiomus litulon. Jor. & Sny.*

Pere, ペレ, 壞ル、開ク. *v.t.* To break. To open.

Pereba, ペレバ, or **Peruba,** ペルバ, 割ル、壞ル. *v.t.* To cleave. To split. To break. To smash.

Pereke, ペレケ, 壞ル、、割ル. *v.i.* To be broken. To be split. **Syn: Yaske. Kone.**

Perepere, ペレペレ, 斤々ニ壞ル. *v.t.* To break into fine pieces.

Peritomi-buri, ペリトミブリ, 割禮. *n.* Circumcision. (Introduced by the compiler).

Peritomi-buri-ki, ペリトミブリキ, 割禮ヲ施ス. *v.t.* To circumcise.

Pero-ni, ペロニ, ナホナラ. *n.* A kind of oak. *Ruercus crispula Bl.*

Pero-ni-karush, ペロニカルシ, シヒタケ. *n.* *Cortinellus Shiitake, P. Henn.*

Peruba, ペルバ, 割ル、開ク. *v.t.* Same as *Pereba,* " to cleave."

Pesakara, ペサカラ, 轉ル(泥中又ハ其

他ノモノ中ニ). *v.i.* To wallow.
Syn: Yaikirukiru.

Pe-san, ペサン, 洪水. *n.* A flood.

Pesh, ペシ, 平ナル山側、崖. *n.* A long mountain or hill with flattish sides. A cliff.

Pesh, ペシ, 懸ル、下ル、底ニ向ツテ、源ニ向ツテ、例セバ、ニベシラン、樹チ下ル. *adv.* and *v.i.* To hang down. To descend. Towards the bottom. Towards the source of a stream or river. As :—*Ni pesh ran,* "to descend a tree." *Pet pesh san,* "to go down a river." *Ehuru pesh,* "to descend a hill."

Peshikambe, ペシカムベ, 浮ベル. *adj.* Floating.

Peshpok, ペシポク, 峡. *n.* A ravine. Gorge. Defile.

Pe-sosh, ペソシ, 雲雨. *n.* Sleet. Rain with snow. As :—*Pe sosh ash,* "to rain sleet."

Pet, ベツ, 片, カケ. *n.* A piece of anything.

Pet, ベツ, 厚キ、濕リタル. *adj.* Thick. Damp.

Pet, ベツ, 水. *n.* Water.

Pet, ベツ, 河, 例セバ、ベットカリ、河ニ沿ヒテ. *n.* A river. As :—*Pet kari,* "along a river." *Pet kashui,* "to wade a river." *Pet au or awe,* "the branch of a river." *Petchiriwei,* "a great bend in a river. *Pet chiu,* "the current in a river. *Pet chiu uwenoye,* "an eddy." *Pet esoro,* "the mouth of a river." *Pet etok,* "a river's source." *Pet iworo,* "all the rivers. *Pet kenash,* "a bend in a river covered with

trees." *Pet nutap,* "the land in the bend of a river without trees. *Pet pana,* "towards the mouth of a river." *Pet pena,* "towards the source of a river." *Pet pesh,* "towards the mouth of a river." *Pet putu,* "the mouth of a river," "a junction of a river." *Pet ramtom,* "that part of a river between its source and mouth." *Pet sam,* "the sides of a river." *Pet toshka,* "a river's bank. *Pet turashi,* "to go towards the source of a river. **Syn: Petchi. Petcha.**

Pet-au, ベッアウ, or **Pet-anu,** ベッアヌ, 支流. *n.* The branch of a river.

Petaru, ベタル, 水チ引キタル處. *n.* A place where water is drawn.

Petcha, ベッチャ, 大河. *n.* A great river ; by some the flat banks of a river.

Pet-chep-ne, ベッチェプネ, 鮮魚. *v.i.* Very fresh fish. Fish just caught.

Petchi, ベッチ, 濕リタレ. *adj.* Wet. Damp.

Petchi, ベッチ, 河. *n.* A river.

Petchine, ベッチ子, 濕ル、ビショビショニシメレ. *v.i.* To be wet through.

Petchish, ベッチシ, 水路. *n.* A water-way.

Petchish, ベッチシ, 貝ノ一種. *n.* The name of a shell fish. By some an oyster ; by others small muscles (*Mytilus sp.*)

Petchish-noka, ベッチシノカ, 銀河. *n.* The milky way.

Pet-inika, ベッイニカ, 濕ス. *v.t.* To moisten.

Pet-kashu, ペッカシュ, 渡河スル. *v.i.* To cross a river.

Petkotchimakani, ペツコッチマカニ, カワカヅカ. *n.* Goby. **Syn: E-shokkui.**

Pet-kutu, ベツクツ, ヨブスマサウ. *n. Senecio sagittatus, Schultz Bip.* Also called *Wakka kuttara.*

Petne, ベツ子, 濕リタレ. *adj.* To be wet. Damp.

Petneka, ベツ子カ, 濕リタル. *adj.* Sloshy. Watery. To be made Damp. Also:—*v.t.* To make wet.

Pet-noka, ベツノカ, 銀河. *n.* The milky way.

Petpaush, ベツパウシ, エゾスゲ. *n. Carex cryptocarpa, C. A. Mey.*

Petpaush, ベツパウシ, 莖ニテ製シタル蓆ノ一種. *n.* A kind of mat made of reeds growing in rivers.

Petpaush-shut, ベツペウシシュツ, 捲カレタルベツパウシュ. *n.* A *pet-paush* rolled up.

Petpetke, ベツペツケ, ギザギザナル、(木ノ葉ノ緣ノ如ク). *v.i.* To be indented (as a leaf).

Petpo, ベツポ, 小河. *n.* A little river.

Pet-susu, ベツスス, キヌヤナギ. *n.* A kind of willow. *Salix viminalias, L.* **Syn: Yaiyaisusu.**

Pet-tat, ベッタツ, シラカンメ. *n. Betula alba, L. var. vulgaris, DC.*

Pet-uturuibe, ベツツルイベ, or **Pet-uturu,** ベツツル, 河中島. *n.* Any land lying between two rivers.

Pet-yau, ベツヤウ, 支流. *n.* A river's tributary.

Peure, ベウレ, 若キ. *adj.* Young. **Syn: Upen.**

Peure-humsei, ベウレフムセイ, カ、又ハ力聲. *n.* The strength or gruff of a young man. The noise a young man makes when pulling with all his might.

Peure-kina, ベウレキナ, ムラサキ. *n. Lithospermum Erythrorhizon, S. et Z.*

Peurep, ベウレブ, 若キ物. *n.* A young thing. The young of animals. **Syn: Upen. Pa pon.**

Pe-ushte, ベウシテ, 濕ラス. *v.t.* To make wet. To mix water with.

Peutange, ベウタンゲ, or **Peutange-hawe,** ベウタンゲハウェ, 救ヲ呼ブ、救ヲ呼ブ聲. *n. and v.i.* A call for help. A call in case of fire or danger. **Syn: Haukotpare. Kimak-hau.**

Peutange-hawe-ash, ベウタンゲハウェアシ, 救ヲ呼ブ. *v.i.* To call for help.

Peutange-ki, ベウタンゲキ, 救ヲ呼ブ. *v.i.* To call for help.

Pewa, ベワ, 兇兆ト認メラレ、特種ノ殘紅. *n.* A peculiar red reflection of the setting sun upon the clouds supposed to be the harbinger of trouble.

Pewan, ベワン, 浮雲 (アブナ)キ、(壞レ物ニノミ用ユ). *n. and v.i.* Dangerous. To be in danger. This word is used only of things likely to get spoiled or broken.

Pewan, ペワン, 柔キ、弱キ. *adj.* Soft. Weak.

Pewanka, ペワンカ, 柔カニスル、弱 クスレ. *v.t.* To make soft. To make weak.

Pewapiwak, ペワピワク, 脆キ. *adj.* Crisp. Brittle (as glass).

Pi, ピ, 種. *n.* Seed. Kernel. Pip. **Syn : Piye.**

Pi, ピ, 抜刀スル、例セバ、タムピハムカ ンナイコサムバ、抜刀ノ音. *v.t.* To draw or unsheath as a sword. Thus :—*Tam pi humkan naikosamba,* "the sound of unsheathing swords."

Pi, ピ, 解ク、トク. *v.t.* To undo or untwist.

Pi, ピ, 少キ、細微ナル、例セバ、ピイタク. 唄、サ、ヤキ. *adj.* Small. Fine. As: —*Pi itak,* "a whisper." *Pi ota,* "fine sand."

Piba, ピバ, or **Pipa, ピバ,** カハガイ. カラスガイ. *n.* A kind of shell fish found in rivers and lakes.

Pichiribe, ピチリベ, 蛆. *n.* A maggot.

Pichish, ピチシ, 忍ビ泣キスル. *v.i.* To weep softly.

Pichitche, ピチッチェ, 剥ゲル、ムケル. *v.i.* To be worn out. To come off. **Syn : Pitche.**

Pikan-no, ピカンノ, 速ニ. *adv.* Quickly.

Pikai-shipini, ピカイシビニ, 旅仕度 スル、例セバ、ピカイシビニアヤイコ カラカラ、我ハ旅裝セリ. *v.i.* To prepare for a journey. To dress for a journey. As:—*Pikai-shipini ayaikokarakara,* "I dressed myself for a journey."

Pikan, ピカン, 速ナル、活溌ナレ、敏捷 ナル、例セバ、ピカンウムマ、駿馬. *adj.* Quick. Active. Agile. Swift of foot. Fast. As :—*Pikan umma,* "a fast horse." **Syn : Nitan.**

Pikata, ピカタ, 西南風. *n.* A southwest wind.

Pikahi, ピカヒ, 搾デル、(指チ以テ濕レ タル外套ノ水分チ去ラン爲). *v.t.* To stroke out (as water from a wet cloth by means of the thumb and fingers).

Pinai, ピナイ, or **Pinnai, ピンナイ,** 壕、谷. *n.* A ditch. A trench. A valley.

Pindoro, ピンドロ, 硝子. *n.* Glass. Through the Japanese word *biidoro* from the Portuguese vidrio.

Pine, ピ子, 砂ノ如ク疎キ、例セバ、ピ 子ナタ、粗砂. *adj.* Coarse as sand. As :—*Pine ota,* "coarse sand."

Pinka, ピンカ, or **Pinkai, ピンカイ,** キハダ、木ノ皮ノ詰物. *n.* A kind of tow made of bark and used in caulking boats.

Pinkishut, ピンキシュツ, or **Pinkushutu, ピンクシュツ,** 股ノ上部. *n.* The upper part of the thighs.

Pinnai, ピンナイ, or **Pinai, ピナイ,** 谷、壕. *n.* A valley. A ditch. A trench.

Pinne, ピン子, 雄. *adj.* Male. This word is often placed before nouns when it is necessary to give them a distinctive masculine gender, but is used principally of animals.

Pinne-rau, ピン子ラウ, 牡鹿. *n.* A buck. Male deer.

Pinne-shibe, ピンチシベ, 善瓦ナル、美ナル. *adj.* Good. Fine. Beautiful.

Pinne-top, ピンチトプ, チマガリダケ *n. Sasa paniculata, mak. et Shib.* **Syn : Okne-top.**

Pinnerau, ピンチラウ, 二歳ノ牡鹿. *n.* A two year old buck. A buck with straight horns, i.e. with horns without branches.

Pin-ni, ピンニ, ヤチダモ. *n.* The ash tree. *Fraxinus mandshurica, Rupr. var. japonica, Maxim.*

Pinne-noya, ピンチノヤ, チトコヨモギ. *n. Artemssia japonica, Th.*

Pinu, ピヌ, 嘱聲、サヽヤキ. *n.* A whisper. **Syn : Chapish-chapish.**

Pinu-no, ピヌノ, 嘱聲ニテ、忍ビ音ニ. *adv.* In a whisper. Quite privately or stealthily.

Pinu-no-heheba, ピヌノヘヘバ, 竊ニ覗フ. *v.t.* To peep stealthily at.

Pinu-no-ye, ピヌノイェ, 嘱ク、ササヤク. *v.t.* To whisper.

Pinu-pukara, ピヌプカラ, 覗ク. *v.t.* To peep at.

Pinu-pinu, ピヌピヌ, 甚ダ柔和ナル嘱聲. *n.* A very soft whisper.

Pio-pio-omke, ピオピオオムケ, 重キ風邪. *n.* A heavy cold. **Syn : Shiunu omke.**

Pip, ピプ, 沼. *n.* A swamp.

Pipa, ピバ, or **Piba, ピバ,** カハガイ. *n.* A kind of fresh water shell fish. *Anodonta sp.* In Saghalien an oyster."

Pipok, ピポク, 沼地. *n.* A swamp.

Pipa-sei, ピバセイ, カハガイノ貝. *n.* The shell of *anodonta.*

Pipo, ピホ, 沼地ノ. *adj.* Swampy. Miry.

Pira, ピラ, 開ケタル、擴リタル. *adj.* Open. Spread out.

Pira, ピラ, 斷崖. *n.* A cliff.

Pirakka, ピラッカ, 下駄. *n.* Clogs.

Pira-ni, ピラニ, ブナノキ. *n.* Beech tree. *Fagus sylvatica, L var. Sieboldi, Maxin.*

Pirapira, ピラピラ, 散布シタル、微塵トスル. *adj.* Scattered. Torn to pieces.

Pirasa, ピラサ, 緩ク、ヒモドク、披ク、ヒラク. *v.t.* To open as a book. To spread open.

Pirasare, ピラサレ, 咲カシム、擴ゲル. *v.t.* To cause another to open.

Piraske, ピラスケ, 咲ク、破レル. *v.i.* To be opened out. To be spread out. To be torn.

Piraspa, ピラスバ, 披ク、擴ゲル. *v.t.* To spread open. To open as a book. *Pl. of Pirasa.*

Piraspare, ピラスバレ, 披カスル. *v.i.* To cause another to open.

Piri, ピリ, or **Piripiri, ピリピリ,** 渦、ウズ. *n.* An eddy. **Syn : Piri-shimoye.**

Piri, ピリ, 傷、キズ、例セバ、ピリリコカラカラ、繃帶スル. *n.* A wound. As :—*Piri-kokarakara,* "to bind up a wound."

Piriba, ピリバ, or **Piruba, ピルバ,** 拭フ、ヌグフ. *v.t.* To wipe.

Pirika, ピリカ, 善キ、善ガル. *adj.* or *v.i.* Good. To be good. Sufficient. Adequate. Well. Safe. Sure. Admirable.

Pirika-irenga, ピリカイレンガ, 好意. *n.* Good will.

Pirika-manuhi-anreika, ピリカマ ヌヒアンレイカ, 喜ンデ承知スレ. *ph.* To assent to with pleasure.

Pirika-mintuchi, ピリカミンツチ, 善性ノ人魚. *n.* A fairy. A well disposed mermaid.

Pirika-no, ピリカノ, 善ク. *adv.* Well. Admirably.

Pirikap, ピリカプ, 善瓦ノ物. *n.* A good thing.

Pirikapo, ピリカポ, 善キ、(復數). *adj.* Good. (*pl*).

Pirikare, ピリカレ, 改善スル. *v.t.* To ameliorate. **Syn: Epirikare.**

Pirika-wa, ピリカワ 宜シ. *ph.* All right. It is well. That will do.

Pirikep. ピリケプ, 打チ落シタル粟. *n.* Thrashed millet.

Pirikere, ピリケレ, 粟ヲ搗ク. *v.t.* To beat millet in a mortar.

Piri-kokarakara, ピリコカラカラ, 繃帶スル. *v.t.* To dress a wound.

Piri-omap, ピリオマプ, 負傷者. *n.* A wounded person.

Piripiri, ピリピリ, or **Piri, ピリ,** 渦. *n.* An eddy.

Piri-seshke-kane, ピリセシケカ子, 船釘. *n.* Iron used for seaming boats.

Pirishinoye, ピリシノイェ, 渦. *n.* An eddy. **Syn: Piri.**

Piru, ピル, or **Piruru, ピルル,** 拭フ、平スル、均スレ、ナラス. *v.t.* To wipe. To level off as grain in a measure.

Piruba, ピルバ, 拭フ. *v.t.* To wipe anything which needs cleaning. **Syn: Piriba.**

Piruturu, ピルツル, 峽. *n.* Between the cliffs.

Pisash-sei, ピサシセイ, ムイ. *n.* Mollusk. *Chiton sp.*

Pise, ピセ, 身內ノ胞. *n.* The bladder.

Pise-kikiri, ピセキキリ, 獸類ノ身內ノ胞ニ時トシテ見ユル蟲. *n.* A worm sometimes found in the bladders of animals.

Pisene-kombu, ピセ子コムプ, クロツノマタ. *n.* Fucus or Rockweed.

Pise-nonno, ピセノンノ, ハマベンケイサウ. *n. Mertensia maritima, Don.*

Pise-pise, ピセピセ, or **Pisepse, ピセプセ,** フノリ、フクロフノリ. *n.* A kind of red seaweed growing on rocks. *Gloiopeltis furcata, Post. et Rupr. var. coliformis, (Harv.)*

Pish, ピシ, 數ノ後ニ用ユレ語、例セバ、チカプツッピシ、二羽ノ鳥. *part.* A classifier used after numerals. As :— *Chikap tup-pish,* "two birds."

Pishakku, ピシャック, or **Pishako, ピシャコ** 柄杓. *n.* A large water ladle.

Pishi, ピシ, 檢査スル、尋問スル、例セバ、クヒシワクイヌ、余ハ檢査セシ. *v.t.* To examine. To inquire. As :— *Ku pishi wa ku inu,* "I will make enquiries.

Pishkane, ピシカ子, 近ク、邊ニ、種種ニ. *adv.* Near. Close. About. Diverse.

Pishkaneke, ピシカ子ケ, 寄リ添ヒテ、周圍ニ. *adv.* Close by. Near to. Around. By. Surrounding.

Pishkaneketa, ピシカ子ケタ, 近ク、例セバ、エンヒシカチケタア、我ニ

近ク坐セヨ. *adv.* Close by. Near to. As:—*En pishkaneketa a*, "sit near me."

Pishkan-moshiri, ピシカンモシリ, 此處其處. *adv.* Here and there.

Pishkanta, ピシカンタ, 此處其處. *adv.* Here and there. To and fro.

Pishkanta-pishkanta, ピシカンタピシカンタ, 此處ヘ其處ヘ、此處其處. *adv.* Hither and thither. Here and there.

Pishkara, ピシカラ, 燒确ノ處. *n.* Rocky, rugged, places.

Pishki, ピシキ, 數、數フレ、例セバ、タムベ ピシキ ヘムパクベアン、是等ノ物幾何アリヤ. *n. & v.t.* A number. To count. As:—*Tambe pishki hempakbe an?* "How many of these things are there?

Pishkipa, ピシキパ, 數フレ. *v.t.* To count.

Pishki-wa-nukara, ピシキワヌカラ, 數フル. *v.t.* To count.

Pishne, ピシ子, 海岸. *n.* The sea-shore.

Pishno, ピシノ, 甚タ、例セバ、コタンヒシノ、各村. *adj.* Every. As:—*Kotan pishno*, "every village."

Pishoi, ピショイ, 魚ノ腹. *n.* The belly of a fish.

Pishto, ピシト, 海岸. *n.* The sea-shore.

Pishto-yomomke, ピシトヨモムケ, 燥ル、ハゼレ(鍋中ノ油ノ如ク). *v.i.* To splutter about (as fat in a frying pan).

Pishunkitesh, ピシュンキテシ, ハマヒルガホ. *n. Calystegia Soldanella, R, Br.*

Pit, ピツ, 小石. *n.* A small stone; flint.

Pita, ピタ, 解ク、説明スル. *v.t.* To untie. To undo. To explain. To loosen.

Pitara, ピタラ, 河床ノ名アル處ノ乾ケル部分. *n.* The dry stony sides of the bed of a river. Also, rarely, "a plain." **Syn: Piuka.**

Pitara-an, ピタラアン, 石多キ. *adj.* Stony.

Pitatke, ピタツケ, 垂ルル. *v.i.* To hang down. To dangle. To become unrolled or unraveled.

Pitche, ピッチェ, 剝ゲル、破レル. *v.i.* To come off. To be worn out. To wear out. **Syn: Pichitche.**

Pitke, ピツケ, 癲癇スル. *v.i.* To be subject to fits. **Syn: Cheachiushiyeye.**

Pitke-tashum, ピツケタシュム, 癲癇. *n.* Fits.

Pito, ピト, 人若クハ神ヲ數フル時數ノ後ニ付ク語、例セバ、アイヌピト、カムイピト、人モ神モ. *adj.* A kind of classifier for men and gods. As:—*Ainu bito, kamui bito*, "gods and men."

Pitoromun, ピトロムン, 青草. *n.* Herbage. Young green grass.

Pitpo, ピツポ, 小石、燧石. *n.* Small stones. Flints.

Pitpoturuse, ピツポツルセ, 石ノ如ク隕ツル、例セバ、ピッポツルセ シコパヤラ、其ハ石ノ如ク隕チタリ. *v.i.* To fall as a stone. As:—*Pitpoturuse shikopayara*, "It fell down like a stone.

Pittarane, ピッタラ子, 誇ツテ膨レル. *v.i.* To swell with pride.

Pittok-kina, ピットクキナ, ハナ ウド. *n.* The cow-parsnip. *Heracleum lanatum, Michx.*

Pituru, ピツル, 新鮮ナル、例セバ、ピ ツル チェプ, 鮮魚. *adj.* Fresh. As:—*Pituru chep,* "fresh fish."

Piuchi, ピウチ, 火打金. *n.* A steel for striking fire.

Piuchi-op, ピウチオプ, 燧箱. *n.* A flint and steel box or bag.

Piuchi-shuma, ピウチシュマ, 燧石. *n.* A flint.

Piuka, ピウカ, 石多キ河床. *n.* A stony river-bed.

Piuka-chishka, ピウカチシカ, or **Piuka-chishkara,** ピウカチシカラ, *n.* A sandpiper.

Piukep, ピウケプ, 砂礫. *n.* Course sand. Grit. Gravel.

Piuki, ピウキ, 攻撃スル、敵フ、例セバ、 セタエンヒウキ、犬我ニ敵ヘリ. *v.t.* To attack. To set upon. To aggress. As:—*Sata en piuki,* "the dog set upon me." **Syn: Chorauge. Otekna.**

Piukire, ピウキレ, 攻撃スル. *v.t.* To set at. To cause to attack.

Piukitoiru, ピウキトイル, 攻撃スル. *v.t.* To attack.

Piukosamba, ピウコサムバ, 鼻ロリ吹 ク、(獣ノ如ク). *v.i.* To blow through the nostrils as an animal. **Syn: Shiukosamba.**

Piwe, ピウェ, 押ス. *v.t.* To push. **Syn: Oputuye.**

Piwiuse, ピウィウセ, 呼吸音. *v.i.* To wheeze (as in breathing with a cold).

Piwiwitki, ピウィウィツキ, 音スレ (鳥 飛プ時ニ). *v.t.* To make a whirling noise with the wings as a wood cock when shooting through the air.

Piyapa, ピヤパ, 粟. *n.* Millet.

Piye, ピイェ, 種子、例セバ、ピイェナプ、 種子入器. *n.* Seeds of any kind. As:—*Piye op* "a seed vessel."

Piye, ピイェ, or **Piyehe,** ピイェヘ, 脂肪. *n.* The fat of living creatures such as birds and beasts.

Piye-kara, ピイェカラ, 投ゲル、例セバ、 シュマアリ ピイェ カラ、投石スル. *v.t.* To throw at. As:—*Shuma ari piye kara,* "to throw stones at. **Syn: Kopiye kara.**

Piye-o, ピイェオ, 肥エタル. *adj.* Fat.

Piye-sak, ピイェサク, 瘠セタル. *adj.* Lean.

Piye-toi, ピイェトイ, 白キ土. *n.* White clay.

Piye-ush, ピイェウシ, 肥エタル. *adj.* Fat.

Po, ポ, 此語ハ時ニ名詞ノ後ニ用キテ 細少チ示ス接尾語トナル、例セバ、チ エプポ、小魚. *part.* This word is sometimes suffixed to nouns as a diminuative particle. As:—*Chep po.* "a little fish." It is also used as an adjective, "small" "little."

Po, ポ, 此語ハ時ニ柔ゲルカチ有ス、例 セバ、プイチポオマンエアイカプ、猫ニ テハ行ケヌ. *part.* Sometimes this particle has a kind of softening power. Thus:—*Puine po oman* *eaikap,* "we cannot go alone" (meaning that the speaker would prefer others to go as well). *Orowa no po,* "And then." "After that."

Po, ポ, 時トシテ此語ハ（特ニ、チプカ ナル語ニ前立タル時）ヘ、即チ物ナル 語ニ似寄タル事アリ、例セバ、チプカ アヱランナクポ、必要ナキ種々物. *part.* Sometimes the word po, especially when preceded by the words *nep ka,* is equivalent to *pe,* "a thing," or "article" Thus:—*Nep ka aerannak po,* "any kind of thing that is not required."

Po, ポ, **Poho,** ポホ, 子供. *n.* A child. The young of anything. A son or daughter.

Po-apa, ポアパ, 子宮. *n.* The womb. **Sya: Po-pukuru. Makun-apa. Sange apa.**

Poat, ポアツ, 臍緒、ヘソノチ. *n.* The navel cord. **Syn: Chaat.**

Poho, ポホ, or **Po,** ポ, 小兒、何ニテ モ若キ者、子息. *n.* A child. The young of anything. A son.

Poekanu, ポエカヌ, 胎兒生命ヲ受クル 事. *n.* The quicking of a child.

Poeyairatki, ポエヤイラツキ, 受胎ス レ・ *v.i.* To conceive a child.

Poi, ポイ, 抜キ出ス. *v.t.* To pick out.

Poi, ポイ, 少サキ. *adj.* Small. Little. **Syn: Pon.**

Poeinonno-itak, ポエイノンノイタ ク, 小兒ノ生レシ後ノ祝. *n.* A religious ceremony performed on or about the sixth day after a

child has been born in which the welfare of the child is prayed for.

Poiba, ポイバ, 啄ム、ツイバム、錐リ 穴ヲ大ニスル、引キ抜ク、搔キ出ス. *v.t.* To pick out as birds pick seeds out of the ground. To enlarge a hole by boring. To shell. To extract. To scratch out. **Syn: Puyapuya.**

Poina, ポイナ, 大石. *n.* Stones of a larger size.

Poi-poi, ポイポイ, 甚ダ小キ. *adj.* Very little.

Poipoi, ポイポイ, 丸メル. *v.t.* To roll about in the hands.

Poishiknupo, ポイシクヌポ, 敗ル、殆 ド呪ヒ殺ス. *v.t.* To defeat. To nearly kill by cursing.

Poi-shitat-ni, ポイシタツニ, カバノ キノ一種. *n.* A kind of birch.

Poiyaumbe, ポイヤウムベ, 北海道ノ 山地ニ住メリト云フ獰猛ナル人種、恐 クハアイヌノ軍人ナラン. *n.* A fierce race of people said to have inhabited the mountainous parts of Yezo, possibly Ainu warriors.

Pok, ポク, 上ニ. *adv.* Under. Beneath. Underneath. **Syn: Po-ke. Chok.**

Poka, ポカ, ドウニカ、例セバ、ネウムポ カクキルスイ、余ハ其ヲ如何様ニカ為 サント欲ス. *adv.* By some means or other. Some how or other. Even. As:—*Neum poka ku ki rusui,* "I desire to do it somehow or other."

Pokap, ポカブ, 脱落膜. *n.* The thin external membrane within the womb thrown off ofter childbirth. *Decidua. Uterus.*

Pokai-iki, ポカイ, 斯程、例セバ、アニボカイ イキイエアシユカイ、彼ノ語ルナ斯クモ賢ク. *adv.* To such a degree. As:—*Ani pokai iki ye eashkai,* "he is thus clever at speaking."

Pokash, ポカシ, 鬱ク、フサク、例セバ、サムベボカシ、鬱ギテ. *v.i.* To be lowspirited. As:—*Sambe pokash,* "downhearted."

Pokashnu, ポカシヌ, ヨリ少ク、例セバ、カスノ シヨモ子、ボカシヌ カ シヨモ子、多クモナク、少クモナク. *adj.* Less. As:—*Kasu no shomo ne, pokashnu ka shomo ne,* "neither more nor less."

Pokashte, ポカシテ, 困ラスル、鬱悶サセル、例セバ、ヤイサムベボカシテ、人ヲ困ヲス. *v.t.* To cause to be downhearted. To give trouble to. As:—*Yaisambe-pokashte,* "to make one downhearted or unhappy."

Pokba, ポクバ, 憎ム、迫害スル、嫌フ. *v.t.* To hate. To persecute. To dislike. **Syn: Epokba.**

Poke, ポケ, 下ニ. *adv.* Under. Underneath. Beneath. **Syn: Pok.**

Pokegeta, ポケゲタ, or **Poketa, ポケタ,** 下ニ. *adv.* Underneath.

Pokep, ポケプ, 處女膜. *n.* Hymen. The virginal membrane at the orifice of the vagina.

Poki, ポキ, 底、陰門. *n.* The bottom of anything. The vagina.

Pokinipeka, ポキニベカ, 子供. *n.* Children. Boys, girls and women.

Pokin-nitai, ポキンニタイ, 小樹. *n.* Small trees.

Pokinoropeka, ポキノロペカ, 子供. Children. Boys, girls and women. **Syn: Pokinipeka.**

Pokipui, ポキプイ, 陰門. *n.* Vagina.

Poki-shiri, ポキシリ, 底、臀、例セバ、チクニ ボキシリ、木ノ底. *n.* The bottom. The hips. Side. The floor. The ground. As:—*Chikuni poki-shiri,* "the bottom of a tree." *Aiai poki-shiri kata ashikoyupu, penram kata aechopnure,* "she held the child upon her side and kissed its bosom."

Pokishiri, ポキシリ, 身體ノ下部、特ニ脚. *n.* The lower part of the body especially the legs.

Pokna, ポクナ, 下. *adv.* Under. Beneath.

Pokna-moshiri, ポクナモシリ, ：冥府. *n.* Hades.

Po-koro, ポコロ, 子ヲ産ム. *v.i.* To bear a child. **Syn: Aiai shikore.**

Pokotchaketa-mat-ahup-kara, ポコッチャケタマツアフブカラ, 嫁ヲ取ル. *v.t.* To take a wife for one's son.

Pon, ポン, 小キ、例セバ、ボン カシユイ、餘リ小キ. *adj.* Small. Little. As:—*Pon kashui,* "too small."

Pon-amushbe, ポンアムシベ, 小蟹. *n.* A small crab.

Pon-apka, ポンアブカ, 三歳ノ牡鹿. *n.* A three year old buck.

Ponbake, ポンバケ, 前布、マエカケ. *n.* An apron.

Ponbaki, ポンバキ, エビ. *n.* Prawns.

Ponbe, ポンベ, 小ナル物. *n.* A little thing.

Ponbepo, ポンベポ, 極小ナル物. *n.*
A very little thing.

Ponchikaman, ポンチカマン, タカ子
メラ. *n.* *Rosa acicularis, Lindl.*

Pon-chimaka-ni, ポンチマカニ, or
**Pet-kot-chimaka-ni, ペッコノチマ
カニ,** . *n.* The father lasher.
Syn: Chimaka-ni.

Ponde, ポンデ, 減ズル、縮少スレ. *v.t.*
To lessen. To abridge. **Syn:
Taknere.**

Ponde-i, ポンデイ, 縮少. *n.* Abridgement. **Syn: Taknere-i.**

Pone, ポ子, 骨. *n.* Bones.

Ponechi, ポ子チ, ペニパナノヘウタン
ポク. *n.* *Lonicera Maximowiczi,
Rupr.*

Pone-ik, ポ子イク, 關節. *n.* A
joint.

Pone-ik-pui, ポ子イクブイ, 脊髓骨. *n.*
The spine. The backbone.

Ponekakanu, ポ子カカヌ, 死體ト共ニ
葬ル上衣. *n.* The outer clothing
buried with the dead. **Syn: Shirikamup.**

Po-ne-kara, ポ子カラ, 養子ニスル.
v.t. To adopt a child.

Pone-kara-i, ポ子カライ, 養子ニス
ル事. *n.* Adoption.

Pone-kem, ポ子ケム, 端舟ノ修繕スレ
ニ用ユル骨ノ針. *n.* A bone needle
used in mending boats.

Pone-o, ポ子オ, 骨アレ. *adj.* Bony.

Pone-op, ポ子オブ, 骨アル物. *n.* A
bony thing.

Po-nere, ポ子レ, 養子スル. *v.t.* To
adopt.

Pone-tum-araka, ポ子タムアラカ,
僂麻質斯、リウマチス. *n.* Rheuma-
tism. Aching bones.

Pongi, ポンギ, ヤマアハ. *n.* *Calamagrostis Epigejos, Roth.*

Pon-guru, ポングル, 子供、例セバ、ポ
ングルコラチ、子供ノ如ク. *n.* A
child. As:—*Pon guru korachi,*
"childlike." **Syn: Heikachi
ramkoro.**

Pon-humbe, ポンフムベ, 海豚.
n. The porpoise.

Pon-itak, ポンイタク, 冤術. *n.*
Witchcraft.

Pon-itak-ki, ポンイタッキ, 冤スレ、
（ロ又ハ語ニテ）、呪フ、調伏ノ爲ニ祈
ル. *v.t.* To bewitch (by word of
mouth). To curse. To worship
demons in order to bring evil
upon another.

**Pon-itak-ki-guru, ポンイタッキグ
ル,** 冤法者. *n.* A witch. One who
bewitches by word of mouth.

Poni-une-mat, ポニウ子マツ, 季女.
n. One's youngest daughter.

Poni-une-po, ポニウ子ポ, 末子. *n.*
Youngest son or children.

Ponkapiu-sei, ポンカピウセイ, カイツ
ムリ. *n.* *Tellina roseas, Speng.*

**Pon-kishimkishim, ポンキシムキシ
ム,** or **Pon-kishunkishun, ポン
キシュンキシュン,** カザカノ類. *n.* A
kind of sculpin.

Pon-kopecha, ポンコペチャ, カイツム
リ. *n.* Little grebe. *Podiceps
L. Minor (Gm.)*

Pon-machi, ポンマチ, 妾. *n.* A
concubine.

Pon-mokrap, ポンモツクラブ, 臀鰭.
n. Anal fins.

Ponpa, ポンパ, 少キ（複数）. *adj.*
Small (*pl*).

Pon-no, ポンノ, or **Pon-nu, ポンヌ,**
少ナキ、僅ノ、例セバ、ポンノパテク、

ホンノ僅ノ. *adj.* A little. A few. As :—*Pon no patek,* "only a little." "just a little." *Pon no po,* "a very little or few." *Pon no pon no,* "a very little or few."

Pon-parumbe, ボンパルムベ, 會厭(ノ ドヒコ). *n.* The uvula.

Pon-pekanbe, ボンペックアンベ, ヒ メ ヒ シ. *n. Trapa bispinosa, Roxb. var. incisa, Wall.*

Ponra-ita, ボンライタ, オ ホ バ ダ イ コ ン サ ウ. *n.* A kind of weed. *Geum strictum, Ait.* **Syn : Kinaraita.**

Pon-ram, ボンラム, 若 キ、少 キ. *adj.* Young. Small. As :—*Pon-ram ita,* "while young."

Pon-no-ka, ボンノカ, 極少 キ. *adj.* A very little.

Pon-nu-pan-nu, ボンヌパンヌ, 少量. *adj.* In small quantities.

Pon-rei, ボンレイ, 渾名、(アダナ). *n.* A nickname.

Pon-sereke, ボンセレケ, 半 バ ヨ リ 少 ク. *adj.* Less than half.

Ponshinsep, ボンシユンセブ, メ ド ハ ギ. *n. Lespedeza sericea, Miq.*

Ponyaumbe, ボンヤウムベ, 北海道ノ 深山ニ住メリ ト云フ 獰猛ナル人種、多 分アイヌノ軍人ナラン. *n.* A fierce kind of people said to have inhabited the most mountainous parts of Ezo, possibly ancient warriors. This word is often used of the singular number.

Pon-yuk, ボンヤク, 鹿ノ子. *n.* A fawn.

Poon, ボオン, 極僅 ニ. *adv.* A very little.

Poon-makke, ボオンマッケ, 少シク開 ケ テ. *adv.* Ajar.

Pop, ボブ, 水胞、ミヅブク レ、例セバ、ポ ブ ア シ、水胞ス ル. *n.* A swelling. A blister. As :—*Pop ush,* "to have blisters."

Pop, ボブ, 沸騰ス ル、タ ギ レ. *v.i.* To boil. To bubble up.

Popai, ボハイ, 管. *n.* A tube. A pipe.

Popekot, ボベコツ, 暑サニ死ス. *v. i.* To die of heat.

Popera, ボベ ラ, 鳩尾(ミヅオチ). *n.* The pit of the stomach. The epigastrium.

Popiuka, ボビ ウ カ, 沸騰ス ル. *v.i.* To bubble up. To rise in bubbles.

Popke, ボブケ, 熱 キ. *adj.* Hot.

Popke-kina, ボブケキナ, オ ホ カ サ ス ゲ. *n.* A kind of sedge. *Carex rhynchophysa, B. A. Mey.*

Popke-no, ボブケノ, 熱 ク. *adv.* Hotly.

Popke-no-okai-yan, ボブケノ オカイ ヤン, 左様 ナ ラ. *ph.* Goodbye. (lit : keep yourselves warm).

Popo, ボボ, 兄. *n.* An elder brother.

Popokichiri, ボボキチリ, オ ヨ ホ シ キ リ. *n.* Reed warbler. *Acrocephalus orientalis, (T. & S.)*

Popokochiu, ボボコチユウ, ベ ニ ヒ ハ. *n.* Mealy red-pole. *Fringilla linaria, Linn.*

Porokutu, ポロクツ, エゾニウ. *n.*
Angelica ursina, Max. A very
large species of Umbelliferous
plants.

Poporaige, ポポライゲ, 發汗スレ. *v.i.*
To perspire much.

Poppe, ポンペ, 汗、アセ. *n.* Perspiration. Sweat.

Poppe-ashin, ポンペアシン, 發汗スレ.
v.i. To perspire.

Poppe-nu, ポッペヌ, 發汗スル. *v.i.*
To perspire.

Poppenuok, ポンペヌオク, 大ニ發汗ス
ル. *v.i.* To perspire profusely.

Poppe-nure, ポンペヌレ, 發汗セシム
ル. *v.t.* To make perspire.

Popporose, ポンポロセ, 病ノ流行地.
n. Spots brought about by disease.

Popte, ポプテ, 沸カス. *v.t.* To make
boil.

Po-pukuru, ポプクル, 子宮. *n.* The
womb. **Syn: Po apa. Makun
apa. Sange apa.**

Pop-ush, ポプウシ, 水胞ニ惱ム. *v.i.*
To be afflicted with blisters.

Porapora, ポラポラ, 振リ廻ス. *v.t.*
To shake about. **Syn: Hopora-
pora. Shiporapora.**

Poro, ポロ, 大ナル、例セバ、ポロカシユ
イ、餘リ大ナル. *adj.* Large. Big.
Great. As:—*Poro kashui,* "too
large."

Poro-ashikepet, ポロアシケペツ, 拇
指. *n.* The thumb. **Syn: Rui-
ashikepet.**

Porokituye-i, ポロキツイェイ, 砦、トリ
デ. *n.* A fort. **Syn: Uorogitu-
yei.**

Porokut'tapne, ポロクノタプ子, 大ナ
ル人、又ハ老人. *n.* A big or old
person. **Syn: Netobake poro
guru. Pa poro guru.**

Poron-no, ポロンノ, 多クノ. *adv.*
Many.

Poron-no-an, ポロンノアン, 多クノ、
豐ナル. *adj.* Plenteous. Abundant.

Poropa, ポロパ, 大ナル. *adj.* Great.
Large.

Porore, ポロレ, 増大スル. *v.t.* To
augment. To make larger.

Poro-sereke, ポロセレケ, 大抵. *adv.*
For the most part. More than
half.

Poru, ポル, 洞穴. *n.* A cave.

Po-sak, ポサク, 子ナキ、孕マヌ. *adj.*
Childless. Barren.

Poshita, ポシタ, or **Poshumta, ポシ
ュムタ,** 小童. *n.* A little boy.

Poso, ポソ, 通テ行ク. *v.t.* To go
through.

Poso, ポソ, 通ジテ. *adv.* Through.

Poso-ingara, ポソインガラ, 見トホス.
v.i. To look through.

Posokayatki, ポソカヤツキ, 澄ミタル.
adj. Clear. **Syn: Pekashnu.**

Potara, ポタラ, 診察スル. *v.t.* To
treat for sickness. To treat a
disease. **Syn: Epotara.**

Potara-guru, ポタラグル, 醫者. *n.*
A doctor. One who treats the
sick in any way with a view to
recovery.

Potoki, ポトキ, or **Potoki-noka, ポ
トキノカ,** 偶像. *n.* An idol. *(Jap).*

**Potrat, ポツラッ, or Potraat, 又ハ
ボツラアツ, クロッノ マタ. n. A
kind of rock-weed. Fucus evanes-
cens.**

**Poukokuchiuchiu, ポウコクチウチ
ウ, コヨシキリ. n. Reed-warbler.
Acrocephalus bistrigiceps, Sw.**

**Poyepoye, ポイェポイェ, 引キ抜ク. v.t.
To extract. To pick out. Syn:
Poiba.**

**Pu, ブ, 堆積、或ル名詞ニ複數ヲ示ス爲
ニ用ユ. n. A heap. Also a plural
suffix to some nouns.**

**Pu, ブ, or Puhu, ブフ, or Pui, ブイ,
納屋. n. A storehouse, or godown.**

**Pui, ブイ, 穴、例セバ、ブイオ、穴ヲ穿ル.
n. A hole. As:—Pui-o, "to
make a hole." Pui oma, "to
have holes." Pui omare, "to bore
or make a hole."**

**Pui, ブイ. クウキンクツ. n. The
marsh marigold. Caltha palustris,
L. var typica, Regel.**

**Pui, ブイ, or Pu, ブ, or Puhu, ブフ,
納屋. n. A godown or storehouse.**

**Pui-ne, ブイ子, 彼等自身、獨リニテ、
例セバ、ブイネポオマンエアイカブ、
彼等ハ獨ニテ行ケヌ. adv. By them-
selves. Alone. As:—Pui ne po
oman eaikap, "they cannot go
alone."**

**Puipui, ブイブイ, 鰻. n. An eel.
Syn: Ukuribe.**

Puira, ブイラ, 急流. n. Rapids.

**Puiraush-surugu, ブイラウシスルグ.
ブシノ雑リタル毒. n. Some kind
of poison having aconite in it.**

**Pukuro, ブクロ, or Pukuru, ブクル,
袋. n. A bag.**

**Pukusa, ブクサ, ヤウウシャニニク.
n. A kind of wild garlic.**

Allium victoriale, L. Also called
hurarui-mun.

**Pukusa-kina, ブクサキナ, フク ヘラ. n.
Anemone flaccida Fr. Schm. This
plant is much used by the Ainu
as an article of diet.**

**Pumba, ブムバ, 揚ゲル (複數). v.t.
(pl). To lift up. To raise.**

**Pumma, ブムマ, or Pummaha, ブム
マハ, 給料、報酬. n. Wages. A
reward.**

**Pummakore, ブムマコレ, 給料ヲ拂フ.
v.t. To give as wages. To pay
wages.**

**Pumma-koro, ブムマコロ, 給料ヲ取
ル. v.t. To take as wages. To
accept as a reward.**

**Pungara, ブンガラ, 蔓. n. A vine
of any kind.**

**Pungau, ブンガウ, ハシドイ. n. The
Japanese lilac. Syringa amurensis, Rupr. var. japonica, Max.**

**Pungau-karush, ブンガウカルシ, ハ
シドイ木耳. n. Polyporus sp.**

**Pungine, ブンギ子, 護ル、番スル. v.t.
To guard. To watch.**

**Pungine-guru, ブンギ子グル, 番人、
酋長. n. A watchman. A guard.
Chief.**

**Puni, ブニ, 揚ゲル、待スル、(單數).
v.t. To lift up. To wait upon.
(sing.)**

**Puri, ブリ, or buri, ブリ, 習慣、風俗.
例セバ、ブリピリカ、善キ風俗. n. A
habit. A custom. Manners. As:
—Puri-pirika, "of good manners." Puri rainatara, "of gentle habits."**

Puri-kanda, ブリカンダ, 荒キ. adj.

Wild. Rough. **Syn : Puri-yup-ke. Puri-o. Nukoshne.**

Puri-koro, プリコロ, 耽ル. *v.i.* To be addicted to. As :—*Ikka buri koro,* " to be addicted to theft."

Puri-o, プ リ オ, 荒キ. *adj.* Wild. Rough. **Syn : Puri-yupke. Puri-kanda. Nukoshne.**

Puri-sama-ayanasapbe, プリサマアヤナサブベ, 暴飲者、ノンダグレ. *n.* A riotous person. A person given to excessive wickedness.

Puri-wen, プリウェン, 荒キ、惡シキ. *adj.* Wild. Bad.

Puri-yupke, プリユプケ, 荒キ. *adj.* Wild. Rough. **Syn : Puri-kanda. Puri-o. Nukoshne.**

Purupuruge, プルプルゲ, 沸騰スル、湧キ出ツル. *v.i.* To bubble up. To gush forth.

Purupuruse, プルプルセ, 湧キ出ル. *v.i.* To gush forth (with a sound). as water.

Puruse, プルセ, 噴水スル. *v.t.* To blow out (as water).

Pusa, プサ, 總(フサ)、刀ノ下緒ノ飾. *n.* The lower ornamental part of a swordsash. A tassel.

Pusari, プサリ, 旅籠. *n.* A travelling bag.

Puse, プセ, 口ヨリ噴キ出ス. *v.t.* To blow out of the mouth.

Push, プシ, 箙、(エビラ)、豆ノ莢、麥ノ種、葡萄ノ朶. *n.* A quiver. The pods of peas or beans. An ear of wheat. A bunch of grapes.

Push, プシ, 爆ル (燃木ノ如ク) 噴火ズル. *v.t.* To jump as burning wood. To burst as a volcano. To go off

as a gun. To snap as a spring. To click. **Syn : Patke.**

Pushi, プシ, or **Push, プシ,** 穀物ノ穗. *n.* An ear of wheat, rice or millet.

Pushkosamka, プシコサムカ, 音スル (水ノ迸水スル). *v.i.* To send forth a gushing sound.

Push-ni, プシニ, ホヽノキ. *n. Magnolia hypoleuca, S. et Z.*

Pushpushke, プシプシケ, 柔キ、クチャクチャニナル. *adj.* Soft. Crumpled. **Syn : Pususke.**

Pushpusu, プシプス, 心チ知ラス. *v.t.* To make known things one has kept in his heart and mind.

Pushte, プシテ, 輕キ、容易ナル. *adj.* Light. Easy.

Pushtotta, プシトツタ, 簇並ニ毒チ入ル、袋. *n.* A small bag made of skin in which hunters carry their arrow heads and poison.

Pusu, プス, 抽キ出ス. *v.t.* To draw out. To take out.

Pususke, プススケ, 柔キ、クチャクチャニナル. *adj.* Soft. Crumpled. **Syn : Pushpushke.**

Putu, プツ, 蓋、河口、小河ノ大河ヘ流入ル口. *n.* A lid. The mouth of a river. The entrance of a small river into a larger one.

Pututke, プツッケ, 膨レ出ル. *v.i.* To swell out. **Syn : Shipushke.**

Puya-puya, プヤプヤ, 錐ル、啄ム. *v.t.* To bore a hole. To peck out as a bird seed from the ground. **Syn : Poiba. Soiba.**

Puyara, ブヤラ, or **Purai, ブラ1,** 窓、例セバ、ブヤラオッタ、窓ノ側. *n.* A window. As:—*Puyara otta,* " by the window." *Puyara range,* " to open a window." *Puyara shi,* " to shut a window." *Puyara otbe ashte* or *puyara otbe shi,* " to shut a window." *Puyara otbe sarare,* " to open a window."

Puyara-attep, ブヤラアッテブ, 窓掛. *n.* A window blind.

Puyara-otbe, ブヤラオッベ, 窓ノ戸. *n.* A window shutter.

Puyara-otki, ブヤラオツキ, 菜製ノ窓 掛. *n.* A window blind made of rushes or straw.

Puyara-shikrap, ブヤラシクラブ, 窓 框. *n.* A window-sill.

Puyara-uimak, ブヤラウイマク, 窓 框. *n.* A window-sill.

Puyuise, ブユイセ, 立登ル(淡キ煙ノ). *v.i.* To ascend as thin smoke. *Usei paha anak ne shupuya korachi puyuise ruwe ne,* " the steam from the hot water ascends like smoke." **Syn : Rikin.**

R (ラ).

Ra, ラ, 下、例ヘバ、ラオロツノ、下カラ. *adv.* Below. As:—*Ra orowa no,* " from beneath." *Rata,* " beneath." *Rata wa,* " from beneath it."

Ra, ラ, 草ノ葉. *n.* A blade of grass.

Ra, ラ, 魚ノ腹中ニ在ル白キ脂肪(鮭ヲ 除ク)、魚ノ肝臟. *n.* A kind of white fat found in the inside of any fish other than salmon. A fish's liver. The corresponding term for that of the larger animal as bears, horses, deer etc, is *huibe.*

Rachichi, ラチチ, 垂レル、吊ラレル(單 數). *v.i.* To hang down. To be suspended. (*sing*).

Rachitke, ラチツケ, 垂レル、吊ラレル、 (複 數). *v.i.* To be suspended. (*pl.*)

Rachitkere, ラチツケレ, 吊ル. *v.t.* To suspend. *Sing. Ratkire.*

Rachiurikikuru, ラチウリキクル, 目 ヲ擧ケル(人ニ話シ掛ケル時ノ如ク). *v.i.* To raise the eyes towards one as when about to speak.

Rachonrashte, ラチョンラシテ, 翼ヲ 張ル(鳥ナドノ). *v.i.* To spread the wings as a bird.

Ra-i, ラ1, 卑キ場處、地獄. *n.* The lower place. Hades.

Rai, ラ1, 死ヌ、例ヘバ、ライヮイサ ム、死ンダ. *v.i.* To die. As:— *Rai wa isam,* " dead." *Rai tek,* " dying." **Syn : Ekot. Aishi-riekot.**

Rai, ラ1, 降ル. *v.i.* The same as *ran,* " to descend."

Rai-ambe, ライアムベ, 死. *n.* Death.

Rai-chish-hawe, ライチシハウェ, 泣 ク、哀悼スル. *n.* A weeping. Wailing.

Rai-chish-kara, ライチシカラ, 哀悼
ス ル. *v.i.* To weep for the dead.
To lament the dead.

Rai-ehange, ライエハンゲ, 死ニ瀕ス
ル. *v.i.* To be at the point of
death.

Rai-etokooiki, ライエトコオイキ, 死
ニ瀕スル、覺悟スレ. *v. i.* To be
about to die. To prepare for
death.

Raige, ライゲ, 殺ス. *v.t.* To kill.

Raigepa, ラ イ ゲ バ, 殺ス. *v.t.* To
kill.

Raigere, ライゲレ, 殺サセル. *v.t.* To
cause to kill.

Rai-guru-korachi, ライグルコラチ,
死人ノ樣ナ、此語ハ侮辱ニ用キラレ屢
屢婦女子ノ中ニ於テ之ヲ耳ニス. *ph.*
Like a dead person. This phrase
is sometimes used in contempt
and is often heard among women.
It is equal to the word "abominable."

**Rai-guru-tekumbe, ライグルテクム
ベ,** 死者ニ用ユル手套. *n.* Gloves
worn by the dead.

Rai-i, ライイ, 死. *n.* Death.

Rai-korachi, ライコラチ, ヤット、困
難シテ. *adv.* Hardly. With difficulty. Like one dead.

Rai-korachi-ok, ライコラチオク, 甚
タ嫌惡スベキ. *adj.* Very abominable.

**Rai-kamui-irushka-tashum, ライ
カムイイルシカタシュム,** or **Rai-ka-
mui-tashum, ライカムイタシュム,**
中風症. *n.* Paralysis.

Rai-kamuikina, ライカムイキナ, キジ
カクシ. *n. Asparagus schoberioides,
Kunth.*

Rai-koro, ライコロ, 死ニ瀕スル. *v.i.*
To be about to die.

Raikosanu, ライコサヌ, 死ヌ、氣ヲ失
フ. *v.i.* To die. To faint.

Raikotenge, ライコテンゲ, 號呼スル
（困難又ハ失望ニ陷リタルトキノ如ク）.
v.i. To call after as in severe
trouble. To call out in distress.

Raimik, ライミク, 婦女子ノ挨拶. *n.*
The salutation of women. This
salutation consists of drawing the
hands from the temples down the
face, and ending with drawing
the index finger across the upper
lip.

Raimik-kara, ライミクカラ, 挨拶ス
ル（婦女子ノミノ）. *v.i.* To make
salutation. (Only used of females).

Rainatara, ライナタラ, 順瓦ナル. *adj.*
Gentle. **Syn : Ratchitara.**

Rainokor'ambe, ライノコルアムベ,
薄命ナル. *adj.* Miserable.

Raiochi, ライオチ, or **Raochi, ラオ
チ,** 虹. *n.* A rainbow.

Raiomap, ライオマブ, or **Rau-o-
map, ラウオマブ,** 魚筌. *n.* A
kind of fish basket trap.

Rai-paraparak, ライパラパラク, 哭
スル、泣ク: *v.i.* To cry aloud. To
weep.

Raishike-an, ライシケアン, 數多ノ.
adj. Very many.

Raita-mun, ライタムン, キンミツヒ
キ. *n. Agrimonia pilosa, Ledeb.*

Raitoshka, ライトシカ, 數多ノ、澤山
ナル. *adj.* Very many. A superabundance. **Syn : Roron-no-an.
Raishike an.**

Raitukunne, ライツクン子, 人事不省.
n. Anaesthesia.

Rai-tush, **ライツシ**, 縊首ニ用キタレ
繩. *n.* A rope with which one
has hung himself.

Rai-wa-oman, **ライワオマン**, 死ヌ.
v.i. To die.

Rai-wa-paye, **ライワパイ**エ, 死ヌ. *v.i.*
To die. **Syn: Moshir'hoppa.**

Raiyaise, **ライヤイセ**, 聲ヲ放チテ泣ク、
例セバ、アイアイライヤイセワアン、小
兒が泣テイ. *v.i.* To cry loudly.
To weep aloud. As:—*Aiai raiyaise wa an,* "the baby is crying." **Syn: Rayayaise. Rai-
paraparak.**

Raiyaiyaise, **ライヤイヤイセ**, ライヤ
イセノ強キ意義ヲ示ス. *v.i.* An in-
tensified form of *raiyaise.*

Rak, **ラク**, 沈澱物. *n.* Sediment.

Rak, **ラク**, 澄マセル (水垢ナドヲ). *v.i.*
To settle as rubbish in water.

Rak, **ラク**, 散スル (雲カ空ニ). *v.i.* To
pass away as clouds from the
horizon. See *Rak-rak.*

Rak, **ラク**, 香ヒスル、例ヘバ、シュムラ
ク、油ノ香ヒスル. *v.i.* To smell of
a thing. As:—*Shum rak,* "to
smell of oil."

Raka, **ラカ**, 必要、有益. *n.* Useful-
ness.

Raka-an, **ラカアン**, 益ニ立ツ、川途.
adj. Useful. Use.

Raka-isam, **ラカイサム**, 無益、陋劣.
adj. Useless. Abject.

Raka-isam-no, **ラカイサムノ**, 益ニ立
タザル、陋劣ナル. *adv.* Uselessly.
Abjetly.

Rakakke, **ラカッケ**, 視界ヨリ遠ザカル
(雲ノ消散スル如ク又人影ノ没スル如
ク)、消滅スル、(紙ナドノ). *v.i.* To
gradually go out of sight as

clouds. To disappear as a man out
of sight. To die out as spots in
a disease. **Syn: Uwepaketa i-
sam.**

Rakakse, **ラカクセ**, 消ユル. *v.i.* To
go out. To die out.

Rakan, **ラカン**, 魚ノ名. *n.* Name of
a fish.

Rakan, **ラカン**, 手足ナモガク. *v.i.* To
flounder. **Syn: Upokte.**

Raka-sak, **ラカサク**, 無益ナル. *adj.*
Useless.

Rake, **ラケ**, 下. *adv.* Below. The
next below. The lower.

Rakesara, **ラケサラ**, 吊サレル. *v.i.* and
adj. To be hanging down.

Rakishke, **ラキシケ**, 吊サレル. *v.i.*
and *adj.* To be hanging down.

Rakka, **ラッカ**, 澄マセル (泥水ヲ). *v.t.*
To put to settle as muddy or thick
water.

Rakko, **ラッコ**, 膃肭虎. *n.* A sea otter. *Lutra marina, Cuv.*

Rakoro-tashum, **ラコロタシュム**, 便
秘. *n.* Constipation.

Rakotesu, **ラコテス**, 淩ヘル (鷲ナドカ
餌ヲ). *v.i.* To swoop down upon
(as an eagle upon its prey). **Syn:
Raotesu.**

Rakrak, **ラクラク**, 棚引ク (雲ガ)、除々
ニ視界ヨリ遠ザカル. *n.* A sky
having soft mackerer looking
clouds upon it. A steady floating
out of sight. A gradual clearing away of the clouds.

Rakrak-paye, **ラクラクパイ**エ, 散スル
(雲ガ)、例セバ、アツパケラクラクパ
イェ、アツイヶシラクラクパイェ、東西ノ
空ニ在ル雲ガ晴レマス. *ph.* To float

gently out of sight as the clouds. As :—*Atui pake rakrak paye, atui gesh rakrak paye*, "the clouds upon the east and west horizon are passing away."

Rakuda-chikoikip, ラクダチコイキプ, 駱駝. *n.* A camel. (*Jap.*)

Rakup, ラクブ, 消ユル、死ヌ、例セバ、イタクエムコラクブ、話聲カ消エタ(聞取レヌ意). *v.i.* To die. To wane. As :—*Itak emko rakup*, "part of his speech died (i.e. could not be heard).

Rakup-wa-isam, ラクブワイサム, 死セル. *adj.* Dead.

Rakuru, ラクル, 霧、小雨、例セバ, ラクルアシ、霧降ル. *n.* Mist. Very fine rain. As :—*Rakuru ash*, "to drizzle."

Ram, ラム, 精神、心、魂. *n.* Mind. Heart. Soul.

Ram, ラム, 卑キ、幼キ、例セバ、ボンラムナロワ、幼キ時カラ. *adv.* Low. Young. As :—*Pon ram orowa*, "from childhood."

Ram, ラム, 獣ナドノ語尾ニ於テ此語ヲ耳ニス蓋シ其意義ヲ強ムルナリ. *part.* A particle sometimes heard at the end of words in songs to intensify their meaning.

Rama, ラマ, or **Ramat, ラマツ**, 精神、靈魂. *n.* The mind. Spirit. Soul.

Ramachi, ラマチ, or **Ramat, ラマト**, 生命、魂. *n.* Life. Soul. Spirit.

Ramai, ラマイ, 幼蟲 (ワカジラミ). *n.* A young louse.

Ramaita, ラマイタ, 美シキ、綺麗ナル. *adj.* Nice. Pretty. Beautiful.

Ramakakke, ラマカッケ, or **Rammakakke, ラムマカッケ**, 快活ナル、

愉快ナル. *adj.* Jolly. Pleased. Joyful.

Ramande, ラマンデ, 狩獵スル、例セバ、ニシヤッタコペチヤクラマンデルス、イグスツナシノエンモソ、ワエンコレ明日鴨撃ニ行キタイカラ早ク起シテ下サイ. *v.t.* To hunt. As :—*Nishatta kopecha ku ramande rusui gusu tunashino en mososo wa en kore*, "please wake me early tomorrow morning as I desire to go and hunt ducks."

Ramat, ラマツ, 心、魂、物ノ素、言語ノ意義. *n.* Spirit. Soul. The mind. The essence of a thing. The meaning of a word.

Rambara, ラムバラ 柳ノ種. *n.* A kind of willow.

Rambash-koro, ラムバシコロ, 人ト交リテ厚クスル. *v.i.* To be on friendly terms with a person.

Rambash-ne, ラムバシ子, 落付カザレ、漂泊スル、行商スル. *adj. and v.i.* Restless. To be a wanderer. To rove about. To peddle.

Rambash-ne-guru, ラムバシ子グル, 落付カザル人、漂泊者、商人. *n.* A wanderer. A restless person. A rover. A pedlar. A merchant.

Rambe, ラムベ, 卑クスル、默ラセル. *v.t.* To make low. To lower. to silence. To bring down.

Ramepakari, ラメバカリ, 考ヘヲ凝ヲシテ物ヲ發明スル、熟考スル. *v.t.* To discover a thing by thinking of it. To think out. To think well over.

Rametok, ラメトク, 勇シキ、又激烈ナル語、例セバ、ネブラメトククゴロワグスチイエヤイラメカシユレエチイエカラカラルウェタアン、汝ハ私ニ掛リマスが私ハ何ノ失敗ナ言ヲ云ヒマシタカ

adj. Brave. Also strong language. Saucy. As:—*Nep rametok
ku goro wa gusu chieyairameka-
shure echi iyekara kara ruwe ta an y*
" What strong language (sauce)
have I used that you should pitch
upon me? " (or " that I should
be called in question by you.")

Rametok-i, ｛ラメトキ, 勇敢. *n.*
Bravery. •

Rametok-koro, ラメトクコロ, 勇シ
キ、例ヘハ、ラメトクコロケル、勇者.
adj. Brave. As:—*Rametok koro guru,* " a brave person."

Rametok-o, ラメトクオ, 勇敢ナル. *adj.*
Brave. Bold.

Ram-i, ラムイ, 卑キ處又ハ物. *n.* A
low place or thing.

Ramka, ラムカ, 卑クスル、縮小スル.
v.t. and *v.i.* To lower. To diminish. To cease. To die out.
To become extinct. **Syn : Aara-
kere.**

Ramkopashtep, ラムコパシテプ, 大
刀. *n.* A sword. As:—*Aram-
kopashtep shitomushi,* " we put on
our swords."

Ram-koro-guru, ラムコログル, 葬式
ニ泣ク人. *n.* A mourner at a
funeral.

Ramkoshkashke, ラムコシカシケ, 恒
心ナキ、薄ナル、曲言スル. *v.i.* To be
fickle. To prevaricate. **Syn :
Maunmaun.**

Ramma, ラムマ, 常ニ、度々. *adv.*
Always. Again and again.

Rammakakke, ラムマカッケ, or Ramakakke, ラマカッケ, 快活ナル.
adj. To be jolly. Joyful. Happy.

Ramma-kane, ラムマカ子, or Ramma-ramma, ランマランマ, 常ニ.
adv. Always.

Ramma-korachi, ラムマコラチ, 例ノ
如ク. *adv.* As usual.

Ramma-ramma, ラムマラムラ, 常ニ、
恒久ニ. *adv.* Continually.

Ramma-shomo, ラムマショモ, 嘗テ
有ラザル、常ニ無シ. *adv.* Never.

Rammaun, ラムマウン, 常ニ、何時モ.
adv. Always. At any time.
When you please. Any time
will do.

Rammakka, ランマッカ, 滑稽. *n.*
Fun. A joke.

Ramne, ラム子, 全體、充満、例セハ、
ラムネト、終日. *adj.* Whole. Full.
As:—*Ramneto,* " the whole day."

Ramnep, ラム子プ, 充満セル物. *n.*
Anything full. A full vessel.
Anything whole.

Ram-no, ラムノ, or Ram-no-kane,
ラムノカ子, 風ンデ. *adv.* Stooping-
ly. Low.

Ramokka, ラモッカ, 世話焼キチスル、他
人ノ過チヲ探ス. *v.i.* To act the
busybody. To endeavour to find
out the faults of other people.

Ramoro, ラモロ, 凝脂、腎臟. *n.* Suet.
Kidneys. **Syn : Chokokoi.**

Rampashkoro, ランパシコロ, 沈着ナ
ル. *adj.* Tranquil. Even-tem-
pered.

Rampokashte, ラムポカシテ, 満足セ
ヌ. *v.i.* To be dissatisfied. **Syn :
Ehoshki.**

Rampoken, ラムポケン, 憫ミ. *n.*
Mercies.

Rampoken-wa-kore, ラムポケンワ
コレ, 憐ム, *v.t.* To have mercy
upon.

Rampokiwen, ラムポキウェン, 憐レナ
ル. *adj.* and *v.i.* Pitiable.

Rampokiwen-wa-kore, ラ ム ポ キ
ウェンワコレ, 憐ム. *v.t.* To have
mercy upon. To pity.

Ramram, ラ ム ラ ム, 鱗、蛇皮. *n.*
Fish scales. A snake's skin.

Ram-satsat, ラムサツサツ, 渇ク. *v.i.*
To be thirsty. **Syn: Iku-rusui.**
Ku-rusui.

Ramtom, ラムトム, 川ノ源ト河口ノ間
ヲ云フ. *n.* That part of a river
between its mouth and source.

Ramtutanu-guru, ラムツタヌグル,
死者ノ最近親. *n.* The chief
mourner at a funeral.

Ramu, ラム, 精神、魂. *n.* and *v.i.*
The mind. The soul. The seat
of the feeling. To think. To
understand. To consider. As:
—*Iteki anun shiri ne ramu wa
kore wa en kore,* "please do not
consider me a stranger."

Ramu-an, ラムアン, 怜悧ナル、智キ.
adj. Astute. Wise. Clever.
Knowing. Learned.

Ramu-an-no, ラムアンノ, 上手ニ.
adv. Cleverly, Knowingly.

Ramu-ashitnere-wa-monraigere,
ラムアシツチレワモンライゲレ, 壓制
ス.レ. *v.t.* To oppress.

Ramu-aye, ラムアイェ, 賞メラル丶. *v.i.*
To be praised.

Ramuchuptek, ラムチュプテク, 寂シ
ク感スル、恟怖スル. *v.i.* To feel
lonely and afraid. To fear. To
be moved with fear.

Ramu-ehorokare, ラムエホロカレ,
馬鹿ニスレ. *v.t.* To make a fool
of.

Ramu-esam, ラムエサム, 解ラヌ. *v.i.*
Not to understand.

Ramu-eunin, ラムエウニン, 輕卒ナル、
不注意ナル. *adj.* Careless. Inattentive. To forget.

Ramu-haita, ラムハイタ, 不知不識、誤
テ. *adv.* Unwittingly. By
mistake.

Ramuhauge, ラムハウゲ, 憐ミアル、親
切ナル. *adj.* and *v.i.* Merciful.
Kind.

Ramu-hokamba, ラムホカムバ, 解
シ難キ、憐ムベキ. *adj.* Difficult
to be understood. Pitiful.

Ramu-hokahoka, ラムホカホカ, os
Ramu-okaoka, ラムオカオカ, 慰メ
ル、鎮メレ. *v.t.* To comfort. To
quiet. **Syn: Omaoma.**

Ramu-hokasush, ラムホカスシ, or
Ramu-hokasusu, ラムホカスス, 惑
ハセレ. *adj.* and *v.i.* To be confused. To be puzzled.

Ramu-isambe, ラムイサムベ, 赤子、
愚人. *n.* A baby. A fool.

Ramu-isam-guru, ラムイサムグル, 愚
人. *n.* A fool. **Syn: Yaieram-**
peutek.

Ramukara, ラムカラ, 嘲弄スル、困ラ
セル、ジラス. *v.t.* To poke fun at.
To make angry. To tease. To
annoy. To make cry. **Syn:**
Iramkara.

Ramukari, ラムカリ, 妄言スル、眩暈
スレ. *v.i.* To rave. To be giddy.

Ramukarikari, ラムカリカリ, 耐ヘ切
レス、狂氣スレ. *v.i.* and *adj.* To
be impatient. To rave. **Syn:**
Katu-karikari.

Ramu-maun-maun, ラムマウンマウン, 遁辞スレ、變心スレ、二心ナル. *v.i.* To prevaricate. To be fickle. To be doublefaced.

Ramu-nin, ラムニン, 氣絶スル、失望ニ陷ル. *v.i.* To faint. To be in dispair.

Ramu-nishte, ラムニシテ, 強顔ナレ、冷淡ナレ. *adj.* Hardhearted. Coldhearted.

Ramu-niutek, ラムニウテク, 意地惡キ、怒リ易キ. *adj.* Cross. Out of temper. Peevish.

Ramu-okaoka, ラムオカオカ, or Ramu-hokahoka, ラムホカホカ, 慰メレ、鎮メレ. *v.t.* To comfort. To quiet.

Ramu-oknatara, ラムオクナタラ, 不幸ナレ. *adj.* and *v.t.* To be unhappy.

Ramu-orooroge, ラムオロオロゲ, 感動スル. *v.t.* To feel for. To become affected. To be touched. **Syn: Erampokiwen wa kore. Epuriwen.**

Ramu-osh, ラムオシ, 心底. *n.* The bottom of the heart. As:— *Ramu-osh wano,* "from the bottom of the heart."

Ramu-oshitchiu, ラムオシッチウ, 決心セシ、安固ノ、果斷ノ. *adj.* and *v.i.* To be determined. Stable. Resolute. **Syn: Katu-shineatki.**

Ramu-oshma, ラムオシマ, 賛成、共贊. *v.t.* and *n.* To assent. To accede. To abet. To acquiesce. To approve. To accord. Complaint.

Ramu-oshma-i, ラムオシマイ, 受納. *n.* Acceptance.

Ramu-oshma-no, ラムオシマノ, 意ニ適ヘル、快ヨキ. *adv.* Acceptably. Agreeably.

Ramu-oshmap, ラムオシマプ, 合意. *n.* Agreement. Accord.

Ramu-oshmare, ラムオシマレ, 合意スレ、一致サセル. *v.t.* To make agree. To cause to accord.

Ramu-pase, ラムパセ, 温厚ナル、自若ナレ. *adj.* Good tempered. Composed. Even tempered. **Syn: Irushka moire.**

Ramu-pekamam, ラムペカマム, 哀シキ. *v.i.* To be troubled. To be sorrowful. **Syn: Shirikirap.**

Ramu-pekamamka, ラムペカマムカ, 哀シマシムレ. *v.t.* To render sorrowful. **Syn: Ramu-sarakka.**

Ramu-pekamamo, ラムペカマモ, 哀シキ. *v.i.* To be sorrowful.

Ramu-pekere, ラムペケレ, 放蕩. *adj.* and *n.* Abandoned. Given up to badness. Unfaithful. Wanton. Wantonness.

Ramu-pekere-guru, ラムペケレグル, 姦夫. *n.* An Adulterer.

Ramu-pirika, ラムピリカ, 上機嫌. *adj.* and *v.i.* To be in good spirits.

Ramu-pirikare, ラムピリカレ, 慰メ. *v.t.* To comfort.

Ramu-rai, ラムライ, 氣脱シタル. *v.i.* To have lost spirit. To be troubled.

Ramu-rara, ラムララ, 舞フ(塵埃ナドノ). *v.i.* To circle around as dust or snow in the air.

Ramu-ratki, ラムラツキ, 健時ナレ. *adj.* and *v.i.* To be in good health and spirits. **Syn: Shikun wa an.**

Ramurakke, ラムラッケ, 幸福ナレ. *adj.* Happy.

Ramu-rikkush, ラムリックシ, 激昂ス レ. *v.i.* To be agitated in mind. To be restless.

Ramu-riten, ラムリテン, 氣ノ浮キ立 チタレ、喜ベレ. *adj.* High spirited. Pleased. Joyful.

Ramu-ritenga. ラムリテンガ, or **Ramu-ritenka, ラムリテンカ,** 喜バセ レ. *v.t.* To please. To make joyful.

Ramu-ritetke, イムリテツケ, 善ベル. *v.i.* and *adj.* Pleased. Joyful.

Ramu-ritetkere, ラムリテツケレ, 喜 バセル. *v.t.* To please.

Ramu-rotcha, ラムロッチヤ, 謙遜ナ ル、柔和ナル、從順ナレ. *adj.* Meek. Mild. Patient. Tender of spirit. Free from haughty self-sufficiency. Enduring things with an even temper.

Ramuru, ラムル, 内臓ノ凝脂. *n.* The fat over the intestives.

Ramu-sak, ラ ム サ ク, 愚 カ. *adj.* Foolish.

Ramu-san, ラムサン, 奇巧ナル. *adj.* Fanciful.

Ramusarak, ラムサラク, 困ル、怒ル. *v.i.* To be troubled. To be in bad spirits. To be angry. To be discouraged.

Ramu-sarakbe-koro-yainu, ラムサ ラクベコロヤイヌ, 困ル. *v.i.* To feel troubled.

Ramu-sarakka, ラムサラッカ, 困ラ セレ、怒ラセレ. *v.t.* To trouble. To make angry. To tease.

Ramu-satsat, ラムサツサツ, 渇スレ. *v.i.* To be thirsty. **Syn: Iku rusui.**

Ram-ush, ラムウシ, 學者、賢人. *adv.* Learned. Wise.

Ramu-shikarun, ラムシカルン, 記憶 スレ. *v.t.* To remember. **Syn: Eshkarun.**

Ramu-shinne, ラムシンチ, 満足セシ ムレ. *v.t.* To be satisfied.

Ramu-shiroma, ラムシロマ, 満足セシ ムレ、忠實ナレ、行儀正シキ. *v.i.* and *adj.* To be satisfied. To be even tempered. Faithful. Complacent. Polite.

Ramu-shiromare, ラムシロマレ, 慰 メレ. *v.t.* To comfort.

Ramushka, ラムシカ, 馴ラス. *v.t.* To train. To domesticate. As:— *Umma hene seta hene ramushka,* "to train a horse or dog."

Ramu-shuye, ラムシュイェ, 欺ク、取リ 込ム. *v.t.* To deceive. To take in.

Ramu-tanak, ラムタナク, 心痛ノ事 ノ為メニ眠ラレヌ. *v.i.* To be unable to sleep for trouble or other causes. **Syn: Mokoro-koinu.**

Ramu-tattariki, ラムタッタリキ, or **Ramu-tattarake, ラムタッタラケ,** 短氣ナル. *adj.* and *v.i.* Irritable. To be impatient. **Syn: Sambe takne. Nukoshne.**

Ramutoine, ラムトイチ, 驚ク. *v.i.* To be surprised. **Syn: Enushkari. Erayap.**

Ramu-tui, ラムツイ, 驚ク、恟怖スレ. *v.i.* and *adj.* To be frightened. To be awed. To be taken aback. To be startled. **Syn: Homatu.**

Ramu-tuika, ラムツイカ, 驚カス. *v.t.*
To frighten. To startle.

Ramu-tunash, ラムツナシ, 唐突ノ、急
遽ナル. *adj.* Abrupt. Quick.

**Ramu-unin, ラムウニン, or Ramu-
unun, ラムウヌン,** 注意スレ、忘却ス
レ. *v.i.* and *adj.* To be inattentive.
To forget. To be careless. Forgetful. To become unconscious.

Ramu-utura, ラムウツラ, 遠慮スル、
躊躇スレ. *v.i.* Diffident. **Syn:**
Yatu-utura. Ekatupase.

Ramuturu, ラムツル, 胸、懷. *n.*
The chest. The bosom.

Ramu-ye, ラムイエ, 賞メル. *v.t.* To
praise. **Syn: Ramye.**

Ramuyupu, ラムユブ, 慫慂スル. *v.i.*
To exhort. To coax.

Ramye, ラムイエ, 譽メレ. *v.t.* To
praise.

Ran, ラン, 下ル、降ル (雨ノ如ク). *v.i.*
To descend. To come down as
rain. To alight. As :—*Ran ap,*
"he has gone down."

Rangarap, ランガラブ, 挨拶. *n.* A
salutation.

Rangarap-itak, ランガラブイタク, 挨
拶ノ辭. *n.* The words of a salutation.

**Rangarap-itak-ki, ランガラブイタ
クキ,** 挨拶スル. *v.t.* To salute.

Range, ランゲ, 卸ス. *v.t.* To let
down. To unload.

Range, ランゲ, 此語ハ他語ニ附加シテ
副詞トナスカアリ、例ヘバ、ケストラ
ンゲ、日々ニ、ヘンバラネヤツカエモ
イレランゲ、彼ノ人ハ毎ニ此ノ樣ニ
遲イ. *part.* This word has an
adverbial force. As :—*Kesto range,* "daily." *Hembara ne yakka*

ene moire range, "he is always
thus late." *Shinen range,* "one
by one."

Range-kando, ランゲカンド, 最下天
(傳說ニ據レル天ニ六階アリランゲカ
ンドハ其最下ナリ). *n.* The lowest
skies. **Syn: Urara kando.**

Range-kut, ランゲクツ, 峥嶸. *n.*
Impassable crags.

Rangetam, ランゲタム, 神ノ劍. *n.*
The sword of the gods.

**Ranko-ni, ランコニ, or Rango-ni,
ランゴニ,** カツラ. *n.* *Cercidiphyl-
lum japonicum, S. et Z.*

Ran-nish, ランニシ, 眉ノ內端. *n.*
The inner corner of the eyebrows.

Ran-no, ランノ, 滴り落ツル. *adv.*
Trickling down.

Rannuma, ランヌマ, 眉. *n.* The
eyebrows. **Syn: Raranuma.**

Ranrewerewe, ランレウェレウェ, 瞬キ
スレ. *v.i.* To blink the eyes.
**Syn: Shikrewerewe. Shikchu-
puchupu.**

Ranrikochiuwe, ランリコチウェ, 眉ナ
上ゲル、(驚キシトキ). *v.i.* To raise
the eyebrows.

Rantom, ラントム, 河流. *n.* The
course of a river.

**Rantupep, ランツベブ, or Rantupe-
pi, ランツベビ,** 帽子ノ紐. *n.* Hat
strings. Bonnet strings.

Raochi, ラオチ, 虹. *n.* A rainbow.

Raoraye, ラオライエ, 下ケル. *v.t.* To
lower down. To put lower as
anything suspended.

Raoshma, ラオシマ, 沈メレ. *v.i.* To
To sink down. To sink into.

Raotereke, ラオテレケ, 降ル、潜ル.

v.i. To descend. To dive. **Syn: Raoshma. Horaochiwe.**

Raotesu, ラオテス, 摑ム(鷲カ餌チ). *v.i.* To swoop down (as an eagle upon its prey). **Syn: Rakotesu.**

Rap, ラブ, 降ル. *v.i.* (*pl*). To descend.

Rap, ラブ, or **Rapu, ラブ,** 羽毛、羽翼. *n.* Feathers. Wings. As:—*Rap porapora*, "to flutter the wings as a bird. **Syn: Rapparappa. Shirapparappa.**

Rapapse, ラバブセ, 脱ケ落チル、例セバ、オトブラバブセ、髪カ脱ケレ. *v.i.* To drop off. To fall off. As:— *Otop rapapse*, "the hair is falling off."

Rapapse-an, ラバブセアン, 神膳チ捧ゲル儀式. *n.* The ceremony of offering food to the gods and manes of the dead. **Syn: Icharapa. Shinnurappa. Arapapse.**

Rapembe, ラペムペ, ガマ. *n.* Cat-tail or Reed Mace. *Typha latifolia, L.*

Rapoke, ラポケ, 何々シツ、アル間ニ. *adv.* Whilst. During.

Rapoketa, ラポケタ, 何々シツ、アル間ニ. *adv.* Whilst. During.

Raporapora, ラポラポラ, 羽バタキスル. *v.i.* To flap the wings (as a bird). **Syn: Rapparappa.**

Rappa, ラツパ, 喇叭. *n.* A trumpet. As:—*Rappa rekte*, "to blow a trumpet."

Rapparappa, ラツパラツパ, 羽バタキスレ. *v.i.* To flutter the wings as a bird. **Syn: Shirapparappa. Rapoarapora.**

Raprap, ラブラブ, 動物ノ乳房(雌雄共ニ用ユ). *n.* The breast of an animal (male or female).

Raprap-pone, ラブラブポチ, 體側、胸骨. *n.* The side and breast bones.

Raptek, ラブテク, 泡チ澄マセル. *v.i.* To settle as froth or foam.

Rapterapte, ラブテラブテ, 吊ルス(藍褸又ハ糸ナドチ). *v.t.* To make hang down as rags or pieces of string.

Rapuchupki, ラブチュプキ, 馬蠅. *n.* A horsefly.

Rapuhu, ラブフ, 羽毛. *n.* Feathers. **Syn: Rap.**

Rapu-piru, ラブピル, 脱ケ替ハル(鳥ノ毛ナドノ). *v.i.* To moult as a bird. **Syn: Urupiru.**

Rapush-ni, ラブシニ, ニシキギ. *n.* *Evonymus alatus, Th.*

Rapush-chep, ラブシチェプ, トビウオ (方言). *n.* *Draciseus sachi, Jor and Sny.*

Rara, ララ, 鍔ノ緣. *n.* The edge of a sword guard.

Rara, ララ, 潜レ. *v.i.* To dive. **Syn: Raotereke.**

Rara, ララ, 眉. *n.* The eyebrows. **Syn: Raru. Rannuma.**

Rara, ララ, 惡戯、愚カ. *adj.* Naughty. Silly. **Syn: Irara.**

Rara, ララ, 馬鹿ニスル、愚弄スレ. *v.t.* To make fun of. To mock. To make a fool of.

Rarachik, ララチク, 戯レル. *v.t.* To sport with.

Raraiba, ララバ, 撫デル、(小兒ノ頭ナドチ). *v.t.* To stroke as the head of a child when fondling it. **Syn: Raruiba.**

Rarak, ララク, 滑カナル. *adj.*
Slippery. Smooth.

Rarakka. ララッカ, 清クスレ、善クス
ル. *v.t.* To refine. **Syn : Shipi.**

Rara-kuma, ララクマ, 雪ノ吹溜リ. *n.*
A snowdrift.

Rarama-ni, ララマニ, オンコ. *n.*
The yew tree. *Taxus cuspidata,*
S. et Z.

Rara-numa, ララヌマ, 眉, *n.*
Eyebrows.

Rara-okesh, ララオケシ, 眉ノ外端. *n.*
The outside corner of the eyebrows.

Rarapa, ララパ, 押付ケレ、撺ル、爭鬩
スル. *v.t.* To press down. To
squeeze. To fight with. **Syn :**
Rari.

Rarapare, ララパレ, 押合フ. *v.t.* To
press together.

Rararaktek, ラララクテク, 滑カナル、
水平ノ. *adj.* Smooth. Level. Slippery.

Rarempok, ラレムポク, 眉ノ下、例セ
バ、ラレムポインガラ、眉ノ下カラ覘ク.
n. The space immediately under
the eyebrows. As :—*Rarempo*
ingara, " to look out from under
the eyebrows."

Rari, ラリ, 何々セラレ、. *v.i.* To be.
Syn : Horari. An.

Rari, ラリ, 押付ケラレ. *v.i.* To be
pressed down. **Pl. Rarapa.**

Raribe, ラリベ, 潜レ（水鳥ナドガ餌チ求
メテ）. *v.i.* To dive for one's food
as various sea-fowls.

Rarire, ラリレ, 押付ケル. *v. t.* To
press down. **Syn : Numba.**

Rariu, ラリウ, 棹チ以テ舟チ漕ク. *v.t.*
To push a boat along with a
pole.

Raru, ラル, 眉. *n.* The eyebrows.
Syn : Rara.

Raru-kara, ラルカラ, 眉毛チ剃ル. *v.t.*
To shave the eyebrows.

Raruiba, ラルイベ, 撫デル（馬、犬、又ハ
小兒ノ頭ナドチ）. *v.t.* To stroke, as
a horse or dog, or a child's head.
Syn : Raraba.

Raruma-ni, ラルマニ, or **Rarama-**
ni, ララマニ, オンコ. *n.* The yew.
Taxus cuspidata, S. et Z.

Raruturu, ラルツル, 眉ト眉ノ間. *n.*
The space between the eyebrows.

Rasu, ラス, 出逢フ（椽ノ端カ棟ノ邊ニ
テ）. *v.i.* To meet as the end of
rafters at the top of a roof.

Ras, ラス, 割木、木片. *n.* Splinters
of wood. A crumb. Pieces of
cleft wood. **Syn: Chipereba ni.**

Ras-chashi, ラスチヤシ, 樯. *n.* A
post and rail fence.

Rashke, ラシケ, 剃レ. *v.t.* To shave.
Syn : Tuye. Erashke.

Rashne, ラシ子, 堅キ、脆キ、例セバ、
カシケラシ子ウパス、雪ハ上層ガ堅イ
ケレド毛下層ハ柔カイ. *adj.* Hard.
Brittle (as frozen snow). As :—
Kashike rashne upas, " snow hard
on the top but soft beneath."
Syn : Uka.

Rash-rashpa, ラシラシパ, 細カニ碎
ク. *v.t.* To break or cleave up
into fine pieces.

Rashtara, ラシタラ, 物チ荷フトキニ
用ユル組. *n.* A thong with a

wooden head-piece used for carrying bundles.

Rashupa-bashui, ラ シュバ バ シュイ, 葬式ニ用ュ レ鬢上ケノ器 (箸). *n.* A moustache lifter made of *Hydrangea pami-culata* and used only in death feasts.

Rashupa-ni, ラシュバニ, ノ リウツギ サビタ. *n.* *Hydrangea paniculata, Sieb.*

Rasu, ラス, 欠キ取ル、削リ取ル. *v.t.* To break a small piece off anything. To chip off.

Rasu-meshke, ラスメシケ, 削ル. *v.i.* To be chipped.

Rasupa, ラスバ, 矢ノ根ヲ繋クニ用ュ ル. *n.* A piece of wood sometimes used next an arrow head when bone is not procurable.

Rat, ラツ, 失望スル、物ヲ失ヒテ迷惑 スル. *v.i.* To feel disappointed. To feel troubled on account of missing anything. To miss.

Rat, ラツ, 痰、動物ノ脂肪. *n.* Phlegm. The thick fat of animals. Blubber.

Rata, ラタ, 下. *adv.* Below. Beneath.

Ratashkep, ラタシケブ, or **Rataskep,** ラタスケブ, 草、野菜. *n.* Herbs. Vegetables. Any kinds of herbs, vegetables and fruits used as food. See, *Kamui ratashked; toi ratashkep.*

Ratchako, ラツチヤコ, 燈. *n.* A lamp.

Ratchi, ラツチ, 温順ナレ. *adj.* Gentle.

Ratchire, ラツチレ, 宥ル、恕スル. *v.t.* To quiet. To assuage. To forgive.

Ratchitara, ラツチタラ, 温順ニ. *adj.* Gently.

Ratchitara-no-oman, ラツチタラノ オマン, 訣別ノ辞(左様ナラ、お静カニ、 等). *adv.* (sing). Adieu. Go gently.

Ratchitara-no-paye, ラツチタラノ バイェ, 訣別ノ辞. *adv.* (*pl*). Adieu.

Ratchitarare, ラツチタラレ, ナダメ ル. *v.t.* To quiet.

Ratchitara-shiomapara, ラツチタ ラシオマバラ, 馴レル. *adj.* Tame. **Syn: Epuntek, Ahomokka.**

Ratchitara-shiomaparare, ラツチ タラシオマバラレ, 馴ラス. *v.t.* To tame.

Ratchitke, ラツチツケ, 吊サレタレ. *adj.* Suspended.

Ratchitkere, ラツチツケレ, 掛ケル、 吊ス. *v.t.* To hang up. To suspend. **Sing: Ratkire.**

Rat-hese, ラツヘセ, 喘息. *n.* Asthma.

Ratki, ラツキ, 吊サレル. *v.i.* To be suspended.

Ratki-osoro-kam, ラツキオソロカム, 臀. *n.* The buttocks. The fleshy part of the posteriors.

Ratkire, ラツキレ, 吊ス、掛ケル. *v.t.* To suspend. To hang up. *Pl. Ratchitkere.*

Rat-o-omke, ラツオオムケ, 喘息. *n.* Asthma.

Rattopotopo, ラットポトポ, 眉ヲ動カ ス. *v.i.* To move the eyebrows.

Ratushne, ラツシ子, 負傷シタル. *adj.* Wounded.

Rau, ラウ, 下、秘密. *adv.* Below. Under. Secret. Hidden.

Rauge, ラウゲ, Rauke, ラウケ, 深處、險阻. *n.* A deep place. A steep place.

Rauge-sak-no, ラウゲサクノ, 偽リナキ、眞實ナル. *adv.* Without prevarication. Truly. Plainly. **Syn:** An korachi.

Rau-ke-an-sak-no, ラウケアンサクノ, 決定シタル、變スベガラザル. *adj.* Settled. Determined. Unchangeable.

Rauke-mina, ラウケミナ, 心中ニテ嗤フ. *v.i.* To laugh inwardly.

Rauke-sapse, ラウケサプセ, 心中ニテ嘲ル. *v.i.* To scorn inwardly.

Raukotapu, ラウコタプ, 捕ヘル. *v.t.* To seize. To take.

Raukushte, ラウクシテ, 潜ル. *v.i.* To dive.

Raun-apa, ラウンアバ, 子宮口. *n.* The entrance of the womb. **Syn:** Makun apa.

Raune, ラウ子, 深キ、例セバ、ラウ子シュイ、深キ穴. *adj.* Deep. As: —*Raune shui*, "a deep hole"; "a steep narrow precipitous place." *Raune piri*, "a deep wound."

Raune-no, ラウ子ノ, 深ク. *adv.* Deeply.

Raunkami, ラウンカミ, 樹木ノ心. *n.* The wood of a tree near the pith; heart-wood.

Rauomap, ラウオマプ, or Rai-omap, ライオマプ, 魚筌. *n.* A kind of wicker fish trap.

Rau-osh, ラウオシ, 沈没. *v.i.* To sink into.

Raupeka, ラウペカ, 密カニ. *adv.* Secretly.

Raurau, ラウラウ, テンナンセウ. *n.* Jack in the pulpit. *Arisaema japonicum*, *Bl.*

Rauraugetoi, ラウラウゲトイ, 泥沼. *n.* **Syn:** Raworawok ushke.

Rauta-ande, ラウタアンデ, 片寄セル、藏フ. *v.t.* To put on one side. To put away out of sight.

Rawe, ラウェ, 爲スコトヲ欲シテモ自カラ行フコトヲ欲セザルコト. *v.t.* To desire to do but not to act.

Rawe-chiu, ラウェチウ, 鞘ヲ被セル. *v.t.* To sheathe as a knife or sword.

Rawekatta, ラウェカッタ, 沈ム. *v.i.* To sink.

Raworawok-ushke, ラウォラウォクウシケ, 泥深キ場處. *n.* A boggy place.

Rawo-ahun, ラウォアフン, 靜ニ水ニ潜ル. *v.i.* To dive gently in water.

Rayahase, ラヤハセ, 怒鳴ル. *v.i.* To call out as in anger.

Rayap, ラヤプ, 驚カサレル. *v.i.* To be surprised at.

Rayapkara, ラヤプカラ, 驚イタ. *Excl.* of surprise.

Rayayaise, ラヤヤイセ, 撃ヲ放チテ泣ク. *v.i.* To weep aloud. To cry.

Raye, ライェ, 捧呈スル. *v.t.* To offer up. To give to a superior.

Rayepash, ライェバシ, 死ニ瀕スル、断末魔. *v.i.* To be at the point of death. The death struggles.

Rayoki, ラヨキ, ケジラミ. *n.* A kind of louse. *Pediculus pubis.*

Rayottemushi, ラヨノテムシ, 辛フシ
テ、漸ク. *adv.* Scarcely. Hardly.
Syn : Rai-korachi.

Re, レ, 此語ヲ動詞ニ附加スルトキハ動
詞トナル. *part.* A causative particle suffixed to intransitive verbs
to make them *transitive.* As :—
Pirika, "to be good;" *pirikare,*
"to better."

Re, レ, or **Rehe, レヘ,** 魚ノ頭ニ在ル
軟カキ部分. *n.* The soft part in
the head of a fish. **Syn : Kaka-
we.**

Re, レ, 三. *adj.* Three.

Reaiush-chep, レアイウシチェブ, トゲ
ウオ. *n.* Three spined stickle-
back. *Gasterosteus cataphractes*
(*Pallas*).

Re-a-ush-op, レアウシオブ, 三歯䰩.
n. A trident. (lit :—Spear with
three tines). **Syn : Urenbe.**

Reep, レエブ, 犬. *n.* A dog. **Syn :
Seta.**

Rehamush, レハムシ, ゴゼンタチバナ.
n. Cornus canadensis, L.

Re-hotne, レホツ子, 六十. *adj.* Sixty.

Rei, レイ, or **Reihei, レイヘイ,** 名. *n.*
A name.

Reihei, レイヘイ, 魚ノ頭ニ在ル肉. *n.*
The meat on the top of a fishes
head. **Syn : Kakewe.**

Rei-iwai, レイイワイ, 小兒ノ命名式.
n. The ceremony of naming a
child.

**Re-ikashima-wan, レイカシマワ
ン,** 十三. *adj.* Thirteen.

Reika, レイカ, 賞メル. *v.t.* To praise.

Rei-kore, レイコレ, 名ヲ附ケル. *v.t.*
To name.

Rei-koro, レイコロ, 何々ト稱セラル、
例セバ、タンコタンレイコロカツサモ
ロモシリネ此處ハ日本國ト稱セラル.
v.i. and *adj.* To have the name
of. To be called. Popular. As :—
Tan kotan rei-koro katu, '*Samoro moshiri*' *ne,* "This place is
called *Samoro moshiri.*" *Usa rei-
korobe moshit'tapan,* "there are
various names for the countries."

Reine, レイ子, or **Rene, レ子,** 四肢ノ
痛ミテカイダルキ感覺. *v.t.* A heavy
dull feeling of pain in the limbs.
To feel weak. **Syn : Keorosak.**

Rek, レク, 頰髯. *n.* The whiskers.
Syn : Reki.

Rek, レク, 音ヲ發スル. *v.i.* To give
forth a sound. To creak as
wheels. To rattle. To sing as a
bird.

Reka, レカ, 賞揚スル. *v.t.* To praise.
to approve with pleasure. **Syn :
Iramye. Omonre.**

Reki, レキ, or **Rek, レク,** 頰髯. *n.*
The whiskers. See *Rek.*

**Reki-otekpeshbari, レキオテクペシ
バリ,** 髯ヲ撫デル (挨拶ノトキニ). *v.i.*
To stroke the beard as in salutation.

Rek-kuttara, レックタラ, ヨブスマ
サウ. *n. Senecio sagittatus Schultz,
Bip.* Also called *Petkutu* and
chirekte-kuttara and *wakka-kuttara.*

**Rek-kuru-poka-eara-ehaita, レッ
クルポカエアラエハイタ,** 頰髯ノ未ダ
生ゼザル壯者. *n.* A young fellow
whose whiskers have not yet begun to sprout.

Rek-sak-ita, レクサクイタ, 幼キ時. *adj.* When young. *Met.* (Lit. "the time when he was without whiskers").

Rekte, レクテ, 彈奏スル. *v.t.* To play as a flute or whistle. To play any musical instrument.

Rekuchi, レクチ, 咽喉. *n.* The throat.

Rekuchi-anumba, レクチアヌムバ, 窒息スル. *v.i.* To be choked or throttled.

Rekuchi-iun, レクチイウン, 躬ラカ窒息スル. *v.i.* To choke one's self.

Rekuchi-orunbe, レクチオルンベ, 首飾リ、軛. *n.* A necklace. A yoke. **Syn : Rekutunbe.**

Rekuchi-tuiba, レクチツイバ, 首ヲ斬ル. *v.t.* To cut the head off.

Rekush-chep, レクシチェプ, 魚ノ名, *n. Alectria beujamini, Jor. and Sng.*

Rekut-koni, レクツコニ, 馬脾風. *n.* Croup.

Rekut-mayamaya-omke, レクツマヤマヤオムケ, 喉ノ感冒. *n.* A cold in the throat.

Rekut-umbe, レクツウムベ, 首飾リ、軛. *n.* A necklace. A yoke. **Syn : Rekuchi orunbe.**

Rekutumbe-kot, レクツムベコツ, or **Rekutumbe-shu,** レクツムベシュ, 首飾ヲ造ル鑄型. *n.* A mould for melting metal for necklaces.

Rekut'umbe-shu, レクツウムベシュ, 首飾リヲ造ル鑄型. *n.* A mould for making necklace patterns.

Ren, レン, or **Rere,** レレ, 沈メル. *v.i.* To sink.

Ren, レン, or **Re-niu,** レニウ, 三人. *n.* Three persons.

Rende, レンデ, 沈メル. *v.t.* To sink.

Rene, レネ, or **Reine,** レイ子, 弱キ、穉カナル. *adj.* Weak. Calm. Quite. **Syn : Tumsak.**

Renga, レンガ, 親切. *n.* Favour. Kindness.

Rengaine, レンガイ子, 欲スル儘ニ、場合ニ從フテ. *adv.* As one likes. According to circumstances. As : —*Ku rengaine hawe an !* "is it my fault (is it owing to me).

Rengaine-iki, レンガイ子イキ, ドーデモヨイ、意ニ介セヌ. *v.i.* To be indifferent. Regardless.

Rengaine-mondum, レンガイ子モンツム, 自由. *n.* Liberty. Freedom.

Rengap, レンガプ, 何々ノ故ニ. *adv.* On account of. Because of.

Rengap-ani, レンカブアニ, 何々ノ故ニ. *adv.* On account of.

Rengap-gusu, レンガブグス, 何々ノ爲ニ. *adv.* Owing to. Through. For the sake of. On account of.

Re-niu, レニウ, or **Ren,** レン, 三人. *n.* Three persons.

Rennatara, レンナタラ, 疲勞スル. *v.i.* To be very tired and drowsy or weak.

Rep, レプ, 三ツノ物. *n.* Three things.

Rep, レプ, 海, 例セバ、レプペカ、海カラ、レプタ、海ニテ. *n.* The sea. As :—*Rep peka,* by sea. *Rep ta,* in the sea. At sea. **Syn : Atui.**

Repa, レパ, 海上遠カニ出漁スル. *v.i.* To be far out at sea for the purpose of fishing.

Repa-gusu-oman, レパグスオマン, 海上ニ出漁スル. *v.i.* To go out to sea to fish.

Repa-op, レパオプ, 魚叉(モリ). *n.* A harpoon.

Rep-ikashima-hotne, **レブイカシマ、ホツ子**, 二十三. *n.* Twenty three.

Rep-ikashima-wanbe, **レブイカシマワンベ**, 十三. *n.* Thirteen.

Repke, **レブケ**, 海＝テ. *adv.* At sea.

Rep-ni-hat, **レブニハツ**, テウセンゴミシ. *n.* *Schizandra chinensis, Bail.*

Rep-ni-hat-pungara, **レブニハツプンガラ**, テウセンゴミシノシル. *n.* The vine of the above.

Repoiki, **レポイキ**, 魚ヲ釣リテ行ク. *v.i.* To go fishing.

Repoparase, **レポパラセ**, 小舟ニテ漂フ、難船スル. *v. i.* To drift in a boat. To be lost at sea.

Repotbe, **レポツベ**, 海魚. *n.* The fishes of the sea. **Syn : Atui or-un chep.**

Rep-pish, **レブピシ**, 三ッノ物. *n.* Three things.

Repta, **レブタ**, 海＝テ. *adv.* At sea.

Rep-un-ekashi, **レブウンエカシ**, 海中ノ怪物常ニ舟ヲ呑ムト言ヒ傳フ. *n.* A fabulous sea monster said to be in the habit of swallowing up ships.

Rep-un-guru, **レブウングル**, 海ヲ渡リテ來リシ人、島人、外國人、(主トシテ樺太及ヒ滿州人ヲ云フ). *n.* A person from beyond the seas. Islanders. Foreigners. Chiefly applied to the inhabitants of Saghalien and Manchuria.

Rep-un-kamui, **レブウンカムイ**, 海神. *n.* The sea gods.

Rep-un-kontukai, **レブウンコツカイ**, 人魚 (龜ノ形ヲナスト云フ). *n.* The name of a mermaid supposed to be in the form of a tortoise.

Rep-un-moshiri, **レブウンモシリ**, 島、外國. *n.* An island. Foreign countries.

Rep-un-riri-kata-inao-uk-kamui, **レブウンリリカタイナオウクカムイ**, 海ノ主神. *n.* The name of the chief of the sea-gods in the Ainu pantheon.

Rep-un-shiri, **レブウンシリ**, 島. *n.* An island.

Repushbe, **レブシベ**, 河中ニ在ル巨岩. *n.* Large stones found in rivers. **Syn : Taktakbe.**

Rera, **レラ**, 風. *n.* The wind. As : —*Rera humi,* "the sound of wind." *Rera humi shem korachi hum ash,* "it sounded like the blowing wind. *Rera nitne,* "a bad wind."

Rera-an, **アラアン**, 風多キ. *adj* Windy.

Rera-ash, **レラアシ**, 吹ク. *v. i.* To blow.

Rera-ash-shiri, **レラアシシリ**, 風多キ日. *n.* Windy weather.

Rera-ash-shiri-an, **レラアシシリアン**, 風多キ. *adj.* Windy.

Re-rai, **レライ**, 三. *adj.* Three.

Rera-kaikai, **レラカイカイ**, 荒灘. *n.* A short choppy sea.

Rera-kare, **レラカレ**, 風ニアテル、風ニアテル爲ニ戸外ニ出ス. *v.t.* To air. To put out of doors to air.

Rera-mau, **レラマウ**, 空氣. *n.* Air.

Rera-oshma, **レラオシマ**, 風アル. *adj.* Airy.

Rerara-kotukbe, **レララコツクベ**, 胸鎧. *n.* A breastplate.

Rerari, **レラリ**, or Reraru, **レラル**, 胸. *n.* The chest. The bosom.

Rera-rui, レラルイ, 吹ク. _v.i._ To blow.

Rera-shiu, レラシウ, 旋風、強風. _n._ A whirlwind. A strong wind. **Syn: Hopoye-rera.**

Rerayupke, レラユブケ, 烈シク吹ク. _v.i._ To blow severely.

Rere, レレ, or **Ren, レン,** 沈メル. _v.i._ To sink.

Rere, レレ, 三. _adj._ Three. **Syn: Re. Rep.**

Rereka, レレカ, 沈メル. _v.t._ To sink.

Rereko, レレコ, 三日. _n._ Three days.

Re-shike, レシケ, 六十尾ノ魚. _adj._ Sixty fish.

Re-shikkeu, レシッケウ, 三角形ナル. _adj._ Triangular.

Reshke, レシケ, 養育スル. _adj._ Brough up. (_pl._)

Reshpa, レシバ, 養育スル. _v.t._ To bring up. To rear. To nourish. _Pl. of Resu._ **Syn: Shukupte.**

Reshpa-guru, レシバグル, 養父母・ _n._ A foster parent.

Re-shui-ne, レシュイネ, 三倍. _adj._ Three times.

Resu, レス, 養育スル. _v.t._ To bring up. To rear. _Sing. of Reshpa._

Resuka, レスカ, _v.t._ To bring up.

Retan-noya, レタンノヤ, エゾノコギリサウ. _n._ _Achillea Ptarmica, L._

Retara, レタラ, 白キ. _adj._ White.

Retara-ambe, レタラアムベ, 白、白キ物. _n._ Whiteness. A white thing.

Retara-i, レタライ, 白. _n._ Whiteness.

Retara-kina-amauri, レタラキナアマウリ, シロバナノエンレイサウ. _n._ _Trillium kamtschaticum, Pall._

Retar'ambe, レタルアムベ, 白キ物、白キ. _n._ A white thing. Whiteness.

Retarape, レタラベ, 白キ物. _n._ A white thing. The whites.

Retara-shik-num, レタラシクヌム, 眼球ノ白キ部分. _n._ The white of the eye.

Retara-tom, レタラトム, 白. _adj._ White.

Retar'o-shikambe, レタルオシカムベ, アホウドリ. _n._ _Diomedia albatrus, Pall._ Steller's albatros. **Syn: Onne chikap.**

Retat'chiri, レタッチリ, ハクテフ. _n._ Swans. _Cygnus musicus, Bechst._

Retat-taskoro, レタノタスコロ, 霜. _n._ White frost.

Retat-tope-ni, レタトトペニ, メイゲツカヘデ. _n._ A kind of maple. _Acer japonicum, Th._

Retat'turu, レタッツル, 頭垢. _n._ Dandruff.

Rettek, レッテク, 老衰スル、酔潰レル、疲勞スル. _v.i._ To be old and infirm. To be decrepit. To be hopelessly drunk and incapable. To be very tired. **Syn: Katutoranne. Katu ikashishba. Rennatara.**

Reu, レウ, 止ル (烏カ枝ニ). _v.i._ To settle as a bird.

Reu, レウ, 膓膓. _n._ A sausage.

Reuge, レウゲ, 曲ゲル、凹形ナル. _adj._ Bent. Concave.

Reukashi, レウカシ, 刀背. _n._ The back of a sword.

Reunashi, レウナシ, 臼ニテ搗ク三人.
v.i. Three persons to pound in a
mortar. **Syn: Utunashi. Yaitunashi. Autunashi. Inereyunashi.**

Reupoki, レウポキ, 物ノ下面. *n.* The
under side of anything.

Reushi, レウシ, 止宿スレ. *v. i.* To
stop or lodge at a place. To
abide at a place.

Reushire, レウシレ, 止宿サセル. *v.t.*
To allow another to lodge at a
place. To lodge a person.

Reu-ushike, レウウシケ, or **Reushi-
ushike,** 止宿所. *n.* A stopping
place. An abode.

**Reushi-wa-shimgehe, レウシワシム
ゲヘ,** 滯留ノ翌日. *adv.* The day
after staying at a place.

Rewe, レウェ, 曲ゲル. *v.t.* To bend.

Reye, レイェ, 這フ. *v.i.* To creep.
To crawl. **Syn: Honu.**

Reye-wa-oman, レイェワオマン, 手足
デ這ヒ廻ル. *v. i.* To crawl along
upon the hands and toes.

Ri, リ, 高キ. *adj.* and *v.i.* High.
To be High.

Ria, リア, or **Riya, リヤ,** 栖息スレ.
v.i. To dwell at a place.

Ria-chikap, リアチカプ, 鳩、鷸ナドノ
如ク遷移セス鳥類. *n.* Non-migra-
tory birds such a pigeons and
some kinds of snipe.

Richara, リチャラ, 擴ゲル. *v.i.*
Spread out on the top. To
spread out as the waves when
beating on the sea-shore.

Richi, リチ, 筋. *n.* Sinews. Tendons. **Syn: Rit.**

Ri-i, リイ, 高キ場處或ハ物. *n.* A
high place or thing.

Rik, リク, 上ニ. *adv.* Above. Over.
High.

Rikan, リカン, 潤カサレル. *v. i.* and
adj. To be soaked. To be soft.

Rikande, リカンデ, 潤カス、濕ラス.
v.t. To soak. To damp.

Rikani, リカニ, 梁、椽. *n.* A beam.
A rafter.

Rikanka, リカンカ, 潤カス. *v.t.* To
soak. To dampen.

Rikanki, リカンキ, 上ゲル. *v.t.* To
send up.

Rikanu, リカヌ, 膠着スル. *v.i.* and
adj. Adhering together. To stick
together. As:—*Rikanu chiporo,*
"fish-roe sticking together."

Riki, リキ, 高處. *n.* Height. An
elevation.

Rikin, リキン, 登ル. *v.t.* To ascend.

Rikin-chiri, リキンチリ, ヒバリ. *n.*
Japanese skylarck. *Alauda arvensis japonica,* (*T. & S.*)

Rikinge, リキンゲ, 上ゲル. *v.i.* To
be lifted up. (*Pl. of the aljeet.*)

Rikinde, リキンデ, 上ゲル. *v.t.* To
send up.

Rikin-kamui, リキンカムイ, 梁、チボ
シカ. *n.* A moose deer.

Rikinno, リキンノ, 跳返ル. *v.i.* To
bounce.

Riknapuni, リクナプニ, 上ゲレ、捧ゲ
ル. *v.i.* and *v.t.* To ascend. To
send up. To offer up.

**Rikochiripo-chikap, リコチリポチカ
プ,** ヒバリ. *n.* Japanese skylark.
Alauda arvensis japonica, (*T.* and
S.)

Rik-oma-kando, ククオマカンド, 天、
空. *n.* Heaven. The skies.

Rikoma-tom-be, リ,オマトムベ, 日又ハ月. *n.* The sun or moon. **Syn:** Tokap chup.

Rikop, リコブ, 星、上方ニ在ルモノ. *n.* A star. Anything over-head.

Rikoraye, リコライェ、ヨリ高ク掛ルル、扛ケル、巻ク、晴ルル. *v.t.* To hang up higher. To raise. To roll up. To send up. To clear up.

Rikoro, リコロ, 上ヨリ. *adv.* From above.

Rik-oshma, リ,オシマ, 扛ケル. *v. t.* To lift up. To raise.

Rikotte, リコッテ, 掛ケル. *v.t.* To hang up.

Rik-peka, リクベカ, 上方. *adv.* The direction above.

Rikta, リクタ, 上. *adj.* Above. Aloft.

Rikta-kamui-hum, リクタカムイフム, 雷. *n.* Thunder.

Rik-un, リクウン, 上ニ. *adv.* Above. In the heights.

Rikun-shiri, リクンシリ, 小屋ノ西側ノ棟ニ在ル窓(烟出ナリ). *n.* The window in the west end angle of the roof of an Ainu hut.

Rimnu, リムヌ, 鳴ル、響ク. *v.i.* To rattle. To sound. To resound.

Rimnu-rimnu, リムヌリムヌ, リムヌノ強キ意チ表ハス語. *v.i.* Intensitive of *rimnu.*

Rikup, リクブ, 地上ニ建テラレタル(穴居ニ反スルコトチ示ス). *n.* A house on the surface of the earth in contradistinction to a pit-dwelling.

Rimse, リムセ, 舞踏スル、跳飛スル. *v.i.* To dance. To jump up.

Rimsep, リムセブ, 舞踏. *n.* A dance.

Rimuse, リムセ, 舞踏スル、跳飛スル. *v.i.* To dance. To jump up.

Rin, リン, 波、例セバ、リンルイ、荒海. *n.* Waves. As:—*Rin rui,* "a rough sea." **Syn:** Riri.

Ringo, リンゴ, 苹果、リンゴ. *n.* An apple. (From the Japanese).

Ripa, リバ, 高(複). *adj.* To be high (*pl*).

Riri, リリ, 波. *n.* The waves.

Rinkosan, リンコサン, 鳴レ(金物カ). *v.i.* To clank. To ring. To clang.

Ririkekke, リリケッケ, 礒浪. *n.* Breakers.

Riri-kopirika, リリコピリカ, 幸運ナル. *adj. and v.i.* To be fortunate. Lucky. **Syn:** Maukopirika.

Riri-puni, リリプニ, 浪ニ揺リ上ゲヲレル. *v.i.* To be lifted up by the waves of the sea. As:—*Chip riri puni iki, ahun iki,* "the boat rises and falls with the waves."

Riri-rui, リリルイ, 高浪. *n.* High waves. A rough sea.

Riri-shietaye, リリシエタイェ, 退潮. *n.* The ebb of tide.

Riri-yan, リリヤン, 満潮. *n.* The flow of the tide.

Risassara, リサッサラ, 高ク生茂ル(荻ノ如ク). *adj.* Thick and tall (as a plot of rushes or reeds). As:—*Ririsassara,* "a thick plot of high reeds."

Risei, リセイ, 引抜ク(甲)(草又鳥ノ毛ノ如キモノチ). *v.t.* (*Sing*). To pull up as weeds. To root up. To pluck as a fowl.

Risesseri, リセノセリ, Kisesseri, キセッセリ, Nisesseri, ニセッセリ, アイヌワサビ. *n.* A kind of water cress. *Ca damine dezoyensis, Maxim.* This plant is used as an article of food by the Ainu.

Rishpa, リシパ, 引拔ク(複). *v.t.* (*pl*). To pull out as weeds. To pluck as a bird.

Rit, リツ, 筋、腱、軟骨. *n.* Sinews. Tendons. Gristle. **Syn: Richi.**

Rit, リツ, 血管. *n.* The veins.

Riten, リテン, 柔カキ、柔カニナル、平癒スル. *v.i.* and *adj.* Soft. To become soft. To improve in health. As:—*Tambe e ko anak tunashi no e riten kusu ne,* "you will soon improve in health if you eat this."

Ritenka, リテンカ, 柔クスル、痛チ鎮メル. *v.t.* To soften. To allay pain.

Riten-kina, リテンキナ, ハコベ. *n.* Chickweed. *Stellaria media, L.*

Riten-nun, リテンヌン, 草ノ一種. *n.* A kind of grass. *Glyceria sp.*

Riten-ni, リテンニ, ムシカリ. *n.* *Viburnum furcatum, Bl.*

Riten-saranip, リテンサラニプ, 木皮又ハ葦ニテ造レル籠. *n.* A kind of basket made of soft reeds or bark.

Riten-toi-shu, リテントイシュ, 陶器. *n.* An earthenware vessel. A crock. **Syn: Sei-shintoko.**

Riterite, リテリテ, 伸サスル、運動スル. *v.i.* To stretch one's self. To take exercise.

Riteush-guru, リテウシグル, 男ノ兒若クハ、胎兒. *n.* A male child either

in the womb or immediately after birth.

Ritne, リツ子, 困難ナル、哀シキ. *adj.* Troubled. To be in sorrow.

Ritutta, リツタ, 途中ニテ. *adj.* On the way.

Riya, リヤ, or Ria, リア, 滯在スル. *v.i.* To dwell at a place. To sojourn.

Riya, リヤ, 古キ、蓄ヘタル. *adj.* Old. Stowed away.

Riya-aep, リヤアエプ, 蓄ヘタ食物. *n.* Old stores of food.

Riya-chikap, リヤチカプ, アブラシギ、遷移セサル鳥類. *n.* A woodcock. Also any other kind of non-migratory bird.

Riya-chikuui, リヤチクウイ, 貯ヘタル木. *n.* Stores of wood.

Riya-ham, リヤハム, 落葉ノ未タ腐敗セザルモノ. *n.* Leaves which have fallen but not rotted.

Riya-ham-ush, リヤハムウシ, エゾユヅリハ. *n.* *Daphniphyllum humile, Maxim.*

Riyamush-punkara, リヤムシプンカラ, ツルマサキ. *n.* *Evonymus japonicus, Th. var radicans Miq.*

Riya-no, リヤノ, 貯ヘタル. *adj.* Stowed away.

Riya-no-ande, リヤノアンデ, 貯ヘル. *v.t.* To store up.

Riyap, リヤプ, 二才熊. *n.* Bear cubs in their second year.

Riya-seshma, リヤセシマ, 五才ノ牡鹿. *n.* A five year old buck.

Ro, ロ, *aux. n.* Sign of the emperative voice.

Roise, ロイセ, 發聲スル. *v.i.* To make a noise with the voice.

Rok, ロク, 坐ル(複數). *v.i.* To sit. *Pl of A.* As:—*Rok an*, "to be sitting." *Rok okai*, "to be sitting." *Rok wa okai*, "they are sitting." *Rok yan*, "sit ye."

Rok, ロク, 此語ハ時トシテ過去ノ自働詞ノ複數チ示スニ用キラル、例セバ、カンロクオカイ、仕上テシマウタ、キロクオカイ、シテシマウタ. *part.* This word is sometimes used as a plural past tense intransitive particle, thus:—*Kan rok okai*, "to be finished." *Ki rok okai*, "to have been done." *Ye rokbe*, "a thing that has been said."

Rokom, ロコム, イルカ. *n.* The dolphin. **Syn: Okom.**

Rokrok, ロクロク, 鳥ノ啼聲(巣ニ附ク前ニ發スル). *n.* The noise a bird makes when about to sit.

Rokrok-ki, ロクロノキ, 啼ク(牝鶴ノ巣ニ附ク前ニ發スル啼聲). *v.i.* To make a noise as a hen when about to sit.

Rokte, ロクテ, 坐ラセル(アレ Are ノ複數). *v.t.* To cause to sit down. *Pl. ed of Are.*

Ronnu, ロンヌ, 殺ス(ライゲ Raige ノ複數). *v.t.* To kill. *Pl. of Raige.*

Ronnupa, ロンヌバ, 殺ス. *v.t.* To kill. *Pl* of the person as well as the object.

Ronronge, ロンロンゲ, or Roronge, ロロンゲ, 痙攣. *n.* A kind of cramp. A twitching of the nerves.

Roram, ロラム, 温順. *adj.* Gentle. **Syn: Noram.**

Roram-no, ロラムノ, 温順ニ. *adv.* Gently.

Roramne, ロラム子, 完ク、健カナル. *adv.* Clear. Entirely. Quite. Healthy. As:—*Roramne kane tereke*, "he jumped clear over." *Roramne an*, "to be in health." **Syn: Irammakaka.**

Roro, ロロ, 爐ノ東側.(即チ上座ナリ). *n.* The head or eastern end of a fireplace. That part of the inside of a hut which lies between the east window and a fireplace. **Syn: Rot. Hoka etok.**

Rorogeta, ロロゲタ, or Roro-keta, ロロクタ, 小屋ノ東ノ外側、又小屋内ノ東北隅即チ主人此處ニ坐シ或ハ寶物チ陳列ス. *adv.* The outside of the east end of a hut. Also the north eastern part of the inside of a hut; the chief and most sacred part of an Ainu hut where the master sits and the treasures are kept.

Roronge, ロロンゲ, or Ronronge, ロンロンゲ, 痙攣. *n.* A kind of cramp. A twitching of the nerves.

Roropa, ロロバ, 入ル. *v.i.* To enter.

Rororogeta-an-guru, ロロロゲタアングル, 亭主、其人. *n.* One's husband. As:—*En rororogeta an guru*, "my husband."

Roroun, ロロウン, 爐ノ上坐ニテ. *adv.* At the head of a fireplace.

Roro-un-puyara, ロロウンブヤラ, 東窓. *n.* The east window. **Syn: Rorun puyara.**

Rorumbe, ロルムベ, 戰爭、哀シミ. *n.* War. Affliction. Sorrow. Distress. **Syn: Tumi.**

Rorumbe-apkash, ロルムベアプカシ, 一列ニナリテ步ム(サラク カムイノ儀式ヲナストキノ如ク). *v.i.* To walk in single file as when performing the ceremony called *Sarak kamui.*

Rorumbe-niwen, ロルムベニウェン, サラクカムイノ儀式. *n.* The ceremony of *Sarak kamui.* **Syn: Niwen horobi.**

Rorun, ロルン, or **Rorui, ロルイ,** 小屋ノ東窓ニ接シタル處. *n.* That part of an Ainu hut nearest to the east window.

Rorun-inumbe, ロルンイヌムベ, 東窓ニ近キ爐端. *n.* That edge of a fireplace nearest the east end window.

Rorun-puyara, ロルンプヤラ, 東窓. *n.* The east window.

Rorun-so, ロルンソ, or **Rorui-so, ロルイソ,** 爐ノ上坐並ニ東窓ニ近キ床. *n.* That part of the floor of an Ainu hut nearest to the head of a fireplace and east window.

Roshki, ロシキ, 建テル(柱ヲ). *v.i.* and *v.t.* To set up (as posts). To stand.

Roshkire, ロシキレ, 建テレ. *v.t.* To set up.

Rosoku, ロソク, 蠟燭. *n.* A candle. (Japanese).

Rot, ロツ, ロヽニ同シ. *n.* The same as :— *Roro.* **Syn: Hoka etok.**

Rotcha, ロッチャ, or **Rotchaot, ロッチャオツ,** 温順ナル、馴レタル. *adj.* Gentle. Tame. Honest.

Rotek, ロテク, 除々ニ、倒レル(木ヲ伐ルトキノ如ク). *v.i.* To fall slowly as a tree when cut down.

Rotta, ロッタ, 前面ニ、例セバ、チセ イロツタ、家ノ前ニ. *adv.* In front. Before. As :— *Chisei rotta,* " in front of the house." **Syn: Rupshi, Erupshita.**

Rottek, ロッテク, 精力盡ル. *adj.* and *v.i.* Exhausted. To drop down through exhaustion. To tumble down as a house. **Syn: Rotek. Yottek.**

Ru, ル, 道路、線、例セバ、ルチュブカ 道路ノ東側. *n.* A way. A path. A line. Road. As :— *Ru chup ka,* " the east side of a road." *Ru chup pok,* " the west side of a road." *Ru hontomta,* " in the road." " Upon the road."

Ru, ル, 凍氷(コンレト義相同シ). *n.* Ice. **Syn: Konru.**

Ru, ル, 融ル、溶ル、碎ケル. *v.i.* To melt. To crumble.

Ru, ル, 毒. *n.* Poison.

Ru, ル, 半分、一部分. *adj.* Half. Partly.

Ru, ル, 雪隱. *n.* A water-closet.

Ruashpa-guru, ルアシパグル, 蛇ノ 一種. *n.* A kind of snake.

Ru-aturainu, ルアツライヌ, 迷フ. *adv.* Astray.

Ruchi, ルチ, 半熟. *adj.* Half cooked. Under cooked. **Syn: Rufu.**

Ruchikaye, ルチカイェ, 峠. *n.* A mountain pass. **Syn: Ruchish.**

Ruchire, ルチレ, 半熟ニスル. *v.t.* To partly cook. **Syn: Aruchire.**

Ruchish, ルチシ, 峠、道、羊腸(ナヽマガ リ). *n.* A mountain pass. A

path. A crooked or winding path. **Syn: Ruchikaye.**

Ruchish-koro, ルチシコロ, 山ヲ踰エテ旅行スル. *v.i.* To take a journey across the mountain.

Ruchup, ルチュプ, 一月. *n.* January.

Rue, ルエ, 遑キ、大キイ. *adj.* Thick. Large.

Rue-kankan, ルエカンカン, 大腸. *n.* The large intestines.

Rue-rit, ルエリツ, 足腱. *n.* The large tendons of the feet.

Rue-san, ルエサン, 水汲場. *n.* A place where one draws water. **Syn: Petaru.**

Rue-shutu-inao, ルエシュツイナオ, イナオノ一種 (疫癘ヲ祓フニ用ユ). *n.* Peculiar kinds of inao made of elder and *chikapeni* (i.e. cladrastis) and used as charms against disease. **Syn: Chikappo. Chikomesup.**

Ru-etok, ルエトク, 先頭ニ. *adv.* Ahead. On in front.

Rue-tui, ルエツイ, 大腸. *n.* The large intestines.

Ru-eukopi, ルエウコピ, 數條ノ道路ノ交叉點. *n.* A place where several paths or trails meet.

Ru'u, ルフ, or **Ruhe, ルヘ,** 牛熟. *adv.* Half cooked. Soft-boiled (as eggs).

Ruhe, ルヘ, 跡. *n.* A footprint.

Ru-homakashi, ルホマカシ, 道ノ左側. *adv.* The left hand side of a road or path.

Ru-hotke, ルホッケ, 牛眠. (ウツヽ). *v.i.* To be half asleep.

Rukumi, ルクミ, 一部分、一片. *n.* A piece. A part.

Rui, ルイ, 黑甲蟲. *n.* A black-beetle.

Rui, ルイ, 砥石. *n.* A whetstone. A grindstone.

Rui, ルイ, 燃ル、吹ク、降ル、(雨ノ如ク)、例セバ、アベルイ、レラルイ、アプトルイ、火ガ燃ル、風ガ吹ク、雨ガ降ル. *v.i.* To burn. To blow. To come down as rain. As:— *Abe rui, rera rui, apto rui,* "the fire burns, the wind blows, and it is raining."

Rui, ルイ, 大ナル、高價ナル. *adj.* Great. Expensive. Loud. Large. Rough. Coarse. As:—*Aya rui ni,* "coarse grained wood."

Ru-ibe, ルイベ, 雪中ニ氷凍セシ魚. *n.* Fish which has been caught in the winter and hung in the air.

Ruibe, ルイベ, 甚ダ、烈シキ、此語ハ屢々語意ヲ強ムル爲ニ動詞ニ附加セラル. *adj. and adv.* Very. Severe. Very much. Severely. This word is often used as a suffix to verbs to indicate intensity or severity. As:—*Oripak ruibe sone gusu,* "for she was exceedingly polite or respectful."

Ruibe, ルイベ, 凍死スル. *v.i.* To freeze to death. **Syn: Me-ekot. Rupushrai.**

Ruige, ルイゲ, 磨ク、刃ヲ付ケル. *v.t.* To sharpen. To grind on a grindstone.

Ruika, ルイカ, 橋. *n.* A bridge. As:—*Ruika ka kush,* "to cross over a bridge."

Ruika, ルイカ, 燃ヤス (吹イテ). *v.i.* To make burn. To blow into a flame.

Rui-no, ルイノ, 大イニ、高聲ニ. *adv.* Greatly. Much. Loudly.

Rui-no-hauge-no, ルイノハウゲノ, 高聲ニ又低聲. *adv.* Loudly and softly.

Rui-rute, ルイルテ, 握手スル. *v.i.* To shake hands.

Ruituye, ルイツイエ, or **Ru-tuye, ルツイエ,** 撫デル. *v.t.* To stroke.

Rui-yupke, ルイユプケ, 最モ力強ク. *adv.* Very strongly or powerfully. As:—*Rui no yupke kishima,* "hold it very tightly."

Ruka, ルカ, 橋. *n.* A bridge.

Rukane, ルカ子, 有毒ナル. *adj.* Poisonous. As:—*Rukane wakka,* "poisonous water."

Ru-kari, ルカリ, 小便スル(女子ニノミ用ユ). *v.i.* To make water (used only of women). **Syn: Hangea.**

Ruki, ルキ, 嚥下スレ. *v.t.* To swallow. **Syn: Hamneruki.**

Ru-ko, ルコ, 綺麗ニ. *adv.* Beautifully. Prettily.

Ru-kopi, ルコピ, or **Ru-eukopi, ルエウコピ,** 數條ノ道ノ交叉點. *n.* A place where several paths meet.

Ru-koro-kamui, ルコロカムイ, 雪隱ノ神. *n.* The demons of watercloosets.

Rukot, ルコツ, 逕. コミチ. *n.* A foot path.

Rukotchi, ルコッチ, 足跡. *n.* A footprint. A trail. **Syn: Ru-yehe.**

Rum, ルム, 矢ノ根. *n.* An arrow head.

Rumaibe, ルマイベ, ハコトコ. *n.* *Agrammus agrammus (Schleigel).*

Rumne-top, ルム子トプ, ネマガリザサ. *n.* A kind of bamboo. *Sasa paniculata, Mak. et Shib.*

Ru-mokoro, ルモコロ, 牛眠(ウツイ). *v.i.* To be half asleep.

Runne-shu, ルン子シュ, 汁鍋. *n.* A soup kettle or saucepan.

Runne-shu-kara, ルン子シュカラ, 食物ヲ煮ル. *v.t.* To prepare food.

Runnu, ルンヌ, 鹽ノ. *adj* Salt. Salty. Salty. As:—*Runnu wakka,* "salt water."

Runnu-shippo, ルンヌシツポ, 強鹽. *n.* Powerful salt.

Ru-o-ashpa-guru, ルオアシパグル, or **Ru-ashpa-guru, ルアシパグル,** 蛇ノ一種. *n.* A kind of snake.

Ru-ohariki-sam, ルオハリキサム, 道ノ左側. *n.* The left hand side of a road. **Syn: Ru-homaka-shi.**

Ru-okake, ルオカケ, 相續. *v.t.* To inherit. **Syn: Ikeshkoro.**

Ru-okopi, ルオコピ, 二條ノ道ノ交叉點. *n.* A place where two roads meet.

Ruop, ルオプ, シマネヅミ. *n.* A ground squirrel. Tamias asiaticus, Pall.

Ru-o-sei, ルオセイ, バカガイ、ハバノテ. *n.* Any kind of shell fish with either radiating ribs or concentrically striated.

Ru-oshimon-sam, ルオシモンサム, 道ノ右側. *n.* The right hand side of the road.

Ru-oyake, ルオヤケ, 道端. *adv.* The side of a road.

Rup, ルプ, 黟多ナル. adj. Very many. As:—*Chikap rup, chep rup,* "very many birds and fish." **Syn : Rupi.**

Rupeshpe, ルペシペ, 小山ノ峯、渓流、又小粒岩石. n. A rill. A small water-course running down a steep place. By some, broken up rock and gravel.

Ru-pishkan, ルピシカン, 道ノ兩側. av. On both sides of a road.

Rupne, ルプ子, 高層ナル、大ナル、成長シタル. adj. Bulky. Large. Adult. Full grown. As:—*Rupne ainu,* "a full grown man."

Rupne-chimat, ルプ子チマツ, 老媼. n. An old woman.

Rupne-guru, ルプ子グル, 成生シタル者. n. An adult.

Rupne-koro, ルプ子コロ, 成長シタル. adj. Full grown.

Rupne-no, ルプ子ノ, 高層ニ. adv. Bulkily.

Rupne-pakno-arikiki, ルプ子パクノアリキキ, 成年ニ達スル迄養育スル. v.t. To bring up until full grown.

Rupne-shiwentep, ルプ子シウェンテプ, 女. n. A woman.

Ruppa, ルッパ, 呑ム. v.t. To swallow. As:—*Hamne no ruppa,* "to swallow whole."

Ruprupse kiripu, ルプルプセキリプ, 脂肪ノ片. n. Lumps of fat.

Rupshi, ルプシ, 前面. adv. The front. Before. As:—*Chisei rupshi,* "in front of the house." **Syn: Rotta.**

Rupush, ルプシ, 水結スル. v.i. To freeze. To be frozen.

Rupushka, ルプシカ, 水結スル. v.t. To freeze.

Rupush-ka-rai, ルプシカライ, 凍死スル. v.i. To be frozen to death. **Syn : Me ekot.**

Rura, ルラ, 借用物ヲ返ヘス、見逆ル. v.t. To return anything that has been borrowed. To see one off on a journey.

Rura, ルラ, 舟積ミスル. v.t. To load a boat. As:—*Chip rura,* "to load a boat."

Ru-rai, ルライ, 牛死. adj. Half dead.

Rure, ルレ, 溶カス. v.t. To melt.

Rurirui, ルリルイ, 我儘、吝嗇. adj. Selfish. Stingy. **Syn : Ibe unara. Epyupke.**

Rurirui-yupke, ルリルイユプケ, 甚ダ我儘或ハ吝嗇ナル. adj. Very selfish or stingy.

Ruru, ルル, 海、鹹. n. The sea. Salt. The ocean.

Ruru, ルル, 野菜又ハ肉ヲ入レザル汁. n. Clear soup. Gravy.

Ruru-o-epaketa, ルルオエパケタ, 波止場. n. A landing place.

Rurukka, ルルッカ, カズナキノ一種(方言). n. A kind of blenny. *Ernogrammus hexagrammus (Schlegel).*

Rurumbe, ルルムベ, or **Rorumbe, ロルムベ, 溺死スル.** n. An accidental death by drowning. **Syn: Yupkep,**

Ruru-omap, ルルオマプ, 鹹(シホカラ)キ. adj. Brackish.

Ruru-sak-keutum-koro-guru, ルルサッケウツムコログル, 愚人、馬鹿者. n. A fool. A stupid person.

Rnrupish, ルルピシ, 砂利、小石. n. Shingles. Pebbles.

Ruru-sam, ルルサム, 海濱. *n.* The sea side.

Ruru-samta, ルルサムタ, 海邊ニテ. *adv.* By the sea side.

Ruru-seppa, ルルセッバ, ハスノハカイ. *n.* A sand cake, *Clypeaster.* **Syn : Atui-seppa.**

Rurushpe, ルルシペ, 杭. *n.* A stake.

Ruru-unkotuk, ルルウンコツク, 琥珀. *n.* Amber.

Ruru-wakka, ルルワッカ, 鹹水、海水. *n.* Salt water. Sea-water.

Rusak, ルサク, or **Ruru-sak, ルルサク,** 愚カナル. *adj.* Stupid. Silly. As :—*Ru-sak keutum koro guru,* "a stupid fellow."

Rush, ルシ, 獸皮. *n.* The skins of animals.

Rushka, ルシカ, 怒ル. *adv.* Angry. As : — *Rushka itak,* "angry words."

Rushka, ルシカ, 怒ル、腹立テル. *v.t.* To be angry with. Not to like. To fall in to a rage. As :—*Ibe ka rushka,* "not to like to eat."

Rushtara, ルシタラ, 荷ヲ背負フトキニ用ユル紐. *n.* A thong with a leather headpiece used for carrying bundles.

Rusui, ルスイ, 欲スレ. *v.t.* To desire. To wish for.

Rutke, ルツケ, 崩レル(山ナドガ)、喧嘩スル. *v.i.* To slip (as land). To quarrel. To rush out as mud from a volcano. As :—*Nupuri orowa no shinrutke,* "the land has slipped from the mountain." **Syn : Charange.**

Rutke, ルツケ, 他ノ喧嘩ヲ引受ケル. *v.i.* To take up the cause of another.

Rutke-guru, ルツケグル, 喧嘩ヲ引受ケル人. *n.* An advocate in a bad sense.

Rutke-i, ルツケイ, 山崩レ. *n.* A land slip. **Syn : Soshke-i.**

Rutom, ルトム, 履キ物ヲ脱グ場處. *n.* The bare space left just inside a floored hut upon which to leave one's foot gear when entering. **Syn : Aun mindara.**

Ru-turainu, ルツライヌ, 途ニ迷フ. *v.i.* To lose one's way.

Rutuye, ルツイェ, 撫デル. *v.t.* To stroke. **Syn : Ru-ituye.**

Ru-umbe, ルウムベ, or **Tu-umbe, ツウムベ,** 刺繍シタル衣服. *n.* A fancy needlework dress.

Ru-utomoshma-i, ルウトモシマイ, 横逕. *n.* Cross roads. **Syn : Ru-ukoopi-hi.**

Ruwe, ルウェ, 然リ. *adv.* Yes. It is. So. *Ruwe* is sometimes used after a person has been speaking as a kind of doubtful affirmative particle. Thus :—*Ruwe ?* "is it so" ? **Syn : A. E. Ruwe ne. Ruwe ne wa. Opunki.**

Ruwe, ルウェ, 此語ハ屢々動詞ノ意義ヲ確定スル爲ニ用キラルネ (ne) 又ハタプアンナ (tapanna) ノ語ヲ附加ス、例セバ、アイヌネルウェヲ、彼ハ人ナリ. *part.* This word is often used as an affirmative ending to verbs, and is usually followed by *ne* or *tap an na.* After nouns *ruwe* is preceded by *ne.* As :—*Ainu ne ruwe ne,* "it is a man."

**Ruwe-shomo he an, ルウェショモヘ
アン,** 左ニ非サルカ. *ph.* Is it not
so ?

Ruwe-un, ルウェウン, 然リ. *adv.* Yes.

Ruyambe, ルヤムベ, 海ノ波、小雨. *n.*
Waves of the sea. Fine rain.
Rain.

Ruyambe-an, ルヤムベアン, 雨天. *n.*
Bad weather. (Principally so
used by the Ainu who inhabit
the Saru district).

Ruyambe-rui, ルヤムベルイ, 雨降ル、
小雨降ル. *v.i.* To rain. To rain
fine mist.

Ruye, ルイェ, 太キ、例セバ、ルイェツシ、

太キ縄. *adj.* Thick. As :—*Ruye
tush,* "a thick rope." *Ruye chikuni,* "a thick tree."

Ruye, ルイェ, 擦ル. *v.t.* To rub. To
stroke the hands (as in salutation).

Ruye-ashikepet, ルイェアシケベツ,
拇. *n.* The thumbs.

Ruyehe, ルイェヘ, or **Ruwe, ルウェ,**
線、跡. *n.* A line. A footprint.
Syn : Ruwehe.

Ruyeruye, ルイェルイェ, 撫デル(他ノ頭
ヲ). *v.t.* To stroke the head of
another as in affection and salutation.

S (サ).

Sa, サ, 前ニ、近クニ. *adv.* In front
of. At hand.

Sa, サ, 擴がル、開ケタル、平地. *v.i.*
Spread out. Open. Exposed.
Also a noun meaning "plain."

Sa, サ, or **Saha, サハ,** 姉. *n.* An
elder sister. **Syn : Sapo.**

Saha, サハ, 平野. *n.* A plain.

Sai, サイ, or **Saye, サイェ,** 島ノ飛行. *n.*
A flight of birds.

Saikonoye, サイコノイェ, 捲キ付ケル.
v.t. To wind round.

Saimon, サイモン, 瞽探ニヨル審問. *n.*
Trial by ordeal.

Saimon-epirika, サイモンエピリカ,
瞽探ヲ以ツテ赦サレ. *v.i.* To be acquitted by trial by ordeal.

Saimon-ewen, サイモンエウェン, 瞽探

ヲ以ツテ罪セラレ. *v.i.* To be condemned by trial by ordeal.

Saimon-ki, サイモンキ, 瞽探ヲ以ツテ
審問セラレ. *v.i.* To be tried by
ordeal.

Saimon-kire, サイモンキレ, 瞽探ヲ以
テ裁ク. *v.t.* To try by ordeal.

Saipake, サイバケ, 先ニナツテ飛ブ鳥.
n. The leader in a large flight
of birds.

Saiturashte, サイツラシテ, 継アル(衣
ノ上ニアルガ如シ). *v.i.* To have
upon a garment as an ornament.

Sak, サク, 夏. *n.* Summer.

Sak, サク, or **Sak-no, サクノ,** 無シニ
例セバ、オトブサク、禿頭. *adv.*
Without. Not having. This

word is often used with nouns to help form negative adjectives. As:— *Otop sak*, " bald."

Sakange, サカンゲ, 牛ハ料理シタルチ日ニ乾シ〻ル. *adj*. Partially cooked and then sun dried.

Sakanram, サカンラム, 喧嘩好ノ性質. *n*. A quarrelsome disposition. **Syn : Nukoshne.**

Sakanram-koro, サカンラムコロ, 喧嘩好ノ. *adj*. Quarrelsome.

Sakanram-koro-guru, サカンラムコログル, 喧嘩好ノ人. *n*. A quarrelsome person.

Sakayo, サカヨ, 喧騒、喧嘩. *n*. An uproar. A quarrel.

Sakayo-kara, サカヨカラ, 騒グ. *v.i.* To make a disturbance. To quarrel.

Sake, サケ, 酒. *n*. Rice beer.

Sake-hau, サケハウ, 酒宴ノ騒音. *n*. The sound of people drinking. Bacchanalian songs.

Sake-hauki, サケハウキ, 酒飲ノ歌ヲ謡フ. *v.i.* To sing the song of drunkards.

Sak-hosh, サクホシ, 草製ノ夏脚胖. *n*. Summer leggings made of grass.

Sak-ibe, サクイベ, 春又ハ夏ノ鮭. *n*. Spring or summer salmon.

Sakiri, サキリ, 木串、塀、竿. *n*. A wooden spit for holding food. A fence. A rail.

Sakkai, サッカイ, 箸. *n*. Chop-sticks. **Syn : Ibe-bashui.**

Sakma, サクマ, 木柵、竿. *n*. A wooden rail. A bar.

Sakne, サク子, 昨、例セバ、サク子チュプ、先月. *adv*. Last. The previous. As:—*Sakne chup*, " last

month." *Sakne pa*, " last year."

Sak-no, サクノ, 無シニ. *adv*. Without. Not having.

Sak-noshike, サクノシケ, 仲夏. *n*. Midsummer.

Sak-pa, サクパ, 夏. *n*. Summer time. Summer.

Sak-un-pa, サクウンパ, 夏. *n*. Summer.

Sakuri, サクリ, 土堤. *n*. An embankment. **Syn : Toi-chashi.**

Sakusa, サクサ, 香. *n*. Smell. Scent.

Sam, サム, or **Sama, サマ**, or **Samake, サマケ**, or **Samaba, サマバ**, 側ニ. *adv*. By the side of anything. Near to. Besides.

Sama, サマ, 横ハル. *v. i.* To lie along. To lie stretched out.

Samai-moshiri, サマイモシリ, 日本. *n*. Japan. **Syn : Samoro moshiri.**

Samai-un-guru, サマイウングル, 日本人. *n*. A Japanese. **Syn : Samoro un guru.**

Samake, サマケ, 側ニ. *adv*. By the side of. Adjacent. As:—*Samake kush*, " to pass close by."

Samakeketa, サマケケタ, 側ニ. *adv*. By the side of.

Samaketa, サマケタ, 側ニ、又. *adv*. By the side of. Again. Besides this.

Samambe, サマムベ, カレイ類ノ總稱. *n*. Any kind of flat fishes.

Samambe, サマムベ, 陰門ノ俗稱. *n*. A slang word for the vagina.

Samamni, サマムニ. or **Samau-ni, サマウニ**, 朽木、洪水ニ流サレ海岸ニ打上ゲラレテ朽チシ木. *n*. Rotten wood. Wood which has floated

down a river during a flood and
been cast upon the sea shore to rot.

Samata, サマタ, 又、其他、側. *adv.*
Again. Besides this. By the side
of.

Samatki-itak, サマッキイタク, 早言、
ハヤゴト、痴言. *n.* Hasty words.
Foolish words. **Syn : Oheuge
itak.**

**Samatki-keutum-koro, サマッキケ
ウツムコロ,** 短気ナル、愚ナル. *adj.*
Easily angered. Foolish.

Samatki-no, サマッキノ, 横様ニ、例セ
ズ、サマツキノアブカシ、横様ニ歩ム
adv. Sidewise. As :—*Samatki no
apkash,* "to walk sidewise."

Sama-un, サマウン, 側ニ. *adv.* At
the side of.

Samau-ni, サマウニ, 朽木. *n.* Rotten wood. See *Samamni.*

Samba, サムバ, ノ如ク. *adj.* Like.

Samba, サムバ, サメ. *n.* Mackerel.
Scomber colias, Gmelin. (*Jap.*)

Samba, サムバ, 側. *n.* Side. The
side of anything. As :—*Ine samba,* "four sided" or "square."

Sambas, サムバス, or **Sambash, サ
ムバシ,** 大又ヘ狐ノ如ク走ル. *v.i.* To
canter. To run as a dog or fox.
Syn : Chaira. Mopash.

Sambe, サムベ, 心臓、脈膊、神経. *n.*
The heart. The pulse. Nerves.

Sambe-aotke, サムベアオッケ, 其心ニ
責メラル. *v.i.* and *adj.* To be
conscience struck.

Sambe-chinoiba, サムベチノイバ, 空
腹ヲ感スル. *v.i.* and *adj.* To be
hungry.

Sambe-etara, サムベエタラ, 其心ニ
責メラレ. *v. i.* To be conscience
stricken.

Sambe-hauge, サムベハウゲ, 親切ナ
ル. *adj.* Kind.

Sambe-horaraise, サムベホララライセ,
晴朗ナル、心穏ニ惑スレ. *v.i.* and *adj.*
To be serene. To be calm and
unpurturbed in mind. To be
restful and quiet. To feel safe
and happy.

Sambe-horipiripi, ホムベホリピリピ,
動悸. *n.* Palpitation of the heart.

Sambe-kokuruse, サムベコクルセ, 混
迷スル. *v.i.* and *adj.* To be confounded. Purturbed in mind.
To be in fear and suspense. **Syn :
Kimatek.**

Sambe-kurukush, サムベクルクシ, 神
経痙攣. *n.* A twitching of the
nerves.

**Sambe-murumruse, サムベムルムル
セ,** 動悸. *n.* Palpitation of the
heart.

Sambe-muruse, サムベムルセ, 愈悪
シクナル、(病ノ). *v.i.* To grow worse
as in sickness.

Sambe-nishkut, サムベニシクツ, 血
管. *n.* A blood vessel.

Sambe-nishte, サムベニシテ, 無慘ナ
ル. *adj.* Hard hearted.

Sambe-oikereke, サムベオイケレケ,
其心ニ責メラル. *v.i.* To be conscience stricken.

Sambe-otke, サムベオッケ, 押シ當ル
(心ニ). *v.i.* To touch one's heart.

Sambe-rikoshma, サムベリコシマ, 吐
氣ヲ催ス. *v.i.* To retch.

Sambe-shipirasa, サムベシピラサ, 親
切ナル、親切ニスル. *adj.* and *v.i.*
To be generous and kind.

Sambe-shituri, サムベシツリ, 清涼ナ
ル心地スル、爽快ヲ感スル. *v.i.*

To feel better in health. To be glad. To feel refreshed.

Sambe-takne, サムベタク子, 短氣ナ ル. *adj.* Irritable. Quick tempered. **Syn : Nukoshne.**

Sambe-tokse, ザムベトクセ, 心臓ノ皷 動、又ハ脈膊. *n.* The beating of the pulse.

Sambe-tokse-tokse, サムベトクセト クセ, or **Sambe-toktok, サムベトク トク,** 心臓ノ皷動又ハ脈膊. *n.* The beating of the heart or pulse.

Sambe-toranne, サムベトラン子, 癲 癇ヲ起ス. *v.i.* To be seized with epilepsy.

Sambe-tuitui, サムベツイツイ, 斷腸 ノ思スレ. *v. i.* To be cut to the heart.

Sambe-yukram, サムベユクラム, 肺. The lungs. **Syn : Yukram.**

Same, サメ, サメ. *n.* A shark. (Japanese).

Same-tuntun, サメツンツン, サメノ 胎兒. *n.* Embryo of shark.

Samoro-moshiri, サモロモシリ, 日 本. *n.* Japan. **Syn : Samai moshiri. Shamoro moshiri.**

Samoro-un-guru, サモロウングル, 日 本人. *n.* A Japanese. **Syn : Samai un guru.**

Samoro-uimam, ザモロウイマム, 敬 禮スレ(昔松前ノ領主ニアイヌが爲セ シ如ク). *v.i.* To pay respects to the Japanese as the Ainu used to do in ancient times to the Governor of Matsumai.

Samta, サムタ, 側ニ、近ク. *adv.* By the side of. Near to. **Syn : Samata.**

San, サン, 下 ル. *v.i.* To descend. To flow along as a river. To go down.

San, サン, 下リ、坂. *n.* A descent. A slope. *Pl. Sap.*

San-assange, サンアスサンゲ, 取リ下 ス. *v.t.* To take down. **Syn : Sa-ta sange.**

Sanekop, サ子コブ, 脂鰭. *n.* Adipose fin.

Sange, サンゲ, 下ス、引證スル. *v. t.* To send down. To adduce. *Pl. Sapte.*

Sange-amunin, サンゲアムニ ン, 腕 ノ下部. *n.* The lower part of the arm.

Sange-apa, サンゲアパ, 陰門ノ入口、 子宮. *n.* The entrance of the vagina. The womb. **Syn : Po-pukuru. Makun-apa. Po-apa.**

Sanike, サニケ, 子孫. *n.* Descendants.

Santa, サンタ, or **Santa-moshiri, サンタモシリ,** or **Santan, サンタン,** 満洲. *n.* The Ainu name for Manchuria.

Sanikiri, サニキリ, 子孫. *n.* Descendants.

San-ita, サンイタ, 甲板. *n.* The deck of a ship.

San-itak, サンイタク, 命令、宣言. *n.* An order. A word handed down. A message from a superior to an inferior. A proclamation.

San-kararip, サンカラリブ, 第二番目 ノ雪. *n.* The second snow. See *Toruru-kararip.*

San-mitpo, サンミツポ, 曾孫、ヒマゴ. *n.* A great grandchild.

Sannakoro, サンナコロ, 鯨ノ尾. *n.* A whale's tail. **Sarakanda.**

San-ne, サンチ, 傾斜セル. *adj.*
Sloping. As :—*Sanne nupuri,* or
san-ne shitu, " a sloping mountain."

Sanniyo, サンニヨ, 決心スル. *v.t.*
To think that. To determine.
To consider. To add up.

San-notkeu, サンノツケウ, 頤. *n.*
The jaws.

**San-notkeu-ka-karari-guru, サンノ
ツケウカカラリグル,** 枕. *n.* A pillow.

San-o-butu, サンオブツ, 河口. *n.*
The mouth of a river. As :—
San-obutu oroge, "to be at a river's
mouth."

San-ota, サンオタ, 砂濱. *n.* A
sandy sea shore.

Sanru, サンル, 下ル. *v.i.* To descend. Descending.

Sanru-konna, サンルコンナ, サンル
ノ可成法、例セバ、ヒリカポンペツサ
ンルコンナマクナタラ、美ナル川ノ流
下ルノガ見エシ. *v. i.* Poetical
form of the above. As :—*Pirika
pon pet sanru-konna maknatara,*
" a beautiful stream was seen to
run down."

Santa-guru, サンタグル, 滿洲人. *n.*
A Manchurian.

Santek, サンテク, 子孫. *n.* Posterity. Descendants. **Syn : Sanikiri. Sanike.**

Santeke, サンテケ, 腕ノ全體. *n.*
The whole of the arm.

Saot, サオツ, 走セ去ル. *v.i.* To run
away.

Saotte, サオッテ, 走セ去ラスル. *v.t.*
To make run away.

Sap, サブ, 下ル. *v.i.* To go down.
To descend. *Pl. of san.*

Sap, ザブ, 無シ、例セバ、ワヤサブ、無
智ナル. *adj.* Without. As :—
Waya-sap, " unwise." (Lit. " without wisdom). **Syn : Sak.**

Sapa, サバ, or **Sapaha, サパハ,** 頭.
The head. As :—*Sapa araka,*
" headache." *Sapa eshirotke,* " to
fall on one's head." *Sapa kankitai,*
" the crown of the head." *Sapa
kara,* " to tidy the head," " to
cut or comb the hair." *Sapa karakara,* "to comb the hair." *Sapa
ruyeruye,* "to stroke one's head
by way of salutation." *Sapa
shuyeshuye,* " to shake the head."
See also *pake* and *pa.*

Sapa-anuye, ザバアヌイェ, 署名スル.
v.i. To be enrolled. To have
one's name written down.

Sapa-kapke, サバカブケ, カザカノ一
種. *n.* A kind of scupin.

Sapane, サバ子, 統率スル、君臨スル.
v. t. To govern. To rule. To
be head.

Sapane-an, サバ子アン, 勝 (マサ) ル.
v.i. To be superior.

Sapane-an-guru, ザバ子アングル, or
Sapane-guru, サバ子グル, 優者、長
上、酋長、司令者. *n.* A superior.
Headman. Chief. Commander.

Sapa-num, サバヌム, 頭ノ頂、頭蓋骨.
n. The top of the head. The
cranium.

Sapa-shina-ambe, ザバシナアムベ, 頭
布 (ヅキン). *n.* A head cloth. A
cloth worn round the head. **Syn :
Matamboshi.**

Sapa-unbe, サバウンベ, 冠、帽子、
轡、オモガイ. *n.* A crown. A
bridle. A hat or cap.

Sapa-un-guru, ザパウングル, 酋長. *n.* A chief. A headman.

Sapke, サブケ, 加減チキク. *v. t.* To try the taste or flavour of any-thing.

Sapke-nu, サブケヌ, 味フ. *v. t.* To taste.

Sapo, サポ, 姉. *n.* A elder sister.

Sapte-wa-ingara, サプテワインガラ, 味フ. *v.t.* To taste.

Sapsap, サブサブ, 一人宛降ル. *v.i.* To come one after another.

Sapse, サブセ, チ笑フ. *v.t.* To laugh at.

Sapte, サブテ, 下ロス. *v.t.* To send down. To cause to descend. *Pl. of sange.*

Sapte, サブテ, 産ム. *v. t.* To give birth to. *Pl. Usapte.*

Sap-wa-ariki, サブワアリキ, 下ル(複数). *v.i.* To come down. *Pl.*.

Sara, サラ, or Saraha, サラハ, 鹿ト熊トノモノヲ除キ一般獣ノ類ノ尾. *n.* The tail of any kind of ani-mal with the exception of that of the deer or bear. A bear's or deer's tail is properly called *okishka,* though *sara* or *saraha* is some-times applied to them.

Sara, サラ, 原野、(莎草ノ生エタル). *n.* A plain covered with a kind of sedge.

Sara, サラ, 開クル、擴ガル. *v.i.* To be open. Spread out. **Syn : Sa-ra wa an.**

Sarageseta, サラゲセタ, 端ニ於テ. *adv.* At the end.

Saragesh, サラゲシ, 最下端、又最後. *n.* The very lowest or hindmost.

Saraha, サラ ハ, 尾. *n.* A tail. See *sara.*

Sarak, サラク, 變死. *n.* An ac-cidental death.

Sarakene-ni, サラケ子ニ, ハンノキ. *n. Alder. Alnus japonica, S. et Z.*

Saraki, サラキ, ヨシ. *n.* Rushes. *Phragmites communis, Trin.*

Sarakka, サラッカ, 震ハス. *v.t.* To cause tremble to.

Sarak-kamui, サラッカムイ, 異變ノ神. *n.* The god or demon of ac-cidents.

Sarakkata, サラッカタ, 憐ミノ叫. *interj.* An exclamation of pity.

Sarakanda, サラカンダ, 鯨ノ尾. *n.* A whale's tail. **Syn : Sanna-koro.**

Sarakop, サラコブ, 脂鰭. *n.* Adipose fin of salmon.

Sara-kushbe, サラクシベ, 鞦、シリガイ. *n.* A crupper. **Syn : Op-asam-i.**

Sarama, サラマ, 擇ブ. *v.t.* To choose. **Syn : Numge.**

Sarambe, サラムベ, 柔キ衣、柔キ地(衣類ナド). *n.* Soft clothing. Soft material.

Sarambe-tat-ni, サラムベタツニ, タケカンバ. *n.* A kind of birch. *Betula Ermani Cham.*

Sarampa, サラムバ, サラバ、左樣ナラ(長キ旅ノ別レノ時ニ用ユ). *excl.* Goodbye. Adieu. Used only when going on a long journey.

Saranip, サラニブ, 籠. *n.* A basket.

Sarapoki, サラポキ, スナガレイ. *n. Limanda sp.*

Sarare, サラレ, 開ク、白狀スル. *v.t.*
To open. To confess. To lay
bare. As:— *Wen buri sarare,* "to
confess one's faults."

Sara-ush, サラウシ, 尾ノアル. *adj.*
Having a tail.

Sar'ush, サルウシ, or **Saro, サロ,** 猿.
n. A monkey.

Sarorun-chikap, サロルンチカプ, 鶴.
n. The crane.

Sar'ush, サ ル ウ シ, 尾ノアル. *n.*
The same as *sara-ush,* "having
a tail."

Sarawatore, サラワトレ, 片付ケル.
v.i. See *Charuwatore,* "to put
in order."

Sash, サシ, 海草ノ類. *n.* A kind of
seaweed.

Sash, サシ, or **Sas, サス,** 蛭(ヒル). *n.*
A leech.

Sash, サシ, 轟ク音、沙々タル音.
n. A low heavy sound. A
rumbling noise. A rustling sound.
A roar. As:—*Ni sash humi ash
newa ruyambe sash humi ash,* "the
rustling sound of the trees and
the roaring of the waves."

Sashnu, サシヌ, 反響スル、沙々ト鳴ル.
v.i. To resound. To rustle.

Sashnu-sashnu, サシヌサシヌ, 反響
スル、沙々ト鳴ル. *v.i.* To resound.
To rustle.

Sat, サツ, 乾ケル. *adj.* Dry. Arid.
Dried.

Sata, サタ, 此處ニ. *adv.* Here. As:
—*Sata ande,* "put it here." *Sata san,* "come here."

Sat-chep, サッチェプ, 乾魚. *n.* Dried
fish. There are various names

given to dried fish according to
the manner in which they are
prepared. Thus:—*Chinana chep,*
are fish with only their entrails
taken out and then dried whole.
Nikerui chep, are fish with their
heads cut off, split down the middle as far as the tail, the backbone taken out, and then dried
in the sun without being salted.
Kerenop chep, are fish with their
heads cut off, their backbone
taken out, and then dried in the
sun; these fish are not divided
in the middle. It is of the skins
of fish thus prepared that the
Ainu make their boots. *Atat chep*
are fish cut up into pieces and
dried in the sun.

Satchiri, サツチリ, ヤマセミ. *n.* Spotted kingfisher. *Ceryle guttata,*
(*Vigors*). **Syn: Ainu satchiri.**

Satka-i, サツカイ, 砂溜、スナダマリ.
n. A sand bank. A spit of
sand or dry earth.

Sat-kam, サツカム, 乾魚. *n.* Dried
flesh.

Satke, サツケ, 乾ス. *v.i.* To dry.
To air. **Syn: Satte.**

Sat-kepa, サツケパ, 乾ス. *v.t.* To
dry.

Sat-kuruki, サツクルキ, 呃逆スル、シ
ヤクリスル. *v.i.* To have hiccups.

Satpe, サツペ, 肺病. *n.* Consump-
tion.

Satpe-koro, サツペコロ, 肺病ヲ患フ.
v.i. To be afflicted with consump-
tion.

Sat-ruyambe, サツルヤムベ, 暴風. *v.i.*
A storm of wind.

Satsatge, サツサツゲ, 乾ケル. *adj.* and *v.i.* Dry. Parched.

Sat-shuke, サツシュケ, 蒸ス. *v.t.* To cook by steaming.

Satte, サツテ, 乾カス. *v.t.* To dry. To air. **Syn: Satke.**

Sattek, サツテク, 瘠セタル、凋メル. *adj.* Thin. Lean. Withered. Dried. Dried up. As:— *Sattek chep,* "dried fish." *Sattek kam,* "dried meat."

Sattumam, サンマム, 身體. *n.* The body. **Syn: Netobake.**

Saune, サウネ, or **Saunu,** サウヌ, 柔キ. *adj.* Soft. **Syn: Hapuru.**

Saure, サウレ, 輕少ノ、緩キ. *adj.* Trifling. Insignificant. Loose.

Saurere, サウレレ, 輕視スレ、赦免スル、許ス、緩ムル. *v.t.* To treat as a mere trifle. To pardon. To absolve. To loosen. To allow.

Sausauge, サウサウゲ, 緩キ (釘ノュルキガ如ク). *adj.* Loose (as a nail in its hole). **Syn: Osausauge.**

Sa-wa-an-atui, サワアンアツイ, 南海. *n.* The southern sea.

Saya, サヤ, 鞘、サヤ. *n.* A sword or knife sheath.

Saye, サイェ, 鳥ノ群. *n.* A flight of birds. As:— *Chikap saye hopuni,* "a flight of birds has got up from the ground."

Saye, サイェ, 繩ノ捲. *n.* A coil of rope.

Saye, サイェ, 珠ヌク、タマヌク: *v.t.* To thread. As:— *Tama saye,* "to thread beads." *Yam saye,* "to thread chestnuts."

Saye-kara, サイェカラ, 卷ク (繩ノ如ク). *v.t.* To coil (as a rope).

Sayekari, サイェカリ, 急ギテ攫ム. *v.t.* To seize in haste.

Sayo, サヨ, 穀物又ハ野菜ノ蒸料理. *n.* A corn or vegetable stew.

Sayo-oro-op, サヨオロオブ, 雑セタル蒸料理. *n.* A mixed stew.

Sayo-shu, サヨシュ, 蒸鍋. *n.* A stew-pot.

Se, セ, 叫ブ. *v.i.* To squeal. To squeak. To make a noise.

Sechiri, セチリ, 側. *n.* The flank. The side.

Seenne, セエンネ, 否定ノ動詞、例セバ、セエンチクメライゲアンカキ、否余寒カラズ. *adv.* Not. No. As:—*Seenne ku meraige an ka ki,* "no, I am not cold." *Seenne ka ki,* "I have not done it."

Seenep-eshikarun-no, セエンブエシカルンノ, 偶然ニ. *adv.* Accidentally.

Sei, セイ, 陶器、皿. *n.* Earthenware. A plate.

Sei, セイ, 介類. *n.* Shells or shellfish of any kind.

Sei, セイ, 背負フ. *v.t.* To carry on the back. As:—*Sei wa arapa,* "carry it away on your back." *Sei wa ek,* "bring it on your back."

Sei-itangi, セイイタンギ, 貝殻ノ椀. *n.* A shell cup. An earthuare cup.

Seikachi, セイカチ, or **Heikachi,** ヘイカチ, 若者. *n.* A lad.

Sei-kap, セイカブ, 貝殻. *n.* Shells. (*Mol.*)

Seikapara, セイカバラ, アサダ. *n.*
Ostrya japonica, Sarg.

Sei-kara, セイカラ, or **Seireka, セイ
レカ,** 火傷スル、熱湯ニ浸ス. *v.t.* To
scald. To steep in hot water.

Seikui, セイクイ, 切歯(ハガミ)スル. *v.i.*
To gnash the teeth. **Syn : Nimaki ukerere.**

Sei-net, セイチツ, 土偶. *n.* An
earthenware figure or idol.

Sei-nima, セイニマ, 土盆. *n.* An
earthenware tray.

Sei-noka, セイノカ, 土偶. *n.* An
earthenware image.

**Seirarak-pekambe, セイララクペカ
ムベ,** ヒメビシ. *n.* *Trapa bispinosa, Roxb. var. incisa, Wall.*

Seire, セイレ, 脊負ハスレ. *v. t.* To
cause to carry on the back.

Seireka, セイレカ, 火傷スル. *v.t.* To
scald. To heat in hot water.

Seisek, セイセク, 暑キ. *adj.* Hot.
As :—*Seisek ekot,* "to die of heat."
"To die through sunstroke."
Syn : Sesek.

Seisekka, セイセッカ, 熱スル. *v.i.*
To heat. To warm up.

Seisek-mau, セイセクマウ, 暑キ息、暑
キ風、熱病. *n.* Hot breath. Hot
wind or air. Fever.

**Seisek-mau-tashum, セイセクマウ
タシュム,** 熱病. *n.* Fever.

Seishintoko, セイシントコ, 陶器. *n.*
An earthenware vessel. A crock.

Seiututke, セイウツッケ, 吐息スレ.
v.i. To sigh.

Sekachi, セカチ, or **Seikachu, セイカ
チュ,** 若者. *n.* A lad.

Sekitan, セキタン, 石炭. *n.* Coal.
Jap.

Sekitan-poru, セキタンポル, 石炭礦.
n. A coal mine.

Sekor'ambe, セコルアムベ, ト云フ
者. *pro.* That kind of thing.
That which is. That which is
called.

Sekoro, セコロ, 誰、所ノソレ、所ノ
誰. *pro.* Who. Which. He who.
That which. So. This here. As :
—*Sekoro ayep,* "that which is called." "So it was said." *Sekoro
itak,* "So he said." "He said
so." "That which he said." *Sekoro iki, sekoro iki,* "to do this
way and that." *Shibe chep otta
iyotta pon chep aye-hi inao-kotchep sekoro ayep ne,* "the small-
est fish among the salmon are
called *inaokot-chep.*"

Sekoro-anak-ne, セコロアナク子, 若
シ然ラバ. *ph.* If it is so. It being like that. As it is such a
thing. That being so.

Sekukke, セクッケ, 膨レル. *v.i.* To
swell out (like a frog). **Syn :
Shipushke.**

Sekumtarara, セクムタララ, or **Shikumtarara, シクムタララ,** 上ノ方
ヘ傾ク. *adj.* To slant upwards.
Syn : Eraot.

Sem, セム, or **Shem, シェム,** 玄関.
n. A porch to a house. An
antechamber.

Sem, セム, or **Shem, シェム,** ノ如
ク、同シ. *adv.* As. Like. The
same.

Semash-chishpo, セマシチシポ, or
Semean-chish, セメアンチシ, 泣キ

眞似スル、啜泣スル. *v.i.* To sniffle as in weeping. To pretend to weep.

Sem-echutkunu, セムエチュックヌ, 其如ク. *adv. ph.* Like that. The same as that. **Syn: Nei ambe ukorachi.**

Sem-korachi, セムコラチ, ノ如ク. *ph.* Like as. Like that. After the same manner.

Semokkaiyoram, セモッカイヨラム, 卑怯ナレ. *adj.* Cowardly. To be afraid. **Syn: Turamkoro.**

Semokkaiyoram-kore, セモッカイヨラムコレ, 卑怯視スレ. *v.t.* To think another cowardly.

Sempi, セムピ, 楔、針、栓. *n.* A wedge. A nail. A peg. As:—*Sempi omare,* "to knock a wedge into wood."

Sempirike, セマビリケ, 陰、後. *n.* Shade. Behind. As:—*Ni sampirike,* "the shade of trees."

Sempirike-oitak, セムピリケオイタク, 譏ル. *v.t.* To slander. To abuse. To backbite. **Syn: Iyohaikara.**

Sempirike-ta-wen-no-ye, セムピリケタウェンノイェ, 誹ル. *v.t.* To slander. To backbite.

Sempiri-oitak, セムピリオイタク, 誹ル. *v.t.* To abuse. To slander. **Syn: Ohaigekara. Sempiripa-omare.**

Sempiri-oitak-i, セムピリオイタクイ, 誹、ソシリ. *n.* Abuse.

Sempiri-pa-omare, セムピリバオマレ, 誹ル. *v.t.* To slander. To abuse. **Syn: Ohaigekara. Sempiri oitak.**

Senkaki, センカキ, 日本ノ布. *n.* Japanese stuffs. Japanese clothing.

Senko, センコ, 線香. *n.* Incense.

Semramush, セムラムシ, 噫. *interj.* Ah. Oh. Alas. This word expresses contempt, pity, surprise, admiration etc., the meaning being determined by the tone of vóice and features.

Sep, セブ, 小サキ谷. *n. geo.* A dale. A small or short valley.

Sep, セブ, 廣キ. *adj.* Broad. **Syn: Para.**

Sepepatki, セペパツキ, 高ク響キテ. *adv.* To sound loudly. To roar as wind.

Sepka, セブカ, 開キタル處、罅隙. *n.* An opening. A crack in a door. As:—*Sepka uturu ashikoturi,* "to peep through an opening."

Seppa, セッバ, 刀ノ鍔. *n.* A sword hilt.

Seppa-rara, セッバララ, 鍔ノ緣. *n.* The edge round a sword guard.

Sepu, セブ, 谷. *n.* A place were there are small vallies.

Sereash, セレアシ, 有ル、(複數). *v.i.* To be. (*pl*). **Syn: At.**

Sere-hum, セレフム, 音、(物ヲ切リ割ル又ハ鼠ノ物ヲ搔ク音). *n.* A noise as of being cut in two. A noise as of a rat scratching.

Sereke, セレケ, 部分. *n.* A part. As:—*Poro sereke,* "for the most part," "the larger half." *Pon sereke,* "the lesser part."

Sere-kosanu, セレコサヌ, 軋ル. *v.i.* To creak (as in opening a door).

To snap or make a noise (as in shaking a cloth). To sound (as when being broken or cut asunder). The sound made in tearing cloth. The clash of arms.

Serekotukka, セレコツッカ, 居ル. *v.i.* To be present. As :—*Nishpa serekotukka guru sange,* " he produced it because the master was present."

Serema, セレマ, 魚ノ臓腑. *n.* Fish entrails.

Seremak, セレマク, 後ニ、(普通嘲笑ノ意味ニ用ユ). *adv.* Behind one. At one's back. Generally used in a bad sense, as speaking of a person behind his back.

Seremak, セレマク, 身體ノ有様、生命、健康. *n.* The disposition of the body. One's circumstances. Life. Health.

Seremaka-tumashnu, セレマカツマシヌ, 健康. *adj.* and *v.i.* To be whole and hearty. Fortunate. Strong. Healthy. **Syn : Seremak koro.**

Seremaka-ush, セレマカウシ, 忠義ス ル. *v.i.* To be faithful to. As : —*Nishpa seremaka ush,* " To be faithful to one's master."

Seremak-kore, セレマクコレ, 健康チ 與フ. *v.t.* To give health to.

Seremak-koro, セレマクコロ, 健康. *v.i.* and *adj.* To be hale and hearty. To be in good health and spirits. To be lucky. Fortunate. **Syn: Kashkamui oshitchiu.**

Seremak-shiknakte, セレマクシクナ

クテ, 欺ク. *v.t.* To deceive. To behave hypocritically toward another. To take one in.

Seremak-ushte, セレマクウシテ, 信頼スル、善クシテヤレ. *v.t.* To rely upon. To do good to.

Serembo, セレムボ, 煙管、例セバ、セレムボウフイェカ、煙管ニ點火スル. *n.* A tobacco pipe. As :—*Serembo uhuyeka.* To light one's pipe. **Syn: Serumbo.**

Seri, セリ, セリ. *n.* *Oenanthe stotonifera, D.C.*

Serikosamba, セリコサムバ, 拔ク (庭丁チ). *v.t.* To draw (as a knife).

Serima, セリマ, 臓. *n.* The bowels. **Syn : Kuroma.**

Serumbo, セルムボ, 煙管. *n.* Same as *serembo.*

Sesek, セセク,
Seisek, セイセク,
Sheshek, シェシェク, } 暑キ. *adj.* Hot.

Sesek-i, セセキ, or **Sesek-u, セセク,** 火ノ熱. *n.* Fire heat.

Sesek-ka, セセッカ, 熱スル. *v.t.* To heat.

Sesek-kara, セセッカラ, 熱セシムル *v.t.* To cause another to heat.

Sesh, セシ, カヅアイサ. *n.* Goosander, *Mergus merganser, Linn.*

Seshke, セシケ, 閉ス. *v.t.* To shut. To cover up. To stop up as a hole. **Syn : Ashi.**

Seshmau, セシマウ, 四歳ノ雄鹿. *n.* A four year old buck.

Sessereke, セッセレケ, 嗚咽(シヤクリナキ)ノ音. *n.* The noise of stifled weeping. **Syn : Pi-chish.**

Set, セツ, 巣、足臺、椅子、卓子. *n.* A nest. A seat. A stool. A chair. Table.

Seta, セタ, 犬. *n.* A dog. **Syn:** Reep.

Seta-amam, セタアマム, エノコロサウ. *n.* Wild Timothy. *Setaria viridis, Beauv.*

Seta-atane, セタアタ子, エゾタイセイ. *n. Isatis tinctoria, L.*

Seta-buri-koro, セタブリコロ, 犬ノ習慣アレ. *adj.* Beastial.

Seta-ando, セタアンド, ナギナタカウジュ. *n. Elsholtziar cristata, Willd.*

Setai-ni, セタイニ, ズミ. *n.* A kind of prickly fruit bearing tree. *Pyrus Toringo, sieb.* Also called *Setan-ni.*

Seta-koro-ni, セタコロニ, ゴバウ. *n.* The burdock. *Arctium Lappa, L.* Also called *Setakorokoni.*

Setak, セタク, 速ニ、今、早ク (時ヲ示ス). *adv.* Quickly. Now. In a moment. Directly. Early. As: —*Setak piyapa,* "early millet."

Setakbe-kina, セタクベキナ, オミナヘシ. *n. Patrima scabiosæfolia, Link.*

Setakko, セタッコ, 永キ間. *adv.* For a long time. **Syn: Ohon no uturuta.**

Setakko-isam, セタッコイサム, 永キ間留守ナアケル. *ph.* To be absent for a long time.

Setakorokoni, セタコロコニ, ゴバウ. *n.* The burdock. *Arctium Lappa, L.* Also called *Setakoroni.*

Seta-munchiro, セタムンチロ, エノコロアサ. *n.* Wild Timothy. *Setaria viridis, Beauv.*

Setan-ni, セタンニ, ズミ. *n. Pyrus Toringo, Sieb.* Also called *Setai-ni.*

Seta-pukusa, セタプクサ, キミカケサウ. *n.* Lily of the valley. *Convallaria majalis, L.*

Setara, セタラ, ズミノミキ. *n.* The stem of the *Pyrus Toringo, Sieb.*

Seta-paragoat, セタパラゴアツ, 犬ニ祟ラレ. *v.i.* To be possessed or punished by dogs. Hydrophobia.

Seta-raita, セタライタ, ダイコンサウ. *n. Geum japonicum, Th.*

Seta-surugu, セタスルグ, カブトギクノ一種. *n.* A kind of aconite.

Seta-sara, セタサラ, クガイサウ. *n. Veronica sibirica, L.*

Setamba, セタムバ, 埋葬地. *n.* A cemetery.

Set-sambe, セツサムベ, 鳥ノ巣ノ眞中. *n.* The middle part of a bird's nest.

Setsetke, セツセツケ, 河縁ノ下部. *n.* The under or hollow part of a river's bank.

Seturu, セツル, or **Saturuhu, サツルフ,** 背. *n.* The back.

Seturuka-yairarire, セツルカヤイラリレ, 後ヲ離レズ從フ. *v.i.* To follow close after one.

Seunin, セウニン, 冷キ(湯ノ). *adj.* Cool (as hot water).

Seuri, セウリ, 咽喉. *n.* The throat. The windpipe. Gullet.

Seuri-sapa, セウリサパ, 結喉、ノドボトケ. *n.* The Adam's apple of the throat.

Sewakuttanne, セワクッタン子, 空虚ナレ. *adj.* Hollow.

Sewashi, セワシ, ホザキナナカド. *n.*
Spiraea sorbifolia, L.

Sewat-ni, セワツニ, タラノキ. *n.*
Aralia sinensis, L.

Seyepo, セイエホ, 蝸牛. *n.* A snail.
Syn : Mokoriri.

Sham. シャム, 側. *n.* Same as
Sama, " side."

Shamo, シャモ, 日本人. *n.* A
Japanese. **Syn : Shisam.**

Shan, シャン, 棚. *n.* A shelf.

Shancha, シャンチャ, 顔ノ下部. *n.*
The lower part of the face. The
countenance. As :—*Shancha otta
mina kane,* " he has smiles upon
his countenance."

Shaot, シャオツ, 走セサル、兩親ヲ見
捨テ. *v.t.* To run away from.
To leave one's parents. **Syn :
Kira.**

Shaotte, シャオッテ, 走リ去ラセレ. *v.t.*
To make run away. **Syn : Kirare.**

Shashuishiri, シャシュイシリ, 昔ヨリ、
常ニ. *adv.* From ancient times.
Always.

**Shashuishiri-pakno, シャシュイシリ
バクノ,** 昔ヨリ今マデ. *ph.* From
ancient times till now.

Shashuishirun, シャシュイシルン, 昔
ヨリ. *adv.* From ancient times.

Shem, シェム, or **Sem, セム,** ノ如ク、
同ジク. *adv.* As. Like. The
same. See *sem.*

Shem-korachi, シェムコラチ, ノ如
ク、同ジク、其如ク. *adv.* Like as.
After the same manner. Like
that.

Shi, シ, 或ル語ニ接頭語トシテ用ユレ
バ、シ、ハ自動法又ハ再歸法ノ意ヲ有
ス. *part.* Used as a prefix to
some verbs *shi* has the sense
of the intransitive or reflexive
mood.

Shi, シ, 獸ノ糞. *n.* The dung of
animals. **Syn : Osoma.**

Shi, シ, 閉ス. *v.t.* To shut. As :—
Apa shi, " shut the door."

Shi, シ, 眞ナル、甚ダ、大ナル. *adj.*
True. Very. Great. As :—*Shi
no wen ruwe ne,* " it is very
bad."

Shi, シ, 發育十分ナル. *adj.* Fullgrown.
As :—*Shi etaspe,* " fullgrown sea
lion." *Shi nitumam,* " the trunk
of a fullgrown tree."

Shiambap, シアムバブ, 經帷 (ケウカ
タビラ)ノ類. *n.* The clothes in
which the dead are dressed before burial As :—*Shiambe hosh,*
" the leggings "; *shiamba tekum-
be,* " the gloves "; *shiamba tush,*
" string used to tie the clothes
on the dead."

Shiamkirara, シアムキララ, 紹介ス
ル. *v.t.* To introduce to one
another.

**Shiampokorare-guru, シアムポコラ
レグル,** 不正直ナル人. *n.* A dis-
honest person.

Shi-amushbe, シアムシベ, 爪アリト稱
セラル、海中ノ怪物. *n.* A kind of
sea monster said to have claws.

Shiankush, シアンクシ, 誠ニ. *adv.*
In truth. Truly.

Shi-an-no, シアンノ, 誠ニ. *adv.*
Truly. In truth. Exceedingly.
Syn : Son no.

Shi-apka, シアブカ, 發育十分ナル牡鹿、老イタル牡鹿. n. A fullgrown buck. An old buck.

Shiara, シアラ, 開ク. v.i. To open. To uncover.

Shiarikiki-no, シアリキキノ, 全力ヲ以テ. adv. With all one's might and main. Syn : Arikiki. Kiroroashnu no.

Shiarikiki-yuptek-no, シアリキキユブテクノ, 全力ヲ以テ. adv. With all one's might and main.

Shiashpare, シアシバレ, 聞エヌ振スレ. v.i. To pretend to be deaf.

Shiassuru-ashte, シアッスルアシテ, 有名トナレ. v.i. To be famous.

Shiassuru-ashte-rusui, シアッスル アシテルスイ, 大望ヲ抱ク. v.i. To be ambitious of fame.

Shiattemshuye, シアッテム シュイェ, 步ム(馬ノ如ク). v.i. To pace (as a horse).

Shibe, シベ, サケ. n. Salmon *Oncorhynchus keta.* (Walbaum).

Shibe-kina, シベキナ, タネツケバナ. n. *Cardamine hirsuta, L.*

Shibekuttara, シベクッタラ, シモツケサウ. n. *Filipendula kamtschatica, Max.*

Shichikap, シチカブ, オジロツシ. n. White tailed eagle. *Haliætus albicilla Linn.*

Shichimichimi-yara, シチミチミヤラ, 不注意ナレ. adj. Careless. Sloven. Syn : Shikatnukarara.

Shichoropok-un-ingara, シチョロボ クウンインガラ, 瞰下ス. v.i. To look down.

Shichupka, シチュブカ, 東. n. The East.

Shichuppok, シチュッポク, 西. n. The West.

Shichupu, シチュブ, 亡ブレ. v.i. To die out. As:—*Ainu shichupu an,* "the Ainu are dying out." Syn : Wenba. Yuk-uturu otbe.

Shichupu-chupu, シチュブチュブ, 眩ユカル、マバユカル. v.i. To be blinded or dazed (as by light).

Shieiwangeyara, シエイワンゲヤラ, 奉公スル、仕フレ. v.t. To serve. To minister to. Syn : Yaieiwangere.

Shieminayara, シエミナヤラ, 笑ハレ、嘲ラル. v.i. To be laughed at. To be derided. Syn : Aemina.

Shienka-un-ingara, シエンカウンイ ンガラ, 仰ク. v.i. To look upwards.

Shiesapse-yara, シエサブセヤラ, 輕蔑セラル. v.i. To be despised. To be held in derision. Syn : Shikuriande yara.

Shietaye, シエタイェ, 引退スル、引退 セシム、減水スル、短縮スレ. v.t. and v.i. To withdraw. To draw in (as a snail its horns). To abate (as water in a river). To contract.

Shietayere, シェタイェレ, 引退セシム レ. v.t. To cause to withdraw.

Shietok-ashongo-kushte, シエトク アションゴクシテ, 傳言スレ. v.i. To send word. Syn : Ekamsakte.

Shietoko, シエトコ, 前面ニ、未來. adv. In front of. The future.

Shietoko-ramu, シエトコラム, 未來 ヲ思フ. v.i. To think of the future.

Shietok-sam, シエトクサム, 前面ニ. *adv.* Ahead. In front of one. As :—*Shietok-sam shikuiruke ingara,* "to look about ahead."

Shietu-uina, シエツウイナ, オヤ、驚 キノ叫, *excl.* Dear me! How surprising! I am surprised!

Shihapapu, シハパプ, 病氣、(烈シク 內部ニ苦痛アリ大抵ハ死スト云ハレ一 種ノ). *n.* A disease which is said to consist chiefly in severe internal pains, and which most often terminates in death.

Shihekote-hotuyekara, シヘコテホ ツイェカラ, 呼ビ集ムレ. *v. t.* To gather together by calling to. To call together to a person.

Shihon, シホン, or **Shion, シオン,** 赤 子・*n.* A baby. **Syn : Tennep. Teinep. Shikoteine.**

Shihontak, シホンタク, or **Shion, シ オン,** 小童. *n.* A small boy. **Syn : Sontak.**

Shihopinuppa, シホピヌツパ, 惜ム. *v.t.* Not caring to spare. Disinclined to let go as one's child or possessions.

Shihoroka, シホロカ, 下方ニ. *adv.* Downwards.

Shihumnuyara, シフムヌヤラ, 咳一 咳スル(家ニ入ル時). *v.i.* To make a noise with the throat as a warning before entering a hut. **Syn : Shimushishka.**

Shik. シク, Shiki, シキ, Shikihi, シキヒ, 眼. *n.* The eyes. As : *Shiki maka,* "to open the eyes." *Shikinum,* "the eyeballs." *Shiki tokoko,* "to fix the eyes on." *Shik-etoko raikosanu,* "to be dazzled." *Shik-kamuktek,* "to shut the eyes."

Shikabekushte, シカベクシテ, 狡 猾 ナル. *adj.* Sly.

Shikaeshinayara, シカエシナヤラ, 秘 スル、否ム、隱ス、結ブ. *v.i.* To keep secret. To deny. To hide. To bind up. **Syn : Eshina.**

Shikai, シカイ, 釘、鋲、留針. *n.* A nail. A peg. A pin. As :— *Chikuni shikai,* "a wooden peg."

Shikakapa, シカカパ, 病氣. *adj.* Sickly. Ailing.

Shikama, シカマ, 貯フ、共ニ置ク. *v.t.* To store. To put together. To lay up.

Shikamare, シカマレ, 隔、例ヘバ、シチ トシカマレンランゲキ、彼ハソレヲ隔 日ニ爲セリ. *adv.* Every other. A jumping over. As :—*Shine to shikamare range ki,* "he does it every other day."

Shikamare, シカマレ, 隱ルヽ. *v.i.* To be hidden.

Shikambe-chikap, シカムベチカプ, 信天翁、アホウドリ. *n.* The albatross. **Syn : Oshkambe. One-chikap. Isho-kapui.**

Shikannatki, シカンナツキ, 環、圓キ. *n.* and *adj.* A circle. Round.

Shikannatkip, シカンナツキプ, 車輪. *n.* A wheel.

Shikannatki-no, シカンナツキノ, 圓 ク. *adv.* In a circle.

Shikaobiukiyara, シカオビウキヤラ, 救ハレ. *v.i.* To beg. To be saved. To be helped. **Syn : Kashichiobiuki.**

Shikaobiukire, シカオビウキレ, 救ハレ. *v.i.* To be saved by. As :— *Kamui otta shikaobiukire*, " to be saved by God."

Shikapashte, シカパシテ, 救ヲ呼プ. *v.t.* To call to another for help. **Syn : Shikashiure.**

Shikap-ekushte, シカプエクシテ, 知ラヌ振スル、惡事ヲ隱ス. *v.i.* To pretend not to know. To do evil things and pretend to know nothing about it. To hide one's evil deeds.

Shikapkapa, シカプカパ, 病身. *n.* A person who is always ill. An invalid. A weakling.

Shikapneka-no, シカプ子カノ, 何處デモ. *adv.* Everywhere.

Shikari, シカリ, 圓キ. *adj.* Round. Winding.

Shikari-chup, シカリチュプ, 滿月. *n.* A full moon.

Shikari, シカリ, 無キ. *adv.* Without. Not having.

Shikarikari, シカリカリ, 圓ク、圓ク. *adv.* Round and round.

Shikarimba, シカリムバ, 圓キ. *adj.* Round. Winding. To spin.

Shikarimbare, シカリムバレ, 絡ム、カラム. *v.t.* To turn round. To twist.

Shikarip, シカリプ, 車輪. *n.* A wheel.

Shikarire, シカリレ, 廻ス. *v.t.* To make go round.

Shikarun, シカルン, 學問アレ. *adj.* Learned. Also *v.t.* To notice. To perceive.

Shikashishte, シカシシテ, 冷遇スレ. *v.t.* To treat with unconcern. To treat with indifference. **Syn : Shikashte. Katchiu. Pange.**

Shikashiure, シカシウレ, 救ヲ呼プ. *v.t.* To call to another for help. **Syn : Shikapashte.**

Shikashke, シカシケ, 否ム. *v.t.* To deny a charge brought against one. To deny. To defend against a charge.

Shikashkere, シカシケレ, 否マスレ. *v.t.* To cause to deny. **Syn : Ikooroshuke.**

Shikashnukara, シカシヌカラ, 幸運ナレ. *adj.* Lucky. Fortunate.

Shikashte, シカシテ, 輕蔑スル. *v.t.* To despise. To treat with disdain. **Syn : Shikashishte. Katchiu.**

Shikashuire, シカシュイレ, 助手ヲ用ユル. *v.t.* To employ as a help. **Syn : Nishuk.**

Shikashuite, シカシュイテ, 助ケシム レ. *v.t.* To cause to help.

Shikatkare, シカツカレ, or **Shikat-kari, シカツカリ,** 罹ル、憑カル. *v.t.* To be seized with a disease or devil. **Syn : Ituren.**

Shikatnukarara, シカツヌカララ, 粗末ニスレ. *v.t.* To be careless. **Syn : Shikopaotteyara.**

Shikatori-kamui, シカトリカムイ,
Shikatori-shiyeye, シカトリシイェイェ,
Shikatori-tashum, シカトリタシュム,
腸窒扶斯. *n.* Typhoid fever. Small-pox by some.

Shikatorushi, シカトルシ, 憑カル. *v.i.*
To be possessed (as by a devil).
Syn : Shikatkari.

Shikaye, シカイエ, 閃メカス. *v.t.* To
flash about.

Shikaye-at, シカイエアツ, 閃ク、輝ク.
v.i. To flash. To glitter. To
shine.

Shikaye-atte, シカイエアッテ, 閃カス、
輝カス. *v.t.* To cause to shine or
glitter. To flash about.

Shikayekaye, シカイエカイエ, 閃カス、
輝カス. *v.t.* To shine. To glitter.
To flash.

Shikayere, シカイエレ, 閃カス、輝カス.
v.t. To case to shine, glitter, or
flash.

**Shik-chupuchupu, シクチュプチュ
プ,** 瞬ク. *v.i.* To wink the eyes.
Syn : Shik-rewerewe.

Shike, シケ, 擴ケル. *adj.* Spread out
flat. **Syn : Seshike.**

Shike, シケ, 二十ノ魚. *adj.* Twenty
fish.

Shike, シケ, or Shikehe, シケヘ, 荷物.
n. Luggage. Baggage. As :—
Shike wa apkash, " to carry a
load. *Shike apkash oman,* " to
take a load." *Shike kooktariri,* " to
carry a very heavy load." (Lit :
to stretch out the neck to a
load). **Syn : Kinkai.**

Shikeka, シケカ, 甲板. *n.* The deck
of a ship. **Syn : San-ita.**

Shikekamup, シケカムプ, 死者ト共ニ
葬ル最上ノ晴衣. *n.* The very best
ornamental and festive garments
buried with the dead. **Syn :
Shirikamup.**

Shike-ni, シケニ, 物ヲ乗セテ荷負フ器.
n. A wooden frame upon which
to pile bundles for carrying.

Shike-ni-eshike, シケニエシケ, 重ネ
タル荷物ヲ運ブ. *v.i.* To carry
bundles of luggage piled one on
the top of another.

Shikepuni, シケプニ, 仰ギ見ル. *v.t.*
To look up to. As :—*Kamui
shikepuni,* " to look up to God."

Shik-eraige, シクエライゲ, 屹ト見ル.
v.t. To look steadily at.

Shikere, シケレ, 背負セル. *v.t.* To
help a person to place a load
upon his back.

Shikerebe, シケレベ, キハダノ實. *n.*
The fruit of the *Phellodendron
amurense.* The fruit of this tree
is used both for food and medicine.

Shikerebe-kina, シケレベキナ, ザゼ
ンサウ. *n.* The skunk cabbage.
Symplocarpus fœtidus, Salisb.

Shikerebe-ni, シケレベニ, キハダ、シ
コロ. *n. Phellodandron amurense,
Rupr.* Both the fruit and bark
of this tree are used as medicine.

Shikesara, シケサラ, 野蠻ナル、悪口
スレ. *adj.* and *v.i.* Of wild habits.
To speak evil of others.

Shikesara-guru, シケサラグル, 叱責.
n. A virago. A scold.

Shikeshke, シケシケ, 虐待スレ (單數)、
悪口スル. *v.t.* (*sing*). To illtreat.
To speak evil of. To speak
against.

Shikeshpare, シケシパレ, 悪口スレ
(複數). *v.t.* (*pl*). To speak evil of.
To speak against. To illtreat.

Shi-ki, シキ, ヲギ. *n.* The larger kinds of reeds. *Miscanthaes sacchariflorus, Hack.*

Shiki, シキ, 眼. *n.* The eyes. Same as *shik*. As:—*Shiki fure,* "to have blood-shot eyes."

Shikihi, シキヒ, 眼. *n.* The eyes. **Syn: Kerup.**

Shiki-kara, シキカラ, 色目ヲ使フ. *v.i.* To make eyes at.

Shi-kina, シキナ, ガマ. *n.* Bulrushes. *Typha japonica, Miq.*

Shi-kina-shup, シキナシュプ, ガマニテ製セシ蓆. *n.* A mat made of bulrushes (but rolled up).

Shiki-okerunne, シキオケルンチ, 張目シテ凝視スレ. *v.t.* To look with staring enlarged eyes.

Shikipip, シキピプ, or **Shikkipip, シッキピプ, 見ルヲ得ズ.** *v.i.* To be unable to look at.

Skikiporo-chep, シキポロ チュプ, ガズナキノ一種. *n.* *Stichæus nozawæ Jor. and Sny.*

Shikirara, シキララ, 知ル、認識スレ. *v.t.* To know. To recognize. **Syn: Kiri.**

Shikiriba, シキリバ, 轉ガル、(馬ノ如ク). *v.i.* To roll (as a horse).

Shikiru, シキル, 廻ル、曲ル. *v.i.* To turn or twist about.

Shikirukiru, シキルキル, 休マヌ、曲リタレ. *adj.* Restless. To turn about.

Shikisakisa, シキサキサ, 身ヲ振フ、(犬ノ如ク). *v.i.* To shake one's self (as a dog).

Shikishoksho, シキショクショ, 寝ラズ. *adj.* Wakeful. **Syn: Mokoro etoranne.**

Shikittektek, シキッテクテク, 急ギ顧. *v.i.* To turn about quickly. To face about in a hurry.

Shikiuta-chup, シキウタチュプ, 五月. *n.* The month of May.

Shikkamare, シッカマレ, 隱ス. *v.t.* To conceal. To hide. To keep out of sight.

Shikkap, シッカプ, 瞼、マブタ. *n.* The eyelids.

Shikkashima, シッカシマ, 支持スル、捉フル、制御スレ. *v.t.* To seize. To govern.

Shikkashimare, シッカシマレ, 制御セシム、捉エシムル、支持セシメレ. *v.t.* To cause to govern. To make seize. To give to another to hold.

Shikkaruru, シッカルル, 横目デ見レ. *v.i.* To look out of the corner of one's eyes.

Shikkemrit-oshma, シクケムリツオシマ, 血眼トナレ. *v.i.* To have bloodshot eyes.

Shik-keruru, シクケルル, 眼ヲ轉ズレ. *v.i.* To turn the eyes about. To turn the eyes round.

Shikkesh-ani-ingara, シッケシアニインガラ, or **Shikkesh-san-ingara, シッケシサンインガラ, 横目デ見レ.** *v.i.* To look out of the corners of the eyes.

Shik-kesh, シクケシ, 頬骨ト眼トノ間. *n.* The space between the cheekbone and the eye.

Shikkeu, シッケウ, 隅、家ノ西端ノ戸ニ近キ處. *n.* A corner. That

end of a hut near the west end door.

Shikkikip, シッキキプ, or **Shikkipip, シッキピプ,** 見ルヲ得ズ. *v. i.* To be unable to look at.

Shikkotesu, シッコテス, 熱心ニ見ル、熟視スル. *v.t.* To look at attentively.

Shiknak, シクナク, 盲シタレ. *adj.* Blind. **Syn : Emuitane.**

Shikno, シクノ, 充チタル. *adj.* Full.

Shikno-ambe, シクノアムベ, 充満. *n.* Fullness. To be full of anything. As :—*Yachi shikno ambe tereke-ibe ne ruwe ne,* " the marsh is full of frogs."

Shikno-an, シクノアン, 充チタレ. *adj.* To be full.

Shiknu, シクヌ, 生ケレ. *v.i.* To be alive. To live.

Shik-num, シクヌム, 眼球. *n.* The eyeballs.

Shik-numumu, シクヌムム, 慼ム、ヒソム. *v.i.* To frown. **Syn : Shikchupupu.**

Shiknu-no, シクヌノ, 生キタレ. *adj.* Living. Alive. As :—*Shiknu no toi tumu ao,* " they were buried alive."

Shiknu-wa-an, シクヌワアン, 生ケレ. *v.i.* To be living. To be alive.

Shiknure, シクヌレ, 生カス、補助スル、救フ、蘇生セシムル. *v.t.* To cause to live. To save. To revive. To assist. Used in matters connected with life and death.

Shiko, シコ, 生ル、カマル、目ヲ開ク. *v.i.* . To be born. To open the eyes.

Shik-o, シクオ, or **Shiki-o, シキオ,** 莩 (ヨシ) アル. Containing reeds.

Shikoba, シコバ, 信頼スレ. *v.t.* To rely on. To depend upon. To get another to do.

Shikoba-eaikap, シコバエアイカプ, 信頼セラレズ. *v.i.* Not to be able to depend upon. Unreliable.

Shikoetaye, シコエタイェ, 引キ入ル(縄ノ如ク)、抜刀スル. *v.i.* To draw in (as a rope). To draw out as a sword from a sheath. **Syn : Ehekem.**

Shikohewehewe, シコヘウェヘウェ, 蹌踉ク、ヨロメク. *v.i.* To tumble about. To stagger. To draw round one's body (as a quiver ready for use). As :—*Kush shikoheweheve wa ai etaye,* " he drew the quiver round his body and drew an arrow." **Syn : Shikoruihewe.**

Shikohorire, シコホリレ, 追ヒ遣ル. *v.t.* To drive away. To dismiss.

Shiko-ingarara, シコインガララ, 偽善スル. *v.i.* To show off. To be hypocritical. **Syn : Aeshikkoingara.**

Shiko-irushka, シコイルシカ, 怒ル. *v.i.* To be angry with another.

Shiko-irushkare, シコイルシカレ, 怒ヲ催サスル. *v.t.* To make angry with another.

Shikomewe, シコメウェ, 攻撃スル. *v.t.* To fall upon. To attack.

Shikom-ni, シコムニ, カシハ. *n.* A kind of oak. *Quercus dentata,* Th.

Shikoni, シコニ, 吸ル、シナブル. *v.t.* To suck. .

Shikoniwen, シコニウェン, 荒キ、怒レ ル. *adj.* Wild. Angry. Fierce.

Shikoniwende, シコニウェンデ, 窘ム ル、イヂメル. *v.t.* To tease (as a dog).

Shikonokka, シコノッカ, 愛スル. *v.t.* To love. To gain the affections of another.

Shikonun, シコヌン, 吸ヒ込ム. *v.t.* To suck in.

Shikonunnun, シコヌンヌン, 吸ヒ込 ム. *v.t.* To suck in.

Shikopa, シコパ, 似ル. *v.i.* To be like. To resemble.

Shikopa-atteyara, シコパアッテヤラ, 注意セヌ. *v.i.* To be careless. **Syn : Shikatnukara.**

Shikopakoita-kara, シコパコイタカ ラ, 不潔ナル. *adj.* Sloven. Filthy.

Shikopayara, シコパヤラ, 似スル. *v.i.* To pretend. To liken.

Shikopop, シコポプ, 錆ル. *v.i.* To rust.

Shikopuntek-yara, シコプンテクヤ ラ, 賞讃ヲ欲シテ爲ス、他ヲ喜バセン トテ爲ス. *v.t.* To do for praise. To do in order be give pleasure to another.

Shikorara, シコララ, 彷徨フ. *v.i.* To wander about. To be a busybody. **Syn : Katukari.**

Shikoraye, シコライェ, 儲クル、得ル. *v.i.* To gain for one's self. To get. To obtain. To take.

Shikore, シコレ, 産ム. *v.t.* To bear. To bring forth (as a child).

Shikorogeta-ye, シコロゲタイェ, or **Shikkorota-ye, シッコロタイェ,** 面 前ニテ語ル. *v.t.* To say in front of another. To say when another is present.

Shikoruihewe, シコルイヘウェ, 蹌跟ス ル. *v.i.* To stagger. To tumble about. **Syn : Shikohewehewe.**

Shikoruiruye, シコルイルイェ, 愛撫 スル. *v.t.* To pat. To fondle (as a child).

Shikotan-kon-ni, シコタンコンニ, 太 ク大ナル木. *n.* A very thick and large tree. **Syn : Poro chikuni.**

Shikotchane, シコッチャチ, 仲立スレ. *v.t.* To speak for or on behalf of another.

Shikotchane-guru, シコッチャチグ ル, 仲立. *n.* A mediator.

Shikotchanere, シコッチャチレ, 仲立 サスル. *v.t.* To cause a person to act as mediator for one.

Shikotchane-yara, シコノチャチヤラ, 仲立ヲ願フ. *v.t.* To ask another to act as mediator.

Shikoteinep, シコテイチプ, 赤子. *n.* A very small child. A baby.

Shikoyaiiraigere, シコヤイライゲレ, 多謝ス. *pp.* I thank you much.

Shikoyupupu, シコユプブ, 抱ク、(子 供ヲ). *v.t.* To hold in the arms (as a baby).

Shikrap, シクラプ, 眉. *n.* The eye-lashes. The eyebrows.

Shik-rapa, シクラパ, or **Shik-rapa-rapa, シクラパラパ,** 瞬ク. *v.i.* To wink or blink the eyes.

Shikrewerewe, シクレウェレウェ, 瞬 グ. *v.i.* To blink the eyes. **Syn : Shik-chupuchupu.**

Shik-sak, シクサク, 盲目ナル. *adj.* Blind.

Shiksei, シクセイ, 眼ノ上皮. *n.* The film of the eyes.

Shik-tarara, シクタララ, 吃驚シテ見上ゲレ. *v.t.* To look up as when startled by something unexpected.

Shikte, シクテ, 充ス. *v.t.* To fill.

Shiktere, シクテレ, 充サシ厶. *v.t.* To cause another to fill.

Shiktokoko, シクトココ, 凝視スル. *v.t.* To stare at. **Syn : Keruptokoko.**

Shiktu, シクツ, 網ノ目. *n.* The meshes of a net.

Shikuiruke, シクイルケ, 彼方此方へ、頭ヲ彼方此方へ向クル. *v.i.* and *adv.* Hither and thither. Here and there. To turn the head this way and that. As :—*Shikuiruke wa ingara*, "to look about." *Chisei upshoro shikuiruke*, "to look about the inside of a house."

Shikukka, シクッカ, 増大スル. *v.t.* To enlarge. **Syn : Porore.**

Shikuma, シクマ, 山ノ集合、峯. *n.* A group of mountains. Also a mountain ridge.

Shikumtarara, シクムタララ, 飛ビ上リタレ. *adj.* To start upwards.

Shikupramta-kara, シクプラムタカラ, or **Shukupramta-kara, シュクプラムタカラ**, 壓サル、. *v.i.* To have nightmare.

Shikuriande-yara, シクリアンデヤラ, 輕蔑セラル. *v.i.* To be despised. To be held in derision. **Syn : Shiesapse yara.**

Shikurukasam, シクルカサム, 躯. *n.* The body.

Shikutkesh-makaraye, シクッケシマカライエ, 咳拂(家ニ入ル時知ラセノ). *v.i.* To make a noise as of clearing one's throat as a warning to the inmates of a house that one is near.

Shikuturu, シクツル,
Shikutut, シクツツ,
Shukuturu, シュクツル,
Shukutut, シクツツ,
エゾネギ. *n.* The common chive. *Allium schoenoprasum, L.*

Shik-uturu, シクウツル, 兩眼ノ間. *n.* The space between the eyes.

Shimachichi, シマチチ, 身ヲ伸バス、(寢覺ノ時ノ如ク). *v.i.* To stretch (as after sleep.)

Shim, シム, or **Shima, シマ**, 明日、次ノ日. *adv.* Tomorrow. The next day.

Shimaima, シマイマ, 蛞蝓、ナメクジ、虱. *n.* Slugs. Also lice.

Shimaka, シマカ, 失セ去ル. *v.i.* To have passed away.

Shimakorai, シマコライ, 過ヤ去ル、出發スル、休厶. *v.i.* To pass away. To go away. To depart. To cease.

Shimakoraiba, シマコライバ, 休厶、止マル、休業スル. *v. i.* To cease. To stop. To leave off work. *Pl. of Shimakorai.*

Shimakmak, シマクマク, 極ノ後方. *adv.* Most behind ; hinder-most.

Shimasa, シマサ, 開ケテ. *adj.* Open.

Shimak-un, シマクウン, 後方. *adv.* Behind.

Shimatnera, シマッチレ, 女ノ眞似ス

ル、慢ズル. *v.i.* To pretend to be a female. To be proud.

Shimaugesh-eot, シマウゲシエオツ, 結婚スレ. *v.t.* To marry. To live together as husband and wife. **Syn: Umurek guru ne·**

Shimaugesh-eotte, シマウゲシエオッテ, 結婚セシムレ、側ニ置ク. *v.t.* To cause to marry. To place by the side of.

Shimauta-chup, マウタチュプ, 七月. *n.* The month of July.

Shimbi, シムビ, シビ. *n.* The tunny fish. *Germo sibi* (*J. & S.*) **Syn: Hokush chep.**

Shimechike, シメチケ, or **Shumichike, シュミチケ,** ス丶キ. *n.* Kind of perch. *Lateolabrax japonicus.* (*C. & V.*) Also called *Airo; aioro;* and *ayoro.*

Shimemke, シメムケ, 剪リタル. *adj.* Shaven.

Shimemokka, シメモ丶カ, 喧嘩ヲ好ム. *v.i.* To be quarrelsome. To desire to quarrel. To stir up a fight. To challenge. To tease. To sow seeds of strife. To try to find out the faults of another person. **Syn: Ramokka.**

Shimge, シムゲ, 次ノ日、次. *adv.* The day following. The next.

Shimibe, シミベ, or **Shin-ibe, シンイベ,** 朝餐. *n.* Breakfast.

Shimma, シムマ, 明日、次ノ日. *adv.* Tomorrow The next day.

Shimokore, シモコレ, 空寢入スレ. *v.i.* To pretend to be asleep.

Shimon, シモン, 右. *adj.* The right.

Shimon-omai-so, シモンオマイソ, 爐邊ノ右. *n.* The right-hand side of a fire-place.

Shimon-sam, シモンサム, 右側. *adv.* The right hand side.

Shimon-samata, シモンサマタ, or **Shimon-samta, シモンサムタ,** 右側. *adv.* The right hand side.

Shimontek, シモンテク, 右側ニテ. *adv.* On the right hand.

Shimoye, シモイェ, 動ク、震フ. *v.i.* To move. To shake. **Syn: Moimoige.**

Shimoyeka, シモイェカ, 動ク. *v.i.* To move.

Shimpitoi, シムピトイ, 遲キ(足ノ). *adj.* Slow of foot. As:—*Shimpitoi umma,* "a slow horse." **Syn: Shiwende.**

Shimpui, シムプイ, 井戸. *n.* A well.

Shimushishka, シムシシカ, 咳拂(家ニ入ル前ノ報知). *v.i.* To make a noise with the throat as a warning to people before entering a house or hut. **Syn: Shihumnuyara. Shirekutkara. Shihaunuyara.**

Shin, シン, 地、陸、世界、山地. *n.* The earth. The ground. Land. The world. Mountain land as opposed to plains. As:—*Shin ratchi wa an,* "the world is at peace." This word is short for *shiri.*

Shina, シナ, 結ビ付クレ. *v.t.* To lace up. To tie up. To bind. **Syn: Tupetupe. Shinashina.**

Shinai, シナイ, 本流. *n.* A main stream.

Shinan-chup, シナンチュブ, or **Shi-nau-chup, シナウチュブ,** 十一月. *n.* The month of November.

Shinankush, シナンクシ, 誠ニ. *adv.* Truly. In truth.

Shinashina, シナシナ, 結ビ付ケル. *v.t.* To lace up. To tie up. To bind. **Syn : Shina. Tupetupe.**

Shinau-chup, シナウチュブ, or **Shi-nan-chup, ナナンチュブ,** 十一月. *n.* The month of November.

Shinchi-chup, シンチチュブ, 六月. *n.* The month of June, by most Ainu called *Momauta chup.*

Shinchike, シンチケ, スケトウタラ. *n. Alakanpollack. Theragra chalcogramma.*

Shinda, シンダ, 搖籃. *n.* A cradle.

Shine, シチ, 一. *adj.* One. As : —*Shine anchikara,* " one night." *Shine to,* " a day." *Shine to paye an,* " a day's journey." *Shine to tori,* " every other day."

Shine-an, シチアン, 一. *adj.* One. As :—*Shine an guru,* " one person." *Shine an toho ta,* "one day ; " " once upon a time."

Shine-anda, シチアンダ, 嘗テ某時. *adv.* Once upon a time. One day. At one time.

Shine-atki, シチアッキ, 同ジク思スル. *adj.* and *v.i.* To be of one mind. To be by themselves. To be alone. As :—*Shine atki no kara,* " to put by themselves."

Shine-atki-no, シチアッキノ, 一致シテ. *adv.* Unitedly.

Shine-chupta, シチチュブタ, 月々.

adv. Monthly. As:—*Shine chupta shine ichi ryo ku sange,* " I will give him one yen per month."

Shine-ikashima-wanbe, シチイカシマワンベ, 十一ノ物. *n.* Eleven things.

Shine-ikinne, シチイキンチ, 一致シテ. *adv.* With one accord. Altogether.

Shine-keutum-koro, シチケウツムコロ, 一致スレ. *v.i.* To be unanimous. To accord.

Shinen, シチン, 一人. *n.* One person.

Shinen-ne-an, シチンチアン, 獨ノ. *adj.* To be alone.

Shine-not, シチノッ, 一口. *adj.* A mouthful.

Shinen-shinen, シチンシチン, 一人宛. *adj.* One by one.

Shine-otutanu, シチオツタヌ, 第一ノ. *adj.* The first.

Shinep, シチブ, 一物. *n.* One thing.

Shine-pa, シチバ, 一盃、一服. *n.* One cupfull. Once full. As :— *Tonoto shine pa,* " one cup of wine." *Tambako shine pa ku ku,* " I shall smoke one pipe full."

Shinepesambe, シチペサムベ, 九. *adj.* Nine.

Shinep-ikashima-arawan-hotnep, シチブイカシマアラワンホツチブ, 百四十一. *adj.* One hundred and forty one.

Shinep - ikashima - ashikne - hot-nep, シチブイカシマアシクチホツネブ, 百一. *adj.* One hundred and one.

Shinep-ikashima-ine-hotnep, シヂ
ブイカシマイ子ホツヂブ, 八十一. *adj.*
Eighty one.

Shinep-ikashima-re-hotnep, シヂ
ブイカシマレホツヂブ, 六十一. *adj.*
Sixty one.

Shinep-ikashima-wanbe, シヂブイ
カシマワンベ, 十一. *adj.* Eleven.

Shinep-ikashima-wan-e-ashikne-
hotnep, シヂブイカシマワンエアシ
ク子ホツヂブ, 九十一. *adj.* Ninety
one.

Shinep-ikashima-wan-e-ine - hot-
nep, シヂブイカシマワンエイ子ホツ
ヂブ, 七十一. *adj.* Seventy one.

Shinep - ikashima - wan - e - iwan-
hotnep, シヂブイカシマワンエイワン
ホツヂブ, 百十一. *adj.* One hundred and eleven.

Shinep - ikashima - wan-e-re-hot-
nep, シヂブイカシマワンエレホツヂ
ブ, 五十一. *adj.* Fifty one.

Shinepe-sambe, シヂベサムベ, 九ツ
ノ物. *n.* Nine things.

Shinepe - sambe - ikashima - ara-
wan-hotnep, シヂベサムベイカシマ
アラワンホツヂブ, 百四十九. *adj.*
One hundred and fortynine.

Shinepe-sambe-ikashima - ashikne-hotnep, シヂベサムベイカシマア
シク子ホツヂブ, 百九. *adj.* One
hundred and nine.

Shinepe-sambe-ikashima-ine-hot-
nep, シヂベサムベイカシマイ子ホツ
ヂブ, 八十九. *adj.* Eighty nine.

Shinepe - sambe-ikashima-re-hot-
nep, シヂベサムベイカシマレホツ
ヂブ, 六十九. *adj.* Sixty nine.

Shinepe-sambe-ikashima- wanbe,

シヂベサムベイカシマワンベ, 十九.
adj. Nineteen.

Shinepe-sambe-ikashima -wan-e-
ashikne-hotnep, シヂベサムベイカ
シマワンエアシク子ホツヂブ, 九十九.
adj. Ninety nine.

Shinepe-sambe-ikashima-wan-e-
ine-hotnep, シヂベサムベイカシマ
ワンエイ子ホツヂブ, 七十九. *adj.*
Seventy nine.

Shinepe-sambe-wan-e-iwan- hot-
nep, シヂベサムベワンエイワンホツ
ヂブ, 百十九. *adj.* One hundred
and nineteen.

Shinepe-sambe-ikashima -wan-e-
re-hotnep, シヂベサムベイカシマワ
ンエレホツヂブ, 五十九. *adj.* Fifty
nine.

Shinepe-san-shui, シヂベサンシュイ,
九度. *adj.* Nine times.

Shine-raine, シヂライ子, or Shine-
rai-no, シヂライノ, 或時. *adv.*
One at a time.

Shinere, シヂレ, 假裝スレ. *v.i.* To
pretend to be. To take another
form. **Syn : Ishinere.**

Shine-set-orunbe, シヂセツオルンベ,
鳥ノ一腹. *n.* A brood of birds.
Syn : Ukosetorunbe.

Shine-shui-ne, シヂ シュイ子, 一度.
adj. Once. **Syn : Arashuine.**

Shine-shike, シヂシケ, 二十ノ魚. *adj.*
Twenty fish.

Shine-tui-orun, シヂツイオルン, 一家.
n. One family.

Shineupa, シヂウバ, 遊ブ、戯ムル. *v.i.*
To take amusement. To play.
To amuse one's self.

Shine-ushbe, シヂウシベ, 一對ノモノ.

n. One pair of anything such as boots or leggings or gloves.

Shine-utara, シネウタラ, 朋友、親類. *n.* Friends. Relations. **Syn: Apa-utara.**

Shinewe, シネウェ, 遊戯、遊戯スレ. *n.* and *v.i.* Amusement. To amuse one's self.

Shingep, シンゲプ, or **Shinkep,** シンケプ, ハギ. *n.* Lespedeza bicolor, Turcz.

Shingi, シンギ, or **Shingi-humi,** シンギフミ, 疲レル. *v.i.* To be tired. To feel tired.

Shingi-kashpa, シンギカシパ, 仕事シテ疲レル. *v.i.* To be tired or worn out with work.

Shini, シニ, 休ム、健康トナレ. *v.i.* To rest. To adjourn. To be better in health.

Shinibe, シニベ, or **Shimibe,** シミベ, 朝饗. *n.* Breakfast.

Shinin, シニン, 涙 (岩＝打上グル). *n.* Breakers in the sea.

Shinire, シニレ, 休マスル. *v.t.* To cause to rest. To give rest to. To adjourn.

Shinish-kando, シニシカンド, 最高ノ天. *n.* The highest skies.

Shiniuka, シニウカ, 疲レル. *v.i.* To be tired. To have sufficient of a thing. To become impatient.

Shini-wa-an, シニワアン, 休ム. *adj.* To be at rest.

Shinkep, シンケプ, or **Shingep,** シンゲプ, シンゲプ＝同ヴ. *n.* Same as *Shingep.*

Shinkop, シンコプ, 鎖、滑結 (ツサ). *n.* A chain. A slipknot.

Shinna, シンナ, or **Shinnai,** シンナイ, 相違. *n.* A difference.

Shinna-an, シンナアン, 相違セル. *adj.* Different.

Shinna-are, シンナアレ, 區別スル. *v.t.* To distinguish.

Shinnai, シンナイ, 相違スル、相違セル、獨リ. *v.i.* and *adj.* To be different. To be abnormal. By themselves. Alone.

Shinnai-kat-iye-unu, シンナイカツイイェウヌ, 孕ム. *v.t.* To conceive.

Shinnai-ramat, シンナイラマツ, 亡魂、幽靈. *n.* A departed spirit. A ghost.

Shinnai-kane, シンナイカ子, 相違セル、獨リ. *adj.* and *v.i.* Different. To be by themselves. To be in a separate place.

Shinnam, シンナム, 寒冷、霜. *n.* Cold. Frost.

Shinnatoi, シンナトイ, 他處＝於テ. *adj.* At another place.

Shinne, シン子, ノ代リ＝. *adv.* Same as *shirine*; instead of. In room of. For. In place of.

Shinnetush, シンチツシ, 妨グル. *v.t.* To hinder.

Shinnoshke, シンノシケ, 眞中ノ. *adj.* The very middle. The central.

Shinnu, シンヌ, 善キ、美ナル、安全ナル. *adj.* Good. Beautiful. Safe. **Syn: Oshinnu.**

Shinnu-kuri, シンヌクリ, 老ユル、不能トナル. *v.i.* To become old or incapable.

Shinnukuri-an, シンヌクリアン, 病氣ノ爲衰弱スル. *v.i.* To have become very fatigued through illness.

Shinnurappa, シンヌラッパ, 祖先崇拜ノ式. *n.* The ceremony of ancestor worship. **Syn: Icharapa. Irappa.**

Shinnuye, シンヌイェ, 彫刻スル. *v.t.* To engrave. To cut into. To carve.

Shi-no, シノ, 誠ニ、非常ニ. *adv.* Truly. Exceedingly. Greatly. In truth.

Shi-no-inao, シノイナオ, 幣ノ一種. *n.* A kind of *inao*.

Shinonruki, シノンルキ, 唾ヲ飲ム. *v.i.* To swallow one's saliva.

Shinonde, シノンデ, 呑ミ込ム. *v.t.* To gulp down.

Shinontuk, シノンツク, 呑ミ込ム. *v.t.* To swallow. To gulp down.

Shinontukpa, シノンツクパ, 呑ミ込ム. *v.t.* To gulp down. (*pl*).

Shinoro, シノロ, 河口. *n.* As estuary. **Syn: Shiretu.**

Shinoshbare, シノシバレ, 攻擊スル. *v.t.* To attack.

Shinoshke-ashikepet, シノシケアシケペツ, 中指. *n.* The middle finger.

Shinot, シノツ, 遊戲. *n.* and *v.i.* Amusement. To amuse one's self. **Syn: Shinewe.**

Shinotcha, シノッチャ, 歌. *n.* A song. A hymn.

Shinotcha-ibe, シノッチャイベ, 歌詞. *n.* The words of a song.

Shinotcha-ki, シノッチャキ, 歌ヲ唱フ. *v.t.* To sing a song.

Shinotcha-oroitak, シノッチャオロイタク, 歌詞. *n.* The words of a song.

Shinot-mindara, シノツミンダラ, 遊ビ場所. *n.* A play ground.

Shinot-rui, シノツルイ, 遊ビ好キノ. *adj.* Playful.

Shinoye, シノイェ, 絡ム、絡メル. *v.i.* and *adj.* To wind. To become twisted.

Shinraun-seisek, シンラウンセイセク, 蒸暑キ. *adj.* Close weather. Damp and hot.

Shinrim, シンリム, or **Shinrim-nu, シンリムヌ,** 大騷音. *n.* A great noise. As:—*Ukattuima no shinrim,* "a great noise at intervals."

Shinrit, シンリツ, 古人、根. *n.* Ancestors. Roots of plants.

Shinrit-oiwak-moshiri, シンリツオイワクモシリ, 死人ノ魂ノ行ク處. *n.* The place of the dead.

Shinrupush, シンルプシ, 凍ラセレ. *v.t.* To freeze.

Shinrush, シンルシ, 苔. *n.* Moss. Lichen.

Shinrutke, シンルツケ, 山崩、大爭鬪. *n.* A landslip. A very great quarrel.

Shintoko, シントコ, 漆器. *n.* Lacquer ware.

Shintoko-emko, シントコエムコ, 洗濯盤. *n.* A washing basin for clothes.

Shinu, シヌ, 匍フ、匍ヒ上ル、匍ヒ寄ル. *v.i.* To crawl. To sidle up to.

To creep near to. As :—*En he-kote shinu yan*, "crawl up to my side." **Syn : Reye.**

Shinuinak, シヌイナク, 隱レル. *v.t.* To hide one's self.

Shinuka, シヌカ, 疲レタル. *adj.* Tired.

Shinu-shinu, シヌシヌ, 匍フ. *v.i.* To crawl.

Shinuma, シヌマ, 彼、其. *pro.* He. She. It.

Shinuwap, シヌワフ, 産痛、吟ク. *adv.* The pangs of childbirth. To groan.

Shinuwap-an, シヌワフアン, 産ム. *v.i.* To be in the act of giving birth to a child.

Shinuye, シヌイェ, 入墨スル、彫刻スレ、染ムル. *v.t.* To tattoo. To carve. To paint. To dye.

Shioarawenrui, シオアラウェンルイ, *v.t.* 爲ス、増ス、善クナリ悪クナル. *v.i.* To be enhanced. To become better or worse. To increase! As :— *Toan shiwentep tane an shiretok shioara wenrui*, "that woman's beauty has become enhanced." *Nei guru tane an wen buri shioara wenrui*, "that person's wickedness has greatly increased."

Shiocha, シオチャ, アイメ風ニシタル髪. *n.* Hair trimmed Ainu fashion.

Shiok, シオク, 悲シキ. *n.* Sorrow. Trouble.

Shioka, シオカ, or **Shiokake, シオカケ,** 後. *adv.* Behind. After. Hindermost.

Shiokaehotara, シオカエホタラ, 殘シタル物ヲ氣遣フ. *v.i.* To feel

anxious about things one has left behind.

Shiokamge-no, シオカムゲノ, 態ト. *adv.* Advisedly.

Shioka-opotara, シオカオポタラ, 殘シタル物ヲ氣遣フ. *v.i.* To feel anxious about things one has left behind.

Shiokaun, シオカウン, 後. *adv.* After. Behind. As : — *Shiokaun hosari*, "to turn the head back."

Shiok-wa-an, シオクワアン, 悲シカル. *v.i.* To be in sorrow.

Shiokerepa, シオケレバ, 終結スレ、(複數)、仆レル. *v.i.* and (*pl.*) To be finished. To come to an end. To fall down.

Shiokunnure, シオクンヌレ, 高慢ス レ. *v.i.* To be proud. **Syn : Shiomunnure. Shiokunre.**

Shiokunre, シオクンレ, 高慢スレ. *v.i.* To be proud. **Syn : Pakesara.**

Shiomonnure, シオモンヌレ, 慢スレ. *v.i.* To be proud.

Shiompiara, シオムピアラ, or **Shiompiyara, シオムピヤラ,** 寡婦、寡夫. *n.* A widow or widower.

Shion, シオン, 子供. *n.* A child. As :—*Pon shion*, "a little child ;" *poro shion*, "a large child." **Syn : Aiai.**

Shioni, シオニ, 痙攣. *n.* Cramp. As:—*Yontekkam shioni*, "to have cramp in the calves of the legs."

Shiontek, シオンテク, 赤子. *n.* A small child.

Shioro, シオロ, 悲シム. *v.i.* To be grieved. To feel concerned about a thing. **Syn : Okunnure.**

Shioro, シオロ, 喜ブ. *v.i.* To feel glad about. **Syn: Erayap.**

Shioshmak-ne, シオシマク子, 帯ノ 後ノ方ニサス. *v. t.* To stick into one's girdle behind.

Shiotemshuye, シオテムシュイェ, 歩ム (馬ノ如ク). *v.i.* To walk (as a horse).

Shioya-itak-yara, オシヤイタクヤラ, 嘲ル、馬鹿ニスレ. *v.t.* To make a fool of. To ridicule. **Syn: Shi-emina yara.**

Shioyapkire, シオヤブキレ, 怠惰ナル、 干渉スル、頑固ナレ. *adj.* and *v. i.* Idle. To meddle. To work in a slovenly manner. Stubborn. To dislike to do a thing.

Shioyapkire, シオヤブキレ, 敗ル. *v.t.* To frustrate.

Shipashipayara, シバシバヤラ, 罰セ ラル. *v.i.* To be condemned. To have one's faults made manifest.

Shipashnu, シバシヌ, 甚ダ多ク. *adv.* Too much. **Syn: Mashkinno.**

Shipaskuru, シバスクル, ワタリカラ ス. *n.* Japanese oriental raven.

Shiperam, シペラム, 鯲. *n.* A minnow.

Shipero-ni, シペロニ, ミヅナラ. *n.* A kind of oak. *Quercus grosseserrata, Bl.*

Shipeshte, シペシテ, 凋メル、延ビタ ル. *v.i.* Withered. Stretched out.

Shipet, シペツ, 本流. *n.* A main river.

Shipi, シビ, 回轉スル. *v.i.* To turn round.

Shipi, シビ, 圓キ小石、(河床又ハ海岸 ニテ見ル). *n.* Small round stones sometimes seen in river beds and along the sea shore. **Syn : Shishirup.**

Shipi, シビ, 雅美ニスル、ミヤビニスル. *v.t.* To refine. **Syn: Rakka.**

Shipi, シビ, 搔キ廻ス. *v.t.* To stir up.

Shipikemchi, シビケムチ, 小貝ノ一種. *n.* A kind of small shell fish.

Shipimba, シビムバ, 用意スル. *v. t.* To make ready. To prepare. **Syn : Shipine.**

Shipine, シビ子, or **Shipini,** シビニ, 用意シテ. *adv.* Ready Prepared.

Shipine-wa-okai, シビ子ワオカイ, or **Shipini-wa-okai,** シビニワオカイ, 用意セラル. *v.i.* To be ready. To be prepared for a journey.

Shipirasa, シビラサ, 花開ク、擴ガル. *v.i.* To blossom out as a flower. To spread out.

Shipirasare, シビラサレ, or **Shipiraspare,** シビラスバレ, 巡環スル. *v.t.* To circulate. To scatter.

Shipirasasare, シビラササレ, 花ヲ開 カス. *v.t.* To cause to blossom.

Shipire, シビレ, 廻ス. *v.t.* To turn round.

Shipitatpa, シビタツバ, 脱ク (衣ヲ). *v.t.* To undress. To untie one's clothes (especially leggings or trousers).

Shipita, シビタ, 緩クナル. *v.t.* To become unloose.

Shipita-pita, シビタビタ, 緩クナル. *v.i.* To become unloose.

Shipopkep, シボブケブ, 器. *n.* Tools. Instruments.

Shiporapora, シポラポラ, 振ル、動ク.
v.i. To move or shake about.
Syn : Porapora.

Shipoyepoye, シポイェポイェ, 曲ゲル、
廻ル. *v. i.* To twist about. To
turn round.

Shipoyepoye-rera, シポイェポイェレ
ラ, 旋風. *n.* A whirlwind. Gusts
of wind. **Syn : Hopoye rera.**

Shippo, シッポ, 鹽. *n.* Salt.

Shippo-sak-guru, シッポザクグル, 愚
人. *n.* A fool. **Syn : Kamdachi
sak guru.**

Shippo-ush, シッポウシ, 鹽ノ. *adj.*
Salted.

Shipship, シプシプ, トクサ. *n.* E-
quisetum or scouring rush. *Equisetum hyemale L. var. japonicum,
Milde.*

Shipuine, シプイ子, 少シノ. *adj.* Few.
Scarce. **Syn : Moyo.**

Shipuinere, シプイ子レ, 扣ユル、減
シム、カラ取ル. *v.t.* To withhold.
To keep back. To decrease. To
take from.

Shipuri-mukesara, シプリムケサラ,
頑固ナレ、我儘ナル. *v.i.* and *adj.*
Self-willed. Obstinate.

Shipushke, シプシケ, 増加スル、膨
上ル. *v.i.* To increase. To swell
up. To rise as dough.

Shipushkep, シプシケプ, 膨レン物.
n. Anything swollen.

Shipushkere, シプシケレ, 膨ラス. *v.t.*
To cause to swell.

Shipushkerep, シプシケレプ, 酵母.
n. Barm. Yeast.

Shipusu, シプス, 内ヨリ上ル、表面ニ
上レ. *v.i.* To rise out of. To come
to the surface.

Shipusure, シプスレ, 抜ク. *v.t.* To
draw out.

Shiraire, シライレ, 死セル振スレ.
v.i. To pretend to be dead.

Shirakkari, シラッカリ, 過ゲル. *v. t.*
To pass. To go beyond. As :—
*Nishpa tan ukuran shirakkari
an ?* "Is the master going further to-night ?"

Shiramborore, シラムボロレ, 憂ヒテ
坐スル、頑固ナレ. *v.t.* To sit still
in a dejected manner. To be
stubborn.

Shiramgiri, シラムギリ, 知ル. *v.t.*
To know. **Syn : Shiru onnere.**

Shiramkore-guru, シラムコレグル,
朋友、知己. *n.* A friend. An acquaintance.

Shiramniukesh, シラムニウケシ, or
Shiramniukesh-yara, シラムニウ
ケシヤラ, 反對スル、承知セヌ. *v.t.*
To dissent from. To disagree
with. To be hard upon another.
To lord it over one.

Shiramsamte, シラムサムテ, or **Shi-
ramuisamte,** シラムイサムテ, 顧ミ
ヌ、聞カヌ振スル. *v.t.* To take no notice of. To pretend not to hear. To
ignore the presence of another.

Shiramu-isamde, シラムイサムデ, 知
ラヌ振スレ. *v.i.* To pretend not to
know. As :—*Ainu itak ku erampeutek nei no shiramu-isamde ku
ki,* "I am going to pretend not
to understand Ainu."

Shiramyeyara, シラムイェヤラ, 鼾濤

ヲ欲ス. *v.i.* To do for praise. To desire praise.

Shiran, シラン, 空間、時間. *adv.* Space. Time. Whiles. **Syn:** **Shiri an.**

Shiran-shiran, シランシラン, 時トシ テ. *adv.* Sometimes.

Shirante, シランテ, 暴風. *n.* A storm.

Shirap, シラプ, 鷲ノ羽. *n.* The wings of an eagle.

Shirapa, シラバ, 漏ル(屋根). *v.i.* To leak from above as the roof of a house. To drip.

Shirapipi, シラピピ, 喜ブ. *v.i.* To rejoice. To be glad.

Shirapok-unu, シラポクウヌ, 自慢ス ル. *v.i.* To boast.

Shirapparappa, シラッパラバ, 羽バ タキスレ. *v.i.* To flap the wings as a bird.

Shirara, シララ, 岩. *n.* Rocks. Boulders. Very large stones. Curds. Thick soup.

Shirara, シララ, 厚キ. *adj.* Thick. Stiff as stew. As :—*Shirara no kara,* "to make thick as soup." *Shirara sayo,* "a thick soup."

Shirara, シララ, 潮. *n.* The tide. As :—*Shirara ha,* "the ebbing of the tide." *Shirara pesh,* "the flow of the tide," *Shirara ika,* "a full tide."

Shirara-kokari, シララコカリ, or **Shirara-paskuru,** シララパスクル, ハシボリカラス. *n.* Carrion crow. *Corvus corone, Linn.*

Shiraraye, シラライェ, 脱衣スレ. *v.t.*

To put off as one's clothes. To undress.

Shirarihi, シラリヒ, 屑. *n.* Dregs. Rubbish.

Shirari-korari, シラリコラリ, ハシボ ツカラス. *n.* Carrion crow.

Shirat-chimakani, シラッチマカニ, オコピカジカ. *n.* Stone-sculpin. *Enophrys, claviger, (Cuv. & Val.)*

Shiratki-kamui, シラツキカムイ, 守 リ神. *n.* A guardian god, especially the skulls of foxes and birds which the Ainu carry in their luggage when travelling.

Shirau, シラウ, 虻(アブ). *n.* A gadfly. As :—*Shirau oi,* "a place of many gad-flies."

Shiraura, シラウラ, 鴉. *n.* A crow. **Syn: Paskuru.**

Shirekutkara, シレクツカラ, 咳拂ス レ(家ニ入ル前). *v.t.* To clear one's throat as in entering a house.

Shiren, シレン, 誘導スル. *v.t.* To lead away. To entice. To lead to. To take with one. This word is used both in a good and evil sense.

Shireok, シレオク, 甚ダ少シ. *adj.* A very little. As :—*Urara poka shireok,* "there was just a very little fog."

Shirepa, シレバ, 某處へ着スル. *v.i.* To arrive at a place. This verb takes *ta* or *otta* before it.

Shireske-an, シレスケアン, 晴ヲ祈ル 祭. *n.* A ceremony for making fine weather.

Shiretok, シレトク, 美ナル(人ニ用ユ). *adj.* Beautiful. Used when speaking of human beings.

Shiretokbe, シレトクベ, 美ナル物. *n.* A beautiful thing.

Shiretok-koro, シレトクコロ, 美ナル. *adj.* Beautiful.

Shiretok-korobe, シレトノコロベ, 美ナル物. *n.* A beautiful thing.

Shiretu, シレツ, 岬. *n. geo.* A cape. Headland. Promontory.

Shiri, シリ, ノ代リ=. *adv.* Instead of. In place of.

Shiri, シリ, 陸地. *n.* The earth. Land. As:—*Shiri kata*, "on the ground." *Shiri mo*, "the world is at peace." *Shiri otettereke*, "to stamp upon the ground."

Shiri, シリ, 敏捷ナル. *adj.* Swift. Very. Well. Much. As:— *Shiri wen*, "very bad."

Shiri, シリ, 天氣. *n.* The weather. As:—*Shiri an no*, "fine weather." *Shiri an noto*, "a calm sea." *Shiri chak*, "to clear as the weather." *Shiri kutek*, "close, calm weather." *Shiri men*, "cool weather." *Shiri popke*, "warm weather," "hot weather." *Shiri seisek*, "hot weather." *Shiri tontek*, "close, warm weather." *Shiri uwande*, "to examine the sky to see what the weather is likely to be." *Shiri wen*, "bad weather." *Shiri wen wa gusu*, "since it is bad weather."

Shiri, シリ, 此語ハ動詞ノ後ニ用ヒ未ダ動作ノ終ラヌヲ示ス、例セバ、クヌカラシリチ、我ハ見ツヽアリ. *part.* This word is used after verbs to indicate that an action is still going on. As:—*Ku nukara*

shiri ne, "I am looking." *Ushungesh kotan un ku hoshipi shiri ne na*, "I am now returning to Hakodate." *Shiri* also makes the frequentive form of a verb. As:—*Ahun shiri, soyui shiri*, "coming in and going out."

Shiri, シリ, or **Shiru,** シル, 時間、空間. *adv.* Time. Space. As:— *Naa pon no shir'an ko*, "after a little while"; "a short time hence."

Shiri-an, シリアン, サテモ多數ノ. *interj.* Dear me how many! How great; how many! As:— *Chep at shiri an*, "Dear me, what a number of fish"!

Shiri-buri, シリブリ, 普通ノ習慣. *n.* A universal custom. **Syn: Kotan buri.**

Shirichieshiri-kikkik, シリチエシリキッキク, 鳴ラス、衝突スル. *v.t.* To knock against. To rattle.

Shirieiuninpa, シリエイウニンバ, 反響スル. *v.i.* To echo. To resound.

Shiri-eiyunimba, シリエイユニムバ, 反響スル. *v.i.* To resound. To echo. To have sounds in the head. **Syn: Eiyunimba. Shirieiuninpa.**

Shiri-epachiu, チリエパチウ, 煙ダフケ. *adj.* Full of smoke. Smoky.

Shiri-eshik, シリエシク, 澤山ノ. *adj.* Plenteous. Abundant. Multitudinous. **Syn: Nuye an.**

Shiri-eshikbe, シリエシクベ, 夥多、群集. *n.* Plenty. Abundance. A multitude. **Syn: Nuye an.**

Shiri-eshik-no, シリエシクノ, 澤山=. *adv.* Abundantly.

Shiri-etu, シリエツ, 岬. *n.* A cape.

Shirihi, シリヒ, ノ代リ二. *adv.* Instead of.

Shirihi-ki, シリヒキ, 代テ爲ス. *v.t.* To do instead of another. As: —*E shirihi ki wa ku arapa,* "I will go instead of you."

Shiri-hine-ye, シリヒ子イェ, 代テ爲ス. *v.i.* To speak for another.

Shiri-hine-ye-guru, シリヒ子イェグル, 辯護人. *n.* An advocate.

Shirihomara, シリホマラ, 朧トナル. *v.i.* To be dim.

Shirihomara-wa, シリホマラワ, 朧二. *adv.* Dimly.

Shirihurarakka, シリフララッカ, 地チ臭グ(獵犬ノ如グ). *v.t.* To smell the ground as a dog in hunting. To scent out.

Shirihutne, シリフツチ, 狭キ. *adj.* Narrow.

Shiri-iki, シリイキ, ト見ユル. *v.i.* To appear to be. Ought to be. As:—*Chish shiri iki,* "he ought to be doing it."

Shiri-ka, シリカ, 地表. *n.* The surface of the earth.

Shirika, シリカ, 上表、床、土. *n.* The upper side of anything. The ground. As:—*Shirika hachiri,* "to fall to the ground." *Nikara shirika hachiri,* "to fall downstairs." *Amip shirika,* "the upper or outer side of a garment."

Shirika, シリカ, 上、地上. *adv.* and *n.* Over. Above the earth. The upper part. Top. Tiptop. Summit. As:—*Shirika wa,* "from above."

Shirika, シリカ, 鞘、サヤ. *n.* A scabbard. A sheath.

Shirikamu, シリカム, 面チ地二伏シテ横ハル. *v.i.* To lie upon the ground face downwards.

Shirikamup, シリカムプ, 死體ト共二葬ル晴衣. *n.* The very best ornamented and festive garment buried with the dead. **Syn: Shikikamup.**

Shirikap, シリカプ, カヂキ. *n.* A swordfish. *Xiphius gladius, Linn.*

Shirikap-haye, シリガプハイェ, カヂキノ上顎. *n.* Upper jaw of sword fish.

Shirikappo, シリカッポ, サヨリ. *n.* Half beak. *Hyporamplus sajori,* (*F. and S*).

Shirika-sak, シリカサク, 哀レナル、醜キ. *ph.* Poor. Without beauty. Without use.

Shirikashike, シリカシケ, 外表. *n.* The outside of anything.

Shirikata, シリカタ, 地上二. *adv.* Upon the earth. On the ground.

Shirikawause, シリカワウセ, 焦ゲタル. *adj.* Parched.

Shirikepkepu, シリケプケプ, 嚙ム. *v.t.* To gnaw.

Shirikerekerip, シリケレケリプ, 熊手. *n.* A rake. **Syn: Mataburip.**

Shiri-keurototke, シリケウロトツケ, 大音. *n.* A very great sound or noise. **Syn: Yupke humi.**

Shiriki, シリキ, 模様. *n.* A pattern. As:—*Retara shiriki,* "of a white pattern."

Shiriki, シリキ, 為シツヽアル. *v.i.*
and *v.t.* To be in the act of
doing.

Shirikikbe, シリキクベ, 鞭. *n.* A
whip.

Shiriki-o, シリキオ, 模様アレ. *ph.*
Having patterns. As:—*Kunne
shiriki-o amip*, "a garment with
black patterns."

Shirikirap, シリキラブ, 悲シム. *v.i.*
To be in trouble or sorrow.
Syn: Ramupekamam.

Shirikirapte, シリキラブテ, 悲シマス.
v.t. To make sorry.

Shiriki-ush, シリキウシ, 斑ナレ. *adj.*
Spotted. Variegated.

Shiriki-ya, シリキヤ, 詠嘆ノ詞. *interj.*
Dear me! Now great! How
much! As:—*Ohaine yuk poron
no at shiriki ya!* "Dear me,
what a number of deer there
are!" **Syn: Shiri an.**

Shiriko, シリコ, 殊シク. *adv.* Severely. Mightily. As:—*Shiriko otke*,
"to spear badly or thoroughly."
Syn: Toiko.

Shirikohopoktara, シリコホボクタ
ラ, 地ニ拜伏スル. *v.i.* To bow
down to the earth.

Shirikokaptek, シリコカブテク, 恐レ
テ地ニ蹲ム. *v.i.* To crouch to the
earth in fear.

Shirikonumba, シリコヌムバ, 詰メ込
ム. *v.t.* To press down.

Shirikomuru, シリコムル, 強ク墜ツル.
v.i. To fall down heavily.

Shirikomuruse, シリコムルセ, 烈シ
ク打チ仆ス. *v.t.* To knock down
with violence.

Shirikopiwe, シリコピウェ, 押ス. *v.t.*
To push.

Shirikorare, シリコラレ, 詰メ込ム.
v.t. To press down.

Shirikot, シリコツ, 縛ケ, ツナゲ. *v.i.*
To be tied as horses.

Shirikote, シリコテ, 縛ケ. *v.t.* To
tie up as an animal.

Shirikotereke, シリコテレケ, 跳ビ廻
レ, 攀ヂ登レ. *v.t.* To jump about.
To climb up as a steep mountain.

Shirikoteye, シリコテイェ, 踏ミ込マレ.
v.i. To press the earth down as
in walking or jumping, or as an
animal in lying down.

Shirikuba, シリクバ, or **Shirikuba-**
ba, シリクババ, 嚙ム. *v.t.* To bite.
Syn: Ikubaba.

Shirikunne, シリクンネ, 暗キ. *adj.*
Dark.

Shirikuri-an, シリクリアン, 曇天. *n.*
Dull. Foggy weather. As:—
Shirikuri an to, "a dull day."

Shirikurok, シリクロク, 暗キ. *adj.*
Dark. Obscure.

Shirikurok-o, シリクロクオ, 暗クナ
リタル. *v.i.* and *adj.* To have
become dark or obscure.

Shirikuru-un, シリクルウン, 曇天ノ.
adj. Dull weather.

Shirikush, シリクシ, 行キ過グル. *v.t.*
To pass by. As:—*Shirikush ran-*
ge, "in passing by."

Shirima, シリマ, 澗, 滓(オリ). *n.* Sediment.

Shirimautum, シリマウツム, 氣候. *n.*
Climate. As:—*Shirimautum pi-*

rika, " a good climate." *Shiri-mautum wen,* " a bad climate."

Shirimo, シリモ, 美トナル、安ニナル. *v.i.* To become fine. To be in peace.

Shirinam, シリナム, 寒キ. *adj.* Cold.

Shiri-obitta, シリオビッタ, 何處デモ. *adv.* Everywhere.

Shirine-koro, シリ子コロ, 代理スル. *v.i.* To act as substitute.

Shiri-onuman, シリオヌマン, 夕暮、昏黄. *adv.* Evening. During twilight.

Shiriori, シリオリ, 土ニ穴ナカキ開ケル. *v.t.* To scratch a hole in the earth (as a dog).

Shiripekere, シリペケレ, 白日. *n.* Daylight. As:—*Nishatta shiripekere echi nukare,* " I will shew you to-morrow by daylight."

Shiripekere-koropoki, シリペケレ コロポキ, 丁度曉ニ. *adv.* Just at the time of daybreak.

Shiripene, シリペ子, 泥ノ. *adv.* Muddy. Slushy. **Syn: Shitichitek. Shiripeyese.**

Shiripo, シリポ, ノ如ク見ユル. *v.i.* and *adj.* To have the appearance of. To look like. As:—*Okkaiyo shiripo an oshmare,* " to have the appearance of a man." *Shiwentep shiripo an oshmare,* " to have the appearance of a woman."

Shiripok, シリポク, or **Shiripuk, シリプク,** アブラコ. *n.* Rock trout. *Hexagrammus aburaco, Jor.* and *Sny.*

Shiripok, シリポク, 物ノ下部又ハ内部. *n.* The under part or inside of

anything. As:—*Amip shiripok,* " the under part or inside of a garment."

Shiripokige, シリポキゲ, 物ノ底. *n.* The bottom of anything.

Shiripokinipeka, シリポキニペカ, 子供ト女. *n.* Children and women. Boys, girls, and women. **Syn: Pokinoropeka.**

Shiripopke, シリポプケ, 炎天. *n.* Hot weather.

Shiripuk, シリプク, シリポクニ同ジ. *n.* Same at *Shiripok.*

Shirisashnu, シリサシヌ, 沙々ト鳴ル (木ノ葉又ハ衣ノ如ク). *v.t.* To rustle as a dress or leaves.

Shirisep, シリセプ, 廣キ. *adj.* Broad.

Shirishimoye, シリシモイェ, 地震. *n.* An earthquake. As:—*Shirishimoye nu,* " to feel an earthquake."

Shirishiru, シリシル, 拂フ. *v.t.* To brush. Same as *Shirushiru.*

Shirishirup, シリシルプ, or **Shirushirup, シルシルプ.** *n.* A brush.

Shirishun, シリシュン, 刷毛. *n.* Frost. Wet cold weather.

Shirishut, シリシュツ, 山麓. *n.* The foot of a mountain.

Shiri-taratarak, シリタラタラク, 石多キ處. *n.* A stony place. **Syn: Shuma o-i.**

Shiritesu, シリテス, 打チ込ム (雨ノ風ノ爲メ). *v.t.* To penetrate as rain driven by the wind through a window.

Shirittore, シリットレ, 一息ニ行ク (旅行スルニ). *v.i.* To go all the way without stopping (as in taking a journey).

Shiri-uhui, シリウフイ, 山火事、大火. *n.* Mountain fire. A conflagration.

Shiri-uhuika, シリウフイカ, 山へ放火 スル. *v.t.* To set fire to a mountain.

Shiriupakbare, シリウパクバレ, 穩ニ スル. *v.t.* To make peace.

Shiriupakbare-guru, シリウパクバ レグル, 平和ヲ為ス者. *n.* A peacemaker.

Shiriwen, シリウェン, 嵐、雨天、惡シ キ天氣. *n.* A storm. Rainy weather. Bad weather.

Shiriwen-hokki-guru, シリウェンホ ッキグル, 雨ヲ降セル人 (呪ニヨリ). *n.* A rain maker. **Syn : Ruyambe ekanok.**

Shiriwen-hokki-marapto, シリウェ ンホッキマラプト, 雨乞祭. *n.* The ceremony of producing wet weather.

Shirokani, シロカニ, 銀. *n.* Silver.

Shirokani-ikayop, シロカニイカヨ プ, 銀裝セル箙. *n.* Quivers having silver ornamentations.

Shirokari, シロカリ, 圓キ. *adj.* Round.

Shirokari-oman, シロカリオマン, 廻 ス. *v.i.* To go round.

Shirokshirok, シロクシロク, 訥ル、ド モル. *v.i.* To stumble or hesitate in speaking. **Syn : Eshirok-shirok.**

Shirokundeu, シロクンデウ, 大舟. *n.* A very large boat or ship.

Shiroma, シロマ, 平和ニ住フ. *v.i.* To abide in peace. To dwell in safety. To go along steadily, as a ship with a fair wind. To be. To abide.

Shiroma, シロマ, 此語ハ時トシテ、人 代名詞ニ用キラル、例セバ、クシロマ 私. *pro.* This word is sometimes used as a personal pronoun. Thus *Ku shiroma,* " I." *E shiroma,* " you." *Shiroma,* " he," " she," " it."

Shiroma-chisei, シロマチセイ, 住家. *n.* A dwelling house.

Shiroma-i, シロマイ, 住居、平和ノ宿. *n.* An abode. A place of peace.

Shiroma-no, シロマノ, 平和ニ. *adj.* Peaceably.

Shiroma-no-okai, シロマノオカイ, 安全ニアル. *v.i.* To be in safety or in peace.

Shirorapakka, シロラパッカ, or Shirorepakte, シロレパクテ, 止ル. *v.i.* To stop. To restrain.

Shirosh, シロシ, or Shiroshi, シロシ, 印、證據. *n.* A sign. A proof. As :—*Nei shirosh tap an,* " this is its sign " or " proof."

Shirosh-asangep. シロシアサンゲプ, 手附、質. *n.* An earnest.

Shirosh-kambi, シロシカムビ, or Shirosh-hunda, シロシフンダ, 旅 行券. *n.* A passport.

Shirosh-omare, シロシオマレ, 印ヲ為 ス. *v.t.* To make a sign.

Shirotatpa, シロタツパ, 撒キ散ラス. *v.t.* To drop about. As :—*Wakka shirotatpa kor'an,* " he is dropping water about."

Shirotektereke, シロテクテレケ, 足ニ テ踏ム. *v.i.* To stamp with the feet.

Shirotereke, シロテレケ, 踏ム. *v.t.* To stamp.

Shirotke, シロツケ, 剥ス、貫ク. *v.t.* To stick. To pierce. To sit down upon any thing with a thud.

Shiru, シル, 擦ル、磨ク、ヒク. *v.i.* To rub. To grind. To chafe. Abrade. **Syn: Ishiru.**

Shiruita, シルイタ, 彼方へ、後へ. *adv.* Off. Away. Behind. As:— *Shiruita ukao*, "to put away." **Syn: Makta.**

Shirun, シルン, 惡シキ、哀レナル、意情ナル. *adj.* Bad. Poor. Wicked. Idle. Destitute.

Shirun-guru, シルングル, 哀レナル人. *n.* A poor person. An unprincipled person.

Shirunbe, シルンベ, 惡シキ人. *n.* A bad person.

Shirunin, シルニン, 反響. *n.* An echo. **Syn: Shirieiuninpa.**

Shiruoka, シルオカ, 側へ投ゲル. *v.t.* To throw on one side.

Shiruonnere, シルオンチレ, 知ル. *v.t.* To know.

Shirupakbare, シルパクバレ, 平和ヲ爲ス者. *v.t.* Same as Shiriupakbare.

Shirush-chiri, シルシチリ, ムクドリ. *n.* Grey starling. *Sturnus cineraceus, Tem.*

Shiru-shiru, シルシル, 刷フ、擦ル. *v.t.* To brush. To rub. To chafe.

Shirushnoya, シルシノヤ, カハラハハコ. *n.* *Anaphalis yedoensis, Maxim.*

Shirutne, シルツ子, 狭キ. *adj.* Narrow. **Syn: Shirihutne.**

Shirutpa, シルツパ, 行ク、匍フ. *v.i.* To go. To glide along. *Pl: of shirutu.*

Shirutu, シルツ, 行ク、匍フ. *v.i.* To move along by degrees. To go. To glide away. To shuffle along. To crawl.

Shiruturu, シルツル, 眞中ニ. *adv.* In the middle. **Syn: Humuturu.**

Shiruturu-wende, シルツルウェンデ, 仲ヲ惡クサセレ. *v.t.* To set at variance.

Shiru-uhui, シルウフイ, 大火. *n.* A conflagration. Same as *shiri uhui.*

Shiru-umomare, シルウモマレ, 荷造スル. *v.t.* To pack up. As:— *Amip shiru-umomare wa ukau*, "to pack up and put away clothes."

Shiruwande, シルワンデ, 番スル、見張リスレ. *v.t.* To watch.

Shiruwe, シルウェ, 酒ノ泡. *n.* The froth of rice beer. Yeast. Barm.

Shiruwe, シルウェ, 世帯ヲ持ツ. *v.i.* To keep house.

Shiruwe-guru, シルウェグル, 家ノ番人. *n.* A house watchman.

Shisak, シサク, 老ヒタレ、美味ナレ、善瓦ナル. *adj.* Old. Sweet. Good.

Shisakbe, シサクベ, 寶. *n.* A treasure. A good or sweet thing.

Shisam, シサム, 日本人、外邦人. *n.* A Japanese. A foreigner.

Shisamchashnure, シサムチャシヌレ, 反抗スル、入ルチ拒ム. *v.t.* To resist. To keep away. To keep from entering.

Shisamoingara, シサモインガラ, or

Shisamoingara, シサモインガラ, 検
査スル (家ノ如ク). *v.t.* To go to
inspect. (as a house). To spy at.

**Shisamoingara-guru, シサモインガ
ラグル,** 間牒. *n.* A spy.

Shisarun-guru, シサルングル, アイヌ
ノ山人. *n.* Ainu mountaineers.

Shiseipere, シセイペレ, 更生スレ. *v.i.*
To pass from one state to another as butterflies.

Shisesh-mau, シセシマウ, 六才以
上ノ牡鹿. *n.* A buck of six years
of age and over.

Shiseku, シセク, 延ビル. *v.i.* To
stretch.

Shiseturuka, シセツルカ, 背負フ. *v.t.*
To carry on the back.

Shish, シシ, 蛾. *n.* A moth. **Syn:
Heporap.**

Shish, シシ, 擴ガレ. *adj.* Spread
out.

Shishi, シシ, 獅子. *n.* A lion.
(Japanese).

Shishiki, シシキ, or **Shishki, シシキ,**
小便スル. *v.i.* To make water.

Shishiki, シシキ, 變形スレ. *v.i.* To
be transformed.

Shishipnoye, シシブノイェ, 顧ル. *v.i.*
To turn back. To turn round.

Shishirikire, シシリキレ, 代理スル.
v.i. To do instead of another.
Syn : Shirihine ki.

Shishiri-kunne, シシリクンネ, 甚ダ
暗キ. *adj.* Very dark.

Shishirimuka, シシリムカ, 沙流川ノ
名. *n.* The name of the Saru
river.

Shishiripa, シシリパ, 轉ガレ (馬ガ土
=). *v.i.* To wallow. To roll as
a horse.

Shishirup, シシルブ, 輕石. *n.*

Pumice stone. Also by some
Ainu pebbles at the bottom of
a river or stream. **Syn : Shipi.**

Shishki, シシキ, or **Shishiki, シシキ,**
小便スル. *v.i.* To make water.

Shishitomap, シシトマブ, or **Chishitomap, チシトマブ,** 恐ル可キ物、妖
怪. *n.* Something to be frightened
of. A bogey.

Shisho, シショ, or **Shiso, シソ,** 爐ノ左
側、即チ主人席. *n.* The lefthand
side of a fireplace, i.e. the master's
side.

Shishouninumbe, シショウニヌムベ,
爐ノ左側ノ端. *n.* The edge of the
hearth along the lefthand side of
a fireplace.

Shishte, シシテ, 擴がル. *v.i.* To
spread out. To set as a sail.

Shishungu, シシュング, エゾマツ. *n.*
Picea ajanensis, Fisch. A kind
of spruce.

Shishuye, シシュイェ, 振フ. *v.i.* To
shake. To wave.

Shishuyepa, シシュイェパ, 振ヒ週ル.
v.t. To wave about. (*pl*).

Shishuyere, シシュイェレ, 振ル. *v.t.*
To shake. To wave.

Shishuyeshuye, シシュイェシュイェ, 振
ル. *v.t.* To shake. To quiver.

Shisoya, シソヤ, 大黄蜂. *n.* A hornet.

Shit, シツ, シリノ畧語. Short for
shiri. In composition shiri is
often shortened into shit.

Shit, シツ, ウペユリノ葛ヲ取リタルア
トノ粕. *n.* The course dregs left
after pounding arrowroot.

Shitaigi, シタイギ, 織レ、紡グ. *n.*
To weave. To spin.

Shitaigi, シタイギ, 打ツ. *v.t.* To strike.

Shitappa, シタッパ, or **Shitatpa, シタツパ,** 痛ム、硬バル (筋肉が仕事又ハ馬乗ノ爲ニ). *v.i.* To become stiff from work or riding. To ache.

Shitashke, シタシケ, 熊ニ害セラレ. *v.i.* To be bitten or torn by a bear.

Shitashumre, シタシュムレ, 假病チツカフ. *v.i.* To pretend to be sick.

Shitat-ni, シタツニ, サイハダカンバ. *n.* A kind of birch. *Betula Maximowicziana, Regel.*

Shitatpa, シタツパ, 用意スル. *v.t.* To prepare. To make ready.

Shit'chak, シッチャク, 晴ルル. *v.i.* To clear away (as clouds).

Shitchashitcha, シッチャシッチャ, 鋸引スレ. *v.i.* To saw. This word is only used when the object is not mentioned.

Shitchashnure, シッチャシヌレ, 整理スレ. *v.t.* To arrange.

Shitchatnure, シッチャツヌレ, 整理スレ. *v.t.* To set in order. To tidy up.

Shitchimchimi, シッチムチミ, 注意シテ見廻ス、番ス、レ. *v.i.* To look carefully about. To watch.

Shitchimichimi, シッチミチミ, 聞キタガリ見タカル. *adj.* Inquisitive. To enquire into carefully.

Shitchire, シッチレ, 乾サル. *v.i.* To be dried up.

Shitchiri-chikap, シノチリチカプ, カハセミ. *n.* The kingfisher. *Alcedo ispida, Linn.* **Syn: Satchiri. Ainu satchiri.**

Shitchiu-ush, シッチウウシ, 激流ノ. *adj.* Having a very strong current.

Shiteksam, シテクサム, 側ニ於テ. *adv.* By the side of.

Shitemnukoro, シテムヌコロ, 胃. *n.* The stomach.

Shitere, シテレ, 待ツ. *v.i.* To wait.

Shiterere, シテレレ, 待タス. *v.t.* To cause to wait.

Shito, シト, 粟菓子. *n.* Cakes made of millet. A clot. Congealed blood. As:—*Kem-shito*, "a clot of blood."

Shito-kara-bera, シトカラベラ, 粟菓子チ造ルニ用ユル匙. *n.* A spoon used in making millet cakes.

Shitoki, シトキ, 垂下セル飾チ有スレ首飾. *n.* A kind of necklace having a large ornament depending from it.

Shitokihe, シトキヘ, シマヨコタイ. *n.* *Oplegnathus fasciatus (T. and S).*

Shitom, シトム, 身體ノ側、身體ノ上部. *n.* The side of body. The upper part of the body. As:—*Shitom ushi*, "To stick into the girdle." **Syn: Tumama.**

Shitoma, シトマ, 恐ル. *v.t.* To fear. To be afraid. To be in dread.

Shitomare, シトマレ, 不思議ナレ. *adj.* and *exclam.* Amazing. Strange. Astonishing.

Shitomatek, シトマテク, 恐シキ. *adj.* Fearful.

Shitomkote, シトムコテ, 人ノ體ニ結ビ付クル. *v.t.* To tie to one's body.

Shitomushi, シトムシ, 帯ブレ. *v.t.* To wear in the belt. As:—

Emush shitomushi, "to wear a sword."

Shitope-ni, シトペニ, イタナ、トキハカヘテ. *n.* *Acer pictum, Th.* A kink of maple.

Shitotkere, シトツケレ, 勉ムル、盡力ス. *v.t.* To endeavour. To attempt to do.

Shitreppo, シツレッポ, 小サキ河鰌. *n.* A small river tout.

Shittachitek, シッタチテク, 泥ノ. *adj.* Muddy. **Syn : Shiripene.**

Shittap, シッタプ, 少ナレ鶴嘴. *n.* A small mattock.

Shitteksama, シッテクサマ, 海ノ側ニ. *adv.* The seaside. **Syn : Atui sam.**

Shitteshke, シッテシケ, 滑ラカナレ. *adj.* Slippery. **Syn : Rarak.**

Shitto, シット, 甚ダ. *adv.* Very.

Shittomo, シットモ, 海岸ノ急ニ曲レル處, *n.* A sharp bend in the sea-coast.

Shitto-yara, シットヤラ, or **Shitto-ara**, シットアラ, 甚ダ甚ダ. *adv.* Very very. Very much.

Shittok, シットク, 肱. *n.* The elbow.

Shittososo, シットソソ, 八釜シキ. *adj.* Noisy.

Shittu, シッツ, or **Shiktu**, シクツ, 網ノ目. *n.* The meshes of a net.

Shittuima, シッツイマ, 甚ダ遠キ. *adv.* Very far.

Shittuitui, シッツイツイ, 掃ク. *v.t.* To sweep.

Shittum-kunne, シッツムクンネ, or **Shittum-pepere**, シッツムペペレ, 薄光. *n.* Twilight.

Shittumu-nam, シッツムナム, 凉シキ. *adj.* Cool.

Shittununatki, シッツヌナツキ, 憂々トナレ. *v.i.* To tick as a clock.

Shittununitara, シッツヌニタラ, 鑰鑰ト鳴ル. *v.i.* To rattle as pieces of metal when shaken together.

Shitturainu, シッツライヌ, 道ヲ失スレ. *v.i.* and *adj.* To lose one's way. Lost. Abberrant. With reference to this word note that when the Ainu intend to say " went astray from such and such a place," The word used is *orota*, "at," as in English, not *wano*, "from." Thus :—*Nishpa orowa no ek tempo anak ne Poropet kotan orota shitturainu wa Tomakomai kotan oroat oman*, "the telegram which the master sent me went astray at Tomakomai."

Shitturainuambe, シッツライヌアムベ, 道ヲ失フ事. *n.* Aberration.

Shitturainu-wa-an, シッツライヌワアン, 失ヘル. *adj.* Lost. Aberrant.

Shitturimimse, シッツリミムセ, 地上ニ響ク (車ノ如ク). *v.i.* To rumble along the ground (as a carriage).

Shitu, シツ, 山脈ノ支山. *n.* A name given to mountains which protrude further than others in the same range.

Shitu, シツ, or **Shitu**, シツ, 棍棒、(武器). *n.* A war-club. A club with notches cut in the end formerly used as a war-club but now used in a game called *ukikkara.*

Shitube, シツベ, or **Shitumbe, シツ
ベム,** 黑狐. *n.* A fox (principally
the black fox).

Shitukari, シツカリ, アサラシ. *n.*
Seal. *Phoca foetida, Fabr.*

Shitumam, シツマム, 身體. *n.* The
body. **Syn : Netobake. Etumam.
Tumam. Shitom.**

**Shitumbe-marapto, シツムベマラプ
ト,** 狐ノ頭骨ニ依テ罪人ヲ發見スル儀
式. *n.* The ceremony of finding
out a culprit by means of the
skull of a fox.

Shitumkanere, シツムカチレ, 慢ズ
レ. *v.i.* To be proud. **Syn : Pakesara.**

Shiturare, シツラレ, 伴フ. *v.i.* To
take as company. To lead. To
take along with one.

Shituri, シツリ, 延ビル、延ビタル. *adj.*
and *v.i.* Stretched out. **Syn :
Chishituriri.**

Shituriri, シツリリ, 身ヲ延バス. *v.i.*
To stretch one's self out.

Shiturupakbe, シツルパクベ, 銀色ナ
リキト云ハレ、傳説上ノ蛇. *n.* A
fabulous snake said to be of a
silver colour.

Shiturupak-no, シツルパクノ, マデ.
adv. As far as.

Shitushkoro-ni, シツシコロニ, カク
ヤナギ. *n. Salix sp.*

Shitushmak, シツシマク, 急ゲル. *adj.*
Hurried.

**Shitushmak-no-kara, シツシマクノ
カラ,** 急キテ爲ス. *v.t.* To do in a
hurried manner.

Shitutanure, シツタヌレ, 前後シテ、
伴ヒテ. *adv.* To be side by side or
one behind the other. Next to.

Shiu, シウ, 苦キ、ニガキ. *adj.* Bitter.

Shiube, シウベ, 膽汁. *n.* The gall.

Shiuk, シウク, or **Shiuk-an, シウクア
ン,** 盛裝スレ. *v.i.* To dress (as
for a feast). To put one's best
clothes and ornaments on.

Shiuk, シウク, or **Shiyuk, シユク,** 雄
熊. *n.* A he-bear.

Shiu-karush, シウカルシ, エブリコ.
n. Polyporus officinalis, Fr. Also
called *Kui-karush.*

Shiukina, シウキナ, エゾニウ. *n.*
Angelica ursina, Maxim.

Shiukina-kuttara, シウキナクッタラ,
エゾニウノ空虛ナル幹. *n.* The hol-
low stems of the *shiukina.*

Shiukosamba, シウコサムバ, 鼻ヨリ
吹ク. *v.t.* To blow through the
nose as an animal. As:—*Hussa
shiukosamba,* " to sigh " (lit : to
send forth breath ").

Shiu-ni, シウニ, ニガキ. *n. Picrasma ailanthoides, Planch.* Also
called *Yuk-raige-ni.*

Shiunin, シウニン, 黃ナレ、綠ナレ.
adj. Yellow. Green.

Shiunin-kando, シウニンカンド, 青
空. *n.* The blue skies.

Shiunin-kani, シウニンカニ, 眞鍮. *n.*
Brass.

**Shiunin-kani-ikayop, シウニンカニ
イカヨプ,** 眞鍮ノ飾アル箙. *n.* Quivers ornamented with brass.

Shiunin-soi, シウニンソイ, シマソイ.
n. Sebastodes trivittatus (Hilgd).

Shiunu-omke, シウヌオムケ, 甚ダ重
キ風邪. *n.* A very heavy cold.

Shiure, シウレ, 注意スル. *v.t.* To
take care of. As:—*Chisei otta*

shiure, "to take care of a house."
Syn : Oha-shirun.

**Shiurepok-eshitaigi, シウレポ゛エシ
タイギ**, 敵ノ首ニ足ヲ置ク. *v.i.* To
place the foot on the neck of one's
enemies.

Shiuri, シウリ, シウリ、ミヤマイヌザク
ラ. *n. Prunus Ssiori, Fr. Schm.*

Shiusaraye, シウサライェ, 分ツ. *v.t.*
To divide. **Syn : Usaraye.**

Shiushiuwatki, シウシウワツキ, 風聲、
(樹間ノ). *n.* The sound of the
wind whistling through the trees
of the forest.

Shiu-susu, シウスス, エゾヤナギ、ナガ
バヤナギ等. *n.* A kind of willow.
*Salix Caprea, L., S. daphnoides,
Vill., S. opaca, Anders., etc.*

Shiutoro-karire, シウトロカリレ, 否
ム. *v.t.* To deny. To send out
of the way. To lay off to another.
Syn : Eshkashke.

Shiuto, シウト, 姑、岳父. *n.* Mother
or father-in-law.

Shiuto-habo, シウトハボ, 姑女. *n.*
Mother-in-law.

Shiuto-katkimat, シウトカツキマツ,
姑女. *n.* Mother-in-law.

Shiuto-machiribe, シウトマチリベ,
夫或ハ妻ノ妹. *n.* A younger sister-
inlaw.

Shiuto-michi, シウトミチ, 岳父. *n.*
·Father-in-law.

Shiuto-sapo, シウトサボ, 夫或ハ妻ノ
姉. *n.* An elder sister-in-law.

Shiwen, シウェン, 謙遜ナル. *adj.*
Humble.

Shiwengun-nere, シウェングンチレ,
謙遜スル. *v.i.* To humble one's
self. **Syn : Yaiwenhunnere.**

Shiwende, シウェンデ, 徐行スル、緩キ
(足ノ). *v.i.* and *adj.* To walk
slowly slow of foot.

Shiwentep, シウェンテプ, 女. *n.* A
woman. As :—*Shiwemtep shiripo
auoshmare*, "to have become a
woman."

Shiwentep-kuwa, シウェンテブクワ,
女ノ墓標. *n.* A woman's grave
mark. **Syn : Mat-kuwa.**

Shiyapke, シヤブケ, 剃髪スル(喪ノ爲).
v.t. To shave the head in mourning.

Shiyara, シヤラ, 清キ、純ナル、善瓦ナ
ル. *n.* Unadulterated. Pure.
Good.

Shiyeye, シイェイェ, 病氣、病氣ノ、病氣
スル. *n.* and *adj.* and *v.i.* Sickness. Disease. Sick. To be ill.
As :—*Shiyeye guru*, "a sick person."

Shiyeyepa, シイェイェバ, 病氣、病氣
ノ、病氣スル. *Pl.* of *shiyeye*. As :
—*Shiyeyepa utara okai*, "there are
some sick persons."

Shiyokunnere, シヨクンチレ, 高慢ス
ル. *v.i.* To be arrogant. To be
boastful. To be proud. **Syn :
Pakesara.**

Shiyompiyara, シヨムピヤラ, 寡夫、
寡婦. *n.* A widow or widower.

Shiyoni, シヨニ, 縮マレ. *v.i.* To
contract. To shrink.

Shiyuk, シユク, or **Shiuk, シウク**, 雄
熊. *n.* A he-bear.

Shiyuk-koro-okai, シユクコロオカイ,
盛装スル. *v.i.* To be dressed smart-
ly.

Shiyuppa, シユッバ, 勉ムル. *v.t.* To

attempt. To try. To brace one's self up. To do diligently. To put forth one's strength.

Shiyuppa-no-ye, シユッパノイェ, 誓フ. *v.t.* To swear. To say earnestly.

Sho, ショ, or **So,** ソ, 露岩、例セバ、ショヤ、露岩ノ土地. *n.* Bare rocks. As :—*Sho ya,* " rocky land." " A place of rocks."

Sho, ショ, 借金、負債. *n.* A debt.

Sho-ataye, ショ アタイェ, 負債. *n.* A debt. As :—*Sho ataye kara,* " to pay off a debt." *Sho uk,* " to contract a debt." *Sho ukte,* " to bring into debt."

Shochakte, ショチャクテ, or **Sochakte,** ソチヤックテ, 宴散ズレ. *v.i.* To arise as from a feast.

Shok, ショク, 逸リ出ス. *v.t.* To send out. **Syn : Oashinge.**

Shoka, ショ カ, 凡テ、全體. *adj.* All. The whole. **Syn : Ebitta.**

Shokai, ショカイ, 水神. *n.* A water-nymph. **Syn : Kappa.**

Shokai-ratush, ショカイラツシ, 水神ニ殺サレ. *v.i.* To be killed by a water-nymph.

Shokata, ショカタ, 全體ニ於テ. *adv.* On the whole. As :—*Iworo shokata,* " on the whole mountains."

Shokisara, ショキサラ, 暗處. *n.* A dark place. On one side. As : —*Shokisara ta ande,* " put it on one side."

Shokkara ショッカラ, 長キ席 (林ニ敷ク). *n.* A long mat used to spread upon the floor.

Sho-kontukai, ショコンツカイ, 第貳位ノ酋長. *n.* The second or under chief.

Shokuruka, ショクルカ, 頂ヲ越ヘテ. *adv.* Over the top of anything. As :—*Iworo shokuruka,* " over the mountain tops."

Shomo, ショ モ, 否、然ラズ、例セバ、ショモネプクイェ、余ハ何モ云ハヌ. *adv.* No. Not. It is not. *Shono nep ku ye,* " I said nothing."

Shomo-ekottanu, ショ モエコッ タヌ, 注意セヌ. *v.t.* To take no notice of. Not to care about.

Shomo-itak, ショモイタク, 啞ノ. *adj.* Dumb.

Shomo-itak-ashpa-uopuk, ショモイタッアシパウォプク, 聾啞ノ. *adj.* Deaf and dumb.

Shomo-ka-ene-kawash-kuni-ra-mu-ai, ショモカエ子カワシクニラムアイ, 余ハ斯ノ如ク云ハレントハ思ハザリキ. *ph.* I had no idea that such a thing would have been said.

Shomoki, ショモキ, 慎ム、断ツ. *v.t.* To abstain. Not to do. As :— *Shomoki ya,* " will he not ? Is he not ? Does he not ?"

Shomo-no, ショモノ, 無シ、持タズ. *adv.* Not. Without.

Shomo-okaibe, ショモオカイベ, 無ナル物、新物. *n.* A thing which does not exist. A new thing. As :— *Shomo okaibe etaraka buri ki ne na,* " do not disgrace yourself in any new manner." *Shomo okaibe tonoto kuruka ko-nukoshne ne na,* " do not go taking too much wine and getting extraordinarily angry."

Shomo-ramnu-ki, ショモラムキ, 断食スル. *v.t.* To abstain from food. To fast.

Shomo-ruwe-un, ショモルウ゛ウン, 實＝然ラヌ. *adv. ph.* Dear me, no! Certainly not.

Shomo-tashnu, ショモタシヌ, 默ス. *v.i.* To be silent. Not to speak. Syn: Sh_{omo} itak.

Shomo-yaikatanu, ショモヤイカタヌ, 輕ンジテ. *adj.* Disrespectful.

Shomo-yak-anak-ne, ショモヤッアナク子, ＝アラザレバ. *adv.* Unless. If there is not.

Shonabi, ショナビ, 堆. *n.* A heap. Heaped up.

Shonep, ショ子プ, 敷物. *n.* A carpet. A mat for laying on the floor.

Shongo, ションゴ, 音信. *n.* A message. News. Tidings. As:— *Shongo koro,* "to bear a message." *Shongo an guru, Shongo koro guru,* "a messenger," "a bearer of tidings." *Pirika shongo,* "good news." *Wen shongo,* "bad news." *Shongo atte or shongo pita,* "to explain a message."

Shonoki, ショナキ, 損スレ (商賣シテ). *v.t.* To lose as in a bargain.

Sho-ottena, ショオッテナ, 第一位ノ酋長. *n.* A head chief. Syn: Poro-ottena.

Shopki, ショブキ, 待遇スル (友人ヲ). *v.t.* To receive (as a friend). To receive into one's own house or family. To receive with favour. To cause to sit down as to a meal.

Shopki-ainu, ショブキアイヌ, 客人(宴會＝招ギタル). *n.* A friend brought in to a feast.

Shose, ショセ, or Shosei, ショセイ, 負債. *n.* A debt.

Shosei-kara, ショセイカラ, 借債. To contract a debt. To buy on trust.

Shoseire, ショセイレ, or Shosere, ショセレ, 借債セシム. *v.i.* To cause to contract a debt.

Shoseire-guru, ショセイレグル, 債權者. *n.* A creditor.

Shosho, ショショ, or Soso, ソソ, 皮ヲ剥ク. *v.t.* To skin. Syn: Kapu-arisei.

Shotki, ショツキ, 寝床. *n.* A bed. As:—*Shotki chupu,* "to get up from bed." Syn: Hotke-i.

Shotki, ショツキ, 爐ノ眞中ノ灰. *n.* The ashes in the middle of a fireplace.

Shotki-i, ショツキイ, 寝室. *n.* A bedroom.

Shotki-tumbu, ショツキツムブ, 寝室. *n.* A bedroom.

Shta, シタ, 犬. *n.* A dog. Syn: Ceta.

Shu, シュ, 鍋. *n.* A saucepan. A porridge pot. A stew pot.

Shu-at, シュアツ, 鍋ノ柄. *n.* A pot handle.

Shuat-ni, シュアツニ, タラノキ. *n.* The angelica tree. *Aralia sinensis,* L. Also called *Enenge-ni* and *eninge-ni.*

Shuenenge-sei, シュエチンゲセイ, イガイ. *n.* Mussel. *Mytilu crassitesta,* L.

Shui, シュイ, 穴、罅隙. *n.* A hole. An aperture.

Shui, シュイ, 再ビ、復. *adv.* Again.

Yet again. More. As :—*Shui pon,* "yet a little" or "a little more."

Shuikere, シュイケレ, 戰ノ如ク終結スル. *v.i.* To have finished as a war. **Syn : Tumi okere.**

Shui-kot-chep, シュイコッチェブ, or **Warantuka,** ワランツカ, ガズナキノ一種(方 言). A kind of blenny. *Lumpenus anguillaris, (Pallas).*

Shuine, シュイ子, 數詞ノ後ニ付ク語. *part.* An adverbial ending to numerals.

Shui-oyashim, シュイオヤシム, 明々後日ノ其次日. *adv.* The third day from tomorrow.

Shui-oyato, シュイオヤト, 明後日. *adv.* The day after tomorrow.

Shuk, シュク, 酸キ. *adj.* Sour. **Syn : Shukkake.**

Shukarasei, シュカラセイ, カキ. *n.* Oysters. Shells used to cook food in. An earthen-ware saucepan. **Syn : Petchist. Akkesh sei.**

Shuke, シュケ, 煮ル. *v.t.* To boil. To cook by boiling. *Pl : of the object.*

Shuke-guru, シュケグル, 料理. *n.* A cook.

Shuke-iwai, シュケイワイ, 婚禮. *n.* A marriage ceremony. **Syn : U-wechiu marapto.**

Shuke-nima, シュケニマ, 俎板. *n.* A cook's board or tray.

Shukepa, シュケバ, 料理スル. *v.t.* To cook. *Pl. of both person and object.*

Shuke-tashiro, シュケタシロ, 庖丁. A kitchen knife.

Shukkake, シュッカケ, 酸キ、スキ. *adj.* Sour. Acid.

Shukkake-no, シュッカケノ, 酸キ. *adj.* Acetous. **Syn : Shuk.**

Shukkake-no-kara, シュッカケノカラ, 酸クスレ. *v.t.* To acidify. To acetify.

Shukkakep, シュッカケブ, 酸、ス. *n.* Vinegar. Anything sour.

Shu-kohui, シュコフイ, or **Shu-kou-hui,** シュコウフイ, 燒カル(鍋ニテ). *v.i.* To be burnt as food in a saucepan or as fat when being boiled.

Shukoyan-mat, シュコヤンマツ, 火ヨリ取り去リタル鍋チ置ク竈ノ或ル部分. *n.* The place upon the hearth where the pots are put after taking them off the fire. Also the name of a god supposed to look after the place where the pots are placed after being taken off the fire, and said to be the grand-child of the fire.

Shukup, シュクブ, 生育スル、若キ. *adj.* and *v.i.* Growing. Increasing in size or bulk. Adolescent.

Shukupashnu, シュクバシヌ, 速ニ生育スル所ノ. *adj.* Quick growing. Of quick growth. Healthy. Well.

Shukup-enininge, シクブエニニンゲ, 緩徐ニ生育スル所ノ. *adj.* Slow growing. Of slow growth.

Shukup-ikoro, シュクブイコロ, 增ス寶. *n.* Increasing treasures.

Shukup-moire, シクブモイレ, 緩徐ニ生育スル所ノ. *adj.* Of slow growth.

Shukupramta-kara, シュクブラムタカラ, or **Shikupramta-kara,** シクブラムタカラ, 宛サレ. *v.i.* To have nightmare. **Syn : Shukup-turashi.**

Shukupte, シュクブテ, 育ツレ. *v.t.*
To bring up. To nourish. **Syn:**
Reshpa.

Shukup-tuikata, シュクブツイカタ, 若
キ時. *adv.* Adolescence.

Shukupturashi, シュクブツラシ, 寃サ
ル. *v.i.* To have nightmare. **Syn:**
Shukupramta kara.

Shukus, シュクス, 日光、天氣. *n.*
Sunshine. The weather.

Shukus-chire, シュクスチレ, 太陽ニ
干ス. *v.t.* To dry in the sun.

Shukus-pirika, シュクスピリカ, 好天
氣. *n.* Good weather. *Shukus
wen,* "bad weather."

**Shukus-toi-kunne, シュクストイクン
子,** ヨク輝キ且ツ澄メル(天氣). *v.i.*
and *adj.* Very bright and clear
(as weather). Very clear. Exceedingly light. As :—*Skukus toi
kunne to,* "a very bright day."
Shukus toi kunne anchikara, "a
very bright night."

**Shukuturu,
  シュクツル,
Shukutut,
  シュクツツ,
Shikuturu,
  シクツル,
Shikutut,
  シクツツ,** } エソネキ. *n.* The
  common chive.
  *Allium schoenop-
  rasum, L.*

Shum, シュム, 油. *n.* Same as *Sum.*
"drowned."

Shum, シュム, 南. *n.* The south.
As :—*Shum-rera.* A south wind."

Shum, シュム, 瘠セタル. *adj.* Thin.
Poor. As :—*Shum aman,* "poor
corn."

Shum, シュム, 油. *n.* Oil. Fat.
Scum. *Shum etayep,* "an oil
pump."

Shuma, シュマ, 石. *n.* A stone.
As :—*Shuma piyekara,* "to throw
stones."

**Shuma-ari-piyekara, シュマアリピ
イェカラ,** 投石スル. *v.t.* To stone.

Shuma-kiroru, シュマキロル, or **Shu-
ma-o, シュマオ,** 石アレ. *adj.* Stony.

Shuma-potoki, シュマポトキ, 石像.
n. A stone idol.

Shumari, シュマリ, 狐、阿諛者. *n.*
A fox. A flatterer.

**Shuma-sekkoro-chikap, シェマセッ
コロチカブ,** シギノ一種. *n.* A small
kind of sandpiper.

Shumaune, シュマウ子, 死獸. *n.*
Dead animals.

Shuma-ush, シュマウシ, 石アル. *adj.*
Stony.

Shum-etuyep, シュムエツイェブ, 油ノ
ポンプ. *n.* An oil pump.

Shumke, シュムケ, 肪ヲ掬ヒ取ル. *v.i.*
To skim the fat off soap.

Shumnu-kash, シュムヌカシ, 灌木ノ
一種. *n.* A kind of shrub *Lindera
sericea, Bl.* A decoction is sometimes made of this shrub and
given to children. It is said to
be of special efficacy in cases of
stomach-ache.

Shum-rera, シュムレラ, 西風. *n.*
The west wind.

Shumumge, シュムムゲ, 凋ム. *v.i.*
To wither. As :—*Shumunge wa
isam,* "withered away."

Shum-ush, シュムウシ, 油ノ如ク、肪
ノ如ク. *adj.* Oily. Fatty. Greasy.

Shunan-chup, シュナンチュブ, or
Shinan-chup, シナンチュブ, 鱒ノ漁

期. *n.* The space of time comprising the latter part of November and the first part of December during which time the Ainu catch salmon by first attracting them with lights or torches called *shune.*

Shunapa, シュナパ, or **Sunapa,** スナパ, マダイワゥ. *n.* *Rumex aquaticus, L.,* var. *japonicus, Max.* The fruit of this plant is used as food by the Ainu.

Shunchikam, シュンチカム, 動物ノ脇ノ肉. *n.* The flesh on the sides of animals.

Shunchike, シュンチケ, スゞキ. *n.* A kind of perch. *Lates labrax japonicus, T. & S.*

Shune, シュチ, 灯松. *n.* A torch. As:—*Shune ni,* "a torch handle." Syn: **Shimechike. Airo.**

Shune-chup, シュチチュブ, 鮭ノ魚期. *n.* The same as *shunan chup.*

Shunge, シュンゲ, 偽言. *n.* A lie. Frawd. Deceit.

Shungu-ni, シュングニ, エゾマツ. *n.* A kind of spruce. *Picea ajanensis. Fisch.*

Shungu-orun-pon-chikap, シュングオルンポンチカプ, 鳥ノ一種. *n.* A kind of bird.

Shuunin-soi, シュウニンソイ, シマゾイ. *Sebastodes trivittatus, (Hilgd).*

Shu-ni, シューニ, ニガキ. *n.* *Picrasma ailanthoides,* Planch.

Shunumaush, シュヌマウシ, 老鹿、老人ヲ輕蔑シテ云フ言葉. *n.* An old deer. A word of contempt sometimes applied to old people.

Shu-okkara, シュオッカラ, 鮭又鱒ノ腹

中ノ脂肪. *n.* The inside fat of salmon and salmon trout.

Shuomki, シュオムキ, or **Shuongi,** シュオンギ, 籠ノ一種. *n.* A kink of plaited basket.

Shuop, シュオブ, or **Shuyop,** シュヨブ, 箱. *n.* A box.

Shupa, シュパ, 料理スレ. *v.t.* To cook.

Shupki, シュブキ, ヨシ. *n.* A kind of reed. *Phragmites communis, Trin.*

Shuppa, シュッパ, 束、タバ. *n.* A bundle.

Shuppa-kara, シュッパカラ, 束ヌル. *v.t.* To make a bundle of anything.

Shuptomo, シュットモ, 内部. *n.* Near the bottom of a place. The inside. As:—*Nupuri shuptomo,* "the inside of a mountain."

Shupun-chep, シュブンチェプ, ウクビ. Roach, *Leuciscus hakuensis, Gthr.*

Shupun-imok, シュブンイモク, 蟲ノ名. *n.* A grub (so named because it is a good bait for *shupun,* or roach).

Shupunkuruki-na, シュブンクルキナ, クサフヂ. *n.* A kink of vetch. *Vicia Cracca, L.* var. *japonica, Miq.*

Shupuya, シュブヤ, or **Shupuyapa,** シュブヤパ, 煙. *n.* Smoke.

Shupuya-at, シュブヤアツ, 煙ル. *v.i.* To smoke.

Shupuya-ekot, シュブヤエコッ, 煙ノ爲ニ死ス. *v.i.* To die through smoke.

Shupuya-ekote, シュブヤエコテ, 燻ベ殺ス. *v.t.* To smoke to death.

Shupuya-nup, シュプヤヌプ, キツチ ノチヤプクロノ類. *n.* The puff ball. *Lycoperdon sps.*

Shusam, シュサム, チカ. *n.* Surf smelt. *Mesopus olidus,* (*Pallas*).

Shusamna, シュサムナ, 一方ニ於テ. *adv.* On one side. Away. As: —*Shusamna tereke,* "to jump to one side."

Shusan, シュサン, or Shusam, シュサ ム, 共通ノ、賤キ. *adj.* Common. Cheap. As:—*Shusambe Shusan ikoro,* "common riches."

Shusan-no, シュサンノ, 不注意ニ. *adv.* Without care. Carelessly. Cheaply.

Shushupopun-kina, シュシュポプン キナ, 草ノ名. *n.* A kind of sedge found growing under trees only and used by the Ainu for making mats.

Shut, シュツ, 束、タバ. *n.* Anything rolled up into a bundle. **Syn : Shuppa.**

Shut, シュツ, 麓. *n.* The foot of a mountain or hill. The edge of anything. As:—*Amsho shut,* "the floor of a house." *Nupuri shut,* "the foot of a mountain."

Shut, シュツ, or Shutu, シツ, 祖母、先 祖、根. *n.* Grandmother. Ancestor. As: — *Ainu-shut,* "the Ainu ancestor. Roots. **Syu : Shinrit. Shinrich.**

Shutu, シュツ, or Shitu, シツ, 根棒 (武器). *n.* A war-club.

Shutu, シュツ, 根、先祖. *n.* Roots. Ancestors.

Shutu-atuye, シュツアツイェ, 子ヲ産マ ズナル. *v.i.* To cease from childbearing.

Shutukap, シュツカプ, 葡萄蔓ノ皮. *n.* The bark of grape vines.

Shutu-keire, シュツケイレ, 葡萄蔓ノ皮 ニテ製セシ履. *n.* Sandles made of the bark of grape vines.

Shutukeire-kina, シュツケイレキナ, コメニツタリ. *n.* *Scopendrium vulgare, Sm.*

Shutu-tuye, シュツツイェ, 死スル. *v.i.* To die.

Shutu-tuye-wa-isam, シュツツイェワ イサム, 死シタレ. *adj.* Dead.

Shuwash, シュワシ, ホザキナナカマド. *n.* *Spiraca sorbifolia, L.*

Shuwat, シュワツ, 自在鍵 (木製ニシテ 爐ニ用ユ). *n.* A wooden pothook.

Shuwonte, シュウォンテ, シホテ. *n.* The carrion flower. *Smilax herbacea, L. var. Oldhami, Max.*

Shuye, シュイェ, 煮ル. *v.t.* To cook by boiling. **Syn : Shuke.**

Shuye, シュイェ, 振リマワス、尾ヲ振レ. *v.t.* To wave about. To wag as a dog its tail.

Shuyepa, シュイェバ, 料理スル (複数). *v.t.* To cook. (*pl*).

Shuye-shuye, シュイェシュイェ, 振リマ ワス、尾ヲ振レ. *v.t.* To wave about. To shake up. To wag (as a dog its tail). As :—*Seta sara shuyeshuye,* "the dogs wags its tail."

Shuyop, シュヨプ, or Shuop, シュオ プ, 箱. *n.* A box.

Shuwanu, シュワヌ, ホドシギノ飛降ノ 音. *n.* The noise snipe make when coming down through the air.

So, ソ, 瀧. *n.* A waterfull.

So, ソ, 林. *n.* The floor of a house. As:—*So ita*, "boards laid upon the floor of a house." *So kara*, "to put a house in order." *So kara gusu ye yan.* "tell her to put the house in order." *So gesh*, "the southern end of the floor above the fireplace." *So-pa*, "the northern end of the floor above a fireplace."

So, ソ, 露岩. *n.* Bare rocks. Also *sho*. As:—*So-ya*, "rocky land. "A place of rocks."

So, ソ, 失フ事. *n.* Loss. As:—*So no ki*, "to lose in business."

Sogesh, ソゲシ, 家ノ南隅. *n.* The southern corner of a house.

Soi, ソイ, ソイ. *n.* *Sebastodes variabilis*, (*Linn*).

Soi, ソイ, 外部. *n.* The outside.

Soiba, ソイバ, 摘マミ出ス、取リ出ス. *v.t.* To pick out. To take out.

Soige, ソイゲ, 外. *adv.* Without. Outside.

Soigeta, ソイゲタ, 外部. *adv.* Outside.

Soimashke, ソイマシケ, ソイノ一種. *n.* A large kind of sea-bream.

Soina, ソイナ, 物ノ外部. *n.* The outside of a place or thing.

Soine, ソイ子, 外ヘ行ク. *v.i.* To go outside.

Soi-oro, ソイオロ, 外. *adv.* Without. Outside.

So-ita, ソイタ, 端舟ノ林. *n.* The boards used as a floor to boats.

Soi-ta, ソイタ, 外部. *adv.* Outside. Abroad.

Soita-koro-same, ソイタコロサミ, シュモクザツ. *n.* The hammer-headed shark. *Sphyrna zygœna* (*Linn*).

Soi-ta-an, ソイタアン, 外ニ居ル. *v.i.* To be outside.

Soiwasama, ソイワサイマ, or **Soiwasamma-aoshiraye**, ソイワサムマアオシライェ, 外ニ行ク、旅立スル. *ph.* and *v.i.* To go out. To set forth on a journey.

Sokaparakasa, ソカパラカサ, 帽子 (廣キ縁アル草製). *n.* A broad-brimmed hat made of grass.

Sokarabe, ソカラベ, 蓆、數物. *n.* A mat. A carpet.

Sokaramat, ソカラマツ, 酋長ノ妻. *n.* The chief wife (the name as *somat*).

Sokkara, ソッカラ, 積ル(雪ノ如ク). *v.i.* To lay as snow.

Soko-ni, ソコニ, ニハトコ. *n.* The elder tree. *Sambucus racemosa, L.* Syn: **Oshpara-ni**.

So-kontukai, ソコンツカイ, 第三位ノ酋長. *n.* The third chief of a village. See *Kontukai*.

Somat, ソマツ, 酋長、酋長ノ妻. *n.* The chief, or principal wife.

Son, ソン, 眞ノ. *adj.* True.

Son-ambe, ソンアムベ, 眞實. *n:* Truth.

Sone, ソ子, 實ニ、誠ニ. *adv.* Truly. In truth. It is truly so.

Soni, ソニ, 舟ノ進水ニ用ユル轆子. *n.* A roller used for launching boats.

Son-i, ソンイ, 事實. *n.* Truth.

Son-no, ソンノ, 誠ニ. *adv.* Truly. Very much. Accurately. Actually.

Son no an, ソンノアン, 眞ノ. *adj.* True.

Sonnonewa, ソンノチワ, 眞ニ. *adv.* Truly. Actually.

Son-no-poka. ソンノポカ, 眞ニ. *adv.* In truth.

Sontak, ソンタク, 小童. *n.* A little boy.

So-nuyep, ソヌイェブ, 帚(家内ノ). *n.* A indoor broom.

So-ottena, ソオッテナ, 第一位ノ酋長. *n.* The head chief of village. See *Kontakai.*

Sopa, ソパ, 家ノ北隅、(最モ神聖ナル場所)・ *n.* The northern corner of a hut. The most sacred part of a hut.

Sopa-un-kamui, ソパウンカムイ, 家ノ北隅ノ神. *n.* The gods of the northern corner of a hut.

Sopesh-ni, ソペシニ, 梁(ウツバリ). *n.* The long poles to which the lower ends of the side rafters of a hut are tied. **Syn: Anan-ni.**

Sori, ソリ, 橇. *n.* A sleigh. **Syn: Nuso.**

Sorokoni-samambe, ソロコニサマムベ, アブラカレイ. *n.* *Pleuronectes sp.*

Soroma, ソロマ, クサソテツ. *n.* A kind of fern. *Onoclea Struthiopteris, Hoffmn.*

Soroma-utare, ソロマウタレ, ワラビ ンシダ. *n.* A kind of fern. *Davallia Wilfordii, Bak.*

Sosh, ソシ, 木皮ノ層、頁、岩層. *n.* A layer of bark. The page or leaf of a book. A layer or strata of earth or rock.

Sosh, ソシ, 木ノ轡(オモガイ). *n.* A wooden bridle.

Sosh, ソシ, 下ル(水又ハ雪雨ノ如ク). *v.i.* To descend as water or sleet.

Soshi, ソシ, 剥ク、ムク. *v.t.* To peel off. (*sing*). To skin.

Soshi-oma, ソシオマ, 剥ガレタレ、ムカレタレ. *adj.* Peeled off.

Soshipi, ソシビ, 再婚スレ. *v.t.* To re-marry.

Soshke, ソシケ, 剥ク、ムク. *v.i.* To peel.

Soshma, ソシマ, ケミ. *n.* *Elaeagnus.*

Soshma, ソシマ, 迂鳴ッテ語ル. *v.i.* To speak in a gruff voice.

Soshne, ソシ子, 層ノ. *adj.* In layers. In companies.

Soshnu, ソシヌ, 層、片. *n.* A layer. A flake.

Soshnu-soshnu, ソシヌソシヌ, 層ノ. 片ノ. *adj.* In layers. In flakes.

Soshpa, ソシパ, 剥ク、ムク、剥ク、ハク. *v.t.* To skin. To bark. To peel. To uncover.

So-un-turuba, ソウンツルバ, 内庭ノ中戸. *n.* An inner porch door.

Soya, ソヤ, 岩多キ地. *n.* Rocky land. A place of rocks.

Soyai, ソヤイ, 黄蜂. *n.* A wasp. A bee. A hornet. As:—*Soyai chotcha,* "to be stung by wasps *Soyai set,* "a wasp's nest." As:—*Ka-soyai,* a bee; *shi-soyai,* a hornet. *Toi-soyai,* a wasp.

Soyai-wakka, ソヤイワッカ, 蜜. *n.* Honey. **Syn: Soyai ninge.**

Soye, ソイェ, 錐ル. To bore.

Soyep, ソイェブ, 錐. *n.* A gimlet. An auger.

Soyekatta, ソイェカッタ, 追ヒ出ス. *v.t.* To drive out. As:—*Seta soyekatta wa apa shi*, "drive the dog out and shut the door." **Syn: Soyukuta.**

Soyemba, ソイェムバ, 外出ス. レ. *v.t.* To go out. **Syn: Soyumba.** *Pl: of Soine and soyun.*

Soyokari-tashum, ソヨカリタシュム, 下痢病、赤痢. *n.* Diarrhoea. Dysentery.

Soyomba, ソヨムバ, 外出スル (次ノ語ノ複數). *v.i.* To go out. Plural of the following word.

Soyone, ソヨ子, 外出スル. *v.i.* To go out. Same as *Soine*. For the plural see *soyemba* and previous word.

Soyoshma, ソヨシマ, 突然戸外ニ突出スル、迸出スレ. *v.i.* A rush suddenly out of doors. To gush out. To drop out as the bottom from a bucket or basket. As:—*Niwatush asama soyoshma*, "the bottom of the bucket has fallen out. **Syn: Osoyoshma.**

Soyotereke, ソヨテレケ, 突然戸外ニ突出スレ. *v.i.* To rush suddenly out of doors. To run suddenly out of a house.

Soyui, ソユイ, 出入口. *n.* A going out of. An exit (of a person). As:—*Soyui-shiri shui-shiri*, "a going out and coming in."

Soyukuta, ソユクタ, or **Soyekatta, ソイェカッタ**, 追ヒ出ス. *v.t.* To drive out.

Soyum-apa, ソユムアバ, or **Soyun-apa, ソユンアバ**, 外戸. *n.* An outer or porch door.

Soyumba, ソユムバ, 外出ス. レ. *v.i.* To go out of doors. *Pl. of soine.* **Syn: Soyemba.**

Sum, スム, 溺レル、洗ヒ去ラレ. *v.i.* To be drowned. To be washed away. As:—*Mungi obitta sum wa okere*, "the barley has all been washed away." *Nei seta sum wa rai*, "the dog was drowned."

Sunapa, スナバ, or **Shunapa, シュナバ**, マダイワウ. *n.* *Rumex aquaticus, L. var. japonicus, Max.* The fruit of this plant is used as an article of food by some Ainu.

Sura, スラ, 邪寇セヌ. *v.t.* To let alone. To cast away.

Surugu, スルグ, 毒、カブトギクノ毒. *n.* Poison. Aconite poison. *Aconitum Fischeri, Reich.*

Suruguiberewaraige, スルグイベレワライゲ, 毒害スレ. *v.t.* To poison.

Surugu-kusuri, スルグクスリ, シャウブ. *n.* The sweet flag. *Acorus Calamus, L.*

Surugu-musa, スルグムサ, 矢ノ毒(貯藏ノ爲束ネラレシ). *n.* Arrow poison done up in a bundle for preservation.

Surugu-ra, スルグラ, ブシ. *n.* The monk's hood or aconite plant.

Sus, スス, 浴スル. *v.i.* To bathe.

Sus-mau, ススマウ, or **Susu-mau, ススマウ**, アキグミノ實. *n.* The fruit of the *Elaeagnus umbellata, Thunb.*

Sussuru-an, スッスルアン, 惡天氣. *n.* Bad weather.

Susu-ni, ススニ, 柳. *n.* Willow of any kind. *Salix.*

Susu-at, ススアツ, バツコヤナギ. *n.*
Salix Caprea, L. Called also
Thush-ni.
Susu-mau-chikum, ススマウチクム,

or Susu-mau-ni, ススマウニ, or
Sus-mau-ni, ススマウニ, アキグミ.
n. Elæagnus umbellata Thunb.

T (夕).

Ta, 夕, ニ於テ、ニマデ、例セバ、夕ア
ン、此處ニ在リ. *post.* At. To. In.
As:— *Ta an,* "it is here." *Ta
an un to an un,* or *ta ani un,*
"here and there."

Ta, 夕, 打ツ. *v.t.* To strike. As:
— *Chikuni ta,* "to strike a tree."
Syn: Tauge.

Ta, 夕, 掘リ出ス、吸ム、クム. *v.t.* To
dig up. To draw as water. As:
— *Emo ta,* "to dig potatoes.
Wakka ta, "to draw water."

Ta-a, 夕ア, 何. *interj.* and *pro.* What.
As:— *Nekon a akara kuni ta a?*
"what ought to be done with
it"?

Taaba, 夕アバ, 此處ニ、其處ニ. *adv.*
Here. There. Syn: Pishkan
moshiri.

Taada-orota, 夕アダオロタ, 此處ヘ、
迄. *adv.* Hither. So far. As:—
Taada pakno, "thus far." "So
far."

Taada-toada, 夕アダトアダ, 其處此處
ニ. *adv.* Here and there.

Taada-un, 夕アダウン, 此處ニ. *adv.*
Here.

Taada-un-toada, 夕アダウントアダ,
其處此處ニ. *adv.* Here and there.

Taan, 夕アン, 此. *adj.* This.

Taanda, 夕アンダ, 此處ニ. *adv.* Here.
Same as *taada.*

Taanda-orota, タンダオロタ, 此方ヘ.
adv. Hither. As:— *Taanda pakno,* "thus far," *Taanda toanda.*
"here and there."

Taanda-un, 夕アンダウン, 此處ニ.
adv. Here. As:— *Taanda un
toanda un,* "here and there."

Taani, 夕アニ, 此處ニ. *adv.* Here.

Taani-toani, 夕アニトアニ, 其處此處
ニ. *adv.* Here and there.

Taani-un, 夕アニウン, 此處ニ. *adv.*
Here.

Tai, 夕イ, 森. *n.* A forest.

Taiki, 夕イキ, 蚤ノミ. *n.* A flea.

Taiorush-mun, 夕イオルシムン, ハ
ク 〃. *n. Mentha arvensis*, L. *var.
piperascens, Holmes.*

Taipe, 夕イベ, 濃キ汁. *n.* A thick
soup. The thick sediment of
soup.

Taishikutkes, 夕イシクツケス, 喉ノ
ド. *n.* The throat. As:—
Taishikutkes amaknaraye, "he
cleared his throat" (as before
entering a house). Syn: Rekut.

Tak, 夕ク, 固キ. *adj.* Hard. A
Taku.

Tak, タク, 束ヲ持チ來ル. *v.t.* To fetch or bring a thing which has previously been tied up into a bundle or otherwise prepared.

Taka, タカ, 鷹. *n.* Hawks.

Takara, タカラ, 夢、寢リ. *n.* A dream. To sleep. **Syn: Wendarap.**

Takasara, タカサラ, or **Takaisara, タカイサラ**, 酒盃ノ臺. *n.* A wine cup saucer. A cup stand.

Takataka, タカタカ, 蟋蟀、蝗. *n.* A grasshopper. A locust. **Syn: Pata. Patapata.**

Takayara, タカヤラ, 持チ來サスル. *v.i.* To send and fetch. **Syn: Tak yara.**

Takbe-kina, タクベキナ, アゼスゲ. *n. Carex vulgaris, Fr.*

Take, タケ, 今、只今、數日以前. *adv.* Now. Just now. A few days ago. **Syn: Nahun. Pon no etoko.**

Takkara, タッカラ,
Tak-ne-kara, タクチカラ,
Tak-no-kara, タクノカラ, } 固ムル. *v.t.* To harden.

Takne, タクチ, 短キ. *adj.* Short. Curt.

Takne-hike, タクチヒケ, 短キ物、蝮、マムシ. *n.* A short thing. A viper. **Syn: Nitne hike.**

Takne-no, タクチノ, 短ク. *adv.* Shortly. In a brief manner.

Takne-no-kara, タクチノカラ, 短縮スル. *v.t.* To shorten.

Takne-no-ye, タクチノイェ, 短縮スル. *v.t.* To abbreviate.

Taknere, タクチレ, 短縮スル. *v.t.* To shorten. To abridge. **Syn: Ponde.**

Taknere-i, タクチレイ, 短縮. *n.* Abridgement. **Syn: Ponde-i.**

Taknere-re, タクチレレ, 短縮セシム. *v.t.* To cause another to shorten.

Taktak, タクタク, 固キ、固キ塊. *adj.* and *n.* Hard. A hard lump. A clot. As:—*Ye-taktak,* "a hard lump of matter or puss.

Taktakbe, タクタクベ, 大石(河中ノ). *n.* Large stones found in rivers. **Syn: Repushbe.**

Taktak-kara, タクタクカラ, or **Taktaku-kara, タクタクカラ**, 固ム ル. *v.t.* To harden.

Taku, タク, 塊、球. *n.* A mass. A ball.

Taku-akara, タクアカラ, 混リタレ. *adj.* Agglomerated. **Syn: Ataku kara.**

Taku-chine, タクチチ, 球根. *n.* A bulb.

Taku-kara, タクカラ, 混ズレ. *v.t.* To agglomerate.

Taku-ne, タクチ, 混リタル. *adj.* Agglomerated.

Takupi, タクビ, 謙遜ノ語. *n.* A term of humiliation. As:—*Tan okkai takupi poku erampokiwen wa en kore,* "please have mercy upon this worthless fellow."

Takupi, タクビ, 肩. *n.* The shoulder.

Takupi, タクビ, 只一ッ. *adj.* One only. Just one. Only. **Syn: Patek.**

Takusa, タクサ, 染. *n.* A bunch of

anything. Sometimes a bunch of herbs or an *inao* used to wave over the sick to drive away disease. As :—*Nuttat takusa*, "a bunch of bamboo grass."

Tak-yara, タクヤラ, 持チ來ラシム. *v.t.* To send and fetch. **Syn : Takayara.**

Tam, タム, 刀. *n.* A sword. As :—*Tam etaye*, "to draw a sword." *Tam koterekere*, "to flourish a sword." *Tam kuri*, "to cut with a sword." *Tam kuri yainutumnu*, "to be cut with a sword." *Tam kuru*, "to draw a sword." "To flash a sword." *Tam kutpokichiu*, "to wear a sword, *Tam sep ukohopuni*, "to fight with swords." *Tam sopkere*, "to strike at with a sword." *Tam tui*, "a strike of the sword."

Tam, タム, or **Tan, タン**, 此. *pro.* This.

Tama, タマ, 球、珠. *n.* A ball. Beads. As :—*Tama saye*, "to thread beads."

Tamane, タマ子, 球、球ニナリシ. *v.i.* and *n.* A ball. To have become a ball.

Tambako, タムバコ, 煙草. *n.* Tobacco. As :—*Tambako iku*, "to smoke." *Tambako kotukka*, "to light a pipe." *Tambako ku*, "to smoke."

Tambako-op, タムバコオブ, 煙草入. *n.* A tobacco pouch or box.

Tambe, タムベ, 此物. *n.* This thing. As :—*Tambe nei no shomo ne*

ya ? "is it not so." *Tambe tashi ne ine*, "it being so."

Tambe, タムベ, 陰門. *n.* The vagina. **Syn : Achike. Chinunuke-ike. Nuina korobe.**

Tambe-gusu, タムベグス, 此故ニ. *adv.* Therefore. For this reason. As :—*Tambe gusu okaibe*, "on account of these things."

Tambe-imakake, タムベイマカケ, 今ヨリ. *adv.* From now. Henceforth.

Tambe-imakake-ta, タムベイマカケタ, 暫時ノ後. *adv.* By and by.

Tambu, タムブ, 龜ノ甲. *n.* Carapace of turtle.

Tambushi, タムブシ, 補綴スレ. *v.t.* To mend, as a hole in clothes.

Tam-chash, タムチャシ, 受ケ流ス. *v.t.* To ward off (as in fencing).

Tam-here, タムヘレ, 刀ノ光. *n.* The flash of a sword. The glitter of a sword.

Tam-kik-humbe, タムキクフムベ, 楯. *n.* A shield.

Tampaketa, タムバケタ, 此側. *adv.* This side.

Tampaneba, タムバ子バ, 今年. *adv.* This year.

Tampara-cheppo, タムバラチェッポ, 魚ノ名. *n.* A perch.

Tamparaparak, タムバラバラク, 泣ク. *v.i.* To weep. **Syn : Hawe ashte wa chish.**

Tampata, タムバタ, 此側. *adv.* This side. As :—*Pet tampata*, "on this side of the river.

Tampota, タムボタ, 暫時ノ後、一兩日ノ後. *adv.* By and by. In a day or two.

Tampush, タムブシ, 刀、鞘. *n.* A sword sheath.

Tamsep, タムセブ, 鳴ル (兩物チ打合セタル時). *v.i.* To sound, as when one thing is knocked against another.

Tamtui, タムツイ, or **Tamtuye, タムツイ,** 腸. *n.* The intestines. **Syn : Kankan-okotbe.**

Tamu, タム, ヨコノミ. *n.* Sand fleas.

Tamunde, タムンデ, 搖レル (木ノ枝ノ如ク). *v.t.* To wave from one side to the other as a branch of a tree.

Tamun-tamun, タムンタムン, 打チ合フ、受ケ流ス. *v.t.* To fence. To ward off.

Tan, タン, 此. *pro.* This. As :— *Tan anchikara,* "this night." *Tan chup,* "this month." *Tan guru,* "this person." Tan to, "today." *Tan ukuran,* "this evening."

Tanak, タナク, 氣絶スル、弱キ. *v.i.* and *adj.* To be faint. To faint away. Weak. Faint. As :— *Tanak koro keutum guru,* "a faint hearted person."

Tanak-tanak, タナクタナク, 氣絶スル、弱キ (前ノ語ヨリ強ク且ク屢シカスル事). *v.i.* and *adj.* Frequentive and intensitive of the previous word.

Tande, タンデ, 今. *adv.* Now.

Tando-oro, タンドオロ, 今ヨリ. *adv.* Henceforth.

Tande-pota-an, タンデポタアン, 殆ド、近ク. *adj.* Nearly. Close at hand. As :— *Tande pota an guru,* "the person near by."

Tane, タ子, 今. *adv.* Now. As : — *Tane pukno,* "until now." *Tane wano,* "from now," "henceforth."

Tane-ankesh, タ子アンケシ, 黎明. *adv.* The break of day.

Tane, タ子, 種子. *n.* A seed. As :— *Tane op,* "a seed basket." This is really a Japanese word but now always used by the Ainu ; the native word is *Piye.*

Tanebo, タ子ボ, 今、只今. Now. Just now. Now for the first time.

Tane-ru, タ子ル, 列 (植エタル植物ノ). *n.* A row (as vegetables in a garden).

Tanne, タンチ, 長キ. *adj.* Long. As :— *Tanne chinika,* "a long step."

Tanne-cheppo, タンチチェッポ, 鰻. *n.* An eel. **Syn : Ukurube.**

Tanne-eremu, タンチエレム, エゾイタチ (夏毛ノ者ノ). *n.* An ermine. *Putorius erminea, Linn.*

Tanne-hesei, タンチヘセイ, 喫息. *n.* A sigh.

Tanne-hesei-ki, タンチヘセイキ, 嘆息スル. *v.i.* To sigh. **Syn :, Yaitasarapare.**

Tanne-hush-arapare, タンチフシアラパレ, or **Tanne-hushta, タンチフシタ,** 吐息スル. *v.i.* To blow as when tired or hot. **Syn : Hesei turiri.**

Tannepuikoro, タンチブイコロ, 重代ノ長劍. *n.* Long swords kept as heirlooms.

Tanne-ushi, タンチウシ, 長サ. *n.* Length.

Tannu, タンヌ, 海豚. *n.* A dolphin. (Including several species).

Tantaraki, タンタラキ, or **Tanta-ratki, タンタラツキ,** 徐歩スル. *v.i.* To canter. To go jogingly along. To trot along gently as a dog or fox. **Syn: Chairak. Sambash.**

Tanto, タント, 今日. *adv.* Today. This word is often followed by *otta*. As :—*Tanto otta,* " today," or during this day."

Ta-okkaiyo, タオッカイヨ, 驚又ハ賞讃ノ叫. *excl.* Expression of surprise or praise.

Tap, タプ, 圓頂丘. *n.* A single hill with a round top. A cone.

Tap, タプ, 此、斯ク、今、只今. *pro.* This. Thus. So. Just now. This moment. As :—*Tap moire,* " so late." *Tap an noshike,* " thus late at night." *Tap soine,* " he has just gone out."

Tap-ambe, タッアムベ, 此物. *n.* This thing.

Tapan, タパン, 斯ク、此種. *adv.* Thus. It is so. This kind. *Tap an,* sometimes lengthened into *tap an na,* is often used as an affirmative ending to verbs. As:— *Tapan orushpe,* " this news." *An ruwe tapan na,* it is so."

Tapan-ta, タパンタ, 此處ニ. *adv.* Here. At this place.

Tapakno, タパクノ, 充分ナル. *adj.* Sufficient. Enough. As :—*Tapakno yainu,* " to be satisfied with." **Syn : Tepakno.**

Tap-chikiri, タプチキリ, 前胛脚. *n.* The fore feet of animals.

Tapera, タペラ, or **Tapere, タペレ,** 肩. *n.* The shoulder.

Tapera-pone, タペラポ子, or **Tapere-pone, タペレポ子,** 肩骨. *n.* The shoulder blade.

Tapip, タビプ, 爪ノ根ノ腫物. *n.* Oynchia.

Tapka, タプカ, 山頂. *n.* The top of a mountain.

Tapkanni-kara, タプカンニカラ, 擴ガル (木ノ枝ノ如ク ニ上方ニ向ッテ). *v.i.* To spread out in an upward position like the branches of trees.

Tapkara, タプカラ, 踊ル. *v.i.* To dance. **Syn : Rimsei.**

Tapkara-kina, タプカラキナ, オミナヘシ. *n.* *Patrinia sceliosoefolia, Link.*

Tapkara-tapkara, タプカラタプカラ, 踊ル. *v.i.* To dance.

Tapkiri, タッキリ, 皮ノ剝ゲタル獸ノ前脚. *n.* The skinned fore legs of animals.

Tapkop, タプコプ, 一峯ノ山. *n.* A single peak of a mountain. A mountain of one peak, standing by itself.

Tapne, タプ子, 斯ク. *adv.* Thus. So. As :—*Tapne an chiki,* " if that is so." *Tapne an,* " it is so." *Tapne an koro,* " it being so." *Tapne an kane,* " it being so."

Tap-okai, タプオカイ, 斯ク、此ノ種. *adj.* Thus. This kind. Such.

Tapshut-umbe, タプシュツウムベ, 肩上ノ物. *n.* Anything upon the shoulders.

Tapsutu, タプスツ, 肩. *n.* Th shoulders.

Taptapu, タプタプ, 塊トナス. *v.t.* To gather up into a lump or ball.

Tara, タラ. 附加物、垂下物. *n.* An appendage. Affixed to, Holding on to. Dangling from.

Tara, タラ, 背負フ為ノ器. *n.* A sling used for carrying bundles. As:—*Tara ari chikuni shuppa kara*, "to make wood into a bundle with a sling."

Tara-at, タラアツ, タラノ繩. *n.* The string of a *tara*.

Tara-ibe, タライベ, タラノ繩ノ額ニ附ケル部分. The head piece of a sling.

Tarai, タライ, 盥、犬ノ食器. *n.* A trough. A dog trough.

Taraiush, タライウシ, or **Tarai-ushike, タライウシケ**, 腰ノ挾キ部分. *n.* The small of the back. By some, the crux.

Tarakin, タラキン, 搖レル. *v.i.* To be jolted. To be bumped up and down as when riding horseback upon a packsaddle.

Tarakin-tarakin, タラキンタラキン, 烈シク搖レル. *v.i.* To be severely shaken or bumped.

Taranton, タラントン, ターレント (量目ノ名). (編者ノ輸入語). *n.* A talent (introduced by the compiler).

Tara-pe, タラペ, 布團. *n.* A matress. **Syn: Atarape. Chita-rape.**

Tarape-nuni, タラペヌニ, 全財産. *n.* One's entire belongings. As:— *Tarape nuni eotuyetuye oara isam*, "his entire furniture and ornaments were completely taken away."

Tara-ush, タラウシ, 背負フ器械ヲ附ケタル. *adj.* Having a sling attached to it. As:—*Tara-ush ikayop*, "a quiver with a sling attached to it."

Tarara, タララ, 捧ブル. *v.t.* To hold out. As:—*Rikta tarara*, "to hold out above one."

Tarara, タララ, 捧グル. *v.t.* To hold up. **Syn: Rikta puni. Rik peka turiri.**

Taratarak, タラタラク, 石多キ. *adj.* Thick as with stones. Stony. Lumpy. Uneven. As:—*Shiri-taratarak*, "a stony place." **Syn: Toksetokse.**

Taribe, タリベ, 背負フ器械ノ額ニ付ケル部分. *n.* The headpiece of a sling.

Taritari, タリタリ, 搖レル、(馬ニ乘ル如グ). *v.i.* To be tossed up and down as when riding.

Tarush, タルシ, 背負フ器械ヲ附ケタル. *adj.* Having a sling attached to it. As:—*Tarush ikayop*, "a a quiver having a sling attached to it."

Tasa, タサ, 横ギリテ、横切ル. *adv.* A cross. Also *v.t.* To cross. Returned as, *Tasa kambi*, a return letter.

Tasa, タサ, 登ル. *v.i.* To ascend. **Syn: Hemesu.**

Tasap, タサブ, 罰金. *n.* A fine. As:—*Makiri tasap*, "a knife given as a fine." *Chip tasap*, "a boat given as a fine." **Syn: Ashimbe.**

Tasaske, タサスケ, 裂ケタル (河ノ氷ノ)、粗キ. *v.i.* Broken up (like the ice in a river)! Rough cracked Turned up on edge.

Tasaske, タサスケ, 苛酷ナル. *adj.* Bitter tempered.

Tashi, タシ, 有ル. *v.i.* To be. Is.

Tashi, タシ, 小刀. *n.* A knife.

Tashi, タシ, 理由. *n.* A reason. As :— *Tambe tashi,* "for this reason."

Tashiro, タシロ, 大ナル小刀. *n.* A large knife. A chopper.

Tashiro-kupushbe, タシロクブシベ, 小刀ノ鞘. *n.* A knife sheath. **Syn: Saya.**

Tashiro-nit, タシロニツ, or **Tashiro-nip, タシロニブ,** 大ナル小刀ノ柄. *n.* A large knifehandle.

Tashmak-hesei,タシマクヘセイ, 喘ク. *v.i.* To gasp.

Tashmak-tashmak-no-hesei, タシマクタシマクノヘセイ, 喘ク. *v.i.* To gasp for breath.

Tashnu, タシヌ, 語ル. *v.i.* To speak. **Syn: Itak.**

Tashui, タシュイ, 暴風. *n.* A storm of wind.

Tashum, タシュム, 病氣. *n.* Sickness.

Tashumki, タシュムキ, 病ム. *v.i.* To be sick. To be ill.

Taskoro, タスコロ, 霜空、大氣. *n.* Frost. Air. Atmosphere. As :— *Retat'taskoro,* "white frost."

Taskoro-mau, タスコロマウ, 露. *n.* Dew. **Syn: Kinape.**

Tasu, タス, 息、イキ. *n.* The breath. Air. **Syn: Hesei.**

Tasu-eshkari, タスエシカリ, 窒息ス ル. *v.i.* To suffocate.

Tasu-tuye, タスツイェ, 窒息スル. *v.t.* To suffocate.

Tat, タツ, 樺ノ皮. *n.* Birch bark.

Tata, タタ, 截ル, *v.t.* To hack. To chop.

Tata, タタ, 此ノ. *adj.* This.

Tata-otta, タタオッタ, 其時、其後、其前. *adv.* Then. Afterwards. Before that. Upon this.

Tata-tata, タタタタ, 大ニ截ル、打ツ. *v.t.* To hack much. To strike. To chop.

Tat-ikayop, タツイカヨブ, 箙ノ一種(樺ノ皮ト金具チ鏤メタル). *n.* A kind of quiver ornamented with birch bark and metal.

Tat-ni, タツニ, 樺. *n.* Birch.

Tattarake, タッタラケ, 激昂スル. *v.i.* To be excited. **Syn: Patpatke.**

Tat-ni-karush, タツニカルシ, 樺木耳. *n.* *Polyporus sp.* Growing on birch.

Tattatse, タッタツセ, 沸ユル. *v.i.* To boil up as water.

Tauge, タウゲ, 截ル. *v.t.* To chop. To beat with an edged tool.

Tauge-tauge, タウゲタウゲ, 多ク截ル. *v.t.* To chop much.

Tauke-sanu, タウケサヌ, 音テ立ル(何物カ チ打ツテ). *v.t.* To make sound as in striking anything.

Tat-ushbe, タッウシベ, 灯松. *n.* A torch.

Te, テ, 此語ハ他動詞ト共ニ用キテ其チ使役相トナス、例セバ、ウック、取ル、ウックテ、取ラスル、ノ如シ、又此語ハ或ル自動詞ト共ニ用キテ、其サ他動詞トナス、例セバ、サブ、下ル、サブテ、下ス、ノ如シ. *part.* The particle *te* is used with some transitive verbs, to give them a causative force. Thus :— *Uk,* "to take ;" *ukte,* "to cause to take."

Te is also used with some intransitive verbs to make them transitive. As:—*Sap*, "to go down"; *saple*, "to send down."

Te, テ, 此處ニ. *adv.* Here. As:— *Te oro*, "here," "from here," "to here." *Te oro pakno*, "thus far." *Te orota*, "to this place." *Te oro wa*, "from here." *Te pakno*, "thus far." *Te peka*, "this side," "here." *Te un*, "here," "to this place," "at this lace." *Te wa no*, "hence," "henceforth."

Teda, テダ, 此處ニ. *adv.* Here. As:—*Teda an*, "it is here." *Teda an a matkachi*, "the girl who lives here."

Teeda, テエダ, 古代、以前ニ. *adv.* Ancient times. Previously. Before.

Tehuru, テフル, 魚ノ腎. *n.* The kidney of fish.

Teike, テイケ, 中ニ墜ツル (家ノ屋根ノ如ク). *v.i.* To fall in as the roof of a house.

Teine, テイ子, 濕レル. *adj.* Wet. Damp.

Teine-pokna-moshiri. テイ子ポクナモシリ, 地獄. *n.* Hell, i.e. Gehenna.

Teinep, テイ子プ, or **Tennep,** テン子プ, 赤兒. *n.* A very young child.

Tek, テク, 此語或ル詞ト共ニ用井テ、其ヲ形容詞トナス、例セバ、ハプンノ又ハ、アプンノ、穩ニ、ハプンテク、又ハ、アプンテク、穩ナル. *part.* When the particle *tek* is used with

some words it gives them an adjectival force. Thus:—*Hapun no* or *apunno*, "gently;" *Hapuntek* or *apuntek*, "gentle." *Monreige*, "to work," *monraiyetek*. "laborious." As, just. As:—*Irukai tek*, "just a moment," It is also used as a conjunction "as;" "for;" "because;" and expresses "reason."

Tek, テク, **Teke,** テケ, **Tekene,** テケ子, 手、腕、木枝、爪 (海老ノ). *n. and adv.* The hands. The arms. A branch of a tree. The claw of a crab or lobster. Near. Close at hand. As:—*Kotan tek*, "the district round a village." *Tek ani.* "to take in the hands." *Tek ani wa arapa*, "to lead by the hand." *Tek kake koro* "to place the hand above the eyes." *Tek kake koro wa ingara*, "to look at by shading the eyes with the hands." *Tek kotoro*, "the outside of the hand." *Tek numba* or *tek ruiruiba*, "to rub the hands together as in salutation." *Tek omare*, "to take in the arms." *Tek tui poki*, "the palms of the hands." *Tek umbe*, "gloves." *Tek un kani*, "a finger ring." *Tek utomo ekik*, "to clap the hands." *Tek uwekik*, "to clap the hands." *Tek wa po echararase*, "to walk along by means of the hands." *Teke koshne guru*, "a light fingered person." *Tek eushbe*, gloves. *Tek sambe*, "the pulse of the hand."

Tek-chashnu-no, テクチャシヌノ, 故障ナク. *adv.* Without impediment.

Tek-chashnu-no, テクチャシヌノ, 故障ナク. adv. Without impediment.

Teke, テケ, or Tekehe, テケヘ, テク, ニ同シ、手. Same as *tek*. Hand or hands.

Teke-aya, テケアヤ, 掌ノ條. n. The lines of the hands. Syn: Tek ru.

Teke-eokok, テケエオコク, 手デ打チ付クレ. v.t. To strike against with the hand.

Tekehe, テケヘ, テクニ同シ、手. *Same as tek*. The hands. A hand.

Teke-iyokok, テケイヨコク, 盗スル. v.i. To commit a theft.

Teke-koshne-guru, テケコシチグル, 盗賊. n. A thief. A light fingered person.

Tek-epakita-aeiwange-guru, テケエパキタアエイワンゲグル, or Tek-epak-un-aeiwange-guru, テケエパクゥンアエイワンゲグル, 少キ僕. n. A small servant.

Tekepashte, テケパシテ, 奪フ、運ビ去ル. v.t. To snatch. To take away. To transport.

Teketanne, テケタンネ, (トビウオ) n. A kind of fish (probably flying fish).

Teke-ushbe, テケウシベ, 手袋. n. Gloves.

Teke-u-ekikkik, テケウエキッキク, 拍手スル. v.i. To clap the hands. Syn: Tek-orari.

Tekka, テッカ, n. An eagle with a white body and a red head.

Tekkakipo, テッカキポ, 手ニテ眼ヲ庇シテ見ル. v.i. To look at by shading the eyes with the hand. As:—*Tekkakipo rik uiruke ran uirike*, "to look up and down with the hand shading the eyes."

Tekkese, テッケセ, 遥ニ. adv. Far off. The end.

Tekkesean, テッケセアン, 距リタルヽ不充分ナレ. adj. and v.i. To be far off. To be insufficient.

Tekkese-kara, テッケセカラ, 不充分ニ仕上ゲル. v.t. To make up an insufficiency.

Tekkese-ne-kara, テッケセネカラ, 不充分ニ爲ス. v.t. To make insufficient.

Tekka, テッカ, or Tekko, テッコ, 手籠. n. A hand basket.

Tekkoro, テッコロ, 手ニ持ツ. v.t. To have in hands. To grasp.

Tek-koshne-guru, テッコシチグル, 盗人. n. A thief.

Tekkup, テックブ, 翼. n. Wings.

Tek-kuwapo-koechararase, テックワポコエチャララセ, 四ツニ匍フ. v.i. To walk along upon the hands and feet.

Teknumgere, テクヌムゲレ, 撰リ出ス. v.t. To choose out.

Teknumteke, テクヌムテケ, 拳. n. The fists. As:—*Teknumtek aeshitaige*, "to strike with the fists."

Tekokbare, テコクバレ, 手ヲ通ス (袖ニ). v.t. To put the hands through as through the sleeves of a garment.

Tek-orari, テッオラリ, 拍手スレ. v.i. To clap the hands. Syn: Teke uwekikkik.

Tek-orun-kane, テクオルンカネ, 腕環、指環. n. A bracelet. A finger-ring.

Tek-pake, テクバケ, 近ク. adv. Near at hand.

Tek-pake-ta, テクパケタ, 近ク. *adv.* Near to. Close at hand.

Tek-paruparu, テクパルパル, 手招ギ ス レ. *v.t.* To beckon with the hand.

Tek-pira, テクピラ, 乾魚(開キニシタ レ). *n.* Fish cut down the centre and spared out to dry. **Syn: Kerekap.**

Tekram-yupu, テクラムユプ, 攫ミ付 ク. *v.t.* To cling to. **Syn: Kotekramyupu. Eyupke kishma.**

Tekrarakare, テクララカレ, 手ヲ突キ 込ム. *v.t.* To thrust the hands into.

Tekriki-guru-pumba, テクリキグル ブムバ, 擧手スル (禮儀トシテ). *v.t.* To lift up the hands as in salutation.

Tek-ru, テクル, 掌ノ條. *n.* The lines of the hands. **Syn: Tek aya.**

Tek-saikare, テクサイカレ, or **Teksayekare, テクサイェカレ,** 捉フ、近 ク. *v.t.* To seize with the hands.

Teksam, テクサム, 近ク. *adv.* Close at hand. Near to. Adjacent.

Tek-sambe, テクサムベ, 手ノ脈. *n.* The pulse of the hands.

Teksamta, テクサムタ, 近ク. *adv.* Close at hand. Near to. As:— *Teksam ta ande,* "to place near or before one."

Teksam-ta-an, テクサムタアン, 近ク ノ. *adj.* Adjacent.

Teksamata-an-no, テクサマタアンノ, 近ク. *adj.* Adjacently.

Teksambe, テクサムベ, or **Teksayekare, テクサイェカレ,** 捉フ. *v.t.* To seize with the hands.

Tek-shikiru-guru, テクシキルグル, 姦 淫者. *n.* An adulterer. (Met: Lit:—One who turns the hands over).

Tek-shito, テクシト, 拳. *n.* The fist.

Tek-shitu, テクシツ, 格闘スレ. *v.i.* To box.

Tek-tereke, テクテレケ, 踉蹌スレ. *v.i.* To reel about as a drunken or sick person.

Tek-tuikashi, テクツイカシ, 手ノ甲. *n.* The back of the hands.

Tekuishipship, テクイシプシプ, メマ ドクサ. *n.* *Equisetum limosum, L.*

Tek-ukot, テ,ウコツ, 手首. *n.* The wrists.

Tek-umshi, テ,ウムシ, 肱、ヒヂ. *n.* elbow. **Syn: Shittok.**

Tek-un-shiship, テ,ウンシプシプ, ト クサノ一種. *n.* A kind of horset. **Syn: Otashipship.**

Tekutapire, テクタピレ, 拳. *v.i.* The fists. The closed hand.

Tek-utomutasare, テクウトムタサレ, 拱手スレ. *v.i.* To fold the arms.

Tem, テム, 一哩、一尋. *n.* A mile. One stretch of the arms.

Tem, テム, 腕. *n.* The arms.

Temari-kik, テマリキク, 球(マリ)ナツ ク. *v.i.* To bounce a ball.

Temba, テムバ, or **Temba-temba, テムバテムバ,** 觸レレ. *v.t.* To touch.

Tem-eshirikik, テムエシリキク, 手ニ テ牀ヲ打ツ (悲ノ爲、特ニ死人ノ有リ タル時、又葬式後ニテ). *v.i.* To beat the floor with the hands as when in great distress (this is especially done at the time of death and after a funeral.

Temi, テミ, 紐. *n.* A loop.

Temka, テムカ, 蘇生スル. *v.t.* To revive.

Temkakonna, テムカコンナ, 振リマワス（刀ノ如ク）. *v.t.* To wave about as a sword. As:—*Temkakonna shikayekaye,* "to fight with swords." "To fence."

Temko-omare, テムコオマレ, 看護スレ、抱擁スレ. *v.t.* To nurse. To embrace in the arms.

Temkoro, テムコロ, 抱擁スレ. *v.t.* To embrace.

Temkoro-sam, テムコロサム, 抱擁スレ. *v.t.* To embrace.

Temmun, テムムン, 屑（海底ヨリ跳子アゲラレタル）. *n.* Rubbish washed up from the bottom of the sea.

Temmun-chimakani, テムムンチマカニ, コモワラカザカ. *n.* Sculpin *Myxocephalus* (inculding several sp).

Temnikoro, テムニコロ, 抱擁スレ、握レ. *v.t.* To embrace. To clasp. **Syn: Oupshoro-omare.**

Tempirasa, テムピラサ, 手チ差シ延バス. *v.i.* To stretch the arms out.

Temtem, テムテム, 闕ルル、模索（テサグリ）スレ. *v.t.* To touch. To feel. To fumble about.

Temu, テム, 削フ（手チツキテ）. *v.i.* To creep along by the help of the hands.

Temui-chep, テムイチェブ, カズナキ. *n.* Gunnels (*including several species of Pholis.*)

Tenki, テンキ, 籠（藁製ノ）. *n.* A kind of woven basket made of fine reeds or straw.

Tennep, テンチブ, 嬰兒. *n.* A baby. **Syn: Teinep. Hachako.**

Tentenge, テンテンゲ, 柔キ. *adj.* Soft.

Tentenge-nok, テンテンゲノク, 無殻ノ卵. *n.* A shelless egg. **Syn: Kapsek nok.**

Te-oro, テオロ, 此ヨリ. *adv.* Henceforth.

Tepa, テパ, 腰卷. *n.* A loin cloth.

Tepeshkeko, テペシケコ, 豐饒. *adj.* Superabundance. Plenty. As:—*Tepeshkeko an ap, aokere,* "I thought there was plenty but it is all gone." **Syn: Poron no.**

Teppo, テッポ, 鐵砲. *n.* A gun. (*Jap.*)

Tere, テレ, 待ツ. *v.i.* To wait. As:—*Tere wa an.* "to be waiting." **Syn: Uhuye.**

Tereke, テレケ, 跳ブ. *v.i.* To jump To spring upon as an animal upon its prey.

Tereke-ibe, チレケイベ, 蛙. *n.* A frog. **Syn: Ooat. Tereke ibe. Okiorumbe. Uimamyaptep.**

Tereke-ikon, テレケイコン, 傳染病. *n.* A contageous disease.

Tereke-iwashi, テレケイワシ, コヒシコ. *n.* Anchovy. *Engraulis japonicus T. & S.* The same as *Hontomo-parochep.*

Tereke-tereke, テレケテレケ, 跳ビ趣ル. *v.i.* To jump about. To skip about.

Teretanne-sei, テレタンチセイ, オホノカイ. *n.* *Mya arenaria var. japonica,* Jay.

Tese, テセ, 織ル、編ム、結ブ. *v.t.* To weave. To make basket work. To bind. To tie together. **Syn: Teshkau.**

Tesh, テシ, 網代, アジロ. *n.* A kind of fence work made across streams to enclose fish.

Teshbare, テシバレ, or **Teshpare,** テシバレ, (テセ、ノ複數)、織ル. *v.i.* The plural form of *tese,* "to weave."

Teshkas, テシカス, 編ム (蓆ヲ). *v.t.* Weave as a mat.

Teshkara, テシカラ, 音信スル、音信ヲ持タセ遣ス. *v.i.* To send a message. To send with a message. Thus :—*Nei guru teshkara un omande yan,* "send that person with the message."

Teshkara-kore, テシカラコレ, 音信ヲ他人ニ托シテ遣ス. *v.t.* To send a message by another. This form is generally preceded by *otta* "to," "by." As :—*Nishpa otta teshkara ku kore,* "I send a message by the master."

Teshkau, テシカウ, 織ル、結ブ. *v.t.* To weave. To bind. **Syn: Tese.**

Teshke, テシケ, 上方ニ曲ル (橇ノ如ク). *v.i.* To be bent upwards as the ends of a sleigh. To shrink. To crumple up. To glance off.

Teshke, テシケ, 不平均ノ、傾ケル. *adj.* Uneven. Slanting.

Teshke-teshke, ルシケテシケ, 捻ル、子ヂル. *v.i.* To writhe about.

Teshma, テシマ, 雪靴、(カンヅキ). *n.* Snow shoes.

Teshma-ni, ラシマニ, クハ. *n.* The mulberry tree. *Morus alba, L.* Also called *Turep-ni.*

Teshnatara, テシナタラ, 滑ナル、平ナル、美ナレ. *adj.* and *adv.* Smooth. Level. Beautiful.

Teshnatarare, テシナタラレ, 滑ニスル、平ニスレ. *v.t.* To smooth. To make level.

Teshtek, テシテク, 療ユル (傷ノ如ク)、減ル (腫物ノ). *v.i.* To heal as a wound. To go down as a swelling.

Teshteshke, テシテシケ, 捻ル. *v.i.* To writhe about. **Syn: Teshke-teshke.**

Teshu, テシュ, 輕打スル、掠メ去ル. To hilt slightly. To hit and glance off. To just touch (as in shooting at an object).

Teske, テスケ, and **Teske-teske,** テスケテスケ, 逸スレ、ソレレ. *v.i.* To glance off (as oars off water in rowing).

Teshu-teshu, テシュテシュ, 手ニテ觸ル レ. *v.t.* To touch with the hand.

Tetarabe, テタラベ, 麻衣. *n.* A kind of rough cloth made of hemp.

Tettereke, テッテレケ, 跟蹌ク. *v.i.* To stagger. To reel about.

Teuna, テウナ, 手斧. *n.* An adze. A chopper.

Teunin, テウニン, 光ル(暗ニ獸ノ目ノ). *v.i.* To sparkle as the eyes of an animal in the dark.

Tingeu-pone, チンゲウポ子, or **Chingeu-pone,** シンゲウポ子, 尻骨盤. *n.* The pelvis.

To, ト, 胸、乳頭、チクビ. *n.* The breasts. A nipple. As:—*To iku,* "to suck the breasts." *To ikure,* "to suckle." *To num,* "the nipples of the breast." *To nunde,* "to suckle." *To nun nimaki,* "the front teeth." *To nunnun,* "to suck the breasts." *To nun-nunde,* "to suckle." *To sura,* "to cease sucking the breast." *To surare,* "to wean."

To, ト, 湖、水溜. *n* A lake. A puddle of water.

To, ト, 彼方、其處ニ. *adv.* Yonder. There. As:—*To umma an a,* "a horse is there."

To, ト, or **Toho, トホ**, 一日. *n.* A day. As:—*To ebitta,* "all day." *To enkota,* "part of a day," "the latter part of day." *To kes,* "evening." *To noshike,* "noon," "midday." *To pirika,* "a fine day." *To wen,* "a bad day." *To ukotte,* "every day."

Toada, トアダ, 其處ニ、彼方. *adv.* There. Yonder. **Syn : Toanda.**

Toambe, トアムべ, 其、其等ノ. *n.* That. Those. **Syn : Nei-ambe.**

Toan, トアン, 其ノ. *pro.* That. As:—*To an guru,* "that person." He. Him.

Toanda, トアンダ, 其處ニ、彼方. *adv.* There. Yonder.

Toanda-taanda, トアンダタアンダ, 其處、此處ニ. *adv.* There and here.

Toani, トアニ, 其處ニ. *adv.* There. As:—*Toani peka,* "that way."

Toani-ta, トアニタ, 其處ニ、彼方ニ. *adv.* There. Yonder.

Toani-un, トアニウン, 其處ニ. *adv.* There. At that place. To that place.

Toanush, トアヌシ, 其處ニ、彼方ニ. *adv.* There. Yonder.

Tochi-ni, イチニ, トチノキ. *n.* The horse-chestnut tree. *Aesculus turbinata, Bl.*

Toda, or **toto, トダ**, 又ハ **トト**, アシカ. Sea-lion. *Otaria stellersi Less.* (lit : Milk carrier).

Todanup, トダヌプ, ハヒマツ. *n.* *Pinus pumila, Regel.* Also called. *Henekkere.*

Toe, トエ, or **Toye, トイェ**, 多クノ. *adj.* Many.

Toi, トイ, 動詞ノ反復スル動作又強力ナル動作ヲ示ス語、例セバ、トオンガミトイウコケシバレ、屢々手ヲ舉ゲテ大ニ挨拶スレ. *part.* This particle is sometimes placed after verbs to express frequency or severity. Thus :—*Toi ongami-toi ukokesh-bare,* "to salute much by lifting up the hands often."

Toi, トイ, 甚ダ惡シキ. *adj.* Very. Bad. **Syn : Wen.**

Toi, トイ, 庭園、地. *n.* A garden. Soil. Land. Clay. Earth. As:—*Toi kara,* "to work in a garden."

Toi, トイ, 墓、埋葬地. *n.* A grave. **Syn : Tushiri.**

Toi-chisei, トイチセイ, 穴居、土ノ家. *n.* A pit dwelling. An earthen house.

Toi-chisei-kotcha-guru, トイチセイコッチャグル, 穴居人. *n.* A pit-dweller. **Syn : Koropok-guru.**

Toieremu, トイエレム, 大黑鼠. *n.* A large black rat.

Toi-haru, トイハル, 野菜. *n.* Vegetables.

Toihekunra, トイヘクンラ, 幽霊、幻. *n.* Ghosts. Apparitions.

Toi-hoku, トイホク, 指間ノ焮(ホテ). *n.* A sore between the toes. **Syn: Poppise.**

Toiko, トイコ, 烈シク. *adv.* Severely.

Toi-kohoppa, トイコホツパ, 遙ニ取残ス. *v.t.* To leave far behind.

Toikunne, トイクン子, ノ如ク. *adv.* Like. As.

Toimok, トイモク, 蚯蚓. *n.* An earthworm. **Syn: Tonin.**

Toiorush-mun, トイオルシムン, 薄荷. *n.* The peppermint. *Mentha arvensis, L. var. piperascens, Holmes.*

Toirai-wen-rai, トイライウェンライ, 悶死スル. *v.t.* To die a hard and painful death.

Toiratashkep, トイラタシケプ, or **Toi-rataskep, トイラタスケプ**, 凡テノ野菜. *n.* All kinds of vegetables.

Toiren, トイレン, 荒レタル. *adj.* Barren. As:—*Toiren toi*, "barren land."

Toiru, トイル, 小路、道. *n.* A path. A road.

Toi-sei, トイセイ, 土器. *n.* Earthenware.

Toi-shinrush, トイシンルシ, タウゲシバ. *n.* *Lycopodium serratum, Th.*

Toi-shokkara, トイショッカラ, 其人ヲ稱シタル熊ノ頭ヲ下ニ敷キテ葬レ(復讎ノ爲ナリ). *v.t.* To bury a person on the top of the head of a bear which has killed him.

Toi-shu, トイシュ, 土鍋. *n.* An earthen pot. **Syn: Kamui-shu.**

Toi-soya, トイソヤ, 黄蜂、大黄蜂. *n.* A wasp or hornet.

Toi-susu, トイスス, シカヤナギ. *n.* A kind of willow. *Salix cardiophylla, Trautv. et Mey.*

Toi-ta, トイタ, 植ユル、播種スル、畑仕事スル. *v.t.* To plant. To sow. To work in a garden.

Toitanne-chup, トイタン子チュプ, 二月. *n.* The month of February.

Toitoi, トイトイ, 土、地. *n.* Earth. Soil. The ground.

Toitoi-ne, トイトイ子, 土トナレ. *v.t.* To crumble into earth.

Toitoi-taktak, トイトイタクタク, 土塊. *n.* A clod of earth.

Toitoi-tarush, トイトイタルシ, 木茸ノ一種. *n.* A toad stool. Fungi.

Toitomne, トイトム子, 黒土ノ如ク黒キ. *adj.* Black (like black earth.)

Toi-upas, トイウパス, 火山灰. *n.* Volcanic dust. As:—*Toi upas hetuku*, "to rain volcanic dust or ashes."

Tok, トク, or **Tuk, ツク**, 上方ニ延ビル. *v.i.* To extend upward. To protrude. To project. To grow.

Tokaorap, トカオラプ, ドクセリ. *n.* The cowbane or water hemlock. *Cicuta virosa, L.*

Tokap, トカプ, 日、乾ケル. *n. and adj.* Day. Dry. Dried up. As:—*Tokap eush no mokoro*, "to sleep late." *Tokap noshike*, "noon," "midday." *Tokap pirika*, "a good day," *Tokap, to*, "daytime." *Tokap wen*, "a bad day."

Tokapchi, トカプチ, 乾ケル. *n. and adj.* Parched. Dried up. Withered. A famine. Scarcity.

Tokap-chup, トカプチュブ, 太陽. *n.*
The sun.

Tokba, トクバ, 啄ム、ツツク. *v.t.* To
peck (as birds). *pl.*

Tokes, トケス, 夕暮、昏黄. *adv.*
Evening. At the time or sunset.

Toki, トキ, or **Tokihi, トキヒ,** 時. *n.*
Time.

Toki, トキ, 記標、條. *n.* A mark.
A line. A dash.

Toki, トキ, 啄ム、ツツク. *v.t.* To
peck (as birds). *Sing.* See *Toppa.*

Tokikara, トキカラ, チカ. *n.* Surf
smelt. *Mesopus olidus, Pallas.*

Tokina, トキナ, サジオモダカ. *n.*
Alisma Plantago, L.

Tokitokik, トキトキク, 粗ナル. *adj.*
Rough. Uneven.

Tokitto, トキット, ヨタカ、カスイドリ.
n. Goat-sucker. *Caprimulgus
jotaka, (T.* and *S).*

Tokkara, トッカラ, トキカラ、ニ同ジ.
n. Same as *Tokikara.*

Tokkoni, トッコニ, マムシ. *n.* A
poisonous snake. *Trigonocephalus
blomhoffii, Boie.*

Tokkoni-pakko, トッコニパッコ, 蛇
ニ祟ラレシ女. *n.* A woman subject
to attacks of hysteria supposed
to be caused through the influence
of snakes.

Tokkoni-parachi, トッコニパラチ, 蛇
ニ祟ラル. *v.i.* To be possessed by
a snake. **Syn: Kinashut-kari.**

Tokkuri, トックリ, 瓶. *n.* A bottle.

Toko, トト, 蛇. *n.* A snake.

Tokom, トコム, 取手、(抽出ノ). *n.* A
handle, as of a bowl or drawer.

Tokompo, トコムポ, ヤマゴバウ. *n.*
Phytolacca acinosa, Roxb. var.
esculenta, Max.

Tokom-pone, トコムポ子, 踝ノ骨. *n.*
The ankle bone.

Tokon, トコン, 小峯. *n.* A small
mountain peak. **Syn: Tapkop.**

Tokon, トコン, 踝、カ、ト. *n.* The
ankles.

Tokpa, トクバ, or **Tokpa-tokpa, ト
クバトクバ,** 啄ム、ツ、ク. *v.t.* To
peck, as a bird.

Tokse, トクセ, 丘. *n.* A rise in a
plain. A little hill.

Tokse, トクセ, 木瘤. *n.* A knot in
a tree. A knob.

Tokse-tokse, トクセトクセ, 粗キ、皺
寄リタレル. *adj.* Crumpled. Rough.
Uneven. Lumpy.

Toktok-kikiri, トクトクキキリ, 木蠹
ノ一種 *n.* The deathwatch.

Toktokse, トクトクセ, 脈ツ、叩ク、憂
憂ト鳴ル. *v.i.* To beat, as the
pulse. To knock. To rap. To
tick. As:—*Sambe toktokse,* "the
pulse beats."

Tokui, イクイ, 友. *n.* A friend
**Syn: Akateomare guru. Ao-
shiknukara guru.**

Tokum, トクム, 木瘤. *n.* A knot in
a tree. A knob. The handle of
a cup or basin, or door.

Tokum-pone, トクムポ子, 踝. *n.*
The ankles.

Tokushish, トクシシ, アメマス. *n.* A
kind of trout. *Salvelinus kunds-
ha (Pallas.)* **Syn: Tokushish.**

Tom, トム, 花. *n.* A flower. **Syn:
Nonno.**

Tom, トム, 輝ケル. *adj.* Bright.
Sparkling.

Tom, トム, 色. *n.* Colour.

Tom, トム, 輝ク. *v.i.* To shine.

As:—*Chup kamui ku shiki un tom,* "the sun shines in my eyes."

Toma, トマ, 蓆 (死體ヲ包ム). *n.* A mat used for rolling the dead in.

Toma, トマ, エンゴサク. *n.* *Corydalis ambigua, Cham. et Shlecht.*

Tomak, トマク, 沼地、滓泥(ハチ)、粘土. *n.* Slime. Mire. Silt. **Syn : Tomau.**

Tomakmak, トマクマク, 沼地ノ、甚ダ粘土ノ多キ、滓泥(ハチ)ダラケノ. *adj.* Very slimy. Miry. Full of silt.

Tomak-ush, トマクウシ, 沼地ノ、粘土ノ多キ. *adj.* Miry. Slimy.

Tomam, トマム, or **Toman, トマン,** 沼、沼地. *n.* A swamp. Soft boggy land. A quagmire. **Syn : Yachi. Nitat.**

Tomamashi, トママシ, or **Tomamash, トマンナシ,** インツ、ジ. *n.* *Ledum palustre L. var. dilatatum, Wahl.* Also called *Hashipo.*

Tomari, トマリ, 港. *n.* A harbour. **Syn : Moi.**

Tomau, トマウ, 沼地、滓泥(ハチ)、粘土. *n.* Slime. Silt. Uire. **Syn : Tomak.**

Tombe, トムベ, 月、又ハ日. *n.* The sun or moon.

Tombe-kunne-soi, トムベクンチツイ, クロツイ. *n.* A kind of rock-fish. *Sebastodes inermis (Cuv, & Val.)*

Tombi, トムビ, 寳. *n.* Treasures.

Tomka, トムカ, 輝カス. *v.t.* To make to shine. To beautify.

Tomkokanu, トムコカヌ, 爲スチ委任スル. *v.t.* To commit to others to do.

Tomo-aekokanu, トモアエコカヌ, or **Tomoakokanu, トモアコカヌ,** 干渉セヌ. *v.t.* To leave to others. To abstain from inferfering in a matter.

Tomo-oitak, トモオイタク, 和解スル. *v.t.* To pacify.

Tomo-oshma, トモオシマ, 觸ルル. *v.t.* To touch.

Tomo-oush, トモオウシ, 下ル(楷段又足場ヲ傳ヘテ). *v.i.* To come down by means of steps or spikes stuck into a tree.

Tomotarushi, トモタルシ, 繩 (大ナル束ヲ運ブ爲ノ). *n.* A rope for carrying large bundles.

Tomototush-chep, トモトツシチェブ, カツヲ. *n.* Bonito. Gymnosarda affinis. Cantor.

Tomotuye, トモツイェ, or **Tomtuye, トムツイェ,** 幅、横切リテ. *n. and adv.* Width. Breadth. Across. As:— *Tomotuye ande* "to lay across." *Tomotuye wa oman,* "to cross."

Tomo-un-itak, トモウンイタム, 會話ニ加ハル. *v.i.* To join in the conversation of others.

Tomo-ure-eroshki, トモウレエロシキ, 足ニテ押ス (猶力強クスル爲). *v.t.* To push by placing the feet against an object so as to get more purchase.

Tompa, トムバ, 輝ク. *v.i.* To shine.

Tompo, トムボ, 星. *n.* A star.

Tomta, トムタ, 遲ク(時)、只今. Of late times. Just now.

Tomte, トムテ, 美ナル. *adj.* Beautiful. Pretty.

Tomte-i, トムテイ, 美、輝. *n.* Beauty. Brightness.

Tomte-no, トムテノ, 善シ、注意シテ. *adv.* Well. Carefully.

Tomte-no-kara, トムテノカラ, 善ク 爲ス、美化スル. *v.t.* To do well. To beautify.

Tomte-wa-an, トムテワアン, 美ナル. *adj.* Beautiful. Pretty.

Tomtere, トムテレ, 飾ル、美化スル. *v.t.* To adorn. To beautify.

Tomtom トムトム, 輝ク. *v.i.* To glitter.

Tomtom-ush, トムトムウシ, (アゴ) 付ケタル. *adj.* Barbed.

Tomtuye, トムツイェ, or **Tomotuye,** トモツイェ, 半鼓スル、止ムル. *v.t.* To cut off in the middle. To stop. As :—*Hau-tomtuye,* " to stop talking or singing."

Tomtuye, トムツイェ, 横切リテ. *adj.* Athwart. Across.

Tomun, トムン, ニ、方ニ. *adv.* To. Towards. As :—*En tomun ek yan,* "come to me." **Syn : Orota.**

Tonakkai, トナッカイ, 馴鹿. *n.* A reindeer. (*Saghalien*).

Tonam, トナム, 甚敷濕リタル. *adj.* Swampy. very wet.

Tonam-i, トナムイ, 沼ノ如キ. *n.* A swamp.

Tonchi, トンチ, 穴、凹ミ. *n.* A hollow. A pit. A sunken place in the earth.

Tonchikama-ni, トンチカマニ, 戸ノ 直外. *n.* The region just out the door-sill (outside).

Tonchi-kamui, トンチカムイ, 昔シ穴 居シタリシアイヌ. *n.* A term applied to such of the Ainu as formerly dwelt in lodges built over pits. **Syn : Koropok-un-guru. Tonchi-un-guru.**

Tonin, トニン, 蚯蚓. *n.* An earthworm. **Syn : Toimok.**

Tone, ト子, 湖水ノ如ク. *adj.* Lakelike. Having lakes.

Tonke, トンケ, 平靜ナル. *adj.* Calm.

Tonnatara-ki, トンナタラキ, 輝ク. *v.i.* To shine. **Syn : Tom.**

Tono, トノ, 殿、トノ、役人. *n.* A chief. A government officer. An official. The government.

Tonoge, トノゲ, 親愛ナル. *adj.* A term sometimes found suffixed to certain nouns to express tenderness and love. As :—*Aak-tonoge,* " my dear younger brother." *A poho-tonoge,* " my dear child."

Tonon-nimaki, トノンニマキ, 前齒. *n.* The front teeth.

Tono-nishpa, トノニシパ, 官吏. *n.* An official.

Tono-para-ru, トノパラル, 殿ノ御道、 (國道). *n.* The Emperor's highway.

Tono-ru, トノル, 公道. *n.* A highway.

Tonoto, トノト, 酒. *n.* Rice beer. Wine. As :—*Tonoto noye,* "sleeping through the effects of drinking too much wine." *Tonoto rak,* " to smell of wine." *Tonoto ewekatkara,* " to tempt to drink wine." *Tonoto mimtum oma* or *tonoto iporo oma,* " To shew the effects of drinking in one's face." *Tonoto iporo eipottumma shinna kane,* " he shews the effects of drinking in his face."

Tonoto-hauki, トノトハウキ, 醉者ガ 歌フ謠. *n.* A drunkard's song.

Tonoto-konka, トノトコンカ, 酒ノ 大桶. *n.* A wine vat.

Tonoto-mau, トノトマウ, 酒精. *n.* Alcohol.

Tonoyan-ush, トノヤンウシ, 上陸場. *n.* A landing place.

Tonra, トンラ, 水草ノ類. *n.* A kind of water weed found in the bottom of rivers. **Syn : Toponra.**

Tonru, トンル, 煮凝ノ類. *n.* A clear jelly.

Tonru-chep, トンルチェプ, 海月、クラゲ. *n.* Jelly fish. Medusa. **Syn : Etoropo.**

Tontek, トンテク, 平穏ナル. *adj.* Calm. Peaceful.

Tonto, トント, 柔皮. *n.* Leather.

Tonto-kamu, トントカム, 氣絶スル. *v.i.* To be in a trance.

Tonto-ne, トント子, 禿ゲタル. *adj.* Hairless.

Tontoneppo, トントチッポ, 井ノシシ. *n.* A wild boar. *Sus leucomystax, Temma.* A term of reproach.

Top, トプ, タケ、サヽ. *n.* Bamboo.

Top, トプ, 笛. *n.* A flute. As :— *Top rekte.* " to play a flute."

Topa, トパ, or **Topaha, トパハ,** 多クノ、群集. *adj.* and *n.* Many. A crowd. A multitude.

Topa-saipake, トパサイパケ, 群鹿ノ長. *n.* A leader deer.

Topan-topan, トパントパン, 振リマワス. *v.t.* To move or shake about.

Topat-tumi, トパツツミ, 夜襲 (人殺、強盗ナドノ). *n.* A night raid for the purpose of murder and rapine.

Tope, トペ, 乳. *n.* Milk.

Topembe, トペムベ, クハ. *n.* Mulberries. Anything sweet. *Morus alba, L.*

Topempira, トペムピラ, スナムグリツメメ. *n.* A sand martin. *Cotyle riparia, (Linn).*

Topen, トペン, 味ヨキ. *adj.* Sweet.

Tope-ni, トペニ, トキハカヘデ. *n.* The maple tree. *Acer pictum, Th.*

Topeseku, トペセク, 乳ノ脹レル、(子チ生ム前)・ *v.i.* The swelling up of the breasts with milk immediately before having young, as in animals. This word is also applied to women. **Syn : Iseku.**

Topipa, トピパ, カハカイ. *n.* A kind of fresh water shell fish.

Topishki-mun, トピシキムン, キジカシク. *n.* *Asparagus schoberioides Kunth.*

Topishki-tashum, トピシキタシュム, 瘧、オコリ. *n.* The ague. **Syn : Iko-san.**

Topiro-an, トピロアン, or **Topiroro-an, トピロロアン,** 蒸暑キ天氣(暴風ノ前ノ)・ *n.* Close, clear weather immediately preceding a storm.

Topki, トプキ, ノガリヤス. *n.* *Calamagrostis robusta, Fr. et Sav.*

Topmuk, トプムク, ツルニンジン. *n.* *Codonopsis lanceolata, Benth. et Hook.*

Topo, トポ, アサリ. *n.* *Tapesphilippinarum Ad. and Rv.*

Topo, トポ, 水溜. *n.* A pool. A puddle.

Topochi, トポチ, 水溜. (複數)・ *n.* Pools. Puddles of water.

Toponra, トポンラ, 水草. *n.* A kind of water weed found in the bottom of rivers.

Topopke-ni, トポプケニ, 弩ノ引金、蹄係チオトス物. *n.* A crossbow lock. The wooden trigger in any trap.

Toppa, トッパ, 啄ク、(複數)、啄キ壊ス. *v.t.* To peck at. To break by knocking. **Syn: Tokba.**

Topse, トブセ, 唾. *n.* Spittle. Saliva.

Topse-kara, トブセカラ, 吐痰スレ. *v.i.* To expectorate.

Topse-op, トブセオブ, 唾壺. *n.* A spittoon.

Topui, トブイ, 蓮ノ一種. *n.* A kind of water lily. (The kingcup). Marsh mallow.

Torai, トライ, 河ノ大ナル部分、(沼ニ似テ). *n.* A large place in a river resembling a lake.

Toranne, トランチ, 怠惰ナル. *adj.* Idle.

Torara, トララ, 皮紐. *n.* Leather thongs. Thongs made of the skins of sea lions, or other animals. A strap.

Toruru, トルル, 魚 (乾ス前積ミ上ゲタル). *n.* Fish caught and laid in heaps before drying.

Torurukararip, トルルカラリブ, 初雪. *n.* The first snow.

Torush, トルシ, 穢レタル、朧ナル. *adj.* Sullied. Tarnished. Dim.

Toshipship, トシブシブ, ヌマトグサ. *n. Equisetum limosum, L.*

Toshiri, トシリ, 河岸ノ下部. *n.* The under part of the bank of a river.

Toshka, トシカ, 岸. *n.* A bank. As :— *Ota toshka,* "a bank of sand." *Pet toshka,* "a river's bank." *Toshka paruru,* "the side of a bank."

Toshka, トシカ, 群集. *n.* A crowd. As :— *Ainu toshka,* "a crowd of men."

Tososo, トソソ, 散布スル、驚カス. *v.t.* To scatter. To frighten.

Totche, トッチェ, 膕(打タレシ爲ノ). *n.* A swelling caused by a blow. **Syn: Hup.**

Totek, トテク, 清純ナル、平穏ナル、健全ナル. *adj.* Serene. Calm. In good health. Hale.

To-to, トト, 藪. *n.* Bushes. Thick underwood.

Totoot, トトオツ, 藪メケテ、叢然トシテ. *adv.* Bushy.

Totonupsara, トトヌブサラ, 藪. *n.* A thicket. **Syn: Pon chikuni tai.**

Totto, トット, 母. *n.* Mother. **Syn: Habo.**

Toye, トイェ, or **Toe,** トエ, 多クノ、(時トシテ動詞ノ複數ヲ示ス). *adj.* Many. Sometimes used as a plural in verbs.

Toyekurok, トイェクロク, 黒キ、(雲ノ如ク). *adj.* Black (as clouds). As :— *Toyekurok nishkuru,* "black clouds."

Toyeran, トイェラン, or **Toyesak,** トイェサク, 瘠セタレ. *adj.* Thin. Lean.

Tu, ツ, 縁、縫物ノ巾廣キ線. *n.* A line. The broad lines in fancy needlework.

Tu, ツ, 二、此語ハ時ニ動詞ノ前ニ用ヰテ、酷酷、至誠、壓等ノ意ヲ示ス、例セバ、ツオンガミ、キルウェチ、彼ハ誠實ニ、或ハ壓敬禮セリ. *adj.* Two. This word is sometimes used before verbs to express severity,

sincerity and frequency. As :
—*Tu ongami ki ruwe ne,* " he
saluted sincerely " or " frequently."

Tu, ツ, 時トシテ名詞ニ附シテ複數ヲ示
ス、例セバ、クツツ、多クノ斷崖. *n.*
Sometimes used as a plural suffix
to nouns. As :—*Kuttu,* "crags"
or " ragged rocks."

Tuchi, ツチ, 槌、ツチ. *n.* A hammer. A mallet.

Tu-otne, ツホツ子, 四十. *adj.* Forty.

Tui, ツイ, 切ラレタル、裂ケタル. *adj.*
Cut. Torn.

Tui, ツイ, 休ム、(雨ノ如ク), *v.i.* To
cease ; as wind or rain. Thus
Upas ash a, " does it snow ? "
Tane tui, " it has ceased."

Tui, ツイ, 物ノ内部. *n.* The inside
of anything. As :—*Chashi tui,*
" the inside of a fort."

Tui, ツイ, 腹、腸、臟、臍. *n.* The
stomach. The intestines. As :—
Tui araka, " the stomach ache."
Tui wen iun, " to have the
stomach ache." *Tui shiri kamu,*
To lie upon the stomach."

Tui, ツイ, or **Tuye,** ツイェ, 切ル. *v.t.*
To cut.

Tuiba, ツイバ, 切ル(ツイノ複數). *v.t.*
To cut (*pl : of tui*).

Tuika, ツイカ, 制御スル、拘束スル、滿
飲スレ. *v.t.* To strain. To draw
off. To drain. As :—*Ichari orun
aohare wa pe tuika,* " he emptied
into a sieve and drained off the
water."

Tuika, ツイカ, 空間. *n.* Space.

Tuikantara, ツイカンタラ, 仰向ニ寢
ル. *v.i.* To be flat upon one's
back.

Tu-ikashima-arawan-hotne, ツイ
カシマアラワンホツ子, 百四十二. *adj.*
One hundred and forty two.

Tu-ikashima-ashikne-hotne, ツイ
カシマアシク子ホツ子, 百二. *adj.*
One hundred and two.

Tu-ikashima-ine-hotne, ツイカシマ
イ子ホツ子, 八十二. *adj.* Eighty
two.

Tu-ikashima-re-hotne, ツイカシマ
レホツ子, 六十二. *adj.* Sixty two.

Tu-ikashima-tu-hotne, ツイカシマ
ツホツ子, 四十二. *adj.* Forty two.

Tu-ikashima-wanbe, ツイカシマワ
ンベ, 十二. *adj.* Twelve.

**Tu-ikashima-wan-e-arawan-hot-
ne,** ツイカシマワンエアラワンホツ子,
百三十二. *adj.* One hundred and
thirty two.

**Tu-ikashima-wan-e-ashikne-hot-
ne,** ツイカシマワンエアシク子ホツ
子, 九十二. *adj.* Ninety two.

Tu-ikashima-wan-e-ine-hotne, ツ
イカシマワンエイ子ホツ子, 七十二.
adj. Seventy two.

Tu-ikashima-wan-e-iwan - hotne,
ツイカシマワンエイワンホツ子, 百十
二. *adj.* One hundred and twelve.

Tu-ikashima-wan-e-re-hotne, ツ
イカシマワンエレホツ子, 五十二. *adj.*
Fifty two.

Tuikata, ツイカタ, 然ルニ、間(時間)、
其他、此上、内ニ、上ニ. *adv.* Whilst.
During Besides. Above this.
In. Upon. As :—*Mokot tuikata,*
" whilst sleeping." *Moshiri tuikata,* " in the world."

Tui-kikiri, ツイキキリ, 懷蟲. *n.* A
stomach worm. Ascaris.

Tui-kisara, ツイキサラ, 胃ノ側面. *n.*
The side of the intestines.

Tuikosanu, ツイコサヌ, 肩下ノ痛、又
ハ痛ム. *v.i.* and *n.* To be seized
with pain between the lower part
of the shoulders. A kind of
muscular rheumatism. Lumbago.

Tuima, ツイマ, 遙ニ. *adv.* Far.
Distant. Afar. As :— *Tuima
esoine,* "to go to relieve one's
self."

Tuima-a, ツイマア, 便所ニ行ク（婦人
ニノミ用ユ）. *v.i.* To go to stool
(used only of women).

Tuima-esoyun-oman isam, ツイマ
エソユンオマンイサム, 便秘. *n.*
Stoppage of the bowels.

Tuima-mimdara, ツイマミムダラ, 塵
堺. *n.* A rubbish heap.

Tuima-no-an, ツイマノアン, 遠ク.
adv. Distant. Far.

Tuimashitta, ツイマシッタ, 遙ニ. *adv.*
A distance away.

Tui-onnai-kenuma, ツイオンナイケ
ヌマ, 産毛、ウブゲ. *n.* The hair
found on a child's body when
first born.

Tuirak-humi, ツイラクフミ, 片々ニ
切リ割ル音. *n.* The sound of
being cut to pieces.

Tuirukumi, ツイルクミ, 片々ニ切レ.
v.i. A piece cut off of anything.

Tuisama, ツイサマ, 側ニ於テ. *adv.*
By the side of.

Tuisamake, ツイサマケ, 側ニ. *adv.*
By the side of. The place by
one's side.

Tuitak, ツイタク, 命令、律法. *n.* A
commandment. Law.

Tuite, ツイテ, 兩断スル、切ル. *v.t.*
To break asunder. To cut.

Tuitak-kainon-yaikoruki, ツイタ
クカイノンヤイコルキ, 呑ミ込ム（言葉
ヲ）. *ph.* To swallow one's words.
To speak indistinctly.

Tuitek, ツイテク, 裂ケタル. *adj.*
Torn. Cut off.

Tui-tui, ツイツイ, 散布シテ. *adj.*
Scattered. Unconnected. Broken.
Separate. Cut up. As :— *Tui-
tui nishkuru,* "scattered clouds,"
"broken clouds."

Tuituye, ツイツイェ, 簸ル. *v.t.* To
winnow.

Tui-un, ツイウン, 下腹ノ. *adj.* Abdominal.

Tuk, ツク, or **Tok,** トク, 上方へ擴ガル.
v.i. To extend upwards. To arise.
To come up. To project. To grow.
To bud. To sprout out. As :—
Tuk no an, "extending upwards."
Tuk ewen, "to grow badly."
Tuk no, "to grow well."

Tuk, ツク, 癒合スル. *v.i.* To heal
up, as a wound. To get well.

Tukan, ツカン, 射ル. *v.t.* To shoot
at.

Tukap, ツカプ, 幽靈、幻. *n.* A
ghost. An apparition.

Tukap, ツカプ, 釣針. *n.* A fish
hook.

Tukap-kane, ツカプカ子, 針金. *n.*
Wire.

Tukara, ツカラ, アザラシ. *n.* Seal.
Phoca fœtida, Fabr.

Tukari, ツカリ, 此側ニ、近ク. *adv.*
This side of. Near to. Part way.
Syn : Samta.

Tukarike, ツカリケ, 遠カラヌ、近ク. *adv.* Not far from. Near to. Part way. As:—*Tukarike pakno oman*, "to go near to."

Tuk-ewen, ツクエウェン, 惡シク發育 スル. *v.i.* To grow or sprout out badly.

Tuki, ツキ, 盃、椀. *n.* A cup. A wine cup.

Tuki-num, ツキヌム, 盃ノ下部. *n.* The lower part of a wine cup.

Tukkari, ツッカリ, アザラシ. *n.* Seal. *Phoca fœtida, Fab.*

Tuk-no, ツクノ, 善ク發育スル. *v.i.* To grow well.

Tuk-no-pinni-korachi-an-guru, ツ クノピンニコラチアングル, 巨人. *n.* A giant. **Syn: Kewe poro.**

Tukunne, ツクンネ, 痺(シビレ)ノ類. *n.* A kind of cramp known as pins and needles," affecting the legs and feet only.

Tukushish, ツクシシ, or **Tokushish, トクシシ,** アメマス. *n.* Charr. *Sal-velinus kundscha (Pallas)*. (*Walb*).

Tum, ツム, 力. *n.* Strength.

Tumak, ツマク, 壞レタレ. *adj.* Broken.

Tumak, ツマク, 疝氣. *n.* A general name for pains in the loins, back and testicles.

Tumak, ツマク, 背ノ痛、(病)、傴人ナ レ. *n.* and *v.i.* A kind of disease of which backache is a prominent feature. To be humpbacked.

Tumam, ツマム, 抱卵スル. *v.i.* To sit,.(as a hen).

Tumam, ツマム, 看護スレ、守スル. *v.t.* To nurse.

Tumam, ツマム, or **Tuman, ツマ ン,** 腰、幹、璧(家ノ). *n.* The waist. The body. The trunk of a tree. The wall of a house. The stem of a pipe.

Tumam-koshaye, ツマムコシャイェ, or **Tumama-koshaye, ツママコ シャイェ,** 裙ヲ端折レ. *v.i.* To gird up the loins.

Tumamma-hotke, ツマムマホツケ, 抱キ込ム、抱キ寢スレ. *v.t.* To hold in one's embrace. To lie down and hold in one's arms as a mother her child.

Tumam-noshke, ツマムノシケ, 腰. *n.* The loins.

Tumashi, ツマシ, ノ間ニ. *adv.* Whilst. As:—*Apto tumashi ku ek,* "I came whilst it was rain-ing."

Tumashnu, ツマシヌ, 强キ. *adj.* Strong. Able-bodied. **Syn: Ki-roroashnu.**

Tumba, ツムバ, 鍔. *n.* A sword guard.

Tumbu, ツムブ, 室、地球、胞(エナ). *n.* A room. An apartment. A divisionin a cave. Also the womb by some and placenta by others.

Tumbu-kara, ツムブカラ, 清播スレ (室ヲ). *v.t.* To tidy a room.

Tumbu-kara-guru, ツムヅカラグル, 家僕. *n.* A house servant.

Tumi, ツミ, 戰、喧嘩. *n.* War. A quarrel. **Syn: Ukoiki-ambe.**

Tumi-eshipopkep, ツミエシホブケブ, 武器. *n.* Arms. Weapons of war.

Tumikoro, ツミコロ, 戰爭スル. *v.t.* To engage in war.

Tumikoro-guru, ツミコログル, 兵士. *n.* A soldier.

Tumi-ram, ツミラム, 激戰. *n.* A very severe war.

Tumi-sange, ツミサンゲ, 戰ヲ起ス. *v.t.* To cause war. To wage war.

Tumi-shimaka, ツミシマカ, 體操スル. *v.i.* To take exercise as with dumb bells or in drilling.

Tumi-shuikere, ツミシュイケレ, 軍ヲ 終ル. *v.i.* To have finished a war.

Tumiwentoiru, ツミウェントイル, 戰 爭ヲ眞似シテ手足ヲ動シテ行ク、事變 ニ死セル者ノ爲御祓ノ儀式ナスレ. *v.i.* To go along exercising the arms and legs as if in war. To act the ceremonies pursued when a person dies through accident.

Tumma, ツムマ, 其中ニ. *adv.* Amongst.

Tum-no, ツムノ, 強キ、荒キ. *adj.* Strong. Wild.

Tumot-ushi-chep, ツモッウシチェツ ブ, カツオ. *n.* Bonito. *Gymno-sarda affinis, Cantor.*

Tum-o, ツムオ, 強キ. *adj.* Strong.

Tumotneka, ツモツ子カ, 惑カメス、疑 フ. *v.i.* To be uncertain.

Tumsak, ツムサク, 弱キ. *adj.* Weak.

Tum-sakka, ツムサッカ, 弱ムル. *v.t.* To weaken.

Tumshi, ツムシ, 房. *n.* A tassel.

Tumshikot, ツムシコツ, 飾リ(木ニテ 作リ種々ノ物ニ用ユ). *n.* Small wooden ornaments attached to various instruments.

Tumshikot-kashup, ツムシコツカシ ュブ, 木匙. *n.* A wooden spoon ornamented with pieces of wood.

Tumta, ツムタ, 中ニ、間. *adv.* In. Among. As:—*Toi tumta,* "in the ground." *Mun tumta,* "among the leaves."

Tumu, ツム, 力、感情、元氣. *n.* Strength. *Power.* One's feelings. As:—*Tumu nu,* "to feel better in health." *Tumu sak,* "weak." *Tumu wen wa hotke,* "he lies down because he is ill." *Tumu an,* "to be strong or well."

Tumu, ツム, 空間ノ、間. *adj.* Space. Between whiles. Among.

Tumu, ツム, 獨樂、絲卷. *n.* A top. A reel.

Tumu-an, ツムアン, 強ガル、善ガル. *v.i.* To be strong or well.

Tumu-an, ツムアン, 多クノ. *adj.* Many.

Tumu-an-no, ツムアンノ, 多クノ. *adj.* Many. As:—*Tumu an no okai,* "there are many." *Tumu an no isam,* "a few."

Tumu-aishirika, ツムアイシリカ, 醜 キ. *adj.* Ugly. Not good. **Syn:** Mashkin no shomo.

Tumuge, ツムゲ, 間、中. *n.* Among.

Tumugeta, ツムゲタ, 間ニ. *adv.* Among.

Tumuge-un, ツムゲウン, 間ニ. *adv.* Among.

Tumumaukush, ツムマウクシ, 罰ス ル、罪スル. *v.t.* To condemn. **Syn:** Katpak kore.

Tumun, ツムン, 腐レシ草、糞屋、糞. *n.* Rotten vegetation. A house which has tumbled down and become rotten. Manure. Dung.

Tumunchi, ツム'ンチ, 惡冤、惡鬼. *n.* The devil. Evil spirits. **Syn :** **Iwende kamui.**   **Wen kamui.** **Kamuiyashi.**   **Nitne kamui.** Also sometimes called *Tumunchi kamui.*

Tumuorepini, ツムオレビニ, 重着ヲ ス ル. *v.i.* To wear many garments one over the other.

Tumutot-un-same, ツムトッウンサメ, オナカザメ. *n.*   Thresher shark. *Alopecias vulpes (Gmelin).*

Tumuturu, ツムツル, 眞中ノ. *adj.* Middle. Centre. **Syn : Shiru-turu.**

Tun, ツン, 二人. *n.*   Two persons. As:—*Tun chi ne,* "we two." *Tun ren,* "two or three persons." **Syn : Tu niu.**

Tun, ツン' 胚. *n.* Fœtus.

Tuna, ツナ, 爐邊ニ掛ヶシ器具. *n.* The apparatus which hangs over a fireplace.

Tunangara, ツナンガラ, 逢フ. *v.t.* To meet.

Tunan-o-guru, ツナンオグル, 兩面人 （日本語ノ兩枚ノ舌ヲ使フ人). *n.*   A double faced person. **Syn : E-nan-o-guru.**

Tunash, ツナシ, or **Tunashi,·** ツ ナ シ, 速ナル、突然ノ. *adj.* Quick. Abrupt.

Tunashi-no, ツナシノ, 速ニ. *adv.* Quickly.

Tunashi-no-tunashi-no, ツナシノツ ナシノ,甚ダ速ニ. *adv.* Very quick-ly.

Tunashka, ツナシカ, 急グ. *v.t.*   To hasten. To accelerate. **Syn : Chashte. Tunashte. Muchina-shnure.**

Tunashka-i, ツナシカイ. 急ギ. *n.* Acceleration.

Tunashte, ツナシテ, 急グ. *v.t.*   To accelerate. To hasten. **Syn : Tunashka.**

Tunatunak, ツナツナク, 搖レル(牀ノ 上ニ跳ル時家ノ). *v.i.* To tremble as a house when one jumps on the floor.

Tunchi, ツンチ, 通事、通譯. *n.*   An interpreter.

Tunchikara, ツンチカラ, 通譯スル. *v.t.* To interpret. **Syn : Eep-akita.**

Tunchikara-guru, ツンチカラグル, 通 事. *n.*   An interpreter.

Tune-nishkuru, ツ子ニシクル, 雲、 層雲. *n.* Clouds. Stratus.

Tun-ikashima-wa-niu, ツンイカシ マワニウ, 十二人. *n.* Twelve per-sons.

Tun-nai, ツンナイ, 海峽. *n.*   A channel. A fairway.

Tunnai, ツンナイ, 矢頃. *n.*   The distance of a bow shot.

Tunne, ツン子, 怠惰. *n.* Idleness.

Tun-ni, ツンニ' カシワ. *n.* A kind of oak. *Quercus dentata, Th.*

Tun-ni-karush, ツンニカルシ, シヒ タヶ. *n.*   A kind of mushroom found growing chiefly upon oaks. *Cortinellus shiitake, P. Henn.* Also called *Kom-ni-karush* and *Pero-ni-karush.*

Tuntum, ツンツム, 太鼓. *n.*   A drum.

Tuntun, ツンツン, 魚卵. *n.* Row. Fish eggs.

Tunun-hawe, ツヌンハウェ, チンチント鳴ラス. *v.i.* To chink or jingle. **Syn: Ukere-humi.**

Tunru-o, ツンルオ, 斑ナル. *adj.* Speckled. **Syn: Keso.**

Tuntek, ツンテク, 反響. *n.* An echo. **Syn: Eiunimba.**

Tuntu, ツンツ, 大黒柱. *n.* A piece of wood used in building huts and which forms the main support of the roof. Pillars. A post. Column. It is to a hut what a corner stone is to a house, or a key stone to a vault or arch, or pillar to a balcony. Hence this word is sometimes applied to God when He is spoken of as the support, pillar, sustainer or upholder of the universe.

Tuntun, ツンツン, 鮫ノ胎子. *n.* Embryo of sharks. **Syn: Same tuntun.**

Tununi, ツヌニ, 呻ク. *v.i.* To groan. **Syn: Tashmak! Kechi.**

Tununitara, ツヌニタラ, 鳴ル (金属チ共ニシテ振リ週ス時ノ). *v.i.* To rattle as metal when shaken together.

Tup, ツプ, 流ル (星ノ)、移轉スル. *v.i.* To shoot, as a star. To migrate.

Tup, ツプ, 二物. *n.* Two things.

Tupa, ツパ, 永續スル (悪クナル事ナク). *adj.* and *v.i.* To keep for a long time without becoming bad. As:— *Tupa chep,* "fish which will keep a long time."

Tupe, ツペ, 結フ. *v.t.* To bind. To tie up. **Syn: Shina. Tupetupe.**

Tupep, ツペプ, 結. *n.* Bonds. Bands.

Tupep, ツペプ, 蹄係、(ワナ). *n.* A slip knot. A bond. Anything one is bound up with. As:— *Tupep kara,* "to make a slip knot."

Tupesambe, ツペサムベ, 八. *adj.* Eight.

Tupetupe, ツペツペ, 結フ. *v.t.* To bind. To tie up. **Syn: Shinashina. Shina. Tupe.**

Tupetupep, ツペツペプ, 結. *n.* Bonds. Bonds.

Tup-ikashinia-hotne, ツプイカシニアホツネ, 二十. *adj.* Twenty.

Tup-ikashima-wanbe, ツプイカシマワンベ, 十二. *n.* Twelve.

Tupiri, ツピリ, 瘢痕. *n.* A scar. **Syn: Piri.**

Tup-ne-rep-ne, ツプネレプネ, 二回又ハ三回. *adj.* Twice or thrice. A phrase often used in songs and legends to express killing or hurting very much. Also, doing with ease.

Tup-rep, ツプレプ, 二又ハ三. *n.* Two or three.

Tupshi, ツプシ, 吐唾スル、タンチハク. *v.t.* To expectorate.

Tupte, ツプテ, 追放スル、輸出スル、送リ出ス. *v.t.* To banish. To transport. To send away.

Tupunetoine, ツプチトイチ, 互ニ踏ミ合フ. *v.i.* To trample on one another. **Syn: Ukata tereke.**

Tupunetoine-re-punetoine, ツプチトイチレプチトイチ, 屢互ニ踏ミ合フ. Frequetive of the previous word.

Tura, ツラ, 物ノ列. *n.* A row of things.

Tura, ツラ, 導ク、伴フ. *v.t.* To lead. To take as company.

Tura-an, ツラアン, 伴フ. *v.i.* To be with. To accompany.

Tura-guru, ツラグル, 案内者. *n.* A guide.

Tu-rai, ツ ラ イ, 二回. *adj.* Twice. As :—*Kurukashike okomomse, turai ongami, re-rai ongami ukakushte,* "upon this he bowed down and worshipped two or three times."

Turainu, ツ ラ イ ヌ, 失フ. *v.t.* To lose.

Turamkoro, ツラムコロ, 卑怯ニ. *adv.* Cowardly. **Syn : Utchike.**

Turamkoro-guru, ツラムコログル, 卑怯者. *n.* A coward.

Tura-no, ツ ラ ノ, 共ニ. *adv.* Together with.

Tura-no-an, ツラノアン, 伴フ. *v.i.* To be with. To be in company with.

Tura-no-ki-guru, ツラノキグル, 伴侶. *n.* An accomplice.

Tura-no-oman, ツラノオマン, 伴フ. *v.i.* To accompany.

Turashi, ツラシ, 間. *adv.* While. During. As :—*Shukup turashi,* "while growing up." **Syn : Tuikata.**

Turashi, ツラシ, 登ル. *v.t.* To ascend. To go up hill. To climb. As :—*Pet turashi oman,* "to ascend a river." *Ni turashi nimu,* "to climb a tree."

Turen, ツレン, 神来スル、特寵ヲ蒙ル (神ヨリ). *v.i.* To be inspired, as by God. To receive special blessings from God. To have God's special protection. To be possessed with a devil. As :—*Kamui turen,* "to be inspired by God," "to be blessed by God." *Nitne kamui turen,* "to be possessed with a devil." *Ashkanne Kamui turen,* "to be inspired by the Holy Spirit."

Turep, ツレプ, オホウバユリ. *n.* A kind of lily. *Lilium Glehni, Fr. Schm.*

Turep-akam, ツレプアカム, オホウバユリノ菓子. *n.* Lily cakes.

Turep-chiri, ツレプチリ, オトシギ. *n.* A wood-cock.

Turep-irup, ツレプイルプ, オホウバユリノ粉. *n.* Lily flour.

Turep-ni, ツ レ プ ニ, クワ. *n.* A mulberry tree. *Morus alba, L.* Also called *topembe.*

Turep-onga, ツレプオンガ, オホバユリノ菓子. *n.* Lily cakes.

Turepshit, ツレプシツ, オホバユリノ粉ヲ取リタル屑. *n.* The dregs left after extracting the flour from lily barlbs.

Turesh, ツレシ, 妹. *n.* A younger sister. **Syn : Mataki. Machiribe.**

Tureshnu, ツレシヌ, 姉妹. *n.* Sisters.

Tureshpo, ツ レ シ ポ, 妹. *n.* A younger sister. Dear sister.

Turi, ツリ, 轉子 (端舟ヲ轉ス). *n.* A pole used to push boats along.

Turi, ツリ, 延バス. *v.t.* To stretch out. **Syn : Turu.**

Turire, ツリレ, 延バサセル. *v.t.* To cause to stretch out.

Turimimse, ツリミムセ, 轟々ト鳴ル. *v.i.* To rumble. To rattle. To make a noise.

Turiri, ツリリ, 延ビタル、延ブ. *v.i.* and *adj.* Stretched out. To be stretched out.

Turiri, ツリリ, 與フ. *v.t.* To give. To hand over. To push out.

Turu, ツル, 淵、埃. *n.* Filth. Dirt.

Turu, ツル, 延ハス. *v.t.* To stretch out. **Syn : Turi.**

Turumbe, ツルムベ, 釣瓶. *n.* A well bucket. **Syn : Niwatush.**

Turupa, ツルバ, 延ハス. *v.t.* To stretch out. To cast, as a net in the sea.

Turusak, ツルサク, 清潔ナル. *adj.* Clean. Pure.

Turuse, ツルセ, 落ス. *v.t.* To drop. As :—*Tekehe wa turuse,* " to drop from the hand."

Turuse, ツルセ, 傳染ノ. *adj.* Contagious.

Turuse, ツルセ, 滴下スル. *v. i.* To drop down.

Turush, ツルシ, 痘瘡. *n.* The small-pox. **Syn : Kamui turush. Shikatoi shiyeye. Kamui paha.**

Turushittok, ツルシットク, 曲リ角. *n.* The turnings in a path.

Turu-tashum, ツルタシュム, 傳染病. *n.* A contagious disease.

Turu-ush, ツルウシ, 淵レル、汚レタル. *adj.* Filthy. Dirty.

Tusa, ツサ, 袖. *n.* A sleeve.

Tusa, ツサ, 快氣スル. *v.i.* To recover from sickness.

Tusa-imaka, ツサイマカ, 袖裏. *n.* The back of a sleeve.

Tusa-pui, ツサブイ, 袖ノ穴. *n.* A sleeve hole. An arm hole.

Tusare, ツサレ, 赦ス. *v.t.* To forgive. To absolve. To acquit. To animate. To cure. To heal.

Tusare-ambe, ツサレアムベ, 赦免. *n.* Absolution.

Tusare-i, ツサレイ, 赦免. *n.* Acquittal.

Tush, ツシ, 速ニ. *adj.* Fast. Quick. Swift. Rapid. **Syn : Tushtek.**

Tush, ツシ, 本妻ト共ニ居ル他ノ妻、(即チ亭主ノ妾). *n.* A woman's fellow wife.

Tush, ツシ, 繩. *n.* A rope. As : —*Tush kote,* " to tie up." *Tush saye,* " a coil of rope." *Tush saye kara,* " to coil a rope."

Tush-ani, ツシアニ, 捕フ (馬ノ如ク). *v.t.* To hold, as a horse.

Tusheka-guru, ツシェカグル, 繩製造人. *n.* A rope maker. **Syn : Tush kara guru.**

Tush-honnere. ツシホンチレ, 赦ス. *v.t.* To pardon. To forgive. To absolve.

Tu-shike, ツシケ, 四十. *adj.* Forty.

Tushik-e, ツシクエ, 兩眼ノ上ニ斑チ持ツ (或ル犬ノ如ク). *adj.* To have a spot over each eye as some dogs.

Tushiri, ツシリ, or **Tushiri-kot,** ツシリコツ, 埋葬地. *n.* A grave. **Syn : Iyuruikot.**

Tushiri-oro-omare, ツシリオロオマレ, 葬ル. *v.t.* To bury.

Tushiri-otta-omare, ツシリオッタオマレ, 葬ル. *v.t.* To bury.

Tushiyok-humi, ツシヨクフミ, 死ニ

シ軍人ノ叫. *n.* The cry of departed warriors.

Tushkote, ツシコテ, 結ビ附ケル. *v.t.*
To tie up.

Tush-ni, ツシニ, ヤマチコヤナギ. *n.*
Called also *Susu* and *Susu-at.* A
kind of willow. *Salix Caprea, L.*

Tush-ni, ツシニ, 釣竿. *n.* A fishing rod. **Syn: Ap-nit.**

Tush-ni-koro, ツシニコロ, 木ニ結ビ
付ク. *v.t.* To tie up to a tree with
a rope.

Tushre, ツシレ, 濁レル (汁又ハ乳ノ肪
ノ如ク). *adj.* Thick (as soup or
cream).

Tush-saurere, ツシサウレレ, 赦ス. *v.t.*
To absolve. To pardon.

Tushtek, ツシテク, 沈默セル. *adj.*
Silent.

Tushtek, ツシテク, 速キ、狂氣ノ、烈シ
キ、惡戲ノ、惡キ. *adj.* Quick.
Rapid. Mad. Fast. Abusive.
Severe. Mischievous. **Syn: Katun-katun.**

Tushtek-korachi, ツシテクコラチ, 惡
シク、狂氣ノ如ク、速ニ. *adv.*
Abusively. Madly. Quickly.

Tushtek-no, ツシテクノ, 狂氣ノ如ク、
急ギテ、惡シク. *adv.* Madly.
Quickly. Hurriedly. Abusively.

Tu-shuine, ツシュイ子, 二回. *adj.*
Twice.

Tusu, ツス, 謠言スル. *v.i.* To prophecy.

Tusu-guru, ツスグル, 法術者. *n.* A
medicine man. A wizard. A
witch doctor.

Tusunabanu, ツスナバヌ, アイヌ人ノ
傳説ノ名. *n.* Name of an Ainu
legend.

Tusuninge, ツスニンゲ, or **Tusu-
nunge, ツスヌンゲ,** リス. *n.* A
squirrel. *Sciurus lis, Temm.*

Tusurepni, ツスレブニ, 法術ナスル時
ニ用ユル木. *n.* A piece of wood
the Ainu wizards use when exercising their craft.

Tusushke, ツスシケ, 振フ. *v.i.* To
shake.

Tusushke-tashum, ツスシケタシュム,
中風症、癱. *n.* Palsy. Ague.

Tut, ツッ, 二. *n.* Two. As:—*Tut
ko,* "two days." *Tut ko rereko,*
"two or three days." *Tut ko rereko shiranak,* "two or three days
hence."

Tutanu, ツタヌ, 第二、次ノ. *adj.*
The second. The next. The next
following.

Tutkopak, ツッコパク, 袂別スル. *v.t.*
To take leave of.

Tuttarep, ツッタレブ, or **Tutturep,
ツッツレブ,** ホツキガイ、ウバカイ. *n.*
Clam. *Mactra sacharinensis, Schrenk.*

Tutturi, ツッツリ, 解ク、皺ノバス. *v.t.*
To straighten out. To unravel.

Tutturep-sei, ツッツレブセイ, ホツ
キガイ、ウバカイ. *n.* *Mactra as-
charinensis, Schrenk.*

Tutturuse, ツッツルセ, 跟蹌ク、(醉漢
ノ)、仆ルル. *v.i.* To stagger and
reel about as when under the influence of strong drink. To fall
down.

Tutukko, ツツッコ, 小包. A parcel.
As:—*Pon tutukko,* "a little parcel."

Tutukkokara, ツツッコカラ, 包裝スル、縛ル. *v.t.* To pack up baggage. To tie up as baggage. To make into a parcel.

Tutut, ツツツ, ツツドリ. *n.* Himalayan cuckoo. *Cuculus intermedius.*

Tu-umbe, ツウムベ, or **Ru-umbe, ルウムベ,** 縫箔ノ衣. *n.* A fancy needlework dress.

Tuwa, ツワ, ワラビ. *n.* The common Bracken. *Pteris aquilina, L.*

Tuwara, ツワラ, 涼シキ、冷キ. *adj.* Cool. **Syn: Nam.**

Tuwaraka, ツワラカ, 冷ス. *v.t.* To cool.

Tuwara-kara, ツワラカラ, 冷ス. *v.t.* To cool. To put to cool.

Tuwarake, ツワラケ, 冷ス. *v.t.* To cool.

Tuwayuk, ツワユク, カマイルカ. *n.* A kind of dolphin. *Lagenorhynchus acutus, Gray.*

Tuyashkarap, ツヤシカラプ, 宥ムル (子供ヲ)、憐ム. *v.t.* To caress. To fondle. To be merciful to. To take pity on. **Syn: Erampokiwen. Epuriwen.**

Tuye, ツイェ, 切ル. *v.t.* To cut. **Syn: Tui.**

Tuye, ツイェ, 母. *n.* One's mother. As :— *Tuye oro,* "of one family."

Tuyehewa-chikannari, ツイェヘワチカンナリ, 倒ニナル (魚ノ泳ゲ時屢見ルモノ). *v.t.* To turn upside down as a fish sometimes does in swimming.

Tuyepa, ツイェバ, 切ル. *v.t.* To cut.

Tuyepap, ツイェバプ, 切ラレシ物. *n.* Things cut.

Tuyepushpushke-an, ツイェプシブシケアン, 下痢病. *n.* Diarrhoea. **Syn: Soyokari tashum.**

Tuyetek, ツイェテク, 引キ抜ク、切リ. *adj.* and *v.t.* To pluck off. Cut.

Tuyetuye, ツイェツイェ, 振フ、簸ル. *v.t.* To shake. To winnow. To shake the dust off anything.

Tuyo, ツヨ, 家族. *n.* A family. **Syn: Tuye oro.**

Tuyokotbe, ツヨコツベ, 魚ノ臟. *n.* The entrails of fish.

U (ウ).

U, ウ, 此語ハ屢動詞ノ前ニ用キテ、交際、親熟、複數ヲ示ス、斯ル時ニハ、ウタサ、横切リテ、ウタシバ、彼日ヲ是ニ、又ハ互ニ、ト同樣ノ意味ヲ有ス、例セバ、オンテレ、知ル、ウナシテレ、知リ合フ、ナシバイェ、從フ、ウナシバイェ、互ニ從フ、サレド此語ハ常ニ正シク其ガ屬スル動詞又ハ副詞ノ直前ニ來ル事ナク、中間ニ他語ヲ挿入ス、例セバ、ウコタンオロコバハワヌシロモキ、我等ノ村々ノ間ニハ交際ナカリキ *part.* This particle is often placed before verbs to indicate association mutuality or plurality, and has at such times the same meaning as *utasa*, "across;" *utashpa*, "from one to the other;" or "one another." As:—*Onnere*, "to know;" *uonnere*, "to know one another." *Oshi paye*, "to follow;" *uoshi paye*, "to follow one another." However this particle does not always immediately precede the verb or adverb to which it rightly belongs, other words may intervene. As:—*U kotan oro kopahaunu shomoki*, there has been no intercourse between our villages."

U, ウ, 場處、ウハ時トシテ名詞ノ接頭語トシテ場所ヲ示スニ用キラレ、斯ル場合ハ、ウシケ、場所ト同樣ノ意味ヲ有ス、例セバ、シキウ、葦ノ生セシ處、其ハ特ニ地方ノ名ニ用キラル. *adv.* U is sometimes used as a suffix to nouns to indicate "place," and as such has the same meaning as *ushike*, "place." As:—*Shiki-u*, "the place of reeds." It is chiefly so used in the names of localities.

Uainu, ウアイヌ, 尊敬. *n.* . Honour. Respect. Reverence. **Syn: Oripak.**

Uainu-an, ウアイヌアン, 尊敬セラレ、例セバ、子イグルアナクチソンノウアイヌアンケルチ、其人ハ大ニ尊敬セラレタリ. *v.i.* To be honoured. To be respected. As:—*Nei guru anak ne son no uainu an guru ne*, "that person is very much respected." **Syn: Eoripak an. Ko-oripak an.**

Uainu-an-no, ウアイヌアンノ, 恭々

敷. *adv.* Reverentially. Respectfully.

Uainu-koro, ウアイヌコロ, 敬フ、例セバ、子ブグスエアニシヌマウアイヌコロショモキヤ、何故ニ汝ハ其人ヲ敬セヌヤ. *v.t.* To honour. To treat with respect. As:—*Nep gusu eani shinuma uainu koro shomoki ya?* "why do you not treat him with respect?" **Syn: Eoripak. Ko-oripak. Ko-uainu koro.**

Uakkari, ウアッカリ, 行キ違フ. *v.i.* To pass one another.

Uamkiri, ウアムキリ, 見知ル、知己トナル. *v.t.* To know one another. To be acquainted with each other. **Syn: Uonnere.**

Uanunkopa, ウアヌンコバ, 見知ラヌ. *v.t.* To deny knowing one another.

Uao, ウアオ, 日本ノ綠鳩. *n.* Japanese green pigeon.

Uarakaraki, ウアラカラキ, 譏ル、罵ル. *v.t.* To speak evil of another.

Uarakarase-itak, ウアラカラセイタク, 無禮ノ詞. *n.* Impolite language.

Uarashota, ウアラショタ, 爐ノ兩側、例セバ、ウアラショツタロク、爐ノ兩邊ニ坐ル. *adv.* On either side of (on each side of) a fireplace. As:—*Uarashota rok*, "to sit one on each side of a fireplace."

Uare, ウアレ, 増加スレ、子ヲ有ス、例セバ、ウアンモシリ、此世界、(直譯、増加スル世界). *v.i.* To increase. To multiply. To have children. As:—*Uare moshiri*, "this world;" (lit: the multiplying world).

Uare-an, ウアレアン, 豐カナレ. *adj.* Productive. Prolific.

Ubas, ウバス, or **Upas,** ウパス, 雪. *n.* Snow.

Ubas-shiri-an, ウバスシリアン, 雪天. *n.* Snowy weather.

Ubas-uka, ウバスウカ, 固雪、カタユキ、積リシ儘春マデ消エヌ雪. *n.* Hardened snow.

Ucharunpash, ウチャルンパシ, 兩人ノ間. *adv.* Mouth to mouth. *Tete-a-ete.* Between two persons.

Uchashkuma, ウチャシクマ, 說教、講義. *n.* A lecture. A sermon. **Syn: Ubaskuma or upaskuma.**

Uchashkuma-an, ウチャシクマアン, 講義スル. *v.t.* To lecture.

Uchashkuma-ki, ウチャシクマキ, 說教スル. *v.t.* To preach.

Uchi, ウチ, 肋. *n.* The ribs. **Syn: Ut.**

Uchike, ウチケ, 卑怯ニ. *adv.* Cowardly. **Syn: Turamkoro.**

Uchipiyere, ウチピイェレ, 他人ノ兩親ヲ惡口スル. *v.t.* To remind one of his parent's faults. To speak evil of another person's parents.

Uchish, ウチシ, 悲泣、永ク別レテ再會ノ時互ニ泣ク事. *n.* A wailing. A weeping over one another upon meeting after having been parted for a long time.

Uchish-an, ウチシアン, 互ニ泣ク事. *n.* A weeping over one another.

Uchish-kara, ウチシカラ, 互ニ泣ク、婦人ガ永ク別レテ再會ノ時互ニ泣ク. *v.i.* To weep over one another. To weep together as Ainu women in meeting one another after a long absence.

Uchiu, ウチウ, 閉ス. *v.i.* To shut. To close. To heal. To mend.

Ue, ウェ, 人肉ヲ食フ. *v.t.* To practice cannibalism.

Ue-guru, ウエグル, 食人々種. *n.* A cannibal.

Uekap, ウエカプ, 互ニ挨拶スレ. *v. i.* To salute one another.

Uekemuram, ウエケムラム, 人肉ヲ喰フ饑饉. *n.* A famine in which people commit cannibalism.

Uenkata, ウエンカタ, or **Uwenkata,** ウウェンカタ, 重々 (但シ密着セズニ). *adv.* One above another but not in contact.

Uerepak-an, ウエレパクアン, 均シキ. *adj.* Equal. Co-equal. **Syn: Une no.**

Uerepak-no, ウエレパクノ, 一諸ニ. *adj.* In combination. **Syn: Shine ikinne. Utura no.**

Ueyairam-nuina, ウエヤイラムヌイナ, 葬ル. *v.i.* To bury. **Syn: Eyairam-nuina.**

Uhaitarep, ウハイタレプ, 過誤、罪. *n.* A fault. Transgressions.

Uhautaroige, ウハウタロイゲ, or **Uhautaroise,** ウホウタロイセ, 騷々シクスル (子供ノ話ノ如ク)、(複數). *v.i.* To make a noise. To babble (as children) *pl.* **Syn: Uhawepopo.**

Uhautaroige-utara, ウハウタロイゲウタラ, 暴徒. *n.* A rabble. Noisy persons. A mob.

Uhautaroise, ウハウタロイセ, 騷々シク語ル (子供ノ). *v.i.* To babble as children.

Uhawepopo, ウハウェポポ, 騷々シク語ル (子供ノ如ク)、(複數). *v.i.* To babble (as children) *pl.* **Syn: Uhautaroise.**

Uhaweroige, ウハウェロイゲ, 騒音ナナ
ス. *v.i.* To make a noise.

**Uhaweroige-utara, ウハエウェイゲウ
タラ**, 暴徒. *n.* Noisy persons. A
mob. A rabble.

Uhaye, ウハイェ, 失ス、例セバ、ゥハイェ
ワイサム、其ハ失セタリ. *v.t.* To
lose. As:—*Uhaye wa isam,* " it
is lost."

Uhekotba, ウヘコツバ, 共ニ居ル (夫婦
ノ). *v.i.* To live together in
wedlock. **Syn: Eeyairamheko-
to.**

Uhenkotpa-ki, ウヘンコツパキ, 互ニ
愛スル、首叩スル (親カ子チ遊バスル
時). *v.i.* To love one another.
Also to nod the head at (as a
parent at a child to amuse it).
Syn: Ihenkotpa ki.

Uheuba, ウヘウバ, 曲リタル (複數).
adj. Crooked. (*pl*)

Uheupare, ウヘウバレ, 向ケル、例セ
バ、キサラウヘウバレワイヌ、耳チ向
ケテ聽ク. *v.t.* To turn towards.
As: *Kisara uheupare wa inu,*
" turn your ears and listen."

Uhokukore, ウホクコレ, 婚姻. *n.* A
marriage.

Uhonkore, ウホンコレ, 産マス、孕マ
ス. *v.t.* To beget. To render
pregnant.

Uhorokare-an, ウホロカレアン, 顛倒
スル. *v.i.* To upset.

Uhosere, ウホセレ, 顛倒セシム. *v.t.*
To put wrong end first.

Uhui, ウフイ, 燃ユル. *v.i.* To burn.
Same as *uhuye.*

Uhuika, ウフイカ, 燃ヤス. *v.t.* To
burn.

Uhui-nupuri, ウフイヌプリ, 火山. *n.*
A volcano.

Uhoshi, ウホシ, 反對ニ、アベッペニ.
adv. The other way about.
Syn: Uwehoshi.

Uhunak, ウフナク, 少シキ以前、少シ
ク後ニ、只今. *adv.* A short time
ago. A short time hence. In a
little while. **Syn: Nahun. Na-
hunak. Take.**

Uhunake, ウフナケ, 少キ以前. *adv.*
A short time ago. **Syn: Take.
Nahun.**

Uhuye, ウフイェ, 燃ユル. *v.i.* To
burn.

Uhuye-eashkai, ウフイェエアシカイ,
可燃性ノ. *adj.* Combustible.

Uhuyeka, ウフイェカ, 放火スル. *v.t.*
To set on fire.

Uhuye-no, ウフイェノ, 可燃性ノ. *adj.*
Combustible. **Syn: Uhuye eashkai.**

Uhuye-nupuri, ウフイェヌプリ, 火山.
n. A volcano. **Syn: Ekai
nuburi.**

Uibe, ウイベ, 破片. *n.* Pieces of
anything.

Uibe-oshke, ウイベオシケ, 味塵ニ碎
ク. *v.t.* To tear into pieces.

Uikokkare-au, ウイコッカレアウ, 愚
弄スル. *v.t.* To make a fool of.

Uimakta, ウイマクタ, 相前後シテ.
adv. One behind another. **Syn:
Ukattuima ukattuima.**

Uimakta-ande, ウイマクタアンデ, 相
前後シテ置ク. *v.t.* To place one
behind another.

Uimam, ウイマム, 商ヒスル. *v.i.* To
trade.

Uina, ウイナ, 灰. *n.* Ashes.

Uina, ウイナ, 取ル、拾ヒ上ケル. *v.t.* To take. To pick up. **Pl. of uk.**

Uina-takusa, ウイナタクサ, 灰ヲ蒙ル(大ナル悲ノアレ時ニナス). *v.i.* To cover one's self with ashes as when in great trouble.

Uinenashi, ウイチナシ, or **Utunashi, ウツナシ,** 兩人同臼ニテ搗ク. *v.i.* Two persons pounding together in the same mortar.

Uinnere, ウインチレ, 多クノ、一大家族. *adj.* Many. A large family.

Uirikara, ウイリカラ, 友トスル、親類トスル. *v.t.* To make a friend or relation of another.

Uirikara-utara, ウイリカラウタラ, 親類. *n.* Relations.

Uiruke, ウイルケ, 帶ブル(耳環ノ如ク)、置ク. *v.t.* To put on (as earrings, etc). To put. To place.

Uirup, ウイルプ, 住民. *n.* Inhabitants.

Uishui, ウイシュイ, 又、再、次ニ. *adj.* Again. Next. **Syn: Kannashui.**

Uitakkashi, ウイタッカシ, 從ハヌ. *v.t.* To disobey.

Uitaknu, ウイタクヌ, 從フ. *v.t.* To obey.

Uitek, ウイテク, 用ユ. *v.t.* To use.

Uitekbe, ウイテクベ, 僕. *n.* Servant.

Uitek-guru, ウイテクグル, 僕. *n.* A servant. Servants.

Uitek-utara, ウイテクウタラ, 僕. *n.* Servants.

Uk, ウク, 取ル、敢得スル. *v.t.* To take. To acquire. To accept.

Uka, ウカ, 固キ. *adj.* Hardened. Solid. **Syn: Rashne.**

Uka, ウカ, 越エテ、上ニ. *adv.* Over. Above.

Ukachiukachiu, ウカチウカチウ, 突キ合フ(戰フ時). *v.t.* To thrust at one another as with a sword.

Ukaeoma, ウカエオマ, 絞ル. *v.t.* To press. To jam. To squeeze. **Syn: Unumba.**

Ukaeoma, ウカエオマ, 一ツ一ツ置ク. *v.t.* To put one upon another.

Ukaeroshki, ウカエロシキ, 有ル(顔面ノ皺ノ如ク). *v.i.* To have (as wrinkles on the face).

Ukaeshik, ウカエシク, 群集ノ. *adj.* Crowded.

Ukaeyoko, ウカエヨコ, or **Ukaoyoko, ウカオヨコ,** 待伏スル、立番スル. *v.i.* To stand guard. To lie in wait.

Ukakik, ウカキク, 木ノ枝又ハ草ナドヲ持テ、ヒシヒシト奇ナル音ヲ爲シ人ヲ上ヲ打ッテ咒チスル. *v.t.* To exorcise sick persons by means of beating over them with boughs of trees and grass, whilst making a peculiar hissing sound.

Ukakushbari, ウカクシバリ, or **Ukakushpari, ウカクシバリ,** 一ツ一ツ連續シテ速ニ互ニ從フ、横切ル. *v.i.* One upon another. To follow one another in quick succession. To follow one another as when in danger. To go over or across.

Ukakushte, ウカクシテ, 屢手ヲ上ケ(禮ノ爲メ)、彼方此方ヘ行ク、積ミ置ヌ. *v.i.* To lift up often as the hands in salutation. To go to and fro. To do over and over. To pile up.

Ukamu, ウカム, 重々. *adv.* One above another.

Ukao, ウカオ, 貯フ、節スル、除キ去ル. *v.t.* To hoard or save up. To clear away.

Ukaoba, ウカオバ, 除キ去ル、節スル、(復數). *v.t.* To clear away. To save up. (*pl*).

Ukaobiuki, ウカオビウキ, 助ヶ合フ、慰メ合フ、親切ニシ合フ. *v.t.* To help one another. To save one another. To comfort one another. To treat one another kindly.

Ukaobiuki-wa-kore, ウカオビウキワコレ, 助ケル、慰メル、救フ. *v.t.* To help. To save. To comfort.

Ukaoiki, ウカオイキ, 待スレ (老イタル父母ニ). *v.t.* To wait upon or take care of (as one's parents in old age).

Uka-omare, ウカオマレ, 上ニ置ク. *v.t.* To put upon. **Syn : Kashiomare.**

Ukaop, ウカオブ, or **Uka-up, ウカウブ,** 斷岩. *n.* Impassable rocks. Precipitous places.

Ukaerai, ウカエライ, 救フ. *v.t.* To save. To deliver.

Ukaoyoko, ウカオヨコ, or **Ukaoyoko, ウカオヨコ,** 待伏スル、立番スル. *v.i.* To lie in wait. To stand guard. To be hidden for purposes of defence or attack. **Syn : Yongororo. Iyetokush.**

Ukapeka, ウカペカ, 前後ニ. *adv.* Backwards and forwards.

Ukara, ウカラ, 棍棒ニテ打合フ遊戯ノ名. *n.* Name of a game in which the Ainu beat one another with war-clubs.

Ukarari. ウカラリ, 密接ニ互ニ付キ從フ. *v.i.* To follow close after one another in single file.

Ukare, ウカレ, 集メル. *v.t.* To accumulate.

Ukari, ウカリ, 集メル. *v.i.* To accrue. To assemble. **Syn : Uwekari. Uwekarapa.**

Ukarire, ウカリレ, 愚弄スル. *v.i.* To be made a fool of. **Syn : Upaka nere.**

Ukashpaotte, ウカシパオッテ, 法律. *n.* Laws. Rules.

Ukashpaotte-uwesere, ウカシパオッテウウェセレ, 命ズル. *v.t.* To command. To order.

Ukata, ウカタ, 重々. *adv.* One upon another.

Ukata-ukata, ウカタウカタ, 重々. *adv.* One upon another.

Ukatchiu, ウカッチウ, 敵手. *n.* Antagonists.

Ukattuima, ウカッツイマ, 遠ク、遙ニ、永キ以前、永キ間、互ニ相別レテ. *adv.* A long way off. A long time ago. For a long time. To be separated from each other. **Syn : Homaka no.**

Ukattuima-no. ウカッツイマノ, 久シキ以前、遙ニ、永キ間. *adv.* A long time ago. A long way off. For a long time.

Ukattuimare, ウカノツイマレ, 別ツ. *v.t.* To separate.

Ukaukau, ウカウカウ, 縫ヒ合ハス. *v.t.* To sew together.

Uka-up, ウカアブ, or **Ukaop, ウカオブ,** 岩、石ダラケ、斷崖. *n.* Rocky. Stony. Rocks piled up.

Uka-un-akara, ウカウンアカラ, 加フ
ル、雑ユル. *v.t.* To add to. To
mix.

Uke, ウケ, 浮標(錨ノ). *n.* A piece
of wood attached to anchors as
a float to point out where the
anchor lies. **Syn : Pekaot-ni.**

Ukema, ウケマ, 足. *n.* The feet, *pl.*

Ukeonin, ウケオニン, 北海道ニ於ケレ
古代ノ日本政府ノ看守. *n.* The
keepers of the ancient Government stations in Ezo. This is a
Japanese word and appears to be
a corruption of Ukeoinin.

Ukepkeki, ウケプケキ, 喰ミ合フ
(動物ノ如ク). *v.t.* To nibble one
another (as animals).

Ukere, ウケレ, 擦リ合フ. *v.i.* To rub
or scrape together.

Ukere-humi-ash, ウケレフミアシ, リ
ンリント鳴ル、鳴レ. *v.i.* To chink
or jingle. To rattle.

Ukeshke-an, ウケシケアン, 容ムル、冤
罪ニオトス、害スレ. *v.t.* To persecute. To falsely accuse. To
injure another.

Ukeshkoro, ウケシコロ, 相続スル.
v.i. To succeed to one another's
inheritance.

**Uketori-kambi-shirosh, ウケトリカ
ムビシロシ,** 受取. *n.* A receipt.

Ukeuhumshu, ウケウフムシュ, 同情
スル. *v.i.* To condole or sym-
pathize with.

Uk-i, ウクイ, 収得. *n.* Acquisition.

Ukik, ウキク, 戦フ、打合フ. *v.i.* To
fight. To beat one another.

Ukik-an, ウキクアン, 戦闘. *n.* A
battle.

Ukikot, ウキコツ, 半熟ノ. *adj.* Half
ripe.

Ukimatek, ウキマテク, 騒ヶ. *v.i.* To
be agitated. To clamour. To
be in commotion.

Ukimattekka, ウキマテッカ, 騒ヶ. *v.t.*
To agitate.

Ukirikopiwe, ウキリコピウェ, 密着シ
テ坐ル. *v.t.* To sit very close to
one another.

Ukirorouande, ウキロロウアンデ, 力
ヲ角スレ. *v.i.* To strive together
to see who is strongest. **Syn :
Ukomondumuwande.**

Ukishimani, ウキシマニ, 互ニ錯雑セ
ル木. *n.* Trees clinging to one
another.

Uko, ウコ, 共ニ、此語ハ虚動詞トシテ
用キ動作ヲナス人ノ複数ナルヲ示ス.
adv. Together. This word is
often prefixed to verbs to indicate
that the actors are in the plural
number.

Ukoashunnu, ウコアシュンヌ, 交ハ
ル、雑ユル. *v.t.* To hold intercourse
with. To mix with. **Syn : Chieomare. Ukopahaunu.**

Ukoatcha, ウコアッチャ, 侮辱スル.
v.t. To treat with disrespect.

Ukoba, ウコバ, 誤テ取ル. *v.t.* To
take by mistake.

Ukoba, ウコバ, 似ル. *v.i.* To resemble. Like.

Ukobapash, ウコババシ, 論ズル. *v.i.*
To dispute.

Ukocharange, ウコチャランゲ, 試ム
ル、列断スル. *v.t.* To try. To
judge. To argue a point.

Ukochimpuni, ウコチムプニ, 足ヲ揃
ヘ占ムレ. *v.i.* To keep step as in
walking.

Ukochipkuta, ウコチプクタ, 舟ヲ覆

ス (多ク人ガ濱ニテ). *v.t.* Many to turn a boat over.

Ukochiutumu-wen, ウコチウツムウェン, 不仲ナレ、睦マヌ. *v.i.* To be on bad terms with another. **Syn: Ukokeutumu wen.**

Ukoechikiki, ウコエチキキ, 酒瓶最後ノ一滴チシタムレ、(酒宴ニ於テ). *v.i.* To pour out the very last drops of wine as at a feast.

Ukoehunara, ウコエフナラ, 守護スレ. *v.i.* To keep guard over anything.

Ukoenchararage, ウコエンチャララゲ, 刺アル (或球根ノ如ク). *adj.* To be spiked as some kinds of bulbs.

Ukoep, ウコエプ, 副食物. *n.* Any kind of food eaten with millet or rice. Condiments.

Ukoepechituye, ウコエペチツイェ, 山徑. *n.* A mountain pass.

Ukoeyukara, ウコエユカラ, 眞似レ. *v.t.* To imitate. To do like.

Ukohakmahakama, ウコハクマカマ, 囁ク. *v.i.* To speak softly. To whisper to one another. **Syn: Pinu no itak.**

Ukohekiru, ウコヘキル, 彼方此方ヘ同首スル. *v.i.* To turn the head this way and that.

Ukoherarapa, ウコヘララパ, 尊敬シ合フ. *v.i.* To pay respects to one another.

Ukoheraye, ウコヘライェ, 似ル. *v.i.* To resemble one another.

Ukohoiyo, ウコホイヨ, 姦淫スレ. *v.i.* To commit adultery.

Ukohoparata, ウコホパラタ, 陰部チ顯ス. *v.i.* To expose the person.

Ukohopi, ウコホピ, 別ツ. *v.i.* To part asunder. To separate.

Ukohosari, ウコホサリ, 彼方此方ヘ同首スル. *v.i.* To turn the head this way and that. **Syn: Ukohekiru.**

Ukohosarire, ウコホサリレ, 彼方此方ヘ同首セシムル. *v.i.* To cause to turn the head hither and thither.

Ukoiki, ウコイキ, 戰フ、喧嘩スル. *v.i.* To fight. To quarrel.

Ukoiki-ambe, ウコイキアムベ, 喧嘩、戰. *n.* A quarrel. A fight. War.

Ukoikire, ウコイキレ, 戰ハス、喧嘩セシム. *v.t.* To set fighting or quarelling.

Ukoimekare, ウコイメカレ, or Ukoimekari, ウコイメカリ, 馳走ヨリ物チ持チ去ル. *v.t.* To carry things away from a feast.

Ukoiomare, ウコイオマレ, 酒チ注グ、(酒宴ノ際). *v.i.* To pour out wine as in a feast.

Ukoiram, ウコイラム, ト、共ニ. *post.* With. Along with.

Ukoiram-no, ウコイラムノ, 一諸ニ、共ニ. *adv.* Altogether. Together with.

Ukoiram-no-an, ウコイラムノアン, 共ナル、件フ. *v.i.* To be with. To accompany.

Ukoirushka, ウコイルシカ, 怒リ合フ. *v.i.* To be angry with one another.

Ukoisoitak, ウコイソイタク, 會話スル. *v.i.* To converse together. To talk over matters together. **Syn: Uweneu-sara.**

Ukoitak, ウコイタク, 會話スル. *v.i.* To talk together.

Ukoiyuhaikara, ウコイ ユ ハイ カラ, 他人ノ 説 チ 話 ス. *v.t.* To repeat what another says. To tell tales of another person.

Ukokai, ウコカイ, or **Ukookai, ウコオカイ,** 雑ユ、交際スル. *v.t.* To mingle with. To associate with. To come together. **Syn: Uorepa.**

Ukokai-guru, ウコカイグル, 交友. *n.* An associate.

Ukokaikire, ウコカイキレ, 交尾スレ (鹿ノ如ク). *v.i.* To rut (as deer). **Syn: Kaikiri. Ukonupuru.**

Ukokai-utara, ウコカイウタラ, 交友. *n.* Associates.

Ukokandama, ウコカンダマ, 欺シ合フ. *v.t.* To deceive one another.

Ukokara, ウコカラ, 雑ユ、共ニ動作ス ル. *v.t.* To mix. To mingle. Also, to do together.

Ukokarakari, ウコカラカリ, 束ニ マ ルメレ. *v.t.* To roll up into a bundle.

Ukokateaikap, ウコカテアイカプ, 男 色. *n.* Sexual abuse. Abusers of themselves with mankind. Sodomy. **Syn: Uyorupuikoiki.**

Ukokauk, ウコカウク, 智惠ノ輪. *n.* A kind of string puzzle.

Ukokauk, ウコカウク, 和合スル. *v.i.* To be in accord.

Ukokeutum, ウコケウツム, 一心同軆. *n.* One mindedness.

Ukokeutum-an, ウコケウツムアン, 一心タル. *v.i.* To be of one mind.

Ukokeutum-koro, ウコケウツムコロ, 一致スレ. *v.i.* To agree. To be in agreement with.

Ukoki, ウコキ, 共ニナス. *v.t.* To do together. **Syn: Inan no iki.**

Ukokomge, ウココムゲ, or **Ukokomse, ウココムセ,** 拘攣ル、ヒキツル、疎クナル (髪ノ如ク). *v.i.* To be drawn up as one's joints by disease. To be crumpled up. To be rough, as the hair. **Syn: Ukomomse. Komkomse.**

Ukokonchi, ウココンチ, 籤. *n.* Lots.

Ukokonchi-etaye, ウココンチエタ イェ, 抽籤スレ. *v.i.* To draw lots.

Ukokonchi-koro, ウココンチコロ, 抽 籤スル. *v.i.* To cast lots.

Ukokoro, ウココロ, 共有スル. *v.t.* To possess in common with others.

Ukokushippa, ウコ クシッバ, 總テ. *adj.* All. Together. **Syn: Shine-ikinne.**

Ukoman-no, ウコマンノ, 甚ガ多ク、酷 シク、絶エズ、屢. *adv.* Very much. Severely. Continually. Frequently. As:—*Ukoman no charange,* "to argue or scold very much." **Syn: Ramma-ramma.**

Ukomat-ehunara, ウコマツエフナラ, 闘フ (牡鹿ガ牝鹿チ得ンガ爲ニ). *v.i.* To fight for females (as bucks).

Ukomeremerege, ウコメレメレゲ, 煌 ク. *v.i.* To twinkle, as the stars.

Ukomomse, ウコモムセ, 踞ミテ行ク、腰曲ル (老ヒテ). *v.i.* To go stooping. To be bent as with age. To be cramped. To be drawn up as one's joints by disease. **Syn: Ukokomge.**

Ukomondumuwande, ウコモンツム ワンデ, 力チ角スル. *v.t.* To strive together to see who is the best man. **Syn: Akokirorowande.**

Ukomui, ウコムイ, 虱チトレ、(頭又ハ衣ヨリ). *v.t.* To pick out lice from the head or dress.

Ukomuye, ウコムイェ, 結ビ合ス. *v.t.* To bind up together.

Ukoniitukte-shinot, ウコニイツクテシノツ, 根木チ打ツ遊戯. *n.* A game of casting sticks into the earth.

Ukoniki-an, ウコニキアン, 疊ミタル. *adj.* Folded.

Ukoniki-kara, ウコニキカラ, 疊ム、タタム. *v.t.* To fold up, as clothes.

Ukonittupte, ウコニツブテ, or **Ukonitupte, ウコニツブテ,** 遊戯ノ名. *n.* Name.of a game somewhat resembling drafts but played with sticks. **Syn: Chikkiri.**

Ukonken-eokte, ウコンケンエオクテ, or **Ukonkopiyokte, ウコンコピヨクテ,** 釣チカケ合フ. *v.t.* To hook together.

Ukoniuchirande, ウコニウチランデ, 仲惡シカル、睦マヌ. *v.i.* To be on bad terms with another.

Ukonukara, ウコヌカラ, 比較スル. *v.t.* To compare.

Ukoniko, ウコニコ, 疊ム. *v.t.* To fold up.

Ukoniteteye, ウコニテテイェ, 奇貌チ作リ合フ (小兒ガ戯ニ). *v.i.* To make faces at one another.

Ukonumba, ウコヌムバ, 押シ合フ. *v.t.* To press upon. To throng.

Ukonupetne, ウコヌペツ子, 相悅フ. *v.i.* To rejoice together.

Ukonupuru, ウコヌブル, 交尾. *n.* Sexual intercourse of animals and birds.

Ukooiki, ウコオイキ, 補缺スル (他人ノ乏シキチ). *v.t.* To provide for the wants of another. **Syn: Ukaoiki.**

Uko-okai, ウコオカイ, 共住スル、共存ス.レ. *v.i.* To be together.

Ukoopi, ウコオビ, 分レタル、離レタル. *adj.* Seperate. Apart. Also "to part."

Ukoopi-ukoopi, ウコオビウコオビ, or **Ukoopiu-ukoopiu, ウコオビウウコオビウ,** 散亂.スル、分解スル、例セバ、チカプウコオビウウコオビウ ホブムバヤバイェ、鳥散亂シテ飛ヒ去レリ. *v.i.* To scatter. To disperse. As:— *Chikap ukoopiu-ukoopiu hopumba wa paye,* "the birds scattered and flew away." **Syn: Chipasusu.**

Ukoopiure, ウコオビウレ, 散亂セシム、分解セシム. *v.t.* To scatter. To disperse. **Syn: Chipasusure.**

Ukooshikkote, ウコオシッコテ, 相慕フ. *v.t.* To desire or long for one-another.

Ukopahaukoro, ウコバハウコロ, 他人ノ事チ云フ、誹ル. *v.t.* To tell tales of another. To backbite.

Ukopahaunu, ウコバハウヌ, 交際スレ、雜ニ. *v.t.* To hold intercourse with. To mix with. **Syn: Chieomare. Ukoashunnu.**

Ukopaiyaige, ウコバイヤイゲ, 蛆ガ. *v.i.* To move about as maggots in flesh or fish.

Ukopake-koshne, ウコバケコシ子, 讒ル. *adj.* and *v.i.* To slander. To speak evil of another. To lie about someone.

Ukopaktuipa, ウコバクツイバ, 親交チ欲ス. *v.i.* To desire to associate with.

Ukopao, ウコバオ, or **Ukopau, ウコバウ,** 叱ス ル. *v.t.* To scold.

Ukopararui, ウコバラルイ, or **Ukopararorui, ウコバロルイ,** 喋リ合フ. *v.i.* To chatter together. **Syn:** Ukoitakrui.

Ukoparata, ウコバラタ, 侮辱ノ爲他ニ對シテ陰部ヲ顯ス、(複数). *v.i.* (*pl*). To expose the person in insult.

Ukopau, ウコバウ, 叱スル. *v.t.* To scold.

Ukopoye, ウコポイエ, 攪(ミダ)ル. *v.t.* To stir. To admix.

Ukopoyege, ウコポイエゲ, 攪サレル. *v.i.* To be stirred. To be admixed.

Ukopoyepoye, ウコポイエポイエ, 攪ル. *v.t.* To stir.

Ukorachi, ウコラチ, 似ル、ニ依レバ. *v.i.* To be alike. To resemble. According. According to. In accordance with. **Syn:** Upakitara an. Une no an.

Ukorachi-an-no, ウコラチアンノ, 其故ニ. *adv.* Accordingly.

Ukoraiba, ウコライバ, 別ツ、裂キ取ル. *v.i.* To part. To tear away. To separate.

Ukoramba, ウコラムバ, 穩ニ諫ムレ. *v.t.* To reprove quietly.

Ukoramashi, ウコラマシ, 喧嘩スレ (子供ノ如ク). *v.i.* To wrangle, as children.

Ukoramasu, ウコラマス, 好ム (複数). *v.i.* To be fond of. (*pl*).

Ukorambashinne, ウコラムバシン子, 相愛スレ. *v.i.* To love one another. To be friendly.

Ukoramkoro, ウコラムコロ, 協議スル. *v.i.* To hold council. To consult.

Ukoramkoro-guru, ウコラムコログル, 協議者. *n.* A councillor.

Ukoramkoro-utara, ウコラムコロウタラ, 協議者. *n.* Councillors.

Ukoramoshma, ウコラモシマ, 仲直スレ. *v.t.* To be reconciled to one another after a quarrel.

Ukoramoshmare, ウコラモシマレ, 仲直スル. *v.t.* To reconcile.

Ukorampoktuye, ウコラムポクツイエ, 絶交スレ、忘ル. *v.i.* To cut off one's connection with. To neglect.

Ukorampoktuyere, ウコラムポクツイエレ, 絶交セシムル. *v.t.* To cause one person to cut off his connection with another.

Ukorari, ウコラリ, 共ニ. *adv.* Conjointly.

Ukoraye, ウコライエ, 取ル、得レ. *v.t.* To take. To get.

Ukoro, ウコロ, 交接スル. *v.t.* To have sexual intercourse.

Ukosambe-chiai, ウコサムベチアイ, 同心ナル、安心スル. *v.i.* To be of one heart. In peace.

Ukosanniyo, ウコサンニヨ, 算用スレ. *v.t.* To reckon with. To make up accounts.

Ukosetorumbe, ウコセトルムベ, 一巣ノ鳥. *n.* A brood of birds. **Syn:** Shine set orumbe.

Ukoshikushshikush, ウコシクシシクシ, 急遽スル (渦流ノ如ク). *v.i.* To rush together as water in an eddy.

Ukoshuwama, ウコ シュ ワマ, 夫婦喧嘩. *n.* A quarrel between husband and wife.

Ukotama, ウコタマ, 加ヘル. *v.i.* To add together.

Ukotamge, ウコタムゲ, 集合ノ. *adj.* Collectively. Altogether.

Ukotamge-no, ウコタムゲノ, 共ニ. *adv.* Altogether.

Ukotaptap, ウコタプタプ, or **Ukotaptapu,** ウコタプタプ, 球ニマルメル. *v.t.* To roll up into a ball.

Ukotereke, ウコテレケ, 角力スル. *v.i.* To wrestle.

Ukotoisere, ウコトイセレ, 集合スル. *v.i.* To flock together. To congregate together, as carrion birds round the bodies of dead animals.

Ukotokpishte, ウコトクピシテ, 一ツ宛 (目的物チ) 射ル. *v.t.* To shoot one by one.

Ukotomka, ウコトムカ, 化粧シ合フ. *v.t.* To adorn one another.

Ukotte, ウコンテ, 毎、例セバ、トゥコツテ、毎日. *adj.* Every. As :— *To-ukotte,* "every day."

Ukotuikoro, ウコツイコロ, 仲善カレ、家族ノ一員トナレ. *v.i.* To be on good terms. To be members of the same family.

Ukotuk, ウコツク, 上ニ付クレ、附着シ合フ、塞ガレ. *v.i.* To be stuck on. To stick together. To be closed up.

Ukotukka, ウコツッカ, 閉ス、(目チ)、上ニ付クレ、重子合フ、結合スル. *v.t.* To close, as the eyes. To stick on. To couple together. To unite.

Ukotumi, ウコツミ, 戦. *n.* War.

Ukotumi-koro, ウコツミコロ, 戦チ起ス. *v.t.* To wage war with.

Ukotumi-koro-guru, ウコツミコログル, 兵士. *n.* A soldier.

Ukoturire, ウコツリレ, 差出ス. *v.t.* To hold out to.

Ukoturuye, ウコツルイェ, or **Ukouturuge,** ウコウツルゲ, 界、町界、例セバ、コタンウコツルイェ、村又ハ、地方ノ界. *n.* The borders of a place. The outskirts of a town. As :— *Kotan ukoturuye,* "the borders of the district or village."

Ukouturu, ウコウツル, 其内、間、例セバ、マチヤウコウツル、街ニ於テ. *adv.* Amongst. Between. As :— *Machiya ukouturu,* "in the streets."

Ukouturuge, ウコウツルゲ, 場所ノ界. *n.* The border or limits of a place.

Ukouturugeta, ウコウツルゲタ, 間、其内. *adv.* Between. Amongst.

Ukowe, ウコウェ, 此語ハ屢バ働詞ノ接頭語トシテ用井複數チ示ス. *part.* This word is often used as a prefix to indicate the plural number.

Ukowenkeutum-koro, ウコウェンケウツムコロ, or **Ukowensambe-koro,** ウコウェンサムベコロ, 仲善カラヌ、睦バヌ. *v.i.* To be evilly disposed towards one another. **Syn :** Uwepokba.

Ukowepekere, ウコウェペケレ, 會話スル. *v.i.* To converse together. **Syn :** Uweneusara.

Ukoyaihumshu, ウコヤイフムシュ, 事變=逢フ、(複數). *v.i.* To meet with an accident. (*pl*)

Ukoyaisambepokash, ウコヤイサム

ベポカシ, 困難ス ル(複數). *v.i.* To be in trouble. (*pl*).

Ukosambayomba, ウコサムバヨムバ, 摘ミトル. *v.t.* To gather, as in needlework.

Ukoyomiyomik, ウコヨミヨミク, 皺寄ル、萎レル(衣ノ). *v.i.* To be creased or crumpled up as clothes.

Ukte, ウクテ, 與フ. *v.t.* To give.

Uku, ウク, 吹ク、例セバ、アベウク、火ヲ吹ク. *v.t.* To blow. As:— *Abe uku,* "blow a fire." **Syn: Ewara.**

Ukuran, ウクラン, 昨夜. *adv.* Last night.

Ukurerarapa, ウクレララバ, or **Ukoherarapa, ウコヘララバ,** 挨拶ス ル、例セバ、イランガラブテ、イヤイコイルシカレ、ウクレララバアンナ、御機嫌如何ニヤ、君ヨ安カレ、余ハ君ニ挨拶ス. *v.i.* To pay respects to. As:— *Irangarapte, iyaiko-irushkare, ukurerarapa an na!* "how do you do, may you be serene, I pay my respects to you."

Ukuribe, ウクリベ, ウナギ. *n.* Eel.

Ukuru-kina, ウクルキナ, ギバウシ. *n. Hosta coerulea, Lratt.*

Ukururube, ウクルルベ, ウナギ、マアナ ル、ヤツメウナギ. *n.* Name applied to anguilliform fishes. Eel. Lampray. Conger eel.

Ukushish, ウクシシ, 泡ヲ立テル(卽チ 酵母ノ如ク). *v.i.* To work as in ferment.

Ukushpa-i, ウクシバイ, 渡シ場. *n. n.* A ferry.

Ukushpa-uchike, ウクシバウチケ, or **Upushpa-ushi, ウブシバウシ,** 渡シ 場. *n.* A ferry.

Um, ウム, 物ノ後部、例セバ、チブウ ム、舟ノ艫. *n.* The after part of anything. As:— *Chip um,* "the stern of a boat."

Umangi, ウマンギ, or **Umanki, ウ マンキ,** 梁、ウツバリ. *n.* A beam.

Umaratto-koro, ウマラットコロ, 公ノ 宴ヲ開ク. *v.i.* To have a public feast.

Umbe, ウムベ, or **Unbe, ウンベ,** 何 ニテモ頭ニ着クル物、何ニテモ某處ニ アル物、複數ハ、ウシベ、ナリ、例セ バ、サバウムベ、轡、オモガイ、キム ウシベ、山中ニアル物、又ハ動物. *n.* Anything that is worn upon the head. Anything that exists in any given place. The plural form is *ushbe.* As:—*Supa umbe,* "a bridle." *Kim ushbe,* "any things or creatures that live in or exist upon the mountains."

Umbipka, ウムビブカ, 信ゼヌ. *v.t.* To disbelieve.

Umkanchi, ウムカンチ, 小揆(梶ニ用 ユ). *n.* A scull used to steer boats.

Umma, ウムマ, 馬、例セバ、ウムマ カ ワラン、下馬スル、ウムマス、乘馬ス レ、ウムマオロワノラン、下馬スル. *n.* A horse. As:—*Umma ka wa ran,* "to dismount a horse." *Um ma o,* "to ride a horse." *Umma orowa no ran,* "to dismount a horse."

Umma-raige-pagoat, ウムマライゲ バゴアツ, 馬ニ附カレレ. *n.* Horse possession. Horse punishment.

Umma-shi-karush, ウムマシカルシ, マクソタケ. *n.* A kind of toad-stool which grows from horse droppings.

Umomare, ウモマレ, 集メル. *v.t.* To collect. To gather together. **Syn: Uomare.**

Umompokta, ウモムポクタ, 互ニ下ナ
レ、ヨリ少キ. *adj.* One under
another. Less than.

Umontasa, ウモンタサ, 答フ レ. *v.t.*
To answer.

Umpirima, ウムピリマ, 非常ヲ告ゲ
ル、警戒ス. レ. *v.i.* To raise an
alarm of danger. Warning. To
spy. To look out for.

Umshi-no, ウムシノ, or **Umshu-no,
ウムシュノ**, 理不盡ニ. *adv.* Without cause. Of itself.

Umshu, ウムシュ, 貯ヘラレシ、準備
セラレシ. *adj.* Stored up. Prepared. Put away in the best
places.

Umta, ウムタ, 柚. *n.* The stern of
a boat.

Umta-an-guru, ウムタアングル, 舵
取. *n.* A steers-man.

Umuraiba, ウムライバ, or **Umura-
yeba, ウムライェバ**, 悲ノ時互ニ慰メ
テ肩ヤ頭ヲ撫ヅ. *v.t.* To rub the
head and shoulders of one another
as when bewailing the dead or
sympathizing with one another
during grief or trouble.

Umurek-guru, ウムレクグル, 一對、
夫婦、雌雄. *n.* A pair. Husband
and wife. Male and female.

Umusa, ウムサ, 休日、祭、通常、官ノ布
告ヲ聞カセンガ爲ニ、命令ニヨリ或ル
特殊ノ場所ニ人民ヲ集ムル事ニシテ、
此時ニ酒、米煙草其他ノ物ヲ日本ノ官
吏ヨリ分配セラル. *n.* A general
holiday. A feast. Originally an
assembly of the people by order
at particular places that they
might be notified of official edicts.

At these meetings rice, *sake*, tobacco and other things were dis-
tributed by the Japanese officials.
Syn: Umusa iwai.

Umusa, ウムサ, 禮スル、頭ヲ撫ヅル
(相慶シテ). *v.t.* To salute. To
stroke the head as in congratu-
lations. **Syn: Musa. Uruiruye.**

Un, ウン, 此語ハ處、場所、又ハ或ル場
所ニ人或ハ物ノ存在スル事ヲ示ス、例
セバ、キムゥンカムイ、山ニ住ム神、卽
チ、熊、レプゥンカムイ、海神、此ウン
ハ其ガ後ニ來ル詞ヲ支配ス. *part.*
This word is often used to indicate locality or that a person or
thing exists in or at a place.
As:—*Kim un kamui*, "gods of
or residing in the mountains,"
i.e. "bears." *Rep un kamui*, "the
gods of the sea." The particle *un*
governs the word it follows. **Syn:
Op.**

Un, ウン, 時トシテ此語ハ文章ヲ決定ス
ルニ用ユ、例セバ、クアニゥン、其ハ我
ナリ、ルウェウン、然リ. *part.* Sometimes this particle is used as an
affirmative part of speech. As:
—*Kuani un*, "it is I." *Ruwe un*,
"yes."

Un, ウン, 方ニ、迄ニ、於テ、例セバ、チ
セイゥン家ノ方ニ、トアニゥン其處ニ
於テ、チュプカムイクシキウントム、太
陽ハ我ノ眼ニ輝ク. *post.* Towards.
To. At. In. As:—*Chisei un*, "towards home." *Toani un*, "at that
place." *Chup kamui ku shiki un
tom*, "the sun shines in my eyes."

Un, ウン, 我等、例セバ、ゥンコレ、其
ヲ我ニ與ヘヨ、ゥンオハイゲカラニサ、
彼ハ我等ヲ誹レリ. *obj. pro.* Us.

As :— *Un kore*, "give it to us."
Un ohaigekara nisa, " he slander-
ed us."

Una, ウナ, 灰. *n.* Ashes. **Syn :
Uina.**

Unankotukka, ウナンコツッカ, 頰擦ス
ル. *v.t.* To put cheek to cheek.

Unarabe, ウナラベ, 叔母. *n.* Aunt.

Unashke, ウナシケ, 勸誘スル. *v.t.*
To persuade.

Uncha-kina, ウンチャキナ, カサスゲ.
n. A kind of sedge. *Carex dispa-
latha, Boett.*

Unchi, ウンチ, 火. *n.* Fire. Also
called *Unji; Abe; Huchi; Fuji.*

Unchi-kema, ウンチケマ, 火把. *n.*
A fire-brand.

Unchi-omap, ウンチオマブ, 爐. *n.*
A fire-place.

Une, ウネ, 均サレ. *v.i.* To be equal.

Unekari, ウネカリ, 旅先ニテ逢フ. *v.t.*
To meet as during a journey.
Syn : Etunangara.

Une-no, ウネノ, 同ジク、只、多量ニ、
平均ニ、例セバ、ツチノアイメグスイ
テキイシトマ、驚クナカレ、其ハ只人ナ
レバナリ. *adv.* The same. Like
as. To the same degree. Only.
Much. Equal. As:— *Une no ainu
gusu, iteki ishitoma,* "don't be
frightened, for it is only a man."

Une-no-an, ウチノアン, 均クサレ. *v.i.*
To be equal. Coequal.

Unepkoro, ウチプコロ, 同樣ノ. *adj.*
Alike.

Uneu, ウチウ, オットセイ. *n.* A
fur seal. *Otaria ursina, Linn.*

Ungerai, ウンゲライ, 賦與スル、施
與スル. *v.t.* To bestow. To give
alms.

Ungeraitep, ウンゲライテブ, 施與物.
n. Alms.

Uni, ウニ, or Unihi, ウニヒ, 家、例セ
バ、ウニタ、家ニ於テ、ウニウン、家ノ
方ヘ. *n.* Home. As:— *Uni ta,*
"at home." *Uni un,* "towards
home."

Unikoro, ウニコロ, 身繕 (ミツクロヒ)
スル、(坐シテノ後). *v.t.* To draw
one's clothes tidily when sitting
down.

**Unintek, ウニンテク, or Unintek-
ki, ウニンテクキ, or Unintep, ウニ
ンテブ,** オニノヤガラ. *n.* *Gastrodia
elata, Bl.*

Unipa, ウニバ, or Unuipa, ウヌイバ,
入墨スル. *v.t.* To tattoo.

Unisak, ウニサク, 身繕スル. *v.i.* To
let one's clothes down as in sitting.

Unisapka-an, ウニサブカアン, 忙シキ、
忙シカレ. *v.i.* and *adj.* To be busy.
Syn : Imontabire.

Uniwende, ウニウェンデ, ニウェンホリ
ビニ同ジ. *n.* Same as *Niwenhoribi.*

Unkeshke, ウンケシケ, 損スル、熱望
スル、追フ. *v.t.* To spoil. To harm.
To baffle. To desire. To pursue.
Syn : Inonchip.

Unkotuk, ウンコツク, 松脂. *n.* The
resin of the *Picea ajanensis, Fisch*

Unkotuk-chip, ウンコツクチブ, 糊鍋.
n. A glue-pot.

Unotmaka, ウノツマカ, 癲癇ノ人ノ口
チ閉ク. *v.t.* To open the mouth
as of a person in a fit.

Unpirima, ウンピリマ, 發見スル、見
ル. *v.i.* To spy. To observe.
To look out for. To raise an
alarm.

Untemaki, ウンテマキ, 手甲. *n.* A kind of fingerless mitten made to cover the back of the hand. A substitute for gloves.

Untak, ウンタク, 行キテ呼ブ. *v.t.* To go to call.

Untere, ウンテレ, 待ッ. *v.t.* To await. To wait for.

Unu, ウヌ, or **Unuhu, ウヌフ,** 母. *n.* Mother. **Syn: Habo.**

Unu, ウヌ, 置ク、例セバ、ウムマクラウヌ、馬ニ鞍置ク. *v.t.* To put. To place. As:—*Umma kura unu,* "to saddle a horse."

Unuipa, ウヌイバ, 入墨スレ. *v.t.* To tattoo.

Unukaot, ウヌカオツ, セコブマス、エトロフマス. *n.* Hump-back salmon. *Oncorhynchus gorbuscha,* (*Walb.*)

Unukara, ウヌカラ, 見交フ、逢フ. *v.t.* To see one another. To meet.

Unukaran, ウヌカラアン, 見交ハサレ. *v.i.* To be seeing one another.

Unukare, ウヌカレ, 見セ合フ. *v.t.* To shew to one another.

Unumba, ウヌムバ, 絞ル、壓搾スレ. *v.t.* To press together. To squeeze. To jam.

Unum-okoiki, ウヌムオコイキ, 拳闘スレ. *v.i.* To fight with the fists.

Ununuke, ウヌヌケ, 愛撫スル(子供ニナス如ク). *v.t.* To fondle as children.

Unuwapte, ウヌワプテ, 産ニテ呻ク. *v.i.* To groan in childbirth.

Unuye, ウヌイェ, 入墨スル. *v.t.* To tattoo. **Syn: Shinuye.**

Uoitakushi, ウオイタクシ, 呪(マジナ)フ、詛フ. *v.t.* To bewitch. To curse. **Syn: Ishiri-shina. Pon itak-ki.**

Uok, ウオク, or **Uwok, ウゥォク,** 結ブ. *v.t.* To fasten.

Uokkane, ウオッカ子, 鎖、掟. *n.* A chain. Fetters.

Uokkane-kut, ウオッカ子クツ, 帯. *n.* A belt.

Uonnere, ウオン子レ, 知ル、知リ合フ、注意スル、聽ク、例セバ、ヌカラウオン子レプカアン、ヌカラ、エラムシカレプカアン、(見テ)知レル者アリ、(見テ)知ラヌ者モアリ. *v.t.* To know. To know one another. To take heed. To listen. As:—*Nukara uonnerep ka an, nukara eramushkarep ka an,* "there are those I know (by seeing) and those I do not know (by seeing).

Uonnerep, ウオン子レプ, 被知物. *n.* Things known.

Uoraika, ウオライカ, 命ズレ. *v.t.* To command.

Uorepa, ウオレバ, 集マル. *v.i.* To come together. **Syn: Ukokai.**

Uoroge, ウオロゲ, 墻. *n.* A mast.

Uorogituye-i, ウオロギツィェイ, 砦. *n.* A fort.

Uorun, ウオルン, 互ニ. *adv.* One another.

Uorunu, ウオルヌ, 着レ. *v.t.* To put on, as an overcoat. To clothe upon.

Uose-kamui, ウオセカムイ, 狼、エゾヤマイヌ. *n.* A wolf.

Uoshmak, ウオシマク, 相前後シテ. *adv.* One behind another.

Uosh, ウオシ, or **Uoshi, ウオシ,**

相前後 シテ. *adv.* Behind one another.

Uoshmakta, ウオシマクタ, 相前後 シ テ. *adv.* One behind another.

Uottumashi, ウオッツマシ, 亂 レ、亂 レシ. *adj.* and *v.i.* To be disorderly. Out of order. Out of rank. **Syn : Uworokopoyege.**

Uotunanu, ウオツナヌ, or **Uwotutanu, ウウォツタヌ,** 此語ハ直接數詞 ノ根ニ附隨シテ其ヲ番號ニ變ズ、例セ バ、ツウオツタヌ、第二、イワンウオ ツタヌ、第六. *adj.* This word placed immediately after the radical forms of numerals changes them into ordinals. Thus :—*Tu notutanu*, "the second." *Iwan notutanu*, "the sixth."

Uoya, ウオヤ, or **Uwoya, ウウォヤ,** 異レル. *adj.* Different.

Uoyakta, ウオヤクタ, 異所ニテ、此處、 其處ニ. *adv.* At different places. Here and there.

Uoyap, ウオヤブ, or **Uwoyop, ウ ウォヨブ,** 異物. *n.* and *v.i.* A different object. To be different.

Uoyato, ウオヤト, 日々. *adv.* Day after day.

Up, ウブ, 白子. *n.* The soft row of a fish. Milt.

Upaekoiki, ウバエコイキ, 論ズレ. *v.i.* To argue. To dispute. To strive with. **Syn : Upatasare.**

Upak, ウバク, 充分ナル、適當ナル、例 セバ、ウバクセレケ、丁度牛. *adj.* Sufficient. Adequate. As :— *Upak sereke*, "just half."

Upak-no, ウバクノ, 同ジ程ニ、充分ナ レ. *adv.* To the same degree. Sufficient.

Upakashnu, ウバカシヌ, 罰スル. *v.t.* To punish. **Syn : Panakte.**

Upakashnu-chisei, ウバカシヌチセ イ, 牢屋. *n.* A prison.

Upakbare, ウバクバレ, 改其スレ、例 セバ、ケウツムウバクバレヤン、改心 セヨ. *v.t.* To set to rights. To reform. As :—*Keutum upakbare yan,* "rectify your heart."

Upakitara, ウバキタラ, 以前ノ如ク、 變リナク、例セバ、ツバキタラアン、常 ノ如ク. *adv.* As before. Without change. As :—*Upakitara an,* "as usual." **Syn : Upakmaune.**

Upakmaune, ウバクマウ子, 安楽ナレ. *adj.* Comfortable.

Upak-sereke, ウバクセレケ, 牛バ. *adv.* Half.

Upakte, ウバクテ, 平均スル. *v.t.* To make equal.

Upakte-wa-nukara, ウバクテワヌカ ラ, 比較スル. *v.t.* To compare.

Upaore, ウバオレ, 論スル、喧嘩スル. *v.i.* To dispute. To argue. To quarrel. **Syn : Upa-ekoiki.**

Upara, ウバラ, 煤. *n.* Soot.

Upara-kore, ウバラコレ, 呪フ、マジ ナフ、誹ル. *v.t.* To curse another To speak evil of another.

Upara-o, ウバラオ, or **Upara-ush, ウバラウシ,** 煤ケタレ. *adj.* Sooty.

Upare, ウバレ, 延焼. *n.* The flaring of fire. The spreading out of fire as before the wind.

Uparu, ウバル, 延焼スル. *v.i.* To flame. To spread out as fire before the wind. **Syn : Paru.**

Uparoiki, ウバロイキ, 補缺スル、養フ. *v.t.* To provide for the wants of

others. To feed. To keep. **Syn:**
Ukaoiki.

**Uparoiki-shomoki, ウバロイキショモ
キ,** 忘ル. *v.t.* To neglect. **Syn:**
Ukorampoktuye.

Uparonneta, ウバロン子タ, 會話ス
ル. *v.i.* To speak together. To
talk over with another.

Uparo-oshuke, ウバロオシュケ, 馳走
スル. *v.t.* To entertain guests with
food.

Uparoroitak, ウバロロイタク, 探求ス
ル, 審査スル. *v.i.* To enquire into. To make people answer for
themselves respecting something
said of or by them.

**Uparoshuke-iwai, ウバロシュケイワ
イ,** 婚筵. *n.* A marriage feast.

Upas, ウバス, or **Ubas, ウバス,** 雪,
例セバ、ウバスアシ、雪降ル、ウバス
ララクマ、雪片、ウバスルイ、雪降ル、
ウバスシリ、雪天. *n.* Snow. As:
—*Upas ash,* "to snow." *Upas rara kuma,* "a snow-drift." *Upas
rui,* "to snow." *Upas shiri,*
"snowy weather."

Upas-an, ウバスアン, 雪ノ. *adj.*
Snowy.

Upas-ash, ウバスアシ, 雪降ル、例セバ、
ウバスルイ、雪降ル. *v.i.* To snow.
As:—*Upas rui,* "to snow."

Upas-chironnup, ウバスチロンヌプ,
エゾイタチ. *n.* Ermine. *Putorius
erminea, Linn.*

**Upash-hurarakkare, ウバシフララ
ッカレ,** 婦人ガ病ヲ逐ヒ出ス爲ニ入墨
ヲ行フ習慣ノ名, 此語ノ意味ハ、互ニ
入墨ヲ香ハスナリ. *n.* Name of a
custom in which Ainu women

tattoo themselves in order to drive
away disease. The word means
literally "making one another
smell of tattooing."

Upas-kep, ウバスケプ, 雪搔、ユキカキ.
n. A snow shovel.

Upaskuma, ウバスクマ, or **Ubaskuma, ウバスクマ,** 説教. *n.* Preaching. **Syn: Uchashkuma.**

Upaskuma-ki, ウバスクマキ, 説教ス
ル・ *v.t.* To preach.

**Upaskuma-ki-guru, ウバスクマキグ
ル,** 説教者. *n.* A preacher.

Upas-kuru, ウバスクル, 雪雲、積雲.
n. Snow clouds. *Cumulus.*

Upas-ush, ウバスウシ, 雪ノ. *adj.*
Snowy.

Upataiba-an, ウバタイバアン, 爭論ス
ル. *v.i.* To have a quarrelsome
argument.

Upatasare, ウバタサレ, 論爭スル、喧
嘩スル、抗言スル. *v.i.* To argue.
To quarrel. To answer back.
Syn: Upaure.

Upaukoiki, ウバウコイキ, 喧嘩スレ、
論爭スル(直譯、口ニテ鬪フ). *v.i.* To
quarrel. To argue. (Lit: to fight
with the mouth).

Upaure, ウバウレ, 喧嘩スル、論爭スレ.
v.i. To quarrel. To argue.

Upaweotke, ウバウェオツケ, 衝突スレ.
v.i. To collide. To be in contact. **Syn: Utomoshma.**

Upeka, ウペカ, 面ト向ヒテ、相對シテ、
例セバ、ウペカロク、相對シテ坐ル.
adv. Facing one another. As:
—*Upeka rok,* "to sit facing one
another."

Upekare, ウペカレ, 整理スル. *v.t.* To adjust.

Upen, ウペン, 若キ. *adj.* Young.

Upepe, ウペペ, 水(雪ヲ溶シタレ). *n.* Water produced by melting snow. **Syn : Upas wakka.**

Upepe-san, ウペペサン, 洪水(雪消ノ爲). *n.* A flood caused by melting snow.

Upereke, ウペレケ, 少女. *n.* A little girl. **Syn : Opere. Opereke.**

Upeu, ウペウ, イブキバウフウノ一種. *n. Sesebi Libanotis, Kock. var. sibirica, DC.* This herb is very much used as a medicine for colds.

Upibi, ウビビ, or **Upipi, ウピビ,** or **Upibi-upibi, ウビビウビビ,** 単獨ニ. *adv.* Disunitedly. Singly. Intermittently.

Upirima, ウビリマ, 賄賂. *n.* A bribe.

Upish, ウビシ, 數,指定セラレシ,成就スル, 例セバ, アエサンニヨトホタ子ウヒシルウェネ, 指定セラレシ日ヘ今ヤ到來セリ. *n.* Number. Appointed. To be fulfilled. As :—*Aesanniyo toho tane upish ruwe ne,* "the appointed day has now arrived."

Upishkani, ウビシカニ, 各側ニ於テ, 例セバ, ウヒシカニワコトツカ, 兩側ニ附スレ. *adv.* On each side. On either side. As :—*Upishkani wa kotukka,* "to stick on both sides."

Upok, ウポク, 角力スル. *v.i.* To wrestle. To strive together.

Upokte, ウポクテ, 泳ク. *n.* To flounder.

Uporunbe, ウポルンベ, 腰卷. *n.* A loin-cloth.

Uppauppa, ウッパウッパ, 踏ム. *v.t.* To trample on. To tread on. To knead as dough. **Syn : Otettereke.**

Upshi, ウブシ, 顛覆スル、破壞スル(馬車ノ仆レテ). *v.i.* To be upside down. To be turned over. To be broken down, as a carriage.

Upshipone, ウブシポネ, 後頭骨. *n.* The occipital bone.

Upshire, ウブシレ, 顛覆セシムル. *v.t.* To turn upside down. To turn over.

Upshoro, ウブショロ, 物ノ内部、胸、例セバ、チセイウブショロ、家ノ内部. *n.* The inside of anything. The bosom. As :— *Chisei upshoro,* "the inside of a house."

Upshoroge, ウブショロゲ, 懷中ニ、内ニ、例セバ、アイアイニシンダウブショロゲエホラレ、子供ハ揺籃ノ内ニ横ハル、ポロチセイウブショロゲ、大家ノ内部. *adv.* In the bosom of. In the inside of a house. As :— *Aiai nishinda upshoroge ehorare,* "the child lies in the bosom of the cradle." *Poro chisei upshoroge,* "the inside of a large house."

Upshoro-pok, ウブショロポク, 胸ノ下部. *n.* The lower part of the bosom.

Upshororoge, ウブショロロゲ, ウブショロゲニ同ジ. Same as *upshoroge.*

Upsho'un-kut, ウブショウンクツ, 腰卷. *n.* A woman's loin cloth. **Syn : Uporunbe.**

Upumba-shinot, ウブムバシノツ, 遊戲ノ名. *n.* A game of sitting on the floor and trying to lift one another over the shoulder.

Upumbatche, ウブムバッチェ, 積ム(雪ノ如ク). *v.i.* To drift as snow.

Upun, ウブン, 亂飛スル(埃又ハ細雪又ハ水煙ノ如ク). *v.i.* To fly about as dust or fine snow, or a spray of water in the wind.

Upunpatche, ウブンバッチェ, 亂飛スレ(埃又ハ細雪ノ如ク). *v.i.* To fly about as dust or fine snow.

Upunshiri, ウブンシリ, 滅却セラル(雪ノ爲路ノ). *v.i.* To be obliterated, as tracks in the snow).

Upush, ウブシ, 破裂スル、火花チ散ス. *v.i.* To burst. To jump as fire sparks.

Upush, ウブシ, or **Upushi, ウブシ,** 物ノ集合、柴. *n.* A cluster of things. A bunch.

Upushi-kara, ウブシカラ, 束メル. *v.i.* To tie up into bundles or strings as onions or radishes.

Urai, ウライ, 網代ノ類. *n.* Fish traps somewhat resembling arrow heads in shape made by driving stakes into the beds of rivers and filling in the spaces with branches of trees. These traps are always made to point down stream and are fitted each with a net at the arrow-headed end with which the Ainu catch the fish.

Urai-kara, ウライカラ, or **Urai-koro, ウライコロ,** 網代チ守ル. *v.i.* To keep watch over as for fish at an *urai.*

Uraini, ウライニ, 棒、柱. *n.* A stake. A post.

Urai-susu, ウライスス, コリナギ. *n.* A small kind of willow. *Salix multinervis, F. et S.* Also called *ura-susu.*

Uramande, ウラマンデ, 相殺害スルチ望ム(戰ニ於テ)、戰チ熱望スル. *v.t.* To desire to kill one another, as in battle. To be eager to fight one another.

Uramarakare, ウラマラカレ, 怒ラセル. *v.t.* To make angry. **Syn: Irushkare.**

Urametokuwande, ウラメトクワンデ 勝負チ決ス. *v.i.* To see which is the best or bravest man, as in a quarrel.

Urameushi, ウラメウシ, 仲善カル、親シム、睦ブ. *v. i.* To be on good terms with a person. **Syn: U-woshiknuka.**

Uramisamka, ウラミサムカ, 欺ク. *v.i.* To deceive.

Uramkoiki, ウラムコイキ, 諧謔スル. *v.i.* To play with. To joke with.

Uramkopashte, ウラムコバシテ, 撰拔スル. *v.i.* To choose out from among others.

Urammokka, ウラムモッカ, 遊ブ. *v.i.* To play. To have some fun.

Uramshishire, ウラムシシレ, 一致セス. *v.i.* To be in disagreement.

Uramu, ウラム, 賞讚スル. *v.t.* To praise. To think in common.

Urara, ウララ, 霧. *n.* Fog.

Urara-an-no, ウララアンノ, or **Urara-at, ウララアツ,** 霧多キ. *adj.* Foggy.

Uraraattep-sei, ウララアッテブセイ, 卷貝ノ總稱. *n.* Any kind of gastropod.

Urara-kando, ウララカンド, 最低キ天. *n.* The lowest skies. **Syn: Range kando.**

Urarapa, ウララバ, 押シ合フ、搖スリ
込ム. *v.i.* To press against one
another. To shake down. To
throng.

Urar'attep, ウラルアッテプ, 巻貝ノ
總稱. *n.* Any kind of gastropod.

Urare, ウラレ, 搖スリ込ム (穀物チ斗ナ
ド二)、押シ合フ. *v.t.* To shake
down, as grain in a measure. To
press against. To throng.

Urari, ワラリ, 霧. *n.* Mist. Haze.

Urarire, ウラリレ, 搖リ込ム. *v.t.* To
shake down, as grain in a measure.

Urari-utara, ウラリウタラ, 群民. *n.*
A multitude of people.

Ura-susu, ウラスス, or **Urai-susu,
ウライスス,** *n. Salix multinervis,
F. et S.* A kind of willow.

Ure, ウレ, 足、脚、例セバ、ウレアサマ、
足ノ裏. *n.* The feet. The legs.
A foot. Thus :— *Ure-asma,* "the
soles of the feet."

Ure-asama, ウレアサマ, 足ノ裏. *n.*
The soles of the feet.

Ureechiu, ウレエチウ, 蹴ク、尊敬スル
v.t. To strike the feet against.
To hold in great esteem. To reverence. To put on the feet.

Urehe, ウレへ, 足、脚. *n.* A foot.
The feet. The legs.

Urei-pok-chup, ウレイポクチュプ, 十
月. *n.* The month of October.

Urekushte, ウレクシテ, 步行スル. *v.i.*
To walk along.

Uremekka, ウレメッカ, 足ノ甲. *n.*
The insteps.

Uren, ウレン, 兩ノ. *adj.* Both.

Urenashi, ウレナシ, 搗ク(數人者一ツ
臼二テ)、例セバ、アシクチンンウレナ

シ、イワ二ウウレナシ、五六人ノ者一
ツ臼二テ搗ク. *v.i.* Several to pound
in one mortar. Together. As :
—*Ashiknen urenashi, iwaniu urenashi,* "five or six persons pounding in one mortar."

Urenga, ウレンガ, 平穩. *n.* Peace.

Urenga-kara, ウレンガカラ, 鎭ムル.
v.t. To make peace.

Urenga-koro, ウレンガコロ, 鎭マル.
v.i. To be at peace.

Urengare, ウレンガレ, 上梁スル、屋根
チ上ゲル. *v.t.* To place on the roof
of a hut. To bring to a peaceful
issue.

Urepende, ウレペンデ, or **Urepeutok, ウレペウトク,** 足ノ爪尖、例セバ、
ウレペンデエアシ、爪先二テ立ツ. *n.*
The points of the toes. As :—
Urepende eash, "to stand upon the
points of the toes."

Urepet, ウレペツ, 趾. *n.* The toes.

Urepeutok, ウレペウトク, 趾尖、ツマ
サキ. *n.* The points of the toes.
Syn : Urepende.

Urepirup, ウレピルプ, 靴拭席. *n.*
A mat for wiping boots on.

Urepo, ウレポ, 小サキ趾. *n.* The
little toe.

Urepuni, ウレプニ, 步ム. *v. i.* To
walk.

Ureshke, ウレシケ, 育テラレシ(複數).
v.i. I have been reared (*pl*).

Ureshpa, ウレシパ, 育ツル. *v.t.* To
bring up.

Uretaro, ウレタロ, アシカ、トド. *n.*
Sea-lion. *Otaria stelleri, Less.*

Ureu-ka-kush, ウレウカクシ, 疊リ合
ヒテ. *adv.* One above or over another.

Ureu-kuruka-kush, ウレウクルカク シ, 一上一下スル(戦＝於ケルカノ如 ク). *v.i.* To go first one and then another above each other as swords in fighting.

Ureu-kuruka-kushte, ウレウクルカ クシテ, 重リ合ハスル. *v.t.* To place one above another.

Ure-utorosama, ウレウトロサマ, 足ノ 側面. *n.* The sides of the feet.

Uri, ウリ, 上ゲラレタル. *adj.* Cast up. Thrown up.

Uriri, ウリリ, ウ、ツガラス、ハム. *n.* A cormorant. A shag. Diver.

Urok, ウロク, 共＝坐ス. *v.i.* To sit down together.

Urokte, ウロクテ, 共＝坐セシムル. *v.t.* To cause to sit together.

Uru, ウル, 皮. *n.* Skin. **Syn：Kapu.**

Uruiruge, ウルイルゲ, 祝シ合フ. *v.i.* To salute one another as in congratulation. **Syn：Umusa. Musa.**

Urukai, ウルカイ, 別々＝. *adv.* Seperately. One at a time.

Uruki, ウルキ, 閉ス、釦チカクル. *v.t.* To shut as doors, or draw too as partitions. To button up as a coat.

Uruki, ウルキ, シラミ. *n.* A louse.

Uruki-o, ウルキオ, 多虱質ノ. *adj.* Lousy.

Urukire, ウルキレ, 便利チ計ル、便＝ス ル. *v.t.* To accommodate.

Urukire-i, ウルキレイ, 便利. *n.* Accommodation.

Urukire-no, ウルキレノ, 便利＝、適切 ＝. *adv.* Accommodately. Fittingly.

Uruki-wa-an, ウルキワアン, 適スル. *v.i.* To fit.

Urukko, ウルッコ, 魚ノ一種. *n.* A fish of some kind.

Uruoka, ウルオカ, 一ツ終レバ又一ツ、 應報. *adv.* First one and then the other. One's deserts. **Syn：Uokato.**

Uruokata, ウルオカタ, 子孫. *n.* Descendants.

Urup, ウルプ, ベニマス. *n.* Red salmon. Blueback. (*Oncorhynchus nerka, Walb.*).

Uru-uruk, ウルウルク, 慄フ. *v.i.* To shiver. To shake.

Usa, ウサ, 種々ノ、其他ノ. *adj.* Various. Besides. Many.

Usa-are, ウサアレ, 區別スル. *v.t.* To distinguish.

Usa-are-kiroro, ウサアレキロロ, 辨 別ノオ. *n.* The distinguishing faculty.

Usaetasare, ウサエタサレ, 種々＝曲 レ(飛鳥ノ群ノ如ク). *v.i.* To coil in and out. To wind about as a flight of birds.

Usakatneka, ウサカツチカ, 種々ノ、 例セバ、ウサカツネカチパハウサウシカ アエンエカラカラ、余＝就キテ種々ノ 事云ハル. *adj.* Various. As :— *Usakatneka chipahauushka a en ekarakara,* "various things are said about me." **Syn：Usaineka.**

Usachire, ウサチレ, 分解スル. *v.t.* To take to pieces. To pick to pieces.

Usai-mongire, ウサイモンギレ, 試ム ル. *v.t.* To test. To try.

Usaine, ウサイ子, 種々ノ、多クノ. *adj.* Various. Many.

Usaine-usaine-an, **ウサイ子ウサイ子アン**, 多クノ、種々ノ. *adj.* Many. Various.

Usak, **ウサク**, 乾ケル. *adj.* Dry.

Usakka, **ウサッカ**, 乾カス. *v. t.* To dry.

Usampeka, **ウサムペカ**, 相携テ、相並ンテ、例セバ、ウサムペカアブカシ、相携ヘテ歩ム. *adv.* Side by side. As:—*Usampeka apkash,* "to walk side by side."

Usamta, **ウサムタ**, Usamata, **ウサマタ**, 相携ヘテ、相並ンテ、例セバ、ウサムタラツキ、相並ンテ懸ル. *adv.* Side by side. Abreast. As:— *Usamta ratki,* "to hang down side by side."

Usamta-usamta, **ウサムタウサムタ**, 相並ンテ. *v.i.* Side by side.

Usanishoro-yaikara, **ウサニショロヤイカラ**, 天氣ヲ見ル. *v.t.* To study the skies.

Usan-usapki, **ウサンウサブキ**, 造ラル、送クラル、例セバ、オピツタ、ノオカイベカムイウサンウサブキ子、萬物神ニ造ラレタリ. *v.i.* To be made by. To be sent by. As: —*Obitta no okaibe Kamui usan-usapki ne,* "all things were made by God."

Usapishkani, **ウサピシカニ**, 此處其處. *adv.* Here and there.

Usapki, **ウサブキ**, 生長スル. *v.i.* To grow up. To come up.

Usapte, **ウサブテ**, 増ス. *v.t.* To cause to increase.

Usarageta, **ウサラゲタ**, or Usara-keta, **ウサラケタ**, 婦人小兒ノ坐スル席. *adv.* The place in an Ainu hut where the women and children sit. That part of a hut along the centre of the hearth's left hand side."

Usaraye, **ウサライェ**, 分ツ. *v.t.* To divide.

Usat, **ウサツ**, 灰. *n.* Cinders. As: —*Abe o usat,* "live cinders."

Usausa, **ウサウサ**, 種々ノ. *adj.* Various.

Usausak, **ウサウサク**, 疑ハシキ、摸糊タル. *adj.* Ambiguous.

Usayun, **ウサユン**, 縫目ノ開ク、綻ブ. *v.i.* To open, as the seams of a garment.

Use, **ウセ**, 通常ノ、下級ノ. *adj.* Ordinary. The lower class.

Usei, **ウセイ**, 湯, *n.* Hot water.

Usekashne-reushi-ushi, **ウセカシ子レウシウシ**, 野宿. *n.* A camp. **Syn: Inne kash utara.**

Useno, **ウセノ**, 日光. *n.* Sunshine.

Usep, **ウセブ**, 片、例セバ、アッツシシネウセブヘテ ツ ウセブヘ子、衣ノ數片. *n.* A piece. As:—*Attush shine usep hene tu usep hene,* "one or two pieces of cloth."

Usepne-attush, **ウセブ子アッツシ**, 縫ハヌ端物. *n.* Cloth not made up.

Ush, **ウシ**, 着ル、履ク、冠ル. *v.t.* To wear as boots or a hat. To put on.

Ush, **ウシ**, 入ル、例セバ、エルムセエン子ウクランアクベ ウシ、昨夜鼠ハ係蹄ニ入ラザリキ. *v.t.* To go into. To get into. As:—*Erum seenne ukuran akbe ush,* "the rat did not get into the trap last night!

Ush, **ウシ**, 此詞ハ或ル名詞ノ後ニ付シテ形容詞ヲ作ル、例セバ、ウパス、ウシ、

雪アル、ウパルシ、煤ノ如キ. part. This word is used as an adjectival ending to some nouns. As :—Upas-ush, " snowy." Uparush, " sooty."

Ush, ウシ, 此語ハ、ウン、ノ複數ナラン、而シテ某處ニ存在スルノ意チ示ス、例セバ、キムウシブ、山中ノ庫、キムウシベ、森ノ木ト藪、ワッカウシカムイ、水神. loc part. This word appears to be a plural form of un and indicates existence in or at a place :—Kim ush pu, " a storehouse built in the mountains." Kim ush-be, " forest trees and bushes." Wakka ush kamui, " the goddesses of water."

Ushi, ウシ, 擦リ込ム、塗ル. v.t. To besmear. To rub into.

Ushi-acha, ウシアチャ,
Ushi-chikuni, ウシチクニ,
Ushi-ni, ウシニ, } ヤマウルシ. n. A kind of tree. Rhus trichocarpa, Miq.

Ushike, ウシケ, 場處. n. Place.

Ushikeshpare, ウシケシバレ, 譏ル、冷遇スル. v.i. To speak ill of one another. To treat another badly.

Ushikomewe, ウシコメウェ, 挑ム. v.t. To challenge.

Ushikosamba, ウシコサムバ, 終ル、暗クナル. v.i. To finish. To become darkened. To be unable to do more (used particularly of prophecying).

Ushimne, ウシムネ, 翌日. adv. The next day. Syn : Shimge.

Ushimne-ushimne, ウシムネウシムネ, 毎日、日々. adv. Every day. Daily.

Ushinanda, ウシナンダ, 一處ニ於テ. adv. At one place.

Ushinanda-omare, ウシナンダオマレ, 一處ニ置ク. v.t. To put into one place.

Ushinna, ウシンナ, 箇々ニ. adv. Individually. Separately.

Ushinnai, ウシンナイ, 異ル. v.i. To differ.

Ushinna-ushinna, ウシンナウシンナ, 異ナリテ、箇々ニ. adv. Individually. Separately.

Ushipinire, ウシピニレ, 埋葬ノ用意スル(死體チ). v.t. To prepare the dead for burial. Syn : Katu karakaran.

Ushi-pungara, ウシブンガラ, ツタウルシ. n. A kind of climbing plant. Rhus Toxicodendron L. var. radicans, Miq.

Ushiramkore-guru, ウシラムコレグル, 朋友、相識ノ人. n. Friends. Persons who know one another. Syn : Uamkire utare.

Ushirenpa, ウシレンバ, 共ニ行ク. v.i. To go about together.

Ushirikire, ウシリキレ, 代理スル. v.t. To do in place of another. To take the place of another. Syn : Shirihine-ki. Ushishiri-kire.

Ushisi, ウシシ, 蹄. n. The hoof of a horse or cow or deer.

Ushitakonoye, ウシタコノイェ, 角チ交ュ(鬪フ鹿ノ如ク). v.i. To get the horns entangled (as fighting bucks).

Ushiune, ウシウネ, 奴隷トナル、僕トナル. v.i. To be a slave. To be a servant.

Ushiune-guru, ウシウネグル, 奴隷、僕. n. A slave. A servant.

Ushiune-kara, ウシウチカラ, 奴隷ト ス ル・*v.i.* To make slaves.

Ushiune-koro, ウシウチコロ, 奴隷ト ス レ. *v.t.* To make slaves.

Ushiune-utara, ウシウチウタラ, 奴隷. *n.* Slaves.

Ushiush, ウシウシ, or **Usshiush, ウ ッシウシ,** 斑ラナル、彫刻アレ、例セ バ、ウシウシバシュイ、彫刻ノアル鬚 上ケ器. *adj.* Variegated. Speckled. Carved with figures. As: — *Ushiush bashui,* "a moustache lifter with figures carved upon it."

Ushka, ウシカ. 消ス. *v.t.* To extinguish.

Ush-oro, ウシオロ, 澗. *n.* A gulf.

Ushtek, ウシテク, 消ユル、滅亡スル. *v.i.* To go out, as fire. To die out, as a race of people.

Ushtekka, ウシテッカ, 消ス、根絶スル、 撃殺スル. *v.t.* To put out. To extinguish. To exterminate. To massacre.

Usoinapashte, ウソイナバシテ, 共ニ 外出スル. *v.i.* To go out together.

Usoshhamu, ウソシカム, 層チナセル、 (百合根ノ如ク). *adj.* To be in layers, as a lily bulb.

Usshi-kara, ウッシカラ, 漆瘡. *n.* A kind of blood poisoning caused by exposure in the forest. *Lackecrema.*

Usshiu-ne, ウッシウ子, ウレウチニ同 ジ、僕、奴隷. *n.* Same as *ushiune.*

Usshiush, ウッシウシ, 斑ナル. *adj.* Variegated.

Ushte, ウシテ, 靴ヘス、ハカス. *v.t.* To cause to draw on (as boots).

Ut, ウツ, 肋. *n.* The sides of the body. The ribs. **Syn: Uchi.**

Uta, ウタ, ナマコ. *n.* A kind of sea cucumber. *Stichopus japonica, Sal.*

Uta, ウタ, ニ於テ. *post.* In. **Syn: Otta.**

Uta, ウタ, 臼. *n.* A mortar.

Utabure, ウタブレ, 閉ス(手チ). *v.t.* To shut, as the hands.

Utakararip, ウタカラリブ, or **Otakararip, オタカラリブ,** ヒトデ、モミヂ カヒ. *n.* A starfish. **Syn: Ninokararip.**

Utamtesbare, ウタムテスバレ, 互ニ 刀チ擧ゲ、(戰又ハ偶然ニ). *v.i.* To hold up the swords to one another after a quarrel or after an accident.

Uta-ni, ウタニ, 杵. *n.* A pestle.

Utapke, ウタブケ, 修繕スル. *v.t.* To mend.

Utara, ウタラ, **Utare, ウタレ,** **Utari, ウタリ,** 人、朋友、人民、此語ハ屢屢 數ノ接尾語トシテ用ユ. *n.* Men. Comrades. People. Persons. This word is often used as a plural suffix.

Utaragesh, ウタラゲシ, 女、下級民. *n.* A woman. The lowest class or rank of men.

Utarakararip, ウリラカラハブ, タコ ノマクラ. *n.* A starfish.

Utara-nimaraha, ウタラニマラハ, 朋 友、親類. *n.* Friends. Relations. **Syn: Nimaraha.**

Utarapa, ウタラバ, 酋長、主人、同力 同能ノ人. *n.* Chief. Head. Lord. Master. Equals in strength, bravery or skill.

tare, **ウタレ**, 人、朋友、ウタラニ同ジ. *n.* The same as *Utara.*

Utare-kore-wen, **ウタレコレウェン**, 害スル、惡クスル. *v.t.* To injure. To do evil to.

Utari, **ウタリ**, ウタラニ全シ. *n.* The same as Utara.

Utasa, **ウタサ**, 横切リテ. *post.* Across.

Utasa, **ウタサ**, 順番ニ 例セバ、トウタ サ、隔日. *adv.* In turn. Every other. As:—*To utasa,* "every other day."

Utasa, **ウタサ**, 横切ル、横ニ寢ル、訪問 スル. *v.t.* To cross. To lay across. To visit.

Utasa-chikuni, **ウタサチクニ**, 十字架、 例セバ、ウタサチクニオッタ アクンギ コキッキク、十字架ニ架ケラル、ウタサ チクニオッタクンギコキッギク、十字架 ニ付ケル. *n.* A cross. As:—*Utasa chikuni otta a kungi kokikkik,* "to be crucified." *Utasa chikuni otta kungi kokikkik,* "to crucify."

Utasa-keutum-koro, **ウタサケウツ ムコロ**, 睦クセヌ. *v.i.* To be at variance with one another. **Syn: Uwetasaash.**

Utasa-no, **ウタサノ**, 十字形ニ. *adj.* Crosswise.

Utasa-tasa, **ウタサタサ**, 多クノ. *adj.* Many.

Utasa-utara, **ウタサウタラ**, 訪問者. *n.* Visitors.

Utasautasa, **ウタサウタサ**, 横切リ合 ヒテ. *adj.* Across one another.

Utashpa, **ウタシバ**, 横切リテ、此方ヨ リ彼方ニ、交互ノ. *post.* Across. From one to the other. Reciprocal.

Utashpa-upaure, **ウタシバウパウレ**, 論ズル. *v.i.* To altercate.

Utashpa-utashpa, **ウタシバウタシバ**, 互ニ. *adv.* From one to the other.

Utchike, **ウッチケ**, 卑怯ニ. *adv.* Cowardly. **Syn: Turamkoro.**

Utek, **ウテク**, 否定ノ語. *adv.* Not.

Utekkishima, **ウテッキシマ**, 握手ス ル、手ヲ取リ合フ. *v.t.* To shake hands. To seize one another's hands.

Utek-nimba, **ウテクニムバ**, 手引合フ. *v.i.* To lead one another.

Utese-no, **ウテセノ**, 相並ンデ. *adv.* Side by side. **Syn: Usamta.**

Utka, **ウツカ**, 急流. *n.* Rapids.

Utnai. **ウツナイ**, 小川、細流. *n.* A small stream. Rivulet. A brooklet.

Ut-nit-pone, **ウツニツポ子**, 肋. *n.* The ribs.

Utokuyekoro, **ウトクイェコロ** 友トナ ル. *v.i.* To be at one. To be friends. **Syn: Uoshiknuka.**

Utoki-at, **ウトキアッ**, 縄、(死人、死人ト共ニ葬ル物 ヲ縛ル). *n.* A cord used to tie the dead to the bier. Also the cord used to tie up the things to be buried with the dead. Also to lace up the clothing the dead are buried in.

Utomechiu, **ウトメチウ**, or Utom-chiure, **ウトムチウレ**, 重着スル、例 セバ、ウェンヤラッツシャイチナイ ネ カトムチウレ、多クノ古キ濫褸 ヲ着ル. *v.i.* To wear, as many clothes. As:—*Wen yarat tush yaine-naine utomchiure,* "wearing many old ragged garments."

Utomeraye, ウトメライェ, 混淆スル、
結合スレ. *v.i.* To amalgamate.
To unite.

Utomeush, ウトメウシ, 觸リ合フ. *v.i.*
To touch one another.

Utomkokanu, ウトムコカヌ, 媒灼ヲ
立ツル. *v.i.* To commit to another
as to a mediator.

**Utomnukara-guru, ウトムヌカラグ
ル,** 結婚者. *n.* An alliance by
marriage. **Syn : Ikokone guru.**

Utomoraye. ウトモライェ, 列セシムル.
v.t. To set in rows. To place
in order side by side.

Utomoshnu, ウトモシヌ, or **Utomoshma, ウトモシマ,** 當リ合フ、衝突ス
ル,逢フ. *v.i.* To knock together.
To come into contact. To come
into collision. To join together.
To meet together. To collide.
Syn : Upaweotke.

Utomu-oshmare, ウトムオシマレ, 衝
突セシム、當リ合ハス. *v.t.* To
knock together.

Utor-hum, ウトルフム, 足音. *n.* The
sound of walking. **Syn : Ainu
utor'humi.**

Utoro-eotke, ウトロエオツク, 押シテ
ル. *v.t.* To push against.

Utorosam, ウトロサム, or **Utorosa-
ma, ウトロサマ,** 物ノ側面. *n.* The
side of anything.

Utorosamne, ウトロサム子, 横様ニ.
adv. Sidewise.

Utorosamne, ウトロサム子, 横ハレ.
To lie upon the side.

Ut-pone, ウツポ子, 肋. *n.* The ribs.

Uttap, ウッタブ, 魚ノ一種. *n.* The
name of a kind of fish.

Uttara, ウッタラ, 懸ル. *v.i.* To hang
down.

Uttarare, ウッタラレ, 懸ラスル. *v.t.*
To cause to hang down.

Utuka-ni, ウツカニ, ミヅキ. *n.* Dog-
wood. *Cornus macrophylla, Wall.*

**Utukaritaokaire, ウツカリタオカイ
レ,** 戰備ヲ整フル. *v.t.* To set in
battle array.

Utumashi, ウツマシ, 混淆スル、確ナ
ラズ. *v.i.* To be unstable. To
be mixed.

Utumashire, ウツマシレ, 混ズル、疑
ハス. *v.t.* To miss. To put in
doubt.

Utumgush, ウツムグシ, or **Utumkush, ウツムクシ,** 厭フ可キ. *adj.*
Disagreeable. To be of a disagreeable disposition of mind.
Syn : Kuroma.

Utumopashte, ウツモパシテ, 錯雜セ
ル. *v.t.* To complicate.

Utumotnere, ウツモツ子レ, 不能ナル、
爲スヲ知ラズ. *v.i.* To be unable.
Not to know how to do a thing.

Utumotte, ウツモッテ, 語リ間違フ、音
ヲ間違フ. *v.t.* To mispronounce.

Utunashi, ウツナシ, 同白ニテ搗ク(二
人ニテ). *v.i.* Two persons to
pound in a mortar. See. **Autunashi. Yaitunashi. Reunashi.
Inereyunashi.**

Utupa-ibe, ウツパイベ, 葬祭. *n.* The
feast held at the time of death
and burial.

Utupepnu, ウツペプヌ, or **Utupe-
shnu, ウツペシヌ,** 歎ク(死者ノ爲).
v.i. To mourn for the dead.

Utura, ウツラ, 共ニ. *adv.* Together.

Utura-no, ウツラノ, 共ニ. *adj.* In combination. Together. **Syn: Shine-ikinne.**

Utura-no-paye, ウツラノパイェ, 共ニ行ク. *v.i.* To go together.

Uturen, ウツレン, 兩ノ、例セバ、ウツレン チキリ、兩ノ足、ウツレンシキ、兩ノ眼. *adj.* Both. As:—*Uturen chikiri*, "both legs." *Uturen shiki*, "both eyes."

Uturen-bashui, ウツレンパシュイ, 箸. *n.* Chopsticks.

Uturu, ウツル, 空間、爐ノ左側. *n.* Space. The left hand side of the fireplace.

Uturu-at-no, ウツルアツノ, 中央ノ. *adj.* Middling.

Uturu-an, ウツルアン, 減ズル、小降 (コフリ)トナル、少シク快氣ス、例セバ、ホンノアプトウツルアン、雨、小降トナリヌ. *v.i.* To abate, as rain or pain. To feel better in health. As:—*Pon no apto uturu an*, "it is raining a little less heavily" *Pon no uturu an*, "to be a little better in health."

Uturugeta, ウツルゲタ, 間. *adv.* Between.

Uturupak, ウツルパク, 一致ノ、程ノ、等シク. *adv.* In agreement. To such a degree. Equal.

Uturupak-an, ウツルパクアン, 一致スル. *v.i.* To be in agreement.

Uturupak-shomoki, ウツルパクショモキ, 一致セズ、不平均ナル. *v.i.* To disagree. To be unequal.

Uturuta, ウツルタ, 間ニ、其内、間、間 (場所). *adv.* Whilst. Amongst. During. Between.

Uturuta-an-range, ウツルタアンランゲ, 時トシテ. *adv.* Sometimes.

Utushi, ウツシ, 物ノ側面. *n.* The side of anything.

Utushmat, ウツシマツ, 多妻. *n.* A plurality of wives. Polygamy.

Utushmat-koro-guru, ウツシマツコログル, 多妻者. *n.* A polygamist.

Utush-pone, ウツシポ子, 肋、肋骨. *n.* The ribs. Side bones.

Ututanure, ウツタヌレ, 整理スル. *v.t.* To arrange.

Ututta, ウツッタ, 戸際 (屋内ノ). *n.* That part of a house nearest the doorway.

Ututta, ウツッタ, 其中、間、此語ハウツルタ、ノ畧ナリ. *adv.* Amongst. Whilst. This word is short for *uturuta*.

Ututtoni, ウツットニ, 中央. *n.* The middle. Centre.

Utuyashkarap, ウツヤシカラプ, 愛撫スル、愍ム. *v.t.* To fondle. To favour. To pity.

Uwa, ウワ, 知ラヌ. *v.t.* Not to know.

Uwakkari, ウワッカリ, 行キ違フ、見失フ. *v.t.* To pass one another. To miss one another.

Uwanbare, ウワンバレ, 檢査スレ. *v.t.* To examine. To look at carefully.

Uwande, ウワンデ, 檢査スル. *v.t.* To examine. To look carefully at.

Uwapapu, ウワパプ, 叱スル、罰スル. *v.t.* To scold. To punish.

Uware, ウワレ, or **Uare, ウアレ**, 增ス. *v.i.* To multiply. To increase

Uwashte, ウワシテ, 增加セシム. *v.t.* To make plenteous.

Uwatni-koro, ウワツニコロ, 混淆ス
ル、太刀打ス レ. *v.i.* To be inter-
mingled. To roll over one
another. To fight together with
swords.

**Uwatni-koro-eshishuye, ウワツニ
コロエシシュイェ,** 太刀ヲ合ハスル. *v.i.*
To clash swords together, as in
fighting.

Uwato, ウワト, 線、列. *n.* A line.
A row. A straight mark.

Uwato-no, ウワトノ, 線チナシテ、例セ
バ、ウワトノロク、列チナシテ坐スル.
adv. In a line. In lines. As:
—*Uwato no rok,* "to sit in
lines or rows."

Uwatore, ウワトレ, 算スル、登錄スル、
整理スレ. *v.t.* To count. To
enroll. To arrange.

Uwatta, ウワッタ, 一ツ一ツ、單獨ニ.
n. Separately. Singly.

Uwatte, ウワッテ, 合セタル、多クハ.
adj. Aggregated. Many. A
crowd.

Uwe, ウウェ, 均シキ. *adj.* Equal.

Uwechi, ウウェチ, 凍傷ノ、凍傷スル、霜
枯ル、シモガル. *v.i.* and *adj.* To
be frost bitten. Frost-bitten.

Uwechi, ウウェチ, 知己トナル. *v.i.* To
know another. To be Acquainted.

Uwechishkara, ウウェチシカラ, 挨拶
スル (女ノ). *v.i.* To salute one
another, as women.

Uwechiu-ibe,
ウウェチウイベ,
Uwechiu-iwai,
ウウェチウイワイ,
Uwechiu-marapto,
ウウェチウマラプト, 婚禮、此儀式ニ
於テ、花嫁若
干ノ物ヲ料理
シテ、其一部
ヲ花聟ニ興フ
レバ、花聟ハ
其ヲ取リ餘チ花嫁ニ返却シテ食セシ
ム、斯クテ此式ヲ終ル. *n.* The mar-

riage ceremony in which the
bride having cooked some food
gives part of it to the bride-
groom, and he after taking a little
gives back the remainder for her
to eat; and so the ceremony is
finished.

Uwechuure, ウウェチュウレ, 打ヲ合ハ
ス. *v.t.* To knock against another.
To kick one another. To come
into contact.

Uwechutko, ウウェチュツコ, 違フ. *v.i.*
To be abnormal. Different.

Uwechutko-no, ウウェチユッコノ, 不
同ニ、異ナリニ. *adv.* Differently.

Uweekarange, ウウェエカランゲ, 集
合スル. *v.i.* To congregate.

Uweekarangere, ウウェエカランゲレ,
集中セシム. *v.t.* To assemble.

Uwe-ema-no, ウウェエマノ, 常ニ. *adv.*
Continuously. Always.

Uweepaketa, ウウェエバケタ, 漸次.
adv. By degrees.

Uwe-ekasure-an, ウウェエカスレアン,
錯雜スレ、散在スル、例セバ、シサム
チセイ イウウェエカスレアン、日本家
屋其内ニ散在セリ. *v.i.* To be mixed
with. To be scattered among.
As:—*Shisam chisei i uwe-ekasure
an,* Japanese houses are scattered
among them."

Uweeripak, ウウェエリバク, 適合スル.
adj. To agree. To correspond.

Uwe-etasa-ash, ウウェエタサアシ, 背
キ爭フ. *v. i.* To be at variance
with one another. **Syn: Utasa
keutum koro.**

Uwe-hopumba, ウウェブムホバ, 共ニ
立ツ. *v.i.* To rise up together.

Uwehoroka, ウウェホロカ, 反對ニ. *adv.* Opposite.

Uwehorokare, ウウェホロカレ, 顚覆スル・ *v.t.* To upset.

Uwehoshi, ウウェホシ, アベコベニ. *adv.* The other way about. **Syn:** **Uhoshi.**

Uweikashui, ウウェイカシュイ, 背カス. *v.i.* To set at variance.

Uweikinne-no-an, ウウェイキンチノ アン, 絶エザル、槇ケル. *adj.* Continuous.

Uweingara, ウウェンガラ, 豫言スル. *v.t.* To prophesy.

Uweingara-guru, ウウェインガラグ ル, 豫言者・ *n.* A prophet.

Uweinonno-itak, ウウェイノンノイタ ク, 病者ノ爲ニ祈ル. *v.t.* To pray for the sick.

Uweiripak, ウウェイリパク, 等シカル. *v.i.* To be equal. To be even. **Syn : Eiripak.**

Uweiripak-no-kara, ウウェイリパク ノカラ, 等シカラシム. *v.t.* To make even. To make equal.

Uwekap, ウウェカプ, 禮儀、挨拶. *n.* Salutations.

Uwekarange, ウウェカランキ, 集マル. *v.i.* To come together.

Uwekarapa, ウウェカラパ, 集マル. *v.i.* To collect. To congregate. To accrue. To accumulate.

Uwekarapa-i, ウウェカラパイ, 集合. *n.* Accumulation.

Uwekarapare, ウウェカラパレ, 集ムル. *v.t.* To assemble. To accumulate.

Uwekarapa-utara, ウウェカラパウタ ラ, 集會. *n.* Congregation.

Uwekari, ウウェカリ, 集會スル、集ムル.

v.i. To congregate. To accrue. Accumulate. **Syn: Uwekara-pa.**

Uwekari, ウウェカリ, 集會. *n.* A congregation.

Uwekarire, ウウェカリレ, 集合セシム. *v.t.* To assemble.

Uwekata, ウウェカタ, 漸次. *adv.* By degrees. **Syn : Uwepaketa.**

Uwekatairotke, ウウェカタイロツケ, 相慕フ、相愛ス. *v.t.* To love one another.

Uwekata-uwekata, ウウェカタウェカ タ, 漸次. *adv.* By degrees.

Uwekatki, ウウェカツキ, 近ヅク、含ム、 完成スレ. *v.i.* To approach. To go to. To comprehend. Complete. To be at one. To agree.

Uwekatki-shomoki, ウウェカツキショ モキ, 一致セズ、喧嘩スレ. *v.i.* To disagree, To quarrel.

Uwekatu, ウウェカツ, 互ニ. *adv.* Mutually.

Uwekikkik, ウウェキッキク, 擊チ合ハ ス. *v.t.* To knock together.

Uwekoramkoro, ウウェコラムコロ, 協議スレ. *v.i.* To confer together. To consult together.

Uwekoppa, ウウェコッパ, 分袖スル、別 レ. *v.i.* To part off from one another. To separate.

Uwekota, ウウェコタ, 相並ンデ、共ニ、 例セバ, ウェコタ アン チセイ、家 家相並ンデ. *adv.* Side by side. Together. As:— *Uwekota an chisei,* "houses side by side."

Uwekota-uwekota, ウウェコタウウェ コタ, 相並ンデ. *adv.* Side by side

Uwekote, ウウェコテ, 結ビ合ハス. *v.t.*
To tie together.

Uwekuchikanna, ウウェクチカンナ,
惡口チ云フ、誹ル. *v.i.* To speak evil
of another. **Syn: Uwohai-
kara.**

Uweman, ウウェマン, 訪フ. *v. t.* To
visit.

Uweman-no, ウウェマンノ, ウウェオマ
ンノニ同ジ. *adv.* Same as *uweoman
no.*

**Uweman-no-tuima-ru-otta-oman,
ウウェマンノツイマルオッタオマン,** 下
痢チ病ム. *v.i.* To be afflicted with
diarrhoea. **Syn: Soyokari tashum.**

Uwen, ウウェン, 慟哭スレ. *v.i.* To
wail. To weep together for the
dead.

Uwenangara, ウウェンアンガラ, 相逢
フ. *v.i.* To meet one another. To
greet one another.

Uweneusara, ウウェチウサラ, 喋々ス
ル、昔噺、譚. *v.i. and n.* To chat
together. Ancient tales. A
story.

Uweneutasa, ウウェチウタサ, 出逢フ、
(旅先ナドニテ). *v.t.* To meet, as
when travelling.

Uwenitomon, ウウェニトモン, 見交ハ
ス. *v.i.* To look at one another.
Syn: Unukara.

Uwenkata, ウウェンカタ, or **Uenkata,
ウエンカタ,** 重ツテ. *adv.* One
above another.

**Uwenkata-uwenkata, ウウェンカタ
ウウェンカタ,** 重ツテ. *adv.* One
above the other.

Uwenkurashpa, ウウェンクラシバ, 喧

嘩スル、(複數). *v.i. pl.* To quarrel.
To fall out with one another.

Uwentasa, ウウェンタサ, 此ヨリ彼ニ、
互ニ. *adv.* From one to the other.
One another. **Syn: Uwonuitasa.**

Uwenukara, ウウェヌカラ, 近キ未來チ
考察スレ. *v.i.* To surmise almost
the near future (e.g. as to whether it will rain to-morrow or
not).

Uwe-no, ウウェノ, 均. *adv.* Equally.

Uweo, ウウェオ, 適合スル. *v.i.* To fit
together.

Uwe-oma, ウウェオマ, 成ル、履行セラレ.
v.i. To be fulfilled. To come
to pass.

Uweokokba, ウウェオコクバ, 縺(モツ)
レル. *v.i.* To be entangled.

Uweoman-no. ウウェオマンノ, 常ニ.
adv. Without cessation. Straight
on. Always. Continuously.

Uweomare, ウウェオマレ, 履行スレ. *v.t.*
To fulfil.

Uweonipa, ウウェオニバ, 總テノ. *adj.*
All together. Collectively.

Uweore, ウウェオレ, 適合セシムレ. *v.t.*
To fit together.

Uweoriro, ウウェオリロ, 衣ノ縞. *n.*
The striped figures in cloth.

Uweoriro, ウウェオリロ, 混消スル. *v.t.*
To compound. To mix.

**Uweoriro-no-akara, ウウェオリロノ
アカラ,** 縞ニ織ラル. *v.i.* To be
worked in striped figures.

Uweoriro-o, ウウェオリロオ, 種々ノ色
アル、縞ニ織ラル、染色セラル. *v.i.* To
be painted in divers colours. To
be worked in stripes of divers
colours.

**Uweoriro-wa-kara, ウウェオリロワカ
ラ**, 縞ニ織ル. *v.t.* To work striped
figures in cloth.

Uweorok-kani, ウウェオロクカニ, 鎖.
n. A chain.

Uweoshke, ウウェオシケ, 網ニ編ム. *v.i*
To be netted. To be made into
a net. **Syn: Aoshke.**

Uwepaketa, ウウェバケタ, 漸次. *adv.*
By degrees.

**Uwepaketa-uwepaketa, ウウェバケ
タウウェバケタ**, 漸次. *adv.* By degrees.

Uwepare, ウウェバレ, 快氣スレ、蘇生ス
ル、終ル. *v.i.* To become well.
To revive, as from unconscious-
ness. To have finished what
one was doing.

Uwepekennu, ウウェペケンヌ, 尋ヌレ.
v.t. To inquire.

**Uwepekennu-guru, ウウェペケンヌグ
ル**, 尋問者. *n.* An inquirer.

**Uwepekennu-katuhu, ウウェペケン
ヌカツフ**, 問答. *n.* Catechism. A
questioning.

**Uwepekennu-oma-kambi-sosh, ウ
ウェペケンヌオマカムビソシ**, 問答. *n.*
A catechism.

Uwepekere, ウウェペケレ, 譚、逸話、會
話、報知、昔噺. *n.* A tale. An
anecdote. Conversation. News.
Ancient tales. A story.

Uwepekere-nu, ウウェペケレヌ, 消息
ヲ聞ク、尋ヌル. *v.t.* To listen to
news. To inquire.

Uwepetchiu, ウウェペッチウ, 蹴合フ.
v.i. To kick against one another.
To stumble over one another.

Uwepe-utara, ウウェペウタラ, 朋友、同
居人. *n.* Friends. People who
live together.

Uwepokba, ウウェポクバ, 憎ミ合フ、審
メ合フ. *v.i.* To hate one another.

Uwepokin, ウウェポキン, 漸次. *adv.*
By degrees.

**Uwepokin-uwepokin, ウウェポキン
ウウェポキン**, 漸次. *adv.* By degrees.

Uwepotara, ウウェポタラ, 病人ノ衣ヲ
切リ取ル、是ハ病ヲ癒ス爲ニシテ、ア
イヌが盛ニ行フ儀式ナリ. *v.i.* To cut
up the clothes of sick persons in
order to cure them of disease, a
ceremony indulged in by the
Ainu.

Uwerangara, ウウェランガラ, 祝ス.
v.t. To greet.

Uwerangarap, ウウェランガラプ, 挨拶.
n. Salutations.

Uweraye, ウウェライニ, 知ヲヌ. *v.t.*
Not to know. Not to understand.

Uwerepap, ウウェレバプ, 均シカレ. *v.i.*
To be equal.

**Uwerusaikari-an, ウウェルサイカリア
ン**, 先取スレ. *v.t.* To forestall.

Uwesaine, ウウェサイ子, 迷ハス. *v.t.*
To lead astray.

Uwesamamba, ウウェサマムバ, 總テ、
全體ニ. *adj.* All. Entirely. **Syn:
Obitta.**

Uwesamanu, ウウェサマヌ, 相並ビテ.
adj. Side by side, in a row.
Also "to place side by side."

Uweshikarun, ウウェシカルン, 會見ヲ
望ム. *v.t.* To desire to meet or
see one another.

Uweshikaye, ウウェシカイニ, 燦ク、キラ
メク. *v.i.* To flash about as a
reflection of light.

Uweshikomarai, ウウェシコマライ, (*sing*). or **Uweshikomaraipa, ウウェシコマライバ,** (*pl*). 相抱ク. *v.i.* To embrace one another.

Uweshineatki, ウウェシチアツキ, 一致ス レ. *v.i.* To be at one. To agree.

Uweshineatkire, ウウェシチアツキレ, 一致セシム. *v.t.* To get together. To cause to be at one.

Uweshinnai, ウウェシンナイ, 違フ. *v.i.* To differ. To be different in kind.

Uweshinnai-an, ウウェシンナイアン, 相違セル. *adj.* To be different.

Uweshinnai-are, ウウェシンナイアレ, 分カツ. *v.t.* To separate.

Uweshiren, ウウェシレン, 伴フ. *v.i.* To accompany another.

Uweshiripa, ウウェシリバ, 病ノ呪トシ テ植物ノ根ヲ嚙ム. *v.i.* Chewing roots as a charm against illness.

Uweshiru, ウウェシル, or **Uweshiru-shiru, ウウェシルシル,** 擦リ合ハス. *v.t.* To rub together.

Uweshishke, ウウェシシケ, 結ビ合ハ ス. *v.t.* To join together.

Uweshopki, ウウェショブキ, 對坐スル. *v.i.* To sit facing one another as at a feast or when praying for the recovery of the sick. **Syn: Uwesoshne no.**

Uwesoshne-no, ウウェソシチノ, ウウ ェショボキ二同ジ. *v.i.* Same as *uwe-shopki.*

Uwetanne-an, ウウェタン子アン, or **Uwe-utanne, ウウェウタン子,** 混ズ レ. *v.i.* To be mixed with. To be together. **Syn: Ukopoyege.**

Uwetantaku, ウウェタンタク, 縫ヒ合 ス. *v.t.* To sew together.

Uwetarap, ウウェタラブ, 夢ムル. *v.i.* To dream.

Uweteshpa, ウウェテシバ, ノ如クニス ル、例セバ、チイグルコロミチウェン ブリウウェテシバ、彼ノ人ハ父親ノ如 ク二悪事ヲ爲ス. *v.i.* To take after. As :—*Nei guru koro mich wen-buri uweteshpa,* "that person takes after his father in bad deeds.

Uwetoita, ウウェトイタ, 特發ノ、流行ノ. *adj.* Self-planted.

Uwetoita-tashum, ウウェトイタタシュ ム, 流行病. *n.* An epidemic disease.

Uwetonrane, ウウェトンラ子, 凝結ス レ. *v.i.* To curdle.

Uwetuangara, ウウェツアンガラ, or **Uwetunanguru, ウウェツナングル,** 相逢フ. *v.i.* To meet one another.

Uwetunuise, ウウェツヌイセ, 鳴レ. *v.i.* To sound. To ring. To resound. **Syn: Mayun-mayun.**

Uweturashte, ウウェツラシデ, 同居メ レ. *v.i.* To live in company with.

Uweturembe, ウウェツレムベ, 二物. *n.* Both things.

Uweturen, ウウェツレン, 二ツノ. *adj.* Both.

Uweturirige, ウウェツリリゲ, 凝結セ レ. *v.i.* Curdled.

Uwetushmak, ウウェツシマク, 競走ス レ. *v.i.* To race. To strive.

Uwetushmakte, ウウェツシマクテ, 競 走セシム. *v.t.* To cause to race.

Uwetushmakushi, ウウェツシマクシ, 競走場. *n.* A race course.

Uwetutkopak, ウウェツッコバク, 告別 スル. *v.t.* To bid adieu.

Uweun-no, ウウェウンノ, 全體＝. *adj.* Entirely.

Uweunu, ウウェウヌ, 結合スル、適合ス ル. *v.t.* To join together. To fit together.

Uweushi, ウウェウシ, 撚(ヨ)ル. *v.t.* To twist. To twist together.

Uweutanne, ウウェウタンチ, or **Uwe-tanne, ウウェタンチ,** 共ニ有ル、又ハ 居ル、例セバ、チカプイウェウタンチワ アン、鳥ハ共ニアリ. *v.i.* To be together. As:—*Chikap iueutanne wa an,* "the birds are together."

Uweyairam-ikashure, ウウェヤイラ ムイカシュレ, 位ヲ爭フ. *v.t.* To strive for the mastery.

Uwoeroshki, ウウォエロシキ, 他物ノ 上ニ立ツル、例セバ、カパラベイタンギ カパラベオッチケウウォエロシキ、盆ノ 上ニ杯ヲ立ツル. *v.t.* To stand one thing in or upon another. As:— *Kaparabe itangi kaparabe otchike uwoeroshki,* "to stand cups upon a tray."

Uwo-humse-chiu, ウウォフムセチウ, 雀ガ蛇ヲ見シ時ノ鳴聲. *n.* The peculiar noise of warning or defiance sparrows make when they see a snake. **Syn: Aru-wo-humse-chiu.**

Uwok, ウウォク, 堅靭ナル. *adj.* Strong. Tough.

Uwok, ウウォク, or **Uok, ウオク,** 結 ビ合ハス. *v.t.* To fasten together. **Syn: Ukonkopishte.**

Uwokamba, ウウォカムバ, 一ツ宛、例 セバ、ウウォカムバ、アフプ、一人宛入 ル. *adv.* One after another. As:—*Uwokamba ahup.*.

Uwok-kani, ウォクカニ, 結ビ. *n.* A fastening. "To enter one after another.

Uwokarapa, ウウォカラバ, 順番＝爲 ス. *v.t.* To do in turns.

Uwokarapa-uwokarapa, ウウォカ ラバウヲカラバ, 順番ニ爲ス. *v.t.* To do in turns.

Uwokari, ウウォカリ, 順番ニ. *adv.* In turns.

Uwokari, ウウォカリ, 順番ニ爲ス. *v.t.* To do in turn.

Uwokari-uwokari,ウウォカリウウォカ リ, 順番ニ爲ス. *v.t.* To do in turn.

Uwokari-wa-kara,ウウォカリワカラ, 順番ニ爲ス. *v.t.* To do in turn.

Uwokbare, ウウォクバレ, 冷遇スル、妻 子ヲ冷遇スレ. *v.t.* To treat badly. To neglect one's wife or parents or children.

Uwokishi, ウウォキシ, 裁縫スレ. *v.t.* To make clothes.

Uwokok, ウウォコク, 縺レタル. *adj.* Untidy. Entangled.

Uwoma, ウウォマ, 整フ. *v.i.* To be placed or put.

Uwomare, ウウォマレ, 集ムレ. *v.t.* To collect. **Syn: Umomare.**

Uwondasa, ウウォンダサ, or **Uwo-nuitasa, ウウォヌイウサ,** 横切リテ. *adj.* Across. Athwart.

Uwondasa-uwondasa, ウヲンダサウ ウォンダサ, 補フ. *v.t.* To make up defects.

Uwonuitasa, ウウォヌイタサ, 横切レ. *adj.* Athwart.

Uwonnere, ウウォンチレ, 知ル. *v.t.* To know.

Uwonnuitasa, ウウォンヌイタサ, 行キ 違フ、見外ス、(互ニ). *v.i.* To pass

one another. To miss one another.

Uwonnutasa, ウウォンヌタサ, 轉居ス ル. *v.t.* To change places.

Uwonuyetasare, ウウォヌイェタサレ, 飜譯スル. *v.t.* To translate.

Uwopaketa, ウウォパケタ, 漸次. *adv.* By degrees. **Syn: Uwepaketa.**

Uworo, ウウォロ, 内部. *adv.* Inside.

Uworoge, ウウォロゲ, 内部、例セバ、チ セイ ウウォロゲ、家内. *adv.* The inside, as of a house. As:— *Chisei uworoge,* "the inside of a house."

Uworokopoyege, ウウォロコポイェゲ, 不順序ニ、混雑スル. *adj.* and *v.i.* Disorderly. Mixed up together.

Uworo-omare, ウウォロオマレ, 浸ス. *v.t.* To put to soak.

Uworush-ande, ウウォルシアンデ, 二 重ニモ三重ニモ入器ニ入レレ. *v.t.* To put things into one another.

Uworushbe, ウウォルシベ, 二重ニモ三 重ニモ入器ニ入レタレ物. *n.* Things put one into another. **Syn: Iworushbe.**

Uworushte, ウウォルシテ, 二重ニモ三 重ニモ入器ニ入レル. *v.t.* To put things one inside another.

Uwosakari, ウウォサカリ, 順々ニ爲ス. *v.t.* To do in turn. To do alternately.

Uwoshi, ウウォシ, 追ヒ付ク. *v.t.* To overtake.

Uwoshikkote, ウウォシッコテ, 相愛ス ル. *v.i.* To be in love with one another. To desire one another.

Uwoshiknuka, ウウォシヌカ, 相愛ス ル. *v.i.* To be fond of one another.

Uwosurupa, ウヲスルパ, 離緣スル. *v.t.* To divorce.

Uwotutanu, ウウォツタヌ, 一ツ宛. *adv.* One after another.

Uwoush, ウウォウシ, 結ビ合ス. *v.t.* and *v.i.* To join together. To follow one another. To last.

Uwoya, ウウォヤ, or **Uoya, ウウォヤ,** 違ヒタレ. *adj.* Different.

Uwoyakta-ande, ウウヤクタアンデ, 分カツ. *v.t.* To separate.

Uwoyap, ウウォヤブ, or **Uoyap, ウオ ヤブ,** 互ニ異ナリタル物, *n.* Things different from one another.

Uwoyawoya, ウウォヤウォヤ, 種々ノ、 例セバ、ウウォヤウウォヤアカラベ、種 々ノ人々ニ依ツテ造ラレシ物. *adv.* Various. As:— *Uwoyawoya aka-rape,* "things made by various or different people."

Uyaikotukkare, ウヤイコツッカレ, 附 ケ合フ. *v.i.* To cleave to one another. To be made to stick together.

Uyaishirubare, ウヤイシルバレ, 擦 リ合フ. *v.i.* To rub against one another.

Uyake, ウヤケ, 搖ク、動ク、例セバ、ウ ヤケトマム、搖ク沼地. *v.i.* To tremble. To move. As:— *Uyake-tomam,* "a trembling quagmire."

Uyepnu-an, ウイェプヌアン, 協議スル. *v.i.* To consult with. To make an agreement with.

Uyoropui-koiki, ウヨロブイコイキ, 男色スル. *v.i.* To abuse one's self with mankind. Sodomy. **Syn: Ukokatesikap.**

Uyotsak, ウヨツサク, 力チ失フ. *v.i.* To have lost strength. To tremble from weakness. **Syn: Tumsak.**

Uyuige, ウユイゲ, 慄フ. *v.i.* To shiver.

W (ワ).

Wa, ワ, (wa) ナル語ガ直チニ動詞ニ續ク トキ又ハ動詞ト動詞ノ間ニ置カレルト キハ現在ノ意チ表明ス. *part.* When the particle wa is placed directly after one verb and is immediately followed by another, it gives the sentence a present meaning. The particle itself represents the English "ing" and may well be rendered by "*and.*" As:—*Ek wa,* "coming." *Oman wa ye,* "go and tell him." *Koro wa ek,* "take it and come," i.e. "bring it."

Wa, ワ, ワナル語カアン (an) ナル語 ニ續クトキハ過去ノコトチ表明ス. 例 セバ、エチヌワアン、汝等ハ聞キタリシ. When followed by *an,* wa has a perfect or past tense. As:— *Echi nu wa an,* "ye have heard."

Wa, ワ, ワグス (wa gusu) トナリテ動 詞ニ續クトキハ、ガ爲ニト云フ義ナ リ、例ヘバ、タムベネイノキワグス、コ ロニシパイルシカルウェネ、彼ガ之チナ シタルガ爲ハ主人ハ立腹シテ居ル. *n.* When preceeded by a verb and followed by *gusu,* wa gusu means "because." As:—*Tambe nei no ki wa gusu koro nishpa irush ka ruwe ne,* "the master is angry because he has done this."

Wa, ワ, (wa) ワナレ語ガウン (un) ナル副詞ニ連ナルトキハ然リノ意チ表 ハス、例セバ、ネイノルウェ、ッウン、 其ノ通リナルヤ、然リ、左樣. When followed by *un* the affirmative adverb "yes" or "it is so" is

meant. As:—*Nei no ruwe!* wa un, "Is it so? Yes."

Wa, ワ, 何々ヨリ、例ヘバ、パワ、頂 上ヨリ. *post.* From. By. As:— *Pa wa,* "from the top." *Gesh wa.* "from the bottom."

Wa, ワ, 杯叉ハ壺ノ蓋ノ如キ圓形ナルモ ノノ緣チ云フ. *n.* The rim of anything round as of a cup or pot lid.

Wa, ワ, or **Wan, ワン,** 十. *adj.* Ten. **Syn : Wanbe.**

Wachirewe, ワチレウェ, or **Watchirewe, ワッチレウェ,** 四角. *adj.* Square. **Syn : Ineshikkeu. Ine sambe.**

Wa-gusu, ワグス, 故ニ. *adv.* Inasmuch as. Because. As:—*Chi nukara wa gusu,* "we see that."

Wairu, ワイル, 過チチスル. *v.i.* To make a mistake. By way of accident. Pretence.

Waise, ワイセ, 大聲ニテ泣ク. *v.i.* To cry aloud. To cry out, as a child. **Syn : Chayaise.**

Wak, ワク, 分チ. *n.* A division.

Wak, ワク, 驚キチ表ハス語、鴨ノ鳴 聲. *adv.* An exclamation of surprise. The cry of a duck.

Wakka, ワッカ, 水. *n.* Water. **Syn : Aka.**

Wakchi, ワクチ, ヤットコ. *n.* A pair of pincers.

Wa-kina, ワキナ, サガレン苔. *n.* Sagalien word for moss.

Wakka, ワッカ, 水. *n.* As :—*Chi-koro kotan otta wakka anak ne* "water" *ani ayep ne ruwe ne, wakka* is called "water" in our country."

Wakka-ashin-ushike, ワッカアシンウシケ, 泉. *n.* A water-spring.

Wakka-chish-chish, ワッカチシチシ. 水ノ雫. *n.* Drops of water.

Wakka-ke. ワッカケ, 水チ汲ミ出ス. *v.i.* To scoop water out of a root. To ladle out water.

Wakka-kuttara, ワッカクッタラ, ヨブスマサウ. *n.* *Senecio sagittatus, Schultz Bip.*

Wakka-o, ワッカオ, 水多キ. *adj.* Watery. Containing water.

Wakka-op, ワッカオブ, 水チ盛ル器. A water vessel.

Wakka-oshimpui, ワッカオシムブイ, 井戸. *n.* A well. **Syn : Shimpui.**

Wakka-ran-nai, ワッカランナイ, 流レノアル谷. *n.* A valley with a stream in it.

Wakka-seru, ワッカセル, 溺レル. *v.i.* To drown.

Wakka-serure, ワッカセルレ, 溺レル. *v.t.* To drown.

Wakka-ush, ワッカウシ, 水多キ.· *adj.* Watery.

Wakka-ush-kamui, ワッカウシカムイ, 川ノ神. *n.* The gods of rivers. These gods are very numerous and are supposed to be of the feminine gender. The chief of them are these :—*Chiwash-ekot-mat,* "the goddess of the mouths of rivers." *Petru-ush-mat,* "the goddess of courses of rivers." *Pet-etok-mat,* "the goddess of the sources of rivers."

Wakte, ワクテ, 分ケル、割譲スレ. To divide. To apportion. To send away.

Wak-wak, ワクワク, 鴨. *n.* A duck.

Wan, ワン, 器ノ緣, 小山ノ端. *n.* The rim of a vessel. The top edges of hills. The round edges of the sea-coast.

Wan, ワン, or **Wa,** ワ, 十. *adj.* Ten. **Syn : Wanbe.**

Wanbe, ワンベ, 十ノ物. *n.* Ten things.

Wande, ワンデ, 吟味スレ、見廻ハス. *v.i.* To examine. look about. To know. To understand. As:— *Uwande utara,* persons one knows.

Wan-e-arawan-hotne, ワンエアラワンホッチ, 百三十. *adj.* One hundred and thirty.

Wan-e-ashikne-hotne, ワンエアシクチホッチ, 九十. *adj.* Ninety.

Wan-e-ine-hotne, ワンエイチホッチ, 七十. *adj.* Seventy.

Wan-e-iwan-hotne, ワンエイワンホッチ, 百十. *adj.* One hundred and ten.

Wan-e-re-hotne, ワンエレホッチ, 五十. *adj.* Fifty.

Wan-e-shinepesan-hotne, ワンエシチペサンホッチ, 百七十. *adj.* One hundred and seventy.

Wan-e-shinewan-hotne, ワンエシチワンホッチ, 百九十. *adj.* One hundred and ninety.

Wan-e-tu-hotne, ワンエツホッチ, 三十. *adj.* Thirty.

Wan-e-tupesan-hotne, ワンエツペサンホッチ, 百五十. *adj.* One hundred and fifty.

Wa-no, ワノ, 何々ヨリ. *adv.* From.

Wao, ワオ, or **Wawo, ワウォ,** アォ ペト (烏). *n.* Green pigeon. *Treron sielboldi,* (*Tem*).

Wappa, ワッパ, 圓形ノ箱. *n.* A round box.

Wappo, ワッポ, 小兒. *n.* A young child. **Syn: Ton-guru. Warapo.**

Warambi, ワラムビ, ワラビ. *n. Pteris aquilina, L.*

Waranratuka, ワランラツカ, ワラツ カ (魚ノ名). *n.* A kind of fish. *Lumpenus anguillaris,* Pallas. **Syn: Shui-kot chep.**

Wara, ワラ, 少年. *adj.* The young-est. **Syn: Upen.**

Wara, ワラ, 吹ク. *v.t.* To blow.

Warapo, ワラポ, ワッポニ同ジ. *n.* A young child. Same as *Wappo.*

Wash, ワシ, 磯邊ノ涙. *n.* Surf.

Wata, ワタ, 毛、綿. *n.* Wool. Flatx Cotton.

Watambushi, ワタムブシ, 綿帽子(男 子ノミ用ユ). *n.* A kind of thick head-gear worn by men.

Watara, ワタラ, 岩、哨壁. *n.* A rock. A cliff.

Watashi, ワタシ, 侮辱ノ語. *n.* A half-breed. A term of reproach.

Watchirewe, ワッチレウェ, or **Wachi-rewe, ワチレウェ,** 四角. *n.* Square.

Wattesh, ワッテシ, 藁. *n.* Straw.

Wauwause, ワウワウセ, 戰慄スレ. *v.t.* To shiver. **Syn: Wotta-tawauwause.**

Wawo, ワウォ, or **Wao, ワオ,** アナパ ト (烏). *n.* Green pigeon. *Treron sieboldi,* (*Tem*).

Waya, ワヤ, 智惠、材能. *n.* Wisdom. Ability.

Wayashi, ワヤシ, 智惠. *n.* Wisdom.

Waya-ashnu, ワヤアシヌ, 智キ. *adj.* Wise.

Waya-sap, ワヤサプ, 愚カナレ. *adj.* Foolish. Injudicious. Stupid.

Wayashnu, ワヤシヌ, 智キ. *adj.* Wise.

We, ウェ, 何々ヨリ、例セパ、ナクウェエ ク、彼ハ何處ヨリ來レルカ. *post.* From. As:—*Nak we ek,* " where did he come from." **Syn: Wa. Orowa.**

Wei, ウェイ, 惡キ. *adj.* Bad. Evil. **Syn: Wen.**

Wen, ウェン, 死ヌ. *v.i.* To die. As:— *Wen nisa,* "he has died." *Wen ehange,* "to be at the point of death."

Wen, ウェン, 惡キ、憎ムベキ. *adj.* Bad. Abject. Abominable. Adverse. Evil.

Wen-ambe, ウェンアムベ, 惡、惡事. *n.* Badness. A bad thing. An evil thing.

Wenbe, ウェンベ, 惡事. *n.* A bad thing. The devil. Abaddon.

Wenbe-buri, ウェンベブリ, 葬儀. *n.* Funeral ceremonies. **Syn: Wen ibe. Wen ikai.**

Wenbe-sani, ウェンベサニ, 侮辱ノ語、 怪物、蛇ナドト云フ. *n.* A term of reproach. A demon. A snake.

Wendarap, ウェンダラプ, 夢. *n.* A dream. As:—*Wendarap nu,* "to dream."

Wende, ウェンデ, 惡クスル、傷フ. *v.t.* To render bad. To spoil. **Syn: Wente.**

Wendere, ウェンデレ, 惡クサセル. *v.t.* To cause another to spoil.

Wene, **ウェチ**, 水多キ. *adj.* Watery.
Syn: Tene.

Wen-ehange, **ウェンエハンゲ**, 死
ニ瀕ル. *v.i.* To be at the point
of death.

Wen-guru-ko-shungep, **ウェングル
コシュンゲブ**, 貧乏人騙シ(此語ハ朝ノ
天氣惡クシテ後ニ晴トナル日ニノミ用
ユ). *phr.* A deceiver of the poor.
This phrase is used only of a day
which begins badly and afterwards turns out clear and fine.

Wen-hosh, **ウェンホシ**, 死人ニ被セル脚
半. *n.* The leggings in which
the dead are clothed before being
buried.

Wen-i, **ウェンイ**, 惡、惡所. *n.* Badness. A bad place.

Wen-i, **ウェンイ**, 小雨. *n.* Fine rain.
As :— *Wen-i ash,* " to drizzle."

Wen-ibe-wen-iku, **ワェンイベワエン
イク**, 葬禮ノ饗宴. *n.* A funeral
feast.

Wen-iki-guru, **ウェンイキグル**, 暴人.
A violent person.

Wen-ituren-koro, **ウェンイツレンコ
ロ**, 鬼ニ憑カレル. *v.i.* To be possessed with a demon. **Syn: Nitne kamui shikatkari. Nit ne kamui
shikatorush. Katuish.**

Wen-kamui, **ウェンカムイ**, 見捨ル、惡
鬼. *n.* Abaddon. The devil. **Syn:
Nitne kamui. Kamiyashi.
Iwendep.**

Wen-kamui-ashishpe, **ウェンカムイ
アシシペ**, 癰. *n.* A carbuncle.

Wen-kamui-kisara-pui-op, **ウェン
カムイキサラプイオブ**, 筋肉. *n.*
A muscle.

Wen-kamui-nitnep, **ウェンカムイニ**

ツチブ, 見捨ル、惡鬼. *n.* Abaddon.
The devil.

Wenkarashpa, **ウェンカラシパ**, 怒鳴リ
付ケル. *v.t.* To storm at. To
speak against. To blaspheme.
Syn: Koatcha.

Wenkatcham, **ウェンカッチャム**, 惡性.
n. An evil disposition.

Wenkoenratki, **ウェンコエンラッキ**, 罵
ル、不親切ニスル. *v.t.* To scold.
To despise. To treat unkindly.
**Syn: Wenkoshipashnu. Pako-
enratki.**

Wenkuriki, **ウェンクリキ**, 雨雪. *n.*
A rain cloud.

Wen-no, **ウェンノ**, 惡シク、賤テ.
adv. Badly. Abjectly. Adversely.

Wen-no-ye, **ウェンノイェ**, 虐待スル、讒
言スル. *v.t.* To abuse. To speak
evil of. To slander.

Wen-no-ye-i, **ウェンノウェイ**, 讒言、虐
待. *n.* Slander. Abuse.

Wen-oyashi, **ウェンオヤシ**, 惡シ鬼. *n.*
A spiteful demon.

Wen-oyashi-huchi, **ウェンオヤシフ
チ**, 火ノ神. *n.* The evil genius of
fire. Fire demon.

Wen-oyashi-kara-ainu, **ウェンオヤ
シカラアイヌ**, 外道. *n.* A demoniac.

Wenpa, **ウェンパ**, 減スル. *v.i.* To
diminish. **Syn: Shiepupu an.
Yukuturu otbe an.**

Wenpa, **ウェンパ**, 惡シキ. *adj.* A
Bad.

Wenparo-sange, **ウェンパロサンケ**, 譴
シメル. *v.t.* To censure. To
reproach.

Wenpipok, **ウェンピポク**, 語リ傳ヘノ有
ル所ノ名. *n.* The name of some
legendary place.

Wenrui, ウェンルイ, 多數ノ(生物ニ用ユ). *n.* Many (used of living beings).

Wen-sapa-koro, ウェンサパコロ, 髪ヲムシル(死ヲ悼ムトキノ如ク)、哀悼スレ. *v.i.* To wear the hair cut as when in mourning. To mourn for the dead.

Wen-shieara-koro, ウェンシエアラコロ, 徒黨ノ. *adj.* Factious.

Wen-shiri, ウェンシリ, 岩山. *n.* Craggs. Very rocky mountains. Rough rocky places. **Syn : Kutchituye.**

Wentek, ウェンテク, 荒ス. *v. t.* To devastate. To ravage. To lay waste.

Wentoi-kantoi-kokiru, ウェントイカントイコキリ, or **Wentoi-kiru,** ウェントイキル, 荒ス. *v.t.* To devastate. To ravage. To lay waste.

Wenuirushka, ウェヌイルシカ, 互ニ怒レ. *v.i.* To be very angry with each other. To scold one another badly.

Wen-yuk, ウェンユク, 人ヲ食フ熊. *n.* A man-eating bear. **Syn : Hokuyuk.**

Wo, ウォ, or **Wowo,** ウォウォ, 栂ト食指ニテ測リシ距離. *n.* A span. Also a quarter.

Wo, ウォ, 犬又ハ狼ノ鳴聲. *n.* An onomatopœa for the howl of a dog or wolf.

Wooi, ウォオイ, 危難ニ逢ヘルトキニ助ケチ呼ブ聲. *exclam.* A call for help when in danger or distress, or warning of great danger.

Woriworik-nupuri, ウォリウォリクヌプリ, 各々谷ニ依リテ分離セラレタレ山々ノ集マリタル處. *n.* A place where there are clusters of mountains with a valley round each separate mountain perfect in itself.

Woro, ウォロ, 濕潤セレ. *adj.* Damp. Wet. Softened by wetting.

Woro, ウォロ, 國ノ内部、山川. *n.* The interior of a country. Mountains and rivers. The midst of the sea. **Syn : Iworo.**

Woro-chironnup, ウォロチロンヌプ, カワウソ. *n.* A common otter. *Lutra vulgaris, Erxl.* **Syn : Esaman.**

Woroge, ウロゲ, or **Woroki,** ウォロキ, 石ノ下ノ穴、壕. *n.* A hole beneath stones. A moat.

Worogetuye-i, ウォロゲツイェイ, or **Worogituye-i,** ウォロギツイェイ, 砦. *n.* A fort.

Woroke, ウォロケ, or **Woroge,** ウォロゲ, 石ノ下ノ穴、壕. *n.* A hole beneath stones. A moat.

Worokushte, ウォロクシテ, 泥濘ナレ. *adj.* Sloshy. Muddy. **Syn : Petneka.**

Woro-omare, ウロオマレ, 潤カス. *v.t.* To put to soak.

Wororatkip, ウォロラツキプ, 舵. *n.* A rudder. **Syn : Shiwororatkip.**

Woro-un-chironnup, ウォロウンチロンヌプ, カワウソ. *n.* A river otter. **Syn : Esaman.**

Woroshma, ウォロシマ, 沈ム. *v.i.* To sink into.

Worumbe, ウォルムベ, 水蟲ノ一種ニシテ害甚ダシ、此蟲ヲ捕ヘ附子ト搗キ交セ熊ル他ノ獸ヲ射ルトキ矢ノ根ニ用フルナリ. *n.* A kind of water insect said to be very poisonous. This insect is caught and smashed up with aconite and used for shooting bears and other animals.

Wosa, ウォサ, 機綜ニ用ユル道具. *n.* An instrument consisting of three bars used in weaving cloth.

Wose, ウォセ, 吠ヘル. *v.i.* To howl, as a dog or wolf.

Wose-kamui, ウォセカムイ, エゾヤマイヌメ. *n.* A wolf. *Canis familiaris,* (*Yessoana*). A word sometimes applied to howling dogs. **Syn: Horokeu.**

Woya, ウォヤ, 違フ、別ナレ. *adj.* Different. **Syn: Aja. Woya.**

Y (ヤ).

Ya, ヤ, 此語ハ言語ノ終リニ在ルトキハ問ヒトナリ問ニ答ヘテ言フトキハ然定ノ意ヲ表ス要ハ唯發音ノ如何ニ在リ例セバ、オマンヤ、彼ハ往キシヤ、オマンヤ彼ハ行キタリ. *part.* This particle is often used at the end of a sentence to express interrogation ; but when used after an answer to a question it becomes an affirmative particle, the difference in meaning being indicated by the tone of voice. Thus :— *oman ya ?* "has he gone," *Oman ya,* "he has gone."

Ya, ヤ, 何方、孰レ. *post.* Whether. Or.

Ya.........ya, ヤ.........ヤ, 何方カ、例セバ、タンベネヤ、ネイアムベネヤ、ヌヤン、此レカ夫レカ何方ナルカ尋ネヨ. *post.* Whether.........or. As :— *Tambe ne ya, nei ambe ne ya ? nu yan,* "ask whether it is this or that." *Anukarape hene ya-wendarap hene ya, ku eramushkari,* "I do not know whether it was a thing seen (vision) or a dream."

Ya, ヤ, 網, *n.* A net. As :— *Ya amba,* "the floats attached to a fish net." *Ya shittu,* "the meshes of a net." *Ya oshke,* "to net." *Ya tambushi,* "to mend a net." *Ya ereba,* "to set a net in the sea." *Ya turuba,* to set a net from the seashore.

Ya, ヤ, 陸、(海ニ對シテ云フ)例セバ、ヤヘカエクア、レプヘカエクア、汝ハ陸ヨリ來リシカ又海ヨリセシカ. *n.* Land. (as opposed to sea). A high rock. As :— *Ya peka ek a, rep peka ek a ?* "did you come by land or sea" ? *Ya sosh,* "strata or layers of earth."

Yachi, ヤチ, 沼澤. *n.* A swamp. **Syn: Opuruse-i.**

Yachi-an, ヤチアン, 泥ノ、谷地カ、リタレ. *adj.* Muddy. Swampy.

Yai, ヤイ, 自己、此語ハ獨立シテ用キラルルハコトナシ、例セバ、ナイライゲ (自殺スレ) *reflex. pro.* Self. This word is only used as a compound. As :— *Yai-raige,* "to kill one's self." ; "to commit suicide."

Yai, ヤイ, 人ニ注意ヲ與フル爲メニ呼ビ掛ケル語. *exclam.* An exclamation used in calling to a person to attract attention. Ho! As:— *Yai ek!* " ho come." ?

Yaiamkire, ヤイアムキレ, 知ル. *v. i.* To know.

Yaian, ヤイアン, 獨立スル. *adj.* Independent. Of one's self.

Yai-arakare, ヤイアラカレ, 自カラヲ傷メル. *v.i.* To hurt one's self. As:—*Nei no e ki chiki e yai arakare nangoro gusu, iteki ki yan,* " do not do so for you will probably hurt yourself if you do."

Yaiashin, ヤイアシン, 自カラ脱出スル. *v.i.* To come out of one's self.

Yaiashish, ヤイアシシ, 嫌フ. *v.t.* To avert. To ward eff.

Yaiateraige, ヤイアテライゲ, 縊首スル. *v.i.* To hang one's self.

Yaiattasa, ヤイアッタサ, or **Yaiyattasa, ヤイヤッタサ,** 貰ヒ物ニ返シチスル、返禮スル. *v.t.* To give in return for something received. To recompense. To requite. To punish. As:—*Aikorep an gusu yaiattasa ku ki na,* " I will recompense him for his gift." *Nei no okai wenbe en otta e ki gusu, ku yaaitasa ku ki kusu ne na,* " I will requite you for doing such evil things to me."

Yaiattasap, ヤイアッタサブ, 報酬. *n.* A recompense.

Yaichepekote, ヤイチェペコテ, 餓死スル. *v.i.* To die of hunger. Syn: Yaikemekote. Kem-ekot.

Yaichinane, ヤイチナ子, 小便スル. *v.i.* To make water. To urinate.

Yaichishte, ヤイチシテ, 哀悼スル. *v.t.* To mourn for the dead. To bewail the dead.

Yaichishte-guru, ヤイチシテグル, 死チ哀ム人. *n.* A mourner.

Yaieashkaire, ヤイエアシカイレ, 學ブ. *v.t.* To learn. **Syn: Eyai-hannokkara.**

Yaieashpa, ヤイアエシパ, 人ノ過チノミナ擧ケテ己レノコトヲ忘レル. *v.i.* To forget one's own faults especially when remembering or speaking of those of others. As:— *Iteki yaieashpa toan wen guru!* " you bad person, do not forget your own faults!" (Lit:—To be deaf to one's self.

Yaieattarashi, ヤイエッタラシ, 無頓着ナル. *v.i.* To be indifferent. Regardless. Careless. **Syn: Rengaine iki.**

Yaiehororose, ヤイエホロロセ, 自カラ勵ム. *v.i.* To stir one's self up to do anything. (Lit: to set one's self at).

Yai-eihok-guru, ヤイエイホクグル, 娼、(身ヲ賣ル人). *n.* A harlot. (Lit: a self seller). **Syn: Yai eiyok guru.**

Yaieinukuri, ヤイエイムクリ, 謙遜スル、遠慮スル. *v.i.* To be diffident about something.

Yaietunnap, ヤイエツンナブ, 嫉ム. *v.t.* To envy. To be jealous of another.

Yaieiwangere, ヤイエイワンゲレ, 仕ヘル. *v.t.* To minister. To serve another. **Syn: Shieiwangeyara.**

Yaiekatuwen, ヤイエカツウェン, 侮蔑スル. *v.t.* To insult. To treat

with disrespect. **Syn: Yaika-tuwen.**

Yaiekeshui, ヤイエケシュイ, 失望ス
ル. *v.i.* To lose hope.

Yaiekimatek, ヤイエキマテク, 痛ム、
病ム. *v.i.* To suffer pain. To be
very ill. To be in trouble. To
fear."

Yaiekimatekbe, ヤイエキマテクベ, 艱
難. *n.* Sufferings. Troubles.

Yaiekoramkoro, ヤイエコラムコロ, 依
賴スル. *v.t.* To ask a favour.

Yaekote, ヤイエコテ, 爲ル. *v.t.* To
do. As:— *Tu chish wenbe yaiekote,*
"she wept very bitterly." **Syn:**
Yaiyekote.

**Yaieku-suri-kara, ヤイエクスリカ
ラ,** 手療治ヲスル. *v.i.* To doctor
one's self.

Yaiekush, ヤイエクシ, 失望サセル.
v.i. To be disappointed.

Yaienichitne, ヤイエニチツ子, 病ノ
爲メニ弱ル. *adj.* and *v.i.* To be
incapable through illness. To be
of a weakly disposition.

**Yaieorushpe-ye-yara, ヤイエオルシ
ペエヤラ,** 報告スレ、陳述スル. *v.i.*
To give an account of one's self.

Yaiepase, ヤイエバセ, 姙マセル. *v.i.*
To be pregnant. To be with
child. **Syn: Honkoro.**

Yaiepirika, ヤイエビリカ, 惠マレタ
ル、幸ヒナル. *v.i.* and *adj.* Blessed. To have gained. To be
fortunate.

**Yaiepirika-ambe, ヤイエビリカアム
ベ,** 利得. *n.* Gain. Profit.

Yaiepirika-i, ヤイエイビリカイ, or
Yaiepirikap, ヤイエビリカプ, 利得.
n. Gain. Profit.

Yaiepirikare, ヤイエビリカレ, 儲ヶ
ル. *v.t.* To gain. To get profit.

Yaiepirikarep, ヤイエビリカレプ, 利
得. *n.* Gain. Profit.

Yaierampoken, ヤイエラムポケン,
失望サセル. *v.i.* To be disappointed.

Yaiesanniyo, ンヤイエサンニヨ, 富
ム. *v.i.* To be rich. To be
careful over one's property. As:—
Yaiesanniyo guru, "a rich or
careful person." **Syn: Nishpa
ne guru.**

**Yaiesanniyorire, ヤイエサンニヨリ
レ,** 高慢ナル. *adj.* and *v.i.* High-
minded. **Syn: Yaikeutum-
karire.**

Yaieshikorap, ヤイエシコラプ, 病ノ
爲ニ弱ル. *v.i.* and *adj.* Incapable
through illness. To be of a
weakly disposition. As:— *Yaieshikorap ki,* "to become ill and
incapable." "To become weakly."
Syn: Yaienichitne.

**Yaieshinniukesh, ヤイイエシンイヌ
ケン,** 貧シキ、窮乏セレ. *adj.* Poor.
Destitute. **Syn: Irapokkari.**

Yaieshirepa, ヤイエシレバ, 撫ル. *v.t.*
To coax. To rub one's cheeks
against another as children in
affection.

Yaieshiwende, ヤイエシウェンデ, 姙マ
セル. *v.i.* To be pregnant.

Yaietaye, ヤイエタイェ, 湧出スル、(穴
カラ外ニ=). *v.i.* To draw one's self
out, as out of a hole.

Yaietokye, ヤイエトクイェ, 已レノ仕
事ヲ鼻ニ掛ケル. *v.i.* To boast of
what one is going to do.

**Yaietushiri-kara, ヤイエツシリ
カラ,** 己レノ墓チ掘ル、(好ンテ危キニ
近ツクコトチ云フ)・ *v.t.* To dig
one's own grave.

Yaietushtek, ヤイエツシテク, 己レチ
傷フ. *v.i.* To abuse one's self.

Yaiewen, ヤイエウェン, 卑シキ、貧シ
キ、跛. *adj.* Humble. Poor.
Lame. Crippled. **Syn : Hera.**

Yaiewende, ヤイエウェンデ, 商買シテ
損スル. *v.t.* To lose as in a
bargain. To waste. As :—*Korobe yaiewende,* "to suffer the
loss of one's goods." **Syn : Koshini.**

Yaiewendere, ヤイエウェンデレ, 損サ
セル. *v.t.* To cause to lose. To
make lose, as in a bargain.

Yaieyashitoma, ヤイエヤシトマ, 同
情ナク感ズル. *v.i.* To feel out of
place. To feel out of sympathy
with one's surroundings.

Yaiibere-wa-rai. ヤイイベレワライ,
毒チ仰キテ死ス. *v.i.* To poison
ones' self.

Yaihaitare, ヤイハイタレ, 避ケ、狙
ヒチ外サセレ. *v.t.* To avoid. To
cause to miss. To dissent. **Syn :
Yaikopashte.**

Yaihumshu, ヤイフムシュ, 不慮ノ出
來事. *n.* An accident. As :—
Yaihumshu kara gusu rai, "he
died through meeting with an
accident." **Syn : Nikuru.**

Yaihumshu-wa, ヤイフムシュワ, 不
意ニ. *adv.* Accidentally.

Yaiikire, ヤイイキレ, 悪口スル、罵ル.
v.t. To blaspheme. To act
wickedly. To mock. **Syn : Yaitombuni. Irara.**

Yaiikire-no, ヤイイキレノ, 獨リ. *adv.*
Alone. As :—*Yaiikire no apkash,*
"to walk alone."

**Yaiikire-no-an-guru, ヤイイキレノ
アングル,** 獨栖者. *n.* A recluse.
A person living alone.

Yaiimine-no, ヤイイミ子ノ, 衣ル、例
セバ、クン子コソンデヤイイミ子ノ、
ウツムチウレグル、黒小袖チ衣タル人.
v.i. To be dressed in. As :—
*Kunne kosonde yaiimine no utom-
chiure guru,* "a person dressed in
black garments."

Yaiipokashka, ヤイイポカシカ, 醜ク
スレ. *v.i.* To make one's self
ugly."

Yaiiraige, ヤイイライゲ, or **Yaiiraigere, ヤイイライゲレ,** 難有. *adv. ph.*
Thank you.

Yaiiraige-an, ヤイイライゲアン, 難有
ク思フ. *v.i.* To be thankful.

**Yaiiraige-an-keutum-koro, ヤイイ
ライゲアンケウツムコロ,** 恩ニ感ズル.
v.i. To be grateful. To be
thankful.

Yaiiraige-ki, ヤイイライゲキ, 謝ス、
禮チ云フ. *v.t.* To thank. To express thanks.

Yaiiraige-koro, ヤイイライゲコロ, 難
有ク. *adv.* Thankfully.

Yaiisam, ヤイイサム, 消滅スレ. *v.i.*
To dwindle away. To come to
nought.

Yaiisamka, ヤイイサムカ, 自殺スレ.
v.i. To commit suicide. To
absent one's self.

Yaiitasasa, ヤイイタササ, 自カラ傷ケ
レ. *v.i.* To hurt one's self. **Syn :
Yaiiuninka. Yaiarakare.**

Yaiiuninka, ヤイイウニンカ, 不慮ノ 災ニ罹ル. v.i. To meet with an accident. To hurt one's self. Syn: Yaiitasasa. Yaiarakare.

Yaikahawashpa, ヤイカハワシバ, 獨言チイフ. v.i. To talk to one's self.

Yaikamui, ヤイカムイ, 怪物. n. A demon.

Yaikane, ヤイカ子, 鉛. n. Lead. As:—Yaikane ikayop, " quivers ornamented with lead."

Yaikannama-wa-hoshipi, ヤイカン ナマワホシピ, 忘レ物チ爲スタメニ立 歸ル. v.i. To turn back to say or do something one has forgotten.

Yaikaobiuki, ヤイカオビウキ, 自カラ チ助ケル. v.i. To help or save one's self.

Yaikaokuima, ヤイカオクイマ, 寢小 便スル. v.i. To wet one's bed.

Yaikaomare, ヤイカオマレ, 懺悔スル. v.t. To confess. To own to.

Yaikara, ヤイカラ, 摸擬スル、眞似ス ル. v.t. To assume. To imitate. To do. As:—Chikap ne yaikara, " to imitate a bird."

Yaikarakarasere, ヤイカラカラセレ, 轉ゲレ. v.i. To roll one's self, as an animal.

Yaikaramu, ヤイカラム, 遲疑スル. To be diffident. To dislike to go to a place.

Yaikarap, ヤイカラブ, 辯解スル、謝 スル. v.i. To apologize. To beg pardon.

Yaikata, ヤイカタ, 恐レ. n. Dread.

Yaikata, ヤイカタ, or Yaikota, ヤイ コタ, 己レ、例セル、ヤイカタチブキ、

己レノ職業. per. pro. One's self. One's own. As:—Yaikata nep ki, " one's own work or business."

Yaikata, ヤイカタ, or Yaikota, ヤイ コタ, 個々別々ニ. adv. Individual- ly. For one's self.

Yaikatchipi, ヤイカッチピ, ヤイカツ シピニ同ヅ. n. Same. As:—Yai- katshipi.

Yaikatan, ヤイカタン, 恥ル. adj. Ashamed. Diffident.

Yaikatanu, ヤイカタヌ, 行儀正シキ. adj. Polite. Well behaved. Syn: Yaioripakka an. Oripak an. Also " to honour " or " re- spect," " to esteem."

Yaikateaikap, ヤイカテアイカプ, 迷 惑チ掛ケラレル. v.i. To be troubled about. To feel concern. To feel compunction.

Yaikateaikapte, ヤイカテアイカプテ, 遲疑スル、恥カシク感ズル. v.i. To feel diffident. To feel ashamed.

Yaikatekara, ヤイカテカラ, 望ム、俟 ツ、慕フ、心配スル. v.t. To yearn after. To long for. To feel anxious about. As:—A poho nukan rusui wa yaikatekara ku ki na, " I desire to see my child and feel anxious about it."

Yaikatekarap, ヤイカテカラプ, 心配. n. Anxiety.

Yaikatshipi, ヤイカツシピ, 蘇生スレ. v.i. To return to life. To revive. To regain one's health or fortune. Syn: Hetopo shik- nu.

Yaikatshipire, ヤイカツシピレ, 蘇カ ヘル. v.t. To raise to life. To revive.

Yaikatuwen, ヤイカツウェン, 辱カシ
ク思フ、赤面スレ. *v.i.* To feel
ashamed. To have been put out
of countenance. **Syn: Nanu-
isam. Yainikoroshma.**

Yaikeshnukara, ヤイケシヌカラ, 迷
惑ヲ掛ケラレル. *v.i.* To feel concerned about. To be troubled
about. To feel anxious.

Yaikeuhumshu, ヤイケウフムシュ,
災難ニ罹ル. *v.i.* To meet with an
accident. **Syn: Yaihumshu.**

Yaikeukoro, ヤイケウコロ, 難儀スレ、
疲労スレ. *v.i.* To be in great
straits. To be in difficulties.
To be very tired. As:—*Yaikeukoro koro sap,* "he has been
made very tired indeed."

Yaikeurura, ヤイケウルラ, 身ヲ危ク
スレ. *v.i.* To jeopardize one's
self.

Yaikeururare, ヤイケウルラレ, 危ク
スル. *v.t.* To jeopardize. To bring
into danger.

**Yaikeutumkarire, ヤイケウツムカリ
レ,** 愚カナル. *v.i. and adj.* To be
foolish. **Syn: Yaiesanniyorire.**

**Yaikeutum-oihunara, ヤイケウツム
オイフナラ,** 考へ出ス. *v.i.* To think
out for one's self.

**Yaikeutum-oshitchiure, ヤイケウツ
ムオシッチウレ,** 己レヲ制スル. *v.i.*
To restrain one's self. To persevere.

Yaikiki, ヤイキキ, 身ヲ搔キムシレ.
v.i. To scratch one's self.

Yaikimatekka, ヤイキマテッカ, 急ク.
v.i. To be in a hurry.

Yaikipte, ヤイキプテ, 危キ. *adj. and
v.i.* Dangerous. To be careful.

Yaikiptep, ヤイキプテプ, 危険物. *n.*
A dangerous thing.

Yaikiru, ヤイキル, 寝返リスレ. *v.i.*
To turn one's self, as when
sleeping.

Yaikirukuru, ヤイキルクル, 泥中ニ轉
ガレ. *v.i.* To wallow. **Syn:
Hota-hota.**

Yaikoan-ainu, ヤイコアンアイヌ, 無
妻人. *n.* A bachelor.

Yaikoan-guru, ヤイコアングル, 妻ヲ
娶ラヌ男、嫁カサル女. *n.* A bachel-
or. A spinster.

Yaikoan-mat, ヤイコアンマツ, 嫁カ
ザル女. *n.* A spinster.

Yaikoan-no, ヤイコアンノ, 自身デ.
adv. By one's self. By itself.
By himself. By herself.

Yaikoanu, ヤイコアヌ, 片側ニ置ク.
v.t. To put on one side. To
place by themselves, as a child
or one's clothes.

Yaikoatcha, ヤイコアッチャ, 汚レタレ.
不潔ナレ. *v.i. and adj.* Dirty.
Sloven. Filthy. Wasteful.

Yaikochipkuta, ヤイコチプクタ, 舟
ヲ顚覆スル. *v.t.* To turn a boat
over. To upset a boat. **Syn:
Chip koupshi.**

Yaikoechupu, ヤイコエチュプ, 衣物ヲ
被ル. *v.i.* To cover one's self up
with clothes. To wrap one's
clothes around one.

**Yaikoechupchupu, ヤイコエチュプチ
ュプ,** 被セル. *v.i.* To wrap one's
clothes about the person. To cover one's self up with clothes.

Yaikoeshina, ヤイコエシナ, 内證ニス
レ. *v.i.* To keep secret.

Yaikoirushkare, ヤイコイルシカレ, 困ラセル、ヅラセレ. *v.t.* To annoy. To weary out.

Yaikokanu, ヤイコカヌ, 熟考スル. *v.i.* To think. To consider.

Yaikokarakara, ヤイコカラカラ, 持ツ、所持スレ. *v.t.* To have. To hold. To possess.

Yaikokatpak, ヤイコカツバク, 悔ュレ. *v.t.* and *n.* To repent. Compunction.

Yaikokishma, ヤイコキシマ, 抱キ合フ. *v.t.* To hug. To embrace. **Syn : Yaiturashte.**

Yaikokotukbare, ヤイココツクバレ, 仲間ニ入ル. *v.i.* To join one's self to.

Yaikonere, ヤイコ子レ, 流産スレ. *v.t.* To cast one's young. **Syn : Honyaku.**

Yaikoniukesh, ヤイコニウケシ, 爲シ得ザル、爲スチ厭フ. *v.t.* To be unable. To dislike to do. To do with difficulty.

Yaikonoye, ヤイコノイェ, 裝ル. *v.i.* To wear, as clothes. **Syn : Amip mi.**

Yaikonrusui, ヤイコンルスイ, 欲シガル. *v.t.* To desire for one's self.

Yaikookere, ヤイコオケレ, 縮少スレ、仕舞フ. *v.i.* To wane. To come to an end.

Yaikooknatara, ヤイコオクナタラ, 哀シム. *v.i.* To mourn. To grieve. To be down-hearted. To have lost courage.

Yaikooniwen, ヤイコオニウェン, 偽善チ爲フ. *v.i.* To be hypocritical. **Syn : Kashi-oniwen.**

Yaikooriknere, ヤイコオリクチレ, 飲干ス. *v.t.* To drink up.

Yaikopash, ヤイコバシ, 寄リ掛ル、寄セ掛ケレ. *v.i.* To lean against. To be set against.

Yaikopashte, ヤイコバシテ, 信任スル、依頼スレ. *v.t.* To trust. To lean against. As :—*Kamui irenga yaikopashte,* "to trust one's self to God."

Yaikopumba, ヤイコプムバ, or Yaikopuni, ヤイコプニ, 發スル(聲チ). *v.t.* and *v.i.* To send forth, as the voice. To rise up.

Yaikopuntek, ヤイコプンテク, 嬉シキ. *v.i.* and *adj.* To be glad. Joyful.

Yaikoramratkire, ヤイコラムラッキレ, 忘レ易キ. *v.i.* and *adj.* To be forgetful. **Syn : Ioira.**

Yaikorange, ヤイコランゲ, 贐ス、落ス、例セバ、ツベケンヌペヤイコランゲ、彼女ハ二ツノ珠ナス涕チ落セリ、換言スレバ甚ダシク泣ケリノ意. *v.t.* To shed. To send down. As :—*Tu peken nupe yaikorange,* "she shed two bright tears" i.e. "she wept bitterly" (found only in legends and songs).

Yaikorapte, ヤイコラプテ, 流ス(涕チ). *v.t.* To shed, as tears. To send down. *Pl. of Yaikorange.*

Yaikore, ヤイコレ, 何々ニナル、例セバ、イルシカケカツムヤイコレ彼ハ怒ッタ. *v.i.* To have. To be. To become. As :—*Irushka keutum yaikore,* "she was angry."

Yaikorobe, ヤイコロベ, 己レノ職業. *n.* One's own business. As :— *Yaikorobe ki,* "to attend to one's own business."

Yaikoropiki, ヤイコロピキ, 考ヘ出ス. *v.i.* To think a thing out. To find out by one's self. **Syn: Yaikeutum oihunara.**

Yaikoruki. ヤイコルキ, 嚥ム. *v.t.* To swallow.

Yai-korusha, ヤイコルシャ, 恤ム. *v.t.* To have mercy upon.

Yaikorushka, ヤイコルシカ, 嫌惡ス ル、悲シム. *v.i.* To feel disgusted. To be in sorrow. **Syn: Ok.**

Yaikosange, ヤイコサンゲ, 産ム. *v.t.* To bear. To bring forth, as young.

Yaikoshaye, ヤイコシャイェ, 帶ビル. *v.t.* To buckle on. To wind round as a belt or band.

Yaikoshikarimba, ヤイコシカリムバ, 振向グ、向ヶ直ス. *v.i.* To turn round. To turn one's self round.

Yaikoshina, ヤイコシナ, 身ニ縛リ付 ケレ. *v.t.* To tie round one's self.

Yaikoshiramse, ヤイコシラムセ, 熟 考ス レ. *v.t.* To think. To consider. To set one's mind on.

Yaikoshiramse-i, ヤイコシラムセイ, 思想. *n.* A thought. A consideration.

Yaikoshiramshuiba, ヤイコシラムシ ュイバ, 考ヘレ. *v.t.* To consider. To think.

Yaikoshunge, ヤイコシュンゲ, 已レチ 欺グ. *v.i.* To deceive one's self.

Yaikota, ヤイコタ, or **Yaikata, ヤイ カタ,** 已レ. *per. pro.* One's self. One's own.

Yaikota, ヤイコタ, or **Yaikata, ヤイ カタ,** 個々ニ. *adv.* Individually. For one's self.

Yaikomekare-aep, ヤイコメカレアエ プ, 反芻. *n.* Cud.

Yaikotcha-kara, ヤイコッチャカラ, 吝カナル. *v.i.* To be stingy.

Yaikotcha-kara-guru, ヤイコッチャ カラグル, 吝嗇家. *n.* A miser. A stingy person.

Yaikotchaotte, ヤイコッチャオッテ, 先 立ツ. *v.t.* To precede.

Yaikotomka, ヤイコトムカ, 好ム. *v.t.* and *v.i.* To desire. To wish for. To desire to obtain. To be pleased. To be happy. To desire in marriage. To be bettered. To be better for.

Yaikotuima-shiramshuye, ヤイコ ツイマシラムシュイェ, 靜思スル. *ph.* To think over quietly.

Yaikotukkare, ヤイツッカレ, 味方ス ル、左袒スル. *v.i.* To side with.

Yaikowayashnu, ヤイコワヤシヌ, 生 意氣ナル、智シコキ振リチスレ. *v.i.* To be wise in one's own conceits.

Yaikoyupu, ヤイコユプ, 縛ル. *v.t.* To fasten. To tie as hat strings. To fasten on. As:—*Kasa rantupepi yaikoyupu,* "to tie the strings of a hat."

Yaikurukata, ヤイクルカタ, 已レノ力 デ. *adv.* By one own exertions.

Yaikush, ヤイクシ, 恥チル. *v.i.* and *adj.* Ashamed. To be ashamed. **Syn: Yashitoma.**

Yaikushkare, ヤイクシカレ, 恥ラハセ ル. *v.t.* To make ashamed. To abase. To degrade.

Yaimechiure, ヤイメチウレ, 痙攣カ息 ム. *v.i.* To have a relapse during convalescence.

Yaimemanka, ヤイメマンカ, 涼ム. *v.i.* To cool one's self.

Yaimire, ヤイミレ, 裝フ. *v.i.* To dress. To put on one's clothes.

Yaimonakte, ヤイモナクテ, 支度ス ル、用意ス レ. *v.i.* To be on the alert. To be ready. To be prepared.

Yaimonasap, ヤイモナサブ, or **Yai-mosak, ヤイモサク,** 繁忙ナル. *v.i.* To be busy. To have business.

Yaimonoro-eyam-eaikap, ヤイモノ ロエヤムエアイカブ, 己レチ制スルコ トガ出來ヌ. *v.i.* To be unable to restrain one's self.

Yaimonpok-tushmak, ヤイモンポク ツシマク, 急ギテスル、急ガセル、例セ バ、シュケヤイモンポクツシマク、急イ 料理スレ. *v.t.* To do in haste. To hurry in doing anything. As:— *Shuke yaimonpok-tushmak,* "to cook quickly."

Yaimosak, ヤイモサク, or **Yaimon-sak, ヤイモンサク,** 忙シキ. *v.i.* To be busy. To be engaged.

Yaimukmuke, ヤイムクムケ, 陸部チ 匿クス. *v.i.* To cover up the person.

Yaimunkopoiba, ヤイムンコポイバ, or **Yaimuntumashbare, ヤイムン ツマシバレ,** 彷徨スル、(避難所チ尋子 テ). *v.i.* To wander about, as when hiding from some enemy or danger.

Yainanka, ヤイナンカ, 人ノ顔. *n.* One's own face. As:— *Yainanka piruba,* "to wipe one's own face."

Yainekonnakare, ヤイ子コンナカレ, 謙遜セル. *v.t.* To make humble.

Yainenaine, ヤイ子ナイ子, 同樣ナル. *adv.* Of the same kind. As:— *Yainenaine utomchiure,* "to dress in garments of the same kind."

Yaineusaraka, ヤイ子ウサラカ, 昔話 シチスレ. *v.i. and n.* To chat of ancient things. To tell stories.

Yaineusaraka-an, ヤイ子ウサラカア ン, 散歩或ハ話ニ出掛ケル. *v.i.* To go out for a walk and chat.

Yaine-yaine, ヤイ子ヤイ子, 全ク. *adv.* Entirely. Quite.

Yai-ni, ヤイニ, ドロ. *n.* The poplar tree. *Populus suaveolens, Fisch.*

Yainikonnakare, ヤイニコンナカレ, or **Yainikorooshma, ヤイニコロオ シマ,** 恥チレ. *v.i.* To be ashamed. To be put out of countenance. **Syn: Aiporosakka. Yaishito-ma. Yainekonnakare.**

Yainino, ヤイニノ, ガヒ. *n.* Sea urchin.

Yainipesh, ヤイニペシ, オホバホダイ ジコ. *n. Maximowlcziana, Shira-sawa.*

Yainomare, ヤイノマレ, 驚ク. *v.i. and adj.* To be surprised. To be astonished. Astonishing. As:— *Yainomare ta hau an!* "what an astonishing thing"! **Syn: Yainumare.**

Yainonepta, ヤイノ子ブタ, or **Yai-nunepta, ヤイヌ子ブタ,** 漸々ニ、徐 徐ニ. *adv.* By degrees. Gradual-ly. As:— *Yainonepta irushka,* "he gradually became angry."

Yainonnenu, ヤイノン子ヌ, 頭チ搔マ ム (深ク考ヘゴトナスルトキ無意識ニ ナス所作). *v.i.* To pick the head, as when thinking deeply.

Yainu, ヤイヌ, 考ヘ レ. *v.i.* To think. To consider.

Yainua-ambe, ヤイヌアアムベ, 思想. *n.* A thought.

Yainuchattek, ヤイヌチャッテク, 幸ヒナレ、嬉シキ. *adj.* Happy. Merry. Joyful. Cheerful.

Yainuchattekke, ヤイヌチャッテッケ, 幸ヒニスレ. *v.t.* To make joyful. To make happy.

Yainu-hi, ヤイヌヒ, 思想. *n.* A thought.

Yainu-humi, ヤイヌフミ, 心地、例セバ、ヤイヌフミエン、心地カ悪イ、ヤイヌフミピリカ、心地カ好イ. *n.* The state of the feelings as regards health. As :— *Yainu humi wen,* "I feel poorly." *Yainu humi pirika,* "I feel well."

Yainu-i, ヤイヌイ, 考ヘ. *n.* A thought.

Yainu-nashke, ヤイヌナシケ, 辯疏スレ. *v.i.* To apologize.

Yainuina, ヤイヌイナ, 匿レル、逃亡スレ. *v.i.* To hide one's self. To abscond.

Yainumare, ヤイヌマレ, 驚ク. *v.i.* and *adj.* To be surprised. To be astonished. Astonishing. **Syn:** Yaiomare.

Yainunepta, ヤイヌ子ブタ, or Yainonepta, ヤイノ子ブタ, 漸々ニ. *adv.* By degrees. Gradually.

Yainunuke, ヤイヌヌケ, 身體ニ注意スル、靜養スル. *v.i.* To take great care of one's self. To rest as when ill.

Yainup, ヤイヌブ, 思想. *n.* A thought.

Yainusaraka-ki, ヤイヌサラカキ, or Yaineu-saraka-ki, ヤイ子ウサラカキ, 話チスレ、昔譚リチ話ス. *v.t.* To tell stories. To speak of ancient things. To tell traditions.

Yainutumnu, ヤイヌツムヌ, 氣絶スレ. *v.i.* To swoon away.

Yaiokapashtere, ヤイオカパシテレ, 修正スレ. *v.t.* To amend, as one's ways.

Yaiokkainere, ヤイオッカイ子レ, 打勝ツ. *v.i.* To exult. To triumph.

Yaiomanambe, ヤイオマナムベ, 彷徨スレ. *v.i.* To ramble about.

Yaiomare, ヤイオマレ, 入ル(市ニ). *v.i.* To enter, as a town. (Lit: To put one's self in.)

Yaiomonnure, ヤイオマンヌレ, 誇ル. *v.i.* To boast. To glory in one's self.

Yaiorai, ヤイオライ, 謙遜ナル、尊重ナル. *adj.* and *v.i.* To be humble. To be respectful.

Yaioiraika, ヤイオライカ, 謙遜スル. *v.i.* To make one's self humble or respectful. **Syn:** Yaieori-pakka.

Yaioraire, ヤイオライレ, 謙遜スル. *v.i.* To humble one's self. **Syn:** Yaishiwennere.

Yaiorampeshishte, ヤイオラムペシシテ, 同情チ表スレ. *v.i.* To express sympathy towards.

Yaioraye, ヤイオライエ, ニ行ク. *v.i.* To go to.

Yaioshkuru, ヤイオシクル, 死ニトモナキ. *adj.* Desire not to die. **Syn:** Rai kopan.

Yaiossereke, ヤイオッセレケ, 途方ニ暮レレ. *v.i.* To be perplexed.

Yaiosshiwen, ヤイオッシウェン, or **Yaiyeosshiwen,** ヤイイェオッシウェン, 自傷スレ. *v.i.* To harm one's self.

Yaiosshiwen-keutum-koro, ヤイオッシウェンケウツムコロ, 根生ガ悪クナレ. *adj.* To be possessed of a very bad disposition. Wicked. Bad.

Yaiotupekare, ヤイオツベカレ, 節制スル、貯蓄スル. *adj.* Abstemious. Faithful. Saving. Stingy.

Yaiotupekare-no, ヤイオツベカレノ, 適度ニ、倹約ニ. *adv.* Abstemiously. Faithfully. Savingly.

Yaipakari, ヤイバカリ, 自殺スレ. *v.i.* To commit suicide.

Yaipakashnu, ヤイバカシヌ, 學習スレ、悔ユル. *v.i.* To learn. To repent. **Syn: Yaikokatpak.**

Yaipaopichi, ヤイバオピチ, 立聞キスレ. *v.i.* To be caught saying something one would rather not be heard by a third party.

Yaipapirushte-an, ヤイバビルシテアン, 遠慮スレ、前ニ出ルヲ憚カレ. *v.i.* To be backward. To dread coming forward.

Yaipapirushte-sak-no, ヤイバビルシテサクノ, 大膽ニ. *adv.* Fearlessly. With confidence. **Syn: Utumkush sak no.**

Yaiparaka-hok-guru, ヤイバラカホクグル, 食物ヲ買フ人. *n.* One who buys food for himself. To provide for one's self.

Yaiparakosai, ヤイバラコサイ, 我儘ナル. *v.i.* To be selfish.

Yaipararoki, ヤイバラロキ, 他人ノ厄介ニナラヌ人. *n.* One well able to sustain himself.

Yaiparo-oshiribe, ヤイバロオシリベ, 理ノ解カラヌコトヲ云フ人. *n.* A person who talks nonsense.

Yaiparoshuiba-guru, ヤイバロシュイバグル, 食物ヲ買フ人. *n.* A person who buys food for himself.

Yaiparaparu, ヤイバラバル, or **Yaiparuparu,** ヤイバルバル, 扇ク. *v.i.* To fan one's self.

Yaiparaparup, ヤイバラバルプ, 扇子. *n.* A fan. **Syn: Aponki or Apunke.**

Yaiparush, ヤイバルシ, 多辯ナル. *adj.* Talkative. Loquacious. By some "to be greedy."

Yaipauchire, ヤイバウチレ, 毒ヲ仰ク. *v.i.* To poison one's self.

Yaipasere, ヤイバセレ, 孕ム. *v.i.* To be with child.

Yaipaye, ヤイバイェ, 思ハズ口外スレ. *v.t.* To let out (as one's thoughts) by mistake.

Yaipekap, ヤイベカプ, 掴ム. *v.t.* To grasp at.

Yaipekare, ヤイベカレ, 出入スル. *v.i.* To pass in or out. To go through, as through a doorway or window. To sally forth.

Yaipokashte, ヤイボカシテ, 避ケル. *v.t.* To avoid. To dissent.

Yaipokishiri-karakara, ヤイボキシリカラカラ, 旅裝スレ. *v.i.* To dress one's self as for a journey.

Yaipopkere, ヤイボブケレ, 暖ヲ取ル. *v.t.* To warm one's self.

Yaiporo-isamka, ヤイポロイサムカ, 面皮ヲ失ハセル. *v.i.* To be put out of countenance. To be cast down. To be troubled.

Yairaige, ヤイライゲ, 自殺スレ. *v.t.* To commit suicide.

Yairamande, ヤイラマンデ, 自殺スル. *v.i.* To commit suicide. **Syn:** Yairaige.

Yairamatte, ヤイラマッテ, 注意スル. *v.i.* To be careful. To watch over one's self. To be circumspect. To be cautious. To pay attention.

Yairamattere, ヤイラマッテレ, 謹慎ナラシムレ. *v.t.* To mend one's ways. To cause to be circumspect.

Yairamchuptekka, ヤイラムチュプテッカ, 淋シキ. *v.i.* To feel lonely. **Syn:** Mishmu. Nishmu.

Yairamde, ヤイラムデ, 辭宜スル(己レヲ下ゲスノ意). *v.i.* To curtesy.

Yairamhekomo, ヤイラムヘコモ, 煩懣. *v.i.* To be in anguish. To suffer pain. **Syn:** Ikoarakomo.

Yairamhekote, ヤイラムヘコテ, 己レヲ養フ、自活スル. *v.i.* To keep one's self.

Yairamkikkara, ヤイラムキッカラ, 中止スル. *v.i.* To cease doing something.

Yairamkoiki, ヤイラムコイキ, 哀シム、失望スル. *v.i.* To be in sorrow. To be distressed. To be out of spirits.

Yairamkote, ヤイラムコテ, 再婚スル、(單). *v.i.* To remarry. (*sing*).

Yairamkotpa, ヤイラムコツパ, 再婚スル、(複). *v.t.* To remarry. (*pl*).

Yairamkuru-shitotkere, ヤイラムクルシトツケレ, 更ニ力ヲ出ス. *v.i.* To put forth renewed strength. To do with renewed energy.

Yairampekamama, ヤイラムベカママ, 落膽スル. *v.i.* To be dejected. To be in low spirits. **Syn:** Aun-kinra.

Yairampeutek-guru, ヤイラムベウテクグル, 愚者. *n.* A fool. An ignoramus. A worthless or bad person.

Yairampekash, ヤイラムベカシ, 哀シム、失望スル. *v.i.* To be sorrowful. To be downhearted. To be in low spirits.

Yairampokashte, ヤイラムポカシテ, 哀ム(朋友親戚ナドノ不幸ニ付テ). *v.i.* To sit in sorrow, as a person upon the loss of a friend or relation. To be downhearted.

Yairamshitne, ヤイラムシツ子, 患ム. *v.i.* To suffer.

Yairamuatte, ヤイラムアッテ, ヤイラマテニ同シ. *n.* Same as *Yairamatte,* to be careful. To pay attention.

Yairamure, ヤイラムレ, 卑キ、憐ミ深キ. *v.i.* and *adj.* Humble. Compassionate.

Yairamure, ヤイラムレ, 卑下スレ. *v.t.* To humble one's self. **Syn:** Yaitukareushte.

Yairamure-kunne, ヤイラムレクン子, 氣質ノ宜キ. *adj.* Of a pleasant disposition.

Yairap, ヤイラプ, 歌. *n.* An ode.

Yairap, ヤイラプ, 災難ニ遭フ. *v.i.* To meet with an accident.

Yairarire, ヤイラリレ, 從フ. v.t. To follow. To go after. As:— *Seturu kashike yairarire,* "he followed close behind him."

Yairat, ヤイラツ, or Yarat, ヤラツ, 孕ム. v.t. To conceive. **Syn: Honkoro.**

Yairawere, ヤイラウェレ, 口ノミニテ 行ハサル人. v.i. One who talks of doing something but leaves it undone. **Syn: Monrawere.**

Yairenga, ヤイレンガ, 喜フ. v.i. To be pleased. To rejoice. As:— *Shi no ku yairenga,* "I am very pleased."

Yairenga, ヤイレンガ, 挨拶スレ. v.i. To salute.

Yairengane, ヤイレンガ子, 喜ンデ. adv. With pleasure. Joyfully. **Syn: Ikopuntek.**

Yairiki-guru-pumba, ヤイリキグルブムバ, 風又ハ雲ニ乘ル. v.i. To be lifted up upon the clouds or wind. To get up in a hurry. (*pl*).

Yairiki-guru-puni, ヤイリキグルブニ, 雲又ハ風ニ乘ル. v.i. To be lifted up upon the clouds or wind. To get up in a hurry. (*pl*).

Yairiki-pumba, ヤイリキブムバ, 上ル、上ケラレル. v.i. To rise up. To be lifted up. (*pl*).

Yairiki-puni, ヤイリキブニ, 上ル、上ケラレル. v.i. To rise up. To be lifted up. (*pl*).

Yairikotte, ヤイリコッテ, 縊首スル. v.i. To hang one's self. **Syn: Yaiateraige. Yaiotusheotte.**

Yairire, ヤイリレ, 達スル、伸ビスル. v.i. To reach up for anything. To stretch one's self. To. be proud.

Yairiterite, ヤイリテリテ, 手足ヲ伸ベル、運動スレ. v.i. To stretch one's legs and arms. To take exercise, as after an illness. **Syn: Yaikotande.**

Yaisannyo, ヤイサンニヨ, 怜悧ナル. adj. Prudent.

Yaisambepokash, ヤイサムベポカシ, 幽鬱ナレ、心配ナル. adj. Down-hearted. Troubled. Pitiable.

Yaisambepokashte, ヤイサムベポカシテ, 心配チサセシ. v.t. To give trouble to. To render down-hearted.

Yaisamne, ヤイサム子, 單ニ、意介セヌ. adv. Merely. Without any special object. Never mind. It is nothing.

Yaisantapka, ヤイサンタブカ, 人ノ腕及ヒ肩. n. One's arms and shoulders. As:—*Yaisantapka riterite,* "to stretch" or "exercise one's arms and shoulders."

Yoisarama, ヤイサラマ, 高慢ナル. adj. Proud. Boastful.

Yaishikakushte, ヤイシカクシテ, 被レ (衣ナドチ). v.i. To throw over one's self, as a garment.

Yaishikashke, ヤイシカシケ, 防衛スレ. v.i. To defend one's self against a charge.

Yaishimattarire, ヤイシマッタリレ, 殘ス、息メレ. v.t. To leave. To cease. **Syn: Shiokere.**

Yaishinire, ヤイシニレ, 休ム、隠退ス

ル. *v.i.* To rest. To retire. To go into retirement from active life.

Yaishinnaire, ヤイシンナイレ, 身ヲ退ク. *v.i.* To separate one's self from.

Yaishinniukesh, ヤイシンニウケシ, 謙遜ス レ. *adj.* and *v.i.* To be humble. Lowly. To underrate one's own abilities. To be unable to do anything. **Syn : Yaieshinniukesh.**

Yaishiporore, ヤイシポロレ, 忍耐ス レ. *v.i.* To persevere.

Yaishirushiru, ヤイシルシル, 身體ヲ 擦ル. *v.i.* To rub one's self.

Yaishitoma-shomoki, ヤイシトマシ ョモキ, 倨傲ナレ. *adj.* Insolent.

Yaishitomkuru, ヤイシトムクル, 此 年又ハ大サニ達シタレ、例セバ、セモ ノカイヨラ△ヤイシトムクレ、一人 前ノ年又ハ大サニナツタ. *v.i.* To have attained to the age or size of. As :—*Semokkaiyoram yaishitomkuru*, "to have attained to the age or size of manhood."

Yaishittekka, ヤイシッテッカ, 監禁ス レ. *v.i.* To curb one's self. To hold one's self in.

Yaishiwen, ヤイシウェン, 卑キ. *adj.* Humble. **Syn : Yaiorai.**

Yaishiwennere, ヤイシウェンヂレ, 卑 下スレ, *v.i.* To humble one's self. **Syn : Yaioraire.**

Yaishukupka, ヤイシュクブカ, 記憶ス レ、決シテ忘レヌ、(恨ミチ). *v.i.* To keep in memory, as a grudge. Never to forget or forgive.

Yaishukupkap, ヤイシュクブカブ, 骨 髄ニ徹シタル恨ミ. *n.* A grudge never forgotten or pardoned.

Yaitapapa, ヤイタパパ, 横臥スレ. *v.i.* To lie down.

Yaitapkuruka, ヤイタプクルカ, 肩. *n.* One's shoulders. As :—*Yaitapkuruka, riterite,* "to exercise one's shoulders."

Yaitasarapare, ヤイタサラバレ, 溜 息スル. *v.i.* To sigh. **Syn : Tanne hesei ki.**

Yaitektek, ヤイテクテク, 小便スル. *v.i.* To make water. To urinate.

Yaito, ヤイト, 艾、例セバ、ヤイトオ マシ、灸ヲ點ヘレ. *n.* Moxa. As :— *Yaito omare*, to apply moxa (Japanese).

Yaitobare, ヤイトバレ, or **Yaitubare, ヤイツバレ,** *v.i.* To be careful. To take care.

Yaitobare-no, ヤイトバレノ, or **Yaitubare-no, ヤイツバレノ,** 注意シ テ. *adv.* Carefully. With care.

Yaitobare-kuni-ita, ヤイトバレクニ イタ, 危機一髪. *n.* A crisis. A time of danger.

Yaitobare-yan, ヤイトバレヤン, 注 意セヨ. *v.i. imp.* Be careful. Take care.

Yaitokoiki, ヤイトコイキ, 準備スル. *v.i.* To prepare. **Syn : Yaietokooiki.**

Yaitombuni, ヤイトムブニ, 模擬スレ、 眞似スル. *v.t.* To imitate. To mimic. To make fun of.

Yaitomte-kara, ヤイトムテカラ, 飾ル. *v.i.* To adorn one's self.

Yaito-omare, ヤイトオマレ, 灸ヲ點 ヘル. *v.t.* To apply moxa.

Yaitopake, ヤイトバケ, 腋下. n. The armpits.

Yaitubare, ヤイツバレ, 注意シテ. adv. Carefully. With care. **Syn:** Yaitobare.

Yaitukapte, ヤイツカプテ, 尊敬スレ. To treat with respect. To do with decency.

Yaitukka, ヤイツッカ, 自然ニ成長スル. v.i. To grow up naturally.

Yaitumam, ヤイツマム, 人身. n. One's body. As :— *Yaitumam karukara*, "to tidy one's self up." **Syn : Yaitumama.**

Yaitumnu-anu, ヤイツムヌアヌ, 容體ヲ問ク. v.t. To inquire after one's health. As :— *E oman wa yaitumnu anu*, "go and inquire after his health."

Yaitumnunu, ヤイツブヌヌ, 氣分降レ、平癒スル. v.i. To feel better in health. To feel in better spirits. To revive after illness.

Yaitunashka, ヤイツナシカ, 急ク. v.i. To be hasty. To be in a hurry.

Yaitunnap, ヤイツンナプ, 嫉ム. v.t. To envy. To be jealous of. **Syn : Yaiyeitunnap.**

Yaitupekare, ヤイツベカレ, 吝嗇ニ. adv. Miserly. Covetously.

Yaitupok ヤイツポク, 腋下. n. The armpits.

Yaitura, ヤイツラ, 孤獨ノ. adj. Alone.

Yaiturare, ヤイツラレ, 同行スレ. v.t. To go with. To accompany.

Yaiturashte, ヤイツラシテ, 抱キ合フ. To hug. **Syn : Yaikokishma.**

Yaituriri, ヤイツリリ, 伸ヒスル. v.i. To stretch one's self out.

Yaiturukotachi, ヤイツルコタチ, 身體ヲ汚ス. v.i. To make one's self dirty.

Yaituyetuye, ヤイツイェツイェ, 身體ノ埃ヲ拂フ. v.i. To shake one's self. To brush one's self.

Yaituwashkara, ヤイツワシカラ, 哀ム. v.i. To mourn. To grieve.

Yaituwashkarap, ヤイツワシカラプ, 哀ミ、悼ミ, n. A grieving. A mourning.

Yaiukauka, ヤイウカウカ, 心ヲ入レ (綿ナド). v.t. To quilt for one's self.

Yaiunashi, ヤイウナシ, 自身ニ臼ク. v.i. To pound in a mortar by one's self. **See Utunashi. Inereyunashi. Autunashi. Reunashi.**

Yaiunashke, ヤイウナシケ, 謝罪スレ. 詫フレ. v.i. To ask to be excused. To beg pardon.

Yaiupshoro-chari, ヤイウプショロチャリ, 淫ヲ竊ク. v.i. To play the whore. To act the harlot.

Yaiupshoro-mukmuke, ヤイプショロムクムケ, 胸ヲ覆フ, 衣ヲ纒フ. v.t. To cover up the chest. To draw one's clothes round one's self. **Syn : Yainumatka seshke.**

Yaiutaratuye, ヤイウタラツイェ, 己レノ友ヲ殺ス. v.t. and v.i. To slay one's own friends. To run amuck.

Yaiusere, ヤイウセレ, 露出スル (刺ナドノ傷口カラ). v.i. To come out of one's self, as a splinter from a wound.

Yaiwende-tope-ni, ヤイウェンデトペニ, クロビイタヤ. n. A kind of maple, *Acer miyabei, Maxim*.

Yaiwennukara, ヤイウェンヌカラ, 失
望スレ: *v.i.* To despair. To be
in great want. To feel discouraged.

Yaiyai, ヤイヤイ, 人ヲ呼ブ叫聲. *excl.*
An exclamation used in calling
a person.

Yaiyainukoro, ヤイヤイヌコロ, 満足
スレ. *v.i.* To be contented. **Syn :**
Aiainukoro.

Yaiyainuwere, ヤイヤイヌウェレ, 満
足スレ. *v.i.* To be contented.

Yaiyaisusu, ヤイヤイスス, 柳ノ一種.
n. A kind of willow.

Yaiyan-kina, ヤイヤンキナ, 陸生ノ蘆.
n. Reeds which grow on land.

Yaiyan-noya, ヤイヤンノヤ, モヨギ.
n. Mugwart, *Artemisia vulgaris,*
L.

Yaiyantop, ヤイヤントブ, チシマザ.
n. A kind of bamboo. *Sasa
kurilensis, Mak. et Shib.*

Yaiyapapu, ヤイヤパブ, or **Yayo-
papu, ヤヨパブ,** 詫ル、辨疏スル.
v.t. To beg pardon. To apologize.
To make a mistake.

Yaiyattasa, ヤイツッサタ, 返禮スル.
v.i. To give in return for something received or done.
Syn : Yaiattasa.

Yaiyeitunnap, ヤイイェイツンナブ, 嫉
ム. *v.i.* To be jealous. To envy.
Syn : Yaitunnap.

Yaiyekote, ヤイイェコテ, 爲ル. *v.i.*
To do. As :—*Tu chish wenbe yaiyekote,* "she wept bitterly." (Lit,
she did two bad weeps).

Yaiyekush, ヤイイェクシ, 愧チレ. *v.i.*
To be ashamed. **Syn :** Yashitoma.

Yaiyenukuri, ヤイイェヌクリ, 恐レル.
v.i. To dread. To fear. To be
diffident.

Yaiyenukuri-no, ヤイイェヌクリノ,
恐怖シテ. *adv.* With fear or diffidence. Diffidently. As :—*Iteki
yaiyenukuri no ahun yan,* "please
enter without diffidence."

**Yaiyepaweteshu, ヤイイェパウェテシ
ユ,** 己レノ事柄ヲ白狀スレ. *v.i.* To
bear witness against one's self.
To commit one's self.

Yaiyen-furep, ヤイイェンフレプ, エヤ
イチゴ. *n.* Raspberry. *Rubus I-
dueus, L. var. nipponicus, Focke.*

Yaiyeshikorap, ヤイイェシコラプ, 負
傷スレ. *v.i.* To be wounded.
Hurt. **Syn :** Euikuruki. Yayapushkere.

**Yaiyetomkokanu, ヤイイェトムコカ
ヌ,** 信任スル. *v.t.* To trust in
one's self. To rely on one's self.

Yaiyeyashitoma, ヤイイェヤシトマ,
愧チレ. *v.i.* To be ashamed of
one's self.

Yaiyokapashte, ヤイヨカパシテ, 悔
ム. *v.t.* To repent. To change
one's life. *v.i.* To be contrite.

Yaiyomap, ヤイヨマプ, 怒ル. *v.i.* To
be angry.

Yaiyomonnure, ヤイヨモンヌレ, 怒
ル. *v.i.* To be angry.

Yaiyukaukau, ヤイユカウカウ, 修繕
スレ. *v.t.* To mend.

Yaiyupupu, ヤイユブブ, 忍耐スレ.
v.i. To exercise patience.

Yak, ヤク, ト、ナラバ、例セバ、ベツォ
ッタ チ エプ シリ エシク ネ ヤク アイェ、
川ニ澤山ノ (魚ガ有ルトノコトデス).
post. That. If. As :—*Pet otta
chep shiri eshik ne yak aye,* "it

is said that there are many fish in the river." *Nei no ye yak wen ruwe ne,* "if she says so, it is bad." *Yak anak ne,* "if." As:— *Nei no an yak anak ne, pirika,* "if it is so, well."

Yak, ヤク, オヤ、(嫌悪ノ意ヲ表ス). *interj.* Dear me. This word is expressive of disgust.

Yak, ヤク, 毀レル、破レル、破裂スル. To break. To split. To burst. To knock. **Syn: Yaku.**

Yaka, ヤカ, 指ス. *v.t.* To point at. **Syn: Epeka.**

Yakanak, ヤカナク, 鷲キノ語、婦女及ビ小兒之ヲ用ユ. *excl.* An exclamation of surprise specially used by women and children. Also. How be it.

Yakara-kina, ヤカラキナ, オホバセンキウ. *n. Angelica refracta, Fr. Schm.*

Yakaru-kina, ヤカルキナ, オホバセンキウ. *n. Angelica refracta, Fr. Schm.* Also called Moshiu-kina.

Yak-aye, ヤクアイエ, ト言ヒマス、例セバ、ライヤクアイエオルシペショモクヌ、彼人ガ死ンダト言フコトヲ聞キマセヌ. *ph.* It is said that. As:— *Rai yak aye orushpe shomo ku nu,* "I have not heard that he is dead."

Yaki, ヤキ, 蝉. *n.* The cicada.

Yakka, ヤッカ, 何々スルトモ. *post.* Although. Albeit. Though. If. Even if. Nevertheless.

Yakka……yakka, ヤッカ, デモ、彼カ其カ、其モ此モ、例セバ、ウパスアシヤツカレラルイナツカ、雪デモ風デモ、カムイネヤッカアイヌネヤッカ、神モ

人モ. *post.* Although……and. Whether……or. Both……and. As:— *Upas ash yakka, rera rui yakka,* "although it snows and blows." *Inne yakka, moyo yakka,* "whether many or few." *Kamui ne yakka, ainu ne yakka,* "both gods and men."

Yakkai, ヤッカイ, ヤッカニ同シ. *post.* The same as *yakka,* and *akka.*

Yaknatara, ヤクナタラ, 粉々ニ砕レル. *v.i.* To be broken into fragments. To break into fragments.

Yak-ne, ヤク子, 其様ナレバ. *post.* If. If so.

Yaku, ヤク, 獣皮又ハ魚類ニ課セシ税. *n.* Tribute paid in furs or fish. A tax.

Yaku, ヤク, 砕レル、破裂スレ. *v.i.* To break. To burst. To be broken. To smash. **Syn: Yak.**

Yakun, ヤクン, 若、何々スルトキ、何々スレトモ. *conj.* If. When. Though.

Yakura-shuma, ヤクラシュマ, 物見櫓. *n.* A watch stone.

Yam, ヤム, クリ、例セバ、ヤムクシ、栗ノ刺(イガ). *n.* Chestnuts. As:— *Yam kush,* "chestnut burrs." *Yam saye,* "to thread chestnuts on a string for stowing away."

Yambe-sei, ヤムベセイ, 蝸牛. *n.* A snail.

Yam-ni, ヤムニ, クリノキ. *n.* A chestnut tree. *Castanea vulgaris, Lam. var. japonica, DC.*

Yam-ni-karush, ヤムニカルシ, 栗木耳. *n.* A kind of Polyporus which grows upon the decaying trunks of chestnut trees.

Yan, ヤン, 動詞ニ附加シテ命令ノ意ヲ表ス、例セバ、アリキヤン、來レ、(複). *part.* An imperative plural particle used after verbs. Imperative of the verb *an*, "to be." As:—*Ariki yan*, "come." *Oman wa ye yan*, "go and tell him." *Yan* is sometimes used in a singular sense also.

Yan, ヤン, 登ル. *v. i.* To ascend. To go up. As:—*Wakka orowa no yan*, "to ascend out of water."

Yange, ヤンゲ, 捧呈スル、曳揚ケル. *v.t.* To give to a superior. To offer up to the gods. To haul up, as a boat from a river. Thus: *Chip yange*, "to haul a boat ashore."

Yange-kunip, ヤンゲクニプ, 供物、貴人ヘノ贈物. *n.* Offerings to the gods. Things given to a superior.

Yangere, ヤンゲレ, 上ゲル、捧ゲレ. *v.t.* To send up. To cause to offer to the gods. To cause to give to a superior.

Yan-guru, ヤングル, ヤウングルニ同ジ. *n.* Same as *Ya-un-guru*.

Yani, ヤニ, 殆ンド. *adv.* Almost. Nearly. **Syn: Yaani. Nanihungo.**

Yani-yani, ヤニヤニ, 殆ンド. *adv.* Almost. Nearly. Very nearly. Same as *yani*, but more intense.

Yanrash-kamu, ヤンラシカム, 濕疹. *n.* Eczema universale.

Yanro, ヤンロ, 自己ニ命令スレ語、例セバ、バエアンロ、イザ行クベシ. *part.* An imperative particle meaning "let us." As:—*Paye yanro*, "let us go." **Syn: Anro.**

Ya-oshke, ヤオシケ, 網ヲ編ム. *v.i.* To net. To make nets.

Yap, ヤプ, 登ル. *v. i.* To ascend. To go up. *Pl.* of *yan*.

Ya-peka, ヤペカ, 陸テ. *adv.* By land.

Yapoki-koro-chip, ヤポキコロチプ, 船ノ骨組. *n.* The skeleton of a boat or ship.

Yapte, ヤプテ, 上方ニ行カシムル(複). *v.t.* To send up. To cause to ascend. *Pl.* of *yange*.

Yara, ヤラ, 蔽種. *n.* Rags. **Syn: Yarape.**

Yara, ヤラ, 裂ク. *v.t.* To tear. To rend.

Yara, ヤラ, 木皮ニテ製シタレ籠ノ一種. *n.* A kind of basket made of bark.

Yara, ヤラ, 家根ヲ葺クニ用ユル木皮. *n.* The bark of trees sometimes used in thatching.

Yara, ヤラ, or **Yara-hi, ヤラヒ,** 人ニ為セル、(主人ガ僕ニ言付ケテ事ヲ為サシムレガ如シ). *auxil. v.* To do through another, as a superior through his subordinates. A particle expressing reverence to the object of a verb. As:—*Nıshpa otbe anu yara na*, "I let the master know." *Tak yara*, "to send to fetch." *Ronnu yara*, "to send and kill." *Kari asei yara-hi isam*, "there is no one by whom to send it."

Yarage, ヤラゲ, 衣服ノ破穴. *n.* A hole in one's clothes.

Yaraka, ヤラカ, 裂ク. *v.t.* To tear.

Yarape-ni, ヤラベニ, カンボク. *n.* Guelder-rose. *Viburnum Opulus, L.*

Yarapeshit, ヤラペシツ, 甚シキ艦褸.
n. Very ragged clothes.

Yarara, ヤララ, 艦褸ニナリタル. *adj.*
Ragged.

Yarat, ヤラツ, or **Yairat, ヤイラツ,**
孕ム. *v.t.* To conceive. **Syn:**
Honkoro.

Yarui-chup, ヤルイチュブ, or **Yaru-ru-chup, ヤルルチュブ,** 八月. *n.*
The month of August.

Yarupe, ヤルペ, 衣服、小兒ノ衣物.
n. Clothes. Infants clothing.

Yaruru-chup, ヤルルチュブ, or **Ya-rui-chup, ヤルイチュブ,** 八月. *n.*
The month of August.

Yasa, ヤサ, 裂ク. *v.t.* To tear.

Yasamge-no-an, ヤサムゲノアン, 孤
獨. *adj.* Alone. To be alone.
Not to mix with others.

Yasara, ヤサラ, 爲セル. *v.t.* To
cause another to do. To get done.

Yasaske, ヤサスケ, 裂レル(岩ナドノ).
v.i. To be rent, as rocks.

Yash, ヤシ, 網ヲ曳ク. *v.t.* To drag
a net along in fishing.

Yashitoma, ヤシトマ, 恥チレ. *v.i.*
To be ashamed.

Yashitomare, ヤシトマレ, 恥シメル.
v.t. To make ashamed. To abash.

Yashitukkari, ヤシツッカリ, 脊髄病.
n. Spinal disease. Paralysis.
Myelitis. **Syn: Ikkeu kamui**
koro tashum.

Yashiya, ヤシヤ, 曳網. *n.* A haul
seine.

Yashkara, ヤシカラ, 攔ム、川デ魚ヲ
網スル. *v.t.* To clutch. To seize.
To take up by the hand. To
make a grab at. To grapple. To
fish with a net in a stream.

Yashke, ヤシケ, 顔又手ヲ洗フ. *v.t.*
To wash the face and hands.

Yashke, ヤシケ, 破レ. *v.t. and v.i.*
To be cracked or broken. **Syn:**
Kone.

Yashke-batchi, ヤシケバッチ, 盥. *n.*
A wash basin.

Yashkep, ヤシケブ, 身體ヲ洗フ. *n.*
Ablutions.

Yashkep, ヤシケブ, 盥. *n.* A wash
hand basin.

Yashpe, ヤシペ, 投網. *n.* A hand
fish net.

Ya-sosh, ヤソシ, 地層. *n.* Layers
or strata of earth.

Yaspa, ヤスバ, 裂ク(複). *v.t.* To
tear. *Pl.* of *yasa.*

Yasu, ヤス, 銛. *n.* A spear with
three forks used for fishing in the
sea. *Jap.*

Yata, ヤタ, 陸デ. *adv.* By land.

Yatchitarabe, ヤッチタラベ, 網袋.
n. A mat used for carrying things
in.

Yatoro, ヤトロ, or **Yatotta, ヤトッタ,**
鷹ノ一種. *n.* A kind of hawk.
Syn: Yattui.

Yattui, ヤッツイ, 蓆ノ子. *n.* A mat
made of reeds which the Ainu lay
upon their floors. **Syn: Aputki.**
Toma.

Yattui, ヤッツイ, トビ、トンビ. *n.*
Black kite. **Syn: Yatotta. Ya-**
toro.

Yatu, ヤツ, or **Yatui, ヤツイ,** カモ
メ. *n.* A sea gull.

Yatupok, ヤツポク, or **Yatupake,**
ヤツパケ, 腋ノレ爲. *n.* The armpits.

Ya-un, ヤウン, 内地、(國ノ内部). *adv.* Inland. The interior.

Ya-un-guru, ヤウングル, アイヌ人. *n.* An Ainu. The Ainu as distinguished from their neighbours the Japanese, Russians, or present kamtchatdales.

Ya-un-kontukai, ヤウンコンツカイ, フクローノ一種. *n.* The eagle owl (lit: the servant of the world).

Ya-un-kotchane-guru, ヤウンコ, チヤ子グル, フクロノ一種. *n.* The eagle owl (lit: the mediator of the world).

Ya-un-moshiri, ヤウンモシリ, 蝦夷地. *n.* Ainu land. The country inhabited by the Ainu.

Yaushukep, ヤウフケブ, クモ. *n.* A spider.

Yautek, ヤウテク, 固クナル. *adj.* and *v.i.* To become hard, as the ground in winter by frost. To become solid or firm. To become stiff and cramped, as the limbs of a dead person if not laid out properly.

Yauyause, ヤウヤウセ, 唸ル. *v.i.* To growl. To snarl.

Yawauge, ヤワウゲ, 皸破レル(ヒヽヤレル). *v.i.* To chap as the hands through exposure to the cold wind.

Yaya, ヤヤ, 智惠. *n.* Wisdom.

Yayaini-emauri, ヤヤイニエマウリ, ナメシロイチゴ. *n.* A kind of raspberry. *Rubus parvifolius, L.*

Yayainu, ヤヤイヌ, 考ヘル. *v.i.* To think. To consider.

Yayainukoro, ヤヤイヌコロ, 威張ル、己レチバ智トスル. *v.i.* To be proud.

To consider one's self better than others. To be vainglorious.

Yayaisurugu, ヤヤイスルグ, 附子毒. *n.* Aconite poison.

Yayamkiri, ヤヤムキリ, 知心、會得スル. *v.t.* To know. To know one's self.

Yayapapu, ヤヤパプ, or Yaiyopapu, ヤイヨパプ, 過チスル、辨疏スル. *v.t.* To make a mistake. To apologize. To beg pardon. As: *Yayapapu ku ki,* "I made a mistake."

Yayai-susu, ヤヤイスス, ナガバヤナギ. *n. Salix stipularis, Sm.*

Yayapte, ヤヤプテ, 爲スコトチ嫌フ. *v.i.* To dislike to do.

Yayapushkere, ヤヤプシケレ, 頁傷スル. *v.i.* To be wounded. To be hurt. **Syn: Yaiyeshikorap. Euikuruki.**

Yayapushte, ヤヤプシテ, 驚ク. *v.i.* To be surprised. To be astonished.

Yayasap, ヤヤサブ, 愚カ. *adj.* Unwise.

Yayashish, ヤヤシシ, 穢キ. *adj.* Dirty.

Yayashnu, ヤヤシヌ, 智コキ. *adj.* Wise.

Yayattasa, ヤヤッタサ, 返禮スル. *v.i.* To make a return present to a person. To return thanks.

Yayekatuwen, ヤイェカツウェン, 愧ハル、哀シム. *v.i.* Ashamed. Sorrowful.

Yayemontasa, ヤヤイェモンタサ, 復讐スル. *v.t.* To take vengeance on.

Yayepataraye, ヤイェパタライェ, 己レニ克ツ. *v.i.* To exercise self-restraint.

Yayepkara-guru, ヤイェブカラ グル, 饕餮、大食. *n.* A glutton.

Yayoparasechui, ヤヨ パラセチュイ, 譽メル. *v.i.* To exult. To say hurrah. To cheer.

Yayakoetaptapu, ヤヤコエタブタブ, 卷ク. *v.t.* To roll up. To wrap up.

Yayunpa, ヤユムパ, 不意ニニ災罹ル. *v.i.* To meet with an accident.

Yayepupu, ヤイェププ, 脛カ痛ム. *v.i.* To have aching calves.

Ye, イェ, 膿. *n.* Matter. Humour. Pus. Fat. The matter of a boil. Fine pumice from volcanoes. White clay. As:—*Ye-ush,* "mattery." "Having pus." "Fatty." **Syn: E.**

Ye, イェ, 告ケレ、知ラセル. *v.t.* To tell. To say. To adduce. To announce. To attest. To acknowledge. As:—*Ye wa ambe,* "that which was said."

Ye, イェ, 仕事、(談話チ專ラトスル仕事チ云フ). *n.* Business. (This word can only refer to business of word of mouth).

Ye-hi, イェヒ, 言ヒシ、例セバ、エチイェヒ、彼が此ク言ヒシ. *v.i.* To be said. Said. He spake. As:—*Ene ye-hi,* "he spake thus."

Yep, イェブ, 話. *n.* A thing spoken. A speech.

Yepe, イェペ, 汚水、油ウミタル水. *n.* Discoloured water. Fatty water.

Yepi, イェヒ, エブニ同シ. *n.* Same as *yep.*

Yoikiri, ヨイキリ, 整ヘル. *v.t.* To arrange.

Yokane, ヨカ子, 後ロ. *adv.* Behind. Following. After. As:—*En yokane ek,* "follow me." *Yokane ambe,* "a person following after."

Yokkata, ヨッカタ, 熱心ニ、偏ヘニ. *adv.* Earnestly. Mostly. **Syn: Eunkashi no.**

Yoko, ヨコ, 狙フ(投鎗スルトキノ如ク). *v.t.* To aim at, as with a spear.

Yoko, ヨコ, 俟ツ. *v.i.* To wait.

Yokore, ヨコレ, 掛ケル(ツナナドチ). *v.t.* To set, as a trap. As:—*Eremu akbe yokore,* "to set a rat trap.

Yomi, ヨミ, 縮ム. *v.i.* To shrink.

Yomiyomik, ヨミヨミク, 皺ヨル. *v.i.* and *adj.* To be wrinkled. To become contracted. Crumpled.

Yomikyomikte, ヨミクヨミクテ, 皺寄セル. *v.t.* To crumple up. To wrinkle.

Yomne, ヨム子, 止メル、仕上ケル、忠告. *v.t.* To cease. Completed. To warn.

Yomne-ki, ヨム子キ, 止メル、忠告スル. *v.t.* To cease. To warn.

Yomomke, ヨモムケ, 火傷スル、過傷スル. *v.i.* To burn or scald.

Yompa, ヨム パ, 縮ム. *v.i.* To shrink.

Yongoro, ヨンゴロ, or Yongororo, ヨンゴロロ, 俟伏スル. *v.t.* To lie in wait. To go in quest. To look for. To crouch as a cat to catch a mouse. To watch for.

To aim at. To look straight at. Thus :—*Meko anak ne erum eyongororo wa kopiye kuni korachi an ruwe ne,* "the cat is lying in wait ready to spring upon the mouse." \Syn: **Oyokoush.**

Yoni, ヨ二, 縮ム. *v.i.* To contract. To shrink.

Yontekbe, ヨンテクベ, or **Yontek-kam, ヨンテッカム,** 腨、カカト、腕ノ肉. *n.* The calf of the leg. The muscle of the arm.

Yop, ヨプ, 主タル兩親、酋長、例セバ、ヨプコダン、首府. *adj* Chief. Principal. Parent. Head. As: ——*Yop-kotan,* "the chief city or capital of a country."

Yopbe, ヨプベ, 先考、(死ンタル親). *n.* One's dead father.

Yoruki-puni, ヨルキプ二, 煽動スル、例セバ、ウェンケウトムヨリキプ二、惡感情ヲ起サセル. *v. t.* To stir up. To raise up. As:—*Wen keutum yoriki puni,* "to stir up evil feelings."

Yorokomne, ヨロコム子, 皺寄ル. *v.i.* To be shrunk up as the body of an old person or the hand or leg of a sick person.

Yoropui, ヨロプイ, 肛門. *n.* The anus. **Syn : Otompui.**

Yorun, ヨルン, 乞フ. *v.t.* To beg. **Syn : Yorun-ki.**

Yorun-guru, ヨルングル, or **Yorun-ki-guru, ヨルンキグル,** 乞食. *n.* A beggar.

Yoshpe, ヨシベ, 大腸. *n.* The large intestines.

Yot, ヨツ, 眩ヒスル、當惑スル. *v.i.*

To be made dizzy. To be perplexed.

Yottek, ヨッテク, 疲レル. *adj.* Tired. Exhausted.

Yu, ユ, 硫黄質ノ温泉. *n.* Sulphur springs. Mineral water.

Yu-be, ユベ, or **Yu-pe, ユベ,** 冷礦泉. *n.* Cold mineral water. Sulphur water.

Yube, ユベ, テフサメ. *n.* A sturgeon. *Asipencer nikadoi,* Hilgd.

Yubin, ユビン, 文字. *n.* A letter. Also *yubin kambi.* (**Jap.**)

Yuk, ユク, 鹿、シカ. *n.* A deer. *Cervus sika,* Temm.

Yuk-apiri, ユクアピリ, 鹿逕. *n.* A deer track.

Yukara, ユカラ, 昔譚. *n.* A legend. A tradition.

Yuk-chikap, ユクチカプ, 鴟梟ノ一種. *n.* The screech owl.

Yuk-emauri, ユクエマウリ, タチイチゴ. *n.* A kind of raspberry. *Rubus crataegifolius,* Bunge.

Yuk-eremu, ユクエレム, エゾイタチ. *n.* Ermine.

Yuki, ユキ, 斜柱、スッカイ. *n.* A building brace.

Yukke, ユッケ, 夥シキ. *adj.* Very many.

Yukki, ユッキ, ダニ. *n.* A tick.

Yuk-nonno, ユクノンノ, コンロンサウ. *n. Cardamine macrophylla,* W.

Yuknumau-ni, ユクヌマウ二, クロウメモドキ. *n. Rhamnus japonica,* Max.

Yukkarush, ユッカルシ, マヒダケ. *n.* A kind of edible polypus.

Yuk-kuttasa, ユックッタサ, ナニシモ

ツケサウ. *n.* *Filipendula kamts-chatica, Max.*

Yukoikire, ユコイキレ, 邪寃スル、口出シスル. *v.t.* To interfere. To intermeddle. To stir up strife. To spread a false report about one. As :— *En orushpe yukoikire,* " he spread a false report about me."

Yukoikire-guru, ユコイキレグル, 口出シスル人. *n.* A meddler.

Yuk-pungara, ユクブンガラ, ツルアヂサキ. *n.* *Hydrangea scandens, Max.*

Yukram, ユクラム, 肝臓. *n.* The liver. Kinop.

Yuk-raige-ni, ユクライゲニ, ニガキ. *n.* *Picrasma ailanthoides, Planch.* Also called *shiu-ni.*

Yuk-topa-kina, ユクトパキナ, フツキサウ. *n.* *Pachysandra terminalis, S. et Z.*

Yuk-uturu-otbe-an, ユクウツルオツペアン, 減ル. *v.i.* To diminish. As :— *Ainu yukuturu otbe an,* " the Ainu are decreasing. **Syn : Wenpa. Shiepupu kor'an.**

Yupi, ユピ, or **Yupihi, ユピヒ,** or **Yupo, ユポ,** or **Yubi, ユビ,** 兄. *n.* An elder brother.

Yupke, ユブケ, 強キ、荒キ. *adj.* Strong. Wild. Severe.

Yupke-no, ユブケノ, 烈シク. *adv.* Severely. Wildly. Earnestly.

As :— *Yupke no ye,* " to speak earnestly." *Yupke no kik,* " to beat severely."

Yupkep, ユブケプ, 不慮ノ死. *n.* An accidental death. As : *Yupkep an,* " to die by accident.

Yupkere, ユブケレ, 強クスル. *v.t.* To strengthen.

Yupkiri, ユブキリ, 播ク. *v.t.* To sow broadcast. **Syn : Iyama.**

Yuppa, ユッパ, 捏ル、(粉ヲ). *v.t.* To knead, as dough.

Yuptek, ユブテク, 勉強ナレ. *adj.* Industrious. Active. Assiduous.

Yuptek-i, ユブテクイ, 活澄ナレコト. *n.* Activity. Assiduity.

Yuptek-no, ユブテクノ, 活澄ニ. *adv.* Actively. Industriously.

Yupu, ユブ, 熱心ニ為ス、精出シテナス、例セバ、キロロユブワキワエンコレ、精出シテ為シテ下サレ. *v.t.* To do earnestly. To do with might. As :— *Kiroro yupu wa ki wa en kore,* " please do it with all your might."

Yusa, ユサ 立腹シテ立去ル. *v.i.* To turn away in anger. To go off in a huff. **Syn : Ikeshu.**

Yuta, ユタ, 白. *n.* A mortar. **Syn : Uta.**

Yuta-ni, ユタニ, 杵. *n.* A pestle used for pounding in a mortar. **Syn : Uta-ni.**

Yutara, ユタラ, 傳言スル. *v.t.* To send a verbal message.

A GRAMMAR

OF THE

AINU LANGUAGE.

アイヌ語文典

PREFACE.

The Grammar contained in the following pages has been worked out during the last stages of the decay of the Ainu race and tongue, and not during the growth or full vigour of either. The merest *tyro* in philological research will therefore realize that the difficulties encountered have not always been of a light nature. Searching for and collating words, reducing them to what seemed to be to the author the most convenient form of writing,—analizing and comparing them, —defining them,—classifying them,—weeding out or noting the known Japanese and even Russian words which had crept in, and studying the laws of the grammatical construction of the language has each in its turn had its own special difficulties. There were also obstacles and difficulties of quite another kind cast in my way at the beginning of my career among the Ainu which, though I do not forget them, it is not necessary to mention in this place. And, however much amid rough living, and hard study one has sometimes longed and looked for the Clue of an Ariadne to guide himself by withal, such a help has not yet been found. Nor should it be forgotten that inasmuch as this language has never been tamed and fixed by any attempt of the people themselves to produce a native literature, what little is left of it is still, as ever it was, in its natural barbaric state. Hence the Author hopes that due allowances will be made for the many imperfections and oversights which must naturally occur in this work.

An edition of the Grammar appeared in September 1903. That little book was thrown out for the purpose of inviting criticisms by which the author might profit in the prosecution of his studies, and with the view of its forming a part of the introduction to what he ventures to deem a somewhat important work, namely, the preceding Ainu Dictionary. But there appear to be so few people truly interested in Ainu, or such a small number thoroughly acquainted with this tongue, that no help was given except to confirm him in his present belief that in so far as construction is concerned the Ainu language belongs as much to the Aryan tongue as Latin, French, Greek, and English do. Nor could the Author lay his hands on any other Ainu Grammar which would serve as a basis to work upon. The present work should therefore be regarded as original and quite independent. Still the Author must acknowledge his great indebtedness to Dr August Phizmaier for his *Kritische Durchsicht der von Davidaw verfassten Worter-sammlung aus der Sprache der Aino's (Wien 1852)*, for on studying this book he has derived great benefit from the critical and analytical method therein followed.

Sapporo, August, 1905.

TABLE OF CONTENTS.

[1] The Author has thought it best to give the headings of the separate sections
contained in the introductory chapter in case any Reader should desire to study
any one of them in particular, while for the rest, the bare subject only has been
announced as a heading.

PART II.

A

GRAMMAR

OF THE

AINU LANGUAGE.

CHAPTER I.

INTRODUCTION.

§ I. WORKS ON AINU GRAMMAR.

In the year A.D. 1851 Dr. A. Pfizmaier of Vienna published a small work called *Untersuchungen über den Bau der Aino-sprache*.[1] This appears to have been the first attempt ever made to submit the Ainu language to a grammatical analysis. This

---

[1] Other works by Pfizmaier are Kritische Durchsicht der von Davidow verfassten Woertersammlung aus der sprache der Aino 1852. Erörterungen und Auklärungen üeber Aino 1882. Also his Beiträge zur kenntnis der Aino-Poesie and vocabulaire der Aino sprache.

work was founded on a small vocabulary collected by two Japanese and called *Moshiogusa*.[1] I have studied the book through very carefully, testing its contents word by word throughout among the Ainu themselves, the result being that I fully agree with Prof. Chamberlain who writes of it as follows :[2]

"Considering that this grammar was founded on little else than one imperfectly printed Japanese vocabulary, the "*Moshiogusa*," the results obtained by the Austrian *servant* are truly marvellous. One only regrets, when perusing it, that a fraction of the vast trouble taken in collating each passage, comparing each word, noting each apparent grammatical phenomenon, should not have been devoted to a journey to Ainu[3] land itself, where a few months' converse with the natives would have abridged the labour of years,—would indeed not only have abridged the labour, but have rendered the result so much more trustworthy. As it is, Dr. Pfizmaier's "*Untersuchungen*" is rather a monument of learned industry, than a guide calculated to lead the student safely to his journey's end. The circumstances under which Dr. Pfizmaier worked were such as to render success impossible."

In 1875 M. M. Dobrotvorsky published his Ainsko-Russkiŭ Slovar. This look is a revision of his brother's original work on the Ainu language and includes the "*Untersuchungen*" here referred to. Unfortunately the work has been spoiled in part by comprehending in it words from too many sources, some of which

---

[1] By Uehara Kumajiro and Abe Chōzaburō; 1804.

[2] Memories of the Literature college, Imperial University of Japan. Vol. I. Page 1.

[3] Prof. Chamberlain always wrote *Aino* but I have taken the liberty of changing the spelling into Ainu (which means "man") wherever I have quoted him in this book so as to bring it into uniformity with the rest of this Grammar; for the people always speak of themselves as *Ainu* not *Aino*. *Aino* is an old Japanese way of calling this race. Dobrotvorsky also notes that the word *Aino* is a corruption of *Ainu* which he defines as "man." With regard to this it is interesting to remark that the Eskimo call themselves *innuit*, "man"; the Moki Indians of Arizona call themselves *hopi*, "man," and that Delaware Indians apply to themselves the term *lennilenape*, i.e. "men of men." All Japanese official documents now have *Ainu* instead of *Aino*.

are not Ainu at all but perhaps Tartar, Oroko, Chuckchi, Yakut, Ziliyak, Aleutean, or some kindered tongue. A full list of the Authors referred to by Dobrotvorsky will be found in the preface to his Slovar.

From the appearance of this work till the year 1883 there is a further gap; but in that year Prof. J. M. Dixon, then of the Tokyo Engineering College, published a small sketch of Ainu Grammar founded on earlier European notices and his own short studies carried on chiefly among the Ainu of Tsuishkari; who, by the by, had a few years before come down from Saghalien. This sketch appeared in a Magazine then published in Yokohama and named *The Chrysanthemum*. After careful perusal of those articles I once more fully agree with Prof. Chamberlain who says :—

" Unfortunately, the results obtained by this conscientious worker were impaired to some extent by the want of that intimate acquaintance with Japanese, which, in the absence of a thorough practical knowledge of Ainu itself, is the first condition to the successful investigation of any subject connected with the Island of Yezo."[1]

The next work to appear on this subject was my own Grammar which is included in the Memoirs referred to above. It will be found introduced by Mr. Chamberlain's excellent *brochure* on the Language, Mythology, and Geographical Nomenclature of Japan viewed in the light of Ainu[2] studies. The present Grammar is a thorough revision of that and also of the one which appeared next as an introduction to my Ainu-English Japanese Dictionary published by the Hokkaidō-cho in 1889.

§ II. AINU AND JAPANESE COMPARED.

That, gramatically speaking, the Ainu language has no general affinity with present Japanese has already been conclusively

[1] Memoirs page 2.
[2] See footnote 2 on page 2.

proved by Prof. Chamberlain in the Memoirs. Taking my
Grammar as a basis, and comparing it with the results of his
own personal studies of the subject among the Ainu themselves
he has pointed out fifteen major points in which the two languages differ. In order not to mar what the Prof. has so well
put I will take the liberty of quoting the passage *in extenso*.

He says :—(1) Japanese has postpositions only. Ainu, besides
numerous postpositions, has also the two prepositions *e* " to,"
" towards," and *o* " from ; " thus : *E chup-pok-un chup ahun*,
" The sun sets to the West." *O chup-ka-un chup hetuku*, " The
sun rises from the East."

(2) The Ainu postpositions are often used independently, in
a manner quite foreign to Japanese idiom, thus : *Koro habo*,
" His mother," more literally " Of [him] mother."—*Tan moshiri
ka ta pakno utari inne utara isambe paskuru chironnup ne
ruwe ne*, " The creatures *than which* there is nothing so numerous in this world are the crows and foxes."

(3) Connected with the Ainu use of prepositions, is that of
formative prefixes. Thus the passive is obtained by prefixing *a*
to the active, as *raige*, " to kill ; " *a-raige*, " to be killed." A
transitive or verbalizing force is conveyed by the prefix *e*, as
pirika, " good " *e-pirika*, " to be good to," *i.e.*, generally, " to
benefit oneself " ; *mik* " to bark," " *e-mik*," to bark at ; *a-e-mik*,
" to be barked at." The signification of verbs is sometimes intensified by means of the prefix *i*, as *nu*, to hear ; " *i-nu*, " to
listen." All this is completely foreign to the Japanese grammatical system, which denotes grammatical relations by means
of suffixes exclusively.

(4) The Ainu passive has been mentioned incidentally under
the preceding heading. Note that it is a true passive, like
that of European language,—not a form corresponding (as does
the so-called Japanese passive) to such English locutions as " to
get killed," " to *get* laughed at." In fact, the habit of looking
at all actions from an active point of view is one of the charac-
teristics of Japanese thought, as expressed in the forms of Japanese grammar. By the Ainu, on the other hand, the passive is

used more continually even than in English, although the abundant use of the passive is one of the features distinguishing English from all other Aryan tongues. Thus an Ainu will say *Ene a-kari ka isam*, "There is nothing to be done," literally "Thus to-be-done-thing even is-not," where a Japanese would say *Shi-kata ga nai*, literally "There is not a way to do." Again, such a sentence as "In any case you must go viâ Sapporo," would be in Ainu *Neun neyakka Satporo a-kush*, literally, "In any case Sapporo is traversed." In Japanese it would be hard to turn such phrases passively at all. Much less would any such passives ever be employed either in literature or in colloquial.

(5) Ainu has great numbers of reflective verbs formed from transitives by means of the prefix *yai*, "self." Thus *yai-erampoken*, "to be sorry for oneself," i.e., "to be disappointed"; *yai-raige*, "to commit suicide"; *yai-kopuntek*, "to be glad" (conf. *se réjouir* and similar reflectives in French). Japanese has no reflective verbs.

(6) Whereas in Japanese those numerous but rarely used words, which foreign students term personal pronouns, are in reality nothing but honorific and humble locutions, like the "thy servant" of Scripture, and such expressions as "Your Excellency," "Sire," etc., Ainu has true pronouns. (*E* is "you"; *kani*, *ku*, and *k'* are "I" in the following examples.) As a corollary to this, the Ainu pronouns are used at every turn, like the pronouns of modern European languages, thus:—

E koro shike, "Your luggage."

Kani k'eraman, "I know;" more literally "*Moi je sais.*"

Satporo-kotan ta ohonno k'an kuni ku ramu yakun, ku koro eiwange kuru ku tura wa k'ek koroka, iruka k'an kuni ku ramu kusu, ku sak no k'ek ruwe ne, "Had I known that I should stay so long in Sapporo, I would have brought my servant with me. But, as I thought I should be here only a short time, I came without one."

In Japanese, all these sentences would be expressed without the aid of a single word corresponding to a personal pronoun; thus:—

Go nimotsu, literally " August luggage."

Wakarimashita, literally " Have understood."

Kahodo nagaku Sapporo ni todomaru to shirimashita naraba, kerai wo tsurete kuru hazu de arimashita ga, wazuka bakari orimashō to omoimashita mon' desu kara, tsurezu ni kimashita.

This last Japanese sentence is impossible to translate literally into our language, English (like Ainu) idiom insisting on the constant iteration of personal pronouns, which in Japanese would be, not merely inelegant, but ridiculous and confusing.

(7) Some traces of the use of " case," as understood in Aryan grammar, exist in the Ainu first personal pronoun. The declension is as follows :—

	NOMINATIVE.	OBJECTIVE.
Singular.	**ku,** " I."	**en,** " me."
Plural.	**chi,** " we."	**un,** or **i** " us."

Japanese is devoid of everything of this nature.

(8) Some traces of a plural inflection are found in the conjugation of Ainu verbs. For Ainu verbs turn singular *n* into plural *p,* viz :—

SINGULAR.	PLURAL.	ENGLISH.
ahun,	**ahup,**	" to enter."
oashin,	**oaship,**	" to issue."
ran,	**rap,**	" to descend."
san,	**sap,**	" to descend."

In a few cases the *p* (or *b*) appears in a less regular manner. They are :—

heashi,	**heashpa,**	" to begin."
hechirasa,	**hechiraspa,**	" to blossom."
hopuni,	**hopumba,**	" to fly."

In the following instances, different verbs have been assigned by usage to a singular or plural acceptation :—

arapa,	**paye,**	" to go."
ek,	**ariki** (or **araki**),	" to come."

Probably further search would reveal the existence of more such plural forms.[1] Indeed, the Saghalien dialect, if we are to trust Dobrotvorsky as quoted in Pfizmaier's "*Erörterungen und Aufklärungen über Aino*," retains fragments of a plural formation in a few of its substantives as well. Thus *kema*, "foot;" *kemaki*, "feet;" *ima*, "tooth;" *imaki* "teeth." Be this as it may, not only has Japanese no plural forms, whether inflectional or agglutinative, but the whole idea of grammatical number is as foreign to it as is that of person.

Thus far we have noted phenomena that occur in Ainu, and are absent from Japanese. We now turn to such as are found in Japanese, but not in Ainu, and observe that:—

(9) Japanese conjugates its verbs by means of agglutinated suffixes, which in certain moods and tenses, combine so intimately with the root as to be indistinguishable from what are termed inflections in the Aryan tongues. Thus, from the root *ot* and the stem *otos*, "to drop," we have such conjugational forms as *otosu* the present, *otose* the imperative, *otoshi* the "indefinite form" (a sort of gerund or participle), where no analysis has hitherto succeeded in discovering the origin of the final vowels. In Ainu there is nothing of this kind. Save in the rare cases mentioned under heading 8, the whole conjugation is managed by auxiliaries. The original verb never varies, excepting when *r* changes to *n* according to a general phonetic rule which affects all classes of words indiscriminately.

(10) A grammatical device, on which much of Japanese construction hinges, is the three-fold division (in the classical form of the language there is a fourth) of verbal adjective forms into what are termed "attributive," "conclusive," and "indefinite."

---

[1] Mr. Batchelor adds to the list sing. *raige*, plur. *ronnu*, "to kill." But the present writer ventures to think that the difference is rather one of signification than of mere number, *raige* meaning "to kill," and *ronnu* "massacre."

[To this I must reply that I still have no reason to doubt that *ronnu* is really what I have represented it to be. To "massacre" would be *ushtekka*. Anyhow, to be understood both the Ainu and I are obliged to use *ronnu* as if it were the plural of *raige*; I know of no other word to take its place.]

This system, which is peculiar and complicated, cannot well be elucidated without entering into details beyond the scope of the present Memoir. The curious in such matters are referred to pp. 39, 47, 86, and 94 of the present writer's "Simplified Grammar of Japanese" (Trübner & Co., London, 1886). Suffice it here to say, that each tense of the indicative mood of Japanese verbs and adjectives is inflected so as to point out the nature of its grammatical agreement with the other words of the sentence, and that one of the results of the system is the formation of immensely long, sentences, all the clauses of which are mutually interdependent, in such wise that the bearing of any one verb or adjective as to tense and mood is not clinched until the final verb has come to round off the entire period. Of such distinctions of "attributive," "conclusive," etc., forms, Ainu knows nothing. They are not represented even by the help of auxiliaries.

(11) The whole Japanese language, ancient and modern, written and colloquial, is saturated with the honorific spirit. In Japanese, honorifics supply to some extent the place of personal pronouns and of verbal inflections indicating person. Ainu, on the contrary, has no honorifics unless we give that name to such ordinary expressions of politeness as occur in every language.

(12) A rule of Japanese phonetics excludes the consonant r from the beginning of words.[1] In Ainu no similar rule exists. Those who have most occupied themselves with the Japanese language, will probably be the readiest to regard the aversion to initial r as being, not the result of accident (if such an expression may be allowed), but truly a radical characteristic; for it is shared, not only by Korean, but by other apparently cognate tongues as far as India.

---

[1] Those whose knowledge of Japanese is limited may be startled by this statement, taken in conjunction with the appearance of hundreds of words beginning with r in the pages of Dr. Hepburn's Dictionary. The explanation of the apparent contradiction is, that all such words are borrowed from the Chinese. In the latter language, the initial is l. But a very soft r is the nearest approach to l of which the Japanese vocal organs are capable. This Chinese li becomes Japanese ri, Chinese liang becomes Japanese ryō, etc.

(13) Japanese constantly use what (to adopt European terminology) may be called genitives instead of nominatives. Thus, *Hito ga kuru*, literally "The coming of the man," for "The man comes." This is foreign to Ainu habits of speech.

Passing on to further points of contrast between the two languages, we notice that :—

(14) Japanese and Ainu treat the idea of negation differently. Ainu uses an independent negative adverb. *shomo* or *seenne*, which corresponds exactly to the English word "not." It also possesses a few curious negative verbs, such as *isam*, "not to be ;" *uwa*, "not to know." In Japanese, on the contrary, the idea of negation is invariably expressed by conjugational forms. Each verb and adjective has a negative "voice," which goes through all the moods and tenses, just as Latin and Greek verbs have an inflected passive voice.

(15) The system of counting in the two languages is radically dissimilar. In discussing this point, we must of course set aside the Chinese system now current in Japan, and which, owing to its superior simplicity, is beginning to make its way even into Ainu-land. The original Japanese system of counting consisted of independent words as far as the number ten. After ten, they said ten plus one, ten plus two, ten plus three, twenty plus one, thirty plus one, and so on up to hundreds, thousands, and myriads. In fact, the old Japanese numeration was not very unlike our own. The complicated nature of the Ainu method of counting will only be properly appreciated by those who will very carefully peruse Mr. Batchelor's chapter on the subject. The salient points in it are the invariable prefixing of the smaller number to the larger, the mixture of a denary and a vigesimal system, the existence of a unit corresponding to our "score," and the absence of any unit higher than the score. The idea of such units as "hundred" and "thousand" is foreign to the Ainu mind. They can say "five score" (100), and "ten taken away from six score" (110). But much higher than that, they cannot easily ascend. To take a concrete instance, if a man wishes to say that he is twenty-three years of age, he must express himself

thus :—" I am seven years plus ten years, from two score years
(!)." Not only is the method of combining different numerals
totally unlike in the two languages. The manner in which the
elemenatry numerals up to " ten " were originally formed, is also
quite dissimilar. In Japanese, as in some other languages of the
North-east of Asia, the even numerals seem to have been obtained
by altering the vowel of the odd numerals of which they are the
doubles ; thus :—

hito,[1]	" one ";	it(s)u,	" five ";
futa,	" two ";	mu,	" six ";
mi,	" three ";	ya,	" eight ";
yo	" four ";	to,	" ten."

In Ainu, on the other hand, the first four numerals *shine* (1), *tu*
(2), *re* (3), *ine* (4) seem independent. *Ashikne* (5) is possibly " new
four " (*ashiri*[2] *ine*). The next four numerals are obtained by a
process of subtraction from the higher number " ten " Compare :—

    ine, " four," with **iwan,** " six " (i.e. four from ten),

    re, " three," with **arawan,** " seven " (i.e. three from ten),

    tu, " two," with **tupesan,** " eight " (i.e. two from ten),

    shine, " one," with **shinepesan,** " nine " (i.e. one from ten),

    wan, " ten."

There might be room for doubt as to the derivation of *iwan*,
" six," and *arawan*, " seven," did they stand alone. Indeed,
doubt is still permissible on their score. But *tupesan* is un-
questionably " two (*tu*) things (*pe*) come down (*san*) [from ten] ";
and *shinepesan* is as evidently " one thing come down [from ten]."

---

§ III. WORD BUILDING.

Besides the dissimilarities in Grammar as set forth in the
preceding paragraph, there are also other important differences

---

[1] *Hito* and *futa* probably stand for earlier *pito* and *puta*, where the correspondence is more apparent.

[2] The author of the present work cannot agree to this, for there is no other
case know where *k* changes into *ri* or *vice versa*.

existing between the two languages which Prof. Chamberlain has not noted in his essay. What he has given, however, are fully sufficient to prove that the present Japanese tongue has no grammatical connection with Ainu. This fact may be fully and very interestingly emphasized by considering the manner in which the Ainu build up their words, illustrations of which it is now proposed to give.

(1) *Aeiyukoikireyara.* This word means " he sent him to set them at variance with each other over something." The following is a chemical analysis of the word :—

ki, root meaning " do."

i, an intensifying root meaning " severely ;" " intently."

iki, " to do intently " or " severely."

ko, a root meaning " to " when used before some verbs.

koiki, " to scold ;" " to beat ;" " do severely to."

u, root meaning " together " or " union " or " mutually."

ukoiki, " to quarrel with each other."

re, used as a suffix to verb expresses " cause."

a, a root expressive of the past tense.

ukoikire, " to make quarrel."

i, expressive of 3rd personal pronoun " he."

aiyukoikire, " make them quarrel with each other."

The *y* is added after the *i* for the sake of euphony only.

e, expressive of the objective case.

aeiyukoikire, " he made them quarrel with each other over something."

yara, " to do through another ;" " to send to do."

aeiyukoikireyara, " he sent and set them at variance with each other over something."

(2) Take now the word *i(y)eyaikoemakbare* " to forsake," " to backslide." It may be analized thus :—

i, 3rd, per. pro. nom. " they."

e, (euphonically *ye*), 2nd, per. pro. obj. " him."

yai, reflex. prop. " self " (from the root *a,* " to exist ").

ko, root meaning " to ;" " with regard to."

e, objective of the verb, " it."

mak, root of *maka* " open."

ba, a plural personal root to verbs (as *cha* a plural ending to some nouns).

re, a causitive ending to verbs.   Hence, *eyaikoemàkbare*, " to forsake " (lit. " they made him cast himself away (from) with reference to it "). E. g. *Koro shinrit ekashi ki buri gusu eiyaikoemakbare nisa ruwa ne,* " they made him forsake the customs of the ancients." It would perhaps be super-fluous to remark that the chief root of this long word is simply *mak,* " open," the transitive of which is *emaka,* " to open."   *λ ꙗꙗꙗ*

Thus do many roots cluster round the little verbs *ki,* " to do ;" and *mak,* " open." Every root always retains one or other of its meanings though of course modified in each as the subject and object require. This kind of—I was going to say *vivisection,* but substitute *postmortem* examination instead proves, I think, that the Ainu language has grown from a monosyllabic to an agglutinative or combinatory one ; and shows that it has not only been highly developed in years long past, but that it was also capable of greater developement had the race survived, come into the arena of civilization, and cultivated it. Indeed, such words as the above show how the Ainu language has passed from the " Rhematic " into the " Dialectic " stage of developement.

In the above examples verbs only have been given ; let us now take an adjective and adverb as further illustrations of this matter.

Thus :—

(a) **Pirika,** " good."
    Pirikap, " a good thing."
    Pirika-hi, " goodness."
    Pirikare, " to better."
    Epirika, " to gain."
    Epirikap, " something gained."
    Epirikare, " to make another gain."

Yaiepirika, " to gain of oneself."

Yaiepirikare, " to make oneself gain."

Eyaiepirikare, " to make one gain something for himself."

Eyaiepirikarep, " that which one causes himself to gain for himself."

(b) **Ioyapa,** " the year after next."

I, an intensifying particle both as regards place, time, and state.

Oya, " other " " next ;" " different."

Pa, " year ;" " season."

Hence, *ioyapa,* " the year after next."

The word *ioyashimge* belongs to the same class.

Thus:

Ioya, as given above.

Oyashim, " the day after to-morrow."

Oyashimshimge, " the morrow following the day after to-morrow."

Ioyashimge, " the third day after to-morrow."

The word *oyaketa,* " elsewhere," is also of peculiar interest when dissected. Thus:—**O,** a separating particle whose root meaning is " off "; " from "; **(y)a, a,** " to be," the verb of existence, the *y* being merely euphonius ; **ke,** a particle meaning " place "; and **ta,** " at " a " in." Hence, *o-ya-ke-ta,* " at another place "—i.e. " elsewhere."

But even nouns of apparently two syllables only may in some instances be shown to be derived, through the process of agglutinization, from three roots. Nay, a one syllable word is sometimes seen to be derived from two several roots. Thus:—

(a) **Amip,** " clothing." This is compounded from *a,* passive particle " is "; *mi,* " to wear "; and *pe,* " an article." Hence, *amip,* " articles worn "; " clothing." Another way of saying the same word is *mi-am-be,* " clothing."

(b) **Pet,** " a river." One would naturally suppose this to be a simple word, yet careful consideration shows it to be a compound. Thus:—*Pe,* " water "; *t,* a contraction of *chi* a plural suffix in common use. Hence, *pet,* "waters," i.e. a "stream" or "river." *Pe-chi* is often heard when reciting traditions or singing songs.

But perhaps one of the most interesting methods of building up words and one which may not for a moment be ignored or overlooked by the student of this language is exemplified in the following examples. But first let it be understood that *He* has the sense of "facing"; "fore"; "looking inwards"; "tending towards one"; "in front." *Ho* has the opposite meaning of "off"; "away from"; "behind"; "back." *Shi* has a reflexive and intransitive force and perhaps represents the infinitive mood. With these words as keys we will take the three following compounds as illustrations.

(1) **Maka,** *v.t.* To open ; to clear away.

Shimaka, *v.i.* To have cleared away of itself.

Hemaka, *v.i. & adj.* To turn from but with the face looking upwards and forward.

Homaka, *v.i. & adj.* To clear off ; to go away entirely and leave an open space.

(2) **Noye,** *v.t.* To wind ; to twist.

Shinoye, *v.i.* To twist by its own power.

Henoye, *v.i. & adj.* To be twisted ; wound up.

Honoye, *v.i. & adj.* Twisted back out of place.

(3) **Pirasa,** *v.t.* To spread out.

Shipirasa, *v.i.* To spread out of itself.

Hepirasa, *v.i. & adj.* To open up as a flower from the bud.

Hopirasa, *v.i. & adj.* To fall apart as one's coat or dress as when blown by the wind.

Such words as these show great developement of speech and the nicities shown in them will be duly appreciated by any lover of philological research.

§ IV. ROOT AFFINITIES BETWEEN ANCIENT JAPANESE AND AINU.

But although, as has thus been pointed out, the Ainu language differs so much in point of grammatical structure from present Japanese, is there not, it may be inquired, some resemblence to be observed when, placing the accident of grammar on one side, ancient unexplained Japanese words are collated, examined, and compared with Ainu? The answer to this question must, in quite a number of cases, be in the affirmative, for there is certainly a root affinity in some of these relics, instances of which will be given later on.

As regards Japanese, in the year 1868 Mr. Edward Harper Parker of China wrote a paper on the relationship of Chinese with ancient Japanese, the object of which was to show " before Chinese was imported into Japanese, (1) directly, and (2) indirectly, through Corea—say before A. D. 1—the Japanese spoke a language the great majority of words in which came from the same language-stock as Chinese."[1] And from anything appearing to the contrary he seems to have pretty well established his point. We must, however, presume to take off a few years from his estimate, for the oldest written books of Japan can carry us back no nearer to the source of time than the year 712 A. D., it being in this year that the *Kojiki* was committed to writing, the *Nikongi* following a few years later. Even linguistically speaking all before this time is pure oral tradition, and the only safe guides in such a matter as this are the written books.

That Chinese and therefore present Japanese are Turanian is, I believe, now admitted. In speaking of Chinese Prof. Max Muller says:[2]—"Taking Chinese for what it can hardly any longer be doubted that it is, viz. the earliest representative of Turanian speech," etc. And again:[3]—"People wonder why

[1] Transactions of the Asiatic Society of Japan, vol. xv., page 13 *et seq.*
[2] Introduction to the Science of Religion, page 155.
[3] Ibid., page 160.

students of language have not succeeded in establishing more than three families of speech—or rather two, for the Turanian can hardly be called a family, in the strict sense of that word, till it has been fully proved that Chinese forms the centre of the two Turanian branches, the North Turanian on one side, and the South Turanian on the other ; that Chinese forms, in fact, the earliest settlement of that unsettled mass of speech, which, at a later stage, became more fixed and traditional,—In the north, in *Tungusic, Mongolic, Tartaric,* and *Finnic,* and in the south, in *Taic, Malaic, Bhotiya,* and *Talmulic.*" And yet again, amid much more to the same effect our Author adds :[1]— " In the Turanian class, in which the original concentration was never so powerful as in the Aryan and Semitic families, we can still catch a glimpse of the natural growth of language, though confined within certain limits. The different settlements of this great floating mass of homogeneous speech do not show such definite marks of relationship as Hebrew and Arabic, Greek and Sanskrit, but only such sporadic coincidences and general structual similarities as can be explained by the admission of a primitive concentration, followed by a new period of independant growth. It would be wilful blindness not to recognise the definite and characteristic features which pervade the North Turanian languages: it would be impossible to explain the coincidences between Hungarian, Lapponian, Esthonian, and Finnish, except on the supposition that there was a very early concentration of speech from which these dialects branched off. We see less clearly in the Turanian group, though I confess my surprise even here has always been, not that there should be so few, but that there should be even these relics, attesting a former community of these divergent streams of language. The point in which the South Turanian and North Turanian languages meet goes back as far as Chinese ; for that Chinese is at the root of Mandshu and Mongolian as well as of Siamese and Tibetan becomes daily more apparent through the researches of Mr. Edkins and other Chinese scholars."

---

[1] Introduction to the Science of Religion, page 162.

But although the Japanese words advanced by Mr. Parker may be from the same language-stock as Chinese, yet no proof has been forthcoming to show that those ancient Japanese words, words which are now quite obsolete so far as the Japanese tongue is concerned, and which are from the same roots as Ainu, are of Chinese origin. Therefore although Chinese and that large and ever increasing proportion of Japanese which has been and is being confessedly borrowed from China may belong to the Turanian branch of language classification, this in no way proves Ainu to be so.   Proofs of this must, it would seem, come from elsewhere if they are to come at all.

But to compare ancient Japanese and Ainu.   It would indeed be very extraordinary were we not to find "sporadic coincidences" of resemblance between these two tongues seeing that one race has now almost displaced the other. . For just as it is known that present day English is made up of fragments of ancient British, so it is only natural to expect to find Japanese, whatever its origin may be, containing fragments of Ainu,—the undoubted aboriginal language of this land.   I will preface my list by reminding the Reader that all works—whether Japanese or Foreign, and dating from A.D. 1730[1] down to the time of writing—which have any Ainu words and phrases in them clearly show that the Ainu tongue has suffered—or rather had suffered till within the last 30 or 40 years—little or no radical change since those books were published.   It should also be remembered that many old Japanese place-names in various parts of Japan prove to be, when stripped of the misleading Chinese characters in which they are written, living, present day, matter of fact, Ainu words.   A list of place-names with their derivations and meanings will be found in a Brochure given later.

The following is a short list of old Japanese[2] and Ainu words carrying the same radical elements in them.

---

[1] Der Word-und Destliche Theil von Europa und Asia by Philipp Johann von Strachlenberg, Stockholm.

[2] The authorities for the ancient and obsolete Japanese words are "List of Ancient Japanese words by Chamberlain and Ueda ; Transactions of the Asiatic Society of Japan. Vol. XVI. Part. III.   Also Hepburn's and other Japanese-English Dictionaries.

JAPANESE.	AINU.
A, " I."	**A**, " I." Also the verb of existence ; " is "; " am."
A, " a net."	**ya**, " a net."
A, " a foot."	**A**, " a tine "; " prong of a fork."
Abai, " a shield."	**Apa-kikkara**, " to defend."
Abame, " to despise."	**Apange**, " to despise." The root of this word is *pan*, " insipid."
Ae-mono, " food eaten with rice."	**Ae-p**, " food." The roots are, *e* " to eat," *a*, a passive particle, *p*, " thing." Hence *a-e-p*, food. *P* is the equivalent of *mono*.
Aka, " the holy water of the Buddhists."	**Aka and Wakka**, ordinary " drinking water."

Speaking of water reminds the author that Chief Penri of Piratori once desired to claim relationship because Eng., " water " and Ainu *wakka* were so much alike. But when informed that ship was *chip*, " bone," *pone*, " two," *tu*, and " three," *re*, he was quite certain we were brothers. With regard to the use of *aka* for " water," however, it should be remarked that in Saghalien the Ainu usually employ the word *pe*, and *aka* is nearly obsolete. Still, that the word is of very ancient use among the Ainu on the Siberian continent is proved by Dobrotvorsky who gives the word *akasannai* as the name of " rivulet " there. He does not, however, venture to show the derivation of the name. Yet in plain, matter of fact, present day Ainu, *aka-san-nai* is simply " the valley with water running down it." It corresponds to *Waka-sa* of the South of Japan and *Wakka-o-nai* of Yezo.

JAPANESE.	AINU.
Azuki, " a kind of small red bean."	**Antuki**, a kind of small red bean." The root seems to be *tuk*, " to sprout." Hence it would mean " the sprouter."
Beko, " ox "; " cow."	**Beko or Peko**. *Bek* is the Ainu onomatopœa for the " lowing " of oxen.

JAPANESE.	AINU.
	O means to " hold "; " to carry." The Ainu verb " to low " is *Bek-se, se* by itself meaning " to make a noise."
Bachi, " punishment sent by heaven."	**Pa,** pachi, pashiko, " punishment inflicted by gods or demons."

The Ainu word *pa,* " punishment " is particularly interesting when taken in connection with Latin *poena* and *punis* and this again with the Sanscrit *pu*[1] and *pa.* The analogy becomes more striking and complete when it is remembered that the Ainu word *pa* means " sin " as well as " punishment." It also occurs in the word *katpak,* " sins," but *lit :* " heart punishment."

JAPANESE.	AINU.
Neko, " cat."	**Meko,** " cat." *Mek* is the onomatopœa for the " mew " of a cat, as *bek* is for the " low " of oxen. As *bekse* is " to low," so *mekse* is " to mew."
Ikashi, " prosperous "; " to be in plenty."	**Ikashima,** " over "; " plus "; " too much"; " superabundant." From *i,* an intensifying root, and *kashi* whose root is *ka,* " over "; " top." The same root will be found in the word *kamui,* " god."
Inori, " prayer."	**Inonno,** " prayer." *Inonno-itak,* "to pray."
Inoti, " life."	**Inotu,** " life." From the root *isu* or *ishu,* " to live," " living."
Ipi, " food."	**Ep,** " food "; ibe, " to eat." The roots are *e,* " eat "; and *pe,* article, " thing."
Iro, " colour."	**Iroho,** " colour."
Iso, " the sea-shore."	**Iso,** " a rock off the sea-coast." Note

---

[1] Compare Chips from a German workshop Vol. II. page 254.

JAPANESE.

AINU.

also *so*, a " bare rock," a " boulder,"
a " waterfall."

Kamu, " god."

Kamui, " god." The root of this
word is *ka*, " over "; " above,"
" top." It is like *super* and ὑπέρ.
Ka occurs in *kando*, " heaven ";
" the skies " and in many words
where the sense of *super* is to be conveyed. *Kamu* means " to cover,"
in Ainu and to " over-shadow."
The final *i* is a substantivizing
particle implying " person " or
" thing," " he," " she," or " it."
Here, according to the genius of the
language and the psychological conception of Ainu theological thought
kamui means " he who covers " or
" he who over-shadows "; thus reminding as of Jupiter and Οὐρανος.[1]

Iwa, " a rock."

Iwa, " land as opposed to rivers and
lakes."

Iwai, " a festive celebration.

Iwai, " a festive celebration of any
kind."

Kasa, " a hat."

Kasa, " a hat." *Kasa-tupep,* " hat
strings."

Keire, " shoes." This word
is still used in the Nam-
bu District by Japanese.

Keire, " shoes and sandles whether
made of skin or bark." This word
is said by the Ainu to be Ainu,
and by the Japanese, Japanese.

Kura,
Kuro, } " black"; dark."
Kuru,

Kunne,
Kurokok, } " black "; " dark." *Kuru,*
Ekureok, } " a cloud."

Makiri, " a knife." This word is much used in the Nambu

---

[1] Cpf. Chips from a German workshop Vol. II. page 65.

Province. But the Ainu have no other word for "knife" of the kind intended. It is the common word for knife in Saghalien Island.

JAPANESE.	AINU.
Nobori, "a hill."	**Nupuri,** "a mountain." There is no other word in Ainu by which a great mountain can be designated. The roots of this word are *nup*, "plain," *u*, a plural particle, and *ri*, "high." *Nupuri* may therefore mean either, "cast up from the plains"; or "cast up plains."
Nomi, "to worship."	**Nomi,** "to offer libations."
Nu, "to be."	**Ne,** "is."
Nuru, "to paint."	**Nore,** "to paint."
Nusa, anciently, "pieces of silk or paper or bamboo used as offering to the gods."	**Nusa,** "offerings of whittled sticks and shavings made to the gods and demons." *Nusa* is a plural word the singular of which is *inao*. *Inao* is from the root *ina*, "a message," "a prayer"; and *o*, "to bear." Hence *inao* is simply a "message" or "request "bearer," *nusa* being its plural form.[1]
Ogi, "a fan."	**Anki; Anunki; Aungi,** "a fan." Translated literally *an-un-ki*, means "to do unto," probably referring to the process of drawing the fan to ones'self. Both forms of the word are used in both Yezo and Saghalien.
Omushi, "the place where the Emperor sits."	**Om-ushi,**[2] "a seat." The roots are *om*, the "thighs," and *ushi*, "a putting place."

[1] See the Ainu and their Folklore Cpts. IX.-XII.
[2] Compare also **momo** *Jap.* "thighs."

JAPANESE.	AINU.
Pa, " thing "; " an article."	Pe or Be, " thing " " an article."
Pakaru, " to weigh."	Pakari, " to weigh."
Parara, " to scatter."	Parara, " to makè another scatter "; *Parase, v.i.* " to scatter." The root is *para*, " broad "; " spread out."
Pasi, " chop-sticks."	Pasui or Pashui, " tongs." There are grounds for believing that the *u* is of a dual or plural signification.
Pasu, " to run."	Pash, *v.i.* " to run."
Sa, Sane,} " true."	So, Son, Sone,} " true."
Saru, " a monkey."	Saro, " a monkey." From *sara*, " a tail "; and *o*, " to bear "; hence *Saro* means " having a tail " in Ainu. Compare also *beko* and *meko*.
Sippo, " salt."	Shippo, " salt."
So-shi, " a sheet of paper."	So-shi, " a layer of bark," strata of rock or earth.
Tama, " the soul."	Rama, *ramat*, and *ramachi*, the soul. This word finds its root in *ram, ramu*, " the heart "; " the understanding " of a being.
U, " a cormorant."	U-riri, " a cormorant."
Uku, " to receive."	Uk, (*sing*), uina (*pl*), to take; to receive.
Wappa, " a boy "; (used in scolding).	Wappo, " a young child," " boy " or " girl."
Warabe, " a child," either " boy or girl."	Warapo, " a child," either " boy " or " or girl."

An analysis of words, such as those above given, (and others might be produced were it necessary), go to prove a very close connection between some parts of ancient Japanese and present Ainu speech. No doubt the two races are quite distinct in so far as physical aspect is concerned, allowing of course for that admixture which has been going on from time immemorial through marriage and concubinage. The Ainu have never indeed regarded the Japanese as of the same stock as themselves. Indeed, they know them as *Samorun-guru*, i.e. "Siamese" only. With how much truth, who will now tell us? It is also interesting to remark in this connection that the Ainu distinguish themselves from the Mongolian and Malay type of the human race by calling the latter *Oyashikpuikotcha utara*, "persons having a different class of eye-socket." In speaking of men of their own race and cast of feature they say *Shineshikpuikotcha utara*, "people of the same eye-socket." And just as the ancient Hebrew would say, "thou art *bone* of my *bone*," and the Arab "thou art *eye* of my *eye*" when they wanted to say "you are the *same* as I am," so an Ainu says to-day "you are of the same *eye-socket* as I," when he desires to say, "you and I are of the *same family*" or "descent."

But does the close resemblance between some of the words found in ancient Japanese and Ainu vocabulary tend to unify or in any way prove the two races to have been originally one? The reply is "yes" and "no." In the sense now generally meant by races being *one*, the verdict must, I think, be "no," certainly. If, however, we go back far enough,—if, for example, we travel back to the time of the confusion of tongues,—to the time when people were fewer and the continents as now found not existing—we may reply, "yes." Let us take an example by way of illustrating what is here meant. Ford, in his Handbook for travellers in Spain, tells us that there is a decided element of Sanscrit in Basque, but Max Müller says that Basque is not an Aryan language. So also, then, the few words advanced above, though originally of a common stock language, prove very little as to Ainu and pure Japanese being one as a whole. But there is this to be remembered, Japanese as now known is of Turanian descent, i.e. taking Chinese as the centre of the Turanian stock of language. But the old Japanese words given above as related to Ainu, have not yet been proved to be connected with Chinese whatever their common origin may have been. By means of Chinese therefore, in so far as those examples are concerned, old Japanese and present Ainu are not proven to be Turanian though they are of a common stock.

§ V. PLACE NAMES CONSIDERED.

It has been thought by many that there was a race of men inhabiting, not only Yezo but also Japan Proper, before the Ainu came ; and that just as the Japanese have displaced the Ainu, so the Ainu drove out and succeeded the race preceding themselves. This was a theory I myself formerly accepted—but wholly upon trust like so many others. Laterly, however, I have paid special attention to this subject the result being a little *brochure* entitled **The Koropok-guru** or **Pit-dwellers of North Japan,** a rivision of which I now proceed to append, by way of preface to the Names of Places.

That the Ainu have left remnants of their language in Place names here and there all over Japan goes without saying, for, from the analogies of other lands we are fully prepared to expect such to be the case. Moreover, if any doubts have ever existed on the matter they have now been for ever set to rest by the writings of such men as Prof. Chamberlain ; Mr. Nagata Hōsei and others. In this revision I have written in some names of Japan Proper and also of the Islands north of Yezo so as to extend the range of view. My Brochure was divided into two parts as follows :—*Part I. The Koropok-guru or Pit-dwellers of North Japan ; and Part II. A critical examination of the Nomenclature of Yezo.*

PART I.
THE KOROPOK-GURU OR PIT-DWELLERS OF NORTH JAPAN.

In the " Memoirs of the Literature College, Imperial University of Japan, No. 1." which treats of the " language, mythology,

and geographical nomenclature of Japan viewed in the light of
Ainu studies," including also " An Ainu Grammar " by myself,
Professor Basil Hall Chamberlain wrote on page 57, at the close
of his list of place-names, as follows :—

" The above catalogue may teach several things. First we
learn from it the method followed by the Ainus in their geographical nomenclature, which is simple enough. They describe
the river, village, or cape, as the case may be, by some striking
feature. . . . . Secondly, there is a large number of names
not to be explained in the *present state* of our knowledge. Some
of them have perhaps been corrupted beyond recognition. Some
are possibly pure but antiquated Ainu, no longer understood in
the absence of any literary tradition. *Why should not some have
descended from the aborigines who preceded the Ainus, the latter
adopting them as the Japanese have adopted Ainu names ?* "
(the italics are mine).

Early in March (1904) I had the pleasure of escorting Professor Frederick Starr, of the Chicago University, to some of
the Ainu villages, and while on the journey I found him to be
particularly interested in place names and was on more than
one occasion much struck by the many questions he put with
regard to them, but when he began to speak of the supposed
connection of some of them with the race of men spoken of in
the sentence I have italicised above as the *aborigines who preceded
the Ainus,* I at once saw the drift of his questions. It was after
one of our conversations on these matters that he pointed out
to me Prof. Chamberlain's words :—words which I had not
previously taken into any serious account. The result is the
present brochure.

Now, I must remark at the outset that I am one of those who
has quite abandoned the idea of a race of men existing in Yezo
anterior to the Ainu. I frankly admit that I formerly acquiesced
in the ordinary belief in the existence of such a people in the
ages gone by. The assertions of those who were here many years
before me ; the assurances given me by the Japanese ; the so-called
tradition of the Ainu respecting them, and the remains of pits

in which they are said to have lived, together with the exhibition of certain remnants of old pottery and such like things were too sure and certain proofs to be laid quietly aside by a new comer; and then lastly there were certain difficult place names whose meaning could not at that time be ascertained. In fact, like the famous missing link your aborigine could almost be seen and touched. But none of these foundations of orthodox belief will bear the light, and I have therefore, as in duty bound, abandoned them.

But to examine the matter briefly yet as thoroughly as space will allow. And *first* as regards the pits. They are here in Yezo in great numbers, so that one is constantly coming across them. The Ainu call them *Koropok-un-guru koro chisei kot*, i.e. "sites belonging to people who dwelt below ground," and this equals "Pit-dwellers." Another name they call them by is *Toi chisei kotcha utara kot chisei kot*, i.e., "house sites of people who had earth houses." Thus then we have the "Pit-dwellers" for certain. But who were they who dwelt in the pits? To come down to living present day examples of them we have them on the island of Shikotan. These people have two kinds of houses, one built on the Japanese model and the other on the pit model. The pits are only for winter use while the Japanese houses are used during the summer. These Ainu were brought down from an island in the Kurile group called Shimushir in the year 1885 by the Japanese Government, and they declare that their forefathers originally came from Saghalien. They were Greek Church Christians. There are also some Ainu at present inhabiting Saghalien who live in the same kind of pits during the cold weather. Hence we find that the Ainu are, some of them at least, actual "Pit-dwellers" to-day. I myself am a "Wood-house dweller," for my house is made of wood; my brother in Africa is a "Stone house dweller;" his house being built of that material; another brother used to be a real "Cave dweller" for he, being a Royal Engineer, lived for some time in the Rock of Gibraltar; our mother must be a sort of mongrel for she is living in a house made of brick, wood, and plaster after the Queen Elizabeth style : but for all that we are English to the backbone every ohe of us !

Another very interesting thing connected with these pit-dwellings is the fact that the Ainu have three native names for " roof," two of which seem to imply by derivation that they rested on the ground over holes. The ordinary word now used is *chisei-kitai* and this just means " house-top " and calls for no special remark. But the other two words are *arikari-chisei* and *chirikari-chisei*, both of which mean " the shell over-head " or " the shell set on high " " high " being in contradistinction to " below "; " the place underneath." *A* and *chi* are both *intransitive* and *adjectival* particles, *rik* is " above " as opposed to " below " ; *ari* is a verb meaning " set " or " placed," while *chisei* really means " shell " or " outer covering."

Referring again to the Ainu of the Kurile group, I was very much struck a short time since by reading what Mr. Romyn Hitchcock has said in his Paper entitled " The Ainu of Yezo, Japan," which will be found in the Report of the National Museum for 1890—Smithsonian Institution, pages 429–502. On page 432 will be found this most astonishing remark : " The so called Kurile Ainu are wrongly named. This name is given to the pit-dwellers of Shikotan, who are quite distinct from the Ainu." Well, I have myself spoken with Shikotan Ainu but the language was Ainu and Japanese and nothing else, unless it were perhaps a word or two of Russian thrown in. Moreover, I have this day (March 28th, 1904) been into the Government offices at Sapporo and reinvestigated the whole matter. The results are : *1st* a reaffirmation of the fact that the Kurile islands were ceeded to Japan by Russia in exchange for Saghalien in the 8th year of Meiji ; *2nd* that in the 17th and 18th years of Meiji the pit-dwellers of Shikotan were brought by the Japanese Authorities from the island of Shimushir in the Kurile group and settled there ; *3rd* that these pit-dwellers were Ainu and spoke the Ainu language ; and *4thly* that those who are left of them still have dwelling-pits for winter use. Mr. Hitchcock's remark must therefore be dismissed as misleading because inexact.

Prof. Milne tells us that[1] in the year 1878 he visited some of these Ainu on this very Island of Shimushir, the total number of whom was only 22. "The men," he says, "were short in stature, had roundish heads, and short thick beards. None of those I saw had the long beard which characterizes many of the Ainus in Southern Yezo, nor were their features so well defined. They call themselves Kurilsky Ainu, spoke a language of their an, and also Russian." The Prof. did not know Ainu, so that when he speaks of these Ainu as speaking a language of their own I am sure from what I have heard them speak and from what I have gathered elsewhere, that their language was an Ainu dialect.

Captain Snow, a gentleman of large experience among these Islands and their inhabitants told Prof. Milne that during the winter of 1879 and 1880 some of this tribe were living on *Matua*. Later they were in *Rashua* and *Ushishiri*. He also informed Prof. Milne that the oldest man among them said that he came from Saghalien. This is just what these Ainu told me ; viz., that originally they came from Saghalien. And, what is also very much to the point here, Prof. Milne adds :—" they construct houses by making shallow excavations in the ground, which are then roofed over with turf, and that these excavations have a striking resemblance to the pits which we find farther south. This custom of making a dwelling-place out af an excavation in the ground belongs, I believe, to certain of the inhabitants of Kamschatka and Saghalien."

The existence of such "pits" or "excavations" in Yezo was first brought to the notice of Europe by Captain T. Blakiston in an account of a journey round Yezo, given by him to the Royal Geographical Society of Great Britain, (July 27th, 1872).

Secondly, there is the question of the ancient Japanese name *Tsuchi-gumo*, "Earth-spiders," and *Ko-bito*, "Little people," applied to these pit-dwellers. And besides, the Ainu themselves sometimes talk about the "little men." But nothing of value

---

[1] Transactions of the Asiatic Society of Japan, vol. x, Part I., pages 190-1.

can be made out of the appellation "Earth-spiders," for it implies
no more than what is meant by "pit-dwellers." *Ko-bito* really
means "little people," "dwarfs"; but the Ainu, when speaking
of these so-called "dwarfs" use the word *Ko-bito*, which is pure
Japanese. I have never heard a real native Ainu name meaning
"dwarfs" applied to them. In fact, I am of opinion that they
have none. Were it not for the Japanese words *Tsuchi-gumo*
and *Ko-bito* I find no grounds for supposing that the Ainu
would speak of a race of dwarfs at all. But foregone conclusions
are always hard to kill, so that it will be asked again, "but
were there not the *Koropok-guru* here and does not that mean
the people of the Petasites[1] plant?" Well; *no it does not.*
Koropok cannot mean Petasites: it can only be translated by
"under," "beneath," "below." The full name is *Koropok-un-
guru*, "persons dwelling below," the *un* being a locative particle.
And this it will be seen does not carry the idea of "Dwarfs"
in it at all. But allowing for the sake of argument that *Koropok-
guru* did mean "people under the Petasites" even that would
not dwarf them in the least. I myself stand nearly 5 ft. 8 and
have scores of times not only walked but also ridden on pony
back among the leaf-stalks of the Petasites without touching the
blades. I wonder how big the ancient Japanese and Ainu must
have been! For if because the ancient pit-dwellers could move
among the stalks of the Petasites without touching their over-
shadowing tops they were called "Dwarfs," those who for this
reason first applied this name to them must have been very
Goliaths in stature!

Nor can anything be said for the *third* argument, viz., that
resting on old kitchen middens and flint implements. For (*a*)
when one meets with children—Ainu children—playing at making
pottery out of soft clay and ornamenting their handiwork with

---

[1] I have hitherto called this plant "Burdock." Prof. Miyabe has kindly
shown me it should be *Petasites japonicus, Miq.* Hence I take this opportunity
of correcting my error. I also tender my best thanks to Prof. Miyabe for kindly
reading the proofs and correcting all the botanical names which appear to this
brochure.

patterns found on the samples dug up from the earth instead of
with ordinary Japanese figures, (which ornamentation was done
by means of grass and sticks); and (*b*) when one is emphatically
told by the Ainu that their ancestors used to make pottery and
use flint implements; and when (*c*) we moreover hear in old
Ainu songs and traditions of Ainu stone armour and stone-headed
spears and arrows, all faith in these things as proofs of a race
here anterior to the Ainu finds no place in the mind.

Again, it was shown above that the Shikotan pit-dwellers are
Ainu. There can be no doubt on this matter. Now, I have in
my hands an Officially printed Report on Northern Chishima,
i.e. on the Kuriles. In this report there are a number of photos
of the people, their pits with the roofs on and the entrances
plainly visible, and of their implements:—of implements still
used by them when their photographs were taken. A list of the
implements is also given and the division is as follows. (1) *Stone
implements* :—Axes, hoes, knives, and stone staves. For some
reason the arrow-heads seem to be left out although a photo of
an example is given. (2) *Bone instruments* (whale bone):—
Spears, hooks, needles, combs, mortars. (3) *Earthenware* :—
Saucepans, basins, cups. The photos were taken in the 33rd year
of Meiji (1900), and the report was made up the following year.
Since this paragraph was written a very interesting work by
Mr. R. Torii (in Japanese) on the Chishima Ainu has been placed
in my hands. This book was published in July, 1903, and fully
bears out what I have written. Both it and the Official Report
above referred to independently and fully overthrow Mr. Romyn
Hitchcock's bold assertion. On reading Mr. Torii's book I find
that he has given some interesting comparative lists of Kurile
and Yezo Ainu words and phrases. But this author does not
appear to shine much as an Ainu philologist. Thus, for example,
Mr. Torii gives Kurile *kosuku*, Yezo, *chabe* for " cat "; and
also Kurile *rosot*, Yezo, *umma* for " horse." But neither these
words are traceable to any known Ainu root. What are they
then ? On the very face of them they are Russian. Thus Кожка,
" cat "; and Лошадъ, " a horse."

A question has often presented itself to my mind with regard to the kitchen middens as proof of antiquity. It is this. These pots, jars and cups are made of sun-dried clay, not burnt. I cannot think that sun-dried vessels could last under ground in a damp climate such as this of Yezo for many hundreds of years. Surely the frost and dampness would tend towards their rapid resolution into the soil.

In the Journal of the Anthropological Society for May, 1881, Prof. J. Milne published a paper read by himself in 1879 before the British Association in which he gave it as his opinion that " the kitchen-middens and other spoor of the early inhabitants of Japan were in all probability the traces of the Ainu, who at one time, as is indicated by written history, populated a large portion of this country." Later, in another paper published in Vol. VIII., Part I. of the Transactions of the Asiatic Society of Japan, entitled " Notes on Stone Implements from Otaru and Hakodate, with a few General Remarks on the Prehistoric Remains of Japan," he also shows that these remains extend through Yezo and the Kurile Islands. Prof. Milne may therefore well be reckoned as another independent witness supporting what has been said in the above paragraphs.

But then *Fourthly* there are the Place-names. Yet even these must be given up. In the Memoirs mentioned above Prof. Chamberlain catalogues 210 real native names out of which the meanings for 99 only could then be supplied. Well then might the Professor ask—" *Why should not some have descended from the aborigines who preceded the Ainus, the latter adopting them as the Japanese have adopted Ainu names?* " But this was in the year 1887 when our knowledge of the Ainu tongue was only just beginning. At that time I could have asked the very same question ; indeed, if I remember rightly, Professor Chamberlain and I did talk the matter over together at Horobetsu just before the memoirs were published. Since then some progress has been made in these studies, and I can no longer ask such a question. I have studied Mr. Chamberlain's list very carefully on the spot with the Ainu, the result being that the real root meanings of the whole 210 with more than a hundred others have been given below under the next division.

But *lastly*, one would imagine that if a race distinct from the Ainu once dwelt here some human remains would be forthcoming. I have made very careful inquiries on this point and find that no signs of any have yet been discovered. Old pits and graves have been dug into but the results have always been the same : that is to say, the skulls and bones exhumed have invariably proved to be Ainu. The skeletons of no dwarfs have as yet been found.

Should these graves yield any remains other than Ainu the fact would be at once apparent for in the Russische Revue, 10 Heft. III. Yahrgang, Materialien zur Anthropologie Ostasiens : Anutschin it is written :—" With reference to the anatomy (of the Ainu) it is remarkable that the humerous as well as the tibia have a very striking form ; they are marked by an extraordinary flattening (ausserordentliche Abplattung) such as, up to the present, has never been noticed of these bones in any people at present in existence. On the other hand, this peculiarity of form has been observed in the bones of extinct people found in caves."[1] Such were the people who gave names to many places ranging from the south of Japan to Kamschatha and other parts of Siberia. We will now proceed to consider some of these names briefly.

PART II.
A CRITICAL EXAMINATION INTO TOPOGRAPHICAL NOMENCLATURE.

In making my list of place-names I have partially followed Professor Chamberlain's excellent plan. That is to say, I have first written the present Japanese pronunciation (omitting the Chinese idiographs with which they are written and their meanings as having nothing to do with Ainu), and then given the real Ainu ; then I have parsed it and given its root meaning as well

---

[1] Transactions of the Asiatic Society of Japan, vol. x, Part I., page 196.

as in some cases pointed out its applicability to the place in question. One thing, however, should not be overlooked, and that is the fact that the Japanese have in some cases taken the name and applied it to a locality perhaps some miles away to which it can by no manner of means apply. But this does not spoil the word or name as an Ainu cognomen.

Jap'se Pronunciation.	Ainu Form.	Derivation and Meaning.

Abashiri ....Apa-shiri kotan ....."Fish-spear-head land." *Ap* is the head of a fish spear : *a* is a singular form of the verb of existence. By another derivation this name may mean " Door-land." Possibly the entrance from Saghalien. *Apa* means "door-way" or " entrance," " the open mouth of a river when looked of from the sea."

Abetsu...............A-pet..................." The river tine." *A* is a prong of a fork or " tine " : *pet* is " river."

Abira................A-pira................."Tine cliff." *Pira* is the usual word for " cliff."

Abuta ....Ap-uta kotan ...." The place of fish-spear-heads." *Ap* " fish-spear-head " : *u* a plural form of the verb of existence expressing the idea of mutuality; *ta* a locative particle. This village is so called on account of some prominent rocks close by which much resemble fish spear-heads in shape. There is also an *apu* which means " floe " or " broken up sea ice," and which word is also used in Saghalien.

Ai ....Aikotan ...."Thorn place."

Aibetsu ....There are four places called by this name among the Japanese each of which is different in Ainu. The first is *A-pet* " the river tine " given above. The second is *Ai-pet* " the river arrow " or " thorn." The third is *Aibe-ush-nai* " the stream containing the sea-car (*Haliotis tuberculata*). The fourth is *Ai-pet-ush-nai* " the valley containing the river arrow."

| Jap'se Pronunciation. | Ainu Form. | Derivation and Meaning. |

Aikapubetsu.........Aikap-pet.............."The river *Pecten*."

Ainomanai...........This should be either *Ainu-oma-nai* or *Ai-oma-nai*. The first name means "Ainu-valley" and the second "thorn valley." *Oma* means "to be in" and "to be contained in."

Akan................Akan-pet.............."The made river." The bed of this river is said to have been formed after a volcanic eruption.

Akasannai...........Aka-san-nai...........*Aka* is the same as *wakka*, "water"; *san*, "descend"; *nai*, "valley." Hence *Akasannai* means "valley with water in it." This is the name of a rivulet somewhere in Siberia according to Dobrotvorsky. Cfr. *Wakasa; Wakonai;* and *Wakanai*.

Akkeshi.............Akkesh-i.............."The place of oysters." At this place there are some very extensive oyster fields, hence the name. *Akkesh* is "oyster," and *i* is an ordinary locative particle.

Anekarimbaushi...Ane-karimba-ushi...This name may mean either ."the place of little cherry trees" or "the place with the thin circle." *Ane* means "thin": *ushi* "place:" but *karimba* may be either "a cherry tree" or "to circle."

Awomori ⎫
          ⎬.........A-omori.............{"The protruding hillock"; or "the place bearing the little hill."
Aomori   ⎭

Aoshuma............Ai-ush-oma-i........."The throny place." The addition of *ush* to nouns is one usual way of forming adjectives out of them.

Araomaibetsu......Ara-oma-pet........."Forceps river." *Ara* is also applied to the pinchers of an earwig. There is an *ara* which means "beautiful," and another which means "one of a pair." But in *Kamtchatka* *ara* also means "slow"; "tardy."

Araweotsugawa.....Arawe-ot-pet........."Scum river." *Ot* like *at*

Jap'se Pronunciation.	Ainu Form.	Derivation and Meaning.

is a plural the one of *an*, and the other of *o*, " to be " and to " contain."

Arikawa ....Ara-pet...............Either " the beautiful river " or " forceps river " possibly " earwig river ; " or " the one of two rivers " or " slow river " or " the open river."

Asahigawa ....Chiupet ...." Current river " (see *Chiubetu*). *Chiupet* has been mistaken by the Japanese as if it were *Chup-pet*, " sun-river "; Hence the misnomer *Asahi-gawa* " rising sun river."

Asari ....Asari-pet ...." The open river." The roots of this words are *sara*, *v.i.* " to open up : " *a*, a passive and intransitive prefix : and *i* a locative particle. The final *a* in *asara* is elided according to Ainu grammatical rule.

Asari................Asar-i................." The open place " *i.e.* open to the skies.

Ashibetsu-nobori...Ashbe nupuri........." Dorsal fin mountain"; so called from its form.

Ashoro...............Ash-so-oro-pet ......" The river with the standing waterfall." But *so* may mean simply a " bare rock " as well as " fall."

Atsuchi ....At-chi-kotan........." The place of elms "; *chi* is a plural suffix.

Atsukaripinai......At-kari-pi-nai......"The tiny string-like stream." *At*, " a string "; *kari*, " by way of "; *pi*, " tiny "; *nai*, stream or valley.

Atsubetsu............There are several rivers and streams in Yezo called *Atsubetsu* by the Japanese which are pronounced differently by the Ainu. Thus, one stream is called *A-pet*, another *Ap-pet*, a third *At-pet*, and yet a fourth *At-ush-pet*, every one of which is called *Atsubetsu* by the Japanese. *A-pet*, means " the river tine " or " tooth "; *A-pet* means " the river spear " or " harpoon "; *At-pet* means " the river thong " or " lace " or " string "; and *At-ush-pet* signifies " the river of elm trees."

Atsukarushi ....At-karush-i........" The place of elm mushroom." Fungi are almost always named after the tree or kind of soil they grow on. Thus :—" Oak fungi "; " fir fungi "; " manure fungi " and so forth.

Atsuta ....Ahachita ...." The place of digging up hog-pea-nuts " (*Amphicarpaea Edgeworthii, Benth, var. japonica, Oliver*). *Aha* is the " hog pea-nut," and *chita* means " digging up."

Awonai...............A-o-nai................." A gully," lit : " dug-out-valley."

Azuma...............At-ma..................This may mean either. " The shining lagoon " or " the shining peninsula," *ma* meaning " lagoon " when applied to water, and " peninsula " when applied to land. But *at* may have three meanings, viz, " to shine "; " a thong," " lace," or " string," and lastly it may possibly be the plural form of the verb *a* " to be.', Thus the meaning may be either " the place of the lagoons " or " peninsulas "; or " the shining lagoon " or " peninsula "; or " thong lagoon " or " peninsula."

Azabu ....Asap-nai or Asapp-nai.." Paddle valley " or " paddle stream."

Bakkai...............Pakkai shuma.........*Pakkai* means " to carry a child on the back," and *shuma* is " stone." Hence " The stone which carries a child on its back." This is the name given to a large stone standing upon the sea coast having a smaller one leaning on it after the manner of women carrying their children when travelling. It quite describes the appearance of the stone when seen from a distance.

Bebetsu...............Pepet-kotan........." The wet or marshy place."

Benkei saki.........Penge-not............." The upper cape." *Penge* means " upper " in contradistinction of the " lower "

Jap'se Pronunciation.   Ainu Form.   Derivation and Meaning.

part of a river or mountain or portion of the sea coast. *Not* means "jaw," and is applied to "blunt capes." The correlative term for lower is *pange*.

Betchaku............Pet-chak-kotan........" The dry place," or "the place without a river." *Pet* besides meaning "river" also means "wet." The roots are *Pe*, "water" (almost always undrinkable), and *ot*, "to be." *Chak* means "without" and *kotan* "place" or "village." But this may also mean "the place where the river pops out."

Bibai ....Pipa-i...................This name may mean either "the place of the swamp" or "the place of the bivalve Anodonta."

Bibaushi ....Pipa-ushi-i............." The place of the bivalve Anodonta." *Pipa* is the Anodonta, *ushi* is the "place where anything is." The *pip* in the previous word most likely means "swamp." But *pipa* may also be a shell of the *margaritana* species.

Bibi ....Pip-i or Pepe........If *pip-i*, "swamp place," but if *pepe*, "damp" or "watery."

Biratori.............Piratoru kotan......." The village by the path of the cliff lake." The village is said to have been so called because of a large lake which once existed near the place. The remnant of the lake, which I myself saw some 26 years ago, has now been completely washed away by the floods. But, on very many occasions I have heard this place called *Pir'uturu kotan*, i.e. "the village between the cliffs"; and this name exactly agrees with the situation. Moreover in Saghalien Ainu the very word *Biruturu* occurs which Dobrotvorski translates by "an open space."

Biro.................Piro-nai............." Cliff valley." In full this name would be *Pira-o-nai*.

Birochinai ....Pirochi-nai............The plural form is *Pirot-*

Jap'se Pronunciation.	Ainu Form.	Derivation and Meaning.

nai, " the valley of cliffs." *Chi*, the plural particle is sometimes contracted into *t*, hence this name is sometimes heard as *Pirot-nai*.

Birofune ⎫
Berufune ⎭ ....Piro-puni-kotan......⎧ "The place of raised cliffs."
⎩ *Puni* means " lifted up."

Birotsunai ....Piro-chi-nai ...." The valley of cliffs," the particle *chi* being a plural ending to the noun *pira*. *Cha*, *chi* and *t* are all plural endings.

Byei ⎫
Bici ⎭ ....Piye-pet.............. ⎧ "The river fat." *Piye* is
⎪ the word used for the fat
⎪ of birds and animals, and
⎨ in this instance the name
⎪ has reference to the colour
⎪ and density of the water
⎩ in the river so called."

Chietomai............Chi-etu-oma-i........." The place containing the sharp cape." *Chietu*, " a sharp cape," *oma*, " containing," *i*, " place." A blunt cape would be *chinot*.

Chikabira............Chikap-pira..........." Bird cape."

Chikanai ....Chik-an-nai..........." Dripping valley." *Chik-an* is the intransitive form of *Chik*, " to drip."

Chikaputomushi....Chikap-toma-ushi...." The place of the yellow star of Bethlehem," (*Gagea lutea Roem. et Sch.*)

Chikabumi ....Chikap-uni ...." The home of the birds." Said to have been so named because storks and other large kinds of birds used to breed here in great numbers.

Chikauchi............Chi-a-ot-i ...." The dripping place."

Chikisappu..........Tuk-e-sap............." The projecting descents."

Chinomibetsu.......Chinomi-pet..........." Libation river."

Chin ....Chin-kotan............This may mean either " the stretched out village " or " pelvis village."

Chinshibetsu.........Chin-shipet............" The great river pelvis."

Chiribetsu ....Chiri-pet ...." Ditch river," or " ditch waters."

Jap'se Pronuncation.	Ainu Form.	Derivation and Meaning.

Chirotto...............Chirot-to ...."The lake containing birds."
Chiri, "birds"; *ot*, "containing (plural);" and *to*, "lake."

Chitose...............Shikot-to..............." Rushes lake." *Ot* determines the *shik* "a rush" to be of the plural number.

Chiubetsu ....Chiu-pet..............." Current river." *Chiu* is the same as *Chiwe*, "a current."

Chiuruibetsu ....Chiu-rui-pet ...." Strong current river."

Ebetsu...............E-pet..............." Humour river." So called because of the dirty colour of the water.

Ekikomanai.........U-kik-oma-nai ......" Battle valley." *Ukik* means "to fight one another."

Ekiminenai ....Ekimne-nai ...." The mountain stream."

Eramachi............Erem-at-chi-kotan ..." The village of rats." The *Chi* in this name is a simple duplication of the *t* in *at*—the plural number.

Erimozaki ....Eremu-not ...." Rat cape."

Esan ....E-san-not ...." The projecting cape."

Esashi ....Esash kotan..........." The place of surf" or "the place of surf rumbling."

Etuchikerepu.......Etu-chikere-ushi ....." The cape with the land torn off."

Ezo ....Isho-moshiri..........." The land where there is abundance of game."

Fuji no yama......Hunchi or Unchi nupuri " Mount of fire"; or "mountain, the goddess of fire." *Unchi* or *unji*

Jap'se Pronunciation.   Ainu Form.   Derivation and Meaning.

is applied to fire in Yezo when being worshipped
only ; but in Saghalien it is the usual name for fire.

Furemappu.........Pui-omap-i............" The place with a hole."

Fumbe-kawa........Humbe-pet............This may be either *hum-pe pet*, " river of sounding waters" or *humbe pet*, " whale river."

Fumbetsu ....Humi-pechi-kotan..." The place of the roaring waters."

Furebetsu............Fure-pet................" The red river."

Furan ....Huru-an-kotan......."The village by the hill"; or " the village with a hill."

Furano................ { Huru-an-nu-kotan." The very hilly place." }
                       { Hura-nu-kotan ...." The hilly place." }
The *nu* defines the noun as plural.

Furanu-i ....Huranu-i ...." The place of the dunes " or "hills."

Furubira............Huru-pira............." The hill cliff."

Fushkobetsu.........Fushko-pet ...." The old river."

Futoro...............Pit-oro-kotan........." The place of pebbles." *Pit* is a small stone.

Fuyujima............Pui-shuma............" The stone with a hole " or "cavern " in it.

Garugawa ....Karu-pet............." Uneven river." Probably referring to stones or boulders or rapids in the bed.

Garu-rushi ....Karu-ushi............." The uneven place."

Habomai ....Hap-oma-i............." The place of the herb *Heracleum lanatum, Michx.*" This herb is by some called *Hara*, by some *Hap*, and by some *Pittok*.

| Jap'se Pronunciation. | Ainu Form. | Derivation and Meaning. |

Hakodate............This is Japanese and takes its name " box-fort " from the ancient Japanese fort which used to be here and which is said to have been built by *Aibara-suo-no kami*. The Ainu name of the place was *Ushungesh*, which means " the lower end of the bay."

Hamamashke........Ma-shike..............." The spread out lagoon " or " peninsula."

Hirakishi............Pira-gesh-i............" Cliff end."

Hiramura ....Piratoru..............." See Biratori.

Homme..............Humne-pet ...." The broken river." *Humne* means " small pieces."

Horobetsu............Poro-pet..............." The big river." *Poro* means " big."

Horoizumi...........Poro-eremu-not......" The great rat cape."

Horomombetsu .....Poro-mo-pet..........." The big tranquil river." *Mo* means " quiet " ; " tranquil."

Horomui............Poro-mui ...." The great fan."

Horonai.............Poro-nai..............." The big stream " or " valley." Among the Saghalien Ainu *nai* means a " large river."

Humbetomare......Humbe-tomare ......" Whale harbour " or " water sounding harbour."

Iburi koku ....Ifure-iso-kotan ...." The place of the rock which is red." *Fure* means " red," and *ifure* " very red."

Ikushumbetsu......Ikush-un-pet ...." The trans-river " or " the yonder river," or " the crossing river."

Ikutoro..............Ik-uturu..............." Between the mountain ridges." The word *ik* also stands for the

Jap'se Pronunciation.	Ainu Form.	Derivation and Meaning.

"spine," a "joint," an "inch," or a "division."

Inao-toge ....Inao-pira ...." Inao cliff." *Inao* are pieces of whittled wood used as fetches.

Inuboe ....I-nup-o-i................*I*, an intensifying particle, *nup*, "plain"; *o*, "protrude"; *i* either a locative particle or a substantivizer. Hence, "the protruding plain"; or "jetting table-land."

Ishikari-gawa.......Ishkari-pet ...." The winding river." *I* an intensifying particle; *shikari*, "to go round." Or, "the blocked up river."

Isoya.................*Isoya* by some and *Isoyake* by others......But both have the same meaning, the *ke* being either a locative particle only or a plural suffix. It means "The place of the great bare rock," or "rocks"; or "The land where there is plenty of game."

Itaki.................Itangi-kotan..........." Cup village."

Itaratarage..........Itaratarage-i ...." The shaky place." The district called by this name has some very boggy land about it which trembles very much when walked over.

Iwanai................*Iwanai* by some *Iwau-o-nai* by others......The first name means "rock valley," and the second "the valley having sulphur."

Kabato..............Kapato-kotan........." The place of the water lily *Nuphar japonicum*. Also "mud lake."

Kakkumi............Kakkumi kotan......" Bucket place," so called because of the conformation of the sounding mountains. Or, "the place of the roaring waters."

Kamiiso ....Kamui-so............." The great cascade." The word *Kamui* is often

Jap'se Pronunciation.	Ainu Form.	Derivation and Meaning.

used to express beauty and greatness among other things.

Kamoi kotan .... Kamui kotan......... "The dreadful" or "wild" or "awe-inspiring place." *Kamui* is the ordinary word for "god" but used as an Adjective it may mean "great," "beautiful," "aweful," "pretty" "dreadful" and so on.

Kamoi wakka...... Kamui-wakka .... "Water par excellence."

Kamoi to............ Kamui-to .... "The beautiful" or "great lake."

Kannikan dake ... Kannikan-nupuri.... "Staff mountain."

Karapto .... Karapto moshiri...... "The country of the descending lakes." Probably there are some highland lakes in *Karafto i.e. Saghalien.*

Karifuto .... Karip-butu............ "The mouth of the river wheel," or "the mouth of the hoop."

Karimba yama..... Karimba nupuri .... "Cherry tree mountain."

Kayabe............... Kayabe nupuri ...... "Sail mountain."

Kayanoma........... Ki-moi-kotan .... "Reed bay village." *Moi* really means a "quiet place," and is applied to any quiet, snug place among the mountains as well as to the sea harbours or bays.

Keneushi .... Kene-ushi............. "*Alnus incana* place."

Kemanai .... Kema-nai .... "Foot stream" or "valley."

Ki.................... Ki-i .... "The place of rushes."

Kiitap............... Kitap................. "Reed hill." *Tap* is a single mountain peak.

Kikonai .... Ki-oma-nai........... "Reed valley."

Kinatoshi .... Kanat-ni-ushi........ "The place of the *Cephalotaxus drupacea.*"

Kim un nai......... Kim un nai .... "The mountain valley."

Jap'se Pronunciation.	Ainu Form.	Derivation and Meaning.

Kinaushi ....Kina-ushi ...." The place of grass."

Kiunnai..............Ki-un-nai ...." The stream among the rushes."

Kiyomap.............This is in Ainu *Ki-omap* and means "the place or water containing reeds." *Ki* means "reeds"; *Oma* is a plural verb meaning "to contain"; and *P* may be either "place" or "water," the locality itself determining which is meant.

Kochikabaki ....Ko-chikap-ak-i ......" The place where birds are shot."

Koitoi................Koi-tui-kotan ...."The place torn by waves," *Koi*, "the waves of the sea," *tui*, "to cut," or "tear."

Kokipiru............Pok-pira..............." The under," or "lower cliff."

Kom-nai ....Kom-nai ...." Knuckle glen," or "knob valley"; "hillock glen."

Konoi ....Kombu-moi..........." Sea-weed bay."

Kotanbetsu ....Kotan-pet ...." The village river."

Kotangeshi ....Kotan-gesh ...."The west end of a village."

Kotan-uturo ....Kotan-uturu ...." The space of land between two villages" or "the middle of a village.

Kotoni...............Kot-on-i ...." The place of the dyke."

Kuchaunai ....Kucha-un-nai........." Hunter's lodge valley."

Kuamaru............Ku-ama-ru ...." Any path in which a spring low is placed."

Kudo ....Ku-to ...." Bow lake."

Kumaishi............Kuma-ush-kotan ...." Bar village" or "rail village."

Kunashiri ....Kunna-shiri ...." Black land." " Black island."

Kunnebetsu.........Kunne-pet............." The black river."

Jap'se Pronunciation.	Ainu Form.	Derivation and Meaning.

Kushiro..............Kush-ru..............." A passage." " The way through (presumably from *Apa-shiri* to the South-east coast.)

Kusuri...............Kusuri-kotan ...." The place of hot springs." " The medicine place." *Kusuri* is said by the Ainu to be an Ainu word and not distinctively Japnese.

Makaribetsu.........Makkari-pet..........." The river which circles back." From *Mak*, " back "; *Karip*, " a wheel," and *pet*. The root *kari* also occurs in the name *Ishkari*.

Makunkotan ....Mak-un-kotan........." The hinder village " or " place."

Maonai...............Mau-nai..............." Windy valley " (*Mau* may also mean the ": beach rose " (*i.e. Rosa-rugosa*).

Mashke...............Meshke-i ...." The place of the land-slip."

Matomanai ....Mat-oma-nai..........." The valley with the lagoons " or " peninsulas." Compare *Matsumai*.

Matsukotan ....Mata kotan..........." Winter village " or " winter residence." Probably referring to the pits the Ainu used to inhabit during the winter months.

Matsumai............Mat-oma-i ...." The place of the lagoons " or " peninsulas." The *t* determines *ma* to be plural.

Mauka...............Mau-ka..............." A windy place " Lit : *mau*, " wind " *ka*, " at the head."

Meakan ....Me-akan-pet-nuburi." The mountain of the cold made river." *See akan-pet*. (But the *me* in this name may be Japanese, and if so it means " female.")

Ja'pse Pronunciation.	Ainu Form.	Derivation and Meaning.
Memnai	Mem-nai	" Pond valley."
Mena-mura	Mena-kotan	" The village by the pond," or " pond place." But it may also very well mean " the damp place."
Menashi	Mena-sara-nai	" The valley of the *Lythyrus maritimus.*"
Misomap	Nishomap	" The cloudy place."
Mitsuishi	Pit-ushi	" The place of pebbles."
Moireushi.	Moi-reushi-kotan	" Stopping place bay."
Moiwa	Moiwa-nupuri	The mountain with the gradually sloping sides. Or, " the mountain with the easy rocks " (*i.e.* rocks easy to climb.)
Mombetsu	Mo-pet	" Slow river."
Mori	Mori	" The little hill," or " the gentle slope " or " the hillock."
Mororan	Mo-ru-ran-kotan	" The village of the gently descending road." A very good description of the old road over the mountains to old Moruran.
Mōseushi	Mose-ushi	" Nettle-fibre place."
Motomanai	Mo-to-oma-nai	" Quiet-lake-glen."
Motta	Motta-moshiretu	" Adze cape."
Mukawa	Muka-pet	" The stopped up river." So called on account of the large quantity of sand which collects at its mouth at each rising tide.
Naiporo	Nai-poro-kotan	" The place at the great glen " or " valley."

Jap'se Pronunciation.	Ainu Form.	Derivation and Meaning.

Namewakka ....Nam-wakka-kotan..."The place of cool water."

Naibuto ....Nai-butu ...." Valley mouth."

Nanai ....⎫
Nanaye ....⎭ Nam-nai..............⎰"The cool stream" or
⎱ valley."

Naiyoro..............Nai-oro-kotan........." The village at the·valley."

Neppu ....Nep-u-nupuri ...." Sword handle " or " haft mountain."

Nemoro ....Nem-oro-kotan......." The place of ponds " or " swamps."

Netsuso..............Net-so..................*Net* is the " smooth surface of water "; *so* is " fall." Hence " smooth-surface fall."

Nigori kawa ....Yu-un-pet ...." The river having mineral springs in it."

Niikappu............Ni-kap-kotan........." The place of the tree bark." Bark fibre was formerly used in making Ainu cloth.

Nina..................Nina-kotan............" Sole fish village."

Nioi ....Ni-o-i-kotan ...." Forest place." *Ni* means " trees."

Niptani...............Niptani by some and Miptani by others...The *niptani* is a raised platform the Ainu hunters make in the forests upon which to stow such meat as they are unable to carry away on their return from hunting.

Nishi..................Nish-kotan ...." Cloud village."

Nishitap ....Nish-tap ...." Cloud capped mount."

Nitui..................Nit-u-i.................." The place of thorns."

Niunnai..............Ni-un-nai ...." Tree valley."

Noboribetsu.........Nupuru-pet ...." The turbid river." So

Jap'se Pronunciation.	Ainu Form.	Derivation and Meaning.

called from the colour of its waters.

Noboripo ....Nupuri-po............"A little mountain."

Nokapiri.............Noka-pira............."Image cliff."

Nokkamappu.......Nup-ka-omap........."The place above the plain."

Nopporo ....Nup-oro-kotan........"The village in the plain."

Noshappu ....Nishtap-u............."Cloud capped mount." *U* like *i* is a locative particle.

Notaoi...............Not-ao-i..............."The place bearing a cape" or "cape bourne place." The *A* in this name is a passive particle and is often used to express the objective.

Notorozaki...........Not-oro-kotan ...."The village at the cape."

Notsuke ....Not-ushike..........."Cape place."

Nottozaki ....Not-o-i ...."The place bearing a cape."

Notsamu ....Not-sam..............."Cape-side."

Notu ....Not-o..................."The place of the blunt cape."

Oakan ....O-akan-pet-nupuri..."The mountain at the mouth of the made river" (see *Akan-pet*). But the *o* in this name may be Japanese, and if so it means "male" c.f. *me-akan*.

Obihiro ....Opereperup-nai......"The stream with the broken up mouth."

Obirashibe...........Opiras-pe-kotan ....."The village by the spread out water."

Ochiaibetsu ....Ochi-ai-pet.........."Arrow-mouthed-river." *O* is the lower end *i.e.* "mouth" of a stream or river, or "mouth meeting river."

Jap'se Pronunciation.	Ainu Form.	Derivation and Meaning.

Ochikapaki..........O-chikap-ak-i ...." The place of shooting birds."

Ofuizaki ....Uhui-not..............." The burning cape."

Okamoi-zaki.........O-kamui-not........." The great protruding cape." There are no expletive words or particles in Ainu; the *o* used as a prefix here means "projecting." For *kamui* as meaning "great" see *Kamiiso* and *Kamui wakka.*"

Okompushbe........Ok-un-push-pesh-i..." The descent of the badly exploded" or "errupted place." Said to have reference to an ancient erruption of a volcano in the district. But by some it is *Ok-un-pesh-be*, and this means "the over-hanging neck" referring to the neck of land at the place so called. By other Ainu the true name is said to be *Okom-pesh-i*, and this means "the place of protruding mountain knobs."

Okotsunai............O-u-kot-nai ...." The valleys where the entrances adjoin," *i.e.* the place where two valleys part off into different directions.

Oku-patchi ....Okoi-patche-i........." The place where the waves of the sea are scattered." From *o-koi*, "out of the waves"; *patche*, "scattered"; *i* a locative particle "place." So called on account of the waves beating among the rocks here.

Okushiri.............Ok-shiri..............." Neck island." *Shiri* is sometimes "land," and sometimes "island."

Ombetsu ....O-mu-pet.............." The river with a stopped up mouth."

Omoribama.........Omori-kotan.. ...." The jetting cape" or "hill." (See *Mori*). *Bama* is the Japanese for

Jap'se Pronunciation.	Ainu Form.	Derivation and Meaning.

hama, "sea coast," or "sandy beach."

Onishika............O-nish-ika-kotan ...."The village over the clouds." This means that the village so named is situated very high up in the mountains.

Orito.................O-rit-o-kotan ...." The place having protruding veins."

Osarubetsu ....O-sara-pet ...." The river with the open mouth." (See *Asari*).

Osatsube ....O-sat-nai..............." The valley " or " stream with a dry mouth."

Oshamambe.........Oshamambe-kotan..." The village of the sole." The name is said to be taken from the conformation of the land on one of the hills behind the village. But *Oshamambe* may grammatically mean " place where soles abound."

Oshima..............Oshma-ushi ...." The sunken place."

Oshoro..............Ush-oro-kotan ...." The village at the head of the bay."

Oshunkushi.........Osh-un-kush-i ...." The back crossing place." But this name may possibly be *Oshungu-ushi* and that means " the place of fir trees."

Ota...................Ota-shiri-etu ...." Sand cape land."

Otaru ....Ota-ru ...." The sand road."

Otasami.............Otasam ...." Sand side."

Otōbe ....Ota-o-pe............." Water containing sand."

Otobe ....Ochi-o-pe ...." The stream with several mouths."

Otoshipe ....Ota-ush-pe ...." Sandy water."

Ōtsu gawa ....Ohot-pet ...." Deep river."

Ōtsunai ....Ohot-nai ...." The deep valley " or " stream."

Parato..............Para-to ...." Broad lake."

Jap'se Pronunciation.	Ainu Form.	Derivation and Meaning.
Pekere	Pekere	" Clear."
Pekereat	Pekere-at-pet	" The shining river."
Penakori	Penak-o-ri-kotan	" The high upper village."
Pitarapa	Pitara-pa-kotan	" The village over the stony place."
Piraka	Piraka-kotan	" The village at the top of the cliff."
Pokkirito	Pok-e-rit-o-i	" The place having veins coming from beneath it."
Poromezaki	Poro-me-an-not	" The very cold cape."
Poromoi	Poro-mui	" The great winnow." This place is so named because the distant mountains suggest a winnow by their conformation. Or, " the great creeper."
Poronai	Poronai	See Horonai.
Porosara	Poro-sara-i	" The great sedge plain," or " the great open place."
Poronobori	Poro-nupuri	" The big mountain."
Raiba	Ra-i-pa	" The head of the low or deep place."
Rakko-gawa.	Rakko-pet	Sea-otter river."
Rampoki	Ram-pok-i	" Under the low place." This is the name given to a place low down under some cliffs not far from Horobetsu.
Rebunge	Rep-un-gep	" The sea scoop." This place is so called because the mountains along the coast here are formed somewhat like a " scoop " or " ladle."

Jap'se Pronunciation.	Ainu Form.	Derivation and Meaning.

Rebunshiri ....Rep-un-shiri..........." The island." The word *rep* is " sea," *un* is a locative particle, and *shiri* is " land."

Rishiri...............Ri-shiri................."The high land."

Rokke ....Rutke-i ...." The place of the land slip," or " the place of slipping off."

Ruriran ....Rui-ran-i ...." The steep descent."

Rurumoppe.........Ruru-oma-pe........." Brackish water." But this name may really be *Ruru-nuppe* " Water of the salt plain."

Rusha...............Ru-san-i..............." The place where the path descends."

Sakkotan ....Sak-kotan ...." Summer village." This name has reference to " the summer " residences of the people in contradistinction to the places where pits were dug for winter dwellings.

Samani...............San-mau-ni..........." The place of rotten wood " or " the wood washed up upon the sea coast by the waves."

Samdo ....San-to ...." The descending lake."

Sannoi ....San-nai ...." The descending stream " or " valley."

Sapporo ....Sat-poro-pet.........." The river which gets very dry." So called because this river is very broad at places and during the summer months the bed has consequently many dry places in it. But the name really comes from *Sat-poro-nupuri*, i.e. " dry mountain."

Sarapa...............Sara-pa-kotan........." The village at the head of the sedge " or " plain."

Sara ....Sara-moshiri ...." (See *Saru*.)

Jap'se Pronunciation.	Ainu Form.	Derivation and Meaning.
Saru	Sara-moshiri	"The country open to the skies." (See *Asari*.)
Sarubuto	Sara-pet-putu	"The mouth of the river Sara."
Saruru	Sar-orun-kotan	Either "the place of cranes" or "the place of sedge."
Sashumbetsu	Sash-hum-pet	"Surge sounding river." So named on account of the noise of the billows of the sea along the coast near here.
Satsuma	Sat-ma	"A dry lagoon," or "pond" or "peninsula."
Sawaki	Sara-ki-kotan	"The place of rushes," (*Phragmites communis Trin.*)
Sawara yama	Sarat-nupuri	"The mountain of sedge grass." *At* is the plural of *an* "to be."
Shakotan	Sak-ibe-kotan	"The place of the summer trout."
Shakubetsu	Sak-ibe-un-pet	"The river frequented by the summer trout."
Shari	Sar-i	"The open place."
Shiribeshi Shibetsu	} Shi-pet	{ "The main river" in contra-distinction to an affluent.
Shibuchari	Shipi-chara-pet	"The river with the stony mouth." *Shipi* are small round pebbles.
Shikabe	Shikambe-kotan	"The place of the albatros." Many of these birds may sometimes be seen along the coast called by this name.
Shikerebe	Shikerebe-kotan	"The place of the *Phellodendron amurense Rupr.*"

Jap'se Pronunciation.	Ainu Form.	Derivation and Meaning.

Shikerebe ....Shikerebe.............."Shale" or " broken rocks," or " gravel."

Shikunoppe ....Shiki-o-nup-pe ...." Water rising from the reed plain."

Shikiu ....Shiki-u.............." The place of rushes."

Shikotan.............Shi-kotan.............." Great," or " best, or "true village " or "place."

Shima................Shuma-kotan........." The place of stones."

Shimamaki ....Shimak-mak-i........." The hindermost place."

Shimamaki ....Shuma'map............" The place containing stones." In full this is *Shuma omap.*

Shimushu............⎫
Shimushir ....⎬Shimoshiri............" The great country."
Shumushu...........⎭

Shinekozaki.........Shi-meko-not........." The great cat cape." *Mek* is the native word for " cat," *mek* being an onomatopoeia for the cat's mew.

Shinshiru............Shin-shiru-kotan....." The place with the earth rubbed off" or "earth abraded place." *Shin* is the same as *shiri*, " land."

Shintoko ....Shin'toko ...." The ends or shoulders of the mountains." In full this name is *shiri*, "mountains as opposed to plains ; " *etok*, " the ends ; " *o*, "jutting." *Shintoko* is a place situated above the plains just before entering the pass over the Tokapchi range.

Shiokubi.............Shi-ok-upipi-kotan .." The place of the great sorrow " (perhaps referring to a defeat in battle).

Shipun...............The Ainu inform me that this place is called

Jap'se Pronunciation.	Ainu Form.	Derivation and Meaning.

by themselves *Shupun* and not *Shipun*. *Shupun* means " roach " (Leuciseus hakuensis, Gthr). The full way of writing the name is *Shupun kotan*, " the place of the roaches." It is said to be so called because the streams here-about contain a very large number of roach. But should it turn out, however, that the name is really *Shipun kotan* it may possibly mean " the place of pebbles," or even " the place of the scouring rush." (Equisetum hycmele, L. var. japonicum, Milde).

Shiraito ....Shiri-etu ...." Cape land."

Shirakami ....Shirara-kamu-i......." The place covered by the tide." It is very interesting to remark that the Ainu term for " God " is *Kamui*, and means " He who " or " that which covers." The particle *i* is either masculine or feminine or neuter as best suits the context in which it occurs. The root of *Kamui* is *ka* " top."

Shiranuka...........Shiraraka ...." Over the tide." By some this is *Shirara-ika*. "The over-flowing tide."

Shirao ....Shirara................." The tide."

Shiraoi...............Shira-o-i..............." The place where the tide comes out (over the land)." This well defines the locality for there are extraordinary high tides here on occasion."

Shiretoko...........Shiretok-o-kotan ...." The beautiful place," or " the place of the jetting land."

Shiribeshi..........⎱
Shiribetsu..........⎰Shiri-pet ....⎰ " The great river," or *Shi-pet*, " the great high river " (probably up-land).

Shiriuchi ....Shiru-ot-kotan ...." The abraded places. *Ot* defines the noun to be of the plural number.

Jap'se Pronunciation.	Ainu Form.	Derivation and Meaning.
Shiruturu	Shir'uturu	" Between the mountains."

Shiri, " land," in sometimes used by the Ainu for " mountains " in contradistinction to level places. Compare *shintoko*.

Shitsukari	Shittok-kari	" By the elbow."
Shizunai	Shut-nai	" Mountain foot stream."
Shiunkotsu	Shum-un-kot-kotan..	" The village of scumbelt."

So called on account of scum often seen in a bend of the river here.

Shonai	So-nai	" Cascade stream."
Shuma-kotan	Shuma-kotan	" The place of stones."
Shumaya	Shuma-ya	" The stony land."
Shusushi	Susu-ushi	" Willow place."
Shusushinai	Susu-ush-nai	" Willow valley."
Sorachi	So-rap-chi-pet	" The river of the water-

falls." From *so*, " waterfall ; " *rap*, " to descend " (plural of *ran*); *chi*, a plural particle belonging to the noun *so ; pet*, " a river."

Sounnai	So-un-nai	" Cascade glen."
Soya	So-ya-kotan	" The land of bare rooks."
Sowen-kotan	So-wen-kotan	" The place of the bad " or

" great falls " or " bare rocks."

Suttsu	Shuptu	" The line of the mountain

foot," or "mountain feet."

Takkashima	Tokkara-so	" Fish rock." *Tokkara* is

a kind of salt water fish. It is called *tsuka* by the Japanese.

Tarumai	Taru-oma-i	" The place of the dug out

road." The volcano so called is thought to have this name given to it because there are some very deep path-like gullies in its sides formed by erosion of loose volcanic deretus.

Jap'se Pronunciation.	Ainu Form.	Derivation and Meaning.
Teine yama.........Tei-nei-nupuri		"Damp valley mountain."
Teshio ....Tese-u.................		"Weaving place" or "basket work place."
Teure shima ....Chiure-shuma.........		"Toe stone." *Chiure* and *chieure* mean "toe" in Ainu.
To-asa ....Tuwasa-kotan		"The place of the basket fern.
Tobe.................To-pe.................		"Milk," or "lake water."
Tobetsu..............To-pet		"Lake river."
Tobitsuomai ....To-pit-oma-i		"Pebble lake."
Tohira ....To-pira................		"The cliff of the lake."
Tobuchi.............⎫		
Tobuto.............⎬To-put		"The mouth of the lake."
Tobutsu ....⎭		
Todohokke ....Toto-ot-ke		"Thicket place." From *todo* bushes, *ot* "to be," and *ke*, "place.
To-ne-betsu ....To-ne-pet		"Lake-like-river."
Topui................To-pui................		"Lake hole." But this may be *Top-u-i*, "The place of bamboos."
Togari...............................		See Tokkari.
Toishikari...........Toi-ishkara-pet.......		"The very winding river."

Toi means superlatively. (See *Ishikari*). The final *a* in this name instead of *i* need cause no trouble for *i* is often changed into *a* in Ainu.

| Toitanai..............Toi-ta-nai ....| | "Earth-dug-valley" or "stream." |
| Tokachi ....Tuk-a-chi-moshiri...| | "Upward extending country." or "protruding country." |

Probably so called on account of the numerous mountains in this locality. *Tuk* means "to grow" and to "extend upwards;" "to protrude;" *achi* is the plural of *an* "to be" and is the same as *at* and *ot*.

Jap'se Pronunciation.	Ainu Form.	Derivation and Meaning.

Tokari .... } Tokkari-moi......... *"* Fish bay." *Tokkari* is the same as *Tokikara* and means a kind of fish called *tsuka* by the Japanese. (See *Takkashima*.) Also *Togari* by some.
Tokkari ....

Tokeshimanai ......Tokes-oma-nai.......or *Tokes-ma-nai*. If *Tokes-oma-nai* the word means "the stream at the lower end of the lake" but if *Tokes-oma-nai* it means "the stream of the lake perninsula."

Tokoro...............To-koro-kotan..........." The place of the lake." Or it may be " Nipple place."

Tomakomai..........Some Ainu call this place *To-mak-oma i*, and others *To-mak-onai*. The first form would mean " The place at the back of the lake", and the second " The stream coming from behind the lake." Yet another name for this place is *Tumak-oma-i* or *Tomak-oma-i* both of which words mean " The place of the quagmires," and this quite agrees with the nature of the locality.

Tomanai ....Tumam-a-i..........." The place of the quagmire."

Tonai ....To-un-nai............." Lake valley."

Toshibetsu ....Tush-pet..............." The rope river."

Tsugaru ....Tukara-moi ...." Sea-leopard bay."

Ucmbetsu ....Uwen-pet............." Wailing river." Said to be so named on account of many Ainu having died here through small-pox. But the name may also mean " mutually-badwaters." If so the name is descriptive of the quality of the water.

Uhui-nobori.........Uhui-nupuri........." A volcano."

Uhuitomori.........Uhui-tomori........." The burning harbour or " bay."

Jap'se Pronunciation.	Ainu Form.	Derivation and Meaning.
Uraka	Uraka-kotan	"The rough place."
Urakawa	Urara-pet	"Foggy river."
Uruppu	Urup-pet	"Red salmon river."
Uryu	Uriu	"The high places." The first *u* expresses mutuality and the last is a locative particle.
Usu	Ush-oro-kotan	"The village at the head of the bay."
Usujiri	Ush-un-chiri	"Bay-head-ditch."
Usu-no-yama	Ush-un-nupuri	"Bay-head-mountain."
Utasutsu	Ota-shut	"The sandy mountain foot."
Uyenbetsu	Uwenpet	"The river of bad waters."
Wakasa-nobori	Wakka-san-nupuri	"The mountain down which the water runs." The mountain district so named may be a particularly wet place; or subject to heavy rains.
Wakanai	Wakka-nai	"Water valley."
Wakonai	Wakka-o-nai	"Water-bearing valley."
Waonai	Wa-o-nai	"The valley of the green pigeon."
Wanishi	Wan-ushi	"Rim place."
Washibetsu	Wash-pet	"Surf river." So named on account of the surf at the river's mouth. *Wash* is the same as *sash*, and occurs in the word *chiwash-ekot-mat*, "The goddess of the surf."
Watara	Watara-i & Watara-kotan	"The place of rocks."
Yakoshi	Yak-ushi	"The burst up place."
Yamakoshi	Yam-kush-nai	"The valley of chestnut burs."
Yamani-kotan	Yam-ni-kotan	"Chestnut tree village."
Yambetsu	Yam-pet	"Chestnut river." But if this is *Yan-pet* it means "the descending river,"

Jap'se Pronunciation.	Ainu Form.	Derivation and Meaning.

which I think is the real name.

Yageshiri............Yange-shiri..........." The lifted up land." This island is so called because it sometimes has the appearance of being lifted up out of the water.

Yange-nai............Yange-nai............." The high " or " elevated valley." *Yange,* " to elevate and " *nai,* " a valley."

Yedo or Edo ......Endo kotan...........The place of the herb *Lythrum salicaria ; L.*

Yepeotsu............Yepe-ot................." The village with the dirty or fatty water."

Yoichi................Iyochikotan ...." The dizzy " or " perplexing place."

Yokotsudake ....Yuk-ot-nupuri......." The mountain where the deer are."

Yubari................Yupara-nupuri ...." The mountain of the mineral water scources."

Yubutsu..............Ipot-pet ...." Face river." I believe the real old name was *E-pet put,* " pumice stone river mouth." This description exactly agrees with the river whose bed is covered with volcanic ashes. But there is another meaning to *E-pet* (see *Ebetsu*) which also quite agrees with this name.

Yūni ....Yu-un-i..............." The place where there is hot mineral water."

Yurappu ....Yu-rap-u ...." The place where the hot waters come down."

Yukchisei............Yuk-chisei..........." The deer house."

Zeni-bako ....The Ainu name of this place is *Ota-shupkotan* which means " Sand-spit place." Zeni-bako is a Japanese name meaning " money-box " and was given

Jap'se Pronunciation.   Ainu Form.   Derivation and Meaning.

to the place many years ago on account of immense sums of money brought to inhabitants through the sale of enormous catches of fishes which used to be made here.

---

§ VI. YEZO AND SAGHALIEN AINU.

No one with the least knowledge of the subject would for a moment doubt that the Yezo and Saghalien Ainu are one and the same race. It is perfectly true that the Yezo Ainu sometimes speak as though the language of the two peoples was different, even going so far as to use the words *itak shinnai*, "different language." But when questioned on the matter it turns out that this *itak shinnai*, "different language," simply means, for the most part, *kutcham shinnai*, "different way of pronouncing words." There are numbers of exact analogies to this loose way of speaking among the Ainu of Yezo, for the people inhabiting the various districts of this island speak of one another's speech under the same terms. Thus the Usu Ainu of the Saru; the Saru of the Tokapchi; the Tokapchi of the Apashiri, and so on. A good illustration of this point is found in the following incident which happened to myself some years ago. I was then in the north of Yezo and had just finished addressing a large concourse of people in Ainu. At the conclusion of the lecture a Japanese who was present said to an Ainu standing by,—"Did you understand what was said"? "Yes," replied the man in Japanese—*Ano hito wa Saru no yama no oku no Ainu da*—"that man is an Ainu from behind the Saru mountains"; and then added in Ainu, *itak shinnai koroka Sar'un Ainu itak ambe ne*, "it was a different language, but it was the speech of the Saru Ainu." He meant to say that I spoke the Saru dialect. As a matter of fact I had lately come from Piratori, the ancient capital of Saru.

Though the Ainu language is, as a whole, spoken with considerable uniformity throughout the Island of Yezo, yet there are some slight differences to be noted in almost every village one passes through. These differences are not always so great as to justify one in calling them dialects, provincialisms would be a more appropriate name for them. As for dialects proper, we may say that there are but three spoken in Yezo, viz ; the Saru, Usu and Tokapchi.[1] The Usu, Yurap, Mororan, and Ishikari Ainu (*i.e. the Ainu of the Southern and Western coasts*) only differ from those of the Saru district in that the former pronounce the words in full whilst the latter use certain contractions. The Tokapchi Ainu differ from all the rest both in the contraction of words and names of certain objects. The Apa-shiri, Akkesh, and Kushiro Ainu (*i.e. the Ainu of the northern and north eastern coasts*), though differing from their nearer neighbours, the Tokapchi people, speak very like those of Usu. However the grammer is the same, and when the Saru dialect is spoken but without the contraction of words, one is pretty well understood by all excepting the Tokapchi people, who sometimes miss the meaning.

A few differences in the words used by the northern and southern Ainu are as follows :—

SOUTHERN.	NORTHERN.
Aman-chikap, ...	Aman e-chiri. " a sparrow."
Chikap.................	Chiri, " a bird."
Chup	Tombe, " a luminary " (*Tombe really means, " the shining thing.*")
K, ...	Ku, " I."
Kek, ...	Ku ek, " I come."
Koira, ...	Ku oira, " I forget."
Koropok, ...	Choropok, " under," " beneath."
Paro, ...	Charo, " the mouth."
Poi, po, ...	Pon, " little."
Upaskuma, ...	Uchashkuma, " a lecture,"

---

[1] It may be remarked here that the Saru Ainu confess to having originally come from Tokachi to Saru, while the Usu Ainu declare that their ancestors come from Saru. The Tokachi Ainu also say that they originaly came form Saghalien.

Saghalien → Tokachi

SOUTHERN.		NORTHERN.
Wei,.....................**Wen**, " bad."		
Yakka,.................**Yakkai**, " although."		

There are, however, a few interesting differences well worthy of a passing note and among them are such as these for example. In one district we have the word *nishatta* for " to-morrow," while in another we hear *shimma* used. *Nishatta* really means " dawn " but it has gradually come to stand for " to-morrow " —indeed, so firmly is this meaning now attached to it that in most places *shimma* is quite unintelligible to the people. Yet it is of interest to remark that *shimma* is ordinarily used in Saghalien for " to-morrow " and appears all over Yezo in the words *oyashim*, " the day after to-morrow " and *oyashimshinge*, " the second day after to-morrow." Or again, in the Saru district the ordinary word for " father " is *michi* and for " mother," *habo*. But in some villages in the *Mukawa* district, and not so much as ten English miles away from Piratori, *michi* stands for " mother," and *habo* for " father "! Further, although in Piratori the word *habo* means " mother," yet at Piraka, only four miles lower down the Saru river, the word commonly used for " father " is *iyapo!* This is very strange, but is a fact notwithstanding. In some other places the ordinary word for " father " is *hambe*. In Saghalien also the usual word for " father " is *hambe*. In Yezo the usual word for " rain " is *apto* while in Saghalien and Kamtchatka *peni* or *pene* is used. But *pene* means " aqueous " as a rule and in rare case " rain " among the Yezo Ainu. *Mene*, " fine rain " belongs to the same root.

There is, however, one other difference to be noted. It consists in accents or the pronunciation of words. There are in many village in Yozo, more formerly than now, quite a number of people who speak their words with a slight tonic accent as though the language was originally connected with Chinese or some kindred tongue. But there is this very important difference ; in speaking Chinese it is absolutely necessary to enunciate the *tones* clearly for they are part and parcel of the word itself. Among the Yezo Ainu this is not the case now whatever it may have been formerly. Here the *tonic* accent is quite unimportant and many would hardly notice it. The principal thing is to clearly define every syllable and pronounce it distinctly.

But both the differences in dialect now mentioned are found among the Ainu of Saghalien but in a more emphasized manner. The chief difficulty in a Yezo Ainu understanding a man from Saghalien—and it was at first my own difficulty also—arises from the marked *tones* the people impose upon their words. Thus, while we say in Yezo Ainu *wakka ta wa ek,* " go and draw some watar," smoothly and without accent, a Saghalien Ainu would, though using the identical words, emphatically *intone* or accent every syllable ; indeed, with my eyes closed and no knowledge of Ainu I should, refering to these *tones,* say he was speaking some dialect of Chinese. And I say this advisedly, remembering that before coming to Yezo I had several months study of the Cantonese dialect of Chinese in Hongkong under the guidance of competent teachers. Saghalien Ainu, in so far as pronounciation is concerned, used certainly to remind me of the Chinese language whenever I heard a native speaking it. At the present time, however, the tones are being lost and a Russian sound given to many of the consonants.

But to mention Yezo and Saghalien vocabulary. There is also a marked difference in the use of words here. Thus in Yezo the word for " sun " is *chup,* while in Saghalien it is *tombe. Tombe* is a compound word meaning in Yezo Ainu " the shiner." Further, in Yezo the ordinary word for " fire " is *abe ;* in Saghalien it is *unchi, fuji, unji, hunji* or *funchi,* according to the taste of the speaker, But in Yezo Ainu—*unchi, huchi, unji* or *fuji* is only applied to " fire " when it is being worshipped. Indeed, it stands for the " goddess of fire." Among the Saghalien Ainu the word for fresh-water " ice " is *ru,* while in Yezo the word used is *konru. Apu* is Saghalien Ainu for " sea-ice " or " floe," a word which occurs in place-names in Yezo, amoug whom *apu* seems to mean " broken ice along the sea-coast." Again, among the Saghalien Ainu the words for " hare " are first *Oshuke* and then *kaikuma* while in most parts of Yezo it is almost always *isepo*, though sometimes *epetche*. But among the Tokapchi Ainu *kaikuma* is also used. Once more, the pit-dwellers of Saghalien are called by those of their fellows who do not use pits (for some use pits even now during the cold winter months) by the name of *Toichiseikotchaguru*, " persons having earth dwellings ;" while in Yezo the pits left by those of their ancestors who used them are known as *koropok* or *choropok-un-guru koro chisei kot*, " the house sites of those who lived in pits." Every part of this last word is purely Ainu as also is *toichiseikotchaguru ;* hence, for such like reasons we conclude that the language of Yezo and Saghalien is one.

There are of course many different words used by the Yezo and Saghalien Ainu whose origin one cannot always trace. *Ibebashui*, for example is Yezo Ainu for " chop-sticks," really meaning " eating tongs "; but the Saghalien Ainu say *sakkai*, word whose full meaning has yet to be determind. However, among the Yezo Ainu the words *sakma* and *sakiri* " a rail" or " pole " appear to carry the same root. In the North again *arak* is used for spiritus liquor, but in Yezo this word is known only to those Ainu who have been to Saghalien. It has probably come through Russia.

If a still clearer proof was needed to show that the Yezo Ainu were in early times connected with the Island of Saghalien it may be found in an examination and comparsion of the Place-names of the two Islands, for both are seen to be pure Ainu. Exception is of course taken with respect to such European names as C. Elisabeth ; C. Maria ; B. Espenberg ; Bai d' Estaing, and so forth. The following score of names are taken from C. W. Schebunin's *karte der Jnsel Sachalien oder Karapto* (1868). Schebunin's name is given first, then the present Ainu pronunciation, and after that the English meaning.

	Schebu.	Ainu.	English.
1.	Ekuroki	Ekurok-i	" Black place."
2.	Naiputzj	Nai-putchi	" The glen mouths."
3.	Naitscha	Nai-cha	" The glens " or " glen-side."

Schebu.	Ainu.	English.
4. Ninaussi ....Nina-ushi		" Sole place."
5. Notoro ....Not-oro		" Having a blunt cape."
6. Nubori-Endum.. { Nupuri entom... / Nupuri etomo ... }		" Mountain side."
7. Otassu...............Ota-shut...............		" Sand foot." _Shut_ is " the foot of a mountain."
8. Piro-tzi..............Pirotchi		" The cliffs."
9. Pissjachssam........Pischa-sam		" The sea-side."
10. Po-tomari...........Pon-tomari		" The little harbour."
11. Ssiranussi ....Shiran-ushi..........		" Tide-place" or "rocky place."
12. Ssirepa..............Shiripa		" Land's head," or as we should say in English, " Land's end."
13. Ssoya .... { Soya .... / Shoya .... }		" The land of bare rocks."
14. Ssussucha kotan. { Susucha kotan .... / Shuhucha kotan... }		" The place of willows."
15. Ssussuso-nai ..... { Susu-ush-nai ..... / Shusu-ash-nai..... }		" Willow glen" or "valley."
16. Tomari-nai.........Tomari-nai		" The harbour of the glen."
17. Tomari-po ....Tomaripo............		" Little harbour " (Lit : " the child of the harbour)."
18. Tunaitscha..........Tu-nai-cha...........		" The two valleys "— " double valley."
19. Tyk..................Tuk..................		" Projecting."
20. Uen-kotan ....Wen-kotan		" Bad place." — (sometimes " bad " in the sense of " rocky " or " stony."

Many other names might be given but the fore-going will suffice for the present purpose.

In studying that dialects of Ainu several questions, such as the following present themselves; viz:—

(a). "Does the fact of the Ainu language having traces of tones in it point to China or Chinese Tartary as its place of origin?"

(b). Or, "if it did not take its rise there is it not possible— nay even probable—that it passed through those regions in prehistoric times and so has been made to feel Tartar influence?"

(c). Or, "can any affinity be found by way of comparative philology between Ainu and Tibetian, it being remembered that Tibetian has *tones* very distinctly developed?"

(d). Or, "is there any connection between Ainu and the languages of the Northern or Southern Turanian type, it being remembered that these are inflected?" These and other interesting questions have crossed my mind more than once, and they are, I am fully persuaded questions which should be closely studied by those who have the leisure, inclination, and competence for such a work. The results would, I believe, well repay the time, trouble and patience expended in the inquiry. Perhaps the grammar contained in this book will help to solve the riddle; it is at least hoped so.

§ VII. AGGLUTINIZATION.

Refering again to the resemblance of the Ainu language to those of the Chinese type in respect of *tone*, it is pertinent to remark that in the matter of agglutinazation also there is a strong family likeness, only that in Ainu it is much more developed than in Chinese. Chinese is a preëminently monosyllabic tongue, for each word may be used either as a noun, verb, adverb, adjective or particle according to desire; what part of speech is meant being left to the context and position in the sentence. Indeed, as my old teacher at Hongkong used to try to impress upon me—"every root is a word, and every word a root." Max Muller in the 4th vol. of his work draws special attention to this fact and also points out how that in the *shi-tsé* and *hiu-tsé*, i.e. "full-word" and "empty-word" of Chinese Grammarians we have the beginnings of agglutinization in this extremely monosyllabic language. It is probable that the ideographs with which Chinese is written has kept the language as it is, without radical change, for so many hundreds of years. Without them there would undoubtedly have been more change and much more agglutinization. Illustrations of compound or agglutinated or combinatory Chinese words are very abundant in Japonico-Chinese and many might be given as illustrations. But as the question here refers to Chinese exclusively I will give those only I find have been examined by Max Müller. Thus, *shi*, "an arrow," *jin*, "a man," *shijin*, "master of arrows." *Shui*, "water," *fu*, "a man," *shui-fu*, "a water carrier." *Shui*, "water," *sheu*, "hand," *shui-sheu*, "a steerman." *Kin*, "gold," *tsiang*, "maker;" *kin-tsiang*, "a gold-smith." *Shou*, "writting;" *sheu*, "hand," *shou-sheu*, "a copyist."

The construction of the Ainu language as spoken to-day, and as exemplified in Dobrotvorski's work, clearly points back to a time when Ainu was as monosyllabic in nature and construction as Chinese itself, for in a very large number of words the various component roots may be easily seen. And that Siberian Ainu is of an older form than that spoken in Yezo is sufficiently proved by the fact that the present day Ainu of Saghalien retain many plural particles in their speech which these of Yezo drop altogether. Besides the very long words, such for example as those given in section 3 the shorter ones are also worthy of attention. Take the words e*petke* and *ise-po*; both of which mean "hare," as illustrations. *E-pet-ke ; e* is an objective particle whose root meaning is "towards"; *pet* means "torn"; "slit"; *ke* is sometimes a plural intransitive form of ki, "to do." Hence *epetke* mean "the torn" or "slit one." Why? an examination of the lip of this animal will soon tell us. The same word appears in *epetke-guru*, "a hare-lipped person," and also in *opetpetke*, "ragged." Turn now to *Isepo*. What is its derivation? *I-se-po*. Three roots. *I*, an intensifying prefix ;

se " to make a noise "; hence, *ise*, " to squeal "; *po*, a diminative particle, as for example, *ponbepo*, " a very little thing "; *po* " a child." Hence *isepo*, " a hare," lit : " the little squealler." But why call a hare by this name ! Let anyone wound or catch a hare in a trap and he will soon learn. The squeal of a hare is not easily foregotten any more than the bark of a wolf; and a " wolf is called in Ainu *wose-kamui*, " the divinity who calls *wo*," the *wo* being an onomatpœia for its bark.

Having thus shown the manner in which Ainu words are built up it would be interesting for any person acquainted with some of the many dialects of China or with Tibetian or kindred languages to superimpose the *tones* he knows on each syllable of the Ainu contained in this book and see what the result would be. Let him, if he chooses, write or pronunce the Ainu words as follows :—When *ch* commences a word let it be *tch*, or if found in the body of a word pronounce it as through it was *j*, or *z*, or *tz :* Thus for *chi* write *tchi*, *ji*, or *tzi* ; or for *che*, let it be *je*, *ze*, or *tze*. Again, let him write *k* as though it was *kh* or *hk*, *gh* or *hg* ; or even as *ch* in some cases. *P* too might be aspirated and pronounced like *ph* ; while *t*, like *k*, might even sometimes be changed into *ch*. All of these variations I have heard, and do hear among the Yezo Ainu, both with and without *tones* slightly present. The *tones* however, are much more marked among the women than among the men. And it may also be remarked here that as among other barbarous races, so also among the Ainu, the women speak their language much more clearly and purely than the men. But alas, the language is fast dying out among both sexes ; nay, it is to all intents and purposes dead. The language of to-day is not the same as that of 28 years ago when the present writer first commenced his studies and work among this people.

The gradual weakening of *tones* in Ainu till they have become lost and inessential may be sufficiently accounted for by the combination and assimilation of roots which the language has been undergoing for ages. We have present day examples of this very thing in those Chinese words and phrases adopted and

adapted by the Japanese, for such words and phrases are never
intoned by the people when using them, though in China they
could not be understood without them.

From all this it will naturally be concluded that the writer
supposes the Ainu to have originally come to Japan through
Amur-land or Siberia. Just so. If this be the case are there
no traces of Ainu words in the geographical nomenclature of this
region? Yes, certainly there are. Thus for example, take the
Russian adjectival ending *sk* in *Tomsk* away and what do
we get. Just *Tom*. But *Tom* is distinctly Ainu and also
Tartar! Or again, take *okhots* and eliminate the final *s*. *Okhot*,
oukot or *ok-ot* is left. Again purely Ainu words. There are
many other words and names of a like nature which might be
given, as the rivers *Yenise* and *Ocha*, and also the names *Atchan*,
Avatcha, *Kamchatka*, *Paratopska* and *Utka*, with *Tarinsky*, *Poro-
chinna*, *Paratoonka*, *Ischappina*, *Arapetcha Araumakkota*, and
many other places such as have *kota* after them; but let these
examples suffice for present treatise.

---

§ VIII. HEBREW WORDS RESEMBLING AINU.

Whilst studying the subject presented in this volume, the
Author has been very much struck at times by the great similarity found to exist between certain Ainu and Hebrew words.
And he has accordingly wondered whether or no there can be
any real family connection between them. No doubt one could
make no greater mistake in such a matter as this than to rely
too much on mere sound. But the comparison of the words
given below shows such a peculiar resemblance that it seems too
much to conclude, without proof, that all is pure accident. But
to be perfectly honest in the matter, and it is truth not fiction
the writer is aiming at, one must add here that in so far a mere
grammar is concerned no analogy has so far been found to exist
between the two languages. It must not be supposed that the Author
is building any theory on this matter; the words are simply

appended and compared as being very curious examples of verbal correspondence. They are, it goes without saying, already insufficient to prove either the Ainu to be the ten lost tribes, or their language to be Semitic. Indeed, I have already stated that I believe, speaking from a study of the construction of the grammar of the langage, that it is Aryan. Whether I am right or not others must judge later.

Hebrew and Ainu words compared.

Heb.		English.	Ainu.	English.
1. ¹ *Ani*,	אֲנִי	I	Ani¹ ... Káni	I.
			Eáni...... Yáni	You.
2. *Anoki*,	אָנֹכִי	I	Anokai . Aokai	I. You.
3. *Av*,	אָב	Father	Abo,...... In some places " father " Habo, ... and in others " mother."

[It should here be noted that in Ainu there is no *v* sound properly so called, the nearest approach to it being *b* or *p*. *Po* is often found suffixed to nouns of consanguinity, thus :—*Iyapo*, " father ; " *achapa*, " uncle ; " *mitpo*, " grandchild ; " *matnepo*, " daughter ; " *yupo*, " elder brother ; " *sapo*, " elder sister ; " *tureshpo*, " younger sister." It is curious to remark also that the English word *papa*, " father," is in Ainu, according to the law of letter changes, *chacha*, " uncle," an " old man ; " for in some districts *pa* always becames *cha*].

Heb.		English.	Ainu.	English.
4. *Akh*,	אָח	Brother	Ak, ... Aki, ... Akihi, ...	Younger brother.

---

¹ The *a* in the Ainu word *ani* is the substantive verb of existence. It therefore differs radically from the *aleph* in the Hebrew word. This fact is fully suffices to prove that the similarity is only in sound and not in essence. Moreover, the Ainu *a* may never be used simply as an expletive while *aleph* may. (See Gesenius' Hebew grammar page 61 par: 4 under *ā'leph prosthetcum*.)

5. Arack, אָרַח To travel...Araki,.......To come ; approach.

6. Ba   בָּא Come ....Paye,........To go.

7. Bara,   בָּרָא Create........Kara, ...To make.

8. Esh,   אֵשׁ Fire..........A,.............To burn.
                              Abe..........Fire.

[Mark the א *aleph* in this and the next word but one.]

9. Kala,   קָלַע To carve....Kara, ...To make.

10. *Ur*,   אוּר Fire.......⎰A,..............To burn.
                           ⎪Uhui,..........To burn.
                           ⎨Uchi,.....⎱
                           ⎩Unchi,·...⎰...Fire.

11. Enush, אֱנֹשׁ A human being...Ainu,...Man ; human being.

12. Nahar, נָהָר River...............Nai,.....River ; stream.

---

§ IX. AINU AND BASQUE.

But another very interesting question presents itself to us in this
place. It it this. Is not the Ainu language connected with
Basque ? If so it can of course have no affinity with Heblrew, for
that language has been adjudged outside the Turanian classification
of language, while Basque, being of Tartar origin is included in
it. Max Müller in vol. 111, page 429, quotes Bunsen as saying[1]
—" I have convinced myself from the grammar and dictionary
that Basque is Turanian." And Borrows is also of opinion that
" Basque is of Tartar origin."

It would not be at all surprising to find that the two are
connected, seeing that, as has already been intimated the original
Ainu in all probability came through Tartary to Japan. A very
curious thing about them is that the ancient Basque and Ainu
customs of Couvade, ridiculous as they were, resembled each other
to a great degree. Compare Max Müler vol. 11, page 273 with
" The Ainu and their Folkore " Chapter XXIII.

---

[1] " Chips from a German workshop."

The following are a few Basque and Ainu words resembling one another. The writer culled them out of a copy of Genesis in the Basque language he has by him. The idea of a possible affinity was suggested to him by Mr. Dodson, of Lisbon, himself a Basque scholar. This gentleman also sent him a list of words resembling Ainu which he has unfortunately quite lost in moving from one place to another. They are given here in the hope that some one who knows Basque will compare that language with this grammar and dictionary.

Basque.	English.	Ainu.	English.
Arima, ...	Soul, life,...	Ramat........	Soul, life.
Etche, ...	House, ...	Chisei,.......	House.
Emazte,............	Wife, woman,	Mat,[2] machi,...	Woman. Female. Wife.
Hastea, ...	Begin, ...	Heashi, ...	To begin.
Hatssa,.............	Breath,......	Hussa,.......	To breath, to blow with the mouth.
Passaia, ...	Walk..........	Apkash, . Paye	Walk, go.

§ X. AINU AND THE ARYAN CONNECTION.

Having thus been brought home to Europe let us linger here for a space and consider one or two very curious matters. The Ainu word now usually used for " house " is *Chisei* or *Tchisei* or *Tchse*, or *Tshe*, or *Tise*, just as one choses, while among the Kurile Saghalien Islanders it is *Che*. But the Welsh for " house " is *T*; and the original Cornish name was *Ty*, *Sing* and *Tai* plural. Shuyd's Grammar informs us, however, that in modern Cornish *t* has been changed to *tsh* thus out of *ty* producing *tshey*, " houses." One wonders whether the Ainu word for " house " has any connection. Again in Cornish and Welsh the word for

---

[1] Compare also the Russian мать, " mother."

" head " (caput) is *pen*. In Ainu *pen* means the " source " or
" head " of a river ; " the upper part of a valley ! " It also
appears in *penram* " the chest. The words *tu* for two and *re*
for " three " still keep us at home. So also *tumbu*. *Tumbu*
means in Ainu " an appartment in a dwelling." Thus, *poru* is
a " natural cave " and *tumbu*, first, a " dwelling appartment "
or " division in a cave " and then a " room " in a house. But
further, the word *Tumbu* has very interesting associations. By
some it means " womb," and according to others " the placenta."
Tun means " foetus," and hence comes the word *tuntun*, " fish-row."
All this reminds one of the Anglo-Saxon word *Tûn* " a close "
(German " Zaun "), which afterwards becomes a " Town."[1] *Chisei*, " house," applies to the " home " of many living objects as,
a wasp, bee, man, bear and such like beings, while *tumbu* is only
applied to the living apartment of a human being, whether it
be in a cave, in a pit dug in the side of a hill or in a hole
dug in the level ground ; or whether it is a room in a " house "
or *Chisei*, as that in of my house in Sapporo, or the poky dark
hole 6 feet by 9 in the southeastern corner of Chief Penri's hut
at Piratori which was put up for me to sleep in ; all these
" divisions " or " apartments " are *tumbu*, " rooms " in Ainu.
But it is a well known fact that the English word " tomb " is
from the mediæval Latin *tumba*. But *tumba* first meant " a
hillock," after that " a tomb." Again one therefore wonders
whether there is any family relationship between *tumba* " a
hillock " and *tumbu*, " a apartment in a cave."

Now, *pu* in Ainu is the ordinary word for " godown " or
" store house." Hence *tumpu* or *tumbu* really means " the home "
or " storehouse of the foetus " of living beings. Or, again, this
last word *tumbu* might well be compared with the Russian
Домъ " home," the final ъ of the Russian word being taken for the
Ainu *bu* or *pu*, and thus we are brought to Latin *domus*.

A comparison of the Ainu word *garu* with the Welsh *garu*
is also interesting for both are identical in meaning, which is

---

[1] Max Müller Vol. II. Page 27.

"rough," "uneven." In Yezo there are two place-names in which the word occurs, one near Sapporo, namely *Garu-pet*, "turbulent stream," (a name which quite agrees with the nature of the stream here), and *Garu-ush-i* "the rough place," the name of a locality not many miles from Horobetsu near Mororan. This place also is a very uneven locality having many soft sulpheric hillocks cast up about it by volcanic action with a number of hot water springs among them.

A, also, both in Welsh and Ainu are the same in some instances. Thus :—In both it is used as an interrogative adverb, and in both also as the pronoun, "who," "which," "that." *An* too seems to be alike in some instances in both languages, for in both it is used as a partitive particle. The resemblance also of Ainu *gur'*, *guru* to welsh *gwr* is very curious, for in both languages this word means a "person," a "man." The word *i* too, is another instance of an interesting analogy, for in both languages it is used as the objective pronoun "me," and also by way of emphasis and intensity. So likeness is the vowel *e*. In Welsh this is the pronoun "he," "she," "it"; while in Ainu it is the ordinary objective particle meaning "him," "it," "her." In Welsh *O* means "from," "out of"; So it does in Ainu also.

Speaking of the vowels, *a* carries one thoughts on through *an* "to be" to the sanscrit verb of existence *as*. Speaking of this word Max Müller says :—"You know, of course, that the whole language of ancient India is but a sister dialect of Greek, Latin, of German, Cetic, and Slavonic, and that if the Greek says *es-ti*, "he is," if the Roman says *est*, the German *ist*, the Slav *yeste*, the Hindu, three thousand year ago, said *as-ti*, "he is." This *asti* is a compound root *as*, "to be," and the pronoun *ti*. The root originally meant "to breathe," and dwindled down after a time to the meaning of "to be."[1]

This is all most interesting when viewed in the light of Ainu studies. In Ainu the verb of existence is *a, an, ash, on* for the singular, and for the plural. Compare also the Greek ὸν and

---

[1] Intro: to the Science of Religion page 303.

ὂυτος. Further, if, as is said to be the case the sanscrit word *as* originally meant "to breathe," the similarity between it and Ainu is yet more striking, for the present-day word for "to blow" in Ainu is *as* or *ash*.

The words *chacha* for "papa," *chip*, for "ship," *mat* for "female," *pone* for "bone," *tu* for "two," *re* for "three," and *pak* for "punishment" have already been mentioned, as also has *wakka* or *aka*, *Eng:* "water" sanscrit: *aka*. There are others too which might well be compared such as *poi*, "little," (Italian poço and poi), *sion* "a little boy" (Russian сынъ), but space will not allow this subject to be further persued here.

The chief argument, however, for an Aryan origin of the Ainu language will be found to lie in the Grammar rather than in vocabulary. And to it the Reader is now to be introduced.

CHAPTER II.

ORTHOGRAPHY.

In writing the Ainu language with the Roman alphabet, the following system has been adopted :—

LETTERS	PRONUNCIATION AND REMARKS
a	has the sound of *a* in the word "father"
e	has the sound of *e* in the word "benefit"
i	has the sound of *i* in the word "ravine"
o	has the sound of *o* in the word "mote"
u	has the sound of *u* in the word "rule"
ai	has the sound of *ai* in the word "aisle" or *i* in *ice*.

However, there are some few cases in which both vowls must be distinctly pronounced ; as : *aikka*, "it was stolen."

LETTERS | PRONUNCIATION AND REMARKS

ei has the sound of *e* in the word "they." In some cases, however, both vowels must be distinctly pronounced. As for example, *eikka*, "he stole it."

ao
au
eo In these combinations each vowel must be always clearly
eu   pronounced.
ou

ch has the sound of *ch* in the word "*ch*urch." In some districts *ch* would always be pronounced like *k*.

sh has the sound of *sh* in the word "*sh*ip."

b is pronounced like *b* in any English word. No sentence now properly commences with this letter, but preceded by another word, the letter *p* is often changed into *b*.

c is never written excepting in the combination *ch*, and it is then always soft like *ch* in "church." Many persons, however, upon hearing *ch* as in *Chup*, "the sun," or *Chisei* compare page 73, "a house," for example, would write *tchup* and *tchise* or *tshey*; and they would be quite correct in doing so for the Yezo Ainu are not at all uniform in their pronunciation, And again, some might very well write either *machi*, *matchi*, or *maji*; nay, even *matzi* or *mazi* where I write *machi*, "wife"; and no one would grumble and all would understand.

d like *b* is never heard at the beginning of a sentence, but *t* often becomes *d* in composition. In some places, however, when a word commencing with *t* or *p* stands alone or at the head of a sentence a sort of compromise is made; thus *t* is pronounced neither like *t* nor *d* in English but something between the two. The same may be said of *p* and *b*.

f resembles the true labial in sound, it being softer than the English labiodental *f*. It never occurs excepting followed by the vowel *u* and is often found in words which appear to be of Japanese origin.

g has the sound of *g* in the word "*g*ood." No initial

sentence commences with this letter, but *k* often becomes *g* in composition. It should be noted however, that *g* is often aspirated as though is was *gh* or *kh*.

h has the sound of *h* in the word "*h*ouse;" that is to say, it is always aspirated.

j Some words have something like the sound of *j* in them, e.g. *machi*, "wife"; *unchi*, "fire"; but these have always been written with *ch* because the tendency in Yezo is rather in the direction of *ch* than *j*.

k has the sound of *k* in the word "*k*eep." Sometimes, however, it is pronounced with a kind of aspirate as though it was *kh*.

m
n
p
r }These letters are all pronounced as in English.
[1]*s*
t
u

l
q
v }These letters are not needed in speaking or writing Ainu.
x

z something like the sound of *z* is heard in the word *pensai*, "a junk." Compare also *c*.

None of the consonants *b*, *c*, *d*, *f*, *g*, *h*, *r*, *w*, or *y*, ever properly end a word, but *k*, *m*, *n*, *p*, *s*, *t*, and *sh* often do.

---

[1] As regards the letter *s*, however, it should be observed that in many cases it is difficult to know whether the Ainu say *s* or *sh*; thus *shui* would be *sui* by some and *sa*, *sha*; or *so*, *sho* and so on or *vice versa*.

CHAPTER III.

LETTER CHANGES.

No sonant letter begins a sentence, but in composition surds are sometimes changed into sonants. These changes are as follows :—

K becomes **g.**
P .... **b.**
T .... **d.**

Chi is sometimes changed into *t* before *utara*, the *u* of which is dropped ; thus :—

Heikattara for heikachi utara, "lads."
Matkattara for matkachi utara, "girls."

He or *hei* becomes *se* or *sei* in some places, thus :—
Sekachi for *hekachi*, "a lad."

Ko becomes *cho* in some places and *vice versa.* Thus :—
Choropok for *koropok*, "underneath."

Pa becomes *cha* in some districts : Thus :—
Uchashkuma for *upaskuma*, "preaching."

N becomes *m* before b or m ; thus :—
Tambe for tan be, "this thing."
Tammatkachi for tan matkachi ; "this girl."

Ra and *Ri* become *n* before n and ra, and *t* before *t*, thus :—
Kan nangoro for Kara nangoro, "will make."
Oan-raige for Oara raige, "to kill outright."
Oattuye for ara tuye, "to cut through."
Ashin-no for Ashiri no, "newly."

Ro becomes t before chi and t, and *n* before n.
Ku kot chisei for ku goro chisei, "my house."
Ku kottoi for ku goro toi, "my garden."
Ku konnishpa for ku-goro-nishpa "my master."

Ru becomes *n* before n ; thus : An gun' ne for an guru ne,
" it is a person."

When one word ending with a vowel is immediately followed
by another commencing with a vowel, the final vowel of the
first word is in some cases dropped ; thus :—

    Moshir' ebitta for moshiri ebitta, " the whole world."

    Oya moshir' un guru for Oya moshiri un guru, " a
       foreigner."

    Utar' obitta for Utara, obitta " everybody."

I becomes *y* before *a*, as, *yayamkiri* " to recognize," while *o*
is sometimes heard for *u*, as, *anno* for *annu*, " to defeat."

Care must always be taken to pronounce the double consonants
as in speaking Italian or Japanese.

As :—

    Ine, " where ? " ....Inne, " a multitude."

    Ota, " sand " ....Otta, " in," " to."

    Shina, " to lace up ".........Shinna, " a difference."

    Tane, " now ".................Tanne, " long."

When it is desirable to give special clearness or emphasis to
a noun or adjective ending with a vowel, such final vowel may
be reduplicated preceded by the consonant *h ;* thus :—

    Nimaki or Nimakihi, " a tooth.".

    To or Toho, " a day ; " " a lake."

    Pirika or Pirikaha, " good,"

    Kunne or Kunnehe " black," " dark."

There are some cases in which it is customary to reduplicate
the final vowel, such reduplication being almost universally prac-
ticed by the Ainu. As :—For example :—

    Chaha instead of *cha*, " twigs."

    Hochihi   ,,   ,, *hochi* " a sum."

    Wen-kurihi instead of *wenkuri*, " a rain cloud."

CHAPTER IV.

THE ARTICLE.

There is no article, properly so called, in the Ainu language; but the numeral adjective *shine*, "one," is often used as the indefinite article *a* or *an*, as:—

Shine Ainu, "a man."

Shine chisei, "a house."

Shine chikoikip, "an animal."

But care must be exercised in using the word *shine* as an article, for when it is essential to draw attention to the fact that there is but one of a thing this numeral is used; e.g.

Shine Ainu, "one man."

Shine shiwentep, "one woman."

For the definite article the demonstrative adjectives are sometimes used; e.g.

Nei guru ye, "that (the) person said."

Nei chep pirika ruwe ne, "that (the) fish is good."

Toan kambi koro wa ek, "bring that (the) letter."

CHAPTER V.

THE NOUN.

Nouns, in the Ainu language, are at the present day subject to no changes to indicate either gender, number, or case.

THE GENDER OF NOUNS.

Gender is sometimes designated by a different word; as :—:

MASCULINE.	FEMININE.
Acha, "uncle."	Unarabe, "aunt."
Ainu, "man."	Mat-ainu, "a woman."
Ona, "father."	Unu, "mother."
Shiuk, "a he bear."	Kuchan, "a she-bear."
Shion, "a little boy."	Opere, "a little girl."
Hekachi, "a lad."	Matkachi, "a girl."

When an object has no special masculine or feminine form, as
for instance *Chikap*, "a bird" (cock or hen), or *seta*, "dog" or
"bitch," and it should be necessary to specify to which sex it
belongs, the words *pinne*," "male," and *matne*, "female," "are
placed before it; thus :—

MASCULINE.	FEMININE.
Pinne chikap, "a cock."	Matne chikap, "a hen."
Pinne seta, "a dog."	Matne seta, "a bitch."

For human beings and gods, however, *okkai* or *okkaiyo*, "male,"
take the place of *pinne*.

THE NUMBER OF NOUNS.

The number of the noun is, in the case of animals, generally
indicated by the context or verb, and is therefore mostly left
unexpressed by any addition to the noun. Thus, *aiai*, "baby"
or "babies"; *ainu*, "man or "men." However, when it is
necessary to express plurality *utara*, *utare*, or *utari* is used. e.g.

SINGULAR	PLURAL
Aiai, "a baby."	Aiai-utara, "babies."
Umma, "a horse."	Umma utara, "horses."
Ainu, "a man."	Ainu utara, "men."

[The word *utara* is analyzed thus—*u* a plural prefix meaning
"mutual"; *tara*, "appendages." Hence *utara* is really "comrades."]

With the numerals, however, *pish* is used in enumerating animals :—Thus :—*Umma tuppish, umma reppish*, "two horses, three horses."

But there appear to be quite a number of nouns, now regarded as singular, which inflection proves to be really plural by derivation. Thus :—

SINGULAR	PLURAL.
Am, " a finger-nail."	Amu, " finger-nails."
Ashikipet, " a finger."	Ashikipettu, " fingers."
At, " a tether."	Atu, " reins."
Chep, " a fish."	Chep-nu, " fishes."
Hura, " a hill."	Huranu, " hills.'
Itak, " a word."	Itaku, " words."
Kut, " a crag."	Kuttu, " crags."
Pe, " water."	Pepe, " waters."
Pet, " a river."	Petcha, " rivers."
Nishi, " a cloud."	Nishu, " clouds."

Also such as :—

Ikushpe, " a post."	Ukushpe, " posts."
Iriwak, " a relation."	Uiriwak, " relations."
Kema, " a foot."	Ukema, " feet."
Nimaki, " a tooth."	Unimaki, " teeth."

The word *pe* " an article," " a thing," may well be compared with *pish* the plural particle used in counting animals; and *koro*, " to possess " with *kotcha*, " possessors." The *cha* in this latter word sometimes appears as *chi* and sometimes as at, ot, or simple *t*. The *nu* given often *chep* and *hura* in the above examples is seen to advantage in the word *nuye* which means " abundance."

Pfizmaier, in his *Erörterungen und Aufklärungen über Aino*, quotes Dobrotvorsky as intimating that the Ainu language retains fragments of a plural formation in a few substantives, and quotes *kema*, " a foot " and *kemaki* " feet "; also *ima*, " a tooth," and *imaki* " teeth " as examples. But on turning to Dobrotvorsky. I find he gives, нога, ношка, and even ногн, i.e. " foot " ; " a little foot " and " feet " for *kema* while *kemaki* does not occur at all! There has been a mistake made somewhere. At present I can find no genuine instance where *ki* is used as a plural suffix. Feet is not *kemaki*, but *ukema*. It is quite true that Dobrotvorsky gives *ima* as "tooth" and *imaki* as "teeth"; but I very much doubt the truth of this definition. "Tooth" is *nimak* or *nimaki* as one pleases, while teeth" is *unimak* or *unimaki*. Moreover, I find lower down in his work that Dobrotvorsky writes Нмакъ which he translates by зудъ "tooth." The final hard mute ъ may represent the *i*. Examples showing that ъ does sometimes represent *i* in Dobrotvorsky might easily be given were it necessary, but one clear instance only shall here be produced. It is зáнъ, "you," which is unmistakably *eani* in Ainu.

THE CASES OF NOUNS.

The case or relation of the noun to other words in a sentence, though generally left to be gathered from the context, may, when necessary, be expressed by certain particles; thus:—

Nom : by *anak* or *anakne*. As, *Ainu anakne ek kor'an,* "the man is coming.

Obj : by *e* preceding a *v.i.* or without any particle when the noun is followed by the passive voice of a verb. As, *seta ainu emik,* "the dog barked at the man." *Ainu araige,* "the man was killed." Before a *v.t.* the particle *ko* "to" is at times found to represent the objective case. Thus :—*kik,* "he strikes," *en kokik,*" "he strikes me."

Gen : by *koro, goro, kot* following the pronoun or noun; as :— *ku goro makiri,* "my knife"; *ainu kot chisei,* "a man's house"; *a koro michi,* "our father."

But although *koro,* expressed or understood, is often used as a possessive factor (*koro* really means to possess), yet this word is very often dropped and the case is expressed by the verb "to be" like the Aryan languages, but preceded in many instances by *otta,* "to." The reason of this is evident. If instead of saying *michi ku goro,* "I possess a father," one says, *en otta michi an,* "to me there is a father," the word "father" is no longer a possessed object, but a subject who indicates his possessor. Compare the Russian, French, and Latin constructions: *У него отецъ есть; tibi est pater, mihi est uxor;* and *ce livre est a moi,* and so on.

Dat : by *otta* or *orun.* As :—*Satporo orun karapa,* "I am going to Sapporo." *Seta otta kore,* "give it to the dog."

Abla : by *orowa* and *orowa no.* Thus: *Habo orowa no,* "from mother"; *Michi orowa,* "from father"; *Moruran orowa ku ek na,* "I have come from Moruran."

Instru : by *ani* or *ari.* As: *Op ani chep raige,* "he killed a fish with a spear"; *makiri ari koro ashikipet tuye,* "to cut one's finger with a knife."

There are certain prepositional particles such as *e, o, ko,* (each in its turn always retaining its own special definite root-meaning—for in the Ainu language there are no expletives) which in a way, may be regarded as indicating case. Thus:

Pishne, "the sea-shore,"   epishne, "to the sea-shore."
Pishne, "the sea-shore,"   opishne, "from the sea-shore."
Kira, "to run away,"   kokira, "to flee to."
Kira, "to run away,"   ekira, "to run away with.

When addressing relations the words *po* and *tonoge* and *nishpake* are sometimes heard used in a complimentary or carressing way. Thus :—

(1) Ak-po, "dear younger brother."
    Turesh-po, "dear sister (younger)."

(2) Aak-tonoge, "my dear younger brother."
    Apoho-tonoge, "my dear child."
    Anish-tonoge, "my dear master."
    Ayupo-tonoge, "my dear elder brother."
    Aturesh-tonoge, "my dear younger sister."
    Asaha-tonoge, "my dear elder sister."
    Amichi-tonoge, "my dear father."

Atotto-tonoge, " my dear mother."

(3) Ayupo-nishpake, " my honoured elder brother."

Aak-nishpake, " my honoured younger brother."

Atono-nishpakehe, " my honoured master."

The root meaning of *po* is " little " and shades off into various interpretations of a diminutive character. Such as, " tiny ; " " small ; " young ; " " child," e.g.

Emush, " a sword " ....*Emushpo,* " a dirk."

Chikap, " a bird "..............*Chikap-po,* " a young bird."

Okkai, " male " ....*Okkai-po,* " a boy."

The word also enters into geographical nomenclature sometimes. As :—

Chi-ika-nai-po, " the little over-flow stream."

Chishnai-po, " the little precipitious valley," " glen," or " stream."

Nai-po, " the little glen " or " stream," or " the little stream " (the meaning being that it comes out of a larger one).

Nupuri-po, " the little mountain."

Poronai-po, " the little *Poronai* " (the meaning being that there is another *Poronai* near at hand, or that the one *Poronai* river flows out of the other).

Tokompo, " the little knob."

Tomaripo, " the small harbour."

Tukarapo, " the little sea-leopard."

Soya-nai-po, " little stony glen."

THE ABSTRACT NOUNS.

Nouns expressing abstract qualities are formed by adding *i* or *hi* or *ambe* to adjectives and verbs, thus :—

Nupeki, " bright "......Nupeki-i (hi or ambe) " brightness."

Itak, " to speak." ......Itak-i (hi or ambe) " a speech."

Care must be exercised in using *ambe* for expressing abstract qualities, for that word when used with adjectives sometimes makes concrete nouns.

THE COMPOUND NOUN.

Compound nouns are extensively used by the Ainu and are formed as follows :—

(a) By compounding two substantives together.

To, " the breast "
Pe, " water " } Tope, " milk."

(b) By compounding verbs with nouns.

Uhui, " to burn."
Nupuri, " a mountain." } Uhui-nupuri, " a volcano."

E, " to eat."
Pe, " an article." } Ep, " food."

(c) By compounding adjectives with pe " an article " contracted into p : e.g.

Pase, " heavy,"   Pasep, " a heavy thing."
Poro, " large "   Porop, " a large thing."

(d) By adding p to the passive forms of the verbs, thus :—

VERB.	NOUN.
Ae, " to be eaten."	Aep, " food."
Aye, " to be spoken."	Ayep, " the thing said."

(e) By compounding verbs with katu " shape," " mode," " way " and ambe " a thing," thus :—

An " to be "   An-katu, " existence," " mode of being.
                  An-ambe, " existing thing."
Itak, " to speak,"   Itak-katu, " language."
    „   „   „   Itak-ambe, " a speech."

Variety and diversity of subjects are expressed by prefixing usa or usaine an or neun-neun to nouns ; Thus :—

Usa-wenburi, " a variety of bad habits."
Usaine an itak ambe, " various or many diverse speeches."
Neun-neun ambe, " various or many things."

Diminutives are formed by prefixing pon or poi or suffixing po to nouns : thus :

Poi-shisam, " a Japanese child."

Pon-umma, " a colt."

Pon-beko, " a calf."

Chikap-po, " a little bird."

The Ainu have, as one would naturally expect, adopted a number of Japanese words, most of which are affected by the peculiarities of pronunciation which distinguish the northern dialects of Japanese. Especially to be noted is the tendency to nasalization ; e.g.

JAPANESE.	AINU.
Kami, " paper."	Kam*b*i.
Kogane, " gold."	Ko*n*gane.
Kosode, " a short sleeved garment."	Koso*n*de.
Kugi, " a nail."	Ku*n*gi.
Tabako, tobacco.	Ta*m*bako.

The following are a few samples of Hybrid Compounds. The words which are italicised are Japanese :—

Chikuni-*potoke*, " a wooden idol."

Mama-po, " a step-child."

Niwatori-chikap, domestic fowls."

Pon-*umma*, " colt."

Shiuto-habo, " a mother-in-law."

Shiuto-michi, " a father-in-law."

Shuma-*potoke*, " a stone idol."

Tera-kamui, " a priest."

Tono-nishpa, " a government official."

Tono-ru and *Tono*-para-ru, " a government road."

Yaku-etaye, " to collect taxes."

Yo-an, " to have an engagement, to have business."

PROPER NOUNS.

The following are a few examples of the way in which proper nouns are formed :—

(a) *Names of the Gods.*

(These are given according to their order of dignity and importance).

Kotan kara kamui moshiri kara kamui kandokoro kamui, "the creator" (lit: *the maker of places and worlds and possessor of heaven*).

Abe kamui, "the goddess of fire" (also called *Huchi* or *Fuji kamui* and *Iresu huchi* (lit: *divine grandmother*).

Tokap chup Kamui, "the sun god;" "the sun" itself; (lit : *day luminary Deity*).

Kunne chup Kamui, "the moon god;" "the moon;" (lit. *black luminary Deity*).

Wakka-ush Kamui, "the goddess of the water;" (lit : *watery Deity*).

Chiwash ekot mat, "the goddess of the mouths of rivers;" (lit : *The female possessor of the places where fresh and salt waters mingle*).

Shi-acha Kamui, "a sea-god;" not worshipped; (lit : *wild Uncle Deity*).

Mo-acha Kamui, "a sea-god;" worshipped; (lit : *quiet Uncle Deity*).

Shi-acha and mo-acha are together termed *Rep un Kamui*, "the gods of the sea."

(*b*). *Names of Men.*

Ekash oka Ainu, "the heir of the Ancients."
Hawe riri Ainu, "the eloquent man."
Nupeki san Ainu, "the sender down of light."

(*c*). *Names of Women.*

Ikayup, "the quiver."
Konru san, "the sender down of ice."
Shine ne mat, "the belle."
Shuke mat, "the female cook."
Parapita Ainu, "the mouth loosener."
Ramu an Ainu, "the wise man."
Yuk no uk Ainu, "the deer catcher."
Usapte, "the prolific one."
Yaikoreka, "the selfish one."
Yaitura mat, "the female misanthrope."

(*d*). *Names of Places.*

Erem not or nottu, "the rat cape." (*Cape Erimo*).

E-san-i-not or notu, "the cape where volcanic matter descends." (*Cape Esan*).

Mopet kotan, "village by the quiet river." (*Jap. Mombetsu*).

· Otaru nai, "the brook by the sand road."

Poropet kotan, "the village by the great river." (*Jap. Horobetsu*).

Riri shiri, "the high land," or "the high island."

Satporo kotan, "the village of much dryness." (*Jap. Sapporo*).

CHAPTER VI.

THE ADJECTIVE.

The adjective now undergoes no declension or change to express either case, gender, or comparison, or to point out its relation to other words in a sentence. They may be conveniently classed under two heads, viz, simple and compound.

§ I. SIMPLE ADJECTIVES.

The simple adjectives end in a variety of ways, as for instance in *ai, ak, chi, ka, m, n, p, ra, re, ri, ro, ru, sh, te, tok,* Thus:—

Hekai, "old."	Ratchi, "gentle."
Shisak, "sweet."	Pirika, "good."
Ram, "law."	Pon ; "little."
Retara, "white."	Shiretok, "beautiful."
Poro, "large."	

§ II. COMPOUND ADJECTIVES.

The compound adjectives end in *an, koro, ne, nei, o, sak, tek, un,* and *ush.* Thus :—

Kera an, " sweet."
Haro koro, " fat."
Ashkanne, " clean."
Wayashnu, " wise."
Ki-o, " lousy."

Ramu-sak, " foolish."
Nuchaktek, " merry."
Paro-un, " eloquent."
Kem-ush, " bloody."

Other adjectives appear to be transitive verbs rendered intransitive by prefixing *shi* to them, which particle gives them a reflexive force. Thus :—

Maka, " to open."

Shimaka, " opened ; " " cleared away."

Noye, " to twist."
Pirasa, " to spread out."

Shinoye, " twisted."
Shipirasa, " spread out."

Some adjectives are simply transitive verbs rendered into the passive voice or past tense by having the particle *chi* prefixed to them. Thus :—

Ama, " to place."
Kuba, " to bite."
Pereba, " to cleave."
Tereke, " to jump."
Ye, " to say."

Chiama, " placed."
Chikuba, " bitten."
Chipereba, " cleft."
Chitereke, " jumped."
Chiye, " spoken."

Adjectives may be made plural if necessary by suffixing the ordinary plural particle *pa* to them. Thus :—

SINGULAR.	PLURAL.
Pirika, " good,"	Pirikapa, " good."
Wen, " bad,"	Wenpa, " bad."
Pon, " small,"	Ponpa, " small."
Harokoro, " fat,"	Harokoropa, " fat."

§ III. COMPARISON OF ADJECTIVES.

The comparative and superlative degrees of adjectives are not so extensively used as in English, the meaning being often left to be gathered from the context; but should it be necessary to be explicit, the comparative degree is formed by placing the word *naa*, " yet; " more," and the superlative by placing, *iyotta*, " most " before the positive degree; e.g.

POSITIVE.	COMPARATIVE.	SUPERLATIVE.
Pirika, " good."	Naa pirika, " better."	Iyotta pirika, " best."
Pon, " small."	Naa pon, " smaller."	Iyotta pon, smallest."

"The comparative with " than " may be expressed in six different ways :—(*a*) with the word *akkari ;* (*b*) with *akkari and eashka ;* (c) with *akkari and eitasa ;* (*d*) with *akkari* and *mashkinno ;* (*e*) with *akkari* and *naa ;* (*f*) with *kasu no.* One illustration of each method is here given as an example.

(*a*). The comparative with *akkari.* *Akkari* originally means " to surpass," and may be translated by " than ; " e.g. *E akkari, ku nitan ruwe ne,* " I am faster than you " (lit. *than you, I go fast.*)

(*b*). The comparative with *akkari* and *eashka. Eashka* means " very," " more," e.g. *Ya akkari rep anak ne eashka poro ruwe ne ;* " the sea is greater than the land " (lit. *than the land, the sea is more great.*)

(c). The comparative with *akkari* and *eitasa. Eitasa* means " excess " :—

Toan kotan akkari, tan kotan anak ne eitasa hange no an kotan ne ruwe ne," this village is nearer than that " (lit. *than that village, this village is a nearer village.*)

(*d*). The comparative with *akkari* and *mashkinno. Mashkinno* means " surpassingly "; e.g.

Umma akkari, isepo mashkinno nitan ruwe ne, "a hare is swifter than a horse " (lit. *than a horse, a hare is surpassingly swift of foot.*)

(*e*). The comparative with *akkari* and *naa ;* e.g.

En akkari, eani naa shiwende ruwe ne. " you are a slower walker than I " (lit. *than me, you go more slowly*).

(*f*). The comparative with *kasu no. Kasu* no means " surpassing," e.g.

En kasu no, e ri ruwe ne, " you are taller than I (lit. *surpassing* me, you are tall.)

---

§ IV. DEMONSTRATIVE ADJECTIVES.

The demonstrative adjectives " this," " that," " these " and " those," are as follows :—

SINGULAR.	PLURAL.
Ta an or tan, " this."	Tan okai, " these."
Nei a, " that."	Nei okai, " those."
Nei an, " that,"	(*a short distance off*).
(*a short distance off*).	To an okai, " those."
To an, " that."	(*a good distance off*).
(*a good distance off*).	

The singular form of these adjectives may be prefixed to plural nouns ; but the plural forms can never be placed before singular nouns. The reason is that *okai* is really a plural verb meaning " to dwell at " or " be in " a place. It is the plural form of *an,* " to be."

---

§ V. THE INFLUENCE OF CERTAIN PARTICLES AND WORDS UPON SOME OF THE ADJECTIVES.

When the particle *e* is prefixed to certain adjectives it has the power of changing them into verbs ; e.g.

ADJECTIVES.	VERBS.
Hapuru, " soft."	E hapuru, " to be unable to endure."
Nishte, " hard."	E nishte, " to be able to endure."

Some adjectives, by taking *no* after them, become adverbs ;
e.g.

ADJECTIVES.	ADVERBS.
Ashiri, " new."	Ashin'no, " newly."
Son, " true."	Sonno, " truly."

A few adjectives become adverbs by taking the word *tara*
after them ; e.g.

ADJECTIVES.	ADVERBS.
Moire, " slow."	Moire-tara, " slowly."
Ratchi, " gentle."	Ratchi-tara, " gently."

When the letter *p* is suffixed to some of the simple adjectives
which end in *a, e, i,* or *o,* or to any of the adjectives compounded with *ne* or *nu* they become nouns. thus :—

SIMPLE.

ADJECTIVES.	NOUNS.
Atomte, " neat."	Atomtep, " a neat thing."
Ichakkere, " dirty."	Ichakkerep, " a dirty thing."
A-ekatnu, " delicious,"	A-ekatnup, " a delicious thing."
Ashkanne, " clean."	Ashkannep, " a clean thing."

The letter *p*, which is here compounded with the adjectives,
is a contraction of *pe* " a thing." This should be carefully
borne in mind lest, in construing, mistakes should arise. The
p converts the adjective to which it is attached, into a concrete,
not into an abstract, noun. Thus *kaparap* is not " thinness,"
but " a thin thing ;" and *porop* is not " largeness," but " a large
thing ;" nor is *wayashnup* "wisdom," but " a wise person " or
" thing."

As the other adjectives, namely a few of the simple, and all
of the remaining compound adjectives, are incapable of taking
the contracted form *p* after them, they are followed by the word
in full, that is, *pe* softened into *be*, thus :—

Hekaibe, " an old person."	Sakanramkorobe, " a quarrel-
Kumi-ushbe, " a mouldy thing."	some person."
Paro unbe, " an eloquent person."	Tum sakbe, " a weak thing."

CHAPTER VII.

THE NUMERALS.

The numerals assume four forms in the Ainu language, viz. ; first, the Radical form ; second, the Substantive form ; third, the Ordinal form ; fourth, the Adverbial form.

---

§ I. THE RADICAL FORMS.

The radical forms of the numerals are as follows :—

Shine	1	Arawan ikashima wa (n)..	17
Tu	2	Tupe-san ikashima wa (n).	18
Re	3	Shinepe-san ikashima wa	
Ine	4	(n)	19
Ashikne	5	[2]Hot ne	20
Iwa (n)	6	Shine ikashima hot ne ...	21
Arawa (n)	7	Tu ikashima hot ne	22
Tupe-san	8	Re ikashima hot ne	23
Shinepe-san	9	Ine ikashima not ne	24
'Wa (n)	10	Ashikne ikashima hot ne..	25
Shine ikashima wa (n) ...	11	Iwan ikashima hot ne	26
Tu ikashima wa (n)	12	Arawan ikashima hot ne...	27
Re ikashima wa (n)	13	Tupe-san ikashima hot ne.	28
Ine ikashima wa (n)	14	Shinepe-san ikashima hot	
Ashikne ikashima wa (n)..	15	ne	29
Iwan ikashima wa (n) ...	16	Wan e, tu hot ne	30

---

[1] But in counting fish 10 is *carasamne no wan*; while in counting animals 10 is *shine atuita*.

[2] In counting fish 20 is *shine shike*, i.e. one bundle, or "one load."

Shine ikashima, wan e, tu hot ne	31	Iwan ikashima, wan e, tu hot ne	36
Tu ikashima, wan e, tu hot ne	32	Arawan ikashima, wan e, tu hot ne	37
Re ikashima, wan e, tu hot ne	33	Tupe-san ikashima, wan e, tu hot ne	38
Ine ikashima wan e, tu hot ne	34	Shinepe-san ikashima, wan e, tu hot ne	39
Ashikne ikashima, wan e, tu hot ne	35	Tu hot ne	40

Twenty, more literally a "score," is the highest unit ever present to the Ainu mind when counting. Thus, forty is "two score" (*tu hot ne*); sixty is "three score" (*re hot ne*); eighty is "four score" (*ine hot ne*); and a hundred is "five score" (*ashikne hot ne*).

Numbers may be framed by means of scores to an indefinite extent; but in actual practice the higher numbers are rarely, if ever, met with. At the present day, the simpler Japanese method of numeration is rapidly supplanting the cumbrous native system.

In order to arrive at a clear comprehension of the Ainu system of counting, the student must carefully note the following two particulars :—

(*a.*)—The word *ikashima* commonly means, "excess," "redundance;" but with the numerals it signifies, "addition," "to add to." It is always placed after the number which is conceived of as added.

(*b.*)—The particle *e* signifies "to subtract," "to take from," and follows the number which is supposed to be taken away. Care must therefore be taken not to confound this particle with the *e* which is used as a preposition, and which means, "to," "towards." Thus *tu ikashima wa(n)* is, "two added to ten," i.e. 12; and *shinepe-san ikashima, wan e, tu hot ne*, is, "nine added to, ten taken from, two score;" and so on.

Note also the following expressions :—*E-tup*, "one and a half;" *e-rep*, "two and a half;" *e-inep*, "three and a half."

Shine ikashima, tu hot ne. 41
Tu ikashima, tu hot ne ... 42
Re ikashima, tu hot ne ... 43
Ine ikashima, tu hot ne... 44
Ashikne ikashima, tu hot
ne 45
Iwan ikashima, tu hot ne. 46
Arawan ikashima, tu hot
ne 47
Tupe-san ikashima, tu hot
ne 48
Shinepe-san ikashima, tu
hot ne 49
Wan e, re hot ne 50
Shine ikashima, wan e, re
hot ne 51
Tu ikashima, wan e, re
hot ne 52
Re ikashima, wan e, re hot
ne 53
Ine ikashima, wan e, re
hot ne 54
Ashikne ikashima, wan e,
re hot ne 55
Iwan ikashima, wan e, re
hot ne 56
Arawan ikashima, wan e,
re hot ne 57
Tupe-san ikashima, wan e,
re hot ne 58
Shinepe-san ikashima, wan
e, re hot ne 59
Re hot ne 60
Shine ikashima, re hot ne. 61
Tu ikashima, re hot ne ... 62
Re ikashima, re hot ne ... 63

Ine ikashima, re hot ne... 64
Ashikne ikashima, re hot
ne 65
Iwan ikashima, re hot ne. 66
Arawan ikashima, re hot
ne 67
Tupe-san ikashima, re hot
ne 68
Shinepe-san ikashima, re
hot ne 69
Wan e, ine hot ne 70
Shine ikashima, wan e, ine
hot ne 71
Tu ikashima, wan e, ine
hot ne 72
Re ikashima, wan e, ine
hot ne 73
Ine ikashima, wan e, ine
hot ne 74
Ashikne ikashima, wan e,
ine hot ne 75
Iwan ikashima, wan e, ine
hot ne 76
Arawan ikashima, wan e,
ine hot ne.................. 77
Tupe-san ikashima, wan e,
ine hot ne.................. 78
Shinepe-san, ikashima, wan
e, ine hot ne 79
Ine hot ne 80
Shine ikashima, ine hot ne. 81
Tu ikashima, ine hot ne... 82
Re ikashima, ine hot ne... 83
Ine ikashima, ine hot ne.. 84
Ashikne ikashima, ine hot
ne 85

Iwan ikashima, ine hot
ne 86
Arawan ikashima, ine hot
ne 87
Tupe-san ikashima, ine hot
ne 88
Shinepe-san ikashima, ine
hot ne 89
Wan e, ashikne hot ne ... 90
Shine ikashima, wan e,
ashikne hot ne 91
Tu ikashima, wan e, ashikne
hot ne 92
Re ikashima, wan e, ashikne
hot ne 93
Ine ikashima, wan e, ashik-
ne hot ne 94
Ashikne ikashima, wan e,
ashikne hot ne 95
Iwan ikashima, wan e,
ashikne hot ne............ 96
Arawan ikashima, wan e,
ashikne hot ne............ 97
Tupe-san ikashima, wan e,
ashikne hot ne............ 98
Shinepe-san ikashima, wan
e, ashikne hot ne......... 99
Ashikne hot ne 100
Shine ikashima, ashikne hot
ne 101
Wan e, iwan hot ne 110
Shine ikashima, wan e,
iwan hot ne 111
Iwan hot ne.................. 120
Shine ikashima, iwan hot
ne 121

Wan e, arawan hot ne ... 130
Shine ikashima, wan e,
arawan hot ne 131
Arawan hot ne............... 140
Shine ikashima, arawan hot
ne 141
Wan e, tupe-san hot ne... 150
Shine ikashima, wan e,
tupe-san hot ne 151
Tupe-san hot ne 160
Shine ikashima, tupe-san
hot ne 161
Wan e, shinepe-san hot
ne 170
Shine ikashima, wan e, shi-
nepe-san hot ne 171
Shinepe-san hot ne 180
Shine ikashima shinepe-san
hot ne 181
Wan e, shine wan hot ne. 190
Shine ikashima, wan e,
shine wan hot ne 191
Shine wan hot ne 200
Ashikne hot ikashima, shine
wan hot ne 300
Tu shine wan hot ne 400
Ashikne hot ikashima, tu
shine wan hot ne 500
Re shine wan hot ne 600
Ashikne hot ikashima, re
shine wan hot ne......... 700
Ine shine wan hot ne...... 800
Ashikne hot ikashima, ine
shine wan hot ne......... 900
Ashikne shine wan hot
ne 1,000

The radical form is always placed before the noun to which it refers; e.g.

Shine itangi, one cup.

Tu ai, two arrows.

Re kuiop, three wild geese.

Ine retat'chiri, four swans.

Shine isepo, one hare.

Tu ichaniu, two salmon trout.

Re nok, three eggs.

Ine yaoshkep, four spiders.

The radical form *shine* is also often used as the indefinite article *a* or *an*. See Chapter IV. The Article.

---

§ II. THE SUBSTANTIVE FORM.

The substantive form of the numeral is two-fold. For persons it is formed by adding *niu*, in some of the numbers abbreviated to the single consonant *n*. For things and animals it is formed by adding *pe*, *be*, or the letter *p* alone. *Niu* means "person," and *pe* means "thing," e.g.

Niu, "a person."

Shinen, one person.

Tun, two persons.

Ren, three persons.

Inen, four persons.

Ashikne niu, five persons.

Iwa niu, six persons.

Arawa niu, seven persons.

Tupe-san niu, eight persons.

Shinepe-san niu, nine persons.

Wa niu, ten persons.

Shinen ikashima wa niu, eleven persons.

Tun ikashima wa niu, twelve persons.

Hot ne niu, twenty persons.

Wa niu e tu hot ne niu, thirty persons.

Shinen ikashima wa niu e tu hot ne niu, thirty-one persons.

Ashikne hot ne niu, one hundred persons.

Pe, *be*, *p*, "thing."

Shinep, one thing.

Tup, two things.

Rep, three things.

Inep, four things.

Ashiknep, five things.

Iwanbe, six things.

Arawanbe, seven things.

Tupe-sanbe, eight things.

Shinepe-sanbe, nine things.

Wanbe, ten things.

Shinep ikashima wanbe, eleven things.

Tup ikashima wanbe, twelve things.

Hot nep, twenty things.

Wanbe e tu hot nep, twenty-one things.

Shinep ikashima wanbe e tu hot nep, thirty-one things.

Ashikne hot nep, one hundred things.

[N.B.—Note carefully the repetition of the noun after each numeral.]

With the numbers two and three, quadrupeds and sometimes even inanimate objects are counted with the word *pish*, e.g.

Seta shinep, one dog.

Seta tup pish, two dogs.

Seta rep pish, three dogs.

Seta inep, four dogs.

Niu, pe and *pish* may be considered to correspond in some degree to the so-called "classifiers" or "auxiliary numerals" of Chinese, Japanese, and many other Eastern languages; but no further trace of such "classifiers" exists.

The radical form can never be used in answer to a question. In such a case one of the substantive forms must be employed.

Some nouns are excluded by their nature from both the above categories. The following are a few such words. *Kamui* "god or gods; *To,* "a day;" *Tokap* "day;" *Kunne* "night," "black."

Kamui is counted as follows :—

Shine kamui, one god.

Tu kamui, two gods.

Re kamui, three gods.

Ine kamui, four gods.

Ashikne kamui, five gods.

Iwan kamui, six gods.

Arawan kamui, seven gods.

Tupe-san kamui, eight gods.

Shinepe-san kamui, nine gods.

Wan kamui, ten gods.

Shine kamui ikashima wan kamui, eleven gods.

Tu kamui ikashima wan kamui, twelve gods.

Hot ne kamui, twenty gods.

And so on.

To is counted as follows :—

Shine to, one day.

Tut ko, two days.

Rere ko, three days.

Ine rere ko, four days.

Ashikne rere ko, five days.
Iwan rere ko, six days.
Arawan rere ko, seven days.
Tupe-san rere ko, eight days.
Shinepe-san rere ko, nine days.
Wan to, ten days.
Shine to ikashima wan to, eleven days.
Tut ko ikashima wan to, twelve days.
Rere ko ikashima wan to, thirteen days.
Hot ne to, twenty days.
Wan to e tu hot ne to, thirty days.
Tu hot ne rere ko, forty days.
Wan to e re hot ne rere ko, fifty days.
Re hot ne rere ko, sixty days.
Ashikne hot ne to, one hundred days.

Tokap is counted as follows:—

Tokap shine to, one day.
Tokap tut ko, two days.
Tokap rere ko, three days.
Tokap rere ko ine rere ko, four days.
Tokap rere ko ashikne rere ko, five days.
Tokap rere ko iwan rere ko, six days.
Tokap rere ko arawan rere ko, seven days.
Tokap rere ko tupe-san rere ko, eight days.
Tokap rere ko shinepe-san rere ko, nine days.
Wan to, ten days.
Tokap shine to ikashima wan to, eleven days.
Tokap tut ko ikashima wan to, twelve days.
Tokap rere ko ikashima wan to, thirteen days.
Tokap rere ko ine rere ko ikashima wan to, fourteen days.
Hot ne to, twenty days.

And so on.

Sometimes *tokap* is counted thus:—

Tokap to shine to, one day.
Tokap to rereko, three days.
Tokap to tutko, two days.

And so on.

Kunne is counted as follows:—

Shine anchikara, one night.
Tu anchikara, two nights.
Re anchikara (*also kunne rere ko*), three nights.
Kunne rere ko ine rere ko, four nights.

Kunne rere ko ashikne rere ko, five nights.

Kunne rere ko iwan rere ko, six nights.

Kunne rere ko arawan rere ko, seven nights.

Kunne rere ko tupe-san rere ko, eight nights.

Kunne rere ko shinepe-san rere ko, nine nights.

Wan anchikara, ten nights.

And so on ; i.e. adding. *kunne* and *kunne rere ko* wherever *tokap* and *tokap rere ko* would be added to express " day."

Sometimes *kunne* is counted thus :—

Kunne .to shine anchikara.   One night.
Kunne to tu anchikara.   Two nights.
Kunne to re anchikara.   Three nights.
                And so on.

---

§ III. THE ORDINAL FORM.

The ordinal numerals are expressed in two ways. The first is as follows :—

Shine ikinne, first.

Tu ikinne, second.

Re ikinne, third.

Ine ikinne, fourth.

Ashikne ikinne, fifth.

Iwan ikinne, sixth.

Arawan ikinne, seventh.

Tupe-san ikinne, eighth.

Shinepe-san ikinne, ninth.

Wan ikinne, tenth.

And so on ; adding *ikinne* to the radical form wherever *pe*, *be*, or *p* would be placed for the substantive form.

The second way is as follows, but goes no higher than ten. Above ten the first method alone is in use :—

Shine otutanu, first.

Tu otutanu second.

Iye e re ikinne, third.

Iye e ine ikinne, fourth.

Iye e ashikne ikinne, fifth.

Iye e iwan ikinne, sixth.

Iye e arawan ikinne, seventh.

Iye e tupe-san ikinne, eighth.

Iye e shinepe-san ikinne, ninth.

Iye wan ikinne, tenth.

The ordinals are rarely met with. When they are used, the noun is preceded by *no an*, e.g.

Shine ikinne no an ainu, the first man.
Shine tutanu no an chisei, the first house.

And so on.

§ IV. THE ADVERBIAL FORM.

The adverbial form of the numeral is formed by adding *shui-ne* to the radical, e.g.

Ara shui-ne, or a-shui-ne once.
Tu shui-ne, twice.
Re shui-ne, thrice.
Ine shui-ne, four times.
Ashikne shui-ne, five times.

Iwan shui-ne, six times.
Arawan shui-ne, seven times.
Tupe-san shui-ne, eight times.
Shinepe-san shui-ne, nine times.
Wa shui-ne, ten times.

And so on.

The word *shui-ne* is compounded from *shui*, "again" and *ne*, part of the verb "to be;" *shui-ne* would therefore mean, "to be again."

§ V. MISCELLANEOUS.

The following miscellaneous expressions may be conveniently here noted.

Pairs of articles are expressed by the word *uren*, "both," placed before the noun, e.g. :—

SINGULAR.	PLURAL
Chikiri, the leg ; foot.	Uren chikiri, both legs or feet.
¹Huyehe, a cheek.	Uren huyehe, both cheeks.
Keire, a shoe.	Uren keire, both shoes.
Kema, a foot ; a leg.	Uren kema, both feet or legs.
Kesup, a heel.	Uren kesup, both heels.
Kisara, an ear.	Uren kisara, both ears.
Kokkasapa, a knee.	Uren kokkasapa, both knees.
Noyapi, a jaw.	Uren noyapi, both jaws.

¹ This word is often pronounced *Fuyehe*.

One of a pair is expressed by prefixing the word *oara* to the noun, e.g. :—

Paraori, insteps.	Oara[1] paraori, one instep.
Patoi, lips.	Oara patoi, one lip.
Raru, eyebrows.	Oara raru, one eyebrow.
Shiki, eyes.	Oara shiki, one eye.
Tapsutu, shoulders.	[2]Oara tapsutu, one shoulder.
Teke, hands.	Oara teke, one hand.
Tokumpone, ankles.	Oara tokumpone, one ankle.

It may be found useful to note also the following phrases :—

(*a.*) Shinen shinen, one by one.
      Tun tun, two and two. } Used only of persons.
      Ren ren, three and three.

And so on.

(*b.*) Shinen range, singly.
      Tun range, by twos. } Used only of persons.
      Ren range, by threes.

And so on.

(*c.*) Shinep shinep, one by one
      Tup tup, two and two.
      Shinep range, singly. } Used of animals and things.
      Tup range, by twos.

And so on.

(*d.*) Chup emko e tu chup, a month and a half.
      Chup emko e re chup, two months and a half.

And so on.

---

[1] Oara is from *a* which also becomes *ara*.

[2] Before *t* the final *ra* may be changed into *t*, thus making *oat-tapsutu*.

CHAPTER VIII.

THE PRONOUN.

The Pronouns are divided into Personal, Possessive, Relative, Indefinite and Interrogative. What are generally termed "Demonstrative Pronouns" will be found under the Adjective Chapter VI.

SECTION I.

The personal pronouns are as follows, their forms differing according to the context.

THE FIRST PERSON SINGULAR.

K, Ku, Kuani, Kani, Anokai and *Chokai*, " I."

(*a*.) *K*, is particularly used with verbs commencing with a vowel as :—

Kek, " I come." Koira, " I forget."

(*b*.) *Ku* is probably the original word whence *K* is contracted. It is better to use *Ku* than *K*, for the contraction *K* is not always understood whereas *Ku* is known all over Yezo.

(*c*.) *Kuani* may be derived thus; *Ku.* " I ;" *an*, " to be ;" *i* a substantivising particle. *Kuani* and *ku* are sometimes used together in a sentence ; as for instance :—

Kuani ku nukara,
Moi je vois, } " I see."

(*d*.) *Kani* is a simple contraction of *ku-ani*, and is now considered by some to be a somewhat impolite mode of speech.

(*e*.) *Anokai* may be derived from *an* " to be," and *okai*, a plural form of *an*. It is supposed to be only used by superiors to inferiors when speaking of oneself.

(*f.*) *Chokai* is sometimes heard for " I " ; it is a contraction of *chi* which means " we," and *okai*, which signifies " to be " or " to be at a place." *Chokai* is principally used by low class Japanese when attempting to speak Ainu, and by Ainu only when addressing Japanese or persons but imperfectly acquainted with the Ainu language. It has come to be pigeon Ainu.

THE SECOND PERSON SINGULAR.

The pronouns of the second person singular are :—

E, eani, yani, aokai and *anokai.*

(*a.*) *E* appears to be the original word from which *eani* has been formed ; thus :—

E-an-i, as shown in *Ku-an-i* above.

(*b.*) Y*ani* is now a very contemptuous expression, and is a corruption of *eani.* It is in fact pigeon Ainu, and equals c*hokai* of the 1st. person.

(*c.*) *Aokai,* which is a contraction of *anokai,* is, like *anokai,* a more polite form of speech than *eani,* but neither are so often used. *Aokai* and *anokai* were originally plurals, and are still so used in certain contexts.

Sometimes the words *ku shiroma* and·*e shiroma* are heard for the first and second person singular respectively, but not often. *Shiroma* is a verb meaning " to abide," " to stay." Thus *ku sh·roma* really means " I who am here ; " and *e shiroma* " you who are there."

THE THIRD PERSON.

There is no proper third personal pronoun. Its place is supplied by the word *Shiroma, Shinuma,* and the demonstrative adjectives.

Tan guru, " this person." (man or woman).

Tambe ; " this thing."

Nei ambe or guru, " that thing or person " (a little way off.)

To ambe or guru, " that thing or person " (a greater distance off).

Tap, "this thing" (whether far off or near).

Ne a ikiyap, "that thing or fellow" (a word of contempt).

Shiroma, he, she, it.

Shinuma, he, she, it.

Sometimes, however, the particle *a,* contracted from *anun,* "another person," or "the person" is used as an honourable way of speaking of one's own master or a superior; thus :—

A e hotuyekara, "he is calling you." *Anun,* pronounced in full, is sometimes used by a servant when addressing his master.

In such cases *anun* means "you;" thus :—

Hunna? "who?" *Anun,* "the other person," i.e. "you."

The above forms are used only at the beginning of sentences, and are never immediately prefixed to verbs. Before verbs, "we" is expressed by *chi,* and "ye" by *echi;* and after verbs "we" is *ash.*

The following are examples.

Chi utara anak ne Ainu chi ne, "we are Ainu."

Echi utara anak ne Ainu echi ne, "ye are Ainu."

Chi kara, "we make."

Kara ash "we make."

The plurals of the third personal pronouns are as follows :—

Tan utara or tan okai utara, "these persons."

Nei utara or nei okai utara, "they" (persons a little way off).

To an utara or to okai utara, "they," (persons farther off).

Tan okai be, "these things," "these."

Nei okai be, "those things," "they" (a short ·distance off).

To an okai be⎱"those things," "they" (a greater distance
To okai be ⎰ off).

Shiroma utara, "they" or "those."

[N.B.] Care should be taken not to use *pe* or *b* when persons are intended; for *pe* or *b* can only be correctly applied to the lower orders of creation.

Thus the pronouns are :—

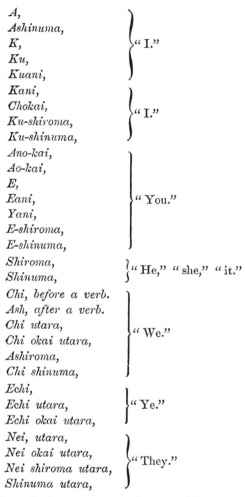

A,
Ashinuma,
K,
Ku,
Kuani,
} "I."

Kani,
Chokai,
Ku-shiroma,
Ku-shinuma,
} "I."

Ano-kai,
Ao-kai,
E,
Eani,
Yani,
E-shiroma,
E-shinuma,
} "You."

Shiroma,
Shinuma,
} "He," "she," "it."

Chi, before a verb.
Ash, after a verb.
Chi utara,
Chi okai utara,
Ashiroma,
Chi shinuma,
} "We."

Echi,
Echi utara,
Echi okai utara,
} "Ye."

Nei, utara,
Nei okai utara,
Nei shiroma utara,
Shinuma utara,
} "They."

The reflexive pronoun *yaikota,* " self," is used as follows :—

Kuani yaikota or *kuani kuyaikota ;* " I myself."

Eani yaikota or *eani eyaikota ;* " you yourself."

Nei guru yaikota ; " he himself" or " she herself."

Before verbs a kind of double reflexive is sometimes used ; thus :—

Yaikota yai-raige ; " he killed himself."

---

§ II. THE CASES OF PRONOUNS.

The various forms of the first and second persons mentioned above in Sect. I, may be termed nominatives. The following examples will illustrate this :—

Kuani tanebo *ku* ek ruwe ne, *I* have just come (i.e. come for the first time.)

Eani e arapa ya ? " have *you* been ? "

Eani nepka *e* ye ya ? " did *you* say something ?

Ku oman, " *I* am going."

The following is an example of the longer form of a pronoun used without the corresponding short one, e.g. :—

Eani nekon a ramu ya ? " what do you think ?"

The first person, moreover, has forms corresponding to the English objective case. They are :—

> *En,* " me."
> *E,* " you."
> *Un,* " us."
> *I,* " us."
> *Echi,* " ye." e.g. :—

> Nei guru *en* kik, " he struck *me.*"
> Kamui *un* kara, " God made *us.*"
> *I* omap, " he loves *us.*"

In the second person the objective case is rendered by *e* for the singular, and *echi* for the plural ; never by the longer forms given in Section I ; e.g. :—

Seta *e* kuba, " the dog will bite *you.*"

Kuani *echi* uitek ash, " I will employ *you* " (*plural*).

The action of the first person upon the second is indicated by placing the objective of the person before the verb, and the word *ash* after it ; thus :—

Kuani echi kik ash, " I will beat you " (*plural*).

Kuani e omap ash, " I love you " (*singular*).

When construed with passive verbs, the second person takes the substantive verb *an* after the verb ; e.g. :—

E omap an, " you are loved."

Echi kara an, " ye are made."

The third person has as a rule no special forms for the objective case ; but *a* the passive particle is sometimes used as an objective of the 3rd person, thus :—

Tan utara or shinnma utara a-kik nangoro, " they will probably be struck."

Nei ainu a-ronuu wa isam, " those men have been killed."

Set akara ? " shall I prepare the table " ?

Postpositions sometimes take the objective case of pronouns, and sometimes the full form ; e.g. :—

En orowa oman, " he went *from* me.

Un osh ek, " come *behind us.*"

Eani orowa no arapa guru, " the person who went *after you.*"

---

§ III. THE POSSESSIVE PRONOUNS.

The possessive forms of pronouns are obtained by adding *koro*, sometimes softened into *goro*, to the personal pronoun. *Koro* means, " to possess ; " e.g. :—

SINGULAR.	PLURAL.
Ku koro, " my "	Chi koro " our."
E koro, " thine "	Echi koro, " your."
Tan guru koro. ⎫ " his "	Tan okai utara koro. ⎫
Nei guru koro. ⎬ or	Nei okai utara koro. ⎬ " their."
To an guru koro. ⎭ " her."	To an okai utara koro. ⎭

The double form may be used ; thus :—

SINGULAR.	PLURAL.
Kuani ku goro, " my."	Chi utara chi koro, " our."
Eani e koro, " thy."	Echi utara echi koro, " your."

The following use of *koro* should also be noted.

Heikachi koro, " to nurse a child."

Heikachi koro guru, "a nurse." *Toi-chisei kotcha guru*, "pit-dwellers" or "persons living in earth houses" *kotcha* being a plural form of *koro*.

Sometimes *a-koro* is used instead of *chi koro*, but not often; When there is no likelihood of ambiguity, the word *koro* is dropped. e.g. :—

SINGULAR.	PLURAL.
Ku michi, "my father."	Chi uni, "our home."
E habo, "thy mother."	Echi ottena, "your chief."

§ IV. THE RELATIVE PRONOUNS.

The relative pronouns may be expressed in the following manner :—

(*a.*) With the words *sekoro, ani* or *ari* thus :—

Ainu sekoro aye utara, "the people who are called Ainu."

Yuk ani aye chikokip, "the animals called deer."

Shirau ari aye kikiri, "the insects called gadflies.

(*b.*) With the verb used attributively; e.g. :—

A-raige-guru, "the person who was killed" (lit. the killed person).

Ainu raige guru, "the person who killed a man" (lit. the person killing man).

Umma o guru, "the person who rides the horse" (lit. the horse riding person).

§ V. THE INDEFINITE PRONOUNS.

The Indefinite Pronouns are as follows :—

Nen neyakka,
Nen nen neyakka, } "Anyone," "everyone," "whosoever."
Nen ne kuru ka,

Nep neyakka, } "Either," "whatever," "whichever."
Nep nep neyakka,

Nepka, "something."

Nenka, "someone."

§ VI. THE INTERROGATIVE PRONOUNS.

The interrogative pronouns are :—

> Hunna or hunnak, " who ? "
> Hemanda or makanak, " what ? "
> Inan or inan ike, ⎱ " which ? "
> Inambe,   ⎰
> Nekon a, " what kind ? "

CHAPTER IX.

THE VERB.

§ I. PRELIMINARY REMARKS ON THE VERB.

Verbs, in the Ainu language, have but one mood, namely, the indicative. The imperative and all the indirect or oblique moods, as well as the desiderative forms and all the tenses, are expressed by means of separate words. No verb, therefore, can be conjugated without the use of various auxiliaries.

These auxiliaries are, for the present tense, as follows :—

(*a.*) *Ruwe ne.*

These words indicate that a subject is concluded, or a sentence finished. They therefore equal what is commonly called " the conclusive form."

(*b.*) *Shiri ne.*

Shiri is a verb meaning " to be doing." When placed after other verbs, it indicates that the action is still going on.

(*c.*) *Kor'an.*

Kor'an is short for *koro an,* and means " to be possessing."

When used as an auxiliary to verbs, it, like *shiri ne*, signifies that the action is still in progress. It expresses, so, to speak, "the very act."

(*d.*) *Tap an.*

The words *tap an* mean "it is so," and, added to verbs, they give them an emphatic force. It is as though one said, "it is so, and no mistake."

For the past tense the following auxiliaries are used :—

(*a.*) *Nisa.*

This word seems to be the proper auxiliary for the past tense. Its real meaning is doubtful.

(*b.*) *Okere.*

Okere is a verb meaning "to finish;" and, when added to other verbs, gives them a conclusive force. When so used, it resembles the English perfect tense.

(*c.*) *Awa.*

This word is a passive participle meaning "being," "having been." When placed after a verb, it indicates that one thing having been done, another was commenced, e.g.

Ki awa, oman ruwe ne, having done it, he went away.

(*d.*) *A-eramu shin'ne.*

For the past tense the words *a-eramu shin'ne* are sometimes used ; e.g.

Ibe a-eramu shin'ne, "I have eaten," or "finished eating."

Iku a-eramu shin'ne, "I have drunk," or "finished drinking."

Kara a-eramshinne, I have finished doing it.

The auxiliaries used to express future time are as follows :—

(*a.*) *Kusu ne*, "will be." Before the verb *ki* the final *ne* is dropped and *kusu* is changed into *kush*, and thus is made the future participle. As :—kush ki, "about to do."

Kik kush ki, "about to strike."

(*b.*) *Nangoro*, "probably will be." This word expresses doubt and never amounts to more than probability. As :—Oman nangoro "he will probably go."

The words *ruwe ne* my be added to the root or to either of the above auxiliaries; and the particle *na*, which has also a conclusive force in it, may follow them.

Both the past and future tenses may be indicated by adverbs of time being placed before the person of the verb. In such cases the auxiliaries may be retained or omitted at pleasure.

It will be seen by reference to the passive voice, that, with the second person singular and plural, the verb *an* always follows the chief verb. *An* is the substantive verb " to be."

The verbs of the Ainu language naturally resolve themselves into two divisions, viz :—

(*a*.) Those of unchanging stem. To this class belong all verbs ending otherwise than in *ra* or *ro*.

(*b*.) Those whose stems change. These verbs end only in *ra* and *ro*. The two verbs *kik*, " to strike," and *kara*, " to make," have been given as illustrations of these two categories.

---

§ II. PARADIGMS OF VERBS.

CLASS I.—VERBS OF UNCHANGING STEM.
THE VERB KIK, "TO STRIKE."

INDICATIVE MOOD.

Present Tense.

(*a*.) The first Present tense.

SINGULAR.	(ACTIVE.)	PLURAL.
Ku kik, I strike.		⌠Chi kik, we strike.
		⌡Kikpa,[1] ,,
E kik, you strike.		Echi kik, ye strike.
Kik, (he) strikes.		Kik, (they) strike.

---

[1] *Pa* is a plural suffix of the person of the verb, which in some localities would be pronounced *cha*.

| SINGULAR. | (PASSIVE.) | PLURAL. |

A-en kik, I am struck.   A-un kik, we are struck.

E kik an, you are struck.   Echi kik an, ye are struck.

A-kik, (he) is struck.   A-kik, (they) are struck.

(*b.*) The present tense with the auxiliary *ruwe ne*.

| SINGULAR. | (ACTIVE.) | PLURAL. |

Ku kik ruwe ne, I strike.   {Chi kik ruwe ne, we strike.
                          {Kikpa ruwe ne,   ,,

(PASSIVE.)

A-en kik ruwe ne, I am struck.   A-un kik ruwe ne, we are struck.

(*c.*) The present tense with the words *shiri ne*.

| SINGULAR. | (ACTIVE.) | PLURAL. |

Ku kik shiri ne, I am striking. {Chi kik shiri ne,} we are strik-
                                {Kikpa shiri ne, } ing.

(PASSIVE.)

A-en kik shiri ne, I am being   A-un kik shiri ne, we are being
struck.   struck.

(*d.*) The present tense with *koro an*.

| SINGULAR. | (ACTIVE.) | PLURAL. |

Ku kik kor'an, I am striking. {Chi kik kor'an,} we are strik-
                              {Kipa kor'an,   } ing.

(PASSIVE.)

A-en kik kor'an, I am being   A-un kik kor'an, we are being
struck.   struck.

- (*e.*) The present tense with *ruwe tap an*.

| SINGULAR. | (ACTIVE.) | PLURAL. |

Ku kik ruwe tap an, I strike. {Chi kik ruwe tap an, we strike.
                                {Kikpa ruwe tap an,   ,,

(PASSIVE.)

A-en kik ruwe tap an, I am   A-un kik ruwe tap an, we are
struck.   struck.

Past Tense.

(*a.*) The past tense with *nisa*.

SINGULAR.   (ACTIVE.)   PLURAL.

Ku kik nisa, I struck. {Chi kik nisa, we are struck.
                       {Kikpa nisa,   ..

(PASSIVE.)

A-en kik nisa, I was struck.   A-un kik nisa, we were struck.

(b.) The past tense with *okere*.

SINGULAR.   (ACTIVE.)   PLURAL.

Ku kik okere, I struck. {Chi kik okere, we struck.
                        {Kikpa okere,   ,,

(PASSIVE.)

A-en kik okere, I was struck.   A-un kik okere, we were struck.

(c.) The past tense with *awa*. In certain combinations this form is equal to the English perfect tense :—

SINGULAR.   (ACTIVE.)   PLURAL.

Ku kik awa, I have struck, {Chi kik awa,} we have struck,
or I struck.   {Kikpa awa,   } or we struck.

(PASSIVE.)

SINGULAR.

A-en kik awa, I have been struck, or I was struck.

[It would be equally correct to translate *awa* by "having been," as :—*e kik an awa*, you having been struck."]

PLURAL.

A-un kik awa, we have been struck, or we were struck.

The future tense.

(a.) *Kusu ne.*

SINGULAR.   (ACTIVE.)   PLURAL.

Ku kik kusu ne, I will strike. {Chi kik kusu ne,} we will
                               {Kikpa kusu ne,   } strike.

(PASSIVE.)

A-en kik kusu ne, I shall be   A-un kik kusu ne, we shall be
struck.   struck.

(b.) *Nangoro.*

SINGULAR. (ACTIVE.) PLURAL.

Ku kik nangoro, I shall prob- { Chi kik nangoro, } we shall probably strike. { Kikpa nangoro, } ably strike.

(PASSIVE.)

A-en kik nangoro, I shall prob- A-un kik nangoro, we shall
ably be struck. probably be struck.

The Imperative is expressed thus :—

SINGULAR. (ACTIVE.) PLURAL.

Kik, } strike thou. { Kik yan or ara, strike ye.
Kik ara, } { Kikpa yan or ara, „

Kik yara, to strike through another.

(PASSIVE.)

E-kik an, be thou struck. { Echi a-kik an, be ye struck.
{ A-un kik anro, let us be struck.

Desire is expressed by the word *rusui;* e.g.

SINGULAR. (ACTIVE.) PLURAL.

Ku kik rusui, I desire to strike. { Chi kik rusui, we desire to strike.
{ Kikpa rusui, ..

(PASSIVE.)

A-en kik an rusui, I desire to A-un kik an rusui, we desire
be struck. to be struck.

The Potential Mood may be expressed in three ways; (a) by
the word *etokush;* (b) by the word *kusu ne ap;* (c) by the
words *shomoki ko wen.*

(a.) The Potential with *etokush.*

SINGULAR. (ACTIVE.) PLURAL.

Ku kik etokush, I must strike. { Chi kik etokush, } we must
{ Kikpa etokush, } strike.

(PASSIVE.)

A-en kik etokush, I must be A-un kik etokush, we must be
struck. struck.

(b.) The Potential with *kusu ne ap.*

(ACTIVE.)

SINGULAR.

Ku kik kusu ne ap ruwe ne, I ought to strike.

PLURAL.

Chi kik kusu ne ap ruwe en, we ought to strike.

(PASSIVE.)

SINGULAR.

A-en kik kusu ne ap ruwe ne, I ought to struck.

PLURAL.

A-un kik kusu ne ap ruwe ne, we ought to be struck.

(e.) The Potential with *shomoki ko wen.*

SINGULAR.	(ACTIVE.)	PLURAL.

Ku kik shomoki ko wen, I $\left\{\begin{array}{l}\text{Chi kik shomoki ko wen,}\\ \text{Kikpa shomoki ko wen,}\end{array}\right\}$ we must must strike. strike.

Concession, condition, and hypothesis are expressed in the following ways:—

Ku kik koroka, though I strike. $\left\{\begin{array}{l}\text{Ku kik yak un,}\\ \text{Ku kik ko,}\end{array}\right\}$ If I strike.

$\left.\begin{array}{l}\text{Ku kik chiki,}\\ \text{Ku kik yak,}\\ \text{Ku kik yak anak ne,}\\ \text{Ku kik yak ne,}\end{array}\right\}$ If I strike. $\left.\begin{array}{l}\text{Ku kik ita,}\\ \text{Ku kik koro,}\end{array}\right\}$ When I strike.

Ku kik yakka, even if I strike.

Any part of the conjugation of a verb, the imperative mood excepted, may be made negative in either of the following ways:—

(a.) By placing the word *shomo* or *seenne* before the person of a verb, thus:—

Shomo (or seenne) ku kik ruwe ne, I do not strike.

Shomo (or seenne) a-un kik nisa ruwe tap an, we were not struck.

(b.) By placing *shomoki* after the verb in any of the present tense forms, and between the verb and *kusu ne* for the future or *nangoro* of the probable future tense, thus:—

Ku kik shomoki ruwe ne, I do not strike.

A-en kik shomoki nangoro, I shall probably not be struck.

The negative imperative is :—

SINGULAR. (ACTIVE.) PLURAL.

Iteki kik yan, do not strike. Iteki kikpa yan, do not strike.

Doubtfulness is expressed by the word *kotoman* being placed after the verb, thus :— ·

Kik kotoman, he will probably strike ; or, it is thought that he will strike.

A-un kik shomoki kotoman, it seems that we shall not be struck.

The English participles may be rendered as follows :—

PRESENT. (ACTIVE.) PAST.

Kik wa ⎫
Kik ine ⎬ striking.   Kik awa, having struck.
Kik hine ⎭

FUTURE.

Kik kusu ne or kik kushki, will strike.

CLASS II.—VERBS WITH STEM ENDING IN "RA AND RO."

THE VERB KARA "TO MAKE."

For the sake of brevity this paradigm is given in an abridged form :—

SINGULAR. (ACTIVE.) PLURAL.

Ku kara, I make, etc. ⎰Chi kan ruwe ne, we make.
                              ⎱Kara ash ruwe ne,   „

SINGULAR. (PASSIVE.) PLURAL.

A-en kara, I am made, etc.   A-un kara, we are made, etc.

(ACTIVE.)

Ku kan ruwe ne, I make, etc. ⎰Chi kan ruwe ne, ⎱ we make,
                                    ⎱Kara ash ruwe ne,⎰ etc.

(PASSIVE.)

A-en kan ruwe ne, I am made   A-un kan ruwe ne, we are
etc.   made, etc.

It should be noted here that before *ruwe*, ra and ro are
always changed into *n*. *Shiri ne* and *kor'an* take the full form
kara before them.

It will be seen in the past and future tenses that *ra* and *ro*
also become *n* before *n ;* thus :—

| SINGULAR. | (ACTIVE.) | PLURAL. |

Ku kan nisa, I made.   {Chi kan nisa, we made,
                                             {Kara ash nisa,   ,,

Ku kan nangoro, I will prob-   Chi kan nangoro, we will probably make, etc.   ably make, etc.

(PASSIVE.)

A-en kan nisa, I was made.   A-un kan nisa, we were made.

All the other parts of verbs ending in *ra* and *ro* are conjugated
exactly like Class I ; the student is therefore referred to the verb
kik.

---

§ III.   VERBS HAVING A SPECIAL PLURAL FORM.

Many verbs have a special form which is used when the object is of the plural number. The words *reshpa*, " to bring up
many," and *uina*, " to take many," have been selected as examples of them ; and one form of the present tense is here given
to show the manner in which such verbs are conjugated.

(*a.*)   The verb *reshpa*.

| SINGULAR. | (ACTIVE.) | PLURAL. |

Ku reshpa, I bring up many. {Chi reshpa, } we bring up many.
                                           {Reshpa ash,}

(PASSIVE.)

A un reshpa ash, we are brought up.
Echi reshpa an, ye are brought up.
A reshpa (they) are brought up.

(*b.*) The verb *uina*.

SINGULAR.	(ACTIVE.)	PLURAL.
Ku uina, I take many.		{Chi uina, we take many. {Uina ash, ..

(PASSIVE.)

A un uina ash, we are taken.

Echi uina an, ye are taken.

A uina, (they) are taken.

Intransitive verbs, which have a plural inflection, are conjugated thus :—

SINGULAR.	PLURAL.
Ku ahun, I enter.	Ahup ash, we enter.
E ahun, you enter.	Echi ahup, ye enter.
Ahun, (he) enters.	Ahup, (they) enter.

The following list contains many of the verbs which belong to this category. It should be remembered that *pa* is usually (though not always) the plural of the person of the verb, while the special forms are the plural of the subject.

SINGULAR.	PLURAL.	
A,	at,	" to be."
A,	rok,	" to sit."
Ahun,	ahup,	" to enter."
Akonere,	akonerepa,	" smashed."
Ama,	amapa,	" to put," " to place."
Amuchichi,	amuchitpa,	" to scratch," " to pinch."
An,	at, achi, okai, at, ash,	" to be."
Ani,	amba,	" to carry."
Arapa,	paye,	" to go."
Arupa,	paye,	" to go."
Ash	ashpa	" to come down (as rain)."
Ashinge	ashingepa,	" to extract."
Ashte,	roshki,	" to set up."
Aship,	ashippa,	" to flower."
Chimi,	chimba,	" to search for."
Chimi-chimi,	chimba-chimba,	" to search diligently for."

Ek,.................{ araki, " to come."
                    { ariki,   ,,
Eok,................eokok, " to strike against."
Heashi, ...heashpa, " to begin."
Hekatu, ...hekatpa, " to be born."
Hekomu,...........hekomba, " to return."
Hepirasa,..........hepiraspa, " to blossom,"
Hetuku, ...hetukba, " to come forth."
Hopiwe, ...hopiuba, " to pull by placing the foot against an object."
Hopuni, ...hopumba, " to fly."
Horikiraye,.........horikirayepa, " to tuck up one's clothes."
Hoshipi, ...hoshippa, " to return."
Hotuikara, ...hotuipakara, " to call."
Hoyupu, ...hoyuppa, " to run."
Ki, ...kichi, " to do."
Mesu, ...meshpa, " to break."
Mi, ...utomichure, " to wear many garments."
O,...................ot, " to be," " having," " containing."
Oashin, ...oaship, " to go out."
Oboso, ...oboshpa, " to pass through."
Oresu, ...oreshpa, " to bring up."
Pirasa,..............piraspa, " to open out."
Puni, ...pumba, " to lift."
Rai, ...Raipa, " to die."
Raige, ...ronnu, " to kill."
Ran,................rap, " to descend."
Resu, ...reshpa, " to bring up."
Ri, ...ripa, " to be high up."
Rise, ...rishpa, " to root out."
San,................sap, " to descend."
Shinewe, ...shineupa, " to take pleasure."
Shipirasa, ...shipiraspa, " to increase."
Shirutu, ...shirutpa, " to go " " to glide along."
Soso, ...soshpa, " to flay."
Tui,.................tuiba, " to cut."

Turi, ...turuba, " to stretch out."
Uk, ...uina, " to take."
Unu, ...uiruke, " to put."
Utasa, ...utashpa, " to cross one another."
Utumashi, ...utumashpa, " to be mixed."
Yan, ...yap, " to ascend."
Yasa, ...yaspa, " to tear."

§ IV. TRANSITIVE AND CAUSATIVE FORMS.

Intransitives are made transitive and causative in the following ways.

(*A.*) Word ending in *ra*, *ri*, and *ro*, change the final vowel into *e*, e.g. :—

INTRANSITIVE.	TRANSITIVE.
Eishokoro, to believe.	Eishokore, to cause to believe.
Hachiri, to fall.	Hachire, to throw down.
Kara, to make.	Kare, to cause to make.
Koro, to possess.	Kore, to give.
Mokoro, to sleep.	Mokore, to put to sleep.
Nukara, to see.	Nukare, to show.

(*B.*) Other words add *ge*, *ka*, *te*, *de*, or *re* to the stem, usage alone deciding in each case which of the suffixes shall be employed ; e.g. :—

(1) Verbs which take *ge* :—

INTRANSITIVE.	TRANSITIVE.
Ahun, to enter.	Ahunge, to put in.
Rai, to die.	Raige, to kill.
Ran, to come down.	Range, to let down.
San, to go down.	Sange, to send down.
Yan, to go up.	Yange, to take up.

(2) Verbs which take *ka* :—

INTRANSITIVE.	TRANSITIVE.
Isam, there is not.	Isamka, to annihilate.
Iunin, to suffer pain.	Iuninka, to agonise.

Kotuk, to touch or stick.   Kotukka, to stick on.
Mom, to float.   Momka, to send adrift.
Ush, to go out.   Ushka, to extinguish.
Uhui, to burn.   Uhuika, to light.

(3) Verbs which take *te* :—

INTRANSITIVE.	TRANSITIVE.
Ash, to stand.	Ashte, to set up.
Ash, to rain.	Ashte, to cause to rain.
At, to shine.	Atte, to cause to shine.
Chish, to cry.	Chishte, to make cry.
Eshirikopash, to lean against.	Eshirikopashte, to set against.

(4) Verbs which take *de* :—

INTRANSITIVE.	TRANSITIVE.
An, to be.	Ande, to put down, to place.
Oman, to go away.	Omande, to send away.
Rikin, to ascend.	Rikinde, to cause to ascend.

(5) Verbs which take *re* :—

INTRANSITIVE.	TRANSITIVE.
Arapa, to go.	Arapare, to send.
Hekatu, to be born.	Hekature, to cause to be born.
Hetuku, to grow.	Hetukure, to make grow.
Oma, to be inside.	Omare, to put in.
Ru, to melt.	Rure, to melt down.

(6) Some intransitive verbs may be made transitive by placing the particle *e* before them. Thus :—

Kira, " to run away."   Ekira, " to run away with."
Mina, " to laugh."   Emina, " to laugh at."

Other verbs become transitive when *ko* is prefixed to them. Thus :—

Irushka, " to be angry."   Ko-irushka, to be angry with."
Kira, " to run away."   Ko-kira, " to flee unto,
Oman, " to go."   Ko-oman, " to go to."

Some transitive verbs are made causative by adding *re* to them :—

TRANSITIVE.	CAUSATIVE.
E, to eat.	Ere, to cause to eat, to feed.
Ibe, to eat.	Ibere, to cause to eat, to feed.
Iku, to drink.	Ikure, to make drink.
Ki, to do.	Kire, to make do.
Shikkashima, to seize.	Shikkashimare, to make seize.
Ta, to draw (as water).	Tare, to make draw.

Sometimes verbs are made doubly causative. The following are a few examples :

Ahun, to enter ; *ahunge*, to send in ; *ahungere*, to cause to send in.

Ash, to stand ; *ashte*, to set up ; *ashtere*, to cause to set up.

Ibe, to eat ; *ibere*, to feed ; *iberere*, to cause to feed.

San, to go down ; *sange*, to send down ; *sangere*, to cause to send down.

Causatives, like the root form of verbs, admit of both an active and passive conjugation, as :—

Ku sangere ruwe ne, I cause to send down.

A-en sangere ruwe ne, I was caused to be sent down.

Wakka a-tare, he was caused to draw water.

In some instances the plural of the object of a verb is formed by adding *ke* to the stem. Thus :—

Ande, "to put a single thing on one side."   *Amke*, "to put many things on one side."

The plural of the person would be *andepa* and *amkepa* respectively.

Shuwe, "to cook a single thing" as rice.   *Shuke*, "to cook several things as rice, fish, vegetables."

Thence *shuke guru*, "a cook." The plural of the person of the verb is *shuwepa* and *shukepa*. The words *memke*, "to shave ;" and *eraske* to clip the hair " belong to the same category; for it is not "a hair " but many "hairs " which are shaved and clipped.

Some transitive verbs are made intransitive by prefixing *shi*, *he* or *ho* to them, the shade of meaning being determined by the particle used. Such compounds often become adjectives. Thus :—

(*a.*) Maka, "to open."

Shimaka, "to have become open."

Hemaka, "to be open from the outside towards the centre."

Homaka, "to be open from the centre towards the outside."

(*β.*) Pirasa, "to spread."

Shipirasa, "to spread out as a blossom."

Hepirasa, "to spread out like a chrysanthemum with the ends of its petals inclined inwards."

Hopirasa, "to spread out like a chrysanthemum with the ends of its petals inclined outwards."

Some adjectives, like a certain class of verbs (see section 4), (page 123)—admit of the suffix *ka*, such suffix having the power to change them with verbs, thus :—

ADJECTIVE.	VERB.
Fure, red ;	Fureka, to dye red.
Moire, slow ;	Moireka, to slacken speed.
Nam, cold ;	Namka, to make cold.
Nisap, quick ;	Nisapka, to quicken.
Nupuru, very dark or black ;	Nupuruka, to blacken deeply.
Ramutui, frightened ;ˈ	Ramutuika, to frighten.
Retara, white ;	Retaraka, to make white.
Riten, soft ; soaked ;	Ritenka, to soften ; to soak.
Sarak, troubled ;	Sarakka, to give trouble to.
Tumsak, weak ;	Tumsakka, to weaken.
Tunash, quickly ;	Tunashka, to hasten.
Tuwara, cool ;	Tuwaraka, to cool.
Usak, dry ;	Usakka, to dry.

Compare also the following compounds.

Ouhuika. O, the bottom of any vessel. Hence *ouhuika* means "to allow food to get burned to the vessel it is being cooked in."

Ramusarakka. Ramu, " the heart ; the seat of the feelings " or " understanding." Hence *ramusarakka* means, " to make one feel troubled."

Iramusarakka. I, a reflexive pronoun, self. *Iramusarakka,* " to be personally troubled."

Ramuritenka, to comfort.

Ramutuika. Tui, " to snap in two ; " " to break asunder ; " *tuika,* " to break off." Hence, *ramutuika* " to frighten ; " " to startle one with fright." Or as one sometimes hears in English " to take one's breath away."

Many verbs ending in *se* have to do with the breath or voice, or with sound produced by wind or water or by both combined. Hence I conclude that *se* is a root which means " breath ; " " voice ; " " noise."

Thus :—Charase, " to slip " (with the sound of a sudden rush).

Chishrimmise, " to weep aloud " (or with a sniffle).

Epururuse, " to blow out of the mouth " (as water).

Ese, " to answer in an ordinary manner."

Horopse, " to sip up."

Hose, " to answer by calling to."

Husse, " to breathe ;" " to blow from the mouth."

Ise, " to squeal."

Kotoise, " to swarm " (as flies with a buzzing sound).

Opuruse, " to sink into with a gurgling sound " (as into a bog).

Parase, " to drift " (as a boat before the wind).

Pururuse, " to well up with a gurgling sound " (as water from a spring).

Puse, " to blow with the mouth."

Wose, " to howl (as a dog or wolf)."

Words with the root *chak* in them as a rule express suddenness of action like the going off of a bow-string or the popping out of water as from the spout of a kettle just beginning to boil. Thus :—

Chak, " to pop out "; " to shoot out." As :—*Kama etu wano usci chak nisa,* " the hot water shot out of the kettle spout."

Chakchak, " a wren ; " (so called because of its note and quickness of action).

Chakka " to be caught " (as in a snare).

Chakte, " to let off " (as a snare).

Ichakka, " to start up suddenly " (as from a quiet to an excited or frightened condition of mind or body).

Nuchaktek, " merry " ; " mirthful ; " " happy and vivacious " ; " brightly happy." Compare also.

Katchak " weak " ; i.e. " heart suddenly gone out."

§ V. MISCELLANEOUS.

Some verbs may be made reflexive by prefixing the word *yai,* " self," to them. This again may, in cases where it is necessary to express emphasis or make a sentence more clear, be preceded by the word *yaikota,* which means ones'self; e.g. :—

Yai-kik or yaikota yai-kik, to strike ones'self.

Yai-eoripakka or yaikota yai-eoripakka, to humble ones'self.

Yai-raige or yaikota yai-raige, to kill ones'self; to commit suicide.

Yai-tui or yaikota yai-tui, to cut ones'self.

Thoroughness of action may be expressed by placing the word *oara* or *toiko* before some verbs, thus :—

OARA.	TOIKO.
[1]Oan-raige, " to kill outright."	Toiko-kik, " to hit hard."
Oara-erampeutek, " not to understand at all."	Toiko-otereke, " thoroughly to trample under " ; " to kick hard."

Many nouns are turned into verbs by taking *kara* or *koro* after them.

(Kara, to do.)

NOUNS.	VERBS.
Ikiri, " a seam."	Ikiri-kara, " to sew."

---

[1] *Oan* is contracted from *oara* which has its root *a* and *ara.*

Attush, " cloth."

Chisei, " a house."

Attush-kara, " to weave."

Chisei-kara, " to build a house."

(*Koro, to possess.*)

NOUNS.	VERBS.
Hau, " the voice."	Hau-koro, " to crow ; to bark ; to neigh."
Honi, " the stomach."	Honi-koro, " to conceive."
Kaya, " a sail."	Kaya koro, " to sail."

A careful analysis of the following words shows very clearly that *ko* is a radical. Indeed, it is a radical which must be variously translated into English according to the meaning of the principal verbal root contained in the compound in which it is found, no one English word representing its whole force. Yet, although many shades of meaning may appear when it is rendered into English, as is only natural, when spoken by the Ainu it is found to carry one meaning throughout. The secret of this lies in the different point of view from which the Ainu look at things. Thus in English *ko* must be rendered by, " to "; " towards "; " at "; " against "; " from "; " off "; some of which words are, according to our ideas, exactly the opposite of one another. Nor after glancing at the examples now to be given will the grammarian be surprised to find that *ko* used prepositionally may sometimes represent what is called the objective case. Nay ; it even comes to be a *double objective :* Thus :—*en*, per : pro: obj. " me "; *ko* as given below ; *kik*, " to strike "; *en-ko-kik*, " he struck me "; lit : " me " " to " " strike." The examples are :—

Charange, " to argue " ....*Ko*-charange, " to argue against ; (lit : " put the mouth out of the way to "; or as might be said in English " to shut one's mouth up," the " one's mouth " being the other mans', of course).

Etaye, " to pull ";.................. *Ko*-etaye, " to pull from "; (lit: " pull to ").

Etun, " to borrow "; .... *Ko*-etun, " to borrow from "; (lit : " to borrow to ").

Hopuni, "to jump up" from   *Ko*-hopuni "to jump up to"
a reclining position;

Iki, "to do severely"; ....   *Ko*-iki, "to scold," "to hit";
(lit: "do hardly to").

Kandama, "deceipt";............   *Ko*-kandama "to deceive" (lit:
"deceive to").

Karakari, "to roll"; ....   *Ko*-karakari "to roll up (as a
mat) lit: "to roll to."

Kira, "to run away"; ....   *Ko*-kira, "to flee to."

Mekare, "to divide"; ....   *Ko*-mekare, "to apportion,"
(lit: "divide to").

Meshpa, "to chip"; ....   *Ko*-meshpa, to chip off," (lit:
"chip to").

Niki, "to fold";..................   *Ko*-niki, "to fold up" (lit:
fold to).

Ninka, "to lessen"; ....   *Ko*-ninka, "to make less" (as
water in a pot when cooking
rice etc.).

Nukara, "to look"; ....   *Ko*-nukara, "to compare" (lit:
look to).

Pak, "punishment"; ....   *Ko*-pak, "to punish" (lit:
punishment to ").

Pakte, "measure";................   *Ko*-pakte, "to compare" (as
length or measure) lit:
" measure to."

Reika, "to praise"; ....   *Ko*-reika "to praise another
(lit: "make a name to)."

Rishpa, "to pull up"; ....   *Ko*-rishpa "to pull up" (lit:
pull up to).

Sakayokara, "quarrel";.........   *Ko*-sakayokara "to quarrel
with " (lit: quarrel to).

Samba, "like"; ....   *Ko*-samba, "to liken."

Taptapu, "agglomerated";......   *Ko*-taptapu, "to make into a
ball."

Tereke, "to jump"; ....   *Ko*-tereke, "to jump to;"

Tomka, "to beautify"; ....   *Ko*-tomka, "to adorn" (as a

Uk, " to take "; .... Ko-uk, " to take from," (lit : take in respect of).

woman her child with ornaments.)

Yaspa, " to tear "; .... Ko-yaspa, " to tear from" (lit : tear to).

An examination of many words which have *u* pre-fixed to them shows that this word is really a *radical* or *root* expressive as *mutuality*, or *association* and may be translated by " one another " or " together " in English, Thus:—

Chishkara, " to bewail the dead," U-chishkara, " to weep together for the dead."

E, " to eat," .... U-e, "to eat one another."

Ekap, " to salute," .... U-ekap, " to salute one another."

Kepkepi, " to nibble" (as a horse), U-kepkepi ; " to nibble one another " (as animals).

Kerekere, " to scrape," .... U-kerekere, " to scrape one another."

Keshke, " to persecute,"......... U-keshke, " to persecute one another."

Memke, " shave," .... U-memke, " to shave one another."

Musa, " to stroke the head,"... U-musa, " to salute one another by stroking heads."

Pashte, " to make run." ...... U-pashte, "to chase one another."

Peka, " facing "; " pointing towards." U-peka, " to face one another.

Pirikare, " to benefit another," U-pirikare, " to benefit eachother."

Ramuoshma, " to consent,"...... U-ramuoshma, " to consent together."

Tasa, " across,"..................... U-tasa, " from one to the other ; across each other."

Tereke, " to jump,".............. U-terekere, " to jump one another up and down."

Wende, " to harm," .... U-wende, "to harm one another."

[It is not at all unreasonable to suppose therefore that *un*, the personal objective pronoun plural "us" is composed of this *root*, viz, *u* and the *root an*, the verb of existence "to be," the *a* being elided. Thus ; = *u'n*, *u-an*, "us."]

When *u* is added to verbs having *ko* prefixed to them a kind of double plural is sometimes the result thus :—

Ukocharange, "to argue together."
Ukohopuni, "to jump up together."
Ukoiki, "to fight together."
Ukokarakari, "to roll up."
Ukokandama, "to deceive one another."
Ukonukara, "to compare things."
Ukotomka, "to adorn one another."
Ukotereke, "to wrestle."

When *u* is followed by *e*, which is used as an objective to verbs, the *e* is preceded by *w*, the *w* appearing for the sake of euphony, thus :—

Ekote, "to tie up"; .... *Uwe*-kote, "to tie together" (as two pieces of string).

Emik, "to bark at"; .... *Uwe*-mik, "to bark at each other."

Emina, "to laugh at"; .... *Uwe*-mina, "to laugh at each other."

Eo, "to set on"; "to be on"; *Uwe*-o, "to fit together" (as beams in building a house).

Erangara, "to greet one"; ... *Uwe*-rangara, "to greet each other."

Etoita, "to plant," .... *Uwe*-toita, "to spread as epidemic disease" *i.e.* "to plant one another"; or "self sown."

Ekuba, "to bite"; .... *Uwe*-kuba, "to bite one another."

Eramunishte, "to be cruel to"; *Uwe*-ramunishte, "to be mutually cruel."

Etutkopak, "to bid adieu to"; *Uwe*-tutkopank, "to say good by to each other."

Kik, "to strike"; .... *Uwe*-kik, "to knock together as sticks," or "the hands."

Kokanda, "to deceive";......... *Uwe*-kokandama, "to deceive one another."

Neusara, ambe, "news" "a *Uwe*-neusara, "to chat together." chat";

It appears that it would be a mistake to suppose that *uwe* is in every case the *u* (*w*) *e* as shown in the last paragraph, for it will not always submit to such an analysis. There are therefore grounds for believing that there is also a *root* word *uwe*. Thus :—

Uwe-ingara, "to foretell future events"; "to prophecy."
Uwe-inonno-itak, "to pray for the sick."
Uwe-nukara, "to surmise about the near future" (as to whether it will rain to-morrow and such like.)
Uwepaketa, "by degrees."

CHAPTER X.

THE ADVERB.

Some adverbs are merely adjectives followed by the particle *no ;* e.g. :—

ADJECTIVES.	ADVERBS.
Ashiri, " new."	Ashin no, " newly."
Hoshike, " previous."	Hoshike no, " previously."
Oupeka, " upright."	Oupeka no, " uprightly."
Nukara, " to see."	Nukan no, " seeing."
Poro, " great," " large."	Poro no, " many."[1]

[1] In some districts the word applied to animals is always *wenrui,* " many " and never *porm no.*

Many verbs may be turned into adverbs or adverbial phrases by placing the word *kane* or *koro* after them; thus:—

VERBS.	ADVERBS.
Apkash, " to walk."	Apkash kane, " whilst walking."
Arapa, " to go."	Arapa kane, " whilst going."
E, " to eat."	E kane, " whilst eating."
Nina koro, " whilst carrying wood."	Tapkara koro, " whilst dancing."

Verbs may be changed into adverbial phrases by putting the word *koro* after them; thus:—

VERBS.	ADVERBS.
Ahun, " to enter."	Ahun koro, " when or whilst entering."
Eiwange, " to use."	Eiwange koro, " when or whilst using."
Iku, " to drink."	Iku koro, " when or whilst drinking."

The following are a few adverbs of time.

Hembara ne yakka, " at any time ; always."	Numan onuman, " last night."
	Okaketa, " afterwards."
Hoshike an numan, " the day before yesterday."	Oyashim, " the day after to-morrow."
Ita, " when " (*relative*).	Oyashimshimge, " the day following the day after to-mor-row."
Kanna kanna, " often ; again and again."	
Kanna shui, " again."	Ramma, " always."
Kesto, " daily."	Rapoketa, " whilst."
Kesto kesto, " daily, every day."	Shiri onuman, " evening."
Nei orota, " then."	Tane, " now."
Nei ita, " then."	Tanto, " to-day."
Nishatta, " to-morrow."	Teëda, " in ancient times."
Numan, " yesterday."	Teoro, " henceforth."

The following are some adverbs of place :—

Choropoketa, " beneath."	Hangeko, " far."
Hange, " near."	Herikashi, " upwards."

Horikashi, "downwards."
Ikushta, "beyond."
Koehange, "near."
Kotchaketa, "in front of."
Kushta, "yonder."
Na an un ne yakka, "every-where," "anywhere."
Nei ita ne yakka, "anywhere," "everywhere."
Oshiketa, "inside."

Oshimake, "behind."
Rikta, "above."
Samata, "beside."
Setak, "quickly."
Setakko, "for a long time."
Teda, "here" (*at this place.*)
Tepeka, "here" (*this side.*)
Toada, "there" (*at that place.*)
Topeka, "there" (*that side.*)

The following are a few adverbs of degree :—

Ebitta, "all, every."
Mashkin no, "too much."
Naa, "more, yet."
Naani-hungo, "almost."
Nimara, "half."
Obitta, "all, the whole."
Ouse, "only."

Pakno, "sufficient, as far as."
Patek, "only, all."
Poro-sereke, "for the most part."
Ukotamge, "about."
Upakno, "sufficient, as far as."

The following are adverbs of manner :—

Arikinne, "positively."
Eyam no, "carefully."
Hetopo-hetopo, "backwards and forwards."
Inne no, "in crowds."
Keutum atte no, with a fixed purpose."
Kuttoko, "upside down."
Nei no, "thus."
Nitan, "fast."

Oheuge sak no, "rightly."
Ratchitara wa, "peaceably."
Shine ikinne, "unitedly."
Shinen shinen ne, "singly."
Shiwende, "slowly" (*used of walking.*)
Ukoiram no, "conjointly."
Utura no, "together."
Uwatte no, "in multitudes."

The following are some adverbs of interrogation :—

Hemanda gusu, "why?"
Hembara, "when?"
Hempak, "how much, how many?"

Hunakta, "where?"
Hunak un, "whither?"
Ine, "whither?"
Nakwe, "whence?"

Nei pakno, "how far? How much?"

Nekon a, "how? What kind?"

Nep gusu, "why?"

Nep pakno, "how much?"

The following are the adverbs of affirmation:—

E, "yes" (*locally* "*a*").

Ohaine, "just so," "so it is."

Opunki, "yes."

Ruwe, "yes."

Ruwe un, "yes."

Yak'un, "yes."

The negative adverbs are:—

Seenne, "no," "not."

Shomo, "no," "not."

The following expressions should be noted:—

Naa shomo, "not yet."

Hembara ne yakka shomo, "never."

Ramma shomo, "never."

Questions are often asked with the particle *he* and the verb *an*, "to be;" e.g.:—

Hunak un e arapa ruwe he an? "Where are you going?"

Nep gusu ariki ruwe he an? "Why has he come?"

Questions may also be asked by means of the particle *a* or *ya*:—

E koro michi okai ya? "Is your father at home?"

E oman a? "Have you been?"

Nekon a a-kara kunip ne? "What ought I to do?"

Very often no particle is used to express a question, the adverb itself being sufficient to indicate that a question is being asked. The voice is also raised, as in speaking English; e.g.:—

Nakwe ek? "Whence has he come?"

Ine un? "Where are you going?"

Hemanda ki? "What is he doing?"

Hemanda a-ye? "What is it called?"

CHAPTER XI.

THE INTERJECTION.

The chief Ainu interjections are as follows :—

Ainu bota! ah me!

Ayo! a cry of pain.

Chôtara! hurrah!

Eyororope! an exclamation of pleasure sometimes used after a song, but especially on the receipt of some present.

Etu-kishma! *excl.* of surprise.

Haye! a cry of pain.

Haye ku ramu! *excl.* of surprise ; dear me!

Hut! *excl.* of surprise or disgust. Used chiefly by men.

Irambotarare! you noisy one!

Iramshitnere! fidgetty! restless!

Ishirikurantere! well I never!

Isenramte ; at it again!

Kik-kik! *excl.* of surprise. Used chiefly by women.

Wooi! a call for help when in distress.

Parasekoro! hurrah!

The words for "thank you" are :—

Haphap or hap, used chiefly by women and girls.

Yaiiraigere, used chiefly by men and boys.

CHAPTER XII.

ON THE VOWELS A, E, I, O, AND U.

It has been thought advisable to treat the particles *a, e, i, o* and *u* separately, because their meanings differ very widely according as they are used as prefixes or suffixes.

The student need scarcely be warned against confounding, for instance, the *i* which is a suffix to turn verbs into abstract substantives with the *i* which is prefixed to verbs to intensify their meaning, or the *e* meaning "you" with *e* meaning "to." Etymologically, no doubt, such words are quite distinct; but, for practical purposes, the several usages of each particle may best be treated under a single heading.

§ I. THE VOWEL "A."

A is very extensively used as a particle, and has a variety of meanings.

When prefixed to verbs in general, *a* has a passive signification; e.g. :—

ACTIVE.	PASSIVE.
Nu, "to hear."	A-nu, "to be heard."
Nuye, "to write."	A-nuye, "to be written."
Raige, "to kill."	A-raige, "to be killed."

But, as a passive particle, *a* does not always precede the verb as the following example will show :—*nei guru ek a koroka shimo ku nukara,* "he came but I did not see him."

A, used as a passive signification sometimes comes to stand for the objective case to verbs. Thus :—*set akara,* "to set a table" as for food.

When prefixed to the verb *koro*, "to possess," *a* and *koro* combined express the possessive plural of the first personal pronoun ; thus :—

Akoro michi, " our father."   Akon nishpa, " our master."
Akoro ekashi, " our ancestors."   Akorope, " our things."

Sometimes, however, *akoro* is used as the second person singular of the possessive pronoun. It is considered to be a polite mode of expression ; thus :—

Akoro michi may stand for *e koro wichi*, "your father," and *akoro habo* for *e koro habo*, "your mother," though not so commonly used ; nor is the word *koro* so often used with *e* as without it. Thus *e koro michi* is less often heard than *e michi*, and *koro habo* than *e habo*. But *a* can never be used as a personal pronoun, whether singular or plural, without the addition of *koro*.

In a few rare cases the particle *a* is used for the 3rd person singular of the personal pronoun.

After verbs the particle *a* often denotes interrogation ; thus :—

E oman a? Have you been?   Ek a? Has he come?
Shisam ne a? Is it a Japan-   Tan okaibe e koro pe a? Are
ese?   these things yours?

Used after a verb which is spoken in answer to a question, *a* signifies either affirmation or past time ; thus :—

E oman a? Ku oman a. Have you been? I have been.
Ek a? Ek a. Has he come? He has come.

The distinction between the two *a*'s is indicated by the tone of voice. The second *a* is, in all probability, a corruption of *an*, which, added to the root form of a verb, has a conclusive of affirmative force.

§ II. THE VOWEL " E."

The particle *e* is of extensive use as the following examples will show :—

Prefixed to verbs in general, *e* is the second person singular of the personal pronoun ; e.g. :—

E kik, "you strike."   E oman, "you go."
E raige, "you kill."   E apkash, "you walk."

Used with the verb *koro*, "to possess," *e* and *koro* together become the possessive pronoun of the second person singular;
thus :—

> E koro sapa (also *e sapa*), "your head."
> E koro makiri (also *e makiri*), "your knife."

[N.B.—It is always better to drop the *koro*, when there is no
fear of ambiguity.]

Prefixed to some verbs the particle *e* has the power of turning an intransitive into a transitive; thus :—

INTRANSITIVE.	TRANSITIVE.
Kira, "to run away."	Ekira, "to run away with."
Mik, "to bark."	Emik, "to bark at."
Mina, "to laugh."	Emina, "to laugh at."

Similarly prefixed to certain adjectives, it gives them so to
speak, a transitive power; thus :—

Hapuru, "soft."	Ehapuru, "unable to endure."
Nishte, "hard."	Enishte, "able to endure."
Pirika, "good."	Epirika, "bent on gain."
Toranne, "idle"	Etoranne, "not caring to do."

In a few cases the particle *e* is used as a preposition meaning
" to ;" thus :—

> Ekim ne, "to the mountains" (to work).
> Ekim un, "to the (particular place in the) mountains."
> Epish ne, "to the sea-shore" (for work or business).
> Echup pok un chup ahun, "the sun sets in the west."
> Enon, "whither"; from *e* and *un*.

Used with the numerals *e* means " from ":—

> Wan *e* tu hotne, 30 (lit. ten from two score.)
> Wan *e* re hotne 50 (lit. ten from three score.)

§ III. THE VOWEL "I."

The word *i*, used as a separate particle, has the following significations :—

Prefixed to some verbs it has an intensifying power ; thus :—

Nu, " to hear."   Inu, " to listen."

Nukara, " to see."   Ingara, " to look at."

Chim-chimi, " to search after   Ichim-chimi, " to search very
by feeling."   carefully after."

But some verbs are intensified by prefixing *ane* rather than *i* to them. Thus :—

Ane-ongami, " to honour much."

Ane-koyaiiraige, " to thank much."

Ane-oshkoro, " to prize very highly."

Prefixed to other verbs *i* indicates the first person plural objective case :—

I kik an, " he struck us."   I noshpa, " they follow us."

I kara an, " he made us."   I pa, " they found us."

Kikiri i pa ko orowa i noshpa, " when the insects have found us, they will follow us."

When suffixed to verbs, *i* has the power to turn them into nouns ; thus :—

VERB.	NOUN.
Yainu, to think.	Yainu-i, a thought.

The particle *i* has also the idea of time and place in it ; thus :—

Nei i pakno ne yakka, " for ever."

Nei i-ta pakno ne yakka, " what place soever."

Shine an i-ta, " at one place " (once upon a time.)

Pet otta san i-ta ichaniu chep a-nukara, " when he went down to the river he saw a salmon-trout " (*a salmon-trout was seen*).

Sometimes *i* stands for the 2nd per ; sing : obj.: case Personal Pronoun " you ":—

Nei guru *i* nukan rusui, "that person wishes to see you."

I tak gusu ku ek, "I have come to fetch you."

---

§ IV. THE VOWEL "O."

The particle *o*, like *e*, is sometimes used as a preposition to nouns. Its signification is "from;" thus:—

Okim un, "from the mountains."

Opish ne, "from the sea-shore."

O-chupka un chup hetuku, "the sun rises from the east."

Onon, "whence"; from *o* and *un*.

When the particle *o* is placed immediately after some nouns it changes them into adjectives, e.g. :—

Kesh-o chikoikip, "an animal of different colours."

Shiriki-o sarambe, "a soft material with a pattern."

Shiriki-o nonno, "a variegated flower."

When the verb *ika*, "to run over" (as water), is immediately preceded by *o*, its meaning is changed, thus :—

Ika, "to run over."

O-ika, "to step or jump over."

Nupuri o-ika, "to cross mountains."

Sakiri o-ika, "to jump a fence."

Wattesh o-ika, "to step over a straw."

Atui o-ika ingara, "to look across the sea."

Pet o-ika hotuyekara, "to call to across a river."

When *o* is used after *shui*, "a hole" or *pui*, "a hole," it must be translated by "to make" or "to bore;"

Erum shui o kor'an, "the rat is making a hole."

Ainu pui o kor'an, "the man is boring a hole."

---

§ V. THE VOWEL "U."

Prefixed to verbs the particle *u* gives the sense of mutuality ; e.g. :—

Koiki, "to fight."	Ukoiki, "to fight one another."
Onnere, "to know."	Uonnere, "to know one another."
Oshi arapa, "to go behind."	Uoshi paye, "to go behind each other."
Raige, "to kill."	Uraige, "to kill one another."

The vowel *u* does not always immediately precede the verb to which it refers. Thus, for *Kotan oro u-kopahaunu* we sometimes hear *U kotan oro kopahaunu*, " there is intercourse between the villages ; " and so on.

CHAPTER XIII.

POSTPOSITIONS.

Under the term *Postpositions* are comprehended such words as in English are generally termed Prepositions and Conjunctions. They are here given in alphabetical order, irrespective of the category under which their European equivalents would be classed. As will be seen, there are some words for which there are no exact English equivalents, and others again whose meaning varies according to the different connections in which they are used. It has therefore been considered advisable to give a fair number of examples, in some cases, as illustrations. It should also be remarked that some of the following words are used before as well as after the words they govern and should therefore be sometimes called prepositions whilst a few are used only before the words they govern.

Aige, " as ; " " and so ! " " with reference to which ; " " there upon ; " e.g. :—*Ku ye aige, a-en kik*, " as I spoke, he struck me."

Nei orushpe ku ye ; aige, Ukomotte Ainu ene itakhi :—" I told him the news ; thereupon Mr. Ukomotte spoke thus."

Usaine usaine an wenkatcham kon ruwe ne, sekoro, uwepaketa ku inu ; aige, Mopet ta san wa nei orushpe ku uwepe-kennu, " by degrees I heard that he had committed various misdemeanours ; and so I went down to Mopet to inquire into the matter."

Aine ; " thereupon," " upon which."

Heikachi a wakka tare yakka kopan ; aine, Kamui irushka gusu, chup kamui samata a-ande ruwe ne; " the lad even disliked to be made to draw water ; thereupon, the gods being angry, they placed him in the side of the moon."

Rai, aine, utare obitta chish nisa ruwe ne na, " he died, upon which the Ainu all wept.

Anak, anakne ; " as regards." " in reference to."

These particles serve to isolate a word or sentence, and to give emphasis to a subject.

When both *anak* and *anakne* are used in the same sentence *anak* is more emphatic than *anakne*. *Anakne,* however, when standing alone need not always be translated :—

Chikap anakne chikuni ka reu, " the bird settled upon a tree."

Otteëda anakne seta reëp iporose, " in ancient times dogs were called reëp."

Amam an, chep anakne an, yuk kam anak pon no ka isam ruwe ne, " there is vegetable food and there is fish ; but as for venison, there is none at all."

Anko, ankoro ; " when " (if).

An is the substantive verb " to be," and *ko* is a contraction of *koro,* which means " to possess."

Chikap reu anko ku tukan. " I will shoot the bird when (if) it settles."

Ru hotom ta reushi anko aep oro omarep, " a vessel in

which to put food (for) when one stays (to rest) on the road."

Ani (locally ari); " with," " by means of," " taking."

The word *ani* is a compound whose parts are *an* " to be," and the particle *i*. In many places *ani* is corrupted into *ari*, so that, generally speaking, it matters little which form of the word is used :—

> Ai ani (ari) yuk raige ruwe ne, " he kills deer with arrows."
>
> Kuwa ani (ari) akpash, " he walks by means of a stick."
>
> Orowa, pishako niwatush ani wa pet otta san ruwe ne, " and taking the ladle and bucket, he went.down to the river."

Awa (a past passive participle); " being."

Wherever the particle *awa* is used past time is signified. It appears to be the passive participle of the verb " to." It is always used conjunctively :—

> Panata kotan un san ita, Ainu tunangara, awa, otta ene itak-hi : " when he went down to the lower village he met an Ainu, and spake thus to him." (lit. *When he went down, an Ainu being met, he spoke thus to him.*)
>
> Teëda ne yakka usa-pirika mi-ambe a-satke ruwe ne, awa, ikka-guru ikka wa isam, " so formerly, when we hung out our wearing apparel to air, a thief stole it." (lit. *In ancient times also various good clothing being hung out to air, a thief stole them.*)

Chiki; " if."

> Ku arapa chiki echi nure ash ha, " I will let you know if I go."
>
> Ki chiki pirika ruwe ne, " it will be well if you do it. '

Choropok, choropok-i, choropok-i-ta, choropok-un, " under," " beneath."

The particles *i, ita,* and *un,* which are here used with *choropok,* have a locative sense in them. Either of them therefore has the power to turn the post position *choropok* into an adverb of place.

Set choropok, " under the seat,"
Shuop choropoki, " the place under the box."
Chikuni choropokita, " beneath the tree."
Mun choropok un, " under the grass."

Ekopash ; " against," " leaning against."

Tuman ekopash kina, " the mat against the wall."
En ekopash, " against me."
Ikushpe ekopash ainu, " the man leaning against the post."

Ene ; " thus," " so," " this or that kind," " such."

En otta 'ene hawashi, " he spoke thus to me."
Ene okaibe isam, " there is no such kind of thing."
Teëda ne yakka ene shiri ki, " it was also so done formerly."

Enka, enkapeka, enkata ; " over," " above."

The word *enka* means " over," " above "; *enkapeka*, " the place above," and *enkata*, " at the place above." *Peka*, like *ta*, is an adverbial particle ; it means " place " or " side."

En enka ; " over me."
Atui enkapeka chikap hoyupu, " a bird is flying over the sea."
Pet enkata chikap an, " there is a bird over the river."

Hekota ; " facing," " towards."

En hekota ; " facing me."
Chisei hekota hosare wa ingara, " to look towards the house."
Ekeshne hekota hosare ; " to look about from place to place."
Atui orun hekota hosare ; " to face the sea."
Nai hekota apkash, " to walk towards the stream."

Hemhem ; " and." *Hemhem...hemhem ;* " both...and."

The word *hemhem* may be used either once or twice in a sentence. When used once, it equals the conjunction " and "; when used twice, it means " both...and "; thus :—

Tambe hemhem nei ambe ; " this and that."
Tambe hemhem nei ambe hemhem ; " both this and that."

Hene ; "and." *Hene...hene ;* both...and."

Hene and *hene...hene,* have the same meaning as *hemhem... hemhem,* and are used in the same way ; thus :—

>   Apto hene urara ; "rain and fog."
>   Seta hene, chironnup hene ; "both dogs and foxes."

Hike ; "as regards," "in reference to."

This word is only suffixed to verbs ; thus :—

>   Ku nukar' hike ; "in reference to what I see."
>   Ku inu hike ; "as regards what I hear."

Ikushta ; "beyond" (*a long way off*).

The particle *i,* which is here used before *kushta,* is an intensifier. Thus, *ikushta* means "a long way off":—

>   Pet ikushta, "beyond the river" (*but far from it*).
>   Pet kushta, "beyond the river" (*but near it*).

Imakake, imakaketa ; "then," "after that."

>   Aige, imakaketa arapa wa ye ruwe ne, "so after that he
>   went and told him."
>   Orowa, imakake pet otta san ruwe ne na, "and afterwards
>   he went down to the river."

Ine, or *hine* " ...ing," "when," "being."

The word *hine* has a participial force and always follows a verb ; thus :—

>   Orowa, kira hine paspas kara guru orota arapa, "and,
>   running away, he went to a charcoal-burner."
>   Ariki hine shirikap eshirikootke, "when they came, they
>   speared a sword-fish."

Ka ; "even." *Ka...ka,* "both...and "; "neither...nor."

Ka, when used only once, means "even." When used twice with an affirmative verb, the two *ka's* mean "both...and"; but when used with a negative, they mean "neither...nor ;" thus :—

>   Chiramantep isam, yuk ka isam, "there are no bears or
>   even deer."

Ep ka isam, anip ka isam, "there is neither food nor clothing." Chep ka an, amam ka an, "there is both fish and vegetable food.

Ka ; kata ; "top," "upon the top."

Pira ka, "the top of a cliff."
Chisei kata, "on the top of the house."
Shiri kata, "on the ground."

Kashi, kashike, kashiketa, kashike-peka, kashikeketa ; "over," "upon." *Kashi* and *kashike* mean "over," "above ;" *kashike-peka* means "the direction above ;" *kashikeketa* and *kashiketa* mean "at the place above ; "upon ":—

E kashi or e kashike, "over you."
Atui kashikepeka kopecha hoyupa wa okai, "the wild ducks are flying over the sea."
Chisei kashiketa paskuru at, "there are some crows upon the house."

Ko, koro ; "if," "when," "whilst."

The word *ko* is probably a corruption or contraction of the verb *koro*, "to possess."

Arapa ko wen, "it will be bad if you go."
Arapa koro hachin nisa "he tumbled as he went."

When the verb *koro* is used as an auxiliary to other verbs it signifies that the action is still going on ; thus :—

A-ki kor'an. "It is being done."

When the particle *ko* is prefixed to some verbs it is a preposition meaning "to," Thus :—

(*a.*) *Ko* with intransitive verbs.

Ko-ahun, "to go in to."   Ko-kira, "to flee to."
Ko-ek, "to come to."   Ko-oman, "to go to."
Ko-san, "to go down to."

(*b.*) *Ko* with transitive verbs.

Ko-ingara, "to compare."   Ko-nukara, "to compare."
Ko-ki, "to do to."   Ko-ongami, "to worship."

Used as a suffix to a few words *ko* has the power of reversing their meaning, thus.

Hange, " near ;" hangeko, " distant ;" setak, " quick," " now ;" setakko, " slow," for a long time."

Kuni ; " likely," " probably."

The word *kuni* seems to express " likelihood," " probability," and " purpose ;" thus :—

> Ek kuni aramu, " he is likely to come " (lit : *it is to be considered (that) he will come*); or " I think, he will come."
>
> Ku iku kuni tambako. " The tobacco for me to smoke."
>
> Ek kuni ku ye, " I told him to come."

Kuni gusu ; " in order that," " in order to," " so that."

> Nu kuni gusu ek, " come so that you máy hear."
>
> A-ki kuni gusu ye, " command that it be done."
>
> Iteki soine kuni gusu kara yan, " make it so that they do not get out " (*i.e. don't allow them to go out*).
>
> Iteki a-en kik kuni gusu ye wa en kore, " please ask him not to strike me " (lit : *please speak to him that I be not struck*).

Kushta ; " beyond," " yonder," (*but not far off*).

> To kushta, " beyond the lake " (*but near it*).
>
> Kushta an, " it is younder."

Kusu or *gusu ; ne gusu ;* " because," " as," " to the effect that," " to."

After a verb *kusu* or *gusu*, but after a noun *ne gusu* :—

> A-hotuyekara gusu ek, " he came because he was called."
>
> Kuani Ainu ne gusu ku erampeutek, " being au Ainu, I do not understand it."
>
> Wakka atare gusu aye yakka etoranne, " though told to draw water, still he was idle " (lit : *though it was said that water was to be drawn, he was idle at it.*)
>
> Ku etutkopak gusu, orota ku arapa, I shall go to bid him farewell.

It should also be noted that *gusu* sometimes acts as an accusative, thus :—

Chi-utara gusu, " for us."

En gusu, " for me."

Newa ; " and." *Newa...newa ;* also *Newa...kane ;* " both... and."

Humirui newa kopecha an, " there is a hazel-hen and a wild-duck."

Tokap newa kunne newa, " both day and night."

Itunnap newa soyai kane shi no yai-sanniyo kikiri ne ruwe ne, " both ants and bees are very prudent insects."

Ne yakka ; " even," " and," *Ne yakka...ne yakka ;* " both... and."

After nouns always *ne yakka,* but after verbs *yakka.*

In an affirmative sentence *ne yakka,...ne yakka,* or *yakka... yakka* mean " both...and ;" but in a negative " neither...nor," and " whether...or :" thus :—

Kuani ne yakka tambe ki eashkai, " even I can do this."

Eani ne yakka kuani ne· yakka, " both you and I."

Tambe ne yakka nei ambe ne yakka shomo, " neither this nor that."

Apkash yakka umma o yakka, " whether I walk or ride."

Okake, okake an ko, okaketa ; " after," " afterwards," " by and by."

Arapa, okake rai nisa ruwe ne, " he died after he went away."

Rai, okake an ko, tushiri otta a-omare, " he died, afterwards he was buried."

Okaketa ku ek na, " I will come by and by."

Okari ; " around."

To okari, " around the lake."

Kotan okari, " around the village."

Oma. The particle *oma* means " having," " containing,"

"with," "holding;" and is sometimes found in Place-names.
Thus :—

Mat-oma-nai, "the stream having lagoons" or "spits of land in it."

Toi-oma-i, "the place where the gardens are."

Tokesh-oma-nai, "the stream" or "glen" at the end of the lake."

To-oma-i, "the glen" or "stream with a lake."

Oro ; "in," "upon," "at," "by," "situated in." *Oro* follows the word it governs."

Oro ahunge ; "put it in."

Aep oro omarep ; "a vessel to put food in."

Amip oro omare kuma, "a pole to hang clothes upon."

The word *oro* is sometimes found to enter into the construction of Place-names. Thus :—

Nai-oro, "by," or "upon" the "glen or stream."

Nup-oro, "situated upon the plain."

Not-oro, "situated at the blunt cape."

Shirar' oro, "situated by" or "among the boulders."

Tomari-oro, "situated at the harbour."

To-oro, "situated by the lake."

Ush-oro, "situated on the bay."

Orota, orun, otta ; "to," "into," "to which," "to this," "in which," "by," "of." The word *otta* is a contraction of *orota.*

Puyara otta shirikush, "to pass by a window."

Pet orota (*otta*) san, "he has gone down to the river."

Shu orota (*otta*) wakka an, "there is water in the pot."

Chisei orun ahun, "he has gone into the house."

Orota (*otta*) ene itak, "to which (to this) he spoke thus."

Ota-taiki otta okai shui, "holes in which sand-flies live."

En otta nu, "he enquired of me."

Otta ahun ushike isam, "there is no place in which to go."

The following peculiar use of *otta*, as expressing "purpose," should be carefully noted :—

Amip a-satke otta a-iwange, "it is used for drying clothes."
Chep a-satke otta neyakka a-iwange, "it is also used for
drying fish."

Orowa ; " and," " then." *Orowa no ;* " from," " by," " after."
Orowa ene itak-hi, "and thus he spake."
Ene itak-hi, orowa paye, "they spake so, then went away."
Ye orowa no kira, "after he told•us he ran away."
Nishpa orowa no akik, "he was struck by the master."

Oshike, Oshiketa ; " the inside," " inside."
Chip oshike, "the inside of a boat."
Chisei oshiketa okai, "they are inside the house."

Pakno ; " sufficient," " enough," " until " (the extreme limits).
Pakno ku e na, "I have eaten enough."
Ek pakno ku tere, "I will wait till he comes."
Atui pa pakno atui gesh pakno ; moshiri pa pakno moshiri
gesh pakno, "from one end of the sea to the other ; from
one end of the world to the other," (*A phrase meaning
" the whole world over "*).

Rata ; " below."
Kando rikta an, shiri rata an, "heaven is above and earth
is below."

Ri, rikta, rikpeka ; "high," "above."
Ri, means "high ;" *rikpeka,* "the direction above," and *rikta,*
"at the place above ;" thus :—
Chikap ri ruwe ne, "the bird is high."
Paskuru rikpeka hoyupu, "the crow flies in the heights above."
Rikta an, "it is above."

Sama, samaketa, samata ; "beside," "by the side of," "before" (*in the sight of*).
Pet sama, "the river's side."
Apa samaketa okai ikushpe ; "the posts by the side of the
doorway."
Kamui tek samata ; "before God " (lit: *by the side of the
hand of God.*)

Shirikata ; this word properly means "upon the earth," but it is very often used for "below" or "beneath," instead of *rata ;* thus :—

> Kando rikta an, moshiri shirikata an, "heaven is above, the earth is beneath."

Ta ; "to," "at," "in."

> Mopet ta san, "he is going to Mopet."
> Chisei ta okai, "they are in the house."
> Shine an ta, "at one place."

Tumugeta, tumuta ; "amongst."

> Chikuni tumugeta ; "among the trees." Mun tumuta ; "among the grass."

Un ; "in," "to," "towards," "at," "of," "among."

The postposition *un* is of very extensive use, and has a great variety of meanings. Its use as a locative particle should be particularly noted. It should be noted that it governs the word it follows.

Chisei un, "in the house."	Oya moshir'un guru, "a foreigner."
Uni un ku arapa, "I am going home."	Kim un, "to the mountains," or "in the mountains."
Te un, "here."	Kim un kamui, "the gods of the mountains."
Eani un, "you."	Rep un kamui, "the gods of the sea."
Kuani un, "I."	Paro un guru, "a man of mouth" (i.e. eloquent).

The particle *un* is found to sometimes enter into the construction of Place-names. Thus :—

> Ki-un-nai, "the stream among the reeds."
> Kin-un-nai, "the mountain stream."
> Kush-un-kotan, "the village yonder ;" meaning that a "river," "lake," or "arm of the sea" intervenes.

Kush-un-nai, " the stream " or " glen over yonder ;" here again something must be understood to intervene.

Mak-un-kotan, " the village back behind."

So-un-nai, " the glen of rocks," or " the stream with a fall."

Uturu, Uturugeta, Uturuta ; " between," " among."

Ikushpe uturugeta, " between the posts."

Nupuri uturuta, " among the mountains."

Wa ; " and."

The present particle of *an* " to be ;" used also as a copulative :—

Koro wa ek, " bring it," (lit : *possessing come*).

Arapa wa uk, " go and fetch it," (lit : *going take it*).

Wano, we ; from.

The word *we* is now only heard in the following sentence *Nak we ek?* " Where have you come from?" But *wano* is very often used ; thus :—

Sara wano ku ek. " I came from Sara."

Nupuri wano sap ash, " we came down from the mountains."

Ya ; " whether," " or."

Ek ya shomo ya ? " Will he come or not."

Ki ya shomo ya, ku erampeutek. " I do not know whether he has done it or not."

Yak, yak anak, yak anakne, yakka, yakun ; " if," " though," " in case," " by."

Arapa yak pirika, " he may go," (lit : *it is good if he goes*).

Arapa yak anak ne, " if upon his going," or, " if when he goes."

Ki yakka, " though he does it."

Uwepekennu yakun, " in the case of his making inquiry."

CHAPTER XIV.

SYNTAX.

In speaking the Ainu language the following rules are to be observed :—

The subject of the verb is always placed at the beginning of the sentence, the verb itself at the end, and the object immediately before the verb ; thus :—

Ainu ek, "a man is coming."

Moyuk raige, "he killed a racoon."

Heikachi umma o, "the lad is riding a horse."

The genitive always precedes the word it defines ; thus :—

Ku makiri ; "my knife."

Chikoro uni ; "our home."

Chiramantep maratto ; "a bear's head ;" "a bear feast."

Seta nimaki ; "the dog's teeth."

Adjectives are used either attributively or predicatively.

(a) When used attributively the adjective is placed before the noun it qualifies ; thus :—

Atomte chisei ; "a beautiful house."

Wen guru ; "a bad person," "poor person."

(b) When an adjective is used predicatively, it is placed after the noun and is itself followed by the verb "to be ;" thus :—

Nonno eramasu ne ruwe ne, "it is a pretty flower."

Seta nimaki tanne ruwe ne, "the dog's teeth are long."

Very often, particularly when the word *anakne* is used, the noun is mentioned twice, once with and once without the adjective ; thus :—

Toi anakne pirika toi ne ruwe ne, "it is a good garden,"
or "the garden is a good one," (lit: *as for the garden,
it is a good one*).

Umma anakne nitan umma ne, "it is a swift horse," or
"the horse is a swift one."

The pronouns are very much used in speaking Ainu, and sometimes occur twice or even thrice in one short sentence ; thus :—

Kuani Ainu ku ne, "I am an Ainu."

Kuani ku arapa wa ku ye, "I will go and tell him."

Aokai e meraige ya, "are you cold ?"

It should also be noted that *en* "me" is sometimes used where
I would be found in English ; thus :—

Nei guru anakne en pak no shomo pa ruwe ne, "he did
not find so many as I."

Prepositions are usually placed after the words they govern
and are therefore, in this work, called postpositions ; thus :—

Uni un arapa, "he is going home."

Chisei orun ahun, "to enter a house."

Kama otta wakka omare, "put some water into the kettle."

Endo kotan orowa no ek, "he came from Tōkyō."

Apparent exceptions will often be heard in the words *otta*,
"to," "and *oro*," "in ," thus :—

Otta ene itak-hi, "to which he said."

Otta okai shui, "holes in which they dwell."

Oro omare, "to bring in," or "to put in."

These exceptions are not real ; for the subject to which these
postpositions refer, though not expressed, is always understood.
Otta should therefore in such sentences as those given above,
always be translated by some such phrase as—"in which," "to
which," "to it," "to that," or "this." *Oro* always means "in"
or "upon."

The adverb always precedes the verb :—

Tunashi no ye. "Say it quickly."

Naa moire oman. "Go more slowly."

Conjunctions are placed at the end of the clause to which
they belong; thus :—

> Shiyeye an gusu, tane ku hoshipi, "I am now returning
> because I am sick."
> Nishpa ikashpaotte chiki, ku ki, "I will do it if the
> master commands."

A conjunctive clause ending in *gusu* may be placed at the
end of sentence; thus :—

> Tane ku hoshipi, shiyeye an gusu ne na, "I am now re-
> turning because I am sick."

The common conjunction "and" is expressed by the particle
wa; thus :—

> Ek wa ibe. "Come and eat."

Interrogative adverbs are placed at the beginning, and interrogative particles at the end of a sentence; thus :—

> Hembara pakno teda e shiroma ruwe he an? "How long
> shall you stay here?
> Nepi ye ya? "What did he say?"

All dependent clauses and participial phrases precede the chief
verb; thus :—

> Orowa, niwatush ani pet otta san wa wakka ta, "and taking
> the bucket, he went down to the river and fetched water."

The following construction with the negative verb *isam*, "it
is not," should be carefully noted. It helps to form a phrase
of which the English equivalent is not negative but affirmative;
thus :—

> Ikka guru ikka wa isam, "a thief stole it away."
> Arapa wa isam, "he is gone;" "also, he is dead."
> A-e wa isam, "it is all eaten."
> Imok auk wa isam, "the bait has been taken away."

As a rule, the Ainu are very fond of using the passive forms
of verbs where one would expect to find the active voice, thus :—

> Pet otta san wa chep anukara, "going down to the river

he saw a fish," (lit: *going down to the river, a fish was seen.*)

Umma a-o wa oman, "he went on a horse," (lit: *he went, a horse being ridden.*)

Chep asatke otta neyakka a-eiwange, "it is also used for drying fish," (lit: *it is also used for fish to be dried.*)

The passive particle *a* is not, in every case, immediately prefixed to the verb to which it belongs; e.g.

A-wakka tare yakka kopan, "he disliked even to draw water."

The *a* really belongs to *tare;* thus, *Wakka atare yakka kopan,* is quite as correct as, *a-wakka tare yakka kopan,* and either may be used.

In compound passive verbs the particle *a* is placed in the middle; thus:—

Kashiobiuki, "to save."

Kashi-a-obiuki, "to be saved."

A polite way of asking for things is with *en kore;* thus:—

Wakka en kore, "please give me some water."

Ye wa en kore, "please tell me."

In prayer the following peculiar idiom is often heard."

Nekon ka newa.........en kore wa un kore. Please give us (lit: *please giving me give us.*)

The way in which pretence is expressed is worthy of special attention. Thus:—

(*a.*) Nouns take the word *shi* before and *nere* after them, e.g.

Shi-chironnup nere, "to pretend to be a fox."

Shi-nishpa nere, "to pretend to be a gentleman."

Shi-okkai nere, "to pretend to be a man."

(*b.*) Qualified nouns take *shi* before the adjective. Thus:—

Shi-pirika gun, nere, "to pretend to be a good person."

Shi-ponbe nere, "to pretend to be a small thing."

Shi-shiretokbe nere, "to pretend to be a handsome person."

(c.) Intransitive verbs take *shi* before and *re* after them, e.g.

Shi-ashpa-re, " to pretend to be deaf."

Shi-ihoshki-re, " to pretend to be drunk."

Shi-ne-re, " to pretend to be."

Shi-rai-re, " to pretend to be dead."

(d.) Verbs which are made transitive by changing the final vowel into *e* do not add *re*. Thus :—

Shi-hachire, " to pretend to throw down."

Shi-kore, " to pretend to give."

Shi-mokore, " to pretend to be asleep."

(e.) Verbs which are made transitive by the addition of any of the particles mentioned under Sec. IV. (B). Page 123, take *re* after them. Thus :—

Shi-raige-re, " to pretend to kill."

Shi-isamka-re, " to pretend to annihilate."

Shi-ashte-re, " to pretend to set up."

Shi-ande-re, " to pretend to put down."

Shi-arapare, " to pretend to send."

(f.) Causative verbs are treated in the same manner. Thus :—

Shi-ere-re, " to pretend to feed."

Shi-kire-re, " to pretend to make do."

LIST OF ERRATA TO PART II.

Page   2. Write Savant for servant.

,,   15. Write Nihongi for Nikongi.

,,   42. Strike out the word "sounding" under *kakkumi*.

,,   56. Write *is* for *in* after "land" under *shiruturu*.

,,   ,,   Under *Soya* write rocks for rooks.

,,   67. 14th line from top write *and* for ard.

,,   71. Write achapo for achapa, and in the foot note write sufficient for sufficies.

,,   74. Strike out *of* in the 18th line from the top.

,,   75. In the last line read "and *at* or *on* for the plural" after the word singular.

,,   83. In line 9 from the bottom read *after* for *often*.

,,   132. In the bottom line write *uwetutkopak* for uwetutkopank.

,,   139. In line 8 from the top write *Michi* for *wichi*.

THE END.

發行兼大賣捌所

東京市京橋區銀座
四丁目三番地

教文館

明治三十八年十月十六日發行
明治三十八年十月十三日印刷

著作權所有

印刷所　株式會社東京築地活版製造所
　　　　東京市京橋區築地二丁目十七番地

印刷者　野村宗十郎
　　　　東京市京橋區築地三丁目十五番地

發行者　堀田達治
　　　　東京市京橋區銀座四丁目三番地

著作者　ジョン、バチラー
　　　　東京市京橋區銀座四丁目三番地
　　　　札幌區北三條四七丁目一番地

CPSIA information can be obtained
at www.ICGtesting.com
Printed in the USA
BVHW06s1553300418
514824BV00014B/346/P